"A LIVING HISTORY...A SPLENDID ACHIEVEMENT...DRAMATIC AND CONVINCING FROM BEGINNING TO END"
—CHICAGO SUN-TIMES

"Did Freud's personality, particularly his 'puritanism,' color his theories? Did he have an erection after an analytic hour with an attractive female patient? Did his ambivalent interest in the occult contribute to his break with Jung? Did he analyze his own daughter? Did the 'Wolfman's' second analyst have a drug problem? Affirmative answers to these questions indicate the range and fascination of this new contribution.... The issues the author raises are of major importance"—THE NEW YORK TIMES BOOK REVIEW

"A work of real importance.... I know of no other portrait that is so unpolemical, carefully developed and convincing.... A major piece of news is Freud's strong interest in the occult, and his acceptance in later life of some varieties of psychic experience.... Though Freud's intellectual heroism retains its power to move and impress, this book decisively returns the Freud of legend to the realities of history" —SATURDAY REVIEW/WORLD

PAUL ROAZEN received his A.B. and Ph.D. from Harvard, did further graduate work at the University of Chicago and Magdalen College in Oxford, and currently is Professor of Political and Social Science at York University, Toronto. His books include *Freud: Political and Social Thought* and *Brother Animal: The Story of Freud and Tausk.* Ten years of research and writing went into FREUD AND HIS FOLLOWERS.

FREUD
AND HIS
FOLLOWERS

by Paul Roazen

A MERIDIAN BOOK
NEW AMERICAN LIBRARY
TIMES MIRROR
NEW YORK, LONDON AND SCARBOROUGH, ONTARIO

Library of Congress Catalog Card Number: 73-20782

Since this page cannot legibly accommodate all acknowledgments,
they appear on pages 601-2.

Portions of I, 1 appeared in the *Virginia Quarterly Review;* portions
of VII, 8 & 9 appeared in *Social Research; portions* of IV, 5 appeared in
Saturday Review; and portions of IV, 5 appeared in *Dissent.*

This is an authorized reprint of a hardcover edition published by Alfred
A. Knopf, Inc. The hardcover edition was published simultaneously in
Canada by Random House of Canada Limited, Toronto.

 MERIDIAN TRADEMARK REG. U.S. PAT. OFF. AND FOREIGN COUNTRIES
REGISTERED TRADEMARK—MARCA REGISTRADA
HECHO EN CLINTON, MASS., U.S.A.

SIGNET, SIGNET CLASSICS, MENTOR, PLUME and MERIDIAN
BOOKS are published in the United States by The New American
Library, Inc., 1301 Avenue of the Americas, New York, New York
10019, in Canada by The New American Library of Canada Limited,
81 Mack Avenue, Scarborough, 704, Ontario.

First Printing, March, 1976

1 2 3 4 5 6 7 8 9

PRINTED IN THE UNITED STATES OF AMERICA

TO

Deborah, Jules, and Daniel

CONTENTS

III

IV

V

VIII
OTTO RANK:
SONS AND FATHERS   391

IX
THE WOMEN   419

ILLUSTRATIONS

PREFACE

WHY ANOTHER BOOK on Freud and his followers? The main outlines of Freud's career have apparently been securely established, and his achievement in founding psychoanalysis is by now a matter of history. To be sure, Freud continues to be blamed for many ills of contemporary life, and Pope Paul VI is only the most recent prominent figure to have criticized him as a prime source of modern sexual libertinism. During this century attitudes toward sexuality have in fact undergone a revolution, which is immediately apparent if we consider a casual case illustration of Freud's and contrast it with the way women dress nowadays: "supposing . . . that a hysterical woman has a phantasy of seduction in which she is sitting reading in a park with her skirt slightly lifted so that her foot is visible. . . ."[1] But Ernest Jones's massive three-volume biography of Freud, published from 1953 to 1957, should have put to rest the outstanding misconceptions about Freud's contribution to science and intellectual life. Jones concluded his long career as a famous British analyst by spending seven years working to unfold the story of Freud's genius. He had the full cooperation of the Freud family, especially Anna Freud, the only child of Freud to follow his professional path and by now his leading disciple. Jones also relied on the aid of many other psychoanalysts, who sent him their memories of the master, lent copies of Freud's correspondence, and commented on early drafts of the manuscript. In the end, Jones's books succeeded not only in superseding all previous accounts of Freud's life but also in presenting a history of the psychoanalytic movement as well.

By and large, however, the perspective Jones brought to Freud's life and its many controversies remained that of Freud himself. Jones fulfilled his central task as an official biographer, settling hosts of factual matters and enlarging on Freud's own conception of his accomplishments. As with other notable authorized biographies, much of what future historians will ever know about Freud has been supplied by Jones's documentation.

Talking about Freud within his own categories is one way of beginning to come to terms with him; an effective approach to evaluating a great thinker is to work at first within his own framework. Much of my own understanding also derives from Freud's work, and it is a tribute to the power of his mind that even without uncritical intentions it is so hard to think about the early days of psychoanalysis in concepts other than his own. Yet the greater any writer, the more diverse are the possible interpretations of his work; and a man's own view of his life is bound to be, at the very least, limited.

In order to get a fresh perspective on what had already appeared in books, I set out in the fall of 1964 to interview and meet as many of Freud's patients and pupils as I could find. I did not begin with the aim of correcting any partisanship in Jones; on the contrary, I was uncertain about comprehending Freud because, as an outsider to those events long past, I feared I might be unappreciative of nuances surrounding the written accounts of Freud's world. By coming in contact with as many of the early analysts as I could find, I hoped to understand the human context in which Freud's ideas first arose and were disseminated.

From 1964 to 1967 I managed to interview over seventy people who knew Freud personally, in addition to another forty or so who either were professionally interested in the history of psychoanalysis or had themselves participated in the early psychoanalytic movement. Eventually I succeeded in meeting twenty-five of Freud's analytic patients, his surviving sister-in-law, two daughters-in-law, as well as three of his children. Unfortunately more than forty-three of these people have already died. The names of all of those who granted me interviews are listed in the Appendix, but I want to record here my indebtedness for their patience, hospitality, and stimulation, even though few among them can be expected to be in agreement with many of my interpretations.

My travels in search of Freud's patients and pupils completed my apprenticeship in psychoanalytic thinking. I had earlier, in 1963, begun a book on the moral and philosophical implications of Freud's ideas (later published as *Freud: Political and Social Thought*[2]). As a political theorist interested in the history of ideas, I felt that Freud's revolutionary work had not yet become part of the common discourse of my professional colleagues. All the while I pursued my interviewing and continued my reading, the future uses to which modern psychology could be put in understanding political and social life were very much on my mind.

Gaining access to Ernest Jones's papers in the summer of 1965 represented a crucial stage of my work. Jones had died shortly after seeing the final volume of his biography published (and before completing his own autobiography). No one had had the foresight to sift through (or censor) all the raw material which had gone to make up his biography. The psychoanalyst in charge of the Jones archives at the London Institute of Psychoanalysis was quite casual with me about these papers, which he himself had not gone through. These archives turned out to be a fascinating storehouse of informal letters and memoranda. Dozens of original Freud letters were scattered about, unreturned to the Freud family until I put them together.[3]

The Jones archives helped not only my first book, but also my *Brother Animal: The Story of Freud and Tausk.*[4] Preconceived ideas, I came to believe, obstruct almost everyone's vision of the history of psychoanalysis. With Victor Tausk, a neglected but important figure, I thought it might be easier to persuade people to reconsider their view of Freud. Since the Freud-Tausk story seemed to me a moving tale in its own right, I decided to publish it separately, apart from the present full-scale study of Freud and his circle; in order to avoid repeating myself, I necessarily have had to exclude many details of *Brother Animal* from this present book.

The following account of Freud and his world pays as much attention to the human dramas involved as it does to the theories that the participants developed. I have not attempted a thorough examination of all the ideas Freud's dissenting pupils later elaborated, but have discussed only those of their concepts which bear directly on an effort to understand their relationship to their former master. Although there has recently been a good deal of convergence among all schools of depth psychology, at the time of their origins theoretical differences stirred passions of the deepest sort. Without some knowledge of the self-understanding and the personalities of the early analysts one cannot fully appreciate their ideas and what their intellectual commitments meant to them. It was not possible for me to discuss every member of Freud's circle, nor all those who may have learned from an encounter with Freud; but I have tried to examine the lives and work of the most important people in Freud's career.

To the hospitals, clinics, and professional associations that have invited me to speak about Freud, I am very grateful. Each time I have given a talk, I have had to ask myself: "Now, for those who do not really know Freud as a man, what needs to be said to describe him?" Freud had many facets to him: the bold adventurer, a revolutionary in psychology; the cautious man of science evolving his technique; the social philosopher, a modern prophet; the teacher and hard-working therapist; the leader of a growing movement; the bourgeois gentleman with many prejudices of his day; the constant cigar smoker; the witty conversationalist, a master story-teller of Jewish jokes; and also a demonic side, for Freud could sometimes be as irrational as he could be superlatively rationalistic. I am indebted for what I learned from the give-and-take at the Beth Israel Hospital in Boston, the Boston State Hospital, the Canadian Psychoanalytic Association (Ontario), the University of Cincinnati Medical School, the Clarke Institute of Psychiatry in Toronto, the Harvard University Health Service, the Massachusetts Mental Health Center, McLean Hospital in Belmont, Massachusetts, the Department of Psychiatry of McMaster University, the National Institute of Mental Health, the New England Medical Center, Roosevelt Hospital in New York, St. Michael's Hospital in Toronto, and the Washington Psychoanalytic Society.

For financial assistance, I am grateful to the Foundations' Fund for Research in Psychiatry, the Faculty Research Grants Committee of the Social Science Research Council, the National Institute of Mental Health, the Boston Psychoanalytic Society, the Foundation for Psychoanalytic Research, and Harvard University's Canady and Milton Funds.

For the editing of this book I am, once again, fortunate in having had the talent of my wife, Deborah Heller Roazen. My editor, Ashbel Green, has been unfailingly helpful in his assistance.

INTRODUCTION:
Meeting Freud's Patients
and Pupils

WHAT WAS FREUD really like? This was a central question I set out to answer when I began to interview those of his patients and pupils who were still alive. It was clear to me that these witnesses of that revolution in the history of ideas would not have many more years to live. Each profession has its oral traditions, stories and ways of thinking about the past which are never included in the textbooks that introduce students to a field; sharing in these teachings and sayings forms a part of every psychoanalyst's identity.

In the tradition of Freud's own psychological system of thought, I talked with his surviving followers, listening to what they had to relate of their experiences. One very elderly analyst brushed aside my youthful hopes of understanding the early days of psychoanalysis: "How can you write about it? You weren't there!" All who participated in this historical event shared an understandable degree of self-congratulation. Yet these disciples, I soon came to believe, had not begun to ask some of the most elementary questions about Freud or their own involvement in his movement.

Many obvious queries seemed strange to those who had lived through the development of psychoanalysis. It was difficult for them to assess the validity and emphasis of what had already been published, since they came to these books with minds already well stocked with their own recollections. If, for example, Jones neglected a particular figure in his biography, this might not be immediately apparent to someone who took that person's place for granted.

An outsider's advantage in such interviews may be illustrated by what happens in modern psychotherapeutic treatment. An observer gains certain insights by his lack of involvement in the material. What to a participant may seem trivial, can, to an outsider, point to important but unexpressed aspects of the matter.

Over the course of about two years, I tried to meet all the living members of the early psychoanalytic movement and some of Freud's immediate family. Usually I spent a few hours with each person, discussing his or her association with Freud. One analyst, however, gave me almost two hundred hours of her time, and in a few other cases I received over twenty hours. Although at times I was able to see an individual only once, I could usually arrange new visits to expand or correct my impressions. Sometimes an exchange of letters would be sufficient, and in a few cases a lengthy correspondence on Freud ensued. Throughout I continually tried to cross-check the information I gathered. (These people could be mistaken about certain facts, such as dates and sequences of events; an unusual number of elderly analysts, for example, thought Freud's cancer had preceded his theory of the death instinct.) In general, what I gained from one interview I would try to use in the next.

My interviews were as open-ended as possible, yet not without structure. Since no one had ever talked to all these people with the same aims in mind, I felt unsure at the beginning about the questions to ask.[1] Although as time went on I grew more confident about what I should inquire, my queries were always designed as much to keep the flow of memories continuing as to elicit responses to specific questions. When my informant's interest or energy began to flag, a question or two might stimulate his thoughts once more.

The interviews varied greatly in how much they taught me. After a while I learned enough to more or less standardize my questions. Before then, I was still so much in the process of gaining new insights that my questions were constantly changing; therefore they differed considerably between the very early period of my interviewing and the end of the first year or so of my work.

In the beginning of the second year my questions were stabilized enough so that I can give an illustration here of the kind of notesheet I used. The woman I interviewed was an American physician, then about seventy years old (now deceased), living in New York City. She had been in analysis with both C. G. Jung (in 1925) and Freud (in 1930), which made her a particularly interesting person to meet. She had formerly practiced analysis in Boston but had been retired for some years when I saw her. Unlike most of her European contemporaries, she had no photographs, etchings, or other mementos of Freud around her apartment.

This rough background may help to explain some of my questions. In addition to these I shall include much-abbreviated examples of her responses, and sometimes my own commentary on them, to make the encounter seem less one-sided and to give a rough idea of how we interacted. I shall not attempt, however, to set down a full account of all her answers throughout the interview.

When had she first come across psychoanalytic ideas? As a student at Johns Hopkins Medical School in 1917. *How was her analysis with Freud arranged?* Through an old friend, already in analysis with Freud. *And how was the analysis with Jung arranged? Did Freud ask her anything about Jung?* Although Jung had spent a good deal of time criticizing Freud in 1925, Freud did not much concern himself with Jung by 1930. The feelings had not died down, but it did not seem a very important issue for Freud. *Did Freud discuss any of the history of psychoanalysis with her? Did he know any psychiatrists from Boston? Who were his favorite pupils when she knew him? Whom did Freud like least?* (This last question had been raised for me by an earlier informant, who found it far easier to answer, and more important, than the previous question.)

Did she know any other patients of Freud's at the time? Or anyone else ever analyzed by Freud? What sort of therapist was he? How was his spoken English? His command of English was very elegant and encompassed all the slang. As for his pronunciation, you would have thought he had lived in England for a time. His speech—like his mind—covered everything; he never lacked a word to express something.

Was he very interested in her? He was so attentive that she might have been his first patient—yet not because of her personally. When she returned to America she would be able to do something for him and his cause; in addition to her practice as an analyst, she performed little jobs like seeing families of former patients of his, collecting money for his publishing house, and making sure that special pupils of his were properly received when they arrived in the United States. Her husband was the nephew of an early supporter of psychoanalysis, and this sort of association was always important to Freud. She herself had an immensely favorable attitude toward Freud; she admired his open-mindedness and willingness to explore and discover new things. (From other sources I later found out that after her analysis Freud had sent enthusiastic letters back to America about her. It should be added that there were many reasons why she and

Freud got on so well together: she was extremely intelligent and intellectual, upright, conscientious, rich and well connected socially; she was also an independent-minded woman, devoted to Freud and his psychoanalysis.)

How much did she pay him? Twenty-five dollars an hour. (His pupils in Vienna would then have been getting about ten dollars an hour from American patients.) *Who helped her more, Jung or Freud, and in what ways?* There could not have been any two people more different than Freud and Jung; at least it would be hard to believe that two people in the same field could be more dissimilar. Freud's analysis definitely helped her. It set her on the track of learning more about herself, and he expected her to take responsibility for everything in her life. *Did she know anything about Victor Tausk? Siegfried Bernfeld? Wilhelm Reich? Herbert Silberer? What did she know about Freud's wife? Or his sister-in-law Minna?* (Freud's relationship with Minna was an obvious subject of inquiry even before the publication of the story of a supposed sexual liaison between Freud and his sister-in-law.) *What did she know about Anna Freud? Or Freud's sisters? Did she think Freud discussed his patients with his wife? Or with anyone else? Who in the family read his books? Did she ever discuss thought-transference or telepathy with him? Or child analysis? Did Freud seem sensitive about priorities? Or about plagiarism? How would he be with psychotics? What sort of a diagnostician was he?*

Did she ever see any signs of neurosis in him? Never, although she looked for them. (Whatever was going on in Freud's soul, he was exceedingly self-controlled and little would have been visible.) *What is the best book on him? What did she think of Jones's books?* Just not the man she knew. *When did she see Freud the angriest? Or the most depressed? Or the happiest? Did he discuss Otto Rank with her? Or Sandor Ferenczi? Was his physical illness apparent? In what ways would she consider Freud's psychological theories outgrowths of his personality? How does psychoanalysis reflect his idiosyncrasies?* It must have been so, it is inevitable, and one would look for signs; yet she never felt any lack of objectivity in him. *What were his relationships with his sons? Did she know how Isidor Sadger and Sandor Rado had their fallings out with Freud? Did she ever treat any of Freud's former patients? With what types of cases would he be best?*

Did his lack of "orthodoxy" in technique help or hurt him as a therapist? In general, Freud talked about everything under the sun—but he analyzed her too. By then it was clear that she was going into psychoanalytic practice when she returned home. He never tried to justify what he did; it all happened naturally. Yet the analysis was conducted in the strictest fashion, there was nothing social about it, nothing was introduced that was not relevant. *Which nationalities did he admire? Has she known emotional symptoms to follow certain cultural patterns?*

How did Freud feel about the Vienna psychoanalytic group? Did he give her any photographs? Did he ever rap on the couch? Did he mention any novels to her? Did he give her any advice about her child? How did he view masturbation? Did he ever discuss politics? Was there a split between his family life and his medical practice? Did she know any of his family friends? Did his Jewishness strike her? Were any children of her friends named after members of his family? What do people mean when they refer to Freud's "intolerance"? On the one hand, Freud would ask her what she thought would last in analysis. He remained his own best critic. But, at the same time, if somebody proposed something destructive to his ideas, he would be considered intolerant. "Today I feel strongly that this is so and this not so"—that was his way.

Was Melanie Klein like Jung and Alfred Adler to Freud? Did she have any letters from him? Did she know of Freud's having analyzed his daughter Anna himself? Yes, how unorthodox can one be! *What was his attitude toward homosexuality? Who was his favorite among his pupils in America? Did he look on psychoanalysis as an empire? Was he money-minded? In what ways was he generous? How did he feel about women having nonmarital sex? Was he discreet? Could she recommend anyone else for me to see? What have I failed to ask?*

It is, of course, difficult to convey the tone of such an interview, not to mention what I learned from it. The questions represent roughly what I came prepared with, and the handful of answers I have selected provide at least a flavor of her responses. But this account necessarily excludes most of the spontaneous give-and-take between us, as we sipped the sherry she graciously served. I was able to pose freely other queries on the basis of the information she supplied. The best kinds of questions were those that came not entirely as a surprise to her and that linked up with what she was already partly familiar with—yet not so well acquainted with as to have a pat answer for. It was ideal for me to watch her mind at work as she tried to think through alternatives. I relied on the list of prepared questions more toward the latter part of the interview as her own material about the past began to dry up.

Perhaps the main purpose of having questions prepared in advance was to keep the interview moving before her patience came to an end. I have chosen this set of questions as an illustration because this interview went approximately according to plan, and I moved from point to point as she seemed to have finished what she had to contribute. Yet even though this list is roughly representative, within a month or so some issues seemed so well settled in my mind that I did not ask about them again. But I can remember looking over this group of questions on several occasions as I prepared for other interviews. As certain subjects became standard topics of conversation I could try to evaluate the slant which each interviewee's character and experience imposed on his perspective.

In retrospect this particular interview was unusually orderly. My preliminary stage of groping was over and I had begun to concentrate on certain problems which I thought deserved attention and which this person was especially qualified to discuss.

It was not just the literal response to a question that interested me, but also her tone of voice, gestures, and the accompanying expression in her eyes. (I remember how telling was the response, her eyes dancing in her head, of an analyst who exclaimed of Freud: "Oh, how he could hate!") I wanted facts, but above all understanding. Therefore every shade of free association was my aim. If I had wanted an exact verbal reproduction of the interview, a tape recording would have been necessary. But since I was dealing with fairly intimate human material, a tape recorder might have stiffened the interviewee and made me defensive. (Instead of using a tape recorder,[2] my practice was to jot down notes and then reconstruct the interview afterwards. But for many people, and for certain topics, even note taking was not possible, and it was only immediately after an interview that I was able to write down the conversations.)

Any scholar, no matter how unbiased, must evaluate in order to know what is worth reporting. So my questions were based on what I had learned up to then and were designed to help my future research. And for this purpose every nuance of expression, every pause or laugh, registered in my mind as part of an answer. I wanted to learn all I could in a given space of time, in this case about three hours of an afternoon.

As my interviews proceeded I began to understand Freud, and in a way that is not possible by merely reading his books. After a period of extended interviews I found myself responding to reported comments of his by remarking to myself: "He would have said that." Gradually I was able to think of Freud as a person.

Even if I were now to produce the complete record I have kept of this interview, it would be far less lively than I remember it. What I

Freud in the Tatra mountains in 1917

learned from that cooperative lady in one afternoon was certainly important. But it was most valuable to me in terms of my reaction to her total personality and how that enabled me to integrate her information with what I was told in my other interviews. (To illustrate further my way of proceeding, after the interview I got in touch with her once again, to settle an uncertainty in my mind and to thank her. She answered my inquiry, and mentioned that she had written to an old friend of hers to recommend that she cooperate with me.)

At the outset I did not expect to be able to secure the cooperation of all the people who eventually saw me. The analysts among them were well known for being extraordinarily defensive toward outsiders. Any movement looks monolithic at a distance, but from the inside all the stresses and strains, contrasting viewpoints and rival perspectives, can readily be seen. Still, those who participated in the early battles for Freud and psychoanalysis were bound to share a lingering insecurity about whether his place in history had been finally established, and to retain a group cohesiveness which would work powerfully against anyone's betraying the cause. (Former patients and retired analysts were more or less exempt from these restraints—as well from the pressures of economic self-interest, for they had no income from psychoanalysis that otherwise might have been jeopardized by speaking their minds.)

Nevertheless, these people had motives for speaking freely with me. Many of them, sometimes explicitly, felt that they were repaying a debt of gratitude to Freud. It took little effort to convince them that their memories were valuable historical sources. Furthermore, it is only human to feel that one's importance is being appreciated. It would be understandable if many cooperated because it flattered their legitimate vanity to do so.

Speaking with me also gave these people an opportunity to express some of their ambivalent feelings, conscious as well as unconscious, about their connection with Freud. To an outsider they could vent grievances which years of piety had kept in check. Freud, as he later admitted, had been reluctant to analyze the negative reactions of his earlier patients.[3] To flatter Freud would have been, at any date, impossible. Confident of his stature in intellectual history, he would have interpreted the utmost devotion and appreciation in a follower as justified by the reality of his greatness.

Freud's attitude was understandable. As a misunderstood and unappreciated genius, and a hard-working therapist, he felt entitled to the undivided approval of his patients. There was also an antagonistic side of his pupils' relationship with him, however, which built up and turned against the outside world; the enemy became the public which for so long inadequately appreciated Freud's contributions. What Freud failed to analyze was displaced onto others, and these uninterpreted emotions grew to tremendous, frightening proportions. Here one can find a source of his pupils' protectiveness about his private life: once they had transformed their hostilities toward Freud into resentments against the external world, thereby denying their own ambivalent feelings, it was easy to overestimate the readiness of outsiders to seize on any of Freud's human weaknesses.

Talking with me was for some a license to express, if only in oblique ways, the resentful feelings they may have had about their involvement with the master and his circle. It took me some time to realize this. I began my research so much in awe of Freud that I did not recognize that some of his pupils might want me to return so that we could speak further. For a time their reverence for Freud only increased my own inhibitions. Yet as soon as I was given some handles for discussing the less constructive sides of their ties to Freud, I could help my informants to become less reticent; at the same time my own shyness in probing about him began to dissipate and I could pursue a more objective course.

They recognized immediately that they would be talking with someone who had profound respect for Freud's significance. His pupils could make critical comments about Freud and his psychoanalysis because they felt I fully appreciated his genius and therefore would be unlikely to misunderstand them. My admiration for Freud extended to them, and they must have sensed my respect for their lives and work.

At times I worried about pushing these people so far into their pasts. But one of the most endearing aspects of their motivation in helping me was their sense that they were contributing to history. If recounting these distant events could help instruct a young man, and through him those who had had no personal contact with Freud, then their expense of time and effort seemed worthwhile. Most of them were quite elderly and many had already partially retired; almost all were in their seventies and eighties.

As social events these interviews were relatively uninhibited. In order to establish the extent of my knowledge, and skip over various formulas for talking about Freud, I often interposed early in an interview some new piece of information that I had recently learned from someone else. The more Freud's followers took me into their confidence, the easier it was to ensure that a future interview would be informative. I was willing to learn whatever they had to teach, without the restrictions that would have come from having participated in past feuds.

Although a few interviews were superficial, on the whole they were remarkably intense exchanges. For myself, it was an exciting intellectual adventure. For my subjects, the issues raised had real meaning. These interviews touched them. Two people, for example, afterward mentioned that they had been unable to sleep the night after I had seen them. And yet in both cases they seemed not to resent what I had stirred up in them. The trailing-off of my interviewing was signaled by a tendency to a reversal of our roles; the information and interpretations that I brought began to teach my interviewees as much as I was learning in return.

The interviews also had their strains. First of all, I began without a clear idea of what I would eventually do with what I found out. If I had known the crucial questions at the outset, there would have been little point in undertaking the work at all. In scholarship as in life, knowing the right questions is always the hardest problem. It was burdensome, however, to be as much at sea as I was at the beginning, and it added to the problems that were inherent in my research.

My interview subjects were even less sure about what ought to be of interest. Many of them were bent on protecting some bit of personal data, certain private experiences of trivial concern to a historian. But it was often difficult to clear up the confusion about what I was after, since I myself was more than a little unsure. Inevitably I came across scandal; but although it was often important for me to be aware of some explosive material, it is not necessary to publish various human calamities and disasters.

Frequently what one person would not wish to discuss at all, another would bring up quite freely. As my interviewing progressed I acquired a feel for who would know something about a particular matter. As my skill increased, even within a given interview I could steer the conversation in a different direction in order to reach a productive area. What an individual may refuse to discuss in one context he can be encouraged to talk about in another.

Although each interview posed special problems, some general conclusions can be drawn about the difficulties I encountered. For certain purposes the mavericks tended to be the best sources of information, and this would be in accord with a principle well known in sociological or anthropological field work. Those who feel they have been given a raw deal are usually willing to talk about subjects others would consider indiscreet, and to offer interpretations which the more loyal might consider seditious. However, today's malcontents may also have been on the outside in the past, and their perspective may be at the expense of intimate familiarity.

The less a person really knew about Freud and his circle, the more easily he could organize his thoughts for the interviewer. One of my difficulties was the readiness of individuals to talk away incessantly. At the start of an interview I had to give a cue as to how much I already knew, lest too much time be wasted. Here it was often the odd or casual fact which suggested that I was someone they would consider worth talking to, and which encouraged them to speak from their own experience instead of from whatever the conventional wisdom might ordain.

My demands were the greatest on those who knew the most about the history of psychoanalysis. It was hardest for them to objectify their experiences for an outsider, to make some sense out of the welter of their personal recollections. They found it difficult to accept simple explanations of past events, and were forced to rethink their own knowledge in the light of what I brought to them. On some topics it was hard for them to review their ideas; almost without exception they were credulous about distant aspects of the history of psychoanalysis, while exact and unblinkered about what they themselves experienced. Most of them were more adaptable in their private thoughts than one would expect from their public commitments. Not surprisingly, the better they knew Freud personally, the more open they were to new suggestions of possible explanations.

My interviewing strategy consumed an enormous amount of time. The main principle was: The greater my exposure to these people, the more valuable the insights that would eventually emerge. I had to travel widely, and it could be a weird experience to go several thousand miles only to resume with one person the same discussion I had just left off with another. Freud had an almost hypnotic effect on his patients and pupils; some of them, living far apart, would discuss the same issue in exactly the same words, and one knew they were using Freud's own phrases. For all of them my work put a strain on their hospitality. Although their receptivity to my questions varied, and I could be bolder with some than with others, on the whole they were remarkably open, cooperative, and generous. Their intelligence and emotional range differed, but the interviews were almost without exception a pleasure to conduct. Nevertheless, one has to concede that the Viennese in particular are expert at using charm while remaining quite distant.

The most important watershed I found among those who knew Freud personally came at 1923—the year he contracted the cancer which harrowed the last sixteen years of his life and gradually forced him to withdraw from the world. Those who met Freud after his illness saw markedly less of him than those who had known him earlier, and after his sickness Freud was in many ways a different man. Yet psychoanalysts who were heads of the movement in their countries, or played a strategic role in a psychiatric center, or were accepted for personal analysis with Freud— even when they appeared on the scene relatively late—were still likely to be excellent sources of information.

To those who knew Freud, as intimately as any of them could enter into the life and mind of this reserved man, many of my preoccupations were bound to seem questionable. Life has its trivial chatter whose distortions are justifiably suspect. With Freud, however, as with any important historical subject, our standards of relevance must be broad. (Freud himself once complained that a piece of oral information about Dostoevsky had been withheld: "Biographers and scientific research workers cannot feel grateful," he wrote, "for this discretion."[4]) Knowing how much has been deliberately omitted from the written record about Freud, and how even more could not have been put into words by those who lived through these events, I had to conclude that undue respect for published evidence would be misplaced.

I also had to be on guard against being misled by the vagaries of human memory about the past. But as long as it was possible for me to double-check the inevitably selective memories of my informants, I could absorb the nuances of contact with those who had had direct communication with Freud. They could tell much that was fresh about the periods in which they were personally involved. Such research can be somewhat wayward and is subject to eccentricities. Yet the alternative would be to declare the history of psychoanalysis "respectable" only after no one is left alive who can reliably contradict anything.

Work such as mine can threaten privacy. Nevertheless, a few people discussed readily the sexual symptoms that had disturbed them before their analyses with Freud, and many people talked freely about the kinds of issues that came up in their treatment with Freud. I did not set out in search of secrets about the early analysts. I aimed to find out what was not in the books—either the details which no one had taken the trouble to nail down or anything that would have been so much taken for granted as not to have been considered worth recording. Somehow, though, the search for the unspoken meshes with the quest for the consciously withheld. It soon became apparent that much information had been left out of the books because some people did not want it there.

I did fail to see a few of Freud's students; for one reason or another their schedules could not be fitted to my own. Among those willing to see me,

in only one instance did I run into an absolute stone wall. This interview
with an old Viennese analyst went disastrously. He was so pious as to have
a fresh bouquet of flowers before an etching of Freud in his waiting room.
I considered my opening question as harmless as possible: "When did you
join the Vienna Society?" He replied that it was none of my business and
he would not tell me. The rest of the interview was about as productive.
"You are not going to get our secrets!" he exclaimed at one point. It
seemed to me striking that, although he carried on in this way, he had
nonetheless agreed to see me. But thanks to my persistence and the intervention of another interviewee who was an old friend of his, he saw me
once again. And this time I succeeded in obtaining a few answers to some
pressing questions. Although my contact with this man was exceptional,
a certain air of uneasiness did sometimes hang over my interviews, which
might be summarized by the feeling on their part: "What have you
learned?"

Perhaps the most valuable result of my interviews was simply getting
to know these people. For me, being acquainted with those who were
part of history gave plausibility and human meaning to published accounts.
Contact with them provided models in my mind for understanding what
had happened in the past. Gradually a rounded sense of reality replaced
what had seemed so flat in the books.

Their sense of history, and what this interviewing could mean to me,
spanned a wide range of sophistication. Some considered everything within
their personal knowledge "private" material which did not belong in
books. While almost everyone used the stop sign "personal" when we
approached what he wanted to omit, some gentle and kindly souls were intent on putting the best face on everything. They were balanced, however,
by the nastier types who did not have a good word to say about anyone.

Many were more ignorant of the published literature than one might
have naïvely expected: one had only read a few pages of Jones's biography,
others just one of his three volumes. On the other hand, the woman whose
interview I have partially described was so industrious as to read a book
she expected me to ask about. Some were aware that all I could count on
from them was their own version of what had happened. For others, distance in time and changes in psychiatric thinking often gave a measure of
objectivity to their accounts of the past. As one analyst put it, she was
looking at her past through two windows: one, when she was involved
with Freud's circle, and the other, now that she was away from it all. In
almost every instance, though, however enlightened their sense of histori-
ography, rapport between us was possible simply on the basis of what the
history of psychoanalysis amounted to.

When Freud set out in the 1890's to describe the role of repressed feelings and especially suppressed sexuality in the origin of neurosis, he felt he was reporting nothing essentially new. When one of his teacher's maxims showed that the older man already knew about the role of sexual frustration, Freud thought: "Well, but if he knows that, why does he never say so?"[5] Freud's commitment to science implied that all significant knowledge should be made available and used. A great deal has been known among Freud's pupils about the inadequacies as well as the strengths of his approach; yet much of this information has not been communicated to the general public. Freud has become such a hero that many do not want to entertain any discussion of the human, personal sources of his contribution to history. Yet Freud himself was a revolutionary in the world of ideas, an inveterate foe of lies and hypocrisy. And it was in that spirit that I tried to proceed with my work.

In publishing as much as possible of the material about Freud and his circle that I collected, I have tried not to burden my narrative with too many interpretations. I would hope that with the information my research uncovered others might be stimulated to think through basic issues anew, and even to arrive at conclusions different from my own. I have aimed not to find the "secret" of Freud's genius, but rather to tell the story of his relation to his followers. We are all Freud's pupils. By abandoning our unrealistic versions of the past we can be more confident in our ability to live in the present.

FREUD AND HIS FOLLOWERS

I

THE ORAL
TRADITION IN
PSYCHOANALYSIS

1. The Legend of Freud

SIGMUND FREUD, unquestionably one of the greatest psychologists of history, has revolutionized how we think about ourselves. His ideas have permeated our world in so many ways, both obvious and subtle, that to acknowledge his importance hardly requires a declaration of faith. His impact on the United States in particular, where the general public has for the last few decades been raising its children according to Dr. Spock's manuals, has been enormous.

Freud's work is of course still being debated. But whereas the critiques of his theories are personalized and exactly labeled, the acceptance of various parts of his system of thought is so widespread as to be almost anonymous.[1] He discovered for science the meaningfulness of dream life and thereby exposed the mechanisms by which we habitually deceive ourselves. Through a series of concepts about our unconscious life, such as transference, infantile sexuality, aggression, defense, identification, regression, and by means of the technique of free association, Freud transformed our image of man. Even if we estimate his significance at its most conservative, anyone whose mistakes have taken this long to correct remains a dominant figure in intellectual history.

Few would dispute that psychoanalysis has been enormously successful in a worldly sense. In America psychoanalysts have been leaders of the psychiatric profession, charging the highest fees and attracting the most ambitious therapists to their fold. But the men and women who have been concerned with the inner life of psychoanalysis, not just with its triumphs in popular folklore and medical psychiatry, have known a variety of disappointments. So many creative people were involved in the beginnings of psychoanalysis as a movement, and their aims were so high, that some disenchantment was inevitable.

Psychoanalysis began with the bold hope of freeing us from our mental conflicts. Its history, however, records a series of retreats in its claims for therapeutic efficacy. Originally Freud proposed to apply depth psychology to all the human sciences. But by now psychoanalysts are largely content to restrict their profession to a medical specialty. Whereas Freud and his immediate followers were radical in their expectations and their promises, and considered themselves at odds with conventional society, success has now bred a very different group of psychoanalysts.

In old Vienna psychoanalysts had an uncertain income and little social prestige. In fact, a few of Freud's students paid a heavy price, in terms of their academic psychiatric careers, for their new beliefs. But they had a pride, which came from their own daring assessment of the significance of the master's teachings. In America, however, where the majority of psychoanalysts now live, the psychoanalytic profession automatically places its practitioners financially and socially in the upper middle class. Not surprisingly, the American adherents of psychoanalysis have tended to be conservative in their professional thinking and lacking in the daring which inspired their forefathers.

It is tempting to look back to those early days as a heroic era. Even discounting the possibility of romanticizing the past, psychoanalysis as a field is now incapable of attracting people as original and, it should be said, as undisciplined as those who joined it half a century ago. One need only look through the old membership lists of the Vienna and the Berlin psychoanalytic groups to gain an impression of how high their caliber must have been.* When Hitler came to power, the Continental analysts began to flee to safety, most of them eventually settling in America. Whereas in Europe they had been members of an underground movement, outcasts from academic psychiatry and university appointments, in America they rapidly rose to positions of psychiatric power and intellectual esteem.

The way had been well prepared in the United States for the coming of the European analysts; Freud's ideas were already becoming accepted in both psychiatric and lay thinking. The Continentals' superior conceptual skills and their special therapeutic experience, combined with their deep sense of dedication to a common cause, placed them in the forefront of American psychiatry. Within the psychiatric world it was as if Napoleon's marshals had been sent to govern in various outposts across the country.

---

* For example, the membership list in the early 1930's of the Vienna Society included August Aichhorn, Lou Andreas-Salomé, Edward Bibring, Helene Deutsch, Erik Erikson, Paul Federn, Anna Freud, Heinz Hartmann, Ernst Kris, Herman Nunberg, Wilhelm Reich, Theodor Reik, and Paul Schilder. Around 1930 the Berlin Society had Franz Alexander, Otto Fenichel, Erich Fromm, Frieda Fromm-Reichmann, Georg Groddeck, Karen Horney, Melanie Klein, Sandor Rado, Hanns Sachs, and René Spitz.

Psychoanalysts who in Vienna or Berlin had been relatively undistinguished became leaders of hospital psychiatric departments in America. Writers who had once been on the margins of the psychoanalytic community found a responsive American audience for their work. Within the psychoanalytic training centers themselves, the Europeans joined with American analysts who had earlier gone to Europe to study with them. American psychiatrists who had formerly been reluctant to embark on psychoanalytic training now were eager to learn from this small band of Freud's followers.

Many factors were responsible for the success of psychoanalysis in America. Certain well-known American character traits—optimism and the belief in individualism, for example—must have contributed to the acceptance of a therapy founded on the hope that it is possible for people to change themselves by their own efforts. A child-centered culture responded enthusiastically to the notion that infantile patterns affect adult behavior and to the tendency to idealize childlike spontaneity in the face of civilization's restraints. America's affluence and leisure, and lack of a coherent national culture, must also have helped psychoanalysis; a poorer society, or one with more rigidly institutionalized centers of learning, would have been less receptive to a new influence such as Freud's. And to the extent that America is a nation of immigrants, cut off from foreign roots, each American must construct an individual history to make up for the uncertainty of his collective past. Finally, Americans, unlike the French or the Swiss, lacked a thriving psychiatric tradition of their own. And it should go without saying that the genuine abilities of these students of Freud also helped ensure their immense success.

Since Freud's pupils, who helped spread the teachings that were to alter world opinion about human psychology, had such a powerful impact on twentieth-century cultural life and modern psychiatry, it becomes the more interesting to try to understand what being close to the master meant to them. Looking back at other historical instances of teacher-pupil relationships, it is difficult to extract any pattern that applies to all. In recent years Ludwig Wittgenstein had his group of devoted followers. Earlier Karl Marx and Jeremy Bentham had their circles of students; in ancient times Plato and Aristotle were surrounded by disciples.* Even in today's academic life we find that an established teacher tends to draw a following. The relationship between teacher and pupil, the ways in which the latter

---

* Speaking of Freud's books, Fritz Wittels wrote that "we fully understood their significance, and we were as proud of ourselves as the pupils of Aristotle in the days before that philosopher's works had become widely known."[2]

learns and grows, as well as the frustration and stifling of talent—none of these are so well known or agreed upon as to provide easy formulas for understanding Freud and his pupils.

Freud was an inspiring teacher, on the model of a Greek philosopher or a great rabbi. His writings, his lectures, and his therapy, added to the magnetism and force of his personality, attracted and retained loyal followers, not only in his own lifetime but today as well, over thirty years after his death. And although historical parallels to the relationship between Freud and his students cannot exactly illuminate what was, after all, a unique experience, they do remind us that discipleship, a normal part of the learning process, has occurred repeatedly in times of creativity.

Freud's relation to his pupils and his own experience as a student were obviously important to him, for he discussed them repeatedly. In his articles and books about the development of psychoanalysis, Freud recounted how he made his discoveries and identified the teachers who were crucial to his work. And he told and retold the tale of his defecting students, those who proved unworthy allies and supporters.

Freud got his own version of these struggles into the history books before it seemed particularly important to anyone else. He knew the power of legend. Even to patients who came to him for therapy, not to mention those who undertook training, Freud recounted the saga of the origins and struggles of his early ideas.[3] If Freud became a living legend in his lifetime, he himself had contributed to the stories that grew up around him.

At the same time, Freud strove to distinguish between his own personality and the science he had discovered. He wrote and spoke about his early career, not for the sake of petty self-glorification, but for the larger purpose of establishing the practice of psychoanalysis in the world. Freud rightly believed that psychoanalytic concepts had to be understood in the context of their historical development. He wanted people to remember the errors of his "deviating" pupils, lest their mistakes be repeated. But mythologizing and legend weaving can be unfair and misleading. Freud's difficulties were not just scientific but also temperamental. Although he presented it as the relentless march of science, the history of his ideas was in fact colored by a highly personal component.

In a sense Freud was frank about the origin of his concepts in his own personal experience. *The Interpretation of Dreams* is one of the great autobiographical studies in the history of mankind; in it Freud drew freely on his inner life in an effort to construct a psychological system relevant for all of us. Yet at the same time he tried to draw a clear line between his work and his personality. Psychoanalysis was his own creation; he wanted, however, to maintain that his early struggles were not personal

biography but the history of a new science. So he strove to set limits to biographical speculation about himself. "It seems to me," he wrote in a letter in 1923, "that the public has no concern with my personality, and can learn nothing from an account of it. . . ."[4] By 1935, four years before his death, he wrote bitterly about intrusions into his personal life:

> The public has no claim to learn any more of my personal affairs. . . .
> I have . . . been more open and frank in some of my writings . . .
> than people usually are who describe their lives for their contem-
> poraries or for posterity. I have had small thanks for it, and from my
> experience I cannot recommend anyone to follow my example.[5]

There have been few fields in which one mind has loomed larger, and even fewer where the personal characteristics of the founder played a more critical role. It should not have been surprising, therefore, that one of Freud's followers undertook to write an official biography of him. Ernest Jones had been seeking this job for some years.[6] The Freud family's reluctance to act against their father's known aversion to a biography was eventually overcome by the accumulation of unauthorized studies which drew portraits that his followers considered misleading.[7] Whatever Freud's own injunctions against a biography of himself, he taught us to respect the past because of the control it can exert over the future. Cultures live by myths about their histories, and Freud understood man's need to respond to experience in terms of established symbols. So Jones, with the full cooperation of the Freud family, sought to wield the power of historical reconstruction.

No one who studies Freud's life or the history of psychoanalysis can fail to acknowledge how much Jones accomplished, part of it in spite of failing health. His books succeeded in presenting an enduringly fascinating account of Freud's life and struggles. Jones's achievement can be instructive for history writing in general. Like other official biographers, he saw parts of Freud's correspondence that will not be released (for reasons of tact as well as censorship) for decades to come. Jones filled the biography with a wealth of valuable details. He was so thorough as to inhibit all others who write afterward. One measure of the stature of a biography may be the length of time it takes to go around it, or the amount of energy one must summon to surmount its interpretations.

Freud in his middle years

Yet Jones's work had its limitations. Despite what a reader of the biography might be led to think, Jones's own relation to Freud was relatively distant. Jones was first of all a Gentile, and Freud could be suspicious of non-Jews. (He could also overvalue their support, which is the other side of the coin.) Furthermore, Jones was in London and therefore an outsider to events in Vienna. He was close to Freud, though, in the politics of the psychoanalytic movement. But by and large Jones lacked the intuitive psychological talent of those whom Freud dearly loved and cherished for the sake of the future of psychoanalysis. Among the group of six chosen by Freud around World War I to advance the cause of psychoanalysis (Jones, Sandor Ferenczi, Otto Rank, Karl Abraham, Hanns Sachs, and Max Eitingon), Jones would not rank high in terms of the originality of his psychoanalytic contributions. His special talent lay in popularizing Freud's ideas and in helping the movement as an organization.

History gets written by accident. Jones lived the longest of those six men, and as a survivor had the last word. His pen was tireless, and his capacity to hate considerable. But his approach to Freud's life was too dogmatic to encompass the full complexities of a man like Freud. As Jones maintained somewhat righteously, "I tried to present as impartially as possible both strong and weak features in his own personality as well as of the people he had most to do with. Since there have been many criticisms of Freud's relationship to other people this was a topic where nothing but the full truth, good or bad, could justify my task."[8] Jones was tempted by the illusion that he—or anyone—could write the definitive version of Freud's life. By publishing large extracts from Freud's letters, Jones hoped to block any attempts to publish the Freud correspondence in full.[9]

Curiously enough, Jones's biography is not very sophisticated psychologically. For example, despite all the evidence for supposing that, in varying degrees, everyone lacks perspective in self-understanding, Jones accepted wholeheartedly Freud's own account of his childhood and his relation to his parents. And Jones always looked at Freud's struggles with his students from the master's own point of view; Jones ignored, in other words, the perspective of the pupils who were struggling to fulfill themselves. Throughout Jones wrote with a set of unconscious taboos. On any other man's life he would have been freer to use the insights that Freud bequeathed to us. (Of what other human being would Jones have proclaimed that at the age of forty-five he had attained "complete maturity,"[10] whatever that might mean?)

Jones did point out various neurotic trends in Freud's life, many of which had been unknown before; the material about Freud now embraces about the most penetrating and precise data on any one person that has ever been amassed.[11] But whatever Jones found of neurosis he isolated from Freud's relationships with other people. For example, Jones never considered Freud's human frailties as important as the unresolved emotional problems of his students. Others in Freud's circle shared Jones's blinders. They needed to see Freud as the master of the conflicts that could interfere with their own lives.

One might think that Freud's pupils must have already written virtually everything that could be said about the early days of psychoanalysis. And it is true that a flood of material about the history of psychoanalysis has appeared. Yet relatively few of Freud's students wrote of their association with him. In studying history it is wise to remember who wrote and who chose to remain silent.

Those who wrote about Freud generally did so when they were in a marginal position or at some distance from the master himself. A separation of time or space appeared to help, as did "defection" from the ranks of Freud's psychoanalysis. Those who remained silent were sometimes the ones who had stayed closest to Freud. Not surprisingly, they found it especially difficult to write about the deeply felt experiences they had lived through. Freud had become so much a part of their lives, and that portion so sacred, that to try to objectify the emotionally charged relationship on paper might have frozen the life out of the memories themselves.

Other obstacles kept his students from writing about Freud as a person. To some degree loyalty to Freud meant respecting his wish for privacy. And in order to retain the esteem of their colleagues, analysts needed to be careful in exploiting their association with Freud. His pupils would certainly try to suppress any interpretations they considered objectionable. More basically perhaps, potential authors were restrained by the extent to which their own private lives would have to be exposed. Throughout the history of psychoanalysis the scientific and the personal so intermingle that it is difficult to talk about the one without entering into a discussion of the other.

Everyone who has written about Freud since his death, and who was in good standing within the psychoanalytic movement, has had to compose with his youngest daughter, Anna, in mind. She looked over Jones's books on her father line by line; without her help and cooperation his work could not have gone forward. But families of great men have often hoped that they could have it both ways: their hero deserves his place in history and yet they fully expect to be able to hold him within the family confines. It invariably turns out, however, that it is impossible to establish a man in history without compromising his privacy.

Freud himself was under no illusions on this point. When Arnold

Zweig suggested that he become Freud's biographer (which would inevitably entail reopening the discussion of some of the famous public squabbles in Freud's career), Freud was aroused to reply in horror:

You who have so many more attractive and important things to do, who can appoint kings and survey the brutal folly of mankind from the height of a watch tower! No, I am far too fond of you to allow such a thing to happen. Anyone turning biographer commits himself to lies, to concealment, to hypocrisy, to flattery, and even to hiding his own lack of understanding, for biographical truth is not to be had, and even if it were it couldn't be used. Truth is unobtainable; humanity does not deserve it, and incidentally, wasn't our Prince Hamlet right when he asked whether anyone would escape a whipping if he got what he deserved?[12]

Freud not only predicted what would become of biographical studies about himself, but also understood how partisan history can be. As he once wrote about the beginnings of a group's consciousness,

It was inevitable that this early history should have been an expression of present beliefs and wishes rather than a true picture of the past; for many things had been dropped from . . . memory, while others were distorted, and some remains of the past were given a wrong interpretation in order to fit in with contemporary ideas. Moreover, people's motive for writing history was not objective curiosity but a desire to influence their contemporaries, to encourage and inspire them, or to hold a mirror up before them.[13]

In interpreting the written accounts about Freud, one must take into account the reliability and position of the witnesses, the unconscious inhibitions on their thinking, as well as their possibly partisan purposes. In addition, however, Anna Freud has been deliberately (and perhaps understandably) protective of her father; her possessiveness about his manuscripts may reflect a legitimate fear of exploitation, as well as a desire to devote her time to the scientific future of psychoanalysis. James Strachey, however, shared her reverence for her father's memory, and therefore based his invaluable standard edition of Freud's works on the published versions of his writings; with very few exceptions Strachey did not consult the manuscripts in Anna Freud's possession.[14] Other pupils of her father routinely submitted to her copies of their manuscripts before publication; and some papers about her father have been withdrawn in conformity with her wishes.[15] Anna Freud's position in modern psychotherapy, both as a theorist and as a clinician, is by this time firmly established; she is almost certainly the leading child therapist in the world today. Yet her generosity and tact, when they concerned her father, have bordered on historical disingenuousness.

Since Freud's letters in English to Jones were not elegant or wholly grammatical, Anna Freud thought it would be appropriate to correct the most disturbing mistakes.[16] Strachey, however, let out a howl to Jones at her suggestion: if they were to start improving on the old man's works, Strachey said, then he had a number of suggestions of his own to make.[17] There is little way, however, of telling just where her standards of propriety have taken their toll on her father's letters. For example, for the sake of the psychoanalytic movement she agreed with Jones to avoid publishing her father's adverse remarks about America.[18] Such hanky-panky makes it hard not to question Jones's claim to have aimed at the whole truth. Although Jones was capable of being extraordinarily honest in his biography, in the end he could not escape cooperating in the deceptions Freud himself had anticipated.

On the other hand, the Freud family, with Anna at its head, was bold in encouraging, so soon after his death, what has now appeared. Any other great man's family might have been far more defensive against the intrusions of outsiders. Freud himself, for example, had not wanted his intimate correspondence with his friend Wilhelm Fliess to appear, yet the family cooperated in its publication. They even made available his love letters to his future wife for the biography he had scorned. But if they defied their father's wishes they did so with a clouded conscience. The letters to Fliess were bowdlerized; Freud is not even permitted to joke at his own expense.[19] Throughout Freud's published correspondence* it is not always made clear where cuts have been made; deletions, without any marks of omission, have been introduced, and one can discern no consistent principle, such as that of medical discretion.[20]

In the late 1920's Freud collaborated with Ambassador William C. Bullitt on an obviously controversial book about President Woodrow Wilson, and when the manuscript finally surfaced in 1965, the Freud family's first impulse was to have the hitherto unpublished book edited into better shape. When Bullitt rightly rejected any tampering with the text, since one of the authors was dead, loyal followers of Freud thought that the way to show their devotion to the master was to dissociate him from his part in the book. Freud stood for the ideal of honesty. Psychoanalysis as a therapy rests on the conviction that the truth can set men free. Such a defensive attitude toward Freud's works only demonstrates a lack of confidence in his ability to withstand historical scrutiny.

---

* In the recently published volume of the Freud-Jung letters, Freud's correspondence has been presented intact for the first time.

*   *   *

To the extent that Freud deserves to be a hero for our time, we have been deprived of his full possibilities as a model. As Freud once lamented, "thanks to their own discretion and to the untruthfulness of their biographers, we learn little that is intimate about the great men who are our models. . . ."[21] Jones unfortunately presented us with such a rationalized version of Freud's struggles that we have seen less of his depths. Yet to minimize what Freud had to overcome only limits the stature of his achievements. And to mythologize Freud as a man in full control of all his emotions is to deprive us of the opportunity of identifying with him as a struggling innovator.

What is so surprising about the use of Freud in contemporary psychiatry is the way in which he is invoked to justify the status quo. No one seems very eager to identify with the Freud who ignored everything that had been said and written before, who dared to try to understand what had previously been considered utterly meaningless. Freud wrote and thought shocking things. The Freud of history, with his large mistakes as well as his great intellectual victories, is a far more interesting figure than the Freud of legend, and it can do his memory no service to see him smaller and more life-sized than the courageous genius he was.

2. Finding Out about
Freud the Man

ANY HISTORIAN seeking to understand Freud as a man must begin with the fact that he was relatively along in years, in his forties, before he made his greatest discoveries. Born in 1856, Freud was almost fifty years old, an age that half a century ago was very much older than it is today, before any of his followers knew him. The earliest patient of Freud's whom I interviewed was in treatment with him in 1908, when Freud's ideas were already highly developed. What he was like in his period of greatest creativity has to be inferred from indirect sources of evidence.

An imaginative leap is necessary to understand what Freud was like even sixty years ago. The Western world has changed so much since then that it requires a special effort to reconstruct the climate in which Freud worked at that fairly late date in his career. Although Freud wrote openly about the role of sexuality in mental conflicts, he never quite divorced himself from many Victorian attitudes. When one of his adolescent sons came to him with worries about masturbation, Freud warned the boy against the practice. The talk upset the son, and prevented him, he has said, from having as close contact with his father as his oldest brother had.[1] Presumably Freud saw masturbation as a symptom, the outcome of unconscious conflicts, even if not a vice. And yet when confronted with the same problem at a greater distance, Freud could seem emancipated from conventional pieties: the problem with masturbating, he is reported to have said, is that one must know how to do it well.[2]

Freud could certainly joke; his wit was a reflection of his enjoyment of life. So much of his career was taken up with battling for the acceptance of his ideas that it is easy to forget his remarkable sense of humor. He shared the mordant irony of the best Viennese satirists. For example, before the Nazis would permit him to leave Vienna in 1938 they demanded that he sign a statement to the effect that he had been well treated. Freud did so, and then added the postscript, at once defiant and ironic: "I can heartily recommend the Gestapo to anyone."[3]

For all the dry-sounding technical rules he put forward for others, Freud's own practice as an analyst was enlivened by wonderfully funny illustrations. The examples he used in his book *Jokes and Their Relation to the Unconscious* provide a glimpse of this aspect of his mind. (A Viennese Jewish analyst, Hanns Sachs, on moving to America and treating more Gentile patients than he had in Europe was worried how he could continue to analyze without Jewish stories. The solution he found was to substitute a minister for the rabbi in the tales: "I baptize the stories.") Patients still recall with pleasure how Freud could illustrate human dilemmas by means of Jewish anecdotes.

Few of those close to Freud ever dared to view him objectively. For his immediate followers and (to a decreasing extent) for successive generations of psychoanalysts, Freud had to be free from human imperfections.[4] At the time his pupils knew him they blotted out whatever signs of neurosis they saw. And although the publication of much of Freud's correspondence in recent years has made it harder to remain unaware of some of his inner conflicts, such as his anxieties about death, the need to believe in a figure who knew all the answers persists. Any detached observer would agree that a central objective of research on Freud's life is to determine to what extent and in what ways the precepts of psychoanalysis may have been colored by his own personal problems. Nevertheless, several interviewees declared they really thought that nothing in Freud's psychology reflects a subjective bias on his part.

In his lifetime Freud was known in his circle as "Professor." Today, more than thirty years after his death, those who were close to him, even some of his relatives, still speak and think of him as "Professor." (To invoke that word, moreover, means that one was on relatively intimate terms with Freud.) No outsider might guess with what regal authority rang his every word. As Theodor Reik put it, "in retrospect, words he had spoken in everyday conversation acquired undreamed-of significance; casual remarks echoed in our minds for years afterwards."[5] There is no doubt that Freud changed these people's lives.

Nowadays much of this respect has shifted to Anna Freud. By a series of accidents all of Freud's leading pupils managed to neutralize or expel each other. In the end his youngest child became his chief support for the future of psychoanalysis. As Freud was "Professor," with all the magic and capacity to infantilize that being the head of a movement entails, so Anna Freud is now "Miss Freud." She reigns in his place; for some, "Miss Freud" communicates exactly the same aura that "Professor" did.

Others have recognized the elements of a cult in psychoanalysis. But writers on Freud have had difficulty being simultaneously pro and con, balancing their admiration with the critical insight that distance can provide. Those involved in psychoanalysis may have been driven by the same religious impulses that others channel in more conventional ways, but psychoanalytic workers have also made real scientific contributions.

The fact that it is possible to go from Anna Freud's clinic in London to centers for the treatment of children in New York or Cleveland, without realizing one has moved at all—the approach to children is that consistent—is a tribute not only to her pupils' emotional involvement in what she offers but also to her substantive understanding of childhood emotional conflicts. From the beginning psychoanalysis has had the dual aspect of subjective distortion along with objective discovery. Freud's achievement has been such that we must take great care in coming up with alternative formulations.

To the extent that psychological treatment can be likened to an educational experience, our understanding of therapy will be enhanced by the study of Freud and his pupils. Freud himself resorted to educational

Freud in his seventies

analogies to explain his new therapeutic technique. As he said more than once, analysis "acts as a second education of the adult, as a corrective to his education as a child."[6]

The more we understand Freud as a teacher, the better we can comprehend his intentions as a therapist. To Freud, patients were "students" for whom the analyst was a "guide." The analytic process was itself an educative activity; psychoanalysis sought to educate the ego.[7] To be sure, some patients were not educable and therefore were less suitable for the analyst's attention. Freud thought that in all analyses points would arise at which the analyst had to act as a model for his patients and sometimes directly as a teacher. But he cautioned against indiscriminate instruction: "the patient should be educated to liberate and fulfill his own nature, not to resemble ourselves."[8]

In investigating psychoanalytic thinking, it would be difficult to exaggerate the importance of interpreting Freud's character. Among those who were in personal contact with him a preconscious screening process has been at work. When reading Freud's writings or discussing his concepts, they take for granted some separation between what is worth talking about as science and what is the result of his own idiosyncrasies. But as that early generation of psychoanalysts gradually disappears, it becomes all the harder for us to pierce through whatever was subjective in Freud's system. His mantle has fallen on every subsequent psychotherapist. Each has in part, consciously or not, identified with him. For the sake of both patients and therapists our minds should be as clear of illusion as possible.

We can safely assume that understanding Freud personally will have inevitable consequences for psychoanalytic theory and therapy. It might otherwise seem strange that there should be so much interest in Freud's personality. After all, should not a science be independent of the character of its originator? Is not the term "genius" somewhat misleading when applied to a scientist? Scientific, as opposed to literary, creation presupposes that a particular discovery will be made sooner or later, if not by one man then by another.

Yet Freud's work, in part surely a literary accomplishment, was intimately related to his own character from the outset. To say that his thinking was self-revelatory and an outgrowth of his self-understanding does not detract from what he achieved; that a theory originates from a subjective source need say nothing against its objective validity. Freud's strength as a psychologist lay in his use of self-knowledge in his writings; he wrote feelingly, for the sake of impersonal science, about some of his most intimate experiences. As with other great writers, it required a rich self to enable him to re-create a version of human experience out of his autobiography. Had he been any other man he would never have been able to make the discoveries that he did.

Once we concede that Freud's work was at least partly autobiographical, research about the history of psychoanalysis requires a special approach. We must, for example, acknowledge the role Freud's personal history played in the development of analysis while he was still alive. At times, however, Freud strove mightily to separate his own personality from what he discovered. In a telling anecdote, one of his students remarked to Freud in the 1930's that he was a great man. "I am not a great man," Freud replied, "I made a great discovery."⁹ Freud was not being falsely modest. The same detachment had enabled him to make his own life the matrix of his psychology. Of course, Freud worked with patients; it was their problems which he set out to understand and alleviate. Yet through his patients he was better able to master himself. By objectifying parts of himself through his therapeutic efforts for others, he could overcome some of his own inner resistance to self-knowledge.

Freud had to insist on the distinction between his personality and his work; he did not want to be regarded primarily as a literary figure. Otherwise his science might not survive his death. And therefore, as we have seen, he believed that biographies of him were unnecessary. He wanted to establish that his own personality had nothing to do with psychoanalysis as a science. In a speech at the Vienna Psychoanalytic Society in 1936, on the occasion of Freud's eightieth birthday, Anna Freud brought a message from her father: that his students should not think of analysis as identified with him but should regard it as an independent body of knowledge.¹⁰

Freud's fear that psychoanalysis would seem too closely associated with his own life has proven to be not unrealistic, and his own accounts of the founding of psychoanalysis have been partially to blame. There is still an enormous amount of interest in Freud's life, even if the biographical material has not yet been used systematically to illuminate his psychological system. As any thinker's works rise in stature we tend to regard them as a person and not just as a collection of volumes. We speak of Plato and Aristotle, as well as lesser thinkers, when we mean to refer to their writings. No matter how hard it may be to find Freud's personality in his work, one always feels in it the distinctive stamp of his mind. Precisely because his system was so intensely personal, and yet at the same time of such great relevance for others, he was capable of attracting a wide following.

All of this was burdensome to his pupils; it was possible to be lured by the immortality of Freud's discoveries and yet alienated by the fallible man. For an early generation of analysts Freud *meant* psychoanalysis, and it was impossible to think of one without the other. To quarrel with Freud was to cease to be an analyst, and this was a matter of definition rather than a question of how one practiced therapy. It was too easy for him to think that personal disagreement represented scientific difference, and that a scientific dispute constituted personal disloyalty. It could be as hard for Freud as for his pupils to keep straight which was the science and which the man.

Freud's strength as a writer and a psychologist lay in his ability to appeal from one soul to the hearts of all men. Examine yourself, Freud said, look within your own depths, and see whether what is true for me is true for you too. And the world reacted to Freud in as personal a way as he had made his appeal. One psychiatrist I interviewed spoke of having first met Freud in the early 1920's; he meant that he had first read a book by Freud then. (This was particularly striking since he did not actually meet Freud until 1936.) Similarly, people have spoken of foes of Freud and usually meant individuals who disagreed with him scientifically, not personal enemies. To his pupils Freud could have the most intense personal meaning; they came to remember dates in his life better than most children do for their own parents.

Yet psychoanalysis eventually did become something quite different from Freud personally. As the movement expanded, changes were introduced into psychoanalytic thinking which would have been utterly alien to Freud himself. Working with the method he gave them, later investigators revised some of his most cherished positions. Too much concern with Freud's personal point of view and prejudices might blind one to the possibilities for revision that are inherent in his ideas.

II

BACKGROUND AND CHARACTER

1. "All the defiance and all the passions"

> I have often felt as though I had inherited all the defiance and all the passions with which our ancestors defended their Temple and could gladly sacrifice my life for one great moment in history.

In autobiographical reflections and with disciplined self-scrutiny, Freud paid more attention to his past than most figures who stimulate the imagination of historians. This fact, together with his insistence on the central importance of the first few years of life for all later personality development, at the least suggests a starting point for approaching Freud's own biography. Yet the mystery of talent remains, and it is never easy to distinguish biographical fact from elaborate fiction. What is mythical can so often, over the course of a lifetime, become historical.

Freud was born in 1856 of Jewish parents who were members of a tiny religious minority in Freiberg, Moravia, then an overwhelmingly Catholic section of the Austro-Hungarian Empire and now part of Czechoslovakia. It seems fitting, or at any rate not incongruous, for a Jew to have founded psychoanalysis. A suffering minority is well placed for understanding the plight of outsiders like neurotics, and a marginal social position encouraged Jews to take the initial risks involved in entering the new profession of analysis. In later years Jews formed a disproportionately large share of the psychoanalytic movement. Jews seem to have had a special affinity for Freud's psychology. It is impossible to overemphasize Freud's Jewishness, since it was the single most important part of his background.[1]

In his mature years Freud was outspokenly atheistic, although he remained sensitive to his identity as a Jew and often asserted its importance to him. He never lost interest in the psychology of religious belief; along with other writings, Freud devoted three books (*Totem and Taboo* in 1913, *Future of an Illusion* in 1927, and *Moses and Monotheism* in 1938) to the elucidation of religious emotions.[2] Usually he stressed the infantile element behind religion, arguing that people need faith in God and ceremonial practices as a crutch for human helplessness. Freud saw religion as a wish-fulfilling compensation for childhood weaknesses that were never outgrown. He knew that religion could assuage guilt feelings, especially those connected with aggressive impulses, and could provide a means for coming to terms with the problem of death. But to Freud this seemed a neurotic way of handling inevitable human conflicts. His bold denunciation of religion was an expression of his stringent hopes for mankind. Surely men could do better than in the past, if only they would give up superstition, ignorance, and neurosis.

Freud's understanding of religious motivation was not without its inadequacies; the fearful and defensive aspects of religious belief, rather than the loving, loomed largest in his mind. However, Freud was forced to confront the powerful role of religion in previous history and the problematic consequences for Western life of the breakdown of previously accepted standards of behavior. Despite his skepticism, with individual

Freud's birthplace in Freiberg, Moravia

patients in treatment Freud felt that religion might serve as a constructive resolution of inner conflicts. He even sometimes regretted the increasing inability of modern men to believe in God; this was, he thought, a source of widespread mental anguish.

Freud's work, however, represented a challenge to traditional religious thought. He explicitly saw psychoanalysis as a scientific (and rival) way of meeting issues on which previously religion had used magic. As a Jew, Freud stood at some distance from conventional Christian values. In *Civilization and Its Discontents*, for example, he picked the maxim "Thou shalt love thy neighbor as thyself" to show it psychologically unrealistic and undesirable; Freud was opposed to denying the inevitability of self-centeredness and the legitimacy of aggression.[3]

Freud blamed Gentile culture for some of the obstacles his ideas had to encounter. To the charge that his concepts were narrowly culture-bound and that Viennese sexuality was not to be found anywhere else, Freud said that "between the lines you can read further that we Viennese are not only swine but also Jews."[4] At the beginning of his psychoanalytic career Freud was sometimes ridiculed for his concepts, and this left him with a confirmed suspicion of Christian culture. As he wrote to a fellow Jew, Karl Abraham, when trying to dampen down a conflict between his own loyal adherents and the Swiss (and Gentile) analysts, including Carl G. Jung:

> I nurse a suspicion that the suppressed anti-Semitism of the Swiss that spares me is deflected in reinforced form upon you. But I think that we as Jews, if we wish to join in, must develop a bit of masochism, be ready to suffer some wrong. Otherwise there is no hitting it off. Rest assured that, if my name were Oberhuber, in spite of everything my innovations would have met with far less resistance.[5]

Whatever his tendency to exaggerate opposition, anti-Semitism, though not the sanguinary variety, played a real role throughout Freud's life. One of his intimate memories was his father's description of his passive reaction to an insult inflicted on him in the street:

> I may have been ten or twelve years old, when my father began to take me with him on his walks and reveal to me in his talk his views upon things in the world we live in. Thus it was, on one such occasion, that he told me a story to show how much better things were now than they had been in his days. "When I was a young man," he said, "I went for a walk one Saturday in the streets of your birth-place; I was well dressed, and had a new fur cap on my head. A Christian came up to me and with a single blow knocked off my cap into the

mud and shouted: 'Jew! get off the pavement!' " "And what did you do?" I asked. "I went into the roadway and picked up my cap," was his quiet reply. This struck me as unheroic conduct on the part of the big, strong man who was holding the little boy by the hand. I contrasted this situation with another which fitted my feelings better: the scene in which Hannibal's father . . . made his boy swear before the household altar to take vengeance on the Romans. Ever since that time Hannibal . . . had a place in my phantasies.[6]

Freud was greatly disappointed by his father's response to this Sabbath insult, and nothing of this passivity to social pressure remained in Freud when he grew up. His son Martin recorded an incident in which Freud bravely charged into a hostile crowd which had been shouting anti-Semitic abuse, an uncanny reversal of Freud's father's behavior.[7] Freud remained sensitive to anti-Semitism and wary of all Gentiles. He believed that basically there was no one who was not anti-Semitic.[8]

In his writings Freud did not pay much attention to the emotion of shame, although he treated the problem of guilt extensively; he thought that shame was a specifically feminine trait. It would be easy to believe, however, that he incorporated within himself some of the low valuation which society had placed upon being Jewish. To be a Jew meant, among other things, to be passive, unheroic, weak, and these characteristics could not be a part of an adult sense of self that Freud would have been comfortable with. In 1935 a cruel joke had it that Jews in Berlin were parading with placards reading "Throw us out." Freud misinterpreted this savage piece of Jewish self-irony—aimed at the Jews who accepted everything the Nazis ordered them to do—as a literally true story, and he was bitterly indignant at what he took to be Jewish self-abasement and lack of dignity.[9]

Freud's psychology takes little account of the role of national character; for him any differences between peoples had racist connotations. Raised in a religion which emphasized separateness, Freud had difficulty appreciating the work of those, such as cultural anthropologists, who did not need to insist on psychological uniformities.[10] (Karl Marx was another Jew who underestimated the force of nationalism in the modern world.)

At the same time Freud was always quick to affirm his Jewishness, even if he did not practice Judaism and his allegiance to it sometimes had a willed quality. Aside from his fondness for Jewish stories, Freud attributed his intransigence—his ability to stand aside from commonly held opinions as he independently pursued his ideas—to a pride and detachment derived from being Jewish. As he declared in a speech in 1926 to his chapter of B'nai B'rith: "Because I was a Jew I found myself free from many prejudices which restricted others in the use of their intellect; and as a Jew I was prepared to join the Opposition and to do without agreement with the 'compact majority.' "[11]

In Central Europe at that time, the Jewish organization of B'nai B'rith was an elite group, whose members had considerable social standing. Freud regularly attended its meetings and even delivered some psychoanalytic papers before the group. "You were my first audience," he recalled to them in that same speech in 1926. He belonged to the organization specifically because it was Jewish, and this participation represented a declaration of his continuing involvement with Judaism.

Freud's life followed some traditional Jewish patterns. He became the official head of his family; children, in-laws, aunts, uncles, nieces, nephews, and cousins were closely knit together. Freud's family mattered a great deal to him, and he was always ready with money or advice for its members. (The psychoanalytic movement was an extension of Freud's family, and he ruled this new profession in much the same way.) It may be significant that none of his children converted or married Gentiles; and his son Ernst was a Zionist. However, despite his wife's feelings on the matter, Freud did not believe in observing traditional Jewish practices. A holiday such as Passover was ignored, even though Freud's parents would have celebrated it. (His mother "did not speak in high German but Galician Yiddish."[12])

Politically, too, Freud stood with the Jews, apart from the typical attitudes of his countrymen. It is true that at the outset of World War I Freud for a time sided jingoistically with Germany and the Central Powers; on July 26, 1914, he wrote that "for the first time for thirty years I feel myself to be an Austrian and feel like giving this not very hopeful Empire another chance."[13] To a Viennese, England and France were the accomplices of the Czar, and the Austrians, freer than the Russians, looked down on them as barbarians. Yet when Freud later asked one of his Italian pupils, who was then in the Austro-Hungarian army, what he thought of the whole war, the man, in his reply, detached himself from the conflict: "Oh, Professor," he excused himself, "you know I am Jewish." And Freud was pleased at this response, for he too felt somewhat removed from the contending military powers.*[14]

---

* While in Paris in 1886 Freud reported a political conversation in which someone predicted a "most ferocious war" between France and Germany. "I promptly explained," Freud wrote at the time, "that I am a Jew, adhering neither to Germany nor Austria." "But," he added, "such conversations are always very embarrassing to me, for I feel stirring within me something German which I long ago decided to suppress."[15]

An incident with religious overtones from Freud's early childhood seemed to him later to have been of major importance. When he was a small child, before he had been brought to Vienna, Freud was in the charge of a Catholic nurse who made a great impression on him. She was "ugly, elderly but clever," provided him "with the means for living and surviving," and gave him, he wrote, "a high opinion of my own capacities." She took him regularly to church services and taught him about Catholicism, and from her he picked up the meaning of heaven and hell. His mother later remembered his little speeches to his family about "how God conducted His affairs."[16]

When Freud was two and a half this nanny was abruptly dismissed, despite his great affection for her, because she had been caught stealing from the family. She had made him hand over to her the small amounts of money he had received as presents, and she "encouraged him to steal money for her."[17] The nurse was reported to the police by one of Freud's older half brothers, Philipp, and served a ten-month sentence. The little boy might well not have ceased to love her no matter what was said to him after she was sent away. This may have been the first of what Freud later wrote were his repeated disappointments with people; he suffered from many feelings of desertion during his struggles in the cause of psychoanalysis. Or had Freud been disappointed even earlier, on finding that the Catholic God of his nurse was not the same as his Jewish God? The issue of theft, transmuted to the level of a concern for scientific priorities and the charge of plagiarism, played an important part in Freud's later scientific relationships.

Freud's family left Freiberg for Leipzig, Saxony, in October 1859, and after a few months moved on to Vienna. The reasons for these shifts are not entirely clear. While the family had once been prosperous, long-term economic changes on top of a major financial setback (Freud's older half brothers Emanuel and Philipp had made unsound investments in South African ostrich-feather farms[18]) finally ruined Freud's wool merchant father, Jakob. In later years Freud was tempted to look back on this Freiberg period as a pastoral idyl of economic and emotional security.

With three men of military age in the family the Freuds may also have been trying to avoid army service by these moves. The family left Austro-Hungarian territory for Leipzig after the outbreak of the war between Austria and Italy, and moved back to Austria (Vienna) after peace was declared. Then Freud's two half brothers settled in England. Conscription was a great hardship for Jews at this time; army life not only meant specially harsh treatment by the officers but also made it impossible to live according to traditional Jewish customs.[19]

*   *   *

Despite the relatively severe economic privations Freud's immediate family was now to undergo, Vienna was in its cultural heyday. From the middle of the nineteenth century to World War I the city underwent a cultural renaissance; in music, philosophy, literature, mathematics, and economics, there were memorable achievements. In this general intellectual ferment, the search for realities behind the façade of a decaying empire, the educated and emancipated Jews were in an ideal position to discern hypocrisy, for they had little to gain from accepting the official view.[20]

The intellectual elite of Vienna was notably cosmopolitan. Like Freud, many of those who became outstanding representatives of the culture of old Vienna had not actually been born there. As the center of the sprawling and ancient Hapsburg Empire, Vienna was a magnet for aspiring talent. The vigorous cultural conflict between East and West that had its vortex in Vienna, the sense that liberal culture was on the verge of being undermined, and the use of irony to pierce the veil of the structure of formal beliefs, were reflected throughout Freud's later thought. Much of his sense of doom, of civilization having played itself out, can also be found in other writers of the period.

Historically the Jews had been driven from Vienna three times. With the industrialism of the nineteenth century, however, the Jews returned, and in the 1850's, 1860's, and 1870's they rose to prominence. Constituting about 10 per cent of the approximately two million Viennese, the Jews came to control much of the banking as well as almost all the newspapers. Overcoming religious discrimination, they also received many academic appointments at the University of Vienna, and filled the ranks of doctors and lawyers. Anti-Semitism grew worse as time passed and the Jews prospered, in part because of their evident successes. The old Emperor, Franz Josef, detested anti-Semitism: Karl Lueger (one of Hitler's heroes) was elected burgomeister three times in 1895–96, but the Emperor refused to confirm his election. In honor of the Emperor's stand at the time, Freud overindulged in smoking, an addiction he was then trying to overcome. Only after being assailed in the streets as the "Emperor of the Jews" did Franz Josef capitulate, in 1897, and confirm Lueger in his office.

Under the restrictive circumstances in which Freud grew up, Jews necessarily had special difficulties in handling their aggressiveness. Freud possessed a powerful need for independence, and his later achievements were indebted to his courage as well as his belligerence. Freud "loved contest, and was a born revolutionist . . . [He] loved to play the part of the devil's advocate."[21] Freud picked up little of Viennese urbane insincerity; his manner was rather gruff and brusque, though like others he could, especially for the sake of his cause, be charming and even hypocritical. A letter to his future wife describes the nature of Freud's aspirations in the context of his special upbringing. He tells how one of his most beloved teachers (Josef Breuer)

> discovered that hidden under the surface of timidity there lay in me an extremely daring and fearless human being. I had always thought so, but never dared tell anyone. I have often felt as though I had inherited all the defiance and all the passions with which our ancestors defended their Temple and could gladly sacrifice my life for one great moment in history.[22]

Much evidence can be found throughout Freud's life of his profound urge to become a mighty warrior. In his early forties he had a dream which reminded him of early prophecies about himself. "At the time of my birth an old peasant-woman had prophesied to my proud mother that with her first born child she had brought a great man into the world." "Could this," Freud asked himself, "have been the source of my thirst for grandeur?"[23] When he was a boy of eleven or twelve, a poet in a park had foretold that the child would grow up to be a cabinet minister. (There were then some Jewish ministers.) Such predictions about a child are not unusual; it is striking, however, that after many years they still had a place in Freud's dream life.

Around the period of *The Interpretation of Dreams* (1900) Freud confessed, in a moment of extravagance, that he was "not really a man of science, not an observer, not an experimenter, and not a thinker. I am nothing but by temperament a *conquistador*—an adventurer, if you want to translate the word—with the curiosity, the boldness, and the tenacity that belongs to that type of being."[24] When the Nazis finally drove Freud from Vienna in 1938, he was eighty-two years old, feeble and ill, yet during the night journey from Paris to London he dreamed he was landing at Pevensey. As Freud explained to one of his sons, Pevensey was the spot where William the Conqueror had landed in 1066.[25]

Hannibal and Napoleon were two of Freud's lasting heroes, and were important to him in the context of his Jewish background. Hannibal was a Semite who hated Rome and almost destroyed it. Freud had ambiguous feelings about Rome, and for years he was reluctant to visit the seat of Catholicism. Yet once he traveled there he went back again and again with immense enjoyment.

Napoleon, who like Hannibal had crossed the Alps, also fulfilled Freud's martial ideal. As a boy Freud stuck labels on the backs of his toy soldiers with the names of Napoleon's marshals; Freud's favorite was Masséna, then thought to have Jewish origins. The mature Freud consciously patterned some of his dicta on those of Bonaparte. "One might say here," Freud remarked once about sexuality, "varying a well-known saying of the great Napoleon: 'Anatomy is destiny.' "[26] More than once Freud referred to "the great Napoleon," "who, incidentally," like Freud himself, "was an extremely sound sleeper. . . ."[27] To a patient Freud explained that one needed three things to succeed in an analysis—the first was courage, the second was courage, and the third was courage. (Freud believed that Napoleon had said three things were required to fight a war—money, money, and money;[28] Danton had thought it was a matter of daring, daring, and daring.) Freud wrote of a trip to the Acropolis with his younger brother that he was reminded of a comment of Napoleon's to a brother, probably (Freud conjectured) Joseph, whose Biblical namesake was an interpreter of dreams: "So too, if I may compare . . . a small event with a greater one, Napoleon, during his coronation as Emperor in Notre-Dame . . . remarked: 'What would *Monsieur notre Père* have said to this, if he could have been here today?' "[29]

Napoleon might seem an odd hero for someone who led as sedentary a life as Freud's. And no doubt Napoleon's name is to some synonymous with autocracy. But to Freud—as to many others—Napoleon was the son of the French Revolution, the liberator of the Jews, and the model for self-made men. (Another hero of Freud's was Cromwell, who, in addition to standing for parliamentarianism and British liberties, had allowed the Jews to return to England. Freud named his son Oliver for him.) Napoleon had forced the Austrian Emperor to hand over his daughter in marriage, and to someone like Freud any humiliation of the Hapsburgs was to Napoleon's credit. A cultivated Viennese at that time would be deeply insulted by being called a patriot, for patriotism implied hypocrisy, subservience to a rotten monarchy, and blindness to evils. The Austrian form of government was an absolutism mitigated only by inefficiency and negligence.

Freud chose to do his fighting in the world of intellect. To accomplish a great intellectual (rather than military) achievement was not only far more in accord with Jewish culture but also was in itself enough to establish the superiority of the Jewish spirit over the philistine Gentile world. Freud's general outlook was reflected in a passage from a letter written during his long engagement: "For the rest of my time in the hospital I will live like the *goyim*, modestly, learning the ordinary things without striving after discoveries or reaching to the depths. What we shall need for our independence can be attained by honest steady work without gigantic striving."[30] Freud founded a great movement, by which, in a sense, he sought to undermine Gentile values. We need not doubt that once Freud could see himself in the line of such great scientific discoverers as Darwin, Copernicus, and Kepler, he had at last fulfilled his dream of having his "one great moment in history."

Freud would have been the first to agree that his own fighting temperament must have had its origins in his early familial setting. He singled out one childhood relationship that is relevant here, although, as with his account of his nurse, we must remember that it was the adult Freud who was finding the meaning of events of his childhood. Freud had a nephew John, one year older than he, the son of his half brother Emanuel, and Freud thought his relationship with John had been fateful for his whole development. "Until the end of my third year we had been inseparable. We had loved each other and fought with each other; and this childhood relationship . . . had a determining influence on all my subsequent relations with contemporaries." "There must have been times," Freud felt sure, "when he treated me very badly and I must have shown courage in the face of my tyrant. . . ." Freud remembered "scenes of quarreling" with John "from my very early childhood."[31] Freud was the "weaker" of the two boys; but his fortitude in the face of outer tyranny prepared him for later years when he had to encounter what he came to call his inner "tyrant," psychology.

Freud asserted that this early tie to John "had become the source of all my friendships and all my hatreds."

All my friends have in a certain sense been reincarnations of this first figure. . . . My emotional life has always insisted that I should have an intimate friend and a hated enemy. I have always been able to provide myself afresh with both, and it has not infrequently happened that the ideal situation of childhood has been so completely reproduced that friend and enemy have come together in a single individual—though not, of course, both at once or with constant oscillations, as may have been the case in my early childhood.

Freud found it a source of satisfaction that he could always find successive replacements for that figure from his childhood—"no one," therefore, "was irreplaceable."[32]

Despite the attention Freud gave in his *Interpretation of Dreams* to this one unusual family relationship, he wrote nothing about most of his siblings. Five of the seven were girls. It is known that Freud disliked his oldest sister, Anna, who was born when he was two and a half. It was during his mother's confinement with Anna that his nurse's thefts were discovered, and it is possible that Freud's memory telescoped the significance of his nurse's departure with the temporary loss of his mother. Shortly thereafter the family set out for Leipzig and then Vienna, Freud's nephew John going with his parents to live in England. Hate can be a result of the anxiety occasioned by such separations, and Freud might well have had to tell himself that no one is "irreplaceable."

Freud did mention his two younger brothers and their significance for his emotional life. One, Julius, was born when Freud was eleven months old but lived only eight months. Freud wrote in a letter that he thought he had "welcomed my one-year-younger brother . . . with ill wishes and real infantile jealousy, and . . . his death left the germ of guilt in me."[33] Freud was more in control of his emotions when his mother's last child, a son, was born, for Freud was then ten years old; the name of Alexander was chosen at Freud's suggestion, in memory and honor of Alexander the Great. (In writing his *Introductory Lectures on Psychoanalysis*, Freud later duly noted that "when Alexander the Great started on his conquests, his train included the most famous dream-interpreters."[34]) Naturally some rivalry grew up between the two brothers; Freud worried, for instance, over which of them would get a professorship first.[35] But Freud and his brother (who died at a ripe age in Canada) got on harmoniously; as adults they often traveled together on vacations. With Alexander in mind Freud used to say that their family was like a book: "we are the covers and the girls are the leaves between."[36] Such protective gallantry fit in with the rest of Freud's Old World make-up.

It is not surprising that, as an eldest son with five sisters, he acted as a big brother, for example deciding what was proper literary fare for the girls. Nor was it unusual for Jewish parents of that time to show favoritism toward their sons. As a young student Freud took his studies very seriously. He had a photographic memory and invariably came out at the head of his class. But when his sister Anna started taking piano lessons at home, Freud found this a great annoyance and an interference in his studying.

Freud had a strange attitude toward music; it irritated him, yet he loved opera, with its words and dramatic interest, and had a sophisticated operatic taste. The Mozart operas *Don Giovanni*, *The Marriage of Figaro*, and *The Magic Flute* were his favorites. Even though he despised Richard Wagner he loved *Die Meistersinger*, and in the late 1920's could point out many aspects of it which had escaped the notice of at least one highly musical patient.[37]

Freud became much more interested in the magic of words than in the power of nonverbal means of communication. Of all the arts music is perhaps closest to the id, and without a guide from the more rational part of his mind Freud felt uneasy. Unable to analyze the effects of music on him, Freud could not enjoy it; this block was similar to his inability to appreciate certain mystic religious states. For a Viennese to dislike music was unusual, and Freud made a point of telling people of his defect. As for his sister Anna and her youthful music lessons, the piano itself was removed from the apartment and subsequently none of Freud's own children were allowed to be musical at home either.

In order to fathom Freud's adolescent years we have to rely mainly on his own accounts; but he was sufficiently introspective so that from his own words it is possible to sketch at least a plausible picture. There is no sign of a tempestuous upheaval in Freud during these years. Later, in a letter to his future wife, Freud talked about his "inaccessibility and gruffness with strangers," and remarked that "I believe people see something alien in me and the real reason for this is that in my youth I was never young and now that I am entering the age of maturity [thirty] I cannot mature properly."[38] Freud was out of tune with "age-appropriate" experiences throughout much of his life, and though a source of pain this also helped to ensure his alertness and productivity.

One of Freud's great talents, which he exercised throughout his life, was the ability to write. Despite his lack of appreciation for music, in writing he displayed a strong sense of rhythm. Even as a schoolboy he was a fascinating writer, perhaps because he drew from his inner loneliness. Some letters from that adolescent period have survived, and whatever his sense of alienation from the world around him, he was a master storyteller of what he saw. A passage in a letter written at the age of seventeen is particularly memorable, for what it reveals about Freud's distinctive writing capacities as well as for what it communicates about his early glimmerings of immortality. Freud wrote to a friend just after concluding the written part of the *Matura* (the qualifying examination required for entrance to the university):

> my professor told me—and he is the first person who has dared to tell me this—that I possess what Herder so nicely calls an *idiotic* style—i.e. a style at once correct and characteristic. I was. suitably impressed by this amazing fact and do not hesitate to disseminate the happy event, the first of its kind, as widely as possible—to you, for instance, who until now have probably remained unaware that you have been exchanging letters with a German stylist. And now I advise you as a friend, not as an interested party, to preserve them—have them bound—take good care of them—one never knows.[39]

2. Childhood and Youth

AT THE END of his school days Freud intended to be a lawyer so that he could become a public figure. "Under the powerful influence," he explained in 1924, "of a school friendship with a boy rather my senior who grew up to be a well-known politician, I developed a wish to study law like him and to engage in social activities."[1] When this former friend died in 1927, his widow wrote to Freud for help in preparing a commemorative volume. Freud wrote back that he remembered that he had

made the acquaintance of Heinrich Braun during the first year at the gymnasium on the day when we got our first "report card" and that we were soon inseparable friends. All the hours of the day which were left after school I spent with him, mostly at his home, especially as long as his family was not yet in Vienna and he lived with his next oldest brother . . . and a private tutor. This brother tried to interfere with our relationship. We ourselves, however, got along marvellously. I hardly remember any quarrels between us or times during which we were "mad" at each other, which happens so frequently during such young friendships. What we did all those days and what we talked about is difficult to imagine after so many years. I believe he reinforced my aversion to school and to what was taught there; he awakened a multitude of revolutionary trends in me and we reinforced each other in the overestimation of our criticism and of our superior knowledge. He turned my interest to books like Buckle's *History of Civilization* and to a similar work by Lecky, which he admired greatly. I admired him: his self-confident poise; his independent judgment; I compared him secretly with a young lion and I was firmly convinced that sometime in the future he would assume a leading position in the world. A scholar he was not, but I did not mind that, though I myself soon became *Primus* and remained it; in the vague feeling of those years I understood that he possessed something which was more valuable than all success in school and which I have since learned to call "personality."

Neither the goals nor the means of our ambitions were very clear to us. Since then I have come to the assumption that his aims were essentially negative ones. But one thing was certain: that I would work with him and that I would never desert his "party" . . .

Our relationship experienced its first interruption—I think it was during . . . the next to the last grade—when he left school, unfortunately not voluntarily. During the first year at the university he was there again. But I had become a student of medicine and he a student of law . . . Our ways separated slowly: he always had more relationships to people than I had and it was always easier for him to establish new ones. Contact with me had probably ceased to be a need to him long before. So it happened that I completely lost sight of him during the later years of study.[2]

Even long after that "powerful influence" in his life was over, as late as *The Interpretation of Dreams*, Freud's dream life showed him identifying with a successful parliamentarian and also wondering if he would prefer to exchange places with the head of the Cabinet. Freud did not, however, study law. Just before entering the university he heard an essay on nature, then thought to be written by Goethe, read aloud at a public lecture. This settled his hesitations in choosing a career, and he decided to "take up the study of natural science."[3]

At the University of Vienna, Freud was a "slave" to his books; he developed an urgent need to buy and collect them. Afterward Freud repudiated this bookish streak, and claimed to have "held fast to the habit of always studying things themselves before looking for information about them in books. . . ."[4] Freud always was a hard worker; later on he was as conscientious at his therapy and devoted to his writing as he had once been diligent in his studies.

However, Freud dragged out his stay at the university for eight years. Perhaps his many interests prevented him from going forward more quickly.

The five years which are prescribed for medical studies were . . . too few for me. I quietly went on with my work for several more years; and in my circle of acquaintances I was regarded as an idler and it was doubted whether I should ever get through. Thereupon I quickly decided to take my examinations and I got through them in spite of the delay.[5]

Freud never lost his wide-ranging curiosity, but he now tried to focus his mind on particular areas—a trait which later led him to worry about his "one-sidedness."[6] By 1924 he observed that his single-mindedness had struck others as well: "In complete contrast to the diffuse character of my studies during my earlier years at the University, I was now developing an inclination to concentrate my work exclusively upon a single subject or problem. This inclination has persisted and has since led to my being accused of one-sidedness."[7]

In tracing the development of his interests in his autobiographical sketch of 1924, after mentioning how he was "decidedly negligent in pursuing my medical studies," Freud referred to the wise advice of an admired teacher (Ernst Brücke) who, in the light of his student's financial situation, urged him to abandon a theoretical scientific career in favor of therapeutic practice as a doctor. In Freud's view this advice corrected his father's "generous improvidence."[8] Evidently Freud considered that his father had been remiss in failing to give more practical direction to his career.

This implicit criticism of Jakob Freud by his son is only partly borne out by the evidence. A much earlier essay of Freud's relates that when he was nineteen his father and his half brother Emanuel had "concocted a plan by which I was to exchange the abstruse subject of my studies for one of a more practical value. . . . No doubt when they saw how absorbed I was in my own intentions the plan was dropped. . . ."[9] This "plan" included Freud's marriage to Emanuel's daughter and a life in England. But Jakob Freud, kindly and gentle as well as impressed by his son's giftedness, was hardly the type ever to have offered too much direction to his son, or to have insisted that he get through the university sooner. In the matter of taking one's examinations, as in meeting anti-Semitism, Freud afterward reversed his father's behavior; Freud's son Oliver was grateful to his father for having firmly encouraged him to take his final exams without delay.[10]

Freud was dissatisfied with his home and family, as he increasingly realized that he would have to fashion himself out of his own resources. He could not suppress the thought that "if only I had been the second generation, the son of a professor or Hofrat, I should certainly have got on faster."[11] As Freud once described his father, he had been "in business" and "had had no secondary education. . . ."[12] A niece reports that Jakob Freud spent a good deal of his time as an old man studying the Talmud.[13] But in his mature theoretical work Freud regarded a father as an obstacle to be surpassed.

Freud saw ambitiousness as the conquest of the father. "[T]he essence of success," he once wrote, is "to have got further than one's father . . . as though to excel one's father was still something forbidden."[14] Two memories of Freud's childhood reminded him of his ambition and its association with his father. "[W]hen I was two years old I still occasionally wetted the bed, and when I was reproached for this I consoled my father by promising to buy him a nice new red bed in N., the nearest town of any size." Freud reported this incident, not for its charm, but to show how it interlocked with a humiliation that had a painfully lasting meaning for his future aspirations:

> When I was seven or eight years old there was another domestic scene, which I can remember very clearly. One evening before going to sleep I disregarded the rules which modesty lays down and obeyed the calls of nature in my parents' bed-room while they were present. In the course of his reprimand, my father let fall the words: "The boy will come to nothing." This must have been a frightful blow to my ambition, for references to this scene are still constantly recurring in my dreams and are always linked with an enumeration of my achievements and successes, as though I wanted to say: "You see, I *have* come to something."[15]

(According to Jung, urinary incontinence continued to trouble Freud well into adulthood.[16])

Freud went on to make a great deal of the father's place in personality development. In his early years, even after others considered the idea old-fashioned, Freud thought it likely that neurotics had syphilitic fathers.[17] This implicit criticism of fathers was only the other side of Freud's idealization of them: "I cannot think of any need in childhood as strong," he wrote in 1929, "as the need for a father's protection."[18] Freud also emphasized how frequently little boys are afraid of being eaten and even castrated by their fathers. Freud traced the tendency to exalt the father's importance to an underlying wish to get rid of him and be one's own father. For the boy is "far more inclined to feel hostile impulses towards his father than towards his mother and has a far more intense desire to get free from *him* than from *her*."[19] Any apparent underevaluation of fathers is traceable, Freud thought, to the overevaluation of early childhood.

In reality Jakob Freud was hardly the powerful man one might expect as the father of the discoverer of the Oedipus complex. Nor was he the potent ego ideal whom Freud might sometimes have wished him to be. The desire for a strong father may have played a role not only in Freud's formulation of the Oedipus complex but also in its acceptance by many who have been in a position parallel to Freud's, uneasy about their past and yet ashamed of repudiating it.

Jakob Freud was not a good provider for his family, though there seems to have been no real want in Freud's childhood. His mother's family also contributed to keep the household going. Financial details are hard

to come by, so it is not clear what the Freud family lived on after the
move from Freiberg to Vienna; at one point they had to take in a lodger,
and Jakob seems to have received help from his sons in England. Consequently, as a young man Freud was poor, though certainly proud. As he
wrote many years later:

> Anyone who has tasted the miseries of poverty in his own youth and
> has experienced the indifference and arrogance of the well-to-do,
> should be safe from the suspicion of having no understanding or good
> will towards endeavors to fight against the inequality of wealth among
> men and all that it leads to.[20]

Although as an adult Freud was generous with money, the commercial
imagery of his writing reflects the poverty of his youth and the middle-
class character of his strivings: for Freud wrote in terms of psychological
"sacrifices," "compensations," mental "balances," "investments," "expendi-
tures," "depreciation," "speculators" and "speculations," "amortization,"
"transfer," "loss," and even spoke of "leasing" an analytic hour.

If Jakob lost his business in Freiberg partly because he felt he had
to bail out his two oldest sons, Emanuel and Philipp, from their business
failure, it would be in accord with what we know of his good-naturedness.
Freud himself once described his father in "rather Micawber-like terms
as 'always hopefully expecting something to turn up.' "[21]

Freud knew his father as a relatively old man; Jakob was just over
forty when Sigmund was born. He had been married twice before, first
at the age of seventeen; he had a son (Emanuel) the first year of this
marriage—a sign of "improvidence" in that era. Little is known of his
second wife.[22] Jakob made his third marriage to Amalie Nathansohn,
Freud's mother, in 1855, three years after his first wife had died.

Whatever the strengths and deficiencies of Freud's father, in accord
with Jewish custom of that time Freud showed filial piety toward him.
It must have been brave of Freud to have reported and interpreted a dream
he had the night after Jakob's death. Freud held that the death of a man's
father inflicts on him a special trauma. Freud was forty when his father
died in 1896 at the age of almost eighty-one, and still Freud thought that
it had "revolutionized" his soul.[23] As a result, he felt free to write *The
Interpretation of Dreams*, and he reflected afterward that the death of a
man's father was "the most important event, the most poignant loss, of a
man's life."[24]

Freud remembered in the course of a dream that it had seemed remarkable "how like Garibaldi" his father "had looked on his death-bed."

To Ernest Jones this literally meant that Jakob Freud "bore a resemblance to Garibaldi," an example of how any fancy in Freud's head could emerge in books as historical fact.*[25] It is more likely that this memory of Freud's represented some aspect of his own conception of himself, or what he might have wanted Jakob to have been. Dates were always important to Freud, and as the year of Freud's father's birth (1815) was the same as Bismarck's, Bismarck was especially fascinating to him.† Freud explained his own preference for Napoleon's marshal Masséna "by the fact that my birthday fell on the same day as his, exactly a hundred years later."[28] And Ambassador Bullitt, in giving the background for the book about President Wilson on which he and Freud had collaborated, mentioned that Freud "had been interested in Wilson ever since he discovered that they were both born in 1856."[29]

Freud's mother, at least on the basis of Freud's writings, is more an enigma than his father. In the autobiographical study Freud wrote in his late sixties, he passed over his childhood and the personalities of his parents in order to get on with recounting the growth of psychoanalysis. In numerous other autobiographical remarks that are scattered throughout Freud's work, Amalie Freud is referred to far less frequently than Jakob. Perhaps this omission is a matter of nineteenth-century reserve about women, and mothers in particular. Yet more can be found out, independently of Freud's comments, about his mother than his father, since she was a girl of nineteen when she married and lived until the age of ninety-five; she died in 1930, and people are still alive who have memories and personal impressions of her, at least in her old age.

Evidently Amalie Freud was a very maternal woman. She gave birth eight times within ten years, and earned the devotion of all her children. We can only speculate what it was like for the first-born son of this young mother to have had little intruders appearing so regularly. Since Freud grew up to be fiercely competitive it is perhaps not farfetched to attribute some of this tendency to the presence of all these siblings, even if most of

---

* Even such sophisticated critics as Lionel Trilling and Stephen Marcus accepted unquestioningly Jones's version of the matter in their abridgment of his biography.[26]

† Freud included in a revised edition of *The Interpretation of Dreams* the following passage from a paper of Hanns Sachs's: "Bismarck must have found it easy to liken himself to a horse; and in fact he did so on many occasions, for instance, in his well-known saying: 'A good horse dies in harness.' "[27] Freud adopted Bismarck's saying as one of his own favorites.

them were girls, who (in addition to the tender husband she loved) demanded so much of his mother's attention. Freud's ambitiousness must have been abetted by his early family life, though the presence of younger siblings may have only provided scope for his conquering tendencies. He was able to retain the position he held with his mother even vis-à-vis his younger brother, Alexander, for if he was not the only son he was still the first. Much of this line of reasoning about Freud and his siblings would make less sense were it not for his later anxieties that others might succeed in taking away from him that which, intellectually, rightfully belonged to him.

But Freud described his relation to his mother as being free of insecurities or doubts. He considered himself his mother's favorite, and found in this as in his Jewishness a source of his self-confidence. "I have found," he wrote, "that people who know that they are preferred or favored by their mother give evidence in their lives of a peculiar self-reliance and an unshakeable optimism which often seem like heroic attributes and bring actual success to their possessors."[30]

Freud took for granted a dated (and yet noble-sounding) conception of a mother's feelings for a son. "[T]he relation between . . . mother and son . . . provides the purest examples of an unchangeable affection, unimpaired by any egoistic considerations."[31]

A mother is only brought unlimited satisfaction by her relation to a son; this is altogether the most perfect, the most free from ambivalence of all human relationships. A mother can transfer to her son the ambition which she has been obliged to suppress in herself, and she can expect from him the satisfaction of all that has been left over in her of her masculinity complex.[32]

Freud repeatedly worried, as he grew old and was afflicted with cancer, that he might die before her. As early as 1918, even before his sickness, he wrote: "I sometimes think I shall feel a little freer when she dies, for the idea that she might have to be told that I have died is a terrifying thought."[33] Freud was hoping to protect his mother from suffering. Yet his comment can perhaps also be interpreted on another level as a deep-seated feeling that if he died, then she too, with whom he felt so intimate, ought not to live.

Such a wish, though not necessarily conscious to Freud, would be consistent with his emotions and behavior at her death in 1930. Early in 1929 he had written that "my mother who will soon be ninety-four years old remains in good health, even though this blocks the way that an old man should have open to him."[34] Before finally succumbing in the next year she had endured painful suffering. In a letter to Sandor Ferenczi, Freud wrote that

> it has affected me in a peculiar way, this great event. No pain, no grief, which probably can be explained by the special circumstances —her great age, my pity for her helplessness towards the end; at the same time a feeling of liberation, of release, which I think I also understand. I was not free to die as long as she was alive, and now I am. The values of life will somehow have changed noticeably in the deeper layers.[35]

Freud wrote in a similar vein to Jones, adding: "I was not at the funeral; again Anna represented me as at Frankfurt. Her value to me can hardly be heightened."[36] The month before, Anna Freud had read an address of Freud's in acknowledgment of his receipt of the Goethe Prize for literature from the city of Frankfurt. At seventy-four Freud was no longer in good health and travel would not have been easy. Freud's mother's funeral, however, unlike this formal, public occasion, was held in Vienna; despite his glowing description of mothers and sons, Freud chose not to attend and considered it suitable to send his daughter to "represent" him.

In Freud's account of the mother-son tie, and of his own mother in particular, he stressed largely what the mother does for her son, though to be sure a son could fulfill, indirectly, a mother's ambition. His feeling of increased personal freedom after his mother's death fits Freud's general orientation on the subject, which was, behind all the idealism, rather egoistic. Freud did not conceal his own narcissism; on the contrary, he held that "a high degree of . . . self-love constituted the primary and normal state of things."[37] "My love is something valuable to me which I ought not to throw away without reflection."[38] His theory of dreams expressed the belief that everyone desired to satisfy egoistic wishes; he was singular in the courage and honesty with which he was able to acknowledge some of these less savory motives. Even compassion, he believed, had a narcissistic origin.[39] Freud had a tough core of hardness in him. "I may say of myself," he wrote during World War I, "that I have given the world more than it has given me."[40] It is difficult to say whether the crusty aspect of Freud's character (which did so much to buoy him in his innovations) indicates maternal overindulgence as a child or an obscure deprivation.

Freud recorded an anxiety-ridden dream of his mother's death, from his seventh or eighth year; correspondingly, she too once reported a dream of her son's death. By then she was an old woman, for whom dying was not a distant prospect. In her dream she was at Sigmund's funeral, and around his casket were arrayed the heads of state of the major European

The Freud family,
around 1876.
From left to right,
standing: Pauline,
Anna, (?), Sigmund,
(?), Rosa, Mitzi,
Simon Nathanson.
Sitting: Adolfine,
Amalie, Jakob.
In front: (?), Alexander

nations.[41] For an old mother, even a Jewish one, to experience such a dream is not implausible, but to permit an account of having dreamed of such a catastrophe to cross her lips because it depicted the fame her beloved son had achieved, does reveal something about the nature of her own yearnings which had been satisfied through her son's career.

Amalie must have cherished the heroic prophecies that were made

about Freud in his early years. More personally for her, this dream, at least
according to her son's theory, may also have expressed a hidden meaning
through a thematic polarity. For through the multiplication of father
figures she may have been accentuating the opposite of the dream's manifest content—that Freud really belonged to her alone and that he was
more her son and less his father's. Simultaneously, for dreams can have

many levels, this dream may have been an attempt at compensation for the loss of her son; she might no longer have him, but she was assured that the world did.

Jones declared that "never in his life did Freud accuse any woman of betraying or deceiving him." He speculated about Freud's childhood past that "it must have been a man who knew the secrets and only pretended to impart them to him," and therefore a woman was unlikely as a model of a rival.[42] Freud had great trouble acknowledging to himself any hostility toward his mother (and for that matter any antagonism to women or envy of them). Freud tended in an old-fashioned manner to idealize and yet also denigrate women. He never wrote about a son's matricidal wishes. In Freud's world women are treated as objects, rarely as subjects; yet they never appear either as bad mothers or as bad daughters. Freud's belief that he was his mother's favorite, and that this was the source of his self-confidence, may have been self-deceptive, a cover for positive feelings of indebtedness to his father. Freud could admit publicly many of his worst traits; yet whereas he could go so far as to describe his parricidal impulses, acknowledging conflicted feelings about his mother, including his dependencies, was more difficult.

One of the heroes Freud wrote a book about, Leonardo da Vinci, also had a young mother. The theme of the great man who grows up fatherless fascinated Freud; both Oedipus and the Moses of legend were raised, like Leonardo, apart from their natural fathers. In Freud's fantasies the true father turns out to be a man of high rank; as with Oedipus he was a king, so with Moses Freud made him into an aristocrat. Freud also believed that Shakespeare was not a man of humble origins but rather the Earl of Oxford. These models sustained Freud in his work.

In discussing Leonardo, Freud recounted the Egyptian legend of vultures being impregnated by the wind; Leonardo was a vulture child in being raised in early childhood by his mother alone, supposedly in accord with an early childhood fantasy of Leonardo's about a vulture having stuck his tail into his mouth. Yet Freud had made a slip here. The connection between the ancient Egyptians having chosen the vulture as a symbol of motherhood and the circumstances of Leonardo's life was irrelevant, though perhaps of meaning to Freud personally. In the German books on Leonardo the bird is correctly given as *Hühnergeier*—kite—but Freud must have seen only the last part of the word, *Geier*, which does mean vulture.[43] (Some of the translations Freud relied on also mistakenly used the word *Geier* for the Italian word for kite.)

Straightforwardly oedipal feelings, love for the parent of the opposite sex and hostility to the parent of the same sex, can be defensive, masking very different emotions. In fact, Freud, with hindsight and the help of his own concepts, seems to have been fearful of his own dependencies, and in particular of his submissiveness to women. He had difficulty in accepting the maternal in him, and even though there is an inevitable maternal core in the art of psychotherapy, Freud tended to minimize the importance of this side of his activities as an analyst. The maternal is also inextricably linked to the infantile, and here (as with his attitude toward music) Freud was quite standoffish. In any deep human relationship there is a danger of engulfment; the mother-son bond is not so one-sidedly glorious as Freud would have us believe.

There is every indication that Amalie Freud was—to use her son's vulture imagery in his study of Leonardo—a tough old bird. Despite the conditions of those times she managed to overcome tuberculosis.[44] She was, at least in her later years, self-willed, fastidious if not vain about her clothes, a tyrant to her daughters—in short, a classic Jewish matriarch. One of her grandsons remembered her as "not easy to live with." Amalie had "great vitality and much impatience; she had a hunger for life and an indomitable spirit."[45] She retained enough zest so that at the age of ninety she was still having her furniture reupholstered. Her sense of humor reminds one of Freud's irony. On her ninety-fifth birthday a photograph of her appeared in a newspaper; she objected that she did not like it: "it makes me look one hundred."[46]

Freud's mother was probably the prototype for the regal and self-sufficient type of woman whom Freud was able to admire and understand in his adult life. One granddaughter in particular resented her tyrannical and selfish ways, and other grandchildren agree that she was a disciplinarian, at least to close relatives; many in the family suffered from her authoritarian character.[47] According to family lore, her middle daughter, Dolfi, was not allowed to have a life of her own; she gave herself up to taking care of her mother, who even as an old woman was "a tornado." For Dolfi, as Freud's son Martin related it, "constant attendance on Amalie had suppressed her personality into a condition of dependence from which she never recovered."[48] (Freud once described Dolfi as "the sweetest and best of my sisters, . . . [with] a great capacity for deep feeling and alas an all-too-fine sensitiveness."[49]) Perhaps Freud and his brother Alexander could have arranged for some other provision for their mother; only what they said would have carried weight in the family, but neither of their wives wanted to take care of her.

There is no evidence that Amalie was ever directly dictatorial to

Freud, whose beauty as a young man she was fond of recalling. But such a woman could well call forth from Freud the intense kind of emotions he would later call oedipal. She is said to have had a court around her. Not only did the family come to see her on Sundays; Freud also brought some of his favored pupils to be introduced to her. Freud's seventieth birthday in 1926 was the occasion for open-house festivities at his apartment in his honor. Although it was taxing on him since he was already ill, Freud was visibly moved as he greeted guests in his morning coat. His mother was there, and had brought as a birthday present a wicker basket full of fresh eggs; it was a human and fitting gift, among the many others that had been made. She announced simply to at least one student of Freud's: "I am the mother."[50]

Freud and Alexander helped support their mother and visited her regularly on Sunday morning. It was a family joke that Freud's stomach would be out of sorts on these visits; this "attack of indigestion," as Jones calls it,[51] may have also been a result of the "chronic constipation" which Jones elsewhere describes Freud as suffering from. He himself attributed his recurrent minor intestinal ailment to the heavy dinner he ate regularly at a card-playing friend's house the Saturday evenings before. Perhaps a psychologically oriented observer with more detachment might have seen in this disorder a sign of Freud's allowing himself to go back to being a little boy in his mother's presence, an invitation to her tenderness. Later on Sunday his mother and all his sisters would come to Freud's house for the evening meal.

Any man's childhood and youth provide many contradictions and surprises, and it is mainly in the light of what we know of the grown man that we see much of anything in his past at all. One is, after all, seeking not so much for determinants, in a cause-and-effect way, as for patterns, configurations, parallels, or even inconsistencies. It is only suitable that our search should be guided by what we know was later important to Freud. He himself once questioned "whether we have any memories at all *from* our childhood: memories *relating to* our childhood may be all that we possess. Our childhood memories show us our earliest years not as they were but as they appeared at the later periods when the memories were aroused."[52]

Obviously, however, some assertions about Freud's early years are more supportable than others, and it is fortunate that he provided us with as much self-observation as he did, and that there are still members of the family alive who can give their own versions of the people involved.

The child is father to the man, without being the same as the man. It is only as we get further into Freud's life that his many-sidedness can become more comprehensible.

3. Love and Marriage

MOST OF WHAT CAN BE KNOWN of Freud's love life centers on his relationship with his wife, Martha. Any discussion of this aspect of Freud's personality has to be extremely tentative. Although more than nine hundred of Freud's letters from his four-year engagement to Martha have survived, only a small fraction of them have been released for publication. But at least the externals of his courtship can be clearly set down. Freud was twenty-six years old and still living in his parents' home when he proposed to Martha; some of his love letters to her were written on Jakob Freud's personal stationery, although Freud became engaged without consulting his father. Having spent eight years as a medical student and more than one year in research, in 1882 Freud became officially engaged to Martha Bernays.

Five years younger than he, Martha had also been brought to Vienna by her parents at an early age. Middle-class Viennese Jewish circles constituted a small world. Six months after Freud and Martha became engaged, her brother Eli, who was a friend of Freud's, announced that he and Freud's sister Anna planned to marry. To round out the picture of that tight little universe, Martha's younger sister Minna also was engaged to a Viennese friend of Freud's.

Martha's family was of a higher social status than Freud's, in terms of culture, both German and Jewish, as well as of money. Her grandfather had been the Chief Rabbi of Hamburg, an intellectual and a friend of Heinrich Heine's. One uncle was a professor of modern languages at the University of Munich, and another taught Greek and Latin at Heidelberg. According to a daughter-in-law of Martha's, her family was shocked that she should marry Freud, who, though a doctor, was someone without a fortune or a particularly promising future.[1] Martha must, therefore, have had some spirit.

Precise in manner and speech, in her later years (when Freud's pupils knew her) she seemed rather boring, a pedantic housewife; by then the great love was long over. She was, however, cultured, and as a young woman had been delicate and pretty. She was also very much Jewish-oriented, and it was only after a good deal of pressure that Freud overcame her allegiance to traditional Jewish ceremonials. (Freud's own father had been a freethinker, and although his mother observed the important Jewish holidays, she did so in a casual way, as they did not mean much to her.) In 1938 Martha and Freud were still carrying on a long-standing humorous (and yet serious) argument over the issue of lighting candles on Friday evening; Martha joked at Freud's monstrous stubbornness which prevented her from performing the ritual, while he firmly maintained that the practice was foolish and superstitious.[2] At her funeral in 1951 her children arranged to have a rabbi speak (as they did not at Freud's); presumably this meant that their mother would have wanted it so.

A self-contained and proud person, Martha was not likely to show much emotion in public. Freud himself commented in print on her bashfulness, even as a mature woman.[3] She was, in other words, very unlike the domineering mother he may have needed to escape from. Freud thought that "for every person, there are certain prerequisites, usually unknown to him, whose fulfillment is the precondition to falling in love."[4] As an opposite type from his mother, Martha may have helped allow Freud to break away from Amalie.

Freud's courtship of Martha was single-minded and possessive, and lasted so long only because of his poverty. The possessiveness in Freud's nature can be seen in the fiery letters he sent her. Freud had all the warmth of an essentially shy person. He could be jealous, and he enormously resented Martha's attachment to her mother, who stood for all the traditional Jewish customs and beliefs Freud was trying to persuade his fiancée to renounce. He put incredible demands on her, asking Martha to break with her family, on whom she was financially dependent, when he was not prepared to take responsibility for her himself. Once in making living arrangements she had thought first of her mother, not Freud:

> If that is so, you are my enemy: if we don't get over this obstacle we shall founder. You have only an Either-Or. If you can't be fond enough of me to renounce for my sake your family, then you must lose me, wreck my life, and not get much yourself out of your family.[5]

Freud knew the immoderate demands of one's infantile self: "childhood love is boundless; it demands exclusive possession, it is not content with less than all . . . it is doomed to end in disappointment and to give place to a hostile attitude."[6] Freud's claims for Martha's love were successful. At the time, she succeeded in meeting his needs for attention while keeping on good terms with her family, and Freud in turn admitted his tendency to be overbearing: "I do have a tyrannical streak in my nature and . . . I find it terribly difficult to subordinate myself."[7] Perhaps Freud had to dominate so in order to cover some of his fears—of women in general or of Martha in particular. It has been shrewdly suggested by Erich Fromm that what was going on in Freud's relation to Martha was a manifestation of Freud's "dependence on his mother," and the same pattern was also to repeat itself in his relationships "to men, older ones, contemporaries and disciples, upon whom he transferred the same need for unconditional love, affirmation, admiration and protection."[8]

Such a hypothesis need not obscure all that Freud brought to Martha in his life. The literary quality of Freud's letter-writing capacity was in itself notable; in letters to Martha he demonstrated his great talent as a born psychologist. One lengthy letter about the suicide of a friend reads like a memorable short story by a creative writer.[9] Martha was obviously so important to Freud that he was eager to share with her serious ideas and important experiences.

Jones was almost certainly right in describing Freud as chaste and puritanical in his engagement to Martha. Freud gave his permission for Martha to go skating (he himself did not skate) with the proviso that she be unaccompanied. In 1885 Martha wanted to stay with an old friend who, though she had just been married, had "married before her wedding."[10] Freud forbade her to do so. Later, in 1915, Freud wrote that he stood "for an infinitely freer sexual life, although I myself have made very little use of such freedom." Freud then added an ambiguous qualification to this disclaimer—"only so far as I considered myself entitled to"—which invites appropriate caution in biographical hypothesizing.[11]

In the beginning of their relationship, Freud's ardor, sometimes outgoing and sometimes jealous, was evident; his letters allow no doubt on this score. One could probably safely hazard the guess that at the outset of their marriage in 1886 Freud's tenderness fully accompanied his sexual passionateness. Freud's view of Martha's side of things may have been expressed in an essay he wrote in 1917:

> Whoever is the first to satisfy a virgin's desire for love, long and laboriously held in check, and who in doing so overcomes the resistances which have been built up in her through the influences of her milieu and education, that is the man she will take into a lasting relationship, the possibility of which will never again be open to any other man.[12]

Freud liked to highlight the loss of self in a love relationship, which was certainly true for him with Martha. Lovers are selfless. At the same time, to be in love presupposes a secure sense of self. Freud took such a secure self for granted, focusing instead on the loss, and this point of view may tell something about his own personality.

Jones's treatment of Freud's marriage was curious; although he maintained that the bond between Freud and Martha was perfection itself ("Freud's unsurpassable tenderness towards his wife was never marred in the fifty-three years of their married life"[13]), Jones also noted in passing that it was "likely that the more passionate side of married life subsided with him earlier than it does with many men." The passage is worth citing in full:

> His wife was assuredly the only woman in Freud's love life, and she always came first before all other mortals. While it is likely that the more passionate side of married life subsided with him earlier than it does with many men—indeed we know this in so many words—it was replaced by an unshakeable devotion and a perfect harmony of understanding.[14]

Jones's tact was at war with his honesty. In a letter from Emma Jung to Freud on November 6, 1911, which Jones cited in his text but quoted only in a letter, she referred to Freud's having told her that his marriage had long been "amortized" and that there was now nothing more left but death. Jones had inferred a similar meaning from parts of Freud's correspondence in the 1890's, and privately thought that an early falling off in Freud's sexuality was related to his neurotic horror of old age and death.[15]

In 1887, a little over a year after their marriage, Freud and his wife had their first child, a girl. Their first son was born in 1889, their second in 1891, their third in 1892; another daughter was born in 1893, and a last child, Anna, in 1895. In 1898 Freud wrote:

> it would be one of the greatest triumphs of humanity, one of the most tangible liberations from the constraints of nature to which mankind is subject, if we could succeed in raising the responsible act of procreating children to the level of a deliberate and intentional

Freud and his future wife,
Martha Bernays, in Berlin, 1885

activity and in freeing it from its entanglement with the necessary satisfaction of a natural need.[16]

In 1908 Freud thought it unfortunate that "all the devices hitherto invented for preventing conception impair sexual enjoyment, hurt the fine susceptibilities of both partners and even actually cause illness."[17]

Freud's potency may have been influenced by his dislike of available contraceptive methods. Since Martha was very easily impregnated, failing to withdraw was likely to produce children, and this probability no doubt made the couple anxious about intercourse. In 1897 (at the age of forty-one) Freud wrote to his most intimate friend, Wilhelm Fliess, that "sexual excitation is of no more use to a person like me."[18] Evidently a couple of years earlier Martha had been expecting (or hoping) to enter menopause, even though she was only in her mid-thirties. Instead, she turned out to be pregnant with Anna. Nevertheless, Martha apparently did have a premature menopause soon thereafter.[19]

During the period when he collected pupils around him, Freud did not seem to care especially for sex. From today's perspective he was decidedly on the prudish side. Freud once spoke of "the harm that is inherent in sexuality in general, sexuality being one of the most dangerous activities of the human being."[20] And in a letter Freud wrote that "anyone who promises to mankind liberation from [sic] hardship of sex will be hailed as a hero, let him talk whatever nonsense he chooses."[21] In his book on Leonardo, which contains many other autobiographical hints, Freud saw his hero "as a man whose sexual need and activity were exceptionally reduced, as if a higher aspiration had raised him above the common animal need of mankind."[22]

In line with his conversation with Emma Jung connecting his feelings about death with the state of his marriage, in 1898 Freud had cited a "colleague's" story of a patient's equation of impotency and death: "*Herr*, you must know, that if *that* comes to an end then life is of no value." The story itself, Freud wrote with candor,

> was also intimately bound up with trains of thought which were in a state of repression in me. . . . That this was really true at the time of the topic of "death and sexuality" I have plenty of evidence, which I need not bring up here, derived from my own self-investigation.[23]

Although Freud might like to feel that there was, as in his portrait of Leonardo, some transfer of energy behind talent and therefore some inner connection between reduced sexuality and genius, he also retained his capacity for occasional sexual high-spiritedness. In 1901, when Freud was forty-five, he mentioned having met "in the house of some friends . . . a young girl who was staying there as a guest and who aroused a feeling of pleasure in me which I had long thought was extinct. As a result I was in a jovial, talkative and obliging mood."[24]

There is evidence on the other side of the matter, in favor of a lengthier continuance of Freud's sex life. In 1908 Freud commented at the Vienna Psychoanalytic Society on a paper that "endeavored to fathom the nature of love." "It was a correct hunch," Freud complimented Fritz Wittels, "to attempt this via the study of perversions. In fact, however, the problem was solved long ago." Freud said he himself was "planning a paper on this topic, but for practical reasons will keep it until the time when his own sexuality has been extinguished."[25] But two years later Freud published the first of three essays eventually collectively entitled "Contributions to the Psychology of Love."

Freud had certain inhibitions that would not be inconsistent with a relative curtailment of his sex life after Martha stopped having children. "We . . . describe a sexual activity as perverse," he wrote during World War I, "if it has given up the aim of reproduction and pursues the attainment of pleasure as an aim independent of it."[26] Jones mentioned Freud's "personal puritanical predilections"[27] without seeing the implications of these for Freud's theories; for example, Freud's commitment to his work led him to see science somehow at odds with the pleasure principle. Freud austerely thought that "the opposite of play is not what is serious but what is real,"[28] and for all the playfulness of his own mind he consistently underrated play as a constituent of maturity.

Freud was pessimistic about the possibility of sexual gratification: "something in the nature of the sexual instinct itself is unfavorable to the realization of complete satisfaction." "An obstacle," he believed, was "required in order to heighten libido. . . ."[29] He even wrote that one of the aims of analytic therapy was to set "the neurotic free from the chains of his sexuality."[30] At the same time Freud well knew that "the feeling of happiness derived from the satisfaction of a wild instinctual impulse untamed by the ego is incomparably more intense than that derived from sating an instinct that has been tamed."[31] And he also wrote:

Sexual love is undoubtedly one of the chief things in life, and the union of mental and bodily satisfaction in the enjoyment of love is one of its culminating peaks. Apart from a few queer fanatics, all the world knows this and conducts its life accordingly; science alone is too delicate to admit it.[32]

Freud was daring in recognizing the role that infantile sexuality could play in adult life. He contended, for example, that masturbation was the "primal addiction" for which later ones—such as smoking, morphine, or gambling—were substitutes. Popular mythology, he wrote, has often agreed in finding "a permanent reduction in potency as one among the results of masturbation," and on the basis of his medical experience Freud could not rule out the possibility. But he sounded dry and cynical about the advantages of such a reduction in potency:

Some diminution of male potency and of the brutal aggressiveness involved in it is much to the purpose from the point of view of civilization. It facilitates the practice by civilized men of the virtues of sexual moderation and trustworthiness that are incumbent on them. Virtue accompanied by full potency is usually felt as a hard task.[33]

Freud thought that "with the advance of civilization, it is precisely the sexual life that must fall a victim to repression,"[34] at the same time that he shared mankind's discontent with civilized restraints.

Whether or not he himself was suffering from any reduction in his potency, he gave us at least several possible explanations for this condition. He once mentioned, for example, "a man suffering from occasional sexual impotence, which originated from the intimacy of his relations with his mother in childhood. . . ."[35] An unsatisfied mother could take "her little son in place of her husband, and by the too early maturing of his eroticism [rob] . . . him of a part of his masculinity."[36] At the same time Freud held that "even a marriage is not made secure until the wife has succeeded in making her husband her child as well and in acting as a mother to him,"[37] a questionable prescription for a mature sexual relationship. Martha actually came to treat Freud as a boy, and this could have resulted in his infantilization as a man. It did not help him as a father either; Freud's relative lack of success with his sons may have stemmed from the combination of his stature in the world, which was a burden to them, and his diminished role at home, which deprived them of a strong male model.

The death of Freud's father in 1896 also coincided with what he wrote at the time of his decreased interest in sex. Freud once mentioned a man who "was the most pronounced rebel imaginable . . . ; on the other hand, at a deeper level he was still the most submissive of sons, who after his father's death denied himself all enjoyment of women out of a tender sense of guilt."[38] Freud's momentous theory of the meaning of dream life came during this same period of the 1890's. After his great discoveries it might be plausible to believe, according to his own theory of the transfer of human energies, that his libidinal interests then went into forwarding his cause.

4. Family Life

ONCE THE PSYCHOANALYTIC MOVEMENT was under way the arrangements of Freud's family life become easier for the historian to verify. The Freuds lived in an apartment on the second floor of a building on the Berggasse, No. 19; a butcher shop occupied the ground floor. In 1892 Freud personally chose this apartment to live in, and he and his family stayed at this address until 1938. From 1892 to 1908, for his practice Freud used a separate apartment of three rooms on the mezzanine, only a few steps up from the ground floor. In late 1907 his sister Rosa gave up her suite on the second floor, adjacent to the Freud family apartment; Freud could now use this for his work and he took the whole second floor.

Martha brought to Freud's household some of her own family's reserve, which contrasted to the petit-bourgeois atmosphere of Freud's mother's home. The Sigmund Freuds had an abundance of servants: "a cook who did no work outside her kitchen . . . a housemaid who waited at table and also received . . . patients. . . . a governess for the elder children and a nanny for the younger, while a charwoman came each day to do the rough work."[1] Martha must have been a good manager, for this establishment seems to have run smoothly. In household matters she was thrifty, especially toward herself. Although "Frau Professor," as she came to be called, did not do any of the cooking, she was a fine housekeeper and always had good food on hand. Jones's account of Freud at the dinner table should remind one how busy his days were, and how preoccupied with his work he usually was.

> The family lunch was at one o'clock. This was the only time when the whole family would usually be together; the evening meal was often so late that the younger members had already retired to bed.

It was the chief meal of the day . . . [Freud] enjoyed his food and would concentrate on it. He was very taciturn during meals, which would sometimes be a source of embarrassment to strange visitors who had to carry on a conversation alone with the family. Freud, however, never missed a word of the family intercourse and daily news . . . He would point mutely at . . . [a] vacant chair with his knife or fork and look inquiringly to his wife at the other end of the table. She would explain that the child was not coming in to dinner or that something or other had detained him, whereupon Freud, his curiosity satisfied, would nod and silently proceed with his meal.[2]

Martha was hardly a "perfect social hostess."[3] The Freuds never gave parties, since the couple disliked them.[4] They had numerous guests—and one room in their apartment was eventually set aside for visitors—but such hospitality tended to become more rare as the years passed. Freud was not a mixer and Martha not much of an entertainer; she was a fussy housewife, always cleaning up spots in the house and worrying where Freud's cigar ashes might land. More and more, company overwhelmed her with petty anxieties.

Once a year she would make formal calls on the wives of Freud's close friends and Viennese pupils. Tea would be served, and perhaps the hostess would have also prepared some embroidery to give to Martha as a token of appreciation for her visit. While Martha was concerned that foreign pupils, especially the women, got well situated in Vienna, it was Freud's eldest daughter, Mathilda, who usually helped them find apartments (and who sometimes even obtained theater or concert tickets). The movement comprised a family, and the family was itself a part of the movement.

From an early date Martha fully appreciated who her husband was, and enjoyed his fame. To her, as to Freud's mother, he was a great man and she glorified him. Sometimes she wondered why their problem in finding a house for the summer was not solved by a generous donor. (Freud is said to have once ironically sent her a letter posing as such a benefactor.[5])

Martha arranged the life of the house so as not to disturb her husband. The apartment was unusually quiet, especially considering the number of people it housed, and the family's life revolved around his work. Martha did far more for Freud than was usual even in those times. Much of Freud's own fastidiousness may have come from Martha's compulsive orderliness; she laid out his clothes, chose everything for him down to his handkerchiefs, and even put toothpaste on his toothbrush. "If I had had such a wife," joked one of his pupils, "I too could have written all those books." But while everything was done for Freud at home and Martha was indulgent as far as his work was concerned, the women ruled the roost. Because of his habit of smoking, Freud wrote, his "reputation for tidiness was not of the highest with the authorities in my own house. . . ."[6]

Freud once mentioned that he tried to carry over his theoretical principles from his work to his family: "When a member of my family complains to me of having bitten his tongue, pinched a finger, or the like, he does not get the sympathy he hopes for, but instead the question: 'Why did you do that?' "[7] The evidence, however, indicates that his clinical practice and his writing were kept separate from the life of the

*The Freud family sitting room; at the right is one of
the twelve coal-fired porcelain stoves in the Freud apartment*

household. This was partly because of Martha's refusal to allow psychoanalytic ideas to invade the nursery, although it has been said that she permitted him to use psychoanalysis more in the upbringing of the younger children. According to Freud's eldest daughter, as well as others, he never discussed his ideas with his wife.[8] Theodor Reik's memories seem to bear this out:

> From conversations on walks on the Semmering, near Vienna, I got the decided impression that she not only had no idea of the significance and importance of psychoanalysis, but had intensive emotional resistances against the character of analytic work. On such a walk she once said, "Women have always had such troubles, but they needed no psychoanalysis to conquer them. After the menopause they become quieter and resigned."[9]

It was not simply that Frau Professor did not allow Freud to apply psychoanalysis to the raising of her children; he himself declined to practice his depth psychology at home. He was not always peering deeply into human motives, and with his own family he could be completely unpsychological. His sons were sent to a family doctor to find out about the facts of life. When a pupil once excitedly pointed out that one of Freud's chows was obviously having a dream, he remarked: "I've told them they feed her too much, I've told them they feed her too much, but they do not listen."[10] And when in the 1920's a visitor to Freud's apartment went through an elaborate explanation of a public slip of the tongue that had occurred at a memorial service for a colleague, Frau Professor commented (with some irony) on how interesting the reasoning had been: "We never hear such things."[11] She probably understood the gist of more of her husband's work than his pupils cared to think.

As the years went on and she grew old, Martha was slighted within the family—by her husband and the circle around him, as well as by her daughter Anna, though not by the rest of the children. Raising the six of them had worn her out early. She felt tired, and Mathilda helped take over the social side of things. Frau Professor was self-contained and a lady, so it is not clear whether her pride prevented her from seeing—or simply from showing that she saw—how she was pushed into the background in Freud's life. Her composure was that of a rich personality and not simply the result of her inhibitions. On their golden wedding anniversary in 1936 Freud wrote to a female pupil, Marie Bonaparte: "It was really not a bad solution of the marriage problem, and she is still today tender, healthy and active."[12]

Whatever had or had not gone on between them physically or intellectually, Martha was still, as an acquaintance of Freud's put it, the bride of his youth. One particularly sensitive observer, a patient close to Freud and his family, remarked that Martha remained the mother of his children, and that she and Freud had a beautiful, simple relationship; for him she was the family.[13] According to another follower, during summer vacations (when Freud was not off traveling) they could not bear a single night away from each other's side, even if it meant the inconvenience of a tiny room.[14]

None of this affection was incompatible with his evident irritation with her. As one pupil put it, "there was an air of understanding forgiveness for her increasingly pedantic attitudes."[15] Freud spent less and less time with his wife as Anna came to replace her. But Anna grew bitter toward her mother for not having the strength to fulfill all of Freud's needs. After he contracted cancer of the jaw, Anna looked after his physical condition; she was the one to see that his mouth, with its prosthesis for a part removed by operations, was adequately rinsed. Martha was jealous of her youngest child, and there grew up an antagonism between them. In 1939, when Freud's suffering had finally overcome his endurance and he and his doctor agreed that it was enough, and that euthanasia was called for, Freud instructed his physician to "tell Anna about our talk,"[16] not his wife.

By this time Anna had not only taken over her mother's role, but that of her Aunt Minna as well. For Martha's sister, who had come to live with the Freud family in 1896[17] at the age of thirty-one and stayed until her death in 1941, was no small figure in Freud's life. Freud, Martha, and "Tante Minna" came to form a remarkable triangle. Physically Minna Bernays was large and heavy, much more like Freud's imperious mother than his wife; like Amalie Freud, Minna wore a little old-fashioned cap on the top of her head. Martha and Minna were very close as sisters —as one pupil put it, emotionally "a pair of Siamese twins." Both were artists at needlework, and both (like others at the Freuds') suffered from migraine headaches and vomiting.[18] Even if Freud had not regarded migraine as an "organic suffering" instead of a psychogenic symptom,[19] he operated on the assumption that neurosis did not exist within his own family. Minna's youthful engagement had ended with the death of her fiancé; afterward she seemed to Freud's pupils an archetypal spinster.

Once she came to live with Freud's family she was a member of the entourage which he supported financially. Earlier she had been a governess and a lady's companion, and she participated actively in the raising of

Freud's children. He referred once in a letter to "the two mothers—
my wife and my sister-in-law."[20] Whatever the children gained from
Minna's presence, they also suffered from this double maternal authority; for either both women were in agreement, which made it hard for
the children to assert themselves, or Martha and Minna disagreed, which
could also be difficult. It has been said that the children were jealous of
the preoccupation of the two sisters with each other.

The more caustic-tongued of the two, Minna was also the stricter
with the children. When one of Freud's daughters-in-law (Martin's wife,
Esti) married into the family, she resented the role Tante Minna played
in her husband's life. Minna disapproved of Martin's marriage; she said
of him when he had just been released from a World War I prisoner-of-
war camp: "He is betaking himself from one imprisonment to another."

*Floor plan of the
Freud apartment,
described as it
was used in 1938*

Sharp and bitter as she could be, her outspokenness never alienated her sister Martha; when Esti (then separated from her husband) visited Frau Professor years after Minna's death, Martha was hurt and astonished that she had not asked after Minna.

Minna was far more intellectual than Martha, read foreign languages easily, was quite literary, and became a real support to Freud in his work. Some have said that Martha, in the early days, listened to stories about some of Freud's patients; but she never actively helped in his work. Minna, however, really understood his ideas, and he was far more likely to discuss his cases with her than with Martha. According to family legend, Freud dictated one of his translations to Minna.[21] In conversation Freud remembered that in his loneliest and yet most creative years, the 1890's, only Minna and his friend Wilhelm Fliess had been able to sustain his faith in himself, for they believed in his intellectual achievement.[22] Minna was exempt from Freud's competitiveness with intellectual men; she was more a listener, a projective screen for his ideas, than anything like a collaborator.

A favorite card partner of Freud's, Minna also frequently traveled with him over the summer holiday. Martha went to her own spa. (When the Freud family took a vacation together, Freud traveled "alone and in comfort."[23]) Freud was an energetic traveler, and Martha was scarcely up to his pace. But many different explanations are given for why Freud traveled with Minna rather than Martha.

Freud did not enjoy traveling alone. One version has it that Freud liked high mountains, but that heights disturbed Frau Professor;[24] of course, Freud also loved Italy, and Martha never went there with him either. Once Jones explained Martha's inability to accompany her husband on vacation by her need to recuperate from an illness; another year, Jones said, Martha had to take care of an ailing child; and Jones mentions another occasion when Freud went to Bad Gastein with Minna because she "also needed treatment there."[25] Whatever the conflicting reasons, it is indisputable that Freud and Minna regularly enjoyed traveling with each other.

In 1969 an article appeared asserting that Jung had claimed that Minna had spoken to him of her anxiety about Freud's love for her and the intimacy of their relationship.[26] It might be attractive to think of Freud and Minna having had a grand passion for each other. Freud once wrote that, unlike Minna's fiancé and Martha, who were completely good people, he and Minna were, in Jones's gloss, "wild passionate people, not so good."[27] Supposedly Freud meant to explain why he was suited to Martha, and Minna to her beau, by the contrast in their natures. But an entirely different (and prophetic) construction might be put on this characterization.

The evidence for the premature falling off in Freud's sex life might be interpreted in quite a different light; instead of merely the cooling of his ardor for Martha, what may have happened is that he transferred his physical and/or emotional needs to another woman, Minna. (An old neighbor of the Freuds thought Minna was prettier than Martha.) In the case of such a prolific and self-investigating writer as Freud, it may well be that if an affair with Minna ever took place evidence for it exists somewhere in unpublished letters.

There are signs of Freud's sexual dissatisfaction; one time he recorded that on a trip to Italy he found himself walking involuntarily again and again to the prostitutes' section.[28] Freud's puritanism could be construed as a reaction formation to his own passions having burnt very brightly. It is difficult to reconcile the vibrant man we know from his works and letters with the man who responded to his self-analysis in the 1890's with a relative loss of potency.

On balance, however, and in a tentative spirit, I would be inclined to reject the notion that a physical relationship existed between Freud and Minna. She did indeed speak to Jung about Freud's involvement with her; his attentions did worry her. But according to Jung's account it was Freud's affection for her that was worrisome, not an actual affair.[29]

To Freud's pupils Minna seemed scarcely a woman—asexual and a neuter. On at least one occasion Freud raised the issue of his relationship with Minna in an analysis; Freud chided the patient, "So you believe in my famous love affair with Minna." But when the patient disavowed the idea, Freud seemed a bit miffed, as much offended for Minna's sake as for his own.[30] Freud hated disorder, and the discord of jealousy would probably have made life in the Berggasse impossible. Perhaps out of his feelings for Minna, Freud's sexual enthusiasm had waned; loss of potency could have been an unconscious device for preventing himself from being unfaithful to Martha.

The important matter is what Minna meant to Freud, the power she gained over him, and not so much the specifics of a possible sexual liaison between them. Freud seemed to have a split in his love life, his sexuality remaining with Martha and his spiritual involvement shifting to Minna. It may be that his tie to Martha might not have survived as well as it did were it not for Minna's presence in the household. As far as we know, Freud found little difficulty in keeping his sexuality under control in his contacts with his many female followers.[31] It is hard to know which of the available alternatives would have been better for Freud as a person; for to have continued to make love to a woman who held as little interest for him as Martha did may have been worse than being unfaithful or lacking in potency.

In Freud's last years, Minna, like Martha, was edged out by Anna. Whatever feeling he still had for Martha, it was Minna who helped make sure that Freud took his medicine on time and who poured his second cup of coffee. Minna was full of admiration for his stoicism in the face of cancer; any "ordinary" man, she once remarked, would have made an end to himself long before.[32] Cataracts in her eyes gave Minna a great deal of trouble in her old age. Of the three women closest to Freud at the time of his death—Anna, Martha, and Minna—Jones believed it was the last, already in poor health, who took the blow the hardest.[33]

III

A SCIENCE
OF DREAMING

1. "Struggles for recognition"

THE PAST IS OF SPECIAL IMPORTANCE to both the biographer
and the psychoanalyst, as they share an interest in reconstructing history
for the sake of better understanding the human being. Although Freud
was more than usually concerned with unraveling the meaning of his own
beginnings, it would be a mistake simply to extract the autobiographical
element in everything he wrote. For above and beyond his search for
self-understanding he had a passionate commitment to science. Jean-Paul
Sartre has remarked[1] that the Jew in particular has learned to distrust
intuition and empathy as forms of magic and hocus-pocus not open to
rational discussion, therefore legitimating discriminations among men.
Intelligence, on the other hand, is a universal capacity, available in varying degrees to all.

As we have seen, Freud's career as a scientist was initially blocked by
his relative poverty and his desire to marry Martha, which led the physi-
ologist Ernst Brücke to advise Freud to enter medical practice. (Years
later Freud recalled Brücke's having remonstrated with him over his
lack of punctuality: "No one who can remember the great man's eyes,
which retained their striking beauty even in his old age, and who has ever
seen him in anger, will find it difficult to picture the young sinner's
emotions."[2] To his own pupils Freud was later known for being extraordinarily punctual, and his own eyes and capacity for anger were no
less notable.) Jakob Freud had not thought much of his son's future as a
doctor, since for all his brilliance he seemed horrified at the sight of blood.[3]
As Freud recalled in 1914, "I . . . had only unwillingly taken up the
profession of medicine, but I had at that time a strong motive for helping people suffering from nervous affections or at least for wishing to
understand something about their states."[4] In his autobiographical study
a decade later, Freud remarked of his choice of a career that "neither at

that time, nor indeed in my later life, did I feel any particular predilection for the career of a doctor. I was moved, rather, by a sort of curiosity, which was, however, directed more towards human concerns than towards natural objects. . . ."[5]

Several years later Freud again spoke of his motivation in becoming a physician, this time in support of the practice of psychoanalysis by non-medical analysts:

> After forty-one years of medical activity, my self-knowledge tells me that I have never really been a doctor in the proper sense. I became a doctor through being compelled to deviate from my original purpose; and the triumph of my life lies in my having, after a long and roundabout journey, found my way back to my earliest path. I have no knowledge of having had any craving in my early childhood to help suffering humanity.

Freud had a striking sense for the way opposites go together, and paused at this point to add an explanation for the absence of any "craving" in his early childhood "to help suffering humanity." "My innate sadistic disposition was not a very strong one," he wrote, in words which must have startled readers in 1925, "so that I had no need to develop this one of its derivatives."

> In my youth I felt an overpowering need to understand something of the riddles of the world in which we live and perhaps even to contribute something to their solution. The most hopeful means of achieving this end seemed to be to enrol myself in the medical faculty. . . .[6]

In letters to Martha in the early days of his medical research and during their betrothal, there is evidence of what he called his "struggles for recognition."[7] To have made a scientific discovery early on not only would have advanced his career but also would have ensured his financial future and made possible an early marriage to Martha. "It is hard to find material for publication," he lamented, and "it infuriates me to see how everyone is making straight for the unexploited legacy of nervous diseases."[8]

In 1884 Freud began experimenting—on himself, Martha, his sisters, as well as others—with the way cocaine could relieve anxiety and depression. Freud wrote "a paper which introduced cocaine into medicine."[9] Despite his intolerance of drugs in general, Freud was so enthusiastic about this work that he was not adequately cautious with regard to cocaine's addictive qualities. Once the real dangers became known Freud's earlier use of the drug did little to enhance his standing in solid Viennese medical circles, but instead, as he wrote, earned him "serious reproaches."[10]

Freud missed becoming famous in the exploration of the uses of cocaine. A fellow Viennese physician, Karl Koller, discovered that cocaine can act as a local anesthetic in eye surgery. Koller had no doubt benefited from Freud's early work with cocaine, but he rightly won all the honor for making the special discovery of cocaine's value in eye surgery, a field far removed from Freud's. At the time Freud thought that Koller's contribution would be only an aspect of the many possible uses of the drug, but in fact it became the central therapeutic one.[11]

Although Freud publicly gave Koller due credit, he could not help blaming someone for what seemed to him a missed opportunity, an understandable even if fanciful notion. At the time of his interest in cocaine Freud had wanted to visit Martha in Berlin, and he hurriedly completed his first essay on cocaine. But Jones later established that there was in fact no such reason for hurrying.[12] Freud concluded his article by predicting that the anesthetizing action of cocaine would be utilized in various ways. As he later wrote in 1897, "the expectation voiced at the end of the work that the property of cocaine for producing local anaesthesia would find further applications was soon afterwards fulfilled by K. Koller's experiments in anaesthetizing the cornea."[13]

Before leaving on his trip to see Martha, Freud had suggested to Leopold Koenigstein, an ophthalmologist friend, that he try cocaine's effects on diseases of the eye. Koenigstein had used a commercial solution from a druggist which had too much alcohol in it and therefore failed to achieve the desired effect, whereas Koller made up his own solution and attained the success that earned him world fame.[14] As Freud wrote in 1899, "I had myself indicated this application of the alkaloid in my published paper, but I had not been thorough enough to pursue the matter further."[15] These then were the grounds on which, in 1926, Freud looked back and wrote that it had been "the fault of my *fiancée* that I was not already famous at that youthful age. . . . but I bore my *fiancée* no grudge for the interruption."[16] This incident is reminiscent of Freud's having blamed his father's "generous improvidence" for not giving him strong advice against pursuing a career in pure science; Martha may have seemed the occasion for a missed opportunity precisely because he had chosen medicine in the first place for the sake of marrying her.

Freud always worried lest a discovery of his be prematurely snatched away by someone else. For example, Wittels reported that in 1906 the Koller incident was still very much on Freud's mind:

Koller, said Freud, had had . . . a fixed idea that he would make an ophthalmological discovery, and had endeavored to apply to the opthalmological field all that he heard and all that he read. That was why Koller, though not a man of any marked ability, had rushed off to drop some cocaine solution into his eye the instant he had read Freud's essay . . . So mechanical an explanation of a discovery seems to me inadequate. Koller did not become an opthalmologist until after his achievement. Before that, his aim had been to study general surgery. . . .[17]

In a 1924 letter to Wittels, Freud objected to this account of the cocaine story:

The reader would . . . have gained a different impression of my attitude to Koller's discovery had he been told, which indeed you couldn't have known, that Koenigstein (it was *he*, not I, who so deeply regretted having missed winning these laurels) then claimed to be considered the co-discoverer, and that both Koenigstein and Koller chose Julius Wagner *and myself* as arbitrators. I think it did us both honor that each of us took the side of the opposing client. Wagner, as Koller's delegate, voted in favor of recognizing Koenigstein's claim, whereas I was whole-heartedly in favor of awarding the credit to Koller alone. I can no longer remember what compromise we decided on.[18]

Hanns Sachs, too, remembered a discussion by Freud of the cocaine incident, in which, however, he attributed to Koller a method similar to his own single-minded style of discovery. Freud had said:

Among my friends, when I was a young internee at the General Hospital, was one who seemed obsessed with the idea of finding a new ophthalmological therapy. Whatever medical problem was discussed, his thoughts and questions went in the same direction: Could this be used for the eye?—so that he became occasionally a bit tiresome by his monomania. Well, one day I was standing in the courtyard with a group of colleagues of whom this man was one, when another internee passed us showing the signs of intense pain. I said to him: "I think I can help you," and we all went to my room where I applied a few drops of medicine which made the pain disappear instantly. I explained to my friends that this drug was the extract of a South American plant, the coca, which seemed to have powerful qualities for relieving pain and about which I was preparing a publication. The man with the permanent interest in the eye, whose name was Koller, did not say anything, but a few months later I learned that he had begun to revolutionize eye-surgery by the use of cocaine, making operations easy which till then had been impossible. This is the only way to make important discoveries: have one's ideas exclusively focused on one central interest.[19]

In 1909 or 1910, perhaps on the occasion of a newspaper article about Koller's discovery of cocaine's surgical uses, Freud explained to a young analytic patient how he, Freud, had rightly made the real discovery, not Koller. Freud then regarded the cocaine episode as a triumph rather than a defeat, since the real discovery was his own.[20] He stressed that when he had mentioned the use of cocaine to Koenigstein he was perfectly aware of the great present he was making him; Koenigstein had simply botched the job.[21] Koller was, however, perfectly entitled to his recognition, although Freud himself claimed the credit for the discovery. In turn, Koller maintained that Freud's work had not influenced his own discovery at all.[22]

Regardless of the controversy with Koller, in relation to his own teachers Freud was more than generous in acknowledging their influence on his development. To be a great teacher it helps to have once been an unusually devoted pupil; for Freud, "to teach an old teacher something" meant "a pure, unmitigated satisfaction."[23] Even in his forties Freud reported vivid dreams of sitting for old school examinations. He paid tribute to his mentors in the names chosen for his children. "I had insisted on their names being chosen, not according to the fashion of the moment, but in memory of people I have been fond of. Their names made the people into *revenants*. And after all, I reflected, was not having children our only path to immortality?"[24] Jean Martin was named for Jean Martin Charcot, Ernst for Ernst Brücke, Mathilda for Josef Breuer's wife, and Anna for the daughter of an old schoolteacher of Freud's. In the 1920's Freud arranged for a grandson to be named for a deceased but valued pupil, and his followers similarly acknowledged his importance as a mentor in their lives by naming their children after his.

Jones astutely accounted for Freud's tendency to hero worship as a projection of "his innate sense of capacity and superiority onto a series of mentors on some of whom he then became curiously dependent for reassurance." In reaction against this tendency to idealize people, however, Freud could be touchy about being dependent or "having his freedom of action restricted. . . . Freedom and independence were life-blood to him."[25] Freud's sensitiveness toward helpers, his need for them as well as his fear of losing them, was poignantly clear to him. In a passage that Freud later dropped from *The Psychopathology of Everyday Life*, he wrote:

> There is scarcely any group of ideas to which I feel so antagonistic as that of being someone's protégé. . . . the role of the favorite child is one which is very little suited to my character. I have always felt an unusually strong urge "to be the strong man myself."

Yet as a young man, Freud wrote, he entertained "the phantasy of my own rescue" through a powerful benefactor; at the same time he felt obliged "to make my longing for a patron and protector tolerable to my pride . . . in my conscious life I myself was highly resistant to the idea of being dependent on a protector's favor, and . . . I found it hard to tolerate the few real situations in which something of that nature occurred."[26] With his family background, needing to create himself and be his own father, Freud wanted to be cared for and at the same time passionately desired to be independent.

Freud was explicit about the immense role certain parental figures came to play in his life. For four and a half months in 1885–86, as part of his neurological training, Freud studied in Paris with Charcot. As Freud recalled it, he "frequently walked about the streets, lonely and full of longings, greatly in need of a helper and protector, until the great Charcot took me into his circle."[27] In 1899 Freud described himself as a "pupil of Brücke" and a "pupil of Charcot,"[28] and it would be hard to overestimate Freud's lasting identification with Charcot. As Freud wrote in a report to the University of Vienna medical faculty after his trip to Paris, Charcot was a "great man." Freud said he left Paris "as Charcot's unqualified admirer,"[29] and somewhat later wrote that he still retained "the memory of the Master's voice and looks."[30] Ever after Freud kept a photograph of this "sage" (signed and given by Charcot, at Freud's request) on his walls: "No one has ever affected me in the same way."[31]

The personal qualities that Freud admired in Charcot were compatible with Freud's conception of himself and he could readily aspire to emulate them. Charcot "had the feeling of those who believe they carry a field marshal's baton in their knapsack."[32] The encounter with Charcot, to Freud "a famous discoverer," was a landmark in the young man's career. In his sympathetic essay on Charcot, Freud—who himself frequently employed pictorial images—admired in his former teacher "the transparent clarity of his diction and the plasticity of his descriptions."

He was not a reflective man, not a thinker: he had the nature of an artist—he was, as he himself said, a "*visuel*," a man who sees . . . He might be heard to say that the greatest satisfaction a man could have was to see something new—that is, to recognize it as new. . . .

Freud remembered objecting to one of Charcot's clinical innovations: "That can't be true, it contradicts the Young-Helmholtz theory." Charcot had not replied: " 'So much the worse for the theory, . . . clinical facts come first' or words to that effect; but he did say something which made a great impression . . . : '*La théorie, c'est bon, mais ça n'empêche pas d'exister.*' " This remark ("Theory is good; but it doesn't prevent things from existing") was one that Freud would repeat throughout his lifetime. Charcot "never tired of defending the rights of purely clinical work, which consists in seeing and ordering things, against the encroachments of theoretical medicine."[33] Freud said he had "learnt to restrain speculative

A demonstration by Jean Martin Charcot
at the Salpêtrière, Paris

tendencies and to follow the unforgotten advice of my master, Charcot: to look at the same things again and again until they themselves begin to speak."[34] According to Freud, Charcot (like Freud himself in his later years) "took an honest, human delight in his own great success and used to enjoy talking of his beginnings and the road he had travelled."[35]

As a teacher Charcot had been (again, like Freud later on) "positively fascinating," and had left behind him "a host of pupils." Charcot welcomed students into his family, and exhibited a "life-long loyalty to them." By "giving the most detailed account of his processes of thought and by showing the greatest frankness about his doubts and hesitations, he had thus sought to narrow the gulf between teacher and pupil." Another parallel between them was that Charcot also had "a highly-gifted daughter who was growing up in the likeness of her father. . . ."[36]

Charcot's originality lay in his scientific respect for neurotic sufferers; in Central Europe at that time the discredit attaching to nervous disorders "extended not only to the patients but to the physicians who concerned themselves with the neurosis."[37] Charcot, as well as being a "great physician and friend of man," was "not pessimistic in his therapeutic expectations. . . ."[38] It is true that Charcot emphasized the role of heredity as a cause of neurosis, placing less importance on the factor that Freud at this time held responsible—parental syphilis; nevertheless, Charcot had set out to try to make rationally understandable clinical phenomena which others had until then ignored.

Charcot found that it was possible through hypnosis to evoke symptoms which previously had seemed purely organic in origin. He perceived "the presence of regularity and law . . . [whereas] other people saw only malingering or a puzzled lack of conformity to rule,"[39] and this was bound to appeal to the scientist in Freud. He proceeded to translate into German one of Charcot's textbooks, but, as Freud later admitted, "I really did infringe the rights of property that apply to publications. I added notes to the text which I translated, without asking the author's permission, and some years later I had reason to suspect that the author was displeased with my arbitrary action."[40]

Charcot inspired not only Freud but also a whole school of French disciples, chief among them Pierre Janet.[41] Whereas Charcot had been immersed in clinical work at his hospital, the famed Salpêtrière, Janet started out with laboratory rather than clinical aims; Charcot's work was like "a bustling kitchen, alive with noise, smells, explosions and excitements, like the great Salpêtrière itself. Janet's was a neat, well stocked pantry with everything in cans."[42] Janet, however, had the foresight to pursue Charcot's lead in the psychological understanding of mental symptoms, particularly states of dissociation ("multiple personalities"). Indeed Janet seems modern and post-Freudian in his emphasis on the role that weakness in a person's higher integrative capacities plays in releasing more primitive reactions below.[43]

But despite this stress on ego processes, Janet did not see as clearly as Freud would the role of psychological conflict in mental disease, the way even the "normal" mind can be permanently at odds with itself. Nevertheless, Janet's work was sufficiently close to Freud's so that in later years they became explicit rivals. One of the reasons Freud preferred the term "unconscious" to "subconscious" was that Janet had used the latter. In 1917 Freud paid him respect, admitting that Janet could "claim

Pierre Janet

priority of publication." However, Janet had not traveled the path Freud took, and Freud said he had "ceased to understand Janet's writings."[44] In 1911 it had been reported to Freud that Janet had "made a real attempt to read your books but finds it well nigh impossible."[45] By the 1920's Janet was bluntly saying that Freud had plagiarized his ideas and simply altered the terminology. "I read," Freud wrote, "that I made use of my visit to Paris to familiarize myself with the theories of Pierre Janet and then made off with my booty."[46] Freud resented "the libel" being "spread by French writers that I had listened to . . . [Janet's] lectures and stolen his ideas."[47] According to Freud, he had "always treated Janet himself with respect. . . . But . . . Janet behaved ill, showed ignorance of the facts and used ugly arguments."[48]

2. Early Mentor: Josef Breuer

IN FREUD'S VIEW, Janet, unlike their master Charcot, had had no influence on him and became simply an opponent of psychoanalysis. Josef Breuer, however, was a teacher and intimate friend of Freud's who exerted on him at least as much, if not more intellectual impact than Charcot, and who certainly played a far more personal role in his life. Breuer was a kindly man with an immense Viennese practice in internal medicine; he also had a fine scientific mind, and "discovered the function of the labyrinth of the ear and the mechanism which controls normal breathing (Breuer-Hering law)."[1]

In the course of treating a clever patient between 1880 and 1882 (and therefore before the publication of Janet's first book), Breuer had discovered that pathological symptoms of at least some types of neurotic patients are not senseless but have a meaning. Breuer had adopted the procedure of investigating the history of each symptom, for it seemed to relieve the young woman's suffering (in her case history she was named "Anna O."). As Freud put it, "Breuer [had] learnt from his first [psychotherapeutic] patient that the attempt at discovering the determining cause of a symptom was at the same time a therapeutic maneuver." Breuer had not investigated this train of ideas further, but he and Freud in collaboration undertook a broader inquiry: "our procedure was to take each separate symptom and inquire into the circumstances in which it had made its first appearance. . . ."[2] Therefore "Breuer's discovery supplemented Charcot's;

or it may be regarded as Charcot's discovery inverted. Charcot had shown that by instilling suitable ideas it was possible to cause hysterical symptoms. Breuer showed that hysterical symptoms vanish when the pathogenic idea can be disinterred from the unconscious."[3]

Breuer was Freud's guide and mainstay for over ten years, lending money, referring patients, and generally being solicitous about his young protégé's career. Freud recognized that the older man was concerned for his welfare; when Freud turned to explore the role of sexuality in the origins of neuroses, he mentioned in a letter that "Breuer will say that I have done myself a lot of harm."[4] Freud tried to repay his obligation to Breuer, persuading him to publish their findings and dedicating his own neurological treatise on aphasia to his mentor.

It is remarkable how slow Freud was to acknowledge the real differences between Breuer's position and his own; Freud turned out to be a reluctant conqueror as a scientific discoverer. In 1896 Freud wrote in a paper that he owed his "results to a new method of psychoanalysis, Josef Breuer's exploratory procedure. . . ."[5] Yet long after Breuer probably would gladly have dissociated himself from the findings of what Freud had come to call "psychoanalysis," Freud still paid tribute to Breuer's priority. Even after their personal break, Freud, writing about himself in the third person, mentioned in 1903 that "as the result of a personal suggestion from Breuer, Freud revived this procedure [used with Anna O.] and tested it on a considerable number of patients."[6]

It would seem that Freud's work was so startling to him that for some time he could not bring himself to assume full responsibility for it, and needed to shield himself behind Breuer's reputation. Even as late as 1909, in his lectures at Clark University in America (where he received his only honorary degree), Freud went so far as to assert that "no doubt I owe this honor only to the fact that my name is linked with the topic of psychoanalysis. . . . If it is a merit to have brought psychoanalysis into being, that merit is not mine."[7] In 1914, however, after the loss of his pupils Adler, Stekel, and Jung, Freud made a different reference to his words about Breuer in the Clark lectures: "some well-disposed friends have suggested to me a doubt whether my gratitude [to Breuer] was not expressed too extravagantly on that occasion."[8] As Freud later put it, in 1914 he felt able to assume "the entire responsibility for psychoanalysis."[9] Nevertheless, Freud continued to pay special deference to Breuer and in the middle of World War I still maintained: "I follow Breuer in asserting that every time we come upon a symptom we can infer that there are certain definite unconscious processes in the patient which contain the sense of the symptom."[10]

Breuer and Freud developed serious differences, for the younger man was more eager to explore thoroughly this new vein of thought. Breuer, among others, had intimated to Freud the role sexuality sometimes played in neurotic suffering. Freud later protested that "the idea for which I was being made responsible had by no means originated with me." But here Freud drew a distinction:

> it is one thing to give utterance to an idea once or twice in the form of a passing *aperçu*, and quite another to mean it seriously—to take it literally and pursue it in the face of every contradictory detail, and to win it a place among accepted truths.[11]

Freud had postulated that patients become ill when they are unable to accept certain aspects of their past. Whereas Breuer assigned a pathogenic role to so-called "hypnoid states" (in which otherwise unexceptional experiences took on a special import), Freud, more thoroughgoing as a psychologist, was "inclined to suspect the existence of an interplay of forces and the operation of intentions and purposes such as are to be observed in normal life."[12] They agreed, however, on the therapeutic aim of relieving memories which were capable of being aroused under hypnosis and which when remembered and acknowledged expressively (the method of "catharsis") had a curative impact.

None of their intellectual differences would seem sufficient to account for the final "breach" in the relations between Freud and Breuer.[13] Freud went out of his way in 1914 to express his gratitude that there had been no squabbles over priority of scientific discovery between them. For example, in their collaborative work the concept of "conversion" was introduced to describe how psychological symptoms "represented an abnormal employment of amounts of excitation which had not been disposed of. . . ."

> Whenever Breuer, in his theoretical contributions to the *Studies on Hysteria* (1895), referred to this process of conversion, he always added my name in brackets after it, as though the priority for this first attempt at theoretical evaluation belonged to me. I believe that actually this distinction relates only to the name, and that the conception came to us simultaneously and together.[14]

According to Freud's editor and translator James Strachey, however, "there seems to be some mistake here. In the course of Breuer's contribution he uses the term 'conversion' (or its derivatives) at least fifteen times. But only once (the first time he uses it. . . .) does he add Freud's name in brackets."[15]

Whatever the sources of their falling out, and no matter what role scientific reasons may have played, Freud's admiration for Breuer was transformed into an intense loathing. (Much of this animosity was editorially suppressed, but some relevant material has recently been made available.[16]) Freud's attitude toward Breuer, as toward Martha when their engagement grew troubled, was an either/or one; if Breuer could not follow Freud all the way into his new researches, then Breuer became an enemy and an opponent. Under these new circumstances Freud wanted to repay the money he still owed Breuer, and when Breuer refused the repayment, Freud only felt worse about his early dependency on his teacher. *The Psychopathology of Everyday Life* contains a thinly disguised reference to the change in his relation to the Breuer family. Speaking of "the M. Family," Freud wrote:

> our intimate friendship later gave place to a total estrangement . . . I fell into the habit . . . of also avoiding the neighborhood and the house . . . as if it were forbidden territory . . . money played a part ["a great part," in some earlier editions| among the reasons for my estrangement from the family living in the building.[17]

The question was once suggestively raised by Otto Rank whether Freud's account of the dramatic effect his father's death had on him in 1896, and the past which it stirred up, may not have been partly a self-deception, a regressive evasion of a present-day conflict—a denial of the importance of the separation that was then taking place between Breuer and him.

In later years Freud would speak privately with condescension and contempt of Breuer for his alleged cowardice in the face of the new findings of psychoanalysis.[18] But a pupil like Freud could not detach himself easily from an ego-ideal like Breuer, any more than Freud could readily let some of his own special pupils go. In his publications, however, Freud never ceased to acknowledge his debt to Breuer. "In this relationship the gain was naturally mine. The development of psychoanalysis afterwards cost me his friendship. It was not easy for me to pay such a price, but I could not escape it."[19] Unfortunately Breuer had not had sufficient distance to recognize the "universal nature" of the unexpected phenomena he confronted in the case of Anna O. Apparently this patient had developed an intense erotic attachment to Breuer, who worried about what he might have done to arouse such expectations.[20] Freud, on the other hand, coolly perceived that Breuer "had come up against something that is never absent—his patient's transference onto her physician. . . ."[21]

Each patient, Freud discovered, comes to psychotherapy with an inner world built up out of past relationships, and the psychotherapist

Josef Breuer (1842–1925)

willy-nilly evokes feelings which are seemingly of an irrational intensity but whose character can be understood in terms of the patient's previous history. According to Freud, Breuer had fled from further treatment of Anna O. because he "had not grasped the impersonal nature of the process" of such "transferences" in therapy; Anna O., then, was responding not so much to Breuer himself as to Breuer seen in the light of other important figures in her life. Freud's therapeutic strategy was to interpret transferences, in order to liberate the patient from his past.

When Breuer died in 1925, Freud wrote a warm obituary acknowledging him as "a man of rich and universal gifts." Even though Breuer was fourteen years older, a "friend and helper," Freud referred to their period of collaboration as a time when Breuer "submitted to my influence. . . ."[22] Freud once spoke of this memorial to his own student Karl Abraham: "I exchanged cordial letters with his family, and so brought my fateful relations with him to a dignified conclusion."[23] Yet Freud's qualities as a gentleman should not obscure the intensity of his feelings of betrayal. Breuer's daughter-in-law remembered walking with him as an old man; suddenly he saw Freud coming straight toward him, and Breuer instinctively opened his arms. Freud passed by, pretending not to see him, which gives some idea how deeply the break must have wounded him.[24]

Because Freud had been so involved with Breuer and so influenced by his teacher's report of the case of Anna O., he felt entitled to repudiate any intimation that he had been dependent on Janet's ideas, whatever the many similarities in their formulations. The method of treatment that Freud began to elaborate out of his work with Breuer marked the beginnings of the distinctive aspects of psychoanalytic therapy. As early as 1895 Freud was referring to "the Freudian theory," and "psychoanalysis" as a term first appeared in a paper of Freud's in 1896;[25] what Freudian theory would refer to, however, as well as what constituted psychoanalysis, was to change a great deal over the years.

Freud had started out treating hysterical disturbances which did not follow an anatomical pattern. The hypothesis of Freud and Breuer was that the root trouble was strangulated affect, emotions which were not conscious to the waking mind of the patient. Through attention to the history of the symptoms, the therapist could dissolve the trouble by means of awakened memories. Despite Freud's comments in his old age about having originally lacked "a genuine medical temperament," the indications are that at the outset of his career he was enormously interested in achieving therapeutic successes. It is true that terms such as "observer" and "observations" rather than "helper" or "healing" continued to be used throughout Freud's career; yet his detailed attention to the life histories of his patients' symptoms was supported by more than just scientific curiosity.

Initially Freud found hypnosis to be the best technique for approaching the neuroses. The role of hypnotist seems to have fascinated him:

> Anyone who has assembled a few personal experiences with hypnotism will recall the impression it made on him for the first time he exercised what had hitherto been an undreamt-of influence on another person's psychical life and was able to experiment on a human mind in a way that is normally possible only on an animal's body.[26]

Freud wrote of working in spite of the "protestations" of his patients, as he tried to uncover their self-deceits; in Freud's view of hypnotism, "no contradiction whatever must be permitted."[27] Through the special power of suggestion—"an energetic denial of the ailments of which the patient has complained, or in an assurance that he can do something, or in a command to perform it"[28]—therapeutic improvements could be accomplished. From the therapist's point of view, "the recollection of so many cures brought about by hypnosis will lend his behavior towards his patients a certainty which will not fail to evoke in them too an expectation of yet another therapeutic success."[29] For a time hypnotism seemed to Freud a boon for both the scientific investigator and the clinical therapist.

By the mid-1890's Freud's enthusiasm for hypnotism had tapered off. For one thing, its suggestive element—although "incomparably more attractive than the monotonous, forcible prohibitions used in treatment by [pure] suggestion"[30]—was hardly desirable for research. Freud already realized that the ideal therapeutic goal was to overcome not just painful symptoms but pathological processes themselves. Successful use of hypnotism required, in Freud's view, "enthusiasm, patience, great certainty and a wealth of stratagems and inspirations."[31] But since Freud found it hard to sustain this level of commitment to the technique, he concluded that hypnotism was "a temperamental and, one might almost say, a mystical ally."[32] Hypnotism became "in the long run, *monotonous*,"[33] and furthermore tended to take away the patient's sense of self-reliance.

Freud describes himself in this period of creative flux as being "driven forward above all by practical necessity,"[34] and as one reads his case histories of this time, it does seem that he was making alterations as his clinical experience gradually enlightened him. His account of how he adopted the technique of free association, for example, is touching in its simplicity. A patient appears to have stoutly resisted Freud's interfering with the flow of the clinical material. "I now saw that I had gained nothing by this interruption and that I cannot evade listening to her stories in every detail to the very end." At another point the same patient "said in a definitely grumbling tone that I was not to keep on asking her where this or that comes from, but to let her tell me what she had to say." As Freud quietly put it, "I fell in with this. . . ."[35] Freud found he had to be more patient in his therapy, and instead of starting out from the pressing symptoms and aiming to clear them up, he left it to the patient to choose the subject of the day's work. The couch was a useful remnant from Freud's use of hypnosis, however, since it permitted both analyst and patient to relax and free-associate without the burden (at least to Freud) of direct face-to-face confrontations.

For its time Freud's new technique seemed far less directive than most other methods of treatment. Eventually the too easily hidden manipulative elements in the analytic situation would have to be emphasized; but Freud's was an appeal to the rational strengths of his patients, an effort, through understanding the past, to free their energies for the future. Whereas hypnotic treatment had sought "to cover up and gloss over something in mental life," analysis sought rather "to expose and get rid of something. The former acts like a cosmetic, the latter like a surgery."[36] A self-made man himself, Freud had devised a method of therapy which relied on the individual's ability to transcend rationally the limitations of his private world, and through verbal self-knowledge to attain a detachment from his emotions that would permit genuine self-mastery. Whatever external situations a person might meet, at least he could learn to maximize his control of his inner emotions.

3. Self-Analysis

IN THE 1890's FREUD WAS probably more troubled than in any other decade in his life. It is for that period, at least, that we have the most extensive records of his discontents, fears, and depressions. Freud's creation of psychoanalysis involved not only treating patients but also trying to analyze himself. These two enterprises went together, since with what he discovered about patients he helped himself, and what he learned introspectively he could use to aid neurotics. Also, the theory and practice of psychoanalysis served Freud as instruments of self-concealment as well as self-discovery. The artist in him was able to use his own most intense experiences as the basis on which to communicate with mankind at large. Freud was not usually shy about describing the hell in his own soul; in the 1890's his inner world seems to have been so much in turmoil that when in his later and more settled years he felt affection for creative but relatively disorganized pupils, perhaps he was exhibiting also a special affection for an earlier but now safely submerged self.

In daily life Freud's limitations were hardly noticeable; for in the 1890's he functioned as part of a large family group. Although his pupils later felt his warmth, he seemed to them an absolutely disciplined person. Reserved, dignified, aloof, Freud was also tenacious, independent, and courageous. His eldest son simply could not imagine seeing his father not always immaculately dressed, or even without a tie.

Yet Freud also suffered in middle life from urinary irritability, which meant frequency if not incontinence (perhaps connected to prostatic troubles).[1] In addition, a spastic colon subjected him to irregular bowel movements. We know more about this problem than some others because Freud spoke openly about it in his letters.[2] According to one of Freud's physicians who later became an analyst specializing in psychosomatic medicine, Freud's gastrointestinal symptoms were a regular response to inner tension.[3]

Freud also suffered from migraine attacks throughout his life; according to his public account, they were "mild," but Jones considered them "severe."[4] In the 1890's, when Freud wrote more about the problem than afterward,[5] he related migraines mainly to sexual deprivation. This was the same decade in which Freud and his wife had the last four of their six children, and they were determined not to have any more. The connection between Freud's personal life and his scientific work has to be, at times, hypothetical. But in the 1890's Freud was particularly interested in writing about the consequences of "coitus interruptus" and he gave it "a prominent place among the causes of anxiety neurosis."[6]

It is no novel guess, however, that in the 1890's Freud was suffering from what he termed an "anxiety neurosis." He was especially fearful about his heart,* worried about dying, and speculated about which dates might be especially dangerous. A strain of romanticism in Central European literature had been concerned with the problem of death, but in Freud's

---

* Max Schur has recently hypothesized a cardiac episode in the 1890's, as opposed to Freud's (and Jones's) version of these symptoms as part of a psychoneurosis. Since Schur was aware "how difficult it is to arrive at a valid differential diagnosis some seventy-five years after the events," additional medical opinion may be of help in deciding whether to amend the customary interpretation.[7]

case there were, in addition, personal motives. "The theme of death, the dread of it and the wish for it, had always been a continual preoccupation of Freud's mind as far back as we know anything about it."[8]

As sexual orgasm has been equated with death, both in literature and in popular folklore, it is possible that Freud's sexual inhibitions may have been related to his heart anxieties. When he wrote on the theme of death and sexuality, and the view of a colleague's patient that once sex comes to an end then life has no more value, Freud mentioned how "the heart itself, as a sick bodily organ" had played a part in his own associations and thoughts.[9] Before long Freud was satisfied that the neurotic fear of death was usually to be explained by guilt feelings. But what is as striking as Freud's anxieties about death was the fortitude with which he endured all the real suffering connected with his cancer of the jaw; for Freud bore this death within him with courage and resignation throughout the last sixteen years of his life.

In Freud's earlier years, however, his anxiety neurosis took other forms as well, for instance a fear of open spaces (usually more common in women). Once while crossing a square with Theodor Reik, Freud hesitated, took Reik's "arm and said, 'You see, there is a survival of my old agoraphobia, which troubled me much in my younger years.' "[10] Freud once suggested that "agoraphobia sometimes has the sole purpose of preventing the patient from going to prostitutes."[11] Freud also discussed agoraphobia in connection with phobias of locomotion, and indeed several persons have reported on Freud's anxieties about travel, which caused him to arrive at the train station well ahead of time and to be concerned about counting his pieces of luggage. (In accord with Freud's principle that opposites go together, he was also inordinately fond of traveling.) Freud himself once said that setting out on a journey by train was symbolic of the ultimate separation, death.[12] The outbreak of such fears of special conditions were part of Freud's anxiety neurosis, "of which phobias are," Freud thought, "a psychical manifestation." In the 1890's Freud suggested that "the specific cause" of anxiety neurosis was "the accumulation of sexual tension. . . ."[13] Although these problems by no means prevented him from carrying on his work, Freud's early agoraphobia was consistent with the experience of his more mature years, when he was most at ease in his office.

Freud was also a heavy cigar smoker, and this addiction must have contributed to the development of his cancer. After trying to give up the habit, Freud found that he could not work productively without cigars, even though he acknowledged that his passion for smoking interfered with his exploration of certain psychological problems.[14] But most of his personal difficulties—urinary, gastrointestinal, migraine, sexual, as well as the anxieties and phobias—are known to us in such detail only because he was honest enough to write or talk about them; moreover, he himself has given us some of the concepts that enable us to interpret his autobiographical material.

To acknowledge that Freud had his human troubles, that he suffered, had fears, and was not the master of all his emotions, is only to subscribe to his own psychoanalytic theories. But Freud was hardly the sum of his troubles; indeed, it is a measure of his capacities that he accomplished as much as he did despite his difficulties, or rather that he succeeded in harnessing his neurosis into constructive channels. Freud once wrote that an ideally "normal" person is a mixed type, and has narcissistic, obsessional, as well as hysterical layers to him; here Freud was undoubtedly writing about himself.[15] Any account of Freud's experiences with his innermost difficulties should warn one away from an excessively puritanical conception of "normality."

While Freud was trying to come to terms with himself during these years, he went through a period of withdrawal from the regular intellectual contacts he had enjoyed earlier. Freud had never been the stereotype of the easygoing, sociable Viennese. It was "obvious" to his pupil Hanns Sachs, for example, that "Freud's personality, his way of thinking as well as living," represented "the diametrical opposite of everything that has been described . . . as typical of Vienna."[16] Freud (and Jones after him) chose to stress his ostracism by his Viennese colleagues.[17] Freud certainly made several false starts in his ambitions, and his dispensing of a drug like cocaine did not foster a reputation for reliability. As Freud moved into the treatment of the neuroses, first with hypnotism and then free association, and as he came to his theory of dreams and the unconscious, his techniques were too far ahead of his time for his medical contemporaries to appreciate. Well might Freud reflect that "there is something comic about the incongruity between one's own and other people's estimation of one's work."[18]

Though he may have suffered from his loneliness, Freud also reveled in his isolation. As he remembered it in 1914,

> My "splendid isolation" was not without its advantages and charms. I did not have to read any publications, nor listen to any ill-informed opponents . . . there was nothing to hustle me. . . . My publications, which I was able to place with a little trouble. could always lag far

behind my knowledge, and could be postponed as long as I pleased, since there was no doubtful "priority" to be defended.[19]

Nevertheless, Freud resented the "vacuum" that formed itself around his person.[20] In 1924 he recalled the resistances his ideas had stirred up:

> For more than ten years after my separation from Breuer I had no followers. I was completely isolated. In Vienna I was shunned; abroad no notice was taken of me. My *Interpretation of Dreams* . . . was scarcely reviewed in the technical journals . . . As soon as I realized the inevitable nature of what I had come up against my sensitiveness greatly diminished.[21]

Freud felt that his ostracism during these years could be accounted for by the inevitable "distaste and repudiation" which his unwelcome ideas had evoked, and this reaction was directed against his own person.[22] In 1926 he wrote that "the announcement of my unpleasing discoveries had as its result the severance of the greater part of my human contacts; I felt as though I were despised and universally shunned."[23]

It would be impossible to overestimate how much of himself Freud put into his work:

> My innovations in psychology had estranged me from my contemporaries, and especially from the older among them: often enough when I approached some man whom I had honored from a distance, I found myself repelled, as it were, by his lack of understanding for what had become my whole life to me.[24]

Although Freud had all along been an intrepid explorer in search of discovery, he harked back to his period of isolation to support, as well as explain, the fierceness of his independence. "It was hardly to be expected . . . that during the years when I alone represented psychoanalysis I should develop any particular respect for the world's opinion or any bias towards intellectual appeasement."[25]

While setting himself apart from the world, he nonetheless used his own responses as a means of understanding those of others:

> There runs through my thoughts a continuous current of "personal reference," of which I generally have no inkling, but which betrays itself by . . . instances of my forgetting names. It is as if I were obliged to compare everything I hear about other people with myself; as if my personal complexes were put on the alert whenever another person is brought to my notice. This cannot possibly be an individual

peculiarity of my own: it must rather contain an indication of the way in which we understand "something other than oneself" in general. I have reasons for supposing that other people are in this respect very similar to me.[26]

Thus the psychological system Freud created closely fit his personal peculiarities—demonstrating that the rise of psychoanalysis was far from a coldly neutral scientific advance. Nor was Freud's retrospection uncolored by his sensitivities: research has exploded the myth that Freud's *Interpretation of Dreams* was widely ignored in book reviews.[27]

Freud described the mechanisms of persecutory paranoids who "cannot regard anything in other people as indifferent." Rather like the practicing analyst with his patients, these types "take up minute indications with which these other, unknown, people present them, and use them in their delusions of reference. The meaning of their delusion of reference is that they expect from all strangers something like love." Freud saw "the enmity which the persecuted paranoic sees in others" as the "reflection of his own hostile impulses against them."[28]

It was fortunate that Freud was grandiose, for it gave him the insight that others might be like himself; and on this basis he could generalize about other people's emotions. The further he went in his own self-analysis, then, the better off he would be in understanding his patients. In 1882 Freud had remarked that "it gave him an uncanny feeling whenever he was unable to gauge someone else's emotions through his own. . . ."[29] Freud's self-analysis gave him empathy and knowledge, even if not his ideal of freedom. But Freud did more than enough in psychology for one man. Perhaps he was correct when he wrote of his own achievement that he thought it was "less the result of intellect than of character."[30]

The most notable instance in which Freud's self-analysis intertwined with his clinical work came in his acceptance of his patients' tales of seduction: one of Freud's large mistakes, what he later called "that first great error,"[31] was to think that the source of his patients' troubles was a childhood sexual trauma, usually inflicted on them by their parents. Freud thought his own father guilty in this regard, though not in relation to himself but to his siblings.[32] It took years for him to publicly admit his error, and the interim which he allowed to pass may well have been when he acquired a dubious reputation in Viennese medicine.[33]

Freud's final resolution was to see that these seduction tales were fantasies, products of incestuous infantile desires rather than actual events. Once Freud, by 1897, could treat the issue as part of the inner world of his patients, what we have come to know as most characteristic of psychoanalysis was already under way: the therapeutic aim lay in uncovering childish fantasies beneath neurotic façades. The inner world of Freud's patients, rather than external events, was seen as the chief source of neurotic difficulties. "Traumas" acquire their character through the way in which seemingly innocuous incidents can be experienced subjectively as distressing crises.

Rather than hold that children were seduced into sexuality, Freud discovered that they themselves could be sexual beings. As Freud later put it, "we have rated the powers of children too low and . . . there is no knowing what they cannot be given credit for."[34] His patients' tales of seduction were expressions of infantile desires, of which they were unconscious. These longings were mobilized in the therapeutic relationship, since the patient transferred to the therapist, as the surrogate for parental figures, all those infantile feelings which have since come to be known as the Oedipus complex.

4. Wilhelm Fliess

THE CHANGES IN FREUD'S THINKING during this period are documented in the letters he sent to a Berlin physician, Wilhelm Fliess, who, while studying in Vienna, had been introduced to Freud by Breuer. Throughout his self-analysis Freud was intimately involved with Fliess, though he eventually became estranged from him, as he had from Breuer. Two years younger than Freud, Fliess was a brother-in-law of Freud's Viennese acquaintance Oskar Rie. It is sometimes difficult to discern in Freud's many letters to Fliess when he is consciously exaggerating and when he is being deadly serious; conventions of attitudinizing have shifted greatly since then. But as far as one can tell Freud became extraordinarily intimate with Fliess. This friend in Berlin was of immense importance in his self-discovery and scientific work. At the time Freud was working in seclusion, he still required a listener: "I need you as my audience,"[1] he once wrote to Fliess. By believing in Fliess, Freud reassured himself about some of his own ideas; "when I talked to you, and saw that you thought something of me, I actually started thinking something of myself. . . ."[2]

The two men shared their work and daily lives through their correspondence, in which scarcely any reference is made to their wives; but

Freud is known to have disliked Fliess's wife intensely.[3] He blamed Breuer,* though he claimed that "I no longer despise him" for inspiring her enmity. Freud wrote to Fliess: "What else is your wife doing but working out, under a dark compulsion, the suggestion Breuer planted in her soul when he congratulated her on the fact that I was not living in Berlin and could not disrupt her marriage."[5] Occasionally Freud and Fliess had meetings, sometimes proudly (and teasingly) dubbed "Congresses." Had Freud's last child, Anna, been a boy, she would have been named for Wilhelm Fliess.[6]

In later periods, when Freud was more secure and self-contained, he rarely revealed himself to others. He may have retained the warm feelings of the Fliess period, but he was not so quick to put them into words, at least not on paper. But in the late 1890's Freud was at the peak of his self-analysis. He had for some time been collecting dreams from people he knew as part of his self-understanding as well as his clinical work; Freud's self-analysis would continue throughout his life, but only in this relatively short period was he so intensely in need of his work as a means of curing himself. As he wrote to Fliess, "I can only analyze myself with objectively acquired knowledge (as if I were a stranger); self-analysis is really impossible, otherwise there would be no illness."[7]

Despite Freud's competitiveness and his conflicts over submission and domination, no rivalry—for a time—marred the closeness of his contact with Fliess. However, they lived a good distance apart, and their friendship might not have lasted as long as it did (over ten years) if Fliess's home had been in Vienna. On the one hand, Freud needed his own isolation, even if he grumbled about it; yet he also sought an uncomprehending blank screen in Fliess. The latter could be a helpful alter ego for Freud, and sometimes by his very lack of receptivity encouraged Freud to work out his own ideas.[8]

Freud's intimate revelations may have been a burden to Fliess, though mitigated by the fact that their exchanges took place almost entirely on paper. Freud's expressions of emotion, then, might not have been unsettling, couched as they were in a rational and elevated form. (In later

---

* Freud aired other reproaches against Breuer in his correspondence with Fliess. Freud found fault with him as a physician. In 1894 he wrote: "I am being treated evasively and dishonestly as a patient instead of having my mind set at rest by being told everything there is to tell in a situation of this kind, namely, whatever is known." As an old-fashioned doctor, Breuer had apparently objected to a patient of Freud's going into a fifth year of analytic treatment. When in 1900 Breuer's daughter was about to marry someone close to Fliess, Freud felt excluded. He wrote to Fliess of "the prospect of being pushed still further apart from you and your family through the impending 'Breuerization' . . . ."[4]

years, when Freud had given up this sort of dependency—or rather reversed it by having others depend on him—his friendship for Fliess was replaced by an inner dialogue; repeatedly he resorted to a Socratic technique in his writings. Freud would put the possible objections to his ideas into the mouth of an observer, showing where any concessions would logically lead; always in Freud's books there would be inner self-questioning and interchange, as if with an interlocutor.)

Freud once addressed Fliess as a "magician"; "for me," Freud also wrote, "you remain the healer, the prototype of the man into whose hands one confidently entrusts one's life and that of one's family."[9] Fliess was the "first reader and critic"[10] of *The Interpretation of Dreams*, and Freud took his comments seriously. It is interesting to find through reading these letters to Fliess how early Freud had some of his most characteristic ideas, even though it took years for some of them to emerge in fully rounded scientific papers.[11] Fliess's work, in turn, had a great impact on Freud; on reading one paper, for example, Freud commented: "My first impression was one of amazement at the existence of someone who was an even greater visionary than I, and that he should be my friend Wilhelm."[12] Clearly Freud's idealization of Fliess had to end in some form of disappointment.

Yet good grounds remained for Freud's immense admiration for Fliess's many talents. The concept of "latency period," for example, which later became part of psychoanalytic theory (used to describe the developmental stage of relative quiescence in sexuality, coming between the height of the Oedipus complex at five or six and the onset of puberty), was originated by Fliess.[13] In Freud's view, Fliess had made "a fundamental biological discovery"[14] concerning the role of periodicity (twenty-eight days for women, twenty-three days for men) in human life. Although by 1920 Freud had his doubts about the soundness of Fliess's hypothesis, Freud still paid tribute to the boldness of the attempt:

> According to the large conception of Wilhelm Fliess, all the phenomena of life exhibited by organisms—and also, no doubt, their death—are linked with the completion of fixed periods, which express the dependence of two kinds of living substance (one male and the other female) upon the solar year.[15]

Fliess's periodic laws could supposedly determine the span of one's lifetime. Freud came to share fully in Fliess's numerological fantasies, on which he based some of his superstitions of how many years he had left to live. (In 1909 Freud referred to these beliefs as "confirmation of the specifically Jewish character of my mysticism."[16]) Jones intelligently interpreted Freud's credulity as part of the receptivity and open-mindedness that accompanies genius.[17]

Another of the concepts that Freud and Fliess shared (and ended up rivals for) was that of bisexuality, which has had a long history. At least since Plato, philosophers have spoken of the feminine side of men and the masculine traits of women. Fliess proposed as a generalization that such sexual inversions not only exist and have psychological consequences, but also are at the root of many neurotic difficulties.

In the course of illustrating the human "tendency to forget what is disagreeable," Freud later cited how he had forgotten in 1900 to acknowledge Fliess's notion of the role of repressed bisexuality in neurosis. "It is painful," Freud admitted, "to be requested in this way to surrender one's originality."[18] The theme of "borrowing someone else's ideas" would come up repeatedly in the course of Freud's career. Although his originality is now indisputable and his contributions to psychology were authentically individual, Freud always worried about the possibility of plagiarism —both in his own writing and in that of his collaborators. After his lapse of memory with regard to the concept of bisexuality, Freud claimed that "since then I have grown a little more tolerant when, in reading medical literature, I come across one of the few ideas with which my name can be associated, and find that my name has not been mentioned."[19]

For a time Freud continued to acknowledge his debt to Fliess. In 1905 he wrote: "It is only fair to say that my attention was first drawn to the necessary universality of the tendency to inversion in psychoneurotics by Wilhelm Fliess of Berlin, after I had discussed its presence in individual cases."[20] By 1910, however, when their private falling out had already become part of a larger public controversy, Freud began to restrict his tributes to Fliess. In 1905 Freud had written in *Three Essays on the Theory of Sexuality* that he became "acquainted through Wilhelm Fliess with the notion of bisexuality," but five years later (and in all subsequent editions of the same book) Freud dropped the words "through Wilhelm Fliess,"[21] while retaining the rest of the sentence. As Freud explained elsewhere in the book, "Fliess (1906) subsequently claimed the idea of bisexuality (in the sense of *duality of sex*) as his own."[22] In a 1937 essay Freud thought that he had "already stated" in a paper in 1919 that "it was Wilhelm Fliess who called my attention to the way in which" the attitude proper to the opposite sex can "succumb to repression"; Strachey, however, had to point out in a correction to Freud that "actually Fliess is not mentioned by name in that paper."[23]

Although Freud could be secretive about ideas of his own, he—even by Jones's account—"was not a man who found it easy to keep someone else's secrets."²⁴ Freud's capacity for indiscretions was enough of a problem for him to discuss it in *The Interpretation of Dreams*.²⁵ Freud reports, in connection with an issue of importance to Fliess, having been "given a warning not to discuss the matter with anyone. I had felt offended by this because it implied an unnecessary distrust of my discretion." Although Freud knew that "these instructions had not emanated from my friend but were due to tactlessness or over-anxiety on the part" of an intermediary, still Freud felt "very disagreeably affected by the veiled reproach because it was—not wholly without justification."²⁶

Throughout his work as a psychoanalyst, and perhaps never more so than in the late 1890's, Freud was full of ideas. The scope of his aims, the breadth of his vision, made it hard for others to keep up. In letters to Fliess, Freud openly discussed how it was that he could have made the "mistake" of believing that his patients' seduction stories were literally true. Freud confessed to Fliess that in his own "case my father played no active role, though I certainly projected onto him an analogy from myself. . . ."²⁷—thus admitting that his feelings for his own children had played a part in his "mistake."

In retrospect, Freud showed courage and tenacity in working through this painful and conflict-laden material until he located the source of neurosis in childish fantasies. But to a contemporary like Fliess it seemed that Freud had been misleading his patients. Knowing Freud's unsettled grudge against his father, and Freud's earlier belief that Jakob had seduced his own children, Fliess could well doubt the objectivity of Freud's methods. Freud's treatment procedure rested on listening to the thoughts of patients, and to Fliess this now smacked of magic, not science. Freud protested Fliess's failure to follow him along his newest path: "you take sides against me and tell me that 'the thought-reader merely reads his own thoughts into other people,' which deprives my work of all its value." Freud remained "loyal to thought-reading," as a scientific method of understanding as well as curing, and he repudiated the notion that the "'thought-reader' perceives nothing in others but merely projects his own thoughts into them. . . ."²⁸ And so, without Freud's adequately acknowledging the part he may have played in suggesting the so-called tales of seduction to his patients, the friendship began to break up and the intensity of their exchanges gradually cooled off.

In the version that Jones set forth (following Freud's account), "Fliess . . . had angrily discarded him in spite of Freud's attempts at reconciliation."²⁹ Freud's interpretation was that Fliess had had a paranoid attack, and Freud was bitter about it. According to later psychoanalytic theory, paranoia stems from repressed homosexuality, and Freud more than once said that the "secret" of paranoia had been learned from Fliess;[30] Freud made the connection only after the break in their friendship. However, it also seems reasonable to suppose that Freud would not have wanted to continue with Fliess once "thought-reading" was regarded by him as a species of magic.

At the same time, Freud needed a new audience, and the last friendly, though somewhat formal, correspondence between Freud and Fliess took place in 1902, the year Freud founded the psychoanalytic movement. Although, according to Jones, "all traces of such dependence had vanished for good after the break with Wilhelm Fliess," it would seem that Jones was once again idealizing Freud; for although Freud no longer required a father figure like Breuer or a "magician" like Fliess, he now needed others who were dependent on him.[31]

One portion of the Freud-Fliess correspondence was excluded from the published volume of their letters. In 1904 Freud found himself in a public controversy over priorities which is reminiscent of the cocaine episode and also foreshadowed some of the future battles in his life. Freud discussed Fliess's pet idea on the multiple roles of bisexuality in human life (for instance, how feminine men attract masculine women and vice versa) with a patient in treatment. The patient, Herman Swoboda, then communicated the thought to his friend Otto Weininger, who, as Freud put it, "thereupon struck his forehead and ran home to write down his book." Weininger's book was an immense success, and Fliess interrupted the lapse in his correspondence with Freud and demanded to know how this "burglary" of his idea had taken place.[32]

Freud tried to dodge the issue by pointing to other writers who had stressed the same themes. Yet Fliess forced Freud to admit not only that he had played a greater role than he wanted to acknowledge in giving away Fliess's concept, but also that he had forgotten an early discussion with Fliess on bisexuality. In explaining his behavior Freud conceded that he had been tempted to "steal" from Fliess the "originality" of this concept. "Ideas," Freud argued, "cannot be patented." One can only "hold them back," and one "does well to do so if one places value on priority."[33]

Fliess thereupon encouraged a friend to publicly denounce Swoboda and Weininger for the "theft"; and in doing so the friend published without permission Freud's letters on the subject. Swoboda, in turn, sued Fliess for libel and for unauthorized publication of private letters. The Viennese satirist Karl Kraus took up Swoboda's cause, but with a Viennese lawyer unversed in German libel laws and court procedures, Swoboda lost the case.[34] As Freud summarized the matter in a letter to Kraus, Weininger (who had shot himself in 1903) could not be "spared the reproach of having failed to divulge the source of this idea and, instead, of passing it off as his own inspiration."[35]

It would be a mistake to regard rivalries among scientists only as an expression of human pettiness. For "the institution of science puts an abiding emphasis on significant originality as an ultimate value, and demonstrated originality generally means coming upon the idea . . . first." Fame in the world of science is an "institutionalized symbol and reward for having done one's job as a scientist superlatively well."[36] Another Viennese, the philosopher Ludwig Wittgenstein, was also inordinately sensitive about priorities. His thoughts were his property, and he had "strong feelings about plagiarism"; Wittgenstein was "sometimes visited by the fear that when his work was finally published posthumously the learned world might believe that he had obtained his ideas from philosophers he had taught."[37]

Certainly other figures (for example, Darwin, Spencer, and Disraeli) have been troubled by questions of priority and plagiarism. It is nonetheless striking how quick Freud always was, even in the case of a "manifestly wild accusation,"[38] to repudiate the suggestion that he had merely repeated someone else's ideas. Freud genuinely needed to think through everything for himself, and even though he sometimes benefited from outside influences, once these ideas became inserted into his own chain of thought they became his own.

Despite the unhappy ending to their friendship, Freud always kept a portrait of Fliess hanging on a wall in his apartment.[39] Freud altered many of the passages in his writings that mentioned Fliess; sometimes, in referring to their friendship, he changed the verbs to the past tense.[40] In later years Freud occasionally discussed Fliess with his pupils. For example, Karl Abraham was once treated by Fliess for a medical problem, and though Abraham was full of enthusiasm for Fliess's ideas, Freud continued to be wary of him.*[41] And in a letter in 1910 to Sandor Ferenczi, Freud wrote that he understood the roots of Fliess's "passion for helping":

> the conviction that his father, who died of erysipelas after suffering for many years from nasal suppuration, could have been saved was what made him into a doctor, and indeed into a rhinologist. The sudden death of his only sister two years later, on the second day of a pneumonia for which he could not make the doctor responsible, led—

---

* Fliess, it is said, continued to read Freud's books and referred patients for psychoanalytic treatment until the end of his life.[42] One of his sons became a psychoanalyst.

Freud in the early 1930's

as a consolation—to the fatalistic theory of predestined lethal dates.
This piece of analysis, very unwelcome to him, was the real reason
for the break between us which he engineered in such a pathological
(paranoic) fashion. . . .[43]

Later that year Freud explained to Ferenczi the changes brought about
by the ending of his ties to Fliess: "I *no longer* have any need to uncover
my personality completely. . . . Since Fliess's case . . . that need has been

extinguished. A part of homosexual cathexis has been withdrawn and made use of to enlarge my own ego. I have succeeded where the paranoiac fails."[44]

The stages of Freud's relationship to Fliess and the steps in Freud's self-analysis are an indispensable background to his theories of the unconscious and of dreaming; they are accessible to us now only because of the survival of Freud's letters to Fliess. After Fliess's death, his widow was unwilling to let Freud's letters go with the rest of Fliess's papers to a Berlin library. But when the Nazis came to power and the Fliess family made plans to migrate, it became clear that the letters could be preserved by selling them through a dealer who could get them out of Germany.[45] Although Fliess's widow had not wanted them sold to Freud himself, they were purchased at a nominal price (one hundred pounds) by a devoted pupil of Freud's, Marie Bonaparte. When she informed him that she had the letters, he offered to pay half the purchase price, but she refused for fear he would want them destroyed. Freud did not understand the political background of the sale of his letters, and was indignant at Mrs. Fliess.

5. The Unconscious

A STRIKING CHARACTERISTIC of Freud's writing habits was that he preferred to wait until his ideas were completely thought out before committing them to paper. Not wanting to be hurried in his composition, Freud "postponed the printing of the finished manuscript [of *The Interpretation of Dreams*] for more than a year," until he finally overcame a "feeling of distaste" connected with the work.[1] Freud was forty-three years old when, in late 1899, the printed book at last lay in front of him.

Conceived in the period when he felt "completely isolated," in its first six years after publication *The Interpretation of Dreams* sold only 351 copies.[2] It was one of the two books Freud kept up to date as it went through different editions, adding new material and expanding certain sections. (The other book was *Three Essays on the Theory of Sexuality*.) In 1929 Freud said that in his revisions of the work he had "again treated it essentially as an historic document and . . . only made such alterations in it as were suggested by the clarification and deepening of my own opinions."[3] Two years later, in a preface to another revised edition, Freud considered it "the most valuable of all the discoveries it has been my good fortune to make. Insight such as this falls to one's lot but once in a lifetime."[4] In his work on neuroses Freud's doubts and uncertainties were allayed by the memory of his achievement in *The Interpretation of Dreams,* and with his intransigent spirit he considered that it was "a sure instinct which has led my many scientific opponents to refuse to follow me more especially in my researches upon dreams."[5]

It was Freud's interpretation of dreams "which brought psychoanalysis," in his view, "for the first time into the conflict with official science which was to be its destiny."[6] The ancient popular attitude toward dreams had always accorded them a meaning, and Freud came to think that the masses were in this case "nearer the truth than the judgment of the prevalent science. . . ."[7] Dreams were often thought to come from indigestion;[8] an analogy which the nonmusical Freud was fond of quoting was that "the contents of a dream are like the sounds produced when 'the ten fingers of a man who knows nothing of music wander over the keys of a piano.' "[9]

Freud came to regard himself as one of those who have "disturbed the sleep of the world," and in writing about Leonardo, Freud described him in an "admirable simile" as "like a man who had woken too early in the darkness, while everyone else was still asleep."[10] The motto to *The Interpretation of Dreams—*"If I cannot bend the Higher Powers, I will move the Infernal Regions"—expressed Freud's revolutionary pride. He saw himself as having discovered a "stretch of new country, which has been reclaimed from popular belief and mysticism."[11] Freud said it was a matter of "fortune"[12] or good luck that he had come upon his theory of dreams, and he fancied himself a Columbus of the mind.

Freud postulated that a dream represents "an *attempt*" by the dreamer "at the fulfillment of a wish."[13] Primarily visual in character, dreams were seen by Freud as a sort of picture puzzle whose meaning is subject to distortion, and so he drew "a contrast between the *manifest* and the *latent* content of dreams."[14] Feelings and thoughts may be present as well as wishes, but the "hidden meaning" of a given dream becomes distorted because of the role of "internal conflict, a kind of inner dishonesty."[15] In Freud's view, "dreams really have a secret meaning," and he proposed to interpret them "down to their last secret."[16] In language as uncompromising as it was decisive for the history of ideas, Freud proclaimed that "every dream deals with the dreamer himself. Dreams are completely egoistic."[17] Precisely because "among the unconscious instigators of a dream we very frequently find egoistic impulses which seem to have been overcome in waking life,"[18] the understanding of a dream required the conquest of an inner resistance to self-knowledge.

In subsequent years Freud tried to broaden the theory that at the time had seemed offensive to his contemporaries. For example, in 1925 Freud maintained that "the statement that dreams are entirely egoistic must not be misunderstood . . . [the] possibility is equally open," Freud tried to believe, "to altruistic impulses."[19] In 1901 Freud had written that "most of the dreams of adults are traced back by analysis to *erotic wishes*."[20] And in 1909 he wrote that "the majority of the dreams of adults deal with sexual material and give expression to erotic wishes."[21] In 1919 Freud argued with justice that "the assertion that all dreams require a sexual interpretation, against which critics rage so incessantly, occurs nowhere in my *Interpretation of Dreams*."[22] Nevertheless, despite Freud's later clarifications, the weight of his theory of dreams always pointed away from altruism toward egoism, and remained principally concentrated on the role of erotic impulses. The wishes behind dreams, Freud wrote during World War I, were the "manifestations of an unbridled and ruthless egoism . . . These censored wishes appear to rise up out of a positive Hell. . . ."[23]

Freud's technique for understanding the latent meaning of dreams was to use free associations, with both his own dreams and those of his patients. It was a rule of his that "in a psychoanalysis one learns to interpret propinquity in time as representing connections in subject-matter."[24] The manifest content of a dream is made up of experiences from the previous day, and the mechanisms of dream formation (such as "condensation," "displacement," "representation") are obliged to work in such a way as to combine the past and present "*into a unity*."[25] As a therapist, Freud confidently asserted that the role of suggestion was restricted to the manifest content of dream formation: "one may often influence a dreamer *about* what he shall dream, but never *what* he actually dreams."[26]

It is uncertain what psychopathological status Freud was assigning to dreaming. On the one hand, dreams were to be the key to understanding neurosis, for the line between the normal and the neurotic, Freud felt, was not a hard and fast one, but a question of degree. "Dreams are," Freud therefore wrote, "phenomena which occur in healthy people—perhaps in everyone, perhaps every night. . . ."[27] He believed, however, that in the popular mind intuition had equated "dreams . . . with madness from time immemorial."[28] Freud also considered the dream to be "the first member of a class of abnormal psychical phenomena," and though he sometimes insisted that "dreams are not pathological phenomena," at other times he considered the dream a "pathological product."[29] Rejecting intuitive superstitions about dreaming, Freud began with the scientific premise that the dream is a mental structure with a meaning; for him there was "no such thing as arbitrary determination in the mind."[30] Therefore, "it is always a strict law of dream-interpretation that an explanation must be found for every detail."[31]

It is still not clear how Freud came to focus so much of his attention on dreams. As he put it in 1914, "my desire for knowledge had not at the start been directed towards understanding dreams. I do not know of any outside influence which drew my interest to them or inspired me with any helpful expectations."[32] Freud's book is full of the most personal kind of self-exploration; for example, about one dream Freud found that in his associations

> the idea of plagiarizing—of appropriating whatever one can, even though it belongs to someone else—clearly led on to the second part of the dream, in which I was treated as though I were the thief who had for some time carried on his business of stealing overcoats in the lecture-rooms.[33]

As much as Freud was in quest of the "secret" of dreaming, he was aware of the "reproach that I was unable to keep a secret."[34] The wish fulfillment of one dream, Freud conjectured, "lay in my being recognized as an honest man. . . . There must therefore have been all kinds of material in the dream thoughts containing a contradiction of this."[35]

As Freud knew, "to interpret and report one's dreams demands a high degree of self-discipline. One is bound to emerge as the only villain among the crowd of noble characters who share one's life."[36] It took hard work to see through his self-deceptions, and he had to struggle with himself over publishing *The Interpretation of Dreams* and giving "away so much of my own private character in it."[37] Although Freud could sometimes be cold and distant, and was rarely intimate with patients, through his dream book he shared some of the most private areas of his life with the whole world.

Freud's book is a rich storehouse of material about his character at the turn of the century. For example, in reflecting on his burgeoning theory of the neuroses, and in particular on the role of sexuality, Freud "longed to be away from all this grubbing about in human dirt."[38] He was forced to acknowledge areas of personality which most people of his day would have been reluctant to admit they possessed, much less to expose in a published book. "I am normally," Freud conceded, "rather apt to harbor grievances and can forget no detail of an incident that has annoyed me . . . ."[39] True to his general outlook on the world, Freud felt that he had "always paid dearly for whatever advantage I have had from other people."[40] His dream thoughts also touched on "the future of my family after my premature death," and expressed the "gloomiest thoughts of an unknown and uncanny future."[41]

Nevertheless, it remains a mystery why Freud should have treated the process of dreaming so seriously. Perhaps he offers a clue: "I am an excellent sleeper and obstinately refuse to allow anything to disturb my sleep . . . whereas psychical motives obviously cause me to dream very easily."[42] Freud began with the assumption that "the enigma of the formation of dreams can be solved by the revelation of an unsuspected psychical source of stimulation."[43] Though Freud thought that his dreams were "in general less rich in sensory elements than . . . is the case in other people," the imagery throughout his writing is consistently pictorial; thus his notion that dream thoughts are "transformed into pictorial language" was in keeping with his own characteristic ways of thinking.[44]

Freud's description of the dream's "navel, the spot where it reaches down into the unknown," suggests that his scientific interest was mobilized by those areas in him which were not subject to self-control.[45] He often compared his interest in ancient Egyptology to his work in uncovering the unconscious past; in both instances the obscure and unknown played an important part. Freud once noted "an irritating vagueness which we declare characteristic of dreams because it is not completely comparable to any degree of indistinctness which we ever perceive in real objects."[46] An apparently "clear and flawless" dream would be regarded by Freud as "well constructed"; he once referred to the "gaps, obscurities and confusions which may interrupt the continuity of even the finest of dreams" —revealing something of what he found agreeable in a dream as opposed to what remained "alien" to him.[47] Freud disliked anything which muddied the rationality of his mind; he could thus write of a class of dreams that they "are disagreeable in the same way as examination dreams and they are never distinct."[48] Vividness and coherence were desirable in Freud's hierarchy of dreams, and he preferred that which tended "towards the light—towards elucidation and fuller understanding," rather than that which headed for "darkness."[49]

Whatever the motivations, autobiographical as well as clinical, that led Freud to the study of dreams, his theory was expressed in ways quite typical of him. A tireless walker himself, he invited the reader of *The Interpretation of Dreams* to accompany him on an imaginary journey. In untangling the meaning of dreams, Freud exhibited a Talmudic ingenuity, which caused some readers to find his theses too far removed from reality. But Freud had dared to look at psychological material that others had ignored and gave form to insights never recognized before. Not that

Freud had no predecessors; he conscientiously tried to examine the entire literature on dreaming, and in later years he frequently quoted, in confirmation of his theories, material his pupils had found for him.

After Freud had come up with a "solution" to the problem of dreams, his stubbornness worked to his benefit; for he sought to extract as much meaning from his theory of dreams as he could, in order to build the constituents of a general theory of the mind. Since the dream stands for the concealed fulfillment of a repressed wish, dreams became in Freud's doctrine *"the GUARDIANS of sleep and not its disturbers."*[50] Half a century later we now have experimental evidence on this point—how psychologically disorienting it is to be deprived of one's dreams, even though given an adequate amount of sleep—but Freud was working on a much more fragile intellectual basis. For Freud it was logical that whereas the day's residue of experiences might act to disturb sleep, dreams serve to preserve sleep. Latent dream thoughts represented a person's infantile past, and Freud thought that, for others as for himself, "a humiliation that was experienced thirty years ago acts exactly like a fresh one throughout the thirty years. . . ."[51] Although Freud hoped someday to replace this psychological theory with a physiological one, he had found to his own satisfaction the source of the true "daemonic" element in dreams, the infantile past. His theory might be "crude" but it was "at least lucid."[52] Years later he emphasized that logically there were always at least two parts to his vision of the mental apparatus; he insisted that he had been "exhibiting . . . not only the evil dream-wishes which are censored but also the censorship, which suppresses them and makes them unrecognizable."[53]

There is a sense in which it can be said that Freud never, in his mature years, basically changed his mind. At times, as in his last years, Freud emphasized more the integrative aspects of personality, whereas for most of his psychoanalytic career it was the repressed and the instinctual which fascinated him; yet on the whole his world remains remarkably unified. Freud may have acquired some new insights along the way, and even made advances in technique, but throughout his writing one finds him reworking the same themes anew.

Once he came to his theory of dreams, Freud was quick to connect it with the rest of his therapeutic work. Like dreams, neurotic symptoms had a meaning; they too represented compromise formations between repressed impulses and censoring agents of the mind. "[T]he theory governing all psycho-neurotic symptoms culminates in a single proposition, which asserts that *they too are to be regarded as fulfillments of uncon-*

scious wishes." Or, Freud added, "more correctly, one portion of the symptom corresponds to the unconscious wish-fulfillment and another portion to the mental structure reacting against the wish."[54]

If there was one emotion Freud really understood, and repeatedly wrote about, it is anxiety. In the period of *The Interpretation of Dreams,* he concluded that neurotic anxiety arose from sexual sources.[55] He retained a fixed belief in the literal meaning of his libido theory (libido was the term for the force by which the sexual instinct manifests itself); neurosis had a physical basis in dammed-up sexuality. Through repression (and on the basis of his dream theory Freud felt that he knew about censorship) sexuality is converted into anxiety. Although Freud revised this theory of anxiety in the 1920's, seeing it then primarily as a danger signal for the ego, in most of his theoretical work and almost all of his clinical practice the earlier view prevailed.

Sexuality as the prime source of neurotic anxiety fit in with the seduction tales of Freud's patients, for they seemed to retain fantasies of sexual gratification stemming from early childhood. This observation had led Freud to "the fact of *infantile sexuality,*" the notion that "human sexual life does not begin only with puberty, as on a rough inspection it may appear to do."[56] Freud had discovered the Oedipus complex: "a girl's first affection is for her father and a boy's first childish desires are for his mother."[57] Father-son conflicts were always uppermost in Freud's mind, and he recalled from Greek mythology that "Kronos devoured his children . . . while Zeus emasculated his father and made himself ruler in his place."[58] Freud's Oedipus complex became a broad one: "a person's emotional attitude towards his family, or in a narrowed sense towards his father and mother. . . ."[59]

Freud believed that one had to accept sexuality for what it was. He himself was not completely detached about it, however, and there seems to have been in him the feeling that sex was somehow shameful, as when, in true Victorian spirit, he referred in Latin to the "*vita sexualis.*"[60] But for his time his extension of the usual conception of sexuality was a radical innovation: "a child sucking at his mother's breast has become the prototype of every relation of love. The finding of an object is in fact a refinding of it."[61] Freud's clinical interest in sexuality was spurred by his patients' dishonesty about sexual matters, which he came to think was a major factor in their troubles. "In matters of sexuality we are at present, every one of us, ill or well, nothing but hypocrites."[62]

One implication of Freud's theory of infantile sexuality was that children had immensely complicated emotional lives deserving of the greatest respect. Of course, Freud did not treat children directly, nor even observe his own very closely; his observations were rather reconstructed from the memories and associations of his adult patients. So it was for him "a very great triumph when it became possible years later to confirm almost all my inferences by direct observation and the analysis of very young children. . . ."[63] He felt that childhood "development takes place so rapidly that we should probably never have succeeded in getting a firm hand of its fleeting pictures by direct observations."[64] Freud acknowledged, however, that the indirection of analysis was a disadvantage in the study of children.

Freud shocked many readers by referring to the child not only as a sexual creature but also as being "polymorphously perverse." (A "deviating" pupil, Wilhelm Stekel, later used the milder term "panerotic.") He often discussed childhood sexuality and adult perversion in the same breath: "the sexual activities of children have hitherto been entirely neglected and though those of perverts have been recognized it has hitherto been with moral indignation and without understanding."[65] Adult perversions, Freud held, were simply a special developmental outcome, the failure to integrate the various component drives of childhood in a heterosexual direction.[66] Neurotics were, in one sense, the opposite of perverts, since their anxieties were repressed instead of acted out. Freud strove to derive his understanding of perverts (by which he generally meant homosexuals) from their childhood background: "If . . . the derivation of perversions from the Oedipus complex can be generally established, our estimate of its importance will have gained added strength."[67]

Despite his personal distaste for perverts and his reluctance to accept them for psychoanalytic treatment (which was, he held, most suitable for neurotics), Freud repeatedly insisted on "how inappropriate it is to use the word perversion as a term of reproach."[68] Freud was a deadly opponent of his era's special brand of cant:

> a place must be created in public opinion for the discussion of the problems of sexual life. It will have to become possible to talk about these things without being stamped as a trouble-maker or as a person who makes capital out of the lower instincts. And so here, too, there is enough work left to do for the next hundred years—in which our civilization will have to learn to come to terms with the claims of our sexuality.[69]

Needless to say, none of this broad-mindedness implied advocacy of "free love." On the contrary, Freud thought that "a progressive renunciation of constitutional instincts . . . appears to be one of the foundations of the development of human civilization."[70]

For the world to have linked Freud's name to sexuality was surely no mistake: he stated in 1898 that "the most immediate and, for practical purposes, the most significant causes of every case of neurotic illness are to be found in factors arising from sexual life."[71] When Freud referred to a patient's sexual life, he had in mind his *"contemporary sexual life"* as well as *"important events in his past life."*[72] "[I]n every case of neurosis there is a sexual aetiology; but in neurasthenia it is an aetiology of a present-day kind, whereas in the psychoneuroses the factors are of an infantile nature."[73] Freud knew that it might seem scientifically disreputable to pursue this avenue of thought, but he went so far as to assert that "the differences separating the normal from the abnormal can lie only in the relative strength of the individual components of the sexual instinct and in the use to which they are put in the course of development."[74] At the same time Freud occasionally set limits to how far his sexual theory could be pushed:

> Now it would never occur to me to substitute a sexual aetiology in neuroses for every other aetiology, and so to assert that the latter have no operative force. This would be a misunderstanding. What I think is rather that in addition to all the familiar aetiological factors which have been recognized—and probably correctly so—by the authorities as leading to neurasthenia, the sexual factors, which have not hitherto been sufficiently appreciated, should also be taken into account.[75]

And again:

> Sexual need and privation are merely one factor at work in the mechanism of neurosis; if there were no others the result would be dissipation, not disease. The other, no less essential factor, which is all too readily forgotten, is the neurotic's aversion from sexuality, his incapacity for loving, that feature of the mind which I have called "repression."[76]

In all of Freud's work on dreams and symptoms he relied on one central assumption about the functioning of what he termed the "mental apparatus," namely, that "our total mental activity is directed towards pleasure and avoiding unpleasure."[77]

> [U]npleasure corresponds to an *increase* in the quantity of excitation and pleasure to a *diminution* . . . . the mental apparatus endeavors to keep the quantity of excitation present in it as low as possible or at

least to keep it constant . . . there exists in the mind a strong *tendency* towards the pleasure principle. . . .[78]

Freud held that the main task of the mind was a negative one, to accomplish the release of tension; tensions meant "unpleasure," since drives lead to discharge and relief. As Freud grew old and gradually withdrew from contact with the world, it became more and more true of himself that "*protection against* stimuli is an almost more important function for the living organism than *reception* of stimuli."[79]

At the same time, Freud felt like Mephistopheles emerging from the depths of the human psyche; he frequently referred to himself as an explorer uncovering the remains of buried archaeological treasure. Nietzsche would have approved of Freud's insistence that "our highest virtues have grown up, as reaction formations and sublimations, out of our worst dispositions."[80] It is not known whether or for how long Freud hesitated over naming the human underworld. Janet had preferred the term "subconscious" to distinguish it from the metaphysical connotations in German thought of the "unconscious."[81] But Freud chose the "unconscious" as a term because it emphasized emotions and feelings that were not only beyond ready access but above all *not* conscious. As Freud put it, "we are forced to the inescapable hypothesis that there are purposes in people which can become operative without their knowing about them."[82]

Because of the nature of Freud's ideas in his early years, he may have appeared to many as merely another sexologist and, in the light of his error concerning the seduction tales, not a very reliable one at that. But Freud's special viewpoint was always that of a psychologist. He tried to plumb the mysteries of memory, amnesias, and false recollections ("paramnesias"). The compromises that the mind makes in its constructions of memory are like the compromise formations in dreaming, as well as those underlying neurotic symptoms. Freud looked at the problem of memory from the egoistic perspective of the expenditure of psychic energy; as he asked himself once: "Now what is there in this occurrence to justify the expenditure of memory which it has occasioned me?"[83] He used his psychology of memory in order to understand how the past could live in the present. Freud was so keenly aware of the "effect of a *memory* surpassing that of an actual event" that he asserted that the "traumas" (what we now might call "stresses") of childhood "*operate in a deferred fashion as though they were fresh experiences; but they do so unconsciously.*"[84] Hysterical symptoms in particular "can only arise with the cooperation of memories. . . ."[85] Freud later qualified the power he attributed to "the preponderance attaching in mental life to memory-traces in comparison with

recent impressions. This factor is clearly dependent on intellectual education and increases in proportion to the degree of individual culture."[86]
To Freud psychoanalysis came to mean the exploration of the past.
As he wrote in a case history, "it appeared that psychoanalysis could
explain nothing belonging to the present without referring back to something past. . . . Not until a long détour, leading back over . . . earliest
childhood. . . ."[87] In *The Interpretation of Dreams*, Freud affirmed that
he "had been driven to assume that impressions from the second year of
life, and sometimes even from the first, left a lasting trace on the emotional
life of those who were later to fall ill. . . ."[88] By World War I, Freud put
the matter in a somewhat different way, but it was by no means enough
of a change to make his view any less radical: "The little creature is often
completed by the fourth or fifth year of life, and after that merely brings
gradually to light what is already within him."[89] The lengthy phase of the
child's dependency and immaturity must have lasting effects, since all of
us retain the child within us. Freud's description of the special egoism
of the unconscious—its "insatiability, unyielding rigidity and the lack of
an ability to react to real circumstances"[90]—fits his stress on the persistence
into adulthood of childish modes of reaction.

Not only did Freud turn his psychologist's eye from dreams to
neurosis, but he also found that memory played a part in ordinary slips
of the tongue and pen. Here, too, that which had previously been taken
to be meaningless could be fetched up from the unknown. Slips were, in
Freud's theory, a product of inner conflict:

> I really do not think that anyone would make a slip of the tongue
> in an audience with his Sovereign, in a serious declaration of love or
> in defending his honor or name before a jury—in short, on all those
> occasions when a person is heart and soul engaged.[91]

Counting on the ready agreement readers would bring to at least some
of the examples he produced, Freud was hoping to gain broader support
for the rest of his theories: "people give slips of the tongue and other
parapraxes the same interpretation that I advocate in this book, even if
they do not endorse theoretically the views I put forward. . . ."[92] With his
interpretation of slips, Freud felt that he had discovered another secret
method of the mind.

Freud generalized his examples into the principle that "*in every case
the forgetting turned out to be based on a motive of unpleasure*,"[93] so
the theory of slips fit in well with the theories of neurosis and dreaming.
Unlike neurotic symptoms, however, slips of the tongue are observed in
so-called normal people as well as in the "ill." However, though Freud,

when trying to understand a slip of the tongue, was usually not attempting to overcome a patient's resistances, a certain punitive tone shows up in his choice of imagery, as we can see in an exchange with an imaginary interlocutor:

> When someone charged with an offence confesses his deed to the judge, the judge believes his confession; but if he denies it, the judge does not believe him . . . "Are you a judge, then? And is a person who has made a slip of the tongue brought up before you on a charge? So making a slip of the tongue is an offence, is it?" Perhaps we need not reject the comparison.[94]

6. The Talking Cure

HOWEVER EXPANSIVELY Freud constructed his psychology, however ambitious his ultimate aims may have been, he reminded his readers that "it must not be forgotten . . . that psychoanalysis cannot offer a complete picture of the world."[1] Freud believed that "psychoanalysis is a part of psychology. . . . It is certainly not the whole of psychology, but its substructure and perhaps even its entire foundation."[2] Through the study of the pathological Freud aimed to discern the normal, albeit in exaggerated form: "pathology, by making things larger and coarser, can draw our attention to normal conditions which would otherwise have escaped us."[3]

Freud had a "preference for the fragmentary treatment of a subject, with emphasis on the points which seem to me best established."[4] He frequently admitted being "one-sided" and thought he "must have needed this one-sidedness in order to see what remains hidden from others."[5] He specifically defended psychoanalysis from the charge of narrowness:

> Unintelligent opposition accuses us of one-sidedness in our estimate of the sexual instincts . . . Our one-sidedness is like that of the chemist, who traces all compounds back to the force of chemical attraction. He is not on that account denying the force of gravity; he leaves that to the physicist to deal with.[6]

Whereas writers on aesthetics chose to concentrate on "feelings of a positive nature"—on "what is beautiful, attractive and sublime"—Freud was usually more in touch with "the opposite feelings of repulsion and distress."[7] Patients do not normally pay therapists to discuss areas of their personality that are congenial to them, but rather to deal with problems of a painful and unwelcome nature. As a practicing analyst, Freud could justify his focus on the impediments in people's lives rather than their successes.

Without minimizing the importance of other kinds of motives, Freud stressed the infantile, since "other motivations are commonplace."[8] Therefore he could claim that "our work on the question of the disposition to neurotic affections has added the 'infantile' factor to the somatic and hereditary ones hitherto recognized."[9] And because of the special contribution of his ideas, Freud could justify the exclusiveness of his movement: "psychoanalysis must keep itself free from any hypothesis that is alien to it, whether of an anatomical, chemical or physiological kind, and must operate entirely with purely psychological auxiliary ideas. . . ."[10] At the same time, Freud felt that "the theoretical structure of psychoanalysis that we have created is in truth a superstructure, which will one day have to be set upon its organic foundation."[11]

The scientist in Freud was often cautious about the nature of his findings, and he warned that "we must not deceive ourselves as to the hypothetical nature and insufficient clarity of our knowledge. . . ."[12] He resented the fact that his

> opponents regarded psychoanalysis as a product of my speculative imagination and were unwilling to believe in the long, patient and unbiassed work which had gone to its making. Since in their opinion analysis had nothing to do with observation or experience, they believed that they themselves were justified in rejecting it without experience.[13]

Repeatedly referring to the "factual" findings "which we believe we have established by our painstaking labors,"[14] Freud tried to resist the impulse to "pursue analogies to an obsessional extreme" and wanted to "bow before the evidence" as it came in.[15] He wrote, in what became a virtually stereotyped expression, of waiting "for the future for confirmation."[16]

On the whole Freud shared the scientist's attitude toward the past: "ancestors of ours were far more ignorant than we are."[17] Yet he thought that "a dim knowledge of the overwhelming importance of sexual factors in the production of the neuroses (a knowledge which I am trying to capture afresh for science) seems never to have been lost in the consciousness of laymen."[18] When once the validity of psychoanalysis "ceases to be denied," "it will not be hard to dispute its originality."[19]

I know very well that in putting forward my "sexual aetiology" of the neuroses, I have brought up nothing new, and that undercurrents in medical literature taking these facts into account have never been absent. I know, too, that official academic medicine has in fact also been aware of them. But it has acted as if it knew nothing about the matter. It has made no use of its knowledge and has drawn no inferences from it.[20]

When he wrote about the symptomatology of slips of the tongue, he paused to say, with a touch of irony, that "this is a subject on which I find myself in the exceptional position of being able to acknowledge the value of a previous work," and he then went on to indicate how much its "lines of approach differ widely from my own."[21]

As much as he craved the position of leading a scientific advance, Freud knew that "there is much of interest to be said on the subject of apparent scientific originality," and he acknowledged in his own case that "the originality of many of the new ideas employed by me in the interpretation of dreams and in psychoanalysis" was capable of evaporating.[22] Freud continually paid tribute to the psychological capacities of imaginative writers:

we may well heave a sigh of relief at the thought that it is nevertheless vouchsafed to a few to salvage without effort from the whirlpool of their own feelings the deepest truths, towards which the rest of us have to find our way through tormenting uncertainty and with restless groping.[23]

Freud, who knew how often his thoughts were "occupied with questions of priority," sometimes sought out "illustrious forerunners" in order to rebut the charge that psychoanalysis had made "an assault upon the dignity of the human race."[24]

In the welter of original ideas associated with Freud's name, the hardest to pin down and at the same time the most important for other people was the specific form of treatment that he recommended. Psychoanalysis, in addition to being a psychological theory and a method of observation, meant a new kind of therapeutic setting. Freud spent most of his working day in the rather stuffy-looking suite of rooms next to his apartment. He sometimes felt uneasy about the lack of scientific controls in his clinical sessions, but he reasoned that even in astronomy "experimentation with the heavenly bodies is particularly difficult. There one has to fall back on observation."[25]

Freud often thought that "the future will probably attribute far greater importance to psychoanalysis as the science of the unconscious than as a therapeutic procedure."[26] In his last years he looked back with disappointment at some of his earlier therapeutic results, and he increasingly emphasized the scientific as opposed to the therapeutic aspects of his accomplishments:

> psychoanalysis began as a method of treatment; but I did not want to commend it to your interest as a method of treatment but on account of the truths it contains, on account of the information it gives us about what concerns human beings most of all—their own nature—and on account of the connections it discloses between the most different of their activities. As a method of treatment it is one among many, though, to be sure, *primus inter pares*.[27]

Freud drew a sharp line between the work of his pupils and that of "those physicians whose interests are focused exclusively on therapeutic results and who employ analytic methods, but only up to a certain point."[28]

Yet in Freud's earlier work he was altogether more outgoing and hopeful about the prospects of achieving therapeutic success. Others had pointed to the importance of heredity, but Freud thought that "the discovery of the hereditary element does not . . . exempt us from searching for a specific [psychological] factor. On its discovery, incidentally, all our therapeutic interest as well depends."[29]

For a time in Freud's thinking, syphilis was a bridge between the organic and the psychological. He thought that "a *strikingly high* percentage of the patients whom I have treated psychoanalytically come of fathers who have suffered from tabes or general paralysis . . . [S]yphilis in the male parent is a very relevant factor in the neuropathic constitution of children."[30] In a passage in *Three Essays on the Theory of Sexuality*, originally written in 1905 and not retracted in subsequent editions, Freud said that "in more than half of the severe cases of hysteria, obsessional neurosis, etc., which I have treated psychotherapeutically, I have been able to prove with certainty that the patient's father suffered from syphilis. . . ."[31] Although Freud eventually abandoned the view of the syphilitic father, his theory continued to suggest that parents had somehow done wrong by their children; indeed, this has been a source of its appeal for young people. Freud's assertion that "the chief part in the mental lives of all children who later become psychoneurotics is played by their parents"[32] may sound today obvious, if not almost tautological, but in the era of the publication of *The Interpretation of Dreams* it required unusual boldness to blame neurosis on ordinary family life.

Freud once wrote that "the theory of the neuroses is psychoanalysis itself,"[33] yet it is no easy matter to determine what he meant by neurotic. He stated that "the borderline between the normal and the abnormal in nervous matters is a fluid one, and . . . we are all a little neurotic. . . ."[34] At least that was the basis on which he hoped to establish the universal validity of his clinical findings. At the same time, however, Freud could write of himself in a wholly pre-Freudian way "as a normal individual, free from neurosis."[35] Elsewhere Freud told of the memory of "someone who is not at all or only slightly neurotic."*[36] As a practicing physician, Freud saw "illness" as essentially a practical matter, of more or less suffering. "But if you take up a theoretical point of view, and disregard this matter of quantity, you may well say that we are *all* ill, that is, neurotic. . . ."[37]

According to Freud's theory, symptoms could "be properly viewed as substitutive satisfactions for what is missed in life."[38] The "daemonic" force at work in neurosis was traced to the patient's failure to overcome an initial trauma, and frustrated attempts to do so only made matters worse.[39] Sandor Ferenczi once expressed the psychoanalytic viewpoint: "The patient does in fact 'heal' his mental conflicts through repression, displacement, and transference of disagreeable complexes; unfortunately what is repressed compensates itself by creating 'costly replacement formations' (Freud), so that we have to regard neuroses as 'healing attempts that have miscarried' (Freud). . . ."[40] Freud was not proposing that an instinct such as sexuality should dominate one's life, only that its various components not be needlessly suppressed; therefore he could write that "we associate neuroticism, a term which has become scientifically inexact, with the idea of inhibition."[41]

In his earlier days Freud tended to focus on symptoms in isolation from a patient's character (and even his family setting), but with time he came to feel that the cure of the besetting symptoms was not as important as understanding the underlying processes. "Whereas at the time [1895] we modestly declared that we could undertake only to remove the symptoms of hysteria, not to cure hysteria itself, this distinction has since come to seem to me without substance, so that there is a prospect of a genuine cure of hysteria and obsessions."[42]

It became the aim of psychoanalysis to pass over the patient's superficial presenting difficulties and focus on the key sources of his trouble. During World War I, Freud wrote that "the work of analysis as we carry

---

* In this passage Freud did not identify himself as having the memory, but it is clearly an autobiographical detail.

it out to-day quite excludes the systematic treatment of any individual symptom till it has been entirely cleared up."[43] As Freud began devoting more of his time to training pupils in analysis and less to treating patients, the more he could afford to be detached about his therapeutic results; in his earlier years, when dealing with relatively less healthy people, Freud had had to be more concerned with the origin and cure of particular symptoms.

In 1904 Freud had been broad-minded enough, and sufficiently devoted to therapeutic success, to announce that "there are many ways and means of practicing psychotherapy. All that lead to recovery are good."[44] In psychoanalytic treatment, however, Freud had very specific aims in mind. "Whereas the practical aim of the treatment is to remove all possible symptoms and to replace them by conscious thoughts, we may regard it as a second and theoretical aim to repair all the damages to the patient's memory."[45] Although Freud again said that "the task of the treatment is to remove all the amnesias . . . all repressions must be undone," he nevertheless thought that "the aim of the treatment will never be anything but the *practical* recovery of the patient, the restoration of his ability to lead an active life and of his capacity for enjoyment."[46]

Neurotic illness hobbled Freud's patients, preventing the "free unfolding of their mental powers."[47] Freud did his best to make sure that "advice and guidance in the affairs of life" did not play an integral part in analytic influence:

> we avoid the role of a mentor such as this, and there is nothing we would rather bring about than that the patient should make his decisions for himself . . . Only in the case of some very youthful or quite helpless or unstable individuals are we unable to put the desired limitation of our role into effect. With them we have to combine the functions of a doctor and an educator; but when this is so we are quite conscious of our responsibility and behave with the necessary caution.[48]

Freud admitted that his ideal of analytic influence often had to be compromised to fit the changing needs of clinical realities:

> We cannot avoid taking some patients for treatment who are so helpless and incapable of ordinary life that for them one has to combine analytic with educative influence; and even with the majority, occasions now and then arise in which the physician is bound to take up the position of teacher and mentor. But it must always be done with great caution. . . .[49]

Freud was more pragmatic as a therapist than some of his later (and often more therapeutically ambitious) disciples: "there are cases in which even the physician must admit that for a conflict to end in neurosis is the most harmless and socially tolerable solution . . . It is not his business to restrict himself in every situation in life to being a fanatic in favor of health." Freud went even further in his skepticism of the absolute value of the healthy state, since he thought that "necessity may even require a person to sacrifice his health. . . ."[50] The "formula" Freud devised for psychoanalysis was that "its task is to make conscious everything that is pathogenically unconscious," which meant filling "all the gaps in the patient's memory, to remove his amnesias."[51] However, by 1937 Freud had become even more explicit about the limits he set to the goals of analysis:

> Our aim will not be to rub off every peculiarity of human character for the sake of a schematic "normality," nor yet to demand that the person who has been "thoroughly analyzed" should feel no passions and develop no internal conflicts. The business of the analysis is to secure the best possible psychological conditions for the functions of the ego; with that it has discharged its task.[52]

Freud, who personally resented being dependent and was inclined to distrust the infantile, cherished his own autonomy and sense of freedom and held out the ideal of self-realization. "The neurotic who is cured has really become another man, though at bottom, of course, he has remained the same; that is to say, he has become what he might have become at best under the most favorable conditions."[53] In many ways Freud shared the liberal values of the eighteenth-century Enlightenment: "The liberty of the individual is no gift of civilization. It was the greatest before there was any civilization. . . ."[54] And although Freud understood some of the most intractable obstacles to the achievement of genuine independence, still he adhered to the libertarian principle that "every man must find out for himself in what particular fashion he can be saved."[55]

Austere and intrepid, bent on unveiling self-deceptions, Freud was as obsessed with investigation as was his hero Leonardo and as much "a fanatic for the truth" as he supposed Emile Zola to have been.[56] "[P]sycho-analytic treatment is founded in truthfulness. In this fact lies a great part of its educative effect and its ethical value."[57] Freud tended to treat a patient's present-day anxieties as an evasion of more deep-seated difficulties: "light could only be thrown upon these earlier problems when the course of the analysis led away for a time from the present, and forced us to make a *détour* through the pre-historic period of childhood."[58]

The premises of Freud's initial psychoanalytic labors seem excessively rationalistic today. "Even where psychical health is perfect," Freud wrote, "the subjugation of the *Ucs.* [Unconscious] by the *Pcs.* [Preconscious] is not complete; the measure of suppression indicates the degree of our own psychical normality."[59] A more mature Freud would not have talked about the perfection of health, certainly not in the context of so ambiguous a concept as "normality." But he believed that "the somatic and emotional effect of an impulse that has become conscious can never be so powerful as that of an unconscious one," even though he would not always have been so bold as to claim that "it is only by the application of our highest mental functions, which are bound up with consciousness, that we control all our impulses."[60]

By 1913 Freud conceded that "in the earliest days of analytic technique we took an intellectualist view of the situation."[61] Freud retained the conviction, however, that "symptoms are never constructed from conscious processes," as well as the idealistic faith that "as soon as the unconscious processes concerned have become conscious, the symptom must disappear."[62] For Freud, intelligence was the great unifier and intellect the only safe recourse; "we have no other means of controlling our instinctual nature but our intelligence . . . the psychological ideal [is] . . . the primacy of the intelligence."[63] Like Spinoza before him, Freud considered the intellectual the freest of men, since through the sublimation of instincts "fate can do little against one."[64]

Since Freud held to the idea (expressed as late as 1932) that "understanding and cure almost coincide,"[65] it pays to look closely at how the analyst was supposed to proceed in his therapy. Just as Freud had referred to "the secret meaning of the dream," so each neurotic had a "relation to his secret—to his 'complex'. . . ."[66] To the patient Freud was explicitly saying, "Turn your eyes inward, look into your own depths, learn first to know yourself! Then you will understand why you were bound to fall ill; and perhaps, you will avoid falling ill in the future."[67]

As a clinician, Freud came to believe that in the course of treatment the patient's forces of self-deception are gradually turned against the analyst. He went so far as to assert that the patient's "overcoming of these resistances is the essential function of analysis. . . ."[68] A "resistance" was once sweepingly defined as *"whatever interrupts the progress of analytic work. . . ."*[69] His meaning can be clarified by the example of a typical neurotic who

makes resistances out of his efforts to become independent in himself
and in his judgments, out of his ambition, the first aim of which was
to do things as well as his father or to get the better of him, or out
of his unwillingness to burden himself for the second time in his life
with a load of gratitude.[70]

Perhaps the hallmark of Freud's preferred method of pure analytic
treatment was that transference reactions in patients were to be sought
out, if not deliberately mobilized, and then interpreted by the analyst.
Here Freud meant the "transference of [past] feelings on to the person
of the doctor, since we do not believe that the situation in the treatment
could justify the development of such feelings."[71] By understanding transference the analyst could reach the patient's unconscious, whereas more
old-fashioned treatment by suggestion "achieves nothing towards the uncovering of what is unconscious to the patient."[72] Although by 1912
Freud was careful to distinguish between the patient's positive emotional
feelings for the analyst and his irrationally negative reactions, the real
meaning of transference was that, however reasonable someone may
appear to be, the analytic situation will reveal the presence of infantile
modes of feeling. It is not only in our dreams at night that our childish
past plays a role. In this sense Freud was correct in saying that "psychoanalysis brings out the worst in everyone."[73] And to the extent that the
aim of analysis was conceived of as first the arousal of transference and
then its rational dissolution, Karl Kraus was also correct in maintaining
that analysis was the illness for which it purported to be a cure.

As rationalistic and intellectual as Freud sounds, he was also concerned
to show that "what turns the scale" in a patient's therapeutic "struggle
is not his intellectual insight—which is neither strong enough nor free
enough for such an achievement—but simply and solely his relationship
to the doctor."[74] Freud wanted the analyst to wait for the patient to introduce problems; but he stressed above all that from the analyst's point of
view "one should always be aware of what one is doing."[75]

IV

FREUD AS
A THERAPIST

1. The Technique
of Neutrality

ONE OF THE REASONS for Freud's influence is that his therapeutic procedure was much more disciplined and orderly than anything anybody else has been able to devise. Freud remained highly rationalistic when it came to technique. He had been reluctant to write about his special approach until his quarrels with Adler, Stekel, and Jung, when it seemed advisable to distinguish his own form of treatment from that of other psychotherapists. Freud was too wise to be dogmatic about technique, and above all he wanted his pupils to be good understanders; perhaps he wrote so little on technique in order not to lay down the law too restrictively for his followers.

When Freud published several technical papers in 1914, he explicitly said that he was offering "recommendations" rather than "rules."[1] Freud's over-all approach had been stabilized for some time. Interpretation of dreams and symptomatic slips, unraveling of symptoms through the reconstruction of the past, and elucidation of transferences, remained, through all the changes in Freud's views, the hub of psychoanalytic treatment. He expected other analysts to encourage patients in their free associations, which for Freud continued to be the main therapeutic tool of analysis; he called it the "fundamental rule," which was opposed to the idea of "recommendation."

Freud thought that anything that would loosen up a patient's resistances was valuable, but he advised against the analyst's revealing too much about his own feelings and reactions, lest he interfere with the patient's analytic material. In outlining the basic assumptions of his therapeutic practice for analysts, Freud thought of himself as establishing beginner's guidelines, "as a warning to analysts"; for "although there may perhaps be more than one good road to follow, still there are very many bad ones. . . ."[2] Freud's discussions of technique were designed to help others avoid some of the mistakes he himself had stumbled into earlier. But he did not expect that his pronouncements on technique, or his own way of practicing, would be appropriate for every analyst. A favorite quotation of Freud's came from Goethe's Mephistopheles: "After all, the best of what you know may not be told to boys."[3]

During Freud's lifetime his followers were aware of the distinction between "the living personality and the oral teaching of Freud and that of the rigid printed rules,"[4] though many tended to adhere to the latter. Since his death this trend has become more pronounced and analysts are much more likely to follow his written recommendations instead of his actual practices. Even in 1928 Freud noted, in a letter to Ferenczi, that

> the "Recommendations on Technique" I wrote long ago were essentially of a negative nature. I considered the most important thing was to emphasize what one should *not* do, and to point out the temptations in directions contrary to analysis. Almost everything positive that one *should* do I have left to "tact," the discussion of which you are introducing. The result was that the docile analysts did not perceive the elasticity of the rules I had laid down, and submitted to them as if they were taboos. Sometime all that must be revised, without, it is true, doing away with the obligations I had mentioned.

Yet if Freud complained about the passivity of some of his followers, he was nonetheless uneasy about Ferenczi's own "concessions" in matters of technique:

> All those who have no tact will see in what you write a justification for arbitrariness, i.e. subjectivity, i.e. the influence of their own unmastered complexes. What we encounter in reality is a delicate balancing . . . of the various reactions we expect from our interventions . . . One naturally cannot give rules for measuring this; the experience and the normality of the analyst have to form a decision. But with beginners one therefore has to rob the idea of "tact" of its mystical character.[5]

So many discrepancies arose between what Freud wrote about technique and what he in fact practiced that some might argue that really he had no technique, simply an *ad hoc* way of going about things. But he needed some formal teachings if he was to establish a discipline that could be carried on by others. One way of reconciling the apparent inconsistencies between what Freud said and what he did would be to say that although he was rigid in his adherence to the principles of the analytic situation, he was "elastic" in applications. But for the historian, "elasticity" is not any easier to summarize than "tact" would be for the beginner Freud wrote about.

Freud was devoted to what he called "a strictly regular, undiluted psychoanalysis."[6] He thought that an analyst should maintain a free-floating attitude—what he called an *evenly suspended attention*"[7]—to the material the patient brought to the analysis. Freud was against the analyst's taking notes, and although he sometimes behaved otherwise, he wrote that he did not want to make "use of analytic writings as an assistance to my patients; I require them to learn by personal experience, and I assure them that they will acquire wider and more valuable knowledge than the whole literature of psychoanalysis could teach them."[8] While maintaining a listening ear, the analyst, Freud thought, "must be distrustful and remain on his guard against" the phenomena of resistance.[9]

Although Freud recommended that the analyst be detached and neutral, he was not afraid to be himself. Freud once wrote that "analysts are people who have learned to practice a particular art; alongside of this, they may be allowed to be human beings like anyone else."[10] The choice of books for his waiting room, for example, revealed something about his own taste: before World War I the humorist Wilhelm Busch's books were there. But by 1928, when his patients were mainly American, his choices came to reflect the preferences of his analysands; his waiting room contained copies of *The Nation* and *The New Republic*.[11] Freud surrounded his practice with a good deal of professional discretion. His office was set up in such a way that there was a separate entrance and exit, so that patients would not encounter each other coming in and out, although they might pass on the apartment staircase outside. To friends and acquaintances who became his patients, he might say that for the period of their treatment they would have to sacrifice contact with the Freud family[12]—though he allowed exceptions.

Freud also recommended that the patient undergo the treatment "in abstinence":

> By this I do not mean physical abstinence alone, nor yet the deprivation of everything that the patient desires, for perhaps no sick person could tolerate this. Instead, I shall state it as a fundamental principle that the patient's need and longing should be allowed to persist in her

[*sic*], in order that they may serve as forces impelling her [*sic*] to do work and to make changes, and that we must beware of appeasing those forces by means of surrogates.[13]

Although Freud did not generally expect his patients to interrupt their sex lives for the sake of the analysis, to one woman patient in the 1930's he said it was his rule not to allow female patients to have sexual affairs for a certain period at the beginning of an analysis; perhaps she was one of his few unmarried patients, or there may have been other reasons for his demand (which she complied with, although with resentment).

To some patients Freud seemed the most silent of men, yet compared to later analysts he was almost garrulous.[14] He was capable of being irritatingly quiet and of not saying a word, but he could also chatter; on the whole, he was not as silent as most of today's orthodox Freudians. As one patient reported of an analytic session, "Freud talked most of the hour, or at least half of it."[15] Of course, Freud had a highly individual approach and therefore did not work with everyone in the same manner; but in general he analyzed in a free way, much more so than analysts do now. He is said to have spoken more openly with his students than training analysts today speak with theirs.[16]

His cancer of the jaw, however, made it difficult for him to talk, and he then compressed his thoughts to the briefest of comments; toward the end of his life he grew more impatient with his cases. Yet he always tried to express himself succinctly so that what he said would be remembered. And even in his last years, if a patient asked a valid question he nearly always got an answer.[17]

Freud frequently played with a ring on his finger (some analysts would consider this behavior a form of tic); patients in analysis, however, since they lay on a couch with Freud sitting behind and out of sight, only heard him playing with his watch chain or jingling his keys. But Freud revealed himself to patients not so much through personal idiosyncrasies as through the whole structure of the analytic situation. From his point of view, analysis fit his own insistence on privacy and hatred of publicity: he advised patients not to talk with anyone about their analysis.[18] Freud could listen to his patients, attending to every item in the stream of free associations, and choose when to reveal his own thoughts.

In the analytic task of searching the unconscious minds of others and in regarding nothing they said as indifferent or unimportant, Freud sometimes succumbed to the danger of paying more attention to the unconscious of others than to his own.[19] While the practice of analysis gave the analyst insight into himself, it also provided a new means for the self-

Freud's analytic couch

deception of both patient and analyst. Fliess had leveled that reproach against Freud in the late 1890's.

At times Freud could be quite frank in acknowledging the limited usefulness of the technique he recommended. As dogmatic about therapeutic matters as some of Freud's disciples were to become, he himself admitted:

> I must however make it clear that what I am asserting is that this technique is the only one suited to my individuality; I do not venture

to deny that a physician quite differently constituted might find himself driven to adopt a different attitude to his patients and to the task before him.[20]

Unlike some therapists, Freud chose to rely on the analytic couch so that he would not have to be watched all day; as he explained it,

> I cannot put up with being stared at by other people for eight hours a day (or more). Since, while I am listening to the patient, I, too, give myself over to the current of my unconscious thoughts, I do not wish my expressions of face to give the patient material for interpretations or to influence him in what he tells me. The patient usually regards being made to adopt this position as a hardship and rebels against it. . . .

Freud knew that "many analysts work in a different way, but I do not know whether this deviation is due more to a craving for doing things differently or to some advantage which they find they gain by it."[21] Rituals can serve a positive function, and Freud considered the use of a couch a "ceremonial."[22] But the use of a couch became the touchstone of analysis, and analysts feared that if they did not use a couch they would not be proper analysts.

Freud never altered his commitment to neutrality as the proper analytic approach. Thanks to the use of the couch, Freud felt, the patient does not have too much reality to cope with, and therefore encounters little interference in developing his fantasies about the analyst: hence a more efficient build-up of transference. The analyst's distance from his patients not only facilitates the analyst's rational insight, which might be impeded in a more commonplace setting, but also, Freud thought, expands the range of the kinds of patients accessible to analytic influence. Freud wrote: "I have been able to help people with whom I had nothing in common—neither race, education, social position nor outlook upon life in general—without affecting their individuality."[23]

It is unclear, nevertheless, why anyone should mind being watched all day, unless he was particularly sensitive to examination and inspection, and because of either unacknowledged guilt or the expectation of criticism was fearful of being looked at. If an analyst is afraid that patients will find weak spots and feels that inspection is a hostile act, then there would of course be a strain involved in face-to-face therapy. The use of a couch can also help the analyst avoid emotional intimacy with patients. With certain kinds of patients, who may—for a variety of reasons—be frightened of lying down, a modern analyst would have to contravene Freud's recom-

mendation and permit the patient to sit up. But none of the limitations of
the couch should obscure the general point that it may still be the easiest
method of allowing the patient to relax and free-associate. The impersonality of the analyst can ease the way to the patient's most private and
personal self-disclosures.

Freud never became a conventional psychoanalytic therapist. His analysis of his own daughter Anna,* for example, was only one example of
how unorthodox he could be. With certain patients or on special occasions, Freud was in favor of jettisoning prescribed psychoanalytic technique. But he would want to be sure that such a maneuver was really in
the interest of the patient, and did not merely serve the pleasure of the
analyst. A student of Freud's was once troubled about her procedures with
a patient; the analyst had given the patient money, helped her with her
lessons at Radcliffe College, commissioned a portrait—in short had done
all the "active" things that a good analyst was supposed to avoid. Yet
Freud was entirely sympathetic and said that sometimes one has to be
both mother and father to a patient: "one does what one can."[24] Freud
was capable of flexibility in his own technique: a patient was once embarrassed about something she was discussing and did not want Freud to
watch her. He got up from his chair and walked in front of the couch
and looked straight at her, saying that she had to have the courage to face
him and thereby confront her problem.[25]

If Freud allowed himself privileges which were not for younger and
more inexperienced analysts, it was because he was above all an investigator and would try almost anything once. He did what he thought best,
without following his own rules. Some of his pupils, however, were docile:
a Berlin analyst in the 1920's, wanting to be orthodox, would not let his
patients smoke, whereas in at least one analysis Freud regularly laid out
a cigarette and match for the patient before the beginning of a session.[26]
As one of Freud's patients and pupils once described it, the master's
attitude was: "Do as I say, not as I do";[27] and this dichotomy may have
been one of the sources of Freud's moralism about technique. Many of
Freud's followers mentioned the Roman maxim *Quod licet Jovi, non licet
bovi* ("What is permitted to Jove is not permitted to an ox").

Freud sometimes let his patients know which of them he preferred,
and for years he raised annual contributions to support a favorite former
patient, the "Wolf-Man," who was an impoverished Russian aristocrat.

---

* Cf. pp. 438–40.

Sometimes Freud even asked his patients for a contribution.[28] In contrast to the image of a coldly neutral analyst, Freud welcomed his patients' views about younger people in the movement and by the 1920's and 1930's would directly inquire whether they had noticed any tensions in the Vienna Society.[29]

Bold and unorthodox as an analyst, Freud simultaneously analyzed married couples on at least two occasions. In the case of James and Alix Strachey, if one of them missed a session then the other could have it in addition to his own, thus being analyzed for two hours that day. Freud analyzed people he knew socially, sometimes even when they were—in the summer, for instance—living with him in the same house. Some of his special favorites would be in and out of his family household, even though this would prevent Freud from being the ideal aloof and dispassionate analyst. Freud sometimes intervened for the benefit of a patient; in one case he wrote a prescription for a contraceptive that would give more satisfaction than a condom.

In at least four instances Freud gave patients papers of his to translate.* Despite what he wrote about the inadvisability of patients reading analytic literature, he is reported not to have cared what some patients read.[31] Once he even encouraged a patient, over the patient's objection, to read two of his case histories.[32] Freud would lend books, although he might express anxiety lest the patient mislay them, since every book was precious.[33] If a patient gave him a present of a book, Freud would not only accept the gift but might reciprocate with a choice of his own. Freud lacked the rigidity that many have complained about in other analysts;† he would tell jokes, would compliment a patient on a dress, and if he felt the need to urinate, would get up and leave the room.

When Freud thought an analysis could be helped by changes in the life of the individual, he would intervene. Sometimes he recommended a specific marriage choice or supported a patient in violating a marriage bond. Freud regarded certain dreams as signifying a return to health, and after interpreting a dream could go so far as to remark: "Now you are

---

* As James Strachey remembered it: "after only a few weeks of our analysis [of him and his wife Alix], he suddenly instructed us to make a translation of a paper he had recently written."[30] Edith Jackson and Joan Riviere also did such work for Freud during their analyses.

† As Theodor Reik observed: "You cannot remain a cold fish the way many analysts trained by the New York psychoanalytic do. It is incredible. My daughter was in analysis and gave her analyst a book for Christmas and the analyst said: 'Why did you give me that book?' and did not accept it. It is inhuman."[34]

going to get well." Freud felt in control of the situation even when two patients in analysis, old friends of each other, were discussing their analyses.[35] Perhaps because he wanted to precipitate a reaction (and also to forward his cause), Freud would often mention the divergencies of Adler, Jung, and Rank; when asked, he was not averse to speaking about his former pupils. When he liked an opera, such as Mozart's *Don Giovanni*, he would mention it if it were playing in town.

In the case of a young man who had written a few poems, Freud asked to have a look at them; Freud said the poetry surprised him, since it indicated that the patient was not, as the patient himself had thought, a weak person but very strong. To be so praised was totally unexpected, and Freud's assurance that he had a good mind was essential to the patient, he later thought, in his ability to fulfill himself.[36] In his old age Freud sometimes rapped on the edge of the couch, either because he had not quite heard something or to drive home a point.[37] He often gave his photograph to followers in analysis, even when unasked.

Freud liked to think that psychoanalytic patients came for treatment entirely of their own volition, and as a testimony to this free choice he exacted sacrifices from them. He proposed as a general principle that the analyst should "refrain from giving treatment free, and make no exceptions to this in favor of his colleagues or their families."[38] But Freud did not hold fast to the rule that he laid down for others; it was one of the contradictions in him that along with a certain niggardliness in his theory went real generosity. For although he held that anything given absolutely free is thereby debased in the eyes of the receiver, in at least several cases Freud analyzed patients free of charge.* On the other hand, some patients made financial contributions to Freud's movement and even gave presents to his family. During the hard times in Vienna at the end of World War I, Freud referred in a letter to "the way in which we have been victualled for the past year or so by patients and friendly followers."[39]

Once Freud recommended to a pupil that, in the case of an apparently aloof and detached patient, the analyst should arouse the patient's envy by making some show of approval about another patient in analysis.[40] (The device worked.) In the 1920's Freud started an analysis with an American who spoke in English, but after a month Freud decided to shift to the German he preferred. The patient had known some German from high school and was then taking further lessons, but Freud gave him only a week's notice. The patient wondered if it would not interfere with his

---

* For example, Freud treated without payment Heinz Hartmann, Kata Levy, Eva Rosenfeld, the "Wolf-Man" for a time, and doubtless others.

free associàtions, but Freud said that, on the contrary, it would help; shortly thereafter the patient made a meaningful slip which he would not have made in English.[41] (Years earlier Freud had written that "it is by no means rare for someone who is not speaking his mother tongue to exploit his clumsiness for the purpose of making highly significant slips of the tongue in the language that is foreign to him."[42]) Once Freud thought an American patient was using English as a resistance, so they shifted to German. But Freud could not stand her German, so they went back to English again.[43]

Freud's more politic followers made him out to be a model, stereotyped analyst: Jones suppressed, in relating an incident recounted by a former patient of Freud's, the fact that it took place during an analysis conducted while the patient was staying in Freud's summer house. And there was the hypocrisy of those who knew of Freud's practices and at the same time claimed that such procedures, when carried out by others, were "unanalytic" in character. American analysts in particular tended to be more orthodox than Freud, since European analysts were likely to have more regular contact with him.

Of course, in any account of Freud's lack of orthodoxy in technique it should be remembered that an implicit part of the contract between a patient and Freud was that one could not expect from him an ordinary analysis. As the founder of a new system of treatment, Freud felt entitled to make any alterations that he deemed necessary.

It is debatable whether Freud's failure to abide by his rules of analysis was a strength or a weakness. But most would agree that whatever system of treatment Freud created would have worked, provided that Freud used it. The trouble arose because, as Heinz Hartmann put it, Freud was like Bismarck: as soon as the German chancellor was fired, the whole way of governing Germany had to be changed (this analogy would have appealed to Freud).[44]

But what happens to analysis without its founder? As Georg Groddeck once wrote: "Because two or three great pianists exist, every schoolboy or schoolgirl has to sit at the instrument of torture. But bad piano playing hurts only the ears, the play with psychoanalysis will tear innumerable hearts."[45] Stefan Zweig had similar doubts in the early 1930's about future uses of Freud's work:

Because of the rarity of such a combination of qualities as are needed to form the true master of mental healing by the psychoanalytic method, psychoanalysis should always remain a vocation, a mission, and should never become (as unhappily it often does today) a mere occupation or business . . . I shudder to think how risky an inquisitorial process such as that thought out by a creative spirit like Freud with the utmost refinement and with a full sense of responsibility, might become in clumsy hands. Probably nothing has tended so much to bring psychoanalysis into disrepute as the fact that it has not been restricted to a narrow and aristocratically selected circle of experts, but, though unteachable to most, has been taught in the schools.[46]

Such doubts, Freud wrote, "whether psychoanalysis can be practiced by average human beings . . . leads back to ignorance of technique,"[47] and his likening of analysis to a microscope or a surgical procedure lent support to magical expectations about the scientific status of his work. What to Freud might have been temporary or *ad hoc* measures became, in the hands of some devoted followers, unchangeable rituals. And the technical jargon he created could be used to justify almost anything.

2. Research Aims

UNFORTUNATELY, THE EXPENSE of psychoanalytic treatment has supported the unrealistic hopes of patients. At the outset of Freud's practice as an analyst, however, he earned relatively little; and in 1913 he wrote of the analyst that "hard as he may work, he can never earn as much as other medical specialists."[1] Freud had an unusually honest attitude toward money; in the early days of his medical practice, he "noticed that, out of a fairly large number of visits to patients, I only forgot those to non-paying patients or to colleagues."[2] So when he evolved the arrangements for analytic treatment, Freud was frank about the monetary side of things. He thought that the financial sacrifice involved in the payment would be a privation that would spur the patient to progress in the analytic work.

With the exceptions already noted, Freud liked being paid for his services. When a former patient sent newspaper clippings about the growing success of psychoanalysis in the world, Freud replied only briefly and with no expression of interest in the patient's current life. (Freud may

also have been trying to wean his patient from a dependence on him.)[3]
He encouraged his pupils to be straightforward about money matters, and
was naturally shocked in the 1920's to find that one analyst in Vienna
expected other analysts to give him a percentage of the fees from patients
referred by him. After a troubled discussion it was made clear that Freud
frowned on such practices.*[4]

Freud would be impressed by a rich patient's ability to pay his bills
as well as possibly to help forward the movement as a whole. In the 1920's
he sent the American writer Thomas Wolfe to a follower because of the
novelist's inability to pay Freud's fees; and this analyst referred Wolfe,
on the same grounds, to still another analyst. By the 1930's Freud expected
to receive twenty-five dollars an hour from his patients, although many
were treated at lower rates, and Freud thought that all analysts had an
obligation to take on a certain number of patients free of charge.

Freud customarily saw his patients six days a week, with Sunday as a
day off; he also took a holiday of a month or more during the summer.
The five-day analytic week, which became customary for a time in the
United States, had an accidental origin in 1921. Freud had undertaken to
accept six new patients, but found that he had time for only five of them.
He suggested that one of them go to Rank instead, at a fraction of his own
fees, but they all refused. Abram Kardiner remembered that then

> we each spent a very bad night, because we didn't know what Freud
> intended to do. Was he actually going to seize one of us and throw
> us out, or would he hit upon a more amicable arrangement? We all
> returned the next day at three o'clock. He convened us and announced
> that he had found a happy solution. His daughter Anna, he said, had
> proved herself a mathematical genius. She had discovered that five
> times six was thirty, and that six times five was thirty, so that if each
> of us would renounce one hour a week he could accommodate six
> of us. This was the beginning of the five-hour week.[5]

Freud had a total of nine patients in analysis in 1921, and of those six new
patients five were American; he did not, however, reduce his other
patients from six days to five, and to the Americans it seemed clear that
Freud preferred to spend his time with the Europeans. By 1930 Freud was

---

* A case of malpractice by an analyst came up before a group of Viennese analysts;
after much discussion of the psychological origins of the analyst's breach of ethics,
Freud ended the matter by saying: "This may all very well be so, but malpractice is
none the better morally for having psychological bases."

still seeing patients on a six-day schedule, although in his last years he saw only five patients a day.

Freud had a "sincere hatred of waiting,"[6] and could not have managed to take care of all his cases unless the patients were punctual. He is reported never to have kept a patient waiting and gave each one "fifty-five minutes precisely."[7] Freud regarded a patient's being on time as an important matter; he could scold a patient for being late, as well as interpret it as a sign of resistance. In any event, a patient paid for missed time. His followers went along with him in taking punctuality for granted, and even the radical Wilhelm Reich is said to have been unable to tolerate being kept waiting.[8] The analytic relationship had an element of formality to it and was not intended to be casual or free and easy.

At the outset Freud was capable of treating a patient on a couch only once or twice, and in one instance (with Wilhelm Stekel) nine sessions constituted an analysis. In 1903 Freud thought that an analysis could be expected to last "long periods, six months to three years, for an effective treatment," and he had hopes for preventing future neurotic reactions in his patients.[9] In 1913 Freud explained that "psychoanalysis is always a matter of long periods of time, of half a year or whole years—of longer periods than the patient expects."[10] In 1930 one of Freud's pupils estimated that "the average duration of an analytic treatment is one year."[11] As time passed, the expected duration of an analysis lengthened considerably, and in 1932 Freud remarked that "there are . . . severely handicapped people who are kept under analytic supervision all through their lives and taken back into analysis from time to time."[12]

It is hard to generalize about how long Freud kept patients in analysis, since as early as *The Interpretation of Dreams* he referred to a patient in the fifth year of treatment, and in 1915 he had a patient who had been in analysis for four years.[13] Still, it is fair to say that in his earlier days as an analyst Freud saw patients for relatively short periods; until late in his career, some months of treatment would have often seemed sufficient. Once he referred a case of impotence to Reich with the directive: "impotence, three months."[14]

By the end of his life, however, Freud was seeing patients for longer periods, in some instances six years. In part this was due to his ill health; as he grew old he became less attracted to meeting new people, and if he found a patient who could afford his fees and was interesting but not too troublesome, it was easier for him not to interrupt the treatment. In addition, Freud was disappointed by the results of some of his early cases, which at the time had appeared to be successful; perhaps lengthier analyses might be more reliable. Once he was asked "whether psychoanalysis was a finite or infinite process. After a pause he said hesitatingly and in a low voice: 'I believe—an infinite one.' "[15]

In 1926 Freud wrote in his defense that "analytic treatments take months and even years: magic that is so slow loses its miraculous character."[16] But it is questionable whether extremely lengthy analyses can be justified. If, for instance, a patient is in analytic treatment for eight or ten years, can one not legitimately ask whether, assuming he really needs such extensive help, a more direct form of support than analysis would have been preferable? Long analyses provoke a dependency in the patient that can be hard to overcome. Moreover, once a patient invests a small fortune in an analysis he can scarcely be expected to have an objective attitude toward the benefit he has received; he may be either excessively docile or unnecessarily disappointed. Freud's relatively brief analyses at least enabled the patient to preserve his independence, which was one of the aims of analysis in the first place.

But questions of how long an analysis should last were not really important to Freud. Uppermost in his mind was the advancement of science. He believed that disease can be a road to knowledge and he devised a means of using this knowledge in the cause of science. His main interest lay in promoting the understanding of human psychology—hence the impersonality that characterized psychoanalytic treatment. There was nonetheless a supportive element in Freud's technique. He did show considerable professional interest in his patients and remembered much about their lives. But it should not be surprising to hear patients reporting that they never had any idea whether Freud liked them or not; Freud's aim was to be completely impersonal, and one former patient concluded that he was essentially cold.[17]

For some it was rather unsettling at first to go to see Freud; he had a certain charm, but was brisk in manner.[18] Yet in his technique he was extremely human, and many patients report the good contact they had. He was natural in talking about himself, and his attentiveness was rarely in question. He could be warm and interested in everything. More than one former patient wondered where later New York analysts got their technique.

Freud was too much of a human being to treat patients simply as objects of scientific research. Yet he was the discoverer of so much that he could become fascinated by what he was unearthing, to the exclusion of other factors. Freud wrote that "in its execution research and treatment coincide. . . .";[19] yet he knew that scientific interest could also interfere with clinical work. He worried about the conflict in analysis between research and therapy.[20] In his old age, however, the balance shifted from a concern with therapy to a protectiveness of science: "I only want to feel assured that the therapy will not destroy the science."[21] In the end it was the scientific discoverer in Freud who triumphed over the artist.

He emphasized again and again that the analyst must maintain "the strength to renounce any short-sighted therapeutic ambition."[22] Gradually "scientific research once more [as in his youth] became the chief interest of my life."[23] He was in favor of "the large-scale application of our therapy," and knew that this "will compel us to alloy the pure gold of analysis with the copper of direct suggestion . . . But, whatever form this psychotherapy of the future may take, . . . its most effective and most important ingredients will assuredly remain those borrowed from strict and untendentious psychoanalysis."[24]

Freud thought that his approach was best for research, if not for therapy. Some of his patients concluded that he was not really interested in therapy, but rather in the possibility of making discoveries. Treatment is not the beginning and end of medicine; Freud believed that matters of prevention and cure would solve themselves provided that we understand enough about the nature of disease and the forces at work.* He wrote in a letter as early as 1912: "The therapeutic point of view . . . is certainly not the only one for which psychoanalysis claims interest, nor is it the most important. So there is a great deal to be said on the subject even without putting therapy in the forefront."[26]

Freud's interest in therapy waned in his old age, and some of his students adopted the same detached attitude toward patients. As Robert Waelder wrote: "Freud thought it was fortunate that psychoanalysis had a therapeutic value because that alone made it possible for people to offer themselves for psychoanalytic research."[27] But Franz Alexander concluded that "the classical technique was originally devised for research and not treatment. . . . [The] apparent parallelism between the aims of research and treatment has proved a grave overstatement."[28] Other pupils of Freud claimed not to have identified with Freud as a scientist, and they thought that the therapist must give the patient some immediate relief. Yet almost all Freud's adherents tended to speak of themselves as "observers" rather than "healers." Freud was not really interested in hearing about the therapeutic results of his students, but rather in what they had discovered.

As early as 1912 Freud had described the analyst as a "surgeon" and

---

* According to William M. Johnston, the Viennese medical approach was that "disease comprised part of life: the task of doctors was not to eradicate it but merely to understand it."[25]

the analysis itself as an "operation"; he recommended that the analyst adopt an attitude of "emotional coldness."

> I cannot advise my colleagues too urgently to model themselves during psychoanalytic treatment on the surgeon, who puts aside all his feelings, even his human sympathy, and concentrates his mental forces on the single aim of performing the operation as skillfully as possible.[29]

Freud de-emphasized the human and moral aspects of the psychoanalytic encounter, and compared the curing of souls to a "surgical operation."[30] He insisted that "the technique of psychonalysis has become as definite and as delicate as that of any other specialized branch of medicine," and that "analytic technique has attained a certainty and delicacy rivalling that of surgery."*[31] Freud wrote that "cruel though it may sound, we must see to it that the patient's suffering, to a degree that is in some way or other effective, does not come to an end prematurely."[32]

It might be easier to agree with Freud if only he had not been so outspoken about having "never been a therapeutic enthusiast"; "our attitude to life ought not to be that of a fanatic for hygiene or therapy."[33] Freud did take his own cases seriously, and also wrote that it was "not a good thing to work on a case scientifically while treatment is still proceeding. . . ."[34] But he knew that what mattered for him in his cases were the psychological discoveries they would eventually enable him to make. Freud recognized that therapeutic results were crucial from the patient's point of view, and he too needed them, for the sake of his practice and that of his pupils. From the outset Freud knew that he could not offer treatment unless there was some prospect of therapeutic success; "anyone who wants to make a living from the treatment of nervous patients must clearly be able to do something to help them."[35] He resented the fact that, as he put it, "the world hears nothing of some of the most successful cures. . . ."[36]

It is difficult to believe that technique by itself can ever produce lasting psychotherapeutic results; there have been no advances in analysis comparable to those in surgery. Yet Freud had argued that

> a surgeon does not refrain from examining and handling a focus of disease, if he is intending to take active measures which he believes will lead to a permanent cure . . . [P]sychoanalysis. . . . may make the same claims as surgery: the increase in suffering which it causes

---

* These analogies were bound to have a suggestive impact of their own; they could encourage passivity in patients rather than the analytic ideal of self-reliance.

the patient during treatment is incomparably less than what a surgeon causes, and is quite negligible in proportion to the severity of the underlying ailment.[37]

Freud's urge for investigation and his desire for scientific knowledge led him to favor lay analysis; the relief of suffering was part of the medical profession of healing, and was not Freud's main objective. Freud once noted in a case that

> It was impossible to unravel this tissue of phantasy thread by thread; the therapeutic success of the treatment was precisely what stood in the way of this . . . The scientific results of psychoanalysis are at present only a by-product of its therapeutic aims, and for that reason it is often just in those cases where treatment fails that most discoveries are made.[38]

In 1908 Freud noted in himself "an indifferent attitude towards my patients," and in 1925 he wrote about the more general "crust of indifference" that he saw "slowly creeping around me. . . ."[39] Freud fostered the illusion that the more perfect an analyst's technique, the better the therapeutic results. An analyst can of course base his judgments only on what he sees, but the fact is that much clinical material looks different to different people.

As early as 1896 Freud acknowledged to Fliess that "when I was young, the only thing I longed for was philosophical knowledge, and now that I am going over from medicine to psychology I am in the process of attaining it. I have become a therapist against my will. . . ."[40] And in 1926 Freud wrote:

> I scarcely think . . . that my lack of a genuine medical temperament has done much damage to my patients. For it is not greatly to the advantage of patients if their doctor's therapeutic interest has too marked an emotional emphasis. They are best helped if he carries out his task coolly and keeping as closely as possible to the rules.[41]

In 1916 Freud wrote: "I lack that passion for helping and I see now why: it is because I never lost any loved person in my early youth."[42] And Freud was fond of contrasting "the medical and the psychoanalytic view of dreams,"[43] his ideal being that of the scientist rather than the physician.

Freud always emphasized that the theory of psychoanalysis was "based on observation,"[44] and no doubt Jones was right in thinking that "to one accusation he appeared to be rather sensitive: namely, the idea that he had evolved all his conclusions out of his inner consciousness."[45] Some of Freud's pupils continued to respect his work after they had ceased to admire his personality, and others acknowledged his genius after having repudiated his findings. Freud himself distinguished between what he called "greatness of achievement" and "greatness of personality."[46]

If Freud was not really a healer, he readily resorted to educational analogies to explain his special contribution. "Psychoanalytic treatment may in general be conceived of as . . . a *re-education in overcoming internal resistances.*"[47] Freud wanted to give patients the instruments for self-knowledge. But although he explicitly used an educational metaphor in referring to the analysts' "standard of psychical normality to which they wish to educate their patients,"[48] he at the same time distinguished education from analysis. "Education and therapeutics," Freud wrote, "stand in an assignable relation to each other . . . Education is a prophylaxis . . . ; psychotherapy seeks to undo the less stable of the . . . outcomes and to institute a kind of after-education."[49] Of course, Freud did not lecture his patients, but his Socratic working assumption was that the patient knows everything but lacks awareness.

Freud defended himself against the accusation that his approach to therapy was too narrow: "The charge of one-sidedness made against psychoanalysis, which, as *the science of the unconscious mind*, has its own definite and restricted field of work, is as inapplicable as it would be if it were made against chemistry."[50] He anticipated the time when chemical methods would be used to correct psychological states, and he wanted his pupils to hurry before neurotic problems disappeared from sight; for "neurotic human beings offer far more instructive and accessible material than normal ones. . . ."[51] Freud would advise his disciples that the "man with the syringe" was right behind their backs, and once neuroses were curable by new methods, analysts would have no opportunity to learn. He was apprehensive that "the blind giant, the hormone man, will do a lot of damage if the dwarf psychologist does not take him out of the China shop."*[52]

Freud always sensed the danger of excessive therapeutic zeal in an analyst. He once wrote to a pupil: "I should advise you to set aside your therapeutic ambitions and try to understand what is happening. When you have done that, therapeutics will take care of itself."[54] A therapist who extends himself more than Freud advised may in fact end up by making

---

* Freud also said in this connection that he "felt like someone in a fog who hears steps behind him which come nearer and nearer." In 1929 or 1930 he remarked that he was like someone in the Arctic, who knows that he has only so much more time before the ice closes in.[53]

the patient too dependent, or too guilty, which can provoke new defensive responses; or the patient may later react badly to the loss of the activist therapist. It is possible for a therapist to care too much and be too identified with his patients. But common sense is not always unreliable, and the therapist's desire to help need not interfere with the patient's recovery.

In the 1890's Freud had aimed as a therapist to accomplish something prophylactically, but by the end of his life he was more skeptical.[55] If Freud was not equally great as a discoverer and a healer, he at least knew some of his limitations. He acknowledged to Kardiner three things wrong with himself as an impatient analyst: he became tired of people too fast and did not keep patients for a long enough time in analysis; he was overly preoccupied with theoretical issues and would look for them in every patient; and he too readily took the role of the patriarchal father.[56]

Among the old-guard analysts it became fashionable in later years to say that Freud was a poor therapist. But he had taken people's money on the promise that he would help them and therefore he cared about the results. He liked to contrast the way his own concepts, unlike those of some of his rivals, arose in a clinical context: "I did not start out, like Janet, from laboratory experiments, but with therapeutic aims in mind."[57] For all Freud wrote about not being a healer, many have attested how much his patients mattered to him. As Binswanger wrote, "despite everything he said about his inadequacies as a physician . . . I only half believed him, for I knew only too well how completely he sacrificed himself for some of his patients."[58]

3. Character and Symptoms

AT THE OUTSET of his psychotherapeutic work, Freud had been intrigued by the possibilities of hypnosis and suggestion. He later wrote that he "soon came to dislike hypnosis."[1] Freud partly had moral objections in mind, and it has been said that he "disliked the ethics of suggestive therapy—the deceit, the coercion, the ignorance."[2] The use of hypnosis and suggestive therapy, he further complained, "was hack-work and not a scientific activity, and it recalled magic, incantations, and hocus-pocus."[3] By eliminating everyday defenses, hypnotic treatment did not allow the therapist to witness his patient's self-deceptions at work.

By "following a dim presentiment," Freud "decided to replace hypnosis by free association."[4] And "with the abandonment of hypnosis the applicability of the treatment was assured to an unlimited number of patients"; for "it depends upon the choice of the patient whether he can be hypnotized or not, no matter what the skill of the physician may be, and . . . a large number of neurotic patients can not be hypnotized by any means whatever. . . ."[5] But the reader could be misled by Freud's 1903 claim that once free association was adopted there were no limits to the kind of patients who would be accessible to analysis; in 1898 Freud had more accurately expressed an enduring conviction of his:

Psychoanalytic therapy is not at present applicable to all cases . . . It demands a certain degree of maturity and understanding in the patient and is therefore not suited for the young or for adults who are feeble-minded or uneducated. It also fails with people who are very advanced in years, because, owing to the accumulation of material in them, it would take up so much time that by the end of the treatment they would have reached a period of life in which value is no longer attached to nervous health. Finally, the treatment is only possible if the patient has a normal psychical state from which the pathological material can be mastered. During a condition of hysterical confusion, or an interpolated mania or melancholia, nothing can be effected by psychoanalytic means. Such cases can nevertheless be treated by analysis after the violent manifestations have been quieted by the usual methods. In actual practice, chronic cases of psychoneurosis are altogether more amenable to the method than cases with acute crises, in which the greatest stress is naturally laid on the speed with which the crisis can be dealt with. For this reason, the most favorable field of work for this new therapy is offered by hysterical phobias and the various forms of obsessional neurosis.[6]

In 1904 Freud listed the "various qualifications . . . required of anyone who is to be beneficially affected by psychoanalysis. To begin with, he must be capable of a psychically normal condition," and exhibit "a certain measure of natural intelligence and ethical development. . . ." Freud thought it was pointless for an analyst to try to help someone of a "worthless" character, "because if the physician has to deal with a worthless character, he soon loses the interest which makes it possible for him to enter profoundly into the patient's mental life."[7]

Since Freud's clinical material did "in fact consist of chronic cases derived from the more educated classes,"[8] his patients would be capable of using the verbal means of therapy he preferred. Freud wondered how he had come upon his particular therapeutic technique of encouraging the patient to express every fragment of thought that passed through his mind. He once suggested that one of his childhood books, which by 1920 was the only book "that had survived from his boyhood," so prefigured his concept of the helpfulness of free associations that "this hint may have brought to light the fragment of cryptomnesia [hidden channels of memory] which in so many cases may be suspected to lie behind apparent originality."[9]

Although Freud thought that free association, unlike hypnosis, would be a way of discovering hidden memories without the magic of suggestion, the analytic situation was unusual enough to involve magical elements all its own. For the analyst to remain silent and out of sight, even in the face of a patient's most troubled and intimate revelations, is to impose on the patient a special sort of stress. The psychoanalyst's method of communicating with a patient—relatively short, pithy remarks, with the patient doing most of the talking—is bound to encourage the patient to expect something special. The more silent an analyst, the more likely his comments will assume a disproportionate weight.

Freud preferred to think that analysis was free of the worst dangers of suggestion, such as had occurred when he unknowingly encouraged his patients to believe their early tales of childhood seduction. Freud also thought that one of his patients abandoned her treatment because of his neutrality; he wondered afterward:

> Might I have perhaps kept the girl under my treatment if I myself had acted a part, if I had exaggerated the importance to me of her staying on, and had shown a warm personal interest in her. . . . ? I do not know. . . . I have always avoided acting a part, and have contented myself with practicing the humbler arts of psychology. In spite of every theoretical interest and of every endeavor to be of assistance as a physician, I keep the fact in mind that there must be some limits set to the extent to which psychological influence may be used, and I respect as one of these limits the patient's own will and understanding.[10]

Freud was thus insistent on "how unjust it is to attribute the results of analysis to the physician's imagination and suggestion."[11] Despite his proposal for the future to "alloy the pure gold of analysis" with "the copper of direct suggestion," it is in reality never easy to distinguish between the two.

It is still an open question how much Freud's results were due to his own personal capacities and how much to the technique he adopted.

Since Freud did not seem to realize how impressive his personality could be, and how coercive the analytic situation could become, he does not sound persuasive when he wrote in 1937:

> The danger of our leading a patient astray by suggestion, by persuading him to accept things which we ourselves believe but which he ought not to, has certainly been enormously exaggerated. An analyst would have had to behave very incorrectly before such a misfortune could overtake him; above all, he would have to blame himself with not allowing his patients to have their say.

But Freud was being too rational in ignoring the subtler bases of an analytic patient's suggestibility. Freud's own intransigence does not help to make him more convincing; he concluded that "I can assert without boasting that such an abuse of 'suggestion' has never occurred in my practice."[12]

However detached and aloof Freud became in his old age, in his early work as a psychotherapist he was intensely involved with his patients. His lectures at Clark University, for example, written as late as 1909, show how interested he was in a patient's symptomatology and in tracing each symptom back to the infantile past. Although at the end of his career Freud was primarily concerned with the reconstruction of patients' pasts, he wrote that psychoanalysis had begun "its work on what is, of all the contents of the mind, most foreign to the ego—on symptoms."[13]

At the beginning of his practice as an analyst, Freud tried to focus directly on the problem of curing symptoms. As early as his collaboration with Breuer, Freud thought that each symptom has a history and a structure; he eventually came to believe, however, that the main task of analysis was to help the patient understand his regressions and inhibitions, and that once this was done symptoms could be expected to cure themselves. But, as we have seen, Freud for many years considered a patient's symptoms a significant matter.[14]

Over the years Freud changed his approach. His chief objective became, not the interpretation and cure of symptoms, but the overcoming of defenses and resistances. He realized that in the fascination with symptomatology it is possible to overlook the human being; and so psychoanalysts became interested, partly under the influence of Wilhelm Reich's work, in studying character traits. Freud's view all along had been that psychoanalysis "does not take the symptoms of an illness as its point of attack but sets about removing its *causes*."[15] Otherwise, nothing might be "cured other than the symptoms, which later can appear once again."[16] By 1922 Freud thought that "the removal of the symptoms of the illness

is not specifically aimed at, but is achieved, as it were, as a by-product
if the analysis is properly carried through."[17]

The term "neurosis" is nowadays applied to a specific syndrome, but
when Freud first began writing, it served as a receptacle for virtually
anything from a cause of suicide[18] to a slip of the pen. In general, Freud
meant by the neuroses "those adult forms of infantile, i.e., dependent
life. . . ."[19]

We have seen that Freud's focus on psychological sources of mental
disorders did not preclude his acceptance of the importance of constitutional predispositions. (By "constitution" Freud meant "everything that
is not psychological."[20]) The organic factors were, however, beyond
psychotherapeutic influence.

> Psychoanalysis points to psychology for the solution of a good half
> of the problems of psychiatry. It would nevertheless be a serious mis-
> take to suppose that analysis favors or aims at a *purely* psychological
> view. . . . [T]he other half of the problems of psychiatry are con-
> cerned with the influence of organic factors . . . on the mental
> apparatus.[21]

In view of the fact that science at that time knew relatively little about
hereditary factors, Freud thought it would be imprudent to ignore the
psychological paths he had opened up.

In the most seriously disturbed cases, the disorders called psychoses
—which often, for practical reasons, entail hospitalization—the argument
in favor of biochemical or neurophysiological (or even genetic) causation
is today generally considered the strongest. Although Freud wanted to
exclude psychotics from analytic treatment, he maintained that "there is
no fundamental difference, but only one of degree, between the mental
life of normal people, of neurotics and of psychotics."[22] He thought that

> as so often in biology, normal circumstances or those approaching
> the normal are less favorable subjects for investigation than pathologi-
> cal ones. I expect that what remains obscure in the elucidation of
> these very slight disturbances will be illuminated by the explanation
> of serious disturbances.[23]

What sort of "serious disturbances" could Freud have had in mind?
He once claimed that "in consequence of the novelty of my therapeutic
method, I see only the *severest* cases, which have already been under
treatment for years without any success."[24] In contrast to today, of course,
in the early days of psychoanalysis a different kind of patient presented

himself for treatment: it was recently reported that in one part of the United States the principal presenting symptom for patients who offer themselves to be analyzed by analysts-in-training is the difficulty of completing their Ph.D. dissertations. But historical changes since Freud's time may confuse us, since by the "severest cases" Freud could not have meant to include the psychoses. Although the Swiss never made much of the distinction between neurology and psychiatry, the Germans did; and in Vienna neurologists like Freud were excluded from seeing hospitalized cases.

To all intents and purposes Freud never had any psychiatric experience. His chosen field was psychology, and although he resented the way official psychiatry, especially in Vienna, treated his findings, it was not until the advent of Jung and Freud's American pupils that psychoanalytic ideas began to have an impact on the understanding and treatment of the great mental illnesses. Freud, however, was unlikely (or unwilling) to make a psychiatric diagnosis.*

Late in 1908 Freud commented that a particular case was "of a paranoid character, and therefore . . . unsuitable for psychoanalysis."[26] In 1926 Freud refused to see a paranoiac patient recommended to him, even though other analysts at the time were trying to treat such cases.[27] Freud wrote that "mental patients are split and broken structures," like crystals that have shattered. "Even we cannot withhold from them something of the reverential awe which peoples of the past felt for the insane."[28] In a letter Freud was more personal: "I do not like these patients . . . I am annoyed with them . . . I feel them to be so far distant from me and from everything human. A curious sort of intolerance, which surely makes me unfit to be a psychiatrist."[29]

Freud seems to have thought that in the future such patients as schizophrenics might be accessible to psychoanalytic technique, but although he was willing to consider what other therapists would come up with, he did not want to participate in this work himself. One needs distance in order not to be swamped by these frightening disorders. But some therapists, such as Frieda Fromm-Reichmann, got through to their patients by means of a loving concern, whereas others have resorted to deep, confronting interpretations.

Freud was not flexible enough to adapt his technique to the treatment of psychotics. His standoffishness toward them now looks defensive, a

---

* After one interview Freud once referred a patient to a pupil, explaining in a letter that he did not know the diagnosis; he could not tell anything more than that the woman was a "crazy hen." In fact she was suffering from a manic attack.[25]

reaction to some inner threat. One has to be, at least superficially, more warm and less distant to be concerned with the psychoses. While admitting his "unfamiliarity with schizophrenia," Freud wrote in 1927 that "in general I am skeptical about the effectiveness of analysis for the therapy of psychoses. . . ."[30] Yet he did not modify his general principle that in an analysis a patient's suffering must not "come to an end prematurely" to accommodate the clinical reality of psychotic problems.

A rule of thumb to differentiate between neurosis and psychosis is that the latter arises when a person is no longer able to handle the former. No really satisfactory means has been found to differentiate qualitatively between the two areas. As late as 1923 Freud emphasized that "neuroses and psychoses are not separated by a hard and fast line."[31] Exhibiting his intolerance of religion, Freud once remarked on the way "religious instruction acts upon the lives of Catholic children"; he then observed "how many a germ of psychosis enters the child's brain along this path!"[32] It may have been broad-minded of Freud to think that "hallucinations occasionally occur in the healthy."[33] But to classify psychoses as a neurotic disorder was to confound the problem by making it seem that neurosis, which psychoanalysis presumably could handle, was the more general category of which psychosis was only a part.[34]

For some time Freud discussed psychoses under the label of "narcissistic neuroses," with the implicit assumption that it would not be necessary to regard them as a distinct category, which, however, he later tried to do. But Freud always thought that "in the narcissistic neuroses the resistance is unconquerable. . . ."[35] In ordinary neurotic cases the patient's capacity to "transfer" old loves and hates onto the analyst established the basis for the possibility of a working relationship; but "narcissistic neurotics" reject "the doctor, not with hostility but with indifference . . . They manifest no transference and for that reason are inaccessible to our efforts and cannot be cured by us."[36] But we now know that "the psychotic is far from being incapable of forming a transference relationship; rather, the transference is there in all too great abundance, but the patient is unable to maintain the reality of the doctor-patient relationship."[37]

Freud's difficulties in diagnosing and treating psychotics did not interfere with his ability to elucidate psychotic processes. He made key advances in our understanding of psychoses; for example, his idea that a melancholic—in mourning for a disappointing love object—introjects it into itself, directing inward the rage that should be turned outward.[38] Freud thought that the study of the psychoses would be fruitful, in particular for our knowledge of ego processes. But he had in mind something more

cultured and more elevated than the treatment of psychotics; he wanted
people to be higher and better.

At the beginning of his psychotherapeutic work, Freud had been
sensitive to the fact that "my colleagues are of the opinion that I make
a diagnosis of hysteria far too carelessly when graver things are in question." Although here he was speaking of having treated both a case of
sarcoma of the abdominal glands and a case of multiple sclerosis as
hysterical,[39] and elsewhere feared that he might have overlooked some
organic trouble,[40] the same issue arose in connection with psychosis.
Neurotic symptoms can mask psychoses. Freud commented on an early
patient of his that "some years later her neurosis turned into a dementia
praecox"; and to a pupil he once wrote: "you have had the bad luck
to run into a latent paranoia and through the cure of his neurosis you
may have freed a more serious sickness."[41]

Freud was not the only one to notice this kind of clinical outcome. He
spoke about the problem of

> those cases, so frequent and on which so little research has been done,
> in which for a rather long time the illness is regarded as a hysteria
> and gradually a dementia comes to light . . . Or . . . persons who,
> having had a hysteria for years, suddenly change to a paranoia. . . .[42]

In 1937 Freud defended psychoanalysis against the "warning that we
should let sleeping dogs lie, which we have so often heard in connection
with our efforts to explore the psychical underworld. . . ." Freud gave a
logical reply: "if the instincts are causing disturbances, it is a proof that
the dogs are not sleeping; and if they seem really to be sleeping, it is not
in our power to awaken them."[43] But as an experienced therapist Freud
sometimes believed otherwise. A letter to a colleague in 1935 shows that
Freud already knew enough to be wary of certain problems:

> Like you, I am not satisfied with the diagnosis of schizophrenia in
> his case. I shall impart to you here what I feel that I understand about
> the psychotic mechanism of his illness. He complained of a total loss
> of capacity to work and a decrease of interest in professional and
> business matters. I was able to bring him back to conducting his busi-
> ness, but he was unable to resume his theoretical work. I never made
> him quite normal. The way he treated symbols in his mind, confused
> identifications, falsified memories, and kept to his delusional super-
> stitions made him always psychotic; his mood was always hypo-
> manic . . . Nevertheless, one day I had the opportunity to observe him

more clearly . . . [A] confession impressed me deeply. I felt seduced
to analyze it. He was then oppressed by something he had done
and he was troubled to keep it secret . . . However, I doubted
the advisability of continuing to attempt to lift his denial. With a
neurotic this would have been the only correct way and would have
promised the end of the illness, but I was probably right in doubting
the influence of analysis on a psychotic. In making conscious the conflict I had to fear a new psychotic breakdown which I would then
be unable to manage. Therefore I decided to leave the theme and to

Freud on vacation outside Vienna, August 1935

be satisfied with an imperfect and temporary success . . . My patient was a neurotic criminal, that is, a swindler with a sensitive conscience.[44]

Freud's growing awareness of the usefulness of defenses against psychotic layers was a new justification for his reluctance to try to treat each symptom separately. As Donald Winnicott has pointed out: "One must be able to note symptoms without trying to cure them because every symptom has its value to the patient, and very frequently the patient is better left with his symptom."[45] A neurosis is not the worst thing that one can suffer from. In a discussion about a schizophrenic in the 1920's, Freud is said to have given "special weight to the fact that it was with the re-establishment of the Oedipus complex that the process of recovery set in."[46] Even if Freud's views on psychoses deepened as the years passed, his distaste for treating them never altered; and because of Freud's theoretical positions on the treatment of psychosis, a non-Freudian therapist might well find it easier to allow himself to get closer to a psychotic patient. But despite the importance of theories in psychotherapy, in the end the personality of the therapist remains crucial.

4. Worthiness

IN FREUD'S VIEW, the analyst's respect for the patient's dignity was communicated not through supportive help but by the truth: "Since we demand strict truthfulness from our patients, we jeopardize our whole authority if we let ourselves be caught out by them in a departure from the truth."[1] Freud liked patients who were capable of honesty and frankness about themselves, and he also admired those who took suffering for granted; despite his goal of neutrality, these personal attitudes of Freud came through to his patients. As an analyst, Freud abided by the standards of nineteenth-century gentlemanly conduct, which future generations of therapists might not be able to live up to: "an honorable man readily forgets such of the private affairs of strangers as do not seem to him important to know."[2]

In view of the setting in which Freud was working, an age when neurotic complaints might be dismissed as imaginary nonsense or willful malingering, he must be considered a tolerant therapist; and as long as he was not personally involved in a problem he could maintain this tolerance.

Nonetheless, in 1903 he wrote that "deep-rooted malformations of character, traits of an actually degenerate constitution, show themselves as sources of a resistance that can scarcely be overcome. In this respect the constitution of the patient sets a general limit to the curative effects of psychotherapy." But Freud thought that "in spite of all these limitations, the number of persons suitable for psychoanalytic treatment is extraordinarily large. . . ."[3]

"Worthless" was an important word for Freud, and he tended to view analysis—in his eyes much more than a medical procedure—as a moral medal; those who could be helped by psychoanalysis were the people who were really significant. To some extent, therefore, the neurotic patient was a pioneer of a new standard of ethics, in that he had proven worthy of being healed by analysis. On the other hand, Freud's moral expectations of his patients were limited by his characteristically harsh view of human nature: "The unworthiness of human beings, even of analysts, has always made a deep impression on me, but why should analyzed people be altogether better than others?"[4]

In a letter to the Protestant minister Oskar Pfister, who practiced analysis, Freud wrote that

> ethics are remote from me. . . . I do not break my head very much about good and evil, but I have found little that is "good" about human beings on the whole. In my experience most of them are trash, no matter whether they publicly subscribe to this or that ethical doctrine or to none at all . . . If we are to talk of ethics, I subscribe to a high ideal from which most of the human beings I have come across depart most lamentably.[5]

Some years later Freud wrote to Lou Andreas-Salomé of his own "worst qualities, among them a certain indifference to the world. . . . In the depths of my heart I can't help being convinced that my dear fellow men, with a few exceptions, are worthless."[6] As Hanns Sachs described Freud, "he was kind without softness, benevolent yet not compassionate."[7] There were some class overtones to Freud's attitudes, since by "good-for-nothings" he sometimes meant the "rabble" or "riff-raff" of society. Freud seems to have grown tired of dealing clinically with what he considered the filth of human life. Yet it is still striking to find him referring in passing to "a person even of only moderate worth,"[8] since so much of our culture has paid at least lip service to the sanctity and importance of every human soul.

Despite the nature of his work and perhaps in part because of it, Freud is said to have "disliked pathological types and extremes of any kind."[9] He even had his doubts about Dostoevsky, a rival of Freud's as an explorer of the human depths, whose novel *The Brothers Karamazov* was Freud's favorite. In a letter to Theodor Reik Freud wrote:

> Another objection I might have raised against him was that his insight was so much restricted to abnormal mental life. Consider his astonishing helplessness in face of the phenomena of love. All he really knew were crude, instinctual desire; masochistic subjection and loving out of pity. You are right . . . in suspecting that, in spite of all my admiration for Dostoevsky's intensity and pre-eminence, I do not really like him. That is because my patience with pathological natures is exhausted in analysis. In art and life I am intolerant of them.

Freud added, for the sake of his followers, that "those are character traits personal to me and are not binding on others."[10] It is understandable, then, why Freud could prefer a lesser writer (but a witty and anticlerical one) like Anatole France.[11]

Partly by refusing analysis to patients he found distasteful, Freud could sustain his claim that he did not necessarily have to like his patients in order to be able to help them. Freud thought that "one tries to give the patient human assistance, so far as this is allowed by the capacity of one's own personality and by the amount of sympathy that one can feel for the particular case."[12] In the 1890's, before his many disappointments, Freud considered that his kind of procedure

> presupposes great interest in psychological happenings, but personal concern for the patients as well. I cannot imagine bringing myself to delve into the psychical mechanism of a hysteria in anyone who struck me as low-minded and repellent, and who, on closer acquaintance, would not be capable of arousing human sympathy. . . .[13]

For all of his tolerance for neurotic processes which others of his time would have been far more impatient with, by the standards of our own day Freud must seem decidedly moralistic. In his practice Freud had definite preferences about the kinds of patients he chose to work with. He would be intolerant of patients unable to be honest, and therefore uninterested in treating those with ego disturbances, such as the group called delinquents. (Nonetheless, an analyst in Freud's circle, August Aichhorn, was not prevented from making his study of delinquency, *Wayward Youth*.[14]) About one patient Freud advised a pupil that he was "obviously a scoundrel who is not worth your trouble . . . I assume that you will send him away."[15] Freud spoke of delinquents as if they lacked an ego, and said on one occasion: "Where there is no ego, the analysis has lost its rights."[16]

Freud knew that, at the time he was writing, "sexual perversions are subject to a quite special ban, which has even affected theory and has stood in the way of the scientific consideration of them."[17] In a now famous letter to a mother of a homosexual, Freud reassured her:

> Homosexuality is assuredly no advantage, but it is nothing to be ashamed of, no vice, no degradation; it cannot be classified as an illness; we consider it to be a variation of the sexual function, produced by a certain arrest of sexual development. Many highly respected individuals of ancient and modern times have been homosexuals, several of the greatest men among them (Plato, Michelangelo, Leonardo da Vinci, etc.). It is a great injustice to persecute homosexuality as a crime—and a cruelty, too.

If the woman's son were "unhappy, neurotic, torn by conflicts, inhibited in his social life, analysis may bring him harmony, peace of mind, full efficiency, whether he remains homosexual or gets changed."[18]

Freud would consider homosexuality inoffensive in a person of good character. But to an analyst he knew far better than the homosexual's mother, Freud could be more open in expressing his feelings of distaste. No more than others could Freud fulfill completely the ideal of considering nothing human alien to him. Writing about a male homosexual, Freud commented that "in the most unfavorable cases one ships such people . . . across the ocean, with some money, let's say to South America, and lets them there seek and find their destiny."[19] (However ill Freud thought of such people, he did not go so far as to recommend that the patient be shipped to North America, which Freud hated.)

Freud once referred to the clinical phenomenon that "a good, capable, conscientious woman will speak no better of herself after she develops melancholia than one who is in fact worthless; indeed, the former is perhaps more likely to fall ill of the disease than the latter, of whom we too should have nothing good to say."[20] On another occasion he remarked that a depressed patient was "obviously a valuable person, who deserves to be treated further. . . ."[21] On the whole, however, Freud regretted that he had to conclude that "only a few patients are worth the trouble we spend on them, so that we are not allowed to have a therapeutic attitude, but we must be glad to have learned something in every case."[22] Whereas a depression involves heightened self-reproach, an increase in the internalization of conflicts, the difficulty with homosexuality for Freud as an analyst was that the patient's conflicts were no longer between different aspects of his psyche but between his instincts and society.

Despite his interest in theories of bisexuality, Freud tended to have an either/or attitude toward homosexuality. In discussing his conception of Leonardo, Freud referred to passivity as "a situation whose nature is undoubtedly homosexual," an unproven claim; and to assert that Leonardo was "emotionally homosexual" would seem to paint a one-sided picture of a man who must have had many other aspects to him.[23] Freud had special ideas about the origins of homosexuality in men. It is perhaps surprising to hear him so facilely agreeing that "the assertion that growing up among women does not lead a man to an intensive love for woman but frequently to homosexuality is correct,"[24] when we remember that he himself had five sisters and a dominating mother, with an old father and a much younger brother.

Other analysts in Freud's circle objected to his personal feelings about irregular sexuality. "When Freud declared that perversion is the negative of neurosis, Stekel and Adler disagreed; for them perversion was but another form of neurosis."[25] Whereas Freud was trying to exclude perversion (unless accompanied by unhappiness) from the scope of psychoanalysis, some of Freud's followers were more eager to extend the reach of their therapy.

Freud felt endangered by male homosexuality, and was therefore intolerant of it. For example, Paul Federn once stressed "the likable impression" that a patient of "multiform perversion" made on him.[26] The same man seemed to Freud "an absolute swine, a case of infantile and homologously inflated sexuality; we have so many repressions within ourselves that, when faced with that, we feel aversion."[27] In at least one case of female homosexuality, however, Freud saw it as a private matter. A woman was guilty and depressed about a proposed liaison with another woman, and had made a suicide attempt; after a one-year analysis by Helene Deutsch, she was freed of her anxiety but manifestly homosexual, and Freud considered this a suitable point to terminate the treatment.*

Although Freud was "always loath to interrupt his holidays for any professional work," Jones tells us that Freud "could not refuse a man of Mahler's worth" when the great composer turned to him for help. After

---

* In her published report of the outcome of this case, Helene Deutsch did not mention her own initial trepidation when she went to report the therapeutic result she had achieved; nor did she include Freud's satisfaction with the compromise arrived at. Freud had sent her the case, so she consulted with him about it.[28]

meeting in a hotel, they "spent four hours strolling through the town and conducting a sort of psychoanalysis."[29]

Freud thought that "health," whatever it meant, was to be distinguished from human worth. He argued that "there are healthy people as well as unhealthy ones who are good for nothing in life. . . ."[30] "Good-for-nothings" were not suitable for analysis, Freud held, nor "is the method applicable to people who are not driven to seek treatment by their own sufferings. . . ."[31]

On the one hand, Freud had maintained that "psychoanalytic therapy was created through and for the treatment of patients permanently unfit for existence, and its triumph has been that it has made a satisfactorily large number of these permanently *fit* for existence." Yet he was quick to point out, as one of the contraindications to treatment, that "those patients who do not possess a reasonable degree of education and a fairly reliable character should be refused." Freud thought it "gratifying that precisely the most valuable and most highly developed persons are best suited" for his procedure.[32]

The key distinction Freud drew between analyzable and nonanalyzable patients was the capacity to establish a transference to the analyst. Freud must have felt that the transferences elicited by analysis were less powerful and more manageable than those he had encountered during his early experiments with hypnosis. Although the practice of psychoanalysis is capable of unleashing powerful emotions, he wrote that in treating "one of my most acquiescent patients" by hypnosis, "as she woke up on one occasion, she threw her arms around my neck. The unexpected entrance of a servant relieved us from a painful discussion, but from that time onwards there was a tacit understanding between us that the hypnotic treatment should be discontinued." Unlike Breuer, Freud did not blame himself for what had happened or even see it in personal terms at all:

> I was modest enough not to attribute the event to my own irresistible personal attraction, and I felt that I had now grasped the nature of the mysterious element that was at work behind hypnotism. In order to exclude it, or at all events isolate it, it was necessary to abandon hypnotism.[33]

Freud's method of treatment relied on the strength of human egoism; he considered that it was the patient's self-centeredness which made the aloof analyst such an important figure in his thoughts. Psychoanalysis aimed at internal readjustments in the patient's way of looking at things. When Freud wrote that psychoanalytic cure is "essentially . . . effected by love,"[34] he referred not to the analyst's feelings for his patients but rather the latter's capacity to invest the figure of the analyst with emotional energy. Transference reactions were a repetition of unaccepted frustration situations from the patient's past, and it was Freud's intention that the analytic process be capable of reopening these issues. As a result, "during the progress of a psychoanalysis it is not only the patient who plucks up courage, but his disease as well. . . ."[35]

Sandor Ferenczi and Otto Rank insisted in the 1920's that everything in treatment has a meaning as a transference phenomenon. But Freud had been the first to see transference as an avenue to what he considered the earlier and true:

> the patient does not *remember* anything of what he has forgotten, but *acts* it out. He reproduces it not as a memory but as an action; he *repeats* it, without, of course, knowing that he is repeating it . . . the repetition is a transference of the forgotten past not only onto the doctor but also onto all the other aspects of the current situation.[36]

In an analysis, "transference emerges as *the most powerful resistance* to the treatment"; "all the forces which have caused the libido to regress will rise up as 'resistances' against the work of analysis, in order to conserve the new state of things."[37] It was out of the analysis of the transferences of adults that Freud had constructed his view of human childhood.

Freud preferred to treat a patient when his "pathogenic experiences belong to the past, so that his ego can stand at a distance from them."[38] Especially for the foreign pupils who came to him, the past stood out in contrast to the alienness of their present. Freud tried to take into account the criticism of Jung, who stressed "the inclination of neurotics for expressing their present interests in reminiscences and symbols from the remote past."[39] But Freud did not appreciate how convenient it could be for some patients to project their current troubles into the past, and therefore he could overlook many transference features which therapists now might see. Instead of interpreting the interaction between the patient and himself, it was often easier for both parties to talk about the distant past. Yet by and large Freud took many current realities of his patients into account; for example, he generally knew the social milieu in which they functioned. Yet he did not specifically highlight the realistic contact with his patients.

Freud is said to have, in the 1890's, "permitted himself unrestricted social intercourse with his patients,"[40] and with some patients he continued to exercise liberties as a therapist throughout his life—although he recommended neutrality for others: "The doctor should be opaque to his patients and, like a mirror, should show them nothing but what is shown to him."[41] "[E]motional coldness in the analyst . . . creates the most advantageous conditions for both parties. . . ."[42] Freud might even have a meal served to a patient, but such actions on his part were independent, he thought, of analysis itself; he took for granted that an analyst should be supportive and did not write about this aspect of his technique.

The impact of the individuality of the analyst on the therapeutic process was not discussed in Freud's work until quite late.[43] For to concede the importance of the analyst's real personality, as opposed to his specialized role as devised by Freud, would be to reopen the old question of suggestion. As one analyst wrote in 1956: "Widespread and increasing emphasis as to the part played by the analyst's personality in determining the nature of the individual transference also implies recognition of unavoidable suggestive tendencies in the therapeutic process."[44]

Freud had advised the analyst to pursue an emotionally cool course so that the burden would then be on the patient to engage, with the story of his life, the analyst's attention and interest. Freud himself succeeded in arousing immense transferences immediately. Because of his reputation, without any special activity on his part he became for the patient a force to be reckoned with. In the absence of this involvement on the patient's part, the analyst is bound to be functioning rather strangely, thinking that everything that is said in an analysis relates to him.

Reality, however, can be so overtaken by transference that to a patient even the least talented analyst can become something of a god. It is tempting for the analyst to view the infantilized subordination of patients as justified in reality, whereas a patient's hostile feelings can be seen as an expression of the negative transference. Freud, however, expressed the optimistic thought that "the doctor is modest enough to attribute his patient's high opinion of him to the hopes he can rouse in him and to the widening of his intellectual horizon by the surprising and liberating enlightenment that the treatment brings with it."[45]

Still, the blank-screen analytic approach has obvious advantages, aside from the issue of transference. Analytic neutrality may block the therapist's spontaneity, but it may also protect a patient from the analyst's sadism. A standard of active intervention, if that is the opposite of neutrality, can pave the way for far more extensive damage than any other device. But there are ways in which an analyst's passivity can in fact be aggressive, and the classical analytic situation contains hidden suggestive elements that may be manipulative.

Freud's patients attest to the sense of security they felt as they worked with him. Freud probably got along best with those who had a sensible admiration for him, who were aware of the privilege of being in the presence of a great man. To some Freud seemed a savior. One person suggested that without Freud he would have been a failure or a suicide.

But long analyses over many years are capable of bringing patients into a regressed situation, from which it may take a long time to emerge. Early on Freud had mentioned the "difficult task of dissolving this transference, of making the patient once again independent."[46] One means of overcoming the patient's overevaluation of his analyst is for the analyst to be natural; but though Freud was "free and easy" as an analyst, that was not what he expected of other analysts. In the 1930's Helene Deutsch suggested at a small meeting at Freud's house that toward the end of an analysis it would be a good idea for the analyst to take some active steps to dissolve the transference. "How?" Freud asked. "By showing he is not perfect," she answered. Freud did not like this idea at all, and with irritation he said: "You mean to show not only the patient is a swine, but I too?"[47] Yet a patient Freud admired reports that at a certain point in her analysis Freud upbraided her for losing her critical faculties, indicating that he did not succumb to the most obvious suggestive dangers of his form of treatment.

5. Counter-Transference and the Value of Enlightenment

As EARLY AS 1910 Freud said he had "become aware of the 'counter-transference'" which arises in an analyst "as a result of the patient's influence on his unconscious feelings. . . ." Freud was "almost inclined to insist that [the analyst] shall recognize this counter-transference in himself and overcome it."[1] At the time Freud thought a self-analysis might be adequate for controlling the analyst's biases, although by the 1920's formal training analyses for future analysts had become the rule. At least for a time, Freud believed that for the analyst "it is not enough . . . that he himself should be an approximately normal person. It may be insisted, rather, that he should have undergone a psychoanalytic purification. . . ."[2] But the tendency to counter-transference, no matter how carefully trained the analyst, can never be totally eradicated, for the analyst and patient, as any two human beings, are bound to interact in unexpected and even irrational ways.

Freud's hope was that an analyst's "interpretations will be independent of . . . [his] personal characteristics and will hit the mark." Freud knew that the analyst's personality was not "a matter of indifference," and that the "individual factor will always play a larger part in psychoanalysis than elsewhere." But his analogies were unrealistic, as when he referred to "this individual factor" as "something comparable to the 'personal equation' in astronomical observations."[3] Even when conceding certain analytic limitations he sometimes seemed to base himself on utopian norms; he granted that in treating patients there might arise "places at which one is disturbed by some personal consideration—that is, when one has fallen seriously below the standard of an ideal analyst."[4] At least at the end of his life, however, Freud did recognize that "the special conditions of analytic work do actually cause the analyst's own defects to interfere with his making a correct assessment of the state of things in his patient and in reacting to them in a useful way."[5]

Although Freud had pointed out the existence of counter-transference feelings, he did not develop the idea. Perhaps his view was that the only important emotional troubles were those of his patients, not his own. It may be that the contemporary interest in counter-transference has been excessive, but Freud had gone to the other extreme. Transference was to him a form of error, and logically should not occur in an analyst. As Freud once said: "This counter-transference must be completely overcome by the analyst; only this will make him the master of the psychoanalytic situation. . . ."[6] Psychoanalysis today would be less absolute in demanding such success, but if an analyst becomes seriously subject to counter-transference, his "patient . . . is not a real object but is only used as a fortuitous tool to solve a conflict situation" of the analyst's own. Consequently, the analyst's "ability to understand, to respond, to handle the patient, to interpret in the right away,"[7] will be interfered with.

Freud's most extensive case history, though composed in response to his controversies with Adler and Jung, gives us some insight into his policies as a clinician. The "Wolf-Man," as he came to be known, was in treatment with Freud from 1910 to 1914, after unsuccessful attempts at therapy by other methods. Although the name Freud chose for him may evoke the image of a man turning into a wolf, the patient, in fact, suffered as a small child from an excessive fear of wolves. Freud treated him for severe adult incapacities, but his case history dealt with the man's childhood phobia. In this way Freud sought to prove that the general importance of childhood was not a product of a patient's neurotic desire to evade current realities, but rather that the structure of an infantile neurosis could be understood in terms of Freud's instinct theory.

At the time of his analysis the patient was a rich Russian landowner; later, as a result of the Russian Revolution, he became impoverished. In 1919 he returned to Vienna and Freud recommended a further analysis, which lasted a few months (and was free of charge). In the 1920's the Wolf-Man blamed Freud for having advised him against returning to Russia to rescue his fortune. (Freud considered this desire to be a resistance to the second analysis.) It is not clear, however, whether there was any justification for this complaint. Adjusting to his new financial situation, the Wolf-Man took a lowly job in a Viennese insurance company, and ever since has been a living part of psychoanalysis.

After his two analyses with Freud, the Wolf-Man underwent two more analyses with Ruth Mack Brunswick. Since World War II he has been in therapy with two additional analysts in Vienna, where he still resides; he is in touch with several more analysts interested in the early history of Freud's work, and for the last fifteen years an analyst has come from America every summer to conduct daily sessions with him. A volume has recently been published consisting of autobiographical essays on his childhood and later years, his recollections of Freud, Freud's famous case history, the supplement to Freud's account written by Ruth Mack Brunswick, and essays on the Wolf-Man by Muriel Gardiner.[8]

Of this material the most interesting is still Freud's own fascinating and rich case history. He characteristically analyzed a childhood disorder through the memories of the mature adult, and paid immense respect to the complexities of the child's picture of the world. Freud's dream interpretations are masterful; and his reconstruction of the Wolf-Man's earliest years, if not convincing, at least represents for its day a daring set of hypotheses. As has been well said, "mediocre writers will make a true story seem manufactured, while a great writer can make the most implausible story seem true."[9] Typically, Freud saw the Wolf-Man as beset by ambivalent conflicts with his father and with all later father surrogates. Freud held that the patient's fear of his father, and simultaneous desire for sexual gratification from him, dominated the Wolf-Man's later life. (Yet Freud strangely ignored the Wolf-Man's adult practice of anal intercourse.[10])

Freud had announced the "final clearing up" of the Wolf-Man's symptoms in 1914, and said that he "parted from him, regarding him as cured."[11] Yet Freud conceded—in contrast to the doctrine of some of his later disciples—that with a patient as disturbed as the Wolf-Man, "psycho-

analytic treatment cannot bring any instantaneous revolution or put matters upon a level with a normal development: it can only get rid of the
obstacles and clear the path, so that the influences of life may be able to
further development along better lines."[12]

Freud's initial four-year treatment of the Wolf-Man was unusually
lengthy for its day, and had Freud been merely a rigorous scrutinizer,
intolerant of all irrationality, he would never have won this patient's life-
long gratitude. Despite his own atheism and his conviction that ambivalent feelings toward the father underlay all religions, Freud fully
acknowledged the usefulness of religion in the Wolf-Man's early life.
(Freud once wrote to Pfister that "from a therapeutic point of view I can
only envy your opportunity of bringing about sublimation into religion."[13]) In addition, startled by the Wolf-Man's recollections of his feelings upon his only sister's suicide—he had thought of how much more
money he would now inherit from his parents—Freud generously interpreted this avarice as a defense against other feelings which would have
been at the time intolerable for him.

Ruth Mack Brunswick was one of Freud's most brilliant pupils, and
Freud referred the Wolf-Man to her in 1926 when he was suffering from
a paranoid delusion about his nose. As a psychiatrist with a special interest
in psychosis, she suggested that perhaps the Wolf-Man's first analysis with
Freud had "robbed him of the usual neurotic modes of solution,"[14] making
possible more primitive kinds of reactions. His loss of equilibrium in the
mid-1920's had been set off, she felt, by Freud's becoming dangerously ill
with cancer, suggesting that despite the aims of analysis, the Wolf-Man
had not emancipated himself from the influence of Freud's personality.

Brunswick's case history of the Wolf-Man is rich with ingenious
dream interpretations; yet in retrospect one wonders, for all her interest
in the Wolf-Man's childhood past, how much she understood her own
feelings toward him. It is clear that Freud's referral of this famous case
was a personal gift, a testimony to her standing in his eyes and an invitation to write a supplement to his own lengthy essay. In the analysis she deliberately undermined the Wolf-Man's fantasies of his position as a favorite
son of Freud's; she emphasized his absence from Freud's social life, Freud's
purely professional attitude toward his former patient, the Wolf-Man's
lack of knowledge of the Freud family, and the fact that other patients
had been treated by Freud for longer periods of time. Besides her rational
objectives, Ruth Brunswick, who was herself a long-standing patient of
Freud's, may have had intense feelings of competitiveness with the Wolf-
Man. Her relationship with Freud was so close that she found it hard
to see what part it played in her treatment of this patient.

It is striking that what was probably the major romance in the Wolf-Man's life, that with Freud and psychoanalysis, stands undiscussed and uninterpreted. In reminiscences of his childhood the Wolf-Man found it puzzling that, "with no effort on my part, I discarded my religion so easily. The question is, what filled up the vacuum thus created?"[15] The Wolf-Man suggests perhaps literature or painting, whereas his lifelong immersion in psychoanalysis is not mentioned.

The Wolf-Man has written articles on philosophy and art seen from a psychoanalytic point of view; he has even sold some of his paintings to analysts. For years Freud collected money for this former patient who, as Ruth Brunswick put it, "had served the theoretical ends of analysis so well."[16] (It is conceivable that Freud also had some guilt feelings about the loss of the Wolf-Man's estates.) This money helped the Wolf-Man to pay his rent and medical bills, as well as to take short trips. Even now, as the Wolf-Man's life has grown less harmonious with old age, writing about his experiences with Freud has given a purpose to his life.

Muriel Gardiner has stated that "Freud's analysis saved the Wolf-Man from a crippled existence, and Dr. Brunswick's reanalysis overcame a serious acute crisis, both enabling the Wolf-Man to lead a long and tolerably healthy life."[17] Unlike some of his disciples, however, Freud was enough of a scientist to be interested in therapeutic failure as well as success, and it would be in his best spirit to mention, alongside the advantages the Wolf-Man derived from analysis, the defects he failed to overcome. He did progress better under Freud's care than with other therapists of the day, but can one say that in the end it was analytic insight which helped him, or rather the continuing emotional support of Freud and the psychoanalytic movement?

Freud was willing to learn from his mistakes, and he wrote a lengthy account of a therapeutic standstill, the case known as "Dora." Freud confessed: "I do not know what kind of help she wanted from me, but I promised to forgive her for having deprived me of the satisfaction of affording her a far more radical cure for her troubles."[18]

Since Freud chose to present his case material "in a fragmentary manner," for the sake of elucidating some special problems he might be working on, it is difficult to reconstruct from a given case history what might have been happening clinically. In discussing telepathy, for example, Freud twice referred to a case in which he actively intervened in behalf of a specific marriage choice, one that today might seem bizarre. Freud wrote about "a young man [who] came to me who made a particularly sympathetic impression on me, so that I gave him preference over a number of others."[19] This patient had had a long-standing relationship with his brother's wife (described in print by Freud only as "a married lady in his own circle"). As a result of an analysis with Freud, his case history reports, the man was freed from his current tie to a girl of the lower classes, who "served merely as a whipping-boy on whom he could satisfy all the feelings of revenge and jealousy which really applied to the other lady."[20] The patient then fell in love with his niece, the daughter of his former mistress. Once the man decided to marry the girl, Freud, who could be remarkably emancipated from middle-class values, "supported his intentions, since it offered what was a possible way out of his difficult situation even though an irregular one."[21]

The girl, however, resisted the advances of her uncle. Freud thereupon recommended that she undergo an analysis. (As Freud put the matter, "it was decided that she should be analyzed.") The girl's analyst (Helene Deutsch) was told by Freud that there was a secret to the case and that when the analyst discovered it she should report it to Freud. Within a week or so Deutsch returned with the news that not only was the secret uncovered but there was a secret to the case that Freud himself did not know.

The young girl did indeed know about the long-standing liaison between her suitor and her mother. This is what Freud had wanted to find out. But he did not know that the girl had the fantasy that she herself was the child of the illicit union between her uncle and her mother, which fully explained her hesitancy to become involved with him sexually. (Freud wrote: "The girl had a complete unconscious knowledge of the relations between her mother and her *fiancé*, and was only attached to him on account of her Oedipus complex."[22]) Once Freud was apprised of the girl's inner world, he dropped the idea of the match.

Yet when writing up this case for publication, Freud tried to suppress, no doubt out of discretion, the familial connection between the partners in the proposed union. But at the very end of his account of the case, there was a return of the suppressed. According to Freud, the patient eventually chose as his wife "a respectable girl outside his family circle. . . ."[23] Until this point in the narrative Freud had not hinted that any of the patient's loves had been within the "family circle."[24] For the purpose of what he had to say about telepathy—his patient had had occasion to consult a handwriting expert—Freud's account was complete enough, but as a case history it remained only a vignette. It underlines how active as a therapist Freud could be. As he once wrote, what a patient "can achieve depends, too, on a combination of external circumstances.

Should we hesitate to alter this combination by intervening in a suitable manner?"[25] But Freud's suppression of the details of the family relationship makes it virtually impossible to comprehend what was going on.

In 1915 Freud had enunciated as a principle what he himself was not always able to follow. "Before I continue the account," he wrote parenthetically of another case,

> I must confess that I have altered the *milieu* of the case in order to preserve the incognito of the people concerned, but that I have altered nothing else. I consider it a wrong practice, however excellent the motive may be, to alter any detail in the presentation of a case. One can never tell what aspect of a case may be picked out by a reader of independent judgment, and one runs the risk of leading him astray.[26]

And in 1924 Freud added a footnote to one of his earliest case histories, in which he had disguised his material: "Katherina was not the niece but the daughter. . . . The girl fell ill, therefore, as a result of sexual attempts on the part of her own father. Distortions like the one which I introduced in the present instance should be altogether avoided in reporting a case history."[27]

However such clinical distortions could damage the scientific future of psychoanalysis, Freud's movement would have faced even greater obstacles if its therapeutic technique could be shown to have had negative results. Freud acknowledged the legitimacy of the question whether psychoanalysis could do harm. "[I]f a knife does not cut, it can not be used for healing either."[28] But just as psychoanalysis could accomplish a limited amount of good, so Freud felt it could do only a finite amount of damage. Like surgery, it hurt for a constructive purpose; furthermore, he maintained that

> the activity of an untrained analyst does less harm to his patients than that of an unskilled surgeon . . . In my judgment severe or permanent aggravations of a pathological condition are not to be feared even with an unskilled use of analysis. The unwelcome reactions cease after a while . . . It is simply that the unsuitable attempt at a cure has done the patient no good.[29]

Freud was confident that "no injury to the patient is to be feared when the treatment is conducted with comprehension."[30] Analysts nevertheless know of patients who deteriorate under treatment. Freud thought such patients had strong masochistic urges which defeated the analytic goal; for their behavior he invented the category of "negative therapeutic reaction."[31]

Even a thorough catalogue of the causes of psychotherapy going awry does not contradict the fact that it may still be underused. In assessing problems of technique, senior analysts today often cite rigidities in an analyst's approach as the cause of most psychoanalytic troubles. Negative transferences can pile up, or a refractory negative therapeutic reaction may set in; if the analyst is going to fail it is better not to be defensive about it and honestly tell the patient. Here the character of the individual analyst necessarily plays a role. An analyst who is not too narcissistic might recommend treatment with another practitioner.

In his early period as an analyst, Freud may not have been cautious enough in handling his creation; yet his mistakes were often the result of outgoingness. Freud's impact as a therapist could be immense. He knew his strength: "I have found in myself only one attribute of first quality: a kind of courage that is not affected by conventions."[32] His comments stuck in the memory of his patients for their lifetimes. A remark he made at the end of a short, three-month analysis before World War I is instructive of Freud's attitude: he complimented the patient and said that the reason he had enjoyed working with her was that as soon as she understood something she was able to make use of it. Freud assumed that his patients had basically healthy minds, that like himself they would thrive on criticism when it was necessary. In a letter Freud once stated that "the optimum conditions for . . . [psychoanalysis] exist where it is not needed—i.e., among the healthy."[33]

For all his immersion in the "underworld" of the unconscious, Freud retained the Enlightenment faith in reason of the *philosophes*. "Nothing in life is so expensive as illness—and stupidity."[34] Freud's ideal of the examined life was an exacting one for the analyst:

> What is given to the patient should never be a spontaneous affect, but always consciously allotted, and then more or less of it as the need may arise. Occasionally a great deal, but never from one's own Ucs [Unconscious]. This I should regard as the formula. In other words, one must always recognize one's counter-transference and rise above it, only then is one free oneself.[35]

Freud had begun his work on dreaming with the idea that "the interpretation of dreams is like a window through which we can get a glimpse of the interior of that [mental] apparatus."[36] Although over the years both his terminology and his understanding changed, the basic rational cast of his mind was consistent. In *The Interpretation of Dreams* he wrote that *"psychotherapy can pursue no other course than to bring the Ucs. [Unconscious] under the domination of the Pcs. [Preconscious]."*[37] In the famous words of his old age: "Where id was, there shall ego be."[38]

The "essential tool" of psychoanalytic treatment was "words";[39] through the achievement of rational distance the patient could reach self-mastery. Freud, we have seen, eventually aimed at an inner reordering of a patient's life rather than any behavioral index of change:

> a neurosis would seem to be the result of a kind of ignorance. . . . Knowledge is not always the same as knowledge: there are different sorts of knowledge, which are far from equivalent psychologically . . . there is more than one kind of ignorance. . . . All we have to add is that the knowledge [in psychoanalysis] must rest on an internal change in the patient. . . .[40]

When Freud came to consider problems of social philosophy, he said (in line with his faith in the therapeutic power of rationality) that "the ideal condition of things would of course be a community of men who had subordinated their instinctual life to the dictatorship of reason."[41]

Freud had initially thought that psychoanalysis was "an art of interpreting."[42] As time passed, he gradually turned away from specific memories of events and focused on a patient's resistances. He admitted that in the 1890's "it was my view at that time (though I have since recognized it as a wrong one) that my task was fulfilled when I had informed a patient of the hidden meaning of his symptoms. . . ."[43] Freud concluded that "the patient gains nothing from the physician's confronting him directly with his complexes. . . ."[44] Yet as late as the 1920's we can find Freud making such a stunning reconstruction as to drive a patient out of treatment: "Freud's extravagant story of an event which I had never suspected (at least consciously) turned out to be true . . . Freud had over-estimated me. He believed he could tell me anything."[45]

Freud wanted the best out of people, and his implicit injunction was always to take better care, to be better next time. A patient once purchased for fourteen dollars a beautiful book on Rome and showed it to Freud, who agreed it was marvelous. "See that you deserve it!" was Freud's comment. For all his moralism Freud could be pragmatic, and with the same patient Freud concluded that masturbatory fantasies in intercourse were permissible if they contributed to heterosexuality.

Analysis meant breaking problems apart. "The unity of this world seems to me something self-understood, something unworthy of emphasis. What interests me is the separation and breaking up into its component parts what would otherwise flow together into a primeval pulp."[46] In opposition to the kind of treatment Jung came to prefer, Freud held that "in the technique of psychoanalysis there is no need of any special synthetic work; the individual does that for himself better than we can."[47] Freud felt it was necessary to answer those who were concerned "that the patient might be given too much analysis and too little synthesis. . . ." He thought that "psycho-synthesis is . . . achieved during analytic treatment without our intervention, automatically and inevitably."[48]

Implicit in psychoanalysis was an ethic of its own. As Freud once explained to a patient, "the moral self was the conscious, the evil self was the unconscious." (For his readers Freud explained that this was only approximately true.[49]) Elsewhere he said:

> we liberate sexuality through our treatment, but not in order that man may from now on be dominated by sexuality, but in order to make a suppression possible—a rejection of the instincts under the guidance of a higher agency . . . We try to replace the pathological process with rejection.[50]

Freud saw the analytic situation as the "struggle between the doctor and the patient, between intellect and instinctual life, between understanding and seeking to act. . . ."[51]

6. Words and Power

IN HIS LAST YEARS Freud referred to a patient's "affectionate attitude . . . the positive transference . . . which is the strongest motive for the patient's taking a share in the joint work of analysis."[1] On the whole, however, "Freudian analysts [do not] talk much about positive transference in their practical work. They work, for the most part, on the negative side, trying to liberate hatred and resentments, in order to free the way for unhampered capacity for love."[2] Wilhelm Reich went to the extreme of basing an entire therapeutic program on interpreting negative transferences. Partly under Reich's influence, "repressed aggression" enjoyed a vogue among analysts in the late 1920's and early 1930's.

Freud knew that "it is not so easy to play upon the instrument of the mind."[3] If a patient manages to gain verbal insight into his emotional life, has he lost anything thereby? Perhaps. Self-consciousness can be a heavy price to pay. According to an old Central European ditty, a centipede was once asked how he knew which foot to put forward next; he never walked again. Although Freud could see the merit of such a reservation about psychoanalysis, his system of therapy was inherently a negativistic one. That he was a nay-sayer can be seen in any photograph which shows his deeply piercing eyes. Freud above all directed our interest to the mind at odds with itself, on the assumption that patients knew best how to put things together and live their own lives. He demanded that people grow up; he expected more of mankind.

Even aesthetically he was far from being a romantic. "Real art begins with the veiling of the unconscious."[4] Henrik Ibsen was a writer Freud could admire: "Ibsen with his self-containment, unity, and simplification of problems, along with his art of concentration and concealment is a great poet, whereas Hauptmann is the neurotic who portrays himself alone."[5] Freud was civilized; as he once commented on a play, he

> perceived no poetic beauty in the drama; the hero is a mad dog who belongs in a lunatic asylum . . . the art of the poet does not consist of finding and dealing with problems. That he should leave to the psychologists. Rather, the poet's art consists of obtaining poetic effects out of such problems. . . . the poet's art consists essentially in covering over.[6]

Freud thought that "the essential *ars poetica* lies in the technique of overcoming the feeling of repulsion in us which is undoubtedly connected with the barriers that rise between each single ego and the others."[7] Actors, like poets, had to be at a distance from their material and in control: "It is one of the customary illusions that the actor must identify with his role. In those roles with which he identifies too well, he fails. In a certain sense, he must remain above his role."[8] As Freud had his doubts about Dostoevsky, so he pointed out "the limits set upon the employment of abnormal characters on the stage . . . If we are faced by an unfamiliar and fully established neurosis, we shall be inclined to send for the doctor (just as we do in real life) and pronounce the character inadmissible to the stage."[9]

Freud's rationalism went so far as to try to find "formulas" for describing the human soul. He referred to the "direction in which the rather simple solution of this case should be looked for,"[10] as if a patient were a puzzle capable of being solved. Although at times Freud objected to particular formulas which he considered "somewhat dreary,"[11] he did

Etching of Freud from life by Max Pollak, 1921

not in principle reject the use of formulas. It was this rather mechanical outlook that Jung opposed and that misled some of Freud's patients, who expectantly awaited the solution of their childhood traumas.

Freud's urge to structure clinical material into formulas was of a piece with his therapeutic aim of leading the patient away from primitive emotional reactions. He was more interested in the magic of words than of gestures, and he relied on the patient's ability to verbalize his problems. The use of the couch forced the analyst to rely all the more on the rationalistic power of verbal insight.

> Words were originally magic and to this day words have retained
> much of their ancient magical power. By words one person can
> make another blissfully happy or drive him to despair, by words the
> teacher conveys his knowledge to his pupils, by words the orator
> carries his audience with him and determines their judgments and
> decisions. Words provoke affects and are in general the means of
> mutual influence among men. Thus we shall not depreciate the use
> of words in psychotherapy and we shall be pleased if we can listen
> to the words that pass between the analyst and his patient.[12]

After a good interpretation Freud might say: "Now I deserve a cigar!"
Since Freud's death nonverbal communication in therapy has become
popular, but his aim had been to strengthen a patient's ego by fostering
an ability to *say* what his feelings are.

Freud recognized that the "working through" of a patient's resistances "may in practice turn out to be an arduous task for the subject
of the analysis and a trial of patience for the analyst,"[13] and he was not
particularly interested in this aspect of therapy. He would rather reconstruct a scene from early childhood, as part of making the unconscious
conscious, than pay attention to the details of a patient's overcoming of
his resistances. For example, one patient was frightened by masks, and
Freud would not let him avoid examining this fear; he wanted to know
why masks frightened him. The patient replied that it was the fixity of
expression, to which Freud thought the analytic solution was easy: the
patient must have, at the age of three, seen the face of his dead mother.
Although the patient could not remember having been alone in the room
with her after she died, his sister later confirmed that this had been the
case.[14] It gave Freud great pleasure to solve the origins of a slight phobia
like this.

Even in the 1920's Freud could abruptly terminate an analysis, since
the operative assumption was that it was the patient's task to unscramble
things on his own. Yet the analyst's support, as well as his interpretative
insight, can be advantageous to the patient. As Franz Alexander reported:
"I was not surprised to hear from . . . [Freud] that according to his
experience in the majority of successful cases the success is based on the
continued faithful attitude of the patient to his analyst even though he
may never see his physician again."[15] Patients of Freud's have praised the
supportive element in his treatment, as well as the way analysis set them
on the track of learning more about themselves. A patient's ego can be
strengthened by his identification with the rational insight of the analyst;
the patient uses what he needs from an analysis, and the analyst's lack of

directiveness provides an opportunity for the patient to take what he needs.

A peculiar aspect of Freud's practice, which has colored the work of other analysts, is the degree to which he used imagery of domination and control to describe the form of therapy he created. If old people were "inaccessible" to analysis, Freud held that "youthful persons under the age of adolescence are often exceedingly amenable to influence."[16] Freud used the concept of "conquest" to describe a good relation between analyst and patient. He once wrote as a consultant to a follower that "perhaps you show him too much impatience and therapeutic ambition, instead of concentrating exclusively on his personal conquest."[17]

Freud was blunt and straightforward in asserting that "analysis . . . presupposes the consent of the person who is being analyzed and a situation in which there is a superior and a subordinate."[18] He could speak of a patient being "disobedient," and elsewhere of a late stage in an analysis "when the battle was actually already won. . . ."[19] Freud frequently used the metaphor of warfare. "A battleground need not necessarily coincide with one of the enemy's key fortresses."[20] Was resistance in analysis in some way simply opposition to Freud? From the beginning Americans sensed an authoritarian air in Freud's circle, which, to Freud's Central European patients, simply resembled an enlightened monarchy. Freud had not grown up with democratic conceptions about one man's opinion being just as good as another's.

Many patients were acutely aware of Freud's tyrannical streak, and although the analytic situation seemed to leave the patient in charge, Freud could be quite intimidating. For example, a patient who compulsively masturbated spent seven years in analysis with Freud; he was told in the first month or two of his analysis that he would never progress in treatment until he stopped masturbating. In retrospect, the patient felt that Freud had vitiated the analysis by behaving like the patient's parents. It might have been better for Freud to have taken the opposite tack, but he assumed that there was a physical basis to things and that unless libido was dammed up the road to sublimation would be blocked. Freud explained that masturbatory gratification prevents one's dreaming the way one should for an analysis (it was characteristic of Freud to think that one should give up some pleasure in order to bring out more psychological material). For a patient who was already afraid of women, this analytic injunction only reinforced his inhibitions.

But perhaps more important than the particulars of any one interpretation was the fact that analysis was inherently a one-sided situation.

Since it is the patient who opens up while the analyst remains aloof, it is no wonder that Freud talked in terms of patients "submitting" to an analysis. Perhaps the patient rightly regards the analyst's interpretations as a form of criticism, for they imply that the patient does not know what he is talking about. Submission is built into the use of the couch—the patient is lying down and the analyst is sitting. The implicit authoritarianism of the arrangement makes it hard for the patient to retain his critical judgment, and the aim of the treatment is to promote a temporary regression in the patient for a later constructive resolution. Give-and-take between two partners entails an egalitarianism which Freud's concept of analysis had foreclosed. He was not naïve about power situations; at least he was "not inclined to regard the Caesars as mentally sick. It was their position that drove them to their excesses; we must not give people that unlimited sense of power."[21] As Freud learned about his own profession, "when a man is endowed with power it is hard for him not to misuse it."[22]

With patients Freud liked he could be natural and open, even about making a mistake. As he wrote, under certain conditions "we may conclude that we have made a mistake and we shall admit as much to the patient at some suitable opportunity without sacrificing any of our authority." Freud succeeded in winning the full support of some patients to all his doctrines, and with these patients some give-and-take was possible. But a patient who was competitive with Freud from the beginning could constitute a threat to him. An analysis that began with opposition to Freud soon ran into the ground.

As an old man Freud could be arbitrary. One Christmas vacation a patient went skiing, and Freud took on another patient; when the vacationer came back he was told he would now have to wait his turn. Freud felt justified to do what he did, since a patient was not in his view entitled to prescribe when he should work and when not. But Otto Rank believed that Freud wanted to fasten his followers into dependency, and in particular that Freud's concept of latent homosexuality was one way of tyrannizing people. At least one of Freud's patients ended his analysis in a depression over the issue of unconscious homosexuality.

The analyst's power becomes compounded in the case of a training analysis, for the analyst is in a position to affect the analysand's professional career. How much Freud helped his patients is difficult to judge; one said she came away a different person, many felt less depressed about their inabilities, whereas others retained the same symptoms despite their analysis, and some ended up in mental institutions. But for pupils who went on to be analysts themselves, having been analyzed by Freud was an advantage in their careers.

As late as the early 1920's there was no such thing as "control" analyses, conducted by candidates in training under supervision by more experienced analysts. One could consult with Freud over a difficult problem, but he did not encourage too much of this; he wanted his pupils to learn by themselves and trust to their own judgment.[23] Sometimes analysts would travel from abroad with their intractable patients, hoping that Freud might somehow break the deadlock.

By the late 1920's the Vienna Psychoanalytic Society was more highly organized, with classes and training procedures conducted by members other than Freud; after a few months of analysis, a sort of trial period, a student in training would be invited to the meetings. Since the foreigners might not be able to stay in Vienna very long, they were allowed to go to meetings sooner. Gradually the supervision of analysts in training became more formalized; but the general attitude in Vienna, reflecting Freud's own view, was that these control analyses were not so important as the development of the candidate's therapeutic artistry. Analysts did not supervise the analyses conducted by their own analysands, but a stricter divorce between training and analyzing might have prevented the perpetuation of orthodoxy and minimized the stifling of talent.

Freud thought that training analyses could "not be conducted exactly like therapeutic analyses. . . ."[24] Freud felt that the students were entitled to social ties to him that otherwise might have been unacceptable. Analytic neutrality with pupils is actually rather new. In 1926 Freud wrote that "a period of some two years is calculated for this training."[25] In 1937 Freud thought:

> For practical reasons . . . [training] analysis can only be short and incomplete. Its main object is to enable his teacher to make a judgement as to whether the candidate can be accepted for further training. It has accomplished its purpose if it gives the learner a firm conviction of the existence of the unconscious, if it enables him, when repressed material emerges, to perceive in himself things which would otherwise be incredible to him, and if it shows him a first sample of the technique which has proved to be the only effective one in analytic work.[26]

By Freud's own report, in his "late years" he had "been mainly engaged in training analyses,"[27] and by 1937 he was sufficiently chastened about analysis as therapy, and impressed by the stresses of working with analytic material, for him to recommend that "every analyst should periodically—at intervals of five years or so—submit himself to analysis once more, without feeling ashamed of taking this step."[28] Of course, Freud's recommendation presupposed that the analyses themselves were not interminable, although self-discovery might be unending; as training analyses have tended to lengthen over the years, Freud's proposal, which is nowhere now followed, would entail virtually permanent analysis.

The practice of analysis poses a temptation for the analyst, in that it is not difficult for him to displace private vanity onto analysis itself. If only analyses were longer and deeper, it is easy to think, then they would be more successful. An analyst can believe this without seeming vain, since it is the analytic situation he is offering, something very special, and not just his own personality. But Freud could not have foreseen all the problems of training future analysts, if only because psychoanalysis in his own day was not as bureaucratized as it soon became.

Perhaps a key difficulty with psychoanalysis is its sense of perfectionism. The ideal of the fully analyzed analyst, for instance, who was supposed to be purified of the last traces of neurosis, was a myth born of the uncertainties and insecurities of the early analysts. Then there was a form of virtuous ritualism; it was high treason not to use a couch, or to fail to analyze the negative transference (for fear of a "mere" suggestive, transitory cure). The impression that Freud was a faultless god was the equivalent of the myth of the perfectly analyzed analyst.[29] Analysts are human, and the fulfillment of the aim of neutrality in technique is an impossibility. But by the end of his life Freud was in little mood to compromise about the practice of therapy:

> It is . . . reasonable to expect of an analyst, as a part of his qualifications, a considerable degree of mental normality and correctness. In addition, he must possess some kind of superiority, so that in certain analytic situations he can act as a model for his patient and in others as a teacher. And finally we must not forget that the analytic relationship is based on a love of truth—that is, on a recognition of reality—and that it precludes any kind of sham or deceit.[30]

Freud's writings had contributed to the unrealistic expectations of some of his adherents. In 1913 he had ambitiously held that "the time is not far distant when it will be generally recognized that no sort of nervous disturbance can be understood and treated without the line of approach and often of the technique of psychoanalysis."[31] For all the appreciation of human diversity Freud could at times display, he felt entitled to view diary keeping as a "neurotic trait."[32] And despite his emancipation from many middle-class values, when an early follower of his finally got married in middle age, Freud complimented him by saying: "Now you are normal."

Despite Freud's cautions about the limitations of analytic technique and all the many "contraindications" to analysis that he cited, the early analysts were interested in putting virtually everybody into analysis. At Simmel's sanatorium near Berlin, which lasted five years before going bankrupt, everyone—nurses, even the janitors—was supposed to be analyzed. It was easy to forget that psychoanalysis was a special technique for limited problems. As the Swiss psychiatrist Binswanger wrote Freud in 1911, "no success makes me proud, unless it is achieved by way of analysis, and . . . every cure leaves me unsatisfied, unless it is an analytic one." Binswanger later reflected: "I still believed then . . . that almost every patient must be analyzed. It took ten years of hard work and disappointments before I realized that only a certain number of cases in our institution were suited to analysis."[33]

As a practical matter, Freud knew that health and illness were not to be sharply distinguished from each other. To Karl Abraham, a pupil he liked, Freud wrote that "we all have these complexes and must be careful not to call everybody neurotic."[34] To another favorite, Sandor Ferenczi, Freud wrote: "One should not try to eradicate one's complexes, but come to terms with them; they are the legitimate guiding forces of one's behavior in the world."[35] Does any physician really cure, or does he rather only help the body heal itself? Freud once mentioned that "a surgeon of earlier times took as his motto the words: 'Je le pansai, Dieu le guérit.' ['I dressed his wounds, God cured him.'] The analyst should be content with something similar."[36]

Freud had taste, and he objected to certain aspects of a paper Wittels once presented on the Viennese writer Karl Kraus: "Analysis is . . . supposed to make one tolerant, and such a vivisection could justly be reproached as being inhumane." Freud told his Society that "we have no right to place neurosis in the foreground wherever a great accomplishment is involved."[37] But Freud was far harder on a paper about Heinrich von Kleist by Sadger:

> One simply cannot do justice to a personality if one stresses only its abnormal sexual components and does not make an effort to establish their close ties with the individual's other psychic forces . . . Sadger must also be reproached for having a special predilection for the

brutal . . . our task is not arbitrarily to speak new truths, but rather to show in what way they can be arrived at. A certain degree of tolerance must go hand in hand with a deeper understanding . . . if life is to remain at all bearable.

Freud phrased his reproach for this "repellent" paper in a tactful way: "Sadger has not acquired this tolerance, or at least he is not capable of expressing it."[38]

It is not surprising that in the contradictory maelstrom of ideas which swirled around Freud some people went astray. By what standards of normality can we steer, that of the concepts Freud formally formulated or that of his life as he lived it? At his best Freud might have agreed with the aim of a great artist like Pablo Picasso: "Tension is a lot more important than the stable equilibrium of harmony, which doesn't interest me . . . I want to draw the mind in a direction it's not used to and wake it up."[39] Freud's conception of health, though rarely defined, was not intended to be dry-as-dust.

Psychoanalysis grew so fast as a movement that it has sometimes oversold itself as therapy; Americans in particular have been guilty of this. But others too, like the Kleinians, have emphasized psychological truth as the equivalent of health. The Viennese approach to psychoanalysis, led by Freud, had been a matter of helping people to find their own compromises. As Jung saw earlier than most, psychoanalysis itself cannot be a maturation process, but it can remove some of the obstacles in the way.

In 1904, long before the doctrinal quarrels within Freud's movement, he had simply stated that

there are many characteristics in the analytic method which prevent it from being an ideal form of therapy . . . From the patient it requires perfect sincerity—a sacrifice in itself. . . . I consider it quite justifiable to resort to more convenient methods of treatment as long as there is any prospect of achieving anything by their means. That, after all, is the only point at issue.[40]

In Jones's words, Freud warned against "excessive ambition, whether of a therapeutic or a cultural nature. One should never demand of the patient more than lies in his native capacity."[41]

By the end of his life Freud concluded that the therapeutic efficacy of the analytic process was severely limited by constitutional factors.

Binswanger reported a conversation with Freud in 1936: "Freud, to my surprise, remarked briefly, 'Constitution is everything.' "[42] In 1937 Freud wrote:

> One has an impression that one ought not to be surprised if it should turn out in the end that the difference between a person who has not been analyzed and the behavior of a person after he has been analyzed is not so thorough-going as we aim at making it and as we expect and maintain it to be.[43]

Freud looked upon man's plight with stoicism; "one of Freud's favorite sayings was . . . 'One must learn to bear some portion of uncertainty.' "[44]

To the circle that assembled around Freud, however, the therapeutic possibilities of analysis were as enticing as the ultimate prospects for the understanding that his ideas had created. Yet some of Freud's personal qualities, which left their mark on his technique as well as his theories, would also provide the stimulus for the dissenters in psychoanalysis, as they tried to model themselves after Freud in basing their ideas on their own scientific experiences and their growing self-understanding.

V

PUBLIC CONTROVERSIES: ALFRED ADLER AND WILHELM STEKEL

1. Collaboration

IN THE DECADE after the publication of *The Interpretation of Dreams* in 1900, Freud enjoyed one of the happiest periods in his life. He was able to overcome whatever inadequacies he felt in his own family life by the creation of his new movement, comprising adopted sons and daughters. Freud knew by then how much he had uncovered in psychology, and in the technique of free association he had fashioned an investigatory tool for the future. During the first ten years of the century Freud filled out his earlier ideas, elaborating his doctrines of infantile sexuality and the unconscious. The psychopathology of everyday life, including jokes and humor, found its place within his kingdom.

During this decade Freud emerged from isolation and established his school. Psychoanalysis was not persecuted, but it was by no means generally accepted. Perhaps Freud too much enjoyed being attacked. Despite the myth which has highlighted those who opposed Freud's theories and ignored those who did not, attending Freud's lectures at the University of Vienna was not considered radical.[1] Freud, who always spoke without notes, was, until the illness of his later years, a superb speaker: "His words flew clearly, simply, logically."[2] By 1906 his influence on the younger generation of Viennese intellectuals was immense; as one Viennese observer put it, Freud's popularity with young people was very high despite his reluctance to enter into much personal contact with them.[3]

In those days, his shoulders already in their scholarly stoop and his hands characteristically clasped behind his back, Freud was an inspiring figure. As a teacher he opened up a new world to the growing, but still small, group of devoted followers who gathered about him. He was generous with his teachings, giving of his ideas. Freud was not yet closed off, withdrawn, or suspicious, as he became in his old age. Sitting in cafés after the Wednesday meetings on psychoanalysis, which began to be held at his apartment in 1902, Freud found no subject—whether telepathy or the Almighty—too far afield for speculation.

Even in this pre-World War I period, when psychoanalysis was still isolated from the world at large, Freud was cautious in citing his pupils. It is true that he mentioned their work in his writings, and they played an essential role in the effort to establish his findings on broad scientific grounds. In 1908, before psychoanalysis was widely recognized, he spoke rather grandly of what "every doctor who has practiced psychoanalysis knows. . . ."[4] In new editions of *The Interpretation of Dreams,* Freud interpolated illustrations which his pupils had brought him. As he wrote in a passage added to that book in 1909, "a large number of dreams have been published and analyzed in accordance with my directions in papers by physicians who have decided to adopt the psychoanalytic therapeutic procedure, as well as by other authors." Here Freud paused in a parenthesis to list a few names, such as Carl Jung and Wilhelm Stekel.

But psychoanalysis remained Freud's personal realm. After citing these pupils, he made sure that there could be no misunderstanding about priorities: "But these publications have merely confirmed my views and not added anything to them."[5] Freud made it plain that it was his pupils' job to apply his original findings. Students at the university, unless they were associated with the psychiatric clinic where he spoke, needed Freud's prior permission before attending his lectures; this requirement was unusual at the time, but Freud was not interested in speaking to those who came without seriousness of purpose.

The public controversies with Adler, Stekel, and Jung, which followed so closely on this peaceful and happy decade in Freud's life, are not easy for some to reconsider. Every family has its version of its own history, and for those who have grown up in Freud's debt these quarrels are already mythic. Every social unit thrives on such legends, and the mythology of those early quarrels has become well fixed, not only in the oral history of psychoanalysis but also in books for the general public.[6]

On the whole, history is not well served by concentrating on the dramatic. It is possible, by placing too much emphasis on the early splits in psychoanalysis, to overlook the areas of unspoken agreement which emerged in later years among all schools of psychotherapeutic thought. Nevertheless, these well-known disputes establish the structure of Freud's relation to his pupils and the impact he had on his circle. Too often psychoanalysis has been seen as a monolithic doctrine.

Alfred Adler (1870–1937) became famous as the leader of a divergent movement; he was a "defector" who founded a so-called deviant school of psychology which de-emphasized the role of sexuality. Adler had been one of Freud's most devoted followers. In 1908, when there were fewer than thirty individuals in the group that met at Freud's home on Wednesday evenings (of whom only about half came to any given session), Adler criticized a paper of Otto Rank's on the grounds that in it "sexuality takes up comparatively little space." At the same meeting Adler faithfully assumed that Rank's entire paper had been founded on an idea of "the Professor's."[7] In later years Adler and his friends tried to deny that he had ever been a believing disciple at all, claiming instead that Freud had treated him as a student if not as an equal.[8] But the *Minutes* of the Vienna Psychoanalytic Society allow no doubt about Freud's sovereignty.

Fourteen years Freud's junior, Adler joined Freud's circle in 1902, the year of its inception. In 1897 Freud had been nominated as a "Professor Extraordinarius," an appointment which entitled him to lecture at the University of Vienna, though he received no salary and was not a regular faculty member. The upper university circles were anti-Semitic, but that it took five years for his appointment to be confirmed was probably due to the fact that Freud was "too absorbed in his self-analysis to see to his interests."[9] Freud had to lobby on his own behalf, with the help of two well-connected women—one a patient and the other a former patient—to promote his candidacy. "To arrive at any position of eminence in this society, one required sponsorship from 'above.' "[10] Freud's relative lack of status at the university always irked him. The title he received in March 1902 was a belated and niggardly tribute to his work. But it helped in his professional life and in the dissemination of his ideas.

Later the same year Freud sent out postcards proposing to four men (Alfred Adler, Wilhelm Stekel, Max Kahane, and Rudolf Reitler) that they assemble at his house to discuss issues of common interest. Freud was so sure of his eventual success, and the manner in which it would take place, that the year before he had written:

> One day I discovered to my great astonishment that the view of dreams which came nearest to the truth was not the medical but the popular one, half involved though it still was in superstition . . . Since then, under the name of "psychoanalysis," it has found acceptance by a whole school of research workers.[11]

At the time this was a wish of Freud's rather than a reality. Not yet adequately appreciated or understood, he needed the approval of followers. The group was at first called the Psychological Wednesday Society and met in Freud's waiting room. Like Freud's "poky little study,"[12] it was lined with books and cabinets of antiquities; Freud's collection of art

*Freud, center, at the Weimar Congress of the
International Psychoanalytic Association, September 1911*

objects was chosen for historical and humanistic rather than purely aesthetic reasons. Many educated Jews of Central Europe shared the prevalent admiration for the pagan ideal of classical antiquity.

The discussions at these meetings were wide-ranging, although they remained within the broad circumference of Freud's ideas. Papers by members reviewed recent books, examined historical figures, presented case material, or raised theoretical subjects. Cigars and black coffee were staples of the gatherings. In 1908 the group renamed itself the Vienna Psychoanalytic Society; starting in 1910, as part of the new organization of Freud's International Psychoanalytic Association, they met in a room of a Viennese medical association.

Freud was far more comfortable at these sessions than at the university, where even his faithful followers might be so casual as to bring dates along. In his own smaller group, too, he had much less fear of being misunderstood. No one "read" papers at these meetings—Freud insisted that people speak without notes or reserve. "He believed that . . . reading distracted the attention of the listener and handicapped his identifying himself with the lecturer."[13] "In this circle of intimates, Freud's method was far more audacious than it was in a public lecture . . . Those who know Freud only through the written word will be far more ready to differ from him than were those who listened to the magic of his speech."[14] It was difficult to disagree with Freud, not so much because he would harshly attack deviant ideas, but, more importantly, because the power of his intellect and character readily undermined any alternative formulations. (Many members of this small group also formed a permanent audience of a loyal guard at Freud's public lectures.)

There were various motives for coming to Freud initially; some, like Adler, were physicians, others were writers or students, and some were simply neurotically self-involved. Adler, like the rest, participated in discussions, wrote papers, and helped to further the cause of psychoanalysis. Inevitably the early analysts were enlisted in proselytizing and preaching. In reciprocation for his help, Freud recognized Adler's special talents. He also referred the wife of his brother Alexander to Adler for an analysis.[15] And in justifying making Adler president of the Vienna Society in 1910, Freud remarked that "after all he is the only personality there. . . ."[16]

Temperamentally, Freud and Adler were very different. Freud's manner was restrained and ceremonious, and his mind systematic. Proud, though not personally vain, Freud wrote of himself in the third person as early as 1903.[17] Unlike the "invariably neat and correct"[18] Freud,* Adler was "always the 'common man,' nearly sloppy in his appearance. . . ."[19] Although Adler could be rambunctious, of the two he was more even-tempered, gregarious, and sociable. Adler also loved music and was a good musician.

Freud, however, was a great writer. "Adler was a born talker who refused to give time and attention to writing."[20] Freud was meticulous

---

* Around World War I, Freud came to meetings of the Vienna Psychoanalytic Society in a *fiacre*, wearing a fur-lined and fur-collared coat, a silk hat, and carrying an ivory-handled walking stick.

and exact in pronouncing his words; he spoke slowly and clearly in expressing just what he wanted to say, in a voice more than one person found
rather rough.[21] A lover of literature, Freud cared passionately about issues
which to less literary minds might seem merely a haggle over words.

Within the world Freud had marked out, Adler was able to pursue
some of his prior interests, specifically his special concern with the social
and environmental factors in disease.[22] Adler was the first in Freud's circle
to become interested in problems of education. Shorter than average, and
having endured a sickly childhood, Adler stressed the role of compensations for early defects in his famous study of "organ inferiority"; "under
favorable circumstances, certain defects in a child create a disposition
toward greater performance."[23] Not concerned so exclusively with infantile sexuality, Adler was preoccupied with ego mechanisms and aggressive drives. Along with his psychoanalytic work and his medical practice
as an internist, Adler—in contrast to Freud's lack of interest in politics—
was an active Socialist; he yearned to improve the world through education
and psychotherapy.[24]

Freud was such a great man that his followers had to struggle to be
original, and sometimes they were led thereby to reject what was valuable
in Freud. Even while appointing Adler president of the Vienna Society,
Freud sensed his follower's uneasy tolerance of his subservient role. But
Freud hoped that "possibly in that position [of president] he will feel
an obligation to defend our common ground."[25] According to Freud,
Adler once explained his discontent this way: "Do you think it gives me
such great pleasure to stand in your shadow my whole life long?" Freud
did not react favorably to what he termed this "striving . . . for a place
in the sun."[26] Somehow intellectual ambitiousness seems illegitimate to
many people, and Adler and his supporters—while never denying the
accuracy of the "shadow" quotation—have gone to some pains to explain
it away.[27] If one were to forget what pioneers these men were in the
investigation of depth psychology, and how emotionally charged intellectual controversies can become, the early analysts would seem self-
assertive and quarrelsome.

Even in this period before World War I, Freud was set apart from
his pupils. If one of them wanted to talk to Freud privately, though,
he could be seen in his office by appointment, and he could be relied
upon to appear at certain points along the routes he invariably took on
his walks. Theodor Reik learned Freud's habits, and when he wanted to
chat he would wait for him to come by. Freud's daily life was unusually
orderly and crammed with work. He saw patients from eight or nine
in the morning until precisely one o'clock, when lunch—the big Vien-

nese meal of the day—was promptly served. From two until three in the afternoon Freud went out of the house, normally taking one of his children with him, for his constitutional as well as to run errands (getting cigars, for example). Three to four o'clock in the afternoon was reserved a few times a week for consultations; otherwise Freud saw patients all afternoon and had a late supper in the evening. After this meal Freud would go for another one of his strolls; he was so indefatigable at these that some have described him as "marching" rather than walking. Before retiring at one o'clock in the morning, Freud had time for his correspondence, manuscripts, editing—and often just for a game of cards, usually with his sister-in-law Minna.

This clockwork regularity of Freud's life enabled him to get his work done. He saw patients punctiliously, and once old age and illness restricted his outdoor walks he would regularly stride through the family apartment between analytic sessions. His weekly schedule was also ordered. Every other Tuesday night was set aside for B'nai B'rith meetings; Wednesday evening he spent with the psychoanalytic group; on Thursday and Saturday nights he lectured at the university. Sunday morning included a visit to his mother's, and Saturday night, after his lecture, Freud went to his old friend Dr. Koenigstein's for his favorite card game, four-handed tarok. Even Freud's vacations were well organized; he liked to be either fully at work or completely at rest, and he set aside at least a month at the end of summer for travel (hopefully to Italy or Greece) or rest in the mountains (which always included mushroom gathering).

In Vienna, Freud was well regarded in middle-class circles, but psychoanalysis was equated with Freud, and his pupils were considered pale imitators. Freud rarely spoke about any of them with particular enthusiasm. His pupils might follow his daily life with the greatest care, and interpret his writings and sayings with the utmost devotion, but in everyday life Freud held himself aloof. None of his pupils, all of whom were younger, was a comrade to him, and he rarely permitted any real intimacies. Hanns Sachs wrote of their last meeting in London shortly before Freud died: "fundamentally he remained as remote as when I first met him in the lecture hall [thirty years earlier]."[28]

In his office he was natural and unassuming, but he would not tolerate opposition in public or in print. Speaking of those Wednesday-evening meetings, Max Graf (the father of a famous patient, "Little Hans") later wrote that "there was an atmosphere of the foundation of a religion in that room. . . . Freud's pupils were his apostles. . . . Good-hearted and considerate though he was in private life, Freud was hard and relentless in the presentation of his ideas." This former pupil went on to explain that he himself had been "unable and unwilling to submit to Freud's 'do' or 'don't'—with which he confronted me—and nothing was left for me but to withdraw from his circle."[29]

In his group Freud insisted on absolute loyalty. As Jones admitted, "with all his knowledge of the complex intricacies of the mind Freud was rather apt, when it was a question of conscious judgment, to take a black or white view of a person's character, and it took a great deal to modify it."[30] Although it might not have been so clear before his fight with Adler, afterward his pupils knew with certainty that if you disagreed with Freud he could unceremoniously eject you.

Freud preferred not to polemicize, but when he felt really pressed he could rise to the occasion. Although he admired originality and talent, he had difficulty tolerating anyone with ideas of his own. As he freely admitted, "I have no use for other people's ideas when they are presented to me at an inopportune moment."[31] Thus Freud repeatedly drove away his best pupils. To be sure, the quarrels were mitigated by the cultured atmosphere in which they took place. Freud was a gentleman, though he resented the hypocrisy of civilized manners: "the politeness which I practice every day is to a large extent dissimulation. . . ."[32]

Freud could also hate. "He was a kind, a benevolent, a good man, but he was kind without softness, benevolent without compassion, and good without mercy."[33] Freud's system of thought reflects his fighting stance; he used military language and the imagery of warfare throughout —attack, defense, struggle, enemy, resistance, supplies, triumph, conquest, fight. It was somewhat flat-footed of Jones to write: "I do not think he took the opposition greatly to heart."[34] In some sense Freud obviously quested for the antagonism he stirred up. Once he referred to the "common saying that we should learn from our enemies," and confessed "never" having "succeeded in doing so."[35] Elsewhere he enjoyed quoting Heine's saying: "One must . . . forgive one's enemies—but not before they have been hanged."[36] The resistances to psychoanalysis were, he held, "not very creditable to the scientific men of our day. But," he went on, "it has never occurred to me to pour contempt upon the opponents of psychoanalysis merely because they were opponents—apart from the few unworthy individuals, the adventurers and profiteers, who are always to be found on both sides in time of war."[37]

Had Freud been broad-minded, his insights might have been smothered in intellectual geniality. On behalf of his cause he let loose all his world-shaking defiance. Personal issues could mushroom into theoretical debates, and intellectual differences could be interpreted as personal affronts. Freud's pupils only made the situation worse. In need of a

strong authority, they transformed Freud's wishes into law; it was tempting for them to be more orthodox than the master, more Freudian than
Freud.

2. The Will to Power

IN 1910, THE YEAR Freud installed Adler as president of the
Vienna Society, psychoanalysis was just becoming officially organized
on an international basis. Freud had made Jung, a Swiss and a Gentile,
head of the new International Psychoanalytic Association. Even today
the psychoanalytic movement stresses its transcultural basis. For Freud,
the institutionalization of his movement not only ensured the viability
of his work in the future, but also gave him something outside himself
to which he could devote his energies; and by attaching his vanity to
psychoanalysis at large, he became much less personally vulnerable to
loss or attack.

At a meeting of Freud's followers in Nuremberg (called the "Nuremberg Congress") in March 1910, the Hungarian Sandor Ferenczi
proposed, with Freud's full prior approval, that an international association of analysts be set up with branch societies in various countries.
Ferenczi, again following Freud's wishes, nominated Jung as president
of the new organization, thereby determining that the center of the
movement was no longer to be Vienna, but Zurich. In his speech Ferenczi
echoed Freud's condescending feelings about the quality of his Vienna
group, and proposed that in the future papers and speeches require the
approval of the president of the International Association.

The Viennese analysts were naturally unhappy at these proposed
changes. Adler and the rest felt slighted by Freud's favoritism toward
the Swiss. As Sachs saw it afterward, "the rivalry for . . . [Freud's]
acclaim and approbation was the mainspring of . . . [the] wranglings"[1]
that followed. Adler feared that Ferenczi's proposals implied "censorship and restrictions on scientific freedom."[2] The Viennese at Nuremberg
held a protest meeting in Wilhelm Stekel's hotel room. Freud went there
himself, and

> made an impassioned appeal for their adherence. He laid stress on
> the virulent hostility that surrounded them and the need for outside

support to counter it. Then, dramatically throwing back his coat, he declared: "My enemies would be willing to see me starve; they would tear my very coat off my back."*³

Freud now had to make peace with his Viennese followers. A new monthly periodical was planned, the *Zentralblatt für Psychoanalyse* (*Central Journal for Psychoanalysis*), with Adler and Stekel as editors; Freud was to be the "director." As Freud described it later, "it was obviously intended originally to represent the Opposition: it was meant to win back for Vienna the hegemony threatened by the election of Jung."⁵ Jung was already editor of the *Jahrbuch* (*Yearbook*), the first journal devoted exclusively to psychoanalysis. To further counterbalance the shift in power toward the Swiss, Freud retired from the presidency of the Vienna Society. He remained "scientific chairman," but the Society was to have its own officers and a more independent status; its members were no longer to be simply Freud's guests and its meetings would not be held in Freud's waiting room. Adler was elected president and Stekel vice-president. Freud hoped in these ways to placate the Viennese.

Becoming president of the Vienna Society did not make Adler more tractable; on the contrary, it seems instead to have confirmed him in his strivings for independence. Like the rest of the Viennese, Adler thought Freud was mistaken in exalting Jung. Whereas Freud held that "the anathema which was imposed upon psychoanalysis led its supporters to combine in an international organization," according to Adler's way of thinking Freud had overestimated the "perils" psychoanalysis faced, owing to an unnecessary sense of inferiority.⁶

The difficulties between Freud and Adler were theoretical as well as personal. Freud believed Adler was too much interested in surface psychology and the concept of the ego. Freud admitted that this was a "field hitherto rather neglected by psychoanalysis," but it seemed to him a regression to commonsensical ways of thinking. "Adler can never do justice to the psychoanalytic facts, because his interest is focused on the ego and conscious processes; psychoanalysis, however, takes hold of matters on the basis of the unconscious and the libido, which are . . . what produce a neurosis." From Adler's point of view, his concepts represented an extension of the field of depth psychology. "The feeling

---

* According to another version, Freud said: "They begrudge me the coat I am wearing; I don't know whether in the future I will earn my daily bread." Tears were streaming down his cheeks.⁴

of inferiority," he held, "is not conscious to the neurotic to the degree it is effective. . . ."[7]

Early in 1911 Freud decided to bring his difficulties with Adler to a head. Adler delivered two papers to the Society, on January 4 and February 1, setting forth his views, and Freud replied on February 1 and 22. "Freud . . . was unsparing in his criticism."[8] He had what may now seem a rather primitive conception of the methodology of science. "Facts" existed and were verifiable, entirely distinguishable from "interpretations," which were subject to personal opinion. Freud held that in psychoanalysis he had discovered a set of new facts, and that these observations comprised a body of knowledge. Adler, however, was threatening to repudiate these findings with fresh "speculations." "The stress on arbitrary personal views in scientific matters is," Freud wrote, "bad; it is clearly an attempt to dispute the right of psychoanalysis to be regarded as a science. . . ."[9] One of Freud's followers at the time expressed his own conception of science: "The natural scientist is a dogmatist; he lays down a principle and declares: that is the way it is."[10]

The dispute between Freud and Adler hardly seems to have been a considered discussion of scientific differences. Freud was airing charges against Adler in full public view. Among the Viennese intelligentsia these meetings caused a sensation; for all its cosmopolitanism, the city, like other centers of intellectual life, was a provincial town. Freud outrightly denounced Adler. It was a trial and the charge was heresy. (Although Richard Wagner voted with Freud and Paul Klemperer with Adler, both agreed the meetings were a "trial." They differed, however, in their views of how personal Freud's attack had been.[11]) As Sachs, who voted with Freud, remembered, Freud "did not spare his opponent and was not afraid of using sharp words and cutting remarks. . . ."[12] Freud examined Adler's views, picking over those concepts which Adler claimed to have fostered; what seemed new, Freud said, was trivial, and the rest had been taken from Freud without acknowledgment.[13]

The penalty was excommunication, and Freud set out to ostracize Adler and his sympathizers. As Graf saw it, "Freud—as the head of a church—banished Adler; he ejected him from the official church. Within the space of a few years, I lived through the whole development of a church history."[14] Freud had come to value his discoveries far more than individual friendships. About his doctrines he was harsh and protective. He considered Adler's work a betrayal, deviation from the revealed truth, and by the end of these meetings he was boiling. It was Freud, not his followers, who was responsible for the split. With the sanction of Freud's anger, the loyal guard then stiffened to expel the unfaithful. These were not just personal admirers of Freud; they believed that his psychology was the psychology of the future.

At the outset Adler did not have many real adherents, but by the end of the battle the Society was split almost in half. Adler and Stekel resigned as president and vice-president of the Society a few days after Freud's February 22 remarks. Adler remained a member of the Society until May, when Freud asked for his resignation as co-editor of the *Zentralblatt*. When Adler left the Society to found his own, he took only three members with him. He named it the Society for Free Psychoanalysis, which Freud dubbed, with heavy irony, "tasteful" and which years later Jones stiffly, echoing Freud, considered "rather tasteless."[15] Adler himself may have felt so too, for he soon renamed his group the Society for Individual Psychology.

The issue quickly arose whether a member of Freud's Society could also attend meetings of Adler's (held on Thursday evenings), and this problem dragged on for some time. Freud's position, unlike Adler's, was that a member must choose between the two groups. A resolution to that effect was finally passed by the Vienna Psychoanalytic Society in the fall of 1911, by eleven votes to five; evidently five members abstained from voting on the either/or choice. Thereafter, since every member of the Society had been forced by Freud to take a stand, one way or the other, six more members resigned from Freud's Society. According to Sachs, loyal to Freud throughout, of those who withdrew

> most . . . did not share Adler's views; their decision was influenced by their belief that the whole proceeding violated the "freedom of science." It may well be that Freud's incisive and harsh criticism had hurt soft feelings and made them willing to think that Adler's complaint of intolerance was justified.[16]

Earlier, shortly after Adler had resigned as president but before he had left the Society, Freud sent this account of their controversy to a pupil in Switzerland: "Adler's theories were departing too far from the right path, and it was time to make a stand against them . . . He has created for himself a world system without love, and I am in the process of carrying out on him the revenge of the offended goddess Libido."[17] To Karl Abraham, Freud explained that Adler had erred because he "denies the importance of the libido, and traces everything back to aggression." As a result of the discussions of Adler's views, Freud said he had grown "more severe. A great deal of confusion is concealed behind his abstraction; he dissimulates a much more far-reaching opposition and shows some fine paranoid traits." When the resignations were all in Freud felt relieved: "I have completed the purge of the society and sent Adler's seven [*sic*] followers packing after him. The decrease in numbers is immaterial, and work will be much easier. . . ." Freud felt that he had "forced" the "whole Adler gang" to resign. As early as November 1910 he had written in a letter to Jung of his hope of getting rid of Adler.[18]

The feud broke up long-standing friendships. Wives stopped speaking to each other, and couples disliked being seated near one another at dinner parties.[19] Although some of the children managed to weather the storm and remain friends, psychoanalysis was never to be the same again. Freud was controlled and polite, but his quick eyes and restless and impatient manner had long since given his followers an indication of his inner resources. To a group which had hung on Freud's every word, and which already had fanciful ideas about the master's wishes, it was electrifying to witness such a display of iron will. "A group," Freud wrote a decade later, ". . . is subject to the truly magical power of words. . . ."

A group is an obedient herd, which could never live without a master. It has such a thirst for obedience that it submits instinctively to anyone who appoints himself its master. Although in this way the needs of a group carry it half-way to meet the leader, yet he too must fit in with it in his personal qualities. He must himself be held in fascination by a strong faith (in an idea) in order to awaken the group's faith; he must possess a strong and imposing will, which the group, which has no will of its own, can accept from him.[20]

Despite the disagreeableness of the fighting, especially following such a successful decade, it was understandable of Freud to worry lest the core of his original findings get lost in the tendencies Adler represented. Freud had found that sexuality develops in separate stages, and does not start with puberty; and his central discovery in psychology lay in pointing out the persistence of infantile remnants in adult life. From Freud's point of view, Adler's concern with ego processes was endangering everything Freud had worked on. As Erik Erikson has said in defense of Freud, he "had to establish one thing at a time, and his great contribution was psychosexuality. It is a mark of a great man that he watches jealously over the expansion of his field. He makes sure that certain principles do not get lost before they can be superseded."[21] Adler would have shifted the focus of the Vienna Society away from what had been most distinctive in Freud's work. In 1911 it was by no

means clear that these ideas of Freud's would one day be widely accepted
—at which later time Adler's concepts might provide a much needed
corrective. Psychoanalysis was then confined to such a small group of
people that Freud might well fear that it would get watered down
before making its mark.

Under the circumstances, a renegade seemed to threaten the whole
movement, not merely the Vienna Society. Moreover, Freud found it
hard to tolerate "deviations," not only for personal reasons, but also
because he felt that the organization he headed was not yet successful
enough to permit much range of opinion. Once psychoanalysis became
established, numbering thousands of practitioners and influencing countless others, the limits of the permissible area of disagreement expanded.
Freud fought more bitterly against backsliders than against the outside
world lest psychoanalysis become hopelessly confused with other techniques and theories. We do not need to doubt that "Freud put all the
fire and vigor of his nature into answering . . . Adler and Jung."[22]

Freud was not only the discoverer of psychoanalysis but also Adler's
great teacher. No one knew better than Freud just how much he had
meant to his unfaithful follower, or resented with more justice the
notoriety Adler gained from the fight with him. So Freud burned at
Adler's presumptuousness in challenging his conceptions. He had come
to identify his ego completely with psychoanalysis, and in 1914, while
"fuming with rage,"[23] he wrote of his troubles with Adler (and also of
the subsequent fight with Jung) in "On the History of the Psychoanalytic Movement." It was premature, though prophetic, to think at
that date that such a small collection of people constituted a "movement"
entitled to a "history." But Freud was supremely confident of what
the future would ultimately bring. "Men are strong," he wrote, "so long
as they represent a strong idea; they become powerless when they oppose
it."[24]

In this essay Freud explained how he had grown alienated from his
Vienna group:

> There were only two inauspicious circumstances which at last
> estranged me inwardly from the group. I could not succeed in
> establishing among its members the friendly relations that ought to
> obtain between men who are all engaged upon the same difficult
> work; nor was I able to stifle the disputes upon priority for which
> there were so many opportunities under these conditions of work
> in common.[25]

Freud primarily insisted upon only one point, that Adler's work not be
confused with psychoanalysis:

> I am not concerned with the truth that may be contained in the theories which I am rejecting, nor shall I attempt to refute them . . . I wish merely to show that these theories controvert the fundamental principles of analysis . . . and that for this reason they should not be known by the name of analysis.[26]

This was not simply possessiveness, for if Freud's concepts were ever to be established, they would first have to be kept distinct from alternative ideas.

Once he was in the midst of a public battle, Freud assumed full responsibility for his work: "psychoanalysis is my creation; for ten years I was the only person who concerned himself with it." And "even today no one can know better than I do what psychoanalysis is. . . ."[27] Even in this polemic Freud could at times sound a tolerant note: "There is room enough on God's earth, and anyone who can has a perfect right to potter about on it without being prevented; but it is not a desirable thing for people who have ceased to understand one another and have grown incompatible with one another to remain under the same roof."[28] To Freud the image of a family was hardly farfetched. He suspected, however, that Adler's innovations were "intended to prove that psychoanalysis is wrong in everything. . . ."[29]

Whatever the justifications for what Freud wrote publicly, in private he remained personally bitter. "I have made a pygmy great" is one comment that has come down to us.[30] Freud remarked that Lou Andreas-Salomé had sent him "an exchange of letters with Adler that shows her insight and clarity in an excellent light and does the same for Adler's venom and meanness, and with such trash, etc."[31] Adler's "venomousness" seemed such that Freud considered him "a loathsome individual."[32]

Jones took an elevated view of Freud's quarrel with Adler. "[W]e are told that such and such a person left Freud and his circle not simply because of a difference of opinion but because of Freud's tyrannical personality and his dogmatic insistence on each of his followers accepting precisely the same views as himself." Such a notion Jones considered "ridiculously untrue." Adler was at fault in his "clamor to be the favorite child," which Jones claimed had a monetary motive. Adler was one of those "obliged to perpetuate the rebelliousness of childhood and to keep searching for figures to rebel against." Objectively, Adler was just as Freud had perceived him, "evidently very ambitious and constantly quarreling wth the others over points of priority in his ideas."[33] Turning the tables on Adler, Jones said that the term "inferiority complex," which

Adler did so much to make popular, "was borrowed without acknowledgement from Marcinowski. . . ."[34] It was a part of Freud's feminine side, Jones thought, to overestimate men like Adler.

Sachs, a devoted pupil of Freud's to the last, who witnessed the Adler fight in Vienna (while Jones was in Toronto), was the better psychologist. "In his writing Freud never blotted out a line . . . he cancelled the whole thing and started to re-write it . . . He always hated to patch up things, whether in the intellectual or emotional sphere." Of the fight with Adler, Sachs related that "in the execution of this duty he was untiring and unbending, hard and sharp like steel, a 'good hater' close to the limit of vindictiveness." Yet Sachs could also report of his years with Freud: "I never heard him raise his voice in anger or excitement."[35]

Curiously enough, the man who thought he had had to "blind" himself "artificially in order to focus all the light on one dark spot. . . ."[36] and who advised his students not to squander their creative energies, at the same time accused Adler of being too single-minded. Adler's work, Freud held, was an oversimplification, reductionism; peripheral notions in psychoanalysis—overcompensations for feelings of inferiority, for example —had been prematurely pushed into the center of the stage. Adler's ideas were "twisted interpretations and distortions of the disagreeable facts of analysis. . . ." Adler exhibited "the most serious departures from actual observation and the most fundamental confusion in his concepts."

[E]verything alike is pressed into the service of the masculine protest, self-assertion and the aggrandizement of the personality. The system is complete; to produce it has cost an enormous amount of labor in the recasting of interpretations, while it has not furnished a single new observation . . . The view of life which is reflected in the Adlerian system is founded exclusively on the aggressive instinct; there is no room in it for love.[37]

"In scientific matters," Freud later wrote, "people are very fond of selecting one portion of the truth, putting it in the place of the whole and of then disputing the rest, which is no less true, in favor of this one portion."[38]

In substance Freud was accusing Adler of desexualizing psychoanalysis, to the degree that he emphasized concepts such as the ego or the will to power. Psychoanalysis, on the other hand, was more concerned to show that "every ego-trend contains libidinal components. The Adlerian theory emphasizes the counter-part to this, the egoistic constituent in libidinal instinctual impulses."[39] Libido was not, according to Adler, the essence of neurosis; even sexual behavior could have symbolic meanings. As Freud summarized Adler's approach, "sexual life is merely one of the spheres in which human beings seek to put in action their driving need for power and domination."[40]

At the same time, Adler had, in Freud's opinion, unnecessarily introduced sexual factors, for instance in explaining dreams and symptoms bisexually "as a confluence of two currents described as a masculine and a feminine one."[41] Adler thought that everyone tries to avoid feminine patterns of development and struggles toward masculine "lines"; in Adler's view this was a part of the human tendency to live by goals of which people are unaware. As Henri Ellenberger has recently summarized Adler's position, "all of our public and private institutions rest upon the prejudice of the superiority of the male."[42] Freud objected to Adler's reasoning: "that 'every dream shows an advance from the feminine to the masculine line,' appear[s] to me to go far beyond anything that can be legitimately maintained in dream-interpretation."[43] Adler stressed the importance of the mechanism by which the fear of femininity leads to compensatory behavior, what he called the "masculine protest." Freud thought that this represented a sexualized version of Freud's own concept of repression:

> We must not be misled by the term "masculine protest" into supposing that what the man is repudiating is his passive attitude [as such] . . . [S]uch men often display a masochistic attitude—a state that amounts to bondage—towards women. What they reject is not passivity in general, but passivity towards a male. In other words, the "masculine protest" is in fact nothing else than castration anxiety.[44]

3. Priorities

THE THEME OF PLAGIARISM resounded throughout this controversy between Freud and Adler. The body of work was Freud's, and Adler had taken a part of it. Freud maintained that Adler had proposed "a change of nomenclature through which we lost clarity,"[1] but behind these new names, Freud felt, lay his own prior conclusions. Adler's emphasis on the psychological advantages of being ill, for instance, was really one of Freud's own insights:

> Psychoanalysis is obliged to give its backing to . . . [this] constituent of Adler's theory as it would to something of its own. And in fact it

is nothing else than psychoanalytic knowledge, which that author extracted from sources open to everyone during ten years of work in common and which he has now labelled as his own by a change in nomenclature.[2]

Since Adler traced his idea of the inferiority complex to feelings of being a child, Freud argued that he had found the "disguise under which the factor of infantilism . . . reappears. . . ." "Adler must also be credited with priority," Freud noted with sarcasm, "in confusing dreams with latent dream-thoughts. . . ." Anyone who ignored the factors of resistance and transference in therapy would be guilty of "misappropriation of property by attempted impersonation, if he persists in calling himself a psychoanalyst."[3] With the support of his loyal disciples, Freud repeatedly returned to these charges against backsliding students. Freud often remarked that his pupils were "like dogs. They take a bone from the table, and chew it independently in a corner. But it is my bone!"[4]

Whether or not Freud was right in stating that Adler had "an uncontrolled craving for priority,"[5] Adler did stumble over the task of distinguishing Freud as a man, fallible and with human failings, from psychoanalysis as a body of knowledge. When Lou Andreas-Salomé came to Vienna she initially saw both Freud and Adler. (Freud had granted a special dispensation allowing her to attend meetings of both Societies.) A letter to Lou shows Adler's awareness of some of what had happened:

> I share your appreciation of Freud's scientific significance up to the point at which I further and further parted company with him. His heuristic model is certainly important and useful as such. . . . But in addition to that, Freud's school has taken sexual phraseology for the heart of the matter. It may be that Freud the man has provoked a critical attitude in me. I cannot regret it.[6]

Freud's defecting pupils felt that they had permitted themselves to be seduced into his mode of thinking, and they reacted with anger. Adler coped with his problem with Freud by rebellion, and then by desertion.

Adler fully shared Freud's concern with priorities. Lou Andreas-Salomé recorded that Adler claimed to have discovered "ambivalence" before Bleuler;[7] and in a letter to her, Adler was explicit in his grievance against Freud:

> My position with respect to Freud's school has alas never had to reckon with its scientific arguments. All I ever see, all my friends ever see, is a busy-busy grabbing and pilfering and all the learned shenanigans. . . . Why is it that that school attempts to treat our views

as common property, whereas we have always insisted on the errors of *their* opinions. . . . My opinions might be wrong! But is that a good enough reason to steal them too?[8]

Some colleagues claimed that Adler, while still a member of Freud's Society, had not received the recognition he deserved, whereas others

Alfred Adler (1870–1937)

insisted that he was merely restating, without adequate acknowledgment, Freud's own views.[9]

The problem of due citation of the sources for one's ideas was not a new issue in Freud's life or in his circle. For example, Freud used the term "libido" in his instinct theory for "describing the dynamic manifestations of sexuality." According to Freud, writing in 1922, "libido" was "already used in this sense by Moll (1898) and was introduced into psychoanalysis" by Freud himself.[10] Freud was being more than conscientious here, for he had mentioned the term "libido" in a letter to Fliess in 1894 and in an article the following year. Albert Moll, a Berlin physician, published another book, *The Sexual Life of the Child*, in 1908, and before its appearance he had begun plans for a new journal and persuaded Freud to contribute some articles. Freud was eager for one paper, "On the Sexual Theories of Children," to appear, partly because of the impending publication of Moll's new book, which, it seemed to Freud, was being announced everywhere.[11]

When Moll's book appeared, the Vienna Society spent an evening discussing it. Freud's followers roundly attacked the book, but not mainly for its few criticisms of psychoanalytic theory. Many of Moll's reservations about Freud were balanced and sound. But his deference to Freud's position in the field, though he rejected many of Freud's conclusions, was infuriating. Rather than try to learn from Moll's book or answer those small portions of it devoted to Freud, the Society spent much of its time on the issue of scientific competition. One analyst accused Moll of considering it "an intrusion into his personal domain if another person has also achieved something in this field." Another found in the book "nothing original," merely a "reaction" to Freud's *Three Essays on the Theory of Sexuality* (1905). Freud himself thought it

> an inadequate, inferior, and above all dishonest book . . . infantile sexuality was really discovered by . . . Freud; before that, no hint of it existed in the literature . . . Moll gleaned the importance of infantile sexuality from the *Three Essays*, and then proceeded to write his book. For that reason, Moll's whole book is permeated by the desire to deny Freud's influence.

On the other hand, it was argued, Moll must have read Freud "selectively," since some of his central points were omitted in Moll's argument. In Moll's chapter on perversion, Freud complained, his own name "is not mentioned. Nor does Moll mention the connection of perversion with neurosis and infantile sexuality. This omission can only be intentional— Moll's character is only too well known . . . He is a petty, malicious, narrow-minded individual." Freud even objected that Moll failed to attack what was worth criticizing in Freud's *Three Essays*. Of one of Moll's own concepts, Freud remarked that "it is a great misfortune when a man who is destitute, as Moll is, of original ideas, nevertheless does have an idea for once."[12]

The day after the discussion of *The Sexual Life of the Child* at the Vienna Society, Freud wrote that he thought the book "as pitiful as it is dishonest." By February 8, 1909, he was still exercised at his critic and rival. Freud "did not think," he wrote to Abraham about Moll, that "our relations with him will develop very amicably." A book review of one of Freud's case histories in Moll's journal had made him "suspect that Moll means to oppose us in this journal, and that he uses a show of impartiality as a trimming to his rather underhand character. Several passages in *The Sexual Life of the Child* really merit a charge of libel, but they are best answered with—prudence and silence."[13]

In April 1909, Moll visited Freud in Vienna, but, as Freud records, the "interview ended badly. It came to hard words, and he left suddenly with a great deal of rapidly secreted venom. I almost had the impression that he thought he was patronizing us, and at that I let myself go a little."[14] Freud described Moll's visit more fully in a letter to Jung:

> To put it bluntly, he is a brute; he is not really a physician but has the intellectual and moral constitution of a pettifogging lawyer. I was amazed to discover that he regards himself as a kind of patron of our movement. I let him have it; I attacked the passage in his notorious book where he says that we compose our case histories to support our theories rather than the other way round, and had the pleasure of listening to his oily excuses: his statement was not meant as an insult, every observer is influenced by his preconceived ideas, etc. Then he complained that I was too sensitive, that I must learn to accept justified criticism; when I asked him if he had read "Little Hans," he wound himself up into several spirals, became more and more venomous, and finally, to my great joy, jumped up and prepared to take flight. At the door he grinned and made an unsuccessful attempt to retrieve himself by asking me when I was coming to Berlin. I could imagine how eager he must be to return my hospitality, but all the same I wasn't fully satisfied as I saw him go. He had stunk up the room like the devil himself, and partly for lack of practice and partly because he was my guest I hadn't lambasted him enough. Now of course we can expect all sorts of dirty tricks from him. . . .[15]

By 1914 Freud came to the unlikely conclusion that Moll's Society in Berlin was "designed to achieve recognition for Fliess." Freud thought "we must at all costs remain independent and maintain our equal rights," but he acknowledged that "ultimately we shall be able to come together with all the parallel sciences."[16] Years later, in 1926, Freud withdrew from membership in the International Committee for Preparing the Congress on Sex Research on the grounds that the Congress would be under the direction of Moll; he was, Freud wrote, a person he wanted to avoid. Freud said that he had been told that at a press conference Dr. Moll had made some "spiteful and impertinent" remarks about psychoanalysis. Freud wanted the organization to be aware of the motives for his decision.[17] Freud's pupils also boycotted the meeting, but Adler attended as one of the speakers.[18]

How are we to understand Freud's side of the controversy with Moll and some of the other difficulties in Freud's life? Granting the inevitable hostility which even a paltry innovation can evoke—not to mention a revolution in the history of ideas—it still seems fair to inquire how it came to pass that Freud got himself into so many altercations. He was, first of all, extraordinarily sensitive to criticism, whether from his least important critic or from those he had reason to feel sure of. Ellenberger has written about Freud that even in the 1890's

> There is no evidence that Freud was really isolated, and still less that he was ill-treated by his colleagues during those years . . . [Freud had] a strong intolerance of any kind of criticism . . . When C. S. Freund published an article on psychic paralyses, Freud called it "almost a plagiarism," although the article expressed a theory quite different from that of Freud, whom the author even mentions in that regard.[19]

Freud may have been inadequately appreciated in Vienna, especially in his early years, but by the end of World War I he was world-famous. Max Graf reported of the first decade of Freud's circle that "in those days when one mentioned Freud's name in a Viennese gathering, everyone would begin to laugh, as if one had told a joke."[20] In psychiatric circles in particular, Freud remained an outsider in Vienna. In 1924 Freud said that as a "result of the official anathema against psychoanalysis . . . the analysts began to come closer together."[21] Perhaps there is an analogy here to Freud's attitude toward his Jewishness: "as long as Jews are not admitted into Gentile circles," he is reported to have said, "they have no choice but to band together."[22]

Yet Freud could exaggerate the extent and intensity of opposition to him and his work, just as he had probably made too much of the role anti-Semitism had played in his life. In 1915, when a scientist whom Freud claimed to have "refused to take as a pupil some years ago because he seemed to be too abnormal" received the Nobel Prize, Freud remarked of himself that "it would be ridiculous to expect a sign of recognition when one has seven-eighths of the world against one."[23] At the same time that Freud was so concerned with what his "opponents proclaim to the world" and had so high an estimation of his own importance as to write that "what unites us against the world is our conviction of the importance of the libido"—he was also convinced that "every theory sacrifices something when it becomes popular."[24]

"Long after his work had won widespread recognition Freud continued to act like a man who daily faced the dangerous fire of the enemy."[25] In 1936, when Freud's eightieth birthday was approaching, he did not look forward to the festivities: "what nonsense to try to make up for all the ill-use of a lifetime by celebrating such a questionable date! No, let us rather remain enemies."[26] A few months later Freud noted that Pater Schmidt, whom Freud called his "arch enemy," had

> just been awarded the Austrian decoration of honor for Art and Science for his pious lies in the field of ethnology. Clearly this is meant to console him for the fact that providence has allowed me to achieve the age of eighty. Fate has its own ways of making one altruistic. When my master Ernst Brücke received the award, in the midst of my awe I became aware of my own incipient wish to be similarly honored one day. Today I am content with having been indirectly responsible for another's receiving it.[27]

Like others, Freud believed that his best work would evoke the severest criticism; to him, opposition was a sign of recognition. It is difficult to ascertain which came first, Freud's cosmic provocativeness or the savage attacks on him. "As I have long recognized that to stir up contradiction and arouse bitterness is the inevitable fate of psychoanalysis, I have come to the conclusion that I must be the true originator of all that is particularly characteristic of it."[28]

Freud thrived on opposition—whether it came from teachers, the resistances of patients, deviating pupils, or the outside world. He is said to have remarked to a favorite patient that "open opposition, and even abuse, was far preferable to being silently ignored."[29] "Many enemies, much honor," he wrote. "If the time of 'Recognition' should arrive it would compare with the present as the weird glamor of the Inferno does with the blessed boredom of Paradise. (Naturally I mean this the other way round.)"[30] While for some the existence of enemies would be impractical if not an inferno, for others it might seem like paradise. Being attacked can be, psychologically, a reassurance that one has something worth defending. Having enemies may also be an advantage in handling inner aggressivity; one is able to focus free-floating anger on an external object and at the same time not be burdened with guilt, since the opponent is worthy of anger and yet one does not actually injure him. The existence of enemies can, paradoxically, relieve one of inner stress.

Freud emphasized his isolation because, fundamentally, he liked it; he preferred to "hold back" concepts until they were thought through to completion. But at the time of disclosure he might then renounce his "claim to priority regarding that idea."[31] Freud could forget having fostered ideas in others, just as he had trouble remembering his own sources.

For a psychologist so interested in memory, false recollections (or "paramnesias," as he called them) about the origins of ideas deserved discussion; the illusion of remembering events is complementary to amnesias, gaps in memory. Illusionary memories were, Freud held, rather like *déjà vu* feelings—those strange impressions of having experienced something before; Freud considered "*fausse reconnaissance*,' 'déjà vu,' 'déjà raconté,*' etc., illusions in which we seek to accept something as belonging to our ego, just as in the derealizations we are anxious to keep something out of us."[32] Freud thought that unconscious memories and fantasies lay behind such illusions. Adler, before the break with Freud, described a specific kind of unconscious plagiarism which was relevant to the early analysts' predicament, whatever their good intentions:

> something that the plagiarizer knew seems foreign to him. The mechanism . . . leads back to the same root: to unsatisfied ambition, to the feeling of inferiority, and a feeling that can be verbalized in the following way: I cannot bear not to have been the first to say a certain thing.[33]

Freud tried to keep straight his own relation to predecessors. It was characteristic of his narrative style to begin a book or a paper by citing previous authorities on the subject. This expository technique not only provided a bench mark for his own contributions but also served as a means of subsuming rival views within his own emerging framework.

To such a truth-loving man, the danger of being convicted of intellectual theft was not a trivial matter. "I can never be certain," he wrote in old age, "in view of the wide extent of my reading in early years, whether what I took for a new creation might not be an effect of cryptomnesia [hidden channels of memory]."[34] In the case of a now forgotten Austrian writer, Josef Popper-Lynkeus, Freud was generous in pointing out how

parallel (in timing as well as conception) were their independent accounts
of dreaming; by such means, Freud revealed, "the originality of many of
the new ideas employed by me in the interpretation of dreams and in
psychoanalysis has evaporated. . . ."[35]

Freud also freely acknowledged the philosopher Arthur Schopenhauer
as a forerunner of psychoanalysis. "Probably very few people can have
realized the momentous significance for science and life of the recognition
of unconscious mental processes." In tones similar to those in which he
once would have deferred to Breuer, Freud declared that "it was not
psychoanalysis, however, let us hasten to add, which first took this step."

> There are famous philosophers who may be cited as forerunners—
> above all the great thinker Schopenhauer, whose unconscious "Will"
> is equivalent to the mental instincts of psychoanalysis. It was this
> same thinker, moreover, who in words of unforgettable impressive-
> ness admonished mankind of the importance, still so greatly under-
> estimated by it, of its sexual craving. Psychoanalysis has this advan-
> tage only, that it has not affirmed these two propositions which are
> so distressing to narcissism—the psychical importance of sexuality
> and the unconsciousness of mental life—on an *abstract* basis, but has
> demonstrated them in matters that touch every individual personally
> and force him to take up some attitude towards these problems. It
> is just for this reason, however, that it brings on itself the aversion
> and resistances which still hold back in awe before the great name
> of the philosopher.[36]

It was not Freud who first recognized Schopenhauer as a pioneer in
psychoanalysis, but his loyal follower Otto Rank:

> The theory of repression quite certainly came to me independently
> of any other source; I know of no outside impression which might
> have suggested it to me, and for a long time I imagined it to be en-
> tirely original, until Otto Rank (1911) showed us a passage in
> Schopenhauer's *World as Will and Idea* in which the philosopher seeks
> to give an explanation of insanity. What he says there about the
> struggle against accepting a distressing piece of reality coincides with
> my concept of repression so completely that once again I owe the
> chance of making a discovery to my not being well read. Yet others
> have read the passage and passed it by without making this discovery,
> and perhaps the same would have happened to me if in my young days
> I had had more taste for reading philosophical works.

Friedrich Nietzsche was perhaps an even more obvious antecedent to Freud as a psychologist of the depths, and Freud went on to explain:

> In later years I have denied myself the very great pleasure of reading the works of Nietzsche, with the deliberate object of not being hampered in working out the impressions received in psychoanalysis by any sort of anticipatory ideas. I had therefore to be prepared—and I am so, gladly—to forgo all the claims to priority in the many instances in which laborious psychoanalytic investigation can merely confirm the truths which the philosopher recognized by intuition.[37]

Nietzsche's insights succinctly epitomize many of Freud's most hard-won concepts: the best that is in us being founded on our most primitive selves; inward-turned aggression as a source of the formation of ethics and conscience; and the way we repress memories that conflict with our pride. Patients and pupils[38] usually brought these passages to Freud's attention.

At the Vienna Society's two meetings on Nietzsche in 1908, Freud described his personal manner of working. The *Minutes* report Freud's saying that he wanted to emphasize

> his own peculiar relationship to philosophy: its abstract nature is so unpleasant to him, that he has renounced the study of philosophy. He does not know Nietzsche's work; occasional attempts at reading it were smothered by an excess of interest. In spite of the similarities which many people have pointed out, he can give the assurance that Nietzsche's ideas have had no influence whatsoever on his own work.[39]

Freud thought that "the degree of introspection achieved by Nietzsche had never been achieved by anyone, nor is it likely ever to be reached again." Of course, Nietzsche was a moralist, and Freud took his own stand pre-eminently as a scientist. But Freud reiterated that "he has never been able to study Nietzsche, partly because of the resemblance of Nietzsche's intuitive insights to our laborious investigations, and partly because of the wealth of ideas, which has always prevented Freud from getting beyond the first half-page whenever he has tried to read him."[40] In 1924 he thought that

> the large extent to which psychoanalysis coincides with the philosophy of Schopenhauer . . . is not to be traced to my acquaintance with his teaching. I read Schopenhauer very late in my life. Nietzsche, another philosopher whose guesses and intuitions often agree in the most astonishing way with the laborious findings of psychoanalysis, was for a long time avoided by me on that very account; I was less con-

cerned with the question of priority than with keeping my mind unembarrassed.[41]

At times Freud could be extravagant about his debts. To a patient in 1930 he said he had taken all his ideas from the Russian novelists, especially Dostoevsky; Freud was willing to grant that they knew it all.[42] Yet he felt uncomfortable about being forced to read relevant literature. In his Fliess period Freud had written that "I do not want to read, because it stirs up too many thoughts and stints me of the satisfaction of discovery."[43] To a pupil in 1909 Freud wrote that he was "really very ignorant about my predecessors. If we ever meet up above they will certainly greet me ill as a plagiarist. But," Freud explained, "it is such a pleasure to investigate the thing itself instead of reading the literature about it."[44] "I invented psychoanalysis," Freud used to joke later, "because it had no literature."[45]

The issue of originality, and therefore of priorities, is inherent in the activity of any scientific group. Was it Darwin or Wallace who first discovered evolution through natural selection? What is worse, the most likely channels of plagiarism are not conscious. It is all too easy to misconstrue the sources of ideas without being dishonest. Depth psychology, moreover, is a field in which very little can be objectively proven; innovations come mainly in how we think about mental processes. In the natural sciences, struggles over priorities at least concern more objective discoveries.[46]

On the other hand, the more famous the predecessors Freud could cite, the more credence might be given to his own findings. In line with his early sense of identification with great warriors like Napoleon and Hannibal, Freud conceived of himself in the tradition of grand men in the history of science—Kepler, Newton, Copernicus ("though something similar had been asserted by Alexandrian science"), and Darwin.[47] Yet Freud felt that he himself had labored peculiarly alone. Einstein, for example, "had the support of a long series of predecessors from Newton onward, while I have had to hack every step of my own way through a tangled jungle alone."[48] Freud was acutely conscious that history does not invariably reward its discoverers; as he put it, "success does not always go with merit: America is not named after Columbus."

But Freud's sense of historical grandeur did not interfere with his genuine personal modesty. He always regarded his discovery of psychoanalysis as a piece of good luck: he remained a simple man with a great subject. Repeatedly he would qualify his assertions with cautious clauses

—"if I am not mistaken" or "if the future confirms"—even, sometimes, when he was most sure of himself. He crusaded for the cause rather than for himself. It was not false humility that moved Freud to repudiate the idea that he was a great man.

I have a high opinion of what I have discovered, but not of myself. Great discoverers are not necessarily great men. Who changed the world more than Columbus? What was he? An adventurer. He had character, it is true, but he was not a great man. So you see that one may find great things without its meaning that one is really great.[49]

Nor was Freud posturing when he said that he avoided reading Nietzsche in order to keep his mind "unembarrassed"; he was not simply evading the painful problem of priorities. For Freud to have hunted up his predecessors would have blunted the edge of his mind. Having made his initial intellectual commitments in the 1890's, Freud spent the rest of his life elaborating their implications; protecting his autonomy was essential to his continued development. Freud insisted on being his own man, seeing his ideas through with logic and lucidity. Thus sometimes the contributions of others seemed "foreign" or even unintelligible to him; he could not make use of the ideas of others until he had made himself ready for them. As he once wrote: "I do not find it easy to feel my way into unfamiliar trains of thought, and generally have to wait until I have found a point of contact with them by way of my own complicated paths."[50]

Some great men believe that nothing is real unless they have thought it. Freud did not welcome the original ideas of others, because he wanted to think through everything for himself, as part of his remaking of the world. He had a great need to arrive at new points in his work in his own way, by the continuous development of concepts already assimilated. He could not accept the ideas of others in their original form, but first had to transpose them into his own manner of thinking. Through his organized set of propositions, by means of the structured integrations of his concepts, psychoanalysis gained an intellectual dynamism all its own.

There was, in fact, an inner momentum in the development of Freud's ideas; despite his eccentricities and seeming pettiness, Freud invented something others could build on and use. He created his own world, which was not, however, just for himself, but had objective value as well. It is important to emphasize Freud's scientific accomplishments; fearful of the infantile, he set out to master it.

Freud was not content to live intellectually from hand to mouth, and the consecutive power of his thought has given his work much strength over rival psychologies. Even his extraordinary sensitivity to criticism formed an essential constituent of his work. Nothing in other people was indifferent to Freud. He picked up the most minute indications by which people express themselves, and gave these often overlooked aspects of behavior his greatest attention; by his watchfulness he constructed a far-reaching theory of human psychology. The man who was so attuned to resistances and who sometimes could misinterpret legitimate criticism or exaggerate hostile opposition, was also able to see bravely through some of his own self-deceptions.

4. Revisionism

SIXTY-YEAR-OLD CONTROVERSIES may sound like antiquated the-ological squabbles today. The terminology of that far-off psychoanalytic era is so alien to contemporary ears that it tends to obscure the issues that were in dispute. With the passage of time it is deceptively easy to read back later theoretical and clinical developments into views that Adler and Freud then held. Worst of all, it might seem largely a semantic struggle; as Lou Andreas-Salomé, however, pointed out, "one is sometimes led to suspect that a quarrel over terms results when the real issue is much deeper and not a terminological one at all."[1]

Broadly speaking, Adler stressed the extent to which emotional prob-lems stemmed from current conflicts and cultural disharmonies, rather than from the patient's childhood past. "Adler was not interested in the causes of a neurosis, but in its purposes," which to the biologically oriented Freud smacked of teleology. Adler interpreted "every symptom as a weapon of parasitic self-assertion; anxiety has the unconscious purposes of enforcing attention, it is a cry for help."[2] "Borrowing Hans Vaihinger's theory of fictions, Adler interpreted neurosis not as unconscious repression but as a deliberate ruse whereby one evades some over-whelming task."[3] Freud had distinguished between what he called the "primary gain" in an illness, the advantage the ego acquires from neurosis instead of facing something painful, and "secondary gain," the advantage a person may subsequently obtain through exploiting the neurosis once it is already constituted. In Adler's view, it was the secondary gain that needed attention, and there-fore the practical remedy lay in the therapist's active intervention, en-couragement, and short-term support. Valuable though this was as a complement to Freud's approach, Adler's judgment that schizophrenia can be seen as the outcome of radical discouragement[4] does indicate the relative shakiness of his views.

As opposed to analyzing problems, in the classic Freudian manner, Adler stressed the importance of the patient's synthesizing abilities. According to Lou Andreas-Salomé, Adler talked "about what the *psyche* does with *them* [guiding tendencies], whereas Freud keeps in mind what *they* do with the *psyche*."[5] Adler "always insisted on the patient's 'wholeness' being the key to his symptoms and would indeed attach no value to symptoms apart from the individual personality."[6] Adler stressed this aspect of his thought in the name he chose for his school, Individual Psychology. For him, the individual represented "a unified whole of which all parts cooperate towards a common goal."[7]

Adler proposed to help patients with their feelings of inferiority, and to lead them out of their self-preoccupied isolation into participation in the community. Through the cultivation of social feeling and through service to society, one could subdue egotism. Adler objected to what he considered Freud's egocentric approach to the world; to Adler, Freud's psychology was that of a "pampered child" who does not understand that to give is better than to receive; the Oedipus complex was "considered by Adler the result of faulty education in a spoiled child."[8] Freud conceived of the individual accomplishing great things in solitude and considered culture the result of instinctual frustration. He postulated that sublimated homosexuality played a role in the formation of social bonds: "homosexual tendencies . . . combine with portions of the ego-instincts, . . . thus contributing an erotic factor to friendship and comradeship, to *esprit de corps* and to the love of mankind in general."[9] In 1909, while Adler was still a member of Freud's circle, he presented a paper on a favorite subject, Marxism. At the time Freud said that "his attitude toward such lectures, which enlarge our horizon, can only be receptive."[10] After their split, however, he alluded to Adler's "socialist prehistory"[11] as a cause of their trouble.

Adler's technique of therapy was less clear-cut than Freud's; but Adler saw patients face to face, with greater intervals between sessions, and the therapy itself was shorter. As Lou Andreas-Salomé contrasted the two approaches: "Freud and Adler . . . differ with regard to the therapeutic method as the knife differs from the salve."[12]

In one sense, Freud's aims as a therapist were modest. As he correctly perceived about the Adlerians, "in their retreat from psychoanalysis, a section of Vienna analysts seem to have arrived at a kind of combination of medicine and education."[13] Instead of pedagogy Freud proposed his specific method of treatment, which aimed at enriching a patient from within. Freud regarded Adler's approach as similar to that of the clergy:

> Both of these procedures, which derive their power from being based on analysis, have their place in psychotherapy. We who are analysts set before us as our aim the most complete and profoundest possible analysis of whoever may be our patient. We do not seek to bring him relief by receiving him into the catholic, protestant or socialist community. We seek rather to enrich him from his own internal sources, by putting at the disposal of his ego those energies which, owing to repression, are inaccessibly confined in his unconscious, as well as those which his ego is obliged to squander in the fruitless task of maintaining these repressions.[14]

The Freudian position was that analysts "cannot guide patients in their 'synthesis'; we can, by analytic work, only prepare them for it."[15] Freud drew a sharp line between ethics and science, and Adlerians struck him later as "buffoons . . . publishing books about the meaning of life (!). . . ."[16] Freud thought that "the moment one inquires about the sense or value of life one is sick, since objectively neither of them has any existence. In doing so one is only admitting a surplus of unsatisfied libido. . . ."[17] Preaching to patients indicated a regression to pre-psycho-analytic forms of therapy and interfered with the progress of scientific understanding.

According to Jones, Adler was "a man with considerable gifts of psychological observation of a superficial order; he had little power of deep penetration."[18] Adler, in fact, seems to have possessed an intuitive practical understanding of human nature, whereas everyone concedes that Freud was a poor *Menschenkenner*, a "poor judge of men."[19] Adler, however, had more than a commonsense knowledge of mankind, though one would think any such talent would not be a liability for a psychologist; his contributions to psychology were by no means negligible.

Contemporary analysts, if asked to defend Freud's criticism of Adler, would find themselves in an embarrassing position. Freud's cherished notion of "libido" rarely appears in the professional literature today. By 1954 a leading orthodox analyst maintained that "as compared to the past, we now pay increased attention not only to early childhood but also to events and conflicts occurring in our patients in later life and in the present."[20] Erik Erikson emphasizes what he calls the "prospective aspects of the life cycle." In the early period of psychoanalysis, "regressive pulls in human life were . . . much more emphasized than what pulls a child out of the past, out of the family and out to wider experiences."[21] It is no longer heresy for psychoanalysts to practice short-term, supportive psychotherapy.

A successful movement can appropriate concepts from all sides, and Adler's ideas were swept up by Freud's pupils even though they may not have been aware of what they were doing. Adler was concerned with what are now known as "character problems." But "in 1914 Freud still believed that psychoanalysis could explain nothing but neurotic symptoms, not the total personality."[22] Although Freud pursued his ideas with fervor, and believed he had found "the truth," still he modestly disclaimed having constructed a "complete system"; he was not a comprehensive thinker, but had instead focused on "gaps" others had overlooked.[23] As he once wrote in defense of himself,

> complete theories do not fall ready-made from the sky and you would have even better grounds for suspicion if anyone presented you with a flawless and complete theory at the very beginning of his observations. Such a theory could only be a child of his speculation and could not be the fruit of an unprejudiced examination of the facts.[24]

Adler's theory, on the contrary, "was from the very beginning a 'system'—which psychoanalysis was careful to avoid becoming."[25] Freud criticized Adler for being overly concerned with normal psychology:

> Psychoanalysis has never claimed to provide a complete theory of human mentality in general, but only expected that what it offered should be applied to supplement and correct the knowledge acquired by other means. Adler's theory, however, goes far beyond this point; it seeks at one stroke to explain the behavior and character of human beings as well as their neurotic and psychotic illnesses.[26]

The heresy of that era has become the orthodoxy of today; one of the chief claims of contemporary ego psychology is that Freud's work can be built upon to explain successful adaptation as well as the malfunctioning that shows up in clinical practice.

Adler pioneered with his interest in the ego as an agency of the mind, and thought, prophetically, that this concept would help bridge the gap between the pathological and the normal. According to Lou Andreas-Salomé, Adler spoke of "ego symbols" instead of only sexual symbols disguised as ego.[27] Adler now sounds almost contemporary in the implications he drew from ego psychology for the understanding of children; like Anna Freud many years later, he concluded that it was "enormously difficult to differentiate between childhood defects and neurotic symptoms."[28] And like present-day dream psychologists, Adler was interested in the conflict-resolving function of dreaming.[29] Not surprisingly, when ego psychology became an authorized branch of psychoanalysis, Freud's pupils sensed the possible charge of "becoming Adlerian."[30]

Adler is no small figure in the history of psychotherapy. By 1920 he had directed his efforts to setting up consultations with schoolteachers; he had been intrigued all along with the psychology of the family group, "favored treating children in the home, and broadly speaking his emphasis on social factors is a precursor of today's community psychiatry. (The so-called Neo-Freudians like Harry S. Sullivan, Karen Horney, Erich Fromm, and Clara Thompson were all in this same stream of thought.)"[31] Along with his early work on the "ego instincts," which Freud admitted having neglected up to then, Adler advanced the "instinct of aggression" long before Freud would discuss any such concept[32] (though by the 1930's Adler had abandoned his own earlier theory).

Looking back on the controversy between Freud and Adler, it appears rather like what Freud described as the narcissism of small differences— a dispute between men who are so close to each other that they feel obliged to compare themselves, but who regard their differences as an implied reproach or criticism. The legend of Freud's defecting students later helped to unite his movement. As Freud himself knew:

> It is always possible to bind together a considerable number of people in love, so long as there are other people left over to receive the manifestations of their aggressiveness . . . it is precisely communities with adjoining territories, and related to each other in other ways as well, who are engaged in constant feuds and in ridiculing each other. . . .[33]

Adler was pursued by Freud with all the vengeance of his passionate nature. Freud looked upon Adler contemptuously, as a betrayer and a defector. And whether Adler turned away from psychoanalysis or was expelled makes little difference, since both elements played a part in what happened.

By the 1930's Freud's pupils came mainly from abroad, and his reputation was more secure in the world at large than in his native city. (It has been said that the Viennese Psychoanalytic Society is still singularly unable to attract young people.[34]) In Vienna, Adler became securely established among the working classes, while Freud was pre-eminent as a psychologist of the bourgeois Jewish intellectuals. Adler had always been interested in education, and the Adlerian school for children was admired by many as the best in Vienna. The success of Adler in Vienna, however, meant that his group was more exposed to the devastation of the Nazis, whereas the supranational psychoanalytic movement was better able to survive the European holocaust.

Freud never forgave the members of his Society who left with Adler. Paul Klemperer claimed that Freud would not even look at him in the street, which fits the pattern of Freud's behavior toward Breuer.[35] (When Jones mentions the "storm of opposition" Freud had to endure, and his "being cut in the street, ostracized and ignored,"[36] one can only wonder what the truth actually was.) Klemperer went to America and came back to Vienna after World War I; although his cousin, Paul Federn, was loyal to Freud and interceded in Klemperer's behalf, Freud resolutely refused to receive him.[37] In Freud's mind Adler was a heretic and Klemperer had gone over to the enemy. As Sachs pointed out, "every rupture with a former friend in Freud's life was final."[38]

Yet Freud never completely ignored a former ally. Immediately after the quarrel in 1911, Freud began to take retribution in his footnotes. Ernst Oppenheim was another member of the Society who left over the dispute with Adler. A reference to Oppenheim appeared in a footnote in the 1911 edition of *The Interpretation of Dreams*, but never thereafter. As James Strachey knew, this "omission . . . is no doubt accounted for by the fact that soon afterwards Oppenheim became an adherent of Adler's. . . ."[39] To Freud this was not a petty matter, for he took references in his writings very seriously. Oppenheim had also co-authored a short paper with Freud, "Dreams in Folklore," which disappeared from sight and was finally published only in 1958.

Toward Adler himself Freud was as unrelenting as he had once been considerate. For example, in a footnote to a case history originally published in 1909, Freud referred to "my colleague, Dr. Alfred Adler." In the next edition of this case history in 1913, Freud made a careful change: it was now "Dr. Alfred Adler, who was formerly an analyst. . . ."[40] Freud also eliminated some citations of Adler's work.[41] But this was only a small indication of how much he had grown to despise "little Adler." In a 1912 letter we find Freud saying that "I continually have to calm down my own personal irritations and must protect myself from those I arouse in others." Freud then went on to refer to Adler's "disgraceful defection . . . [he is] a gifted thinker but a malicious paranoiac. . . ."[42]

Freud was furious but self-controlled. In his essay of 1914 "On Narcissism," he paused to comment (as a criticism of Adler) that cases of neurosis existed "in which the 'masculine protest,' or, as we regard it, the castration complex, plays no pathogenic part, and even fails to appear at all." When asked for an interpretation of this sentence in 1926, long after the fight with Adler, Freud said he found himself in "an embarrassing position" over the question "whether there are neuroses in which the castration complex plays no part. . . ." Although it had clearly been part of his polemic against Adler, Freud could "no longer recollect what it was I had in mind at the time. Today, it is true, I could not name any neurosis in which this complex is not to be met with. . . ."[43]

All of Freud's articles and books after 1911 can be understood as part of an interplay with various opponents. But he also explicitly criticized Adler's views. He felt obliged to warn others against this dangerous departure from psychoanalysis, as well as to state his own position. In 1922, for example, Freud discussed Adler (along with Jung) as leading movements of "divergence from psychoanalysis," "evidently with the object of mitigating its repellent features." At the same time, Freud again mentioned that Adler had merely "reproduced many factors from psychoanalysis under other names. . . ." According to Freud, "it soon became clear that [Adler's theories] had very little in common with psychoanalysis, which they were designed to replace." Further, Adler's movement had exerted no "permanent influence on psychoanalysis."[44]

There were other instances of Freud's inability to let Adler go.[45] He continued his criticisms of him; little of worth was new in his work.[46] Egoistic motives were not as central as Adler believed; and narcissism, not the sense of inferiority, was the original primary state of childhood.[47] In a virulent footnote in 1925 Freud examined the "core of truth" in Adler's conceptualization:

> That theory has no hesitation in explaining the whole world by this single point ("organ inferiority," the "masculine protest," "breaking away from the feminine line") and prides itself upon having in this way robbed sexuality of its importance and put the desire for power in its place! . . . On the other hand, one hears of analysts who boast that, though they have worked for dozens of years, they have never found a sign of the existence of a castration complex. We must bow our heads in recognition of the greatness of this achievement, even though it is only a negative one, a piece of virtuosity in the art of overlooking and mistaking. The two theories form an interesting pair of opposites: in the latter not a trace of a castration complex, in the former nothing else than its consequences.[48]

In a letter in 1924 Freud wrote that a pupil showed "too much respect for the poverty of Adler. Just ask yourself what difference it would make to your work if you had never heard of the Adlerian theory."[49] Yet Freud was entitled to assert his priority over Adler: "You charge Adler with responsibility for the connection between ambition and urethral eroticism. Well, I have always believed it was my discovery."[50]

In 1932 Freud reconsidered Adler's ideas at some length, even though

Adler's Individual Psychology had "very little to do with psychoanalysis but, as a result of certain historical circumstances, leads a kind of parasitic existence at its expense . . . Its very name is inappropriate and seems to have been the product of embarrassment."[51] "If only because the inferiority complex . . . [had] become so popular" by then, Freud launched into another discussion of it; to be sure, Freud wrote, "the sense of inferiority which is supposed particularly to characterize neurotics . . . especially haunts the pages of what are known as *belles lettres*" rather than scientific writings. Adler's ideas on inferiority and the goal of perfection could now be more elegantly explained, Freud thought, by his own new concept of the superego; conscience and the sense of guilt can be seen as the consequence of inwardly turned aggression.

> The sense of inferiority has strong erotic roots. A child feels inferior if he notices that he is not loved, and so does an adult . . . But the major part of the sense of inferiority derives from the ego's relation to its superego; like the sense of guilt it is an expression of the tension between them. Altogether, it is hard to separate the sense of inferiority and the sense of guilt. It would perhaps be right to regard the former as the erotic complement to the moral sense of inferiority.[52]

In an interview that same year Freud is reported to have gone as far as he ever did in dismissing Adler's work: "Adler's departure was not a loss; Freud had no regrets for his going for he was never an analyst."[53]

Even at Adler's death in 1937, a quarter of a century after the debates in the Society, Freud remained adamant and unforgiving. Adler had died suddenly on a trip to Aberdeen, and Arnold Zweig mentioned in a letter to Freud that he was very much moved by the news. Freud shot back:

> I don't understand your sympathy for Adler. For a Jew boy out of a Viennese suburb a death in Aberdeen is an unheard-of career in itself and a proof of how far he had got on. The world really rewarded him richly for his service in having contradicted psychoanalysis.[54]

(In 1904 Adler had converted to Protestantism; he is reported to have "resented the fact that the Jewish religion limited itself to one ethnic group, and he wished to belong to a universal one."[55]) Although Jones included Freud's comment on Adler's death in his biography, Freud's son Ernst censored the passage in the volume of Freud's correspondence with Arnold Zweig, published in 1970, with no indication of an omission.

Freud's other pupils shared his antagonism to Adler; and Adler and his friends reciprocated Freud's bitterness. Over the years Adler had repeatedly, while advancing his own concepts, attacked those of Freud.

Adler even prided himself on having "much more than Freud . . . drawn the line sharply between Individual Psychology and psychoanalysis."[56] A year or two before he died, Adler referred to Freud's psychoanalysis as that "filth," "fecal matter."[57] Around this same period, an admirer of Adler's, Abraham Maslow, had a conversation with him in which at one point something was said that implied Adler's discipleship under Freud. Adler "became angry, flushed and talked loudly enough so that other people's attention was attracted. He said this was a lie and a swindle for which he blamed Freud entirely, whom he then called names liked swindler, sly, schemer. . . ."[58]

Few within psychoanalysis today would feel entirely comfortable to be identified with Adler's tradition.[59] The most orthodox have explicitly differentiated Freudian ego psychology from anything stemming from

Adler shortly before he died

Adler.[60] The American ego psychologist Ives Hendrick was exceptional in acknowledging that his idea of an "instinct to master" was "essentially the same as Alfred Adler's will to power."[61] Adler, the great dissenter, laid down an enduring perspective in human psychology. He was especially compassionate toward victims of social injustice, and he thought it of primary importance to help promote human dignity. Like Jean-Paul Sartre many years later, Adler understood how people, out of their own inadequacies and lack of self-esteem, can bolster themselves by degrading others, and how once a group or a class has been treated as inferior, these feelings intensify and can lead to compensatory maneuvers to make up for self-doubts. Adler was ahead of his time in understanding some of the social bases for destructiveness; for instance, those concerned with race as a psychological force in the modern world—men as different as Kenneth Clark[62] and Frantz Fanon[63]—have acknowledged themselves in Adler's debt.

5. Thanatos

THE DIFFICULTIES between Freud and Wilhelm Stekel came to a head a year and a half after the break with Adler. It would be a mistake, however, to regard the struggle with Stekel as a replica of that with Adler. For in all of Freud's confrontations, though there are certain thematic continuities, the specific issues and the personalities involved differed considerably.

Wilhelm Stekel (1868–1940), a practicing physician in Vienna, was one of the more undisciplined people to join Freud's early group. At that time it took a certain lack of balance to be interested in Freud's work at all, for psychoanalysis was a deviant activity. Stekel was a talented and prolific writer, as well as a poet and an excellent musician, and some of his clinical descriptions had great merit. But his work was somewhat journalistic, and his interest in sexuality remained quasi-pornographic; to some in the movement he seemed a dubious character with a dirty-minded interest in case material.

"In view of the courage displayed by their devotion to a subject so much frowned upon and so poor in prospects," Freud wrote in 1914, "I was disposed to tolerate much among the members to which I should otherwise have made objection."[1] In the period when Freud's support was meager he could be gullible about praise for psychoanalysis, and he took an immediate liking to anyone who was interested in his ideas.[2] He was susceptible to flattery—it could never seem too much—and consequently he occasionally misjudged people grossly. On the one hand, Freud did not like those who lacked an ethical or moral character; yet he was so captured by approval and admiration, especially from people of fancy and imagination, that he could easily let himself be taken in.

Stekel had once been Freud's patient, suffering from what on separate occasions Jones described as "a troublesome neurotic complaint" and "a very dangerous condition."[3] Jones related that Freud had been indiscreet enough to talk to him of Stekel's sexual perversion, although Jones thought Freud should not have done so; the biographer himself withheld the clinical details.[4]

It is not entirely clear what Stekel's difficulty was. In a conversation with a pupil Freud himself ruled out homosexuality.[5] In a published letter of Freud's there is at least a hint that what Jones referred to may merely have been masturbation. "One day when I am no more—my discretion will also go with me to the grave—it will become manifest that Stekel's assertion about the harmlessness of unrestrained masturbation is based on a lie. It is a pity that—but this is enough."[6] Freud deliberately, if guardedly, seems to have violated the privacy of this former patient who had by then become an enemy. (But his son Ernst, in his edition of Freud's collected letters, obscured this indiscretion through ignorance. In an editorial slip-up, he inserted a clause in the letter changing its meaning, so that it reads "Stekel's assertion about [my alleged claim of] the harmlessness of unrestrained masturbation," etc. But Stekel had been the only one in Freud's circle who had emphasized the harmlessness of masturbation, certainly not Freud himself, and Freud could not possibly have thought that Stekel had imputed to him a position on an issue which was a public bone of contention between them. Once the inserted clause is dropped, the meaning Freud seems to be implying becomes more plain.)

Whatever Stekel's troubles may have been,* a short psychoanalysis (a matter of weeks) with Freud relieved him, and he became, as he put it, "the apostle of Freud who was my Christ!"[8] It was at Stekel's suggestion that the Wednesday-evening discussion group was first started.[9] Nevertheless, not many years later Stekel can be found in the *Minutes* of the Vienna Society claiming priorities for himself, as well as pointing out Freud's precursors.[10] One follower of Freud's approved of Stekel's "one-

---

* He wrote about later having experienced potency difficulties for two years.[7]

sidedness" as having been "immensely fruitful," at the same time pointing out a passage in Freud which anticipated the content of a paper of Stekel's.[11]

Stekel became noted for his intuitive understanding of unconscious emotions, especially dream symbolism. He possessed, according to Freud, a "scent" for the unconscious.[12] Strachey thought "it was relatively late before . . . [Freud] realized the full importance of dream symbolism, largely under the influence of Wilhelm Stekel. It was not until the fourth (1914) edition of *The Interpretation of Dreams* that a special section was devoted to the subject."[13] Freud always acknowledged Stekel's psychological talent. Considering Freud's reluctance to put himself in the debt of his followers, his mention of Stekel's contribution to the growth of his own work (coming after their falling out) seems generous, even with its qualification:

> the *symbolism* in the language of dreams was almost the last thing to become accessible to me, for the dreamer's associations help very little towards understanding symbols . . . I was able to establish the symbolism of dreams for myself before I was led to it by Scherner's work on the subject. It was only later that I came to appreciate to its full extent this mode of expression in dreams. This was partly through the influence of the works of Stekel, who at first did such very creditable work but afterwards went totally astray.[14]

After the quarrel with Adler, Freud is said to have complimented Stekel: "I have made a pygmy great, but I have overlooked a giant close at hand."[15]

At a series of meetings of the Vienna Society in 1911 and 1912, the psychological and physiological effects of masturbation were debated; it was part of Freud's effort to "at last . . . subject the problems of man's sexual life to a scientific examination."[16] This discussion was part of a longstanding debate on the subject between Freud and Stekel. In 1908 Freud is reported to have declared:

> As far as the old controversy with Stekel about masturbation is concerned, Freud's opinion still differs from Stekel's. Masturbation as such may cause purely somatic damage, what we see as common neurasthenia. It is true, however, that the greater harm of masturbation is done in the psychic sphere—namely, in the character change that is brought about through this short-circuiting between desire and satisfaction, by a bypassing of the external world, and particularly through thus setting up a prototypical pattern for the entire [future] sexual life.[17]

Masturbation was, in Freud's eyes, "an antisocial act" involving "the general debasement of sexual life."[18] For some time Freud had believed that a special class of neuroses ("actual neuroses" versus "psychoneuroses") existed in which the besetting symptoms were the toxic outcome of unsatisfactory sexual practices. In these cases Stekel would instead search for the psychological meaning of the symptoms, which to Freud was to "greatly . . . overstretch psychogenicity."[19]

Freud opened his contribution to the 1912 meeting on masturbation in a spirit of post-Adlerian tolerance:

> It is never the aim of the discussions in the Vienna Psychoanalytic Society to remove diversities or to arrive at conclusions. The different speakers, who are held together by taking a similar fundamental view of the same facts, allow themselves to give the sharpest expression to the variety of their individual opinions without any regard to the probability of converting any of their audience who may think otherwise. There may be many points in these discussions which have been misstated and misunderstood, but the final outcome, nevertheless, is that every one has received the clearest impression of views differing from his own and has communicated his own differing views to other people.[20]

He yielded to criticism of one line of his reasoning (which sounded teleological and therefore too much like Adler), and at another point was able to grant "today what I was unable to believe formerly. . . ."[21]

> As regards the majority of the points of controversy among us, we have to thank the challenging criticisms of our colleague Wilhelm Stekel, based on his great and independent experience. There is no doubt that we have left very many points over to be established and clarified by some future band of observers and inquirers. But we may console ourselves with the knowledge that we have worked honestly and in no narrow spirit, and that in doing so we have opened up paths along which later research will be able to travel.[22]

Freud had long-standing hesitations about how Stekel's character and work might discredit psychoanalysis. He complained that Stekel relied "exclusively on his inspirations, instead of submitting them to the control of conscious thinking."[23] In 1909 Freud agreed with some critical remarks of Jones's about a book of Stekel's: "you have hit the mark. He is weak in theory and thought but he has a good flair for the meaning of the hidden and unconscious. His book cannot satisfy me personally, but it will do immensely good [sic] among the outsiders, his level being so very much nearer to theirs." A few years later Freud wrote of another book of Stekel's that it was "mortifying for us in spite of the new contributions it makes." Elsewhere Freud noted that "the conscious theoretical evaluation of things is not so easy for Stekel as is the tracking down of unconscious symbols, in which one's own unconscious serves as divining rod."[24]

Freud always admired rich imaginative capacities; but apparently Stekel felt free to invent illustrations whenever precise material was lacking.[25] Stekel also published reports of the discussions of the group in a Viennese newspaper, which, while serving Freud's propaganda purposes, was bound to make him uncomfortable.

As the years passed, the discussion group that had begun in Freud's waiting room had grown into the hub of an international movement. Stekel later thought that Freud's troubles with Adler, Jung, and himself stemmed partly from Freud's aspiration to solidify psychoanalysis into a coherent association. As Stekel recalled it, "the former harmony among the Freudians was gone; there was an heir-pretendency and a secret rivalry among the pupils."[26] At the time Stekel said that Freud "seems to harbor deep hatred toward Vienna"[27] and his following there.

We have seen that Freud's preference for Jung stirred up resentment among Freud's more senior pupils in Vienna. Adler's behavior had gone far toward realizing (and therefore justifying) Freud's worst anxieties about his group. As Stekel put it, Freud had the "primitive horde complex. He is the Old Man, afraid of his disciples."[28] (The imagery came from Freud's *Totem and Taboo*.) Stekel's "success in the field of symbolism made him feel he had surpassed Freud," as epitomized in an anecdote which became legendary. Stekel

> was fond of expressing this estimate of himself half-modestly by saying that a dwarf on the shoulder of a giant could see farther than the giant himself. When Freud heard this he grimly commented: "That may be true, but a louse on the head of an astronomer does not."[29]

Freud's private complaints about Adler were sometimes mixed with reproaches against Stekel. In November 1910, Freud wrote in a letter to a foreign pupil that the "tactlessness and unpleasant behavior of Adler and Stekel make it very difficult to get along together. I am chronically exasperated with both of them." With both Adler and Stekel on his hands, Freud had little energy for his writing: "I am having an atrocious time with Adler and Stekel. I have been hoping it would come to a clean separation, but it drags on and despite my opinion that nothing is to be done with them I have to toil on."[30]

Sending such comments abroad not only ensured that the movement as a whole would rally against Adler and Stekel, but at the same time reinforced the· conviction of his loyal followers that more than ever they formed an embattled minority. In February 1910, Freud had written that he could "no longer get any pleasure from the Viennese. I have a heavy cross to bear with the older generation. Stekel, Adler, Sadger. They will soon be feeling that I am an obstacle and will treat me as such, but I can't believe that they have anyone better to substitute for me." Freud also wrote of his "long pent up aversion for the Viennese" analysts.[31] In April 1911, Freud called Adler and Stekel "Max and Moritz," the two bad boys in a book by the humorist and cartoonist Wilhelm Busch. Freud thought Adler and Stekel were "rapidly developing backwards and will soon end up by denying the existence of the unconscious." "Adler is a little Fliess come to life again. And his appendage Stekel is at least called Wilhelm."[32]

When Freud had given up his post of president of the Vienna Society, in favor of Adler, he doubted whether his group would "even be very sorry" at his retirement; "I had almost got into the painful role of the dissatisfied and unwanted old man."[33] When Adler resigned as president on February 22, 1911, Stekel quit his post as vice-president at the same time; Stekel had taken the stand that there was no fundamental contradiction between Freud's views and those of Adler. Stekel also shared some of Adler's theoretical positions; both, for example, liked to interpret dreams bisexually. Freud's understanding of these difficulties was that "father is not doing enough for them. Criticism of the impotent Father. In fact my capacity to distribute patients has declined considerably in this year of continual agitation. With Stekel there will probably be a reconciliation; he is incorrigible, but fundamentally decent, and has done great service to psychoanalysis."[34]

The final break with Stekel came when Freud sided with Victor Tausk after an "ugly scene" between Stekel and Tausk at the Society.[35] Freud had wanted Tausk to supervise the book reviews in the *Zentralblatt*, of which Stekel was co-editor (along with Adler). Stekel stubbornly resisted this encroachment on his editorial powers. Freud wrote to the publisher requesting that Stekel be removed as editor. Stekel still did not budge, and also communicated his side of things to the publisher. Finally Freud arranged for everyone else connected with the journal to resign, leaving Stekel with an almost empty title. The *Internationale Zeitschrift* was then founded to replace the *Zentralblatt*.

Before finally leaving Freud's Society, Stekel seems to have engaged in some plans with Adler, his former ally in what Freud had called the Viennese "Opposition" to his preferential treatment of Jung and the Swiss. Stekel finally resigned from the Vienna Society on November 6, 1912, but later that month was still denying (to Lou Andreas-Salomé) that he "adhered to the Adlerian views . . . and this on the street and with all manner of witnesses." Lou records Adler complaining to her of Stekel's "disloyalty"[36] to him.

On November 3, 1912, Freud wrote of his relief at Stekel's impending departure from the Society:

> Stekel is going his own way. (I am so delighted about it; you cannot realize how much I have suffered under the obligation to defend him against the whole world. He is an intolerable person.) The occasion for the split was not a scientific one, but presumption on his part against another member of the Society whom he wished to exclude from the reviews in "his paper," which I could not permit . . . it is a blessing to have got rid of such a doubtful character. . . .[37]

It seems that the Swiss analysts were especially dubious about some of Stekel's work. Nevertheless, Freud was using grandiose terms (his "obligation to defend" Stekel against "the whole world") to describe what was a relatively minor dispute. Had the intolerable "presumption" been against Tausk, or really against Freud? On November 21 Freud wrote to a follower that "the blessing of having got rid of Stekel is worth some sacrifice," and the next week Freud told another of Stekel's "treason."[38] Shortly thereafter Freud wrote that "Stekel's loss is universally estimated as a great gain."[39]

Afterward, Freud handled the Stekel affair in ways which by now will seem familiar. Although he retained in his *Psychopathology of Everyday Life* some of the illustrative material of Stekel's which he had originally included, in later editions of the book Freud understandably excised the phrase "my colleague"[40] when referring to Stekel; and elsewhere in Freud's writings some direct citations to Stekel were removed. In 1909 Freud had written of Stekel that "for the true explanation of examination dreams I have to thank an experienced colleague," but after their break, in place of the phrase "the true explanation" Freud inserted the more cautious expression "a further explanation."[41] In turn, Stekel dropped a preface which Freud had written for one of his books from subsequent editions of the volume.[42]

As best he could Freud tried to pay his intellectual debts; but, as we have noted, anything not yet incorporated into his own train of thought was likely to seem "incomprehensible," "unintelligible," or "confused" to him. According to Stekel's account, Freud "confessed to me once (in a 'weak' moment) that every new conception offered by others finds him resistant and unreceptive. Sometimes he required two weeks to overcome such resistance."[43] Jones was right in thinking that when it came to the opinions of others, Freud "would listen politely to them, would show interest in them and often make penetrating comments on them, but somehow one felt that they would make no difference to his own."[44] By 1924 Freud considered among the "features well known to myself . . . that I am compelled to go my own way, often a roundabout way, and that I can not make any use of ideas that are suggested to me when I am not ready for them." Yet Freud thought (or hoped) it a "misconception that I deny things merely because I can't as yet judge or digest them."[45]

Stekel was the first to use the term "Thanatos" as an expression for the death wish, and although Freud later wrote more and more about the psychology of death, eventually postulating a death "instinct," his aversion to Stekel kept him from ever using "Thanatos" in his writings.[46] Jones noted only that it was "a little odd" that "Freud himself never, except in conversation, used for the death instinct the term *Thanatos*. . . ."[47]

From the very beginning Stekel laid great stress on the death theme. According to his account in 1910, anxiety was to be looked at as "the reaction to the advance of the death instinct, caused by a suppression of the sex instinct."[48] Stekel was responsible for the first examination of death symbolism in dream life, although Freud objected to the "confusion" that seemed to underlie the "assurance that the idea of death will be found behind every dream." Freud set down his reservations in a typical form: "I am not clear exactly what is meant by this formula. But I suspect that it conceals a confusion between the dream and the dreamer's whole personality."[49] In 1913, describing the origin of morality as a defense against hate —ethics as a means of protecting one's love objects from hostility—Freud realized that "this is perhaps the meaning of an assertion by Stekel, which at the time I found incomprehensible, to the effect that hate and not love is the primary emotional relation between men."[50] And by 1929 Freud could "no longer understand how we can have overlooked the ubiquity of non-erotic aggressivity and destructiveness and can have failed to give it its due place in our interpretation of life."[51]

Despite this awareness, Freud could not refrain from a subtle dig at what he thought had been taken from him, as well as a chance to imply that Stekel's contribution was unscientific. After paying tribute in 1922 to Stekel as the first to have given an account of death symbolism, Freud added in a parenthesis: "We must not omit to fulfill the duty, often felt to be inconvenient, of making literary acknowledgments."[52] Stekel singled out the death instinct when complaining of Freud's having later "adopted some of my discoveries without mentioning my name. . . ."[53]

After the quarrel with Stekel, Freud was perhaps more condescending than bitter. In 1914 he classified Stekel's interpretations as "reckless"; "this author's lack of a critical faculty and his tendency to generalization at all costs throw doubts upon others of his interpretations or render them unusable. . . ."[54] Freud always recognized Stekel's talent for deciphering the unconscious, though he distinguished his own type of work from that of Stekel. In an addition to *The Interpretation of Dreams* in 1925, Freud wrote:

> The analysis of this last . . . dream is clear evidence that I recognized the presence of symbolism in dreams from the very beginning. But it was only by degrees and as my experience increased that I arrived at a full appreciation of its extent and significance, and I did so under the influence of the contributions of Wilhelm Stekel. . . . That writer, who has perhaps damaged psychoanalysis as much as he has benefited it, brought forward a large number of unsuspected translations of symbols; to begin with they were met by skepticism [Freud's?], but later they were for the most part confirmed and had to be accepted . . . Stekel arrived at his interpretations of symbols by way of intuition, thanks to a peculiar gift for the direct understanding of them. But the existence of such a gift cannot be counted upon generally, its effectiveness is exempt from all criticism and consequently its findings have no claim to credibility.[55]

These public assertions were fully consistent with Freud's more private opinions. In 1923 Freud restated his views on Stekel:

> In spite of his unbearable manners and his hopelessly unscientific approach, I stood by him for a long time in the face of attacks from all sides, forced myself to ignore his far-reaching lack of self-criticism and truthfulness—an outer as well as an inner truthfulness—until finally on a certain occasion which revealed his treachery and ugly dishonesty "all the buttons of [even my] trousers snapped off."[56]

Compared to the defection of Adler and Jung, it would be fair to agree with Sachs that "the departure of Stekel stirred no deep feelings; Freud had never taken him quite seriously although he recognized his various gifts."[57] But Freud viewed him, nonetheless, as a despicable character. Stekel was, Freud wrote in 1924, a case of "moral insanity."[58] Freud regularly classed him among those who had defected, without paying much attention to him publicly as he had with Jung and Adler. Stekel could never pretend to be the author of a large-scale or comprehensive doctrine, although Freud thought Stekel might be said to have a "standpoint" toward his former master.[59]

As late as 1927 Freud retained a measure of respect for Stekel's abilities, or at any rate was concerned whether Stekel and he might share certain ideas. He delayed the publication of a paper of his on "Fetishism" until "he could find out whether Stekel had touched on the solution he was now propounding in a book Stekel had recently devoted to the topic."[60] Freud could not bear to read Stekel's book, and he commissioned Wittels (who had returned to the fold after being a follower of Stekel for a time) to read it for him.

Over the years Stekel repeatedly sought a reconciliation, but Freud remained unforgiving. After the onset of Freud's cancer, Stekel wrote to him in late 1923 with good wishes for the improvement of his health. In response to what Stekel wrote about their past relationship, Freud replied, unable to "refrain from contradicting you on a few important points":

> You are mistaken if you think that I hate or have hated you. The facts are that after an initial sympathy—perhaps you still remember how our relationship began—I had reason for many years to be annoyed with you while at the same time having to defend you against the aversion of everyone around me, and that I broke with you after you had deceived me on a certain occasion in the most heinous manner. (You never even mentioned this occasion—*Zentralblatt*—in your letters.) I lost confidence in you at that time and since then you have not provided me with any experience that could help me regain it.

> I also contradict your often repeated assertion that you were rejected by me on account of scientific differences. This sounds quite good in public, but it doesn't correspond to the truth. It was exclusively your personal qualities—usually described as character and behavior—which made collaboration with you impossible for my friends and myself. As you most certainly will not change—you don't need to, for nature has endowed you with an unusual degree of self-complacency—our relationship stands no chance of becoming any different from what it has been during the last twelve years. It will not annoy me to learn that your medical and literary activities have earned you success; I admit that you have remained loyal to psycho-analysis and have been of use to it; you have also done it great harm.

> My friends and pupils will find it easier to value your publications objectively when you begin to voice your criticisms and polemics in a more polite tone.[61]

Stekel, at this point an outsider for over ten years, had expressed many independent views; but though, like Adler and Jung, he used Freud's ideas as a backdrop for his own, his differences with Freud were expressed in more muted form. He may have been hopeful, then, when he tried to

VI

THE "CROWN PRINCE": CARL GUSTAV JUNG

1. The Science of Psychiatry

FROM FREUD'S POINT OF VIEW, Carl Gustav Jung (1875–1961) led the most painful of the "secessions" from psychoanalysis; for of all the pupils in Freud's life, Jung played the most substantial intellectual role. Jung was declared a "heretic" by Freud some time after his troubles with Adler and Stekel, yet the three controversies were historically interrelated. These men established the revolutionary tradition within psychoanalysis. All later psychoanalysts would be both tempted and frightened by the prospect of open rebellion; by the 1920's it would even be possible, as in the case of Otto Rank, for leading pupils to help push another into being a "deviant." Nevertheless, a wide range of evasive strategies existed, enabling an analyst to be his own person and yet a Freudian as well.

Of all possible accusations, "Jungian" is still probably the most devastating among Freud's intellectual descendants. Every subculture has its villains, and Jung is a particularly odious figure, partly because Freud had placed such high hopes on him. His later contact with the Nazis only put the final seal of disapproval on a man Freud's pupils had learned to detest. Jung is still dismissed today, following Freud's lead,[1] as a "mystic," supposedly as unscientific as the Socialist Adler.

The extent of the Freudian bitterness over Jung can be inferred from the difficulties the Jung archives encountered in gaining access to Jung's part of his correspondence with Freud. When, long after Freud's death but while Jung was still alive, the Jung archives offered to exchange with the Freud archives its half of the many letters between the two men, Anna Freud was unable to find Jung's letters to her father. The Jung archives then sent copies of Freud's letters, but without reciprocation. As soon as Jones needed Jung's letters for his biography, however, they somehow turned up, and even to the Freud archives it seemed rather awkward timing.[2]

*   *   *

In order to understand how the career of Jung ·came to occupy such a pivotal place in Freud's life and work, the full extent of Freud's feelings of alienation from the medical science of his day must be appreciated. Trained as a neurologist, Freud regarded the psychiatry of his day as uninterested in psychological processes, merely giving "names to the different obsessions but . . . [saying] nothing further about them."[3] As one of Freud's psychiatrically trained pupils later remembered it, the entries in pre-Freudian case histories were "stereotyped: 'the patient does not talk,' 'the patient talks nonsense,' 'the patient is not clean,' etc."[4]

The most prestigious chair in psychiatry in the Austro-Hungarian Empire, at the University of Vienna, was occupied by an old classmate of Freud's, Julius Wagner von Jauregg. With biting humor and a funereal laugh, Wagner was inclined to make ironic jokes about Freud's work. Although Wagner may have admired Freud personally, and they exchanged some friendly letters, as a leading psychiatrist Wagner had to take a position vis-à-vis psychoanalysis. What to Freud seemed like great discoveries were so much nonsense to him. It was not that Wagner was not scientifically oriented; he later became the only psychiatrist to win the Nobel Prize, for his fever treatment in cases of general paresis. Nor was Wagner uninterested in therapy; although he had a gruff, sometimes rude, manner, he was a kind man and his concern for his patients was evident.

Wagner was more mocking than aggressively hostile to Freud's ideas. But he was fair, and he permitted his assistants to do as they liked about Freud. Most of his staff, however, did not share his private respect for Freud, and they tended to be antagonistic to psychoanalytic work. Freud knew that the clinic at the University of Vienna was in enemy hands and that anyone studying under Wagner was not likely to acquire a friendly attitude toward Freud's innovations.

Freud had all the more reason to be delighted when in the spring of 1906 Jung wrote to him appreciatively from one of Europe's most prestigious centers of psychiatric training, the Burghölzli in Zurich, Switzerland. (Nevertheless, it was a sign of the low esteem in which psychiatry was held at that time that, when Jung decided to specialize in it, well-meaning friends were afraid he was jeopardizing his career.) Jung had been a staff member of the Burghölzli since late in 1900, and shortly thereafter had been asked to give a report on Freud's *Interpretation of Dreams*.

By 1906 Jung had achieved a respectable standing in the scientific community. In addition to his doctoral dissertation on the psychology of occult experiences, he had worked to perfect the technique of word association. The experimenter would call out a word, and then time the verbal reaction to the stimulus; Jung's aim was to detect repressed emotional conflicts, or what he came to call "complexes," through inappropriate responses and trains of associations. The more Jung interpreted associations in patients psychoanalytically, the easier it seemed to find meaning in psychotic symptoms which heretofore had seemed merely bizarre. In November 1906 Jung published a reply to a criticism of Freud's theory of hysteria, and in February 1907 he visited Freud in Vienna. At their first meeting they are said to have spent thirteen consecutive hours talking. Given Freud's status as an outsider in Viennese psychiatry, not to mention the general lack of popular recognition for his work, it is not difficult to understand how Freud succumbed to his occasional tendency to overestimate official recognition.

At this time Jung was the chief assistant to Eugen Bleuler, head of the Burghölzli and one of the world's experts in schizophrenia; he may now be best known for his concept of "ambivalence." Bleuler was interested in psychology and had succeeded in creating a cosmopolitan center for psychiatric training. Future analysts such as Ernest Jones, Sandor Ferenczi, Karl Abraham, and Abraham Brill spent research time there, and even after the final split with Jung, Freud was generous enough to acknowledge in 1914 that "most of my followers and co-workers at the present time came to me by way of Zurich, even those who were geographically much nearer to Vienna than to Switzerland."[5]

Bleuler and Jung represented the best academic psychiatry of their day. For Freud the period from 1906 to 1909 constituted a break with his past, as he emerged from the narrow sphere of Vienna into European psychiatry as a whole. Bleuler, a year older than Freud, was wary of the sectarian character of psychoanalysis. Freud later credited both Bleuler and Jung with having "built the first bridge from experimental psychology to psychoanalysis," through their use of the stopwatch as a tool for studying associations.[6] Bleuler accompanied Jung to the first Congress of analysts at Salzburg in 1908, after which Freud wrote that Bleuler had "made an uncanny impression on me in Salzburg; the situation can't be agreeable for him."[7] When Jung resigned from Bleuler's clinic in order to devote himself entirely to psychoanalysis, Freud, according to Jones, "came away rejoicing."[8]

In 1907 Jung had published a book on the psychology of dementia praecox, in which he attempted to show how this form of madness could be understood in terms of Freud's theory of neurosis. Jung "strove constantly to penetrate the deeper meaning of delusions and to interpret the material presented in schizophrenia which is characteristically rich in symbols, and so became one of the champions of the psychotherapeutic approach to the treatment of schizophrenia."[9] As Bleuler and Jung had worked on the dynamic motivation leading to psychotic conduct, they naturally tried to put this knowledge to therapeutic use.

Freud, since he thought ill of the alleged mediocrities in his Vienna group, wanted to transfer the center of psychoanalysis to Zurich. This attitude was partly a reflection of his over-all dislike of Vienna. Although it is difficult to evaluate Freud's frequent assertions of hatred for Vienna—whether, for example, he was simply adopting a romantic pose, since after all he chose to live there throughout his adult life—Freud once wrote in an anonymous autobiographical account in the 1890's: "I never felt really comfortable in the town."[10]

When, however, at the Nuremberg Congress in 1910 Freud's favorite Hungarian pupil, Sandor Ferenczi, made "some very derogatory remarks about the quality of Viennese analysts and suggested that the center of the future administration could only be Zurich, with Jung as President,"[11] the stage was set for the next few troubled years in Freud's Vienna group. Freud's preference for the Swiss was not only an organizational quest for men with the best brains to advance psychoanalysis, but also an intensely personal effort to achieve a more inclusive identity and to belong to a wider scientific community than had up to then been available to him.

As a Jew, Freud felt keenly the need for the help of the Gentile Jung. The Viennese psychoanalytic group was made up almost entirely of Jews, and Freud wanted psychoanalysis to be something more than a Jewish sect. Once Jung had been, as Freud put it, "formally adopted . . . as an eldest son," and anointed as his "successor and Crown Prince,"[12] Freud had to defend the Swiss against the jealousies of his other followers. As Freud once wrote to Abraham,

> Please be tolerant and do not forget that it is really easier for you than it is for Jung to follow my ideas, for in the first place you are completely independent, and then you are closer to my intellectual constitution because of racial kinship, while he as a Christian and a pastor's son finds his way to me only against great inner resistances. His association with us is the more valuable for that. I nearly said that it was only by his appearance on the scene that psychoanalysis escaped the danger of becoming a Jewish national affair.[13]

Freud felt that Abraham had "a rather excessive distrust" of Jung, "a trace of a persecution complex."[14] To the extent that Freud aimed to fulfill his early dream of founding a great intellectual movement, he could not hope to succeed until he had acquired Gentiles as followers; and as a Jew trying to subvert and overcome Christian standards of morality, Freud had to break out of the constricting confines of Jewish circles in Vienna.

After the split with Freud, Jung's pupils set out (as did Adler's supporters) to deny that their leader had ever been a disciple of Freud's.[15] Freud's language, however, could leave none of his followers in doubt about his own view of the matter. Freud's "face beamed whenever he spoke of Jung: 'This is my beloved son, in whom I am most pleased.' "[16] Freud had long identified himself with Moses, as the leader of a people who would reward him by turning on him with anger and disobedience. "Jung was to be the Joshua destined to explore the promised land of psychiatry which Freud, like Moses, was only permitted to view from afar."[17] Freud called Jung his "son and heir": "When the Empire I founded is orphaned, no one but Jung must inherit the whole thing."[18] The theme of succession was crucially important to a patriarchal man like Freud, and after the loss of Jung, Freud said that the "assurance that the children will be provided for, which for a Jewish father is a matter of life and death, I expected to get from Jung. . . ."[19]

Freud was nineteen years older than Jung and the undisputed leader of a growing movement; Jung did not try to be the organizer Freud was, and did not really like organizations, his own or anyone else's. It was only years later that something approximating a Jungian movement was established, and even then Jung did not take it seriously. So it is unlikely that Jung could ever on his own have aspired to head Freud's movement. Jung repeatedly felt burdened by the organizational demands Freud put on him, and Freud had to chide him about not taking his functions as a leader seriously enough; Jung ultimately came to the conclusion that his own work had to take precedence over his labors for the International Psychoanalytic Association.[20]

Although Freud could be uncritical toward a new supporter, in Jung's case he knew he had found an extraordinarily talented young man. One of Freud's sons described how exceptional was Jung's presence at the Freud family dinner table. Jung

> never made the slightest attempt to make polite conversation with mother or us children but pursued the debate which had been interrupted by the call to dinner. Jung on these occasions did all the talking and father with uncontrolled delight did all the listening. There was little one could understand, but I know I found, as did father, his way of outlining a case most fascinating . . . I think his most outstanding characteristics were his vitality, his liveliness, his ability to

project his personality and to control those who listened to him. Jung had a commanding presence. He was very tall and broad shouldered. . . .[21]

Freud was barely five feet seven inches tall, while Jung was six feet two; Freud was sensitive about his stature, at least when it came to Jung.[22] When Freud was in the United States with Jung in 1909, a photograph was taken in which Freud and Jung are seated together; Jung looks larger than Freud. In a group photograph taken at the Weimar Congress in 1911, however, Freud seems to be the taller of the two men; not only was Freud standing on something to achieve this effect, but Jung can be seen loyally crouching forward in order to permit Freud to stand out as the leader of the movement.

At the time of their first meeting Freud was in his early fifties, possessing not only a settled group of theories but a well-consolidated sense of himself; Jung was in his thirties and still very much the seeker. In 1909 Jung admitted in a letter to Freud that "the high degree of security and serenity, so characteristic of you, is in general not yet my own. . . ."[23] Freud commented admiringly on the differences between them:

> I have invariably found that something in my personality, my words and ideas strike people as alien, whereas to you all hearts are open. If you, a healthy person, consider yourself a hysterical type, then I must claim for myself the class "obsessive," each member of which lives in a world shut off from the rest.[24]

As Freud had earlier needed Fliess as his audience, so now he relied, in a more restrained way, on Jung: "the calm certainty I finally compassed which bade me wait until a voice from beyond my ken would respond. It was yours!"[25] (In later years Freud would write in almost identical language to more than one pupil about how much he needed to hear their voices "from the unknown.")

One key feature in their personalities joined them together for a time but in the end made continued cooperation impossible—their mutual rebelliousness. Jung made much of his own natural affinity for heresy, and Freud's challenge to the accepted psychological wisdom of the day was a source of the attraction that psychoanalysis held for him. "I myself am a heretic," Freud wrote on more than one occasion.[26] Before their first meeting Freud wrote to Jung that "the great names in psychiatry mean very little; the future belongs to us and our ideas, and everywhere youth is actively siding with us."[27] On their trip to America in 1909, a comment of Freud's surprised Jung as they sailed into New York Harbor. Whereas Jung was impressed by the view of the skyline, Freud remarked: " 'Won't

At Clark University in 1909.
From left to right, standing: A. A. Brill,
Ernest Jones, Sandor Ferenczi.
Sitting: Freud, G. Stanley Hall, Carl G. Jung

they get a surprise when they hear what we have to say to them. . . .' 'How ambitious you are,' exclaimed Jung. 'Me?' said Freud. 'I'm the most humble of men and the only man who isn't ambitious.' " As Jung recalled it, he had pointed out to Freud at the time that " 'That's a big thing—to be the only one.' "28

Freud acknowledged that the differences in their temperaments, which eventually made their parting seem inevitable, found a legitimate expression in their contrasting approaches to their work. When it came to studying character formation, for example, Freud thought that "Jung could do it better, as he is studying men from the superficial layers downwards, while I am progressing in the opposite direction."[29] As late as December 1910 Freud noted of a meeting with Jung that "he was magnificent and did me a power of good. I opened my heart to him, about the Adler affair, my own difficulties and my worry about what to do about the matter of telepathy." Freud alluded to his doubts about Jung's interest in mythology, and "bade him return in good time to the neuroses. There is the motherland where we have first to fortify our dominion against everything and everybody."[30]

It was typical of Freud not to strike up intimate friendships readily; yet when he did allow himself to grow dependent on someone, the intimacy was often sustained by letter writing: (For years Freud kept a record of letters sent and received.[31]) Whereas to Jung the correspondence between himself and Freud was not so crucial, to Freud it meant that as long as letters went back and forth the relationship was under his control as a writer.

None of this should becloud Freud's enthusiasm toward his young friend. After Jung brought a contemporary novel to Freud's attention, rather slight in terms of world literature but of interest to someone immersed in Freudian psychology, Freud wrote an essay about it "especially to please Jung."[32] Unlike Freud, who grew up in a bustling city, Jung had gone to school with children of peasants and was the earthier of the two men; when one of Freud's pupils commented that Jung's "jokes were rather coarse," Freud "sharply answered, 'It's a healthy coarseness.' "[33]

Jung's private life was in essential respects quite different from Freud's. Unlike Freud's wife Martha, Emma Jung approvingly understood her husband's work and became a practicing therapist herself. Jung and his wife, with their five children, founded an enormous family, which grew to be far more extensive than Freud's, and to outward appearances Jung remained the upright representative of conventional family behavior. Nevertheless, Antonia Wolff, a psychiatrist and former patient of Jung's, became his long-standing lover; even after the end of the affair their relationship was still friendly and close, and Jung's writings contain many citations to her work.

The dates of Jung's affair are not yet known, but it seems unlikely that Jung ever discussed these two women in his life with Freud. But Jung did allude to his "polygamous" tendencies, and maintained that "the prerequisite for a good marriage . . . is the license to be unfaithful."[34]

Emma Jung discussed with Freud at least some of her marital problems (she also tried to differentiate herself in Freud's life from someone like Fliess's wife: "do not count me among the women who, you once told me always spoil your friendships"[35]).

Austere, aloofly private, and as remote as he often was with pupils, Freud was intimate and unreserved with Jung. He confided in Jung's wife about the gradual termination of sex in his marriage to Martha, and in 1910 he wrote Jung: "My Indian summer of eroticism that we spoke of on our trip has withered lamentably under the pressure of work."[36] In later years—when Freud and his pupils castigated Jung's "cowardice" in the face of the "facts" of infantile sexuality—it must have seemed ironic to Jung that in reality he had lived a far less sexually frustrated life than Freud evidently had. Jung may have rejected Freud's concepts of sexuality, but then he had less personal need to make sex seem so all-important.

2. The Occult

FREUD AND JUNG SHARED an interest in the occult. Freud once wrote that one of the two themes that "always discomposed"[1] him was the problem of occultism, and spiritism and parapsychology were long-standing interests of Jung's. Freud worried that because of his own special interest in telepathy (or "thought-transference," as he preferred to discuss it) the charge of mysticism would be applied to his other work. But Freud and Jung had every reason to persist in this line of inquiry.

Freud's studies of dream life had already aroused the suspicion that he was unscientific if not mystical; but it was only because Freud chose to ignore received scientific wisdom that he was able to confirm some of the folk beliefs about the significance of dreaming. Both telepathy and dreaming had "experienced the same contemptuous and arrogant treatment by official science,"[2] which moved Freud to affirm the legitimacy of inquiries in the (for him) still unsettled of the two areas, telepathy.

In justifying his interest in the occult Freud harked back to his earlier discoveries about dreaming:

one must show one's colors and need bother about the scandal this time as little as on earlier, perhaps still more important occasions. . . .

on a reduced scale I had to repeat the great experiment of my life: namely, to proclaim a conviction without taking into account any echo from the outer world.[3]

As much as Freud wrote of his need for an "audience," he also wanted to stand alone. Freud believed he had reclaimed the intellectual territory of dreams from the swampland of mysticism; and just as dreams have long been associated with madness, in his effort to understand neurosis Freud felt entitled to explore the even murkier area of the occult.

A good deal of the initial interest in Freud's ideas came from people mainly concerned with parapsychological phenomena. Among Freud's pupils, Jung went the furthest in this field, in his attempts to understand graphology and astrology, even alchemy, and in later years flying saucers. Not only did Jung respect religious mysticism, but he even considered communication between the living and the dead a probability. These are some of the elements in Jung's work which enabled an opponent like Jones to dismiss him as "a breezy personality" who "lacked both clarity and stability in his thinking"; Jung had, Jones held, "a confused mind" marked by "mystical obscurantism."[4]

Jones entertained this harsh judgment of Jung's over-all character and work because for a time Jones feared the power which Jung's influence seemed to have over Freud; in later years Jones tried to warn Freud against taking telepathy seriously. Others shared Jones's anxieties; in particular, Karl Abraham was "discontented at what he called the tendency to occultism, astrology and mysticism in Zurich. . . ."[5] Freud told Abraham reassuringly that psychoanalysis would not founder scientifically because of Jung, for "on the whole it is easier for us Jews, as we lack the mystical element."[6]

Although Jones tried to lean over backward in describing Freud's interest in the occult, his own skepticism led him to exclude whatever he could not understand. A glance at the work of some of Freud's other pupils shows how important a role telepathic problems played in Freud's life. For instance, Sandor Ferenczi, a close friend and the most important Hungarian analyst, was an enthusiast in behalf of the reality of telepathy; Freud once singled out Ferenczi's occult studies as evidence that he was able to grow independently within psychoanalysis, succumbing neither to rebelliousness nor undue submissiveness.[7]

Ferenczi seemed to endorse the possibility of the power of prophecy, and once, before World War I, he brought a telepathist to a meeting of the Vienna Psychoanalytic Society. Someone would write something down, and the medium would try to divine what it was.[8] Whenever one of his

Jung in his study in 1945

disciples brought a report of a telepathic dream, or an account of something a specially endowed person seemed able to perform, Freud—without denying the existence of such phenomena—would tell his followers to be cautious. In 1910 the *Minutes* of the Vienna Society report "a long informal discussion" "about the phenomena of spiritism, occultism and clairvoyance. . . ."[9]

In the period before World War I, perhaps because the future of psychoanalysis was too uncertain to permit the inclusion of something like telepathy, Freud remained at least publicly skeptical. Speaking at the end of the 1910 meeting of the Society at which "spiritism, occultism and clairvoyance" were informally discussed, Freud said that "if such things exist at all, they are physiological and not psychological. Besides, it seems that, *subjectively*, the impulse to cheat must always be present."[10] Nevertheless, Freud's most loyal disciples continued to write about telepathy and the occult—as good an indication as any of Freud's own continued interest in the subject.[11]

Although Freud could be open to the possibility of telepathy and "discomposed" by the subject of occultism, he could also be tough-minded about the realm of the mysterious and the miraculous. When Freud wrote of "the general tendency of mankind to credulity and a belief in the miraculous,"[12] he was referring to precisely what he intended psychoanalysis to conquer. And his "suspicion that the interest in occultism is in fact a religious one"[13] points to the worst origin a subject could have, as far as he was concerned. Freud wrote, regretfully, that "when psychoanalysis and occultism encounter each other . . . the former has, so to speak, all our mental instincts against it; the latter is met half-way by powerful and mysterious sympathies."[14] To Freud, opposition signified that one had hit upon a deep truth; to be met halfway meant that one was, intentionally or not, pandering to what people self-deceptively want to believe.

Since Freud held that "the craving of mankind for mysticism is ineradicable, and . . . makes ceaseless efforts to win back for mysticism the territory it has been deprived of by *The Interpretation of Dreams*,"[15] it behooved him at least to try to explain mystical yearnings. In the end he held that mysticism was "the obscure self-perception of the realm outside the ego, of the id."[16] The human feelings Freud saw behind mystical beliefs were linked to other emotions he had difficulty understanding or tolerating. Feelings of "transience," as well as the "oceanic feeling," were not readily assimilated to Freud's ideal of rationality; it would seem that every ecstasy was suspect as an interference in the intellectual control that was so important to him.

To Freud, the essence of science was that it represented "the most complete renunciation of the pleasure principle of which our mental activity is capable."[17] He prided himself on his ability to seek out mental causation where common sense might not perceive even the presence of anything problematic; he repudiated the view that "it is precisely with regard to the unimportant, indifferent decisions that we could just as well have acted otherwise: that we have acted of our free—and unmotivated—will."[18] If Freud wanted his science to bring home unpleasant truths, not likely to please, he also recognized the presence of chance: "I believe in external (real) chance, it is true, but not in internal (psychical) accidental events. With the superstitious person it is the other way round."[19] The cool rationalist in Freud thought it would be superstitious to find causation everywhere, when coincidences do in fact take place. He was against "an exaggerated respect for the 'mysterious unconscious.' It is only too easy to forget that a dream is as a rule merely a thought like any other."[20]

Freud went so far as to deny the legitimacy of intuition in psychology:

there are no sources of knowledge of the universe other than the intellectual working-over of carefully scrutinized observations—in other words, what we call research—and alongside of it no knowledge derived from revelation, intuition or divination . . . Intuition and divination would be . . . [methods of research] if they existed; but they may safely be reckoned as illusions, the fulfillments of wishful impulses.[21]

To link intuition with "revelation" and "divination" was to damn it as a species of hocus-pocus. Elsewhere Freud wrote that " 'empathy' . . . plays the largest part in our understanding of what is inherently foreign to our ego in other people."[22] Yet he was so rationalistic that when writing about processes of constructing theories he commented: "I do not think a large part is played by what is called 'intuition' in work of this kind." And: "From what I have seen of intuition, it seems to me to be the product of a kind of intellectual impartiality."[23]

As one biographer has observed, there were at least two distinct sides to Freud:

One sombre, passionate, inclined to self-torment and superstition, sometimes tender to the point of sentimentality, and yet blessed with a sense of humor . . . ; the other reasonable and somewhat argumentative, always ready to recognize his mistakes, provided they were proved to him, and with a tendency to lay down the law and to draw a lesson from everything.[24]

As Freud grew older, these two aspects—the romantic respecter of the unknown and the rationalistic scientist of the observable—became more and more distinct, and traits that had earlier been seen by Freud's pupils as merely private eccentricities tended to coalesce behind his defense of the existence of telepathy. Oddly enough, this turn toward a belief in thought-transference came at a period in Freud's life, the 1920's, when he was putting more and more stress on the purely scientific, as opposed to the artistic, side of psychoanalysis. Although many of these trends in Freud's thought took place long after Jung left Freud's circle, if one is to understand what had brought the two men together as well as how they came to separate, one has to see Freud's career as a whole.

Freud recorded in 1901 that, at the time of his engagement to Martha,

During the days when I was living alone in a foreign city [Paris]— I was a young man at the time—I quite often heard my name suddenly called by an unmistakable and beloved voice; I then noted down the exact moment of the hallucination and made anxious enquiries of those at home about what had happened at that time. Nothing had happened.

By 1924, however, Freud's attitude toward telepathy had changed enough for him to append a new sentence to the account of what he had called his experiences of "hallucination": "I must however confess that in the last few years I have had a few remarkable experiences which might easily have been explained on the hypothesis of telepathic thought-transference."[25]

Freud participated in at least one telepathic séance,[26] and was as open to the occult as the great, yet sometimes gullible, psychologist William James. Freud principally had in mind, not communing with the dead, but wordless communication among the living. He was both fascinated and repelled by the possibility of two minds being in touch without the help of a conscious bridge. Telepathy was an attractive concept to Freud because with it he might be able to extend the significance of the unconscious. But he feared that it would seem that "after a détour through science, we were becoming superstitious again."[27] And he was once quick to repudiate an apparent instance of telepathy between mother and child, stating that it was a case of their unconscious minds being in such close contact as not to need thought-transference to explain it.

At least as early as 1889 Freud referred in his writing to "the obscure problems bordering on hypnotism (thought-transference, etc.). . . ."[28]

To the extent that he himself had relied on hypnotic technique in his earlier psychotherapy, Freud was familiar with the magic-like susceptibilities of the human psyche. He thought that "the state of sleep seems particularly suited for receiving telepathic messages,"[29] so that the study of thought-transferences seemed to flow logically from his prior writing on dreams. Not only did Freud point to "the incontestable fact that sleep creates favorable conditions for telepathy," but, perhaps thinking of sleep as a temporary form of death, he held that "by far the greater number of all telepathic intimations relate to death or the possibility of death. . . ."[30]

No matter how impartial Freud tried to be about telepathy, his pre-occupation with death was excessive to the point of superstition. If he met someone who resembled him, he was reminded of the folk belief that seeing one's double constitutes a prophecy of death.[31] He wrote openly that in "unconscious thought-operations with numbers I find I have a tendency to superstition. . . ." and invariably these numbers bore on the date of his death: "I generally come upon speculations about the duration of my own life and the lives of those dear to me. . . ."[32] Jones reports that in Freud's sixtieth year he "superstitiously believed he had only another couple of years to live,"[33] and on a trip to Italy, Freud was haunted by the number sixty-two. At various times he believed he was going to die at a fixed age; at eighty-one he entertained the idea that he would die at the same age as his father had.

Freud's distress over telepathy was intimately connected with the problem of mortality. If his "double" was "the uncanny harbinger of death," he also represented "an assurance of immortality. . . ."[34] Freud thought that the belief in "the 'double' was originally an insurance against the destruction of the ego, an 'energetic denial of the power of death,' as Rank says; and probably the 'immortal' soul was the first 'double' of the body."[35]

Whenever a thought of Freud's was precisely duplicated in external reality, his superstitious fears were aroused. In honor of Freud's fiftieth birthday in 1906, his followers struck a medallion for him, with a motto from Sophocles' *Oedipus Rex*—"Who divined the famed riddle [of the Sphinx] and was a man most mighty." These words struck Freud as un-canny, since it turned out that they were identical to the inscription he had, years before, fantasied for his own bust at the University of Vienna. When Freud saw the medallion's message, "he became pale and agitated and in a strangled voice demanded to know who had thought of it."[36]

Freud's acute sensitivity to memory, its selections and distortions, logically supported his interest in "*déjà vu*" feelings. But his research on such illusions was also allied to a more controversial set of private feelings, namely his reaction of distress if not repulsion toward what he discussed under the rubric of the uncanny. To Freud, the uncanny meant the disagreeable, and in an essay he related it "to what is frightening—to what arouses dread and horror. . . ."[37] Freud's curiosity about the uncanny was not untouched by anxiety. Fittingly enough for a man so interested in the problem of the double, he was aware of others who had delved into the supernatural. Significantly, Freud introduced his contribution to an understanding of the uncanny with a disclaimer of originality. As his essay was composed during the isolation imposed by conditions in Vienna during World War I, Freud wrote that he had

> not made a very thorough examination of the literature, especially the foreign literature, relating to this present modest contribution of mine, for reasons which, as may easily be guessed, lie in the times in which we live; so that my paper is presented to the reader without any claim to priority.[38]

It is difficult, thinking back on Freud's troubles with Adler and Stekel, not to conclude that Freud's concern over priorities, however legitimate, also derived from private anxieties. In this connection it is interesting that the second issue that always "discomposed" Freud, in addition to the problem of occultism, was the controversy over the supposed true author of the plays of Shakespeare.[39]

Freud chose to look on the negative side of feelings of the uncanny. He thought that such experiences could be "traced back without exception to something familiar which has been repressed," since the uncanny for him was "that class of the frightening which leads back to what is known of old and long familiar."[40] If Jung's master Bleuler had made an "uncanny" impression on Freud at the Salzburg Congress, that specific incident can perhaps be explained by Freud's more general principle that "we can . . . speak of a living person as uncanny, and we do so when we ascribe evil intentions to him."[41] (Bleuler was a rival leader from whom Freud succeeded in winning Jung away.)

Freud was to have some of the same problems with Jung as he had earlier with Fliess and Adler, at least in their controversies over who had which idea first. Psychoanalytic treatment hinged on the transference of thoughts, conscious as well as unconscious, from the patient to the analyst, so it was not surprising for Freud to try to understand and give a rational explanation for telepathic communications. Perhaps a contemporary analyst might see in Freud's "torment"[42] over thought-transference (as in his number anxieties) a remnant from his childhood past: a panicky fear that someone can take something away from him and a reaffirmation that he was his mother's first if not only child.

At least some such explanation is necessary to account for the fact that a disciplined scientist like Freud went so far toward accepting the reality of telepathy. Before World War I, Freud might, late at night and at a coffeehouse, mention to followers his belief in something mystical of which he did not want to speak. As time passed, however, he grew bolder, and to a small group of adherents in 1921 he read a paper on "psychoanalysis and telepathy," which remained unpublished until after his death. Although he claimed that his "personal attitude to the material" remained "unenthusiastic and ambivalent," as the years passed he grew more outspoken.[43]

In 1932 Freud wrote of occult problems that "when they first came into my range of vision more than ten years ago, I too felt a dread of a threat against our scientific *Weltanschauung*, which, I feared, was bound to give place to spiritualism or mysticism if portions of occultism were proved true. Today I think otherwise."[44] Freud came to believe that he had enough material about telepathy from his clinical experiences to conclude that "the scales weigh in favor of thought-transference."[45] As with his earlier ideas, Freud insisted on describing his contribution as factual, rather than conceptual: "there remains," he now wrote, "a strong balance of probability in favor of thought-transference as a fact."[46] As he wrote in a letter that same year, "behind all so-called occult phenomena lies something new and important: the fact of thought-transference, i.e. the transferring of psychical processes through space to other people."[47] Like dreams, occult phenomena hid their secret meaning behind their manifest content.

Perhaps it is not surprising that Freud should have at times been as much a believer in telepathy as Jung. In explaining the roots of superstitiousness, Freud had noted "the predilection felt by obsessional neurotics for uncertainty and doubt," which led them "to turn their thoughts by preference to those subjects upon which all mankind are uncertain and upon which our knowledge and judgments must necessarily remain open to doubt"; here Freud mentioned death and memories, in addition to paternity and immortality.[48] Whatever may have led Jung to be interested in the occult, Freud's personal obsessionality provided him with sufficient motives.

To be sure, Freud thought that his "own superstition has its roots in suppressed ambition (immortality) and in my case takes the place of that anxiety about death which springs from the normal uncertainty of life. . . ."[49] Both Freud and Jung had their yearnings for immortality, and the quarrel between them is a good illustration of Freud's principle that sometimes one interprets the unconscious motivation of others in order to remain blind to one's own. Freud's method of treatment tended to overestimate the importance of psychical reality, and Freud held that this tendency was at the source of superstition.

Freud wrote in 1901 that in people of "high intelligence"

> superstition derives from suppressed hostile and cruel impulses. Superstition is in large part the expectation of trouble; and a person who has harboured frequent evil wishes against others, but has been brought up to be good and has therefore repressed such wishes into the unconscious, will be especially ready to expect punishment for his unconscious wickedness in the form of trouble threatening him from without.[50]

Such a characterization would fit Freud fairly closely. According to his view, those with obsessive tendencies find that they experience unusual coincidences—such as repeatedly coming across the number sixty-two—which are really projections of their own inner feelings; this also helps to explain the accompanying superstitious belief that thoughts are actualized in the outer world. Freud, however, once claimed that he was "one of those unworthy people in whose presence spirits suspend their activity and the supernatural vanishes away, so that I have never been in a position to experience anything myself which might arouse a belief in the miraculous."[51]

But there can be no doubt of Freud's involvement in occultism; he once wrote, "If I had my life to live over again I should devote myself to psychical research rather than to psychoanalysis."[52] There may be only an apparent paradox in a scientist's going so far in this direction as Freud did. Moved by his own inner needs, Freud had founded a therapeutic technique and a theoretical system; and out of his treatment of patients he had found self-curative help. As neatly as one may structure Freud's personality, however, it was never so easy to understand in real life. But it should be at least possible to recognize how certain inner conflicts in Freud, even if they can be only partially understood, may have been obscure to Freud himself, and at the time played havoc with some of his key human relationships. It was Freud's mystical yearnings, and his uneasy interest in the occult, which, in addition to objective scientific differences, contributed to the falling out between him and his chosen successor.

3. Oedipus

THE CONTROVERSY WITH JUNG fits into an already well-established pattern in Freud's life. He sometimes extended himself to people too enthusiastically and tended to idealize them. He then later blamed them for not having qualities which he himself had imputed to them, for having failed to live up to his fantasied conception of them.

In observing Freud's relationships with his favorite pupils, as well as his mentors, one may be reminded of what Freud had written in *The Interpretation of Dreams* about his childhood relationship with his nephew John:

> All my friends have in a certain sense been reincarnations of this first figure. . . . My emotional life has always insisted that I should have an intimate friend and a hated enemy. I have always been able to provide myself afresh with both, and it has not infrequently happened that the ideal situation of childhood has been so completely reproduced that friend and enemy have come together in a single individual—though not, of course, both at once or with constant oscillations, as may have been the case in my early childhood.[1]

Throughout his life Freud maintained a number of friendships (for example, with Oskar Rie and Leopold Koenigstein) that did not follow this uncle-nephew pattern; but these men knew little or nothing about his work. His loyal pupils publicized the "cowardice," "resistance," and "flight from the unconscious" of those erstwhile colleagues who let Freud down. Although there may be an element of truth in these charges, at the same time one must look at the problem from the perspective of Freud's most talented disciples. To Jung, as to Adler before him, it was intolerable to have a genius block his way, and for the sake of relieving his frustration and continuing his creativity, Jung had to set out on his own.

There were special features of Freud's circle that facilitated these conflicts. For one thing, psychoanalysis was "science" and grounded on objective evidence, and yet at times Freud would point to the autobiographical nature of his discoveries. How was a follower to keep clear which part of Freud's work represented a contribution to neutral science and which merely reflected personal idiosyncrasies? For that matter, how was Freud himself to tell in a given case whether one of his ideas was realistically being threatened with distortion by a follower or whether one of his personal complexes had been activated by an ambitious and rivalrous disciple? Freud thought he had special property rights to his field, and at the same time wanted to think of psychoanalysis as independent of human will and a part of Western science.

In addition, the controversies in psychoanalytic circles have tended from the first to be relatively few in number, although this is probably more true now than before World War I. In view of the divisions that have occurred in psychoanalysis, this statement may seem surprising; but by discouraging controversy and by promoting conformity to the group's will (if not Freud's), psychoanalysis has missed many opportunities for airing its intellectual grievances and settling its differences of opinion; as a result, the blow-ups have tended to be of disproportionate strength. Admittedly, as Freud himself once pointed out, the nature of the evidence in psychoanalysis is such that one can never obtain the same degree of certainty as in other fields;[2] excommunication, then, becomes a more frequently used method of settling a dispute.

At the height of his difficulties with Freud in 1912–13, Jung apparently thought that Freud's kind of leadership was responsible for mobilizing the various rebellions against him. In an unsent letter to Jung, Freud referred to "Your reproach that I abuse psychoanalysis for the purpose of keeping my pupils in infantile dependency and that therefore I myself am responsible for their infantile behavior towards me. . . ."[3] By keeping pupils dependent until their individuality could find expression only in revolt, by making the profession of an analyst a question of either/or, Freud helped create oedipal reactions. Wittels believed that Freud "certainly had a way of treating his pupils like children with an alteration of rewards and punishments, and by keeping them out of bad company."[4] Jung wrote in a letter in March 1913 that "among neurotics, there are not a few who do not require any reminders of their social duties and obligations, but are born and destined rather to be bearers of new cultural ideals."

As long as we look at life only retrospectively, as is the case in the psychoanalytic writings of the Viennese school, we shall never do justice to these persons and never bring them the longed-for deliverance. For in this way we train them only to be obedient children and thereby strengthen the very forces that made them ill—their conservative backwardness and submission to authority . . . the impulse which drives . . . [them] out of their conservative father-relationship is by no means an infantile wish for insubordination; it is a powerful urge to develop their own personality, and the struggle for this is for them an imperative duty. Adler's psychology does much greater justice to this situation than Freud's.[5]

After their falling out Freud described Jung as "a person who was incapable of tolerating the authority of another, but who was still less capable of wielding it himself, and whose energies were relentlessly devoted to the furtherance of his own interests."[6]

Jones took some pains to disabuse the public of the reputation for intolerance that Freud had acquired, and in particular he attacked the analogy that compared psychoanalysis to a religious movement, with Freud a new Pope. According to Jones's version of these misunderstandings,

> Freud was of course the Pope of the new sect, if not a still higher Personage, to whom all owed obeisance; his writings were the sacred text, credence in which was obligatory on the supposed infallibilists who had undergone the necessary conversion, and there were not lacking the heretics who were expelled from the church. It was a pretty obvious caricature to make, but the minute element of truth in it was made to serve in the place of the reality, which was far different.[7]

Although Jones did not think "the general idea of a Pope"[8] was of much help in understanding Freud, the latter's honesty was such as to undermine Jones's later attempts to clarify the master's position. As Ludwig Binswanger remembered it: "I questioned . . . [Freud] as to how it had come about that it was precisely his oldest and perhaps most talented disciples, Jung and Adler, to give examples, who had broken away from him. He replied" not without some self-irony: "'Precisely because they too wanted to be Popes.' "[9] In 1924 Freud again employed the religious metaphor in writing of Jung and Adler as "the two heretics."[10]

Shortly after Jung's introduction to Freud the troubling theme of Oedipus came up. The day after Jung's first visit, in February 1907, Freud is said to have questioned him (along with Binswanger, a fellow Swiss psychiatrist) about their dreams; as Jung's companion remembered it, "I do not recall Jung's dream, but I do recall Freud's interpretation of it, namely, that Jung wished to dethrone him and take his place."*[11] Jung undoubtedly aspired to accomplish at least as much as Freud had, and by

---

* Jung's wife once wrote to Freud about his "father-complex": "do not think of Carl with a father's feeling: 'He will grow, but I must dwindle,' but rather as one human being thinks of another, who like you has his own law to fulfill."[12]

the end of their relationship he may have had death wishes against Freud. But classical mythology, which, Freud felt, so often develops as a conscious theme what is deeply buried within us, relates, in addition to Oedipus' crime, the intended infanticide of his father, and tells, as well, of other fathers who took the initiative against their sons; Kronos destroyed all his sons save one, and he was Zeus.

Even when Freud and Jung were on their most intimate terms, signs of strain and tension between them could be detected. Jung felt "veneration" for Freud, as he built up his " 'religious' crush"; as a boy Jung had been the victim of a sexual assault by a man he had once worshipped, and therefore he felt uneasy about his feelings for Freud.[13] On his part Freud thought that "a transference on a religious basis would strike me as most disastrous; it could end only in apostasy. . . ."[14]

Both were invited to speak at the twentieth anniversary of Clark University in 1909; so (together with Ferenczi) they sailed across the Atlantic. During their voyage they exchanged dreams. In Freud's eyes, Jung and Ferenczi were his psychoanalytic heirs; they told Jones afterward that "the predominant theme running through" Freud's dreams "was

Ludwig Binswanger at the International Congress for Psychoanalysis in Lucerne, Switzerland, August 1934

care and anxiety about the future of his children and of psychoanalysis."[15]
Jung recalled, however, that at certain points Freud refused to provide
his associations to the dream material he offered, on the grounds that it
might undermine his authority as leader of the psychoanalytic movement
to be quite so open; and this refusal of intimacy, for such a reason, was
to weaken Freud's position in Jung's eyes.[16] Jung is said to have thought
the problem with Freud's dreams was that they related to

> the triangle—Freud, his wife, and [his] wife's younger sister. Freud
> had no idea that I knew about the triangle and his intimate relationship
> with his sister-in-law. And so, when Freud told me the dream in
> which his wife and her sister played important parts, I asked Freud to
> tell me some of his personal associations with the dream. He looked
> at me with bitterness and said, "I could tell you more, but I cannot
> risk my authority." That, of course, finished my attempt to deal with
> his dreams.[17]

The most spectacular signs of tension came in two fainting spells of
Freud's. One took place in Bremen, before they set out on their 1909 trip
to the United States. Freud had just succeeded in persuading Jung to
abandon the teetotalism that Bleuler insisted on; it is curious that Freud,
who disliked "the faint mental obfuscation that even a slight drink in-
duces,"[18] should have undertaken to change Jung's attitude toward alcohol.
But Jung's position on drinking was part of the Burghölzli tradition, and
for Jung to have some wine with Freud and Ferenczi meant a shift in the
young Swiss physician's allegiances.

At the time of their discussion of alcohol, Jung spoke of being fas-
cinated by some recent discoveries of "peat-bog corpses" in prehistoric
Copenhagen cemeteries. Jung had confused these corpses with seventeenth-
century mummies preserved in Bremen; Freud made the correction, but
Jung's persistent interest in the subject of corpses "got on Freud's nerves."
Jung recalled Freud's questioning him:

> "Why are you so concerned with these corpses?" he asked me several
> times. He was inordinately vexed by the whole thing and during one
> such conversation, while we were having dinner together, he sud-
> denly fainted. Afterwards he said to me that he was convinced that
> all this chatter about corpses meant I had death-wishes towards him.
> I was more than surprised by this interpretation, I was alarmed by the
> intensity of his fantasies—so strong that, obviously, they could cause
> him to faint.[19]

Then again, at a meeting in Munich in 1912, when the strains between Freud and Jung were far more evident, Freud is said by Jones to have reproached

> the two Swiss, Jung and Riklin, for writing articles expounding psychoanalysis in Swiss periodicals without mentioning his name. Jung replied that they had thought it unnecessary to do so, it being so well known, but Freud had sensed already the first signs of the dissension that was to follow a year later. He persisted and I remember thinking he was taking the matter rather personally. Suddenly . . . he fell on the floor in a dead faint.

Jung carried Freud into the next room, where Freud remarked, "How sweet it must be to die."[20]

The question of priorities, never taken lightly by Freud, had already come up in Jung's contact with psychoanalysis. Jones mentioned the occasion in 1908 of

> one of those stupid little disputes over priority that have so often marred scientific papers. . . . It arose from Abraham's omitting to mention or give any credit to Bleuler and Jung in his Congress paper for their psychological investigations into dementia praecox, which Jung took very much amiss at the time.[21]

Freud usually tried to soothe his followers' "sensitiveness about priority,"[22] and in this instance he was successful. His own concern with the problem, however, did not lessen that of his adherents. When Freud was on good terms with Jung he could half-jokingly refer to his reliance on his leading student's work as a form of plagiarism.[23]

Freud's fainting in Munich—as with his fainting in Bremen—was also closely associated with the issue of Jung's death wishes for Freud. Prior to the fainting spell, Freud and Jung were discussing Abraham's recent paper on the ancient Egyptian Amenophis IV (Ikhnaton); Abraham had been impressed by the "constant emphasis on truth in his ethical teachings," and had mentioned in passing that although Amenophis was not an epileptic he was said to have suffered as a boy from "fits."[24] According to Jung,

> The point was made that as a result of his negative attitude towards his father he had destroyed his father's cartouches on the steles, and that at the back of his great creation of a monotheistic religion there lurked a father complex. This sort of thing irritated me, and I attempted to argue that Amenophis had been a creative and profoundly

religious person whose acts could not be explained by personal resistances toward his father. On the contrary, I said, he had held the
memory of his father in honor, and his zeal for destruction had been
directed only against the name of the god Amon, which he had everywhere annihilated; it was also chiselled out of the cartouches of his
father Amon-hotep. Moreover, other pharaohs had replaced the names
of their actual or divine fore-fathers on monuments and statutes by
their own, feeling that they had a right to do so since they were
incarnations of the same god. Yet they, I pointed out, had inaugurated
neither a new style nor a new religion. At that moment Freud slid off
his chair in a faint.[25]

In Freud's last years he returned to the problem of the origins of Egyptian monotheism, in *Moses and Monotheism*; Freud then raised anew the
problem of priorities, in Moses' having picked up from the Egyptians a
religion he then transmitted to the Jews.*

In 1912, however, the conflict between Freud and Jung involved the
master's concern for the future of his ideas in the hands of his chosen
successor. Freud expressed himself through the dramatic means of fainting.
Jung remembered that after he had carried Freud to the other room Freud
"half came to, and I shall never forget the look he cast at me. In his weakness he looked at me as if I were his father."[26] Freud felt he depended on
Jung, and Jung's interpretation of Amenophis—that he was much more
than a man who had removed his father's name from monuments, that he
could not be so easily dismissed since he was the founder of a great religion
—must have shaken Freud's faith that this was the right man to entrust
psychoanalysis to.

In both fainting episodes it was as if Freud were so overwhelmed by
his anger that he could not tolerate his own emotions. By fainting Freud
was also perhaps trying to show Jung what he considered Jung's underlying motive, namely his wanting Freud to disappear. Perhaps Freud's
fainting can also be seen as a gesture of appeasement on his part, an attempt
to win back what he anticipated he was in danger of losing. Jung, however,
interpreted Freud's fainting as an avoidance and a surrender; on the one
hand, Freud was sensitive to criticism and any challenge to his authority,
and on the other, he was unwilling to engage in face-to-face conflict with
Jung. Freud "could not stand a critical word," as Jung is said to have
remembered the incidents. "Just like a woman. Confront her with a disagreeable truth: she faints."[27]

* Cf. below, pp. 294–96, 528–32.

As a child it was Jung who had fainting spells. But as an adult Freud had at least two other such episodes, both connected with Fliess. In the early 1890's Fliess had operated on the nose of one of Freud's patients, "Irma" (Emma Eckstein); sometime later she suffered a profuse nose bleed in Freud's presence and he fainted at the sight of the blood.[28] Seeing him in a "weak moment," she is said to have "mocked him with her remark: 'This is the strong sex.' "[29] By fainting Freud may have been trying to escape from the situation, so that he would not have to treat the bleeding patient or to acknowledge that his friend might have been in any way at fault.

Once again in the 1890's, when Freud thought he had sensations of heart palpitations that were not organic in origin, he experienced in Fliess's company "similar though not such intense symptoms in the *same* room"[30] in Munich in which he later fainted in front of Jung. Jones thought "the resemblance between the two situations," first with Fliess and then with Jung, was "unmistakeable," and threw "light on Freud's general avoidance of contention; his emotions, if allowed to be fully generated, were apt to be too much for him, hence the iron control in which he habitually kept himself."[31]

In November 1912 Freud wrote to Ferenczi: "I had an anxiety attack at the table" in Munich, "similar to the one I had had . . . in Bremen."[32] And the next month Freud wrote to Binswanger: "I am resigned to being declared a candidate for eternity on the basis of my attack in Munich. Recently Stekel wrote that my behavior was already showing the 'hypocritical feature.' All of them can hardly wait for it, but I can answer them as Mark Twain did under similar circumstances: 'Reports of my death grossly exaggerated.' "[33] Freud did not spare himself self-scrutiny after his fainting episodes:

> My fainting attack in Munich was surely provoked by psychogenic elements, which received strong somatic reinforcements (a week of troubles, a sleepless night, the equivalent of a migraine, the day's tasks). I had had several such attacks; in each case there were similar contributory causes, often a bit of alcohol for which I have no tolerance. Among the psychic elements there is the fact that I had had a quite similar seizure in the same place in Munich, on two previous occasions, four and six years ago. In the light of a most careful diagnosis, it seems scarcely possible to attribute my attacks to a more serious cause, for instance a weak heart. Repressed feelings, this time directed against Jung, as previously against a predecessor of his, naturally play the main part.[34]

What Freud wrote in 1927 about Dostoevsky's seizures (as Freud thought, "long before the incidence of the 'epilepsy' ") may partly explain his mature understanding of his earlier fainting spells:

> These attacks had the significance of death. . . . We know the meaning and intention of such deathlike attacks. They signify an identification with a dead person, either with someone who is really dead or with someone who is still alive and whom the subject wishes dead. The latter case is the more significant. The attack then has the value of a punishment. One has wished another dead, and now one *is* this other person and is dead oneself.[35]

In fainting in Jung's presence then, Freud may have been atoning for his murderous hate, with which he responded to the death wishes toward himself which he detected in his disciple.

By fainting Freud had taken an angry flight from a disagreeable situation. It can be better to die in fantasy than have to bear one's own aggressiveness. At the same time Freud was giving up on his side of the argument, and yet as dramatically as possible indicating to Jung that the matters they were disputing were of the greatest importance.

Freud's emotional involvement with Jung was heightened by the political character of his choice. By favoring a foreigner, Freud had alienated his local Viennese following for the sake of a breakthrough in the world at large. Others in the movement regarded Freud's reliance on Jung as currying favor with the Gentile world.

The year 1912, which Freud later wrote had been "the very climax of my psychoanalytic work," proved to be critical in the separation between Freud and Jung. Freud would think that Jung was cooling toward him whenever Jung failed to answer one of his letters promptly. Freud's nature was a jealous one, and he looked with ill favor on negligence in a correspondent. Freud's love of letter writing was as much due to his need to express thoughts to himself as it was his way of being outgoing to others. Although Freud was extraordinarily reliable about day-to-day aspects of life, Jung could be forgetful, and Freud would be quick to discern elements of unconscious betrayal. When Jones brought a slip of Jung's to Freud's attention, he reacted: "A gentleman should not do such things even unconsciously."[36]

Freud and Jung had such different perspectives on human psychology, each an outgrowth of their own experiences, that their rival viewpoints seem almost inevitably inharmonious. For instance, Freud regarded religious beliefs as a pack of lies put over on a stupid populace. In individual cases in treatment, Freud might appreciate the constructive role religion could play, but when he was writing in general terms, he would have sided with the old saw that the ruler's job is murder and the priest's is fraud.

Freud's conception of religion was primarily patriarchal: "the ambivalent feelings towards the father . . . are an underlying factor in all religions. . . ."[37] Freud ignored the figure of the Madonna; he "saw the religious impulse as a purely negative and fear driven drive, based not on love but on guilt; not on faith but on the need to atone; not on communion with a loved figure but an anxious pacification of a hated figure."[38] His resistance to religious ideas was akin to his more general rejection of dependence and passivity, which he associated with femininity. Whenever Freud sounds intolerant, it is likely that something in him was threatened and he may have been more involved with the problem of religion than he cared to know. If Freud neglected religion as man's way of mastering his anxieties and finding support for his aspirations, it may also be possible to trace his own personal feelings against religion back to the passive meaning Judaism held for him.

The attitude toward religion that Freud adopted was consistent with the rest of his work. Psychoanalytic research was concerned with "the underworld" of human instinctual life, not with traditional religious standards of ethics. And Freud had the biologist's relatively limited conception of what would qualify as an instinct:

> It may be difficult, . . . for many of us, to abandon the belief that there is an instinct towards perfection at work in human beings, which has brought them to their present high level of intellectual achievement and ethical sublimation and which may be expected to watch over their development into supermen. I have no faith, however, in the existence of any such internal instinct and I cannot see how this benevolent illusion is to be preserved. The present development of human beings requires, as it seems to me, no different explanation from that of animals.[39]

As much as Freud may have, as a young man and in his old age, aspired to philosophical understanding, to Jung he stressed the necessity of curbing speculative tendencies, just as with Jung he had to worry lest psychoanalysis be too closely linked with mysticism.

Although Jung was not a great supporter of established religions, he was respectful of religious philosophies, and later in life made a comparative study of world religious beliefs. He tried to prevent psychotherapy from being prematurely rigidified in scientific pretentiousness, and respect for religion was one way, he thought, to keep psychoanalysis humanized.

To Freud, however, any emphasis on the positive functions of religion was abhorrent, and if Freud had come to the conclusion that religion reflected a collective neurosis, Jung went to the opposite extreme when he argued that neurosis was a reflection of the loss of one's bearings: "The neurotic is ill not because he has lost his old faith, but because he has not yet found a new form for his finest aspirations."[40]

Jung was, of course, the son of a pastor—one of the features that had attracted Freud in the first place; but in retrospect Freud singled out "the theological pre-history of so many of the Swiss"[41] as a source of the trouble between him and Jung. It cannot have made it any easier for Freud that he all along suspected Jung of disguised anti-Semitism. Whereas Freud as a Jew sought Jung for the sake of breaking out of the constricting milieu of Viennese Jewry, Jung had chosen to emphasize the way different cultural groups develop different psychological systems, and in particular the way "Aryan" psychology might differ from Jewish psychology. But to Freud anything less than accepting psychoanalysis as universally true for all mankind, whatever the surface differences in national character, seemed like racism.

Freud must have felt considerable horror when, during the break between him and Jung, he reported that "in the latest works of the Zurich school . . . we find analysis permeated with religious ideas rather than the opposite outcome that had been in view."[42] Freud gloried in the ability of psychoanalysis to repudiate "so many conventional ideals," which somehow did not seem to coincide with Jung's aims. In 1907 Freud had written encouragingly to Jung, "we cannot avoid the resistances, so why not rather challenge them at once? In my opinion attack is the best defense."[43]

Freud claimed that in 1912 Jung had "boasted, in a letter from America,* that his modifications of psychoanalysis had overcome the resistances of many people who had hitherto refused to have anything to do with it." Freud resented any such "pushing into the background of the sexual factor in psychoanalytic theory,"[45] and as late as 1919 still maintained that "the theme of sexuality. . . . is our shibboleth."[46] At the height of Freud's troubles with Jung, the founder of psychoanalysis stated the premise of his whole fighting attitude: "We possess the truth; I am as sure of it as fifteen years ago."[47] The quarrel with Jung forced Freud to restate the essential features of his system of ideas: "the theory of repression and resistance, the recognition of infantile sexuality, and the interpreting and

---

* The letter was in fact sent *after* a trip of Jung's to America; but Freud evidently blamed America for awakening what he called Jung's "taste for money-making." Jung had written: "I found that my version of psychoanalysis won over many people who until now had been put off by the problem of sexuality in neurosis."[44]

exploiting of dreams as a source of knowledge of the unconscious."[48] Freud, therefore, had specific advice for his followers about how to disseminate their beliefs:

> One has really to treat doctors as we do our patients, therefore not by suggestion but by evoking their resistances and the conflict . . . one has to be content to state one's point of view and relate one's experiences in as clear and decided a manner as possible and not trouble too much about the reaction of one's audience.[49]

4. The Primal Father

JUNG'S RECEPTION IN AMERICA may have confirmed him in some of his earlier hesitations about Freud's ideas. Freud approved Jung's journey to the New World, but the projected Congress of analysts in 1912 had to be postponed because of Jung's absence. In September of that year Jung delivered a series of lectures at Fordham University in New York City, which marked an important step away from his endorsement of Freud. Jung does not seem to have consciously desired a break with Freud,* and after their final falling out sent a copy of one of his books to Freud with a humble inscription. Jung's view of the philosophy of science, like Freud's, held that it was possible to distinguish rigidly between "facts" and "theories," and as long as Jung felt he was acknowledging psychoanalytic "facts," he could believe that he was not being disloyal to Freud's essential aims.

At Fordham, Jung considered himself to be speaking in defense of Freud; yet it is hard to believe that Jung could have expected Freud, especially after the recent quarrel with Adler, to accept the kind of ideas Jung was now proposing. For example, Jung maintained that "the incest fantasy is of secondary and not causal significance, while the primary cause is the resistance of human nature to any kind of exertion."[2]

I think there is nothing for it but to abandon the sexual definition of libido, or we shall lose what is valuable in libido theory, namely the

---

* As Brill remembered it, "As I have been in the thick of the movement I can definitely state that Jung would have preferred to have remained in the psychoanalytic fold, but his views differed so much from those of Freud that it was best for both parties to separate."[1]

energic point of view . . . Freudians would be wrong not to listen to those critics who accuse our libido theory of mysticism and unintelligibility . . . It seems to me impossible simply to transfer the libido theory to dementia praecox, because this disease shows a loss of reality which can not be explained solely by the loss of erotic interest.[3]

Earlier, in the spring of 1912, Jung had written Freud that "incest is forbidden *not because it is desired* but because the free-floating anxiety regressively reactivates infantile material. . . . The aetiological significance of the incest prohibition must be compared directly with the so-called sexual trauma, which usually owes its aetiological role only to regressive reactivation."[4]

At Fordham, Jung paid tribute to Freud's earlier single-mindedness: "we must be glad that there are people who are courageous enough to be immoderate and one-sided." But Jung held that "*obtaining pleasure is by no means identical with sexuality.*"[5] He therefore objected to "the incorrect terminology and the boundless extension of the concept of sexuality" in Freud's work: "What he calls a disappearance is nothing other than the *real beginning of sexuality*, everything preceding it being but a preliminary stage to which no real sexual character can be attributed." To Jung, "the incorrectness of the conception of infantile sexuality" was "no error of observation . . . The error lies in the conception."[6]

Jung's orientation toward a patient's past was also different from Freud's. Jung found it "very suspicious . . . that patients often have a pronounced tendency to account for their ailments by some long-past experience, ingeniously drawing the analyst's attention away from the present to some false track in the past."[7] He observed the "tendency in our patients to lure us as far away as possible from the critical present," and concluded that "*the cause of the pathogenic conflict lies mainly in the present moment.*"[8] At the same time, Jung respected regression as "the basic condition for the act of creation," and thought that "we yield too much to the ridiculous fear that we are at bottom quite impossible beings, that if everyone were to appear as he really is, a frightful social catastrophe would ensue."[9] These views he presented as the contributions of "the work of the Zurich school."[10]

Some of Freud's critics had all along rejected his work on the grounds that he had placed an exaggerated emphasis on the role of sexuality. And now Jung was saying that "the expression 'polymorphous-perverse' has been borrowed from the psychology of neurosis and projected backwards into the psychology of the child, where of course it is quite out of place."[11] Freud had extended the commonsense meaning of sexuality to cover a variety of spheres, from childhood to mental illness, where science had not widely acknowledged the role of the erotic; and it was just this extension of Freud's which Jung was now repudiating. From the beginning Jung had tried to persuade Freud to use some word other than "sexual,"* but Freud steadfastedly stood by his earlier commitments. To

* Jung had written Freud that "the expression 'libido' and . . . all the terms (no doubt justified in themselves) that have been carried over into the broadened conception of sexuality are open to misunderstanding, or at least are not of didactic value. They actually evoke emotional inhibitions. . . ."[12]

Jung photographed during his 1912 visit to the United States

Jung, Freud seemed unnecessarily reductionistic; but from Freud's point of view, Jung's arguments about the role of incest fantasies, for example, had been laid to rest by the ousting of Adler.

Jung's conviction that patients often invented childhood sexual traumas, as a way of escaping from present-day life tasks, has more than half a century later found its way into psychoanalytic orthodoxy; a past infantile conflict is now recognized as a potential means of overlooking the significance of a current problem.[13] Though most clinicians, and many analysts, would today agree with Jung's conviction that it is often more comfortable to live in the past than to confront the future, at a time when Freud's ideas had not won widespread acceptance, he was afraid that all he had fought for would be swallowed up prematurely in Jung's kind of revisionism.

Once Jung had embarked on the tack of reinterpreting the significance of Freud's Oedipus complex, the way was open to a full-scale repudiation of Freud's conclusions. Freud had tried to force man to confront the instinctual side of his nature. Jung, like Adler in his emphasis on the ego, was in "retreat" from Freud, since Jung stressed the clinical importance of the "higher" task of self-realization on which patients could founder. Freud saw in Jung's new departures "resistance" to the unconscious, and a wish to destroy the father. As Jung wrote Freud in November 1912, "I regret very much that you believe it is resistance only that leads me to make certain changes."[14]

Jung thought that Freud's literalistic approach to the Oedipus complex neglected more subtle aspects of human psychology; for instance, to speak of the little boy's sexual tie to his mother should not be a substitute for acknowledging a son's legitimate dependency need for his mother. And in Jung's work "the mother is viewed as a protective and nourishing figure, not as the object of incestuous wishes."[15] Jung could have called attention to Freud's own uninterpreted relationship of dependency on his mother. As Erich Fromm and others have since pointed out, to see the relation between mother and son in sexual terms is in a sense to be highly rationalistic and to avoid the less rational sphere of the child's lack of early differentiation between the self and the outside world. As Jung was elaborating his ideas he found himself unable to finish the last third of his *Symbols of Transformation*; in the end Freud tried to persuade him not to publish it, and Jung concluded that his difficulties in completing the manuscript lay in his anguish over departing from some of Freud's views.

Jung returned from America more determined to assert his independence. His innovations did, he acknowledged, "deviate in places from the hitherto existing conceptions," but he refused to concede that his ideas entailed that he "be treated like a fool riddled with complexes."[16] Instead, he advocated a policy of "liberalism":

> I propose to let tolerance prevail in the *Jahrbuch* so that everyone can develop in his own way. Only when granted freedom do people give of their best. We should not forget that the history of human truths is also the history of human errors. So let us give the well-meant error its rightful place.[17]

On November 24, 1912, Jung met Freud at a psychoanalytic conference in Munich; although the two apparently got on well enough, Freud had the fainting attack discussed earlier. In his first letter to Jung after their meeting, Freud conceded that "one always finds it rather irritating when the other party insists on having an opinion of his own." As for his fainting, Freud referred to "a bit of neurosis that I ought really to look into."[18]

Jung took this occasion to suggest that Freud's "bit of neurosis" "should, in my opinion, be taken very seriously indeed . . . I have suffered from this bit in my dealings with you. . . ." Jung tried to speak as a friend, but went on to object that "the majority of psychoanalysts misuse psychoanalysis for the purpose of devaluing others and their progress by insinuations about complexes. . . ." Finally, Jung objected that "psychoanalysts are just as supinely dependent on psychoanalysis as our opponents are on their belief in authority. Anything that might make them think is written off as a complex. This protective function of psychoanalysis badly needed unmasking."[19]

Freud still held his peace. In reply to Jung, he suggested "a household remedy: let each of us pay more attention to his own than to his neighbor's neurosis." But Freud objected: "You have not, as you suppose, been injured by my neurosis."[20] To Jones, Freud commented on his fainting at Munich that there was "some piece of unruly homosexual feeling at the root of the matter."[21] Then Freud precipitated a breakdown in his relationship with Jung by pointing out a slip of the pen in one of Jung's letters. On December 14, 1912, Jung had intended to write in defense of himself— "Even Adler's cronies do not regard me as one of theirs"—but through mistakenly capitalizing one word transformed "theirs" into "yours."[22]

Freud had recently written to Jung that he thought that "in relations between analysts as in analysis itself every form of frankness is permissible."[23] But Jung, who had restrained himself in letters from interpreting Freud's fainting spells, responded unexpectedly sharply to his having picked up that slip of the pen:

May I say a few words to you in earnest? I admit the ambivalence of my feelings towards you, but am inclined to take an honest and absolutely straightforward view of the situation. If you doubt my word, so much the worse for you. I would, however, point out that your technique of treating your pupils like patients is a *blunder*. In that way you produce either slavish sons or impudent puppies (Adler-Stekel and the whole insolent gang now throwing their weight about in Vienna). I am objective enough to see through your little trick. You go around sniffing out all the symptomatic actions in your vicinity thus reducing everyone to the level of sons and daughters who blushingly admit the existence of their faults. Meantime you remain on top as the father, sitting pretty. For sheer obsequiousness nobody dares pluck the prophet by the beard and inquire for once what you would say to a patient with a tendency to analyse the analyst instead of himself. You would certainly ask him: *"Who's* got the neurosis?"

You see, my dear Professor, so long as you hand out this stuff, I don't give a damn for my symptomatic actions; they shrink to nothing in comparison with the formidable beam in my brother Freud's eye. I am not in the least neurotic—touch wood! I have submitted *lege artis et tout humblement* to analysis and am much the better for it. You know, of course, how far a patient gets with self-analysis; *not* out of his neurosis—just like you. If ever you should rid yourself entirely of your complexes and stopped playing the father to your sons, and instead of aiming continually at their weak spots took a good look at your own for a change, then I will mend my ways and at one stroke uproot the vice of being in two minds about you. Do you *love neurotics* enough to be always at one with yourself? But perhaps you *hate* neurotics. In that case how can you expect your efforts to treat your patients leniently and lovingly *not* to be accompanied by somewhat mixed feelings? Adler and Stekel were taken in by your little tricks and reacted with childish insolence. I shall continue to stand by you publicly while maintaining my own views, but privately shall start telling you in my letters what I really think of you. I consider this procedure only decent.

No doubt you will be outraged by this peculiar token of friendship, but it may do you good all the same.

Freud, taking unusual pains to draft a belated reply to Jung's "recriminations," finally argued that "one who while behaving abnormally keeps shouting that he is normal gives ground for the suspicion that he lacks insight into his illness," and he proposed that "we abandon our personal relations entirely."[24]

The stage was thus set for a public confrontation between Freud and Jung at the Congress for analysts held in Munich in early September 1913. It was to be the last meeting between the two men. Throughout the spring of 1913 Freud had been thinking about the coming public break with Jung, who had become so "useless" to Freud that "he could scarcely imagine himself on the same terms he had been with him formerly."[25] If the Zurich group was now overestimating its importance to Freud's cause, he acknowledged that his own earlier preference for the Swiss had been responsible for the situation in the first place. On March 27, 1913, Freud wrote that "naturally I am not indifferent to the distortions of my psychoanalysis,"[26] as he tried to separate Jung's recent work from his own. On the same day Freud wrote to another pupil, Karl Abraham, that

> Jung is in America, but only for five weeks, that is, he will soon be back. In any case he is doing more for himself than for psychoanalysis. I have greatly retreated from him, and have no more friendly thoughts for him. His bad theories do not compensate me for his disagreeable character. He is following in Adler's wake, without being as consistent as that pernicious creature.[27]

Freud completed the manuscript of *Totem and Taboo* that spring, and he felt it would be helpful in driving a wedge between himself and Jung. He expected that the book would be published before the meeting at Munich and "would serve to make a sharp division between us and all Aryan religiosity."[28] Freud's thesis in *Totem and Taboo* was concerned with nothing less than the origins of human society; he had found that the Oedipus complex threw "a light of undreamt-of importance on the history of the human race and the evolution of religion and morality."[29]

Since September 1911 Freud and Jung had been working on the same theme of the origin of religion. Fascinated by the uncanny meaning of the double, Freud admitted his uneasiness at having an intellectual twin:

> it is a torment to me to think, when I conceive an idea now and then, that I may be taking something away from you or appropriating something that might just as well have been acquired by you . . . Why in God's name did I allow myself to follow you into this field?[30]

Freud had resisted the efforts of Adler and his followers to remain in the Vienna Society on the grounds that they would do so "to provide themselves parasitically with ideas and with material to misrepresent."[31] Freud's sensitivity to problems connected with plagiarism and priorities was well known to Jung. In 1908, for example, Freud had referred a patient to Jung—a drug-addicted psychoanalyst, Otto Gross.

> I originally thought you would only take him on for the withdrawal period and that I would start analytic treatment in the autumn. It is shamefully egotistic of me, but I must admit that it is better for me this way; for I am obliged to sell my time and my supply of energy is not quite what it used to be. But seriously, the difficulty would have been that the dividing line between our respective property rights in creative ideas would inevitably have been effaced; we would never have been able to disentangle them with a clear conscience. Since I treated the philosopher Swoboda I have had a horror of such difficult situations.[32]

If the subject matter of *Totem and Taboo* had helped to undermine Freud's feelings for his heir, Jung was none too relaxed about it either: "the outlook for me is very gloomy if you too get into the psychology of religion. You are a dangerous rival."[33]

In *Totem and Taboo,* Freud postulated that man first lived in a primordial band or horde, which was dominated by a father who monopolized all the women; the sons banded together and rebelled, slaying and then eating the father. The sons' love for their murdered father, however, soon overwhelmed them with guilt feelings for their crime, and they agreed that never again would any one male have the powers that their father had exercised; once restrictions upon impulses were settled, Freud thought, civilization could be said to have begun.[34]

By tracing the beginning of society back to that primal crime— or, as some have suggested, to a series of such murders—Freud was expanding the significance of the Oedipus complex, which Jung had been trying to put in a different perspective. By interpreting the meaning of totemic religion in terms of the acting out of oedipal wishes, instead of the incestuous fantasies which troubled neurotic patients, Freud thought he had found the "beginnings of religion, morality, social life and art meeting in the Oedipus complex."[35]

Anthropologists have never been able to confirm the existence of these primitive hordes; in such bands that can be verified there is little of the possessiveness Freud described, or the jealousy, or anything like the institution of one dominant male monopolizing the females.[36] Freud relied for his sources on armchair anthropology, which later came into disrepute with the growth of modern field work. But it was a commonplace in nineteenth-century intellectual life to identify the primitive mind with that of "savages." At least as dubious was Freud's emphasis on man's phylogenetic inheritance; for he argued that an acquired characteristic—guilt over the slaying of the primal father—could be inherited.

It is striking that "prior to 1910, hardly any mention of phylogenesis can be found in Freudian teaching."[37] Freud acknowledged that "in 1912 . . . Jung's forcible indication of the far-reaching analogies between the mental products of neurotics and of primitive peoples led me to turn my attention to that subject."[38]

> C. G. Jung was the first to draw explicit attention to the striking similarity between the disordered phantasies of sufferers from dementia praecox and the myths of primitive peoples; while the present writer pointed out that the two wishes which combine to form the Oedipus complex coincide precisely with the two principal prohibitions imposed by *totemism* (not to kill the primal ancestor and not to marry any woman belonging to one's own clan) and drew far-reaching conclusions from this fact.[39]

Jung was far more prone to cite phylogenetic interpretations than was Freud himself, though after their encounter Freud seems to have adopted some of Jung's method of approach. Although Freud thought it "a methodological error" on Jung's part "to seize on a phylogenetic explanation before the ontogenetic possibilities have been exhausted," he himself not only spoke of "organic inheritance" but concluded, according to Jones, that "certain primordial phantasies, notably those of coitus and castration, were transmitted through inheritance in some form or other. . . ."[40]

At the time, however, Freud found Jung's ideas at best confused, if not unintelligible or insane. On June 1, 1913, Freud wrote to Abraham: "Jung is crazy, but I have no desire for a separation and should like to let him wreck himself first. Perhaps my *Totem* paper will hasten the breach against my will."[41] Abraham remained the loyal disciple, and the wording of Freud's gratitude to Abraham for his comments on *Totem and Taboo* gives an idea of what Freud wanted from his pupils. "The way in which all of you try to show me the value of the work," Freud wrote, "by supplementing and drawing conclusions from it is of course the most marvellous."[42] It was Jung's "confusion"[43] that Freud repeatedly objected to. Freud did not so much disagree with Jung; as with other "dissidents" in psychoanalysis, he simply found his work unintelligible. Freud "always intended to understand thoroughly"; and it was by the same logic that "music did not interest him, because he regarded it as an unintelligible language."[44]

Freud was not a depressive person, and therefore not inclined to criticize himself for what he had done to others; it was more like Freud to look for what others had done to him.* But in July 1913, after the completion of *Totem and Taboo* and prior to his final meeting with Jung, Freud experienced a depression which may have allowed him to see what role his personality had played in the failure of his relationship with Jung.[46] By the next winter, however, Freud focused on Jung's behavior as president; the Congress, he reported,

> was conducted by Jung in a disagreeable and incorrect manner; the speakers were restricted in time and the discussions overwhelmed the papers . . . The fatiguing and unedifying proceedings ended in the re-election of Jung to the Presidency of the International Psychoanalytic Association, which he accepted, although two-fifths of those present refused him their support.[47]

Jones reported that Jung had said to him at the end of the Congress, referring to their being on opposite sides now, "I thought you were a Christian."[48] Since Jones was one of the few Gentiles at the Congress, it might seem that Jung expected, for that reason, to have him on his side; but in his autobiography, uncompleted at his death, Jones gave a different and more extended version. "As he said good-bye he sneeringly remarked to me: 'I thought you had ethical principles' (an expression he was fond of); my friends interpreted the word 'ethical' here as meaning 'Christian' and therefore as anti-Semitic."[49] Whether it was Jones or his "friends" on Freud's side who made this interpretation, he reported it in his biography of Freud as Jung's literal comment, which by his own later account obviously was not.

But no one rereading Jung's paper at that Congress could doubt that Freud would find Jung's position an intolerable affront. "A Contribution to Psychological Types" was a brilliant presentation in which Jung introduced his concepts of "introversion" and "extraversion," later to be elaborated extensively as contrasting orientations to the world. It would not have suited Freud, who at that time was still chiefly preoccupied with the understanding and treatment of symptoms, to have looked for such character types. But perhaps most annoying of all to Freud was a passage at the end of Jung's paper in which he treated Adler's work and that of Freud as opposite approaches corresponding to Jung's two psychological types. Jung's concluding sentence—"The difficult task of creating a

---

* As Freud wrote in 1915, "I have never done anything shameful or malicious, nor do I find in myself any temptation to do so. . . . others are brutal and unreliable. . . ."[45]

psychology which will be equally fair to both types must be reserved for the future"—could not really be tolerated, in the light of Freud's controversy with Adler in Vienna.[50]

October 1913 was the last time Freud and Jung exchanged letters, after more than seven years of correspondence.* That month Jung resigned as editor of the *Jahrbuch,* and in a letter Freud wrote that he

> was struck by the complete analogy that can be drawn between the first running away from the discovery of sexuality behind the neuroses by Breuer and the latest one by Jung. That makes it the more certain that this is the core of psychoanalysis.[51]

Few responsible figures in psychoanalysis would be disturbed today if an analyst were to present views identical to Jung's in 1913; for example, years before the rise of ego psychology Jung contended that "the fact that the neurotic seems to be markedly influenced by his infantile conflicts shows that it is less a matter of fixation than of the peculiar use which he makes of his infantile past."[52]

Although Freud later described the "loneliness"[53] that surrounded him, he does not seem to have acknowledged that he himself had brought that state into being. He only knew that he had to

> protect myself against people who have called themselves my pupils for many years and who owe everything to my stimulus. Now I must accuse them and reject them. I am not a quarrelsome person, nor do I share the widespread opinion that a scientific quarrel brings about clarity and progress. However, I am not in favor of sloppy compromises, nor would I sacrifice anything for the sake of an unproductive reconciliation.[55]

If it was to remain Freud's movement, if he was to impose his will on history, paradoxically Freud had to reduce psychoanalysis in talent as well as in numbers.

In 1913 Jung was invited to speak in London "as a representative of the psychoanalytic movement."[56] Lest word get out "that psychoanalysis has changed," Freud wrote, "at the Munich Congress I found it necessary to clear up this confusion, and I did so by declaring that I did not recognize the innovations of the Swiss as legitimate continuations and further developments of the psychoanalysis that originated with me."[57] Instead of writing in terms of his own beliefs, Freud preferred the more impersonal-sounding expression "psychoanalytic teaching"; having driven out dissenters, in

---

* In 1923 Jung referred a patient to Freud by letter, but with no reply.[54]

future years Freud would be able to write of "the unanimous report of all psychoanalysts."[58] "Analysts have long been agreed. . . ."[59] was also a persuasive way to make a case.

In January and February of 1914 Freud wrote his essay "On the History of the Psychoanalytic Movement" for the readers of the *Jahrbuch*, in which he branded Jung as "in full retreat from psychoanalysis."[60] Freud outlined how the work of both Adler and Jung represented scientifically regressive tendencies, and his polemic against them was designed to make sure that the public understood why he regarded them as having "abandoned" and "seceded" from psychoanalysis. Yet it was he who in both cases had felt entitled to take the initiative. Jung should have known that Freud intended the International Psychoanalytic Association to be more than an official licensing body;* it was a political organization as well. Jung did not resign his presidency until April 1914. (Karl Abraham succeeded him on an interim basis.)

When Freud's polemic appeared in print in July 1914, Jung withdrew from the International Psychoanalytic Association, along with almost the entire body of Swiss analysts. As with the Adler resignations, "one of the reasons advanced . . . by the Zurich people was 'the endangering of independent research.' "[62] Despite his increasingly critical attitude toward Freud's work, Jung had wanted to go on with Freud, but the latter seemed intent on expelling him. As Freud wrote at the end of July 1914, "I am dying to receive the official news that we have got rid of the 'independents.' "[63] Freud wrote of psychoanalysis as he had once written of the state of his mind in letters to Fliess: "It is tossed by the waves, but does not sink" (citing the coat of arms of the city of Paris).[64] Freud had at least preserved what he understood to be the integrity of his doctrines, and when his time came his original contributions would win their recognition.

---

* At the beginning of his involvement with Freud, Jung had "advocated the policy of excluding from attendance of meetings all those who did not subscribe to everything in the doctrine."[61]

5. Analytical Psychology

FROM THE ORTHODOX PSYCHOANALYTIC point of view, Jung has seemed "nothing more or less than a pre-Freudian who having at first let himself be carried into the stream of Freudian thought has ever since striven to make his peace with conscious psychology." The danger to Freud's position was Jung's "using Freudian terminology in a way that divests it of its original meaning and so bamboozles the unoriented reader."[1] Jung's writings did lack Freud's unique clarity. In 1914 Freud wrote that

> Jung's modification . . . [of psychoanalysis] loosens the connection of the phenomena with instinctual life; and further, as its critics (e.g. Abraham, Ferenczi and Jones) have pointed out, it is so obscure, unintelligible and confused as to make it difficult to take up any position upon it.[2]

However, Freud was stuck with one of Jung's concepts—"complex" —since it had been embedded for so long in the psychoanalytic vocabulary. Freud's editor, James Strachey, noted the "*début*" in 1906 "in Freud's published writings of the Zurich term 'complex.' "[3] For a time in 1912 Freud, already disengaging himself from Jung, tried to make it seem that the term was superfluous to psychoanalysis, but it was already too late.[4] In later years Jones tried to deprive Jung of credit for the term by referring to a Berlin psychiatrist "who had a proprietary interest in the word 'complex' which he had first introduced. . . ."[5]

Early psychoanalysis focused on conflict. Since Freud's death psychoanalytic writers have been more interested in "conflict-free" areas of the psyche. Jung was as contemptuous of Heinz Hartmann's work on the "autonomous" ego as he was convinced that Freud's concepts were unduly negative. To Jung, orthodox psychoanalysis remained merely a hedonistic account of the human dilemma. For all of Jung's differences with the Adlerian position, he might have agreed that "the Oedipus theory universalizes the disappointing experiences of the pampered child just as the libido theory universalizes its pleasure-seeking propensities."[6] And like Adler, Jung wanted to get away from Freud's concentration on causes from out of the past: "no psychological fact can ever be exhaustively explained in terms of causality alone; as a living phenomenon, it is always indissolubly bound up with the continuity of the vital process, so that it is not only something evolved but also continually evolving and creative."[7]

Freud's concern for the human condition of inner conflict, his empathy for suffering, his appreciation of the inevitability of tragedy, can be seen in the persistent dualism of his ideas. In his earlier writing he thought in terms of libidinal drives versus standards of conscience, and in his last years he hypothesized a life instinct opposed to a death instinct; despite occasional references to psychic unity, it was the dualism of human emotions—what Bleuler had called "ambivalence"—which became Freud's chief interest. Jones reports that "Freud . . . told Jung that were he [Freud] ever to suffer from a neurosis it would be of the obsessional type. That signifies . . . a deep ambivalence between the emotions of love and hate. . . ."[8] Jones knew that Freud had an "almost obsessional determination to confine himself to two sets of instincts only."[9]

Jung departed from Freud's theory in hypothesizing libido as a much broader and all-encompassing psychological force than Freud envisioned. Freud's libido theory held that sublimation was the result of a holding back of sexuality. To Jung, seeing creativity as the result of the denial of other human capacities was merely an expression of Freud's sexual inhibitions.[10]

Freud's view of libido was more narrowly sexual, although sex for him always included the emotions connected with infantile sexuality. Jung objected that "Freud's idea of sexuality is incredibly elastic and so vague that it can be made to include almost anything."[11] Freud thought of libido, for both men and women, as inherently masculine in character, and he used military terms to describe the development of libidinal stages— for example, the mind leaving troops at various strongholds along the road of growth. Freud tried to establish that even egoism was a libidinal problem, and his essay "On Narcissism" was an effort to establish an alternative to Jung's asexual libido (as well as to Adler's notion of masculine protest).[12] But Freud included so much in his concept of narcissism that to a modern reader it may be difficult to understand how Freud is really differing from the monism of which he accused Jung.

But there was an ineluctable conflict in the outlooks that Freud and Jung eventually came to represent. For example, Freud was consistently suspicious of the human capacity for regression, whereas Jung tended to see the nonrational as a profound component of human vision. Freud could sometimes speak in romantic terms, and once complimented a patient's short story: "Well, usually what the unconscious does, it does well."[13] But on the whole Freud's work as a therapist and his own rationalistic temperament led him to distrust that which could not be made rationally explicable, and both in patients and in his own life he was wary of apparent lapses of maturity or control. Jung reported that Freud had once said to him: " 'I only wonder what neurotics will do in the future when all their symbols have been unmasked. It will then be impossible to have a neurosis.' He expected enlightenment to do everything."[14] According to the point of view Jung had developed by 1934:

> We should not try to "get rid" of a neurosis, but rather to experience what it means, what it has to teach, what its purpose is. We should even be thankful for it, otherwise we pass it by and miss the opportunity of getting to know ourselves as we really are. A neurosis is truly removed only when it has removed the false attitudes of the ego. We do not cure it—it cures us. A man is ill, but the illness is nature's attempt to heal him.[15]

Jung thought that "the conscious mind is even more devilish and perverse than the naturalness of the unconscious," and he repudiated "the totally erroneous supposition that the unconscious is a monster."[16]

For Jung, regressions could serve positive and not merely neurotic functions, and this insight would eventually be incorporated in the work of orthodox psychoanalysis, chiefly through the writings of Ernst Kris.[17] A later analyst, Ronald D. Laing, would go so far as to stress the positive aspects even of psychosis, the way the mentally ill may be more perceptive than so-called sane people.

The difference in Jung's and Freud's attitudes toward regression extended to their conception of the function of the unconscious itself. To Freud, the unconscious was primarily regressive; when Jung challenged this view, it seemed to Freud that Jung was in flight from accepting the concept of the unconscious at all. But it could just as well be said that Jung simply had a different conception of the unconscious; Jung had more appreciation of the creative potentials of the unconscious, and saw in the unknown at least as much of life forces as of death forces. The difference in Freud's and Jung's views of the unconscious is reflected in their contrasting attitudes toward fantasy. Freud had felt that he could "lay it down that a happy person never phantasies, only an unsatisfied one."[18] Jung, on the other hand, wrote: "I have no small opinion of fantasy. To me, it is the maternally creative side of the masculine man . . . As Schiller says, man is completely human only when he is at play."[19]

Jung held that "between conscious and unconscious there exists a compensatory relationship, and . . . the unconscious always tries to make whole the conscious part of the psyche by adding to it the parts that are missing, and so prevent a dangerous loss of balance."[20] For Jung, the psyche was therefore "a self-regulating system that maintains its equilibrium just as the body does . . . Too little on one side results in too much on the other."[21]

Jung discerned Freud's distrust of the unconscious in his theory of dreams. Freud thought that "it would be quite incorrect to ascribe any 'creative' character"[22] to the mind's "dream work." Jung's experience led him "to think of . . . [dreams] as functions of compensation" instead of wish fulfillment.[23] Wish fulfillment stressed the gratification achieved through the release of instinctual drives, whereas compensation implied that through dreams the patient might be seeking ethical direction. According to Jung, Freud "too ascribes a compensatory role to dreams in so far as they preserve sleep."[24] Jung rejected Freud's distinction between the manifest and latent content of dreams, maintaining that the former, which to Freud seemed merely the surface of a dream, contained the dream's message as well:

> I was never able to agree with Freud that the dream is a "façade" behind which its meaning lies hidden—a meaning already known but maliciously, so to speak, withheld from consciousness. To me dreams are a part of nature, which harbors no intention to deceive, but express something as best it can, just as a plant grows or an animal seeks its food as best it can.[25]

"When Freud asserts that the dream means something other than what it says, this interpretation is a 'polemic' against the dream's natural and spontaneous presentation of itself, and is therefore invalid."[26] Jung thought that "dreams may contain ineluctable truths, philosophical pronouncements, illusions, wild fantasies, memories, plans, anticipations, irrational experiences, even telepathic visions, and heaven knows what else besides."[27]

One of Jung's Swiss associates, Alphonse Maeder, discussed the "prospective tendency of dreams," which, like Adler's notion of masculine and feminine elements in dreams, was a move away from Freud's early theory of wish fulfillment. Freud felt he had to refute the usefulness of rival dream theories. By attributing to these so-called "discoveries" the claim of universality (which Jung had been careful not to make), Freud attempted to dismiss them: "The reason why I have mentioned all these discoveries of fresh universal characteristics of dreams is in order to warn you against them or at least to leave you in no doubt as to what I think of them."[28]

Jung made at least one innovation in dream psychology that is generally accepted by analysts today; namely, his suggestion that one can interpret characters in dreams as standing for aspects of the dreamer's own ego. A man who dreams of a girl who is very sad may be expressing his own sadness; and it was typical of Jung to think that a man might be out of contact with his femininity ("anima"), just as many women suffer from lack of access to their masculine side ("animus"). "In man the unconscious has feminine features, in women masculine. . . ."[29]

To Freud, dream figures stood, when interpreted in their latent meanings, for people in the dreamer's past life. Whereas today many psychologists would agree with Jung and even, like Erikson, speak of "ego symbols" in dreaming, Freud was adamant in rejecting this part of what he deemed Jung's mistaken path: "I should reject as a meaningless and unjustifiable piece of speculation the notion that *all* figures that appear in a dream are to be regarded as fragmentations and representations of the dreamer's own ego."[30]

Jung's emphasis on the need to understand the "life-task" of the dreamer, and his concern with the current (rather than the hidden or disguised) conflicts of his patients, may have stemmed from a peculiarity of his original clinical practice. For if it became "one of the main principles of Jungian psychotherapy" to bring "the patient back to reality,"[31] instead of encouraging Freud's kind of detour through the past in order to understand the present, this was a consequence of Jung's having had so much more familiarity than Freud with the most disturbed kind of mental patients. Freud took for granted that his patients had egos which were more or less intact, whereas more disturbed patients quite often project portions of themselves onto others. Through his hospital position in Switzerland, Jung had observed cases Freud would not have had the opportunity to see; and Jung was more tolerant toward psychosis than Freud was ever able to be.* In his earlier years Jung treated cases of psychoses, and he was more fascinated by the material brought by a schizophrenic than, for instance, a garden-variety obsessional neurotic.

Jung was less defensive than Freud about psychosis, and this may explain many aspects of their differences. Dealing with a schizophrenically disturbed person, the analyst cannot take for granted the patient's day-to-day sense of reality and may have to intervene to ensure that the most mundane daily tasks (getting washed, dressing, and so on) are performed. In addition, those who have worked with the severe mental illnesses are

---

* Jung was, however, "notoriously intolerant of male homosexuals." In addition, he wrote relatively little about the positive aspect of the "animus" in women: "a recurrent theme . . . is the disastrous effect which he thought universities—especially American universities—had upon the personality of women. He called them 'animus incubators'. . . ."[32]

more sensitive to the possibility that biochemical disorders are involved, and therefore are more likely to retain a respect for the physician's special competence in the field of psychotherapy. Although Jung was not opposed to the practice of lay analysis, his fear of the presence of latent psychoses in patients led him to argue that "a lay analyst should . . . always work with a doctor."[33] When he was still in Freud's circle, Jung accepted Freud's image of the analyst as a mental surgeon, and he wrote in 1913 that "I should deceive myself if I thought I was a practising physician. I am above all an investigator. . . ."[34] But by 1942 Jung thought that "the important thing is not the neurosis, but the man who has the neurosis. We have to set to work on the human being, and we must be able to do him justice as a human being."[35]

Freud disagreed repeatedly with those who were greatly interested in psychotic cases. It was under the impact of his association with Jung that Freud wrote his case history of Schreber (a psychotic), although Freud worked from a book of memoirs rather than clinical material of his own. Freud expected his essay to earn "scornful laughter or immortality or both."[36] It has been suggested that "Jung's most vital contribution" to psychoanalysis was that he pointed out "that Freud had failed to distinguish between neurotic and psychotic phenomena in the Schreber case."[37] Freud acknowledged "the striking light thrown upon the most obscure symptoms of what is known as dementia praecox by C. G. Jung," yet Freud added that this had been accomplished "at a time when he [Jung] was merely a psychoanalyst and had not yet aspired to be a prophet. . . ."[38] Freud, however, had his own prophetic side, as he showed in his denunciation of religious belief and his criticism of traditional religious morality. But accounts of modern depth psychology have too often omitted Jung's great practical achievements as a therapist.

Jung's early experience and interest in understanding psychosis was matched by an apparent opposite, his fascination with the supranormal, the genius. The hero theme was central in Jung's thinking, and in order to enrich his understanding of mythology, Jung turned to the study of comparative religion. In 1912 Freud thought that Jung had "excellent grounds for his assertion that the mythopoeic forces of mankind are not extinct, but that to this very day they give rise in the neuroses to the same psychical products as in the remotest past ages."[39]

But by 1914 Freud complained that in Jung's new theories "the investigation of individuals was pushed into the background and replaced by conclusions based on evidence derived from anthropological research."[40] While Freud was using prehistory in *Totem and Taboo* to re-emphasize the importance of the Oedipus complex, Jung found an avenue in anthropology for using nonliterate religion, symbolism, and mythology to forward his own special interests. In later years he visited the Indians of the American Southwest and traveled to India, Egypt, North Africa, and the Sahara, to add to his knowledge of man.

In keeping with Jung's religious orientation, he saw "life as a succession of metamorphoses, the central one being 'the turning of life' around the age of thirty-five."[41] In the course of the individual's metamorphoses, it was, Jung held, the last half of life which, for the exceptional few, was "a period of confrontation with the archetype of the spirit and of the self."[42] Jung's concept of archetype had "nothing whatever to do with inherited ideas, but with modes of behavior."*[43] Freud had distinguished primarily between childhood and adulthood, interpreting the latter according to unique characteristics of the former. Freud had been wary of analyzing older patients, but Jung became especially interested in their problems. The difficulties of older people were different from those of the young; they were less concerned with the vicissitudes of sexuality and more with problems of meaning.

In discussing a person's fundamental attitudes toward being, Jung was back in the religious realm that Freud had tried to supersede. Freud conceded the legitimacy of the direction of Jung's thinking, at least with reference to "the phantasy of rebirth, to which Jung has recently drawn attention and to which he has assigned such a dominating position in the imaginative life of neurotics." But, Freud added in criticism, "this would be all very well, if it were the whole story."[45] Half a century later, however, analysts would not only be treating patients older than those Freud considered accessible to therapeutic influence, but also would be following Jung's lead (without always knowing it) by discussing the psychology of stages of life other than those that specifically interested Freud.

Jung's immersion in philosophical quests was plainly a source of disharmony between him and Freud. Jung held that the therapist must be prepared to meet the patient on all levels, including the moral. Although in many ways a conformist in daily life, Freud was cynical about traditional morality; as late as 1921 he argued that "it has long been our contention that 'social anxiety' is the essence of what is called conscience."[46] Freud believed that we control our unconscious instinctual impulses, "in

---

* Anthony Storr has recently suggested that Jung had in mind inherited predispositions; for example, "one has to take into account 'archetypal' images of the good and bad mother, which . . . become projected upon the real mother in such a way that she may appear as a kind of divinity or else as a kind of witch."[44]

which all that is evil in the human mind is contained as a predisposition," out of fear of the outside world.[47] By 1930 Freud gave his most extensive understanding of the origins of conscience in his *Civilization and Its Discontents*, but he had earlier dismissed the idea of "an instinct towards perfection at work in human beings" as a "benevolent illusion."

Jung tried to deal directly with the philosophic dimensions of depth psychology, and he was more willing than Freud to discuss the implications of these ideas for a modern conception of individualism. Everyone, Jung thought, has a "persona," a means of presenting himself to the external world. But from Jung's "viewpoint the so-called well-adjusted personality may lead a rather mask-like existence."[48] For a patient to break through what he may have become in order to please others, Jung thought he had to come in contact with his "shadow" side, which lies behind the "persona." By "shadow" Jung "meant the 'negative' side of the personality, the sum of all those unpleasant qualities we like to hide, together with the insufficiently developed functions and the contents of the personal unconscious."[49]

In Jung's concepts of persona and shadow, he was again carrying an aspect of Freud's work further than Freud himself wanted, though later students of Freud have come to feel comfortable with Jung's distinction. Without using Jung's terminology, Donald Winnicott was designating similar philosophical (as well as clinical) entities when he distinguished between "the true and the false selves," the latter being built "on reactions to external stimuli." The defensive function of the "False Self," Winnicott thought, "is to hide and protect the True Self, whatever that may be."[50]

Jung also thought that the analyst's own irrational susceptibilities played a significant role in psychotherapeutic treatment. His concern for the importance of the analyst's own neurosis may have begun with his insight into Freud's limitations; by 1912 he concluded that self-analysis was impossible and therefore every analyst should undergo a personal analysis.[51]

In 1912 Jung said that "it is quite impossible, even by the subtlest analysis, to prevent the patient from taking over instinctively the way in which his analyst deals with the problems of life"; in order to avoid "the unacknowledged infantile demands of the analyst" identifying "themselves with the parallel demands of the patient," the analyst should submit "to a rigorous analysis at the hands of another."[52] That same year Freud wrote: "I count it as one of the many merits of the Zurich school of analysis that they have laid increased emphasis on this requirement, and have embodied it in the demand that everyone who wishes to carry out analyses on other people should first himself undergo an analysis by someone with expert knowledge."[53] It was not until 1918 that Freud encouraged one of his pupils, Herman Nunberg, to introduce the proposed rule that every analyst be analyzed; the motion was finally adopted in 1926 as the official policy of the International Psychoanalytic Association.[54] More than Freud, however, Jung considered "the great healing factor in psychotherapy" to be "the doctor's personality."[55] In 1934 he expressed his disapproval of artificial rigidity in therapeutic technique; speaking of the analyst's analysis, Jung wrote:

> Freud seconded this requirement, obviously because he could not escape the conviction that the patient should be confronted by a doctor and not by a technique. It is certainly very laudable in a doctor to try to be as objective and impersonal as possible and to refrain from meddling with the psychology of his patient like an overzealous saviour. But if this attitude is carried to artificial lengths it has unfortunate consequences. The doctor will find that he cannot overstep the bounds of naturalness with impunity. Otherwise he would be setting a bad example to his patient, who certainly did not get ill from an excess of naturalness. Besides it would be dangerously to underestimate the patients if one imagined that they were all too stupid to notice the artifices of the doctor, his security measures and his little game of prestige.[56]

Jung's early concern with the analyst's unconscious interference with the progress of his patients distinguished his form of therapy from the more antiseptic ideal of Freud's written recommendations about analytic technique.* As Jung wrote in 1935 of an analyst's reaction to his patient (in words one cannot imagine Freud agreeing with): "If I wish to treat another individual psychologically at all, I must for better or worse give up all pretensions to superior knowledge, all authority and desire to influence. I must perforce adopt a dialectical procedure consisting in a comparison of our mutual findings."[58]

In placing so much importance on the patient's current life, Jung necessarily had to consider directly the doctor-patient relationship.[59] For Jung, "the therapist is no longer the agent of treatment but a fellow

---

* In 1911 Freud had objected to the technique of Jung and Pfister: "you still get involved, giving a good deal of yourselves and expecting the patient to give something in return. . . . this . . . is invariably ill-advised . . . it is best to remain reserved and purely receptive.[57]

participant in a process of individual development."[60] By a process of "individuation" the "patient becomes who he really is"; this takes place "by means of reconciling the opposing factors within."[61] But

> the psychotherapist should no longer labor under the delusion that the treatment of neurosis demands nothing more than the knowledge of a technique; he should be absolutely clear in his own mind that the psychological treatment of the sick is a *relationship* in which the doctor is involved quite as much as the patient.[62]

To Jung, Freud's method of treatment seemed to encourage the neurotic desire to return to the past, which Jung regarded as an evasion of the present; "it makes an enormous difference in practice whether we interpret something regressively or progressively."[63] Jung thought "it matters little that, even today, the view prevails in many quarters that analysis consists mainly in 'digging up' the earliest childhood complex in order to pluck out the evil by the root. This is merely the aftermath of the old trauma theory."[64] Jung considered that "we cannot simply extract his [a patient's] morbidity like a foreign body, lest something essential be removed along with it, something meant for life. Our task is not to weed it out, but to cultivate and transform this growing thing until it can play its part in the totality of the psyche."[65]

Freud objected that Jung's approach represented, as had Adler's, a scientific regression "by reverting to the current conflict, in which . . . the essential thing was on no account to be what was accidental and personal, but what was general—in fact, the non-fulfillment of the life-task."[66] However, Jung's conception of the "actual conflict," he insisted, referred not to "*the petty vexation of the moment*" but to "the problem of adaptation."[67] But according to Freud, "the first piece of reality which the patient must deal with is his illness. Efforts to spare him that task point to the physician's incapacity to help him overcome his resistances, or else to the physician's dread of the results of the work."[68]

For Freud, Jung's difference in technique flowed from his inability to adopt what was then the accepted psychoanalytic framework. Freud complained that for Jung

> the Oedipus complex has a merely "symbolic" meaning: the mother in it means the unattainable, which must be renounced in the interests

Carl G. Jung

of civilization; the father who is killed in the Oedipus myth is the "inner" father, from whom one must set oneself free in order to become independent.[69]

Freud concluded that Jung's theories of independence had an autobiographical source in Jung's need to be free of Freud.

Jung came to believe that patients need not only analysis but also synthesis; and here religious and philosophical doctrines might have some relevance. But, to Freud, analysis automatically entailed synthesis, and he took for granted the patient's ability to decide for himself what kind of life to lead. The psychoanalytic viewpoint has held that "whoever ventures to teach or guide his patients has, whether he knows it or not, usurped the privileges of the minister of religion."[70] As close as Jung came to traditional religion, he too drew back: as he wrote in 1935: "I have chiefly to do with people in whom I cannot implant any values or convictions. . . . The pastor of souls is naturally not in this position as a rule; he has to do with people who expressly demand to be spiritually arranged from above downwards."[71] For all Jung's stress on the importance of helping neurotic patients with problems of philosophical meaning, he could correct a disciple's overzealousness: "You *wanted* to help, which is an encroachment upon the will of others. Your attitude ought to be that of one who offers an opportunity that can be taken or rejected."[72]

Like Adler, Jung abandoned the use of the analytic couch and did not rely on the analyst's neutrality to evoke transferences. As a matter of fact, Jung would have been dubious about permitting the transference reactions, which Freud considered the essence of psychoanalytic treatment, to build up. By 1935 Jung contented himself "with a maximum of four consultations a week. With the beginning of synthetic treatment it is of advantage to spread out the consultations. I then generally reduce them to one or two hours a week, for the patient must learn to go his own way."[73] Following through on his early principle that "psychoanalysis is only a means of removing the stones from the path of development. . . . ,"[74] Jung believed in breaking off

> the treatment every ten weeks or so, in order to throw . . . [the patient] back on his normal milieu. In this way he is not alienated from his world—for he really suffers from his tendency to live at another's expense. In such a procedure time can take effect as a healing factor, without the patient's having to pay for the doctor's time.[75]

To provide short-term psychotherapeutic help, instead of full-scale analyses, was not short-changing patients, for it might sometimes be the best means of treatment.

*   *   *

Freud's supreme achievement was the development of his technique of free association, for this was something he could hand on to others; he may have been unduly stubborn in ruling out certain types of cases from treatment, but at least his followers were later able to adapt his approach to a wider range of patients. Jung was more accepting as a therapist, more willing to treat some cases Freud might have considered "unworthy" of analysis, and more flexible with regard to the kind of interventions in a patient's life that might be possible or desirable. Yet Jung was so interested in the interaction between himself and his patient that he did not evolve as firm a set of therapeutic principles as Freud and therefore did not train as many followers. Consequently, Jungian circles have had an undisciplined quality to them, and in the end Freud's rigidity paid off in the success of his movement. Though "the consensus is that Jung was an unusually skilled psychotherapist who took a different approach with each one of his patients according to their personality and needs,"[76] his example was not enough to overcome the momentum of Freud's followers.

With historical perspective, most observers today would find that on many issues of technique Jung was often more right than Freud. While Freud charged Jung with cowardice in the face of sexuality, it is also true that some early analysts were unrestrained advocates of sexual license. In the case of Otto Gross, who later died of starvation, Jung was undoubtedly sound when in 1909 he wrote that "the extreme attitude represented by Gross is decidedly wrong and dangerous to the whole movement . . . Both with students and with patients I get on further by not making the theme of sexuality prominent."[77]

Freud and his early followers were too inclined to look for deep interpretations, ignoring current conflicts, and it cannot be said simply that Jung confused the secondary gain from an illness (in the avoidance of a life task) with the primary source (the travails of instinctual life).[78] For the Jungians were right in thinking that Freud looked on the "primary" as somehow more real than the "secondary," whereas most therapists now might regard depth interpretations as conjectural and of limited therapeutic importance.

Freud dismissed the Jungian contribution, as he had the Adlerian, with regal hauteur:

> We have recently received a piece of advice, purporting to represent one of the latest developments of psychoanalysis, to the effect that the current conflict and the exciting cause of illness are to be brought into the foreground in analysis. Now this is exactly what Breuer and I used to do at the beginning of our work with the cathartic method.[79]

Breuer and Freud had aimed at the dissolution of current symptoms through a revival of the past by means of hypnotism, whereas Jung was interested in the way the past could be used in analysis for defensive purposes, unless the therapist takes the initiative in examining the realities of the patient's life situation.

Freud was afraid that this approach might lead to the kinds of "philosophic" questions he wanted to exclude from psychoanalysis. In 1932 Freud restated his objections to Jung's ideas:

> When the differences of opinion had gone beyond a certain point, the most sensible thing was to part and thereafter to proceed along our different ways—especially when the theoretical divergence involved a change in practical procedure. Suppose, for instance, that an analyst attaches little value to the influence of the patient's personal past and looks for the causation of neuroses exclusively in the present-day motives and in expectations of the future. In that case he will also neglect the analysis of childhood; he will have to adopt an entirely different technique and will have to make up for the omission of the events from the analysis of childhood by increasing his didactic influence and by directly indicating certain particular aims in life. We for our part will then say: "This may be a school of wisdom; but it is no longer analysis."[80]

Freud's willingness to allow his patients to set their own goals in life was admirable. It was well and good to emphasize that patients should take responsibility for everything in their lives, and instead of looking for faults in others should be concerned with self-criticism. Freud would hold that, even if someone else were at fault, what counts is what the patient is able to do with the situation.

Yet in more serious cases (or in the treatment of children) it would not be enough to simply analyze a patient's problems, leaving him to resolve them himself. The patient may require the analyst's continued emotional support and direction. Even by 1930, it is said, Freud's pupils would have put too much of a burden on a child in treatment.[81] Although child analysts have by now changed their technique, in the beginning they often ignored the realities of a family situation. Jung, however, had used his notion of the collective unconscious to stress that an individual always exists in the context of an environment. He thought that "the psychology of an individual can never be explained from himself alone; a clear recognition is needed of the way it is also conditioned by historical and environmental circumstances."[82] He considered that "a neurosis is more a psychosocial phenomenon than an illness in the strict sense," and he proposed to look upon "the neurotic person as a sick system of social relationships."[83] These ideas led to the opposite of the early Freudian approach in treating children, for Jung put the responsibility for the child's welfare on the parents or their substitutes. Later therapists would agree not only that one cannot take for granted a patient's capacity to integrate new insights, but also that the environment, whether of adult or child, cannot be safely neglected.

6. Afterward

JUNG HAD A STRONG TEMPER, but he was not likely to hold his anger against anyone for long. He resented Freud's followers after his separation from psychoanalysis, claiming they ruined his practice for years; and he spread stories about Freud's neurosis.* But when Ernest Jones was working on his biography of Freud and wrote to Jung to inquire about his side of the controversy, he replied that since so many years had passed, and Freud was long dead, he declined to carry on the feud further. (Jung seems to have forgotten this request for help, since when he saw Jones's biography he blamed Jones for not having adequately checked with him.) Freud was a more controlled person than Jung, but once his anger was aroused it could endure. In the polemic he wrote against Adler and Jung in 1914, Freud noted that he could be "as abusive and enraged as anyone. . . ."[2]

Freud's bitterness toward them never disappeared, and although he retained many references to Jung's works in his writings, he also sometimes suppressed an earlier citation.[3] A suggestion of Wittels's about Freud's antagonism toward Stekel can also be applied to his hatred for Jung and Adler: Freud "wanted to shake off part of his own ego, and succeeded in doing this when he began to hate Stekel. Projection explains the affective hatred with which, for years now, Freud . . . regarded his ex-disciple."[4]

Whenever Freud recounted the history of psychoanalysis, he felt obliged to refer to what he regarded as the principal secessionist move-

---

* In 1941 Jung wrote in a letter: "Freud himself was a neurotic his life long. I myself analyzed him for a certain very disagreeable symptom which in consequence of the treatment was cured."[1]

ments which had abandoned it. Freud held that each of the dissidents in psychoanalysis (he sometimes referred to them with irony as "independents") either "took their own paths, or turned themselves into an opposition which seemed to threaten the continuity of the development of psychoanalysis."[5] Each of these groups was organized around its respective leader, view, and theories; but the defectors' ideas were marred, according to Freud, by one-sidedness:

> From a highly composite combination one part of the operative factors is singled out and proclaimed as the truth; and in its favour the other part, together with the whole combination, is then contradicted. If we look a little closer, to see which group of factors it is that has been given the preference, we shall find that it is the one that contains material already known from other sources or what can be most easily related to that material. Thus, Jung picks out actuality and regression, and Adler egoistic motives. What is left over, however, and rejected as false, is precisely what is new in psychoanalysis and peculiar to it. This is the easiest method of repelling the revolutionary and inconvenient advances of psychoanalysis.[6]

Freud was entitled to his bitter feelings toward Jung to the extent that Jung, like the rest of Freud's pupils, had gained far more from contact with psychoanalysis than Freud had gained in return. Publicly Freud put a good face on the matter, and in 1914 he claimed: "I had not expected gratitude nor am I revengeful to any effective degree. . . ."[7] It cannot be entirely an accident, however, that in 1913 Freud alluded in an essay to the "tragedy of ingratitude."[8] When in 1920 Freud began to discuss his concept of the repetition compulsion, and his impression that "we have come across people all of whose human relationships have the same outcome," his first example was "the benefactor who is abandoned in anger after a time by each of his *protégés*, however much they may otherwise differ from one another, and who thus seems doomed to taste all the bitterness of ingratitude. . . ."[9]

Freud thought that the "disappointment" Adler and Jung had caused him

> might have been averted if I had paid more attention to the reactions of patients under analytic treatment. I knew very well of course that anyone may take to flight at his first approach to the unwelcome truths of analysis. . . . But I had not expected that anyone who had reached a certain depth in his understanding could renounce that understanding and lose it . . . the very same thing can happen with psychoanalysts as with patients in analysis.[10]

Part of Freud's immediate response to the loss of Jung was to minimize the importance of the Swiss support: "it was not the support of the Zurich school which first directed the attention of the scientific community to psychoanalysis at that time. What had happened was that the latency period had expired. . . ."[11] Freud was so close to the event that his emotions were naturally mixed at the loss of Jung, but even today the accounts of his most orthodox followers make the whole story seem lifeless and artificial. "If anything," as one such version has it, "one may reproach Freud with having continued to dote on undeserving disciples."[12]

Freud's repeated caution against "an analytic worker [who] may . . . attempt to emphasize some single one of the findings or views of psychoanalysis at the expense of all the rest"[13] was a veiled reproach of plagiarism. At other times Freud went so far as to imply that Jung had stolen merely the name of analysis:

It may be said . . . that by his "modification" of psychoanalysis Jung has given us a counterpart to the famous Lichtenberg knife. He has changed the hilt, and he has put a new blade into it; yet because the same name is engraved on it we are expected to regard the instrument as the original one.[14]

A "knife" would fit Freud's own conception of psychoanalysis as a form of mental surgery.

Freud was specific about how Jung, like Adler, had borrowed concepts from psychoanalysis and simply put new labels on them. For instance, Freud felt that Jung's "specialized 'psychical inertia' is only a different term, though hardly a better one, for what in psychoanalysis we are accustomed to call a 'fixation.' "[15] Freud once referred to the view (not mentioning Jung by name) that

the importance of childhood is only held up before our eyes in analysis on account of the inclination of neurotics for expressing their present interests in reminiscences and symbols from the remote past . . . scenes of early infancy . . . as products of the imagination, which find their instigation in mature life, which are intended to serve as some kind of symbolic representation of real wishes and interests, and which owe their origin to a regressive tendency, to a turning away from the tasks of the present.[16]

To counteract this position, Freud wrote the lengthy case history of the Wolf-Man, in which he tried to show the force of infantile experience on a child's neurosis. He thought he could fairly weigh the merits of Jung's point of view, since "I was the first—a point to which none of my opponents have referred—to recognize both the part played by phantasies in symptom-formation and also the 'retrospective phantasying' of late impressions into childhood and their sexualization after the event."[17] Jung reciprocated Freud's concern with priorities, mentioning that Jung's pupil Sabina Spielrein (Jean Piaget's analyst) had developed "her idea of the death instinct, which was then taken up by Freud."*[18]

Of the two movements, Adler's and Jung's, Freud thought in 1914 that Adler's was "indubitably the more important; while radically false, it is marked by consistency and coherence. It is, moreover, in spite of everything, founded on a theory of instincts."[20] Freud complained that Jung's ideas were unclear: "Wherever one lays hold of anything, one must be prepared to hear that one has misunderstood it, and one cannot see how to arrive at a correct understanding of it."[21]

Jung conceded some truth to both Adler's and Freud's viewpoints; as he once wrote, "each of these methods and theories is justified up to a point, since each can boast not only of certain successes but of psychological data that largely prove its particular assumption."[22] But Freud disliked compromises and did not want halfhearted supporters. He objected that Jung's ideas were

> put forward in a peculiarly vacillating manner, one moment as "quite a mild deviation, which does not justify the outcry that has been raised about it" (Jung), and the next moment as a new message of salvation which is to begin a new epoch for psychoanalysis, and, indeed, a new *Weltanschauung* for everyone.[23]

Freud did not know whether what he took to be Jung's inconsistencies were due to a "lack of clearness" or to a "lack of sincerity." But he could point out that the Jungians were "now disputing things which they themselves formerly upheld, and they are doing so, moreover, not on the ground of fresh observation. . . ."[24]

The charge Freud leveled against Adler and Jung was that they had offered only what he sometimes called "fresh interpretations" and at other times "twisted re-interpretations"; he had no use for what he considered "new interpretations of the facts of psychoanalysis."[25] When Freud credited Adler with "unusual ability, combined with a particularly speculative disposition,"[26] he was paying him a backhanded compliment; for speculation was high on Freud's list of intellectual sins. To Freud, Jung

---

* In "Beyond the Pleasure Principle," Freud mentioned that "a considerable portion of these speculations have been anticipated by Sabina Spielrein (1912) in an instructive and interesting paper which, however, is unfortunately not entirely clear to me."[19]

suffered from the same defect: he "first forms a theoretical conception of the nature of the sexual instinct and then seeks to explain the life of children on that basis . . . But these problems cannot be got rid of by speculation; they must await solution through other observations or through observations in other fields."[27] When Freud presented his own ideas, he tried to make sure that the reader would not be misled as to the nature of psychoanalytic propositions: "you should not for a moment suppose that what I put before you as the psychoanalytic view is a speculative system. It is on the contrary empirical. . . ."[28]

Freud thought that Jung had undergone a nonrational "illumination"[29] requiring an answer. In Freud's eyes the deviations led by Adler and Jung constituted a new emotional resistance to his ideas: "people are now adopting," he wrote in the winter of 1914–15, "another plan—of recognizing the facts, but of eliminating, by means of twisted interpretations, the consequences that follow from them, so that the critics can still ward off the objectionable novelties as efficiently as ever."[30] Jung in particular "attempted to give to the facts of analysis a fresh interpretation of an abstract, impersonal and non-historical character. . . ."[31] In essence Freud's view of Jung's work was that

> a new religio-ethical system has been created, which, just like the Adlerian system, was bound to re-interpret, distort or jettison the factual findings of analysis. The truth is that these people have picked out a few cultural overtones from the symphony of life and have once more failed to hear the mighty and primordial melody of the instincts.[32]

Freud thought that Jung was guilty of watering down psychoanalysis, and for poor motives. "[I]n an endeavor to conform to ethical standards," Jung "divested the Oedipus complex of its real significance by giving it only a *symbolic* value, and in practice neglected the uncovering of the forgotten and, as we may call it, 'pre-historic' period of childhood."[33] Jung, like Adler before him, had succumbed to the temptation "to free human society" from what Freud in 1926 rather puritanically considered the "yoke of sexuality":

> a few of those who had at that time been my followers gave in to the need to free human society from the yoke of sexuality which psychoanalysis was seeking to impose on it. One of them explained that what is sexual does not mean sexuality at all, but something else, something abstract and mystical. And another actually declared that sexual life

is merely one of the spheres in which human beings seek to put in action their driving need for power and domination. They have met with much applause, for the moment at least.³⁴

As early as 1914 part of Freud's bitterness came from his conviction that Adler and Jung would thrive on the opposition he had succeeded in stirring up: "These two retrograde movements . . . both court a favorable opinion by putting forward certain lofty ideas, which view things, as it were, *sub specie aeternitatis*."³⁵ The strength of Adler and Jung "lay . . . not in their own content, but in the temptation they offered of being freed from what were felt as the repellant findings of psychoanalysis even though its actual material was no longer rejected."³⁶

The work which won for Jung his greatest popular fame was his *Psychological Types* (1921); in 1931 Freud answered Jung's huge book on the subject of introversion and extraversion with a short essay. By entitling it "Libidinal Types," Freud was making the point that one did not need to reject libido theory, as Jung had, in order to construct character typologies. By 1923 Freud felt secure enough to write of the Adler and Jung controversies of 1911–13: "it soon appeared that these secessions had effected no lasting damage" to psychoanalysis.³⁷ And in 1932 Freud noted:

People like accusing us psychoanalysts of intolerance. The only manifestation of this ugly characteristic has been precisely our parting from those who think differently from us. No other harm has been done them. On the contrary, they have fallen on their feet, and are better off than they were before. For by their separation they have usually freed themselves of one of the burdens which weigh us down—the odium of infantile sexuality, perhaps, or the absurdity of symbolism—and are regarded by their environment as passably respectable, which is still not true of those of us who are left behind.³⁸

Although both Adler and Jung, "in view of the general hostility to psychoanalysis, could be certain of a favorable reception," in Freud's opinion they both "remained scientifically sterile."³⁹ However, Jung successfully pioneered in short-term psychotherapy, and the use of projective tests as well as self-help institutions such as Alcoholics Anonymous can be traced to his inspiration. Child analysts have "adopted Jung's techniques of therapy through drawing and painting."⁴⁰

In the fall of 1913, Freud completed an essay entitled "The Moses of Michelangelo." His study of a statue of Moses holding the Ten Commandments is most revealing of his feelings about Jung. For Freud identi-

Jung in 1922

fied with Moses as the leader of his people who liberated them from oppression. Although Freud did not return to the Moses theme until the 1930's, the earlier essay is important in itself. Composed around the time the break with Jung became public, and originally published anonymously, the essay reveals autobiographical concerns through a subject dear to Freud's heart.

Freud had admired the statue for years, writing that "no piece of statuary has ever made a stronger impression on me than this," and he singled out for the reader's attention "the angry scorn of the hero's glance." It was, of course, Freud himself who was angry at the backsliding Jung, and when he fancied the sight of "the mob upon whom his eye is turned—the mob which can hold fast no convictions, which has neither faith nor patience, and which rejoices when it has regained its illusory idols,"[41] it is clear that Freud had in mind those faithless followers of his who turned out to be less staunch than he had anticipated. Freud identified with Moses descending Mount Sinai at "the moment when he perceives that the people have meanwhile made themselves a Golden Calf and are dancing around it and rejoicing."[42]

He could appreciate Moses' "wrath," as well as "the conflict which is bound to arise between such a reforming genius and the rest of mankind." Freud thought that "the great secret of the effect produced by the Moses lies in the artistic contrast between the inward fire and the outward calm of his bearing."[43] Typically examining apparently insignificant details, Freud argued that the statue represented Moses' having overcome the temptation to smash the Commandments, "and he will now remain seated and still, in his frozen wrath and in his pain mingled with contempt."[44] Moses checked his passion, "he remembered his mission and for its sake renounced an indulgence of his feelings."[45]

According to Freud, "the Moses of legend and tradition had a hasty temper and was subject to fits of passion." But Michelangelo had carved out a different character for Moses, a being superior to the historical Moses. The statue was to be placed on the tomb of Pope Julius II: "so that the giant frame with its tremendous physical power becomes only a concrete expression of the highest mental achievement that is possible in a man, that of struggling successfully against an inward passion for the sake of a cause to which he has devoted himself."[46] There may seem something incongruous about the short and slight Freud identifying with the tremendous heroic figure of a man that Michelangelo had carved. But Freud had chosen Jung, a taller and larger man, as his successor; for this reason, perhaps, the statue was an appropriate vehicle for expressing his feelings on losing his pupil.

Freud had long before been secure as a spiritual warrior; and in writing about how Michelangelo's relationship to the Pope helped explain the nature of his statue, he was able to surmount his own emotions. For what Freud wrote about the personalities of Michelangelo and Pope Julius could also apply to Freud himself.

Julius II was akin to Michelangelo in this, that he attempted to realize great and mighty ends, and especially designs on a grand scale. He was a man of action and he had a definite purpose, which was to unite Italy under the Papal Supremacy. He desired to bring about single-handed what was not to happen for several centuries, and then only through the conjunction of many alien forces; and he worked alone, with impatience, in the short span of sovereignty allowed him, and used violent means. He could appreciate Michelangelo as a man of his own kind, but he often made him smart under his sudden anger and his utter lack of consideration for others. The artist felt the same violent force of will in himself, and, as the more introspective thinker, may have had a premonition of the failure to which they were both doomed. And so he carved his Moses on the Pope's tomb, not without a reproach against the dead pontiff, as a warning to himself, thus, in self-criticism, rising superior to his own nature.[47]

It must have been a shock for Freud to discover that he tended to undermine his own efforts. However, it was only after the break with Jung that Freud felt certain of his identity. With enemies like Adler and Jung, Freud felt he could lay claim to his historic role, which until then he had not asserted.

In publicly justifying his original choice of Jung, Freud explained: "I wished . . . to withdraw into the background both myself and the city where psychoanalysis first saw the light."[48] Having failed, Freud now moved to the center of the stage; relatively slow in maintaining that psychoanalysis was his creation (instead of Breuer's)—he did not state until 1914 that "psychoanalysis is my creation"—Freud was now confident enough to take full responsibility for his ideas. As part of defining what he was, Freud had to delineate what he was not; and therefore he had to repudiate Jung and Adler. At the same time, Freud carried on his discussion in an impersonal way: "When I come to the points at which the divergences occurred, I shall have . . . to defend the just rights of psychoanalysis with some remarks of a purely critical character."[49]

If Freud could write to Jones after World War I that "your intention to purge the London Society of the Jungish members is excellent,"[50] it was not just personal vindictiveness but state policy. Freud had his own special way of handling controversies. Whenever he had a disagreement with a pupil, he tended to look for the motivation; his conception of "resistance" would tend to shift the discussion away from the merits of the case. Concerning Adler and Stekel, for instance, Freud once wrote that "whatever analytic comment I made about these two men was uttered to others and chiefly at a time when they were no longer in contact with me."[51] But a patient in a training analysis after World War I was unable to draw Freud into a discussion of the split with Jung, as Freud explained that the reasons had been "personal and scientific."[52] Yet it is reported that in the 1930's, "twenty years after the event, a casual visitor was startled by Freud's bitterness about Jung, a bitterness which he said 'was always apparent and extended from [Jung's] person to his countrymen.' "[53]

While still in Freud's circle Jung had tried to minimize the extent of his own innovations, but subsequently he stressed how much he had learned on his own and how little he had gained from Freud. In a letter in 1933 Jung wrote: "I would like to take this opportunity to rectify the error that I come from the Freudian school. I am a pupil of Bleuler's. . . ."[54] As early as 1908 Freud had complained that Jung was "hampered by a spirit of compromise," to which Jung replied: "I am really no propagandist. . . . I always have a little more to do than be just a faithful follower. You have no lack of those anyway. But they do not advance the cause, for by faith alone nothing prospers in the long run."[55] Yet at other times Jung maintained that he was pursuing a deeper understanding of the unconscious, and that "I am only going further along the path taken by Freud. . . ."[56] Yet his backsliding must have been evident to him, if only because of the need he felt to delete certain passages from earlier essays.[57] It cannot have been easy for Jung after the break with Freud. One is reminded of accounts of those who have left the Communist Party. As Jean-Paul Sartre has put it so well,

> It isn't easy to leave a Party. There are all its laws that must be wrenched from oneself before they can be broken. There are all these men whose beloved, familiar faces will become the dirty mugs of the enemy, this somber crowd which will continue to march along stubbornly, and which he will watch marching off to disappear.

But whereas, in Sartre's words, "a lone Communist is lost,"[58] a lone former Freudian need never be. Since Freud had glorified, and indeed exaggerated, his isolation in the 1890's, and was willing to reduce the size of his movement for the sake of purification, a pupil of Freud's could always identify with him in the very act of setting out on an independent course. Jung could be dictatorial himself; "those who have known Jung remember the tone of absolute conviction with which he spoke of the anima, the self, the archetypes, and the collective unconscious."[59] Jung often criticized Freud's theory of the libido as too one-sided and biological, though earlier, in 1906, he had written in defense of Freud that "seldom has a great truth appeared without fantastic wrappings."[60] By 1948 Jung believed that Freud had "directed his attention mainly to the ruthless desire for pleasure," as Adler had to the "psychology of prestige."[61] Jung thought that "Freud began by taking sexuality as the only psychic driving force, and only after my break with him did he take other factors into account"; but for Jung "it was to no purpose that he [Freud] modified the worst aspects of his theories in later years. In the public eye he is branded by his first statements."[62] Jung felt that his own insistence on the importance of man's higher nature had re-emerged in Freud's late concept of the super-ego.

In 1929 Jung denied being an "opponent" of Freud: "I am merely presented in that light by his own shortsightedness and that of his pupils."[63] As Jung had earlier explained his relationship to Freud:

> After having . . . put my finger on the same psychological mechanisms of Freud, it was natural that I should become his pupil and collaborator over a period of many years. But while I always recognized the truth of his conclusions so far as the facts were concerned, I could not conceal my doubts as to the validity of his theories. His regrettable dogmatism was the main reason why I felt obliged to part company from him.[64]

In 1932, although he felt that Freud's psychology had not been "forward-looking" enough, Jung acknowledged that Freud

> is a great destroyer who breaks the fetters of the past. He liberates us from the unwholesome pressure of a world of rotten habits . . . like an Old Testament prophet, he overthrew false idols and pitilessly exposed to the light of day the rottenness of the contemporary psyche.[65]

It was only toward the end of his life that Jung had an association with journals and institutes for training. Many of his followers were women, at least in Switzerland, and they were relatively untrained. Jung was not the writer or teacher Freud was, and he could make fun of his later pupils (for example, for their sexual inhibitions). In a sense, he developed more a cult than a school. However, Jung's pupils did not experience the kind of controversies that harassed the Freudians. For according to Jung's theory of opposites and his concept of the shadow, if one was intensely against anything it was probably because of latent positive feelings; as a result, it was nearly impossible to have a real fight in Jungian circles and problems tended to be driven underground.

In Jung's last twenty years his interests, like those of Freud at the end of his life, tended to transcend his earlier medical orientation and were directed to all of humanity. "Kind and compassionate though Jung was, he was always more interested in ideas than in people. . . ."[66] Although Jung had begun with greater therapeutic ambition than Freud, at the end Freud was more interested in the ill than was Jung; at least Freud continued to practice until a few months before his death, whereas Jung stopped at an earlier age. Some of Jung's ideas about society and art tallied almost exactly with those of Freud: for example, Jung's contemptuous view of the masses and his hostility to contemporary art. In religion, however, they were at opposite ends of the spectrum, and the publication of Freud's *Future of an Illusion* only confirmed Jung's distrust of Freud's devotion to what seemed to him a materialistic conception of science.

Partly because of Freud's tendency to exaggerate opposition, it is hard to assess the anti-Semitism he complained of, and in particular how much Jung's attitude toward Jews contributed to the difficulties with Freud. Publicly Freud mentioned Jung's decision "for my sake to give up certain racial prejudices. . . ."[67] In private Freud complained of Jung's "lies, brutality, and anti-Semitic condescension towards me."[68] Curiously enough, however, in Freud's correspondence with Jung there is not a trace of any such accusation.

During the Nazi ascendancy in Europe, Jung not only assisted Jewish refugees in Switzerland but also helped Jews to get into England. The Nazis put his name on their "black list" and "his works were suppressed by the Nazis in Germany and occupied countries."[69] In a sense, Freud and his followers had to depict Jung as an anti-Semite, since Freud's enthusiasm for Jung in the first place had been essentially anti-Semitic in character. It would not be in keeping with Jung's character or his theories for him to take a wholeheartedly negative position toward any group. Although he made hostile remarks at various times about both the English and the Swiss, for instance, he tried to show that there are good and bad elements in everything.

Whether because of his shadow concept or because of his naïveté about Hitler (which many others shared), Jung first misjudged the real nature of the Nazi phenomenon in Germany. Jung had always thought that different cultural groups had psychologies that were appropriate to them, and in particular he distinguished between Jewish and "Aryan" psychotherapy. For Jung, both Adler and Freud "deserved reproach for overemphasizing the pathological aspect of life and for interpreting man too exclusively in the light of his defects."[70] (Jung, however, tended to err in the opposite direction.) What Jung wrote in 1934 was entirely consistent with his understanding of Freud's own character:

> no psychotherapist should let slip the opportunity to study himself critically in the light of these negative psychologies. Freud and Adler have beheld very clearly the shadow side that accompanies us all. The Jews have this peculiarity in common with women; being physically weaker, they have to aim at the chinks in the armor of their adversary, and thanks to this technique which has been forced on them through the centuries, the Jews themselves are best protected where others are most vulnerable. Because, again, of their civilization, more than twice as ancient as ours, they are vastly more conscious than we of human weaknesses, of the shadow-side of things, and hence in this respect less vulnerable than we are. Thanks to their experience of an old culture, they are able, while fully conscious of their frailties, to live on friendly terms with them, whereas we are still too young not to have "illusions" about ourselves. Moreover, we have been entrusted with the task of creating a civilization . . . and for this "illusions" in the form of one-sided ideals, convictions, plans, etc. are indispensable. As a member of a race with a three-thousand-year-old civilization, the Jew, like the cultured Chinese, has a wider area of psychological consciousness than we. Consequently it is *in general* less dangerous for the Jew to put a negative value on his unconscious. The "Aryan" unconscious, on the other hand, contains explosive forces and seeds of a future yet to be born, and these may not be devalued as nursery romanticism without psychic danger . . . The Jew, who is something of a nomad, has never yet created a cultural form of his own and as far as we can see never will, since all his instincts and talents require a more or less civilized nation to act as host for their development . . . The "Aryan" unconscious has a higher potential than the Jewish; that is both the advantage and the disadvantage of a youthfulness not yet fully weaned from barbarism. In my opinion it has been a grave error in medical psychology up to now to apply Jewish categories—which are not even binding on all Jews—indiscriminately to German and Slavic Christendom. Because of this the most precious secret of the Germanic peoples—their creative and intuitive depth of soul—has been explained as a morass of banal infantilism, while my own warning voice has for decades been suspected of anti-Semitism. This suspicion

emanated from Freud. He did not understand the Germanic psyche any more than did his Germanic followers. Has the formidable phenomenon of National Socialism, on which the whole world gazes with astonished eyes, taught them better? . . . That is why I say that the Germanic unconscious contains tensions and potentialities which medical psychology must consider in its evaluation of the unconscious.[71]

Jung had been a great admirer of Chinese culture; as he protested in a letter, "the mere fact that I speak of a difference between Jewish and Christian psychology suffices to allow anyone to voice the prejudice that I am an anti-Semite. Or, in the opinion of the Swiss Israelite Weekly, my assertion that I am as little an anti-Semite as an anti-Chinese proves my intention to compare the Jews with a Mongolian horde."[72] But just as Jung shared sexist prejudices toward women, it would not be surprising for him to have uncritically adopted many traditional stereotypes about Jews. Jung had, however, allowed his comments on the differences between Jewish and "Aryan" psychology to appear in an article published in Germany; the closeness of Jung's distinction between "Jewish science" and "German science" to the Nazi one is chilling.

In 1934, shortly after the Nazis came to power, Jung concluded in "Wotan" that "things must be concealed in the background which we cannot imagine at present, but we may expect them to appear in the course of the next few years or decades." But to Jung "the impressive thing about the German phenomenon is that one man, who is obviously 'possessed,' has infected a whole nation to such an extent that everything is set in motion and has started rolling on its course towards perdition."[73] In 1939 Jung polemically complained that "introversion is felt . . . as something abnormal, morbid, or otherwise objectionable. Freud identifies it with an autoerotic, 'narcissistic' attitude of mind. He shares his negative position with the National Socialist philosophy of modern Germany, which accuses introversion of being an offence against community feeling."[74]

Unfortunately for Jung's later reputation, in June 1933 the German Society for Psychotherapy had been reorganized by the Nazis into the International General Medical Society for Psychotherapy; its president resigned, and Jung accepted the post.[75] Almost immediately, Jung was publicly denounced by a Swiss analyst, Gustav Bally. Jung had also become editor of the Society's journal, and in 1936 a psychiatrist cousin of Göring was installed as co-editor with him. It was not until 1940 that Jung severed his connections with this Nazi association. Jung wrote a rejoinder to Bally,[76] and for the rest of his life felt called upon to explain his collaboration with the Nazis. In a letter in 1951 Jung wrote about the "slander rumor":

> When . . . the International Medical Society for Psychotherapy was founded my German colleagues were afraid that the Nazis would wipe out Psychotherapy in Germany altogether and they wanted a non-German authority to help them. Well, I stepped in and made it possible for the cast-out Jewish doctors to become immediate members of the International Society . . . The Journal of the Society appeared in Germany, being bound by a contract to a German publisher and I could not change this. The president became automatically its editor and I had to sign it. Soon then the Nazis put Göring in. I wanted to withdraw, but my colleagues insisted that I should stay, in the hope that I could do something for them. Eventually I succeeded to tuck away Psychotherapy in a remote department, where the medical Nazi boss could not reach it. From 1937 on I tried to withdraw, but representatives of the Dutch and of the recently founded British group begged me not to give up and to hold the connection . . . I would not disavow my colleagues and friends. Thus I had to play the game and tread softly (much against my grain!) knowing very well that I was a black sheep on account of my Wotan essay which only a complete ass can misunderstand as a pro-Nazi sentiment. I have never changed my view about the Nazis, nor have I ever been an anti-Semite; but I am convinced of the psychological differences between Jew and Gentile as between French and English and so on.[77]

An extensive literature has grown up concerning Jung's role as a Nazi fellow traveler; to some it seemed that for the sake of a prestigious psychiatric post Jung was willing to do business with the Nazis, and his later version merely an attempt to justify what is bound to be, at the least, distasteful. Responsible people, however, are convinced that Jung's co-editor, the cousin of Hitler's deputy, was truly trying to protect therapists in Germany. The new Society Jung headed could house therapists who had been removed from the earlier organization. Ernest Jones also had dealings with M. H. Göring, and Jones remembered him as "a fairly amiable and amenable person."[78] Jones was trying to protect analysts in Germany, and found Göring pliable enough.[79] However, when in 1935 the Dutch members of the new organization refused to be hosts to a Congress, Jung fell back on the "principle" of neutrality:

> I must resolutely emphasize that our German colleagues were not makers of the Nazi revolution, but live in a state that demands a def-

inite political attitude. If the association with Germany is now to be jeopardized on political grounds, we are falling into the same error we accuse the others of: politics is simply pitted against politics.[80]

We have no evidence of what Freud thought of Jung's activities in connection with the Nazis. He continued to analyze and to write throughout the 1930's, and was again preoccupied with the Moses theme. *Moses and*

Woodcut of Freud by Sidney Chafetz

*Monotheism** was a reconstruction of the Biblical legend. Freud thought there had in fact been two Moseses, the first an Egyptian nobleman, the true founder of monotheism, and a second Moses who was able to govern and implement monotheistic religion thanks to the guilt feelings of the Jews over their having slain the first Moses, against whose severity they had revolted. In his 1914 polemic against Adler and Jung, Freud had mentioned his expectation in the 1890's that "science would ignore me entirely during my life-time; some decades later, someone else would infallibly come upon the same things—for which the time was not now ripe—would achieve recognition for them and bring me honor as a forerunner whose failure had been inevitable."[81]

Though *Moses and Monotheism* had little objective basis in history (Freud himself referred to it as a "novel"), it accurately reflected themes that were important to Freud. As early as his fainting episode in Munich when he was with Jung, Freud had associated the mystery of ancient Egyptology with the unknown territory of the unconscious, and had worried about whether his chosen successor would be true to the innovative ideas that he, like the first Moses, had managed to promote. But by transforming the earlier Moses into an Egyptian—by depriving the Jews of their greatest figure—might not Freud have been unconsciously expressing his discomfort at being a Jew, converting himself to a Gentile in fantasy and thereby helping to ensure what he hoped Jung would accomplish, namely protecting analysis from the charge of being merely a Jewish psychology?

Freud liked to identify with the mythic hero who is an outsider and who does not belong to his people, even if it must remain unsettled whether, as one writer suggests, he felt "resentment, secret and unacknowledged, at being a Jew at all, at being forced to feel inferior when he was convinced of his own superior endowments."†[82] Consistent with the suggestion that *Moses and Monotheism* harked back to Freud's relationship with Jung, and Freud's fears about the future of psychoanalysis after his death, one part of the book comes close to Jung's doctrine of the collective unconscious. In *Moses and Monotheism*, as in *Totem and Taboo*, Freud argued that acquired guilt feelings could be passed on genetically, and the Oedipus complex did in the end assume for Freud archetypal status. Although Freud wrote that "I do not think we gain anything by introducing the concept

---

* Cf. below, pp. 529–32.

† In 1933 Freud wrote of himself: "Here a piece of opposition to one's own Jewishness may still be hiding cunningly. Our great master Moses was, after all, a strong anti-Semite and made no secret of it."[83]

of a 'collective' unconscious,"[84] Jung's theory of archetypes could find support in Freud's theory of symbolism; Freud thought symbols were a phylogenetic inheritance. To Jung, Freud's notion of "super-ego" denoted Jung's collective unconscious, "of which the individual is partly conscious and partly unconscious (because it is repressed)."[85]

In 1936 Harvard University held its tercentenary celebration; an alumnus, Franklin Roosevelt, was President of the United States, and the ceremonial arrangements were elaborate. A committee unanimously decided to offer an honorary degree to Freud. It did not occur to the members that he might refuse. A few days later Erik Erikson informed them that the chances of Freud's accepting were nil.[86] So the committee declined to proceed, for fear Freud would turn down the invitation because of his age and illness; if an offer were rejected the decision would go to a different committee, and the psychologists involved wanted one of their own to get the honor, rather than risk the prize going to, say, an economist. Instead of Freud, then, Jung received the honorary degree. Pierre Janet was also invited to take part in the proceedings, and he lectured as well.

Jung stayed at the home of a distinguished Harvard neurologist, Stanley Cobb. Cobb had befriended many European analysts who were on good terms with Freud. In European fashion, Jung put his shoes outside the door of his room at night, and Cobb obligingly polished them. Cobb had a bad stammer, and when he haltingly introduced Jung in the large amphitheater of the Massachusetts General Hospital, the audience hung on his every word. At the end of his remarks, however, Cobb committed one of the classic slips in the history of psychoanalysis; for he introduced Jung as "Dr. Freud." Some newspaper reporters were roused to ask afterward why, if Jung was Freud's pupil, the master himself had not been invited.

Later Henry Murray, the Harvard psychologist, visited Freud in Vienna. Though an old man, Freud still cared for the world's recognition, and one of the first things Freud brought up was why Jung had received the honorary Harvard degree and not himself. Murray told him about the vote and the reasons for his not being invited. Still at war with Jung, Freud was convinced he had been right in predicting that popularity and fame would come to those who served up psychoanalysis in a more agreeable guise than his own. In 1938 Jung also received an honorary doctorate from Oxford University.

VII

THE LOYAL
MOVEMENT

1. Elder Statesmen

WHENEVER FREUD preferred not to be drawn into a quarrel with any of his students, a variety of arguments (some legitimate, others less so) could stiffen his defensiveness. He usually knew a great deal about their private lives and the ways in which personal problems might impede them in working with a parental substitute. Steadily and unobtrusively, Freud was continually collecting new pupils; if some fell by the wayside, he could be confident that they would be replaced by others. Writing in 1914 of the circle that had grown up around him, Freud remarked that "on the whole I could tell myself that it was hardly inferior, in wealth and variety of talent, to the staff of any clinical teacher one could think of."[1] In defending himself in 1924 against the charge of intolerance, Freud called attention to how many gifted pupils had stayed with him:

the secession of former pupils has often been brought up against me as a sign of my intolerance or has been regarded as evidence of some special fatality that hangs over me. It is a sufficient answer to point out that in contrast to those who have left me, like Jung, Adler, Stekel, and a few besides, there are a great number of men, like Abraham, Eitingon, Ferenczi, Rank, Jones, Brill, Sachs, Pfister, van Emden, Reik, and others, who have worked with me for some fifteen years in loyal collaboration and for the most part in uninterrupted friendship. I have only mentioned the oldest of my pupils, who have already made a distinguished name for themselves in the literature of psychoanalysis; if I have passed over others, that is not to be taken as a slight, and indeed among those who are young and have joined me lately talents are to be found on which great hopes may be set. But I think I can say in my defense that an intolerant man, dominated by an arrogant belief in his own infallibility, would never have been able to maintain his hold upon so large a number of intellectually eminent people, especially if he had at his command as few practical attractions as I had.[2]

By 1924 psychoanalysis was becoming a successful method of making a living. The economic factors in the history of psychoanalysis can easily be overlooked. Most of those who first came to Freud for training as analysts had been none too successful at their previous occupations. Changing a field of work represented self-dissatisfaction and self-questioning, and to join a new movement with an uncertain future entailed the courage to take a risk. Even in 1924 a psychoanalytic background would have been a detriment in academic psychiatry almost everywhere.

Career instability, however, has its less engaging and more earthly sides. Having successfully put all their eggs in a new basket—and by 1924 Freud was internationally well known—the early analysts were inclined to be excessively self-assured, in contrast to (and perhaps in compensation for) their previous frustrations. It is still more or less true of psychoanalysts that to defend Freud is simultaneously to defend their own means of livelihood. By 1924 analysts had vested interests to protect, and to have followed Jung, Adler, or Stekel into rebellion would have ruined most of them, since they were dependent for referrals of patients on either Freud himself or his associates scattered around the Western world. However hazardous psychoanalysis might have been as a profession in its early days, as it began to take hold its prospects as a career brightened disproportionately; paradoxically, today if there are fifty colleagues in a city a psychoanalyst's income is more secure than if there are only a handful.

By the 1920's Freud's circle had acquired not only some of the stability of success but also relative peace. The great ideological quarrels of the prewar years were over; and although minor outbreaks would occur right up to Freud's death in 1939, whatever antagonisms there were would never again be acted out, as, for instance, in Adler's "trial." Freud dominated the scene completely in the 1920's and 1930's, and by then was mostly above such rivalries. One of Freud's talented new students, Franz Alexander, had to hear "from one of the older Viennese psychoanalysts that Freud on one occasion, referring to a younger member of the Viennese group, said: 'I cannot stand the parricidal look in his eyes.' "[3] In Alexander's time Freud was an exalted old gentleman above open clashes.

Whereas in the case of Jung, for example, Freud had sought out and encouraged this brilliant and eager supporter, by now his pupils wooed him. They did not participate in his movement for purely scientific reasons. They revered him like a monarch; he was surrounded by a court, the

members of·which were unlikely to stand up to him on any matter. Erik
Erikson quotes one of Mahatma Gandhi's followers: "I am not going to
Gandhiji with the ambition of achieving success. I want to live like his
shadow. . . .";[4] and many of Freud's followers had exactly this feeling
toward the master. Helene Deutsch recalled:

> All . . . created the same atmosphere about the master, an atmosphere
> of absolute and infallible authority on his part. It was never any fault
> of Freud's that they cast him in this role and that they—so rumor has
> it—became mere "yes men." Quite the contrary; Freud had no love for
> "yes men" and so it fell out that the very ones who proved to be the
> most loyal and the more reliable adherents were not the recipients of
> a warmer sympathy on his part.[5]

Realistically, however, Freud helped his pupils in their work simply
with his presence; any writer needs an audience, and it was for Freud that
they all wrote. At the same time Freud's stature could be intimidating.
Some pupils felt so "hurt" by Freud's reaction to their presentation of
papers that they did not submit them for publication.[6]

The ties that bound Freud's circle together were powerful. Some of
his pupils were highly intelligent and no more naturally docile than others.
Why, then, were they so passive toward Freud? For one thing, their
intense dedication to psychoanalysis was reinforced by their fear of excommunication. Freud needed to dominate and be master, and his pupils
were afraid of being excluded from his community.

Whereas Freud naturally saw the rebellions from his own perspective,
his pupils looked at the situation in another way; for them the danger (and
the temptation) was to assume the role of defiance and revisionism. The
anxiety "of being isolated and of becoming an outcast through having
thoughts and feelings which nobody would share"[7] might be enough to
induce conformism. At any given period orthodox pupils would check
to see whether members of the circle were unobtrusively slipping into the
mistakes of earlier outcasts. To be so stigmatized was to run the risk of
getting lost, being dropped from the movement and thereby forfeiting
a place in history (and this risk was real, for once out of the movement a
heretic's work no longer was cited). Like the early Marxists, the Freudians
felt that the future was on their side.

Freud claimed to dislike giving the impression that analysts were
"members of a secret society and . . . practicing a mystical science."[8] Yet
his was an army on the march, scornful of any "compromise" that might
weaken the cause. "I like to avoid concessions to faintheartedness. One
can never tell where that road may lead one; one gives way first in words,

and then little by little in substance too . . . he who knows how to wait
need make no concessions."[9] Freud held his followers together through
the fighting spirit he communicated to them. As he wrote to a pupil in
1927:

> There is a way to represent one's cause and in doing so to treat the
> audience in such a cool and condescending manner that they are
> bound to notice one is not doing it to please them. The principle should
> always be not to make concessions to those who don't have anything
> to give but who have everything to gain from us. We can wait until
> they are begging on their knees even if it takes a very long time.[10]

Freud's followers could thus be incredibly arrogant, not directly in behalf
of themselves, but for psychoanalysis.

The Professor took many practical steps to hold his group together.
Certain photographs of him amounted to a party membership card, and
Freud passed these out as a sign of welcome and affection. It was an index
of special recognition for Freud to write a preface to a pupil's book. Freud
once described how a group is bound together by the "illusion . . . of
there being a head . . . who loves all the individuals in the group with an
equal love."[11] The tie that united each individual to Freud also was the
source of the tie which united them with one another. With docile pupils,
once Freud gave of his kindness and devotion his friendship would endure
as passionately as his hatred. It was also no minor source of his hold over
his followers that when they (or anyone they cared about) were personally troubled, they could turn to him as a therapist.

Freud's most ardent disciples might privately scoff at the others as
mere believers; but knowing Freud gave meaning to their lives. These
early analysts were in the process of breaking away from their own constricting families, only to settle in a tight family-like milieu. "They were
urban intellectuals, with a deep yearning to be committed to an ideal, to
a leader, to a movement, and yet without having any religious or political
or philosophic ideal or convictions. . . ."[12] The call for faith and sacrifice
can be for some a welcome demand.

In the words of Helene Deutsch, one of Freud's most loyal followers,
"his pupils were to be above all passive understanding listeners," "projection objects through whom he reviewed—sometimes to correct or to
retract them—his own ideas."[13] In the 1920's Freud was delighted by a
paper of Robert Waelder's which systematized some of the master's concepts without suggesting new formulations. Freud said approvingly: "I
feel as if a painter has done my portrait, and when I look at it, it is better
than the original." That was Freud's highest possible compliment; to re-

flect his own ideas back to him, without offering anything disturbingly new, was what he wanted from them. Freud's ideal sons and daughters (he greeted and addressed many of the men as "my son") were embarked on ensuring his scientific immortality. The quality and generality of his ideas were such that a follower had to alter his beliefs in order to function in Freud's world. None of his supporters had to be especially mature or brilliant; anyone, no matter how mediocre, could help Freud by giving back his ideas with only a slightly different twist, or by forwarding the practice of psychoanalysis itself.

It is not clear to what extent all this flattery was corrupting, either to Freud himself or to his pupils.* Though they may have unwittingly encouraged his sense of grandiosity, he kept his distance from them and never lost sight of their usefulness to him. "Everybody around Freud wanted to be loved by him, but his intellectual accomplishments meant infinitely more to him than the people around him. As an inspired path-finder he felt justified in regarding his co-workers as a means towards his own impersonal objective accomplishment. . . ."[14] Freud regarded the youngest pupils in his last phase as "colonists" who would replace the "pioneers" of the early days.[15] To use another of Freud's images, every-one was capable of adding "bricks" to the edifice of psychoanalysis.

Freud expected immense devotion from his adherents. It can be no accident that in his study of group psychology the two examples he dis-cussed were "churches—communities of believers—and armies."[16] Freud thought that it could be "said of psychoanalysis that if anyone holds out a little finger to it it quickly grasps his whole hand."[17]

> As a rule psychoanalysis possesses a doctor either entirely or not at all. Those psychotherapists who make use of analysis among other methods, occasionally, do not to my knowledge stand on firm analytic ground; they have not accepted the whole of analysis but have watered it down—have drawn its fangs, perhaps; they cannot be counted as analysts.[18]

He made a sharp distinction between those who were and those who were not true, full-time analysts, even though from his own point of view "cooperation in medical practice between an analyst and a psychotherapist who restricts himself to other techniques would serve quite a useful pur-pose."[19] Toward those who were in his group, however, Freud was

---

* For example, Freud never realized how much of a suggestive impact he had on his followers, and therefore could be led to think that his findings were being genuinely confirmed by independent observers.

extremely possessive, and in Vienna, for example, it would have been considered an interference in a candidate's training to practice psychotherapy in addition to classical analysis.

The various analytic communities were composed of deeply convinced and highly motivated people. In practical terms, their own special techniques were familiar only to them, and in their inner circle they could safely exchange comments on their therapeutic experiences and give one another practical advice. Freud had warned them against "eclectics," who would not fully endorse their work, "these half- or quarter-adherents," although "they, to be sure, are excused by the fact that their time and their interest belong to other things. . . ."[20] Outsiders were regarded as the equivalent of religious unbelievers. Freud once wrote that

> a religion, even if it calls itself the religion of love, must be hard and unloving to those who do not belong to it. Fundamentally indeed every religion is in this same way a religion of love for all those whom it embraces; while cruelty and intolerance towards those who do not belong to it are natural to every religion.

He went on to predict that other ties, such as political ones, would be able to take the place of religious ones; and "then there will be the same intolerance towards outsiders as in the age of the Wars of Religion; and if differences between scientific opinions could ever attain a similar significance for groups, the same result would again be repeated with this new motivation."[21]

Publicly Freud put a bold face on the scientific rebellions that had once wracked psychoanalysis; yet it was plain in Freud's circle how pained he was by these "desertions." But precisely because Freud admired brilliance and originality, and did not like it if someone (especially a man) became too dependent on him, he had little respect for some followers who stayed with him to the end. As Freud summed up his dilemma to a patient in the late 1920's, "the goody-goodys are no good, and the naughty ones go away."[22] Even in his 1924 list of those who stayed to counterbalance those who had left, Freud could not bring himself to include some of his most well-known disciples. Although he covered himself by saying that "if I have passed over others, that is not to be taken as a slight," it was well known within Freud's circle how contentious a matter it was who counted and who did not. Freud kept some around him because they performed specific functions or exhibited specialized talents; but others remained out of their utter devotion to him, while he tolerated them in gratitude for their services to his cause in its earliest period.

*　　　　*　　　　*

Paul Federn (1871–1950), for example, was not a special favorite of Freud's, even though he played a prominent role in the history of psychoanalysis. Having first come into Freud's circle in 1903, he was one of Freud's oldest adherents; Frau Professor would include Federn's wife among those to whom she would pay a formal call once a year. To the generation of analysts who joined Freud in the 1920's and 1930's, Federn was a bearded patriarch, the St. Peter of the movement. Otto Fenichel, Wilhelm Reich, Edward Bibring, Edoardo Weiss, Heinrich Meng, Smith Ely Jeliffe, and August Aichhorn were analyzed by him. If Federn had not finished a meal, he would offer a patient some food, and he treated Reich free of charge. The poet Rainer Maria Rilke came to him for a brief period, as did the novelist Hermann Broch. Like others of the first generation of analysts, Federn had not himself been analyzed. He often mentioned, with great sadness, his regret and resentment that Freud had not taken him into analysis; for only Freud would have had enough seniority in the group to treat Federn.

Freud always paid Federn the respect due him as an early follower —the oldest pupil Freud still had with him when the Nazis entered Vienna. At that time Freud entrusted to Federn, as a gift to him, the *Minutes* of the meetings of the Vienna Society (Volume I was published in 1962, Volume II in 1967, Volume III in 1974, and IV appeared in 1975). In 1931, at a celebration in honor of Freud's seventy-fifth birthday in Freiberg, Moravia, Freud deputized Federn to accompany Freud's daughter Anna and to make a speech. In 1930, when Freud's mother became dangerously ill just before she died at the age of ninety-five, Federn escorted her back to Vienna from her summer resort.

After Freud was first struck by cancer in 1923, he appointed Federn vice-president of the Vienna Society. Freud made him his personal substitute, and automatically referred to him some patients who had come to Freud himself for treatment.[23] Like other Europeans of that era, Freud could not adjust to the ready use of the telephone; so he would communicate by letter to Federn (as to other pupils) about patients and candidates in training. When Freud asked Federn to act as his personal substitute in 1924, it seemed to Federn that Freud was appointing him his heir, and thereafter he considered himself the true successor to Freud.

With the onset of his illness Freud also ceased to attend the public meetings of the Society, and instead invited a selected group of analysts to his apartment for meetings on Wednesday evening every few weeks. There were regular participants as well as occasional ones, and Freud put Federn in charge of deciding who was to be invited to these private gatherings. In 1938, when the Vienna Society was dissolved, Freud gave Federn a written testimonial of his having been "my substitute in leading the Viennese psychoanalytic group acknowledging him thereby as the most prominent member equally distinguished by his scientific work, his experience as teacher and his success in therapeutics."[24]

Nevertheless, Freud had his doubts about Federn's capacities; Freud described him in a letter, for example, as "not" being "completely reliable."[25] The two men were different types. Federn could be confused, in both his writings and his daily life, though he tried hard to overcome his difficulties as a speaker. His slips of the tongue became famous among the Vienna group, and he told jokes about them himself; he could invite a couple to dinner and then greet them at the door with a bewildered expression, not having remembered the invitation. But the many anecdotes about Federn were told benevolently.

"Federn was a dreamer and a romantic, at times subject to great discouragement and at times over-optimistic. . . . he lacked Freud's realism

Paul Federn (1871–1950)

and scepticism."[26] If Freud was a scientist and a searcher, Federn was a physician and a reformer. Politically, Freud was moderate and pro-establishment, and by the 1930's he was supporting a reactionary regime in Austria. Federn, on the other hand, was an idealist and an active Socialist. Whereas Freud was one of the more cautious of the believers in his own ideas, Federn thought that psychoanalysis was the final message of liberation for mankind. Freud was inclined to think that not much could help improve mankind. Federn co-authored a "people's" handbook of psychoanalysis, still recently being reprinted; for a new edition of the book he wrote a passage about psychoanalysis and society which Freud advised against publishing since it was too optimistic (it was therefore not published until after Federn's death).

Part of Federn's lack of clarity in his writings may have been due to his deference to Freud; for although his ideas followed a relatively different line from Freud's, he wanted to avoid slipping into the role of a deviant and a rebel. He knew some of his limitations and made the most of the gifts he had. His strength came from Freud and the psychoanalytic movement; Federn succeeded in what others could not do, submerging himself in the ethos of a stronger man.

It was said that Federn felt he had betrayed his father, a well-known internist, by not following a similar career; so there was something sacred in his loyalty to Freud. He named his daughter Anna, and commissioned a portrait of Freud which was painted during a short period late in 1908 when Freud was beardless. (The painting was intended as a wedding present for Freud's daughter Mathilda, but since she did not like it Federn kept it himself.) Federn also arranged for a bust of Freud to be sculptured by Oscar Nemon, who later did a statue of Winston Churchill for the House of Commons. Federn observed Freud closely enough to advise others never to approach him when he was alone and immersed in his thoughts, for such an interruption would at first irritate Freud, even though he would be cordial enough after a few minutes.[27]

As a therapist, Federn was more humane and compassionate than Freud, and had less of the scientific investigator in him. Federn, a Jew, was taken with the Christian ideal of charity, and was always on the verge of converting to Protestantism (as his two brothers did; his wife was a Protestant and his children were raised as such). "As therapists . . . Federn was more a physician and would fight harder against greater odds to help the patient than Freud in whom the scientist was always stronger than the healer."[28] Federn treated sicker patients than did others in Freud's circle, and had more suicides (including one of Freud's nieces); he became convinced that "psychoses could only be cured through somatic means, though in combination with psychotherapy. . . ."[29] Like Freud himself, Federn was capable of inspiring the devotion of former students and patients.

Unlike Freud, though, Federn was depressive; laden with guilt feelings, he sometimes coped with potential ill-humor and aggressiveness by means of nobility and sacrifice for others. At the age of almost eighty he decided to take his own life; his wife had already died, and he had had a recurrence of cancer of the bladder. A short time earlier he had undergone an operation for the cancer, which failed in its purpose but had precipitated a temporary psychosis. Such a mental disorder following a serious operation is more common than is popularly known; it can be an organic process, or may even represent a fight for life. When his wound healed, Federn fully recovered. But he was then scheduled for another operation, and he could not face the possibility of a further post-operative breakdown. He transferred his patients to other therapists, and then shot himself (sitting in his analytic chair) the morning he was to be sent to the hospital. In the suicide note he left for his sons, he recurred to his romantic image of himself as a

Freud with Oscar Nemon and his bust of Freud, 1931

soldier, "the long-serving sergeant in the psychoanalytic army." Characteristically, in this note he told his sons to be careful of the gun—for there was still one bullet left. To the very end he had to care for others.

Although Federn's "unwavering devotion to Freud hampered him in expressing his divergencies from Freud in any but an ambiguous way," he was one of the pioneers of modern ego psychology. At the time, Freud "could not give his attention to Federn's findings or grasp their importance."[30] Federn's compassion for the ill lay behind his special interest in the treatment of psychotics, and he fashioned his ideas accordingly. Building on the concept of "identity" first introduced into psychoanalysis by his intimate friend and rival Victor Tausk, Federn proposed that a defect in organizing ability might account for a patient's incapacity in the face of instinctual drives.

Freud had at first held that to make an instinct conscious can only be to weaken it. But the goal of removing self-deceptions presupposes that the patient's ego is capable of integrating the new insight presented to it. Otherwise psychoanalysis may simply strip away a patient's defenses, leaving him worse off than before. Instead of labeling psychotics narcissistic, or too self-involved—as Freud would—Federn, like Tausk, saw them as suffering from a deficiency in ego strength. The psychotic's problem, then, was weakness rather than excess, and the key to his disorder lay in the ego rather than in an underground instinctual life of sex or aggression. Only if the patient's integrating capacities were strengthened could the boundary between his inner and outer world become realistic.

As usual, Freud found "unclear" whatever was different from his own work; and besides Federn was hardly the clearest of thinkers or speakers. At a meeting of the Vienna Society, Freud once passed a note to another student, Helene Deutsch, while Federn was presenting a paper: "Do you know what he is talking about?" Freud joked. "I don't."[31] Federn's work on ego psychology seemed to Freud nothing new, only his own ideas expressed somewhat differently. Although he was unhappy over Freud's silence toward his pioneering in the psychological treatment of the severely ill, at least Freud did not order him to discontinue such work or get out. Federn's desire to remain loyal and devoted obscured even to himself the originality of his conceptions, and it was only a month before he died that he saw that there were more differences in his and Freud's ego psychologies than he had realized.[32]

By the 1930's ego psychology began to be more important to psychoanalytic writers; they diverted their attention from the vicissitudes of the sexual instinct, and scrutinized more closely the mechanisms of coping

(whether defensive or adaptive) which the ego develops for handling conflicts. By the 1950's and 1960's this work would become central to psychoanalysis. Although logicians of psychoanalytic theory maintained that this
new trend represented a return to Freud's formulations of the 1890's on
defenses, the mood of this work was fresh—indeed revisionist, in substance
if not in declaration. From the 1930's on, ways of self-healing would be at
least as important to psychoanalytic theory as mechanisms of self-deception.

Even in the 1930's Federn justifiably felt that his earlier work was
going unrecognized and unacknowledged; so he complained about not
being adequately quoted, especially in Anna Freud's writings. "After
1930 some psychoanalysts close to Freud, who had attended Federn's
seminars, published a series of books and articles on ego psychology without mentioning any of Federn's contributions. This greatly disappointed
and embittered Federn."[33] But the notion of "ego boundaries," designed to
emphasize that ego defects lay behind schizophrenia, was the original
formulation of Victor Tausk. One can only wonder if Federn's own
reluctance in later years to acknowledge the priority of Tausk's contribution may not have in part reflected his shock at the circumstances surrounding Tausk's death.[34]

Federn had fully identified with Freud's attitude toward priorities. In
an article published in 1930, Federn raised the issue of unconscious plagiarism, the "wide unscrupulousness in regard to stealing other people's ideas."
Freud and Bullitt were then collaborating on their book about Woodrow
Wilson, and Federn alluded to Hale's book on Wilson, which Freud
had read: "Hale, Wilson's secretary, felt he had reason to take revenge
on the president for purloining his ideas." In remarks which describe
Freud's own style as a writer, Federn noted that "it is a general practice
to begin a scientific article with the mention of other authors' findings,
explanations and theories"; and what was also true of Freud, "if the cause
of the resistance is unconscious, the reader fails to understand what he
reads."[35]

As Theodor Reik once pointed out, Federn was a pacifist with a belligerent temper. (Freud had laughed at this characterization.) Federn of
course sided with Freud in the controversies with Adler and Jung, although
he played no prominent role. When he moved to America, however, he
was an elder statesman of doctrinal orthodoxy, and became one of the
leaders in the New York Psychoanalytic Society who insisted on pointing
out the heretical lapses of a brilliant Hungarian analyst, Sandor Rado. As
Federn put it at a public meeting, in Italy there are two kinds of artists:

one who sells what he produces and one who digs up old objects and sells them as his own—making a lot of money. "I leave it to you to decide which is Dr. Rado," Federn concluded.[36]

Edward Hitschmann (1871–1957) was another of the early Viennese analysts whom Freud felt somehow saddled with; and yet on emigration to America, Hitschmann became a figure of some importance. As remarkable as Freud's ability to attract followers was his talent for keeping those he did not particularly admire. Although Hitschmann had a witty sense of humor, to Freud he came to seem sarcastic, rigid, and superficial. Freud personally liked a man of Federn's imagination a lot better. Yet both Hitschmann and Federn were typical of those analysts who came to Freud at a time when he had little to choose from.

Shortly before World War I, Freud began to reward favorites by giving them antique stones to be made into rings. Although at first this was a way of recognizing talented workers, by the end of his life the practice represented a mark of gratitude for a personal service performed or even simply a sign of affection. At all times it meant that the recipient was a part of either the psychoanalytic movement as a whole or Freud's personal family, to the extent that these two spheres were ever kept separate. But once Freud had passed over Hitschmann and Federn—for he gave a ring to neither—it would have been an insult to give one to them much later; it would only have underlined the extent to which Freud had all along sought more illustrious supporters.

Hitschmann had been introduced to Freud's group in 1905 by his old friend Federn. Hitschmann was then an established internist, and therefore a welcome addition to a group that was mainly nonmedical. For a time he functioned as the Freud family's doctor, but from Hitschmann's point of view this was a burden. In honor of Freud's sixtieth birthday Hitschmann wrote an address to Freud, which, according to Hitschmann, Freud would have been too impatient to listen to. Freud answered by remarking that "in order to live it is necessary to have a few people who believe I have succeeded."[37] When a psychoanalytic clinic, called the *Ambulatorium*, was opened in Vienna in 1922, Freud appointed Hitschmann its head.

Freud's mildly derogatory attitude toward someone like Hitschmann was not a subject that, in my interviewing, the more politic old analysts wanted to talk about. But by the 1930's there seems to have been a general impatience with Hitschmann, partly out of identification with Freud but also due to the quality of Hitschmann's slow remarks.[38] As the Vienna group expanded, Hitschmann looked more and more old-fashioned in his thinking. But he remained devoted and loyal to Freud, and often took a summer house close to the master. Like others in the circle, the Hitschmanns always observed Freud's birthdays: the couple regularly sent a pineapple which was a rarity in Vienna and which Freud loved. They would order it a month in advance at several stores to be absolutely sure about obtaining one. Like Federn, Hitschmann experienced no reluctance in being dependent on Freud, nor was he to Freud a powerful son capable of slaying a father figure. Hitschmann was an amusing sketcher, and once drew a shield of psychoanalysis which gained some notoriety in sexually conscious psychoanalytic circles at the time; "the longer the better" was emblazoned on the shield, around the edges of which were the flowers of a certain bean to which this saying commonly applied.

Freud judged people according to very high standards. Hitschmann was a cultured and well-educated man, and one of the earliest to work on psychoanalytic biographies, even if he did usually demonstrate in the lives of great men merely the working out of the Oedipus complex. He also wrote an excellent popular summary of psychoanalytic findings, one of the earliest besides Freud's own. Before undertaking this piece of what is described in the *Minutes* of the Vienna Society as "propaganda" to be directed "mainly to the body of physicians," Freud warned that "this work would require that the author refrain from expressing any of his own ideas." Hitschmann replied that "in this book he would never pretend to offer his own ideas; actually he would have to do nothing but copy."[39] On the whole, it was the triumph of psychoanalysis which lifted this man to historical prominence. But to read any of the papers by such a member of the circle written when he was closest to Freud is to read him at his best and also to read Freud at second hand. Freud inspired more from his followers than they might otherwise have accomplished, even though their creativity was often contingent on his continued presence.

2. Victor Tausk
and Lou Andreas-Salomé

VICTOR TAUSK (1879–1919) was one of Freud's most talented early supporters, but although he was a towering figure among pre-World War I psychoanalysts, he became almost completely forgotten. Some of his work is known among those professionally interested in early psychoanalytic papers,[1] but to the extent that Tausk has had a place in history it has mainly been as one of Lou Andreas-Salomé's (1861–1937) lovers.

They had a short affair in Vienna, during her stay there in 1912–13. Supposedly, years earlier in Lou's life, Nietzsche had proposed to her, and she subsequently was intimate with Rilke. When she joined Freud's circle to learn psychoanalysis, Lou could not have Freud himself; but Tausk, who had considerable talent and standing in Freud's eyes, represented second best. And in her *Journal* on Freud she wrote the most penetrating comments on Tausk's character.

Freud himself composed the official obituary of Tausk. "No one," he wrote, "could escape the impression that here was a man of importance." Freud's final judgment was that Tausk was "sure of an honorable memory in the history of psychoanalysis and its earliest struggles."[2] Yet it took half a century for a full account of the difficulties between Freud and Tausk to become public. It is not surprising that Freud's disciples in Vienna kept this story to themselves. We should remember their reverence for Freud, as well as their guilt over a fallen rival. A suicide under any circumstances is a fearful act. But coming after his fight with Freud, Tausk's suicide helped give a sense of reality to the powers that Freud's pupils magically attributed to their leader.

Tausk grew up in Croatia, now a part of Yugoslavia but then an outlying province of the Austro-Hungarian Empire. He was a tender and thoughtful son to his mother, who behaved with self-sacrifice and family devotion to her aggressive and even tyrannical husband. Although she is said to have been beautiful, constant anxiety and the demands of the children left her tired and cheerless, and her husband was unfaithful; he could be charming and women found him fascinating.

Tausk's relationship with his father was strained and antagonistic; he later wrote that he was forever embarrassed to be called by his father's name. Admired by his fellow students, Tausk was a leader among them in behalf of justice and intelligence. He had a row with a teacher of religion whose principles conflicted with his own atheism; just before graduating he led a students' strike over religion. At first he had wanted to study medicine, but since his family could not afford it, he settled on the less expensive prospect of becoming a lawyer.

In 1897 Tausk went to the University of Vienna; the next year he met his future wife, Martha. Tausk's hostile relationship with his father was duplicated with his future father-in-law, a printer; they hated each other passionately. But Martha loved Victor deeply, became pregnant, and they were married in 1900. Together they went to Yugoslavia, where the baby died at birth.

Tausk continued his training as a lawyer, first in Sarajevo and then in Mostar, while his wife gave birth to two sons. Late in the spring of 1905 they decided to separate, she going to Vienna with the children and Victor eventually settling in Berlin. Having been stuck in the provinces for several years, at the age of twenty-six Tausk was still restlessly ambitious. He published some Serbian ballads he had translated into German, wrote short stories and poetry, tried his hand as a playwright, and published literary criticism.[3]

In Berlin, Tausk was able to embark on a new career. He practiced the violin, drew charcoal sketches, and directed plays. The necessity of earning a living, however, forced him to struggle at journalism, which to him seemed degrading. In letters we find evidence of his efforts to earn money, his yearning for creative work, as well as his concern for his boys.

For Tausk, law had been merely the shortest and cheapest academic study leading to a professional title. He felt he had deceived his true self by becoming a lawyer and consequently had behaved badly out of self-hatred, and this contributed to his problems with his marriage. In addition, Tausk seems to have been unable to tolerate his wife's dependent love; she had not been self-sufficient enough to make him comfortable with her. As he once wrote her: "I love only free people, those that are independent of me . . . The way I am living now is truly the best. . . . : independent because nobody depends on me, not a slave because not a master." The grounds for the failure of his marriage would illuminate Tausk's future tie to Freud.

Tausk understood the destructive element in his great capacity for love. The more he loved, the more dependent he became, and hence, by the curious logic of his emotions, also the more cruel. Throughout his life he gave to others, was goodhearted, devoted, and loyal. But when he suddenly realized how enslaved he had become, he would break the relationship, and the whole cycle would begin again with someone else.

In Berlin, Tausk's health was gradually undermined. Frustrated in an effort to win a particular woman's love and suffering from a relapse of lung trouble, he also complained of fatigue and lack of concentration. He obtained a free place at a German sanatorium, in exchange for a promise to write a few promotional articles about it. The diagnosis was mental and physical exhaustion. Unexpectedly, his condition deteriorated rapidly; he slid into a deep depression. He yearned for a profession and a home, but had neither. Yet he functioned admirably as a writer, describing, in letters to his wife, what it means not to function. Tausk's collapse had come on suddenly, and his recovery was equally rapid and spontaneous. But depressive emotions, though never again so debilitating, returned to plague him.

Even after such a terrible collapse, Tausk could pick himself up and try something new. Out of this misery he turned to Freud and psychoanalysis. In Freud he sought the guidance he felt he so sorely lacked. Tausk responded to an article of Freud's with a letter, and Freud—thinking Tausk was a medical doctor—encouraged him to come to Vienna to study psychoanalysis. In the fall of 1908 Tausk moved to Vienna to study medicine; he already planned to become an analyst. But before beginning anew, he determined to put an end to a part of his former life: although he and his wife had been separated since October 1905, only on his return to Vienna in October 1908 did they go through with a divorce.

Tausk had Freud's personal support, and the rest of the Viennese psychoanalytic group did what they could to smooth his way; his superior abilities were immediately obvious to them. With the advantages of hindsight, his choosing to become an analyst may seem a life-saving maneuver. But it was also a natural outgrowth of his talents and interests.

Unlike Freud and most of his medical following, Tausk chose to become a psychiatrist. Freud's Swiss psychiatric adherents had been important to him because they offered his concepts new territory to conquer. Tausk's most original achievements were to be his clinical studies of schizophrenia and manic-depressive insanity.[4] He was the first member of the Vienna Psychoanalytic Society to study the psychoses clinically, at a time when Freud himself was interested in treating only less disturbed persons. Tausk made lasting contributions to psychoanalytic theory which have been incorporated in the works of such contemporary thinkers as Bruno Bettelheim and Erik Erikson;[5] but he could not survive in Freud's circle. For he was to be overwhelmed by his contact with Freud.

The best source on Tausk's relationship with Freud's group before World War I remains Lou Andreas-Salomé's *Journal*. She approached Freud with the aura of past European culture.[6] Fifty-one years old when she came to Vienna in 1912, she had prepared herself beforehand by reading everything Freud had written. She aimed to elicit Freud's interest in her, and she succeeded completely.

Lou was of the genre of women who have a knack for collecting great men. Whatever her earlier good looks, she now had to rely on her psychological resources to arouse the attention of any potential conquests. Vibrantly responsive to ideas, she possessed an extraordinary flair for identifying with men, and especially with that creative part of them most subject to inner uncertainties. But as men fell in love with her they eventually discovered that she had not truly given of herself. She had mirrored them, had helped their creative need, but had withheld herself as a person.

They all needed her, but ultimately they realized that she had eluded them.

Freud liked people of fancy and imagination. Thus Lou Andreas-Salomé was bound to represent an acquisition for him personally as well as for psychoanalysis. Many years later Freud wrote that he had admired Lou immensely and been attached to her "curiously enough without a trace of sexual attraction."[7] Through her, Freud was in touch with the best of German cultural life, and he took her into his confidence to an extraordinary degree. In his letters of later years he discussed with her the emotional problems of his daughter Anna.

In 1912 Lou had ranked Victor Tausk "the most prominently outstanding"[8] among Freud's students, and she actively set out to seduce him. Tausk was handsome, with blonde hair, blue eyes, and a mustache. He was also eighteen years her junior. For the period 1912–13 Freud, Lou, and Tausk established a triangle which had advantages for each. Lou often had had two men in her life simultaneously. For Freud the arrangement had frustrations as well as satisfactions. He was jealous of Tausk's opportunity to have an affair with Lou. Tausk was younger, more virile, and altogether a larger man physically. On the other hand, Lou could give Freud information about Tausk, to help keep this potentially troublesome student under control. For both men she was a buffer.

As a woman, Lou would arouse none of Freud's feelings of rivalry. For such an old-fashioned man, women simply did not exist as competitors. She could flatter him and still believe everything she said. A woman can more easily dissociate her sense of self from her professional work; so to give Freud what he wanted in no way compromised her integrity. But Freud's demand that his students identify with him eventually mobilized rebellion in men; for a man really to be like Freud meant finally for him to be original. Yet originality ended his usefulness to Freud.

Supporting Freud in his quarrel with Adler, Tausk had displayed a degree of malice that Lou considered excessive and unfair.[9] And at the height of Freud's public struggle with Jung, Tausk thundered against Jung's heresy.[10] In these verbal battles Tausk was at his best, though in his articles too he could be truculent. Listening to Tausk lecture on psychoanalysis, Lou had the impression "not only of classical Freudian theory but also of an unusually loving and reverent approach to the essential discoveries of Freud. . . ." She objected only that Tausk was "*too* precisely Freudian; in any case, he is never likely to be reproached with the contrary."[11]

Yet Lou saw exactly the sources of tension between these two men. Freud characteristically wished to transcend all previous limits of knowledge. But he thought that Tausk was seizing problems ahead of their time.[12]

Tausk's work irritated Freud, and a good part of the problem was Tausk's originality.[13] Lou and Freud talked about it repeatedly, while she was still engaged in her affair with Tausk.[14]

Tausk's independence was partly a façade. For worst of all, from Freud's point of view, was that at times Tausk stayed glued to Freud's own preoccupations. In an uncanny way Tausk seemed able to anticipate Freud's own formulations.[15] Freud felt uneasy with Tausk, not just because he had a mind of his own, but also because he dared to use this talent on problems which mattered dearly to Freud himself. Freud's fear that Tausk might steal some of his ideas before he had finished with them also helps explain why Lou could be useful to Freud in keeping an eye on Tausk.* Freud could be sure that she would ultimately be on his side. He did not like the uncertainty of fearing that Tausk might have an idea before he did.

Lou realized that Tausk was self-absorbed and introspective, excessively ambitious and yet passionately loyal to Freud. The situation was such that Tausk could place the blame on Freud for their mutual difficulties. Tausk clung to Freud partly because of his own lack of inner resources.[17] Lou loved in Tausk his helplessness before his inner being, his tortured struggle to use his intellect to master his passions. He was demanding, but his capacity to nurture illusions made him lovable. His self, however, remained the prisoner of the past. "Yet from the very beginning I realized that it was this very struggle in Tausk that most deeply moved me—the struggle of the human creature. Brother-animal. You."[18]

But with World War I everything collapsed around Tausk again. Having completed his medical education, he had begun his new life, but now patients grew scarce and it was almost impossible to practice psychoanalysis. Called up by the army, Tausk acted with genuine heroism in using psychiatric diagnoses for humane ends. He wrote an eloquent article on the psychology of deserters, which was one of the earliest applications of psychoanalytic findings to law.[19] Repeatedly he endangered himself by his kindness and unselfishness in behalf of patients. He also must have cherished the opportunity, it should be added, to defy his superiors.

With the end of the war, Tausk returned to Vienna to resume his practice. The city, however, was in economic chaos. Almost forty, Tausk

---

* Lou claimed that "the entire substance of . . . [Nietzsche's] *Genealogy of Morals* originated with Paul Rée, who had been discussing his conception in a conversation with Nietzsche; Nietzsche carefully listened to Rée, making Rée's thoughts his own, and later became hostile to him."[16]

still had to live like an impoverished student, while supporting a family. He had left himself dependent on Freud's personal favor and acceptance. Many of his friends and associates shared these problems, yet most of them were not in so vulnerable a position. Paul Federn, for example, could easily fall back on his strictly medical practice.

Tausk's productivity in writing during the war encouraged him not only to apply as a *Dozent* at the University of Vienna, but also to ask Freud for an analysis—his great dream was to be analyzed by Freud. Yet Tausk must have known that his presence caused Freud discomfort, and the latter's answer was no. Although this refusal further strained Freud's relationship with Tausk, Freud thought he could hold him within the fold.

Freud tried to work out a compromise with Tausk. He recommended that he go into analysis with a psychiatrist more than five years Tausk's

*Victor Tausk
during World War I*

junior, Helene Deutsch, whom Freud had taken into analysis earlier that fall.[20] She had been with Freud for about three months when Tausk began to go to her for treatment in January 1919. Freud had to discuss the case with Helene Deutsch and explain his reasons for not taking Tausk into analysis himself.* He told her he felt inhibited in Tausk's presence. Freud was restless and uncomfortable with Tausk, as Lou had described earlier. Freud's ideas were still very much in flux, and he told Helene Deutsch that it made an "uncanny" impression on him to have Tausk at the Society, where he could take an idea of Freud's and develop it before Freud had quite finished with it.†

The referral was flattering to Helene Deutsch but a terrible insult to Tausk. Despite her psychiatric experience, as an analyst she was a nobody. Both she and Tausk knew he had done much better work. But Tausk need not have accepted the insult. However, Lou had prophesied his inability to be fully independent, and he partially recognized elements of this weakness in his relations with women. As he could not be independent toward Freud, so Tausk did not want others to be dependent on him. Freud's self-sufficiency, like Lou's, must have been especially attractive to Tausk. Freud had been partially rejecting Tausk for some time; this gave Tausk exactly that combination of support and distance which made him feel at ease.

Tausk swallowed the offense and went into analysis with Helene Deutsch; she could be a bridge between him and Freud. He would lie on her couch six days a week, knowing that she would be on Freud's couch just as often. He could be analyzed by Freud through her. At the same time, he would be re-establishing a triangular relationship with Freud through a woman. It was almost the same story as with Lou; once more an attractive woman would be the channel between the two men. Tausk knew that a woman would be far less threatening to Freud, and through her he could plead his case. For Freud, Helene Deutsch could be a source of information about Tausk, just as Lou had been.

* The grounds Freud gave were exactly the same as in the case of his refusal to treat Otto Gross in 1908. Cf. above, p. 260.

† Oddly enough, in an essay, "The 'Uncanny,' " which Freud completed in the spring of 1919, he wrote that "it is long since he has experienced or heard of anything which has given him an uncanny impression. . . ." Elsewhere in that essay Freud alluded, in discussing the phenomena of the "double" and telepathy, to a problem that beset him and Tausk: "the subject identifies himself with someone else, so that he is in doubt as to which his self is, or substitutes the extraneous self for his own." "[W]hatever reminds us of [the] . . . inner 'compulsion to repeat' is perceived as uncanny."[21] Earlier Freud had hypothesized that "we appear to attribute an 'uncanny' quality to impressions that seek to confirm the omnipotence of thoughts. . . ."[22]

In his analytic sessions with Helene Deutsch, Tausk talked almost entirely about Freud. Whatever Tausk's deeper difficulties, they now centered on Freud. He did not rage against Freud; he rather grieved over the master's attitude toward him. Tausk thought that the trouble between them derived from Freud's own difficulties. He felt that he had had some ideas before Freud, but Freud would not acknowledge them. There is no doubt that Tausk was capable of having ideas of his own, which could in fact correspond to what Freud might eventually think. But Freud's manner of working was bound to elicit Tausk's resentment because it prevented him from ever gaining credit for asserting himself in an original manner.

Freud and Tausk had more or less the same reproach, and part of the interest in the Freud-Tausk struggle stems from the similarity of their personalities. Each thought that the other was taking ideas without due acknowledgment. And each had good grounds for this belief. Freud believed that what his pupils thought of was ultimately his. And to Tausk it seemed that no matter how far his mind ranged, eventually Freud would put his own imprint on Tausk's contributions. Each man believed he was unique and a genius and feared being destroyed by the other. Tausk, however, was the one who sought treatment. Having heard complaints and accusations from both sides, Helene Deutsch thought there was some reality to what both felt.

Whatever Freud's motives in sending Tausk to her, or Tausk's in accepting the humiliation, the arrangement proved unworkable. Impressed with what she considered Tausk's genius, Helene Deutsch's analytic hours with Freud became filled with talk of Tausk. Tausk therefore began to interfere with her own analysis with Freud. Near the end of March 1919, after three months, Freud called a halt to the incestuous situation.

Freud explained to Deutsch that Tausk had become an interference in her own analysis and that Tausk must have accepted her as his analyst with the intention of communicating with Freud through her. Freud forced her to choose between terminating Tausk's analysis with her and discontinuing her own analysis with Freud. To Deutsch it did not constitute a realistic choice, but an order. Tausk's treatment ended immediately.

At this stage of his life Freud could not waste time on people who muddied his waters. Tausk wanted too much from him and was easily offended. Tausk's attitude toward Freud was neurotically dependent, and Freud found it easier simply to get rid of him than to risk being—as Freud saw it—swallowed by him. Of course, he could well afford to dispense with an early supporter like Tausk, now that so many new pupils were flocking to him from all over the world.

Tausk tried to put his private life in order. He had been singularly unsuccessful in firmly establishing a relationship with a woman. With his rejection by Freud and the failure of his attempt to be analyzed, Tausk tried to take a new woman into his life—Hilde Loewi, a concert pianist sixteen years his junior. He had met her as a patient who came to him for therapy. For an analyst to marry a patient was to commit the great crime of his profession. Tausk's elation at falling in love may have masked grief and mourning, and it would not be unknown for a patient to act out his emotional conflicts after such a sudden termination of treatment. In Tausk's choice of a former patient one can see the glimmering of his growing resentment of Freud.

Freud's rejection was so personal that it was difficult to rationalize on scientific grounds. Tausk was not content to be one of Freud's apostles; without a rebellion against Freud, the creative part of Tausk would have been frustrated. Now he had to find out whether he was capable of being creative without Freud. For Tausk to have deserted Freud would surely have been healthier. Why could he not have returned to Berlin or Yugoslavia?

But it is easy to underestimate how readily one could have been checkmated in Central Europe fifty years ago. Psychiatry was Tausk's third career; after having attacked the psychiatric status quo in Freud's behalf, he suddenly found himself losing Freud.

The precipitating cause of Tausk's suicide was his inability to go through with his marriage to Hilde Loewi. The next morning he was to have obtained a marriage license. He must have realized that, although he had fallen in love with her partly to escape from his dilemmas, they were not going to disappear. As so often before, Tausk had fallen passionately in love, and then it had all vanished. In the end he was confronted with his commitment to marry. With Hilde Loewi he had wanted more than ever to succeed in love, yet he knew he had seen it all happening to him before. But this time he was left without Freud as well.

In the early morning hours of July 3, 1919, Tausk determined to kill himself. He wrote a will with a lengthy itemization of all his possessions. The huge inventory was all he had to establish his immortality. He also wrote and sealed two letters and left them on his desk—one to Hilde, the other to Freud. Having decided to kill himself, Tausk found inner reconciliation; with all his aggressive feelings directed inward, he was left with only love for others. While he wrote he sipped slivovitz, the Yugoslav national drink. Then he tied a curtain cord around his neck, put his army pistol to his right temple, and pulled the trigger. Besides blowing off part of his head, he strangled himself as he fell.

*   *   *

Freud wrote the official obituary of Tausk, praising his many contributions to psychoanalysis. But in a letter to Lou, Freud could be far more open concerning his relief that Tausk was finally gone: "I confess I do not really miss him; I had long taken him to be useless, indeed a threat to the future."*[23] Freud was characteristically honest about his feelings, courageous in writing about some of his worst qualities—which is exactly what has laid him so open to criticism. In contrast to Freud's obituary, with its public commendation, in private Freud was left with only pity for Tausk.

Lou was taken aback by Freud's cold reaction to Tausk's death. Yet her reply to Freud was a masterpiece of subtle diplomacy. By and large she agreed with Freud's interpretation of Tausk's character, yet she managed to shift the center of gravity of the post-mortem to Tausk's lovableness. Tausk could trust his character less than his intellect. As Lou remarked of him in a marginal comment in her letter, "even such a *strong* character dwarfs to powerlessness when confronting the inner giants of immoderation." Lou agreed that Tausk was a menace to the future of psychoanalysis. She accepted Freud's flattery that it was because of her friendship with Tausk that Freud had put up with him for so long. She gave him up so readily, defending him so little, that one can only conclude that she may have really used Tausk all along for the sake of her relationship with Freud.

Lou, who became a practicing analyst, never wrote another word about Tausk to Freud. But on returning to Vienna in 1921, and once again attending meetings of the Vienna Society, she recorded in her diary how she was reminded of Tausk's absence: "Freud unaltered; 50 people; one was missing (Victor Tausk). I looked for him everywhere, so that it seemed to me that all the old familiar faces were missing."[24]

Tausk's death remained a skeleton in the psychoanalytic family closet. To Helene Deutsch, the suicide was not her responsibility but Freud's. In retrospect it was not unreasonable for her to have considered her own role negligible, a mere mediator between Tausk and Freud. On the surface, little emotional tie between patient and analyst was established between Tausk and his analyst. However, in a subtle way Tausk had been wooing Helene Deutsch with the story of his conflict with the master; it was the most seductive power Tausk had at his disposal. Helene Deutsch could indulge her interest in this rebellious pupil without acknowledging to herself that she too might have critical feelings about Freud. All her negative impulses toward Freud could be isolated and embodied in the person

---

* Originally this passage in the letter was censored, but now in the English edition the cuts have been restored.

of Tausk. She may even have implicitly encouraged Tausk's interest in her own analysis and his expressions of rivalry. Helene Deutsch never realized that Tausk was flattering her by his tale, or that she might be benefiting by it in Freud's eyes.

Paul Federn, in a letter[25] to his wife written immediately after Tausk's death, saw the motivation exclusively in terms of Tausk's failure to win Freud's human interest. Federn flatly asserted that the motive for the suicide was Freud's rejection. Tausk's quarrel with Freud need never have been kept a secret, except for the need to make Freud seem powerful. Federn, as well as others in that tiny subculture, readily believed that if Freud dropped a man it could lead to his self-extinction. Exclusion from the revolutionary community was an annihilation greater than any physical death.

Lou Andreas-Salomé, however, knew how Tausk's neurosis had involved his whole personality; every piece of him was consumed in the struggle with Freud. But she also saw how power can infantilize those who wield it as much as those who submit to it. Although she remained loyal to Freud until her death in 1937—she had helped Freud's daughter Anna psychoanalytically, and Freud often sent her money during trying times—she could, unlike many of Freud's other followers, acknowledge how his achievements were linked to his limitations. As she once wrote, "confronted by a human being who impresses us as great, should we not be moved rather than chilled by the knowledge that he might have attained his greatness only through his frailties?"[26]

3. Apostles

As a personality, Hanns Sachs (1881–1947) typified Viennese Jewish intellectual life. Clever and intelligent, equipped with an "endless stock of the best Jewish jokes,"[1] he was loquacious and exuberantly optimistic, and with his plumpness and short stature some thought he resembled an owl. He loved good food, wine, and beautiful women, and was a frequent visitor to cafés. He had been unhappily married for a short time, but because he hardly ever spoke of it, few of his associates knew about it. A carefree bachelor with many women in his life, he also enjoyed movies and burlesque shows when he came to America.

Originally Sachs had been dissatisfied with his life as a lawyer; he had been in Freud's circle for nine years when, in 1919, after a bout with tuberculosis, he abandoned the law entirely and decided to practice as a "lay" (nonmedical) analyst. Freud welcomed persons from different fields, for they would be able to apply his work to the humanities and the social sciences. He wanted them to practice analysis so that they could fully understand it; but they had to give up their previous careers, for Freud did not believe one could be a proper analyst unless practicing full time.

In analysis Sachs found meaning for his whole life. "I had found," upon reading *The Interpretation of Dreams*, "the one thing worthwhile for me to live for; many years later [1919] I discovered that it was also the only thing I could live by."[2] Earlier Sachs had had a variety of interests, but once he left law to be a psychoanalyst Freud's world became the center of his life. A prophet more than a scientist, he treated psychoanalysis as a revealed religion.

Freud had taken a great personal interest in Sachs, who was one of the first to receive the cherished ring. Sachs was named, along with Otto Rank, Sandor Ferenczi, Karl Abraham, and Ernest Jones, to a secret committee founded by Freud before World War I (after the loss of Adler, Jung, and Stekel) to forward the cause. Jones had proposed the idea to Freud, who liked it immediately: "This committee would have to be *strictly secret* in its existence and in its actions." Freud was worried about the future of his work; "I was so uneasy about what the human rabble would make out of it when I was no longer alive."[3] The committee first met as a group in the late spring of 1913. "On May 25, 1913, Freud celebrated the event by presenting us each with an antique Greek intaglio from his collection which we then got mounted on a gold ring. Freud himself had long carried such a ring. . . ."[4] As Freud himself once noted, a ring is "an object of . . . rich symbolic meaning," customarily associated with "an erotic tie."[5] His bestowal of rings marked the recipients as specially chosen bearers of his message.

Without previous clinical experience, Sachs became one of the first to devote himself primarily to analyzing future analysts. As Sachs wrote about the purpose of such "didactic" analyses:

> Religions have always demanded a trial period, a novitiate, of those among their devotees who desired to give their entire life into the service of the supermundane and the supernatural, those, in other words, who were to become monks or priests . . . It can be seen that analysis needs something corresponding to the novitiate of the Church.[6]

He moved to Berlin in 1920, where the first psychoanalytic training institute was being established; one of the attractions of psychoanalysis as a career was that it could be practiced anywhere. Sachs always emphasized

Freud and the committee in 1922. For a time this photo hung in Freud's waiting room.

From left to right, standing: Otto Rank, Karl Abraham, Max Eitingon, Ernest Jones.

Sitting: Freud, Sandor Ferenczi, Hanns Sachs

the importance of nourishing the positive aspect of the patient's relationship with his analyst. Among his analysands were Erich Fromm, Franz Alexander, Edwin Boring, Gregory Zilboorg, Karen Horney, and John Dollard. At a time when there was little authoritative work on therapeutic technique, Sachs lectured widely on the subject. In summers in those days it was customary for Sachs, as for a few others, to take along a caravan of trainees (who brought their patients too) when he went on vacation. It helped Sachs with the bills, and from the trainees' point of view—especially those from abroad—it was profitable, since in addition to a subsidized holiday more analysis was available.

Artistic himself (and not much good at the politics of the movement), Sachs was especially interested in applying psychoanalysis to cultural problems, and he produced literary studies and a book on the Roman emperor Caligula. Sachs was also, along with Otto Rank, a founding editor of

Imago (1912), a journal specializing in the nonmedical aspects of psycho-analysis. In 1932 he was invited to Boston as a desperately needed training analyst. He had to be guaranteed eight patients a day before he would agree to come, but they were not difficult for local analysts to find. In a medically traditional city like Boston, Sachs as a lay analyst encountered some problems, but he obtained a teaching appointment at Harvard Medical School.

His last years were gloomy; in addition to suffering heart trouble, he learned that only a few of his friends and relatives had been able to escape the Nazi holocaust. He was also disappointed in his hopes of converting an English patient into a faithful disciple: a writer who calls herself Bryher, she preferred instead to retire to Switzerland. Sachs also had his difficulties with local analysts who were trying to establish a systematic procedure for accepting candidates for training. Sachs identified with Freud's more arbitrary ways, and would accept on the spot a candidate for training and afterward notify the local psychoanalytic institute.

In his relation to Freud, Sachs remained a son. His book about the master, written not long before his own death, was admittedly a love poem. In Berlin his "couch was placed in such a way that the analysand faced a portrait bust of Freud standing on a high wooden pedestal."[7] In his personal habits Sachs became as much like Freud as possible. All the men in the circle smoked, and most of them took to cigars. Some of them even acquired Freud's neurotic traits. For example, Freud never lost his travel anxieties and had to be at the train station well ahead of time; Sachs was obsessional in exactly the same way, and would pace the railway platform long before the train was due.

Among the loyal Viennese apostles of Freud, Theodor Reik (1888–1969) may be the best known to the general reading public today. Throughout Freud's lifetime Reik's writings were serious, sometimes even original. He had a vast knowledge of religion, and Freud encouraged him as a lay analyst. Freud's own book on lay analysis was composed in behalf of Reik, who faced a court case instigated under a Viennese law against quackery.

Reik practiced in Berlin and in Holland. At that time there was a good deal of moving about from one psychoanalytic society to another, because of political upheavals and dissatisfaction with local groups. Even in Vienna, and much more so after coming to America, Reik was a lively figure. In Vienna he was the heel-clicking admirer of every word the Professor uttered. Freud took him into analysis for a short time, after the death of Reik's first wife. When he left Europe for the United States, Reik stressed even more his association with Freud.

Reik could not get on with the New York analysts, however, so he set up his own training group there. He had always sought to imitate Freud—in his smoking, in his style of writing, and even in the way he talked. Once in America he grew a beard like Freud's. His office walls were covered with photographs depicting various stages of Freud's life; toward Freud personally he maintained the adoration of a schoolboy. Reik's writings, however, became raconteurish, although he did much to spread many central parts of Freud's psychology—such as the importance of masochism in psychoanalytic theory.

Herman Nunberg (1883–1970) was one of the more scientific members of the Vienna group, although his sour disposition disqualified him from being a special favorite of Freud's. Relatively late in life, he married Margarete Rie, a friend of Anna Freud and the daughter of Freud's old friend Oskar Rie. While Nunberg had only a brief therapeutic experience with Paul Federn, his wife was for a time analyzed by Freud; she was also the sister of the analyst Marianne Kris, who also had been analyzed by Freud and whose husband, Ernst Kris, was an outstanding student of Freud's last phase. Through Nunberg's marriage, as well as his profession as a psychoanalytic psychiatrist, he became a secure member of Freud's family.

Nunberg was one of the most orthodox analysts, even defending Freud's theory of the death instinct, which many others rejected. At one time or other he trained Lawrence Kubie, Grete Bibring, and Willi Hoffer. Devoted and submissive to Freud, Nunberg probably fits the category of "yes-men" who, Helene Deutsch tactfully wrote, "rumor" had it surrounded Freud at the end.

Nunberg's chief contribution to psychoanalysis derived from his ability to systematize theoretically some of Freud's rather disorderly insights. In a brilliant and professionally well-known paper in the late 1920's on the "synthetic" function of the ego, Nunberg (many years after the rebels Adler and Jung but, unlike them, in a tactful way) attempted to acknowledge the role of psychological factors not incorporated within Freud's earlier instinct theory. Freud was by then interested in ego processes. According to Nunberg's account of Freud's discussion of this paper, presented at Freud's apartment, the Professor said:

> Your paper brings to mind a picture by Schwind (a famous Austrian painter of the end of the nineteenth century). It represents the construction of a chapel on the top of a steep hill. St. Wolfgang, the bishop, who is standing in front of the chapel, makes a magic gesture, while the devil, who is panting, the tongue outstretched, pushes a cart

heavily laden with stones from the bottom of the hill upward. I envy the bishop who merely has to make his magic gesture to force the devil to do the heavy work for him, so that the stones will fall into their proper places. I myself seem to be the devil who does the hard work, while you make a magic gesture, and everything falls into place.[8]

According to Sachs's account of this same meeting, the problem for Freud was not so much his preference for the demonic and the lower compared to the religious and the higher, but rather the speculative (instead of clinical) nature of Nunberg's presentation. Moreover, according to the legend of St. Wolfgang, the devil had made a deal with the saint to supply the stones with which to build the church, but the devil gets cheated of his due reward. Freud said:

Mine was the devil's lot. I had to get the stone out of the quarry as best I could and was glad when I succeeded in arranging them willy-nilly so that they formed something like a building. I had to do the rough work in a rough way. Now it is your turn and you may sit down in peaceful meditation and so design the plan for a harmonious edifice, a thing I never had the chance to do.[9]

Afterward Freud gave Nunberg a lithograph of the picture of the devil and the praying bishop, although there was a trace of ironic reservation in his appreciation of Nunberg's work. Whereas for the largest and more far-seeing figures in the circle, such as Jung or Adler, Freud's position as a god had interfered with their becoming like him, for someone like Nunberg there was little problem. Being a disciple was a great gratification; for the pupil it meant the making of his career. It was always possible to imagine oneself in Freud's position as the discoverer of it all.

Of those who received the rings from Freud, Karl Abraham (1877–1925) is today probably the most respected as a scientist. Freud did not approve of Abraham as enthusiastically as he did Sandor Ferenczi, since Freud preferred persons with less formality and more spark. Freud praised Abraham's "clarity, solidity, and power of carrying conviction"; earlier Freud regretted not being able to "harness" together Abraham's "precision" and Jung's "*élan*."[10] Freud complained that Abraham had "no dash"[11]; but he was fully devoted to psychoanalysis, and his dedication was devoid of self-absorbed passion. In his long and windy letters to Freud, Abraham comes across as a rather boring straight man. He is said to have had a "saner" view of the "dissidents" (Adler, Jung, and later Rank) than Freud himself, but Abraham may often have made a bad situation worse, out of jealousy, as Freud sometimes thought at the time. Abraham had enough of Freud's confidence to succeed Jung as president of the International Psychoanalytic Association in 1914.

Whatever Abraham's faults, he was sound as a thinker and as a clinician. He possessed considerable organizing ability, and was principally responsible for making Berlin the center for psychoanalysis that it became. After World War I analysts began to set up their own centers for training recruits. Very informal then, today such institutes are much more organized—with elaborate regulations, seminars, and committees; nevertheless, the earlier institutes were able to propagate Freud's teachings. From then on it would be feasible to supervise candidates in training without having to rely directly on Freud's personal advice.

In the 1920's Berlin offered the best training apparatus. Sachs had gone there specifically to lift some of the training burdens from Abraham. Vienna might have had the Professor, but Berlin soon had, in addition to Abraham and Sachs, Franz Alexander and Sandor Rado. Although during this period rivalry existed between Vienna and Berlin, Vienna did not have a functioning institute until 1925. The Vienna institute was never as successful as the Berlin institute—in number of candidates, in the quality of its work, or in its financial resources.

The money of Max Eitingon (1881–1943) lay behind the founding in 1920 of the Berlin Polyclinic and the Berlin Psychoanalytic Institute. A Russian physician of independent means, Eitingon was analyzed by Freud in the course of evening walks in Vienna. Eitingon was reported to be "entirely devoted to Freud, whose lightest wish or opinion was decisive for him."[12] Freud had earlier added a sixth member to his secret committee —Anton von Freund, a wealthy Hungarian brewer; when he died in 1920 (some of his money going to found the institute in Berlin), Freud decided to give Eitingon his place on the committee. It is hard to say much about Eitingon, since he was not a good teacher or speaker (he had a stammer) and he wrote next to nothing.* Like the others, he was a

---

* Eitingon opened the Psychoanalytic Congress at Innsbruck in 1927 with a speech whose tone communicates the conquering spirit of the early analysts: "Our Congress this year is a Jubilee Congress. As the Tenth it is the last of a decade of Congresses, silent but ever-increasing mile-stones in a splendid progress, an unchecked march to the conquest of man, of humanity. If the names of Nürnberg, Weimar, Munich, Budapest, The Hague, Berlin, Salzburg, Homburg and Innsbruck do not actually represent the battlefields of Freud and psychoanalysis, they at least bring in review before us what has been achieved and accomplished and they are a buglecall to that onward march which we must always have in mind."[13]

cultured person, though scientifically the least significant on the committee; he concerned himself mainly with establishing training standards for the International Psychoanalytic Association. His wife did not approve of his involvement with Freud; and the attitude of spouses of the members of Freud's circle was no insignificant matter. A passage from one of the many letters Freud sent to Eitingon communicates the flavor of their association in 1922:

> I take this opportunity of answering your friendly reference to the fifteenth anniversary of our relationship. You are aware of the role you have acquired in my life and that of my family. I know that I was not in a hurry to assign it to you. For many years I was aware of your efforts to come closer to me, and I kept you at bay. Only after you had expressed in such affectionate terms the desire to belong to my family—in the closer sense—did I surrender to the easy trusting ways of my earlier years, accepted you and ever since have allowed you to render me every kind of service, imposed on you every kind of task.
>
> Today I confess that in the beginning I did not appreciate your sacrifices as highly as I did later after recognizing that—burdened with a loving and loved wife who isn't too fond of sharing you with others, and tied to a family who fundamentally has little sympathy for your endeavors—you actually overtaxed your strength by making that offer. But do not conclude from this remark that I am ready to release you. Your sacrifices have become all the more valuable to me; if they have become too much for you, then it is up to you to tell me.
>
> So I suggest that we continue our relationship which has developed from friendship to sonship until the end of my days.[14]

Whatever Eitingon (who lost his money in the great crash of the 1930's) had done for the Berlin institute, it was Abraham (and Freud's respect for him) who attracted people from abroad. Of all the early analysts except Freud himself, Abraham had the most eminent future analysts in training analyses—Sandor Rado, Alix Strachey, Edward and James Glover, Helene Deutsch, Theodor Reik, Karen Horney, Melanie Klein, and Ernst Simmel. Abraham's therapeutic technique is said to have been easy, quiet, and standard.[15] His personality and work have drawn praise, not only from his former students but from his friend Ernest Jones. Abraham systematically made Freud's concepts of libidinal stages more compellingly elaborate; and like only a few others in the movement, with an education in Swiss psychiatry, Abraham tried to understand the psychoses. However, in a field that could be as undisciplined as psychoanalysis, categorizing, unfortunately, can be a temptation for some of its theorists. It was one of the merits of the work of Reik and Sachs that they objected to the excessive rigidity and system in Abraham's approach, the "orderly, methodical, surgical approach to the unconscious."[16]

Freud counted on Abraham as a stalwart supporter—until Abraham suddenly became ill and died, probably from lung cancer, late in 1925.[*] Freud was shaken by Abraham's death, especially as it coincided with his own ill health. The memorial meeting of the Vienna Society became legendary among analysts. Freud had long feared that his presence inhibited discussions at the meetings, and with the onset of his first cancer (which interfered with his speaking) Freud had stopped coming to the Society. The meeting in honor of Abraham was the first exception to Freud's decision, and also the last. Reik, who was then a favorite of Freud's, was charged with delivering the eulogy Freud had written for the occasion, but he arrived a few minutes late; Freud was upset at the lack of punctuality. Federn presided at the meeting, and in referring to their departed colleague, substituted Reik's name for Abraham's. (Federn later felt he had to go through a long explanation of this slip of the tongue to Freud.[†]) Freud was angry about having created such ambivalences among his students, and in line with his all-or-nothing way of doing things he never returned to the Vienna Society again. In Freud's published obituary of Abraham, he called him "one of the firmest hopes of our science, young as it is and still so bitterly assailed, and a part of its future that is now, perhaps, unrealizable."[17]

4. The "Wild Hunt"

GEORG GRODDECK (1866–1934) was different from Abraham, as unsystematic, disorganized, and inspired as Abraham was a disciplined man of science. Groddeck, also a German, horrified Freud's followers who were concerned with establishing psychoanalysis as a scientific body of

---

[*] Despite his lung trouble, Abraham had insisted on having a gall-bladder operation. Medically this was so odd that Sandor Rado theorized that Abraham had killed himself to avoid a conflict with Freud, echoing Federn's version of Tausk's death.

[†] Cf. above, p. 58.

knowledge. Yet Groddeck was a man of ideas, with a wealth of psychological intuition and literary talent. It was from Groddeck that Freud, with acknowledgment, took *das Es*, or "it," which is rendered in English-speaking countries by the Latin word "id." (In turn, Groddeck—as Freud pointed out—had borrowed the term from Nietzsche.) As Freud summarized Groddeck's position, he was "never tired of insisting that what we call our ego behaves essentially passively in life, and that, as he expresses it, we are 'lived' by unknown and uncontrollable forces."[1] As a therapist, Groddeck focused on organic symptoms and their symbolic meanings. He was the first to write about psychosomatic problems. He was also a pioneer in stressing the mother's role in child development as well as in emphasizing the generally unacknowledged feminine ambitions of men, such as pregnancy fantasies. Groddeck was a man of fancy, and even if Freud did not entirely respect him, he nevertheless won Freud's love. Freud defended Groddeck, for example, against the strictures of the Swiss pastor Pfister. And in return Pfister conceded that "the state of mind that leads you to encourage Groddeck is exactly the same as that which made you the discoverer and pioneer of psychoanalysis."[2]

Freud felt more personally involved with Groddeck than with the orderly Abraham. Of one of Groddeck's books Freud wrote that it was "the work of a mind on a par with that of Rabelais."[3] Yet to the extent that Freud permitted himself to regard Groddeck with affection, Freud also faced the same threat that had been posed by some of his more famous followers. On June 5, 1917, in response to Groddeck's announcement of his qualified conversion, Freud wrote:

> It is a long time since I received a letter which has pleased and interested me so much; it also tempts me to replace in answering it the normal politeness due to a stranger with analytical candor.
>
> I will do my best: I note that you urge me to confirm to you officially that you are not a psychoanalyst, that you don't belong to the flock of disciples, but that you may be allowed to consider yourself as something apart and independent. I evidently would be doing you a great favor by rejecting you to the place where Adler, Jung and others stand. But this I cannot do; I must lay claim to you, must insist that you are an analyst of the first order who has grasped the essence of the matter once for all. The man who has recognized that transference and resistance are the hubs of treatment belongs irrevocably to the "Wild Hunt." Whether he gives the "UCS" [Unconscious] the name of "Id" as well makes no difference.

Freud liked to think of his followers as a horde on a "Wild Hunt"; it fit his conquistador self-image. Whereas only five years earlier Freud had reproved Tausk for a comment on psychosomatics, on the ground that it was "far too early to talk of these things," Freud was now not only ready to entertain such discussions but also determined to settle the issue of originality, in a way that recalls the cocaine episode:

> Let me show you that the notion of the UCS requires *no extension* to cover your experiences with organic diseases. In my essay on the UCS which you mention you will find an inconspicuous note: "An additional important prerogative of the UCS will be mentioned in another context." I will divulge to you what this note refers to: the assertion that the UCS exerts on somatic processes an influence of far greater plastic power than the conscious act ever can. My friend Ferenczi, who is familiar with this idea, has a paper on pathoneurosis waiting to be printed in the *Internationale Zeitschrift*; it comes very

*Georg Groddeck
(1866–1934)*

close to your disclosures. The same point of view, moreover, has caused him to make for me a biological experiment to show how a consistent continuation of Lamarck's theory of evolution coincides with the final outcome of psychoanalytical thinking. Your new observations harmonize so well with the reasoning of this work that we would be only too glad if we could refer to your already published paper when we are ready to go into print.

Groddeck's letter to Freud had mentioned his envy of what Freud had uncovered. After welcoming this new student into the fold, at the same time pointing out how Groddeck's ideas had already been partially anticipated, Freud went on to discuss his own interest in hidden channels of memory and to disparage his pupil's concern with priorities:

> While I should very much like to welcome your collaboration with open arms, there is one thing that bothers me: that you have evidently succeeded so little in conquering that banal ambition which hankers after originality and priority. If you feel assured of the independence of your discoveries, why should you want to claim originality? And besides, can you be so sure on this point? After all, you must be ten to fifteen, possibly twenty years younger than I (1856). Is it not possible that you absorbed the leading ideas of psychoanalysis in a cryptomnemonic manner? Similar to the manner in which I was able to explain my own originality? Anyhow, what is the good of struggling for priority against an older generation?
>
> I especially regret this point in your communication because experience has shown that a man with unbridled ambition is bound at some time to break away and, to the loss of science and his own development, become a crank.
>
> I very much liked the samples of your observations which you offer and hope that even after severe critical sifting many of them will hold their own. Even though the whole field is not new to us, examples such as that of your blind man have so far never been given.

Freud was justified in worrying lest Groddeck's enthusiasm lead to a form of mysticism; it is reminiscent of his concern about Jung and the dangers of "monism" and "philosophy." It was certainly true that Groddeck was inclined to see the unconscious everywhere; a crash between two trains, after all, need not imply hidden motivation.

And now for my second objection: why do you plunge from your excellent vantage point into mysticism, cancel the difference between psychological and physical phenomena, and commit yourself to philosophical theories that are not called for? Your experiences, after all, don't reach beyond the realization that the psychological factors play an unexpectedly important role also in the origin of organic diseases. But are these psychological factors *alone* responsible for the diseases, and do they call the difference between the psychic and the physical into question? To me it seems just as arbitrary to endow the whole of nature with a psyche as radically to deny that it has one at all. Let us grant to nature her infinite variety which rises from the inanimate to the organically animated, from the just physically alive to the spiritual. No doubt the UCS is the right mediator between the physical and the mental, perhaps it is the long-sought-for "missing-link." But just because we have recognized this at last, is that any reason for refusing to see anything else?

I am afraid that you too are a philosopher as well and have the monistic tendency to disparage all the beautiful differences of nature in favor of tempting unity. But does this help to eliminate the differences?

I don't have to say that I should be very pleased to receive an answer from you! I am very anxious to know how you will greet this letter which may sound far more unfriendly than is the intention behind it.[4]

In spite of Freud's reservations about Groddeck's tendency to see organic problems only as expressions of psychological conflicts, he took Groddeck into his affection. Like others, however, Groddeck put inordinate demands on Freud for encouragement, approval, and support; the closer Freud got to his pupils, the more of a burden to him they became, a trial to his patience.

Paul Schilder (1886–1940) was a brilliant psychiatric practitioner and theoretician who because of his position in the psychiatric department of the University of Vienna played an important part in European psychiatry. From the perspective of the future, "Schilder did more for the propagation of analytic findings among European psychiatrists than, apart from Freud himself, any adherent of psychoanalysis."[5] Formally Schilder was a member of the Vienna Society, knew everyone in the group, and had carefully absorbed Freud's works. But he had refused to become a believer, found the Society stifling, and did not passively surrender to Freud.

Unlike Jung, Schilder never left the academic world of psychiatry; completely devoted to his work, he needed clinical hospital material for his research. Once he became a full professor at the University in 1925, he was fully independent. Emotionally he retained his objectivity toward

Freud, and remained a critical spirit within psychoanalysis. Freud had very much wanted Schilder's wholehearted allegiance, and was annoyed by his independence.

This background helps make comprehensible a formal charge against Schilder, made by Federn at the Vienna Society in 1922, that in a book on hypnotism Schilder had plagiarized Ferenczi and Freud. The members of the Society were usually divided into two groups: the functioning psychoanalysts and the outsiders, who were in effect honorary members. Schilder's position was his own; he was not one of the inner circle and at the same time he could scarcely be considered a dilettante.

To lodge a charge of plagiarism against a man who had not embraced Freud, over an issue sensitive to Freud, was to make a gesture of loyalty to the master. The incident is a good illustration of the manner in which an orthodoxy can influence men. Given an opportunity, Freud's pupils

Paul Schilder
(1886–1940)

would show their devotion to the master by attacking those who had not "fully accepted" his ideas.

Federn might not have seemed the most likely follower to lead the inquisition. Kindly and compassionate as a therapist, romantic and dreamy about serving others, even a trifle fatuous, at the same time he lived on another level, which was hostile and aggressive. To younger analysts in Vienna, the issue of plagiarism seemed an obsession of Federn's, probably even before he had grounds for suspecting that other psychoanalytic writers were not sufficiently citing his work. No matter how frequent was the insistence on priorities in this circle (Nunberg once claimed that Franz Alexander had accused him of plagiarism[6]), it is hard not to think in this instance that Federn knew whom he would please by the charge against Schilder at the Society.

Freud chaired the meeting at which the issue against Schilder was raised. One *ad hominem* point appeared prominently in the discussion: Schilder not only had not been analyzed but did not believe that a "didactic" (training) analysis was necessary. Schilder had the courage to stand up for himself, and turned this charge against Otto Rank, who had not himself been analyzed. The trial against Schilder was petty; he had so many ideas of his own that he scarcely needed to borrow from someone else. But he needed defenders, since he was relatively independent toward psychoanalysis. (Later, in America, his lack of orthodoxy led the New York Psychoanalytic Society to force him to withdraw from the organization.)

Although there are conflicting accounts of this inconclusive meeting, Freud seems to have remained relatively silent throughout. One member thought Freud leaned against Schilder. As another remembered it, Freud grew irritated at the end because he had not been asked what he thought of the matter. If they behaved so while he was alive, how would it be after he was dead? As Freud should have realized, no one dared to question him about his views. For to have involved Freud so directly would have made the quarrel even more blatant than it already was.

In later years Freud continued to acknowledge Schilder's talents. He was an exception to the rule that it was impossible to navigate successfully between Freud's either/or ultimatums, retaining one's independence while at the same time not irrevocably alienating Freud. In the 1930's Freud spoke highly of Schilder to Joseph Wortis; according to this account, Freud told Wortis that he could

> learn a lot from Schilder. . . . Schilder shares most of our views. In some respects, though, he has opinions of his own, to which every

man is certainly entitled, and is thus outside the psychoanalytic group. He does not believe in the necessity of a didactic analysis, for example, and keeps his patients under treatment for only three or four months.[7]

In addition, Schilder adopted an attitude toward Freud's instinct theory which today sounds prescient:

> Schilder took issue with Freud's basic assumption that desires tend to establish a state of rest. On the contrary, Schilder asserted, drives and desires go beyond mere satisfaction. They do not tend simply to bring the individual back to a state of rest; they thrust outward toward the world. Drives do not have regressive tendencies alone. A constructive effort toward the world is already present in the perception and the creation of objects. Schilder reiterated in many forms this positive constructive attitude of the individual toward the world.[8]

If Schilder's career exemplified how one could manage the various stresses of this circle, Herbert Silberer's suicide was the result of frustration and failure. Silberer (1882–1923), whose father was rich and well known in Vienna, entered the Vienna Society in 1910. For some time he was, if not the only non-Jew in the Society, prominent enough to be remembered as such. It was not difficult for analysts, especially after the loss of Jung, to label any Gentile in the movement an anti-Semite, or perhaps this was characteristic of that generation of Viennese Jewry.

From the outset Silberer's work was unorthodox. He was said to have come from "another point of view," though it is not certain whether this meant he disagreed with the conventional wisdom or that his starting point in academic psychology gave him a special perspective. Silberer wrote about hypnagogic phenomena, the images one sees on waking or while falling asleep. Freud thought Silberer had "made important contributions to dream-interpretation by directly observing this transformation of ideas into visual images."[9] Silberer published early papers about such symbolic, "primary process" (as opposed to conscious and verbal) thinking. In addition, he interpreted dreams differently from Freud—that is, ethically ("anagogic" interpretations), in a manner closer to Jung's formulations. Silberer concluded that "certain dream pictures are symbolic self-representations, and he was the first psychoanalyst to be concerned with the symbolic meaning of alchemy."[10]

Freud, as we have seen, found it hard to appreciate work outside his own line of thought; and he preferred to institute changes himself. For many reasons, then, Silberer was not in harmony with the psychoanalytic group in Vienna. For a short time he even edited a periodical with Stekel. The one time Hitschmann ever saw Freud in a deep rage, growing pale, was when Silberer invited the other members of the Vienna Society to contribute to Stekel's *Zentralblatt.*[11]

But Freud admired Silberer's work. Even though he considered Silberer's ideas about understanding dreaming to be too "speculative" and "philosophic," he always took any contribution to the interpretation of dreams seriously; Silberer's demonstration of the role played by "observation" in dreams was in Freud's view "one of the few indisputably valuable additions to the theory of dreams."[12] Repeatedly Freud mentioned Silberer's contributions with respect, though he also pointed out his errors. Then in the early 1920's Freud formally ejected Silberer from psychoanalysis.

It is not possible to reconstruct the sequence of events which culminated in Silberer's suicide. He was, however, depressed over his relationship with Freud. According to one good friend, Silberer felt offended and rejected by Freud's attitude toward him.[13] No one knew for sure why Freud did not like Silberer; he was devoted to Freud and had done important work, but Freud was no longer friendly or receptive to him. It was all quite open, though Silberer apparently had trouble admitting how Freud felt about him. His suicide was no surprise, although perhaps Silberer all along had been expecting too much from Freud.

Freud's dismissal of Silberer was curt and official.* In one short letter we can see in miniature an exaggerated version of Freud's earlier methods of getting rid of troublesome students. The letter from Freud to Silberer is dated April 17, 1922:

Dear Sir,

I request that you do not make the intended visit with me. As the result of the observations and impression of recent years I no longer desire personal contact with you.

Very truly yours,

Freud

Silberer killed himself in a horrible way nine months later; he hanged himself on a set of window bars, leaving a flashlight shining in his face as he strangled so his wife could see him when she came home.

The official obituary summed up Silberer's career in psychoanalysis:

---

* No doubt there are still some unknown controversies in Freud's life. Wittels mentioned, for example, Freud having severed relations with Max Kahane.[14]

On Jan. 12, . . . [1923], at the age of forty, Herbert Silberer put an end to his own life. Silberer was for many years a member of the Vienna group, but in recent years he had attended its meetings only rarely. His scientific writings, particularly on the subject of dream-psychology, have received recognition in psychoanalytic literature from various quarters. Critical objections, however, were made to more than one unjustifiable generalization on his part.

Freud had already referred to "an unjustifiable generalization" of Silberer's, "based on a few good examples, . . . involved in the statement that every dream allows of two interpretations—one which agrees with our account, a 'psychoanalytic' one, and another, an 'anagogic' one, which disregards the instinctual impulses and aims at representing the higher functions of the mind."[15] To interpret dreams anagogically would be, Freud held, to "divert interest from their instinctual roots."[16]

In a 1922 lecture that "for some reason"[17] Freud did not read before the Vienna Society, although he had intended to (it was, however, published that same year), he criticized Silberer's "superficial" concern with ethics, instead of with "the region of the repressed life of the instincts." "Silberer, who was among the first to issue a warning to us not to lose sight of the nobler side of the human soul, has put forward the view that all or nearly all dreams permit . . . a two-fold interpretation, a purer, anagogic one beside the ignoble, psychoanalytic one." The trouble was, according to Freud, that

> the contrast between the two themes that dominate the same series of ideas is not always one between the lofty anagogic and the low psychoanalytic, but one rather between offensive and respectable or indifferent ideas. . . . In our present example it is of course not accidental that the anagogic and the psychoanalytic interpretations stood in sharp contrast to each other; both related to the same material, and the later trend was no other than that of the reaction-formations which had been erected against the disowned instinctual impulses.[18]

Within a few short years, psychoanalysts, including Freud himself, would not speak so casually about the "later" ethics that were "reaction-formations" against instinctual life. The concept of the superego was to be designed specifically to take into account such standards of conscience within Freud's framework. But in Silberer's time, as his obituary had gone on to say, his "interest obviously lay outside the domain of psychoanalysis proper." The obituary also paid Silberer a somewhat uncertain compliment, in saying that "he achieved great success in his work on the psychological understanding of the so-called occult phenomena . . . in the book which was really his principal work . . ."[*][19] To point to a basic interest in occultism was hardly to place him in the mainstream of psychoanalysis, but rather to establish Silberer on the periphery of the Vienna group and the movement as a whole. (Although this obituary notice was unsigned, it sounds very much like an expression of Freud's attitude toward Silberer's work; if Freud did not write it himself, he probably gave the gist of it to Otto Rank.)

Wilhelm Stekel also published an obituary of Silberer: "When I separated from Freud, he was the only one of all the Freudians who remained true to me. (He was to pay dearly for this friendship.)"[21] Basically Stekel felt that Freud, who had complained about Silberer in letters more than ten years earlier,[22] had finished with Silberer once he collaborated with Stekel on their journal. Prior to his death, however, Silberer had been attacked in an article written against psychoanalysis; he had also resigned an editorship because of the publication of an attack on Freud. Nevertheless, Silberer had been bitterly assailed at the presentation of a paper at the Vienna Psychoanalytic Society,[†] and Freud was said to have explained the behavior of his followers on the grounds that "the man is a Jesuit."[24] (Otto Rank "referred to the Professor as having said that he would accept the obligation 'to finish Silberer.' "[25]) Stekel saw Silberer's death in the larger context of the failure of his ambitions, and specifically in terms of his recent distress at not succeeding in being awarded an honorary doctorate.

Anyone interested in psychoanalysis in those early days doubtless had enough personal difficulties to help him to see beyond the commonplace ways of dismissing depth psychology. (Even today, at least in America, the rate of suicide among physicians seems to be high, and that for psychiatrists may be higher than for any other occupational group.) Silberer could have overestimated the value Freud placed on Silberer's relationship with him. Freud might be pleased that a disciple was interested in psychoanalysis, but he was not always happy when such feelings included him personally; he did not feel obliged to return these sentiments. Freud might even have sensed a suicidal outcome, and for that reason held himself back.

---

[*] Jung acknowledged Silberer's work on alchemy, and commented: "Unfortunately, rationalistic psychologism broke his neck for him."[20]

[†] Jones once claimed that Silberer "had broken his relationship with the Vienna group years before his death," and that he had gone "into open opposition."[23]

5. Ernest Jones: Pioneer

OF THE FIRST FIVE RECIPIENTS of rings—who made up the membership of the original secret committee—Ernest Jones (1879–1958) was the only one to lose his; it was stolen from a box in the trunk of his car. Although one can only speculate how Freud would have regarded this loss, since it happened after his death, it is safe to say he would not have been pleased with what he might have considered a symptomatic lapse on Jones's part. A car trunk was a casual place to deposit what was to Jones, as well as the others, a sacred object. Freud had high expectations of the unconscious of a gentleman; an act which was open to rational interpretation in a patient might be unforgivable in a supporter.

Jones joined the psychoanalytic movement, which he described in his autobiography as "by far the most important thing in my life,"[1] after his career as a neurologist had been badly damaged. Neurology was then one of the glories of English medicine, and Jones became well educated in his field. He failed, however, to obtain an academic post he felt entitled to; in disappointment he left for a position in Toronto, Canada. In writing an obituary of his good friend Karl Abraham, Jones singled out Abraham's "rather odd desire" to land an appointment at the University of Berlin:

> With a solitary exception, the nature of which was such as to prove the rule, it was impossible to detect in him a trace of any personal ambition whatever; the exception was a rather odd desire to become a Docent at the University of Berlin, and this was itself obviously bound up with the prestige of psychoanalysis.[2]

It seemed later to Edward Glover that this was "a rather obtuse comment coming from one who in his time experienced the trauma of not achieving academic recognition in the groves of English academic life."[3] Although Jones longed for professional medical prestige, honors did not come to him until late in life.

Jones was a fiery little man, with a staccato, military manner, and at his worst he could be spiteful, jealous, and querulous. His face was said by one psychiatrist to have been pale but pungent—like a salad dressing; his eyes were sharp and his tone imperious. At the same time Jones's view of himself stressed his "tactfulness";[4] "Freud was to say laughingly that my diplomatic abilities might lead to my being taken over by the League of Nations."[5] He described himself as someone "who readily strikes up acquaintances,"[6] which may well have been true, but he did not make friends easily and was much hated.

Jones could be tactless at professional meetings, at times tearing somebody else's paper to shreds. With a patient who came for a consultation, Jones concluded the interview (after referring him to another analyst) by remarking that he was like "a brand plucked from the fire," even though the offended man did not feel he was about to go up in smoke. When the *Psychoanalytic Quarterly*, a rival to the *International Journal of Psychoanalysis*, which he edited, was begun in America, Jones thought the originators of this venture were a little group of restless and ambitious new arrivals.[7] At an international Congress, Jones pushed through a resolution requiring members of psychoanalytic societies in the United States to subscribe to the *International Journal of Psychoanalysis*: essentially it was a British journal, even though most of its subscribers were American, but

*Ernest Jones—
caricature drawn at
the Salzburg Congress
in 1924*

Jones had maintained the "international" label. Glover later commented that the "skill with which he [Jones] maintained the international status of the *Journal* and secured its financial stability by rendering it an obligatory charge on English-speaking membership of the Psychoanalytical Association had to be witnessed to be believed."[8]

Jones was a successful power-seeker. In the 1930's he wanted to make the British Society the psychoanalytic regulating body for the Empire, with other societies (such as the South African) in the status of subordinate groups.[9] To conclude the catalogue of Jones's less attractive qualities, he also had an excessive respect for fame and wealth: both his autobiography and his biography of Freud are marred by namedropping.

A narrower and more constricted human being than Hanns Sachs, Jones had the broader and more expansive mind. His great intellectuality interfered with his human contacts; for he was, besides being opinionated and egocentric, extremely intelligent and erudite. If he was difficult in person, he was equally wonderful in print. Nor did anyone tangle with him in debate without being worsted; Jones was "a gifted controversialist with a quick eye for the soft underbelly of an argument and a sharp edge to his tongue."[10] Jones knew his stuff and was, like Freud, a scientist. He said of himself once, quite rightly, that he had "a curious intolerance of illusion," and needed "the sense of security that the pursuit of truth gives."[11] For example, much as he was distressed at reading Freud and Bullitt's manuscript on Woodrow Wilson, Jones never questioned the authenticity of the text and mentioned to Strachey that perhaps the book belonged in the *Standard Edition* of Freud's works, since *Studies on Hysteria*, which Freud had written with Breuer, had appeared there earlier.[12]

Jones was also brave. As soon as the Nazis entered Vienna he flew there to help rescue Freud and the analytic community. And he finished the final volume of his biography of Freud despite many serious illnesses. For a number of years he had suffered from rheumatoid arthritis, yet he could see ten or eleven patients a day. A good administrator, Jones was enormously industrious and accomplished a great deal. His strengths had caused some of his difficulties with colleagues; precise and efficient himself, the Viennese pace of business struck him as appallingly slack. Before becoming a psychoanalyst Jones had been "drawn to Socialist doctrines; this was more for the orderliness and efficiency they seemed to promise than for the remedying of social injustice."[13]

Jones's private life seems to have been relatively happy, although his first wife died early. Later Hanns Sachs introduced him to a Viennese woman, Katherine Jokl (who, unlike Jones, was Jewish). They were engaged in three days and married within three weeks. One son, a well-known novelist, also writes journalism, and another became a musician; at his death Jones had four grandchildren. His second wife devoted herself completely to him, and by the time of the Freud biography she acted in effect as his secretary. When Freud came to England in 1938 he gave her a stone to be made into a ring, in gratitude for her translating *Moses and Monotheism* into English; he asked her to send him the bill, for a present should not cost anything. Freud was in a great hurry, since he knew it would be his last book.

Jones was Welsh—almost all the early British analysts were outsiders and Gentiles; James and Edward Glover were Scots, and in his autobiography Jones wrote that in England "only two analysts have been Jews (apart from refugee immigrants)."[14] The Swiss analysts constitute probably the only other Western psychoanalytic group notable for its absence of Jews. Jones's own attitude toward Freud's Jewishness was limited by what his generation in England considered its unconventionality toward religion; religions were the product of human superstition, and Freud's Jewishness was (for James Strachey perhaps even more than for Jones) an interesting eccentricity rather than a living (and conditioning) factor in Freud's life. In Freud's movement Jones stood out as one of the few notable Gentiles.

Psychoanalysis in England developed, in contrast to the situation in America, independently of medical psychiatry. Jones ruled over the British Society with a firm hand. A psychoanalytic group existed under his direction in London before World War I, but the war helped to break it up. "Of the fifteen original members only four got so far as the practice of psychoanalysis, the others contenting themselves with a more or less academic interest in it."[15] Jones overemphasized psychoanalytic exclusiveness, and was pleased to see the eclectic prewar group dissolve. The British group reorganized after the war as a branch of the International Psychoanalytic Association, with Jones still in control. (In a letter Jones referred to the mistake they had made at first, in working with uncertain members; and he advised the Japanese to keep their society as small as possible.[16])

The British Society in the early 1920's was substantially nonmedical and somewhat amateurish. Jones invited Melanie Klein from Berlin partly to build up the stature of his society and to help overcome its members' feelings of inferiority; he also wanted her to treat his children. The society, however, had strong ties to Cambridge intellectual circles; and the famous Bloomsbury group took pride in being free of prejudices. James Strachey (Lytton's brother), Alix Strachey, Lionel Penrose, John Rickman, Karen

*James Strachey
in 1934*

Stephen (Clive Bell's sister-in-law, a niece of Bertrand Russell), Adrian Stephen (a son of Sir Leslie Stephen and Virginia Woolf's brother) were, besides being analysts, members of the English intelligentsia.

After World War I the Stracheys went to Vienna for analyses with Freud, who spotted their literary talents as translators. James and Alix Strachey were old friends of Virginia and Leonard Woolf, and when the London analysts were floundering with their publishing ventures, James Strachey approached Leonard Woolf, who was then founding the Hogarth Press, and terms were readily agreed upon. (Sir Allen Unwin had wanted the British Psychoanalytic Society to underwrite the publication of Freud's works with a subsidy.) The British analysts were incompetent businessmen, and out of megalomania had printed 10,000 copies of one of Freud's books which sold only 500 in its first twelve months.

Freud himself was not much of a businessman. He had sold outright to the London Psychoanalytic Institute, for fifty pounds each, the rights to the first volumes of his *Collected Papers*. Once Leonard Woolf had made back this advance, he wrote to Freud and offered him a more straight-forward publishing contract with a normal royalty arrangement of 10 per cent. Although Leonard Woolf played an outstanding role in the dissemination of Freud's ideas in the English-speaking world, it is notable that despite his wife's repeated mental breakdowns (and ultimate suicide), he not only never took her to a psychodynamically oriented therapist (her brother Adrian was an analyst), but even years afterward, in reflecting on her illness, seems to have taken a remarkably rationalistic and unpsycho-analytic view of her difficulties.*[17]

After the dissolution of the Vienna Society in 1938 and the emigration of many of its members to England, the British Society became a more professional group, but at the same time more isolated from outside in-tellectual contacts. Throughout the years Jones retained his sovereignty. As in Vienna, formal meetings were held on Wednesday evenings. Jones, like Freud himself, eventually excluded his potential male rivals. At the time of the Nazi takeover, he kept Theodor Reik (who had been practic-ing in Holland) from coming to England—because he was supposed to be unscrupulous in practice, a lay analyst, not properly speaking a German refugee, and Jones just did not want him.[19] (His attitude toward Reik was all the more striking because of the help Jones afforded other refugee analysts in reaching the United States as well as Britain.) From the incep-tion of his Society, Jones had nourished his jealousies, as he resisted admit-ting those of intellectual eminence to active participation in it. For example, David Forsyth had extensive connections with academic medicine, was the first Englishman to go to Freud after World War I, and felt that any part he played in psychoanalysis in England should be a major one. This aspiration conflicted with Jones's view. Forsyth came from medical societies where it was not unusual to aspire to become president; but Jones held on to the presidency of the British Society until his semi-retirement in 1944.

Jones was also jealous of David Eder, his dictatorial methods caused difficulties with Bernard Hart, and he failed to admit to membership as

---

* Alix Strachey recalled that her husband James "often wondered why Leonard did not persuade Virginia to see a psychoanalyst about her mental breakdowns. There were analysts with sufficient knowledge to understand her illness in those days. Although this knowledge was available, I did not agree with James that it would be of help to Virginia. Leonard, I think, might well have considered the proposition and decided not to let her be psychoanalyzed . . . Virginia's imagination, apart from her artistic creativeness, was so interwoven with her fantasies—and indeed with her madness—that if you had stopped the madness you might have stopped the creative-ness too . . . It may be preferable to be mad and be creative than to be treated by analysis and become ordinary."[18]

promising a psychiatrist as Emanuel Miller. Like Freud, Jones thought that one could not be an analyst unless one practiced full time; so he felt that Lionel Penrose had too many other interests (and Penrose agreed). Also like Freud, in the end Jones collected around him a group of especially talented female psychoanalysts. If Jones accepted a physician for membership he preferred a woman. He also encouraged lay people: Mrs. Joan Riviere, for example, was a brilliant Cambridge graduate, analyzed first by Freud and then by Melanie Klein. A handsome woman with a fine mind, she enjoyed her power behind the throne and once tried to strike a bargain with Jones's second-in-command, Edward Glover (a physician but, in Jones's view, a mere Scot), to govern without Jones; but Glover refused to go along.[20]

Jones, who referred to the British Society as "my promising Society,"[21] considered his position as leader of the British analytic community to be so vital that at the outset of World War I, despite the pressure of patriotic duty to enlist, he at first resisted because he felt "like a sentry at a post."[22] Freud had supported Jones's view of his stature in psychoanalysis when, in 1913, he congratulated Jones for having dueled publicly with Janet: "I cannot say how much gratified I have been by your report of the Congress and by your defeating Janet in the eyes of your countrymen. The interest of psychoanalysis and of your person in England is identical, and now I trust that you will 'strike while the iron is hot.' "[23]

On Jones's fiftieth birthday in 1929, Freud praised him publicly. According to this tribute, Jones

> worked tirelessly for psychoanalysis, making its current findings generally known by means of lectures, defending it against the attacks and misunderstandings of its opponents by means of brilliant, severe but fair criticisms, maintaining its difficult position in England against the demands of the "profession" with tact and moderation, and, alongside of all these externally directed activities, accomplishing, in loyal cooperation with the development of psychoanalysis on the Continent, the scientific achievement to which, among other works, his *Papers on Psychoanalysis* and *Essays on Applied Psychoanalysis* bear witness.

Jones was, in Freud's view, "not only indisputably the leading figure among English-speaking analysts, but . . . also recognized as one of the foremost representatives of psychoanalysis as a whole. . . ." Freud could "not think of Ernest Jones, even after his fiftieth birthday, as other than before: zealous and energetic, combative and devoted to the cause."[24] As with

Marxism and Calvinism, an apparently deterministic system of ideas went hand in hand with great individual activism. Privately Freud wrote to Jones for that same birthday:

> I have always looked upon you as a member of my intimate family circle and will continue to do so, which points (beyond all disagreements that are rarely absent with a family and also have not been lacking between us) towards a fount of affection from which one can always draw again.[25]

Jones had a heart attack in 1944 and went into semi-retirement in the country, where he had first moved in 1940 because of the threat of invasion.

Ernest Jones at the age of fifty-five

He mellowed and could be encouraging to young people's work. He insisted, however, in charging consulting fees for his analytic patients (which was not the customary practice), and therefore his few pupils tended to be rich. By certain standards he could be broad and tolerant; not only did he support and protect Melanie Klein, viewed as a schismatic in Vienna, but he also wrote an introduction to the work of Ronald Fairbairn, at the time the only analyst in Scotland. However, Jones was no friend of the independent Tavistock Clinic in London, since it stood for eclecticism and he was as much opposed to "watering down" Freud's views as he was antagonistic to the old-line anti-analytic neurologists and psychiatrists. (Even in the 1930's psychoanalysis in Britain was segregated and restricted. Jones ruled that no qualified analyst was permitted to give lectures on psychoanalysis to anyone without his express approval; Karen Stephen did not honor this procedure for some talks at Tavistock, and Jones is said to have berated her for it.)

Jones was a superb publicist for psychoanalysis, and his expositions of Freud's ideas are unmatched in their clarity. Good writing is a rare quality, and anyone interested in Freud's life and work must be grateful for Jones's contribution. He saw himself in relation to Freud as Huxley had been to Darwin.[26] Other than Freud, no one better described the psychoanalytic focus on "the deep disharmonies that lie at the center of human nature." The "secrets of the human soul were to be apprehended and understood only in connection with suffering: through being able to suffer oneself and thus entering into contact with the suffering of others."[27]

It is not disparaging of Jones to say that his psychoanalytic writings consisted mainly in popularizing Freud's ideas. Freud was explicit in his needs; in a letter to Jones of February 1, 1927, Freud wrote of wanting "to do the most suitable thing for propaganda purposes." Freud respected Jones as the leader in England, referring patients to him and deferring (if sometimes only halfheartedly) to his judgment in the tangled area of translations and publication rights. Freud typically was cavalier (from a translator's, though not his own, point of view) in the matter of translations; for instance, he might give the rights to a new book to both an American and an Englishman, without telling one about the other, although two such editions in the same language would conflict. As a result, his copyrights became entangled. (There were similar mix-ups with Freud's books in Italy.)

In his own writings Jones naturally leaned heavily on Freud's suggestions. For example, Jones loyally developed a footnote of Freud's in *The Interpretation of Dreams* about the oedipal meaning of *Hamlet*, first into an essay and then into an impressive book. But Jones felt that Freud sometimes spoiled his chances for original work, through indiscretion. Jones

was working on a book about Napoleon, and talked it over with Freud
several times. Freud

> passed on some of the ideas to Ludwig Jekels, who was then in
> analysis with him and who happened to be a rival of mine with a
> certain lady. Jekels seized on them avidly and wrote an excellent essay
> on the subject. The cream was gone, the war and other interests
> supervened, and my book never got written.[28]

It sounds very much like the Fliess-Swoboda-Weininger incident all over
again.

In his idolization of Freud, Jones did his best to suppress anything
from being published about Freud which could be construed in an
unflattering light. In the early 1930's Isidor Sadger, one of Freud's Viennese followers from before World War I, prepared a book on Freud;
Jones was so incensed by some of the interpretations in it that he recommended in a letter to Federn that Sadger (who was Jewish) be put into
a concentration camp,[29] if need be, to make sure the book never appeared.
(It was never published.) Jones later included a nasty (but perhaps fair)
description of Sadger in his own autobiography.*[30] Jones also possessed
an extraordinarily prescient sense of history, and in all his early reports,
book reviews, and obituaries he constantly kept a historical perspective
in mind.

Jones was eminently qualified to become Freud's official biographer.
Anna Freud was a chief source of information, and having all along jealously guarded her father's papers, she had material at her disposal that
could swamp with details any rival studies; but having access to these
resources meant that Jones had to work under the constraints of writing
for his hero's family. The English and the Americans in the movement
were delighted with the outcome of Jones's labors, whereas the Continental
analysts were more aware of Jones's limitations.

At the same time, Jones probably knew more about Freud's irrational
side than he admitted in print. For example, in an essay Jones once published called "The God Complex," he lists some tendencies characteristic
of it which he also later attributed to Freud, although in discussing Freud
he would not have dared to use such a term or develop any of its implications: "a tendency to aloofness. The man is not the same as other mortals,
he is something apart, and a certain distance must be preserved between

---

* In 1908 Freud had written to Jung that Sadger was a "congenital fanatic of orthodoxy, who happens by mere accident to believe in psychoanalysis rather than in the
law given by God on Sinai-Horeb. . . ."[31]

him and them"; such people "rarely invite friends to their home, where
they reign in solitary grandeur"; "the person aims at wrapping himself in
an impenetrable cloud of mystery and privacy. Even the most trivial pieces
of information about himself, those which an ordinary man sees no object
in keeping to himself, are invested with a sense of high importance, and
are parted with only under some pressure"; finally, "as a rule they are
atheists, and naturally so because they cannot suffer the existence of any
other God."[32]

If Jones shied away from discussing some aspects of Freud's character,
he was nevertheless more independent and freethinking than Freud's followers in Vienna. They tended to have no interests whatsoever outside
psychoanalysis. Jones was a fine chess player and figure skater (he even
wrote a book on figure skating). He said himself that his "own contribution
to the Committee was essentially to give them a broader view of the outside world. The Viennese circle had a certain limited outlook, which was
in some ways even rather provincial."[33]

When it came to accusing Jung of anti-Semitism, Jones cited Jung's
"highly colored" view of the Viennese group around Freud:

> Jung had told me in Zurich what a pity it was that Freud had no
> followers of any weight in Vienna, and that he was surrounded there
> by a "degenerate and Bohemian crowd" who did him little credit. . . .
> I soon found that Jung's description was a highly colored one, to put
> it mildly . . . I was obliged to ask myself whether his account had
> proceeded from anything more than simple anti-Semitism. . . .

Yet Jones's own description of the Vienna Society when he first came to
it (only a few pages after this attack on Jung) is no more flattering than
the picture he had ascribed to Jung:

> I was not highly impressed with the assembly. It seemed an unworthy
> accompaniment to Freud's genius, but in the Vienna of those days,
> so full of prejudice against him, it was hard to secure a pupil with a
> reputation to lose, so he had to take what he could get.[34]

As an analyst, Jones was tough with patients, almost ritualistic (perhaps out of fear); the man who poignantly described psychoanalytic
insight as derived from mental suffering did not care if his analysands
suffered a bit. Jones had a fairly standard technique as an analyst; describing his earlier career as a neurologist, Jones explained that he

> did not suffer from the therapeutic obsession—the belief that treat-
> ment is the beginning and end of medicine—that produces so many
> poor doctors and holds up the progress of medical knowledge. On

the contrary, I held—and still do—that the questions of prevention and cure will answer themselves provided only we understand enough about the nature of disease and the forces at work.[35]

Although Freud would have agreed with Jones here, he was less certain than Jones about proper therapeutic technique.* Of the quarrel with Jung at Munich, Freud conceded that "the objections of our spokesman—I think it was Ernest Jones who took the chief part—were too harsh and uncompromising."[37]

The Viennese outlook on psychoanalytic therapy was less uncompromising than Jones's; a patient should be helped to overcome only certain problems, and left free to sort out the rest on his own. And some symptoms, in Freud's view, are best left entirely alone. A famous brain surgeon once discussed with Jones

> a distressing neurotic symptom that afflicted him before each of his great brain operations. He wished me to analyze him for it, but that never proved feasible. I told Freud of it afterwards, and rather to my surprise he said he would not have advised treatment in such a case: it might prove that the surgeon's superb achievements were so closely bound up with the neurotic symptom—in a sense conditioned by it —that to disturb the one might disturb the other. My own opinion is that such an eventuality could only be temporary.[38]

Jones went so far as to describe the novelist James Joyce as a highly pathological case.[39] He considered that "dream analysis is the centre of our practical therapeutic work. . . ." and was impressed with "the value of psychoanalysis for prophylaxis, in preventing slight cases from ever becoming serious."[40] It is typical of the temperamental differences between Jones and Freud that whereas the former feared religion's anti-naturalism, the latter was more afraid of the dangers of medicine's scientific materialism.[41]

Jones made a great display of the extent of whatever doctrinal differences there were between him and Freud, in an effort to establish how tolerant Freud could be. It is true that Freud's openness sometimes horrified Jones; late one night Freud got into a "superstitious" enough mood even to talk about the possible existence of the Almighty. On the whole, however, Jones found it relatively easy to deal with Freud from London.

---

* Freud's first impressions of him were set down in a letter to Jung: "Jones is undoubtedly a very interesting and worthy man, but he gives me a feeling of, I was almost going to say racial strangeness. He is a fanatic and doesn't eat enough. 'Let me have men about me that are fat,' says Caesar, etc. He almost reminds me of the lean and hungry Cassius. He denies all heredity; to his mind even I am a reactionary. How, with your moderation, were you able to get on with him?"[36]

and the members of the committee wrote circular letters to each other. Jones cited Freud's having once said to him that "the simplest way of learning psychoanalysis was to believe that all he wrote was true and then, after understanding it, one could criticize it in any way one wished. . . ."[42] It might prove difficult, however, to emerge from that initial state of belief, and passages can be found in Jones which echo Freud almost word for word.

"I differed completely from Freud in many matters. . . . ," Jones thought, but as one scrutinizes his list the issues seem minor.[43] The sole exception was Jones's support of Melanie Klein, an enemy of Anna Freud. The one time a tone of resentment crept into Jones's account of his relation to Freud came after the death of Jones's first child. When Freud heard of Jones's loss, he wrote "suggesting a piece of Shakespeare research in the hope of its distracting me."[44] (This insensitivity is reminiscent of how Karl Marx reacted to the death of Engels's long-standing mistress— Marx strained his relationship with Engels by suggesting that Engels do some more translating work for Marx's cause.)

As the leader of the British Society, Jones succeeded on an issue particularly dear to Freud's heart: he established, despite private reservations, lay analysis in England. In contrast to the situation in America, orthodox analysis in England has always had a high percentage of lay analysts. When in the late 1920's it was first widely discussed in psychoanalysis whether medical training was necessary or advisable for an analyst, 40 per cent of the British Society was nonmedical. But, Jones wrote, "we did not adopt Freud's extreme position of dissuading intending candidates from studying medicine." It is not true that Freud took the stand Jones imputed to him, but to Jones it seemed that his views on the matter were "enough for Freud to consider me as much an opponent as if I were altogether opposed to lay analysis . . . He could never understand midway positions."[45]

Earlier, while living in Toronto, Jones traveled around America, speaking at meetings and organizing support for psychoanalysis; so that in addition to his services in Britain, Jones helped the cause in the country that eventually became the largest center of analysts in the world. Although Jones shared the anti-American prejudices of a European of his day, he helped hold the movement together. For in the 1920's there was a real danger of a split between Europe and America over the issue of lay analysis. The fight went on and on, for Congress after Congress, as the Americans fought against any infringement on the medical monopoly of psychoanalysis in their country. Jones was a good chairman, and was sympathetic to the special demands of the component societies in the International Psychoanalytic Association, of which he was president from 1920 to 1924 and from 1932 to 1949.

6. Ernest Jones and Sandor Ferenczi: Rivalry

IN THE PERIOD just before World War I, when still a bachelor in Canada and able to travel freely, Jones was in close personal contact with Freud. By the coming of the war Jones was back in England, and after it was over he married and became the leader of a growing British Society. None of the early psychoanalytic pioneers led conventional private lives, and Jones was no exception. In Toronto, Jones paid a blackmailer (a former patient) five hundred dollars to prevent her from accusing him publicly as a seducer; probably innocent of the charge, Jones felt too insecure professionally not to pay the money.[*][1]

Before going to Canada, Jones had met Loe Kann, a young Dutch woman (who was Jewish), and for seven years their lives were "closely linked." Jones described her in his autobiography as having an extraordinarily fine character, and he "got into the habit of sharing her flat. . . ."[3] Unfortunately, Loe suffered from a kidney condition, which required operations. "For the pain she took morphia twice a day and this developed into a heavy drug addiction. In those days the sale of such drugs to the public was quite unrestricted."[4] Her health, mental as well as physical, grew so bad in Canada, where she had gone with Jones, that for a time "she had seldom left her bed." "So in 1912 she decided to go to Vienna and place herself in Professor Freud's hands."[5]

Jones went with Loe to Vienna and stayed there with her awhile.

---

[*] In London, Jones had been accused by two small children of having "behaved indecently during the speech test I had carried out with them. . . ."; he was actually imprisoned for a night, but the magistrate eventually dismissed the case. Later, however, a young girl of ten whom Jones had interviewed clinically "boasted to other children in the ward that the doctor had been talking to her about sexual topics. . . ."; Jones had to resign his position.[2] His career could ill afford any more such scandal.

"Two or three evenings a week would be spent *tête-à-tête* with Freud." Jones wrote that

> He had taken a liking to me, and seemed to wish to open his heart to someone not of his own milieu. He was a magnificent talker, and we ranged over all sorts of topics in philosophy, sociology, and above all psychology. More than once I had to reproach myself for allowing him to continue till three in the morning when I knew his first patient was due at 8 o'clock. Those were the days when I got to know Freud well—his fearlessness of thought, his absolute integrity of mind and character, and his personal lovableness.[6]

Like other converts to psychoanalysis, Jones's initial attraction to the movement had not been based on Freud's personal influence; some, like Stekel, came as grateful former patients, whereas others, like Jones, were originally motivated by the meaning Freud's ideas gave to their scientific understanding.

When Freud returned from his holiday in September 1912, he decided it would be best for Loe if Jones did not remain in Vienna during her analysis. (In Jones's autobiography she is discreetly described simply as Loe, whereas in his biography of Freud she is referred to as Loe Kann, a patient of Freud's and a woman of some importance in his life—with no mention of her intimate relationship with Jones.) Jones returned to Vienna from Canada in May 1913, with the intention of practicing in London again. As a result of Freud's treatment of Loe, Jones and she "decided to part, after which we both married happily."[7]

Freud at this time advised Jones to make use of his temporary freedom from professional commitments by getting himself analyzed. According to Jones, this recommendation had nothing to do with what might seem likely to an outside observer—Loe's analysis and Jones's relationship with her, in short Freud's increased familiarity with Jones through Loe. To Jones, Freud's suggestion was related to his decision to recommend Jones as Jung's successor, "and this was perhaps the reason why he advised me that spring to undergo a didactic analysis."[8]

Freud recommended another bachelor, Sandor Ferenczi (1873–1933) of Budapest, as the analyst.

> My analysis, like the rest of my life, was intensive. I spent an hour twice a day on it during that summer and autumn, and derived very great benefit from it. It led to a much greater inner harmony with myself, and gave me an irreplaceable insight of the most direct kind into the ways of the unconscious mind which it was highly instructive

to compare with the more intellectual knowledge of them I had previously had.[9]

Jones claimed that he was "the first psychoanalyst" to undertake an analysis for purposes of training. Only a thin line separates a therapeutic from a training analysis, especially so in those days; in theory the latter seeks to prepare the patient for the practice of the profession while the former aims to relieve psychological suffering. Former patients of Freud's (Stekel and Ludwig Jekels) had already become psychoanalysts. And it was not unknown for Freud before World War I to recommend to young medical-school candidates who had a serious interest in psychoanalysis that they be analyzed. Jung had already proposed that all future analysts be analyzed.

Jones may have been one of the first of the most prominent early analysts to have been analyzed; of the initial committee, only Sandor Ferenczi had undergone a formal analysis, though his was with Freud, for short stretches—a few weeks—in 1914 and 1916. After his few months with Ferenczi in Budapest, Jones returned to London in the fall of 1913. In June 1914 Freud and Otto Rank went to Budapest to attend Loe Kann's wedding to a man named Herbert Jones. According to Ernest Jones, this marriage ceremony was "one of the two weddings [Freud] . . . ever attended outside his immediate family."[10] (Like the Brunswicks' marriage,* this one also ended in divorce.)

The four months that Jones spent in analysis with Ferenczi had unfortunate consequences for the Hungarian's future historical reputation. For Jones concocted such an extraordinary account of Ferenczi's last years that one is tempted to agree with James Strachey and Edward Glover who both maintained that Jones never forgave Ferenczi for having been his analyst.[11] Perhaps Jones's resentment of this relationship was also compounded by his jealousy of Ferenczi's greater closeness to Freud, and by the fact that Freud had analyzed Ferenczi and not Jones. To be sure, at times Jones could describe Ferenczi at his best in a way that fits other accounts of him and explains why Ferenczi became a great personal favorite of Freud's:

> He had an altogether delightful personality which retained a good deal of the simplicity and a still greater amount of the imagination of the child: I have never known anyone better able to conjure up, in speech and gesture, the point of view of a young child . . . He had a very keen and direct intuitive perception, one that went well with the highest possible measure of native honesty . . . His ideas were

---

* Cf. below, p. 422ff.

far too numerous for more than a small portion of them to be committed to writing, so this quality could be fully appreciated only from repeated conversations with him . . . a boyishly lovable person, rich in vitality and zest for living, simple, direct, and honest to the core, scintillating with interesting ideas that were mostly tossed off for the moment, and with a keen perception of other people's thoughts and motives. This was what he was when I first had to do with him, before the unhappy deterioration that set in some twenty years later . . . As is well known, some very deep layer of mental disturbance began to give trouble a few years before he died, largely in connection with the organic disease from which he suffered, and his character changed in many respects.[12]

According to everyone who knew Ferenczi intimately during his last years, and in contrast to what Jones wrote of as "well known," the notion of an "unhappy deterioration" and "some very deep layer of mental disturbance" was entirely fictional.

Many consider Ferenczi to have been the warmest, most human, most sensitive of the early psychoanalytic group. Short and expressive, poetical and not egotistical, interested in other people and always eager to help, Ferenczi was charming and imaginative. He had the capacity for thinking bold new ideas without being sure he really believed in them. He did not marry until March 1919, when he was in his mid-forties; the consummation of his long courtship (eighteen years) with his bride had been favored by Freud for some time, even though the woman was much older than Ferenczi, married, and the mother of two daughters. Freud later gave Gisela Ferenczi one of the cherished rings; he had once described her to Jung as "thoroughly versed in our lore and a staunch supporter."[13] Like Ferenczi himself, she was kind and sentimental; nevertheless, she divorced her husband in order to enter into this new marriage. Her first husband had been a soft, sad man, unfortunately deaf, who therefore had had great trouble communicating with people.

On the day Ferenczi married his wife, her first husband died (according to some a suicide, while others maintained that it was a heart attack[14]). She had decided not to divorce until her two girls were married. One daughter (Magda) married a younger brother of Ferenczi, and the other (Elma) an American. In 1907 or 1908 Ferenczi, then a doctor in general practice, had arranged for Elma to go to Freud for an analysis, which lasted three months. Elma and Freud got on well together; she remembered her analysis as being pleasant and not an upheaval, and yet felt that she came back to Hungary a different person.

Ferenczi had arranged for Elma's analysis at the beginning of his association with Freud. She must have been important to him beyond being the daughter of the woman he loved. In a 1957 letter Jones reassured Ferenczi's literary executor, Michael Balint, that the Freud biography had been most cautious in avoiding discussing Ferenczi's private life, his relation to Gisela and his intimacy with Elma.[15] Perhaps Jones was emboldened to say whatever he wanted about Ferenczi's final illness and his "mental disturbance" precisely because Balint (who had inherited Ferenczi's ring) knew that Jones was privy to unpublished information about Ferenczi's earlier years.

Freud wrote more letters—approximately 2,500—to Ferenczi than to anyone else. (Jones, for instance, received about 400.) If Ferenczi was ever deeply in love with his future wife's daughter, Freud would not have held such "irregular" behavior against him. Whereas, in a letter to Ferenczi, Freud had praised Jones for his "superb letters, full of victories and fights,"[16] it was what Freud called Ferenczi's "lovable and affectionate personality"[17] that won Freud. The faces of persons who knew Ferenczi still light up at the mention of his name. As Jones understood, perhaps jealously, Freud was "attracted by Ferenczi's enthusiasm and lively speculative turn of mind. . . ."[18] Freud preferred people who were brilliant but not excessively organized.

Jones also knew how much Freud responded to Ferenczi's emotional generosity: "What we saw was the sunny, benevolent, inspiring leader and friend . . . with his open childlike nature, his internal difficulties, and his soaring fantasies, [Ferenczi] made a great appeal to Freud. He was in many ways a man after his own heart."[19] To Freud's credit, Ferenczi was more interesting to him than the more reliable scientists in the movement, such as Abraham. As Freud once wrote, "I cannot help but wish that Abraham's clarity and accuracy could be merged with Ferenczi's endowments and to it be given Jones's untiring pen."[20]

Ferenczi published, to be sure, criticisms of Jung's heresy (and later Otto Rank's), and confidently believed with the others that the "knowledge of the truth can compensate us for much we are deprived of and also for much suffering."[21] But Ferenczi (more than Jones, at any rate) identified with the side of Freud that wanted to avoid unfruitful public discussions of psychoanalysis.[22] Ferenczi's generous nature, his psychological intuitiveness, and his capacity (within Freud's world) to entertain fresh ideas were the source of Freud's deep affection for him. In a tribute to Ferenczi on his fiftieth birthday, Freud praised him for "his originality, his wealth of ideas and his command over a well-directed scientific imagination," and noted that "his friends know that Ferenczi has held back even more than he has been able to make up his mind to communicate."[23]

Sandor Ferenczi (1873–1933)

Ferenczi played a significant role in what Freud called the "external affairs"[24] of psychoanalysis. In Freud's "On the History of the Psychoanalytic Movement," he listed only one Hungarian collaborator, Ferenczi, "but one that indeed outweighs a whole society."[25] The first meeting of the Hungarian Psychoanalytic Society had been held in 1913, with Ferenczi the leader; under his "guidance" it became, in Freud's view, "a center of intense and productive work and was distinguished by an accumulation of abilities such as were exhibited in combination by no other Branch Society."[26] At the Congress of analysts in Budapest in 1918, Ferenczi was elected president of the International Psychoanalytic Association.

The reception that the city of Budapest gave to the assembled analysts in 1918 was a milestone in the history of psychoanalysis. World War I (as later World War II) stimulated psychiatric interest in psychoanalytic concepts; for emotional problems that interfered with a soldier's duties, the "war neuroses," had become a troublesome issue for the military authorities. The Budapest Congress marked a turning point for Freud's movement. For a short time (March–August 1919) Ferenczi held an appointment in Budapest to the first university lectureship on psychoanalysis.

Freud had hopes of accomplishing in Budapest what he had once failed to achieve in Zurich—establishing "the analytic capital of Europe"[27] outside Vienna, thereby ensuring the continuance of psychoanalysis after his death. (Living in England in 1939, Freud complimented Jones that "the events of recent years have made London the principal site and center of the psychoanalytical movement."[28]) However, not only did political difficulties soon isolate Hungary from the rest of the world (at which point Ferenczi resigned as president of the International Psychoanalytic Association, handing over the post to Jones in London), but Anton von Freund, a wealthy Hungarian on whom Freud was relying for financial support and whom Ferenczi had in 1918 appointed secretary of the Association, died in January 1920. During the war von Freund had given the city of Budapest (at a prewar rate of exchange) the equivalent of $300,000, for the purpose of setting up a psychoanalytic institute

> in which analysis was to be practiced, taught and made accessible to the people. It was intended to train a considerable number of physicians in this Institute who would then receive an honorarium from it for the treatment of poor neurotics in an out-patient clinic. The Institute, furthermore, was to be a center for further scientific research in analysis.[29]

Through "a relatively smaller sum" given to Freud by von Freund, an international psychoanalytic publishing house (*Internationaler Psychoanalytischer Verlag*) was eventually set up in Vienna; however, this gift as well as the earlier one amounted, in the end, to less than had been expected, owing to political difficulties in extracting the money from Hungary as well as the general economic inflation.

In this period Freud tended especially to take Hungarians (considered to be even more vivacious extroverts than the Viennese) into analysis, and in addition to Ferenczi and von Freund he analyzed Istvan Hollos (who was later psychotic for five years before his death) and Elisabeth Rado-Revesz, both of whom became analysts. Von Freund was a wealthy brewer with philanthropic interests, and was also a doctor of philosophy. A charming and popular man, his private life, unfortunately, was sorely troubled (his first wife killed herself, his daughter was disturbed, and while married to his second wife he maintained a mistress to whom he bequeathed some money). Von Freund contracted a cancer, recovered, and then died, at almost the same time as Freud's daughter Sophie. "I don't know who I am mourning more for now, Toni or our Sophie," Freud remarked to von Freund's sister, Kata Levy, whom he then took into analysis for a short period (free of charge).[30] Mrs. Levy was married to a physician, Lajos Levy, who was one of the founding members of the Hungarian Psychoanalytic Society and whom Freud occasionally turned to for medical advice; she had been briefly analyzed by Freud during his stay in Budapest, subsequently became a lay analyst, and then, having lost her money by the end of World War II, moved to London, where she lived in a house adjoining Anna Freud's garden. Freud persuaded one of his daughters-in-law to name her son for Kata's brother Anton, and at least one couple of loyal followers, Ernst and Marianne Kris, did likewise.

For all that Budapest meant to Freud as a center for psychoanalysis, it was Ferenczi personally who was most important to him. Normally Freud was torn between his desire for recognition and his need for seclusion. But Ferenczi (aside from Freud's sister-in-law Minna) was his favorite traveling companion; they often spent holidays together in Italy. In his many letters to Ferenczi, Freud regularly discussed his health (Ferenczi had hypochondriacal anxieties of his own), something he would not have done with other members of the committee.[31] Freud rarely received guests from abroad other than Ferenczi, and once said that he wished Ferenczi had married his oldest daughter, Mathilda.[32] In 1926 Ferenczi even offered to come to Vienna to analyze Freud, and it is a tribute to their relationship that Freud was touched by this proposal rather than resentful.[33]

Freud sent his new manuscripts to Ferenczi (as he had sometimes to Abraham) to read and comment on. He rated Ferenczi's scientific work as high as that of Abraham's; in his obituary of Abraham in 1926, he alluded to Ferenczi's special niche: "among all those who followed me along the dark paths of psychoanalytic research, he [Abraham] won so pre-eminent a place that only one other name could be set beside his."[34] In his 1933 obituary Freud declared that Ferenczi's written works had "made all analysts into his pupils."[35]

7. Sandor Ferenczi:
Technique and Historical Victim

WHATEVER THE RIVALRIES between Ferenczi and Abraham, or Ferenczi and Jones, in the history of the psychoanalytic movement its Byzantine politics should not be allowed to obscure its central achievement —the development of a new conception of the mind. But although Ferenczi was as talented a theorist as any of Freud's disciples (he developed a "bio-analytic" theory of genitality in *Thalassa*[1]), his greatest interest lay in therapeutic technique. No one has ever been fully satisfied with therapeutic results, analytic or otherwise. As Freud wrote in his obituary of Ferenczi, "one single problem had monopolized his interest. The need to cure and to help had become paramount in him." Freud had always recommended that his students concentrate their energies, but in Freud's view Ferenczi "had probably set himself aims which, with our therapeutic means, are altogether out of reach today."[2] Ferenczi was inclined to experiment with and improve upon "classical" psychoanalytic technique, and it was only in accord with his impulsive Hungarian nature that his changes were in the direction of "elasticity" and "relaxation" of Freud's more austere recommendations. Where Freud was often intolerant of a patient's regressions in therapy, Ferenczi tended to be unsuspecting of such infantilism. Ferenczi was able to meet a patient at least halfway, to make of the therapeutic relationship a genuine interpersonal encounter.

Eager to exploit his own personality for the sake of a therapeutic gain, Ferenczi gradually came to believe that it was the analyst's task to rectify the mistakes of harsh upbringing in his patients. There were no bad children, he held, only inadequate parents, whereas Freud had abandoned his early environmentalism (the belief in parental seduction) in favor of the view that it was the child's struggle with instinctual problems that led to later neurotic difficulties.[3] Perhaps out of his own childlessness, Ferenczi eagerly assumed the role of the helping parent.[4] (One can only wonder about the part that Ferenczi's relationship with Gisela's daughter Elma may have played here.) As Freud summarized Ferenczi's final position, arrived at shortly before he died in 1933, "one could effect far more with one's patients if one gave them enough of the love which they had longed for as children."⁵

Ferenczi's ideas on technique evolved over a number of years, and it was only at the end of his life that serious difficulties arose between him and Freud. In 1923 Ferenczi had published *The Development of Psychoanalysis* in collaboration with Otto Rank, Freud's special favorite in Vienna and Ferenczi's close friend. Freud knew of the book's impending publication and had a rough idea of its contents, but the other members of the committee did not; with Freud's support Ferenczi and Rank need hardly have worried what the other members of the committee would think. They were unwary, however, for to Jones the book "revealed at once the seeds of divergent tendencies."⁶

In Ferenczi and Rank's account, psychoanalysis had "developed from a therapy into a science and even into an attitude towards life. . . ." But they were fearful of its "remaining fixed . . . in this or that phase," thereby failing to evolve with experience.⁷ Ferenczi and Rank emphasized the importance of current realities in treatment, they aimed to shorten therapy, and they stressed the intercommunication between patient and analyst. To be therapeutically successful, they suggested, an analysis needed to be more than an intellectual reconstruction of the patient's early childhood years; it had also to be a genuine emotional reliving. One "might be tempted to ask oneself, whether our therapeutic analyses have not up to now been too 'didactic,' whereas the so-called didactic analyses taught less analysis than the theory. . . ."⁸ But any improvement in technique entailed, as Ferenczi in particular emphasized, more "actvity" and involvement on the analyst's part than had heretofore been explicitly sanctioned. Abraham, like Jones, suspected heresy, and warned Freud of a revival of Jung's ideas in a new guise. Freud told Rank of Abraham's suspicions, Rank in turn told Ferenczi, and "it is hard to say which of the two got angrier."⁹

Freud did not find the book entirely congenial, and Ferenczi felt blasted by Freud's expressed reservations. But Freud wrote to reassure Ferenczi on February 4, 1924:

As for your endeavor to remain completely in agreement with me, I treasure it as an expression of your friendship, but find this aim neither necessary nor easily attainable. I know that I am not very accessible and find it hard to assimilate alien thoughts that do not quite lie in my path. It takes quite a time before I can form a judgment about them, so that in the interval I have to suspend judgment. If you were to wait so long each time there would be an end of your productivity. So that won't do at all. That you or Rank should in your independent flights ever leave the ground of psychoanalysis seems to me out of the question. Why shouldn't you therefore have the right to try if things won't work in another way from that I had thought? If you go astray in so doing you will find that out yourself some time or other, or I will take the liberty of pointing it out to you as soon as I am myself sure about it.[10]

Since Rank was also at this time putting forward his new ideas on the birth trauma, Freud wrote an official letter to the other members of the committee—to clarify his own thinking and to reassure them about the prospects of any further "deviations" from psychoanalysis. Freud admitted once again that he "did not find it easy to feel my way into alien modes of thought, and I have as a rule to wait until I have found some connection with my meandering ways. So if you wanted to wait with every new idea until I can endorse it you would run the risk of getting pretty old."[11] Freud thought the technical suggestions of Ferenczi and Rank were, as "experiments," "entirely justified. We shall see what comes of it. In any event we must guard against condemning at the outset such an undertaking as heretical." Freud had his misgivings, especially because in the hands of "ambitious beginners" Ferenczi's kind of active therapy might lead to superficial understanding, and therefore present a "risky temptation."

> Naturally, however, I shall bow to experience. Personally I shall continue to make "classical" analyses, since in the first place, I scarcely take any patients, only pupils for whom it is important that they live through as many as possible of their inner processes—one can not deal with training analyses in quite the same way as therapeutic analyses —and, in the second place, I am of the opinion that we still have very much to investigate and cannot yet, as is necessary with shortened analyses, rely solely on our premises.[12]

Whereas Otto Rank gradually drifted out of Freud's world, Ferenczi remained loyal to Freud. In 1926 Ferenczi was invited to lecture in New York at the New School for Social Research; he and his wife stayed eight months, and his course at the New School did much to promote interest in psychoanalysis in America. Ferenczi also gave seminars on technique for members of the New York Psychoanalytic Society and the American Psychoanalytic Association, and conducted some analyses. Many of the local analysts were unhappy with Ferenczi's visit, since he completely shared Freud's own position in favor of training lay analysts. Although Freud had approved of Ferenczi's appointment to the New School, Jones had warned him against going, out of "intuitive foreboding." According to Jones's version, "Ferenczi was never the same man again after that visit, although it was another four or five years before his mental deterioration became manifest to Freud."[13]

Freud had for years tried to keep Ferenczi from being too dependent on him, but on Ferenczi's return from New York

> Freud was piqued that he [Ferenczi] had not come sooner [to Freud] instead of spending three months in Europe first. He suspected it betokened some tendency to emancipate himself (from Freud or from psychoanalysis or, as the event showed, from both); "when one gets old enough one has at the end everyone against one." He found Ferenczi distinctly reserved since his visit to America.[14]

For all of Freud's intransigence in resisting outside "influences," Ferenczi had a great impact on him; they were, for instance, equally fascinated by

Sandor Ferenczi

the possibility of telepathy and thought-transference. But-in 1930 Ferenczi complained to Freud that, in his analysis during World War I, Freud had not looked in Ferenczi for any repressed hostility toward Freud.[15] This complaint might seem childish of Ferenczi, but it was true that Freud had wanted to minimize as much as possible his followers' ambivalence to him. Ferenczi was a master of analytic technique, and Freud brought up this particular technical issue in a paper after Ferenczi's death. Freud conceded that it was "not altogether" to be ruled out, "considering the limited horizon of analysis in those early days," that he had not paid "attention to the possibilities of a negative transference." Freud doubted, however, that, even "if he had not failed to observe some very faint signs" of a negative transference in Ferenczi, he "would have had the power to activate a topic . . . by merely pointing it out, so long as it was not currently active in the patient himself at the time."[16]

The central issue between Freud and Ferenczi was the question of activity in the analyst's technique. The problem of priorities did not, so far as we know from the tiny portion of their correspondence that has been published, disturb their relationship. Freud could acknowledge that Ferenczi was ahead of him on a point, and he even postponed the publication of one of his papers so that Ferenczi could get full credit.[17] In a paper delivered on his trip to America in 1926, Ferenczi had echoed Freud's own attitude toward the different ways his ideas had been "appropriated":

> In Europe it has become customary for people to appropriate a large part of Freud's life-work, to dish it up in a new form and with a new terminology, and publish it as their own original work . . . On the other hand, it seems as though in America . . . people are much readier than we in Europe to accept the watered-down and attenuated view of certain of Freud's former disciples.[18]

Ferenczi thought that "the most usual and most contemptible way of accepting Freud's theories is that of rediscovering them and broadcasting them under new names."[19]

Although Ferenczi did not come to grief with Freud quite as others had, his personal warmth and effusiveness led him to experiment with the standard analytic technique. Jones recorded with "astonishment" how Ferenczi could "burst" into a room and kiss both Jones and Freud on the cheeks.[20] By 1931 Ferenczi evidently was kissing patients and allowing them to kiss him, all part of the motherly affection he thought patients needed; but Freud worried whether "pawing" might not be next on the agenda in the work of future adherents of Ferenczi's views, and then maybe "peeping and showing," and so on to the ultimate sexual act. The "kissing technique" was to Freud an expression of Ferenczi's quiet withdrawal: "the need for definite independence seems to me to be stronger in you than you recognize."[21]

It was probably true that, like Paul Federn, Ferenczi "remained a secret rebel who could not quite allow himself to know of his rebellion." Ferenczi "suffered . . . from a need to be accepted and loved. Because of this need, his personal relationship to Freud was more important to him than his own independent thinking."[22] No final break ever came between Freud and Ferenczi, but their last meeting, on August 24, 1932, was strained. Freud had wanted Ferenczi not to publish his latest paper for a year. "Freud thought the paper Ferenczi had prepared could do his reputation no good and . . . begged him not to read it" at the psychoanalytic Congress that year. From today's perspective, the paper was brimming with fresh ideas, but—in Jones's view—other leaders in the movement "thought it would be scandalous to read such a paper before a psychoanalytic congress."[23]

That Freud took to Ferenczi in the first place, so many years earlier, and held him in the movement as long as he did, should be considered at least as important as Freud's final rejection of him. For Ferenczi, Freud's attitude toward his technical experimentation was a cruel experience.[24] To Freud, Ferenczi was now like so many of the others, but, as he wrote to his Hungarian follower, with even less cause: "Each of those who were once near to me and then fell away might have found more to reproach me with than you of all people. (No, Rank just as little.)"[25] To Ferenczi, Freud's judgment against analytic "activity" seemed a personal slight, and not just the result of a scientific controversy.[26] At their last interview, Freud had warned Ferenczi that he was making a dangerous departure in technique. As the meeting ended, Ferenczi reported of himself that he held out his hand "in affectionate adieu. The Professor turned his back on me and walked out of the room."[27] Ferenczi was grief-stricken and bitter at Freud's behavior, corresponded with him much less frequently, yet to the end remained loyal to Freud and psychoanalysis.

Ferenczi died on May 22, 1933. He had been suffering from pernicious anemia, although because of his hypochondria it is hard to tell for how long. At the psychoanalytic Congress in 1932 he spoke of his illness (to Jones, among others), and to physicians present the external signs of the grave sickness were already obvious. In letters after Ferenczi's death, as well as in his obituary, Freud mentioned this disease. "Signs were slowly revealed in him of a grave organic destructive process which had probably overshadowed his life for many years already. Shortly before completing his sixtieth year he succumbed to pernicious anemia."[28] At his death Ferenczi was bitter; he still wanted to live, but though silent and depressed, he was, at the end, not at all confused.[29]

All sorts of barriers, inner as well as outer, prevented Freud's loyal students from competing with the master; but there was every incentive for their competing with each other for Freud's favor while he was alive, and for stature in the history of psychoanalysis after his death. Jones could be a ruthless infighter with his rivals. All of his hostility was directed at his colleagues, instead of at Freud himself. Jones claimed that at least on one occasion Ferenczi had accused him of plagiarism,[30] and Jones treated all his difficulties with Ferenczi or Rank as precursors of the opposition they later manifested against Freud himself.[31]

Psychoanalysts frequently abuse their science by diagnostic name calling, and Jones's treatment of Ferenczi's last years may well be the most notorious instance of this in print. He not only recounted Ferenczi's last years as if the Hungarian were deteriorating into lunacy, but he also minimized the role of Ferenczi's organic illness. In Volume II of the Freud biography, Jones simply referred to "severe trouble in the depths" of Ferenczi's personality, and to how Ferenczi's "stability began to crumble."[32] By Volume III, Ferenczi was, according to Jones's view, subject to "mental deterioration";[33] Ferenczi "toward the end of his life . . . developed psychotic manifestations that revealed themselves in, among other things, a turning away from Freud and his doctrines. The seeds of a destructive psychosis, invisible for so long, at last germinated."[34] Along with "the progressive deterioration" in his "mental condition," in the final phase of his illness his physical disorder, Jones wrote, "undoubtedly exacerbated his latent psychotic trends."[35] Ferenczi is supposed to have experienced a "final delusional state," to have committed doctrinal "errors of regression," to have had "delusions about Freud's supposed hostility," and just before dying to have exhibited "violent paranoic and even homicidal outbursts."[36] Such was the death, in Jones's account, of "Freud's closest friend."[37]

Yet no one intimately acquainted with Ferenczi during this final period of his life has confirmed any of Jones's version.[38] At the end Ferenczi's anemia had so weakened him that he was bedridden; fearful that his own enthusiasm had led him into mistakes that would cost him forever Freud's respect and that of his colleagues, Ferenczi spoke of reworking his recent papers to eliminate misunderstandings.[39] When the volumes of Jones's biography of Freud were first published, it seemed to the surviving analysts such a miracle that those early days had been recreated (which was also good for business) that few of them were eager to be critical of what he had accomplished. However, Ferenczi's literary executor, Michael Balint, disputed the story of Ferenczi's psychosis in a letter to the *International Journal of Psychoanalysis*.[40] Jones answered with a letter of his own, but beforehand had persuaded Balint to strike from his letter any reference to the fact that Ferenczi had analyzed both of them. Jones claimed to have a direct source for his version of Ferenczi's death, although he refrained from mentioning names. An examination of Jones's correspondence around the time of Ferenczi's death, however, reveals a different picture from the one he presented in the Freud biography. In a letter of June 20, 1933, in which he discussed "madmen" in psychoanalysis who were also troublemakers, Jones referred to Ferenczi's last organic illness; while Jones claimed that Ferenczi became paranoiac, he also discussed the ravages that the pernicious anemia probably effected on Ferenczi's spinal cord. But Jones did not list Ferenczi with the other supposed "madmen" (such as Gregory Zilboorg, Victor Tausk, Wilhelm Reich, and Jenö Harnik).[41]

Freud himself would probably have referred to Ferenczi as "ill" and suffering from mysterious affects. A patient of Freud's once explained Ferenczi's having "gone bad" on the analogy of the early use of X rays, when its developers became overexposed because they did not know its potential dangers.[42] Freud thought this a brilliant explanation, for it fit perfectly with his ambition to treat psychoanalysis as a pure science; he used it himself in discussing the "dangers" of being an analyst. (The analogy was in fact an old one: Stekel had referred to it in his obituary of Silberer.)

Jones's correspondence indicates that his source for his account of Ferenczi's death might have been the master himself. Ferenczi died quite suddenly, and at the time Jones wanted to know more details about Ferenczi's illness. (The Hungarian analyst-anthropologist Geza Roheim told Jones that Ferenczi's death was unexpectedly sudden but without undue suffering.) Jones telephoned Freud in Vienna,[43] and then wrote a letter to Freud which indicates some of what Freud communicated to him. Jones assumed (and later omitted from his biography) that Ferenczi's physical illness had, in its terminal phase, attacked his spinal cord. Jones promised to keep secret one of Freud's remarks about Ferenczi—something about an American woman—but Jones thought that the paranoia was already public, evident to anyone who heard or read Ferenczi's last Congress paper.[44]

Freud might have, in a telephone conversation, used a word like "paranoid" about Ferenczi; although Ferenczi was a mild and unaggressive person, there were real troubles between him and Freud, and Freud (as well as other analysts) sometimes loosely applied the term to touchy or defensive phases in other people's lives. If Jones was relying on the highest authority for some part of his account of Ferenczi's death, one can imagine he might not have wanted to involve Freud by name. However, Freud's obituary of Ferenczi was fair and objective, and stressed the physical illness that afflicted Ferenczi at the end. As a gentleman, Freud would not have publicly resorted to the *ad hominem* line of reasoning Jones adduced to explain Ferenczi's drift away from Freud, Ferenczi's seeming "inaccessibility." (As yet we do not have an explanation of the reference to an American woman, presumably an erotic relationship between Ferenczi and one of his patients or pupils. Or perhaps Freud had in mind Ferenczi's stepdaughter Elma, who was by then an American. Freud may have been aware of something we cannot know; but in the context of his fear that Ferenczi's technical innovations might lead to professional improprieties, it is conceivable that he was receptive to a mere rumor.)

To those who participated in the early days of psychoanalysis, Jones's account of Ferenczi is widely acknowledged as a travesty of the truth. Ferenczi is remembered as an inspiring teacher; it was a big event in the Vienna Society when he delivered a guest lecture. Not only a specialist in analytic technique, Ferenczi pioneered in character analysis. Ferenczi had fewer eminent students than Karl Abraham, largely for linguistic reasons (but Ferenczi's analysand Clara Thompson became one of the most far-seeing of analytic writers). Hungarian is an unusual language, less likely to be available to students than German; and although Ferenczi was able to analyze patients in German or English, going into treatment with Ferenczi in Budapest might involve taking one's whole family, and children would be unable to manage with such a difficult tongue. When Freud wrote in his obituary that Ferenczi had succeeded in making "all analysts into his pupils," that was high praise indeed. Freud found it "impossible to believe that the history of our science will ever forget him."

8. The Americans:
J. J. Putnam and H. W. Frink

FREUD NEVER HAD an undisputed and unqualified favorite in America. Yet nowhere else has any version of psychoanalysis triumphed on such a scale. The reception of Freud in America[1] is an interesting question of comparative history. For example, though translations of Freud's books appeared almost simultaneously in England and America, from the period before World War I and thereafter Freud found to his consternation a far more responsive audience in the United States.

William James, probably America's greatest philosopher, was aware of Freud's writings as early as the 1890's. James initially welcomed Freud's contributions, since his own work on the psychology of the irrational seemed thereby extended. (James was also perhaps the first of the Cambridge, Massachusetts, intelligentsia to make personal use of the psychiatric services of McLean Hospital.) Yet James grew to have his doubts about the early analysts and Freud, having met him in 1909: "They can't fail to throw light on human nature, but I confess he made on me personally the impression of a man obsessed with fixed ideas."[2]

Morton Prince, another Bostonian, was one of the progressive medical leaders of the native psychotherapeutic movement in America who had done much to interest the reading public in the concept of the subconscious and in the technique of hypnotism; he wrote a famous book on a case of multiple personality. Nonetheless, he was regarded by Ernest Jones as a dangerous enemy. In later years Jones put the responsibility for the way he treated Prince on Freud:

> A slight disagreement between us arose over the personality of Morton Prince, a man whom I had known through correspondence in London years before and with whom I always stayed on my visits to Boston. He had been the first American pioneer in psychopathology, a fact which I felt deserved some recognition. Furthermore he freely opened his periodical, *The Journal of Abnormal Psychology*, to papers on psychoanalysis, almost the only one then available for that purpose.

He was a thorough gentleman, a man of the world, and a very pleasant colleague, as I found in cooperation with him for some years in editing his *Journal*. But he had one serious failing. He was rather stupid, which to Freud was always the unpardonable sin.[3]

To Freud, Prince had "no talent at all" and was "something of a schemer"; "he really is an arrogant ass. . . . Jones's criticism is moderate and polite. . . ."[4] Prince bitterly resented what he considered Jones's attempt to "discredit" his work, and dubbed Jones a "fanatic" in behalf of psychoanalysis.[5] Prince found one of Jones's letters "not only bitter but offensive, not to say insolent," and concluded that Jones was "a nervous, high-strung, self-centered young fellow and takes everything one says as personal to himself."[6]

Prince had "insisted that the neuroses were perversions of normal memory processes and that buried memories were best reached by hypnosis," but his view of the unconscious was decidedly not Freud's:

> I conceive of the unconscious not as a wild, unbridled conscienceless subconscious mind, as do some Freudians, ready to take advantage of an unguarded moment to strike down, to kill, after the manner of an evil genii, but as a great mental mechanism which takes part in an orderly, logical way in all the processes of daily life, but which under certain circumstances involving particularly the emotion-instincts becomes disordered or perverted.[7]

As psychoanalysis began to take hold in America (and it was favorably received in medical circles earlier than among the general public), the arguments grew more belligerent. Prince thought the analysts were becoming more a "cult" than a scientific group, and argued that "Freudian literature was sprinkled with such expressions as 'proved,' 'established,' 'well known,' 'accepted.' Such expressions take the place of 'theory,' 'possibility,' 'probability,' to which we are accustomed in progressive science. . . ."[8]

Freud's therapeutic approach, although more hopeful in its pre-World War I form than in later years, seemed too austere to many Americans, and their "tendency to make the unconscious beneficent kept breaking through."[9] Although the analysis of dreams, the technique of free association, and the revival of old memories appealed to the American desire to overcome excessive reticence,[10] the Americans were reluctant to admit that analysis could automatically bring about a synthesis on the part of the patient. They were inclined to believe, along the lines Jung suggested in his lectures at Fordham, not only that the unconscious was less dangerous than Freud thought but also that the analyst should not restrict his activities quite so narrowly as Freud proposed.

A leading proponent of these views was James Jackson Putnam (1846–1918), a founder of the American Neurological Association and a distinguished professor at Harvard Medical School, who had since the 1890's been experimenting with hypnosis and psychotherapy. Like Prince, Putnam was disenchanted with heredity as an etiological factor, and like Jung's, his method of treatment was partly inspirational. As an Emersonian, Putnam was avowedly optimistic and environmentalist, and as a New Englander with a social conscience, he felt, like Adler, that the "social instincts" in neurotics had to be cultivated. For Putnam, Freud's psychoanalysis meant a new burst of hope.

As Freud put it, Putnam represented "altogether a wonderful acquisition"[11] for the psychoanalytic movement, and Freud was willing to overlook many differences between his views and those of Putnam on account of the latter's sterling character, as well as for the sake of psychoanalysis in America. Freud admired Putnam's "high moral character and unflinching love of truth," and after Putnam's death Freud wrote that "he was one of those happily compensated people of the obsessional type for whom what is noble is second nature and for whom any concession to unworthiness has become an impossibility."[12] It is a tribute to American puritanism that it should have been a straight-laced group of New England Brahmins who took up Freud's ideas in America; they knew at first hand what Freud was struggling against. Putnam was not only well connected socially but also a Gentile, a representative of the "English race" Freud admired.

It would be hard to overestimate what psychoanalysis meant to Putnam. He was sixty-three years old when he became an advocate of Freud's cause. Like others who came under Freud's influence, Putnam felt that Freud's visit to the United States in 1909 had "helped to change radically the whole course of my life and thought."[13] Putnam once referred to a patient of his as "a thorough convert" to psychoanalysis.[14] Freud knew Putnam's worth; as he wrote Putnam at the end of 1910:

> I do not want to let this eventful and troublesome year close before having thanked you for many things; for your valuable articles, for the inestimable aid which you have lent our cause, for allowing your name to be used in America as a protection against the possible misunderstandings and abuses to which I otherwise would have been subjected. From the bottom of my egotistical heart I wish you untroubled health and energy.

Freud's reference to his own egotism was somewhat tongue-in-cheek, since Putnam's New England altruism made him uncomfortable. But it was typical of Freud to mention in the same letter that "our cause is doing very well here; the opposition is at its height."[15]

About Freud's trip to America in 1909, one of his relatives noted, "Freud never forgot that at a relatively early stage in his career the Americans gave him the opportunity to present in . . . public addresses the results of his investigations . . . and that they awarded him an honorary doctorate."[16] (According to legend, Freud's cabin steward on the voyage over had been reading *The Psychopathology of Everyday Life*.) Freud stayed at a camp in the Adirondacks owned by Putnam and some of his

James Jackson Putnam (1846–1918)

old friends. He went to the camp with Jung and Ferenczi, only to find that in honor of the visiting "German" doctors—one Austrian, another Swiss, and the third Hungarian—the buildings were decked out with the emblems of Imperial Germany. The intended honor must have taught them something of the state of American understanding of European feelings. Perhaps there had not been enough formality for Freud, since he found the customs and manners barbarous; Freud's diarrhea and stomach aches did not help to make him comfortable, but similar afflictions were not enough to turn Jung against America.[17] Partially in reciprocation of Freud's visit, Putnam went to Weimar for the 1911 Congress of analysts; "the highlight of the Congress was certainly Putnam's appearance."[18] During this European trip Putnam spent six hours in analysis with Freud.[19] Their degree of intimacy was such that Putnam could confide in a letter that "my sexual relations with my wife have been rather infrequent for many years, of late years exceedingly infrequent, and . . . I have 'dreaded' them. . . ."[20]

As a therapist, Putnam seemed to Freud on the "ambitious" side, too eager to find means of helping and curing. When the controversies arose within the psychoanalytic movement over the ideas and personalities of Alfred Adler and Carl Jung, Putnam remained wholly loyal to Freud yet hoped that a compromise arrangement with the dissidents could be worked out. Putnam had long been interested in treating relatively more serious cases than those to which Freud preferred to confine his technique.

Putnam's catholicity comes through in his defense of Morton Prince in a letter to Jones: "I think it would be utterly unfortunate if those of us who really care about psychopathology in the larger sense, should drift apart, no matter what the provocation."[21] As late as the fall of 1912 Putnam could not quite understand the fuss over Jung. A former patient of Putnam's had introduced him to American Hegelianism, and this convinced him that patients need ideals to encourage sublimations. So Putnam sympathized with Jung's view that the analyst should help the patient with his current problems.

Freud tolerated considerable differences between his own position and Putnam's. To the old New Englander, Freud's conception of the unconscious was "too *negative* to be fully satisfactory."[22] Though Putnam appreciated the novelty of Freud's approach, he drew back from some of its consequences: "I cannot convince myself that life, with all that makes it admirable, is to be explained purely and simply through the study of conflicts. . . . we have to reckon all the time with *positive*, rather than with *negative*, factors in the world."[23] In anticipation of later analysts' interest in problems of the superego, Putnam expressed his "longing to get all that metaphysics has to offer," thus moving away from Freud's reductionism.

Putnam hoped and believed that Freud's "terribly searching psychogenetic explanations correspond only to one pole of human life, and that there is another pole in which he takes no interest."[24]

Putnam could not accept Freud's view that religion was an outgrowth of infantile helplessness and the need for an all-powerful father. He objected, as did Jung, that the real " 'unconscious' contained not only the 'shady' side of human nature, but an implicit recognition of the good."[25] Therefore, Putnam held, "no patient is really cured unless he becomes better and broader morally, and, conversely, I believe that a moral regeneration helps towards a removal of the symptoms."[26] In a letter to Freud, Putnam further stressed that "the individual is not to be thought of as existing alone, but should be considered as an integral part of the community in which he lives."[27]

In his answer Freud evaded the substance of Putnam's argument and simply stated "I do not share your great respect for Adler's theories."[28] Putnam then sent a rather abject reply in which he promised to take to heart Freud's reference to the danger of Adlerian heresy. Unlike Putnam, Freud was determined to keep psychoanalysis clear of philosophy, in order to establish his new field on independent scientific grounds. As Freud expressed it, "Putnam's philosophy is like a beautiful table center; everyone admires it but nobody touches it."[29] Putnam's letters could be tedious, and although Freud usually responded immediately to his mail, he was often slow in replying to Putnam's most boring missives.

Freud never held that analysts had to be perfectionists, about either themselves or their patients. Therefore Freud could write to Putnam: "I feel no need for a higher moral synthesis in the same way that I have no ear for music."[30] Freud elaborated his position in his correspondence with Putnam:

> If we are not satisfied with saying, "Be Moral and philosophical," it is because that is too cheap and has been said too often without being of any help . . . Whoever is capable of sublimation will turn to it inevitably as soon as he is free of his neurosis. Those who are not capable of this at least will become more natural and more honest.[31]

Whatever the differences between Putnam and Freud, the American remained steadfast in his defense of psychoanalysis. The early analysts, including Freud, shared a literalistic fear of seducing their children, and Putnam was afraid of holding his daughters on his lap; he even fixed the seat on one daughter's bicycle lest she be unduly stimulated.[32] (Nowadays many analysts would think that without some form of indirect parental seduction infants and children suffer a deprivation.) Evidently Putnam's work in behalf of Freud hurt his own medical practice, and it certainly offended his wife. She regarded him as gullible and too easily taken in, and their daughter reports that she reacted "with tragic bitterness, feeling that he had been mistakenly lured into a false path which would ruin his professional standing."[33] His death on November 4, 1918, was a keen disappointment to Freud, since the American future would now be more uncertain; even a few months before Putnam suddenly died, Freud had, because of the American interest in Adler and Jung, referred to America as a "land . . . which is now so hostile to us. . . ."[34]

Freud considered Putnam's death "a great loss," and later said: "I felt protected behind his personality as behind a shield."[35] After World War I, Freud had about him a flock of young Americans who came to Europe for training, and "in Freud's opinion the most brilliant and promising of the younger Americans" was Horace W. Frink (1883–1935).[36] His psychoanalytic textbook, *Morbid Fears and Compulsions*, was the best of its kind in English at that time. He was an exceptional clinician, a charming man and a fine conversationalist. The contrast between Frink and his American colleagues was especially sharp, since many of them were raw and unsubtle. Frink, who had been orphaned at an early age,[37] was a Gentile, like Putnam. Analyzed by Freud twice, on October 25, 1921, Frink gave an informal talk at the New York Psychoanalytic Society on his experience with Freud.[38]

Earlier Frink had been analyzed by A. A. Brill, who was then the leader of psychoanalysis in America. But not long after Freud met Frink, he turned to him to replace Brill as his deputy in the United States, though he was personally on friendly terms with Brill.* Frink was elected president of the New York Psychoanalytic Society virtually at Freud's direction. Freud's enthusiasm for Frink, and confidence in his capacities, may have inadvertently contributed to Frink's downfall; such expressed, overt admiration from an analyst, who also happens to be Freud, may have been too much for Frink to deal with.

Freud's unrestrained faith in Frink persisted despite the fact that, during his second analysis with Freud, Frink experienced a psychotic episode. He suffered such acute depersonalization that he had to be taken care of for a time by a male attendant.[40] Freud seems to have misinterpreted

---

* In a book review published in 1923, Frink had pointed out some of Brill's short-comings: "The omission of quotation marks from paragraph after paragraph of material taken practically word for word from Freud, creates a bad impression that is by no means wholly deserved."[39]

Frink's difficulties as simply part of the analysis. Freud showed a patient of his, Abram Kardiner (who had earlier been analyzed by Frink), two photographs of Frink, one taken before and the other after his analysis; Frink had lost forty pounds, and in response to Kardiner's sense of shock Freud commented: "That's what analysis does."

Frink had planned to get married upon his return to the United States after his second analysis. His intended wife was a former patient of his, a wealthy Jewish woman. Her husband had been unhappy about her falling in love with her analyst, and had threatened to provoke a scandal. "Actually Freud approved of the step Frink was contemplating; the falling in love was a mistake, but it now had to be accepted."[41] While Frink was in Vienna for his second analysis with Freud, the woman's husband died; then his own wife died; and Frink and his former patient were smitten with guilt. Frink was a shaken man when he returned to New York

Horace W. Frink
(1883–1935)

and did not resume his psychoanalytic practice.[42] But Freud stated, when asked by Frink's bride-to-be, that Frink was well enough to marry. The marriage, however, was short-lived, and it was clear that Frink would be unable to fulfill Freud's expectations. At a psychoanalytic meeting Brill read a letter from Freud to another New York analyst, which declared that it was obvious that Frink could not execute the commission to which Freud had appointed him, because he was suffering from a mental disorder. Although Frink was not present at the meeting, the letter constituted a serious blow to him.

Later Frink went to Johns Hopkins to put himself under the care of the famous psychiatrist Adolf Meyer. There is a special pathos to an analyst's losing his mind, knowing and yet not knowing what is wrong with him. As Frink explained to Kardiner, who visited him with a manuscript of a new book: "I have no awareness of my body—only my lips."[43] Frink turned against analysis, but he did not in the remotest way blame Freud for what had happened to him. He improved enough to remarry in 1935, and then died that same year in Chapel Hill Mental Hospital in a state of manic excitement.[44] His death was untimely and his career a tragedy, and, combined with Putnam's loss, this episode encouraged Freud to speak widely of his disappointment with America.

9. The Americans: A. A. Brill and the Future of the Cause

AFTER FRINK'S BREAKDOWN Abraham A. Brill (1884–1948) continued for years to be the leader of psychoanalysis in America. He wrote a large number of papers and books to expound psychoanalysis, but is perhaps now best known for his early and controversial translations of Freud's works into English. Hungarian by descent, Brill emigrated to America at the age of fifteen; thus neither English nor German was his native tongue. In rendering Freud's German into English, when it came to illustrations of dreams or slips of the tongue Brill simply substituted his own examples for those of Freud. Freud once explained his own agreement with such a manner of proceeding; in criticizing another translation, Freud once wrote:

I understand the difficulties which exist in rendering errors and dreams into another language, but I do not consider that the expedient used of inventing similar examples to be the correct method . . . The only proper thing to do would have been to substitute for the untranslatable examples of slips of the tongue, puns in dreams, etc., other examples *based on his own analytic experience,* and occasionally to annotate the German example.[1]

Brill's reputation has suffered excessively because of his translations; Freud perhaps rightly paid tribute to Brill's work as a translator,[2] since Brill had seen his task as one of popularizing Freud and not of producing the scriptures in a definitive form. (Freud tended to be uninterested in the matter of translations, although he was more concerned for his British readers than his American ones.[3]) In putting together the Modern Library version of Freud, Brill deliberately dropped passages from Freud's books so that the collection would not interfere with the sales of Freud's individual works. Freud certainly gave translators into other languages the right "to make such changes in the examples" as were considered necessary;[4] it would have been better, however, if Brill had indicated in the texts where his own substitutions were being introduced. But when Jones tried to speak to Freud against Brill's translations, Freud became irritated and attributed Jones's position to jealousy of Brill.[5]

Brill was a good organizer; when he founded the New York Psychoanalytic Society in 1911, Jones (who was then in Toronto) countered in May 1911 by starting the American Psychoanalytic Society, which would contain all the analysts in the United States who lived outside New York City. (Eventually the second organization became the parent unit, with member societies, such as New York groups, coming under its aegis.) Although these two early groups were initially somewhat competitive, Brill joined Jones's association within a year. Jones soon returned to Europe, and by the end of World War I, Brill was the acknowledged head of psychoanalysis in America, and often gave interviews to journalists.[6] Although he liked Brill personally, Freud could be annoyed with him; as Freud wrote, "He is totally Americanized, though still a good-natured boy."[7]

Despite Freud's efforts to install Frink as a replacement for him, Brill remained touchingly loyal to Freud. As for many early analysts, Freud was a successful father figure for Brill, who dedicated his first book to "My Esteemed Teacher, Professor Doctor Sigmund Freud, L.L.D., whose ideas are herein reproduced."[8] Brill named his daughter Gioia (Joy), the literal meaning of Freud's name in German. And, like Freud, he attempted to analyze one of his own children. When Freud visited New

York in 1909, Brill was living on Central Park West; Freud was so impressed with the location he said "stay here, don't move from this spot; it is the nicest part of the city, so far as I can see."[9] Today, too, many New York analysts have chosen to live in that area.

By and large Brill has not fared well at the hands of historians. His true stature will not be accorded him until, as in the case of Putnam, his papers have been made available for research scholars if not for publication. The letters of Brill's that are available make extraordinarily interesting reading, revealing an unexpected liveliness of spirit. Freud himself was particularly hard on Brill as a correspondent, since it could be difficult to get a reply out of him.[10] As Jones maintained, Brill had "a heart of gold,"[11] but his offers to Jones to resign his posts appear rather childish. As the early analysts went, he was easygoing; when he first came to the United States "he supported himself by sweeping out bars, giving mandolin lessons, and teaching."[12] Brill was so goodhearted as to be easy to double-cross, and Jones did not always forbear doing so when it came to issues connected with the politics of the International Psychoanalytic Association.

Brill's position was insecure enough, however, for Freud's favorite in Vienna, Otto Rank, to imagine that the leadership of psychoanalysis in the United States was still unfilled. When Rank came to America in 1924 he had the idea of organizing the American analysts, with himself as their leader.[13] Brill, of course, was bitter about another favorite of Freud's trying to push him out, and he protested to Freud. As late as 1933 Jones thought that the New York Society seemed to be so seething with personal intrigue that psychoanalysis itself had to be neglected.[14]

Jones acknowledged that Brill had "rendered far more service to psychoanalysis in America than anyone else."[15] Freud had relied on Brill to take care of the business dealings connected with his books in the United States, and Brill would draw a check for Freud when the occasion seemed right. Brill's mind was agile and quick, and by the 1930's he had become the center for psychoanalytic referrals in New York City. (Ultimately Brill was dependent on Freud's favor; Freud in a sense supported all his followers, as the economic structure of the movement rested on him. Freud's favor was expressed through the referral of patients, citations in the literature, and verbal recommendations; there were analysts dependent on Freud all over the world, and it could be a corrupting influence.) Brill was, however, rather coarse, and although he had studied for a short time at the Burghölzli in Zurich and held an important appointment in psychiatry at Columbia, his manner lacked the kind of polish that could further the acceptance of psychoanalysis in the world of established medicine.[16]

Until around 1922 membership in the New York Society was completely open; subsequently personal analyses were required, but the practice whereby older analysts supervised analyses conducted by students in training had yet to be devised. In 1930 the New York analysts had $50,-000 with which they wanted to start a training institute on the Berlin model. A group of them (Bertram Lewin, Monroe Meyer, and Abram Kardiner) went to Brill and demanded that someone be brought in to head the institute, since in their opinion Brill was not the man for the job. They all agreed to invite Sandor Rado from Berlin, and in 1931 he became the new director, while Brill remained president of the Society.

Although no analyst in America had Freud's unconditional blessing, neither did democracy flourish among analysts; and Rado came to resent the spirit of orthodoxy and traditionalism upheld by an oligarchy in the New York group. The intolerance of the most orthodox lasted well beyond the uninformed attacks.[17] Even today many American analysts share some of Freud's defensiveness toward the outside world, as if they were not now part of the establishment. Freud's model has served many purposes, and can support the pretense of being bold and innovative even among those who are in reality quite conformist. Before Rado left the New York Psychoanalytic Society in 1944 to head Columbia University's College of Physicians and Surgeons school for training analysts, Karen Horney (a Gentile) had already been branded as a traitor. And by the late 1930's, with many new refugee analysts establishing themselves in New York, Brill had encountered a ground swell of opposition, not on account of his orthodoxy but because his individualistic style of leadership was now too old-fashioned.

The old idea of psychoanalytic societies in America had been that eclectic groups of people would meet to discuss issues of mutual interest. But the trend was toward professionalization, and the training institutes acquired organizational lives of their own. Earlier, to become a member of a society one had only to attend meetings. By the late 1930's the institutes had become formidable, and they withstood the challenge of the apprentice tradition that the European analysts were more familiar with. The rise of the institutes was aided by the social receptiveness to new institutions in America, where it was easier for them to acquire prestige than in the Old World.

Many observers of American life have pointed out that alongside the individualistic rhetoric the actual conduct of life has tended to be highly conformist. In fact, these two opposites can be linked together in explaining America's receptivity to Freud. A society relatively lacking in hierarchy and without fixed standards of status is bound to make each individual more dependent on the approval of the group. Psychoanalysis had its appeal to the collectivistic, as well as the individualistic, side of American national character. The fear of being different has often supported an interest in the psychoanalytic emphasis on the exceptional and the abnormal.

Freud never attained the standing in English cultural life that he has long had in the United States; even in terms of fees, an analyst would be better off almost anywhere in North America than in London. At the turn of the century English neurology was among the best in the world, and doubtless this inhibited the rise of a strong psychotherapeutic movement. In addition, England, unlike the United States, possessed an ancient culture and an appreciation of its past. Only at the end of the last century were Americans forced to realize that with the closing of the frontier their future was acutely constrained by the limitations of history.

Even in comparison to Freud's own prudish attitude toward sex, turn-of-the-century Americans seem to have been more puritanical; and a strain of this puritanical interest in sex persists in America today. Nevertheless, America has come far in its conception of sexual morality. For example, "the physician's stereotype of woman became progressively 'purer' from the 1870's to about 1912,"[18] which suggests that women were being newly stigmatized. Perversions were condemned as unhealthy, and both excessive masturbation and too frequent intercourse were deemed dangerous; if Freud himself wondered whether masturbation could lead to a loss of virility, he was only a man of his time.

Despite the acclaim America accorded Freud, he was disdainful and contemptuous of American life; this was partly linked to his hatred of dependency, since in his last years Americans were his most lucrative patients. According to Jones, who fully shared Freud's opinion on this point, Freud had

> a feeling that commercial success dominated the scale of values in the United States, and that scholarship, research, and profound reflection . . . were lightly esteemed . . . he came later to take the rather cynical view that it was a country whose only function was to provide money to support European culture. . . .[19]

The more Freud's practice was confined to American rather than local patients, the more his need for opposition had to change its focus. Earlier,

Freud had "needed the opposition of Vienna psychologically and did not wish to forego the opportunity of making fun of the Viennese."[20]

By the 1920's, in dismissing an American patient he considered tedious and superficial, Freud explained that the fellow "had no unconscious!" To another American, Freud exclaimed about an account of a particularly bizarre dream, "Now that is a real dream." Freud's passion for smoking made him think that the discovery of tobacco was "the only excuse I know for Columbus's misdeed."[21] "America," Freud once joked, "is a mistake; a gigantic mistake, it is true, but none the less a mistake."[22] He denied "hating" America, he merely "regretted" it.[23]

On his memorable trip to America in 1909, Freud's reasons for his difficulties in adjusting to native ways ranged from the absence of public toilets, the quality of the water and food, to the more common complaints about the United States: the lack of respect for privacy, the manners, the sexual hypocrisy, the general lack of culture, alcoholism, and the frantic pace of life. Freud once weighed the possibility of writing some popular articles for the American press, but then drew back at the conditions attached:

> If an author of good esteem offered a contract to a German publisher he would be glad to accept it and would not let it depend on the success of the first article, whether to take a second one or not. This absolute submission of your editors to the rotten taste of an uncultivated public is the cause of the low level of American literature and to be sure the anxiousness to make money is at the root of this submission. A German publisher would not have dared to propose to me on what subjects I had to write.[24]

Freud disliked American ideals of equality, and in particular egalitarianism between the sexes. He once referred contemptuously to "petticoat government" in the United States, and told an American patient that "American women are an anti-cultural phenomenon . . . American men don't know how to make love . . . There must be inequality, and the superiority of the man is the lesser of two evils."[25] He justified his hatred of America with such a shifting variety of reasons that one can be certain only of the existence of the antipathy. Like Marx in his distaste for Russia, Freud detested the country which was to choose him as one of its prophets. By 1952, 64 per cent of the members of the International Psychoanalytic Association were in America.[26]

Freud did admire America's sense of independence, although he assumed most of her freethinkers would be Jews; he kept a copy of the American Declaration of Independence on a wall of his apartment.[27] Per-

haps his most favorable comment about America came in a letter to Arnold
Zweig in 1939, after Freud had moved to London:

> I think you are right to have chosen America instead of England. In
> most respects England is better, but it is very difficult to adapt oneself
> here. . . . America seems an Anti-Paradise to me, but it has so much
> space and so many possibilities and ultimately one does come to be-
> long there.[28]

However, reflecting on the development of the psychoanalytic movement,
Freud feared that the Americans would be too quick to unite psychoanalysis with medical psychiatry. "The essence of his comment" to Martin
Peck shortly before his death "was that in America medical application was
the rule, and contributions to its structure were the exception."[29]

The history of the psychoanalytic movement illustrates Robert
Michels's "iron law of oligarchy," which states that all reform movements
are bound to become bureaucratized and hierarchical, at odds with the
spirit which created them. Before Freud's death it had become apparent
that there was a conflict between creative genius and organizational needs;
Freud's willingness to have foreign students trained in Vienna, whatever
the wishes of the home psychoanalytic societies, made him a menace to a
bureaucratizing movement. His special attitude toward America played
a role here; when Theodor Reik was asked by Freud "whether I would
like to train an American psychiatrist who could only stay a short time
in Vienna and I expressed strong doubt that such a short period of training would be sufficient, he said with a shrug, 'It is only export ware.' "[30]

Freud's fears about the future of psychoanalysis were focused on the
symbol of America, his unwanted heir. He was shocked by the tendency
to commercialize and sensationalize his ideas; and he was convinced that
Americans lacked intellectual creativity: "the contributions to our science
from that vast country are exiguous and provide little that is new."[31]
Freud thought that in America "psychiatrists and neurologists make frequent use of psychoanalysis as a therapeutic method, but as a rule they
show little interest in its scientific problems and its cultural significance."[32]
Freud even worried, characteristically, that the American reception of his
ideas would be intellectually not muscular enough; "the ancient centers
of culture, where the greatest resistance has been displayed, must be the
scene of the decisive struggles over psychoanalysis."[33] Whatever welcome
America gave his ideas could be dismissed as the grasping at straws, the
eagerness for anything new, on the part of an essentially inferior culture.
The American tendency, as Freud saw it, was "to shorten study and

preparation and to proceed as fast as possible to practical application."[34] He had seen, first with Jung and later with Otto Rank, the manner in which visits to America appeared to seduce his followers into abandoning parts of his psychoanalytic edifice. To Freud, new arrivals in the United States seemed to develop a rebellious temperament, and he spoke caustically of American interest in the work of Adler.[35] Jones repeatedly echoed Freud on the dangers of scientific regression posed by the supposedly enervating environment of America.[36] In Freud's presence it could be extremely hard to find the emotional resources to disagree with him; and he may have realized that distance could affect a follower's relationship with him. So Freud's parting sentence to Franz Alexander, as he set out for the United States, was: "I hope America will leave something intact of the real Alexander."[*37]

Freud's distrust of the American response to his ideas was buttressed by the American failure to welcome lay analysis. He harbored an immense antagonism to the medical profession, and felt that fields other than medicine could be appropriate backgrounds for aspiring analysts. Freud realized that "what is opposed to psychoanalysis is not psychiatry but psychiatrists," and was fair-minded enough to acknowledge that "our psychiatrists are not students of psychoanalysis and we psychoanalysts see too few psychiatric cases." He held out the prospect that "a race of psychiatrists must first grow up who have passed through the school of psychoanalysis as a preparatory science," and recognized that "a start in that direction is now being made in America. . . ."[39]

Fundamentally Freud's aim was that of an entirely new profession of analysts, divorced from a medical background as from a clerical one. The best the Americans would do, however, was to enact a grandfather clause which accepted older analysts without medical qualifications, but they made it almost impossible for young candidates to be admitted to first-class training unless they had already completed their education as physicians. Freud took the American position on lay analysis personally; as he once wrote, "I feel hurt by the behavior of American analysts in the matter of Lay-Analysis. They, it seems, are not very fond of me."[40] He thought that "the movement against lay analysis seems to be only an offshoot of the old resistance against analysis in general."[41] While American analysts were, in Freud's view, failing to produce work of fundamental importance, they were also, by opposing lay analysis, undermining one of the sources of future contributions to psychoanalytic thought.

---

* Freud's final words to Hanns Sachs were: "I know that I have at least *one* friend in America."[38]

In the study of Woodrow Wilson on which Freud collaborated with William C. Bullitt, further evidence of the nature of Freud's feelings toward America can be found. Wilson stood for all the pious provincialism that others have seen in America, "God's own Country."[42] Although he tolerated—and occasionally admired—individual Americans, Freud expected that American analysts would someday repudiate his work.[43] The American analysts so opposed the admission of nonmedical members that an American secession from the International Psychoanalytic Association was a real possibility in the late 1920's.[44] Thanks to Ernest Jones, who fully appreciated the Americans' resentment of their cavalier treatment by the Viennese, a compromise was worked out at the Oxford Congress in 1929 whereby Europeans agreed henceforth not to accept anyone for training, whether a lay person or a physician, unless his home psychoanalytic society had first expressed its approval.[45] As late as 1938 Freud still asserted that "probably the American group will secede; we expect it."[46]

Freud's forebodings about what would happen to his ideas in America have been in some measure fulfilled. For example, in the consulting rooms of present-day British analysts, the analytic couch is prominently displayed, sometimes in the very center of the room. When one moves across the Atlantic to New England, the analytic couch, still a distinct entity, is more likely to be inconspicuous, placed against a wall. In Chicago an analyst's couch might be used for social purposes as well as therapeutic ones, and on the West Coast the furniture of the analyst's office—which is likely to include enough chairs for group therapy—makes abundantly clear just what Freud feared, that to the analyst the practice of analysis has become one therapeutic technique among many others.

Contrary to Freud's wishes, the psychoanalytic movement in America became an integral part of psychiatry. As Freud observed, "I am by no means happy to see that analysis has become the handmaid of psychiatry in America and nothing else."[47] American psychiatrists, unlike the English, supported Freud's work. But just as in other areas of American life there has been a minimum of theorizing, so within psychoanalysis pragmatism has triumphed.[48] The American inclination, even in as introspective a field as psychoanalysis, has been to emphasize behavioral changes in therapeutic treatment, rather than to retain Freud's insistence on inner changes in personality.

Freud's practice in his extreme old age, when most of his American disciples knew him, tended to be different from psychoanalysis before World War I. It was the later, dying Freud who trained most of the therapists who carried his technique back to the United States; they were identifying, however, with a man taking leave of his human contacts, whom it pained to talk. More naïve than their European colleagues about what experts can expect to know, the Americans were reassured by Freud's growing aloofness that the science of psychoanalysis, which Freud came to push more and more into the limelight, had a technique which would ultimately serve their own special objectives.

So the Americans, legendary optimists, came to Freud's sepulchral study. As foreigners temporarily cut off from the United States, their past was highlighted for them, since their life in Vienna was limited and insulated. For an American, an analysis with Freud was particularly isolated, in that afterward the patient would go home again. Even if Freud disliked treating Americans, he needed their money, and he could be quite open about this; but he must have known that by choosing to analyze American patients he was eliminating whatever chance there might have been for psychoanalysis to thrive in Vienna.

The early adherents of psychoanalysis were passionately committed to the cause: the initial campaign for the Freudian approach was manned by practitioners quite unlike today's. Yet American psychoanalytic circles are less insistent on doctrinal clarity than has been the case in Europe. Some of the refugee European analysts' insistence on orthodoxy interfered with the scientific development of analysis in America; they succeeded in keeping psychoanalysis more insular than was necessary. But their fervor may have been an indispensable part of the energy which underlay the triumph of psychoanalysis in America.

VIII

OTTO RANK:
SONS AND
FATHERS

1. The Trauma of Birth

OTTO RANK (1884–1939) OCCUPIED an exceptional place in Freud's life; he was important in an intensely personal way to Freud, and no one else filled quite the same role. It is hard to know in retrospect just how much Ernest Jones's envy of Rank's closeness to Freud led him to emphasize the degree to which Rank came merely to follow in the "deviating" path of Adler and Jung. In large part Jones could draw on the conventional wisdom among psychoanalysts, and with a wealth of hitherto unpublished material he filled out an official version of what happened between Freud and Rank. Freud's high expectations, so this account goes, led him to overvalue Rank's talents and potential contributions to psychoanalysis. As soon as Rank gave up the basic findings of psychoanalysis, and not merely its theoretical superstructure, Freud let him fall.

Jones covered the difficulties between Freud and Rank with great care:

> I have related at some length the episode of Otto Rank's leaving Freud because it furnishes the most complete refutation of the myth, still current, of Freud's being a dictatorial person who would not tolerate on the part of his followers the least departure from his own ideas, and who at once drove them out of his circle.[1]

In combating this oversimplification, Jones charged that Rank had had a psychosis brewing within him which helped to alienate him from Freud. Yet it is possible to construct a far more satisfying explanation of what went on between Rank and Freud, one that emphasizes the tragic aspects of the conflict between these two men, without falling back on the old clichés, either of the pupil's resistance or the master's authoritarianism. Although a portion of the truth resides in the Jones account, we can try to make more humanly plausible a controversy which has, I think, been mythologized.

Born in Vienna in 1884, Rank came from relatively low social origins. His father drank and was irresponsible, but "seems to have afflicted his family more with indifference than with brutality."² The family finally split up. "At sixteen or seventeen, Rank and his brother threw off for good the authority of their father."³ The family name had been Rosenfeld, but Otto decided that he could not bear the burden of his father's name. So he picked the name Rank, perhaps out of Ibsen's play *A Doll's House*, retaining only the first letter "R" as a part of his past. (At least one other psychoanalyst, Erik H. Erikson, also invented his own last name.)

At an early age Rank went to work and helped support his mother. According to one version, he labored in a glass blower's factory, but doubtless there were other jobs as well. Somehow Rank also found the time and energy to read widely, and he became enthralled with Freud's writings. Alfred Adler was Rank's family physician, and once while at Adler's office for an examination Rank ventured to discuss Freud. Adler offered to introduce him, and in 1906, at the age of twenty-two, Rank presented himself to Freud with an essay he had written, "The Artist."

Freud, who had had conflicted feelings toward protectors in his own youth, soon became Rank's mentor and patron. As Freud described it in 1914:

> One day a young man who had passed through a technical training college introduced himself with a manuscript which showed very unusual comprehension. We persuaded him to go through the *Gymnasium* and the University and to devote himself to the non-medical side of psychoanalysis. The little society acquired in him a zealous and dependable secretary and I gained in Otto Rank a most loyal helper and co-worker.⁴

The *Minutes* of the Vienna Society were taken down in Rank's handwriting. Evidently Rank was efficient in his work, and he and Freud became intimates. Freud put Rank in charge of the revised editions of *The Interpretation of Dreams*; for the fourth, fifth, sixth, and seventh editions (1914–22) Rank was entirely in charge of the bibliographies. Rank became Freud's "research worker, his proofreader, his adopted son."⁵

Freud was a great believer in the advantages of a teacher's keeping a certain distance from his pupils; inevitably he became much more important to them than any of them could to him. With Rank, though, Freud succeeded at being his most generous and giving. Freud's trust confirmed Rank in his creative aspirations. Part of what Freud could offer was financial; but equally important, Freud's faith in Rank's abilities, his high hopes for this gifted youth, gave Rank the push he needed. With psychoanalytic concepts to work with, buoyed by Freud's personal inspiration, Rank emerged as a writer, intellectual, and scholar.

Freud did as much as any older man can ever do for someone younger, and it would be impossible to overemphasize what Freud meant to Rank. At the time he came to Freud, Rank's only training was from a technical school. With Freud's help he took a Ph.D. from the University of Vienna in 1912. Freud became an ideal substitute for Rank's own father.

Rank's special field of interest was mythology, in which he achieved, according to Jones, "truly vast erudition."[6] Rank's approach to the psychology of myths, as Freud himself summarized it, was to see how mythology was "projected on to the heavens after having arisen elsewhere under purely human conditions."[7] He also continued to develop his interest in creativity and the psychology of the artist. An important essay of Rank's interpreted the role of the "double" in literature. Freud contributed an essay to Rank's book *The Myth of the Birth of the Hero*. Even more remarkably, and one can imagine the impact on Freud's other pupils, Freud permitted two essays of Rank's to appear in new editions of *The Interpretation of Dreams* (which were later dropped after their falling out). Scattered throughout Freud's work can be found indices of Rank's standing, comments like "what follows at this point was written under the influence of an exchange of ideas with Otto Rank" or "as Otto Rank has aptly remarked. . . ."[8]

In 1912 Rank became, with Hanns Sachs, a founding editor of *Imago*, and Freud soon made Rank the most important editor of the *Zeitschrift*, the central periodical of psychoanalytic literature published in German. Rank was also the leading (though youngest) member of the secret committee founded after the loss of Adler and Jung to relieve Freud of some of the burdens of statecraft; in a group photograph taken in 1922 of Freud and his closest supporters (Rank, Ferenczi, Abraham, Jones, Sachs, and Eitingon), it was Rank who was positioned directly behind Freud's throne-like chair. By the early 1920's Freud would stay at the Vienna Society only for the presentation of papers; then an intermission would follow, after which Rank took over from Freud the chairing of the meeting.

Freud's other pupils were understandably envious of Rank, and perhaps such jealousy was eventually responsible for Jones's misconstruing the sources of the difficulties that grew up between Freud and Rank, and minimizing the extent of their prior intimacy. "For years Rank had a close almost day-to-day contact with Freud, and yet"—Jones claims—"the two men never really came near to the other. Rank lacked the charm, among other things, which seemed to mean much to Freud."[9] All the available evidence challenges this interpretation; Freud valued in Rank precisely those qualities that led to spontaneous intimacy.[10]

No matter what Freud may have done for his other pupils, Rank was Freud's personal favorite, indeed far more than a pupil. When Anna Freud fell ill of whooping cough one summer, Freud took Rank traveling with him instead; it was as an adopted son that Rank figured so greatly in Freud's life. Freud's encouragement of Rank in part reflected his dissatisfaction with many of his Viennese pupils; and Freud's recognition of Rank's talents also stemmed, more personally, from his alienation from his sons. (Freud's oldest son, Martin, grew angry at and a bit jealous of Rank's management of Freud's affairs, and was able to take over the care of money matters only after their separation.)

Rank was peculiarly suited, from Freud's point of view, to be his ideal successor. Freud's own sons were not suitable, since their lack of creativity made them unfit to uphold the immortality Freud felt to be his. Other pupils were not appropriate either; for having come to Freud with at least some background of achievement, they could be their own men. But Rank had entered Freud's circle with only his native abilities, and Freud was able, metaphorically, to give him birth. Freud felt that his own genius had sprung full-blown and could be traced to no recognizable familial or social past. In Rank, Freud could have a worthy successor, the product of the master's own will, fashioned out of generosity, encouragement, and inspiration.

Rank's gratitude to Freud in some measure infantilized him in relation to his patron. Jones traced part of Rank's immense respect for Freud to his having come from "a distinctly lower social stratum than the others, and this perhaps accounts for a noticeably timid and even deferential air he had in those days."[11] "Deference" seems too mild a term, and yet "slavery" would miss the eagerness of Rank's collaboration. Before World War I, Rank was known for his servility, even in a culture where respect for fathers and superiors in general was routine. At meetings Rank would be there to fetch a glass of water for Freud or to light his cigar.

Early in 1916 Rank was sent to Cracow to edit the official journal of the Austrian army, the *Krakauer Zeitung*. For the first time he was separated from Freud, and he was able to make only a few short trips to Vienna until the end of the war. He continued to produce *Imago* from Cracow and always managed to send cigars to Freud.

Jones thought that Rank's years at Cracow were "fateful for the rest of his life. . . . [H]e presented two quite different personalities before and after the Great War; I never knew anyone change so much."[12] According to Jones, the war had interfered with Rank's plans to come to Jones for an analysis. Away from Freud, Rank for the first time performed a responsible job on his own. He had to travel in his work and altogether seems to have acquitted himself admirably. At the end of the war, in a quick military ceremony on November 9, 1918, Rank married; two days later he brought his bride to meet Freud in Vienna.

Beata Tola Mincer was in her early twenties when she fell in love with Rank. Being presented to Freud was for this shy and unsophisticated Polish girl like being launched at court. Freud had "become an emperor, one around whom legend began to accrete, who holds enlightened but absolute sway in his realm. . . ."[13] Whereas Tola Rank was beautiful, with more than a touch of elegance, her husband was almost an ugly man. But they made an admirable couple, and she deferred to him with nineteenth-century femininity.

Tola Rank immediately became a member of Freud's family, an adopted daughter-in-law. Almost the same age as Freud's daughter Anna, Tola was welcomed by Freud into his orbit. In a paper he wrote in the spring of 1919, a footnote thanked "Frau Dr. Rank" for a suggestion.[14] Freud's citation was not lost on his followers; Otto's wife obviously had a special niche in Freud's affections. When her daughter was born, she was received as if she were a genuine grandchild of Freud's; the Freud family contributed to the making of a baby carriage, and Freud's sister-in-law Minna was responsible for preparing the mattress. Freud's children had so far produced only sons, so this child was, so to speak, his first granddaughter.

Ultimately Rank's marriage may have led him to interests outside Freud, but for the time being the Ranks functioned smoothly as a couple within Freud's world. Freud's wife rarely received guests, partly because of her difficulties with entertaining, so Tola Rank acted as Freud's hostess. She gave a dinner party for David Forsyth, an important English patient in analysis with Freud. She also gave a dinner party for Lou Andreas-Salomé when she visited Vienna; in addition to the Freuds, the Ranks invited their good friends Helene and Felix Deutsch. In their four-room apartment, the Ranks were able to entertain successfully for Freud. They had at least one Christmas party to which Freud's foreign patients were invited.

Tola helped, as she had in Cracow, with the editing of *Imago* and did proofreading chores. She also had the honor, along with Anna Freud, of taking dictation from Freud when he composed letters for the members of the committee, which were sent over the signatures of both Rank and Freud. Freud and Rank "always wrote together and usually referred to themselves as: 'we.' The text seemed to have been suggested by Freud in conversation with . . . Rank who then formulated the letter from his notes. Freud always assumed full responsibility."[15] (Freud's other letters

THE OXFORD CONGRESS, JULY 27-31, 1929

1. Edoardo Weiss
2. Smith Ely Jeliffe
3. Marjorie Brierley
4. Mrs. Roger Money-Kyrle
5. Melitta Schmideberg
6. Sandor Lorand
7. Prince Peter Bonaparte
8. Otto Fenichel
9. Philip Sarasin
10. Hanns Sachs
11. Rudolf Loewenstein
12. Melanie Klein
13. Joan Riviere
14. Paul Federn
15. Gisela (Mrs. Sandor) Ferenczi
16. Sandor Ferenczi
17. A. A. Brill
18. Mrs. Sandor Rado
19. Karen Horney
20. Marie Bonaparte
21. Max Eitingon
22. Anna Freud
23. Ernest Jones
24. Theodor Reik
25. Istvan Hollos
26. M. B. Herford
27. Sandor Rado
28. Ruth Mack Brunswick
29. Johann van Ophuijsen
30. Ludwig Binswanger
31. Heinrich Meng
32. Sybille Yates
33. Isidor Sadger
34. Felix Boehm
35. Clarence Oberndorf
36. Franz Alexander
37. Gregory Zilboorg
38. John Rickman
39. Bertram Lewin
40. Katherine (Mrs. Ernest) Jones
41. Herman Nunberg
42. A. C. Wilson
43. James Strachey
44. Edith Jacobson
45. Adolph Stern
46. Lajos Levy
47. Helene Deutsch
48. Ludwig Jekels
49. Ernst Simmel
50. Edward Hitschmann
51. Dorian Feigenbaum
52. Caroline Newton
53. Mrs. David Eder
54. Sigmund Pfeifer
55. Maurits Katan
56. Salomea Kempner
57. Roger Money-Kyrle
58. Alix (Mrs. James) Strachey
59. Ella Sharpe
60. M. N. Searl
61. Rene Laforgue
62. Edward Glover
63. Barbara Low

were rarely typed, as he liked to write out everything himself in his characteristic but very difficult German script.) The year after Anna Freud became a member of the Vienna Society, Freud proposed that Tola Rank join also.* Membership did not then imply that one was trained, or expected to practice, but she had to give a paper, which in those days was a requirement for being elected to a psychoanalytic society. On May 30, 1923, Tola Rank spoke about "The Part Played by Women in the Evolution of Human Society" and was duly elected.

After Vienna had begun to settle down following World War I, Rank, with his new family responsibilities, began to practice analysis. Like Freud, he had his office next door to his apartment, though it was smaller. Rank was one of the first lay analysts; with the full support of Freud he was analyzing patients by 1920. In addition, Rank had thrown himself into being managing director of Freud's new publishing house with "truly astounding capacity and energy, both editorial and managerial. . . ."[16]

Rank went regularly to dinner at the Freuds' on Wednesday evening; afterward Freud and Rank would go off to talk before the Society meetings. Freud discussed everything he wrote with Rank, and listened to what his pupil had to say. In the early 1920's there was even a rumor that Rank had analyzed Freud for a short time, and although this sounds extremely unlikely—probably they had merely exchanged accounts of their dreams —still it captures the closeness that had grown up between the two men. Whatever other pupils Freud may have admired, in the early 1920's Otto Rank was not only his personal favorite but also his Prince of Wales.

In explaining the failure of Freud's plans, Jones mentions two heresies of Rank's, one the theory of the trauma of birth and the other a different clinical approach to therapy. In Rank's view, his theory partly grew out of his therapeutic experience as an analyst, and as he outlined his concept of the birth trauma, it had definite clinical implications. These two issues were indeed the crux of an almost philosophical dispute that eventually arose between Freud and Rank.

Jones reports that in March 1919 Rank already maintained that "the essence of life was the relation between mother and child." "[M]arried partners," Rank soon came to believe, "always repeated . . . those [ties] between mother and child. . . ."[17] Psychoanalysis in 1919, however, paid very little attention to the mother's role in the development of the child

---

* A friend of Tola's remembered calling for her on the way to a masquerade ball around this time; Freud was at the Ranks', worrying over Tola as if she were his daughter.

or to the maternal needs of patients in therapy. Freud understood the mother as an object of sexual desire and as a source of sensual pleasure. But he did not emphasize the mother's protective functions or her nurturing role, and he did not even mention the mother as a figure upon whom the child at an early stage establishes a legitimate dependency. (Perhaps this reflects Freud's reluctance to explore his own dependencies on his powerful, domineering mother.)

By and large Freud took for granted the nurturing functions of a mother. The tie that Freud interpreted repeatedly was that of the child to his father. In a case history published as late as 1918, Freud spoke about a male patient's father as "his first and most primitive object-choice, which, in conformity with a small child's narcissism, had taken place along the path of identification."[18] Freud at that time thought that the small boy's "first and most primitive" human bond was to his father, not his mother. Freud did not exclude the mother's part in the psychopathology of his patients; but he saw the mother mainly as either a seductress into an oedipal situation or the source of adult homosexual conflicts.

As Jones pointed out, the practical deduction from Rank's concept of the trauma of birth was that "clinically it followed that all mental conflicts concerned the relation of the child to its mother. . . ."[19] This would now be considered an oversimplification, but since that time psychoanalysis has come more and more to focus on the mother's role in normal as well as pathological development. The work of Donald Winnicott in England and Erik Erikson in America, for example, has been directed toward defining the mother's essential contribution to the growing child's health. Separation anxiety and the child's reaction to the fear of the loss of mothering help have by now received enormous elaboration; even though anticipated by Jung, the bulk of this work had not appeared by the early 1920's, when castration threats of the father were still considered by analysts to be central.

When Rank first presented his new concepts, Freud jokingly commented that "with an idea like that anyone else would have set up on his own."[20] The manuscript of *The Trauma of Birth* was completed in April 1923, and presented to Freud for his birthday on May 6. Freud accepted the dedication of the book, which appeared in print in December 1923; initially he reacted favorably to Rank's new concepts. By February 1924 Freud wrote that he didn't "know whether 66 or 33 per cent of it is true, but in any case it is the most important progress since the discovery of psychoanalysis."[21]

It would be unfair to imply that Rank was the only psychoanalyst of this time to emphasize the neglected role of the mother. Georg Grod-

Otto Rank in 1930

deck also seemed to be coming to that conclusion, and Sandor Ferenczi was inclined to the same point of view. But it was Otto Rank who made the pre-oedipal mother the center of his system. The notion that anxiety stemmed from the trauma of birth, and that that trauma had to be re-experienced in therapy, may have been extreme, yet in the main Rank's conception was designed to drive home the central psychological importance of the mother.* According to an analyst who did some supervisory work under Rank at this time: "Wherever the early view had put the father at the core of emotional conflicts, Rank simply substituted the mother."

Rank's book represented a caricature-like exaggeration of Freud's own method of working, focusing on a single problem at a time. Having discovered the protecting mother for psychoanalysis, Rank tried to elaborate the implications of this insight. To use the notion of birth trauma was in a sense to follow loyally in Freud's own footsteps. At least as early as 1908 Freud had mentioned "the act of birth as a source of anxiety."[22] And on another occasion he wrote:

> Birth is both the first of all dangers to life and the prototype of all the later ones that cause us to feel anxiety, and the experience of birth has probably left behind in us the expression of affect which we call anxiety. Macduff of the Scottish legend, who was not born of his mother but ripped from her womb, was for that reason unacquainted with anxiety.[23]

For Rank to have built his thesis on an idea of Freud's was perfectly in order; it was the way Freud expected his pupils to proceed, by elaborating his own undeveloped contributions. But for Rank to use his theory as an act of independence was to expose himself to the charge of stealing;[24] once more it might be argued that a pupil of Freud's was overstressing one component of psychoanalysis, building a system on the basis of one of Freud's ideas.

The clinical conclusions Rank drew, and which had in part led him to his theory in the first place, conflicted sharply with psychoanalytic thinking of that time. It is all too easy when examining Freud's papers today to read back into them insights from our present state of understanding. At the time Rank was writing, Freud was heavily emphasizing intellectual insight as a curative agent.

---

* Clinically the concept of birth trauma may have played a relatively small role in Rank's practice. At least one patient in analysis with Rank in 1926 never heard anything about the birth trauma. One is reminded here of Karen Horney's having said that whatever the stages of her theoretical convictions her technique as an analyst never altered.

Before writing *The Trauma of Birth*, Rank had collaborated with Ferenczi on *The Development of Psychoanalysis*, which was designed to move away from the more rationalistic early days of Freud's work. Although even in the 1950's Jones considered this book "sinister,"[25] its outlook has become part of the everyday awareness of analysts. Rank and Ferenczi emphasized the importance of keeping current realities in focus throughout an analysis, which was a way of drawing more attention to the analyst-patient interaction in therapy. Freud had generally frowned on the tendency of patients to act out problems instead of recalling them to memory. Rank and Ferenczi, on the other hand, pointed out the possible therapeutic uses of acting out as part of an analysis that should involve an emotional reliving of the past instead of just intellectualized knowledge. Although Ferenczi was to stay with Freud for a decade longer than Rank, their book was one source of the troubles between Freud and his chosen successor. Rank's approach, like that of other dissidents in psychoanalysis, implied that support and not just insight was advantageous to the patient. Like others, Otto Rank stood for a more tolerant attitude toward psychotherapy and its aims. As the essence of Rank's concept of the birth trauma has been well characterized, "the mother appears to the child in the relation of love—and stands for what the child already is, for his natural condition—while the father appears in the relation of virtue— and stands for what the child must become."[26]

2. Premature Grief

THE TENSIONS BETWEEN FREUD AND RANK were exploited by the other students, especially Jones and Abraham. Freud wanted with all his heart to keep Rank. But even Freud became the prisoner of events, the captive of his own greatness, once he had created the psychoanalytic movement and propagated the tales of the heresies of Adler and Jung. Now those who had reason to be jealous of Rank's position, as one analyst remembered it, "fell on Rank like dogs."

The qualities that had made Rank suitable to be Freud's adopted son, and all the favor Freud had shown him, stimulated the rest to attack. Some of Freud's pupils have reported that he could be milder than many of his adherents: "My pupils are more orthodox than I,"[1] Freud is reported to have said, which recalls Marx's disclaimer of being a Marxist. Provisionally

Freud seemed willing to let Rank work out his ideas. Freud had learned something from his earlier struggles with male pupils; and because of his love for Rank he was able to make an exception.

Freud the man might have wanted to keep peace with Rank. But the movement as a whole, or at least some leaders of it, interfered with Freud's personal attitude toward Rank. Psychoanalysis now had a life of its own, and it succeeded finally in coming between Freud and Rank. Since the loyal pupils could not successfully compete with Freud, they did so with each other. The desire to be the favorite son played a role in all of them. Rank's book on the birth trauma came as something of a surprise, and there were good grounds for disputing many of his contentions. But Rank did not think of himself as having "renounced" anything in psychoanalysis. What burst upon him was all the suppressed rivalries and jealousies of Freud's other disciples.

Karl Abraham in Berlin was one of the chief hunters of heresy. As Jones would have it, Abraham had a sane and well-balanced view of Rank's position. Abraham supposedly perceived in Rank signs of scientific backsliding resembling that of Jung over a decade earlier. But simply taking Freud's letters to Abraham at their face value, an alternative interpretation can be posed: Abraham was making the situation much worse. As Freud wrote him in May 1924 about Rank's new theory, "I believe it will 'fall flat' if one does not criticize it too sharply, and then Rank, whom I value for his gifts and the great service he has rendered, will have learned a useful lesson."[2]

Freud repeatedly defended Rank to Abraham, trying to hold off the attack. Abraham was, according to Jones, "bold enough to attribute Freud's changed attitude . . . [to Abraham] to his resentment at being told a painful truth."[3] Freud told Rank of Abraham's suspicions and his references to the trouble with Jung; so Rank had grounds for resenting the faithlessness of a former friend. Ferenczi supported Rank's view of Abraham, and for practical purposes the committee ceased to function. Even after Abraham's death in 1925, Freud still held the Berliner's fanaticism about Rank against him. "Abraham's premature diagnosis certainly hastened and favored the course of events."[4]

Jones not only publicized his own version of these events in his biography of Freud, but had himself played a role in driving Rank out. The strains among Jones, Abraham, and Rank were not apparent to the rest of the psychoanalytic movement until the publication of parts of their correspondence years later. Jones admitted that he was a man with definite ideas of his own, and as he was editor of the *International Journal of Psychoanalysis* in London, antagonisms were bound to arise between him and Rank, who was editor of the *Zeitschrift* and manager of the press in Vienna. Jones had a fine mind, but his account of Rank's separation from Freud is mean and one-sided.

Jones later grew sententious about having had only Freud's own interests at heart. "For three years," Jones claimed, "I lived with the fear lest Rank's 'brother-hostility' regress to the deeper 'father-hostility,' and I hoped against hope that this would not happen in Freud's lifetime."[5] Jones was honest enough, however, to concede that Freud sometimes blamed both Abraham and Jones for what was happening with Rank, though after the final loss of Rank, Freud thought they might have been right. Freud defended Rank against "our [Jones's and Abraham's] supposedly neurotic susceptibilities. We both of course disputed Freud's version."[6] A 1924 letter of Freud's conveys a tone of agony as he still tried to find a way out of the mess:

> I simply don't understand Rank any longer . . . For fifteen years I have known him as someone who was affectionately concerned, always ready to do any service, discreet, completely trustworthy, just as ready to receive new suggestions as he was uninhibited in the working out of his own ideas, who always took my side in a quarrel and, as I believed, without any inner compulsion to make him do so. . . . Which is the real Rank, the one I have known for fifteen years or the one Jones has been showing me in the past few years?[7]

If Freud was torn between his affectionate regard for Rank and the growing reality of losing him, the personal tale is even sadder. All accounts agree that the "separation from Rank . . . was perhaps the most difficult one [of all] for Freud, who had been extremely fond of Rank and thought very highly of his capabilities . . . Freud had seen in him his successor who would further develop his ideas."[8] Although we have pointed out some of the bases for the trouble between Rank and Freud in terms of intellectual and therapeutic issues, and have sketched the ways in which Abraham and Jones in particular made a reconciliation that much harder, there was another precipitating event—Freud's cancer of the jaw. Though Jones conceded that Freud always thought his illness had played a key role in the quarrel, this idea did not become widespread among the rest of Freud's pupils.[9] As Jones put Freud's own view of the matter, he "always maintained later that this news [of his cancer] had had a fateful effect on Rank, who was entirely dependent on him for a living, and that it had stimulated Rank to strike out on an independent path."[10]

Whatever psychoanalysis at that time might have taught about the necessity of a son's overcoming his father, before Freud's illness Rank was not aware of any feelings of rivalry or ambivalence toward Freud. Freud's cancer began in April 1923, the month in which Rank composed his

Trauma of Birth. To Rank, the prospect of losing Freud meant being suddenly deprived of his ideal father substitute. For Freud, his illness was to be a turning point in his life: from then on he would be tormented by physical suffering.

Of all the members of the committee, Rank alone was fully informed of the seriousness of Freud's illness. At the time it was thought that Freud would not survive.[11] Jones claimed that, at a dinner when Freud's name was brought up, "Rank broke out in a fit of uncontrollable hysterical laughter."[12] Rank's immediate response to Freud's illness may have been manic; sudden elation can cover the deepest grief and mourning, and it would be no surprise if the impending death of Freud touched Rank's deepest emotional undercurrents. Moreover, Rank was wholly reliant on the cases Freud had been sending him. But humanly too, Rank was to suffer greatly at the anticipated loss of this figure from his life. Along with his grieving for Freud went a natural detachment of Rank's emotional energies. If Freud was to be no more, then Rank had to prepare himself for what lay ahead.

None of this could have been clear in Rank's mind, nor could it have been as easy then to untangle the skein of complicated emotions as it may be now with the advantages of hindsight. But one unexpected factor was as striking then as it is important to recognize now. Freud did not die; he recovered and managed to live for another sixteen years. Rank's manic outburst suggests that he first reacted to what he thought was going to be the loss of Freud by denying it. Rank increasingly feared what would happen to him after Freud's death; as all psychoanalytic teaching showed, a fear is not unrelated to a wish. Accompanying his anxiety about the loss of his patron there must have been a partial realization of his desire for Freud's removal, and the corresponding guilt feelings. Such grief is not easy to bear. Yet at the end of it, after Rank in his own mind had begun to order his life as if Freud were no more, Freud suddenly came back. To Rank, it must have been as if he had experienced the pain of bearing Freud's death, and then Freud had been resurrected.[13]

Freud's illness was bound to make him look at Rank anew. Shortly after falling ill, he "got a newspaper cutting from Chicago announcing that he was 'slowly dying,' had given up work and transferred his pupils to Otto Rank."[14] It was brought home to Freud that Rank would be ready to take over. For Freud, Rank now became the favorite come to slay the father.

Freud described himself early in 1924 as "an invalid with diminished powers of working and in an enfeebled frame of mind. . . ."[15] Once he had the cancer in him, this death living in his jaw, it was easy to think of all men as his murderers. The trauma of his cancer caused a part of him to die. Rank stood for everything in Freud's life that had been inspiring, giving, sharing, and now it was no longer possible for Freud to be this way. A reconciliation between the two men was obstructed by the extent to which Rank's mere presence only personified to Freud the part of him that was now gone.

The years between 1923 and 1926 marked the drawn-out chapter of Rank's "defection" from Freud. It is true that Rank grew rebellious, and came to repudiate Freud's path as he set out on his own. But just as the motives and events that drove him out of Freud's world were idiosyncratic, so the historical sequence was crowded with departures and reconciliations.

After a good deal of wrangling, mostly on the part of Abraham, Rank accepted an invitation to visit America for six months. He sailed on April 27, 1924, just a few days before his fortieth birthday. The detachment of travel played its part in Rank's exit from Freud's world. "It would be hard to exaggerate the significance of this act of separation in space upon those he [Rank] left behind as well as upon himself."[16]

Over the next few years Rank traveled frequently between Vienna, Paris, and New York, at least partially as a means of coping with his mixed feelings about Freud. When Rank arrived in New York in the spring of 1924, he was set to take over; he tried to organize the American analysts under his leadership, which did not endear him to the established figures there. Freud found himself defending Rank anew; for example, to Freud's nephew in America, Edward Bernays, Rank seemed intolerably overbearing.[17]

The American analysts, almost all of them concentrated in New York City, were desperately in need of training. They flocked to Rank to be analyzed, in order to learn better how to handle their own practice. As far as they knew, Rank came as Freud's most trusted lieutenant. Rank took on a great number of patients, each for a relatively brief period, charged much higher fees than American analysts could obtain, and tried to disseminate his new ideas. While the Americans looked to Rank to explicate Freud's theories, they found that Rank was critical of some of them himself.

Freud tried his best to win back Rank. The letters they exchanged across the Atlantic tell the tale of their difficulties. Rank's notion of the birth trauma became to Freud one more way of escaping the reality of the Oedipus complex. Freud pointed out, quite rightly, a source of Rank's emphasis on the mother: "The exclusion of the father in your theory seems to reveal too much the result of personal influences in your life. . . ."[18] But Rank was able to counter, "You know as well as I do that the accusation that an insight is derived from a complex means very little

... and ... says nothing of the value or truth of this insight."[19] Freud strained mightily to be understanding and tolerant:

> Suppose you had told me one day that you could not believe in the primordial horde and the primordial father, or thought that the separation into Ego and Id to be inexpedient, do you really believe that I would not have invited you for meals or would have excluded you from my circle? ... [Y]ou have my admission that it is never easy for me to follow a new train of thought that somehow does not go my way or to which my way has not yet led me.[20]

In the late summer and early fall of 1924, Freud listed Rank (in order to establish his own tolerance) among those followers who had remained loyal, in contrast to the famous public dissidents such as Adler and Jung.[21]

Freud recognized that Rank needed to grow up, and that this entailed some separation from his spiritual home. As Freud wrote, "I was so delighted that he had mounted to a thoroughly original achievement in the analytic field that I was prepared to make the friendliest judgment about it."[22] Yet Freud was haunted by the memory of earlier betrayals. "Rank is carried away by his discovery, just as Adler was, but if he becomes independent on the strength of it he will not have the same luck. ..."[23] Freud went so far as to tell Rank in a letter that the trouble lay in Rank's neurosis and in Rank's not having been analyzed. "Rank angrily replied that from what he had seen of the analysts Freud had trained he thought he was lucky never to have been analyzed."[24]

Whatever their difficulties, for almost twenty years Freud had filled a deep need in Rank for "a living person on whom he could project the ideal self."[25] Burdened by problems with American analysts, guilty and worried at having disappointed Freud (and not just as a pupil), Rank returned to Vienna in October 1924. Already events in the Vienna Society were pushing Rank out. He had been vice-president, and would have become president after Freud's illness; in Rank's absence Freud had made Paul Federn vice-president and appointed Rank secretary of the Society. Rank decided to transfer his teaching and practice to the United States for at least part of the year, and so he resigned as editor-in-chief of the *Zeitschrift*; in announcing Rank's retirement Freud paid high tribute to Rank's "tireless devotion and exemplary work."*[26] Freud also had to find a new

---

* In private, however, around this time Freud wrote to Lou Andreas-Salomé that Rank "felt his livelihood to be threatened by my illness and its dangers, looked round for a place of refuge, and hit upon the idea of making his appearance in America. It is really a case of the rat leaving the sinking ship."[27]

managing director of the publishing house. As Freud remarked a month after Rank was back in Vienna, "an open break has been averted . . . But all intimate relations with him are at an end. . . ."[28]

Rank set out from Vienna once more in the late fall of 1924, got as far as Paris, and then returned to Freud. He had grown despondent and depressed, and now felt contrite and reconciled to Freud. According to Freud's view, Rank had come out of a psychiatric condition.[29] It is not clear how formal a therapeutic relationship was then established between them. But at the end of many hours with Rank, Freud wrote Abraham that he was "confident he has been cured of his neurosis by this experience just as if he had gone through a proper analysis."[30]

In a letter of penance that Rank sent to the other members of the committee, he tried to absolve himself of any ill will toward either Freud or other analysts; Rank avowed that he

> recognized the actual cause of the crisis in the trauma occasioned by the dangerous illness of the Professor . . . [A] manic state . . . as direct reaction to his illness . . . was intended to spare me the pain of a loss . . . The Professor, of course, knows the story in all its details and I hope that will be sufficient for you, too.[31]

The reconciliation with Freud apparently completed, Rank returned to America in January 1925. But once their closeness had been initially breached, the two men continued to grow more independent of each other. By the end of February, Rank was back in Vienna, and stayed until September. Then Rank once again left for the United States, returning to Vienna in the spring of 1926. In April, three weeks before the celebration of Freud's seventieth birthday, Rank paid him his final respects, and left for good to go to Paris. The same year Rank notified the Vienna Society that he had "permanently settled" in Paris; in 1929 he quietly resigned. Unlike Adler and Jung, he took no other analysts with him.

During this period of strain, Rank had good reason to complain of Freud's other pupils, "noisy ranters . . . [with] their childish jealousy." He quite justifiably considered the "Berlin plans and plots . . . unworthy of a scientific movement. . . ."[32] In Vienna, however, at least one friend and colleague, Helene Deutsch, had interceded with Freud to help effect a reconciliation while Rank was in America.

She did it as much for Freud's sake as for Rank's, since Freud seemed deeply hurt. She explained to Freud that Rank's closeness to him had put the younger man in a state of extreme stress; patience and understanding were in order. She reminded Freud of Rank's attachment to him, and of how he had set out on his own in expectation of Freud's death. But none of this gave any comfort to Freud. He brushed aside her intercession with the final sentence from a Jewish story, "Then why isn't he kissing the hot stove!" A master of Jewish anecdotes, Freud explained his meaning: The Rabbi has a beautiful young wife and many students living in his house. One day the Rabbi returns home to find his favorite student kissing his wife. The Rabbi turns on his wife to accuse her, but she pleads with him that the pupil does not know what he is doing, he is sick. "Then why isn't he kissing the hot stove!"[33]

Freud was angry, not only at Deutsch's intervention but also at Rank. Freud's expectations, which had inspired Rank, also made him feel betrayed. His time was valuable and he would turn elsewhere. Though he conceded that on one level it might have been a question of Rank's premature grief, Freud thought the issue was now much simpler—money. Freud believed there was no need to go deeper; Rank was doing very well by his theories in America.[34]

3. Will and the Artist

THE THEME OF MONEY in Rank's life was new. In Vienna he had lived in the most modest circumstances; in America, however, psychoanalysts from Central Europe were welcomed as celebrities. Not only were the Americans rich and eager to be treated, but Rank was offering shorter analyses, which meant they could afford to pay more per session (though in the long run the way to make money, with less trouble for the therapist, might be extended analyses). By the time the Ranks moved to Paris they were living extravagantly in a lavish apartment, with a butler, cook, and chambermaid. Although he never saw Freud again, and it was already clear that the break was irrevocable, it took Rank several more years before he officially resigned from the Vienna Society. It was good for Rank's status as an analyst in Paris and New York to remain a member of Freud's group even after the cessation of their personal contact.

Jones brought up the monetary issue in an indirect way: "Rank had . . . a keen eye for practical affairs and would assuredly have been very successful had he entered the world of finance; there are rumors that he employed this capacity to good effect in his later years in Paris."[1] Freud, who had once considered Rank "thoroughly honest," now called him both a "roguish boy" and a "mountebank"; "he was one of my most gifted pupils, but a rascal [*gonif*]."[2]

> It looks now as if from the very beginning he had the intention of establishing himself on the basis of his patent procedure. . . . He seems to me now to resemble the employee in Victor Hugo's *Les Travailleurs de la Mer* who achieved great confidence through years of correct behavior so as to be able to embezzle an enormous sum.[3]

Rank followed in Jung's path by becoming a schismatic while in America, a country which had all along offended Freud by its deference to numerical superiority, its belief in statistics, and its worship of brash wealth.

Freud's bitterness must have been all the greater since here, as with his birth trauma theory, Rank was in a sense caricaturing him. Ever since the end of World War I patients had been coming from America to Vienna, and Freud was of course the chief psychoanalytic beneficiary, and dispenser, of the New World's wealth: he sat back and waited for the Americans to visit him. Rank did him one better by going to America, in answer to invitations to lecture and in search of patients. As Freud wrote to Rank in May 1924, "I am so very glad that you found the only rational way of behavior with which you try to live among these savages: To sell one's life as dear as possible to them."[4] When Rank moved to Paris he managed to scoop up American patients headed for Vienna. Just as when Rank first went to America he was still considered the most faithful of Freud's disciples, even after he settled in Paris it was some time before people heard of his fight with Freud.

In none of the published accounts does Rank's wife Tola play any role in the falling out between Freud and her husband. It is known that there were differences between Tola and Otto and that she did not always accompany him on his trips to America. In 1935 she stayed in Paris when he moved permanently to the United States. Shortly before Rank died in 1939 they were divorced, and he remarried. Invited to Boston in the late 1930's by Helene Deutsch, Tola was one of the last nonmedical people to qualify as an analyst in America.

Although Tola Rank may not have known about it, Freud partly blamed her for what happened between him and her husband. "It's her fault, his increasing need of money and importance."[5] Anna Freud then thought it had been Tola's fault, though later she decided that Tola had been victimized.[6] No one could seem less likely to come between Freud and Rank. Tola was devoted to Freud; as Otto's wife, she did not play an independent role in the intimate circle around Freud. At the time she

introduced no new theories or techniques into psychoanalysis. She attended
Anna Freud's seminar on child analysis in Vienna, and as late as November
1925 was lending money to the psychoanalytic press.[7]

The split between Freud and Rank "hit" Tola "very hard."[8] She
never fully understood the theoretical and clinical differences between
them, and she had trouble handling the painful divisions within her that
this controversy created. At the height of the difficulties Freud complained
to her of Otto's ingratitude. Although some estrangement already existed
between her and her husband, she moved with him to Paris in 1926. It
was not yet clear that ultimately she would side with "father" against
husband, but she continued to preserve her ties to Freud. Unlike her husband, she never resigned from the Vienna Society. Every year she traveled
back to Vienna to see Freud and her intimate personal friends. Once Freud
asked her a harsh personal question about Otto, and she tactfully defended
herself, "Why do you ask me that, you know how I think and feel, why
do you make it harder for me?" She pointed out that she had a small child,
and chose to remain loyal to her companion in marriage.[9]

Beata Rank in the 1920's

She later reported that she reminded Rank of what Freud had done for him and how hurt Freud was by his loss. Yet she spoke only rarely with her husband about the problem with the Professor or about any of the bitterness. Both Ranks were reticent, even secretive, about themselves. Tola could not directly side with Freud while she was still living with Otto. Yet by the end, when her marriage was almost over and she was beginning to practice as an analyst, she more openly became a public follower of Freud's.

Tola's loyalty to Freud as opposed to her husband struck some as opportunistic. Freud's affection for her had come only through her marriage to Rank. She had rich psychological talents of her own, and was an intuitive and imaginative woman, a type Freud would cherish; but this had mattered less to Freud than that she was Rank's wife.

Tola's immense admiration for Freud, which persisted throughout Rank's struggle to become independent, may have encouraged Rank's initial strivings to free himself from Freud. If Freud was the kind of man his wife looked up to, then Rank would try to be more like him. In addition, Tola was extravagant with money. Not that money in itself was important to her—she did not seek it—but she spent it with very little anxiety.

In Paris, Rank created an environment for his new conception of himself and for his wife. Their circle included Henry Miller, Anaïs Nin, and wealthy American patients. Tola became the patron of artists. Rank could never earn enough to support their extravagance. "I feel forced," he wrote in 1931, "by financial needs to go to America because I cannot make a living otherwise."[10] Intimate friends saw the same problem: "Rank is talking about his despair. He cannot earn a living in France. He may have to accept an offer from America. He does not want to leave . . . the pressure of reality is terrible, his wife, his daughter, his future."[11]

In Paris, Tola resisted Rank's encouragement to join him in America; he was helping to found a school for social work at the University of Pennsylvania. Otto's sadness about their relationship was apparent. Tola had started to work with children in Paris, although as late as 1934 she was still mainly running the household. She also had an analysis with Mira Oberholzer, a former patient of Freud's. Once settled in Boston in 1939, however, she gradually worked up an analytic practice of her own; in those days it was not unusual for dead analysts' wives to be accepted as analysts themselves. She became outstanding in her own right, specializing in supervising work with children and in training future therapists; at the James Jackson Putnam Children's Center she pioneered in the therapy of "atypical" children. Her professional success in America, all the more remarkable for her lack of formal standing in Europe, followed the failure of her marriage. She died in 1967.

While Tola stayed within psychoanalysis, Rank struggled to be free from Freud's influence. Immediately after leaving Vienna in 1926, Rank sent an elegantly bound edition of Nietzsche's works to Freud for his seventieth birthday; Freud showed it to his pupils when they gathered for the occasion. Freud was, however, annoyed by the lavish gift; he had already blamed Rank for an "extravagant production, in costly leather" of Freud's own collected works.[12] The monetary theme reverberates in Freud's comments about the present which he took to be Rank's bribe. But Rank's choice of Nietzsche's works as a birthday gift must have been a special irritant. On the surface the present was loyal and humble, and yet it also meant that Rank was emphasizing a predecessor and anticipator of Freud's. It was as if Rank's gift were saying, "you accuse me of taking from you, when look what you have taken from Nietzsche."[13]

The process of withdrawing from a teacher who has been an ego ideal, from someone who has become an internalized part of oneself, can be painful, slow, and tortured. The great temptation with Freud's work was either total acceptance or complete rejection. Rank went from one extreme to the other, as he strove to emancipate himself.

One means of breaking away from Freud that Rank chose was to identify with the lost master, to become a teacher himself with pupils to carry on his own work. In Paris, Rank found Anaïs Nin, an artist and writer; Rank's prose was turgid and difficult to read, and he wanted her to rewrite his books, condensing and clarifying them. He analyzed her; she started to practice herself, and helped him as a private secretary.

Her diaries are the most eloquent account of Rank's ascetic character. He is still the man of ideas: "He is a philosopher, not an artist. The poet is in love, a lover. The philosopher is a commentator . . . Rank has to proceed immediately to extract the meaning or the essence . . . *Il pense sa vie.* His true life may be in the analysis of it." She contrasted Rank with their friend Henry Miller:

in life . . . [Rank] is inexperienced. To living he brings nothing. The details of life which so fascinate Henry, he overlooks. The comic face of a passer-by, the color of a house, the savor of small things. Physical, visible life. He disregards appearance, color, detail. His life is in abstractions.

According to her, Rank could be "dark and heavy. He has no *joie de vivre.* His pleasures are of the mind." She had found in "the world of psychoanalysis the only metaphysician in it: Rank."[14]

Rank's course in Paris was increasingly original. He recommended short-term analyses, with time limits set in advance, whereas the older and more experienced (and also the sicker) Freud grew, the more he advocated lengthier treatments. Rank, partly out of self-criticism no doubt, became hostile to what he considered the scientific desiccation of Freudian therapy:

> I believe analysis has become the worst enemy of the soul. It killed what it analyzed. I saw too much psychoanalysis with Freud and his disciples which became pontifical and dogmatic. That was why I was ostracized from the original group. I became interested in the artist. I became interested in literature, in the magic of language. I disliked medical language, which was sterile.[15]

As Anaïs Nin learned from Rank, "if one can get lost in the labyrinth of emotions, one can also get lost in the labyrinth of analysis . . . Objectivity is just as fallible as the instincts, just as self-deceptive."[16] She quoted Rank as saying:

> Half of the effectiveness of analysis lies in the wish of the analyst to heal and to help . . . Every analyst has it at the beginning and then gradually loses it. If analysis becomes mechanical it suffers . . . Freud began to analyze me. He believed every analyst should be analyzed himself. But we could not go on. He was not objective. Or at least, I did not feel he was. Too much wisdom prevented me from living out my natural self.[17]

Rank regarded neurosis not as an illness but as a failed work of art, and the neurotic was to be treated as a "failed artist."[18] The key lay all along in the psychology of creativity. Like many later post-Freudian writers, Rank became convinced that the earlier psychoanalytic formulations had put the individual's ego in too passive a role vis-à-vis instinctual life, whereas the ability to integrate conflicts creatively was the main difference between emotional success and failure. "Rank concluded that the patient's problem is really the problem of learning to assert his will . . . around 1925 Rank was advocating a more active form of therapy designed to encourage the patient to assert himself and find his own individuality."[19] Instead of being suspicious of "resistances," the therapist's job was to help the patient assert his will (creative powers), despite whatever guilts or fears, whether of union or of independence, he might have.

Rank objected to what he considered the excessive rationalism of Freud's approach, which aimed to remove illusions and to expose the "truth":

Science has proved to be a complete failure in the field of psychology. . . . The error lies in the scientific glorification of consciousness, of intellectual knowledge, which even Psychoanalysis worships as its highest god although it calls itself a psychology of the unconscious . . . Intellectual understanding is one thing and the actual working out of our emotional problems another. . . .[20]

For Freud, the reconstruction of the patient's past was the task of therapy as well as of research, and he tended to make rational understanding the test of health, leaving everything nonrational open to the charge of neurosis. According to Anaïs Nin, Rank was opposed to the psychoanalytic emphasis on "the resemblance between people; I emphasize differences between people." Rank was "not practicing mental surgery. He was relying on his intuition, intent on discovering [in her] a woman neither of us knew."[21] Rank yearned to abandon Freud's injunction to self-overcoming. "I really wish I could retire and live a peaceful life-end. I had enough of the 'world' and I have worlds and worlds within myself."[22] The trouble with psychoanalysis was that it did not "accept human nature."[23] Yet Anaïs Nin felt that Rank had not fully emancipated himself from Freud's point of view:

> At times I feel Rank puts too great an emphasis on what ought to be rather than what is; he never accepts experience as a substitute for wisdom. At times I feel the process of accelerated wisdom may become a dangerous short-cut. It eliminates terror and pain. I feel it should only be used in extreme cases.[24]

Despite himself, Rank remained Freud's disciple. Just as Freud had in a sense created him, so he strove to create others:

> When Rank saved people they were his creation. He had to continue to be the figure that saved them, the ideal wise man. He was not permitted to be human, or even to love them. The life of an analyst is tragic. A country doctor, a physical doctor, can be human, fallible. He can be loved for what he is outside of his profession. An analyst does not exist in the mind of his patient except as a figure in his own drama.[25]

In her view, Rank was too much of an "absolutist for life." He felt that "analysis and therapy separated him from life rather than fulfilled his personal needs. Analysis created illusory attachments."[26] Life demands compromise, limitations, whereas in creation Rank could be autocratic and controlling.

Jones not only submerged the distinctive fiber of Rank's life in the parallel with Jung, but went on to accuse Rank of a psychosis. Rank "suffered from cyclothymia (i.e. manic depressive psychosis)."[27] Other writers, accepting Jones's account, have spoken of "Otto Rank's slow descent into madness."[28] It was apparently Freud who privately first put a diagnosis of manic-depressive (though almost certainly of a neurotic rather than a psychotic character) on this pupil he seemed unable to manage. In 1934, for example, Freud commented verbally of Rank that he:

> was . . . my secretary for fifteen years, and was closely associated with me and did very valuable work, practicing psychoanalysis in the way it should be done. Then he went another way and since then we have no longer had relations with each other . . . I cannot go into the reasons why, because I have no right to reveal his personal life, but I can say one thing, because it is generally known: since leaving me, Rank has been having periodic bits of depression, and in between, sort of manic phases—periods in which he does a great deal of work, and others in which he cannot do any at all. He had this tendency before, but now . . . one could call him ill. . . .[29]

But as a psychiatrist has recently observed, "it is important to make a clear distinction between illness and character structure. A man may have a manic-depressive psychopathology without being clinically ill or having any kind of breakdown."[30]

Jones discerned changes in Rank that were "startling" and "remarkable"[31] (Jones frequently used such breathless adjectives as "astonishing," "extraordinary," and "radical"—the well-known British understatement is often accompanied by exaggeration). But the people who knew Rank best—his family, friends, and patients—never perceived any of the signs of "mental breakdown"[32] that Jones tried to document. Rank had his share of human troubles, but he remained a well-consolidated personality, and his depressive moods were contained and never seized hold of him.

Freud's bitterness was reciprocated by Rank, although there may have been more of it in Jones's books than in the two men involved. Rank was resentful of the treatment he received from his former psychoanalytic colleagues. According to his old friend Hanns Sachs (each thought the other had cut him after the quarrel between Rank and Freud), Freud had dismissed the subject of Rank by saying "sternly: . . . 'Now, after I have forgiven everything, I am through with him.' "[33] In his writings Freud often emphasized how hard it could be for anyone ever to withdraw affections, and like much of the rest of psychoanalytic thought, this was true of Freud himself. With Freud nothing was really ever over.

Freud's rejection of Rank's elaboration of the birth trauma as the original source of all anxiety led to a reconsideration of his own position, and the book *Inhibitions, Symptoms, and Anxiety* (1926) was the outcome. Although Freud considered Rank's constructions farfetched and unverified, he wrote "it would be unjust to put his attempt on the same level as Adler's. . . ."[34] Like Adler and Jung, however, Rank was to repudiate Freud's emphasis on the childhood past, and to concentrate instead on the patient's present-day experiences within the analytic situation itself. Rank was developing a psychological theory and technique explicitly at

Hanns Sachs (1881–1947)

odds with Freud's. By 1932 Freud was not only more dubious about the value of Rank's work, but saw him more clearly in the rebellious line of his two most famous dissenters. Criticizing Adler and Jung, Freud then went on to discredit the process by which "someone else"

> may arrive at the view that the experience of anxiety at birth sows the seed of all later neurotic disturbances. It may thereupon seem to him legitimate to restrict analysis to the consequences of this single impression and to promise therapeutic success from a treatment lasting three to four months.[35]

In 1937, two years before they both died, Freud made an uncompromising statement of his position toward the work of his former friend: Rank's attempt to shorten treatment

> was bold and ingenious; but it did not stand the test of critical examination. Moreover, it was a child of its time, conceived under the stress of the contrast between the post-war misery of Europe and the "prosperity" of America, and designed to adapt the tempo of analytic therapy to the haste of American life. We have not heard much about what the implementation of Rank's plan has done for cases of sickness. Probably not more than if the fire-brigade, called to deal with a house that had been set on fire by an over-turned oil-lamp, contented themselves with removing the lamp from the room in which the blaze had started. No doubt a considerable shortening of the brigade's activities would be effected by this means. The theory and practice of Rank's experiment are now things of the past—no less than American "prosperity" itself.[36]

For years Freud had wanted Rank to apply pschoanalytic theories to the legend of Ulysses—the quest of the father for a son, the son for a father. In despair of persuading a successor to take up the interpretation of mythology, in the 1930's Freud himself undertook to examine a myth, the Moses of legend. In beginning his discussion, Freud paused to mention that "in 1909 Otto Rank, who was at that time still under my influence, published, following a suggestion of mine, a book bearing the title *The Myth of the Birth of the Hero*" (and in a footnote Freud qualified his comment by saying that "it is far from being my intention to belittle the value of Rank's independent contributions to the work"[37]). In *Moses and Monotheism*, Freud mentioned the clinical example of

> a young man whose fate it was to grow up beside a worthless father, [who] began by developing, in defiance of him, into a capable, trust-

worthy and honorable person. In the prime of life his character was reversed, and thenceforward he behaved as though he had taken this same father as a model. In . . . the beginning of such a course of events there is always an identification with the father in early childhood. This is afterwards repudiated, and even overcompensated, but in the end establishes itself once more.[38]

Sachs spotted his old friend Rank in this passage, who, according to Freud's reasoning, had found an ideal compensation for a good-for-nothing father but had then regressed back to an identification with the worthless father. On a trip to see Freud just before he died, Sachs was able to confirm that Freud was indeed referring to Rank here.[39]

Only a month after Freud died at the age of eighty-three, Rank suddenly died in October 1939, in his middle fifties and two months after his remarriage to Estelle Buel, his American secretary. Whereas Freud survived sixteen years with his cancer, Rank had merely a throat infection but succumbed a few days later as a result of an allergic reaction to a sulfur drug. Anaïs Nin, stunned by the death of a man she remembered as so full of vitality, has left the most moving post-mortem:

> He had been about to fulfill his wish to live in California. His new wife had a ranch there. She had fulfilled his need of a collaborator, had translated his writings, worked with him. He had been happy, about to escape from individual therapy. He had finished a new book.

Anaïs Nin felt a void:

> But memory can invoke a figure, and because of its own vividness it appears sharp and clear, eyes both soft and penetrating, his curiosity and interest, his abundance of ideas, his fecundity. He did have sorrows, profound depressions, disappointments, frustrations, but he never became bitter or cynical. His faith never died, nor his capacity to feel, to respond. He never hardened, never became calloused.[40]

IX

THE WOMEN

1. Ruth Mack Brunswick:
"The Rabbi May"

AFTER OTTO RANK, Freud never "adopted" another son. Although there were no women on his 1924 list of pupils who had remained loyal to him, from that time on Freud's female pupils stand out prominently. Freud found women less difficult and competitive. His female students constitute, in fact, a long line of adopted daughters: Mira Oberholzer, Eugenia Sokolnicka (André Gide's Polish analyst, whom he put into his novel *The Counterfeiters* and who, though analyzed by Freud, committed suicide by gas in 1934), Hermine von Hug-Hellmuth, Helene Deutsch, Marie Bonaparte, Ruth Mack Brunswick, Jeanne Lampl-de Groot, and the women who came to him primarily through their friendship with Anna Freud—Dorothy Burlingham, Eva Rosenfeld, Anny Katan, and Marianne Kris.

Freud is not the only famous man who, aging and in ill health, attracted a flock of admiring women; Albert Schweitzer, whom Freud regarded highly, did likewise. Freud did not actively seek adulation from these women, nor did he specifically choose his admirers. By and large he passively accepted women as members of the inner circle around him, though the existence of what resembled a royal court did not shock him. Alongside Freud's intense preoccupation with his work and his aggressiveness toward the outside world, went a passive surrender, not to one woman, but to a whole group of them. He did not want to worry about the nuisances of daily life. In his last years these women formed what some called a "camarilla" around him. They shielded him from visitors, arranged his vacations, and watched over his health. Shy and retiring with women,

Freud ended his life surrounded by them; it is perhaps worth remembering that as a child he had five sisters.

These women went on to establish themselves in a profession markedly receptive to feminine talents. Although Ruth Mack Brunswick's place in Freud's life has not yet been adequately recognized, her career illuminates the last decade and a half of Freud's old age. By 1930 Ruth Mack Brunswick (1897–1946) was unquestionably Freud's favorite in Vienna.[1] Her access to him was unique: she came to dinner at his house, would visit him in summers, and was on good terms with his children. She was really a member of Freud's personal family. Loved and also jealously considered a rival by Freud's daughter Anna, Ruth Brunswick was the most important of the last of Freud's adopted daughters.[2]

She also played a role in mediating between the American analysts and Freud's inner circle in Vienna. An American as well as a confidante of Freud's, simultaneously a member of the New York and Vienna Societies, she was in an excellent position to smooth over the natural disharmonies between these two very different worlds. In Freud's private practice, Ruth Brunswick was the channel through which wealthy Americans came to Freud; and in general she looked after the American analytic patients in Vienna.

Although to an outsider it might not always be clear who was "in" and who was not, to those who had been in communication with Freud for some time Ruth Brunswick's stature was well known. Her daughter was also a favorite of Freud and his wife. In his biography Jones did not mention Ruth Brunswick's position, possibly out of jealousy or perhaps out of tact. Unknown to him, she was one of the female recipients of Freud's much-cherished ring.*

Ruth Brunswick had charm and intelligence, and, as a prototypical American, few inhibitions; she was demonstrative and explosive, outgoing, effusive, and warm. She was also an elegant person with cultivated manners, as well as vivacious and possessed of a lively intellect. As a woman, she was neither especially attractive nor unattractive to Freud. As with his sister-in-law Minna, Freud liked to use women as a screen for his ideas; unlike Minna, however, Ruth tended to be domineering and was not a peaceful motherly type satisfied with simply understanding Freud's ideas. She was literate and verbal, well read, and one of the few Americans not stigmatized as an American in Freud's eyes.

---

* According to Jones,[3] only his wife Katherine, Freud's daughter Anna, Lou Andreas-Salomé, and Marie Bonaparte received rings. In fact, Gisela Ferenczi, Jeanne Lampl-de Groot, Ruth Mack Brunswick, Edith Jackson, Henny Freud, and Eva Rosenfeld were among the women to whom Freud gave rings.

Ruth Brunswick had a courageous mind, and this may have been the crux of the matter for Freud. She was not intellectually restricted; she dared to take risks. She could have one idea today and change her mind tomorrow. Few people brought that same intellectual elasticity to Freud. She was proud of her relationship with him, and it was a pleasure for them both.

Ruth Brunswick—then Ruth Blumgart—was twenty-five years old when she came to Freud, and she entered his world with enthusiasm and warmth. Freud became the ideal person for her, scientific mentor as well as father substitute. Her father, Judge Julian Mack, was a distinguished jurist and a well-known Jewish philanthropist. But she had an uncertain relationship with him, and Freud seemed the perfect solution. She knew that, after Frink's demise, he regarded her as his connection to the Americans, and that he trusted her to see that his work was correctly interpreted in American circles.

For a long time Ruth Brunswick was much closer to Freud than his own daughter Anna.[4] He gave Ruth a few pages of the manuscript of the book on Woodrow Wilson, but Anna did not see any of the volume until 1965. As he showered honors upon Ruth and granted her intimacies, she aroused the jealousy of everyone less favored. Some of her male colleagues considered her obnoxious and aggressive.

Ruth Brunswick played a special part in supervising Freud's health. It was she who, through her father's influence on the Board of Overseers at Harvard, arranged in 1931 for a professor of medicine at Harvard to make a special prosthesis for Freud's mouth.[5] She and Marie Bonaparte paid the expensive bill, which Freud ended up resenting; the new prosthesis was not a success, and Freud was touchy about being beholden to anyone financially. Ruth hovered over Freud in his illness and even interfered with his diet.

Ruth had been married to Hermann Blumgart when she first came to Vienna in 1922. Blumgart had been a student of E. B. Holt's at Harvard Medical School, who not only gave one of the first courses on Freud but also wrote an early textbook on psychoanalysis. A graduate of Radcliffe College, Ruth went to medical school at Tufts. Through Hermann's brother Leonard, an analyst who had already been to Vienna for a short analysis with Freud, Ruth made arrangements to go there herself. Her marriage was evidently already in trouble. But she had completed her psychiatric residency, and she went to Vienna not only for help with her personal problems but also for training. Blumgart traveled to Vienna in an effort to bring her back. He was determined to remain a physician, and she wanted to become an analyst. Hermann Blumgart spoke to Freud in an effort to hold the marriage together, but to no avail. So Blumgart left his wife there and returned to America, where, as an expert in heart diseases, he pursued an outstanding career.

Ruth already had another man in mind for a husband, whom Freud too preferred for her: Mark Brunswick was five years younger than she and very much in love with her. He had made up his mind to marry her when as a teen-ager he attended her wedding. Hermann Blumgart was a first cousin of Mark Brunswick's mother. This group of Americans was interrelated by complicated ties: Mark Brunswick's mother later married Judge Mack in the last years of his life.

Ruth arranged for Mark, in addition to herself, to be analyzed by Freud. In 1924, at the age of twenty-two, Mark entered Freud's circle. Freud was then sixty-eight; Mark remembered Freud's remarking at their first interview, "Is it possible for anyone to be so young?" Mark had little formal education; a year at Exeter Academy was the last schooling he ever had. Shy and timid, musically a prodigy and yet emotionally undeveloped, he ultimately became a professor of music and chairman of his department at the City College of New York from 1946 to 1965. He was an open, imaginative, and artistic person, and Freud took to him right away. Mark knew nothing about science or medicine, and cared only for composing and his musical friends in Vienna.[6] Freud had taken him into analysis as a prospective son-in-law so to speak; Ruth and Mark were already in love, and Freud set out to patch up Mark so he could marry Ruth.[7]

Their marriage in 1928 was an event in Freud's life, for he rarely went out publicly in those days. The wedding was held in the town hall, with Freud as one of the witnesses. The second witness at the ceremony was Oskar Rie, the pediatrician of Freud's grandchildren and later of Ruth and Mark's daughter. (This child was named after Mathilda Hollitscher, Freud's eldest daughter, who was a close personal friend of Mark and Ruth's.) Rie's daughter, Marianne Kris, was Ruth's best friend. The Brunswicks' marriage papers had been drawn up by Freud's son Martin, a lawyer. Also present at the town hall for the ceremony were Mark's brother David (who was in analysis with Freud) and his youngest sister (who was in analysis with Nunberg).

Freud had taken Ruth and Mark into analysis simultaneously, and Mark's brother David as well. Between the three of them they made up 60 per cent of Freud's analytic time and income. (In those days Freud regularly carried about five analytic cases.) Today analysts do not, however, like to treat a couple, married or not, and it would be contraindicated by the "rules"; an analyst needs to be able to identify with his patient, and this is made more difficult in treating such closely linked people. But Freud would violate normal analytic procedures in the spirit of "the Rabbi may" —for the Rabbi special exemptions were permitted.[8]

Mark Brunswick saw much of Freud in his family surroundings, since Ruth and he often visited the Freuds socially. Mark later felt that this personal contact did him a lot of good, but also reinforced certain pathological traits. Freud lived in two worlds and was self-protective; he tended to be unpsychological away from his practice. In his family circle Freud was pleasant and unguarded; he once teased his son-in-law, Mathilda's husband, for being so flirtatious with Ruth, when Ruth was Freud's patient at the time.

But Mark would not have dared to communicate to Freud his observations about the disparity between Freud's home and office behavior, or rather, at the time it never occurred to him to say he would not have dared to do so. Before going to Vienna, Mark had read and admired Freud's *Totem and Taboo*, but although he was interested in anthropology he could not develop an interest in medicine. He never considered becoming an analyst himself. He went only once or twice to meetings of the Vienna Society, and then he was shocked at the words that were used in public with both sexes present.

Mark also was acquainted with William Bullitt, then in analysis with Freud, and Marie Bonaparte, who, like Ruth, was intermittently in and out of analysis with Freud over many years; in the 1930's he also knew Edith Jackson, another patient of Freud's. Until the 1930's Freud's patients paid him twenty dollars an hour; then, of their own accord, they decided to raise their payments to twenty-five dollars.

The intimacy of these personal interrelations did not help Mark therapeutically; nor did Freud's indiscretions. For example, after David had been with Freud for some weeks, Freud complained to Mark: "What have you and Ruth done to me! Your brother is the most boring person!" In different ways both Mark and David were intimidated by Freud. David thought that Freud had been prejudiced against him by Mark and Ruth; apparently expecting intellectualized resistances from David, on the second day of his analysis Freud told David to speak in German and to enroll in medical school. David was then a psychologist by training who expected to go into business; he had dropped out of medical school in the United States, and he later did the same in Vienna. Freud assumed that, as an American, David would need a medical degree to qualify as an analyst in the United States. When David began practicing in America, Freud wrote him: "that you have become an analyst is the right punishment for you." It was one of Freud's jokes, but, to David, it also expressed Freud's attitude toward him.

The young Mark Brunswick had come to Freud with severe character disorders. In retrospect Mark believed that if Freud had refused to take him into analysis on the grounds that Ruth was already his patient, it would have been traumatic for him but it might have been better in the long run. (Afterward David too felt that Freud should not have taken him into analysis.) As it was, in September 1924, Mark began his first analysis with Freud, and it continued for three and a half years. At that point Freud pronounced him cured; Mark terminated the analysis and married Ruth. According to Mark, he had not been cured of a single symptom, although he did have better feelings toward his father. Mark adored Freud, although he developed some negative feelings toward him later on. Nevertheless, he had never found anything remotely petty in Freud; he felt that Freud's mistakes had stemmed from good will and had been sins of outgoingness.

Ruth and Mark left Vienna in June 1928 for the United States, where their baby was born; they returned to Europe in 1929 and stayed in Vienna until 1938. Around the end of 1933 or early 1934, Mark told Freud that he still had all his symptoms, but that in some sense he was now worse off, since he was trying to live up to an adult situation. Freud was disturbed at the news, and he took Mark back into analysis.

During his first analysis, when Mark had been a young man in love with a married woman, Freud and Ruth had discussed his case in complete detail. Ruth became almost a mother to Mark. This time, however, Freud explained to Mark that Ruth must not know about his analysis in the same way, and that he had made a serious mistake in discussing Mark's analysis with her before. Freud was natural and open in confessing his earlier error. (With other patients—such as David—he was less easygoing.)

Mark soon fell in love with a young girl. He asked Freud whether it was proper to violate his marriage vow, and Freud said yes. Ruth and Mark were divorced in 1937, but remarried within six months, though Freud was displeased with them for doing so. Mark made considerable progress in his treatment until 1938. By then none of his musical friends were still in Vienna. He had left Vienna in October 1937 and come back in December; he finally departed for good at the end of January 1938. Freud started writing Mark's case history the same month he left Vienna, but it was unfinished at Freud's death.[9] (Some years later Mark underwent another analysis in New York, which he thought was far more successful than the ones with Freud.)

Tensions had already arisen between Freud and Mark, mainly over politics. Both Ruth and Mark were disappointed in Freud when the Socialists in Vienna were violently put down in 1934. Politically, Freud seemed to have completely reversed his position, and argued in favor of supporting Dollfuss, although his was an authoritarian regime. Freud was a dying man, and wanted at all costs to remain in Vienna. In February 1934 Mark and Freud agreed to part for a while, in view of Mark's bitterness over Freud's political attitude. Austria then had an anti-intellectual government, representing the social forces that had failed to accord Freud recognition, and the Socialists were Freud's friends. But Freud could not handle the issue in the analysis, perhaps because of a guilty conscience.

Time and again Mark and Ruth urged him to leave Vienna, but Freud resented this pressure, as he thought their fears were groundless. As early as 1932 he wrote in a letter: "That there is a risk of personal danger [in staying], as Ruth and Mark are never tired of telling me, I can hardly believe. I am pretty well unknown in Austria; the best informed only know that any ill-treatment of me would provoke a great stir abroad."[10] The others in the analytic community in Vienna had difficulties in leaving because they often had to cross Freud to do so, and it seemed to them that they would be deserting a sinking ship.

By the time the Nazis took over Austria, Ruth had made her mark in analysis, largely as a result of Freud's patronage. For he had made one great personal gift to her—the referral of the Wolf-Man, his former patient. In doing so, Freud paid her the highest compliment. In her treatment of the case, however, she overlooked her own transference feelings for the Wolf-Man; since Ruth thought that "for this patient analysis was Freud," she considered that as a therapist "my own role was almost negligible; I acted purely as mediator between the patient and Freud."*[11]

For Ruth, the case and the article she wrote about it constituted a tremendous lift in her self-esteem. She wrote the article in close collaboration with Freud, though one hopes that Freud would not endorse the kind of tautology she ended her account with: the Wolf-Man's future health, she wrote, would be "in large measure dependent on the degree of sublimation of which he proves capable."[12] In Freud's presence she had found herself. Without Freud, few of his followers would be of any importance in the history of ideas. Freud inspired and encouraged more from them than they had ever accomplished before.

---

* Cf. above, pp. 154–57.

2. Ruth Mack Brunswick:
Dependency and Addiction

FREUD HAD DISCERNED a natural psychological ability in Ruth Brunswick. She had an intuitive talent for "smelling" the unconscious.[1] In her technique as an analyst she was always unconventional; within orthodox limits, she was a somewhat active analyst, although considering that Freud had been her analyst it is perhaps surprising that she was not more active than she was. Like Freud, she was more interested in the science of psychoanalysis than in therapy for its own sake. Most of her patients were Dutch, probably because Freud had initially sent her Dutch patients. (Analysis was recognized in Holland very early;[2] it has flourished there, perhaps because the Netherlands is basically a middle-class country. By the 1960's it was the only nation in which analysts complained of having too many students in analytic training.)

The police gave Ruth trouble at one point, since her visa did not permit her to work. Martin Freud tendentiously explained to the authorities that she was working, under supervision, merely for training purposes. In Vienna the Brunswicks had a car and big house with servants. In the eyes of the rest of the analytic community, they lived like millionaires.

Freud gave to Ruth unstintingly, ideas as well as patients; unlike some of his earlier male pupils, Ruth was never a rival. Freud even admired her interest in psychotics. She gave a seminar on psychosis for her colleagues in the Vienna Society; it was not a part of the regular curriculum of the Institute, but rather a "graduate" seminar, and Marie Bonaparte and Paul Federn, among others, attended sessions at her house in Vienna. One might wonder how Freud could have encouraged her work and remained silent about Federn's. It is true that Federn was confused in his ideas; but even if Freud doubted whether the treatment of psychoses was a legitimate application of psychoanalysis, his affection for Ruth won out.

Ruth Brunswick had the intellectual ability to incorporate her findings within Freud's framework. She had a talent for manipulating Freud's theoretical concepts, and she could use them to set forth new ideas of her own. She stressed the importance of the mother in the development of the child, yet so tactfully that it did not seem to Freud to be a revolt against his basic ideas. One of the central trends in analysis since Freud's death has been a concern for cases in which "the etiology of . . . illness goes back behind the Oedipus complex, and involves a distortion at the time of absolute dependence."[3] As Jung had long ago pointed out, Freud had originally been oblivious of the non-oedipal role of the mother-child tie. But Ruth expressed her findings with absolute discretion.

Whereas Rank had built a rival theory around his innovation of emphasizing the importance of non-oedipal factors, Ruth stressed that there were "pre-oedipal" phases of child development. As she cautiously put it, "to the best of my knowledge the term pre-oedipal was first used by Freud in 1931 . . . and by this author in 1929. . . ."[4] She limited herself originally to the psychology of women, but her theories would in future years have implications for men as well. By "pre-oedipal" Ruth meant that an early emotional relationship preceded the triangular conflict in which the little girl longs for the love of father and feels rivalrous toward mother. And this earlier "position," which comes before the Oedipus complex, involves love and identification of the little girl with the mother. This is a far more archaic and primitive emotional involvement than the oedipal, and Ruth hypothesized that it lay at the root of the psychotic problems she was studying.

Ruth Brunswick had succeeded in incorporating ignored phenomena, which Freud's defecting pupils had stressed, within his libido theory; and so he paid high tribute to her work. By casting her theory originally in terms of the psychology of women (where Freud admitted he had not been able to get very far) and by retaining the importance of the Oedipus constellation itself (following Freud's notion that it had a "pre-history"), she was able to re-emphasize the importance of Freud's concepts and at the same time extend them.

As early as 1925, Freud had launched this shift in psychoanalytic thinking by postulating that the existence of a phase of emotional life prior to the oedipal complex meant that, in girls, "the Oedipus complex is a secondary formation."[5] The more Ruth's work fleshed out the theory of pre-oedipal factors, the more important the Oedipus complex seemed to become, for it now had a developmental history of its own. "Our insight," Freud wrote in 1931, "into this early, pre-Oedipus phase in girls comes to us as a surprise, like the discovery, in another field, of the Minoan-Mycenean civilization behind the civilization of Greece."[6]

Freud acknowledged Ruth Brunswick's work on pre-oedipal patterns in women; she "was studying these problems at the same time as I was. . . ."[7] After her death Nunberg claimed that in "her exceedingly important

Ruth Mack Brunswick (1897–1946)

paper on The Preoedipal Phase of Libido Development . . . she asserted that she could not exactly say which were Freud's ideas and which were her own";[8] although this admission cannot be found in Ruth's paper, Nunberg may well have heard her make such a remark, for it is consistent with her intimate collaboration with Freud. Freud conceded that women analysts had been able to discover this earlier attachment to the mother that he himself had not been able to make out "because the women who were in analysis with me were able to cling to the very attachment to the father in which they had taken refuge from the early phase that was in question."[9] Yet Freud still maintained that "the phase of exclusive attachment to the mother, which may be called the *pre-Oedipus* phase, possesses a far greater importance in women than it can have in men."[10] A pre-oedipal fixation in a woman, it was believed, would lead to a lack of libido toward men, whereas a pre-oedipal tie in a man would mean a passive attachment to the father. In this area Freud acknowledged Ruth's priority; she was "the first," he wrote in 1932, "to describe a case of neurosis which went back to a fixation to the pre-Oedipus stage and had never reached the Oedipus situation at all."[11]

Ruth Brunswick worked hard as a clinician and also participated in the politics of the psychoanalytic movement on both sides of the Atlantic. Jones claimed that she sided with Zilboorg against Brill; and Brill thought she had worked against Schilder, until he resigned from the New York Psychoanalytic Society.[12] In Vienna, Ruth was more or less continuously in analysis with Freud, whenever he could fit her in. Her most famous American student was Karl Menninger; she also analyzed Robert Fliess, the son of Freud's former friend.

Despite her scientific productivity and her excellent functioning as an analyst, her health was troubled. She tended to convert emotional problems into somatic symptoms, and her doctors could not diagnose her illnesses as unequivocably organic. At one point they found too much arsenic in her blood; it was not clear whether she had been poisoned by the cook or by the wallpaper, but she had her rooms repapered. (James Jackson Putnam had earlier incriminated wallpaper as a common agent in arsenic poisoning.[13])

Ruth used morphine to cope with the terrible pain of what she thought were gall-bladder attacks. Doctors came and went, and it was known to a few in Freud's inner circle that she seemed to have mysterious illnesses. She underwent surgery, which was unsuccessful, perhaps because she had more than gall-bladder trouble. Max Schur, her doctor, thought she did not have gall stones, but others disagreed. (Ruth had analyzed both Schur and his wife, thereby reproducing her and Mark's situation with Freud.) She also suffered from neuritis. As a doctor she had been able to prescribe for herself—she took sleeping pills and pain killers—and by 1933–34 she had gradually slipped into a serious drug situation. Unhappy and plagued with organic troubles, by 1937 or so she had become an addict. In those days most addictions derived from using drugs for medicinal purposes.

For a time she was weaned from her dependency on drugs. On Freud's advice, she was once, while still in analysis, hospitalized in an effort to overcome her addiction. But Ruth was addicted not only to drugs; as a personality she was clinging and sticky, which may partly explain why in the end Freud became so rejecting toward her. Her life ended tragically; try as she might, she was unable to rise above a sickness which analysts described as pre-oedipal in character.

In Vienna, while Freud was still alive, she did not seem outwardly disturbed or pathological. She functioned effectively until the last part of her life, when she grew heavily dependent on drugs. Up to her sudden death early in 1946, she was regarded as a leading psychoanalyst, an intimate favorite of Freud's in the last years of his life.

Ruth's private misery is important because of her close involvement with Freud. Given Freud's personality, a drug addiction would be especially intolerable to him. In his dying days, despite the pain connected with his cancer, Freud was reluctant even to take aspirin. To use sedation to deaden the pain, to muddle his mind, and—worse still—to allow himself to become dependent in such a way, was unacceptable. He was proud of being able to overcome himself. For Ruth to become dependent on drugs, and finally addicted and enslaved, was a deadly affront to Freud's intolerance. He himself never resolved his own nicotine addiction, although for years he struggled against what he called "my habit or vice." (Curiously enough, Freud did not trace this smoking problem to a pre-oedipal tie to his mother, but even as late as 1929 referred to an identification with his father as a "heavy smoker."[14]) Freud recognized Ruth's addiction as an illness to be understood and treated rather than condemned, yet he found such problems distasteful. Ruth could not have invented her addiction out of unconscious defiance toward Freud, in order to express her ambivalence; she had had something of this problem all along. Yet, to Freud, any addictive problem would be particularly bad, and it was one of the main constituents in his final disappointment in her.

When Ruth first came to Vienna in 1922, training amounted to not much more than being analyzed, ideally by Freud himself. A good deal of make-believe surrounds the early figures in psychoanalysis. From a contemporary point of view, training in those days may seem to be merely a gesture; it has been said that most of Freud's "first adherents had only a purely intellectual experience of analysis and . . . when they had been analyzed their treatment had been too short and too superficial to produce any lasting result."[15] It has been suggested that their problems would have been fewer if only they had been adequately analyzed.

In Ruth's case, however, her analysis with Freud stretched on and on, extending, with some interruptions, from 1922 to 1938. Such a long analysis was in itself an addiction, reminiscent of what Freud had earlier feared would happen in the use of hypnotic technique.[16] Freud's treatment of Ruth helped induce the very dependency which it should have been the task of analysis to dissolve. The main feature of Ruth's sad illness is not that so much analysis with Freud did not protect her from a debilitating disorder, but that the more Freud treated her the closer they became and the less she was helped to overcome her difficulties with dependence.

Freud liked working with Ruth too much; his feelings for her became an interference in her efforts to rise above her troubles. She enjoyed being dependent on him, which should have been treated as a problem and not indulged as a pleasure.[17] Probably Freud should have sent her to someone else.[18] Ruth would have gone to another analyst, and when she returned to America she finally went to Nunberg just before she died. But it was not beyond Freud to have wanted to keep Ruth for himself; their mutual fondness and intellectual exchanges kept them together.

Genius can have a seductive power. Freud was irresistible to many people, even though he might not do anything intentionally to arouse adulation. Freud disliked infatuations, yet he aroused them to an extraordinary degree. Freud had set out to liberate, but sometimes he enslaved. The tenderhearted patients, with the weakest self-defenses, were those who succumbed in contact with Freud. If one cannot agree with an analyst who maintained that Freud had "destroyed" Ruth, it is because she herself lacked the essential narcissism which would have enabled her to withdraw self-protectively from Freud.

As one friend colorfully put it, Ruth always made a big tum-tum over the Professor. Like others, she expected more from Freud than any human being could provide. But then Freud had played a central role in her life and had called forth an enormous transference. Freud first treated Ruth in too close a way, and then tried to make the relationship more distant.[19] Along with her dependency, Ruth tended to be domineering and dictatorial, and Mark Brunswick later remembered observing a conversation between Ruth and Freud on their porch in which she was laying down the law; Mark could not hear what was being said but he saw Freud's face freeze.

Freud's disappointment in Ruth developed as he grew sicker and more frail, and as she became more demanding and jealous of Anna Freud's role in caring for her father. Out of envy, Ruth behaved aggressively. Although some who were intimately acquainted with both Freud and Ruth did not know it, Freud became disillusioned with her. Despite years of analysis with him, she was more addicted than ever. By 1937, when his illness had gotten worse, Freud had more trouble controlling his irritability with her. From the outside, however, she still seemed to be one of his closest favorites.

As Freud's health deteriorated so did their relationship. She visited him in London in the summer of 1938, and was ecstatic about what she had gained from her renewed analysis. But by the winter of 1939, the last in Freud's life, he kept putting her off. She wanted to see him again, but he did not want her to come and watch him die. He reproached her with what he thought of as the "eternal feminine" need to see her father die; his idea that too much concern might be concealing an opposite feeling was perfectly valid, but all of his problems were exacerbated and he was bitter. By January 1939 he was not himself, and he began to act strangely toward her; though disappointed in both Mark and Ruth, if his health had been better he would not have expressed himself as he did. For his seventieth birthday Mark had given him the first volume of the Cambridge ancient history series, and since they discussed archaeology together, as each of the subsequent volumes was published Mark presented Freud with a copy; but when the last volume appeared in 1938, Freud ordered it for himself and then wanted to know who should pay. Areas of his personality were being restricted by his pain and his awareness of the approach of death. He once said of Ruth's daughter, whom he had adored, "I think I've heard of her."[20]

Ruth had not gone to London when Freud emigrated from Vienna. Her father was ill in America, and Mark frequently telephoned her across the Atlantic; his mother was staying in Vienna with Ruth and their daughter. As Ruth's father's eyesight and memory had been affected by his illness, he needed his only daughter. And the Nazis were about to move into Austria. Freud had others to take care of him. Very reluctantly she went back to the United States.

Away from Vienna, however, Ruth gradually went to pieces. Given her tendency to hypochondria, one can only wonder if her illnesses had not, like those of the Wolf-Man in the 1920's, been exacerbated by an unresolved transference to Freud. She had horrible pains in her eyes, and prescribed drugs for herself. Despite her problems Freud had sent her patients over the years, and other analysts continued to do so; apparently there was no overt decline in her ability to analyze until almost the end. She obtained affidavits for all her close friends in Vienna, so that they could go straight to America if they chose to.

When Ruth returned to New York from her last trip to London, Freud was dying. Her worst period of drug addiction occurred in America. In 1940 her mother died, followed three years later by her father. And, as her relationship with Mark had greatly deteriorated, she was under a great deal of stress. Paradoxically, in view of her own problems, she had been against Mark's drinking until the last two years of their marriage, and he drank furtively, though by American standards he did not consume much. She clung to Mark as she did to whatever she was attached to. Still, among the analysts it was Ruth who welcomed Freud's son Oliver when he arrived in the United States with his wife in 1943. Two years later, Mark divorced her, and she went to Nunberg for further analysis. As Mark later put it, "Everything she loved seemed to have crumbled, so she crumbled too."

Toward the end of her life, Ruth—who had always had work inhibitions—developed a real block. She never published as much as Freud or she thought she should, which partly explains why she is so little known to the reading public today. A psychiatrist has recently related creative blocks to the problem of identity: "Some measure of a sense of personal identity quite apart from the work is necessary if the latter is to be carried out effectively."[21] Perhaps Freud overestimated her talents; but if so, it was because of her immense attractiveness to him, which in itself requires some explanation. As sensitive as Freud could be about plagiarism vis-à-vis other students, he at least once made a point of giving Ruth a "present" of an idea; he said he was giving her this insight, that for the development of the aesthetic sense the relation of the infant to the mother's breast is of exceptional importance.* She failed to pursue Freud's suggestion, and in one of his last papers in 1937 he was still hoping that she would publish more material on the Wolf-Man, who had once again been in treatment with her.[23]

One cannot be sure whether Ruth regarded her separation from Freud as a rejection, which may have intensified her demands on him. In fact, by the end of his life Freud had had enough of her. With his death she lost not only a revered man in her life but also a source of gratification for her self-esteem. She may have then realized that she was not as creative as she had once thought. Her premature death ensured that she would publish much less than some of her contemporaries.

---

* Erasmus Darwin had already expressed the idea.[22]

Ruth's death is not technically classifiable as a suicide, but it was the product of at least half-intentional self-destruction. Although originally her illnesses had made her prone to drugs, by the end she was drinking paregoric the way an alcoholic might drink whiskey; she also took barbiturates, and years of drug taking had undermined her health. She did not have fits or exhibit other addiction symptoms, but the Federal Bureau of Narcotics had taken notice of her. Then she contracted pneumonia, which persons with such addictions are prone to. After a difficult time, she seemed to be getting better; but the night before she died she had been unable to attend a party for Marie Bonaparte, another favorite of Freud's, who, however, at the end of Freud's life had pulled well ahead of Ruth in his inner circle.

Ruth's death on January 25, 1946, came as a great shock to everyone; Mark had seen her six hours before. The cause of the death was given out as "a heart attack induced by pneumonia,"[24] but that was concocted. She died of too many opiates, combined with a fall in the bathroom: she had hit her head and fractured her skull. She had been subject to severe diarrhea, and would take morphine for it, falling asleep on the bathroom floor. Possibly this last night of her life she had taken too many sleeping pills, and then fell; it was the fall that killed her.

Despite her importance to Freud and psychoanalysis, no obituary appeared in the *International Journal of Psychoanalysis*; because of her sad end, no one felt happy about writing it. Nunberg did write one for an American quarterly, referring only to her "sudden tragic death."[25]

Any life looked at sympathetically is bound to have tragic features; but it would be as wrong to overemphasize this side as to succumb to the temptation to eulogize. According to Freud, accomplishments are tied to limitations, and even the best we manage is paid for at the price of human loss. But a suicide, or gradual self-destruction, is a different matter. In addition to the deaths of Federn, Stekel, Tausk, and Silberer, one can find other recorded suicides among this early group of analysts: Karin Stephen, Eugenia Sokolnicka, Tatiana Rosenthal, Karl Schrötter, Monroe Meyer, Martin Peck, Max Kahane, Johann Honegger.

Jones ridiculed the legendary "dangers of psychoanalysis; it either drove people mad or sent them to their death."[26] Whatever one may think of the limited therapeutic usefulness of psychoanalysis, such exaggerated polemics are surely out of place. But it remains troubling that these early analysts should so frequently have killed themselves or otherwise come to bad ends. When informed of Honegger's death in 1911, Freud reflected in a letter to Jung: "Do you know, I think we wear out quite a few men."[27] Yet it is questionable whether the group was more disturbed than any other set of people. A number of lives seemed to have been sacrificed for the sake of the triumph of Freud's work, but other great ideas in human history have also taken their toll. And what stands out in this group may be largely the result of the microscopic lens we have turned on it. Examine any human life with enough care and attention, and one will find pathology, pain, suffering, and inner torment. But this need not imply that tragedy is the only human experience. It may be a good deal easier to find words and concepts to describe the failures we endure, than to break through the banalities and clichés with which we usually describe the fulfilling parts of life.

3. Anna Freud:
Child Analysis

THE SERENITY OF ANNA FREUD'S LIFE stands in sharp contrast to the turbulence of Ruth Mack Brunswick's. Yet they were the closest of friends, and for some time competitors for Freud's attention. Anna Freud was jealous of the women who were significant in Freud's life, and she thought that her memories of jealous feelings were a means of gauging the importance of a woman in Freud's life.[1] As so many pupils sought Freud's love, while to him they served mainly to extend psychoanalysis, Anna was proud that her father withheld himself from them all. She adopted her mother's (and paternal grandmother's) tendency to put Freud on a pedestal, and identified with Martha against other women in Freud's life. Anna Freud did not need to compete with her mother since Martha was already excluded; but she was competitive with women like Ruth Brunswick. Mark Brunswick thought that Freud's fondness for their daughter Tilly was an additional cause of Anna's jealousy of Ruth; Anna could give only the devotion and care of an unmarried daughter.

Born in 1895, Anna Freud was the last of Freud's children, and evidently an unwanted one. Perhaps Freud's reluctance to have another child reflected his anxieties about heart troubles of the year before; and Martha

Freud was apparently disappointed at this pregnancy.[2] The girl was named after a friend of the family; yet Anna was also the name of one of Freud's sisters whom he liked least. Around the birth of this child Freud's practice had decisively improved.[3]

As a father, Freud was not active in the day-to-day care of the babies. He never fed them bottles or changed their diapers; they could not go walking with "Papa" until toilet training was completed. However, he occasionally made use in his writings of "material provided by my own children," and referred to one of Anna's dreams in *The Interpretation of Dreams*.[4] Martha Freud put limits on his use of their children as objects of investigation, but he had more freedom when it came to the upbringing of the younger ones.[5] Freud was aware of his own counter-oedipal problems—which came first, Freud's feelings or those of his youngest child?— but Anna Freud's life is a testimony to her father's principle that "a girl's first affection is for her father. . . ."[6]

Physically resembling her father's side of the family, Anna Freud grew up to be an unworldly young lady. Freud wrote her at least one sympathetic letter during her adolescence, encouraging her to be more easygoing, for when unoccupied she was apt to be restless. As Freud imploringly wrote her at the age of seventeen, when, after an illness, she had an opportunity to spend the winter in sunshine:

> Your plans for school can easily wait till you have learned to take your duties less seriously. They won't run away from you. It can only do you good to be a little happy-go-lucky and enjoy having such lovely sun in the middle of the winter . . . I can tell you that we all enjoy your letters very much but that we also won't be worried if you feel too lazy to write every day. The time of toil and trouble will come for you too, but you are still quite young.*[7]

With three daughters Freud could liken himself to King Lear, and the theme of a father's fondness for his daughters appears in his writings.[9] He explicitly referred to Anna in letters as his faithful Antigone, the daugh-

---

*Anna Freud recently reminisced about "an attitude of mine which stems from the remote past. At the age before independent reading, when children are read to or told stories, my interest was restricted to those which 'might be true.' This did not mean they had to be true stories in the ordinary sense of the word, but that they were supposed not to contain elements which precluded their happening in reality. As soon as animals began to talk, or fairies and witches, or ghosts to appear—in short, in the face of any unrealistic or supernatural element—my attention flagged and disappeared. To my own surprise, I have not altered much in this respect."[8] Presumably the fables of Aesop or La Fontaine were beyond her early childhood ken.

ter of the blind and ailing Oedipus.[10] Remaining unmarried and relatively unaware of what life could be like outside the·family, Anna became in a way a victim of the grandiosity of her father's old age.

Since she was shy and pretty as a young girl, it was said at one time or another of every bachelor in Freud's circle that he was seeking to marry Freud's daughter Anna. Concerning Rank especially there were rumors of a match with Anna. In his analyses of his students, Freud frequently would claim to discern a desire to marry one of his daughters; Binswanger remarked on "Freud's interpretation of . . . [a] dream, which I found rather unconvincing . . . was that it indicated a wish to marry his eldest daughter but, at the same time, contained a repudiation of this wish. . . ."[11] Even with an analytic patient, the "Rat-Man," Freud made the same kind of interpretation.

All of Anna Freud's suitors came through her father and her older brothers. She is reported to have been in love at various periods with at least three men in Freud's circle—Siegfried Bernfeld, Hans Lampl, and Max Eitingon—but her tie to her father blocked the way.[12] In 1935 Freud mentioned his "worries" about her: "she takes things too seriously. What will she do when she has lost me? Will she lead a life of ascetic austerity?"[13]

With no scientific training of her own (she did not even finish the Gymnasium), she became a schoolteacher for small children. For five years she taught in an elementary school[14] but earned very little money. She sat in on her father's lectures at the university; she took dictation for him and helped out with secretarial tasks. Though not a member, she attended meetings of the Vienna Society at least as early as November 1918. It was then only a short step to becoming a member of the Vienna Society, before which she presented, on June 13, 1922, a paper, "Beating Phantasies and Day Dreams"; like her father, she spoke without lecture notes. She entered practice as an analyst just before her father fell ill in 1923, initially working with children.

One of the well-established legends among Freud's pupils was that Lou Andreas-Salomé was Anna Freud's analyst;[15] Freud might very well have been dubious about sending Anna to an analyst in Vienna. Lou and Anna became great friends in later years, and Lou dedicated one of her books to her.[16] In view of Lou's notorious successes with men, she no doubt would have been an inhibiting analyst for the retiring Anna Freud. And Anna almost certainly would have been competitive with Lou over Freud himself. But at least one witness was certain that Lou had analyzed Anna while staying at the Freud apartment in Vienna.[17]

In any event, Lou could not have been Anna Freud's first analyst; for earlier, despite the rules of analytic technique that he laid down for others to follow, Freud had analyzed his daughter himself. The analysis must have stretched over a number of years. Freud spent a month in Budapest in 1918, and had brought Anna along; at that time she was already in analysis with him.[18] One of Freud's sons, Oliver, remembered that in the spring of 1921 his sister was going to Freud's study for her analysis.[19] And in Anna's analysis of at least one patient, the fact of her analysis by her father played a great part.[20] Freud could be open about it, and in a 1935 letter to Edoardo Weiss, who had asked his advice about analyzing his own son, Freud answered that with his daughter the analysis had gone well but that with a son it might have been different:

> Concerning the analysis of your hopeful son, that is certainly a ticklish business. With a younger, promising brother it might be done more easily. With one's own daughter I succeeded well. There are special difficulties and doubts with a son. Not that I really would warn you against a danger; obviously everything depends upon the two people and their relationship to each other. You know the difficulties. It would not surprise me if you were successful in spite of them. It is difficult for an outsider to decide. I would not advise you to do it and have no right to forbid it.[21]

Weiss interpreted Freud's letter as a discouragement.

In the light of Freud's taking his own daughter into analysis, all the squabbles about what constitutes proper psychoanalytic technique— whether the patient should be seen three or four or five days a week, whether patients are permitted to read analytic literature or not, whether an analysis requires the use of a couch, how much activity on the part of the analyst is proper—are reduced to trivia. But when Jones was going to America for the centenary celebrations of Freud's birth, Anna suggested he might want to discuss the relationship between psychoanalysis and psychotherapy, with a stiff warning about the latter.[22]

In view of the elaborate and esoteric rules of proper technique that have been developed by Freud's followers, the disclosure of Freud's analysis of his daughter renders their position rather difficult. It was an open secret to a small group of Freud's inner circle, but to others concerned with the history of the movement Freud's analysis of his daughter is a shock; some of the old Viennese analysts either did not know of this analysis or did not want to hear about it when they were told.

From Freud's point of view, there were good reasons for doing what he did. The rules he set down in his papers were not intended for himself, and he did not expect his students to follow them too closely either.

Perhaps Anna Freud would not have gone to anyone else. Surely another analyst would have hesitated before daring to wean Anna from her father, which presumably would have been part of the task of a proper psychoanalysis. Freud must have been afraid that another analyst might hurt her. He might have thought he could conduct the analysis loosely, with limited therapeutic objectives, while teaching her the best he knew. It amounted to his showing his daughter how he did things, without hoping to clarify her relation to him, since that would have been practically impossible.

Freud had analyzed himself, and he may well have thought he was capable of analyzing his daughter. Any other analyst he could turn to would already have some sort of emotional relationship to her, as the master's daughter, so he might well have mistrusted what anyone else could accomplish. If Freud could not take liberties with psychoanalysis, who else could? At the same time, his analyzing Anna and her submitting to it, may have amounted to a mutual agreement between them that he was to keep her with him. Psychoanalysis was so important to both of them that everything else became trivial; the primary consideration might have been whether the analysis would help equip her as a future analyst. But then Anna may have been more afraid of her father than either of them knew.

Freud's motives may have been the very best, but medically and humanly the situation was bizarre. As her analyst, he would inevitably mobilize her feelings of overevaluation, while at the same time invading the privacy of her soul; he added new transference emotions to their relationship, without the possibility of ever really dissolving them. A genius who was also naturally an immense figure in his daughter's fantasy life, as her analyst he tied her permanently to him.

Freud could sharply criticize another analyst's technical liberties. For example, he once wrote to Sandor Ferenczi, "What one does in one's technique one has to defend openly."[23] Taking his daughter into analysis undoubtedly gratified an oedipal tie on his part; and at the same time it was good for the psychoanalytic movement to have Anna as an analyst. But for Anna, the analysis helped to limit the possibilities for personal gratification, although she had a role in her father's life as well as her eventual leadership of the movement, which constituted a rich exchange. Perhaps only by normal standards was her relationship to such a father a tragic one.

In the 1920's, however, and in fact up to her father's death, it was not realized that Anna was destined to become the leader of psychoanalysis. While she was a young woman without formal credentials some of Freud's older pupils could be patronizingly protective about her.

To those who were aware of Anna Freud's presence in the movement,

and how much it meant to Freud, it seemed that his defense of lay analysis
had been devised at least in part to protect Anna's future. (His life's sav-
ings are said to have been wiped out in the postwar inflation.) But lay
persons, without scientific training, are more prone to religiosity; the
requirement of a medical degree at least tended to siphon off those who
came to analysis with an excessive preoccupation with their own psychological difficulties. Freud encouraged some of his pupils to study medicine,
not because it was important in itself but in order to make their careers
as analysts easier.[24]

As late as World War I, Freud had written that "psychoanalysis is a
procedure for the medical treatment of neurotic patients,"[25] and in 1918
he still referred to the psychoanalyst as "the physician." But by 1924 he
thought it was "no longer possible to restrict the practice of psycho-

Anna Freud in the early 1920's

analysis to doctors and to exclude laymen from it."[26] Freud had grounds for resenting his reception in the world of medicine: "Doctors have no historical claim for the sole possession of analysis. On the contrary, until recently they have met it with everything possible that could damage it, from the shallowest ridicule to the gravest calumny."[27]

Freud could tolerate the dispute over lay analysis, and he cited it as evidence that "differences of opinion are allowed even in our own camp."[28] But it enraged him to think that others might disagree with his right to appoint his youngest daughter an analyst, and he viewed opposition to lay analysis as an attack on Anna and an implied criticism of him as well. In 1926 Freud wrote that "my daughter Anna has devoted herself to the pedogogic analysis of children and adolescents. I have never yet referred to her a case of severe neurotic illness in an adult." (He immediately added that "incidentally, the only case with moderately severe symptoms verging on the psychiatric which she has hitherto treated repaid the physician who referred it to her by its complete success."[29]) Medical qualifications are less relevant for working with small children than with adults if only because by the time one can finish analytic training (child analysis being added on to the basic analytic skills) one might be too old to have adequate patience for treating children.

Anna Freud has justifiably earned fame for her observation and treatment of young children. Hermine von Hug-Hellmuth (1871–1924) had preceded her in Vienna in this field, and in Berlin and London Melanie Klein developed a different technique for working with children as well as an elaborate conceptualization of her own. In Vienna, August Aichhorn had been interested in treating delinquents, and both Pfister (in Zurich) and Bernfeld (in Vienna) focused on adolescents. But it was Anna Freud who specialized in small children, and she inevitably aroused the jealousy of Hermine Hug-Hellmuth.

Frau Dr. Hermine von Hug-Hellmuth died shortly after Anna Freud officially entered the psychoanalytic scene. In appearance Hug-Hellmuth was a tiny woman, pinched, tidy, and unelegant; it was easy for others to make jokes about her, but her work was original. She was one of the few Gentiles and one of the few women in the Vienna Society. She originated play therapy as a means of communicating with young children. She seems to have been so imaginative as to have concocted a diary of her youth which is still available in its English translation as *A Young Girl's Diary*, with a preface by Freud.[30] It is generally agreed that the book was a fraud, and its appearance created a scandal; it was withdrawn from publication in German. At the most charitable, she had reworked her childhood reminiscences in the light of the psychoanalytic theories of the 1920's; her book sets forth everything that the Freudians then taught about the nature of female sexuality.

Hug-Hellmuth had not been particularly close to Freud, though she admired him tremendously. About a year before she died, Anna Freud began to practice. As Freud's daughter started to work with children, she rapidly overshadowed Hug-Hellmuth's position. It was only natural for this pioneer in child analysis to feel jealous of her new rival.

Shortly after the Salzburg Congress of analysts, on September 9, 1924, Hug-Hellmuth was murdered by her sister's illegitimate son, whom Hug-Hellmuth had raised. Apparently they had had a quarrel over money. Her death was a great shock to the psychoanalytic community, and the trial of her eighteen-year-old nephew received widespread newspaper coverage. He was convicted and imprisoned.

A week before she died, Hug-Hellmuth had asked that no obituary

Hermine Hug-Hellmuth—
caricature drawn at
the Salzburg Congress
in 1924

be published about her in a psychoanalytic publication.[31] Did she anticipate her own destruction? Her relationship with her nephew seems to have been more that of a therapist than of an aunt or mother substitute. When he was a small boy she made "observations" on him, and he provided illustrative material for her articles. One analyst—convinced that the murder of a therapist by a patient usually represents a self-destructive impulse in the therapist which the patient acts out—referred to Hug-Hellmuth as a suicide.

The young man served his sentence, and when released went to Federn to demand money from the Vienna Society as a victim of psychoanalysis. Hitschmann recommended that the boy go to Helene Deutsch for treatment; he thought it might be good for him to work out his problem with a woman analyst. The boy was bitter that his maiden aunt, instead of giving him love, had used him as case material; Hug-Hellmuth had not merely noted an occasional aspect of his behavior for her work, but had made a systematic study of the child. Their money quarrel may have been only an excuse for the killing, but it was unnerving for Helene Deutsch to be proposed as the second woman analyst for this patient who was now demanding money from the psychoanalytic establishment that his late aunt had represented. In Hitschmann's referral Helene Deutsch detected her colleague's hostility toward her; her husband was so concerned about his wife's safety that he hired a private detective to watch the boy's movements.

Anna Freud's work with children had a distinctive cast from the outset; she was interested in adapting classical psychoanalytic technique to the special capacities and strengths of young children, who will not lie on a couch and free-associate. Her educational experience was helpful; for she held that children need to establish an educative relationship with the therapist before they will accept interpretations.

The key distinction between the analysis of adults and that of children, according to Anna Freud, was that children were not capable of establishing an adult's kind of transference, since they were still tied to their parents in daily life. With children an analyst could get only transference reactions, not a true transference neurosis. Unlike the more analytically puristic Melanie Klein, therefore, Anna Freud suggested that a preparatory phase was necessary before analytic treatment can begin. And she proposed to work therapeutically as much as possible through the parents of the children in treatment (a line of reasoning in which the pediatrician in Freud's circle, Joseph Friedjung, at least in part had preceded her: "In many cases," he had maintained in 1909, "it is sufficient simply to change the milieu or the influence exercised by those around the child, in order to effect the disappearance of symptoms"[32]).

Some Viennese analysts put their children into analysis, though they would not necessarily have consulted Freud about it. However, unlike Melanie Klein, who thought that child analysis was the best prophylactic against neurosis, Viennese child analysts did not by and large hold that every child needed treatment. It was not unknown for a child analyst to refuse to treat a child on the ground that the child was sufficiently normal; but the case of one such three-year-old, who later committed suicide in young adulthood, should underscore how limited is our knowledge in this area.

Freud was proud that analysts had moved from studying childhood through the retrospective memories of adult patients to direct observation: "We had begun by inferring the content of sexual childhood from the analysis of adults. . . . Afterwards, we undertook analyses on children themselves. . . ."[33] But he insisted that though "psychoanalysis can be called in by education as an auxiliary means of dealing with a child . . . it is not a suitable substitute for education . . . One should not be misled by the statement—incidentally a perfectly true one—that the psycho-analysis of an adult neurotic is equivalent to an after-education."[34]

Freud left child analysis completely to Anna. She went her own way, despite Freud's skepticism about the possibilities of therapy with young children; but he was in favor of exploration through the direct observation of children. Freud pointed out that there was no analytic pedagogy, and he did not give patients advice about their children. This was so well known that many patients would not have even ventured to ask for such advice. He was of course aware of the interest in "the application of psychoanalysis to education, to the upbringing of the next generation," and he wrote: "I am glad that I am at least able to say that my daughter, Anna Freud, has made this study her life work and has in that way compensated for my neglect."[35] When one thinks of the James Jackson Putnam Clinic in Boston, or Bruno Bettelheim's University of Chicago Orthogenic School, it is clear how these early efforts of Anna Freud and her co-workers would be built upon and broadened, so that in the future children could be treated who once might have seemed inaccessible to psychotherapeutic intervention.

Despite Freud's disclaimers, he had definite ideas about child rearing. For example, he is reported to have thought that "when a mother is too tender with her child—that is, boy child, homosexuality often develops."[36] And once when one of Freud's daughters-in-law was, in his opinion, cuddling her infant son too much, Freud became angry and chastised her about it;[37] presumably he was worried about a possible oedipal seduction. Years later this daughter-in-law defensively argued that nowadays doctors would tell you the reverse (her baby at the time had been three or four months old, too young to sit up). Although Freud may have rarely given such advice about child rearing, he was not very reliable when he did. There is a paradox here: Benjamin Spock has acknowledged how much he owed to psychoanalysis, and his manuals have been practical and good.

As much as Freud did not want to tell people how to live, he did insist on the advisability of the sexual enlightenment of children. He had sent his sons to a family physician to learn the facts of life, but he proposed that "children should be gradually enlightened from the very beginning. Sexual life must, from the start, be treated without secretiveness in the presence of children."[38] Freud held that "to orient the child in life is among the responsibilities proper to the school, and sexual problems are an important part of this orientation . . . Enlightenment should above all make it clear to them that this is a matter of acts of tenderness. . . ."[39] For "the main damage done by neglecting [to enlighten] children lies in the fact that, for the rest of the child's life, sexuality is afflicted with the character of the forbidden. . . ."[40]

4. Anna Freud:

Ladies-in-Waiting

AFTER FREUD FELL ILL in 1923, Anna Freud played a gradually increasing role as the guardian of her father's time and health. Though he preferred to write his letters by longhand, sometimes she acted as his private secretary. The more her father became an invalid, the more important her position was as the person closest to him.[1] The other women of Freud's family were also there to guard him from unwanted outsiders, but Anna was particularly sensitive to the jealousies in the Vienna Society that tended to grow up around her father.[2] Anyone who had known Freud before his illness might have an already established relationship to fall back on. But the newcomers to Freud's circle tended to come to him through his daughter Anna. Characteristically, these women were either unmarried or separated, or their husbands were somehow not important.

Eva Rosenfeld, for example, entered Freud's world in November 1924 as a friend of Anna's; also the niece of a favorite singer of Freud's, Yvette Guilbert, Eva Rosenfeld was adopted by the family to the extent that they would, for instance, celebrate her birthday. In 1929 Freud took her into analysis, through Anna's mediation; but he did not charge her for the treatment. She was in analysis for two months, six times a week. After the analysis was over, on Sunday afternoons, when Anna went out for a drive with her friend Dorothy Burlingham, Freud would again analyze Eva; in her analysis he once referred to Mrs. Burlingham as "your rival," and it seemed to him that the essence of analysis was getting over rivalries and jealousies.

On summer holidays Freud would analyze Eva Rosenfeld every day. In exchange, she would help arrange lodgings for the Freud family during the summers. Her husband does not seem to have resented her attentions to Freud. Although in later years Eva became an analyst herself, her position in Freud's court was mainly a personal one. He admired the way she bravely coped with private tragedy. But he was through with Eva too one day; for her to go to Melanie Klein for an analysis was an insult to her old friend Anna Freud.

Jeanne Lampl-de Groot was a rich and intellectual (Gentile) Dutch psychiatrist who had been engaged to a member of Wagner-Jauregg's staff. However, she broke the engagement to marry Hans Lampl, who had been in Freud's circle for some years as a friend of his son Martin. But eventually Hans Lampl rebelled against his wife's intimate involvement with Freud; he wanted a wife, but for her everything centered on Freud. When Lampl vigorously protested against the situation, the circle around Anna Freud decided he was paranoid and should have himself analyzed. But the analyst concluded it was realistic jealousy on his part, and though he was not a brilliant man, he had known when to assert himself, lest dedication to Freud deprive him of a wife.

Marianne Kris, as the daughter of Oskar Rie, was accepted into Freud's circle as a matter of course. She was too young to be an influence on psychoanalytic issues, but Anna Freud arranged for her to have an analysis with Freud free of charge. Over the years he would treat her for a few weeks at a time. Freud was very fond of her; her husband Ernst was analyzed by Anna Freud, and their daughter was named Anna.

As a pediatrician, Marianne Kris's father had treated Freud's children free of charge, but he was also a regular member of Freud's card-playing foursome, which for years met on Saturday evenings. Freud cherished these nonanalytic friends of his, who, unlike former patients, would not be a burden to him. One of them was Ludwig Rosenberg, who was married to one of Oskar Rie's sisters and whose family spent summers together with the Freuds; Rosenberg's daughter, Anny Katan, became an analyst herself. In this instance, however, Anna Freud did not arrange for her father to analyze Anny Katan, but conducted the analysis herself, despite the fact that she and Anny Katan were childhood friends.

Dorothy Burlingham also came to Freud and psychoanalysis as Anna's close friend. Leaving her disturbed husband, she moved to Vienna from America with her four children. She was first in analysis with Theodor Reik and then Freud. A relative of Mrs. Burlingham's was also in Vienna with her children for analysis. A member of the Tiffany family, Dorothy Burlingham could afford to pay for the treatment of her whole family; her children were among Anna Freud's first patients.

Freud was happy when Anna found Dorothy as a friend; to him it meant she was now in safe hands. In 1929 he wrote: "our symbiosis with an American family (husbandless), whose children my daughter is bringing up analytically with a firm hand, is growing continually stronger, so that we share with them our needs for the summer."[3] And in 1932 Freud noted that Anna and "her American friend (who owns the car) have bought and furnished . . . a weekend cottage."[4] Anna Freud loved dogs, and in his old age Freud would play "with them as he used to play with his ring."[5] Dorothy, who had a relative in Paris who bred chows, was the main source not only of Freud's dogs but also of the chows that went to others in Freud's circle, such as the Lampls, the Deutsches, and Edith Jackson. Dorothy Burlingham had much extra-analytic contact with Freud and his family, but, unlike Ruth Brunswick's direct access, Dorothy's came through her friendship with Anna Freud. Anna became a second mother to her children, and Dorothy was a recipient of one of Freud's rings.

None of the women around Freud was at all chic. Their total dedication to psychoanalysis seemed to consume their energies. When they gathered together at restaurants they were so noticeably not "smart" dressers that waiters knew they belonged together. Freud tended to rely on Anna's judgment of these women. He held himself discreetly aloof, trying not to gossip about one to the other.

Aside from Anna Freud herself, Princess Marie Bonaparte (1882–1962) was, by the end of Freud's life, the most important of his female pupils. He regularly had five patients in analysis, but he would fit in Marie Bonaparte (like Marianne Kris or Ruth Brunswick) as his time opened up. Marie was known in Freud's circle simply as "the Princess"; she was a direct descendant of Napoleon's brother Lucien. In addition, she was by marriage a member of one of the most respectable royal families in Europe;

her husband, Prince George, was a brother of the late King of Greece and also a member of the royal family of Denmark. As a young girl, Marie had wanted to become a physician, but at that time her father, a geographer and anthropologist, forbade it as unfitting for a daughter of a princely family.

Her husband, a simple and unintellectual man, was much older, and treated her involvement in psychoanalysis as if it were a toy for her; yet at the same time he had great respect for Freud. Marie and her husband had a distant though fond relationship, and often lived apart. Freud was something of a snob, and the rest of his circle relished the prospect of never quite knowing whom they might meet at the Princess's—the King of Norway, perhaps, or other members of the nobility. (Psychoanalysis has had one other princess, the wife of the author of *The Leopard,* Giuseppe di Lampedusa.) If Freud had great respect for money and the rich, it was prompted by his concern for the movement he led.

Marie Bonaparte was a grand personality whose mistakes could be as amusing as her virtues. She came to Freud first in 1925; as she put it, "I went to Vienna in 1925 to undergo an analysis by Professor Freud. . . . I thus had the occasion to make the acquaintance of his family."[6] For the first three months she wrote an account of her analysis, but Freud made her stop. She was a good case for Freud, since he reconstructed an early scene from her life which she could not remember but could confirm through a living witness.[7]

Through Marie, Freud transmitted the initiative for the founding of a French psychoanalytic society in 1926. She had great influence as a supporter of Freud's, yet was herself vulnerable to attack. Although rich and a princess, she was nevertheless a woman and did not have a medical degree. In her own world of the international aristocracy, her credentials were damaged by the fact that her maternal grandfather had been the (Jewish) founder of Monte Carlo's gambling casino. Despite her marriage, she could be snubbed at the Athens court because of the supposedly "tainted" money in her background. Well known in Parisian society, she was somewhat of an outcast in European aristocracy; she then proceeded to join a whole movement of outcasts, the psychoanalysts, in whose eyes she had unequaled social standing. Both she and the analysts felt increased self-esteem by virtue of her involvement in psychoanalysis.[8]

France had excellent psychiatrists and a native tradition of psychotherapy; thus Marie Bonaparte's organizational efforts never made much of an impact. Despite Freud's stature, the French initially regarded him as a German, and therefore alien, influence, and, unlike the British, they would in later years be more interested in the metaphysical than in the clinical side of Freud's teachings. But, in any event, psychoanalysis was not taken very seriously in France until after World War II. Few of the early analysts in France were regarded as really French, and France is nationalistic when it comes to its receptivity to new ideas. In France (as in England) the first analysts were largely outsiders—Swiss, Polish, or Alsatian. Moreover, Princess Marie's family was considered international rather than specifically French.

Marie became a completely devoted disciple of Freud's, rather like Hanns Sachs. She gave up everything for psychoanalysis—her interest in literature, her life as a princess—and in exchange she was lifted by her association with Freud far above her natural intellectual level. Though her involvement with Freud precluded any other interest, at the same time it gave her an approach to understanding psychology.

Marie was unable to match some of Freud's other students in terms of writing or thinking; she was "clearly unable to play her part on the scientific level."[9] She wrote, however, a lengthy study of Edgar Allan Poe,

Marie Bonaparte in 1934

for which Freud composed a preface. To Freud she remained mainly "our Princess" and a benefactor of his cause. She financed an anthropological expedition by Geza Roheim to Australia, but Freud was disappointed by the results of the field work. She also helped the psychoanalytic press whenever it was in financial trouble.

Freud encouraged the transference Marie had set up toward him. She fit into the category of those beautiful and narcissistic women for whom Freud seems to have had a special fascination.[10] Said to have once been the mistress of Aristide Briand, she was attractive and seductive, and had a lively temperament. In the inner circle around Freud, Princess Marie was one of the prime figures. She and Ruth Brunswick were the closest to Freud; when Marie was in Vienna, she could stay at Ruth's house, and Ruth and Mark visited Marie in Paris. Quite often Marie and Ruth took a villa together in the summer. Over summers these women—Marie Bonaparte, Ruth Brunswick, Dorothy Burlingham, Eva Rosenfeld—formed a colony around Freud. Once they took five houses together—one each for Marie, Ruth, Dorothy, Eva, and the Freuds.

Anna always had her own special position as Freud's daughter. On many points a curious distance existed between them, and he never, for instance, discussed thought-transference or telepathy with her. But there was a mutual exchange between Freud and his youngest child, and if someone like Siegfried Bernfeld was important to Anna, that was enough to establish him with Freud.

Anna Freud was a great admirer of Bernfeld's; when she first began to lecture, she looked to him for encouragement and support. Married and much older than Anna, she had helped bring him into Freud's inner circle. With her introduction he became a member of Freud's larger family. Like Hans Lampl, Bernfeld was a big brother for Anna; but unlike Lampl, Bernfeld had a first-class mind and it was said he had a face that revealed the intensity of a Savonarola.

Only at home did Anna seem to be at ease with men. But her regal manner and bearing might have made almost any man anxious. Bernfeld, who became divorced, preferred a more erotic type of woman, and married a former patient of Freud's. Bernfeld had begun practicing only in 1921, but he had been to meetings of the Vienna Society since 1913. Freud, however, grew disappointed in him, and this may in part have reflected Anna Freud's own feelings. Nevertheless, Bernfeld did make striking historical contributions to our understanding of Freud's early career.[11]

Although Anna Freud had entered the field later than some, and had many rivals, especially among the women in Freud's circle, ultimately she displaced all the others. She became a psychoanalyst shortly before the struggle with Rank began, and served to fill the gap he left. Eventually she performed all the functions of Rank's substitute. As Goethe had used his son to represent him at official occasions, so Freud sent Anna to deliver speeches and accept honors. Because of his illness Freud found speaking in public difficult, so Anna not only gave his honorific addresses but also read papers by Freud at the psychoanalytic Congresses in 1925, 1927, and then again in 1938. Freud felt that after his death Anna would be obliged to earn her own living, and her substituting for him was designed partly to build her up in her own right.

Anna's role also included acting as Freud's private nurse. He survived repeated surgery, and she continued to care for him. She helped him through his suffering; without her he would not have survived sixteen years with his cancer. As he wrote in the last year of his life, "I get more and more dependent on her and less on myself."[12]

Anna now accompanied Freud on trips. His sister-in-law Minna, an uncritical admirer, had been a good listener for Freud's ideas; he even discussed his cases with her. Anna took over Minna's functions, except for that of a card partner for Freud. But what Freud's wife had accepted from her sister became a source of antagonism between mother and child; and Frau Professor used to say of Anna that "she *was* such a tender child," but that the hardness in her had come out. Anna was resentful that her mother had placed such a burden on her child and had lacked the strength to fulfill Freud's needs. The more incapable Martha became, the more Anna's feelings of being an unwanted child were reinforced, and thus the more her father meant to her.

Freud was proud of his daughter's work as a child analyst. In 1926 he thought that child analysis was "an excellent means of prophylaxis."[13] Since it was considered proper to train other child analysts, gradually Anna Freud also moved into analyzing adults. By 1935 Freud remarked in a letter that "the one bright spot in my life is the success of Anna's work."[14] By the time of Freud's emigration to London, Anna was in charge of the pursestrings, at least when it came to sensitive family matters.*

Anna Freud's work has in a sense interfered with what might have been her private life. Shunning stylish clothes, she grew into old-maidhood wearing dark, wide, ankle-length dresses; she kept her hair short-cropped; her sport was horseback riding. Her relationship with her father deprived her of what is conventionally thought of as a full life. She could be very

---

* After Esti Freud first left her husband Martin, the money sent her from London came from Anna Freud.

charming, yet the prudishness she absorbed never allowed her to surmount the last barrier of fear when it came to men. Sharing her father's interests, she was to a great degree spiritually united with him. Yet having lived her life this way, she found it intolerable for him to be a mere man. Only the genius in Freud could justify the sacrifice of her life.

5. Anna Freud:
Ego Psychology

FREUD'S DECISION to emigrate to England rather than America in 1938 was clearly a matter of his convenience, and not Anna's. For England was the home of the only rival school of child analysis, that of Melanie Klein. Although Anna was relatively peaceable compared to Klein's kind of belligerence, the long-standing feud between the two women threatened for a time to split the British Psychoanalytic Society.

Before leaving Vienna in the spring of 1938, Freud had expressed the hope for Anna that "in England she will also be able to do much for analysis, but she will not intrude."[1] After World War II she founded, with Dorothy Burlingham, the Hampstead Child-Therapy Clinic, composed of a largely nonmedical group of workers engaged in the observation and treatment of children. It would be hard to imagine Freud himself leading or cooperating in such a clinic, since he was so committed to the practice of individual therapy. But Anna Freud's background as a schoolteacher has enabled her to infuse her clinic with a pedagogic atmosphere that has proved successful. The conferences begin as precisely on time as did Freud's Viennese meetings. In 1956, on the hundredth anniversary of Freud's birthday, money was raised in Freud's honor, especially in the United States, and was channeled to Anna Freud's clinic, much to the resentment of other leaders of the British Psychoanalytic Society.

During Freud's lifetime Anna Freud was never in her own right a leader in psychoanalysis, but by now she has inherited Freud's throne. Her access to Freud's letters and manuscripts (wielded with the help of her brother Ernst, as well as the advice of leading analysts) has also given her a special power. In addition, Anna has been, like her father, a therapist to whom other eminent psychoanalysts turn in time of personal trouble;

she not only analyzed people like Robert Waelder, but has also treated the children of prominent analysts.

Although she has kept the issue of lay analysis alive, Anna Freud has not instigated any major quarrels on the scale of those her father once engaged in. She might be repelled by one of Erik Erikson's papers about her father, or thoroughly despise Theodor Reik, yet her feelings[2] did not initiate new public quarrels in a movement grown to over two thousand fully qualified analysts. She nevertheless continued to share the animosity her father had felt toward his defecting pupils. Instead of considering the loss of Adler and Jung a misfortune which left analysis the poorer, in reading Jones's accounts of those early quarrels Anna Freud preferred to revel in what she considered the fierceness of the "resistance" to her father.[3]

She has tended to resent many of the older analysts who had firm ties to her father that did not extend to herself. And different generations of analysts have in fact had different outlooks toward her. In general, those who knew Freud before the end of World War I are less likely to have the same fealty to Anna Freud as those who arrived in the 1920's and 1930's.

Like Freud himself, she has understood the power of tradition; and so she journeyed to the little-known Clark University in Worcester, Massachusetts, to receive an honorary degree, because it had conferred a similar honor on her father half a century earlier. (Subsequently she received the Hillcrest Children Center's Dolly Madison award at the White House in 1965, as well as honorary degrees from Yale, the University of Chicago, and the University of Vienna.) Like her father, she has endorsed favored pupils by writing prefaces to their articles and books, and given exclusive photographs of herself as a sign of personal approval. In her old age she has even come to acquire Freud's characteristic gestures.

Though Anna Freud lacked her father's genius, she inherited some of his gift for language, his clarity of thought and expression, and his ability to speak extemporaneously. Both were single-minded and felt a sense of mission, and both pushed aside everything that threatened to get in their way.

Under the weight of her statecraft, Anna evolved from the shy, gentle girl of her youth into a great lady. A collected edition of her works has been undertaken, and she is quoted, especially by American analysts, in almost a ritualistic manner. Anna Freud possesses less warmth than her father, and she expresses herself verbally in more polished and even flowery language. Despite the effusive sweetness of her style, however, she is capable of becoming the belligerent leader of an embattled movement.

The site of her work has been 20 Maresfield Gardens, in Hampstead, London, the house in which Freud died. The officially designated homes of great men often bear only a casual relation to their importance in the lives of these men. Freud lived there only about a year; his apartment in Vienna has only recently been recognized as a historic site, and until then half of it was rented out for families to live in and another part had become a seamstress' shop. In the meantime Anna Freud has transformed his house at Maresfield Gardens into a shrine in her father's memory.

Her theoretical as well as her clinical contributions have been important. Although she was initially dubious about Heinz Hartmann's concepts, and has been more than skeptical about the writings of her former pupil Erik Erikson, she was one of the earliest, and certainly one of the most influential, forces within orthodox psychoanalysis to stress the defensive capacities of the ego. Freud's early emphasis had been on instinctual drives; in the 1920's he began to describe the psyche's mechanisms of coping, not only with inner dangers but also with threats from the outside. Although Freud and others in psychoanalysis had anticipated her, and in particular Reich's work on character structure antedated her own contribution, nonetheless her most famous book, *The Ego and the Mechanisms of Defence*, presented to her father on his eightieth birthday, systematized and codified what was then known analytically about ego psychology. In it she discussed such phenomena as regression, repression, reaction-formation, isolation, undoing, projection, introjection, turning against the self, denial, and identification with the aggressor—all from the point of view of how a person's ego can resort to such devices in order to endure.

By and large Freud had taken ego psychology for granted. And even when Anna Freud tried to pull together into an elegant form what might be said about the unconscious ego, she included sublimation as one of the mind's defense mechanisms.[4] From today's perspective, a defense is a neurotic mechanism. One would think that a sublimation would in principle be an alternative to neurosis. Yet Anna Freud still retained so much of the early analytic interest in abnormality and pathology that she included sublimation under the heading of a defense.

During World War II, Anna Freud and Dorothy Burlingham operated a nursery for children whose parents could not be with them. These were normal children, and Anna and her friend were confronted, as others before them, with the limitations of earlier psychoanalytic thinking. Once children were separated from their mothers, developmental inhibitions set in and they regressed. Here was an example of the environment having

*Freud and his daughter, Anna, in Paris
on June 13, 1938, on their way to London*

an effect on instinctual life, through the mediation of the children's egos; for once a stable relationship with a surrogate mother had been established by one of the women at the clinic, the superficial signs of symptomatology disappeared and "the children began to develop in leaps and bounds."[5] Anna Freud later concluded that "with the development of good object relationships, aggression became bound and its manifestations reduced to normal quantities."[6] The use of a term such as "object relationships" may sound like a peculiarly cold and unfeeling way of describing intimate human interactions, but the emphasis on "object relations," developed partly at the Tavistock Clinic in London, marked a big step away from the concentration on classical oedipal problems. Thanks to their work during World War II, Anna Freud and Dorothy Burlingham finally concluded, in silent contrast to Freud's own position, that "the infant's emotional relationship to its father begins later in life than that to its mother. . . ."[7]

Anna Freud's interest in ego processes had implications for her view of psychoanalytic technique. She sounded less severe than Freud in his pre-World War I recommendations to future analysts, even though she may only have been articulating what had been the current Viennese clinical practice:

> so far as the patient has a healthy part of his personality, his real relationship to the analyst is never wholly submerged. With due respect to the necessary strictest handling of the transference, I feel still that we should leave room somewhere for the realization that analyst and patient are also two real people, of equal adult status, in a real personal relationship to each other.[8]

In her approach to the treatment of children, Anna Freud, unlike Melanie Klein, rejected exclusive reliance on play as a technique. It was, she held, like other symbolic interpretations of behavior, too rigid for the full variety of a child's mind. Her accounts of the mental activities of small children are masterful, a testimony to the respect for human psychology which Freud's teachings had imparted.

Anna Freud's work stimulated others in clinical psychology to think about those parts of the psyche which are adaptive rather than merely symptomatic. Although her initial approach to the ego had been to focus on its defensive functions, by 1960 her work with children had made her sensitive to "the bewildering variety of pathological, or seemingly pathological manifestations" which appeared to her to "call for new diagnostic categories based not on symptomatology, but on developmental considerations."[9] She increasingly emphasized an understanding of what may be fitting in a child for a given age level, so that it might be possible to distinguish between disturbances that can be considered only passing developmental phases and serious neurotic problems.[10]

In keeping with a major trend in psychoanalysis since Freud's death, Anna Freud's work has tried to broaden the scope of earlier clinical thinking, so that normal psychological functioning could receive its proper share of attention. Even in dealing with aggression, Anna Freud concluded that "the aggressive strivings, if fused in the normal way with the libidinal ones, are socializing influences, rather than the opposite. They provide the initial strength and tenacity with which the infant reaches out for the object world and holds on to it." Although in 1965 she argued that "there is no antithesis between development and defense. . . ." and that "all defense mechanisms serve simultaneously internal drive restrictions and external adaptation, which are merely two sides of the same picture,"[11] there was an undeniable shift of mood, in child analysis, from the 1930's to the 1960's, which can be seen reflected in Anna Freud's approach.

While in the earlier period the personal characteristics of the mother played little role in an understanding of the psychodynamics of the child, it was not long before the untenability of this approach was apparent. Post-Freudian psychoanalysis then put as much emphasis on the rejecting mother as Freud had earlier put on the castrating father. Anna Freud warned that "in the social services a transitional stage has existed, and partly still exists, where all the blame, which in the more distant [prepsychoanalytic] past had been put on the bad children, is now put on the bad mother."[12] She herself, however, relied more than ever on helping the child by encouraging changes in maternal behavior; as she wrote in 1960,

> I refuse to believe that mothers need to change their personalities before they can change the handling of their child . . . in rearing their children mothers are not only guided by instinct and misled by distorting personal influences, but they are to an even larger degree dependent on tradition and public opinion, both of which are open to change.[13]

Whereas the analyst of adults works with the patient's inner world, and therefore is "a firm believer in psychic, as opposed to external reality," "for the analyst of children, on the other hand, all the indications point in the opposite direction, bearing witness to the powerful influence of the environment."[14]

Although she has taken some steps in the direction of neo-Freudian revisionism, Anna Freud remains today one of the most outspoken defenders of psychoanalytic orthodoxy. More rigidly than her father would have, for example, she has argued that "in psychoanalysis the method of therapy is identical with the method of inquiry."[15] But Anna Freud has stuck to Freud's unwillingness to commercialize psychoanalytic ideas, and her integrity in these matters is much like his own. She has also held high the hopes of what analytic therapy can accomplish: "what they [analysts] have to offer is unique, i.e., thorough-going personality changes as compared with more superficial symptomatic cures."[16] She still harks back to the original "revelations of psychoanalysis."[17] And she has been able to prescribe moralistically for an impulsive adult neurotic: "as much pure analysis as his nature could tolerate while the rest would be child analysis, because on account of his quite infantile character he would deserve nothing better."[18]

Despite her residence in London since 1938, Anna Freud has never, any more than Ernest Jones before her, received her due recognition in England. Paradoxically, considering her own feelings about America—similar to those of her father—she has been given much more support and welcome in the United States than anywhere else in the world. One of her special interests has been psychoanalysis and the law, and for some years

*Anna Freud
lecturing in 1934*

she helped conduct a seminar at Yale Law School. In a recent American survey among both psychiatrists and psychoanalysts to determine who was considered the outstanding living practitioner of their crafts, Anna Freud headed the list for both groups of respondents.[19]

6. Helene Deutsch:
The Black Cat Card Club

ANOTHER WOMAN WHO EARNED Anna Freud's jealousy was Helene Deutsch. Eleven years older, Helene Deutsch entered psychoanalysis from within Viennese psychiatry, a world in which Anna Freud had no standing. Anna Freud's earliest memory of Helene Deutsch was of her coming to one of Freud's lectures straight from Wagner-Jauregg's clinic, still in her psychiatrist's white smock.

Helene Deutsch was one of the first female followers of Freud whom he personally analyzed. Born in 1884 in a Polish town (Przemyśl) within the domain of Austro-Hungary, she grew up in an outlying part of the Empire before moving to Vienna to pursue her professional career. Among her close friends she was always known by her Polish diminutive, "Hala." Her command of German was to remain as idiosyncratic as her English in later years in America; yet her limitations in both languages enabled her to achieve a kind of poetic effect.

Wanting at first to become a lawyer like her father, she considered herself a leader in female emancipation. When she chose the path of medicine it was still an exceptional field for a woman. In 1912, just before finally becoming a doctor, Helene married Felix Deutsch, a physician in internal medicine. In late 1917, she gave birth to a son, Martin, and though she had not yet officially entered Freud's circle, she may well have guessed his pleasure at her boy's receiving the same name as his eldest son.[1] (Her husband Felix had belonged to a Zionist organization with Martin Freud.)

It was unusual for a woman to be a psychiatrist then, but they had less to lose professionally in coming to Freud than their male colleagues. The career of a woman in academic psychiatry would be unlikely to get very far, whereas in a new field like psychoanalysis there would be none of the barriers of established medicine. In the spring of 1918 Helene

Deutsch tried to arrange with Freud for an analysis; she had read, in 1911, *The Interpretation of Dreams,* and she had attended his lectures at the University of Vienna and had even gone to meetings of the Vienna Society. With her genuine talents, she was obviously an acquisition for Freud's movement; moreover, her husband was already a *Dozent.* Nevertheless, Freud asked Deutsch what she would do if he referred her elsewhere for an analysis; when she said she would not go he accepted her for the following fall.

The atmosphere at Wagner-Jauregg's clinic was so hostile to Freud that Helene Deutsch felt she had no alternative but to resign her position there, as part of transferring her full allegiance to Freud. Freud wanted his teachings to penetrate Wagner-Jauregg's clinic and yet he believed that no one could serve two gods simultaneously. Angered by his rejection at the clinic, Freud held himself aloof from Viennese psychiatry; but he hoped to change the official position toward his work. During Helene Deutsch's analysis, which began in the fall of 1918 and lasted about a year, there were hostile things being said about Freud at the clinic. In order not to have to repeat remarks about psychoanalysis to Freud in her analysis, Helene Deutsch informed clinic officials that she had begun her analysis with Freud. When once in an analytic hour she referred to the fact that she never produced unpleasant stories about him in her free associations, he simply said: "That is because you are too decent." Freud could be complimentary, and did not resort to the kind of interpretation which a later analyst might have used, that it was because she was so unconsciously hostile that she could not afford to be consciously aggressive toward Freud.

Helene Deutsch had such an immense emotional transference to Freud that she did not resent his twice falling asleep in her analytic sessions; they had such an easy, friendly relationship that they joked about it. (But in 1937 Freud is reported to have denied ever having fallen asleep in an analytic hour.[2]) Once she left her handbag on the couch; when Freud shook hands, as he did before and after every analytic hour, he held on and gazed into her eyes, until she realized that she had committed what Freud regarded as a symptomatic act. To Freud, the forgotten handbag represented a symbolic sexual invitation. Helene Deutsch felt an active, questing element in Freud's behavior toward her. He had a penchant for attractive women, and she responded with all the devotion of an adoring disciple.

Within the next few years Helene Deutsch reached the peak of her relationship with Freud, and she later regarded the first decade after her analysis as the high point of her productivity. She was remembered from

the early 1920's as a Helen of Troy, brilliant and beautiful, Freud's dar-
ling.[3] For young students of psychoanalysis at that time, Berlin seemed
a better place for training than Vienna. Around Freud, the scientific-
minded, like Nunberg, tended to be dull or crusty, whereas the more interesting people, like Stekel, were volatile and unorthodox.

Helene and Felix Deutsch were probably the liveliest in the Viennese
psychoanalytic circle. Her seminars are still recalled as memorable experiences.[4] She was one of the best teachers in psychoanalysis, and her
classes, which tended to be larger than those in Berlin, were true spectacles.
She could listen to a case presentation for hours, and then be able to pull
the threads together, remembering all the details the analyst had reported.
After a full day's analytic practice, she would conduct a seminar until
late in the evening and would always have the stamina and energy to revive
and go on to another case.

Helene Deutsch was able to cultivate a whole younger generation of
analysts in the 1920's. Having already "arrived" herself, it was possible for
her to be a patroness for others. She founded a Saturday-night group,
called the Black Cat Card Club, which met at her house once a week.
Those who came included the Bibrings, the Hartmanns, the Hoffers, the
Krises, and the Waelders, all of them about ten years younger than Helene
Deutsch and destined to be leading orthodox analysts in later years. She had
the established reputation and an "in" with Freud. Although ultimately
she survived more than half of them, in the end she owed much of her
stature to having been a figure in the early professional lives of those
who carried on Freud's school after his death.

Every Saturday night was set aside for dinner and discussions. Ostensibly they gathered to play cards, but while playing they could concentrate
on psychoanalytic issues. Perhaps the most notable aspect of this group
was its exclusion of some of the older analysts, such as Hitschmann and
Federn. Helene Deutsch got along poorly with both of them, partly out
of identification with Freud's view of their capacities. Federn preferred
motherly women to career-oriented types. Hitschmann too resented her,
and later, in his autobiographical notes, accused her of "dictatorship"[5] of
the Boston Psychoanalytic Society and of being responsible for his exclusion from a governing committee there. In Vienna the younger analysts
did not want to meet socially with the old-line psychoanalysts—they felt
Freud was stuck with them because they had supported him so early.

Freud's pleasure with Helene Deutsch did not prevent him from showing skepticism toward at least one of her contributions. At a meeting of the
Society on November 9, 1921, she presented "an observation" drawn from
two of her nephews. The boys were very different types physically, and

the elder was the mother's favorite. He was killed in the war, however, and the mother was grief-stricken; then, according to Helene Deutsch, the younger boy began to change physically, grew rapidly and darkened as well, until he came to resemble his dead brother. It was reported as follows in an account of the proceedings of the Vienna Society:

> Two brothers quite unlike one another, of which the elder dies. Later the younger brother comes to resemble both physically and mentally the dead brother in a quite remarkable manner: he wished to take the elder brother's place in his mother's estimation; this was the clear motive of his metamorphosis.[6]

Freud couched his skepticism in the most tactful way possible: "If it were not Dr. Deutsch who reported this," he remarked, "we would not believe it."[7] He went on to say, however, that it was possible that the younger boy had been shaded from the mother's sunlight by the older brother, but with the removal of the overhanging tree his mother's love had transformed him. It was characteristic of Freud, like his teacher Charcot, to express himself with such a visual image of a psychological process.

Helene Deutsch was an intimate favorite of Freud's for only a few years in the early 1920's, and then her husband seemed to come between her and the master. At the time Freud first contracted cancer in 1923, Felix Deutsch was his personal physician and chose to conceal from him the nature of the malignancy. Freud blamed Felix for not having told him the full truth, and Felix withdrew as Freud's physician.* There was so much anxiety as well as admiration in the atmosphere around Freud that Helene Deutsch felt she needed another analysis. Freud first recommended that she go to Ferenczi in Budapest, but she ruled him out because of the difficulties her son might have with Hungarian; Freud then suggested Sachs, but she decided on Abraham instead. Even though she left her husband in Vienna to go to Berlin largely because of the difficulties that had arisen between him and Freud, the Deutsches scarcely talked of the matter; like the Ranks they had the kind of marriage in which husband and wife did not discuss some of the most sensitive areas of their lives. Helene Deutsch also hoped to learn how the Berlin Psychoanalytic Institute had been set up, so she would know how to organize the Vienna training facilities she was to head.

She was angry with Freud for speaking so persistently about her husband's conduct, and yet at the same time she was furious with her

---

* Cf. below, pp. 491–96.

husband for having caused the distance between her and Freud. (However, she herself was to a degree a participant in her husband's decision.) Both Felix and Helene Deutsch had carefully cherished their relationship with Freud, but it was she who had initiated their involvement in psychoanalysis, and Freud was immensely important to her; then her husband seemed to her to have somehow upset everything. Freud was later reconciled with Felix Deutsch and did what he could for the Deutsches as a couple. When she was in analysis with Abraham he showed her a letter from Freud saying that hers was a marriage that should not be disrupted by analysis.[8] The split between Felix Deutsch and Freud put a great strain on the marriage, though officially Helene was in Berlin as a distinguished guest, someone in Freud's confidence. Helene Deutsch felt that she developed no transference to Abraham and that after her analysis with Freud no other was possible. Freud's specification to Abraham, which virtually amounted to an order, was also taken to heart by Helene Deutsch; the couple remained married until Felix Deutsch's death in 1964.

While Helene Deutsch was being analyzed in Berlin (patients went with her from Vienna for the year 1923–24), her husband was in analysis with Bernfeld in Vienna. Felix Deutsch was very different from his already famous wife. Whereas many in Freud's circle thought she acted like a prima donna and found her difficult to get along with, her husband was considered by all to be sweet and down-to-earth. Though warm and emotional, he could also be autocratic. Felix was more the healer of the two, more willing to exploit his own personality for the sake of a diagnostic discovery or a therapeutic improvement. Helene was more identified with Freud; she could be satisfied with a paper of hers even if it had nothing essentially new in it, as long as it reflected Freud's ideas.

Helene was far more distinguished as a psychoanalyst and was a better writer. Felix had been an internist, known for complicated diagnoses in medicine, but in psychoanalytic circles he was not considered an intellectual, neither a thinker nor a writer. In fact, he lost prestige in the Viennese medical community because of his contact with Freud's group. It was not until he emerged as a leader of the Boston Psychoanalytic Society that he became prominent as an analyst—in the new field of psychosomatic medicine. He lacked his wife's self-control, but his emotional range and elasticity were perhaps greater.

Although Helene Deutsch held herself more distant from Freud after the trouble between him and her husband, she still felt jealous of those who rose in Freud's firmament; and chief among those she disliked was Ruth Brunswick. One bone of contention was Freud's patient the Wolf-Man. In 1919 Freud had terminated Helene Deutsch's analysis, over her

Helene Deutsch in old age

objections, by abruptly announcing that he needed her hour.[9] The Wolf-Man had returned to Vienna seeking help, and Freud told Helene Deutsch that she had had sufficient analysis. Freud had been fascinated by the Wolf-Man, and evidently was not particularly interested in her case, though he valued her as a part of his circle. She had no conscious regrets at the time, and after her analysis there were some compensations for her; she had increased social contact with Freud, and he sent more patients. But in 1923 she had her first depression, over the disturbance in her relationship with Freud.

When in 1926 the Wolf-Man was again in need of treatment, Freud might have made amends to Helene Deutsch if he had sent the Wolf-Man to her; every time he sent her a patient she took it as a demonstration of his affection. But now, by making a gift of this patient to Ruth Brunswick, Freud seemed to have compounded his offense.

Helene Deutsch regarded Ruth Brunswick as a rival for Freud's favor; but while Ruth drew closer and closer to Freud, Helene stood back. Deutsch probably had the better mind of the two women, and a more stable marriage. She could easily accept as a rival someone like Lou Andreas-Salomé, who had had great beauty and famous lovers, or Marie Bonaparte, a royal princess; but she felt disdainful of less eminent women like Ruth Brunswick or Jeanne Lampl-de Groot, who, as members of Freud's court, developed toward him what she regarded as neurotic clinging transferences. It may have been partly with her own quiet seclusion in mind that she later wrote of Freud's pupils:

> While the less gifted expressed their ambivalence in a reactively in-creased dependence and in the over-evaluation of analysis . . . , the more gifted denied this dependence in a more direct but still scientific form and separated themselves from the group in either a noisy and hostile or in a more veiled and passive manner.[10]

She watched from a distance as Ruth Brunswick, not entirely unlike Victor Tausk before her, drew closer to Freud personally. Compared to her husband Helene Deutsch may have been cool and aloof but next to Ruth Brunswick she seemed more the therapist* than the psychological observer.[11] Ruth Brunswick knew that Freud did not appreciate Helene Deutsch's kind of temperamentalism, but her scientific work was so con-siderable that there were grounds for the women's jealousy of each other.

---

* Helene Deutsch remembered being distressed at Nunberg's detachment about a suffering female melancholic at Wagner-Jauregg's clinic. Preoccupied more with theory than clinical reality, Nunberg wondered aloud: "But where is her libido?"

When Deutsch wrote a psychoanalytic article about Don Quixote, Freud was as pleased and delighted as if someone had given him a present; he wanted to know how she had become interested in the subject.[12] But it was Ruth Brunswick who received a ring from Freud, although Helene Deutsch survived her for over twenty-five years as one of the greatest teachers in psychoanalysis.

It was partly because of the hostility of men like Federn and Hitschmann that she felt she should decline Freud's offer of the vice-presidency of the Vienna Society when he retired because of his illness; the post went instead to Federn. Despite her pride and aloofness, she joined in the celebration of Freud's birthdays; she and her husband would send orchids and a telegram on May 6. (The Freud Lectures of the New York Psychoanalytic Society are now given annually on that date.) When their only son went off to school in Switzerland at the age of seventeen, it was considered fitting for him to go with his father to visit Freud beforehand; Freud gave the boy a telescope and wrote something in a book for him.[13] Afterward Freud reported to Helene Deutsch about her son's activities in Switzerland, on the basis of what he had heard during one of his analyses.[14]

Helene Deutsch considered it a matter of personal honor not to join in Ruth Brunswick's kind of active adoration of Freud. Her self-preservative capacities prevented her from becoming as vulnerable as her rival. Even though she dedicated herself to the forwarding of Freud's cause, in her own mind she did not want to be like the others. She could have had much more direct personal contact with Freud in his later years had she so desired.

7. Helene Deutsch:
The Theory of Femininity

HELENE DEUTSCH'S SPECIAL CONTRIBUTION was in the area of female psychology. Freud acknowledged that she, like Ruth Brunswick, was among those female analysts who had been able to discover, through their role as mother substitutes in analytic transferences, the little girl's early identification with her mother. Deutsch, for example, treated the acts of mothering and being mothered as central to the adult female homosexual relationship, and considered female homosexuality a problem which stemmed from an oral pre-oedipal tie to a mother.[1] Freud had earlier regarded female homosexuality as a result of a woman's identification with her father.

Deutsch's career as a psychoanalyst, however, seemed to contradict her ideas of femininity. According to Freud's theories, which she did much to elaborate, the feminine woman clung to and was dependent on her husband, as opposed to the active and independent ideal more recently advocated by Simone de Beauvoir. Partly due to the traditional prominence of women in Jewish families, but also because of the special intuitive talents of women as psychologists, Helene Deutsch achieved a self-sufficiency in her professional life which tended to belie her conception of womanliness.

Because of the influence of her two-volume study, *The Psychology of Women,* originally published in 1944 and 1945 and subsequently reprinted many times (it was also translated into eight languages and appeared in a dozen countries), her ideas have been widely criticized. To many, her work seemed a rationalization of the social position of women in the past, and Women's Liberation writers have taken her to task.*[2] Her aim was to persuade people to "give up the illusion of the equivalence of the sexual act for the two sexes";[3] some of the specifics of her argument have understandably annoyed feminist critics. For instance, she seemed to depreciate what women had already accomplished: "Many intellectual women are actually only fugitives, with impoverished emotions . . . as a rule such women are intellectualizing rather than intellectual."[4]

Her convictions were in keeping with Freud's approach. He had maintained that "libido is invariably and necessarily of a masculine nature, whether it occurs in men or in women and irrespectively of whether its object is a man or a woman."[5] Freud later modified this position by saying that "there is only one libido, which serves both the masculine and the feminine sexual functions. To it itself we cannot assign any sex. . . ." But then he went on to withdraw his apparent retraction: "Nevertheless the juxtaposition 'feminine libido' is without any justification."[6]

Freud's attitudes toward women have to be evaluated in the light of his own times. He extended himself to the leading women in his movement. Whereas others, such as Sadger, were opposed to admitting women to the Vienna Society, Freud is reported to have said that he "would take

---

* Can the success of women analysts (they are said to be typically far more in demand than their male colleagues) be traced to the nature of our sexually reactionary society, which has acculturated women to be sensitive to emotional nuances, and men to the external world of power?

it as gross inconsistency . . . to exclude women in principle."⁷ He was an old-fashioned man who, though he might believe women belonged in the home, also would honor them in his profession; they possessed finer feelings than men, but as weaker creatures they were in need of protection.

Freud admired loyalty in women, and although he relished stories about unfaithful women he would not have tolerated them in his own family. He could not conceive of a woman as a competitor. He had great success in keeping women in a dependent relationship to him, and he admired his female pupils. Yet in terms of the standards of that era these women tended to be considerably emancipated.

The kind of male narcissism that can be found in Freud's theories about women can also be seen in the writings of other early analysts. Western culture at the turn of the twentieth century generally looked down on women, who were supposed to exist primarily for the sake of gratifying a man's needs, bearing his children, and running his house. In such a milieu it was easy to divorce sex from love. Some psychoanalysts, however—in particular, Karen Horney and Clara Thompson—gradually took a different line from Freud's; they tried to differentiate biological givens from socially sanctioned patterns of behavior. To someone like Jones, and almost certainly to Freud as well, this seemed to be replacing psychoanalysis with a pseudo-sociology.⁸

Freud's ideas became so influential that he has had to bear a great deal of the feminist criticism of our own day. His collection of *Schadchen* (a Jewish marriage broker) stories* reflected the highly dependent social position of the traditional Jewish woman. Although toward the end of his life Freud acknowledged that "we must beware . . . of underestimating the influence of social customs, which . . . force women into passive situations,"¹⁰ in practice he appears to have consistently regarded women

---

* Here are two examples: "The *Schadchen* was defending the girl he had proposed against the young man's protests. 'I don't care for the mother-in-law,' said the latter. 'She's a disagreeable, stupid person.'—'But after all you're not marrying the mother-in-law. What you want is her daughter.' 'Yes, but she's not young any longer, and she's not precisely a beauty.'—'No matter. If she's neither young nor beautiful she'll be all the more faithful to you.'—'And she hasn't much money.' 'Who's talking about money? Are you marrying money then? After all it's a wife that you want.'—'But she's got a hunch-back too.'—'Well, what *do* you want? Isn't she to have a single fault?' "

"The bridegroom was most disagreeably surprised when the bride was introduced to him, and drew the broker on one side and whispered his remonstrances: 'Why have you brought me here?' he asked reproachfully. 'She's ugly and old, she squints and has bad teeth and bleary eyes . . .'—'You needn't lower your voice,' interrupted the broker, 'she's deaf as well.' "⁹

as less sexual than men. He believed that a married woman needs sex for only twenty years.[11] (Perhaps this was based on his experience with his wife, Martha.)

A woman's sexual activity was, Freud held, "essentially of a passive nature," and in general for him "the active was the same as masculine, while passive was the same as feminine."[12] Knowing Freud's personal feelings of distaste for weakness and passivity, it is hard not to find his view of women a patronizing one. He later qualified his stand[13] but he continued to conceive of a woman as a defective man. Penis envy was for him an essential constituent of female psychology, as if a vagina were somehow unsatisfactory; he wrote about penis envy as the feminine equivalent of the man's fear of damage to his genitals, the "castration complex."[14] The decisive developmental step supposedly occurs "when the little girl discovers her own deficiency . . . from seeing a male genital. . . ."[15] Freud reduced the woman's reproductive function to a search for a child as a compensation for a missing penis.

Women possessed a "subtler understanding of unconscious mental processes" and were victims of civilization's tendency to stultify: he noted "all the artificial retarding and stunting of the female sexual instinct."[16] Freud held that women were more predisposed to neurosis than men, especially to hysteria.[17] He considered women generally as intellectually inferior beings;[18] lacking the full libido of a man, they had less energy to sublimate:

> The fact that women must be regarded as having little sense of justice is no doubt related to the predominance of envy in their mental life; for the demand for justice is a modification of envy and lays down the condition subject to which one can put envy aside. We also regard women as weaker in their social instincts and as having less capacity for sublimating their instincts than men.[19]

He thought that "women have made few contributions to the discoveries and inventions in the history of civilization. . . ."[20] Freud even wrote that "women give vent to or appreciate humor so much more rarely than men."[21]

Freud said that a man's love for a woman, what he called "sexual over-evaluation," "only emerges in full force in relation to a woman who holds herself back and who denies her sexuality."[22] There was less ethical development in women: "their superego is never so inexorable, so impersonal, so independent of its emotional origins as we require it to be in men."[23] Freud could write of children that they "behave in the same kind

of way as an average uncultivated woman in whom the same polymorphously perverse disposition persists."[24] His underlying point of view was
that "woman is a breed apart and inferior to man."[25] One source of his
hatred of America was that women were less subservient there, and Freud
did not like the shift away from the Old World conception of the relation
between the sexes. He was one of the last defenders of the sexual double
standard. (We should remember that contraceptive devices were not so
available in his day.)

Freud faced similar stumbling blocks in his quest for a "solution" to
the "problems" of music, religion, and femininity, since in his mind they
were all allied to the primitive and the irrational. He once freely admitted
that "the female side" of a problem was "extraordinarily obscure to me";
he considered that the erotic life of women, "partly owing to the stunting
effect of civilized conditions and partly owing to their conventional secretiveness and insincerity . . . is still veiled in an impenetrable obscurity."[26]
He seemed to be complaining[27] about the inaccessibility of femininity to
his research; for Freud "the sexual life of adult women" remained "a 'dark
continent' for psychology," a "riddle" he had not solved.[28] In 1932 he
concluded one of his few essays on femininity with the greatest caution:

> That is all I had to say about femininity. It is certainly incomplete and
> fragmentary and does not always sound friendly. But do not forget
> that I have only been describing women in so far as their nature is
> determined by their sexual function. It is true that that influence ex-
> tends very far; but we do not overlook the fact that an individual
> woman may be a human being in other respects as well. If you want
> to know more about femininity, enquire from your own experiences
> of life, or turn to the poets, or wait until science can give you deeper
> and more coherent information.[29]

Freud tended to regard himself as independent and self-sufficient and
also regretted outside influences on him; on the other hand, he could
sometimes also resent lack of direction, as in his criticism of his father.
But as resistant as he was to innovations from his male pupils, Freud was
influenced by his women disciples; it was thus that he came to understand
"the prehistory of the Oedipus complex," and to acknowledge the mother
as the original love object for women as well as men.[30] A woman's
tendency to neurosis could then be explained by the fact that she had to
turn from her mother to her father in order to establish an Oedipus
complex.

"With the change to femininity," Freud rather puritanically thought, "the clitoris should wholly or in part hand over its sensitivity, and at the same time its importance, to the vagina. This would be one of the two tasks which a woman has to perform in the course of her development. . . ."*[31] Recent research by Masters and Johnson has denied the existence of the hypothesized vaginal orgasm; but Freud's downgrading of sensations in the clitoris in his preference for the concept of vaginal orgasm emphasized a woman's unique dependence on the man. As Helene Deutsch put it, "the awakening of the vagina to full sexual functioning is entirely dependent upon the man's activity. . . ."[33]

It was through the "phase of their [women's] pre-Oedipus attachment to their mother"[34] that Freud hoped to unravel the mystery of femininity. The prototype was always masculine: "the difference between the sexual development of males and females . . . corresponds to the difference between a castration that has been carried out and one that merely has been threatened."[35] Whereas a boy renounces his oedipal striving under a threat, "in women the Oedipus complex is the end-result of a fairly lengthy development. It is not destroyed, but created, by the influence of castration. . . ."[36] Girls "hold their mother responsible for their lack of a penis and do not forgive her for their being thus put at a disadvantage," and so turn to their father instead.[37] Thanks to his female disciples Freud acknowledged that

> it would seem as though we must retract the universality of the thesis that the Oedipus complex is the nucleus of the neuroses. But . . . we can extend the content of the Oedipus complex to include all the child's relations to both parents; . . . we can take due account of our new findings by saying the female only reaches the normal positive Oedipus situation after she has surmounted a period before it that is governed by the negative complex.[38]

Freud's theories about women can be taken as a defense against his submissiveness toward them. Much of his anxiety can be traced to his inner dependency on his mother, which he transferred not only to Martha but to some of his women pupils as well. "If Freud had not resented, as a husband, the absence of a more mature solace than that which the mother brings to her son, he would never been able to speak of women as he did

---

* Theodor Reik expressed this sort of puritanism in connection with men: "When a man has his orgasm, where is the sensation? I ask them, in the second or third interview. On the tip of the penis or near the testicles? It should be at the tip."[32]

in old age."[39] Freud's horror and fear of the female genitalia can be read in his account of his dream life. Freud saw women as by nature voracious. As he once said to Marie Bonaparte, "the great question that has never been answered and which I have not yet been able to answer, despite my thirty years of research into the feminine soul, is 'What does a woman want?' "[40] Freud thought that women had succeeded in not betraying their secret, which may have been a way of expressing his anxiety about them.

He handled his own femininity at a distance; in some of his writing he drew clear-cut divisions between men and women, which we now see as culturally conditioned rather than as eternal psychobiological truths. In general, Freud feared passivity too much. He hated to lose control, and, for example, refrained from using whiskey or aspirin. At the same time, in his clinical practice Freud could link femininity and creativity; as he said to one highly artistic male patient, "You are so feminine you can't let it out." And Freud intended the interpretation as a compliment.

In Helene Deutsch's last analytic hour with Freud, he encouraged her to retain her identification with her father, which Freud regarded as beneficial to her. To attribute her professionalism to such an identification was more supportive than to see it in terms of bisexuality or envy. Even in her extreme old age she still regarded her mother as a terrible woman.[41] (Despite later sophistication, one suspects that Freud and the early analysts thought of the Oedipus complex in a woman as simply love for her father and hatred for her mother.) She was the youngest of four children, but had been born almost ten years after her next-oldest sibling; so as her father's youngest and third daughter, she was like an only child, the apple of his eye.

Deutsch survived so many other pioneers in psychoanalysis that her identification with Freud led her to view herself as "Freud's ghost." She tried to identify with the spirit of Freud's teachings rather than with psychoanalysis as a bureaucratic movement. In her later years she became skeptical of the therapeutic efficacy of prolonged psychoanalytic treatment; she was disappointed in psychoanalysis as therapy since it too often seemed to serve regressive needs in patients.[42] Some of her best analyses seemed to yield the worst therapeutic results, and some of her best therapeutic changes followed her worst analyses. She concluded, as had Freud earlier in connection with hypnotic technique, that the depth of analysis had little to do with its therapeutic effect. Despite recent trends in psychoanalytic theory, she disliked the emphasis on ego psychology and was inclined to deny the existence of Hartmann's conflict-free spheres.[43]

In spite of her excellent personal relationship with Freud, the issue of priorities had once arisen between them. In the mid-1920's she had sent an article for publication, and then in his office they discussed her recent work on female psychology. Her essay touched on a special developmental problem of little girls—their having to detach their libido from the primary object (the mother) in order to reach a heterosexual choice of a loved one. Freud explained that he had had some of these thoughts himself, before having read her paper, which was scheduled to appear before one of his own.[44] She regarded her failure to insist that she had arrived at her ideas independently as an abdication.

She was sorely disappointed when, in 1925, Anna Freud read her father's paper "Some Psychical Consequences of the Anatomical Distinction Between the Sexes" and there was no mention of any of her prior work.[45] Her paper had appeared on schedule, and she attributed it to Anna Freud's jealousy that there was no reference to her.[46] In the published version of Freud's paper, however, a concluding paragraph, apparently not part of Anna Freud's presentation, acknowledged the work of others in this area. Knowing Freud's earlier anxiety that others might take from him without acknowledgment, one can see how muted the great battles had now become:

> In the valuable and comprehensive studies on the masculinity and castration complexes in women by Abraham (1921), Horney (1923) and Helene Deutsch (1925) there is much that touches closely on what I have written but nothing that coincides with it completely, so that here again I feel justified in publishing this paper. [47]

It is hard to know how realistic Helene Deutsch's resentment against Freud was, and it may well be that her reproach against Anna Freud was unjustified, since Freud's last paragraph might not have been written when she presented his paper to the Congress. Deutsch did not like being cited with two others, although she respected them both as at least her equals. (She also resented being cited by Freud in tandem with Jeanne Lampl-de Groot and Ruth Mack Brunswick.[48]) The incident was so emotionally charged that she suspected that even in citing a monograph of hers he had ignored her earlier contribution which he had discussed in his office.[49] Other pupils of Freud's last years, such as Edoardo Weiss, felt that Freud had lifted concepts from them without acknowledgment.[50]

Yet these pupils were so close to Freud that it was all too easy for them to confuse their ideas with his. In an article published after Freud's death, Helene Deutsch concluded with an "absolutely true anecdote" about the psychology of surgery:

> One early summer morning many years ago, the inhabitants of a small German university town . . . made the horrifying discovery that all the dogs which had been running loose during the night in a certain part of the city had lost their tails. They learned that the medical students had attended a drinking bout that night and that when they left the party one young man had had the highly humorous inspiration to cut off the tails of the dogs. Later he became one of the most famous surgeons in the world.[51]

Yet she had forgotten that this anecdote had been used by Freud at a small gathering of his students, in order to illustrate the concept of sublimation.[52] (Heine too had told this same tale, which presumably Freud also had repressed; Freud reported the story as one he had heard as a child.)

Enjoying a full career as a psychiatrist and psychoanalyst, Helene Deutsch remained passive and receptive toward Freud and his concepts. When Germaine Greer summarized Deutsch's view that a woman's "significance can only be conferred by the presence of a man at her side, one on whom she absolutely depends,"[53] she did not realize that Deutsch's model of how a woman fulfills herself was her relation, not to her husband, but to Freud. As Deutsch put it:

> The narcissistic prerequisite of this identification is psychologic affinity, the similarity of the egos. To the woman falls the larger share of the work of adjustment: she leaves the initiative to the man and out of her own need renounces originality, experiencing her own self through identification. Some of these women need to overestimate their objects, and their narcissistic method of making the man happy can be expressed in the formula, "He is wonderful and I am a part of him."
>
> These women are not only ideal life companions for men; if they possess the feminine quality of intuition to a great degree, they are ideal collaborators who often inspire their men and are themselves happiest in this role. They seem to be easily influenceable, and adapt themselves to their companions and understand them. They are the loveliest and most unaggressive of helpmates and they want to remain in that role; they do not insist on their own rights—quite the contrary. They are easy to handle in every way—if one only loves them . . .

If gifted in any direction, they preserve the capacity for being original and productive, but without entering into competitive struggles. They are always willing to renounce their own achievements without feeling they are sacrificing anything and they rejoice in the achievements of their companions, which they have often inspired. They have an extraordinary need of support when engaged in any *activity directed outward*, but are absolutely independent in such thinking and feeling as relate to their inner life, that is to say, in their *activity directed inward*. Their capacity for identification is not an expression of inner poverty, but of inner wealth.*[54]

When Freud went to a concert Helene Deutsch went too, but she sat with her husband and apart from the women who flocked around the Professor. She did not so identify with Freud that she could not use her own judgment. Once a case of epilepsy was referred to her, and Freud feared that his enemies would charge that psychoanalysis claimed to cure more than the neurotic side of this affliction; Helene Deutsch listened to what Freud had to say about it, but she decided to take the case. Her creative period coincided with the time of her closest contact with Freud, so one can assume that his presence had a catalytic effect on her work.

When she was depressed over her relationship with Freud, after his falling out with her husband, her second analyst, Abraham, wrote her in 1924 that she was exaggerating Freud's rejection out of her feminine masochistic feelings toward her father; he advised her to be more active toward Freud, who was then in the process of losing Otto Rank and therefore would have, in the terminology of that day, a surplus of libido for new objects in his life. Although she could never get over the trauma of the misunderstanding with Freud over his cancer, she could rival Freud's capacity for hard work. Starting at seven in the morning, she saw eleven or twelve patients a day in Vienna, six days a week. An analyst could hope to see relatively few cases in a lifetime, and therefore needed variety; and it was also not then clear that psychoanalysis would endure, so cases had to be taken as they came.

At the end of 1924 Helene Deutsch became Director of the Training Institute of the Vienna Psychoanalytic Society. She was not so much Freud's personal choice as she was the Society's. She communicated with Freud mainly by letter, and never by telephone; there would be interviews

---

* One of her best-known clinical contributions had to do with the vicissitudes of identification in "as-if" personalities and imposters.[55]

to arrange about candidates and patients. She functioned for ten years in her official capacity without needing any bureaucratic backstopping. When she came to the United States in 1934 her successors wrote to her from Vienna because they could not find the records; but there had never been any. Her reputation in Vienna made her an obvious training analyst for Americans when they arrived; in the view of many she was the very best, assuming one could not get Freud himself.

In 1930 she traveled to America on a grant to attend a conference on mental hygiene. Freud gave her money beforehand to buy a present for Brill as a gift from himself; she bought a piece of silver, realizing that such a secondhand present meant that Brill was really no special favorite of Freud's. She traveled first-class, and when she arrived in the United States, she received a Hollywood-like impression of American life. Wittels placed an article about her in a newspaper, describing her, she recalled, as a tall, blonde German beauty (she was short, chestnut-haired, and Polish-Jewish), a representative from Freud's court. She took back to Vienna two boxes of cigars, one for her husband and the other for Freud; when one of them was stolen she was faced with a dilemma, but her husband told her to give the remaining box to Freud.

By the 1930's two-thirds of her patients in Vienna were American. Freud's pupils in Vienna were tempted to emigrate to the United States, for political safety as well as economic security. In 1934 she was invited to Boston by Stanley Cobb, who was interested in psychosomatic medicine. In the fall of 1934 she arrived in Cambridge, Massachusetts, with a great entourage of patients. From across the Atlantic she could see the Nazi threat more clearly, and early in 1935 she persuaded her husband to join her. Like other incoming physicians, Helene Deutsch had to take her medical examinations again; because of her work on women she had kept up an interest in endocrinology, but it took two years' preparation to pass the tests.

Before finally deciding to leave Vienna, Helene Deutsch had consulted with Freud. Felix Deutsch left the decision up to her, even though he preferred that she stay, since there was to be an opening for him as the head of an important medical clinic. Freud did not want her to go. But he would not put the case for her staying in terms of his personal needs, which was the kind of appeal she was looking for. Instead he argued on professional grounds, claiming that the psychoanalytic community in Vienna would suffer from her loss. Although to her it seemed an order that she not go to America, she left Freud's office hurt and more determined than ever to emigrate.[56]

8. Melanie Klein: "The English School"

MELANIE KLEIN (1882–1960), who was trained in Budapest and Berlin before moving to England, had only a slight personal relationship with Freud, yet her ideas were a challenge to his daughter's work on children and have played a notable role in psychoanalytic circles, especially in England and South America. Melanie Klein was one of those creative persons whom a young and unrecognized movement is capable of bringing to prominence. Without academic credentials or scientific training, she added her special stamp to the psychoanalytic thinking of her day.

Klein's main contribution, like that of many other post-Freudian psychologists, was to emphasize the importance of pre-oedipal layers of personality development. Ruth Brunswick had tried, under Freud's personal direction, to formulate the early role of the mother, as had Carl Jung and Otto Rank in defiance of Freud. Harry Stack Sullivan, and in our own time Donald Winnicott and Erik H. Erikson, have also illuminated the child's more archaic ties to the mother.

As a man of the nineteenth century, Freud was not alone in neglecting the mother's nurturing role in child development. John Stuart Mill included no mention of his mother in his *Autobiography*, and Samuel Butler's *The Way of All Flesh* was similarly obsessed with the son's relation to his father. In the nineteenth century, with few exceptions, mothers were not considered fit subjects for novelists. Mothering was not deemed relevant psychoanalytically until the 1920's, and in view of the recent emphasis in this direction it is easy to forget that it was not always an issue of substance to psychoanalysts.

As a result of their more intensive investigation of motherhood, analysts have come to appreciate the importance of preverbal communication. The earliest stages of the child's contact with its mother, or mother substitute, do not involve words, and in adult life nonverbal means of communication play an important, if not always obvious, role. Freud himself emphasized the power of words to free us from what we have not understood, but therapists since his time have been more sensitive to the limitations of the rationalism implicit in his approach.

An important therapeutic task may be to confirm and support talents and capacities already possessed by the patient. The experience of a patient who was in analysis with both Freud and Melanie Klein illustrates the difference in their approaches. This patient said that Freud's analysis had changed the shape of her life, and that years afterward his interpretations sunk in and finally made sense; it was Freud's courage to speak out that impressed her. In contrast to Freud's sharp intelligence, Melanie Klein's was not so stupefying; her particular interpretations were nothing special, and yet in a flexible way she was always helpful. Klein's analysis succeeded in giving the patient more of a sense of being what all along she had known herself to be but had lacked the strength to fulfill.

Melanie Klein also did a good deal to expose Freud's idealizations of women, which ignored their realistic roles as mothers. Freud, who felt safer with women than with men, displayed nineteenth-century gallantry toward women. But this attitude represented also an implicit devaluation of them, in that it obscured the extent to which men and women can be equals. To describe the mother-son tie in as idealistic terms as Freud did is simultaneously to deny a woman the right to have full sexual gratification with her husband.

In her time most of Klein's views met with opposition, and fierce battles over her concepts raged within British psychoanalysis. But however ambitious she may have felt as a critic of more orthodox psychoanalytic ways of thought, she always fitted her ideas within Freud's framework. Instead of saying that human beings were beset by more problems than genital or even oedipal ones—a piece of common sense that the rebels against Freud considered a great discovery—Klein (like Ruth Brunswick) phrased her emphasis on earlier and more primitive stages in terms of precursors of the Oedipus complex.

Melanie Klein seemed intent on being more royal than the king, and said that the Oedipus complex begins to build up in the small child at the age of six months, as a result of the projection of infantile fantasies of rage and aggression. While her emphasis on preverbal fantasies in children has been generally acknowledged as valid, her dating of processes in early infancy has been criticized as being incapable of confirmation. She held not only that Freud's tripartite distinction of the psychic apparatus into ego, id, and superego was valid but also that each of these agencies of the mind was distinct almost from the very beginning of life. She took Freud's concept of the death instinct literally, and claimed to follow its development from

Melanie Klein

infancy onward. Her postulation of inborn emotions in a child, such as
envy, seemed to some a modernized version of original sin.

Although she is said not to have breast-fed her children, in her stress
on the neglected importance of the mothering functions the breast assumed
almost metaphysical significance. Whereas Ernest Jones was once so
chauvinistic as to maintain that "there are probably more symbols of the
male organ itself than all other symbols put together,"[1] Melanie Klein
pointed out the importance in men of breast envy, in addition to castration fear. Freud would not have acknowledged the importance in child
psychology of either envy of the mother or hostile aggression toward her,
but Klein drew early attention to the role of childish destructive impulses
and the various defenses against them.

In contrast to Anna Freud's view of child analysis, Klein believed that
no alteration in technique was necessary to establish the analytic situation
with a small child. The dispute between Anna Freud and Melanie Klein
dated from 1927, when they both delivered papers at the Innsbruck
Congress on their different ways of treating children. Klein was the more
outspoken and self-righteous, puristically applying the same technique to
both children and adults. For her, play material was an exact equivalent of
verbal free associations in an adult's analysis, and the child analyst could
boldly make deep interpretations of psychic life. When she once expressed
her hope that "child analysis will become as much a part of every person's
upbringing as school education is now,"[2] she was carrying forward a
millennial strain within Freud's system of thought. In 1930 she went so
far as to argue that "one of the chief tasks of the children's analyst is to
discover and cure psychosis in children."[3] For a time Melanie Klein advocated universal child analysis, in contrast to the more typical Viennese
analytic view that not every child needed one. But plenty of analysts sent
their children for treatment.

Melanie Klein's approach may have been in some ways more therapeutically supportive than the classical Freudian one, yet she held that
everything in a personality should be subjected to analysis. Reassurance,
she thought, can also be cruel, and she proposed that the analyst find a
patient's anxieties and go after them with interpretations. She emphasized
the extent of childhood suffering, whereas Freud tended to look on human
existence with more stoicism. He took a more medical view of analysis,
and would be willing to leave certain defenses uninterpreted, as long as
the patient could reach a tolerable compromise with himself. Klein tried to
help a person face all his anxieties, leaving nothing untouched, even the
most primitive kind of problems.

Followers of Melanie Klein in England speak of analyses lasting ten years, without questioning what could ever therapeutically justify such a massive intervention in another human being's life.[4] But once the truth becomes its own justification, and research the goal of analytic technique, the foundations are laid for the kind of moralism that led many early analysts to look down on "lesser" forms of psychotherapy.

Klein's stress on the role of inner fantasies was only an extension of Freud's own position; but, for her, unconscious fantasies ("internal objects") became the crux of human life, both normal as well as pathological.* Regression in the course of therapy becomes then not a danger signal but a sign of the deepening of an analysis.[6] Whereas the trend within American psychoanalysis has been toward emphasizing the ego and the healthy-minded aspects of Freud's work, in England Klein was in tune with the characteristically British sensitivity to the role of primitive impulses in life. While the view of normality in American psychoanalytic circles now hinges on Heinz Hartmann's concept of the ability of the "autonomous" ego to resist regressions, in England the Kleinians have emphasized the degree to which the normal developmental process is tied to psychotic layers. Klein's work was relatively uncontroversial as long as she confined herself to children, but in the 1930's she became more interested in adult psychology and even psychoses. As a nonmedical analyst, she might be thought by some to be unqualified to discuss psychotics, but, though she did not treat them, she thought her concepts had implications for how their behavior could be understood.

Freud himself abhorred the direction Melanie Klein took. Once again, as with Rank's concept of the trauma of birth, her views seemed a caricature of his ideas, except this time occasioned by hostility not to him but to Anna. Although Freud once referred to "child analysis as an excellent method of prophylaxis," he grew skeptical of the prophylactic power of analysis.[7] However, Freud was moderate in his public pronouncements about Melanie Klein. He mentioned in print her contributions together with those of Anna, and when he elaborated his concept of aggression he found himself benefiting from her work; in particular, Freud appreciated the idea that the child's superego may reflect its own projected aggressive fantasies as well as actual parental behavior.[8] (It has been said that "when later in his life Freud discussed the reasons which had led him for years to overlook the importance of aggressive impulses in man, he was inclined to make his own unconscious tendencies responsible for this time lag."[9])

---

* "In his description of archetypes and the collective unconscious, Jung may be said to have anticipated the point of view of those psychoanalysts who write in terms of an inner world of 'internal objects.' "[5]

But basically Freud's attitude toward Melanie Klein was that her ideas were "unintelligible," like the other deviations in psychoanalysis.[10] Freud remarked that this was the first time that psychoanalysis was able to hold such a deviation within the movement.[11]

Like Anna Freud, Melanie Klein was trained as a nursery-school teacher; unhappily married and later divorced from her husband, she was first analyzed by Ferenczi in Budapest and later by Abraham in Berlin. Though Abraham is said to have been fascinated by her ideas, she felt isolated as a child analyst in Berlin; in addition, she could not seem to get through to Freud in Vienna. Alix Strachey, then in analysis with Abraham in Berlin, wrote about Melanie Klein to her husband James, who in turn spoke to Jones.

After Abraham died, Melanie Klein accepted Jones's invitation to lecture in London, and in 1926 decided to settle there. Jones had been moved by two considerations, one public and the other private. He wanted to improve the intellectual quality of the London psychoanalytic group, and "Mrs. Klein," as she became known, seemed likely to enhance the prestige of the London Society; she did succeed in setting up a school of child analysis to rival that of Anna Freud in Vienna. At the same time Mrs. Klein was known for her intuition—one of her colleagues admiringly remarked that she would have made a good medium—and Jones wanted to import a child analyst to help his own children.*

Freud thought that Anna was being attacked by Mrs. Klein's supporters, and to a certain extent this was true. The Kleinian position was defended not only by a respectable group of psychoanalysts but also by distinguished academicians. Jones recounted Freud's "complaining strongly about a public campaign I was supposed to be conducting in England against his daughter Anna, and perhaps therefore against himself."[12] To Jones, it seemed that Anna Freud could take the initiative in attacking Melanie Klein.[13] Because of Jones's relation to Mrs. Klein, for a time the whole Freud family turned against him. The best Freud could say for Mrs. Klein to Jones was that child analysis was an alien field to him:

> I do not estimate our theoretical differences of opinion as slight, but as long as there is no bad feeling behind them they can have no troublesome results. . . . Melanie Klein and her daughter erred . . . toward Anna. It is true I am of opinion [*sic*] that your Society has followed Frau Klein on a wrong path, but the sphere from which she

---

* In the British Psychoanalytic Institute in London there is a box marked as containing the toys used in the first child analysis in England.

has drawn her observations is foreign to me so that I have no right to any fixed conviction.[14]

The Viennese and British Societies exchanged lecturers in the 1930's, so that the Kleinian point of view could be presented to the Viennese and the Viennese criticism to the English. Had it not been for the war and the emigration of Viennese analysts to England, it is possible that the British Society might have become isolated enough to be openly schismatic. When the Nazis took over Austria, and Jones and Freud had to decide which Viennese analysts to escort to England, it was clear that the strength of the Kleinian opinion would preclude, for instance, Robert Waelder, the Viennese exchange lecturer on Klein, from being invited to London permanently.[15]

The 1930's had been an exciting and productive period for the British psychoanalysts, but the coming of Freud and his retinue virtually ended it. Anna Freud's appearance on the English scene may have forced Melanie Klein to systematize her ideas. The more traditional Freudians viewed Klein's emphasis on the pre-genital as a flight from the Oedipus complex, like that of earlier dissidents in psychoanalysis. It is hard to say whether or not Anna Freud was really such a threat to Melanie Klein; but to the degree that Mrs. Klein viewed her own work as a major change in psychoanalysis, she could anticipate the reproaches of the orthodox newcomers. The European refugees felt that they had come to a provincial group, whereas the English in the 1930's considered London the center of psychoanalytic creativity; it had the largest Society apart from those of Berlin and Vienna.

After 1938 Melanie Klein shrank back from a free and open discussion of ideas and began to set up her own system with her own followers. Then Edward Glover proceeded to live up to Mrs. Klein's worst expectations, as he publicly attacked her concepts. Glover, for years Jones's second in command, was a good fighter. Jones would send him to professional and public meetings which he could not attend himself. When Jones retired to the country during World War II, Glover was left in charge of the Society. At first he had been interested in Klein's ideas but later came to consider them a heresy; he felt that the British Society's sense of inferiority had helped account for its receptivity to the Kleinian influence, and he feared that the power of transferences built up in training analyses would extend her mistakes far into the future. In an article written after the battle was over, one can hear the thunder of psychoanalytic name-calling:

The Klein group follows Rank in attributing mental development, and all variations in mental disorder, to a traumatic situation occurring, not, it is true, at birth, but shortly after birth; it follows Jung in attributing dynamic and developmental power to archaic phantasies.[16]

(Glover wrote a combative book against Jung, yet was independent enough from orthodoxy also to write a critical essay on Hartmann.)

Whatever Mrs. Klein's weaknesses as a theorist, she had considerable talents as an intuitive therapist; but her severest critics claimed that she— a beautiful regal woman—was too dependent on being idealized and that she ignored the family dynamics of the children she treated. To be primarily interested in getting patients better is not the same as being a scientist, and a public confrontation with the more traditional Freudians showed her at her weakest, for she had to conceptualize what at best was a psychological green thumb. Original and creative, Melanie Klein was not a good expositor of her own ideas. After she became a success in London she could be, in contrast to her earlier modest bearing, very domineering, and she came to believe in every word she had written.

Edward Glover, however, might have been thought the last person to lead an onslaught on Mrs. Klein. Aside from his earlier interest in her work, he was personally mild-mannered. Regarding himself as an intellectual grandson of Freud's, Glover was a clear thinker and a fine writer; no one could have predicted that he would be the instrument in an attempt to break up the British Society.

A key figure was Klein's daughter, Melitta Schmideberg. Earlier she had sided with her mother against Anna Freud in a manner Freud considered distasteful. In 1934 a brother had died in a mountaineering accident which, according to her mother's way of thinking, was an expression of a suicidal wish. Melitta Schmideberg was herself a physician and an analyst (trained first in Berlin and then analyzed by Ella Sharpe in England), and also married to an analyst. She turned against her mother while in treatment with Edward Glover. Like other children of divorced parents, she had gone with her mother but carried along resentments nonetheless. Presumably Glover saw how she had been damaged and meant to do his best for her. From a personal point of view she had scores to settle with her mother, and with Glover's support she had public grounds for doing so. Glover had silently chafed for years as Jones's second in command, and now felt that with Anna Freud and her colleagues in England he would have the support to finally expose Melanie Klein's heresy. For Glover had convinced himself, probably with Melitta Schmideberg's help, that Klein was a deviationist like Adler and Jung.

Mother and daughter criticized each other in public with the aid of their respective allies. To these early analysts ideas were really important, and for them personal salvation was ineluctably linked to intellectual commitments. That the presiding officer, Glover, was a partisan created difficulty for the peacemakers. Jones was rather on Mrs. Klein's side, and he thought that Anna Freud seemed her irreconcilable enemy.[17] The traditional Freudians refused to accept the focus in Mrs. Klein's work on anxieties connected with pre-genital drives. Klein personally suffered terribly under the attack, and in particular from her daughter's behavior. Feeling misunderstood, Melanie Klein could be angry and cruel. In later years her daughter grew alienated from the psychoanalysis for whose sake she had publicly crossed her mother. It was no wonder that Mrs. Klein developed an increasing need in her writings to justify the mother and accuse the child. But she immensely admired pupils of hers, such as John Rickman and Herbert Rosenfeld.

Klein's supporters had formed a distinct group before World War II, but the divisions among British analysts dissipated when the war scattered many members of the Society. Glover then presided over a temporarily

*Edward Glover—
caricature drawn at
the Salzburg Congress
in 1924*

"purified" Society, and although he later claimed to have opposed Melanie Klein as early as 1928–31, it was only as analysts started returning to London in 1943 that the public fight over Klein broke out. The thick of the quarreling lasted about eighteen months, although many members were reluctant to participate. Certain members were willing to combine elements of ideas from all sources, some objected to washing dirty linen in public, and others simply wanted peace.

To those who spoke up, it was a scientific dispute requiring a resolution, although in retrospect the emotions involved seemed more of a religious nature. More Kleinians than Freudians took a public stance in the dispute, leading Glover to fear that the former group would take over the Society. Years later he admitted his wrong estimate of Mrs. Klein's strength, but at the time he decided to resign from the British Society; one or two other analysts went with him. Glover proceeded to join the Japanese Psychoanalytic Society (as far away from London as he could get); he still practiced in London, however, and later became a member of the Swiss Society, Switzerland being a traditional home for spiritual refugees.

The argument within the British Society simply petered out. The Kleinians had resisted being expelled, but Anna Freud insisted on having her own training facilities so that her pupils would not be contaminated by Kleinian ideology. Sylvia Payne was responsible for holding the Society together by her proposal of an organizational compromise: Anna Freud could have her training group (the "B" group) within the regular psychoanalytic Society; the rest of the analysts would belong to a separate faculty (the "A" group). Even today there are in the Society a small group of enthusiastic Kleinians and a somewhat larger group of those who follow Anna Freud. But by far the largest number of analysts, about half the Society, belong to neither group and are therefore known as the "Middle Group" or "Independents." By and large it has been the British analysts who have held the reins between the warring Continentals, and it has been from within these "compromisers" that some of the most original psychoanalytic thinking has come: the best-known representatives would be John Bowlby, Michael Balint, and Donald Winnicott.

The Kleinians were capable of interesting work, for example in aesthetics, but these "heretics" could be as rigid and fanatical as the worst defenders of orthodoxy. Klein's therapeutic aims were idealistic if not utopian. The Kleinian impulse had been a crusading one, and even if this trend was an authentic offshoot within psychoanalysis, it still has to be contrasted to the more sober approach of Freud himself.

Melanie Klein had a greater appreciation than Freud for essentially religious feelings, and her understanding of what she called the "depressive position" in child development was designed to conceptualize how one feels better when one is good than when one is bad. She was especially concerned with a person's problems in tolerating ambivalence, without feeling too anxious lest one's hate overpower one's love.[18] Klein was, however, so outspoken that until she died in 1960 the situation in the British Psychoanalytic Society was tense and difficult. But the fact that psychoanalysis in England is not more intellectually complacent is due in part to her energy and absorption in life.

X

OLD AGE

1. Illness

FREUD WAS EIGHTY-THREE YEARS OLD at his death in 1939; the last years of his life naturally involved a gradual process of shrinkage and physical deterioration. In his rumpled salt-and-pepper tweed suits, Freud's presence was still strong. He had the thin hands of a grandmother and a slightly feminine aspect to his manner.[1] He continued to see patients in the same office, and its old furniture reinforced the heavy atmosphere. (The decorations in the family apartment also looked stodgy and in increasingly old-fashioned taste.) In his consulting room he was surrounded by the gods and goddesses from dead civilizations which he had collected over the years.

For years Freud had consulted medically with a number of his followers and colleagues, but the cancer overshadowed his last sixteen years. The photographs of this period show the suffering around his mouth, and his jaw grew smaller as successive operations removed suspicious-looking tissue. His speech was so gravely impaired that many thought he was suffering from cancer of the tongue.

Once Freud's mouth was damaged he often manipulated his fingers around his prosthesis, readjusting its position. He was naturally preoccupied with his mouth, and it became difficult to express his thoughts orally. He tended to be more expressive with his hands and gestures, to compensate for his difficulties in speaking. In addition, he had eating difficulties. For his dinner, the light meal in Vienna, he would eat a boiled egg. He was more aloof, and did not want to eat with many people around. He ate hastily and often read a newspaper during his meal.

Some patients in analysis around 1930, meeting Freud for the first time, report that they would not have recognized Freud's illness. But for those who had known Freud beforehand, it was noticeable that in his last years he did not talk freely. Toward the end every word caused him pain and he was not easy to understand.

Not counting extraction of teeth, Freud underwent thirty-one surgical procedures from 1923 to 1939.[2] In addition, there were constant attempts to make his prosthesis more comfortable; it could not be out of his mouth for long lest the tissues shrink and necessitate further adjustments. To compound his difficulties, the operations had interfered with his hearing on the right side. When Freud mentions "weeks of pain"[3] in a 1936 letter, it must have been very bad. Freud was constantly in discomfort and dependent on doctors, and his life grew quite restricted. Yet he wrote that "the only real dread I have is of a long invalidism with no possibility of working: to put it more plainly, with no possibility of earning."[4]

His head seemed to shrink, and he grew smaller and thinner, with one side of his face often drawn in pain. Describing himself in 1929 as "old, feeble and tired," Freud said that he would "probably not publish anything further unless I am definitely pressed to do so."[5] Yet he was capable of seeing five patients a day. His energy was intact despite his ill health, and he could startle a pupil by his vigorous walking. Shortly after contracting his cancer Freud made public how

the conditions under which I work have undergone a change. . . . Formerly, I was not one of those who are unable to hold back what seems to be a new discovery until it has been either confirmed or corrected . . . But in those days I had unlimited time before me. . . . But now everything has changed.[6]

In November 1923 he agreed to Federn's suggestion of undergoing a rejuvenatory (Steinach) operation on his testicles, in a bizarre attempt to check his cancer.[7] The idea was to overcome the forces of death by mobilizing the life instinct, although modern medicine holds that cancer thrives on the host and therefore the more vigorous the patient the more virulent the cancer is likely to be. Freud assumed for a time that the operation, which also sterilizes, had rejuvenatory results, but this may have been subjective on his part, for according to him there were no lasting benefits.

In April 1923 Freud had consulted an old acquaintance, Dr. Marcus Hayek, about a growth in his mouth, some "tissue-rebellion." Hayek blamed Freud's smoking, but also remarked that "No one can expect to live forever."[8] An operation for an excision was scheduled at an out-patient clinic; a few days before the surgery, Freud asked Felix Deutsch, who was an expert diagnostician, to examine the growth. Felix Deutsch later specialized (as did Groddeck and Jelliffe) in applying psychoanalysis to organically sick patients, the field of psychosomatic medicine, in which Freud had only a slight interest.[9]

At the time Freud showed Deutsch the growth in his mouth, Freud said: "For what I intend to do I need a doctor. If you take it for cancer, I must find a way to disappear from this world with decency."[10]* For Freud, death was preferable to a life without dignity, and cancer could mean a painful and humiliating, as well as protracted, end. There was no immediate danger from the cancer, but as a physician Felix Deutsch was concerned about the possibility of suicide. Freud had only dropped a hint, but then he would not have done it any other way.

According to Max Schur, who became Freud's personal physician from 1929 on, Felix Deutsch was then in analysis with Bernfeld; Schur was later critical of how Deutsch, already a member of the Vienna Society, had behaved. Although Schur acknowledged that in 1923 Freud's behavior toward his illness was unusually fatalistic, somehow Schur felt confident enough to assert that "the thought of suicide never entered . . . [Freud's] mind. . . ."[12] Schur complained that Deutsch should have spoken to someone in the family about what he suspected would be found in Freud's mouth; they were heartbroken that Freud kept his first operation a secret from them. In addition, Schur thought Hayek was a poor surgeon. But it was Freud, not Deutsch, who had chosen Hayek.

Although Deutsch drove to the hospital with Freud, the operation took place with no one at his side, and it went badly:

> the family were surprised by getting a telephone message from the clinic requesting them to bring a few necessities for him to stay the night. Wife and daughter hurried there to find Freud sitting on a kitchen chair in the out-patient department with blood all over his clothes.[13]

The growth was cancerous, but neither Hayek nor Deutsch reported this to Freud (from the outset Deutsch considered it an obvious advanced cancer). Two X-ray treatments were performed, which "did not accord with the supposed harmlessness of the condition."[14] In addition, a series of radium doses had severe toxic effects on Freud. Hayek had been "cavalier" in treating Freud and had not guarded against a shrinking of the scar; either "he was under the impression that he had accomplished everything possible, and that the growth would probably not recur, or on the other hand it may be that he regarded the case from the start as so hopeless that any special concern would be superfluous."[15]

---

* Freud had already come to emphasize the importance of a primary self-destructive death instinct. He later went so far as to maintain: "It really seems as though it is necessary for us to destroy some other thing or person in order not to destroy ourselves, in order to guard against the impulsion to self-destruction."[11]

Hayek permitted Freud to go on a vacation, but Freud did not want to interrupt his trip to Italy for the examination Hayek wanted at the end of July. A local doctor thought Freud's mouth was all right, but Freud was feeling so bad that his daughter Anna persuaded him to write to Felix Deutsch to visit them in Italy for an inspection. Freud was also depressed over the loss of a beloved grandson who had died in June. Freud had planned a trip to Rome with Anna, and Deutsch knew how much this meant to him. Deutsch, who was by then Freud's physician, was a kindly man who did not like to tell people bad news; he believed in concealing matters from dying patients. Freud's initial appeal to help him to depart life with dignity was all the excuse Deutsch needed. He also had a dictatorial way about him, and could easily imagine that he knew best about a situation. So although he perceived the necessity of a more radical operation, he first confided in his friend Otto Rank and then in the other members of the committee, who had assembled for a meeting; Deutsch did not tell Freud the truth, although he communicated enough to Anna to keep her and her father from extending their stay in Italy, and she guessed what was happening.[16]

In Freud's absence Deutsch found an oral surgeon, Hans Pichler, who performed Freud's subsequent operations. Hayek had assured Freud that the operation and subsequent treatments had been prophylactic in character. On Freud's trip to Rome, however, a stream of blood from his mouth, as tissue loosened, left "no doubt of its significance" to either Freud or Anna.[17] In the fall a malignancy was diagnosed, necessitating a second operation.

Many years later Jones told Freud in London that the members of the committee meeting in Italy had discussed whether to inform Freud of the malignancy. With "blazing eyes" Freud asked: "With what right?"[18] Freud was the most self-disciplined of patients, and for Deutsch not to have told him the truth was terrible: it meant that Freud was in someone else's custody. He was furious with Deutsch, and even though the members of the committee had, whatever their reservations, gone along, Freud blamed his physician for the deception. In the spring of 1939, a few months before his death, Freud complained that "the people around have tried to wrap me in an atmosphere of optimism: the cancer is shrinking; the reactions to the treatment are temporary. I don't believe any of it, and don't like being deceived."[19] Freud's independence was precious to him, and "he insisted on paying Pichler full fees, as he did with all his doctors."[20]

To Freud, Deutsch's behavior meant that he had underestimated Freud's strength to face the truth. Although in later years Deutsch claimed that he would do what he had done over again, Freud could not forgive him. Deutsch withdrew as Freud's physician, although later he and Freud were on good terms again. On August 6, 1924, however, Freud wrote·to Ferenczi that he had known from the beginning that his growth was cancerous.[21]

From Felix Deutsch's point of view it had been a difficult decision.[22] Years later Helene Deutsch remembered how, as Felix and she walked on the beach at Riga on the Baltic Sea, he worried about what he would decide in Italy. He knew in advance that Freud would be unhappy about the truth being kept from him; he asked his wife's help in interpreting

Felix Deutsch at his desk in Cambridge, Massachusetts

Freud's intentions and they both feared a possible suicide. At the same time they appreciated his great longing for Rome; the growth was extremely slow and the trip would place him in no special danger.

Felix Deutsch feared that Freud might prefer to die rather than be operated on a second time, and so he thought it better to make the necessary arrangements for the new operation without Freud's knowledge.[23] Schur later contended that "it was Deutsch who could not 'face reality' when he saw the ugly lesion in Freud's mouth. . . ."[24] But according to Deutsch, Freud was a fighter who could not countenance weakness in himself any more than in others.[25] To Deutsch, it seemed afterward that Freud was angry at him precisely because Deutsch had caught him out at a weak moment;* the physician had seen him as a man whose normal human fears and reactions had to be taken into account. In 1901 Freud had written Fliess: "You have reminded me of that beautiful and difficult time when I had reason to believe that I was very close to the end of my life, and it was your confidence that kept me going. I certainly did not behave either very bravely or very wisely then."[27] The incident in 1923 was also a sign of Freud's vulnerability; once he had resumed his former life and could practice and write again, he was able to live heroically with the knowledge and suffering of his cancer.

Freud continued to complain about his former physician. In a letter to his wife in August 1924, Felix Deutsch explained:

> Just as before Professor speaks in a monomaniac way about my keeping the secret of his illness . . . With time . . . he must see the untenability of his breaking [with me] the more he tries to support it by other motivations . . . His ego has not proved during his illness so worthy of love nor so strong as he would like to pretend. And now, when he is recovering, deeply wounded, he can fulfill the task of ego restoration in the midst of a great organic damage that stays with him, only by taking away the libido from this one who was the witness of his weakness. His unapproachability—he tries to rationalize it with the argument about the uncertainty of his illness. He has to blame someone.[28]

In repeatedly criticizing Deutsch, Freud might well have felt that the initial uncertainty had made it harder to bear his troubles. From Deutsch's point of view, Freud had distorted the whole episode: Deutsch believed that in retrospect Freud thought that he should have known all along

---

* Years earlier "Jung had the clear impression that Freud could not accept the fact that he had exposed what he regarded as his weakness."[26]

what to expect, and so was using Deutsch as a scapegoat, to protect himself from self-criticism.

Deutsch noted in that letter to his wife how Freud was retiring more and more from people, involved with writing his autobiography and an article for the Encyclopaedia Britannica. He may have been depressed; he spent time in his study with a telescope, watching the surrounding hills in the daytime and the moon and stars at night. His family suffered from his withdrawal. After Deutsch bowed out as Freud's physician he was occasionally consulted on medical matters and invited to play cards with Freud. Anna retained him as her physician. Freud later made Felix a personal gift of a ring, and told him that "nothing could have separated us." (Long ago Freud had written Stekel: "I don't know what could ever separate us."[29])

Max Schur has emphasized, as did Jones, the bravery of Freud's reaction to cancer, and whatever the immediate response to the growth which Deutsch witnessed, it was heroic of Freud to endure such suffering. For years, out of resentment at Deutsch, Freud remained without a personal physician. In 1929 Schur, an internist, was close to the end of his personal analysis, begun in 1925 with Ruth Brunswick;* in order to treat Marie Bonaparte, Schur contacted Freud in regard to her illness, and it was she (and probably Ruth Brunswick) who convinced Freud that he needed his own doctor. Freud set up as the "basic rule" of their relationship that Schur not hide the truth from Freud, no matter how grim it might be. Although Freud said he could stand much pain and strongly disliked sedatives, he wanted to be certain that Schur would not let him, when his time came, suffer without necessity. (Near the end, in 1939, Freud would remind Schur of this early "pact.") He also told Schur he expected to pay for whatever treatment he received.

Freud was an easy patient for Schur, although in the face of such a cancer his heavy cigar smoking was frustrating to the physician. For the sake of heart symptoms, but not his mouth, Freud would temporarily try to restrict his smoking; but he could not write without his cigars. Schur's main job, and here Anna helped, was in making constant adjustments in Freud's rather monstrous plate, which was supposed to separate the nasal cavity from his mouth and sinuses; and there was also the sensitive task of detecting new growths which might be malignant. Although Freud would tolerate belladonna for spastic stool, he would only rarely use pyramidon or aspirin. Freud hated to complain, and it took the devotion of Schur and Anna's love to take care of him.

---

* Freud referred in 1931 to Schur and Ruth Brunswick as "'my two *Leibärzte*.' . . . *Leibarzt* was the term which royalty used to designate their personal physician."[30]

        *   *   *

At the time of Freud's initial illness in April 1923, his four-year-old grandson Heinz Rudolf, "Heinerle," had been living in Vienna. Freud's eldest daughter Mathilda was childless and wanted to adopt him. The boy's mother, Freud's daughter Sophie, had suddenly died in 1920 in an influenza epidemic. Starting with an ear infection, the child developed tuberculosis. Freud was good with small children, using any excuse for giving a present. But this was his only grandchild so near at hand, its mother had died, and to Freud in the midst of his own illness the death of the child was a terrible blow.

In Freud's mind, the child may have stood for his successor; his daughter had given him an heir. The child was so intelligent that he seemed to Freud, whatever he thought of his own sons, a worthy symbol of the future. At Heinerle's death Freud was depressed as he had not been since the troubles with Jung in 1913.[31] Heinerle "was indeed an enchanting fellow, and I myself was aware of never having loved a human being, certainly never a child, so much."[32]

Perhaps Freud's depressed feeling had all along found expression in his interest in the past, since he cherished his collection of ancient statuary, ruins of dead civilizations.* But this grief over a grandchild was a watershed for him. As he wrote to Binswanger in 1926: "I lost a beloved daughter when she was 27, but I bore this remarkably well . . . To me this child [Heinerle] had taken the place of all my children and other grandchildren, and since then, since Heinerle's death, I don't care for my grandchildren any more, but find no joy in life either."[33] In 1929 Binswanger lost a son, and Freud's letter of condolence showed him still a master psychologist:

> Although we know that after such a loss the acute state of mourning will subside, we also know we shall remain inconsolable and will never find a substitute. No matter what may fill the gap, even if it be filled completely, it nevertheless remains something else. And actually this is how it should be. It is the only way of perpetuating that love which we do not want to relinquish.[34]

On the whole, Freud was more interested in his psychoanalytic family than his natural one, and it is hard to be sure which came first, his disappointment in his sons or their relative lack of talent. Other sons of great men have found their fathers burdens to them. It was probably not so much that Freud was tyrannical with his family, although he wielded more power and authority than would be conceivable for a father now.

---

* His granddaughter Sophie looked to him like a Chinese doll; he wrote in the little girl's scrapbook: "to the youngest but most precious piece of my Chinese collection."

Though tender, he was remote and perhaps neglectful. For Freud holidays were a time for writing, whereas for other parents they may be the occasion for getting to know their children. Freud could be more patriarchal with students than with his own sons; to the latter he was more the observing analyst than the active father. As a result, he ended up somewhat estranged from his sons, though closest to Ernst.

Freud's pupils enjoyed disparaging Freud's sons. Martin began work at the psychoanalytic publishing house in 1931, and replaced A. J. Storfer as manager in early 1932 when he was dropped for lack of business sense. Freud commented on Storfer's departure: "We feel like subjects who have chased out their sovereign only now realizing what he has done for them." But for Martin to manage the *Verlag* was an indication that he had not been able to make his own way. He lived only a short walk from the Freud apartment, and even before he worked at the press he would visit twice a a day. As a former banker, he looked after Freud's financial affairs and those of some of his pupils; foreigners needed to convert currency and the Viennese wanted their affairs liquidated when they emigrated.

Martin exemplified the difficulties of the son of a great man. Dashing and handsome, married and the father of two children, he had a number of affairs, including one with a pupil in a training analysis with Freud. Martin collected women as his father collected antique statuary. When the Nazis arrived in Vienna in 1938, Martin hid out in his *pied-à-terre*, and his wife realized for the first time what had been going on. The couple split up, each of them taking half of their books. By one of those cruel chances, a booklet of photographs of Martin's lady friends had gone to his wife; taken on various street corners, they were a modern Don Juan's reminder of his conquests. Once Freud reached London and Martin's wife left him, the son was punished; the directorship of psychoanalytic publishing was taken away from him and from then on Ernst was in charge.

The celebration of Freud's seventieth birthday in 1926 was more public than private, despite his personal dislike of such affairs; he was generally "in revolt against . . . conventional expressions of sympathy. . . ."[35] Yet because of his illness Freud consented to hold open house; it might be the last such occasion. He welcomed well-wishers and showed gifts that had arrived. He loved flowers, especially orchids and gardenias, and the apartment was full of such testaments. Freud did not like being photographed, but he sat for an etching, copies of which could later be ordered from the Vienna Society. A small group of his younger students were selected to come to his apartment, and Freud—like a parent addressing his children

—advised them strongly to get along with one another. "At the celebration, he addressed all his 'sons' and warned them that they would henceforth have to be on their own."[36] If they wished to change something in psychoanalysis, that was all right, as long as it was not for the sake of pleasing the public.[37]

In 1929 Freud wrote that "against the suffering which may come upon one from human relationships the readiest safeguard is voluntary isolation, keeping oneself aloof from other people. The happiness which can be achieved along this path . . . is the happiness of quietness."[38] He grew quieter and busied himself with dogs; Freud's attachment to dogs was a substitute for his old relationships with people, as he found it increasingly difficult to start out anew. Chows may have been less bothersome than people to Freud, but they upset his wife Martha. Probably her attitude reflected the traditional Jewish distaste for the animals who patrolled the boundaries of the Central European ghettos. She would be angry when Freud put down his food for them.

He was explicit in comparing dogs favorably with the pettiness of corrupt "civilized" man. For Freud, dogs had qualities humans lack; they were honest and he felt he could trust them. If a dog loves, he shows it; and if he hates, he does so strongly. Dogs are not capable of the deceptions of men. As he wrote to another animal lover, Marie Bonaparte, about the source of his attraction to dogs: "affection without any ambivalence, the simplicity of life free from the conflicts of civilization that are so hard to endure, the beauty of an existence complete in itself."[39] Freud preferred great beauty in a dog even if it had little temperament. In his old age Freud regularly analyzed with a dog in his consulting room; and other analysts also practiced in the presence of their dogs.

Freud's composure and harmony, even in the face of his suffering, should not obscure the fact that he could still harbor old resentments. If anything, his view of human nature grew more grim as the years passed. He maintained his "wholly non-scientific belief that mankind on the average and taken by and large are a wretched lot," and he is said to have had "bitter words of deep disappointment" about the future of analysis.[40] One has to attribute some of Freud's ill humor to the frustrations of an invalid, and if Freud sometimes seems arbitrary, his age may help account for it.

He was impressed with how his creation, psychoanalysis, had "met with plenty of mistrust and ill-will."[41] When he was awarded the Goethe Prize by the city of Frankfurt in 1930, Arnold Zweig wrote that "your deep pessimism about the future of analysis is not quite justified after all."

Freud wrote back: "For a reconciliation with my contemporaries it comes pretty late and I have never doubted that long after my day analysis will finally win through."[42] Freud always had a generally low opinion of mankind: "human beings exhibit an inborn tendency to carelessness, irregularity and unreliability in their work. . . ."[43] And in particular, "men do not always take their great thinkers seriously even when they profess most to admire them."[44]

After Freud's cancer, his anger was inseparable from his resignation. Old and sick, he saw the outside world as more hostile than it really was. As he grew old he may have become personally less hard, and his withdrawal may have reflected his awareness that he could not bear the kind of strains he had earlier undergone. In 1931, according to Jones, Freud wrote to Eitingon that "in his leisure time he had composed what he called a 'hate list' of 7 or 8 people."[45] Even if Freud's psychology did not have a *Weltanschauung* of its own, he thought it had revenge on other world views: "Psychology is a poor Cinderella, and has nothing to give the other *Weltanschauungen*, and that nothing is uncertain. But psychology has the opportunity of revenge. It can examine the other *Weltanschauungen*, and therefore has stopped being harmless."[46]

2. Dissenters

DESPITE WHAT FREUD WROTE about the opposition to his ideas, his conviction of his ultimate triumph sustained him through sickness and old age. Critics have claimed that Freud indoctrinated his patients. Whatever the truth of the allegation, Freud was an undoubted success as a teacher. It has been said that "Freud was aware that in its practical application analysis must undergo dilution,"[1] but he stuck to classical analysis because he felt his earlier findings were tentative and more research was necessary. Because his retinue of needy followers and relatives was so large, and the *Verlag* always required funds, in his last years money helped determine his choice of a case. As he explained to his pupils, he might not have much time left for earning and he had to support himself through his sickness.

Whether he liked to admit it or not, Freud had become the head of a sect. A mutually self-congratulatory society can never expect to make the progress that might come from free and open competition in the intellectual marketplace. On the other hand, as a solid band the analysts reinforced each other with their mutual faith. If one sees psychoanalysis as partly a religious phenomenon, then it is not surprising if the followers were united in their worship of Freud and of the unconscious. But as a historian of religion has observed, "beliefs seldom become doubts; they become ritual."[2]

The responses Freud elicited are enough to make a reader squirm. In thanking Freud for a gift of his collected works, Arnold Zweig wrote of "this splendid gift: the foundation stone of a library as well as of life."[3] Those of Freud's pupils who lived in Vienna followed his comings and goings with care. When Freud's favorite operas were performed, many analysts in Vienna would be sure to be present. Freud's last public appearances were at concerts of Yvette Guilbert, and he would be surrounded by his followers.

Some have suggested that by Freud's seventieth birthday in 1926 "there was more benevolence than respect in the way he spoke of his followers. On the whole, he seemed weary of his school and not in need of it any longer."[4] The Society had grown bigger, and naturally he felt doubtful about some of its members; but he maintained contact with selected pupils. Freud did not really have to retire from the Society for physical reasons, but he felt that young analysts might defer too much to him in settling disputes. As much as he had wanted to conquer, he disliked the idea of his influence and was embarrassed by his effect on others. It irritated him to see his writings treated as a sacred text.[5]

Nonetheless, he found his disciples useful. When Enrico Morselli, a professor of psychiatry at the University of Turin, who was "considered a sensitive and distinguished man,"[6] published a two-volume study of psychoanalysis, Freud wrote his Italian pupil Weiss that Morselli's work "is completely without value, the only value is its undoubted proof that he is a donkey." Freud asked Weiss to write a detailed book review: "I ask you not to spare him any unpleasant truth."*[7] Freud liked to think of himself as an unfailing truth-teller, but Viennese tact meant that Freud would leave the public polemics to Weiss. To Morselli himself, Freud wrote that the books constituted an "important work."[8] To Weiss, however, Freud wrote how pleased he was by the critical review: "I am glad

---

* Weiss had already been disillusioned with Morselli. He had asked Weiss about Freud's work, had invited Weiss to present psychoanalytic views in Trieste, and then had spoken critically of Freud. Betrayed by his own expectations of Morselli, Weiss did not wait for Freud's request that he review the study, and he wrote a criticism of it.

you have shown yourself to be courageous and honest, as always. . . ."[9] In a letter a few months later, Freud used against Morselli invective reminiscent of the great battles of the prewar years: "It would be humanly interesting to learn whether he has always been such a bum or whether he has permitted himself to become that way only under the influence of senility."[10]

By 1926 small meetings assembled about twice a month at Freud's apartment; later they would be held once a month. Ten or twelve analysts sat around an oval table in Freud's waiting room, six of them regular participants and the rest selected from the larger Viennese group. There was such a gulf between Freud and his followers that he towered over them, and he confined himself to aphoristic but weighted remarks. The procedure at these private meetings was the same as at the Society; after the presentation of a paper there would be an intermission before the discussion. It was not unusual, as the discussion period opened, for no one to speak, since everyone wanted to hear from Freud; so he would shrug his shoulders and launch in.

When he was finished speaking, Freud would remark, "Now let me hear what you have to tell me."[11] He felt he had said what he wanted to say, and it was his turn to learn from others. It was clear to them, however, that he was full of ideas and they did not quite believe his disclaimer. But in the light of his earlier concern with priorities, his reluctance to speak too extensively can be interpreted in a different way; as he checked himself he could control his anxiety over having ideas taken from him prematurely. Yet he was so far above his disciples that he was no longer in real danger. What had once been a torment to him was now more of a joke; one of his pupils wrote:

> I remember once meeting Freud when he was reading a book by one of his most heated opponents. Freud pointed to a passage in the book and said to me with a smile: "Look, this man states that I am wicked. . . . Pure plagiarism! I published that myself long ago."[12]

Freud knew that everything he said would be taken up and used. He might be critical of some papers, but he was urbane in his criticism; he tried not to hurt anyone's feelings. He did not have to raise his voice to express his displeasure; he almost growled at Bernfeld's attempt to measure libido quantitatively, and so it was known then that Bernfeld must be on his way out with Freud. There were only unconditional adherents at these seminars, and no one dared oppose him.

An isolated remnant of Freud's earlier concern about plagiarism can be detected throughout his old age, in his involvement with the controversy over the authorship of Shakespeare's works. Freud supported the

Earl of Oxford instead of the man from Stratford. Freud was "almost" irritated by the idea that Arnold Zweig should accept Shakespeare as an authentic figure, but after he talked it over with Zweig the latter was "tempted . . . to create a Shakespeare character of such a kind that in the last weeks of his life he struggles with the shade of Oxford and all the time wishes to confess: My plays are not by me at all, they're by him."[13] Freud was impressed by a book by J. Thomas Looney which "identified" Shakespeare as the 17th Earl of Oxford, and he lent a copy of the book to at least one patient (and to Hanns Sachs as well), mentioned the subject in letters, and even added a footnote about it to a revised edition of his autobiography.[14]

Now and then, troublesome pupils created difficulties in Freud's circle. Wilhelm Reich (1897–1957) was one of Freud's more talented younger pupils, yet too undisciplined (and original) to stay permanently within the psychoanalytic orbit. Freud conceived of neurosis primarily as a memory problem. Like Adler and Jung before him, Reich tried to show that the real issue to be studied and treated was not symptomatology but the whole personality. Even in his later years Freud tended to confine his understanding to the structure and dynamics of interesting, but isolated, symptoms. In his work on "character analysis" Reich succeeded in broadening the earlier conception of what was suitable for an analyst's concern.

If Reich helped to shift the focus of attention to nonverbal means of expression, he failed to convince analysts of the diagnostic significance of orgastic sexual satisfaction. Reich thought that health depended on orgastic potency, and he was in favor of full and free sexual gratification. (Freud did not like these ideas at all.) Reich was especially interested in adolescence as a phase of personality development. As a practical reformer, Reich held that many adult problems would never develop if sexual expression were not prematurely stifled. This liberationist side of Reich has ensured his continuing popularity.

What orthodox analysts called sublimation appeared to Reich as the rationalized product of bourgeois sexual inhibitions. He argued that Freud was betraying, out of conformist pressures, his original revolutionary stand in behalf of the rights of libido. Freud in turn objected that Reich was trying to set psychoanalysis back, to limit the concept of sexuality to what it had been before Freud. When in 1932 Freud mentioned the "secessionist" movements, which had seized hold of only a fragment of the truth, he listed "selecting the instinct for mastery [Adler], for instance, or ethical conflict [Jung], or the mother [Rank], or genitality [Reich]. . . ."[15]

Even as a relative newcomer to psychoanalysis in the early 1920's,

Reich seemed excessively self-assured; at any rate, Freud would not countenance his arrogance. At one of the private meetings at Freud's home he
said to Reich: "You are the youngest here, would you close the door?"
Freud kept his distance from Reich, leaving him to the experienced analysts
in the Society. Reich had insisted that analysts were neglectful of negative
transferences, and he inaugurated a major shift in technique by which
the patient's hostility to the analyst was actively searched for. A continuous
case seminar at the Institute in Vienna was partly invented as a way of
keeping Reich within bounds; he was asked to show, as the clinical material
came up, where the standard technique was misguided.

Reich was also a Marxist and one of the few analysts of his time
capable of building bridges between psychoanalysis and social science.
He proposed to prevent the rise of oedipal problems rather than simply
study and cure them after the fact. The key, he thought, was to ameliorate
human suffering through changes in the traditional Western family structure. To most Freudians, he seemed to have betrayed the purity of their
psychological mission. Reich argued that only the dissolution of the
middle-class family would lead to the disappearance of the Oedipus complex (and the experience of the Israeli *kibbutzim* would later prove him
right).

Freud was skeptical, since he had viewed the Oedipus complex as an
outgrowth of the biological necessity of the family; he wrote his *Civilization and Its Discontents* as an answer to Reich's position. Freud had seen
too many prior attempts to de-emphasize the Oedipus complex, and he did
not want psychoanalysis to seem so much in favor of the liberation of
human instinctual life. It has been suggested that Reich's lecture trip to
Bolshevik Russia in the late 1920's, where he claimed that unless there was
a sexual revolution Communism would deteriorate into a bureaucratic
state, helped convince the Soviet authorities that if this was what psychoanalysis was about they had better close it down.[16] Psychoanalysis, along
with many other cultural movements in Russia at that time, had until then
flourished.

Reich expected something from Freud that Freud was not interested
in: he wanted Freud to be a social reformer. He also wished to be
recognized as a new favorite son. Reich had already been analyzed by
Sadger and Federn, and was later analyzed by Sandor Rado; but he desired
an analysis with Freud himself, which was refused. His first wife held
that "it was the refusal of Freud to take Reich for personal analysis that
led to the serious break . . . Freud had become . . . a father substitute for
Reich. The rejection, as Reich felt it, was intolerable. Reich reacted to
this rejection with deep depression."[17] The twelve letters Freud wrote to

Reich[18] mainly concern themselves with comments about Reich's manuscripts—he found them too copious, in need of clarification—and Reich's difficulties with other analysts (especially Federn), who thought him a troublemaker. Freud shrugged off these quarrels as part of normal family life. In 1931 he declined to write a preface to one of Reich's books.

Reich believed he had been expelled from the International Psychoanalytic Association (1934), whereas to Jones it seemed a resignation.[19] There were a few other members of the Communist Party involved with psychoanalysis (for example, Otto Fenichel), but Jones insisted that Reich

Wilhelm Reich in February 1927

had to choose which was of more importance to him, psychoanalysis or politics.[20] By trying to understand human instinctual life in conjunction with social forms of domination, Reich exposed himself to attack from both ideological flanks. The Marxists thought he was too involved with the mere superstructure of bourgeois society, and in the 1930's Communist organizations got rid of him too.

The latter part of Reich's life is more controversial. After divorcing his first wife, a former analytic patient, he moved gradually away from the mainstream of psychoanalysis until the final break in 1934. Without the moorings of friends and colleagues he was beleaguered and alone. Although he had a legitimate influence on A. S. Neill's Summerhill school, Reich allowed himself to become the leader of a new cult. He became for some "a dictator who could not let others do independent work," and was fearful that "people might steal some of his discoveries. . . ."[21] He created a new terminology, which, to some, is indicative of a religious system of thought. His invention of orgone energy accumulators—he claimed to have discovered "physical orgone energy"—and his use of them in therapy set the U. S. Food and Drug Administration against him. If he was, as seems likely, mentally disturbed by the time of his trial, his prison sentence is an example of the cruelty of which modern society is capable. His writings were destroyed by the American government, and he died in a federal prison in 1957.

Whereas Reich achieved a good deal of popular fame and his books are still in print after many decades, Sandor Rado (1890–1972) was a psychoanalytic "traitor" whose contributions are known mainly within medicine. In 1938 Freud mentioned with distaste that " 'the American group [of analysts] is largely Jewish, dominated by Rado . . . while the Americans'—meaning the Gentiles—'do not seem much better.' "[22] Rado never achieved any such power. But in Nunberg's *Memoirs* he mentioned that "Rado . . . had moved farther and farther away from psychoanalysis, had even given up its basic tenets and yet still called himself a psychoanalyst." Nunberg specifically classed Rado with the more famous dissenters in psychoanalysis, by referring to "what has amounted essentially to the abandonment of psychoanalysis (for example, Adler, Jung, Rado, etc.)"[23]

Rado was once one of the most brilliant lights in psychoanalysis. A Hungarian who was an intimate friend of Ferenczi's, he had a photographic memory which enabled him not only to quote Freud exactly but even to remember page numbers. Rado was analyzed in Berlin by Abraham; in turn, he analyzed such theoreticians as Otto Fenichel, Heinz Hartmann, and Wilhelm Reich, giving some idea of his standing among the most highly intellectual of the analysts. When Otto Rank retired as editor-in-chief of the *Zeitschrift*, Rado took over in his place, which earned him the envy and hostility of many analysts. He was capable of superb work—for example, his professionally well-known article on the problem of melancholia.[24] He edited two volumes in honor of Freud's seventieth birthday in 1926. It is easy to overlook Rado's stature in Freud's lifetime, since the later contributions of others, who remained within the orthodox movement, are now more often cited. But Freud had written him in connection with his work as editor: "You who are doing by far the greatest unselfish work for psychoanalysis." Rado received royal answers from Freud whenever he asked about something in connection with his activities on the journal. When the issue of lay analysis was debated, Rado was silent. He felt he should not oppose Freud yet he could not share his views.

When the Americans needed an exciting and well-trained teacher to direct the training at the New York Institute, Rado was offered the job. Freud gave his blessings to Rado's departure for the United States in 1931. Rado found, however, that after he left Berlin his former ties began to loosen. To have been an early analyst meant that one was a member of a segregated group in which everyone depended on everyone else. In the United States his work was soon recognized as a part of modern medicine. During his first five years in America, Rado spent every summer in Europe, visiting Freud each time. He resisted Freud's plans to build a new international psychoanalytic institute in Vienna even after Hitler had come to power in Germany; Freud was that much afraid of finding himself isolated there.[25]

A turning point in Rado's relationship with Freud was reached in 1935, when Jeanne Lampl-de Groot published a critical review of one of Rado's books, after first discussing it with Freud.[26] In attempting to explain feminine "castration anxiety," Rado had, in her view, succumbed to the temptation to "over-simplify" the complexities of the human soul in terms of an "unproveable" "trauma theory" involving the ego's struggle against masochism. The need to seize on only a fragment of the truth had already appeared in charges against earlier psychoanalytic "deviators," and Otto Rank, Rado's predecessor as editor, had also used a "trauma theory." Lampl-de Groot expressed not only her own opinions but also critical comments raised at a meeting of the Vienna Psychoanalytic Society. Rado was offended at what he considered an insult—that Freud had permitted her to write such a review under his auspices. After all Rado's work in analysis, Freud had treated Lampl-de Groot with more respect. (Evidently Rado wrote to Freud about the review, and then Freud showed her the letter and his reply.) Rado had been the most faithful of disciples, but he felt rejected by Freud and turned away from the traditionalists in psychoanalysis. Having regarded Freud's every word as a serious matter, suddenly Rado had found out how little he meant to Freud personally.*

As had happened when Rank departed, it was in good measure Freud's followers who led the attack on a former favorite of the master's; but Rado had never played as important a role as Rank in Freud's life, and Freud was now more than ten years older. Freud had resented the way

* On a smaller scale, Frederick Perls was similarly shocked and disappointed by his personal contact with Freud.[27]

Sandor Rado (1890–1972) in the United States

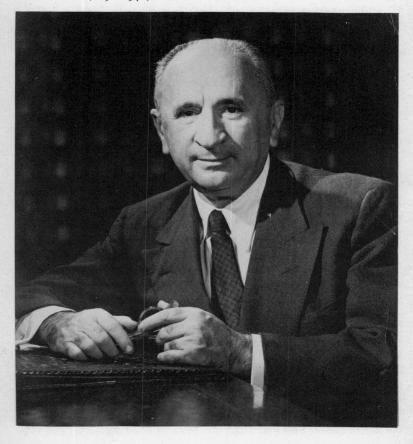

Rado had helped and encouraged some Continental analysts to leave for America. In addition, Anna Freud had not approved of the warmth of a memorial for Ferenczi that Rado had published in 1933;[28] there had also been a quarrel between Anna Freud and Rado over the report of the 1934 Psychoanalytic Congress.[29] Like others, Rado thought a "camarilla" now surrounded Freud; the faithful—out of jealousy, he thought—would try to make him out to be a traitor. With Jeanne Lampl-de Groot's review he felt that the Vienna group had finally triumphed over him.

Rado made significant contributions of his own. He emphasized that id, ego, and superego have to be seen functioning as a unit. He aspired to make psychoanalysis an empirical science, and he wanted to understand the emotions that play a role in motivation; he disliked the abstractness of so much psychoanalytic theorizing, and he emphasized the study of genetics as a legitimate field of inquiry for the psychodynamic psychiatrist. Like others, Rado held that classical psychoanalytic technique was too rationalistic, and that for purposes of therapy more than the overcoming of repressions and the recalling of the past is necessary; the patient's self-reliance can too easily be unknowingly undermined. Like other dissident opinions in the history of psychoanalysis, many of Rado's views showed more common sense than the ideas of those who remained loyal to orthodoxy and who expressed their conformity as members of the official organization.

In 1944 the New York Psychoanalytic Society terminated Rado as a training analyst, although he remained a member. He continued his research as head of Columbia University's Psychoanalytic Institute, and for a time he allied himself with the independent work of Abram Kardiner. Out of his rebellion (and genuine talent) he created new words for everything in psychoanalysis. On his retirement from Columbia in 1957 he helped found the New York School of Psychiatry of the State University of New York.

Franz Alexander (1891–1964), also a Hungarian, was another leader of the radical left in psychoanalysis. Unlike Rado, however, he went to the United States without Freud's approval. As he remembered his initial interest in Freudian psychology, "to turn to psychoanalysis meant to give up every idea of an academic career, for which I had prepared myself since my early school years. . . . In 1921 the decision to become a psychoanalyst placed a physician outside the medical fraternity."[30] In compensation, however, a young analyst was given

> a spiritual haven, a kind of citizenship in a small but devoted group . . . There was scarcely a cultural center in Europe where the young

psychoanalyst, once recognized by his local society, would not have found friendly acceptance by the local psychoanalysts. Among them he found a home at once, with the sensation that he belonged to the chosen few who were enlightened by Freud's teachings about the nature of man and society . . . Whether he was visiting his confrères in Vienna, Zurich, Berlin, Munich, Budapest, Rome, Amsterdam, Paris, or London, the conversation soon turned to the hostility and prejudice which the local analysts met on the part of the medical societies and the universities. Soon a well-told anecdote about a slip of the tongue or an observation about the Oedipal behavior of a little son or daughter, an account of an interesting dream fragment, created the feeling of complete solidarity, the feeling that we all shared the same new knowledge for which the rest of the world rejected us . . . One felt that whatever one's contributions were, one lived for a worthy cause and that the results of one's efforts would continue to live.[31]

Coming from a cultured background, Alexander was an exceptionally brilliant student at the Berlin Institute. Never having had Rado's analytic status in Europe, Alexander needed to go less far in a rebellious direction in America.

Freud was interested in Alexander, and there is an extensive and important correspondence between them which is as yet unpublished (which is also true of Freud's letters to Rado); it is therefore hard to talk about Alexander as Freud's pupil except to say that he was among the very best. First in Boston, then for many years in Chicago and Los Angeles, Alexander breathed life into every psychoanalytic community he participated in. In the tradition of Ferenczi's concern with technique, Alexander wrote about some of the defects in the analytic situation as devised by Freud, in particular about the dangers of dependence and the weakness of intellectual insight and interpretation. The analysis of latent transference emotions makes possible the revival of past memories, which Alexander thought was more an index of therapeutic improvement than anything else. He analyzed Bertram Lewin and was, at Freud's suggestion, Marianne Kris's first analyst; Alexander was also said by some to have treated Freud's son Ernst.[32] Alexander thought that too often etiological research was confused with what was best for the patient. Many of his technical innovations, designed to improve therapeutic results, were in fact anticipated by Jung.

Alexander pioneered in psychosomatic medicine, and tried to develop the implications of psychoanalysis for social philosophy.[33] In some ways his revisionist intentions were similar to Karen Horney's (1885–1952); she was also trained in Berlin, but had no personal relationship with Freud.

Alexander invited her to Chicago, but after a few years they found themselves unable to work together harmoniously. It is perhaps the inevitable
fate of dissidents that they must go their own ways.[34] Alexander was a
psychoanalytic liberal who once wrote a sympathetic essay on Rado; Rado
was "one of the few 'reformers' who have remained in the psychoanalytic
fold and tried to advance psychoanalysis from within the fraternity."[35]
Alexander admired Rado's efforts to end the isolation of the psychoanalytic
institutes and to bring psychoanalysis within the universities; yet Alexander,
though interested in the history of psychiatry, tactfully abstained from
going so far as to discuss the occasion of Rado's falling out with Freud.
Alexander does not really fit into the category of either a dissenter or an
aspostle of Freud's; an expert in metapsychology, he continued to work
within Freud's framework, which did not mean that the more orthodox
refrained from attacking his contributions.[36]

A prolific writer, Erich Fromm may be popularly known as one of
Freud's most trenchant critics, but he never had any personal acquaintance
with Freud. Analyzed by Sachs and trained in the 1920's at the Berlin
Institute, for about ten years he practiced as an orthodox analyst. His
first wife, Frieda Fromm-Reichmann, was a psychiatrist who worked for

*Franz Alexander—
caricature drawn at
the Salzburg Congress
in 1924*

many years in the Weisser Hirch sanitorium in Dresden; earlier she had been an assistant to Kurt Goldstein in Königsberg. In the 1920's German psychoanalysis did not have the kind of strict controls the organization developed later. Not sharing the dominant feeling of the Berlin analytic community which regarded Groddeck as something of a fool, both Erich Fromm and his wife admired his originality and urge to heal. In particular, Freida Fromm-Reichmann was a leader in the psychotherapy of psychotics; but in America, where she worked at Chestnut Lodge, an emissary from the American Psychoanalytic Association came to at least one of her seminars for the purpose of finding out whether she had been teaching unorthodox ideas. She was indignant at what she regarded as an illegitimate intrusion.[37]

Erich Fromm developed outside of what were then the dominant trends among analysts. Earlier than most of his colleagues and partly thanks to his Marxist affiliations, Fromm tried to integrate psychoanalysis with contemporary social thought. He had a Ph.D. in sociology, and his *Escape from Freedom* became a landmark in modern social science. In addition, Fromm was one of the first analysts to confront explicitly the moral implications of psychoanalytic ideas.[38]

Fromm analyzed such prominent Americans as Clara Thompson and David Riesman. (Riesman's notion of "other-direction" fits Fromm's concept of "market-orientation.") Nevertheless, Fromm's pioneering work won him the intense animosity of the most sectarian representatives of psychoanalysis. Although a major social thinker in his own right, Fromm (like Karen Horney) falls outside the scope of this study because of his lack of direct contact with Freud himself.

3. Erikson and Hartmann

ERIK ERIKSON IS ONE OF FREUD'S most important intellectual heirs. Like Reich, Fromm, and Kardiner before him, Erikson has been interested in integrating psychoanalysis with the social sciences, and he has drawn broad implications from Freud's work. Fromm and Erikson have both succeeded in winning a wide audience for psychodynamic thinking; along with Bruno Bettelheim, they illustrate Freud's contention that lay analysts can greatly contribute to the life of analysis.

Erikson first came in contact with the Viennese analytic circle in

1927, when he was an artist hitchhiking around Europe. His old school friend Peter Blos was then a tutor in a school (in Eva Rosenfeld's back-yard) for children of analytic patients and for patients in child analysis with Anna Freud. Dorothy Burlingham's children were being educated there, and without her financial support the school probably could not have existed. Blos put Erikson in touch with Mrs. Burlingham to paint her children's portraits. Blos wanted to go away on holiday for the summer, so Erikson also took over Blos's teaching job. At the end of the summer Erikson was asked if he desired to become a child analyst, a profession whose existence he had not known of before.

Slender and light-haired, Erikson—like Anna Freud—never obtained any formal academic degrees, and later as a professor he was sensitive about being an outsider to university life. Blos and Erikson were exceptional for their time because men in that era were not expected to be skillful with children; a middle-class man in Europe never even wheeled a baby carriage. Eager to attract men into child analysis, both Anna Freud and Dorothy Burlingham spotted Erikson's intuitive capacity with small chil-dren. The stepson of a German-Jewish pediatrician, Erikson found in analysis an identity which was liberating for him. He had assumed his step-father's name of Homburger, and his earliest papers were published under that name. His real parents were Danish, and in analysis he felt that he was committing himself to what seemed to him a German system of thought; later in America, where he thought up the name Erikson, he would focus on the problem of identity formation.

In Vienna, Erikson met his future wife Joan, an American student of the origins of modern dance. She also taught in Dorothy Burlingham's school, and was analyzed in Vienna by Ludwig Jekels. The Eriksons were very poor and slept on a mattress on the floor; Dorothy Burlingham became aware of their situation and gave them a feather quilt. When Joan Erikson, then pregnant, plopped down and stretched out on the top of the quilt, Tante Minna admonished her that one does not lie on a quilt, it damages the feathers.

Erikson's sole professional training was in child analysis, which may account for his sometimes excessive deference to Freud. Whereas others have taken pains to differentiate their work from Freud's, Erikson actually ascribed his own ideas to Freud. Erikson does not always seem to want to acknowledge his own originality.

He was analyzed by Anna Freud and sat in the same waiting room as Freud's students. She scheduled her patients five minutes later than her father's, so while Erikson waited Freud would make a little bow not only to his own patient but to Anna's as well. Soon after, the housekeeper, Paula

Fichtl, would come and say: Miss Freud is ready. Erikson was charged only seven dollars a month for his analysis. Erikson felt indebted to Anna, but he thought she never forgave him for not continuing to be the child analyst he was trained to be. At the time, however, he was welcomed as part of the new movement. When Freud had to go to Berlin for a new prosthesis and Anna wanted to accompany him, she offered her patient lodgings at her brother Ernst's house in Berlin.

Like her father, when she does not like certain ideas Anna Freud tends to protect herself from her hostility by finding them "foreign"; she has repeatedly said of Erikson's work that she could not understand much of it. Nevertheless, Erikson dedicated one of his books to her.

In the last years of Freud's life pupils doubled as servants. It was once Erikson's job to chauffeur Freud in Dorothy Burlingham's car for a four-hour drive. At one point tears were streaming down Freud's face; it was not sobbing, but the prosthesis must have been pressing on his tear ducts.[1]

Erikson found the atmosphere of the Viennese Society stifling. For one thing, the female domination of the field of child analysis made it difficult for such a man to find room to think in. Erikson's own observations on children also contended with the kind of objections that were bound to irritate any self-respecting investigator. He had written an article on children's play and was told it sounded like Melanie Klein. He later commented on "a growing conservatism and especially a pervasive interdiction of certain trends of thought. This concerned primarily any idea which might be reminiscent of the deviations perpetrated by those earliest and most brilliant of Freud's co-workers. . . ." To those around Anna Freud, sounding like Klein was as bad as resembling Adler or Jung. Joan Erikson encouraged her husband to get out of Vienna as soon as possible; "the idea of moving on and working independently seemed . . . invigorating. . . ."[2]

Erikson graduated from the Vienna Institute in 1933, becoming a full member of the Society; and since he had made it known that he wanted to leave, within six months Anna Freud recommended him abroad as a training analyst. He first tried practicing in Denmark, but it would have taken him years to obtain his Danish citizenship and in the meantime it was not clear how he could earn a living.[3] He then decided to emigrate to the United States; the Americans were, however, somewhat offended that the Viennese should consider Erikson competent as a training analyst so soon after the completion of his own training.[4] The feeling was that when it came to "export ware" the Viennese had different standards than for their own Society; and the attitude of "good enough for the Americans" did in fact color the Viennese approach. Yet Erikson was really better than anyone the Americans already had. Erikson saw Brill in New York, but Brill was not much impressed by him.[5] Hanns Sachs encouraged Erikson to settle in Boston, where he worked first at Henry Murray's psychological clinic at Harvard.

Erikson's rise was meteoric. Once outside Vienna, he was freer to be himself. After leaving Freud's presence, a pupil, even a distant one like Erikson, could begin to disagree, though it remained a hard task, laden with feelings of guilt. An analyst who had never been part of the Vienna circle would be more free to proceed along his own way without being torn by conflicts over whether one was being adequately loyal or not. Erikson, unlike Alexander, had been of no known intellectual significance to Freud; whereas Alexander had a greater impact on clinical practice in North America, Erikson has had his effect on the general reading public.

Erikson's concept of identity, like Adler's notion of inferiority, gave people a name for a feeling that was important to them. Other analysts, such as Tausk and Federn, had worked with identity as an element in ego psychology, yet it is clear from Freud's attitude toward their work how alien this idea seemed to him. Nonetheless, as Erikson introduced the concept in his work he would repeatedly cite Freud's speech to B'nai B'rith in which he spoke of his "inner identity" as a Jew. That essay is of slight importance in Freud's canon, and he would have found Erikson's elaboration of identity problems at least as difficult to follow as did his daughter. Yet Erikson has had a great need, while innovating, to stress his lack of rebelliousness toward orthodox analysis; though he shared many of the ideas of the early heretics, the movement had grown large and successful enough so that no one need bother to exile him. Sometimes excessively glorifying the public image of Freud, Erikson has tried to bestow a kind of inevitability on the course he has taken in psychoanalysis. So when asked if he felt "that had Freud been living today he would reformulate his libido theory to conform to recent developments in the fields of biology, biochemistry and physiology," Erikson replied: "I'm reasonably convinced of that,"[6] even in the face of the evidence of Freud's insistence on his autonomy.

One of the central means by which Erikson has revised Freud has been through the use of the concept of "ego strength." Although Erikson put Freud's use of energy metaphors into historical context, he himself was forced to rely on the idea of "strength" to describe how the ego is capable of unifying extremes. In this way Erikson was able to measure health not in negative terms of symptoms—of what has been cut off and sacrificed in a person—but rather by the positive standard of how many extremes a man can unite in himself at the same time. On the grounds of the significance of "higher" functions, as opposed to instinctual drives, Erikson has encouraged the therapist to be sanctioning, confirming, and supportive. Many therapists resist Erikson's way of looking at things, for it is flattering to think that therapeutic success is due to the analyst's skill and understanding rather than to a patient's native health.

Erik Homburger Erikson

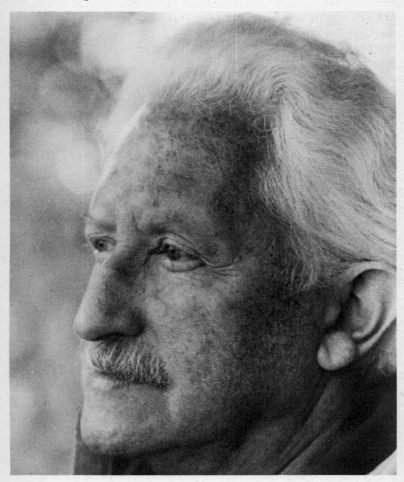

As late as 1922 the Viennese analysts were mainly interested in human sexuality.[7] Although Freud was responsible for introducing ego psychology as a legitimate part of psychoanalysis and his daughter's work became classic in the field, most traditional analysts were still primarily concerned with pathology, even when writing about ego processes.* Erikson was not content to see the ego as a passive mediator between the id, the superego, and the outside world, as it is portrayed even in Freud's later writings. Erikson has tried to sketch a developmental cycle of the ego, which has its own sources of strength, like Freud's conception of libido. Some have seen in Erikson's model of personality development a conformist image of man, to the extent that he thinks it is necessary for everyone to live through these stages in the order he outlines. But defenders of Erikson have suggested that in his view "the individual does not grow smoothly, accumulating maturity and strength in an unbroken linear progression; rather, development proceeds from struggle to struggle, and each struggle focuses on different life problems."[9]

Temperamentally ambivalent, Erikson has moved about as far "left" in the movement as it is possible to go and still be respectfully listened to and influential among analysts. It has been well said that Erikson "suggests, he hints, he insinuates. Unfailingly polite and tactful, his most telling criticisms are gently whispered." Unlike the rebellious Fromm, Erikson has "himself blurred the extent of his divergence from the psychoanalytic movement."[10] As he has explained his own position on technique, an analyst "can really learn only a method which is compatible with his own identity . . . So it isn't just a question of which method is the best for patients, but also of which method the therapist feels most at home with and creative in."[11]

There are purists who suggest that Erikson is no longer an analyst but only a psychotherapist.[12] Although Erikson has had an enormous impact on social science, in particular through his development of "psycho-history," he has not undertaken to train disciples in a manner at odds with the traditional psychoanalytic hierarchy; therefore he has not encountered the hatred that has greeted Erich Fromm. It may be that Erikson's work is no longer representative of Freud's view of psychoanalysis, but what Erikson writes would be inconceivable without its Freudian background.

If Fromm and Erikson helped interest the public in psychoanalysis, Heinz Hartmann (1894–1970) has been perhaps the leading theoretician

---

* Freud once pointed to a collection of Goethe's works and remarked: "All this was used by him as a means of self-concealment."[8]

within orthodox psychoanalysis. Although not much older than Erikson, Hartmann was established enough by the time Erikson came to Vienna to seem like a father to him. Freud's analytic "grandchildren," who had only the most distant contact with him, could be much more freethinking than the older analysts.

Although Hartmann and Fromm were at the opposite ends of the spectrum, with the former ostensibly as loyal to Freud's teachings as the latter was seemingly disrespectful, the work of both includes very few case histories. With Fromm, this is not surprising, since he admittedly favors the social and political perspective over the clinical. But for an analyst writing as explicitly in Freud's tradition as Hartmann, it may seem remarkable that his papers are so lacking in clinical examples. It was the old, dying Freud with whom Hartmann was in contact, and the abstractness of much of contemporary psychoanalytic writing, some of which sounds like a species of metaphysics, stems from the analysts who identified with the withdrawn Freud, in his last years trying to consolidate his findings for the future. The more Freud physically decayed, the more he wanted to make sure he could distill a body of scientific findings.

In his early days Freud needed an audience for the confirmation of his ideas; but this was less necessary by the 1920's, when Hartmann came to him. Hartmann arrived too late to qualify as the kind of son that Freud had in mind when he "adopted" Jung. However, like Jung, Hartmann represented the world of academic psychiatry, and was the Gentile Freud could rely on to keep analysis from being a completely Jewish affair. (Hartmann in fact had one Jewish grandparent.) Because of his association with the psychiatric clinic at the University of Vienna, Hartmann was at first suspect to Freud; the staff there was at best only ambivalently friendly to analysis. In addition, Hartmann's mind was too academic for Freud's taste. But Freud offered him a training analysis free of charge.

Hartmann's interest in methodology was more formalistic than Freud's ever became. Hartmann wanted to elaborate the mind's ego functions, and, although in different ways, it can be said of both Hartmann and Erikson that they were accommodating psychoanalysis to "many of the discoveries made by Freud's old enemies, the men who rejected Freud's emphasis on a human nature dominated by instinct."[13] Instead of seeing the ego as a dependent psychological variable, Hartmann spoke of ego processes that were autonomous from intrapsychic conflict. "Just as *conflict* is the central notion in Freud's work, *adaptation* is central in Hartmann."[14]

Like Erikson, Hartmann tried to demonstrate that his viewpoint was implicit in Freud's way of looking at things. One would think, however, that the emphasis on the conflict-free sphere of the ego, or the autonomous ego, would seem a patent divergence from Freud's interest in psychic division. Hartmann argued that what had happened over the years was merely that one ego function, that of defense, had become all-important at the expense of other functions, such as perception, attention, judgment, and so on, thereby artificially introducing an unbalanced stress in psychoanalysis on pathology as opposed to normal psychology. Freud, however, wrote in 1932: "it was impossible for me to keep this first beginning of an ego psychology back from you, and if we had possessed it fifteen years ago I should have had to mention it to you then."[15] Whether or not Hart-

Heinz Hartmann in 1934

mann's work,[16] as Glover has suggested, is essentially "static," "an armchair exercise directed toward the theoretical extension of ego adaptation,"[17] Freud was right in predicting that for ego psychology "it will be difficult to escape what is universally known; it will rather be a question of new ways of looking at things and new ways of arranging them than of new discoveries."[18]

As the American prime minister of analysis, Hartmann ran things, under Anna Freud's auspices, as though psychoanalysis were still a family; often he published jointly with Ernst Kris and Rudolf Loewenstein, and this triumvirate was probably the most authoritative source of analytic ideas in the 1950's and 1960's. Through their work psychoanalysis came into academic life, not only in medical schools but also in departments of psychology. Hartmann probably knew the extent to which Freud's genius had driven away his best pupils, and realized what this meant for future intellectual productivity in analysis. He mentioned the inhibiting influence of a genius on the men closest to him, and thought this a key aspect of the history of analysis.[19]

Freud's success is due as much to the proselytizing of his followers as to his writings. It is true that in staying close together they quoted each other more than necessary, and they brought a spirit of exegesis to Freud's work; in overestimating the distinctiveness of Freud's approach from that of his seceding pupils they·cultivated a constricting narrowness. By and large they succeeded in avoiding doctrinal feuds, and even if the therapeutic technique they advocated might not be that which Freud himself practiced, they managed to expand the scope of cases that he would have thought accessible to psychoanalytic treatment. It is still too early to assess how rich the Freudian heritage has been, but to have inspired people like Erikson or Fromm is to its lasting credit; neither, however, has proceeded on the assumption that one becomes a good psychologist merely by quoting Freud.

4. Wider Identity

WRITING ABOUT FREUD has become in itself a small industry. His psychology has not ceased to be influential, which may help explain the kind of hold he had over people even in his lifetime. One of his nieces could, long after his death, still refer to him as "Professor," indicating the awe and distance with which even members of his private family treated him.

By 1914 Freud had been "compared to Darwin or Kepler," and in 1924 Freud added Columbus's name as well.[1] The "great Darwin"[2] was a long-standing ideal of Freud's, and he was pleased to compare the opposition to psychoanalysis to previous great efforts of mankind to preserve its own sense of self-importance.

> In the course of centuries the *naïve* self-love of men has had to submit to two major blows at the hands of science. The first was when they learnt that our earth was not the center of the universe but only a tiny fragment of a cosmic system of scarcely imaginable vastness.

The "second blow fell when biological research destroyed man's supposedly privileged place in creation and proved his descent from the animal kingdom and his ineradicable animal nature." Darwin, Wallace, "and their predecessors" were responsible for this "revaluation."

> But human megalomania will have suffered its third and most wounding blow from the psychological research of the present time which seeks to prove to the ego that it is not master in its own house, but must content itself with scanty information of what is going on unconsciously in its mind.[3]

Shortly thereafter Freud again compared his work to that of Copernicus and Darwin, though at the time he offered the analogy (during World War I) it was unlikely that many independent observers would have rated his work as earth-shaking as he did.[4]

For one of Freud's birthdays a daughter-in-law ordered a cake from a famous Viennese baker which depicted different books by Freud being read in various countries of the world; this appealed to Freud's aims and sense of himself. He could complain of not receiving the Nobel Prize, covering his genuine disappointment with the thought that "it is only the money that would matter to me. . . ."[5] By the time Freud wrote his autobiographical study in 1924, his own life and that of psychoanalysis had become so completely identified in his mind that the autobiography became a history of the movement.

Freud's commitment to psychoanalysis was total, and it was awe-inspiring to see "a man who had staked his life on an idea."[6] Since Freud considered it his "destiny"[7] to be an analyst, whenever he had a chance to talk with one of his gifted followers the conversation would always be about analysis. This fascination, which dominated Freud's other interests, accelerated with the passage of years. But even in 1909 he was so dedicated to his work as to spend New Year's Eve writing letters to his pupils abroad. In a 1935 addition to his autobiography Freud wrote:

> Two themes run throughout these pages: the story of my life and the history of psychoanalysis. They are intimately interwoven. This *Autobiographical Study* shows how psychoanalysis came to be the whole content of my life and rightly assumes that no personal experiences of mine are of any interest in comparison to my relations with that science.[8]

Freud's identity was so fused with psychoanalysis that almost anything he did as part of his practice became somehow psychoanalytic. He became increasingly grandiose about the nature and uses of his findings. A few years before his death Freud wrote:

> I perceived ever more clearly that the events of human history, the interactions between human nature, cultural development and the precipitates of primaeval experience (the most prominent of which is religion) are no more than a reflection of the dynamic conflicts between the ego, the id and the super-ego, which psychoanalysis studies in the individual—are the very same processes repeated upon a wider stage.[9]

He stressed his scientific ambitions more and more, and he would even maintain that "the only appropriate preparation for the profession of educator is a thorough psychoanalytic training."[10]

Almost before Freud had a chance to enjoy world fame after World War I, he was stricken with cancer. Thenceforth not only were his physical activities restricted but intellectually he could not afford to expend his resources as he did formerly. Whereas in his younger days, when his work was at its best, the outside world had failed to accord it the proper recognition, his experience after his cancer could only confirm him in his contempt for external acceptance: the more his powers declined, the more the world hailed him as a genius.

Since Freud's death the psychoanalytic movement has cherished certain of his sayings from the last period in his life. After Freud escaped from Vienna in 1938 and settled in handsome new quarters in London, he wrote with a certain gruesome humor of "the enchantment of the new surroundings (which make one want to shout 'Heil Hitler!'). . . ."[11] When the Nazis visited his apartment in Vienna, and he was informed how much they had taken from his safe, Freud said laconically: "I have never taken so much for a single visit."[12] Freud could still joke, even in the face of the upheaval of Nazism; he said that Ernst Kris should not write to him in code, otherwise he would have to give his letters to the Gestapo to get them properly deciphered.[13] Earlier, when the Social Democrats had offered, in behalf of the Vienna municipality, to donate a piece of land on the Berggasse for the Psychoanalytic Institute, but Freud had not enough money for the rest of the project, he said he was in the position of the man who wanted to buy a *lederhosen* outfit and all he had so far were the knees.[14]

In his last years what Freud had to say was no more memorable than before, but until then he was not widely treated as a sage whose every thought was worth pondering; within his own circle, of course, Freud's status had long been acknowledged, but Freud felt cramped and restricted by his milieu and sought an identity in a wider community. His environment was generally not large enough for him. He had wanted a psychoanalytic press for the sake of his independence in promoting ideas; but the firm had never made money, although his own books were profitable. Much of what he earned from his writings was plowed back to subsidize other analytic works, and often authors were asked to help underwrite their books.

By the end of his life Freud was personally in contact with literary figures such as Thomas Mann, Stefan Zweig, and Romain Rolland, and he was himself a European man of letters. The novelist Arnold Zweig was moved to remark in a letter to Freud: "to think that you should have to invent a public for yourself—you who will have set the seal upon this whole epoch by the very fact of your having lived in it."[15] Freud boasted to Stefan Zweig: "I . . . have actually read more archeology than psychology. . . ."[16] Freud admired Thomas Mann, though he felt alien to him because of the novelist's North German manners;[17] Mann wrote some essays in Freud's honor, placing him in European thought. But as much as Freud respected artists and novelists, he feared that they might make his work seem less than pure science.

In 1910 Freud had written a beautiful essay about Leonardo, in which he sketched the conflict between the artist and the scientist in a great man; in the end, according to Freud's version, it was the scientist who won out. For all his admiration for what the artist can see intuitively, Freud had been dubious about his imaginative faculties. In *Studies on Hysteria* he had paused to comment: "it still strikes me myself as strange that the case histories I write should read like short stories and that, as one might say, they lack the serious stamp of science."[18] Yet as Freud grew old, the scientist in *him* overcame the artist, so that by 1926 we find him remonstrating: "do not try to give me literature instead of science."[19]

After Freud's cancer the human being in him began to die, and he tried more and more to take his stand on the neutral ground of science.

But his disciples saw Freud also as a simple and shy human being who did not intentionally surround himself with the aura of greatness; admiration sometimes embarrassed him, and his lonely simplicity could easily be mistaken for its opposite. As much as he aggrandized his ego in placing himself in the line of Copernicus and Darwin, he could be self-effacing about his ideas. His dualistic theory of life and death instincts had not won over most analysts, but Freud was

> all the more pleased when not long ago I came upon this theory of mine in the writings of one of the great thinkers of ancient Greece. I am very ready to give up the prestige of originality for the sake of such a confirmation. . . ."[20]

Pupils of Freud report observing him in many modest moments; he tried to avoid playing the role of the wizard or magician. He wondered aloud what would endure in psychoanalysis: " 'What will they do with my theory after my death? Will it resemble my basic thoughts?' " But as Maryse Choisy remarked, "I have often met with this kind of concern among great writers or artists, but never among scientists."[21] At times Freud sounds so self-abnegating and cautious about his work that it is hard to reconcile this mood with his polemics against his enemies; in 1924 he wrote:

> Looking back, then, over the patchwork of my life's labors, I can say that I have made many beginnings and thrown out many suggestions. Something will come of them in the future, though I cannot myself tell whether it will be much or little. I can, however, express a hope that I have opened up a pathway for an important advance in our knowledge.[22]

Even in Freud's final years he continued to move in unpredictable directions. His illness inevitably upset the equilibrium of his mind, that special combination of theoretical skill and clinical observation he had achieved. As Freud wrote in 1935 of the effects of his illness upon him:

> I myself find that a significant change has come about. Threads which in the course of my development had become inter-tangled have now begun to separate; interests which I had acquired in the later part of my life have receded, while the older and original ones become prominent once more.[23]

He had earlier protested that "only believers, who demand that science shall be a substitute for the catechism they have given up, will blame an investigator for developing or even transforming his views."[24]

Freud's intellectual interests expanded to include a broader understanding of the psychology of the ego and a more comprehensive treatment of the role of social forces. It is possible to date analysts in terms of the ideas extant when they came to analysis, and it should be no surprise that these two directions of Freud's last years—ego and society—have dominated much of the analytic literature since Freud's death. As early as World War I, Freud had wondered of the future "whether it may not be possible . . . to do justice to the part played by the ego in neurotic states and in the formation of symptoms without at the same time grossly neglecting the factors revealed by psychoanalysis."[25] Until the 1920's, however, it was the deviators in psychoanalysis—Adler, in particular—who were interested in ego psychology, whereas Freud had stuck largely to processes of repression and of the repressed.

Ego psychology has been a way of incorporating into psychoanalysis the insights of Freud's "defecting" students, while trying to retain his emphasis on the power of human instinctual life. It is hard to evaluate the change of mood in psychoanalysis which ego psychology brought about, since Freud's contributions in this area had such a deductive air to them. Freud now saw anxiety functioning as a danger signal to the ego, a motive for defense, instead of being, as in his early theory, reactive, transformed libido.

Freud did not feel entirely happy about his late writings, which he once characterized as "a phase of regressive development."[26] He is said to have remarked: "For a short while . . . I allowed myself to leave the sheltered bay of direct experience for speculation. I regret it greatly, for the consequences of so doing do not seem of the best."[27] Freud never wrote another case history after he first contracted cancer, although he collaborated on a study of Woodrow Wilson and wrote a book about the biblical Moses. What he called his "metapsychology" was the philosophical side of his writings, and it was to the broadest expansion of his ideas that he gave himself up in his last years. At the same time his writings after 1923 also represent his taking leave of human relationships.

Freud proposed that the distinguishing feature of the ego was "a tendency to synthesis in its contents."[28] The ego has the task of maneuvering with instinctual energies as a rider does with a horse, and the ego's "three tyrannical masters are the external world, the superego and the id."[29] Unlike later ego psychologists such as Hartmann and Erikson, Freud himself never went so far as to hypothesize an independent role for the ego's functions, and to the end he emphasized the importance of the vicissitudes of instinctual conflicts. For Freud, the ego was "really something superficial and the id something deeper," even though he suggested that "large portions of the ego can remain permanently unconscious."[30] He felt uncomfortable discussing his concept of the superego:

> If we possessed more applications of this kind, the hypothesis of the super-ego would lose its last touch of strangeness for us, and we should become completely free of the embarrassment that still comes over us when, accustomed as we are to the atmosphere of the underworld, we move in the more superficial, higher strata of the mental apparatus. We do not suppose, of course, that with the separation off of the super-ego we have said the last word on the psychology of the ego.[31]

Freud's early patients have reported that, as far as they could tell, he was not at all interested in politics, ethics, or a philosophy of life. Although he continued his clinical practice until shortly before his death, and he had engaged in social speculation (as in *Totem and Taboo*) long before his illness, it is fair to say that in his last years Freud tended to take an abstract view of the human personality, as an object to be investigated rather than treated, and he turned toward social philosophy rather than psychology. Freud felt the need to fill out the implications of his earlier work, especially in regard to religious belief. For all his protestations to the contrary, he had an artistic and synthesizing side to him; but it was in behalf of scientific truth that he denounced religion as an illusion.

Freud had long held that "society . . . is based on sublimated homosexual feelings."[32] As he once wrote, "our civilization is built up entirely at the expense of sexuality. . . ."[33] To be civilized meant to be repressed and less sexual, and therefore civilization had taken something away from the individual. Freud shared the fantasy of others that the lower classes, and nonliterate peoples, enjoyed freer sexual expression: "Among races at a low level of civilization, and among the lower strata of civilized races, the sexuality of children seems to be given free reign."[34] At the end of his life Freud became absorbed in the cultural sciences, not so much on the basis of his original research as through his reading of *belles-lettres*. The sloughing off of medicine did not occur all at once, but was a gradual process. As he wrote in 1935, "My interest, after making a lifelong *détour* through the natural sciences, medicine and psychotherapy, returned to the cultural problems which had fascinated me long before, when I was a youth scarcely old enough for thinking."[35]

In *Totem and Taboo* and *The Future of an Illusion*, Freud was working toward what he fancied as "the solution of the problem of religion."[36]

The application of his psychoanalytic method was "by no means confined," he held, "to the field of psychological disorders, but extends also to the solution of problems in art, philosophy and religion."[37] Sociology was to Freud merely a branch of psychology: "For sociology . . . , dealing as it does with the behavior of people in society, cannot be anything but applied psychology. Strictly speaking there are only two sciences: psychology, pure and applied, and natural science."[38] In Freud's mind he had had nothing less than "the whole human race"[39] as his patient. One has to recall that, during World War I, it was he who referred negatively to Jung's prophetic ambitions. But by 1924 Freud was holding:

> As a "depth psychology," a theory of the mental unconscious, it [psychoanalysis] can become indispensable to all the sciences which are concerned with the evolution of human civilization and its major institutions such as art, religion and the social order . . . The use of analysis for the treatment of the neuroses is only one of its applications; the future will perhaps show that it is not the most important one.[40]

Despite the grounds on which Freud had earlier quarreled with Adler, by 1926 he thought that "there is no reason for surprise that psychoanalysis, which was originally no more than an attempt at explaining pathological mental phenomena, should have developed into a psychology of normal mental life."[41] Increasingly cautious about therapeutic achievements yet nonetheless bold in using clinical insights in social theory, Freud was almost extravagantly committed to the rationalistic path of science:

> The riddles of the universe reveal themselves only slowly to our investigation; there are many questions to which science today can give no answer. But scientific work is the only road which can lead us to a knowledge of reality outside ourselves. It is . . . an illusion to expect anything from intuition and introspection; they can give us nothing but particulars about our own mental life, which are hard to interpret, never any information about the questions which religious doctrine finds it so easy to answer.[42]

This reliance on science was the basis for Freud's optimism about man's future. Arnold Zweig correctly divined Freud's true aims when he wrote Freud that "analysis has reversed all values, it has conquered Christianity, disclosed the true Antichrist, and liberated the spirit of resurgent life from the ascetic ideal."[43] Freud specifically criticized Christianity, since for him "not all men are worthy of love."[44] He hoped for "superior, unswerving and disinterested leaders . . . to act as educators of the future

Freud taking his first airplane flight in Berlin, 1928

generations."[45] Civilization was based on a struggle between life and death instincts, and order was an essential ingredient of man as a social being: as Freud put it, "law was originally brute violence and . . . even today it cannot do without the support of violence."[46]

The book that absorbed Freud's last years, and which he composed between 1934 and 1938, was *Moses and Monotheism*. It was oddly constructed, and Freud's argument did not march with his usual syllogistic skill. Freud admitted the "weakening of creative powers which goes along with old age. . . . ," and knew that he had undertaken this book "with the audacity of one who has little or nothing to lose."[47] He feared that the publication of the book "would probably lead to our being prohibited from practicing psychoanalysis,"[48] and acknowledged how tenuous was the particular thesis he wanted to establish. But the rise of Hitler had impelled a whole generation of emancipated Jews to affirm their Judaism, and in Freud's speculative phase he wanted (having touched on the death instinct, ego psychology, and social philosophy) to confront the origins of the Jews' unique cultural characteristics. Throughout the 1930's Freud could not "shake off" the Moses problem; as he wrote in 1934, "the man and what I wanted to make of him pursue me everywhere."[49] The next year Freud remarked: "it suffices me that I myself can believe in the solution of the problem. It has pursued me throughout the whole of my life."[50]

In Freud's last phase his preference for art objects had shifted from Graeco-Roman to Egyptian-Chinese-Indian, but ancient Egypt had long interested him. Freud found that one of his patient's "mental life impressed one in much the same way as the religion of Ancient Egypt, which is so unintelligible to us because it preserves the earlier stages of its development side by side with the end products. . . ."[51] He was fascinated by Napoleon's trip to Egypt, and when one realizes the multiple grounds for Freud's own identification with the figure of Napoleon,* his comments are worthy of note:

> that magnificent rascal Napoleon, who remained fixated on his puberty phantasies, was blessed with incredible good luck, inhibited by no ties apart from his family, and made his way through life like a sleepwalker, until he was finally shipwrecked by his *folie de grandeur*. There scarcely ever was a genius so totally lacking in distinction, an

---

* Cf. above, pp. 29–30.

absolutely classic Anti-Gentleman, but he was cut on the grand scale.[52]

Freud's most startling contention in *Moses and Monotheism* was that the Moses of legend is in fact a composite of two historical Moseses, and the earlier one, the true founder of monotheism, was not a Jew but an Egyptian aristocrat. Freud's interpretation saw the earlier, supposedly slain leader as ambitious and "of an irascible nature"; he was "jealous, severe and ruthless." In addition, Freud maintained, this Moses was "slow of speech,"[53] and on this one point Freud's conception was in accord with biblical tradition, which has it that Moses was heavy of tongue, a stutterer. And, of course, Freud's cancer gave him speech difficulties.

As Freud had been forced to find his own family from among the immortals—Leonardo, Goethe, Michelangelo, and so on—he thought Shakespeare must have been an aristocrat; conversely, if Freud believed the legend that made Romulus the "offspring and heir of the royal house," then "if any such person existed, he must have been an adventurer of unknown origin, an upstart. . . ."[54] For Freud, things were never what they seemed on the surface, and therefore he transposed the Jew Moses, the son of slaves, into not only a Gentile but an aristocrat as well. Freud was sure that "in a few decades my name will be wiped out and our results will last," and as the Jews accepted the law transmitted to them by Moses, others in the future would harken to Freud's creeds.[55]

According to Freud's reconstruction of the origins of monotheism, it was Amenophis IV who was the real originator. This Pharaoh "with magnificent inflexibility . . . resisted every temptation to magical thought. . . . In an astonishing presentiment of later scientific discovery he recognized in the energy of solar radiation the source of all life. . . ." If this was the "first and perhaps the clearest case of a monotheistic religion in human history. . . ." his people were not ready for it and after his death "the memory of the heretic king was proscribed." In Freud's view, "every novelty must have its preliminaries and preconditions in something earlier," but Amenophis IV had, in the doctrine of exclusiveness, "introduced something new."[56]

The first Moses was a follower of the proscribed Pharaoh, and (like Freud himself in turning to his Swiss followers) "under the necessity of his disappointment and loneliness . . . turned to these foreigners [the Jews] and with them sought compensation for his losses. He chose them as his people and tried to realize his ideals in them." Through Jung, Freud had been the originator who selected a Gentile following; here Freud stripped the Jews of one of their greatest leaders by proposing that Moses was a

Gentile who chose the Jews to carry forward his doctrine. But the old theme of priorities is unmistakable:

> The great religious idea for which the man Moses stood was, on our view, not his own property; he had taken it over from King Akhenaten [Amenophis]. And he, whose greatness as the founder of a religion is unequivocably established, may perhaps have been following hints which had reached him—from near or distant parts of Asia—through the medium of his mother or by other paths . . . Thus it seems unfruitful to try to fix the credit due to an individual in connection with a new idea.

Freud proposed that Moses, like his Pharaoh—and like Freud's own image of himself—failed, having "met with the same fate that awaits all enlightened despots."[57]

His conviction that Moses was an Egyptian, raising "the question of this great man's nationality," turned his hero into an alien. Psychoanalysis had suffered from anti-German animus throughout Europe, while Freud's being Jewish was no asset in Vienna.

Perhaps under the influence of writers such as Wilhelm Reich, in his last years Freud grew more sensitive to sociological factors. In his Moses book he took up cudgels against those who would distort our understanding of historical processes, specifically against the Marxists. In examining the Moses legend, Freud was impressed "how impossible it is to dispute the personal influence upon world-history of individual great men, what sacrilege one commits against the splendid diversity of human life if one recognizes only those motives which arise from material needs. . . ." For "it was this one man Moses who created the Jews," as Freud felt he had created psychoanalysis. Freud could identify with what he saw as "the autonomy and independence of the great man, his divine unconcern which may grow into ruthlessness . . . his wrathful temper and his relentlessness."[58]

As in "all such advances in intellectuality" as monotheism (or, we may add, psychoanalysis), Freud thought the adherent "feels superior to other people who may have remained under the spell of sensuality." The religion of Moses was admirable to Freud precisely because it "condemns magic and sorcery in the severest terms. . . ."; "everything to do with myths, magic and sorcery is excluded from it"—in "contrast to popular religion. . . ." In keeping with his own stoical attitude toward death, Freud approved of the way "the ancient Jewish religion renounced immortality entirely. . . ." However, Freud continued to search for the psychological origins of ethics, and he felt that monotheism's "ethical ideas cannot . . .

disavow their origin from the sense of guilt felt on account of a suppressed hostility to God." In this way Freud was consistent with his dogmatic view that "religious phenomena are only to be understood on the pattern of the individual neurotic symptoms familiar to us. . . ."[59]

If Freud ended his life with a novelistic account of a political leader such as Moses, rather than a case history of a patient or an essay on an artist such as Leonardo, it was in part a reflection of his early ambition to become a lawyer and politician; but it was also clearly a response to the beginnings of the holocaust that was about to descend upon European Jewry.

5. Exile and Death

FREUD HAD STUBBORNLY RESISTED SUGGESTIONS that he leave Vienna; having made so much of anti-Semitism in his life, he nonetheless denied the real danger when it came. Throughout the 1930's his more self-protective pupils fled abroad to safety. Herman Nunberg remembered Freud's anger, and how, during Nunberg's absence in the United States in 1932,

> Freud had talked to my wife; he wanted her to write to me to come back where I was needed, to be satisfied with what Vienna had to offer me. He did not see the threatening danger. When I visited Vienna again in 1934, and implored Freud to leave Austria, he tried even then to convince me that there was no real danger, that the existing government of Austria would protect the Jews and not yield to the Nazis. As for him, he said, he was an old man and a sick one; Vienna was his home, and it was there that his doctors were, men who knew him well and whom he needed.[1]

When Felix and Helene Deutsch went to say their final good-bye to Freud, Frau Professor said their leaving was "pure high-spiritness." The characteristic Viennese attitude was to regard Austrian culture as distinct from that of Germany; according to an old saw, where the heavy-handed Germans might see a situation as "serious but not hopeless," to the more lighthearted Viennese it was "hopeless but not serious."

It was easy for Freud to believe that National Socialism would not affect Austria. In general, Freud had felt alien to the Germans.* As a Jew, Freud detached himself from the fortunes of Germany, whose citizens seemed to him characterized by thoroughness and cruelty. He regarded Hitler as a "German disgrace,"[3] and that was all. When Mark Brunswick once bemoaned the absence of barbarians who could bring freshness to a declining civilization, Freud commented that we already had the Prussians. (According to Brunswick, Freud thought World War I should have ended in a stalemate.[4]) Freud came to hate the Germans, and in 1932 wrote to Arnold Zweig: "I can relieve you of the illusion that one has to be a German. Should we not leave this Godforsaken nation to themselves?"[5] Not long after the Nazis came to power Freud's books were being publicly burned in Berlin.

Politically, Freud could be naïve,† and is earlier reported to have said of Germany that "a nation that produced Goethe could not possibly go to the bad."[8] Yet it is easy, in retrospect, to underrate the difficulty of adjusting to the idea not only that the Nazi revolution had come about in Germany but also that it would threaten all Europe. Increasingly Freud was afraid of being left alone in Vienna as analysts began to flee the Nazi danger. After all his bickering about the special hostility to his ideas in Vienna, only after arriving in London did he acknowledge his love for his native city: "I always greatly loved the prison from which I have been released."[9] Up to the end Freud hoped that by staying in Vienna he could rescue something of psychoanalysis, if only the Society's library.

Politically, Freud was, as he once put it, "a liberal of the old school,"[10] which meant that his sympathies were alien to both the Communist Left and the Fascist Right of his day.‡ His brother Alexander was far more conservative and hated the Socialists, and Freud would listen to him discuss the evils of socialism with an understanding smile.[12] During the first civil war in Vienna in 1927, the Freuds stayed neutral, but "when the second civil war occurred in the summer of 1934 . . . the Freud family were

---

* But Freud is quoted as once having said: "My language is German. My culture, my attainments are German. I considered myself German intellectually, until I noticed the growth of anti-Semitic prejudice in Germany and German Austria. Since that time, I consider myself no longer a German. I prefer to call myself a Jew."[2]

† As evidence of Freud's political credulity, Mark Brunswick recalled that Freud had believed all the stories about Hitler's sexual perversions—in particular, that he got satisfaction from a prostitute's urinating in his mouth.[6] A later psychological study of Hitler accepted this idea as a historical reality.[7]

‡ In February 1918 Freud wrote of the Russian Revolution that he was "sorry" "its radical policies have been so discredited . . . What the human beast needs above all is restraint. In short, one grows reactionary. . . ."[11]

anything but neutral . . . : all our sympathies," wrote Freud's son Martin, "were with the Chancellor Dollfuss and his successor Schuschnigg."[13] The Dollfuss regime was clerical and authoritarian, "a somewhat fascist type administration"[14] although anti-Nazi. According to Martin Freud, who hung a picture of Dollfuss on a wall of the *Verlag*, "the majority of the Viennese population were . . . Socialists who had become hostile to the Dollfuss regime after their defeat in the first civil war."[15] Freud was not the only one to go over to Dollfuss's side. His old critic, the satirist Karl Kraus, now supported the Dollfuss regime even though it "stood for everything that Kraus [like Freud] in his earlier years had bitterly fought against."[16]

Freud could even flatter Mussolini. The leader of the Italian psychoanalytic movement, Edoardo Weiss, brought a patient to meet Freud, after a relatively successful period of treatment.[17] Her father, a high official in Mussolini's government, but described by a recent historian as merely a "mouthpiece" of Mussolini, came along too, and after the interview asked Freud for a present of one of his books for Mussolini. For Freud to have refused would have hurt not only Weiss but also psychoanalysis in Italy, but his inscription in *Why War?*, two open letters by him and Albert Einstein, was perhaps more lavish than absolutely necessary: "Benito Mussolini with the respectful greeting of an old man who recognizes in the ruler the cultural hero."[18]

Freud's interest in archaeology led him to admire Mussolini's new excavations in Rome, but there was more to Freud's action. Perhaps out of naïveté, Freud chose to overrate grossly Weiss's political connections in Italy. On such a slender basis—Weiss's having treated the daughter of an Italian leader—Freud could write in 1934 that "Weiss had direct access to Mussolini. . . ."[19] Weiss was in reality an anti-Fascist with almost no political pull, yet Jones (partly out of identification with Freud) not only exaggerated Mussolini's interest in protecting psychoanalysis in Italy, but also had the fantasy that Mussolini was a real help in getting Freud out of Vienna in 1938.[20] It is true that for a time Mussolini tried to keep Hitler from seizing Austria, which perhaps helps to explain Freud's passing remark in *Moses and Monotheism*: "with similar violence" to that employed by the Russian Communists, "the Italian people are," Freud thought, "being trained up to orderliness and a sense of duty." Freud believed that some good might come of the "experiments" in the Soviet Union and Italy, whereas he found it "a relief from an oppressive apprehension when we see in the case of the German people that a relapse into almost pre-historic barbarism can occur as well without being attached to any progressive ideas."[21]

After the Nazis had taken power in Germany, Felix Boehm (a Gentile) took over from Eitingon (a Polish Jew) as leader of the Berlin Society. The situation was awkward for some time. Boehm visited Freud in Vienna, and said he wanted to invite a lecturer from the Vienna Society to Berlin. He selected a young analyst, Richard Sterba, one of the few Gentiles prominent in the Vienna psychoanalytic group. Sterba said he would go, provided that a Jewish colleague was invited first. Under Boehm's leadership Adler and Jung were being read at the Berlin Psychoanalytic Institute; Freud told Boehm that he was prepared to make sacrifices but not concessions, which amounted to a condemnation of Boehm for having, in Freud's eyes, watered down psychoanalysis.[22]

Anna Freud and Edoardo Weiss in 1934

When the Nazis came to Vienna everyone in Freud's circle was in trouble. After the invasion, at the last meeting of the governing board of the Vienna Psychoanalytic Society, Freud remarked that "we are all used to persecution—from our history, our tradition, and some from personal experience." He then added that there was one exception present, Sterba. In a sentence that later appeared in *Moses and Monotheism*, Freud said to his pupils: "Immediately after the destruction of the Temple in Jerusalem by Titus, the Rabbi Jochanan ben Zakkai asked permission to open the first Torah school in Jabneh."[23] To Freud, the end of psychoanalysis in Vienna marked the beginning of another Diaspora. Although only one Viennese analyst, Sadger—who was already out of favor with Freud— perished at the hands of the Nazis, this was largely because people such as Jones and Marie Bonaparte had been brave, and influential, enough to come to Vienna immediately to protect Freud once the Nazis took over. With their help and money, in addition to the aid of William Bullitt, who was then the American ambassador to France, it was possible to ransom Freud out. Although many analysts in Vienna complained that Freud had stayed too long, without the protection of his prestige it is possible that things might have been even worse for some in his circle.

From the perspective of our own time, Freud seems very much a man from an alien country in another century; although he survived well into the twentieth century, he was really a representative of the preceding one. To cite a trivial but telling feature of his daily routine, "a barber appeared every morning to trim his beard and if necessary his hair."[24] To his Continental followers, in old age he appeared a typical university professor of the 1890's; for Viennese medical circles had by and large stood still, living on the glories of the 1880's and 1890's, when their medical school was the best in Europe.

One must understand these cultural aspects of Freud's character if one is to put his neurotic traits into proper perspective. For example, the obsessive-compulsive aspect of Freud, his clarity as well as rigidity in thinking, became more pronounced as he grew old. Befitting his cultural era, Freud was a man of many rituals, and it was a sure instinct which led one of the members of his Society, Rudolf von Urbantschitsch, when trying to lure Freud into becoming the official head of a new sanitarium in the country, to offer to build him an exact replica of his office in his new home.[25]

Freud once described obsessionality as the way "the expression of intense feelings, which have however become unconscious through repression, is displaced onto trivial and even foolish actions."[26] In his last years anything unexpected or not guarded against would arouse anxiety and discomfort in Freud. Once he knocked at Tante Minna's door because she had left a pencil in his study that he wanted to return. Given these exacting needs, it seems fitting that Freud became a moderately active stamp collector. His sink would usually be full of stamps, and sometimes in the evening Freud would arrange them on sheets.[27]

Intellectual control always meant a great deal to Freud, and this need stimulated him to study dreams, even if it prevented him from understanding emotions like "transience" or the "oceanic feeling." Freud would use the word "uncanny" rather loosely, so that sometimes it seems that anything not purely rational was mysterious to him. And as Freud grew older his personality narrowed.

There may be a lesson here for our conception of normality. What is really wrong about the picture of Freud given us by his most orthodox followers is that it leads to an erroneous and unnecessarily bourgeois conception of the range of normal behavior. As Freud became in some sense greater through his self-mastery, enduring so many years of intense physical suffering, he may have simultaneously become more limited as a person. Self-mastery can have its costs in human openness, and whatever the merits of such control it may also impose restrictions of its own.

Freud's orderliness did smooth his daily life, as his need for structure helped him organize his thoughts and write his books. He was discontented with partial knowledge; "in limiting your aims," he would nevertheless claim, "that's masterly." But if Freud grew so detached in his old age, it was partly because something in him had already died. When in 1928 a young pupil praised *The Future of an Illusion*, Freud replied: "This is my worst book! . . . It isn't a book of Freud . . . It's the book of an old man! . . . Besides Freud is dead now, and believe me, the genuine Freud was really a great man. I am particularly sorry for you that you didn't know him better."[28]

It was this old Freud who became the sage in his last years. He achieved his final great serenity in the face of tormenting suffering. When Stefan Zweig visited him in London, he thought "it was my first experience of a true sage, exalted beyond himself, to whom neither pain nor death longer counted as a personal experience but as a supra-personal matter of observation and contemplation; his dying was no less of a moral fact than his life."[29] Freud's Olympian resignation was the fulfillment of his stoicism; a favorite misquotation[30] of his was: "Everyone owes nature a death" (Shakespeare had written: "Thou owest God a death"). In photographs taken in London, showing his face lined with suffering, Freud looks like many traditional representations of Christ.

He had been persuaded to leave for London* only after the Gestapo had temporarily taken his daughter Anna into custody. After her release she told Freud that they had made it a condition of letting her go that she make a daily visit to the police. " 'You, Anna,' he said, 'have of course refused to obey so humiliating an order.' "[31] There was a rash of suicides at the time, by Austrians unable or unwilling to face life abroad. Freud counseled his daughter Anna against such a course.

In Paris, Freud's former patient Bullitt had contacted President Roosevelt in Freud's behalf, but Bullitt doubted Roosevelt had done anything to intervene. The American consul in Vienna did send a man every day to keep the Gestapo off. The German ambassador to France, according to Bullitt, also helped to secure Freud's release. Once Freud had agreed to leave, there were still steps to be taken with the new political authorities in Austria, and he did not depart until June 4, 1938. Marie Bonaparte and Anna Freud spent part of their time classifying Freud's correspondence, and in the evenings they burned some of his papers. It was necessary, however, to leave much of Freud's library behind; but the money Marie Bonaparte put up (about five thousand dollars, which Freud returned to her in London) helped obtain good treatment for him.

Although the immediate Freud family and the analysts who wanted to go succeeded in getting out, his four surviving sisters stayed behind. Freud and his brother Alexander left their sisters money, but it seemed impossible (according to Jones) to bring them to England and to support them there. Not many realized even then the extent of the Nazi threat. Later that year, however, Marie Bonaparte tried to get Freud's sisters into France, but red tape obstructed her efforts in their behalf. All Freud's sisters were killed in concentration camps during the war.

Freud did bring out his art collection, the antiquities he surrounded himself with; each of them had its personal history of where and when he had found it or who had given it to him. Freud's exactitude always required that the figures of the little gods be in the same order on his desk, and in his home at 20 Maresfield Gardens in London his housekeeper's "memory enabled her to replace the various objects on Freud's desk in their precise order, so that he felt at home the moment he sat at it on his arrival."[32]

Freud had first visited England at the age of nineteen, and for him it

---

* Freud's health might not have permitted him to go to America.

*Freud in Paris on June 13, 1938, being met by
Marie Bonaparte and William Bullitt*

always remained a home for the persecuted. He participated in British psychoanalytic activities to the extent of sitting in on two editorial meetings of the *International Journal of Psychoanalysis*; he would listen, let everyone have his say, and at the end express his opinion, which was then accepted. But essentially Freud was now in full retirement, a guest in a foreign land. His mind was still active, but he could not really rise to any new work; to those who had not seen him for some time he seemed to have shrunk. He did not talk freely, but made a phonograph recording in which he predicted that the struggle for psychoanalysis was not yet over.

Arthur Koestler visited him, and came away thinking that "though small and fragile . . . the dominating impression was not that of a sick octogenarian, but of the indestructible vitality of the Hebrew patriarchs."[33] Leonard Woolf, Freud's London publisher, paid him a call with his novelist wife Virginia, and Freud was extremely courteous in a formal, old-fashioned way; for instance, "almost ceremoniously he presented Virginia with a flower." Woolf thought him "an extraordinarily nice man," who had "an aura, not of fame, but of greatness . . . There was something about him as of a half-extinct volcano, something sombre, suppressed, reserved . . . a formidable man."[34]

Freud retained his sense of humor. Woolf brought a clipping from a London newspaper about a trial; someone had stolen one of Freud's books from the city's largest bookstore, and in sentencing him to three months in jail the judge had added: "I only wish I could sentence you to read all of Freud's books." Freud laughed.[35] There were other visitors, such as Isaiah Berlin, who thought that it would be a good idea just to meet Freud. Throughout the last year of his life, followers leaving the Continent, or coming over from the United States for a visit, paid homage. When Eva Rosenfeld saw him in 1939, she remarked on how his study had been reassembled almost identical to what it had been in his old suite in Vienna. "Everything is here," Freud remarked, "only I am not here."

Freud continued with his letter writing and completed a short "Comment on Anti-Semitism"; in it he quotes a "Gentile's" view of the way much criticism of anti-Semitism is in fact unduly patronizing toward the Jews:

> we have no right to look down on them. In some respects, indeed, they are our superiors. They do not need so much alcohol as we do in order to make life tolerable; crimes of brutality, murder, robbery and sexual violence are great rarities among them; they have always set a high value on intellectual achievement and interests; their family life

is more intimate; they take better care of the poor; charity is a sacred duty to them . . . So let us cease at last to hand them out favours when they have a claim to justice.[36]

Freud could not recall his source—and Ernest Jones and Anna Freud thought that Freud had been engaging in self-quotation, which would be a curious last twist to Freud's long-standing concern for priorities; Freud was asserting his independence and making a gift of his own thoughts to an anonymous Gentile. Jones thought that if Freud invented these paragraphs for the occasion instead of quoting from someone else, then he had "put into words what some Gentile should have, his remark about not being able to find the original constituting an oblique reproach."[37]

One of Freud's chief reasons for hesitating to leave Vienna had been the unpleasant prospect of being dependent on doctors unfamiliar with his case. It turned out that his London doctors were too slow in diagnosing the recurrence of malignancies. Marie Bonaparte thought his doctors in London were afraid of him; his Viennese surgeon, Pichler, had rough ways and operated at the first signs of trouble. By late February 1939 his cancer was for the first time deemed inoperable and incurable. Despite whatever treatments were then available, by May 6, his last birthday, he was in frightful pain. But he still had three or four patients and carried on his practice until the end of July. In June he had written "my world is again what it was before—a little island of pain floating on a sea of indifference."[38] When his personal physician, Schur, made a short trip to the United States to begin the first steps toward citizenship, for a time Freud took it as if Schur, like the rest of Freud's world, was leaving him.

For those who loved Freud it was torture to look at him; the beginning of the end came when he stopped seeing patients. For his last two months he could not work any more.[39] He could still read, however. Jones and Schur have discussed in print the significance of the last book Freud read, Balzac's *Le Peau de Chagrin*; it fascinated Freud because everything for him was shrinking and diminishing as in the novel, and he knew the end could not be far off. (But Jones was disheartened to hear from Anna Freud of Freud's great love for detective stories, especially following operations; Agatha Christie and Dorothy Sayers were special favorites.[40])

Among Freud's pupils the legend has it that Freud's mind was perfectly clear to the end. The evidence for this comes mainly from Max Schur and Anna Freud. Others, such as Frau Professor, found him strange and different.[41] When a friendly Viennese lawyer, Dr. Indra, stopped by to see Freud in May on a trip back to Vienna from America, Freud said:

"Now you are going back to . . . What is the name of the place?" (Jones interpreted this, not, as Indra had thought, as an act of forgetfulness, but as a "pretended amnesia to convey his struggle to forget Vienna."[42])

There is, however, no necessary contradiction between Freud's seeming transformed to some and normal to Anna Freud and Schur. For these two were essentially keeping him alive, while the rest of the world was becoming more remote. With Anna and Schur he would be as alert as possible, and they accurately reported what they witnessed. But Freud did tend to isolate his responses, and one has to take into account the special perspective from which Anna and Schur observed him.

Writing letters until a few days before his death, Freud seems to have been lucid. The main manuscript he left unfinished, *An Outline of Psychoanalysis,* was put aside by Freud in September 1938, so it tells us nothing about the state of his mind at the end. It would not be surprising if he experienced certain toxic symptoms, for, if anyone ever died a real death, it was Freud.

He died after horrible suffering; he was so old and sick that it was a deliverance finally to die. His cheek had had to be pierced from the outside, to allow better medical access to the cancer. A terrible odor of putrefaction from the wound began to develop; in August his favorite dog would not come near him. Freud had great trouble taking nourishment, his appetite had gone; he would awake in the middle of the night, and Anna would see if he could take any food. He was as dependent as a child, but showed his usual courtesy to the housemaid, Paula, who prepared his food. Off and on for years he had been endangered by starvation; now it was becoming a reality.

In all this Freud accepted very little medical assistance. He could tolerate only an occasional aspirin. "I prefer to think in torment than not to be able to think clearly."[43] Toward the end insulfation with a cocaine derivative helped alleviate his misery.

Anna Freud's tender care and nursing, her vigilant and protective watch for precancerous growths over the years, had prolonged her father's life. But in the summer of 1939 his illness was permitted to drag on. Schur, had it been up to him, would have ended the suffering at least a few weeks earlier.[44] It was painful for him to see Freud at rest in his sick bay, an open hole in his cheek, with mosquito netting to keep the flies off. But Anna Freud could not bring herself to allow Schur to act. (Frau Professor's views at this stage did not count at all.) Freud would not or could not take morphia.

Until three days before Freud died he could still read and take an interest in things, but when he put his last book aside it was a sign of the end. On September 21, 1939, he said to his doctor: "My dear Schur, you remember our first talk. You promised me then you would help me when I could no longer carry on. It is only torture now and it has no longer any sense." Schur promised sedation and granted Freud the right of euthanasia. He was so weak and unused to opiates that the small dose of morphia Schur gave him the next morning was enough to send him to sleep. He died on September 23. With the advice of his sons Martin and Ernst, Freud left an estate (20,000 English pounds) to the whole family, from which Martha could draw at will. The analytic library and the collection of antiques went specifically to Anna.[45] Contrary to Jewish custom, Freud was cremated at Golder's Green in London on September 26. Ernest Jones and Stefan Zweig spoke, and Freud's ashes were placed in a favorite Grecian urn that Marie Bonaparte had given him. Ever since his death a small group of his followers, on the anniversaries of his birthday and his death, have gathered in his memory at the crematorium.

NOTES

INDEX

LIST OF PERSONS INTERVIEWED

Dr. Hilda Abraham
Mrs. Karl Abraham
Dr. Alexandra Adler
Dr. Michael Balint
Dr. Therese Benedek
Dr. E. A. Bennet
Sir Isaiah Berlin
Mr. Edward Bernays
Miss Hella Bernays
Dr. Bruno Bettelheim
Dr. Carl Binger
Dr. Smiley Blanton
Miss Berta Bornstein
Dr. John Bowlby
Dr. David Brunswick
Prof. Mark Brunswick
Mrs. Stephanie Dabo
Dr. Helene Deutsch
Dr. H. V. Dicks
Dr. Kurt Eissler
Prof. and Mrs. Erik Erikson
Mr. Ernst Federn
Dr. Michael Fordham
Dr. Thomas French
Mrs. Alexander Freud
Miss Anna Freud
Dr. Esti Freud
Mr. and Mrs. Oliver Freud

Dr. and Mrs. Erich Fromm
Dr. William Gillespie
Dr. Edward Glover
Mr. Geoffrey Gorer
Dr. Roy Grinker, Sr.
Dr. and Mrs. Martin Grotjahn
Dr. Heinz Hartmann
Dr. Leston Havens
Dr. Paula Heimann
Mrs. Judith Bernays Heller
Dr. Ives Hendrick
Mr. Albert Hirst
Mrs. Edward Hitschmann
Dr. Willi Hoffer
Dr. and Mrs. Richard Hoffmann
Mrs. Mathilda Freud Hollitscher
Dr. Otto Isakower
Dr. Edith Jackson
Dr. Jolandi Jacobi
Dr. Elliott Jacques
Dr. Robert Jokl
Mrs. Ernest Jones
Dr. Abram Kardiner
Dr. Anny Katan
Prof. Hans Kelsen
Mr. M. Masud Khan
Dr. Marianne Kris
Dr. Edward Kronold

Dr. Lawrence Kubie

Dr. Jeanne Lampl-de Groot

Prof. Harold Lasswell

Mrs. Elma Laurvik

Prof. Nathan Leites

Mrs. Kata Levy

Dr. John Mack

Mrs. Nada Mascherano-Tausk

Prof. Heinrich Meng

Dr. Emmanuel Miller

Dr. Fritz Moellenhoff

Dr. Roger Money-Kyrle

Mrs. Merrill Moore

Prof. Henry Murray

Dr. Herman Nunberg

Mrs. Ochsner

Prof. Talcott Parsons

Dr. Sylvia Payne

Prof. Lionel Penrose

Dr. Irmarita Putnam

Dr. Marian Putnam

Dr. Sandor Rado

Mrs. Beata Rank

Dr. J. R. Rees

Dr. Annie Reich

Dr. Theodor Reik

Prof. David Riesman

Mrs. Eva Rosenfeld

Dr. Charles Rycroft

Mrs. Hanns Sachs

Dr. Philip Sarasin

Dr. and Mrs. Raymond Saussure

Dr. Melitta Schmideberg

Dr. Max Schur

Dr. Hannah Segal

Dr. Rene Spitz

Dr. Richard Sterba

Dr. Anthony Storr

Mr. and Mrs. James Strachey

Dr. John Sutherland

Dr. Marius Tausk

Dr. Victor Hugo Tausk

Dr. Alan Tyson

Mrs. Helene Veltfort

Dr. Robert Waelder

Dr. Richard Wagner

Dr. Edoardo Weiss

Dr. Allen Wheelis

Prof. Robert White

Dr. and Mrs. George Wilbur

Dr. Donald Winnicott

Dr. Martha Wolfenstein

Mr. Leonard Woolf

Dr. Elizabeth Zetzel

PREFACE

1. "Some General Remarks on Hysterical Attacks," *The Standard Edition of the Complete Psychological Works of Sigmund Freud*, ed. James Strachey (London: Hogarth; 1953-1974), Vol. 9, p. 231. Hereafter this edition of Freud's works will be referred to simply as *Standard Edition*.

2. New York: Knopf; 1968. London: Hogarth; 1969. New York: Vintage; 1970.

3. Some of these have now been published. Cf. "Some Early Unpublished Letters of Freud," *International Journal of Psychoanalysis*, Vol. 50, Part 4 (1969), pp. 419-27.

4. New York: Knopf; 1969. London: Penguin; 1970. New York: Vintage; 1971. London: Pelican; 1973. For a further discussion of Tausk, cf. Paul Roazen, "Reflections on Ethos and Authenticity in Psychoanalysis," *The Human Context*, Vol. 4, No. 3 (Autumn 1972), pp. 577-87. This article was written as a reply to Kurt Eissler's attack.

INTRODUCTION:

Meeting Freud's Patients and Pupils

1. Many years before my project, Kurt Eissler, on behalf of the Freud archives, conducted tape-recorded interviews with surviving early analysts and patients. Partly in order to persuade them to cooperate, he promised that their material would be sealed in the Library of Congress for fifty to one hundred years; as a result, the innocuous as well as the purely private have been made inaccessible. Some people I interviewed claimed not to know of this restriction on their material, and others had no objection to its being made available for scholarly work. Eissler sent to Ernest Jones copies of his interviews with Paul Klemperer and Albert Hirst (Jones archives). For a published example of Eissler's interviewing technique, cf. *Reich Speaks of Freud*, ed. Mary Higgins and Chester M. Raphael (New York: Farrar, Straus & Giroux; 1967), pp. 3-128. I have seen a few of Eissler's other interviews (some people saved copies he had sent them), and I conclude that my own approach as an interviewer was more active than his. There is also a project under way on the history of psychoanalysis at the Columbia University Oral History unit.

2. With one person I did try using a tape recorder, since she had one of her own and suggested that we use it. I promptly purchased a machine, but my next interview subject refused to let it run. I am convinced that elderly Continentals would have looked on a

tape recorder as vaguely a Nazi technique. I had many practical problems with my one tape-recorded interview; in addition to the expense of professional typing, many names were inevitably misspelled, and the long interview produced a bulky manuscript in which I found it difficult to locate specific details.

3. "Analysis Terminable and Interminable," *Standard Edition*, Vol. 23, pp. 221–22. Cf. also James Strachey, "The Nature of the Therapeutic Action of Psychoanalysis," *International Journal of Psychoanalysis*, Vol. 15, Parts 2–3 (Apr.–July 1934), p. 130. It is rather appalling to find Theodor Reik at the end of his life saying: "The positive transference you never interpret at all. Only when it turns negative. The positive transference is the waterfall which drives the mill. Why should you interpret that?" Erika Freeman, *Insights: Conversations with Theodor Reik* (Englewood Cliffs, N. J.: Prentice-Hall; 1971), p. 52.

4. "Dostoevsky and Parricide," *Standard Edition*, Vol. 21, p. 182.

5. "On the History of the Psychoanalytic Movement," *Standard Edition*, Vol. 14 (cited hereafter as "On the History"), p. 14.

I: THE ORAL TRADITION IN PSYCHOANALYSIS

1. The Legend of Freud

1. Cf. Hans Herma, Ernst Kris, and Joel Shor, "Freud's Theory of the Dream in American Textbooks," *The Journal of Abnormal and Social Psychology*, Vol. 38, No. 3 (July 1943), pp. 328, 331.

2. Fritz Wittels, *Sigmund Freud* (New York: Dodd, Mead; 1924), pp. 130–31.

3. For example, in 1909 he told a patient about his claims to priority in the discovery of the uses of cocaine. Interview with Albert Hirst, Jan. 21, 1966. In 1922 Freud told another pa-

tient, the sister of a leader in the psychoanalytic movement, that a young man had just been to see him who years earlier had been the subject of a famous case history ("Little Hans"). Interview with Edoardo Weiss, June 25, 1966. It was common for Freud to comment on phases of his early work that would be of interest to students in training with him. He told James Strachey about Josef Breuer's reactions to "Anna O." Letter from James Strachey to Ernest Jones, Oct. 24, 1951 (Jones archives). Freud discussed his admiration for James Jackson Putnam during an analysis. Interview with Edith Jackson, Aug. 30, 1966. And Freud spoke about Bernheim's demonstration of posthypnotic suggestion during Wortis's analysis. Joseph Wortis, *Fragment of an Analysis with Freud* (New York: Charter; 1963), p. 159. Cf. also Smiley Blanton, *Diary of My Analysis with Sigmund Freud* (New York: Hawthorn; 1971), and Roy R. Grinker, "Reminiscences of a Personal Contact with Freud," *American Journal of Orthopsychiatry*, Vol. 10 (1940), p. 852.

4. "Letter to Fritz Wittels," *Standard Edition*, Vol. 19, p. 286.

5. "An Autobiographical Study," *Standard Edition*, Vol. 20, p. 73.

6. In print Jones sounds reluctant, giving "the reasons why I nevertheless yielded to the suggestion that I should undertake" the biographical task. But in at least one letter to a publisher (which Jones wanted kept private, especially from other analysts) he eagerly gave his qualifications as Freud's biographer. Compare Ernest Jones, *The Life and Work of Sigmund Freud* (New York: Basic Books; 1953) (cited hereafter as *Sigmund Freud*; the pagination differs in the American and English editions), Vol. I, p. xiii, with the letter from Jones to Mr. Bassett, Oct. 1, 1946 (Jones archives).

7. Letter from Ernest Jones to E. Philp, Sept. 13, 1955 (Jones archives).

8. "Letter to the Editor," *American Journal of Psychotherapy*, Vol. 10, No. 1 (Jan. 1956), p. 110.

9. Letter from Ernest Jones to Anna Freud, Mar. 10, 1954 (Jones archives).

10. Jones, *Sigmund Freud*, Vol. II (New York: Basic Books; 1955), p. 3.

11. I am indebted for this point to Henry A. Murray.

12. S. Freud, *Letters,* ed. Ernst Freud, translated by Tania and James Stern (New York: Basic Books; 1960) (cited hereafter as *Letters*; the pagination differs in the American and English editions), p. 430.

13. "Leonardo da Vinci," *Standard Edition*, Vol. 11, pp. 83–84.

14. "General Preface," *Standard Edition*, Vol. I, p. xv.

15. Cf. Felix Deutsch, "Reflections on Freud's One Hundredth Birthday," *Psychosomatic Medicine*, Vol. 18, No. 4 (July–Aug., 1956), p. 279, which refers to a paper about Freud's illness withdrawn from publication. A copy of "Reflections on the Tenth Anniversary of Freud's Death," which was to have appeared in *The American Imago* but for Anna Freud's objections, is in the Jones archives. Letter from Felix Deutsch to Ernest Jones, Jan. 31, 1956.

16. Letter from Anna Freud to Ernest Jones, Apr. 8, 1954 (Jones archives). Cf. also her letter to Jones, Apr. 4, 1954 (Jones archives).

17. Letter from James Strachey to Ernest Jones, May 13, 1954 (Jones archives).

18. Letter from Anna Freud to Ernest Jones, Mar. 4, 1957 (Jones archives).

19. Strachey repaired one piece of the damage in his *Standard Edition*, Vol. I, p. 259. Max Schur undertook to publish additional portions of the Fliess correspondence. Cf. *Freud: Living and Dying* (New York: International Universities Press; 1972).

20. For instance, Jones included in his biography of Freud a sharp comment of Freud's to Arnold Zweig about Alfred Adler's death. Although the rest of that letter has now been published in the volume of the Freud-Zweig correspondence, that particular passage has been expurgated without the benefit of ellipses. Compare Jones, *Sigmund Freud*, Vol. III (New York: Basic Books; 1957), p. 208, with *The Letters of Sigmund Freud and Arnold Zweig*, ed. Ernst Freud, translated by Elaine and William Robson-Scott (New York: Harcourt, Brace & World; 1970) (cited hereafter as *Letters of Freud and Zweig*), pp. 131–33. Cf. Paul Roazen, "Dear Father Freud," *The Nation*, Vol. 210, No. 20 (May 25, 1970), pp. 631–32.

21. "Introductory Lectures on Psychoanalysis," *Standard Edition*, Vol. 16 (cited hereafter as "Introductory Lectures"), p. 260. The reader may be interested in other reflections of Freud on our interest in biography: "it is . . . the need to acquire affective relations with such men, to add them to the fathers, teachers, exemplars whom we have known or whose influence we have already experienced, in the expectation that their personalities will be just as fine and admirable as those works of art of theirs which we possess. All the same, we may admit that there is still another motive at work . . . It is true that the biographer does not want to depose his hero, but he does want to bring him nearer to us. That means . . . reducing the distance that separates him from us: it still tends in effect towards degradation. And it is unavoidable that if we learn more about a great man's life we shall also hear of occasions on which he has in fact done no better than we, has in fact come near to us as a human being. Nevertheless, I think we may declare the efforts of biography to be legitimate." "Address Delivered in the Goethe House at Frankfurt," *Standard Edition*, Vol. 21, pp. 211–12.

2. Finding Out about Freud the Man

1. Interview with Oliver Freud, Apr. 22, 1966.

2. Letter from Edward Hitschmann to Ernest Jones, Mar. 26, 1954 (Jones archives).

3. Jones, *Sigmund Freud*, Vol. III, p. 226. Cf. letter from Franz Bienenfeld to Ernest Jones, Jan. 28, 1956 (Jones archives). Cf. also Martin Freud, *Glory Reflected* (London: Angus & Robertson; 1957), p. 217.

4. Although Freud's most loyal pupils would at the time never have dreamed of analyzing the master's own personality, twice I found analysts absolutely fascinated with a patient of theirs whose character structure they thought resembled Freud's own, in my opinion representing a displacement of their interest in Freud.

5. Theodor Reik, *From Thirty Years with Freud* (New York: Farrar & Rinehart; 1940), p. 27.

6. "Psychoanalysis," *Standard Edition*, Vol. 20, p. 268.

7. "Recommendations to Physicians Practicing Psychoanalysis," *Standard Edition*, Vol. 12, p. 117. "A Difficulty in the Path of Psychoanalysis," *Standard Edition*, Vol. 17, p. 143.

8. "Lines of Advance in Psychoanalytic Therapy," *Standard Edition*, Vol. 17, p. 165.

9. Quoted in Rudolf M. Loewenstein, *Freud: Man and Scientist* (New York: International Universities Press; 1951), p. 17.

10. Interview with Edward Kronold, Sept. 19, 1966.

II: BACKGROUND AND CHARACTER

1. "All the defiance and all the passions"

1. Cf. Ernst Simon, "Sigmund Freud, the Jew," *Yearbook II*, ed. Robert Weltsch (London: Leo Baeck Institute; 1957), pp. 270–305. Cf. also Karl Menninger, "The Genius of the Jew in Psychiatry," *A Psychiatrist's World* (New York: Viking; 1959), pp. 415–24.

2. Cf. Roazen, *Freud: Political and Social Thought*, Ch. 3.

3. "Civilization and Its Discontents," *Standard Edition*, Vol. 21, p. 109.

4. Quoted in Jones, *Sigmund Freud*, Vol. II, p. 116.

5. *A Psychoanalytic Dialogue: Letters of Sigmund Freud and Karl Abraham*, ed. Hilda Abraham and Ernst Freud, translated by Bernard Marsh [pseudonym] and Hilda Abraham (New York: Basic Books; 1965) (cited hereafter as *Letters of Freud and Abraham*), p. 46.

6. "The Interpretation of Dreams," *Standard Edition*, Vol. 4, p. 197.

7. Martin Freud, *Glory Reflected*, pp. 70–71.

8. Jones, *Sigmund Freud*, Vol. II, pp. 163, 44; Vol. III, p. 185.

9. *Ibid.*, Vol. III, p. 198. The passages relating to this incident have been suppressed without any marks of omission in the relevant published edition of Freud's correspondence. Cf. *Letters of Freud and Zweig*, pp. 107–08.

10. Geoffrey Gorer, in *Psychoanalysis Observed*, ed. Charles Rycroft (London: Constable; 1966), p. 41.

11. "Address to the Society of B'nai B'rith," *Standard Edition*, Vol. 20, p. 274. In Marx too can be heard the voice of "a member of a long humiliated race"; "it is the oppression of centuries of a people of pariahs . . . that seems to be speaking in him." Sir Isaiah Berlin, "Benjamin Disraeli, Karl Marx, and the Search for Identity," *Midstream* (Aug.–Sept. 1970), p. 46.

12. Freeman, *Insights*, p. 80.

13. *Letters of Freud and Abraham*, p. 186.

14. Interview with Edoardo Weiss, May 8, 1965.

15. *Letters*, p. 203. Elsewhere Freud referred to "a German-nationalist phase which I passed through during my youth, but have since got over." "The Interpretation of Dreams," Vol. 4, p. 323.

16. S. Freud, *The Origins of Psychoanalysis*, ed. Marie Bonaparte, translated

by Eric Mosbacher and James Strachey (London: Imago; 1954) (cited
hereafter as *The Origins of Psychoanalysis*), pp. 219–21.

17. Schur, *Freud*, p. 120.
18. Interview with Edward Bernays, Nov.
28, 1965.
19. Letter from Leslie Adams to Ernest
Jones, Nov. 29, 1953 (Jones archives).
20. Cf. Roazen, *Freud: Political and Social
Thought*, pp. 257–68.
21. Wittels, *Sigmund Freud*, p. 35.
22. *Letters*, p. 202.
23. "The Interpretation of Dreams," Vol.
4, p. 192.
24. Quoted in Jones, *Sigmund Freud*, Vol.
I, p. 348.
25. *Ibid.*, Vol. III, p. 228.
26. "On the Universal Tendency to Debasement in the Sphere of Love,"
Standard Edition, Vol. 11, p. 189.
27. "The Interpretation of Dreams," Vol.
4, p. 233; Vol. 5, p. 554. "Psychoanalytic Notes on an Autobiographical
Account of a Case of Paranoia (Dementia Paranoides)," *Standard Edition*, Vol. 12, p. 58.
28. Interview with Edoardo Weiss, May
10, 1965.
29. "A Disturbance of Memory on the
Acropolis," *Standard Edition*, Vol.
22, p. 247. Cf. also Jones, *Sigmund
Freud*, Vol. I, p. 342, and Emil Ludwig, "A Visit," in *Freud As We
Knew Him*, ed. by Hendrik Ruitenbeek (Detroit: Wayne State Univ.
Press; 1973), pp. 214–15.
30. Quoted in Jones, *Sigmund Freud*,
Vol. I, p. 171. Cf. also *Letters*, p. 54.
31. "The Interpretation of Dreams," Vol.
5, p. 424; Vol. 4, p. 231.
32. *Ibid.*, Vol. 5, pp. 472, 483, 486.
33. *The Origins of Psychoanalysis*, p. 219.
34. "Introductory Lectures," Vol. 15, p.
86.
35. "The Psychopathology of Everyday
Life," *Standard Edition*, Vol. 6, p.
270.
36. Interview with Oliver Freud.
37. Interveiw with Mark Brunswick, Jan.
25, 1966.
38. *Letters*, p. 202.
39. *Ibid.*, p. 4.

2. Childhood and Youth

1. "An Autobiographical Study," p. 8.
2. Cf. Martin Grotjahn, "A Letter by
Sigmund Freud with Recollections of
His Adolescence," *Journal of the
American Psychoanalytic Association*,
Vol. IV, No. 4 (Oct. 1956), pp. 647–
48. Cf. also *Letters*, pp. 378–80.
3. "The Interpretation of Dreams," Vol.
5, p. 441.
4. "On the History," p. 19.
5. "The Interpretation of Dreams," Vol.
5, p. 450.
6. *Ibid.*, p. 444.
7. "An Autobiographical Study," p. 11.
Cf. Roazen, *Freud: Political and Social Thought*, pp. 91–95.
8. "An Autobiographical Study," p. 10.
9. "Screen Memories," *Standard Edition*,
Vol. 3, p. 314.
10. Interview with Oliver Freud.
11. "The Interpretation of Dreams," Vol.
5, p. 438.
12. "A Disturbance of Memory on the
Acropolis," p. 247.
13. Cf. Judith Bernays Heller, "Freud's
Mother and Father," *Commentary*,
Vol. 21, No. 5 (May 1956), pp. 418–
21.
14. "A Disturbance of Memory on the
Acropolis," p. 247.
15. "The Interpretation of Dreams," Vol.
4, p. 216.
16. Interview with Henry A. Murray,
Nov. 10, 1965. John Bilinsky, "Jung
and Freud," *Andover Newton Quarterly*, Vol. 10, No. 2 (Nov. 1969),
p. 42. Cf. below, p. 83. Schur mentions Freud's "prostatic discomfort
(frequency) while in the United
States." *Freud*, p. 255. For references
to urethral themes in Freud's writings,
cf. "The Interpretation of Dreams,"
Vol. 5, p. 469; "From the History of
an Infantile Neurosis," *Standard Edition*, Vol. 17, p. 76; "Civilization and
Its Discontents," p. 90; "The Acquisition and Control of Fire," *Standard
Edition*, Vol. 22, pp. 187–93.
17. Cf. "Fragment of an Analysis of a

Case of Hysteria," *Standard Edition,* Vol. 7, pp. 20–21. Cf. also Kurt Eissler's interview with Albert Hirst, Mar. 16, 1952 (Jones archives). Cf. also Jones, *Sigmund Freud,* Vol. II, pp. 291–92; Vol. III, pp. 307–08.

18. "Civilization and Its Discontents," p. 72.

19. "Family Romances," *Standard Edition,* Vol. 9, p. 238.

20. "Civilization and Its Discontents," p. 113.

21. Jones, *Sigmund Freud,* Vol. I, p. 2.

22. R. Gicklhorn and J. Sajner, "The Freiberg Period of the Freud Family," *Journal of the History of Medicine,* Vol. 24 (1969), pp. 37–43.

23. Quoted in Jones, *Sigmund Freud,* Vol. III, p. 20.

24. "The Interpretation of Dreams," Vol. 4, p. xxvi.

25. *Ibid.,* Vol. 5, p. 428. Jones, *Sigmund Freud,* Vol. I, p. 2.

26. Lionel Trilling and Stephen Marcus, eds., *The Life and Work of Sigmund Freud,* by Ernest Jones (New York: Basic Books; 1961), p. 4.

27. "The Interpretation of Dreams," Vol. 5, p. 379. Cf. also Ernest Jones, "Book Review of Wittels's *Freud,*" *International Journal of Psychoanalysis,* Vol. 5 (1924), p. 485.

28. "The Interpretation of Dreams," Vol. 4, p. 198. In reality Masséna was born in 1758.

29. S. Freud and William C. Bullitt, *Thomas Woodrow Wilson: A Psychological Study* (Boston: Houghton Mifflin; 1967), p. vi.

30. "The Interpretation of Dreams," Vol. 5, p. 398. Cf. also "A Childhood Recollection from *Dichtung und Wahrheit,*" *Standard Edition,* Vol. 17, p. 156.

31. "Introductory Lectures," Vol. 15, p. 206.

32. "New Introductory Lectures on Psychoanalysis," *Standard Edition,* Vol. 22 (cited hereafter as "New Introductory Lectures"), p. 133. Cf. also "Group Psychology and the Analysis of the Ego," *Standard Edition,* Vol. 18, p. 101.

33. Quoted in Jones, *Sigmund Freud,* Vol. II, p. 196.

34. Quoted in Ludwig Binswanger, *Sigmund Freud: Reminiscences of a Friendship,* translated by Norbert Guterman (New York: Grune & Stratton; 1957), pp. 85–88.

35. *Letters,* p. 400.

36. Quoted in Jones, *Sigmund Freud,* Vol. III, p. 152.

37. "Two Encyclopaedia Articles," *Standard Edition,* Vol. 18, p. 257.

38. "Civilization and Its Discontents," p. 109.

39. "From the History of an Infantile Neurosis," p. 88.

40. Quoted in Jones, *Sigmund Freud,* Vol. II, p. 177.

41. For Freud's dream, cf. "The Interpretation of Dreams," Vol. 5, p. 583. For his mother's dream, cf. Lancelot Whyte, *Focus and Diversions* (New York: Braziller; 1963), pp. 110–11. In a letter to me (Oct. 17, 1971) Whyte expressed the opinion that it was likely that Freud's mother had had a dream during the night, rather than the daydream he reports in his book.

42. Jones, *Sigmund Freud,* Vol. II, p. 434.

43. Letter from Ernest Jones to James Strachey, Jan. 11, 1954. Cf. also letter from James Strachey to Ernest Jones, Jan. 20, 1954 (Jones archives). Cf. Meyer Schapiro, "Leonardo and Freud," *Journal of the History of Ideas,* Vol. 17 (1956), pp. 147–78.

44. Cf. letter from Dorothy Burlingham to Ernest Jones, June 6, 1951 (Jones archives).

45. Martin Freud, *Glory Reflected,* p. 11. Cf. also Martin Freud, "Who was Freud?," in Josef Fraenkel, ed., *The Jews of Austria* (London: Vallentine, Mitchell; 1967), p. 202.

46. Jones, *Sigmund Freud,* Vol. I, p. 3.

47. Judith Bernays Heller, "Freud's Mother and Father." Interview with Edward Bernays, Dec. 2, 1965. Interview with Hella Bernays, Apr. 3, 1967. Interview with Oliver Freud. Interview with Judith Bernays Heller, Dec. 23, 1965.

48. Martin Freud, *Glory Reflected*, pp. 11, 16. Cf. also Martin Freud, "Who was Freud?," pp. 202–03.
49. *Letters*, p. 58.
50. Interview with Otto Isakower, Sept. 20, 1966.
51. Jones, *Sigmund Freud*, Vol. II, p. 391.
52. "Screen Memories," p. 322.

3. Love and Marriage

1. Interview with Esti Freud, Apr. 30, 1966.
2. I am indebted to Sir Isaiah Berlin for this story. Cf. Jones, *Sigmund Freud*, Vol. III, p. 228.
3. "The Interpretation of Dreams," Vol. 4, p. 110.
4. *Minutes of the Vienna Psychoanalytic Society*, ed. Herman Nunberg and Ernst Federn, Vol. II (New York: International Universities Press; 1967) (cited hereafter as *Minutes*), p. 237.
5. Quoted in Jones, *Sigmund Freud*, Vol. I, p. 130.
6. "Female Sexuality," *Standard Edition*, Vol. 21, p. 231.
7. *Letters*, p. 52.
8. Erich Fromm, *Sigmund Freud's Mission* (New York: Harper & Row, 1959), p. 18.
9. *Letters*, pp. 58–66.
10. Quoted in Jones, *Sigmund Freud*, Vol. I, p. 128.
11. *Letters*, p. 308.
12. "The Taboo of Virginity," *Standard Edition*, Vol. 11, p. 193.
13. Jones, *Sigmund Freud*, Vol. III, p. 228.
14. *Ibid.*, Vol. II, p. 386.
15. Cf. *The Freud/Jung Letters*, ed. William McGuire, translated by Ralph Manheim and R.F.C. Hull (hereafter cited as *Freud/Jung Letters*) (Princeton: Princeton University Press; 1974), p. 456. Letter from Ernest Jones to Max Schur, Oct. 6, 1955 (Jones archives). This association of Jones's echoes Freud's own teaching; for example, Freud wrote that "a restriction of sexual activity in a community is quite generally accom-panied by an increase of anxiety about life and of fear of death. . . ." " 'Civilized' Sexual Morality and Modern Nervous Illness," *Standard Edition*, Vol. 9, p. 203.
16. "Sexuality in the Aetiology of the Neuroses," *Standard Edition*, Vol. 3, p. 277.
17. " 'Civilized' Sexual Morality and Modern Nervous Illness," p. 194.
18. *The Origins of Psychoanalysis*, p. 277. In 1894 Freud had written that "the libido has long since been subdued." Quoted in Schur, *Freud*, p. 48.
19. Interviews with Esti Freud, Apr. 30 and Aug. 27, 1966. For confirmation of Freud's early celibacy, cf. Freeman, *Insights*, p. 81.
20. *Minutes*, Vol. II, p. 561.
21. Quoted in Jones, *Sigmund Freud*, Vol. II, p. 151.
22. "Leonardo da Vinci," p. 101.
23. "The Psychical Mechanism of Forgetfulness," *Standard Edition*, Vol. 3, pp. 292–94. Cf. also "The Psychopathology of Everyday Life," p. 3. I am indebted to Meyer Schapiro for pointing out to me that the frescoes in Orvieto, which were an essential part of Freud's anecdote, not only had to do with resurrection as well as death, but also pictured exceptionally virile masculine types.
24. "The Psychopathology of Everyday Life," p. 175.
25. *Minutes*, Vol. II, pp. 60–61.
26. "Introductory Lectures," Vol. 16, p. 316.
27. Jones, *Sigmund Freud*, Vol. II, p. 5.
28. "Creative Writers and Day-Dreaming," *Standard Edition*, Vol. 9, p. 144.
29. "On the Universal Tendency to Debasement in the Sphere of Love," pp. 188–89, 187.
30. "Two Encyclopaedia Articles," p. 252.
31. "Civilization and Its Discontents," p. 79.
32. "Observations on Transference-Love," *Standard Edition*, Vol. 12, pp. 169–70.
33. "Contributions to a Discussion on Masturbation," *Standard Edition*, Vol. 12, p. 252.

34. Quoted in Jones, *Sigmund Freud*, Vol. III, p. 325.
35. "The Psychopathology of Everyday Life," p. 214.
36. "Leonardo da Vinci," p. 117.
37. "New Introductory Lectures," pp. 133–34.
38. "Some Neurotic Mechanisms in Jealousy, Paranoia and Homosexuality," *Standard Edition*, Vol. 18, p. 228.

4. Family Life

1. Martin Freud, *Glory Reflected*, p. 33.
2. Jones, *Sigmund Freud*, Vol. II, p. 382.
3. For this claim of Jones's cf. *ibid.*, p. 387.
4. Dictation from Ernst Freud to Ernest Jones, Nov. 27, 1953 (Jones archives).
5. Interview with Helene Deutsch, Sept. 18, 1965.
6. "The Interpretation of Dreams," Vol. 4, p. 239.
7. "The Psychopathology of Everyday Life," p. 180.
8. Letter from Mathilda Freud Hollitscher to Ernest Jones, Mar. 30, 1952 (Jones archives).
9. Theodor Reik, "Years of Maturity," *Psychoanalysis*, Vol. 4, No. 1 (1955), p. 72. Cf. also René Laforgue, "Personal Memories of Freud," in *Freud As We Knew Him*, ed. Ruitenbeek, p. 342.
10. Interview with Mark Brunswick, Jan. 25, 1966.
11. *Ibid.* Cf. below, p. 331.
12. Quoted in Jones, *Sigmund Freud*, Vol. III, p. 209.
13. Interview with Mark Brunswick, Jan. 25, 1966.
14. Interview with Eva Rosenfeld, Nov. 3, 1966.
15. Max Schur, "The Medical History of Sigmund Freud," p. 44.
16. Jones, *Sigmund Freud*, Vol. III, p. 246.
17. *Ibid.*, Vol. I, p. 153. But according to notes Jones took from Martha Freud in Aug. 1947, Minna moved in with them in 1892.

18. Judith Heller, "My Aunt, Minna Bernays" (Jones archives). Interviews with Esti Freud.
19. *Minutes*, Vol. II, pp. 525, 527.
20. *Letters*, p. 288.
21. Letter from Anna Freud to Ernest Jones, Apr. 24, 1952 (Jones archives).
22. Jones, *Sigmund Freud*, Vol. II, p. 387. Cf. also letter of Marie Bonaparte to Ernest Jones, Dec. 10, 1953 (Jones archives).
23. Martin Freud, *Glory Reflected*, p. 44.
24. Interview with Kata Levy, July 20, 1965.
25. Jones, *Sigmund Freud*, Vol. III, pp. 10, 25, 79.
26. Bilinsky, "Freud and Jung," pp. 39–43.
27. Jones, *Sigmund Freud*, Vol. I, p. 164.
28. "The 'Uncanny,'" *Standard Edition*, Vol. 17, p. 237.
29. Interview with Henry Murray, Nov. 10, 1965.
30. Interview with Eva Rosenfeld, Nov. 3, 1966.
31. Hitschmann once observed through Freud's trousers an erection after an hour with a pretty woman. Letter from Edward Hitschmann to Ernest Jones, Mar. 26, 1954 (Jones archives).
32. Interview with Eva Rosenfeld, Sept. 1, 1965.
33. Letter from Ernest Jones to Max Eitingon, Oct. 21, 1939 (Jones archives).

III: A SCIENCE OF DREAMING

1. "Struggles for recognition"

1. Jean-Paul Sartre, *Anti-Semite and Jew*, translated by George J. Becker, (New York: Grove Press; 1948), p. 114.
2. "The Interpretation of Dreams," Vol. 5, p. 422.
3. Jones, *Sigmund Freud*, Vol. I, p. 24.
4. "On the History," p. 9.
5. "An Autobiographical Study," p. 8.
6. "The Question of Lay Analysis," p. 253.

7. *Letters*, p. 98.
8. *Ibid.*, p. 89.
9. "Autobiographical Note," *Standard Edition*, Vol. 3, p. 325.
10. "The Interpretation of Dreams," Vol. 4, p. 111.
11. Jones, *Sigmund Freud*, Vol. I, p. 88.
12. *Ibid.*, p. 79.
13. "Abstracts of the Scientific Writings of Dr. Sigm. Freud," *Standard Edition*, Vol. 3, p. 233.
14. Another version has it that Koenigstein may have himself added something to make the solution clear, thereby ruining the experiment. Cf. letter from Kurt Eissler to Ernest Jones, Nov. 9, 1953 (Jones archives).
15. "The Interpretation of Dreams," Vol. 4, p. 170.
16. "An Autobiographical Study," pp. 14–15.
17. Wittels, *Sigmund Freud*, p. 25.
18. *Letters*, p. 351.
19. Sachs, *Freud: Master and Friend* (London: Imago; 1945), p. 69.
20. Letter from Albert Hirst to Ernest Jones, Nov. 6, 1953, and letter from Ernest Jones to Albert Hirst, Nov. 10, 1953 (Jones archives). Interview with Albert Hirst.
21. Letter from Albert Hirst to Anna Freud, Oct. 19, 1953, and letter from Kurt Eissler to Ernest Jones, Nov. 9, 1953 (Jones archives).
22. Letter from Siegfried Bernfeld to Ernest Jones, Apr. 27, 1952 (Jones archives).
23. *Letters*, p. 73.
24. "The Interpretation of Dreams," Vol. 5, p. 487.
25. Jones, *Sigmund Freud*, Vol. II, pp. 3, 420.
26. "The Psychopathology of Everyday Life," pp. 149–50.
27. *Ibid.*, p. 149.
28. "Autobiographical Note," p. 325.
29. "Report on My Studies in Paris and Berlin," *Standard Edition*, Vol. I, p. 10.
30. "Preface and Footnotes to the Translation of Charcot's *Tuesday Lectures*," *Standard Edition*, Vol. I, p. 135.

31. Quoted in "Editor's Note," *Standard Edition*, Vol. 3, p. 10.
32. Wittels, *Sigmund Freud*, p. 28.
33. "Charcot," *Standard Edition*, Vol. 3, pp. 17, 15, 12, 13.
34. "On the History," p. 22.
35. "Charcot," p. 11.
36. *Ibid.*, pp. 17, 15, 16, 18.
37. *Ibid.*, p. 19.
38. *Ibid.*, p. 17.
39. "On the Psychical Mechanism of Hysterical Phenomena," *Standard Edition*, Vol. 3, p. 27.
40. "The Psychopathology of Everyday Life," p. 161.
41. Henri F. Ellenberger, *The Discovery of the Unconscious* (New York: Basic Books; 1970), pp. 331–417.
42. Leston Havens, "Pierre Janet," *The Journal of Nervous and Mental Disease*, Vol. 143, No. 5 (1966), p. 397.
43. *Ibid.*, p. 396.
44. "Introductory Lectures," Vol. 16, p. 257.
45. Quoted in *James Jackson Putnam and Psychoanalysis*, ed. Nathan Hale, Jr. (Cambridge: Harvard University Press; 1971), p. 131.
46. "An Autobiographical Study," p. 13.
47. Quoted in E. A. Bennet, "The Freud-Janet Controversy," *British Medical Journal*, Jan. 2, 1965, pp. 52–53.
48. "An Autobiographical Study," p. 31. Cf. Pierre Janet, *Psychological Healing*, Vol. I (New York: Macmillan 1925), pp. 601–40.

2. Early Mentor: Josef Breuer

1. Alfred Schick, "The Vienna of Sigmund Freud," *Psychoanalytic Review*, Vol. 55, No. 4 (Winter 1968–69), p. 543.
2. "On the Psychical Mechanism of Hysterical Phenomena," pp. 35, 30.
3. Wittels, *Sigmund Freud*, p. 38.
4. Quoted in "Editor's Note," *Standard Edition*, Vol. 3, p. 261.
5. "Heredity and the Aetiology of the Neuroses," *Standard Edition*, Vol. 3, p. 151.

6. "Freud's Psychoanalytic Procedure," *Standard Edition*, Vol. 7, p. 249.

7. "Five Lectures on Psychoanalysis," *Standard Edition*, Vol. 11, p. 9.

8. "On the History," p. 8.

9. "Five Lectures on Psychoanalysis," p. 9.

10. "Introductory Lectures," Vol. 16, p. 279.

11. "On the History," pp. 13–15.

12. "An Autobiographical Study," p. 23.

13. "On the History," p. 11.

14. *Ibid.*, pp. 8–9.

15. *Ibid.*, p. 9.

16. Letter from Ernest Jones to James Strachey, Nov. 6, 1951 (Jones archives). Cf. Schur, *Freud*, pp. 204, 216–17.

17. "The Psychopathology of Everyday Life," pp. 137–38.

18. Interview with Abram Kardiner, Apr. 1, 1967.

19. "An Autobiographical Study," p. 19.

20. Ellenberger has done away with some myths. Cf. his "The Story of 'Anna O.,'" *Journal of the History of the Behavioral Sciences*, Vol. 8, No. 3 (July 1972), pp. 267–79.

21. "Josef Breuer," *Standard Edition*, Vol. 19, p. 280.

22. "Josef Breuer," p. 280.

23. *Letters of Freud and Abraham*, p. 386.

24. Letter from Hannah Breuer to Ernest Jones, Apr. 21, 1954 (Jones archives).

25. "A Reply to Criticisms of My Paper on Anxiety Neurosis," *Standard Edition*, Vol. 3, p. 131; "Heredity and the Aetiology of the Neuroses," p. 151.

26. "Review of August Forel's *Hypnotism*," *Standard Edition*, Vol. 1, pp. 98–99.

27. "The Neuro-Psychoses of Defence," *Standard Edition*, Vol. 3, p. 57; "Hypnotism," *Standard Edition*, Vol. 1, p. 112.

28. "Hypnotism," p. 111.

29. *Ibid.*, p. 105.

30. "On the History," p. 9.

31. "Review of August Forel's *Hypnotism*," p. 99.

32. "Five Lectures on Psychoanalysis," p. 22.

33. "Introductory Lectures," Vol. 16, p. 449.

34. "Five Lectures on Psychoanalysis," p. 22.

35. Josef Breuer and Sigmund Freud, "Studies on Hysteria," *Standard Edition*, Vol. 2, pp. 61, 63.

36. "Introductory Lectures," Vol. 16, pp. 450.

3. Self-Analysis

1. Letter from Ernest Jones to Max Schur, Oct. 6, 1955 (Jones archives).

2. Jones, *Sigmund Freud*, Vol. II, p. 391. Cf. also letter from Ernest Jones to Anna Freud, Mar. 18, 1954 (Jones archives).

3. Letter from Max Schur to Ernest Jones, Sept. 30, 1955 (Jones archives). This lengthy letter really amounted to an essay and is revealing of Schur's contact with Freud.

4. "The Psychopathology of Everyday Life," p. 21; Jones, *Sigmund Freud*, Vol. II, p. 392.

5. *The Origins of Psychoanalysis*, pp. 116–18. Cf. also "A Reply to Criticisms of My Paper on Anxiety Neurosis," p. 133.

6. "On the Grounds for Detaching a Particular Syndrome from Neurasthenia under the Description 'Anxiety Neurosis,'" *Standard Edition*, Vol. 3, p. 107.

7. Schur, *Freud*, p. 55.

8. Jones, *Sigmund Freud*, Vol. III, p. 42.

9. "The Psychical Mechanism of Forgetfulness," p. 296.

10. Theodor Reik, *Listening with the Third Ear* (New York: Farrar, Straus; 1948), pp. 15–16.

11. *Minutes*, II, pp. 459, 371.

12. "Introductory Lectures," Vol. 15, p. 153.

13. "Obsessions and Phobias," *Standard Edition*, Vol. 3, p. 81.

14. *Letters of Freud and Abraham*, p. 233.

15. "Libidinal Types," *Standard Edition*, Vol. 21, p. 219.

16. Sachs, *Freud*, p. 34.

17. Jones, *Free Associations* (New York: Basic Books; 1959), p. 213.

18. *The Origins of Psychoanalysis*, p. 84.

19. "On the History," p. 22.

20. *Ibid.*, pp. 12–13.
21. "An Autobiographical Study," p. 48.
22. "On the History," p. 12.
23. "Address to the Society of B'nai B'rith," p. 273.
24. "My Contact with Josef Popper-Lynkeus," *Standard Edition*, Vol. 22, p. 224.
25. "On the History," p. 24.
26. "The Psychopathology of Everyday Life," pp. 24–25.
27. Ilse Bry and Alfred Rifkin, "Freud and the History of Ideas," in *Psychoanalytic Education*, ed. Jules Masserman (New York: Grune & Stratton; 1962), pp. 6–36.
28. "Some Neurotic Mechanisms in Jealousy, Paranoia and Homosexuality," p. 226. Cf. also "Introductory Lectures," Vol. 15, pp. 66–67.
29. Jones, *Sigmund Freud*, Vol. II, p. 227.
30. *Letters*, p. 402.
31. *Letters of Freud and Abraham*, p. 2.
32. Roazen, *Freud: Political and Social Thought*, p. 77.
33. "Three Essays on the Theory of Sexuality," *Standard Edition*, Vol. 7, p. 190. Cf. Frank Cioffi, "Was Freud a Liar?" *The Listener*, Feb. 7, 1974, pp. 172–74.
34. "From the History of an Infantile Neurosis," p. 103.

4. Wilhelm Fliess

1. *The Origins of Psychoanalysis*, p. 275.
2. *Ibid.*, p. 60.
3. Interview with Mrs. Karl Abraham, Nov. 4, 1966.
4. Quoted in Schur, *Freud*, p. 52; Schur, *Freud*, p. 185; quoted in Schur, *Freud*, p. 204.
5. Quoted in *ibid.*, p. 216.
6. *The Origins of Psychoanalysis*, pp. 130, 132.
7. *Ibid.*, pp. 234–35.
8. The analogy of a formal analysis can be pushed too far. Cf., for example, Schur, *Freud*, p. 209.
9. Max Schur, "Some Additional 'Day Residues' of 'The Specimen Dream of Psychoanalysis,'" *Psychoanalysis: A General Psychology*, ed. Rudolf M.

Loewenstein, Lottie Newman, Max Schur, and Albert Solnit (New York: International Universities Press; 1966), p. 67; quoted in Schur, *Freud*, p. 83.
10. "The Interpretation of Dreams," Vol. 4, p. 297.
11. Cf., for example, some comments of Freud's relating mourning to melancholia. *The Origins of Psychoanalysis*, pp. 103, 207.
12. *Ibid.*, p. 130.
13. Jones, *Sigmund Freud*, Vol. II, p. 289.
14. "The Interpretation of Dreams," Vol. 5, p. 663.
15. "Beyond the Pleasure Principle," *Standard Edition*, Vol. 18, p. 45.
16. Quoted in Schur, *Freud*, p. 232. *Freud/Jung Letters*, p. 220. Cf. David Bakan, *Sigmund Freud and the Jewish Mystical Tradition* (Princeton, N.J.: Van Nostrand; 1958).
17. Jones, *Sigmund Freud*, Vol. II, p. 429.
18. "The Psychopathology of Everyday Life," p. 144.
19. *Ibid.*
20. "Three Essays on the Theory of Sexuality," p. 166.
21. *Ibid.*, p. 220.
22. *Ibid.*, p. 143.
23. "Analysis Terminable and Interminable," p. 251.
24. Jones, *Sigmund Freud*, Vol. II, p. 409.
25. Schur, *Freud*, pp. 82, 111.
26. "The Interpretation of Dreams," Vol. 5, pp. 481, 421.
27. *The Origins of Psychoanalysis*, p. 219.
28. *Ibid.*, pp. 334, 337.
29. Jones, *Sigmund Freud*, Vol. II, p. 365.
30. *Ibid.*, pp. 250, 268; *Letters of Freud and Abraham*, p. 103.
31. Jones, *Sigmund Freud*, Vol. III, p. 44; Fromm, *Sigmund Freud's Mission*, pp. 46, 48.
32. Cf. Richard Pfennig, *Wilhelm Fliess* (Berlin: Goldschmidt; 1906), pp. 26–29.
33. *Ibid.*, pp. 30–31.
34. Letter from Siegfried Bernfeld to to Ernest Jones, May 26, 1952 (Jones archives).
35. *Letters*, p. 250.
36. Robert K. Merton, "Making It Scientifically," *The New York Times Book Review*, Feb. 25, 1968, p. 42. Cf. Rob-

ert K. Merton, "Priorities in Scientific Discovery," *American Sociological Review*, Vol. 22, No. 6 (Dec. 1957), pp. 635–59.

37. Norman Malcolm, *Ludwig Wittgenstein* (London: Oxford University Press; 1958), pp. 58–59, 93.

38. Marthe Robert, *The Psychoanalytic Revolution*, translated by Kenneth Morgan (New York: Harcourt, Brace and World; 1966), p. 154.

39. Interview with Oliver Freud.

40. Letter from Alan Tyson to Ernest Jones, Dec. 16, 1954 (Jones archives).

41. Jones, *Sigmund Freud*, Vol. III, pp. 112, 115–16.

42. Schur, *Freud*, p. 70.

43. Quoted in Jones, *Sigmund Freud*, Vol. II, pp. 446–47.

44. Quoted in *ibid.*, p. 83.

45. Letter by Charles Fliess, *London Sunday Observer*, May 2, 1954.

5. The Unconscious

1. "The Interpretation of Dreams," Vol. 5, p. 477.

2. "On the History," p. 20; "Editor's Introduction," *Standard Edition*, Vol. 4, p. xx.

3. "The Interpretation of Dreams," Vol. 4, p. xxxi.

4. *Ibid.*, p. xxxii.

5. *Ibid.*, p. xxvi.

6. "The Claims of Psychoanalysis to Scientific Interest," *Standard Edition*, Vol. 13, p. 169.

7. "The Interpretation of Dreams," Vol. 4, p. 100.

8. "Introductory Lectures," Vol. 15, p. 95.

9. *Ibid.*, p. 87.

10. "On the History," p. 21; "Leonardo da Vinci," p. 122.

11. "New Introductory Lectures," p. 7.

12. "On the History," p. 22.

13. "New Introductory Lectures," p. 29.

14. "The Interpretation of Dreams," Vol. 4, p. 135.

15. *Ibid.*, p. 96; "On the History," p. 20.

16. "The Interpretation of Dreams," Vol. 4, pp. 146, 273.

17. *Ibid.*, p. 322.

18. *Ibid.*, p. 271.

19. *Ibid.*, p. 270.

20. *Ibid.*, Vol. 5, p. 682.

21. *Ibid.*, p. 396.

22. *Ibid.*, p. 397.

23. "Introductory Lectures," Vol. 15, pp. 142–43.

24. "The Interpretation of Dreams," Vol. 4, p. 247.

25. *Ibid.*, p. 178.

26. Quoted in Jones, *Sigmund Freud*, Vol. II, p. 221.

27. "The Interpretation of Dreams," Vol. 4, p. 35.

28. "Constructions in Analysis," *Standard Edition*, Vol. 23, p. 267.

29. "The Interpretation of Dreams," Vol. 4, p. xxiii; "Introductory Lectures," Vol. 16, p. 297; "New Introductory Lectures," p. 15.

30. "The Interpretation of Dreams," Vol. 5, p. 680.

31. "From the History of an Infantile Neurosis," p. 42.

32. "On the History," p. 19.

33. "The Interpretation of Dreams," Vol. 4, p. 205.

34. *Ibid.*, Vol. 5, p. 482.

35. *Ibid.*, Vol. 4, pp. 336–37.

36. *Ibid.*, Vol. 5, p. 485.

37. *Ibid.*, p. 453.

38. *Ibid.*, p. 470.

39. "The Psychopathology of Everyday Life," pp. 136–37.

40. "The Interpretation of Dreams," Vol. 5, pp. 638–39.

41. *Ibid.*, pp. 465–66.

42. *Ibid.*, Vol. 4, p. 229.

43. *Ibid.*, p. 41.

44. *Ibid.*, Vol. 5, pp. 546, 340.

45. *Ibid.*, p. 525.

46. *Ibid.*, Vol. 4, p. 329.

47. *Ibid.*, p. 331; *ibid.*, Vol. 5, p. 464; "New Introductory Lectures," p. 14.

48. "The Interpretation of Dreams," Vol. 5, p. 475.

49. *Ibid.*, p. 511.

50. *Ibid.*, Vol. 4, p. 233.

51. *Ibid.*, Vol. 5, p. 578.

52. *Ibid.*, p. 677.

53. "Introductory Lectures," Vol. 15, p. 147.

54. "The Interpretation of Dreams," Vol. 5, p. 569.
55. *Ibid.*, p. 582.
56. "An Autobiographical Study," p. 33; "Sexuality in the Aetiology of the Neuroses," p. 280.
57. "The Interpretation of Dreams," Vol. 4, p. 257.
58. *Ibid.*, p. 256.
59. "Preface to Reik's *Ritual*," *Standard Edition*, Vol. 17, p. 261.
60. "A Reply to Criticisms of My Paper on Anxiety Neurosis," p. 128.
61. "Three Essays on the Theory of Sexuality," p. 222.
62. "Sexuality in the Aetiology of the Neuroses," p. 266.
63. "On the History," p. 18.
64. "Introductory Lectures," Vol. 16, p. 326. Cf. "From the History of an Infantile Neurosis," pp. 8–9.
65. "An Autobiographical Study," p. 38.
66. "Introductory Lectures," Vol. 16, p. 311.
67. "'A Child Is Being Beaten,'" *Standard Edition*, Vol. 17, p. 193.
68. "Three Essays on the Theory of Sexuality," p. 160.
69. "Sexuality in the Aetiology of the Neuroses," p. 278.
70. "Obsessive Acts and Religious Practices," *Standard Edition*, Vol. 9, p. 127.
71. "Sexuality in the Aetiology of the Neuroses," p. 263.
72. "Heredity and the Aetiology of the Neuroses," p. 149.
73. "Sexuality in the Aetiology of the Neuroses," p. 268.
74. "Three Essays on the Theory of Sexuality," p. 205.
75. "Sexuality in the Aetiology of the Neuroses," p. 270.
76. "On Psychotherapy," *Standard Edition*, Vol. 7, p. 267.
77. "Introductory Lectures," Vol. 16, p. 356.
78. "Beyond the Pleasure Principle," pp. 8–9.
79. *Ibid.*, p. 27.
80. "The Claims of Psychoanalysis to Scientific Interest," p. 190.
81. Ellenberger, *The Discovery of the Unconscious*, p. 413.

82. "Introductory Lectures," Vol. 15, p. 74.
83. "Screen Memories," p. 311.
84. "Heredity and the Aetiology of the Neuroses," p. 154; "Further Remarks on the Neuro-Psychoses of Defence," p. 167.
85. "The Aetiology of Hysteria," *Standard Edition*, Vol. 3, p. 197.
86. "Three Essays on the Theory of Sexuality," p. 242.
87. "On the History," p. 10.
88. "The Interpretation of Dreams," Vol. 5, p. 451.
89. "Introductory Lectures," Vol. 16, p. 356.
90. "Leonardo da Vinci," p. 133.
91. "The Psychopathology of Everyday Life," p. 101.
92. *Ibid.*, p. 94.
93. *Ibid.*, p. 136.
94. "Introductory Lectures," Vol. 15, p. 50.

6. The Talking Cure

1. "A Short Account of Psychoanalysis," *Standard Edition*, Vol. 19, p. 209.
2. "The Question of Lay Analysis," p. 252.
3. "New Introductory Lectures," p. 58.
4. "Contributions to a Discussion on Masturbation," p. 246.
5. *Letters*, p. 307.
6. "A Difficulty in the Path of Psychoanalysis," p. 138.
7. "The 'Uncanny,'" p. 219.
8. *Minutes*, Vol. II, pp. 367–68.
9. "On Psychoanalysis," *Standard Edition*, Vol. 12, p. 209.
10. "Introductory Lectures," Vol. 15, p. 21.
11. *Ibid.*, Vol. 16, p. 389.
12. "Three Essays on the Theory of Sexuality," p. 179.
13. "An Autobiographical Study," p. 50.
14. "Introductory Lectures," Vol. 15, pp. 23–24.
15. "Civilization and Its Discontents," p. 140; "Two Encyclopaedia Articles," p. 243.

16. "Introductory Lectures," Vol. 15, p. 57; "Psychoanalytic Notes on an Autobiographical Account," p. 79.
17. "The Future of an Illusion," *Standard Edition*, Vol. 21, p. 27.
18. "Sexuality in the Aetiology of the Neuroses," p. 265.
19. *Ibid.*, p. 263.
20. "A Reply to Criticisms of My Paper on Anxiety Neurosis," p. 124.
21. "The Psychopathology of Everyday Life," p. 53.
22. "Josef Popper-Lynkeus and the Theory of Dreams," *Standard Edition*, Vol. 19, p. 261.
23. "Civilization and Its Discontents," p. 133.
24. "The Psychopathology of Everyday Life," p. 107; "The Resistances to Psychoanalysis," *Standard Edition*, Vol. 19, p. 218.
25. "New Introductory Lectures," p. 22.
26. "Psychoanalysis," p. 265.
27. "New Introductory Lectures," pp. 156–57.
28. "Some Psychical Consequences of the Anatomical Distinction Between the Sexes," *Standard Edition*, Vol. 19, p. 248.
29. "A Reply to Criticisms of My Paper on Anxiety Neurosis," p. 138.
30. "Fragment of an Analysis of a Case of Hysteria," *Standard Edition*, Vol. 7, pp. 20–21.
31. "Three Essays on the Theory of Sexuality," p. 236. Cf. also interview of Kurt Eissler with Albert Hirst (Jones archives).
32. "The Interpretation of Dreams," Vol. 4, p. 260.
33. "Introductory Lectures," Vol. 16, p. 379.
34. "The Psychopathology of Everyday Life," p. 278.
35. *Ibid.*, p. 152.
36. "Screen Memories," p. 309.
37. "Introductory Lectures," Vol. 16, p. 358.
38. *Ibid.*, p. 300.
39. "Beyond the Pleasure Principle," pp. 35–36; "The Interpretation of Dreams," Vol. 4, p. 185.

40. Sandor Ferenczi, "Contributions to Psychoanalysis," in *Sex in Psychoanalysis,* authorized translation by Ernest Jones (New York: Dover; 1956), pp. 47–48.
41. *Letters of Freud and Abraham,* p. 118.
42. "Sexuality in the Aetiology of the Neuroses," p. 282.
43. "Introductory Lectures," Vol. 16, p. 266.
44. "On Psychotherapy," p. 259.
45. "Fragment of an Analysis of a Case of Hysteria," p. 18.
46. "Freud's Psychoanalytic Procedure," p. 253.
47. "Sexuality in the Aetiology of the Neuroses," p. 284.
48. "Introductory Lectures," Vol. 16, p. 434.
49. "Lines of Advance in Psychoanalytic Therapy," p. 165.
50. "Introductory Lectures," Vol. 16, p. 382.
51. *Ibid.*, Vol. 16, p. 282.
52. "Analysis Terminable and Interminable," p. 250.
53. "Introductory Lectures," Vol. 16, p. 435.
54. "Civilization and Its Discontents," p. 95.
55. *Ibid.*, p. 83.
56. "Introductory Lectures," Vol. 16, p. 260.
57. "Observations on Transference-Love," p. 164.
58. "From the History of an Infantile Neurosis," p. 18.
59. "The Interpretation of Dreams," Vol. 5, pp. 580–81.
60. "On Psychotherapy," p. 266.
61. "On Beginning the Treatment," *Standard Edition*, Vol. 12, p. 141.
62. "Introductory Lectures," Vol. 16, p. 279.
63. "The Future of an Illusion," p. 48.
64. "Civilization and Its Discontents," p. 79.
65. "New Introductory Lectures," p. 145.
66. "Psychoanalysis and the Establishment of the Facts in Legal Proceedings," *Standard Edition*, Vol. 9, pp. 109, 111.
67. "A Difficulty in the Path of Psychoanalysis," p. 143.

68. "Introductory Lectures," Vol. 16, p. 291.
69. "The Interpretation of Dreams," Vol. 5, p. 517.
70. "Introductory Lectures," Vol. 16, p. 290.
71. *Ibid.*, p. 442.
72. "Recommendations to Physicians Practising Psychoanalysis," p. 118.
73. "On the History," p. 39.
74. "Introductory Lectures," Vol. 16, p. 445.
75. "The Handling of Dream-Interpretation in Psychoanalysis," *Standard Edition*, Vol. 12, p. 94.

IV: FREUD AS A THERAPIST

1. The Technique of Neutrality

1. "On Beginning the Treatment," p. 123.
2. "The Interpretation of Dreams," Vol. 5, p. 517; "The Handling of Dream-Interpretation in Psychoanalysis," p. 91.
3. "The Interpretation of Dreams," Vol. 4, p. 142; Vol. 5, p. 453.
4. Walter Schmideberg, "To Further Freudian Psychoanalysis," *The American Imago*, Vol. 4, No. 3 (July 1947), p. 4.
5. Quoted in Jones, *Sigmund Freud*, Vol. II, p. 241.
6. "Observations on Transference-Love," p. 171.
7. "Two Encyclopaedia Articles," p. 239.
8. "Notes upon a Case of Obsessional Neurosis," *Standard Edition*, Vol. 10, p. 159; "Recommendations to Physicians Practising Psychoanalysis," pp. 119–20.
9. "Introductory Lectures," Vol. 16, p. 287.
10. "Analysis Terminable and Interminable," p. 247.
11. Letter from Marie H. Briehl to Ernest Jones, Apr. 28, 1956 (Jones archives).
12. For example, Kata Levy.
13. "Observations on Transference-Love," p. 165.

14. Interviews with Mark Brunswick, Jan. 25, 1966, and Nov. 22, 1967, and with Philip Sarasin, Nov. 30, 1966. Cf. Raymond de Saussure, "Sigmund Freud," in *Freud As We Knew Him*, ed. Ruitenbeek, p. 359.
15. Blanton, *Diary of My Analysis with Sigmund Freud*, pp. 34, 45, 53.
16. Interview with Heinz Hartmann, Oct. 18, 1965.
17. Interview with Smiley Blanton, Jan. 25, 1966.
18. Edoardo Weiss, *Sigmund Freud as a Consultant* (New York: Intercontinental Medical Book Corp.; 1970), p. 37.
19. Freud mentions this sort of mechanism in "Some Neurotic Mechanisms in Jealousy, Paranoia and Homosexuality," p. 226.
20. "Recommendations to Physicians Practising Psychoanalysis," p. 111.
21. "On Beginning the Treatment," p. 134.
22. *Ibid.*, p. 133.
23. "Lines of Advance in Psychoanalytic Therapy," p. 165.
24. Interview with Irmarita Putnam, June 30, 1966.
25. Interview with Edoardo Weiss, Jan. 25, 1966.
26. Interview with Sandor Rado, Jan. 29, 1966.
27. Interview with David Brunswick, Dec. 30, 1965.
28. Interview with Roger Money-Kyrle, Nov. 7, 1966.
29. Interviews with Irmarita Putnam and Philip Sarasin.
30. "General Preface," *Standard Edition*, Vol. I, p. xxi.
31. Interview with Albert Hirst.
32. Interviews with Mark Brunswick.
33. Interview with Smiley Blanton, and with Kata Levy, July 13, 1965.
34. Freeman, *Insights*, p. 32.
35. Interview with Irmarita Putnam, and with Edith Jackson, Aug. 30, 1966.
36. Interview with Albert Hirst.
37. Interviews with Edith Jackson and Smiley Blanton.
38. "On Beginning the Treatment," p. 132.
39. *Letters of Freud and Abraham*, p. 276.

40. Interview with Theodor Reik, Oct. 26, 1965.
41. Interview with Mark Brunswick, Jan. 25, 1966.
42. "Psychopathology of Everyday Life," p. 87.
43. Interview with Edith Jackson.
44. Interview with Heinz Hartmann.
45. Quoted in Carl and Sylvia Grossman, *The Wild Analyst* (New York: Braziller; 1965), p. 61.
46. Stefan Zweig, *Mental Healers* (London: Cassell; 1933), pp. 324–25.
47. *Letters*, p. 403.

2. Research Aims

1. "On Beginning the Treatment," p. 132.
2. "The Psychopathology of Everyday Life," p. 157
3. Interview with Albert Hirst.
4. Interview with Helene Deutsch, Oct. 7, 1967.
5. Abram Kardiner, "Freud," in *Freud and the Twentieth Century*, ed. Benjamin Nelson (New York: Meridian Books; 1957), pp. 48–49.
6. Sachs, *Freud*, p. 81.
7. Jones, *Sigmund Freud*, Vol. II, p. 382.
8. Ilse Ollendorff Reich, *Wilhelm Reich* (New York: St. Martin's; 1969), p. 52.
9. "Freud's Psychoanalytic Procedure," p. 254.
10. "On Beginning the Treatment," p. 129.
11. Max Eitingon, in *Ten Years of the Berlin Psychoanalytic Institute* (Chicago Psychoanalytic Society Library), p. 13.
12. "New Introductory Lectures," p. 156.
13. "The Interpretation of Dreams," Vol. 5, p. 536; Binswanger, *Freud*, p. 59.
14. *Reich Speaks of Freud*, p. 59.
15. Viktor von Weizsaecker, "Reminiscences of Freud and Jung," in *Freud and the Twentieth Century*, p. 66.
16. "The Question of Lay Analysis," p. 187.
17. Cf. Eissler's interview with Hirst.
18. Interview with Lionel Penrose, Aug. 31, 1965.
19. "Recommendations to Physicians Practising Psychoanalysis," p. 114.
20. Lou Andreas-Salomé, *The Freud Journal*, translated by Stanley Leavy, (New York: Basic Books; 1964), p. 130.
21. "The Question of Lay Analysis," p. 254.
22. "From the History of an Infantile Neurosis," p. 10.
23. "An Autobiographical Study," p. 18.
24. "Lines of Advance in Psychoanalytic Therapy," p. 168.
25. William M. Johnston, *The Austrian Mind* (Berkeley: University of California Press; 1972), p. 228.
26. Quoted in Jones, *Sigmund Freud*, Vol. II, p. 125.
27. Robert Waelder, "Historical Fiction," *Journal of the American Psychoanalytic Association*, Vol. 11, No. 3 (July 1963), p. 635.
28. Franz Alexander, "Sandor Rado," in *Psychoanalytic Pioneers*, ed. Franz Alexander, Samuel Eisenstein, and Martin Grotjahn (New York: Basic Books; 1966), pp. 247–48.
29. "Recommendations to Physicians Practising Psychoanalysis," p. 115; "Lines of Advance in Psychoanalytic Therapy," p. 167.
30. "Introductory Lectures," Vol. 16, p. 459.
31. "A Short Account of Psychoanalysis," *Standard Edition*, Vol. 19, p. 203; "Two Encyclopaedia Articles," p. 249.
32. "Lines of Advance in Psychoanalytic Therapy," p. 163.
33. "New Introductory Lectures," p. 151; "The Future Prospects of Psychoanalytic Therapy," *Standard Edition*, Vol. 11, p. 150.
34. "Recommendations to Physicians Practising Psychoanalysis," p. 114.
35. "An Autobiographical Study," p. 16.
36. "On Beginning the Treatment," p. 137.
37. "Five Lectures on Psychoanalysis," pp. 52–53.
38. "Notes upon a Case of Obsessional Neurosis," pp. 207–08.
39. Quoted in Jones, *Sigmund Freud*, Vol. II, p. 166; *Letters*, p. 360.
40. *The Origins of Psychoanalysis*, p. 162.
41. "The Question of Lay Analysis," p. 253.

42. Quoted in Jones, *Sigmund Freud,* Vol. II, p. 446.

43. "Introductory Lectures," Vol. 15, p. 178.

44. " 'A Child Is Being Beaten,' " p. 203.

45. Jones, *Sigmund Freud,* Vol. II, p. 123.

46. *Letters,* p. 287.

47. "On Psychotherapy," p. 267.

48. "Analysis Terminable and Interminable," p. 247.

49. "Introduction to Pfister's *The Psychoanalytic Method,*" *Standard Edition,* Vol. 12, p. 330.

50. "Two Encyclopaedia Articles," p. 252.

51. "The Question of Lay Analysis," p. 254.

52. Interview with Richard Sterba, July 10, 1966.

53. *Ibid.*

54. Quoted in Fredrick Redlich, "The Concept of Schizophrenia and Its Implications for Therapy," in Eugene Brody and Fredrick Redlich, *Psychotherapy with Schizophrenia* (New York: International Universities Press; 1952), p. 35.

55. *The Origins of Psychoanalysis,* p. 71; "Editor's Note," *Standard Edition,* Vol. 23, p. 213. Cf. also "Lines of Advance in Psychoanalytic Therapy," p. 162.

56. Interview with Abram Kardiner, Oct. 12, 1965.

57. "Five Lectures on Psychoanalysis," p. 22.

58. Binswanger, *Freud,* pp. 42–43.

3. Character and Symptoms

1. "Five Lectures on Psychoanalysis," p. 22.

2. Thomas Szasz, "Behavior Therapy and Psychoanalysis," *Medical Opinion and Review,* June 1967, p. 27.

3. "Introductory Lectures," Vol. 16, p. 449.

4. "On the History," p. 19.

5. "Freud's Psychoanalytic Procedure," p. 250.

6. "Sexuality in the Aetiology of the Neuroses," pp. 282–83.

7. "Freud's Psychoanalytic Procedure," p. 254.

8. "Sexuality in the Aetiology of the Neuroses," p. 283.

9. "A Note on the Prehistory of the Technique of Analysis," *Standard Edition,* Vol. 18, p. 265.

10. "Fragment of an Analysis of a Case of Hysteria," p. 109.

11. "From the History of an Infantile Neurosis," pp. 89–90.

12. "Constructions in Analysis," *Standard Edition,* Vol. 23, p. 262.

13. "New Introductory Lectures," p. 57.

14. Cf. Eissler's interview with Hirst.

15. "Introductory Lectures," Vol. 16, p. 436.

16. *Minutes,* Vol. II, pp. 318–19.

17. "Two Encyclopaedia Articles," p. 251.

18. Letter from Alfred von Winterstein to Ernest Jones, Dec. 4, 1957 (Jones archives).

19. Quoted in Binswanger, *Freud,* p. 94.

20. Wortis, *Fragments of an Analysis with Freud,* p. 94.

21. "The Claims of Psychoanalysis to Scientific Interest," p. 175.

22. "On Psychoanalysis," p. 210. Cf. also Ernest Jones in *James Jackson Putnam and Psychoanalysis,* ed. Hale, p. 231.

23. "The Psychopathology of Everyday Life," p. 273.

24. "Fragment of an Analysis of a Case of Hysteria," p. 21.

25. Interview with Helene Deutsch, Sept. 30, 1967.

26. *Minutes,* Vol. II, p. 74.

27. Weiss, *Sigmund Freud as a Consultant,* p. 57.

28. "New Introductory Lectures," p. 59.

29. Quoted in Max Schur, *The Id and the Regulatory Principle of Mental Functioning* (London: Hogarth; 1967), p. 21.

30. "Freud's Letters to Simmel," translated by David Brunswick and Frances Deri, *Journal of the American Psychoanalytic Association,* Vol. 12, No. 1 (Jan. 1964), pp. 103, 106.

31. "A Short Account of Psychoanalysis," p. 204.

32. *Minutes*, Vol. II, pp. 285–86.
33. "A Disturbance of Memory on the Acropolis," p. 244.
34. "The Interpretation of Dreams," Vol. 4, p. 303; "The Claims of Psychoanalysis to Scientific Interest," p. 174; "Introductory Lectures," Vol. 16, p. 415.
35. "Introductory Lectures," Vol. 16, p. 423.
36. *Ibid.*, p. 447.
37. Daniel Yankelovich and William Barrett, *Ego and Instinct* (New York: Random House; 1970), p. 284.
38. "Mourning and Melancholia," *Standard Edition*, Vol. 14, pp. 243–58.
39. "The Psychopathology of Everyday Life," pp. 166, 146.
40. "The Interpretation of Dreams," Vol. 4, p. 107.
41. "Studies on Hysteria," p. 95; Weiss, *Sigmund Freud as a Consultant*, p. 50.
42. *Minutes*, Vol. II, p. 268.
43. "Analysis Terminable and Interminable," p. 231.
44. Quoted in *Psychiatry & Social Science Bookshelf*, Vol. I, No. 1 (Sept. 15, 1966), pp. 12–13.
45. Donald W. Winnicott, *Collected Papers* (London: Tavistock; 1958), p. 86.
46. Herman Nunberg, *Memoirs* (New York: Psychoanalytic Research and Developmemnt Fund; 1969), p. 32. Cf. also Edoardo Weiss, *Agoraphobia in the Light of Ego Psychology* (New York: Grune & Stratton; 1964), p. 6.

4. Worthiness

1. Observations on Transference-Love" p. 164.
2. "On Beginning the Treatment," p. 135.
3. "Freud's Psychoanalytic Procedure," p. 254.
4. Quoted in Jones, *Sigmund Freud*, Vol. II, p. 182.
5. *Psychoanalysis and Faith: The Letters of Sigmund Freud and Oskar Pfister*, ed. Heinrich Meng and Ernst Freud, translated by Eric Mosbacher (New York: Basic Books; 1963) (cited hereafter as *Letters of Freud and Pfister*), pp. 61–62.
6. *Letters*, p. 390.
7. Sachs, *Freud*, p. 146.
8. "Recommendations to Physicians Practising Psychoanalysis," p. 119.
9. Jones, *Sigmund Freud*, Vol. II, p. 406.
10. "Dostoevsky and Parricide," p. 196.
11. Helen Walker Puner, *Freud: His Life and His Mind* (New York: Howell, Soskin; 1947), p. 279.
12. "Studies on Hysteria," pp. 282–83.
13. *Ibid.*, p. 265.
14. August Aichhorn, *Wayward Youth* (New York: Meridian Books: 1955).
15. Quoted in Weiss, *Sigmund Freud as a Consultant*, p. 36.
16. Interview with Edoardo Weiss, conducted by Kurt Eissler, Dec. 13, 1952.
17. "Introductory Lectures," p. 321.
18. *Letters*, pp. 423–24.
19. Quoted in Weiss, *Sigmund Freud as a Consultant*, p. 28. Cf. also Wortis, *Fragments of an Analysis with Freud*, p. 41.
20. "Mourning and Melancholia," p. 247.
21. Quoted in Weiss, *Sigmund Freud as a Consultant*, p. 35.
22. Quoted in *ibid.*, p. 37.
23. "Leonardo da Vinci," p. 98.
24. *Minutes*, Vol. II, p. 311.
25. Ellenberger, *The Discovery of the Unconscious*, p. 598.
26. *Minutes*, Vol. II, pp. 297, 290.
27. *Ibid.*, p. 379.
28. Helene Deutsch, *The Psychology of Women*, Vol. I (New York: Grune & Stratton; 1944), pp. 346 ff. Cf. Paul Roazen, "Psychoanalysis and Moral Values," *Dissent*, Feb. 1971, pp. 77–78; this essay has been reprinted in *Moral Values and the Superego Concept*, ed. Seymour C. Post (New York: International Universities Press; 1972), pp. 197–204.
29. Jones, *Sigmund Freud*, Vol. II, p. 80.
30. "On Psychotherapy," p. 263.
31. *Ibid.*, p. 263.
32. *Ibid.*, pp. 263–64.
33. "An Autobiographical Study," p. 27.

34. *Freud/Jung Letters*, pp. 12–13.
35. "Notes upon a Case of Obsessional Neurosis," p. 223.
36. "Remembering, Repeating and Working Through," *Standard Edition*, Vol. 12, pp. 150–51.
37. "The Dynamics of Transference," *Standard Edition*, Vol. 12, pp. 101–02.
38. "Analysis Terminable and Interminable," p. 232.
39. "From the History of an Infantile Neurosis," p. 49.
40. Jones, *Sigmund Freud*, Vol. II, p. 228.
41. "Recommendations to Physicians Practising Psychoanalysis," p. 118.
42. *Ibid.*, p. 115. Cf. also Elizabeth R. Zetzel, "The Analytic Situation," in *Psychoanalysis in the Americas*, ed. Robert E. Litman (New York: International Universities Press; 1966), p. 87.
43. "Analysis Terminable and Interminable," pp. 247–48. Cf. also Grete Bibring-Lehner, "A Contribution to the Subject of Transference-Resistance," *International Journal of Psychoanalysis*, Vol. 17, Part 2 (Apr. 1936), pp. 181–89.
44. Elizabeth R. Zetzel, "Current Concepts of Transference," *International Journal of Psychoanalysis*, Vol. 37, Parts 4–5 (July–Oct. 1956), p. 369–76.
45. "Introductory Lectures," p. 440.
46. *Minutes*, Vol. II, p. 359.
47. Interview with Helene Deutsch, Aug. 13, 1966.

5. Counter-Transference and the Value of Enlightenment

1. "The Future Prospects of Psychoanalytic Therapy," pp. 144–45.
2. "Recommendations to Physicians Practising Psychoanalysis," p. 116.
3. "The Question of Lay Analysis," pp. 219–20.
4. "Recommendations to Physicians Practising Psychoanalysis," p. 113.
5. "Analysis Terminable and Interminable," p. 248.
6. *Minutes*, Vol. II, p. 447.
7. Annie Reich, "On Counter-Transference," *International Journal of Psychoanalysis*, Vol. 32, Part 1 (1951), pp. 28–29.
8. *The Wolf-Man*, ed. Muriel Gardiner (New York: Basic Books; 1971).
9. Ellenberger, *The Discovery of the Unconscious*, p. 467.
10. Ruth Mack Brunswick, "A Note on the Childish Theory of Coitus A Tergo," *International Journal of Psychoanalysis*, Vol. 10 (1929), p. 93.
11. "From the History of an Infantile Neurosis," pp. 84, 121.
12. *Ibid.*, p. 118.
13. Quoted in Jones, *Sigmund Freud*, Vol. II, p. 458.
14. *The Wolf-Man*, p. 305.
15. *Ibid.*, p. 20.
16. *Ibid.*, p. 266.
17. *Ibid.*, p. 366.
18. "Fragment of an Analysis of a Case of Hysteria," p. 122.
19. "Psychoanalysis and Telepathy," *Standard Edition*, Vol. 18, p. 191.
20. *Ibid.*
21. *Ibid.*, p. 192. Cf. Roazen, "Psychoanalysis and Moral Values."
22. "Psychoanalysis and Telepathy," p. 192.
23. *Ibid.*, pp. 192–93.
24. Cf. also "New Introductory Lectures," pp. 45–47.
25. "Lines of Advance in Psychoanalytic Therapy," p. 162.
26. "A Case of Paranoia Running Counter to the Psychoanalytic Theory of the Disease," *Standard Edition*, Vol. 14, p. 263.
27. "Studies on Hysteria," p. 134.
28. "Introductory Lectures," Vol. 16, p. 463.
29. "The Question of Lay Analysis," p. 233.
30. "On Psychotherapy," p. 265.
31. "Analysis Terminable and Interminable," p. 243.
32. Quoted in Jones, *Sigmund Freud*, Vol. II, p. 183.
33. *Letters of Freud and Pfister*, p. 15.
34. "On Beginning the Treatment," p. 133.

35. Quoted in Binswanger, *Freud*, p. 50.
36. "The Interpretation of Dreams," Vol. 4, p. 219.
37. *Ibid.*, Vol. 5, p. 578.
38. "New Introductory Lectures," p. 80.
39. "Psychical (or Mental) Treatment," *Standard Edition*, Vol. 7, p. 283.
40. "Introductory Lectures," Vol. 16, pp. 280–81.
41. "Why War?," *Standard Edition*, Vol. 22, p. 213.
42. "Beyond the Pleasure Principle," p. 18.
43. "The Interpretation of Dreams," Vol. 4, p. 108.
44. *Minutes*, Vol. II, p. 35.
45. Maryse Choisy, *Sigmund Freud* (New York: Citadel; 1963), pp. 6–7.
46. *Letters*, p. 310.
47. *Letters of Freud and Pfister*, p. 62.
48. "Lines of Advance in Psychoanalytic Therapy," pp. 160–61.
49. "Notes upon a Case of Obsessional Neurosis," p. 177.
50. *Minutes*, Vol. II, p. 89.
51. "The Dynamics of Transference," p. 108.

6. Words and Power

1. "Analysis Terminable and Interminable," p. 233.
2. Edith Weigert, "Dissent in the Early History of Psychoanalysis," *Psychiatry*, Vol. 5 (1942), p. 353.
3. "On Psychotherapy," p. 262.
4. *Minutes*, Vol. II, p. 373.
5. *Ibid.*, p. 194.
6. *Ibid.*, p. 189.
7. "Creative Writers and Day-Dreaming," p. 153.
8. *Minutes*, Vol. II, p. 391.
9. "Psychopathic Characters on the Stage," *Standard Edition*, Vol. 7, p. 310.
10. *Minutes*, Vol. II, p. 300.
11. *Ibid.*, p. 256.
12. "Introductory Lectures," Vol. 15, p. 17.
13. "Remembering, Repeating and Working Through," p. 155.
14. "Kardiner Reminisces," *Bulletin of the Association for Psychoanalytic Medicine*, May 1963, p. 63.
15. Franz Alexander, "Reflections of Berggasse 19," *Psychoanalytic Quarterly*, Vol. 9, No. 2 (1940), p. 202.
16. "On Psychotherapy," p. 264.
17. Quoted in Weiss, *Sigmund Freud as a Consultant*, p. 35.
18. "On the History," p. 49.
19. *Minutes*, Vol. II, p. 133.
20. "Introductory Lectures," Vol. 16, p. 456; "The Dynamics of Transference," p. 104.
21. *Minutes*, Vol. II, p. 90.
22. "Analysis Terminable and Interminable," p. 249.
23. Cf. Siegfried Bernfeld, "On Psychoanalytic Training," *Psychoanalytic Quarterly*, Vol. 31, No. 4 (1962), p. 463.
24. *Letters of Freud and Abraham*, p. 346.
25. "The Question of Lay Analysis," p. 228.
26. "Analysis Terminable and Interminable," p. 248.
27. *Ibid.*, p. 224.
28. *Ibid.*, p. 249.
29. Interview with Edward Glover, Sept. 2, 1965.
30. "Analysis Terminable and Interminable," p. 248.
31. "Preface to Maxim Steiner's *The Psychical Disorders of Male Potency*," *Standard Edition*, Vol. 12, p. 346.
32. *Minutes*, Vol. II, p. 343.
33. Binswanger, *Freud*, pp. 33, 29.
34. Quoted in Jones, *Sigmund Freud*, Vol. II, p. 454.
35. Quoted in *ibid.*, pp. 452, 166.
36. "Recommendations to Physicians Practising Psychoanalysis," p. 115.
37. *Minutes*, Vol. II, p. 391.
38. *Ibid.*, pp. 224–25.
39. Quoted in Françoise Gilot and Carlton Lake, *Life with Picasso* (London: Nelson; 1965), p. 52.
40. "On Psychotherapy," pp. 259, 262; cf. also "American Interview of Freud with A. Albrecht," *Psychoanalytic Review*, Vol. 55, No. 3 (1968), pp. 333–41.

41. Jones, *Sigmund Freud*, Vol. II, p. 235.
42. Binswanger, *Freud*, p. 21.
43. "Analysis Terminable and Interminable," p. 228.
44. Sachs, *Freud*, p. 145.

V: PUBLIC CONTROVERSIES: ALFRED ADLER AND WILHELM STEKEL

1. Collaboration

1. Interview with Richard Wagner, Mar. 25, 1966.
2. *Reich Speaks of Freud*, p. 73.
3. Letter from Franz Bienenfeld to Ernest Jones, Oct. 9, 1955 (Jones archives).
4. "Character and Anal Eroticism," *Standard Edition*, Vol. 9, p. 173.
5. "The Interpretation of Dreams," Vol. 4, p. 93.
6. A notable recent exception is Ellenberger's *The Discovery of the Unconscious*.
7. *Minutes*, Vol. II, p. 66.
8. Phyllis Bottome, *Alfred Adler* (New York: Vanguard; 1957), p. 69. Cf. also Heinz Ansbacher, "Was Adler a Disciple of Freud? A Reply," *Journal of Individual Psychology*, Vol. 18 (Nov. 1962), pp. 126–35.
9. Ellenberger, *The Discovery of the Unconscious*, p. 454.
10. Puner, *Freud*, p. 30.
11. "On Dreams," *Standard Edition*, Vol. 5, p. 635.
12. Sachs, *Freud*, p. 185.
13. Reik, *From Twenty Years with Freud*, p. 15.
14. Wittels, *Sigmund Freud*, p. 134.
15. Interview with Mrs. Alexander Freud, May 12, 1966. Cf. also letter from Harry Freud to Ernest Jones, Jan. 25, 1956 (Jones archives).
16. Quoted in Jones, *Sigmund Freud*, Vol. II, p. 71.
17. "Freud's Psychoanalytic Procedure," pp. 249, 251.
18. Jones, *Sigmund Freud*, Vol. II, p. 386.
19. Carl Furtmuller, "Alfred Adler," in *Alfred Adler: Superiority and Social Interest*, ed. Heinz and Rowena Ansbacher (Evanston, Ill.: Northwestern University Press; 1964), p. 346.
20. Nigel Dennis, "Alfred Adler and the Style of Life," *Encounter*, Vol. 35 (1970), p. 7.
21. Jones, *Free Associations*, p. 169. Interview with Abram Kardiner, Oct. 17, 1964.
22. Ellenberger, *The Discovery of the Unconscious*, pp. 599–603.
23. *Minutes*, Vol. II, p. 260.
24. Jones said of Adler's wife Raissa that "Trotsky and Joffe . . . constantly frequented her house." *Sigmund Freud*, Vol. II, p. 134. But Alexandra Adler disputes this view. Interview with Alexandra Adler, Oct. 19, 1965. Jones may have been relying on Eissler's interview with Klemperer.
25. Quoted in Jones, *Sigmund Freud*, Vol. II, p. 71.
26. "On the History," p. 51.
27. According to Phyllis Bottome, "the whole process of psychoanalysis was inimical to the welfare of mankind. This was the 'shadow' . . ." *Alfred Adler*, p. 77. Cf. also Ansbacher, "Was Adler a Disciple of Freud? A Reply," pp. 126, 131.
28. Sachs, *Freud*, p. 126. Cf. also Jones, *Sigmund Freud*, Vol. II, p. 408.
29. Max Graf, "Reminiscences of Professor Sigmund Freud," *Psychoanalytic Quarterly*, Vol. 11, No. 4 (1942), pp. 474–75.
30. Jones, *Sigmund Freud*, Vol. II, p. 62.
31. "Letter to Fritz Wittels," p. 287.
32. "The Interpretation of Dreams," Vol. 4, p. 142.
33. Puner, *Freud*, p. 253.
34. Jones, *Sigmund Freud*, Vol. II, p. 121.
35. "New Introductory Lectures," p. 139.
36. "Civilization and Its Discontents," p. 110.
37. "On the History," pp. 38–39.

2. The Will to Power

1. Sachs, *Freud*, p. 57.

2. "On the History," p. 44.
3. Jones, *Sigmund Freud*, Vol. II, pp. 69–70.
4. Wilhelm Stekel, *Autobiography*, ed. Emil A. Gutheil (New York: Liveright; 1950), p. 129.
5. "On the History," pp. 44–45.
6. "Two Encyclopaedia Articles," p. 248; *Minutes*, Vol. II, p. 464.
7. *Minutes*, Vol. II, pp. 539, 538, 540.
8. Jones, *Sigmund Freud*, Vol. II, p. 132.
9. "On the History," p. 59.
10. *Minutes*, Vol. II, p. 63.
11. Interviews with Richard Wagner, Dec. 17, 1965, Feb. 11, 1966, and March 25, 1966. Cf. Kurt Eissler's interview with Paul Klemperer (Jones archives).
12. Sachs, *Freud*, p. 51.
13. Eissler's interview with Klemperer.
14. Graf, "Reminiscences of Professor Sigmund Freud," p. 473.
15. "On the History," p. 51; Jones, *Sigmund Freud*, Vol. II, p. 133.
16. Sachs, *Freud*, p. 51.
17. *Letters of Freud and Pfister*, p. 48. But cf. Weigert, "Dissent in the Early History of Psychoanalysis," p. 353.
18. *Letters of Freud and Abraham*, pp. 103, 105, 110. *Freud/Jung Letters*, pp. 447, 373, 403.
19. Interview with Mrs. Hanns Sachs, Dec. 22, 1965.
20. "Group Psychology and the Analysis of the Ego," pp. 80–81.
21. Erik Erikson, *Dialogue with Erik Erikson*, ed. Richard I. Evans (New York: Harper & Row; 1967), p. 16.
22. Sachs, *Freud*, p. 114.
23. Quoted in Jones, *Sigmund Freud*, Vol. II, p. 304.
24. "On the History," p. 66.
25. *Ibid.*, p. 25.
26. *Ibid.*, pp. 49–50.
27. *Ibid.*, p. 7.
28. *Ibid.*, p. 52.
29. *Ibid.*, p. 51.
30. Wittels, *Sigmund Freud*, p. 225.
31. *Letters of Freud and Abraham*, p. 182.
32. *Sigmund Freud and Lou Andreas-Salomé: Letters*, ed. Ernst Pfeiffer, translated by William and Elaine Robson-Scott (hereafter cited as *letters of Freud and Andreas-Salomé*) (London: Hogarth; 1972), p. 19.
33. Jones, *Sigmund Freud*, Vol. II, pp. 127, 129, 128, 130.
34. Jones, *Free Associations*, p. 218.
35. Sachs, *Freud*, pp. 95–96, 115, 42.
36. *Letters*, p. 312.
37. "On the History," pp. 54–55, 57–58.
38. "Introductory Lectures," Vol. 16, p. 346. Cf. also Heinz Hartmann, Ernst Kris, and Rudolph Loewenstein, "The Function of Theory in Psychoanalysis," in *Drives, Affects, Behavior*, ed. Rudolph Loewenstein (New York: International Universities Press; 1953), p. 28.
39. "On the History," p. 52.
40. "The Question of Lay Analysis," p. 208.
41. "Introductory Lectures," Vol. 15, p. 237.
42. Ellenberger, *The Discovery of the Unconscious*, p. 611. But cf. Johnston, *The Austrian Mind*, p. 257.
43. "The Interpretation of Dreams," Vol. 5, p. 397.
44. "Analysis Terminable and Interminable," pp. 252–53.

3. Priorities

1. *Minutes*, Vol. II, p. 433.
2. "On the History," p. 53.
3. *Ibid.*, pp. 56, 57, 16.
4. Interviews with Helene Deutsch, May 22, 1965, Aug. 6, 1966, and April 8, 1967. Cf. also letter from Louis S. London to Ernest Jones, May 15, 1956 (Jones archives), *Reich Speaks of Freud*, pp. 59–60, and interview with Richard Sterba.
5. "On the History," p. 51. Cf. *Freud/Jung Letters*, p. 373.
6. Quoted in Andreas-Salomé, *The Freud Journal*, p. 33.
7. *Ibid.*, p. 127.
8. Quoted in *ibid.*, pp. 160–61.
9. *Minutes*, Vol. II, pp. 251, 580, 510, 579.
10. "Two Encyclopaedia Articles," p. 255.

11. Letter from Sigmund Freud to Max Marcuse, Aug. 17, 1908.
12. *Minutes*, Vol. II, pp. 43–52. For an examination of the climate of ideas in which Freud wrote, cf. Stephen Kern, "Freud and the Discovery of Child Sexuality," *History of Childhood Quarterly*, Vol. I, No. 1 (Summer 1973), pp. 117–141.
13. *Letters of Freud and Abraham*, pp. 58, 73–74.
14. *Ibid.*, p. 78.
15. *The Freud/Jung Letters*, p. 223.
16. *Letters of Freud and Abraham*, p. 171.
17. Letter from Sigmund Freud to Max Marcuse, Sept. 26, 1926.
18. Ellenberger, *The Discovery of the Unconscious*, p. 849.
19. *Ibid.*, p. 448.
20. Graf, "Reminiscences of Professor Sigmund Freud," p. 469.
21. "An Autobiographical Study," p. 50.
22. Wortis, *Fragments of an Analysis with Freud*, p. 144.
23. Quoted in Jones, *Sigmund Freud*, Vol. II, pp. 189–90.
24. *Letters of Freud and Abraham*, p. 352; Binswanger, *Freud*, p. 30; *Letters of Freud and Abraham*, p. 64.
25. Puner, *Freud*, p. 212.
26. *Letters of Freud and Zweig*, pp. 122–23.
27. *Ibid.*, p. 130.
28. "On the History," p. 8.
29. Jones, *Sigmund Freud*, Vol. II, pp. 110–11.
30. Quoted in *ibid.*, p. 45. Cf. *Freud/Jung Letters*, p. 178.
31. *Minutes*, Vol. II, pp. 516, 461–62.
32. "A Disturbance of Memory on the Acropolis," p. 245.
33. *Minutes*, Vol. II, p. 536.
34. "Analysis Terminable and Interminable," p. 245.
35. "Josef Popper-Lynkeus and the Theory of Dreams," p. 261.
36. "A Difficulty in the Path of Psychoanalysis," pp. 143–44.
37. "On the History," pp. 15–16.
38. "Notes upon a Case of Obsessional Neurosis," p. 184; Interview with Heinz Hartmann, Oct. 18, 1965.
39. *Minutes of the Vienna Psychoanalytic Society*, ed. Herman Nunberg and Ernst Federn, Vol. I (New York: International Universities Press; 1962) (cited hereafter as *Minutes*), pp. 359–60.
40. *Ibid.*, Vol. II, pp. 31–32.
41. "An Autobiographical Study," pp. 59–60.
42. Interview with Irmarita Putnam.
43. *The Origins of Psychoanalysis*, p. 126.
44. Quoted in Jones, *Sigmund Freud*, Vol. II, p. 443.
45. Interviews with Helene Deutsch, June 11, 1966, and Jan. 21, 1967.
46. Cf. Roazen, *Brother Animal*, Ch. 3.
47. "Introductory Lectures," Vol. 16, p. 285; "A Difficulty in the Path of Psychoanalysis," pp. 139–41.
48. Quoted in Jones, *Sigmund Freud*, Vol. III, p. 131.
49. Quoted in *ibid.*, Vol. II, p. 415.
50. *Letters of Freud and Abraham*, p. 345.

4. Revisionism

1. Andreas-Salomé, *The Freud Journal*, p. 43.
2. Weigert, "Dissent in the Early History of Psychoanalysis," p. 351.
3. Johnston, *The Austrian Mind*, p. 256.
4. Ellenberger, *The Discovery of the Unconscious*, p. 617.
5. Andreas-Salomé, *The Freud Journal*, p. 88.
6. Bottome, *Alfred Adler*, p. 72.
7. Ellenberger, *The Discovery of the Unconscious*, p. 606.
8. *Ibid.*, p. 613.
9. "Psychoanalytic Notes on an Autobiographical Account," p. 61.
10. *Minutes*, Vol. II, p. 174.
11. "On the History," p. 61.
12. Andreas-Salomé, *The Freud Journal*, p. 62.
13. "On the History," p. 38.
14. "The Question of Lay Analysis," p. 256.
15. Ernst Kris, "Some Vicissitudes of Insight in Psychoanalysis," *International Journal of Psychoanalysis*, Vol. 37, Part 6 (Nov.–Dec. 1956), p. 453.
16. *Letters*, p. 401.

17. Quoted in Jones, *Sigmund Freud*, Vol. III, p. 465.

18. Jones, *Free Associations*, p. 217.

19. Jones, *Sigmund Freud*, Vol. II, p. 412.

20. Rudolph Loewenstein, "Some Remarks on Defenses, Autonomous Ego and Psychoanalytic Technique," *International Journal of Psychoanalysis*, Vol. 35, Part 2 (1954), p. 189.

21. Evans, *Dialogue with Erik Erikson*, pp. 100, 27.

22. Weigert, "Dissent in the Early History of Psychoanalysis," p. 350.

23. *Minutes*, Vol. II, p. 441.

24. "Five Lectures on Psychoanalysis," p. 20.

25. "On the History," p. 52.

26. *Ibid.*, p. 50.

27. Andreas-Salomé, *The Freud Journal*, p. 35.

28. *Minutes*, Vol. II, p. 321.

29. "The Interpretation of Dreams," Vol. 5, pp. 579–80.

30. Ernst Kris, "Book Review of Anna Freud's *The Ego and the Mechanisms of Defence*," *International Journal of Psychoanalysis*, Vol. 19 (1938), p. 142.

31. Ellenberger, *The Discovery of the Unconscious*, pp. 638–39.

32. *Minutes*, Vol. II, pp. 260, 266, 321.

33. "Civilization and Its Discontents," p. 114.

34. Interview with Willy Hoffer, June 29, 1965.

35. Cf. Kurt Eissler's interview with Paul Klemperer.

36. Jones, *Sigmund Freud*, Vol. II, p. 107.

37. Interview with Ernst Federn.

38. Sachs, *Freud*, pp. 120–21.

39. "The Interpretation of Dreams," Vol. 5, p. 621; "Editor's Note," *Standard Edition*, Vol. 12, p. 178.

40. "Notes upon a Case of Obsessional Neurosis," p. 160.

41. Cf. "Three Essays on the Theory of Sexuality," p. 184; "The Psychoanalytic View of Psychogenic Disturbance of Vision," *Standard Edition*, Vol. 11, p. 218.

42. Quoted in Hale, ed., *James Jackson Putnam and Psychoanalysis*, p. 146. Cf. also *Freud/Jung Letters*, pp. 373, 376, 387, 422, 428.

43. "On Narcissism," *Standard Edition*, Vol. 14, pp. 92–93.

44. "Two Encyclopaedia Articles," p. 248.

45. Freud objected to Helene Deutsch's use of the term "As-If" in her work on psychopaths. Unknown to her, Adler had frequently cited Vaihinger's book *The Philosophy of As-If*; hence Freud took exception to the phrase in a loyal pupil's article.

46. "The Interpretation of Dreams," Vol. 5, p. 507.

47. "From the History of an Infantile Neurosis," p. 53; "Totem and Taboo," *Standard Edition*, Vol. 13, p. 90.

48. "Some Psychical Consequences of the Anatomical Distinction Between the Sexes," pp. 253–54.

49. *Letters of Freud and Pfister*, p. 95.

50. *Letters of Freud and Abraham*, p. 364.

51. "New Introductory Lectures," p. 140.

52. *Ibid.*, pp. 65–66.

53. E. A. Bennet, *C. G. Jung* (New York: E. P. Dutton; 1962), p. 56.

54. Quoted in Jones, *Sigmund Freud*, Vol. III, p. 208.

55. Ellenberger, *The Discovery of the Unconscious*, p. 595.

56. Alfred Adler, *Social Interest: A Challenge to Mankind*, translated by John Linton and Richard Vaughan (New York: Capricorn Books; 1964), p. 253.

57. Interview with Emmanuel Miller, Aug. 27, 1965.

58. A. H. Maslow, "Was Adler a Disciple of Freud? A Note," *Journal of Individual Psychology*, Vol. 18 (Nov. 1963), p. 125.

59. Cf. Kurt Eissler's criticism of Franz Alexander's concepts as Adlerian. "The Chicago Institute of Psychoanalysis," *The Journal of General Psychology*, Vol. 42, First Half (Jan. 1950), p. 115.

60. Robert Waelder, "Present Trends in Psychoanalytic Theory and Practice," *The Yearbook of Psychoanalysis*, Vol. I (New York: International Universities Press; 1945), p. 87.

61. Ives Hendrick, "The Discussion of the 'Instinct to Master,'" *Psycho-*

analytic Quarterly, Vol. 12, No. 4 (1943), p. 563.

62. Kenneth Clark, "Implications of Adlerian Theory for an Understanding of Civil Rights Problems and Action," *Journal of Individual Psychology*, Vol. 23 (Nov. 1967), pp. 181–90.

63. Frantz Fanon, *Black Skin, White Masks*, translated by Charles Lam Markmann (New York: Grove Press; 1967).

5. Thanatos

1. "On the History," p. 26.
2. Cf. Kurt Eissler's interview with Edoardo Weiss.
3. Jones, *Sigmund Freud*, Vol. II, p. 7; Jones, *Free Associations*, p. 219.
4. Letter from Ernest Jones to Max Schur, Oct. 4, 1955 (Jones archives); Jones, *Free Associations*, p. 220.
5. Wortis, *Fragments of an Analysis with Freud*, p. 147.
6. *Letters*, p. 352.
7. Stekel, *Autobiography*, p. 123.
8. *Ibid.*, p. 106.
9. "On the History," p. 25; Stekel, *Autobiography*, pp. 115–16.
10. *Minutes*, Vol. II, pp. 112, 248, 551, 560.
11. *Ibid.*, pp. 111–12.
12. *Ibid.*, p. 273.
13. "Introductory Lectures," Vol. 15, p. 149.
14. "On the History," p. 19.
15. Wittels, *Freud*, p. 225.
16. "Contributions to a Discussion on Masturbation," p. 243.
17. *Minutes*, Vol. II, p. 61.
18. *Ibid.*, p. 562.
19. "Contributions to a Discussion on Masturbation," p. 248.
20. *Ibid.*, p. 243.
21. *Ibid.*, p. 249.
22. *Ibid.*, p. 246.
23. *Minutes*, Vol. II, p. 10.
24. Quoted in Jones, *Sigmund Freud*, Vol. II, pp. 62, 135; *Minutes*, Vol. II, p. 401. Cf. *Freud/Jung Letters*, p. 259.
25. Jones, *Sigmund Freud*, Vol. II, p. 136.
26. Stekel, *Autobiography*, p. 125.

27. *Minutes*, Vol. II, p. 466.
28. Wittels, *Freud*, pp. 192–93.
29. Jones, *Sigmund Freud*, Vol. II, p. 136. This saying of Freud's was a paraphrase of one of Heine's dictums; Freud often quoted him admiringly.
30. Quoted in Jones, *Sigmund Freud*, Vol. II, p. 130.
31. Quoted in *ibid.*, p. 71.
32. Quoted in *ibid.*, p. 130. Cf. also *Freud/Jung Letters*, pp. 376, 382.
33. Quoted in Jones, *Sigmund Freud*, Vol. II, p. 71.
34. *Letters of Freud and Pfister*, p. 49.
35. Jones, *Sigmund Freud*, Vol. II, p. 136.
36. Andreas-Salomé, *The Freud Journal*, pp. 53, 67.
37. *Letters of Freud and Abraham*, p. 125.
38. *Ibid.*, p. 127; cf. also Hale, ed., *James Jackson Putnam and Psychoanalysis*, p. 150.
39. Hale, ed., *James Jackson Putnam and Psychoanalysis*, p. 151.
40. "The Psychopathology of Everyday Life," p. 120.
41. "The Interpretation of Dreams," Vol. 4, p. 274.
42. "Preface to Wilhelm Stekel's *Nervous Anxiety States and Their Treatment*," *Standard Edition*, Vol. 9, p. 250.
43. Stekel, *Autobiography*, p. 134.
44. Jones, *Sigmund Freud*, Vol. II, p. 428.
45. *Letters*, p. 346.
46. Letter from Edoardo Weiss to Ernest Jones, Aug. 22, 1956 (Jones archives).
47. Jones, *Sigmund Freud*, Vol. III, p. 273.
48. *Minutes*, Vol. II, p. 395.
49. "Introductory Lectures," Vol. 15, p. 237.
50. "The Disposition to Obsessional Neurosis," *Standard Edition*, Vol. 12, p. 325.
51. "Civilization and Its Discontents," p. 120.
52. "Dreams and Telepathy," *Standard Edition*, Vol. 18, p. 197.
53. Stekel, *Autobiography*, p. 138.
54. "The Interpretation of Dreams," Vol. 5, pp. 353, 357.
55. *Ibid.*, p. 350.
56. *Letters*, p. 346.
57. Sachs, *Freud*, p. 115.

58. Quoted in Jones, *Sigmund Freud*, Vol. II, p. 137.
59. "Letter to Fritz Wittels," p. 286.
60. Jones, *Sigmund Freud*, Vol. III, p. 138.
61. *Letters*, pp. 347–48.
62. Jones, *Sigmund Freud*, Vol. III, p. 102.
63. Bennet, *C. G. Jung*, p. 56.
64. Wortis, *Fragments of an Analysis with Freud*, pp. 142, 163, 30, 41.
65. Weiss, *Sigmund Freud as a Consultant*, p. 39. Cf. also *Reich Speaks of Freud*, p. 90.
66. Jones, *Sigmund Freud*, Vol. III, p. 158.
67. *Ibid.*, p. 234.

VI: THE "CROWN PRINCE": CARL GUSTAV JUNG

1. The Science of Psychiatry

1. Wortis, *Fragments of an Analysis with Freud*, p. 146.
2. Letter from Kurt Eissler to Anna Freud, Sept. 17, 1954 (Jones archives).
3. "Introductory Lectures," Vol. 16, p. 260.
4. Nunberg, *Memoirs*, p. 12.
5. "On the History," p. 27.
6. "Introductory Lectures," Vol. 15, p. 109.
7. Quoted in Jones, *Sigmund Freud*, Vol. II, p. 138. Cf. also *Freud/Jung Letters*, p. 158.
8. Jones, *Sigmund Freud*, Vol. II, p. 50.
9. Jolande Jacobi, "C. G. Jung," *International Encyclopaedia of the Social Sciences*, Vol. 8 (New York: Macmillan–The Free Press; 1968), p. 328.
10. "Screen Memories," p. 312.
11. Jones, *Sigmund Freud*, Vol. II, p. 69.
12. Quoted in C. G. Jung, *Memories, Dreams, Reflections*, recorded and edited by Aniela Jaffé, translated by Richard and Clara Winston (New York: Vintage Books; 1965), p. 361.
13. *Letters of Freud and Abraham*, p. 34.
14. *Ibid.*, p. 62.
15. Jacobi, "C. G. Jung," p. 327; E. A. Bennet, *C. G. Jung*, p. 41.
16. Wittels, *Freud*, p. 138.

17. Jones, *Sigmund Freud*, Vol. II, p. 33. Cf. *Freud/Jung Letters*, pp. 196–97.
18. Jones, *Sigmund Freud*, Vol. II, p. 33; quoted in Binswanger, *Freud*, p. 31.
19. *Letters*, p. 302.
20. *Freud/Jung Letters*, pp. 343, 364, 370.
21. Martin Freud, *Glory Reflected*, pp. 108–09.
22. Interview with Theodor Reik, Apr. 4, 1967. Cf. also Freeman, *Insights*, p. 116.
23. Quoted in Jolande Jacobi, "Freud and Jung—Meeting and Parting," *Swiss Review of World Affairs*, Vol. 6, No. 5 (Aug. 1956), p. 18.
24. *Letters*, p. 256. Cf. *Freud/Jung Letters*, p. 82.
25. Quoted in Jones, *Sigmund Freud*, Vol. II, p. 112.
26. Quoted in Carl and Sylvia Grossman, *The Wild Analyst*, p. 102; Jones, *Sigmund Freud*, Vol. II, p. 46.
27. Quoted in Jones, *Sigmund Freud*, Vol. II, p. 399.
28. Bennet, *C. G. Jung*, p. 41.
29. Quoted in Jones, *Sigmund Freud*, Vol. II, p. 65.
30. Quoted in *ibid.*, p. 140.
31. Sachs, *Freud*, p. 92.
32. "Editor's Note," *Standard Edition*, Vol. 9, p. 4; Jones, *Sigmund Freud*, Vol. II, p. 341.
33. Quoted in Jones, *Sigmund Freud*, Vol. II, p. 86.
34. *Freud/Jung Letters*, pp. 207, 289.
35. *Ibid.*, pp. 467, 452.
36. *Ibid.*, p. 292.

2. The Occult

1. Quoted in Jones, *Sigmund Freud*, Vol. III, p. 391.
2. "Dreams and Telepathy," p. 178.
3. Quoted in Jones, *Sigmund Freud*, Vol. III, pp. 394–95.
4. Jones, *Free Associations*, p. 165.
5. Jones, *Sigmund Freud*, Vol. II, p. 138.
6. *Letters of Freud and Abraham*, p. 46.
7. Jones, *Sigmund Freud*, Vol. II, pp. 166–67.
8. Interview with Edoardo Weiss, May 13, 1965.

9. *Minutes*, Vol. II, p. 422.
10. *Ibid.*
11. Cf., for example, Helene Deutsch, "Occult Processes Occurring During Psychoanalysis," in *Psychoanalysis and the Occult*, ed. George Devereux (New York: International Universities Press; 1953), pp. 133–46; and Edward Hitschmann, "Telepathy and Psychoanalysis," in *Heirs to Freud*, ed. Hendrik M. Ruitenbeek (New York: Grove Press; 1966), pp. 101–20.
12. "New Introductory Lectures," p. 33.
13. *Ibid.*, p. 34.
14. "Dreams and Telepathy," p. 204.
15. "The Psychogenesis of a Case of Homosexuality in a Woman," *Standard Edition*, Vol. 18, p. 165.
16. "Shorter Writings," *Standard Edition*, Vol. 23, p. 300.
17. "A Special Type of Object Choice Made by Men," *Standard Edition*, Vol. 11, p. 165.
18. "The Psychopathology of Everyday Life," p. 254.
19. *Ibid.*, p. 257.
20. "Remarks on the Theory and Practice of Dream Interpretation," *Standard Edition*, Vol. 19, p. 112.
21. "New Introductory Lectures," p. 159.
22. "Group Psychology and the Analysis of the Ego," p. 108.
23. "Beyond the Pleasure Principle," p. 59.
24. Robert, *The Psychoanalytic Revolution*, pp. 63–64.
25. "The Psychopathology of Everyday Life," pp. 261–62.
26. Jones, *Sigmund Freud*, Vol. II, p. 65.
27. "Introductory Lectures," Vol. 15, p. 59.
28. "Review of August Forel's *Hypnotism*," p. 91.
29. "New Introductory Lectures," p. 37; cf. also "Dreams and Telepathy," p. 208.
30. "Dreams and Telepathy," pp. 218–19.
31. Jones, *Sigmund Freud*, Vol. II, p. 21; *Letters*, pp. 339–40.
32. "The Psychopathology of Everyday Life," p. 250.
33. Jones, *Sigmund Freud*, Vol. II, p. 184.
34. "The 'Uncanny,'" p. 235.
35. *Ibid.*
36. Jones, *Sigmund Freud*, Vol. II, pp. 13–14.
37. "The 'Uncanny,'" p. 219.
38. *Ibid.*, pp. 219–20.
39. Jones, *Sigmund Freud*, Vol. III, p. 391.
40. "The 'Uncanny,'" pp. 247, 220.
41. *Ibid.*, p. 243. Cf. Roazen, *Brother Animal*, pp. 77–78.
42. Andreas-Salomé, *The Freud Journal*, p. 169.
43. "Psychoanalysis and Telepathy," *Standard Edition*, Vol. 18, p. 181.
44. "New Introductory Lectures," p. 54.
45. *Ibid.*, p. 54. Cf. also *ibid.*, p. 47.
46. *Ibid.*, p. 43.
47. Quoted in Weiss, *Sigmund Freud as a Consultant*, p. 69.
48. "Notes upon a Case of Obsessional Neurosis," p. 233.
49. "The Psychopathology of Everyday Life," p. 260.
50. *Ibid.*
51. *Ibid.*, p. 261.
52. Quoted in Jones, *Sigmund Freud*, Vol. II, p. 392.

3. Oedipus

1. "The Interpretation of Dreams," Vol. 5, p. 483.
2. Interview with Edoardo Weiss, June 26, 1966.
3. *Letters*, p. 296.
4. Wittels, *Freud*, p. 176.
5. Carl G. Jung, *Freud and Psychoanalysis, Collected Works*, Vol. IV, ed. Herbert Read, Michael Fordham, and Gerhard Adler, translated by R. F. C. Hull (New York: Pantheon; 1961), pp. 284–85.
6. "On the History," p. 43.
7. Jones, *Free Associations*, p. 205.
8. *Ibid.*, p. 206.
9. Binswanger, *Freud*, p. 9.
10. "An Autobiographical Study," p. 53. Cf. also *Freud/Jung Letters*, pp. 42, 301, 400.
11. Binswanger, *Freud*, p. 2.
12. *Freud/Jung Letters*, p. 457.
13. *Ibid.*, p. 95.

14. *Ibid.,* p. 98.
15. Jones, *Sigmund Freud,* Vol. III, p. 44; cf. also *ibid.,* Vol. II, p. 55.
16. Jung, *Memories, Dreams, Reflections,* p. 158. Cf. *Freud/Jung Letters,* p. 526.
17. Bilinsky, "Jung and Freud," p. 42.
18. Jones, *Sigmund Freud,* Vol. II, p. 386.
19. Jung, *Memories, Dreams, Reflections,* p. 156; cf. also Jones, *Sigmund Freud,* Vol. II, p. 146; letter from Lester Bernstein to Ernest Jones, Nov. 26, 1954 (Jones archives).
20. Jones, *Sigmund Freud,* Vol. I, p. 317.
21. *Ibid.,* Vol. II, p. 47. In 1905 Jung had published an article on "cryptomnesia." Cf. also *Freud/Jung Letters,* p. 149.
22. Quoted in Jones, *Sigmund Freud,* Vol. II, p. 48.
23. *Ibid.,* p. 312.
24. Karl Abraham, *Clinical Papers and Essays in Psychoanalysis* (London: Hogarth; 1955), pp. 273, 265.
25. Jung, *Memories, Dreams, Reflections,* p. 157.
26. *Ibid.*
27. Letter from Lester Bernstein to Ernest Jones (Jones archives).
28. Interview with Albert Hirst, Jan. 21, 1966. Cf. Schur, *Freud,* pp. 80–82.
29. Schur, "Some Additional 'Day Residues' of 'The Specimen Dream of Psychoanalysis,'" pp. 55, 77.
30. Quoted in Jones, *Sigmund Freud,* Vol. I, p. 317.
31. Jones, *Free Associations,* p. 222.
32. Quoted in Schur, *Freud,* p. 266.
33. Quoted in Binswanger, *Freud,* pp. 48–49.
34. Quoted in *ibid.,* p. 49.
35. "Dostoevsky and Parricide," pp. 182–83.
36. Jones, *Sigmund Freud,* Vol. II, p. 145. Cf. also Jones, *Free Associations,* p. 221.
37. "From the History of an Infantile Neurosis," p. 65.
38. Puner, *Freud,* p. 239.
39. "Beyond the Pleasure Principle," p. 42.
40. Jung, *Freud and Psychoanalysis,* p. 289.
41. "On the History," p. 61.
42. *Ibid.,* p. 37.
43. Quoted in Jones, *Sigmund Freud,* Vol. II, p. 436.
44. *Freud/Jung Letters,* pp. 436, 515.
45. "On the History," p. 58.
46. Quoted in Jones, *Sigmund Freud,* Vol. III, p. 15.
47. Quoted in *ibid.,* Vol. II, p. 148.
48. "On the History," p. 15.
49. Quoted in Jones, *Sigmund Freud,* Vol. II, p. 124.

4. The Primal Father

1. A. A. Brill, "A Psychoanalyst Scans His Past," *The Journal of Nervous and Mental Disease,* Vol. 95, No. 5 (May 1942), p. 547.
2. Jung, *Freud and Psychoanalysis,* p. 208.
3. *Ibid.,* pp. 118–22.
4. *Freud/Jung Letters,* pp. 505–06.
5. Jung, *Freud and Psychoanalysis,* p. 107.
6. *Ibid.,* pp. 164–65.
7. *Ibid.,* p. 132.
8. *Ibid.,* p. 166.
9. *Ibid.,* pp. 180, 197.
10. *Ibid.,* p. 202.
11. *Ibid.,* p. 128.
12. *Freud/Jung Letters,* p. 25.
13. Schur, *Freud,* pp. 167, 170.
14. Quoted in Jacobi, "'Freud and Jung," p. 19. Cf. *Freud/Jung Letters,* p. 515.
15. Ellenberger, *The Discovery of the Unconscious,* p. 698.
16. *Freud/Jung Letters,* p. 516.
17. *Ibid.,* p. 521.
18. *Ibid.,* pp. 523–24.
19. *Ibid.,* pp. 525–27.
20. *Ibid.,* pp. 529–30.
21. Quoted in Jones, *Sigmund Freud,* Vol. I, p. 317.
22. *Freud/Jung Letters,* p. 533.
23. *Ibid.,* p. 529.
24. *Ibid.,* pp. 534–35, 538–39.
25. Binswanger, *Freud,* p. 53.
26. Quoted in *ibid.*
27. *Letters of Freud and Abraham,* p. 137.
28. Quoted in Jones, *Sigmund Freud,* Vol. II, p. 353.

29. "The Interpretation of Dreams," Vol. 4, p. 263.
30. *Freud/Jung Letters*, p. 459.
31. *Ibid.*, p. 447.
32. *Ibid.*, p. 152. Cf. also *ibid.*, pp. 157, 414.
33. *Ibid.*, p. 460.
34. Cf. Roazen, *Freud: Political and Social Thought*, Ch. 3.
35. Jones, *Sigmund Freud*, Vol. II, p. 360; quoted in *ibid.*, Vol. III, p. 329.
36. Letter from Geoffrey Gorer to Ernest Jones, Dec. 14, 1955 (Jones archives).
37. Wittels, *Freud*, p. 168.
38. "An Autobiographical Study," p. 66.
39. "Two Encyclopaedia Articles," p. 253.
40. "From the History of an Infantile Neurosis," p. 97; "Three Essays on the Theory of Sexuality," p. 225; Jones, *Sigmund Freud*, Vol. III, p. 308.
41. *Letters of Freud and Abraham*, p. 141.
42. *Ibid.*, p. 142.
43. *Letters of Freud and Pfister*, p. 107.
44. Edward Hitschmann, "Freud in Life and Death," *American Imago*, Vol. 2, No. 2 (July 1941), p. 127.
45. Quoted in Hale, ed., *James Jackson Putnam and Psychoanalysis*, pp. 189–90.
46. Letter from Anna Freud to Ernest Jones, June 16, 1954 (Jones archives).
47. "On the History," p. 45.
48. Jones, *Sigmund Freud*, Vol. II, p. 102.
49. Jones, *Free Associations*, p. 224.
50. Jung, *Psychological Types, Collected Works*, Vol. VI, a revision by R. F. C. Hull of the translation by H. G. Baynes (Princeton: Princeton University Press; 1971), p. 509.
51. *Letters of Freud and Abraham*, p. 151.
52. Jung, *Freud and Psychoanalysis*, pp. 246–47.
53. Quoted in Hale, ed., *James Jackson Putnam and Psychoanalysis*, p. 200.
54. *Freud/Jung Letters*, p. 553.
55. Quoted in Hale, ed., *James Jackson Putnam and Psychoanalysis*, p. 176.
56. Jung, *Freud and Psychoanalysis*, p. 243.
57. "On the History," p. 60.
58. "Three Essays on the Theory of Sexuality," p. 165; "Introductory Lectures," Vol. 16, p. 298.
59. "From the History of an Infantile Neurosis," p. 72.
60. "On the History," p. 60.
61. Franz Alexander and Sheldon Selesnick, "Freud-Bleuler Correspondence," *Archives of General Psychiatry*, Vol. 12 (Jan. 1965), pp. 1–9. Cf. *Freud/Jung Letters*, pp. 329, 352.
62. Binswanger, *Freud*, p. 55.
63. Quoted in *ibid.*
64. "On the History," p. 7.

5. Analytical Psychology

1. Edward Glover, *Freud or Jung?* (New York: Meridian Books; 1957), pp. 33, 45.
2. "On the History," p. 60.
3. "Editor's Note," *Standard Edition*, Vol. 9, p. 100.
4. Andreas-Salomé, *The Freud Journal*, pp. 38–39.
5. Jones, *Sigmund Freud*, Vol. II, p. 113.
6. Lewis Way, *Adler's Place in Psychology* (New York: Collier; 1962), p. 291.
7. Jung, *Psychological Types*, p. 431.
8. Jones, *Sigmund Freud*, Vol. II, p. 423.
9. *Ibid.*, Vol. III, p. 306.
10. Cf. Anthony Storr, *The Dynamics of Creation* (New York: Atheneum; 1972), pp. 9–12, 172.
11. Jung, *The Practice of Psychotherapy, Collected Works*, Vol. XVI, translated by R. F. C. Hull (2nd ed.; New York: Pantheon; 1966), p. 156.
12. "Editor's Note," *Standard Edition*, Vol. 14, p. 70.
13. Interview with Albert Hirst.
14. Jung, *The Spirit in Man, Art and Literature, Collected Works*, Vol. XV, translated by R. F. C. Hull (New York: Pantheon; 1966), p. 48.
15. Jung, *Civilization in Transition, Collected Works*, Vol. X, translated by R. F. C. Hull (New York: Pantheon; 1964), p. 170.
16. Jung, *The Practice of Psychotherapy*, p. 152.

17. Ernst Kris, *Psychoanalytic Explorations in Art* (New York: International Universities Press; 1952).
18. "Creative Writers and Day-Dreaming," p. 146.
19. Jung, *The Practice of Psychotherapy*, pp. 45–46.
20. *Ibid.*, p. 123.
21. *Ibid.*, p. 153.
22. "Two Encyclopaedia Articles," p. 241.
23. Jung, *The Development of Personality, Collected Works*, Vol. XVII, translated by R. F. C. Hull (New York: Pantheon; 1954), p. 110.
24. Jung, *The Structure and Dynamics of the Psyche, Collected Works*, Vol. VIII, translated by R. F. C. Hull (New York: Pantheon; 1960), p. 251.
25. Jung, *Memories, Dreams, Reflections*, pp. 161–62.
26. Jung, *The Development of Personality*, p. 88.
27. Jung, *The Practice of Psychotherapy*, p. 147.
28. "Introductory Lectures," Vol. 15, p. 237.
29. Jung, *The Practice of Psychotherapy*, p. 15. Cf. Anthony Storr, *C. G. Jung* (New York: Viking; 1973), pp. 44–45.
30. "Remarks on the Theory and Practice of Dream-Interpretation," pp. 120–21.
31. Ellenberger, *The Discovery of the Unconscious*, p. 664.
32. Storr, *Jung*, p. 48.
33. Jung, *Psychology and Religion: West and East, Collected Works*, Vol. XI, translated by R. F. C. Hull (New York: Pantheon; 1959), p. 351.
34. Jung, *Freud and Psychoanalysis*, pp. 147, 264.
35. Jung, *The Practice of Psychotherapy*, p. 83.
36. Quoted in Jones, *Sigmund Freud*, Vol. II, p. 268.
37. Sheldon T. Selesnick, "Carl G. Jung," in *Psychoanalytic Pioneers*, p. 76.
38. "Introductory Lectures," Vol. 16, p. 269.
39. "Psychoanalytic Notes on an Autobiographical Account," p. 82.
40. "On the History," p. 63.
41. Ellenberger, *The Discovery of the Unconscious*, p. 686.
42. *Ibid.*, p. 711.
43. Jung, *The Practice of Psychotherapy*, p. 124.
44. Storr, *Jung*, p. 41.
45. "From the History of an Infantile Neurosis," p. 100.
46. "Group Psychology and the Analysis of the Ego," pp. 74–75.
47. *Ibid.*, p. 74.
48. Weigert, "Dissent in the Early History of Psychoanalysis," p. 356.
49. Jung, *Two Essays on Analytical Psychology*, translated by R. F. C. Hull (New York: Meridian Books; 1956), p. 313.
50. Donald W. Winnicott, *The Maturational Processes and the Facilitating Environment* (London: Hogarth; 1965), pp. 34, 142.
51. Ellenberger, *The Discovery of the Unconscious*, p. 719.
52. Jung, *Freud and Psychoanalysis*, pp. 198–99.
53. "Recommendations to Physicians Practising Psychoanalysis," p. 116.
54. Nunberg, *Memoirs*, p. 35.
55. Jung, *The Practice of Psychotherapy*, p. 88.
56. Jung, *Civilization in Transition*, pp. 159–60.
57. *Freud/Jung Letters*, p. 476.
58. Jung, *The Practice of Psychotherapy*, p. 5.
59. Clara Thompson, *Psychoanalysis: Evolution and Development* (New York: Grove Press; 1950), p. 15.
60. Jung, *The Practice of Psychotherapy*, p. 8.
61. *Ibid.*, p. 10; Storr, *The Dynamics of Creation*, p. 230.
62. Jung, *Civilization in Transition*, p. 164.
63. Jung, *The Practice of Psychotherapy*, p. 9.
64. *Ibid.*, p. 133.
65. *Ibid.*, p. 138.
66. "On the History," p. 63.
67. *Freud/Jung Letters*, p. 548.
68. "On the History," p. 66.
69. *Ibid.*, p. 62.
70. Glover, *Freud or Jung?*, p. 141.

71. Jung, *Letters*, Vol. I, selected and edited by Gerhard Adler in collaboration with Aniela Jaffé, translated by R. F. C. Hull (Princeton: Princeton University Press; 1972), p. 196.
72. *Ibid.*, pp. 83–84.
73. Jung, *The Practice of Psychotherapy*, p. 20.
74. Jung, *Freud and Psychoanalysis*, p. 278.
75. Jung, *The Practice of Psychotherapy*, p. 27.
76. Ellenberger, *The Discovery of the Unconscious*, p. 681.
77. Quoted in Jones, *Sigmund Freud*, Vol. II, p. 139. On Otto Gross, cf. Arthur Mitzman, *The Iron Cage: An Historical Interpretation of Max Weber* (New York: Knopf; 1970), pp. 280–82.
78. Glover, *Freud or Jung?*, p. 124.
79. "On the History," p. 10.
80. "New Introductory Lectures," p. 143.
81. Interview with Irmarita Putnam.
82. Jung, *Psychological Types*, p. 431.
83. Jung, *The Practice of Psychotherapy*, p. 24.

6. Afterward

1. Jung, *Letters*, Vol. I, p. 302.
2. "On the History," p. 39.
3. For example, cf. "Leonardo da Vinci," p. 79.
4. Wittels, *Freud*, p. 233.
5. "A Short Account of Psychoanalysis," p. 202.
6. "From the History of an Infantile Neurosis," p. 53.
7. "On the History," p. 49.
8. "The Theme of Three Caskets," *Standard Edition*, Vol. 12, pp. 300–01.
9. "Beyond the Pleasure Principle," p. 22.
10. "On the History," pp. 48–49.
11. *Ibid.*, p. 27.
12. Kurt Eissler, "Mankind at Its Best," *Journal of the American Psychoanalytic Association*, Vol. 12, No. 1 (Jan. 1964), p. 212.
13. "An Autobiographical Study," p. 74.
14. "On the History," p. 66.
15. "A Case of Paranoia Running Counter to the Psychoanalytic Theory of the Disease," p. 272.
16. "From the History of an Infantile Neurosis," p. 49.
17. *Ibid.*, p. 103.
18. Jung, *Symbols of Transformation, Collected Works*, Vol. V, translated by R. F. C. Hull (New York: Pantheon; 1956), p. 328. Cf. also Jung, *Letters*, Vol. I, p. 73.
19. "Beyond the Pleasure Principle," p. 55.
20. "On the History," p. 60.
21. *Ibid.*
22. Jung, *The Practice of Psychotherapy*, p. 4.
23. "On the History," p. 60.
24. *Ibid.*
25. *Ibid.*; "Introductory Lectures," Vol. 15, pp. 207–08; "A Short Account of Psychoanalysis," p. 202.
26. "On the History," p. 50.
27. *Ibid.*, p. 19.
28. "Introductory Lectures," Vol. 16, p. 244.
29. "On the History," p. 65.
30. "From the History of an Infantile Neurosis," p. 9.
31. "An Autobiographical Study," pp. 52–53.
32. "On the History," p. 62.
33. "Two Encyclopaedia Articles," p. 248.
34. "The Question of Lay Analysis," p. 208.
35. "On the History," p. 58.
36. "An Autobiographical Study," p. 52.
37. "A Short Account of Psychoanalysis," p. 202.
38. "New Introductory Lectures," p. 144.
39. "Psychoanalysis," p. 270.
40. Ellenberger, *The Discovery of the Unconscious*, p. 732.
41. "The Moses of Michelangelo," *Standard Edition*, Vol. 13, p. 213.
42. *Ibid.*, p. 216.
43. *Ibid.*, p. 221.
44. *Ibid.*, p. 229.
45. *Ibid.*, p. 230.
46. *Ibid.*, p. 233.

47. *Ibid.*, pp. 233–34.

48. "On the History," p. 43.

49. *Ibid.*, p. 50.

50. Quoted in Jones, *Sigmund Freud*, Vol. II, p. 254. Cf. also *Freud/Jung Letters*, p. 372.

51. *Letters*, p. 296.

52. Interview with Abram Kardiner, Apr. 1, 1967.

53. Puner, *Freud*, p. 181. Cf. also Roy Grinker, "Reminiscences of a Personal Contact with Freud," p. 852.

54. Jung, *Letters*, Vol. I, p. 122.

55. *Freud/Jung Letters*, pp. 137, 139, 144.

56. Jung, *The Practice of Psychotherapy*, p. 123.

57. Cf., for example, Jung, *Freud and Psychoanalysis*, pp. 306, 317, 320.

58. Jean-Paul Sartre, "Paul Nizan," in *Situations* (New York: Fawcett; 1969), p. 119.

59. Ellenberger, *The Discovery of the Unconscious*, p. 673.

60. Jung, *Freud and Psychoanalysis*, p. 9.

61. Jung, *The Structure and Dynamics of the Psyche*, p. 50.

62. Jung, *Freud and Psychoanalysis*, p. 337; *The Practice of Psychotherapy*, p. 30.

63. Jung, *Freud and Psychoanalysis*, p. 334.

64. Jung, *The Development of Personality*, p. 67.

65. Jung, *The Spirit in Man, Art and Literature*, p. 36.

66. Storr, *Jung*, p. 10.

67. "On the History," p. 43.

68. Quoted in Hale, ed., *James Jackson Putnam and Psychoanalysis*, p. 189. This passage had previously been omitted from the rest of the letter. Cf. *Letters*, p. 308.

69. Ellenberger, *The Discovery of the Unconscious*, p. 678.

70. Jung, *Freud and Psychoanalysis*, p. 335.

71. Jung, *Civilization in Transition*, pp. 165–66.

72. Quoted in Ernest Harms, "Carl Gustav Jung—Defender of Freud and the Jews," *The Psychiatric Quarterly*, Vol. 20 (1946), pp. 228–29.

73. Jung, *Civilization in Transition*, pp. 192, 185.

74. Jung, *Psychology and Religion: West and East*, p. 481.

75. Jones, *Sigmund Freud*, Vol. III, p. 186.

76. Jung, *Civilization in Transition*, pp. 535–44.

77. Letter from Jung to Parelhoff, Dec. 17, 1951.

78. Jones, *Sigmund Freud*, Vol. III, p. 187.

79. Letter from Ernest Jones to Anna Freud, July 20, 1936 (Jones archives).

80. Jung, *Letters*, Vol. I, p. 205. Cf. also pp. 152–53.

81. "On the History," p. 22. Cf. also letter quoted in Jones, *Sigmund Freud*, Vol. II, p. 400.

82. Puner, *Freud*, p. 61.

83. Quoted in Schur, *Freud*, p. 468.

84. "Moses and Monotheism," *Standard Edition*, Vol. 23, p. 132.

85. Jung, *The Archetypes and the Collective Unconscious, Collected Works*, Vol. IX, Part 1, translated by R. F. C. Hull (New York: Pantheon; 1959), p. 3.

86. Letter from Henry Murray to the author, Sept. 1972.

VII: THE LOYAL MOVEMENT

1. Elder Statesmen

1. "On the History," p. 25.

2. "An Autobiographical Study," p. 53.

3. Franz Alexander, "Recollections of Berggasse 19," p. 200.

4. Erik H. Erikson, *Gandhi's Truth* (New York: Norton; 1969), p. 314. Thomas Mann's novel about Goethe may have been patterned on knowledge of Freud. Cf. *The Beloved Returns: Lotte in Weimar* (New York: Knopf; 1940), p. 75.

5. Helene Deutsch, "Freud and His Pupils," *Psychoanalytic Quarterly*, Vol. 9, No. 1 (1940), p. 189.

6. For example, cf. Nunberg, *Memoirs*, p. 23.

7. Fromm, *Sigmund Freud's Mission*, p. 110.
8. "New Introductory Lectures," p. 69.
9. "Group Psychology and the Analysis of the Ego," p. 91.
10. "Freud's Letters to Simmel," pp. 102–03.
11. "Group Psychology and the Analysis of the Ego," p. 94.
12. Fromm, *Sigmund Freud's Mission*, p. 105.
13. Deutsch, "Freud and His Pupils," pp. 188–89.
14. *Ibid.*, p. 191.
15. "New Introductory Lectures," pp. 145–46.
16. "Group Psychology and the Analysis of the Ego," p. 93.
17. "Introductory Lectures," Vol. 15, p. 193.
18. "New Introductory Lectures," p. 153.
19. *Ibid.*
20. *Ibid.*, p. 138.
21. "Group Psychology and the Analysis of the Ego," pp. 98–99.
22. Interviews with Eva Rosenfeld, Sept. 3, 1965, and Nov. 3, 1966.
23. Edoardo Weiss, *The Structure and Dynamics of the Human Mind* (New York: Grune & Stratton; 1960), p. xii.
24. Quoted in Ernst Federn, "Thirty-Five Years with Freud," *Journal of the History of the Behavioral Sciences*, Vol. 8, No. 1 (Jan. 1972), p. 18.
25. Quoted in Edward Bernays, *Biography of an Idea* (New York: Simon & Schuster; 1965), p. 272.
26. Weiss, *The Structure and Dynamics of the Human Mind*, p. xiii.
27. Interview with Edoardo Weiss, June 26, 1966.
28. Weiss, *The Structure and Dynamics of the Human Mind*, p. xiv.
29. Heinrich Meng, in "Thirty-Five Years with Freud," p. 35.
30. Weiss, *The Structure and Dynamics of the Human Mind*, p. xiv.
31. Interviews with Helene Deutsch, Nov. 28, 1964, and June 18, 1966.
32. Edoardo Weiss, "Federn's Concepts and Their Applicability to the Understanding and Treatment of Schizophrenia," *The Journal of the Nervous and Mental Diseases*, Vol. 133, No. 2 (Aug. 1961), p. 155.
33. Weiss, *The Structure and Dynamics of the Human Mind*, p. xvii.
34. Cf. p. 322.
35. Paul Federn, "The Neurotic Style," *Psychiatric Quarterly*, Vol. 31 (Oct. 1957), pp. 689, 684, 688, 682.
36. Interview with Ernst Federn.
37. "Freud Correspondence," *Psychoanalytic Quarterly*, Vol. 25 (1956), p. 361.
38. Interview with Edith Jackson.
39. *Minutes*, Vol. II, pp. 208, 210, 213.

2. Victor Tausk and Lou Andreas-Salomé

1. Cf., for instance, Henry Brosin, "Contributions of Psychoanalysis to the Study of the Psychoses," in *The Impact of Freudian Psychiatry*, ed. Franz Alexander and Helen Ross (Chicago: University of Chicago Press; 1961), pp. 178–99, Gregory Zilboorg, *A History of Medical Psychology* (New York: Norton; 1941), p. 502.
2. "Victor Tausk," *Standard Edition*, Vol. 17, p. 275. For a much more extensive discussion of Tausk, the reader is referred to Roazen, *Brother Animal*, and Roazen, "Reflections on Ethos and Authenticity in Psychoanalysis."
3. For example, cf. Victor Tausk, *Paraphrase als Kommentar und Kritik zu Gerhart Hauptmanns "Und Pippa Tanzt"* (Berlin: Siegfried Cronbach; 1906).
4. Victor Tausk, "On the Origin of the 'Influencing Machine' in Schizophrenia," in *The Psychoanalytic Reader*, ed. Robert Fliess (New York: International Universities Press; 1948), pp. 31–64. Cf. also Paul Roazen, "Victor Tausk's Contribution to Psychoanalysis," *The Psychoanalytic Quarterly*, Vol. 38, No. 3 (1969), pp. 349–53.
5. Bruno Bettelheim, *The Empty Fortress* (New York: The Free Press;

1967), pp. 233–339; Edith Jacobson, *The Self and the Object World* (New York: International Universities Press; 1964), p. xi; Erik H. Erikson, *Identity: Youth and Crisis* (New York: Norton; 1968), p. 9; and Bertram Lewin's obituary of Federn, *The Psychoanalytic Quarterly*, Vol. 19 (1950), p. 296.

6. H. F. Peters, *My Sister, My Spouse: A Biography of Lou Andreas-Salomé* (New York: Norton; 1962), and Rudolph Binion, *Frau Lou: Nietzsche's Wayward Disciple* (Princeton: Princeton University Press; 1968).
7. Quoted in Jones, *Sigmund Freud*, Vol. III, p. 213.
8. Andreas-Salomé, *The Freud Journal*, p. 57.
9. *Ibid.*, p. 51.
10. *Ibid.*, p. 169. Cf. Carl G. Jung, "A Comment On Tausk's Criticism of Nelken," in *Spring: An Annual* (1973), pp. 183–87.
11. Andreas-Salomé, *The Freud Journal*, pp. 51, 56.
12. *Ibid.*, p. 51; "Victor Tausk," p. 274.
13. Andreas-Salomé, *The Freud Journal*, pp. 97–98.
14. *Ibid.*, pp. 97, 114; cf. also *Letters of Freud and Andreas-Salomé*, p. 215.
15. Andreas-Salomé, *The Freud Journal*, p. 114.
16. Ellenberger, *The Discovery of the Unconscious*, p. 170.
17. Andreas-Salomé, *The Freud Journal*, pp. 166–67.
18. *Ibid.*, pp. 167–68.
19. "On the Psychology of the War Deserter," *The Psychoanalytic Quarterly*, Vol. 38, No. 3 (1969), pp. 354–81.
20. Helene Deutsch, *Confrontations with Myself* (New York: Norton; 1973), p. 135.
21. "The 'Uncanny,'" pp. 220, 234, 238.
22. "Totem and Taboo," p. 86.
23. Compare Sigmund Freud and Lou Andreas-Salomé, *Briefwechsel* (Frankfurt: Fischer; 1966), p. 108, with *Letters of Freud and Andreas-Salomé*, pp. 98–99. Cf. also Binion, *Frau Lou*, pp. 402–03.

24. *Letters of Freud and Andrea-Salomé*, p. 229.
25. Roazen, *Brother Animal*, pp. 153–54.
26. Andreas-Salomé, *Freud Journal*, p. 163.

3. Apostles

1. Jones, *Sigmund Freud*, Vol. II, p. 161.
2. Sachs, *Freud*, pp. 1–2.
3. Quoted in Jones, *Sigmund Freud*, Vol. II, p. 153; quoted in Sidney Pomer, "Max Eitingon," in *Psychoanalytic Pioneers*, p. 53.
4. Jones, *Sigmund Freud*, Vol. II, p. 154.
5. "The Psychopathology of Everyday Life," p. 205.
6. *Ten Years of the Berlin Psychoanalytic Institute*, p. 45.
7. Fritz Moellenhoff, "Hanns Sachs," in *Psychoanalytic Pioneers*, p. 188.
8. Nunberg, *Memoirs*, p. 54.
9. Sachs, *Freud*, p. 168.
10. *Letters of Freud and Abraham*, pp. 91, 47.
11. *Freud/Jung Letters*, pp. 105, 140.
12. Jones, *Sigmund Freud*, Vol. II, p. 161.
13. "Bulletin of the International Psychoanalytical Association," *International Journal of Psychoanalysis*, Vol. 9 (1928), p. 133.
14. *Letters*, pp. 337–38.
15. Interview with Edward Glover, Aug. 25, 1965.
16. Joseph M. Natterson, "Theodor Reik," in *Psychoanalytic Pioneers*, p. 257. Cf. also Ann Leslie Moore and Merrill Moore, "Notes on Re-Reading Dr. Hanns Sachs's Last Book," *The American Imago*, Vol. 11, No. 1 (Spring 1954), pp. 6–7.
17. "Karl Abraham," *Standard Edition*, Vol. 20, p. 277.

4. The "Wild Hunt"

1. "The Ego and the Id," *Standard Edition*, Vol. 19, p. 23.
2. *Letters of Freud and Pfister*, p. 81.
3. Quoted in Schur, *Freud*, p. 312.
4. *Letters*, pp. 316–18.
5. Heinz Hartmann, "The Psychiatric World of Paul Schilder," *Psychoanalytic Review*, Vol. 31 (1944), p. 296.

6. Nunberg, *Memoirs*, pp. 61–62.
7. Wortis, *Fragments of an Analysis with Freud*, pp. 131–32.
8. Isidore Ziferstein, "Paul Schilder," in *Psychoanalytic Pioneers*, p. 465.
9. "The Interpretation of Dreams," Vol. 4, p. 102.
10. Ellenberger, *The Discovery of the Unconscious*, p. 728.
11. Memorandum of Edward Hitschmann (Jones archives).
12. "On Narcissism," p. 97.
13. Interviews with Robert Jokl, Dec. 28 and 30, 1965.
14. Wittels, *Freud*, p. 216.
15. "Introductory Lectures," Vol. 15, p. 237.
16. "The Interpretation of Dreams," Vol. 5, p. 524.
17. "Editor's Note," *Standard Edition*, Vol. 18, p. 196.
18. "Dreams and Telepathy," p. 216.
19. "Obituary of Herbert Silberer," *International Journal of Psychoanalysis*, Vol. 4 (1923), p. 399.
20. Jung, *Letters*, Vol. I, p. 206.
21. Wilhelm Stekel, "In Memoriam Herbert Silberer," *Fortschritte der Sexualwissenschaft und Psychoanalyse*, Vol. I (1924), p. 411. I am indebted to Prof. William M. Johnston for lending me a copy of this obituary.
22. Binswanger, *Sigmund Freud*, p. 40.
23. Ernest Jones, "Book Review of Wittels's *Freud*," *International Journal of Psychoanalysis*, Vol. 5 (1924), p. 482.
24. Stekel, "In Memoriam Herbert Silberer," p. 415.
25. Martin Grotjahn, "Notes on Reading the 'Rundbriefe,'" *Journal of the Otto Rank Association*, Vol. 8, No. 2 (Winter 1973–74), p. 50.

5. Ernest Jones: Pioneer

1. Jones, *Free Associations*, p. 201.
2. Ernest Jones, "Introductory Memoir," in Karl Abraham, *Selected Papers on Psychoanalysis*, translated by Douglas Bryan and Alix Strachey (London: Hogarth; 1926), p. 38.
3. Edward Glover, "Karl Abraham" (manuscript), p. 25.
4. Jones, *Free Associations*, p. 195.
5. *Ibid.*, p. 176.
6. *Ibid.*, p. 172.
7. Letter from Ernest Jones to A. A. Brill, July 15, 1932 (Jones archives).
8. Edward Glover, "In Praise of Ourselves," *International Journal of Psychoanalysis*, Vol. 50, Part 4 (1969), p. 499.
9. Letters from Ernest Jones to Johann van Ophuijsen, March 26 and 28, 1933 (Jones archives). Jones did not want Heinz Hartmann to edit a commemorative volume for Freud's one-hundredth birthday; it would have taken the spotlight away from Jones's own work on Freud. Cf. letter from Ernest Jones to Heinz Hartmann, Feb. 15, 1955 (Jones archives).
10. Edward Glover, "Ernest Jones," *The British Journal of Medical Psychology*, Vol. 31 (1958), p. 72.
11. Jones, *Free Associations*, p. 63.
12. Letter from Ernest Jones to William C. Bullitt, June 7, 1956 (Jones archives).
13. Jones, *Free Associations*, p. 62.
14. *Ibid.*, p. 209.
15. *Ibid.*, p. 229.
16. Letter from Ernest Jones to Max Eitingon, Sept. 26, 1929 (Jones archives).
17. Leonard Woolf, *Beginning Again* (London: Hogarth; 1964), pp. 75–82.
18. *Recollections of Virginia Woolf*, ed. Joan Russell Noble (London: Peter Owen; 1972), pp. 116–17.
19. Letter from Ernest Jones to A. A. Brill, Dec. 2, 1933 (Jones archives).
20. Interview with Edward Glover, Aug. 25, 1965.
21. Jones, *Free Associations*, p. 240.
22. *Ibid.*, p. 244.
23. Quoted in Jones, *Sigmund Freud*, Vol. II, p. 100.
24. "Dr. Ernest Jones," *Standard Edition*, Vol. 21, pp. 249–50.
25. *Letters*, p. 385.
26. Jones, *Free Associations*, p. 60.
27. *Ibid.*, p. 154.
28. Jones, *Sigmund Freud*, Vol. III, p. 191.
29. Letter from Ernest Jones to Paul

Federn, Oct. 10, 1933. Cf. also letter from Ernest Jones to Max Eitingon, Dec. 19, 1932, and letter from Anna Freud to Ernest Jones, Dec. 31, 1932 (Jones archives).

30. Jones, *Free Associations*, p. 169.
31. *Freud/Jung Letters*, p. 130.
32. Ernest Jones, *Essays in Applied Psychoanalysis*, Vol. II (New York: International Universities Press; 1964), pp. 244–60. Cf. Rudolf Blomeyer, "Der Gottmensch-Komplex bei Freud und seine Darstellung bei Jones," *Zeitschrift für Analytische Psychologie und ihre Grenzgebiete* (July 1973), pp. 247–70.
33. Jones, *Sigmund Freud*, Vol. II, p. 162.
34. Jones, *Free Associations*, pp. 166–67, 169–70.
35. *Ibid.*, p. 98.
36. *Freud/Jung Letters*, p. 145.
37. "Lines of Advance in Psychoanalytic Therapy," p. 165. Freud may have been confusing Jones's role with that of Tausk. Cf. Andreas-Salomé, *The Freud Journal*, pp. 168–70.
38. Jones, *Free Associations*, p. 190.
39. Letter from Ernest Jones to Leonard Albert, n.d. (Jones archives).
40. Quoted in Hale, ed., *James Jackson Putnam and Psychoanalysis*, pp. 215, 251.
41. Letter from Ernest Jones to Freud, Jan. 10, 1933 (Jones archives).
42. Jones, *Free Associations*, p. 204.
43. Jones, *Sigmund Freud*, Vol. III, p. xii. Cf. also pp. 196–97.
44. *Ibid.*, p. 140.
45. *Ibid.*, pp. 293–95.

6. Ernest Jones and Sandor Ferenczi: Rivalry

1. Hale, ed., *James Jackson Putnam and Psychoanalysis*, p. 253.
2. Jones, *Free Associations*, pp. 145, 150–51.
3. *Ibid.*, p. 140.
4. *Ibid.*
5. *Ibid.*, p. 197.
6. *Ibid.*
7. *Ibid.*
8. *Ibid.*, p. 224.

9. *Ibid.*, p. 199.
10. Jones, *Sigmund Freud*, Vol. II, p. 106.
11. Interview with James Strachey, June 28, 1965. Interview with Edward Glover, July 29, 1965.
12. Jones, *Free Associations*, pp. 199–200.
13. *Freud/Jung Letters*, p. 271.
14. Interview with Elma Laurvik, Apr. 3, 1967; interview with Kata Levy, July 2, 1965.
15. Letter from Ernest Jones to Michael Balint, Dec. 16, 1957, and letter from Michael Balint to Ernest Jones, Dec. 19, 1957 (Jones archives).
16. Quoted in Jones, *Sigmund Freud*, Vol. II, p. 75.
17. "Sandor Ferenczi," *Standard Edition*, Vol. 22, p. 227.
18. Jones, *Sigmund Freud*, Vol. II, pp. 34–35.
19. *Ibid.*, pp. 157–58.
20. Quoted in Jessie Taft, *Otto Rank* (New York: Julian; 1958), p. 78.
21. Quoted in Jones, *Sigmund Freud*, Vol. III, p. 7. Cf. also Martin Grotjahn, "Notes on Reading the 'Rundbriefe,'" p. 59.
22. Letter of Sandor Ferenczi, *Rundebriefe*, Dec. 15, 1924 (Jones archives).
23. "Dr. Sandor Ferenczi," *Standard Edition*, Vol. 19, p. 269.
24. *Ibid.*, p. 267.
25. "On the History," p. 33.
26. "Dr. Sandor Ferenczi," p. 268.
27. *Ibid.*, p. 267.
28. *Letters*, p. 458.
29. "Dr. Anton von Freund," *Standard Edition*, Vol. 18, p. 268.
30. Letter from Kata Levy to me.
31. Jones, *Sigmund Freud*, Vol. III, p. 89.
32. *Ibid.*, Vol. II, pp. 55, 156.
33. *Ibid.*, Vol. III, p. 120.
34. "Karl Abraham," p. 277.
35. "Sandor Ferenczi," p. 228.

7. Sandor Ferenczi: Technique and Historical Victim

1. Sandor Ferenczi, *Thalassa*, translated by Henry Alden Bunker (New York: Psychoanalytic Quarterly; 1938).

2. "Sandor Ferenczi," p. 229.

3. Clara Thompson, *Interpersonal Psychoanalysis*, ed. Maurice R. Green (New York: Basic Books; 1964), p. 74.

4. Sandor Lorand, "Sandor Ferenczi," in *Psychoanalytic Pioneers*, p. 32.

5. "Sandor Ferenczi," p. 229.

6. Jones, *Free Associations*, p. 228.

7. Sandor Ferenczi and Otto Rank, *The Development of Psychoanalysis*, authorized translation by Caroline Newton (New York: Dover Books; 1956), pp. 50, 53.

8. *Ibid.*, pp. 60–61.

9. Jones, *Sigmund Freud*, Vol. III, p. 65.

10. Quoted in *ibid.*, pp. 57–58.

11. Quoted in *ibid.*, p. 60.

12. Quoted in *ibid.*, p. 61.

13. *Ibid.*, p. 127.

14. *Ibid.*, p. 135.

15. *Ibid.*, p. 149.

16. "Analysis Terminable and Interminable," pp. 221–22.

17. Jones, *Sigmund Freud*, Vol. III, p. 330; Vol. II, p. 231.

18. Sandor Ferenczi, *Final Contributions to the Problems and Methods of Psychoanalysis*, ed. Michael Balint, translated by Eric Mosbacher and others (London: Hogarth; 1955), p. 42.

19. *Ibid.*, p. 305.

20. Jones, *Sigmund Freud*, Vol. III, p. 16.

21. *Ibid.*, pp. 164–65.

22. Thompson, *Interpersonal Psychoanalysis*, pp. 74, 73.

23. Jones, *Sigmund Freud*, Vol. III, p. 173. Cf. Sandor Ferenczi, "Confusion of Tongues Between Adults and the Child," in *Final Contributions to the Problems and Methods of Psychoanalysis*, pp. 156–67.

24. Letter from Izette de Forest to Ernest Jones, Dec. 8, 1954 (Jones archives). Cf. also Izette de Forest, *The Leaven of Love* (New York: Harper & Row, 1954).

25. Quoted in Jones, *Sigmund Freud*, Vol. III, p. 173.

26. Letter from Michael Balint to Ernest Jones, Jan. 22, 1954 (Jones archives).

27. Quoted in Fromm, *Sigmund Freud's Mission*, p. 65.

28. "Sandor Ferenczi," p. 229.

29. Interview with Elma Laurvik.

30. Vincent Brome, *Freud and His Early Circle* (London: Heinemann; 1967), p. 165.

31. Jones, *Sigmund Freud*, Vol. III, p. 129.

32. *Ibid.*, Vol. II, pp. 82, 84.

33. *Ibid.*, Vol. III, p. 127.

34. *Ibid.*, p. 45.

35. *Ibid.*, pp. 166, 176.

36. *Ibid.*, pp. 176, 178.

37. *Ibid.*, p. 178.

38. Cf. Sandor Lorand, "Sandor Ferenczi," pp. 14–34. Erich Fromm, "Psychoanalysis—Science or Party Line?," in *The Dogma of Christ* (New York: Holt, Rinehart & Winston; 1963), pp. 131–44. Letter from Michael Balint to Ernest Jones, May 31, 1957 (Jones archives). Interview with Elma Laurvik.

39. Letter from Michael Balint to Ernest Jones, Jan. 22, 1954 (Jones archives).

40. Cf. *International Journal of Psychoanalysis*, Vol. 34 (1958), p. 68.

41. Letter from Ernest Jones to A. A. Brill, June 20, 1933 (Jones archives).

42. Interview with Mark Brunswick, Jan. 25, 1966.

43. Letter from Ernest Jones to Anna Freud, June 1, 1933 (Jones archives).

44. Letter from Ernest Jones to Sigmund Freud, June 3, 1933 (Jones archives).

45. "Sandor Ferenczi," p. 229.

8. The Americans: J. J. Putnam and H. W. Frink

1. Cf. John C. Burnham, *Psychoanalysis and American Medicine, 1894–1918* (New York: International Universities Press; 1967); David Shakow and David Rapaport, *The Influence of Freud on American Psychology* (New York: International Universities Press, 1964); Marie Jahoda, "The Migration of Psychoanalysis: Its Impact on American Psychology," *Per-*

spectives on American History, Vol. 2 (1968), pp. 420–45; and F. H. Matthews, "The Americanization of Sigmund Freud: Adaptations of Psychoanalysis Before 1917," *Journal of American Studies*, Vol. 1 (Apr. 1967), pp. 39–62.

2. Quoted in Nathan G. Hale, *Freud and the Americans*, Vol. I (New York: Oxford University Press; 1971), p. 19. Cf. also Jones, *Free Associations*, p. 191.

3. Jones, *Sigmund Freud*, Vol. II, pp. 61–62.

4. *Freud/Jung Letters*, pp. 398–99.

5. Hale, ed., *James Jackson Putnam and Psychoanalysis*, pp. 329, 332.

6. *Ibid.*, pp. 328–29.

7. Hale, *Freud and the Americans*, pp. 305, 307.

8. *Ibid.*, pp. 285, 283.

9. *Ibid.*, p. 408.

10. *Ibid.*, p. 463.

11. Quoted in Hale, ed., *James Jackson Putnam and Psychoanalysis*, p. 43.

12. "On the History," p. 31; "James Jackson Putnam," *Standard Edition*, Vol. 17, p. 271.

13. Hale, ed., *James Jackson Putnam and Psychoanalysis*, p. 147.

14. *Ibid.*, p. 140.

15. *Ibid.*, p. 110.

16. Ernst Waldinger, "My Uncle Sigmund Freud," *Books Abroad*, Vol. 15, No. 1 (Jan. 1941), p. 5.

17. C. G. Jung, *Memories, Dreams, Reflections*, p. 336.

18. Jones, *Sigmund Freud*, Vol. II, p. 85.

19. Hale, ed., *James Jackson Putnam and Psychoanalysis*, p. 39.

20. *Ibid.*, p. 127.

21. *Ibid.*, p. 259.

22. *Ibid.*, p. 94.

23. *Ibid.*, pp. 185–86.

24. *Ibid.*, p. 79.

25. *Ibid.*, p. 54.

26. *Ibid.*, p. 118.

27. *Ibid.*, p. 172.

28. *Ibid.*, p. 173.

29. Jones, *Free Associations*, p. 189.

30. Hale, ed., *James Jackson Putnam and Psychoanalysis*, p. 105.

31. *Ibid.*, pp. 121–22.

32. Interview with Marian C. Putnam, Sept. 22, 1966.

33. Hale, ed., *James Jackson Putnam and Psychoanalysis*, pp. xii–xiii.

34. "Lines of Advance in Psychoanalytic Therapy," p. 165.

35. Blanton, *Diary of My Analysis with Sigmund Freud*, p. 50.

36. Hale, *Freud and the Americans*, p. 348. Cf. Jones, *Sigmund Freud*, Vol. III, pp. 85, 105–06, and Clarence P. Oberndorf, *A History of Psychoanalysis in America* (New York: Grune & Stratton; 1953), p. 148.

37. Hale, *Freud and the Americans*, p. 323.

38. Jones, *Sigmund Freud*, Vol. III, pp. 85, 105–06, 111.

39. Horace Frink, "Review of *Psychoanalysis* by Brill," *Mental Hygiene*, Vol. 7 (1923), p. 400.

40. Interview with Abram Kardiner, Oct. 12, 1965.

41. Jones, *Sigmund Freud*, Vol. III, p. 85.

42. Letter from Clarence Oberndorf to Ernest Jones, Dec. 23, 1953 (Jones archives).

43. Interview with Abram Kardiner, Apr. 1, 1967.

44. Letter from Clarence Oberndorf to Ernest Jones, Dec. 23, 1953 (Jones archives). Cf. also the obituary in *Psychoanalytic Quarterly*, Vol. 5 (1936), pp. 601–03.

9. *The Americans: A. A. Brill and the Future of the Cause*

1. Quoted in Bernays, *Biography of an Idea*, p. 259.

2. "The Interpretation of Dreams," Vol. 4, p. xxxii.

3. Jones, *Free Associations*, p. 232.

4. Weiss, *Sigmund Freud as a Consultant*, p. 24.

5. Jones, *Sigmund Freud*, Vol. II, p. 45.

6. Hale, *Freud and the Americans*, pp. 394–96.

7. Martin Grotjahn, "Collector's Items from the Correspondence Between Sigmund Freud and Otto Rank,"

Journal of the Otto Rank Association, Vol. 6, No. 1 (June 1971), p. 27.

8. Hale, *Freud and the Americans,* p. 391.

9. Fritz Wittels, "Brill," *Psychoanalytic Review,* Vol. 35 (1948), p. 398.

10. Jones, *Sigmund Freud,* Vol. II, p. 37; Jones, *Free Associations,* p. 231.

11. Jones, *Sigmund Freud,* Vol. II, p. 46.

12. Hale, *Freud and the Americans,* p. 202.

13. Interviews with George Wilbur, Sept. 24–25, 1965.

14. Letter from Ernest Jones to Anna Freud, Oct. 25, 1933 (Jones archives).

15. Jones, *Sigmund Freud,* Vol. III, p. 111.

16. Paula Fass, "A. A. Brill—Pioneer and Prophet," M.A. dissertation, Dept. of History, Columbia University, June 1968, p. 29.

17. Interview with Sandor Rado, Jan. 29, 1966.

18. Hale, *Freud and the Americans,* p. 39.

19. Jones, *Free Associations,* pp. 190–91. When a Viennese physician living in the United States exhibited unreliable traits, Jones referred to him as "an American psychoanalyst." *Sigmund Freud: Four Centenary Addresses* (New York: Basic Books; 1956), p. 52.

20. Reik, "Years of Maturity," p. 70.

21. Jones, *Sigmund Freud,* Vol. II, p. 183.

22. *Ibid.,* p. 60.

23. Max Eastman, "Differing with Sigmund Freud," in *Einstein, Trotsky, Hemingway, Freud and Other Great Companions* (New York: Collier Books; 1962), p. 129.

24. Bernays, *Biography of an Idea,* p. 263.

25. "Civilization and Its Discontents," p. 49; Wortis, *Fragments of an Analysis with Freud,* p. 98. Cf. Oberndorf, *A History of Psychoanalysis in America,* pp. 148–49.

26. Robert P. Knight, "The Present Status of Organized Psychoanalysis in the United States," *Journal of the American Psychoanalytic Association,* Vol. 1, No. 2 (Apr. 1953), p. 209.

27. Interview with Mathilda Hollitscher, Nov. 5, 1966.

28. *The Letters of Freud and Zweig,* p. 178.

29. Martin Peck, "A Brief Visit with Freud," *Psychoanalytic Quarterly,* Vol. 9, No. 2 (1940), p. 206.

30. Reik, "Years of Maturity," p. 72. Cf. also letter from Ernest Jones to Johann van Ophuijsen, Dec. 14, 1927 (Jones archives).

31. "Introduction to the Special Psychopathology Number of *The Medical Review of Reviews,*" *Standard Edition,* Vol. 21, p. 254.

32. *Ibid.*

33. "On the History," p. 32.

34. "Introduction to the Special Psychopathology Number of *The Medical Review of Reviews,*" p. 255.

35. "New Introductory Lectures," p. 140.

36. Letter from Ernest Jones to Max Eitingon, Feb. 24, 1937 (Jones archives); Jones, *Free Associations,* pp. 218, 221; Jones, *Sigmund Freud,* Vol. III, p. 135.

37. Franz Alexander, *The Western Mind in Transition* (New York: Random House; 1960), p. 101.

38. Sachs, *Freud,* p. 187.

39. "Introductory Lectures," Vol. 16, pp. 254, 423.

40. Quoted in Nolan D. C. Lewis, "Smith Ely Jelliffe," in *Psychoanalytic Pioneers,* p. 227.

41. Quoted in Jones, *Sigmund Freud,* Vol. III, p. 292; cf. also *ibid.,* p. 298.

42. "The Future of an Illusion," p. 19.

43. Interview with Irmarita Putnam.

44. Letter from Johann van Ophuijsen to Ernest Jones, Oct. 31, 1927 (Jones archives).

45. Letters from Ernest Jones to Johann van Ophuijsen, Dec. 14, 1927, and Nov. 28, 1928 (Jones archives).

46. Blanton, *Diary of My Analysis with Sigmund Freud,* p. 108.

47. Quoted in Lewis, "Smith Ely Jelliffe," p. 228. Cf. also letter from Freud to Jacques Schneir, July 5, 1938 (Jones archives).

48. Oberndorf, *A History of Psychoanalysis in America,* p. 2.

VIII: OTTO RANK: SONS AND FATHERS
1. The Trauma of Birth

1. Jones, *Sigmund Freud*, Vol. III, p. xii.
2. Jack Jones, "Otto Rank: A Forgotten Heresy," *Commentary*, Vol. 30, No. 3 (Sept. 1960), p. 219.
3. *Ibid.*
4. "On the History," p. 25
5. *The Diary of Anaïs Nin*, Vol. I, ed. Gunther Stuhlmann (New York: Harcourt, Brace & World; 1966), p. 279.
6. Jones, *Sigmund Freud*, Vol. II, p. 160.
7. "The Theme of Three Caskets," p. 292.
8. "Group Psychology and the Analysis of the Ego," p. 135; "Mourning and Melancholia," p. 249. Cf. also "The Interpretation of Dreams," Vol. 4, p. 160.
9. Jones, *Sigmund Freud*, Vol. II, p. 160. Cf. also *ibid.*, p. 155.
10. Cf., for example, Felix Deutsch, "Hanns Sachs," *The American Imago*, Vol. 4, No. 2 (Apr. 1947), p. 4. Cf. also Sachs, *Freud*, p. 12.
11. Jones, *Sigmund Freud*, Vol. II, p. 160.
12. *Ibid.*, pp. 187, 160.
13. Wittels, *Freud*, p. 18.
14. "The 'Uncanny,' " p. 230.
15. Grotjahn, "Collector's Items from the Correspondence Between Sigmund Freud and Otto Rank," p. 26.
16. Jones, *Sigmund Freud*, Vol. III, p. 31.
17. *Ibid.*, p. 58.
18. "From the History of an Infantile Neurosis," p. 27.
19. Jones, *Sigmund Freud*, Vol. III, p. 58.
20. *Letters of Freud and Abraham*, p. 352.
21. Quoted in Jones, *Sigmund Freud*, Vol. III, p. 59.
22. *Minutes*, Vol. II, pp. 71–72, 323.
23. "A Special Type of Choice of Object Made by Men," p. 173. Cf. also "The Interpretation of Dreams," Vol. 5, pp. 400–01 and "Introductory Lectures," Vol. 16, pp. 396–97, 407.
24. Deutsch, *Confrontations with Myself*, p. 146.

25. Jones, *Sigmund Freud*, Vol. III, p. 55.
26. Jones, "Otto Rank: A Forgotten Heresy," p. 228.

2. Premature Grief

1. Letters from Rudolf Urbantschitsch to Ernest Jones, Feb. 29, 1956, and Sept. 30, 1956 (Jones archives).
2. Quoted in Jones, *Sigmund Freud*, Vol. III, p. 68.
3. Jones, *Sigmund Freud*, Vol. III, p. 66.
4. Quoted in *ibid.*, p. 76.
5. *Ibid.*, p. 47.
6. *Ibid.*, p. 54.
7. Quoted in *ibid.*, p. 69.
8. Nunberg, "Introduction," *Minutes*, Vol. I, p. xxvi.
9. An exception is Schur, *Freud*, pp. 386, 467.
10. Jones, *Sigmund Freud*, Vol. III, p. 55.
11. Cf. Sachs, *Freud*, p. 158; Siegfried Bernfeld, "On Psychoanalytic Training," p. 467.
12. Jones, *Sigmund Freud*, Vol. III, p. 93.
13. Bernfeld, "On Psychoanalytic Training," p. 467.
14. Jones, *Sigmund Freud*, Vol. III, p. 94.
15. Quoted in *ibid.*, p. 65.
16. Taft, *Otto Rank*, p. 94.
17. Bernays, *Biography of an Idea*, pp. 270–71.
18. Quoted in Taft, *Otto Rank*, p. 99.
19. Quoted in *ibid.*, p. 101.
20. Quoted in *ibid.*, p. 107. Cf. also Jones, *Sigmund Freud*, Vol. III, p. 60, and "Letter to Fritz Wittels," p. 287.
21. "An Autobiographical Study," p. 53.
22. Quoted in Jones, *Sigmund Freud*, Vol. III, p. 65.
23. Quoted in *ibid.*, p. 70.
24. *Ibid.*, pp. 69–70. According to Nunberg, in 1918 Rank had joined Tausk in rejecting the proposal that future analysts should have to undergo analyses themselves. "Introduction," *Minutes*, Vol. I, p. 22.
25. Taft, *Otto Rank*, p. 98.
26. "Editorial Changes in the *Zeitschrift*," *Standard Edition*, Vol. 19, p. 293.
27. *Letters of Freud and Andreas-Salomé*, p. 143.

28. Quoted in Jones, *Sigmund Freud,* Vol. III, p. 71.
29. *Ibid.,* p. 72.
30. *Letters of Freud and Abraham,* p. 379.
31. Quoted in Taft, *Otto Rank,* pp. 110, 113, 114.
32. Quoted in *ibid.,* p. 102.
33. Interviews with Helene Deutsch, Sept. 8, 1965, and Feb. 26, 1966.
34. Cf. *Letters of Freud and Andreas-Salomé,* p. 144.

3. Will and the Artist

1. Jones, *Sigmund Freud,* Vol. II, p. 160.
2. *Freud/Jung Letters,* p. 28. Taft, *Otto Rank,* p. 180; *Letters of Freud and Zweig,* p. 107; Jones, *Sigmund Freud,* Vol. III, p. 76; letter from Anna Freud to Ernest Jones, Nov. 7, 1955 (Jones archives); interview with Mrs. Hitschmann, Feb. 28, 1966.
3. Quoted in Jones, *Sigmund Freud,* Vol. III, p. 70.
4. Quoted in Grotjahn, "Collector's Items from the Correspondence Between Sigmund Freud and Otto Rank," p. 22.
5. Interview with Helene Deutsch, Nov. 18, 1967.
6. Letter from Anna Freud to Ernest Jones, Feb. 8, 1955 (Jones archives).
7. Jones, *Sigmund Freud,* Vol. III, p. 113.
8. Interview with Beata Rank, Aug. 22, 1966.
9. Interview with Beata Rank, Feb. 12, 1966.
10. Quoted in Taft, *Otto Rank,* pp. 159–60.
11. *The Diary of Anaïs Nin,* Vol. I, p. 334.
12. Jones, *Sigmund Freud,* Vol. III, p. 113.
13. The more scholarly of Freud's pupils pointed out to him special passages in Nietzsche. For Freud's relation to Nietzsche, cf. Roazen, *Freud: Political and Social Thought,* pp. 84–85, and *Brother Animal,* pp. 33, 43, 92. Cf. also *Letters of Freud and Zweig,* p. 78.
14. *The Diary of Anaïs Nin,* Vol. II, ed. Gunther Stuhlmann (New York: Harcourt, Brace & World; 1967), p. 16; Vol. I, p. 327; Vol. II, pp. 26, 157.
15. *Ibid.,* Vol. I, p. 277.
16. *Ibid.,* Vol. III, ed. Gunther Stuhlmann (New York: Harcourt, Brace & World; 1969), p. 228.
17. *Ibid.,* Vol. II, p. 37.
18. *Ibid.,* Vol. I, p. 270.
19. Thompson, *Psychoanalysis,* p. 177. Cf. also Ruth Monroe, *Schools of Psychoanalytic Thought* (New York: Dryden Press; 1955), p. 581.
20. Quoted in Taft, *Otto Rank,* pp. 149–50.
21. *The Diary of Anaïs Nin,* Vol. I, pp. 271, 276.
22. Quoted in Taft, *Otto Rank,* p. 223.
23. Quoted in Jones, "Otto Rank," p. 227.
24. *The Diary of Anaïs Nin,* Vol. II, p. 34.
25. *Ibid.,* pp. 15–16.
26. *Ibid.,* Vol. III, p. 21.
27. Jones, *Sigmund Freud,* Vol. III, p. 73. Cf. also pp. 45, 47, and Vol. II, p. 187. Elsewhere Jones was more cautious about the meaning of "cyclothymia." Cf. *Papers on Psychoanalysis,* p. 497.
28. Robert, *The Psychoanalytic Revolution,* p. 241.
29. Wortis, *Fragments of an Analysis with Freud,* p. 121. Cf. also Jones, *Sigmund Freud,* Vol. III, p. 74.
30. Storr, *The Dynamics of Creation,* pp. 204–05.
31. Jones, *Sigmund Freud,* Vol. II, p. 187.
32. *Ibid.,* Vol. III, p. 32.
33. Sachs, *Freud,* p. 148.
34. "Inhibitions, Symptoms, and Anxiety," *Standard Edition,* Vol. 20, p. 150.
35. "New Introductory Lectures," p. 143.
36. "Analysis Terminable and Interminable," pp. 216–17.
37. "Moses and Monotheism," p. 10.
38. *Ibid.,* p. 125.
39. Interview with George Wilbur. Sachs mentions this only obliquely. Cf. his *Freud* p. 115.
40. *The Diary of Anaïs Nin,* Vol. III, pp. 20–21.

IX: THE WOMEN

1. Ruth Mack Brunswick: "The Rabbi May"

1. For examples, interviews with Edith Jackson and Irmarita Putnam.
2. Letter from Max Schur to Ernest Jones, Sept. 30, 1955 (Jones archives).
3. Jones, *Sigmund Freud*, Vol. III, p. 18.
4. Interview with Oliver Freud.
5. Jones, *Sigmund Freud*, Vol. III, p. 167.
6. For his obituary, cf. *The New York Times*, May 28, 1971, p. 32.
7. Interview with Mark Brunswick, Jan. 25, 1966.
8. Letter from Max Schur to Ernest Jones, Sept. 30, 1955.
9. "Splitting of the Ego in the Process of Defence," *Standard Edition*, Vol. 23, pp. 275–78. Jones thought the patient was Bullitt, but Ruth and Mark Brunswick thought otherwise. Jones, *Sigmund Freud*, Vol. III, p. 239.
10. Quoted in Jones, *Sigmund Freud*, Vol. III, p. 456.
11. *The Wolf-Man*, p. 306.
12. *Ibid.*, p. 307.

2. Ruth Mack Brunswick: Dependency and Addiction

1. Interview with Anny Katan.
2. "On the History," p. 33.
3. D. W. Winnicott, *The Maturational Processes and the Facilitating Environment*, p. 54.
4. Ruth Mack Brunswick, "The Preoedipal Phase of the Libido Development," *Psychoanalytic Quarterly*, Vol. 9, No. 2 (1940), p. 293.
5. "Some Psychical Consequences of the Anatomical Distinction Between the Sexes," p. 256.
6. "Female Sexuality," p. 226.
7. *Ibid.*, p. 238.
8. Herman Nunberg, "In Memoriam: Ruth Mack Brunswick," *Psychoanalytic Quarterly*, Vol. 15, No. 2 (1945), p. 142.
9. "Female Sexuality," p. 226.

10. *Ibid.*, p. 230.
11. "New Introductory Lectures," p. 130. Cf. Ruth Mack Brunswick, "The Analysis of a Case of Paranoia (Delusion of Jealousy)," *The Journal of Nervous and Mental Disease*, Vol. 70 (1929), pp. 1–22, 155–78.
12. Letter from Ernest Jones to A. A. Brill, Dec. 22, 1933, and letter from Jones to Clarence Oberndorf, Dec. 2, 1933 (Jones archives).
13. Hale, *Freud and the Americans*, p. 371.
14. Quoted in Schur, *Freud*, p. 62.
15. Robert, *The Psychoanalytic Revolution*, p. 235.
16. "Introductory Lectures," Vol. 16, p. 449.
17. Interviews with David Brunswick.
18. Interviews with Mark Brunswick.
19. *Ibid.*
20. *Ibid.*
21. Storr, *The Dynamics of Creation*, p. 222.
22. Ellenberger, *The Discovery of the Unconscious*, p. 504.
23. "Analysis Terminable and Interminable," p. 218. Strachey does not seem to have known that there was supposed to be a second paper by Ruth Brunswick on the Wolf-Man.
24. *The New York Times*, Jan. 26, 1946, p. 13.
25. Nunberg, "In Memoriam."
26. Jones, *Sigmund Freud*, Vol. III, p. 127.
27. *Freud/Jung Letters*, p. 413.

3. Anna Freud: Child Analysis

1. Letter from Anna Freud to Ernest Jones, Feb. 14, 1954 (Jones archives). In addition to Ruth Brunswick, Anna Freud also mentioned Jeanne Lampl-de Groot and Joan Riviere.
2. Interview with Eva Rosenfeld, Nov. 17, 1966.
3. *The Origins of Psychoanalysis*, p. 136.
4. "The Interpretation of Dreams," Vol. 4, pp. 127, 130. Cf. also "Introductory Lectures," Vol. 15, p. 132.

5. Interview with Kata Levy, July 6, 1965.
6. "The Interpretation of Dreams," Vol. 4, p. 257.
7. *Letters*, pp. 294–95.
8. Anna Freud, *Problems of Psychoanalytic Training, Diagnosis, and the Technique of Therapy*, Vol. VII of *The Writings of Anna Freud, 1966–1970* (New York: International Universities Press; 1971), pp. 73–74.
9. Letter from Freud to Bransom (Jones archives). "The Theme of Three Caskets," pp. 293, 296, 298, 301; *Letters*, p. 301.
10. *Letters*, pp. 382, 424.
11. Binswanger, *Freud*, p. 2.
12. Interviews with Abram Kardiner, Oct. 12, 1965, Helene Deutsch, June 5, 1965, and Eva Rosenfeld, Nov. 3, 1966. Cf. dictation from Ernst Freud, Nov. 27, 1953 (Jones archives).
13. *Letters of Freud and Andreas-Salomé*, p. 204.
14. Anna Freud, "The Role of the Teacher," *Harvard Educational Review*, Vol. 22, No. 4 (Fall 1952), p. 229.
15. *Letters of Freud and Andreas-Salomé*, p. 231.
16. *Ibid.*, p. 233.
17. Interview with Beata Rank, Feb. 12, 1966. Cf. also Freeman, *Insights*, p. 82.
18. Interview with Kata Levy, July 13, 1965.
19. Interview with Oliver Freud.
20. Interview with Anny Katan.
21. Weiss, *Sigmund Freud as a Consultant*, p. 81.
22. Letter from Anna Freud to Ernest Jones, Oct. 20, 1955 (Jones archives).
23. Quoted in Jones, *Sigmund Freud*, Vol. III, p. 164.
24. Interview with Anny Katan.
25. "Introductory Lectures," Vol. 15, p. 15.
26. "An Autobiographical Study," p. 70.
27. "The Question of Lay Analysis," p. 229.
28. *Ibid.*, p. 239.
29. "Dr. Reik and the Problem of Quackery," *Standard Edition*, Vol. 21, pp. 247–48.
30. "Letter to Hermine von Hug-Hellmuth," *Standard Edition*, Vol. 14, p. 341.
31. Interviews with George Wilbur. Cf. *International Journal of Psychoanalysis*, Vol. 6 (1925), p. 106.
32. *Minutes*, Vol. II, p. 318.
33. "The Question of Lay Analysis," p. 214.
34. "Preface to Aichhorn's *Wayward Youth*," *Standard Edition*, Vol. 19, p. 274.
35. "New Introductory Lectures," pp. 146–47.
36. Blanton, *Diary of My Analysis with Sigmund Freud*, p. 72.
37. Interviews with Esti Freud.
38. *Minutes*, Vol. II, p. 51.
39. *Ibid.*, p. 230.
40. *Ibid.*, p. 236.

4. Anna Freud: Ladies-in-Waiting

1. Schur, "The Medical History of Freud," p. 11.
2. Letter from Anna Freud to Ernest Jones, July 8, 1935 (Jones archives)
3. Quoted in Binswanger, *Freud*, p. 88.
4. *Letters of Freud and Zweig*, p. 39.
5. Sachs, *Freud*, p. 169.
6. Marie Bonaparte, "Introduction," in Martin Freud, *Glory Reflected*, p. 6.
7. Marie Bonaparte, "Notes on the Analytic Discovery of a Primal Scene," *The Psychoanalytic Study of the Child*, Vol. I, ed. Ruth Eissler (New York: International Universities Press; 1945), pp. 119–25.
8. Interview with Erich Fromm, Jan. 5, 1966.
9. Wladimir Granoff and Victor Smirnoff, "History of Psychoanalysis in France and of the French Psychoanalytic Movement," p. iii (manuscript).
10. "On Narcissism," p. 89. Cf. letter from Max Schur to Ernest Jones, Sept. 30, 1955.
11. Cf. "An Unknown Autobiographical Fragment by Freud," *The American Imago*, Vol. 4, No. 1 (Aug. 1946),

pp. 3–19; "Freud's Earliest Theories and the School of Helmholtz," *Psychoanalytic Quarterly*, Vol. 13, No. 3 (1944), pp. 341–62; with Suzanne Cassirer Bernfeld, "Freud's Early Childhood," *Bulletin of the Menninger Clinic*, Vol. 8 (1944), pp. 107–15; with Suzanne Cassirer Bernfeld, "Freud's First Year in Practice: 1886–87," *Bulletin of the Menninger Clinic*, Vol. 16 (Mar. 1952), pp. 37–49; "Freud's Scientific Beginnings," in *The Yearbook of Psychoanalysis*, Vol. VI, ed. Sandor Lorand (New York: International Universities Press; 1951), pp. 24–50; "Freud's studies on Cocaine, 1884–87," *Journal of the American Psychoanalytic Association*, Vol. 1, No. 4 (Oct. 1953), pp. 581–613; "Sigmund Freud, M.D.," *International Journal of Psychoanalysis*, Vol. 32 (1951), pp. 204–17.

12. Quoted in Jones, *Sigmund Freud*, Vol. III, p. 241.

13. "The Question of Lay Analysis," p. 249.

14. Quoted in Jones, *Sigmund Freud*, Vol. III, p. 195.

5. Anna Freud: Ego Psychology

1. *Letters*, p. 444.

2. Letters from Anna Freud to Ernest Jones, Dec. 25, 1952, April 5, 1955, and Jan. 10, 1956 (Jones archives).

3. Letter from Anna Freud to Ernest Jones, June 6, 1954 (Jones archives).

4. Anna Freud, *The Ego and the Mechanisms of Defence* (London: Hogarth; 1954), p. 56.

5. Anna Freud and Dorothy T. Burlingham, *War and Children* (New York: Foster Parents' Plan for War Children; 1943), p. 160.

6. Anna Freud, "Observations on Child Development," *Psychoanalytic Study of the Child*, Vol. VI, ed. Ruth Eissler (New York: International Universities Press; 1951), p. 24.

7. Anna Freud and Dorothy Burlingham, *Infants Without Families* (New York: International Universities Press; 1944), p. 103.

8. Anna Freud, "The Widening Scope of Indications for Psychoanalysis," *Journal of the American Psychoanalytic Association*, Vol. 2 (1954), p. 618.

9. Anna Freud, "The Child Guidance Clinic as a Center of Prophylaxis and Enlightenment," in *Recent Developments in Psychoanalytic Child Therapy*, ed. Joseph Weinreb (New York: International Universities Press; 1960), p. 37.

10. Anna Freud, *Normality and Pathology in Childhood* (New York: International Universities Press; 1965), p. 119.

11. *Ibid.*, pp. 180, 177.

12. Anna Freud, "The Pediatricians' Questions and Answers," in *Psychosomatic Aspects of Pediatrics*, ed. Ronald MacKeith and Joseph Sandler (London: Pergamon; 1961), p. 39.

13. Anna Freud, "The Child Guidance Clinic," p. 37.

14. Anna Freud, *Normality and Pathology in Childhood*, p. 50.

15. Anna Freud, "Clinical Studies in Psychoanalysis," *Psychoanalytic Study of the Child*, Vol. XIV, ed. Ruth Eissler (New York: International Universities Press; 1959), p. 123.

16. Anna Freud, *Difficulties in the Path of Psychoanalysis* (New York: International Universities Press; 1969), p. 17.

17. *Ibid.*, p. 21.

18. Quoted in Robert Waelder, *Basic Theory of Psychoanalysis* (New York: International Universities Press; 1960), p. 232.

19. Arnold Rogow, *The Psychiatrists* (New York: G. P. Putnam's Sons; 1970), p. 109.

6. Helene Deutsch: The Black Cat Card Club

1. Her article "A Two-Year-Old Boy's First Love Comes to Grief," which Freud is said to have "encouraged her

to publish," was probably written about her son. Cf. Marie H. Briehl, "Helene Deutsch," in *Psychoanalytic Pioneers*, p. 286, and Helene Deutsch, *Neuroses and Character Types* (New York: International Universities Press; 1965), pp. 159–64. Also, cf. *Confrontations With Myself*, pp. 123–24.

2. Blanton, *Diary of My Analysis with Sigmund Freud*, p. 91.

3. Interview with Abram Kardiner, Oct. 12, 1965.

4. Interviews with Ives Hendrick, Richard Sterba, and Irmarita Putnam.

5. Edward Hitschmann, "Autobiographical Notes."

6. *International Journal of Psychoanalysis*, Vol. 3 (1922), p. 135.

7. Interviews with Helene Deutsch, May 22, 1965, and Nov. 18, 1967. Cf. also Deutsch, *Confrontations With Myself*, pp. 60–61, 140.

8. Interview with Helene Deutsch, Sept. 23, 1967.

9. Interview with Helene Deutsch, Sept. 30, 1967.

10. Deutsch, "Freud and His Pupils," p. 192.

11. Interview with Robert Jokl.

12. Interview with Helene Deutsch, Apr. 16, 1966. Cf. "Don Quixote and Don Quixotisms," in Deutsch, *Neuroses and Character Types*, pp. 218–25.

13. Interview with Helene Deutsch, May 14, 1966.

14. Interview with Helene Deutsch, Mar. 30, 1965.

7. *Helene Deutsch: The Theory of Femininity*

1. Cf. Helene Deutsch, in *Neuroses and Character Types*, pp. 165–89.

2. Kate Millet, *Sexual Politics* (New York: Doubleday; 1970), pp. 176–228, and Germaine Greer, *The Female Eunuch* (New York: McGraw-Hill, 1971).

3. Helene Deutsch, *The Psychology of Women*, Vol. II (New York: Grune & Stratton; 1945), p. 84.

4. *Ibid.*, p. 275. Cf. Deutsch, *Confrontations With Myself*, pp. 75, 209.

5. "Three Essays on the Theory of Sexuality," p. 219.

6. "New Introductory Lectures," p. 131.

7. *Minutes*, Vol. II, p. 477.

8. Letter from Ernest Jones to Anna Freud, Dec. 19, 1934 (Jones archives).

9. "Jokes and Their Relation to the Unconscious," pp. 61, 64.

10. "New Introductory Lectures," p. 116.

11. Letter from Edward Hitschmann to Ernest Jones, Mar. 26, 1954 (Jones archives).

12. "Introductory Lectures," Vol. 16, p. 402; "From the History of an Infantile Neurosis," p. 47.

13. "Civilization and Its Discontents," p. 106; "An Outline of Psychoanalysis," *Standard Edition*, Vol. 23, p. 188.

14. "The Taboo of Virginity," p. 204.

15. "Female Sexuality," p. 233.

16. "The Psychopathology of Everyday Life," p. 156; "Civilization and Its Discontents," p. 103; "On the Grounds for Detaching a Particular Syndrome from Neurasthenia under the Description 'Anxiety Neurosis,'" p. 109.

17. "Three Essays on the Theory of Sexuality," p. 221; "Inhibitions, Symptoms and Anxiety," p. 143.

18. "'Civilized' Sexual Morality and Modern Nervous Illness," p. 199.

19. *Ibid.*, pp. 195, 199; "New Introductory Lectures," p. 134.

20. "New Introductory Lectures," p. 132.

21. *Letters of Freud and Andreas-Salomé*, p. 172.

22. "Three Essays on the Theory of Sexuality," p. 221.

23. "Some Psychical Consequences of the Anatomical Distinction Between the Sexes," p. 257.

24. "Three Essays on the Theory of Sexuality," p. 191.

25. Puner, *Freud*, p. 285.

26. *Letters of Freud and Abraham*, p. 376; "Three Essays on the Theory of Sexuality," p. 151.

27. James Strachey, "Editor's Note," *Standard Edition*, Vol. 19, p. 243.

28. "The Question of Lay Analysis," p. 212; "New Introductory Lectures," p. 113.

29. "New Introductory Lectures," p. 135

30. "Some Psychical Consequences of the Anatomical Distinction Between the Sexes," p. 251.
31. "New Introductory Lectures," p. 118.
32. Freeman, *Insights*, p. 47.
33. Deutsch, *The Psychology of Women*, Vol. I, p. 233.
34. "New Introductory Lectures," p. 119.
35. "Some Psychical Consequences of the Anatomical Distinction Between the Sexes," p. 257.
36. "Female Sexuality," p. 230.
37. "New Introductory Lectures," p. 124.
38. "Female Sexuality," p. 226.
39. Puner, *Freud*, p. 288.
40. Quoted in "Editor's Note," *Standard Edition*, Vol. 19, p. 244.
41. Interview with Helene Deutsch, Sept. 30, 1967; Marie Briehl, "Helene Deutsch," in *Psychoanalytic Pioneers*, p. 283. Cf. Deutsch, *Confrontations With Myself*, pp. 62–69, 30–37.
42. Interviews with Helene Deutsch, June 18 and July 2, 1966.
43. Interview with Helene Deutsch, Feb. 19, 1966.
44. Interviews with Helene Deutsch, Feb. 5 and May 14, 1966.
45. Interview with Helene Deutsch, June 3, 1967.
46. Interview with Helene Deutsch, Dec. 31, 1966.
47. "Some Psychical Consequences of the Anatomical Distinction Between the Sexes," p. 258.
48. "Female Sexuality," pp. 226–27; "New Introductory Lectures," pp. 130–31; interview with Helene Deutsch, Nov. 13, 1965. Cf. Deutsch, *Confrontations With Myself*, p. 138.
49. Helene Deutsch, "The Psychology of Women in Relation to the Function of Reproduction," *International Journal of Psychoanalysis*, Vol. 6, Part 4 (Oct. 1925), pp. 405–18.
50. Weiss, *Agoraphobia in the Light of Ego Psychology*, p. 119.
51. Deutsch, *Neuroses and Character Types*, p. 304.
52. Interview with Willy Hoffer.
53. Greer, *The Female Eunuch*, pp. 94–95.
54. Deutsch, *The Psychology of Women*, Vol. I, pp. 191–92.
55. Deutsch, *Neuroses and Character Types*, pp. 262–81, 319–38.
56. Interview with Helene Deutsch, Mar. 5, 1966.

8. Melanie Klein: "The English School"

1. Jones, *Papers on Psychoanalysis*, p. 103.
2. Melanie Klein, *Contributions to Psychoanalysis* (London: Hogarth; 1948), p. 276.
3. *Ibid.*, p. 253.
4. Interview with Hannah Segal, Nov. 12, 1966, and interview with Elliott Jacques, Nov. 17, 1966.
5. Storr, *Jung*, p. 55; cf. also p. 41.
6. Elizabeth Zetzel, "Current Concepts of Transference," pp. 372–73.
7. Compare "Introductory Lectures," Vol. 16, p. 365, with "The Question of Lay Analysis," p. 249. Cf. also "Editor's Note," *Standard Edition*, Vol. 23, p. 213.
8. "An Autobiographical Study," p. 70; "Civilization and Its Discontents," pp. 130, 138.
9. Ernst Kris, "The Development of Ego Psychology," *Samiksa*, Vol. 5, No. 3 (1951), p. 159.
10. Interview with Eva Rosenfeld, Nov. 17, 1966.
11. Edward Glover, "Autobiographical Manuscript," p. 16. Cf. also letter from Mrs. Riviere to Ernest Jones over Ch. 2 of his manuscript for Vol. III of his biography of Freud (Jones archives).
12. Jones, *Sigmund Freud*, Vol. III, p. 137.
13. Letter from Johann van Ophuijsen to Ernest Jones, Oct. 13, 1927 (Jones archives).
14. Quoted in Jones, *Sigmund Freud*, Vol. III, p. 197.
15. Interview with Willy Hoffer.
16. Edward Glover, "The Position of Psychoanalysis in Great Britain," *On the Early Development of the Mind* (London: Imago; 1956), p. 358. Cf. also Edward Glover, *An Examination of the Klein System of Child Psy-*

chology (London: The Southern Post Ltd.; 1945); D. W. Winnicott, "A Personal View of the Kleinian Contribution," *The Maturational Processes and the Facilitating Environment*, pp. 171–78; Hannah Segal, *Introduction to the Work of Melanie Klein* (London: Heinemann; 1964); J. O. Wisdom, "Freud and Melanie Klein," *Psychoanalysis and Philosophy*, ed. Charles Hanly and Morris Lazerowitz (New York: International Universities Press; 1970), pp. 327–62; Harry Guntrip, *Personality and Human Interaction* (London: Hogarth; 1961), Chs. 10–12.

17. Letter from Ernest Jones to Max Eitingon, May 14, 1943 (Jones archives).

18. Elizabeth Zetzel, " 'The Depressive Position,' " in *Affective Disorders*, ed. Phyllis Greenacre (New York: International Universities Press; 1953), pp. 109–10.

X: OLD AGE

1. Illness

1. Jones, *Sigmund Freud*, Vol. II, p. 43; Robert, *The Psychoanalytic Revolution*, pp. 222–23; interview with Smiley Blanton.
2. Schur, "The Medical Case History of Sigmund Freud," p. 12.
3. *Letters of Freud and Zweig*, p. 143.
4. Quoted in Jones, *Sigmund Freud*, Vol. III, p. 121.
5. *Letters of Freud and Zweig*, pp. 5–6.
6. "Some Psychical Consequences of the Anatomical Distinction Between the Sexes," pp. 248–49.
7. Jones, *Sigmund Freud*, Vol. III, pp. 98–99. Cf. also manuscript by Rudolf Urbantschitsch (Jones archives), as well as letters from Urbantschitsch to Ernest Jones, June 12 and July 31, 1956 (Jones archives).
8. Quoted in Jones, *Sigmund Freud*, Vol. III, pp. 89–90.
9. Felix Deutsch, ed., *On the Mysterious Leap from the Mind to the Body* (New York: International Universities Press; 1959), p. 28.

10. Interviews with Helene Deutsch, Aug. 20 and Aug. 27, 1956. Felix Deutsch, "Reflections on the Tenth Anniversary of Freud's Death." Letter from Felix Deutsch to Ernest Jones, Jan. 31, 1956 (Jones archives).
11. "New Introductory Lectures," p. 105.
12. Schur, *Freud*, pp. 353, 187, 38. Jones, *Sigmund Freud*, Vol. III, p. 90.
13. Jones, *Sigmund Freud*, Vol. III, p. 90.
14. *Ibid.*, p. 91.
15. *Ibid.*
16. *Ibid.*, p. 93.
17. *Ibid.*, p. 94. Cf. letter from Anna Freud to Ernest Jones, Mar. 7, 1955 (Jones archives).
18. Jones, *Sigmund Freud*, Vol. III, p. 93.
19. Quoted in Jones, *Sigmund Freud*, Vol. III, p. 241.
20. Jones, *Sigmund Freud*, Vol. III, p. 99.
21. *Ibid.*, p. 93.
22. Letter from Anna Freud to Ernest Jones, Jan. 4, 1956 (Jones archives).
23. Letter from Felix Deutsch to Ernest Jones, Feb. 13, 1956 (Jones archives). However, in her *Confrontations With Myself* Helene Deutsch has recently advanced the new hypothesis that her husband "concealed his diagnosis from fear of precipitating a heart attack. . . ."; cf. p. 169. However, Felix Deutsch himself—in "Reflections on the Tenth Anniversary of Freud's Death" and in letters to Jones—discussed the possibilities of suicide and euthanasia, without mentioning the danger of a heart attack. Cf. also Jones, *Sigmund Freud*, Vol. III, pp. 90, 92–93.
24. Schur, *Freud*, p. 354.
25. Deutsch, "Reflections on the Tenth Anniversary of Freud's Death," p. 7.
26. Bennet, *C. G. Jung*, p. 40.
27. Quoted in Schur, *Freud*, p. 214.
28. Interview with Helene Deutsch, Aug. 27, 1966.
29. Quoted in Stekel, *Autobiography*, p. 142.
30. Schur, *Freud*, pp. 426, 287.
31. Letter from Anna Freud to Ernest Jones, June 16, 1954 (Jones archives).
32. *Letters*, p. 344.
33. Quoted in Binswanger, *Freud*, pp. 78–79.

34. *Letters*, p. 386.
35. "The Psychopathology of Everyday Life," p. 155.
36. Schur, *Freud*, p. 394.
37. Interview with Oliver Freud.
38. "Civilization and its Discontents," p. 77.
39. Quoted in Jones, *Sigmund Freud*, Vol. III, p. 211.
40. *Letters of Freud and Zweig*, pp. 3, 10.
41. "The Future of an Illusion," p. 36.
42. *Letters of Freud and Zweig*, pp. 8–9.
43. "Civilization and Its Discontents," p. 93.
44. "Group Psychology and the Analysis of the Ego," p. 91.
45. Jones, *Sigmund Freud*, Vol. III, p. 159.
46. Interview with Richard Sterba.

2. Dissenters

1. Deutsch, "Freud and His Pupils," p. 194.
2. Herbert W. Schneider, *The Puritan Mind* (Ann Arbor: University of Michigan Press; 1958), p. 98.
3. *Letters of Freud and Zweig*, p. 72.
4. von Weizsaecker, "Reminiscences of Freud and Jung," p. 66.
5. Bernfeld, "Freud's Earliest Theories and the School of Helmholtz," p. 359.
6. Ellenberger, *The Discovery of the Unconscious*, p. 755.
7. Weiss, *Sigmund Freud as a Consultant*, p. 52.
8. *Letters*, p. 365.
9. Weiss, *Sigmund Freud as a Consultant*, p. 53.
10. *Ibid.*, p. 58.
11. Deutsch, "Freud and His Pupils," p. 193.
12. Ernst Simmel, "Sigmund Freud," *Psychoanalytic Quarterly*, Vol. 9, No. 1 (1940), p. 172.
13. *Letters of Freud and Zweig*, p. 144.
14. Blanton, *Diary of My Analysis with Sigmund Freud*, p. 37; Sachs, *Freud*, pp. 106–07; "An Autobiographical Study," pp. 63–64; "Address Delivered in the Goethe House at Frankfurt," p. 211; Jones, *Sigmund Freud*, Vol. III, pp. 457–58.
15. "New Introductory Lectures," p. 144.
16. Interview with Harold Lasswell.
17. Ilse Ollendorf Reich, *Wilhelm Reich* (New York: St. Martin's Press; 1969), p. 14. Interview with Annie Reich.
18. Copies of these are in the Jones archives.
19. *Reich Speaks of Freud*, p. 8.
20. Letter from Ernest Jones to Anna Freud, May 2, 1933 (Jones archives).
21. Reich, *Wilhelm Reich*, p. 46.
22. Blanton, *Diary of My Analysis with Sigmund Freud*, p. 117.
23. Nunberg, *Memoirs*, pp. 65, 46.
24. Sandor Rado, "The Problem of Melancholia," *International Journal of Psychoanalysis*, Vol. 9, Part 4 (Oct. 1928), pp. 420–38.
25. Interview with Sandor Rado, Apr. 4, 1967.
26. Jeanne Lampl-de Groot, "Review of Rado's *Die Kastrationangst des Weibes*," *Internationale Zeitschrift für Psychoanalyse*, Vol. 25 (1935), pp. 598–605.
27. Frederick S. Perls, *In and Out the Garbage Pail* (New York: Bantam; 1972), p. 56.
28. Sandor Rado, "Sandor Ferenczi," *Psychoanalytic Quarterly*, Vol. 2 (1933), pp. 356–58.
29. Letter from Ernest Jones to Anna Freud, Dec. 19, 1934 (Jones archives).
30. Alexander, *The Western Mind in Transition*, pp. 55, 81.
31. Franz Alexander, *The Scope of Psychoanalysis* (New York: Basic Books; 1961), p. 539.
32. Interviews with Robert Jokl and Martin Grotjahn.
33. Cf. Martin Birnbach, *Neo-Freudian Social Philosophy* (Stanford: Stanford University Press; 1961).
34. Cf. Alexander's critique of Horney's *New Ways in Psychoanalysis*, in *The Scope of Psychoanalysis*, pp. 137–64.
35. Alexander, "Sandor Rado," in *Psychoanalytic Pioneers*, p. 240.
36. Eissler, "The Chicago Institute of Psychoanalysis and the Sixth Period of the Development of Psychoanalytic Technique," pp. 103–57. Cf. also Edward Glover, "Freudian or Neo-

Freudian?," *The Psychoanalytic Quarterly*, Vol. 33, No. 1 (1964), pp. 97–109.

37. Letter to me from Erich Fromm, Aug. 27, 1970.

38. Cf. Roazen, "Introduction," *Sigmund Freud* (Englewood Cliffs, N.J.: Prentice-Hall; 1973).

3. Erikson and Hartmann

1. Interview with Erik Erikson, Oct. 31, 1966.

2. Erik Erikson, "Autobiographical Notes on the Identity Crisis," *Daedalus*, Vol. 99, No. 4 (Fall 1970), p. 740.

3. Letter from Ernest Jones to Anna Freud, Sept. 19, 1933 (Jones archives).

4. Interview with Ives Hendrick.

5. Letter from Abraham Brill to Ernest Jones, Nov. 17, 1933 (Jones archives).

6. Evans, ed., *Dialogue with Erik Erikson*, p. 85.

7. Interview with Willy Hoffer.

8. Quoted in Sachs, *Freud*, p. 103.

9. Yankelovich and Barrett, *Ego and Instinct*, p. 138.

10. *Ibid.*, p. 151.

11. Evans, ed., *Dialogue with Erik Erikson*, p. 95.

12. Kurt Eissler, *Discourse on Hamlet and "Hamlet"* (New York: International Universities Press; 1971), p. 518.

13. Yankelovich and Barrett, *Ego and Instinct*, p xi.

14. *Ibid.*, p. 97.

15. "New Introductory Lectures," p. 112.

16. Cf. Heinz Hartmann, *Essays in Ego Psychology* (New York: International Universities Press; 1964).

17. Edward Glover, "Some Recent Trends in Psychoanalytic Theory," *Psychoanalytic Quarterly*, Vol. 30, No. 1 (1961), pp. 90, 87.

18. "New Introductory Lectures," p. 60.

19. Letter from Heinz Hartmann to Ernest Jones, Nov. 11, 1955 (Jones archives).

4. Wider Identity

1. "On the History," p. 43.

2. "Introductory Lectures," Vol. 15, p. 76.

3. *Ibid.*, Vol. 16, pp. 284–85.

4. "A Difficulty in the Path of Psychoanalysis," pp. 139–41.

5. Letter from Rudolf von Urbantschitsch to Ernest Jones, May 29, 1956 (Jones archives). Quoted in Jones, *Sigmund Freud*, Vol. II, p. 189; cf. *ibid.*, Vol. III, p. 234, and *Letters of Freud and Zweig*, p. 163.

6. Henry A. Murray, "Sigmund Freud," *American Journal of Psychology*, Vol. 53 (1940), p. 135.

7. *Letters of Freud and Zweig*, p. 6.

8. "An Autobiographical Study," p. 71.

9. *Ibid.*, p. 72.

10. "New Introductory Lectures," p. 150.

11. *Letters*, p. 446.

12. Quoted in Martin Freud, *Glory Reflected*, p. 211.

13. Interview with Richard Hoffman, June 2, 1965.

14. Letter from Anna Freud to Ernest Jones, Apr. 8, 1954 (Jones archives).

15. *Letters of Freud and Zweig*, p. 51.

16. *Letters*, p. 403.

17. Schur, "Medical History," p. 28.

18. "Studies on Hysteria," p. 160.

19. "The Question of Lay Analysis," p. 198.

20. "Analysis Terminable and Interminable," pp. 244–45.

21. Choisy, *Freud*, p. 5.

22. "An Autobiographical Study," p. 70.

23. *Ibid.*, p. 71.

24. "Beyond the Pleasure Principle," p. 64.

25. "Introductory Lectures," Vol. 16, p. 381.

26. "An Autobiographical Study," p. 72.

27. Deutsch, "Freud and His Pupils," p. 193.

28. "New Introductory Lectures," p. 76.

29. *Ibid.*, p. 77.

30. "The Question of Lay Analysis," pp. 196, 198.

31. "New Introductory Lectures," p. 68.

32. *Minutes*, Vol. II, p. 100.

33. "The Question of Lay Analysis," p. 209.
34. *Ibid.*, p. 217.
35. "An Autobiographical Study," p. 72.
36. "The Future of an Illusion," p. 23.
37. "On the Teaching of Psychoanalysis in the Universities," *Standard Edition*, Vol. 17, p. 173.
38. "New Introductory Lectures," p. 179.
39. "The Resistances of Psychoanalysis," *Standard Edition*, Vol. 19, p. 221.
40. "The Question of Lay Analysis," p. 248.
41. "Psychoanalysis," pp. 266–67.
42. "The Future of an Illusion," pp. 31–32.
43. *Letters of Freud and Zweig*, p. 23.
44. "Civilization and Its Discontents," p. 102.
45. "The Future of an Illusion," p. 8.
46. "Why War?," p. 209.
47. "Moses and Monotheism," p. 54.
48. *Ibid.*, p. 55.
49. *Letters of Freud and Zweig*, p. 98.
50. Cf. *Letters of Freud and Andreas-Salomé*, p. 205.
51. "From the History of an Infantile Neurosis," p. 119.
52. *Letters of Freud and Zweig*, p. 85.
53. "Moses and Monotheism," pp. 32–33.
54. *Ibid.*, p. 13.
55. Quoted in Jones, *Sigmund Freud*, Vol. III, p. 21.
56. "Moses and Monotheism," pp. 59, 20, 21–22.
57. *Ibid.*, pp. 60, 110, 47.
58. *Ibid.*, pp. 52, 106, 109–10.
59. *Ibid.*, pp. 115, 19, 24, 20, 134, 58.

5. Exile and Death

1. Nunberg, *Memoirs*, p. 60.
2. George S. Viereck, *Glimpses of the Great* (London: Duckworth; 1930), p. 34.
3. William G. Niederland and Jacob Shatzky, "Four Unpublished Letters of Freud," *Psychoanalytic Quarterly*, Vol. 25 (1956), p. 154.
4. Interview with Mark Brunswick, Jan. 25, 1966.

6. Interviews with Mark Brunswick.
7. *Letters of Freud and Zweig*, p. 45.
8. Walter C. Langer, *The Mind of Adolf Hitler* (New York: Basic Books; 1972), p. 134.
9. Quoted in Jones, *Sigmund Freud*, Vol. III, p. 151.
10. Quoted in *ibid.*, p. 230.
11. *Letters of Freud and Zweig*, p. 21.
12. *Letters of Freud and Andreas-Salomé*, p. 75. For Freud's feelings about the French Revolution, cf. "Interpretation of Dreams," Vol. 5, pp. 495–96.
13. Letter from Mathilda Hollitscher to Ernest Jones, Feb. 16, 1956, and letter from Ernst Waldinger to Ernest Jones, Jan. 11, 1956 (Jones archives).
14. Martin Freud, *Glory Reflected*, p. 196.
15. Schur, *Freud*, p. 450.
16. Martin Freud, *Glory Reflected*, p. 197.
17. *Minutes*, Vol. II, p. 383.
18. Jones got his details wrong here. Cf. *Sigmund Freud*, Vol. III, p. 180. Interviews with Edoardo Weiss, Apr. 5 and May 8, 1965.
19. Weiss, *Sigmund Freud as a Consultant*, p. 20.
20. *Letters of Freud and Zweig*, p. 92.
21. Jones, *Sigmund Freud*, Vol. III, pp. 192, 220–21. Interview with Edoardo Weiss, May 10, 1965.
22. "Moses and Monotheism," p. 54.
23. Interview with Richard Sterba.
24. "Moses and Monotheism," p. 115.
25. Jones, *Sigmund Freud*, Vol. II, p. 382.
26. Letter from Rudolf von Urbantschitsch to Ernest Jones, May 29, 1956 (Jones archives).
27. "Leonardo da Vinci," p. 105.
28. Letter from Anna Freud to Ernest Jones, Jan. 16, 1956 (Jones archives).
29. Quoted in Choisy, *Freud*, p. 84
30. Stefan Zweig, *The World of Yesterday* (London: Cassell; 1953), p. 422.
31. "Thoughts for the Times on War and Death," *Standard Edition*, Vol. 14, p. 289.
32. Martin Freud, *Glory Reflected*, p. 217.
33. Jones, *Sigmund Freud*, Vol. III, p. 232.

33. Arthur Koestler, *The Invisible Writing* (Boston: Beacon; 1955), p. 408.
34. Leonard Woolf, *Downhill All the Way* (London: Hogarth; 1967), pp. 168, 166, 197.
35. Interview with Leonard Woolf, Aug. 17, 1965.
36. "A Comment on Anti-Semitism," p. 292.
37. Jones, *Sigmund Freud*, Vol. III, p. 240.
38. Quoted in *ibid.*, p. 242.
39. Letter from Anna Freud to Ernest Jones, May 15, 1955 (Jones archives).
40. Letter from Anna Freud to Ernest Jones, June 16, 1954 (Jones archives).
41. Interview with Mark Brunswick, Nov. 22, 1967.
42. Jones, *Sigmund Freud*, Vol. III, p. 230.
43. Quoted in *ibid.*, p. 245.
44. Interview with Max Schur.
45. Letters from Anna Freud to Ernest Jones, Mar. 18, 1954, and Jan. 21, 1955 (Jones archives); Harry Freud, "My Uncle Sigmund," in *Freud As We Knew Him*, ed. Ruitenbeek, p. 312.

ACKNOWLEDGMENTS

*Grateful acknowledgment is made to the following
for permission to reprint previously published material:*

Basic Books, Inc., and The Hogarth Press Ltd.: Excerpts from *The Letters of Sigmund Freud*, Selected and Edited by Ernst L. Freud, translated by James and Tania Stern, copyright © 1960 by Sigmund Freud Copyrights Ltd., London. Excerpts from *The Life and Work of Sigmund Freud* by Ernest Jones, M.D. Copyright © 1953 by Ernest Jones. Excerpts from *Collected Papers of Sigmund Freud* edited by Ernest Jones, M.D. Published by Basic Books, Inc., by arrangement with The Hogarth Press Ltd. and The Institute of Psycho-Analysis, London. Excerpts from *A Psycho-Analytic Dialogue: The Letters of Sigmund Freud and Karl Abraham, 1907–1926*, edited by Hilda C. Abraham and Ernst L. Freud, translated by Bernard Marsh and Hilda C. Abraham.

Basic Books, Inc., and George Allen & Unwin Ltd.: Excerpts from *Interpretation of Dreams* by Sigmund Freud, translated and edited by James Strachey.

Basic Books, Inc., and Katherine Jones: Excerpts from *Free Associations: Memoirs of a Psychoanalyst* by Ernest Jones, copyright © 1959 by Katherine Jones.

Grune & Stratton, Inc., and Helene Deutsch, M.D.: Excerpts from *Psychology of Women*, Volume I, by Helene Deutsch, 1944.

International Universities Press, Inc., and Martin Grotjahn: Excerpts from "A Letter by Sigmund Freud" by Martin Grotjahn, reprinted from Vol. 4, No. 4, of the *Journal of the American Psychoanalytic Association*. Copyright © 1956 by the American Psychoanalytic Association.

Alfred A. Knopf, Inc., and The Hogarth Press Ltd.: Excerpts from *Moses and Monotheism* by Sigmund Freud, translated by Katherine Jones (or by James Strachey) copyright 1939 by Alfred A. Knopf, Inc., and renewed 1967 by Ernst L. Freud and Anna Freud.

Liveright Publishing Corp. and The Hogarth Press Ltd.: Excerpts from *Five Introductory Lectures on Psycho-Analysis, The Future of an Illusion, Introductory Lectures*, and *Beyond Pleasure and Principle* from *The Standard Edition of the Complete Psychological Works of Sigmund Freud*.

W. W. Norton & Company, Inc., and Ernest Benn Ltd.: Excerpts from *Psychopathology of Everyday Life* by Sigmund Freud, translated by Alan Tyson, edited by James Strachey. Copyright © 1965, 1960 by James Strachey, translation copyright © 1960 by Alan Tyson.

W. W. Norton & Company, Inc., and The Hogarth Press Ltd.: Excerpts from *Civilization and Its Discontents* by Sigmund Freud, translated from the German and edited by James Strachey. Copyright © 1961 by James Strachey. Excerpts from *On Dreams* by Sigmund Freud, translated by James Strachey. Copyright © 1952 by W. W. Norton & Company, Inc. Excerpts from *An Autobiographical Study* by Sigmund Freud, translated by James Strachey. Copyright 1935, 1952 by W. W. Norton & Company, Inc., and renewed 1963 by James Strachey. Excerpts from *The Question of Lay Analysis* by Sigmund Freud, translated by Nancy Proctor Gregg. Copyright 1950 by W. W. Norton & Company, Inc. Excerpts from *New Introductory Lectures* by Sigmund Freud, translated and edited by James Strachey. Copyright 1933 by Sigmund Freud, renewed 1961 by W. H. J. Sprott. Copyright © 1965, 1964 by James Strachey.

W. W. Norton & Company, Inc., and Routledge & Kegan Paul Ltd.: Excerpts from *Jokes and Their Relation to the Unconscious* by Sigmund Freud, translated from the German and edited by James Strachey. Copyright © 1960 by James Strachey. Excerpts from *Leonardo da Vinci and a Memory of His Childhood* by Sigmund Freud, translated by Alan Tyson. All rights reserved. First American Edition.

Princeton University Press: Excerpts from *The Freud/Jung Letters: The Correspondence Between Sigmund Freud and C. G. Jung*, edited by William McGuire, translated by Ralph Manheim and R. F. C. Hull, Bollingen Series XCIV (Copyright © 1974 by Princeton University Press).

SURVIVE

SURVIVE

THE ALL-IN-ONE GUIDE
TO STAYING ALIVE IN EXTREME CONDITIONS

BY KY FURNEAUX

ILLUSTRATIONS BY
EMILY SULLIVAN

CIDER MILL
PRESS

BOOK
PUBLISHERS
KENNEBUNKPORT, MAINE

Contents

Introduction

Nothing's Impossible
If You Really Want It

> ## "May you live in interesting times."
> ### ANCIENT CHINESE CURSE

FROM A VERY YOUNG AGE, I started venturing into the outdoors. I spent my early years in the Outback of Australia in a time when it was okay for a group of kids to head off in a direction for the day, taking only some snacks and a sandwich, as long as we were back by dark. We would use only what we found out in the bush to entertain ourselves. Shelter building was a must, with us returning to the same forts every weekend to deck them out with whatever luxuries we had made or discovered during the week. I was learning, even then, how to interact with the wildlife, as we would quite often come across any number of deadly snakes or spiders that also called those places home. I learned that most deadly snakes won't threaten you unless they are hurt or threatened, and it was okay to observe them, give them space, and let them go on their way. And I felt what it was like to have redback spider venom run through my body as I was accidentally bitten by one in my bed. The dry, uninhabitable deserts showed me that they were full of life, you just needed to know where to look.

I was always a bit of a wild child, and as I grew, weekends would often see me vanishing into the Australian bush bareback on my horse for any number of adventures that I would make up as I went. In my mind I was always Indiana Jones or MacGyver, taking what the world would throw at me and dealing with it, using my wits and what I had around me. You could say I was a perfect candidate for the extreme lifestyle I ended up leading.

I was never scared of the outdoors. I never felt in awe of its vastness. Quite simply, I felt most at home with the wide-open spaces, the wind in my hair, and the sun on my face.

At nineteen, I was completing a Bachelor of Business Management, looking at heading into a marketing position in a major hotel chain, and in a moment, my whole life changed. I was the passenger in a car accident and ended up fracturing a bone in my lower back. A doctor told me that I would never be physically active again. I remember thinking that he didn't know me, and how was he giving me a condition that would supposedly follow me around for the rest of my life? In that moment, I decided that I would prove to him that nothing was impossible for me if I really wanted it. That was when the full extent of a lifetime of extremes kicked in.

I became a rock climber in an attempt to get strong and gain my physicality back, and after completing my degree, I left the corporate world behind and became an outdoor guide. I taught rock climbing, rappelling, sailing, kayaking, and hiking to groups of all ages, from schools and businesses to juvenile offenders and the general public. For six years, I barely slept in a bed and only returned to civilization to wash my clothes between trips. I kept people safe in some of the most extreme terrain in the world, from the remote and dangerous West Coast trail in the far reaches of British Columbia to the depths of the Amazon jungle and the barren, deadly high-altitude slopes of Nepal, while participating in high-risk activities that had the potential for disaster.

At twenty-six years of age, I decided that I wanted to push myself even harder and followed a suggestion to become a stunt performer in Vancouver, British Columbia. This really did seem to be the most physical job in the world: putting my life on the line regularly to make flawless, hard-hitting action sequences for some of Hollywood's biggest names. It took me about three years of working hard to finally crack the industry, and it was my fighting skills that got me there. Martial arts and weapons were my specialty, and one of my first big jobs was working as one of the doubles for Sharon Stone in *Catwoman*. For the next sixteen years, I doubled for stars such as Jennifer Garner in *Elektra* and Jaimie Alexander in *Thor* and the NBC series *Blindspot*. A-list names required my help to ensure they remained safe while filming some of the greatest action sequences of the time. My calm and positive attitude on set had me working with the likes of Anne Hathaway, Ellen DeGeneres, Hugh Jackman, Arnold Schwarzenegger, and Chris Hemsworth. I even ended up winning an award for being the Best Female Stunt Performer at the world in the 2012 Taurus Awards; this is the equivalent of an Oscar in our industry and a far greater honor than I ever imagined was possible.

Toward the end of my stunt career, I felt the urge to get back into the outdoors and away from the glitz and glam. I had increasingly been testing myself, heading out into the bush with less equipment until I felt confident in my ability to survive with just a knife. In an effort to test my skills, I produced and documented an extraordinary hundred-mile hike across the Sierra Nevada mountain range. It was this achievement that put me on the radar for the Discovery Channel and led to me being asked to participate in the very first season of their new concept show, *Naked and Afraid*. It was to be the Everest of survival challenges: twenty-one days with only one item to keep me alive and not even the clothes on my back to protect me from the elements. Never one to back down from a challenge, I was in. This was the start of three of the most extreme adventures I've had. Louisiana swamps can be hard to survive at the best of times, but my partner, Billy Berger (pictured), and I lived through the coldest May on record, with nine days of flooding where we had no dry land to stay on at all. My next challenge was the Bahamas, where there was no food on the island, and I had to compete with sharks for my sustenance. And, finally, my last challenge was the most desperate of all: the Amazon in the wet season, alone.

I have also braved a twelve-thousand-foot mountain climb and minus 22°F temperatures in China to be the only female competitor in the second season of Discovery's *Ed Stafford: First Man Out* and conquered grueling terrain in over sixty-five other countries. I am very passionate about my country's unique landscape and wildlife and have shared the beauty of the Aussie bush in my Discovery and 7mate series, *Outback Lockdown*.

As hard as I have pushed my mind and body, I have never reached a place where I have fallen down and not been able to get back up to put one foot in front of the other again. I am curious as to what that would take and plan to continue to push my boundaries until I find out.

I've always tried to live my life in interesting times—a curse to someone who wants peace, but a blessing to someone who wants adventure.

"As hard as I have pushed my mind and body, I have never reached a place where I have fallen down and not been able to get back up to put one foot in front of the other again."

1

My Approach to Survival

WHEN IT COMES TO ALL THINGS SURVIVAL, I'm a nerd and have been since I first ventured out into the Australian Outback at a young age. I was a guide as my first career, taking a variety of groups into the outdoors for rock climbing, hiking, kayaking, and sailing. As time progressed, I reduced my gear, eventually heading out for multiple days with nothing but a knife. I have since challenged myself to more extreme trips into varied locations around the world, including high-altitude mountains in China and Nepal, deep swamplands in Louisiana, and dense Amazon jungles. I realized that there was a vast difference between knowing theories and putting your body on the line to test what really works. I wanted to find out for myself the most effective methods of surviving in extreme conditions.

I explore my environment and experiment with survival skills and bushcraft at every opportunity, and as a result, my approach to survival is slightly different from the traditional ways of looking at it. Survival has been thought of as a scenario that requires the biggest, strongest, and most skilled person to make it through, and also requires certain gear to make your time in the emergency survivable. And if you don't have that strength and gear, then you might as well curl up and die. I don't believe that and have fought against those opinions for years. I believe that anyone can survive with the right mindset and attitude. It's why eighty-year-old grandmothers have walked out of three months of being lost in the woods with barely a scratch on them, and why trained army survivalists have died in days. Will knowledge help get you through? Absolutely, if applied with the right attitude. Will being prepared with the right gear help get you through? Definitely. But nine times out of ten, we aren't expecting to be put in a survival situation, which is why it becomes a life-or-death struggle rather than an extended camping trip.

Through my experimentation, I have discovered that some of the knowledge that has been passed down to me by my peers has limited me, and that the best way to learn something is to try it for myself without bias. I encourage you to do the same. Doing the very thing that someone has told you isn't possible may just save your life.

I acknowledge that the variations of what your survival scenario could look like are too numerous to address. I can't prepare you for every element of what your struggle will contain. I can prepare your mindset, though. I will provide you with ways of looking at your specific situation that will have you understanding what *your* priorities are and how best to deal with them. I can't list every tree and every plant you will encounter, but I can give you some easy-to-remember, general clues about what to look for in assets and what to avoid that might make you ill, or even kill you.

I haven't written this book to instill fear in you about all the possible horrible things that could happen to you in this world. Quite the opposite, actually. I want you to know that whatever unexpected event happens, with the right mindset, a bit of preparation, and some general knowledge, you have a good chance of making it out the other side of a disaster with merely some memorable stories to show for it.

This book is a survival book, rather than a bushcraft book. The difference is that bushcraft is the practice of skills you can use to make your situation more comfortable out there, such as carving bowls and cups and weaving bags, whereas survival addresses your basic needs of how to live through a bad situation and get rescued as soon as possible. It means that most of the time I will be assuming you have only the clothes on your back, and anything else will be a bonus. It changes the teachings from "let's use this tool you should have" to "what do you have out there that you can use for your survival?"

There will be some crossover, since making tools will make your life out there easier, and sometimes a piece of natural rope may just be the thing that allows you to live another day. But generally, we will be addressing skills that help with your basic survival needs.

I am writing this assuming it will probably be a reference book for you, rather than a book that you will read cover to cover. This will lead to some areas of repetition, as things like avalanches are an issue in both polar ecosystems and backcountry ski trips but not so common in the tropics, and I want to make sure that you gain all the relevant information you need in the section you turn to. If there is information that I feel as a survivalist you should know and that will be relevant to every location and situation, I will simply refer to the technique once rather than repeat it, in the hope that this will inspire you to memorize it. This is the case for such things as the toxin test (see page 110) and plants to avoid (see page 108).

Don't let this repetition discourage you from reading *Survive* cover to cover, though, because you may learn some interesting facts that you never knew you needed to know.

I want you to become flexible with your thinking—sometimes trying to remember and follow a rigid set of rules will be more detrimental to you than observing what is going on in the moment and finding **your** best mode of moving through the situation. I will teach you the properties of assets to look for, rather than specific resources, and I'll explain the theories behind what works and why, rather than giving you endless methods to memorize.

I want to empower you to know the difference between your **wants** and your **needs** and focus on what you can change rather than obsessing over what you can't. I want you to understand why some people give up in a survival scenario and why others manage to beat the odds, in the hope that you can train your mindset to get you through any range of unexpected circumstances. I will give you tools to help you do this.

Above all, I want you to learn to be proactive in doing what you need to do in your specific scenario to keep you and your loved ones safe and alive.

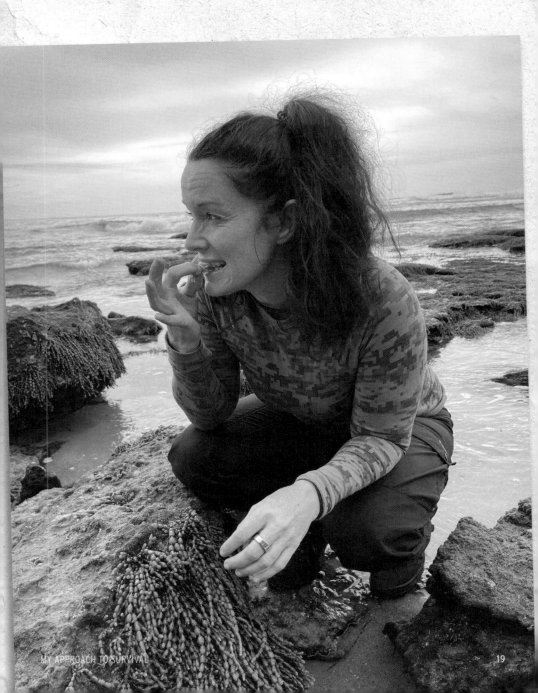

2

The Psychology of Survival

SURVIVAL HAS BAFFLED PEOPLE FOR CENTURIES. Why, in the same given circumstances, does one person survive when another doesn't? Terms such as "the will to live" are thrown around, but, when broken down, they seem to suggest that the mind has such a strong influence over our body that it can simply decide it doesn't want to go on, and all necessary bodily functions will cease. This seems to defy logic, yet time and time again, survivors of multiple-person scenarios have described the light fading in someone's eyes as they give up when other people in the same situation push through.

There have been scenarios where people have had access to food, water, and shelter, but the desperation of their situation has caused them to perish before they should have. There is a view that people die because they become depressed and simply give up, unable to adapt to this new way of life. In order to look at how to endure the mental aspect of survival, we need to learn what happens when a life-or-death emergency is suddenly thrust upon us, and come up with tools to combat that.

Our eyes pick up about ten million bits of information per second. Our brain works to keep us sane by filtering most of that down to a manageable fifty bits per second for our conscious mind to process. This is made easier when the information that the brain is processing is largely familiar.

Researchers talk about "intrinsic" survival versus "extrinsic" survival, and suggest that intrinsic survival is our day-to-day living, where our survival is supported by our daily routine and known behavior. Extrinsic survival is when we need to change our behavior or adopt new behaviors in order to survive in an environment or situation that hasn't been previously experienced. When we are participating in intrinsic behavior, our brain doesn't experience an overwhelming amount of stress. The danger arises when we are forced outside our typical environment.

As soon as an unexpected scenario arises, there is an increase in anxiety in our brain due to the adrenaline triggered by the fight-or-flight mechanism. This adrenaline can give you a burst of energy to escape a life-or-death moment, but as that moment extends into minutes, it can actually inhibit your ability to make good decisions. The working memory can only process so much information, and when it gets overloaded with anxiety, it can become restricted, leading to an inability to think or make decisions, essentially freezing a person into inactivity when faced with a dangerous scenario.

This might be okay if this dangerous scenario is short-lived, such as a fender-bender car accident or a near miss on the crosswalk, but if it stretches into hours or days, this lack of flexibility with your thinking can become deadly.

It has been recorded that during trauma, people regularly experience:

- **Cognitive paralysis:** complete inaction

- **Perseveration behavior:** repeating a particular response, regardless of what is happening around you

- **Stereotypical behavior:** repeating a behavior that might not be suitable to the situation, without being able to change it

- **Hyperactivity:** constant activity, with a tendency to impulsive and aggressive behaviors

- **Hypoactivity:** the inability to motivate yourself to action

These behaviors can lead to people being disorganized, inappropriate to the circumstances, and/or too slow to respond to changing conditions.

Survival requires the ability to cope under conditions of environmental distress, and therefore requires you to have a capacity to interact flexibly within that environment. In other words, it is imperative to be adaptable.

Some behaviors that have been identified as contributing to survival success include:

- **Goal-directed behavior:** making a list of tasks you can complete, and then working to complete them

- **Managing emotions:** calming yourself down to avoid descending into panic is a must; the higher your emotional arousal, the worse your judgment and decision making become

- **Identifying assets:** noting what skills and abilities you have that will help you in this scenario, as well as material possessions that will contribute to your survival

- **Perseverance:** knowing that you are capable of far more than you think you are and putting one foot in front of the other, taking every step you can to prove it to yourself

It is understandable to be fearful when you are catapulted from the familiar into the desperate. It is also important to distinguish real fear from perceived fear. Your body will react the same way whether the fear is real or not, and fear will quite often lead to panic, and panic leads to making decisions based on emotions rather than facts. The best way to dispel fear is with knowledge. Take control of your thoughts, and begin to look at what you are afraid of. A lot of people won't visit Australia because of the abundance of venomous spiders, yet the reality of the situation is that no one has died from a spider bite in Australia since 1979, whereas the last recorded death by spider in the United States was in 2019. Having the facts is a good way of dispelling fears.

As a short-term scenario stretches into a long-term scenario, knowing what to expect with your physiological changes (how your body responds) also helps to manage fear.

THE PHYSIOLOGY OF SURVIVAL

The average amount of time that a person can survive without food is about twenty-one days. I think this is one of the most important facts I can give you to dispel fear about what is happening to your body. We are conditioned to having three regular meals a day, plus snacks, and are guided to think that we won't function any other way. If you can dispel the expectation of food, then immediately you will be in a better place.

The first day or two of a survival scenario is okay as your body works with what it has in its stomach and stored in its tissues. After that, it begins to crave all the things that you are addicted to without even knowing it. This causes all kinds of withdrawal symptoms that people misdiagnose as "starvation" or dehydration. If you are getting enough water, these headaches and shivers and nausea are most probably caused by things such as coffee, alcohol, tobacco, and sugar cravings. Day three to five will probably be the worst, as your body demands access to these substances that you can't deliver. You might even feel like you are going to die, but trust me, things will get better.

Men usually struggle more in the first days of survival scenarios because, in general, they have more muscle and are used to a greater calorie intake than women. Women also have pockets of fat designed by evolution to get them through the harder times in their role as child bearers. This eventually balances out, though, as time moves on.

If you are getting enough water, you will continue to urinate, but your ability to defecate will probably become almost nonexistent with the lack of regular food. Don't be alarmed by this, unless your body really aches to go and is unable to. Women will probably menstruate in the first three or four days of going without regular meals, as their body shuts down in a primal response of not wanting to bring a child into the world where there is not enough food to feed them. These are all normal bodily responses to food scarcity.

It is important that you establish your fire, shelter, and water situation in the first few days of your emergency. If you manage to reach a satisfactory state with these needs, then it leaves you free to focus all your energy on gaining calories to extend your ability to survive.

The body has an amazing way of adapting to the harshness of whatever situation you find yourself in, and I have found that even twenty-one days in, surviving on small handfuls of insect larvae, I still have had the energy and stamina to trek great distances and perform feats of endurance. Everybody will respond differently to a survival situation, but the important thing is to know that we are designed to be adaptable, and your body will fight for you to find a way to stay alive.

The distractions of an emergency can cause a victim to move away from proactive, positive behaviors and toward impulsive, reactive behaviors that are more likely to decrease their chances of survival. Your attitude toward the situation you are in may be the very thing that saves your life.

3

The Attitude
of Survival

I HAVE COMPLETED NUMEROUS CHALLENGES in many different environments, and watched countless people succeed or fail when placed in survival scenarios. My experiences have taught me that, nine times out of ten,
it is your attitude of survival that will be the difference between survival or
death. I'm not saying that skills won't help—the person most likely to survive
will be the one who has both the skills to suit the scenario and the right attitude to get them through. But I am saying that I would rather be in a survival
situation with someone who has a good attitude over the right skills.

THE ATTITUDE OF SURVIVAL

So, what is an attitude of survival? Over the years, I have tested out what I see as the most important traits that will ensure my success in extreme challenges. I have documented these attitudes and taught them to many people who have used them successfully throughout their lives, in both physical outdoor hardship and also in their everyday experiences. They are very simple and have been talked about forever, and yet many people fail to remember or use them when life throws unexpected scenarios at them. I believe that using these attitudes will make for a more proactive experience and, where possible, ensure your survival. I suggest beginning to practice them in everyday life before you are tested in the extreme, so they become second nature rather than something you aim to remember under stress.

The four I have identified as being the most important are:

1. **Educate yourself**
2. **Be prepared**
3. **Be positive**
4. **Be adaptable**

3.1

EDUCATE YOURSELF

KNOWLEDGE

There is an old Latin saying: *Scientia potentia est* or "knowledge is power." But I prefer to think of it as "knowledge is empowerment."

When I learn skills and am confident that I know what to do in a given situation, I feel empowered. What you don't know could kill you. In everyday life, not knowing the answer to a question might result in something as simple as a B grade on an exam paper rather than an A, or another trip around the block while you search for the restaurant where you are meeting friends. In a survival situation, not knowing something could result in illness, injury, or death. The problem is knowing what is important to learn, and this is where a little bit of research comes into play.

IDENTIFY YOUR NEEDS

Wherever possible, look at what your likely survival scenarios are going to be. If you live in an area of dense woodland in an arid state, then wildfires are a probability, so research the best way to prevent them, and know what to do if one should disrupt your daily life. If you live in an area that has earned the nickname of "Tornado Alley," then you have a different set of scenarios to prepare for. Hunting on the plains of the Serengeti is going to require a knowledge of desert climates should something go wrong, and if you are taking a tour of the Bayou, I suggest you brush up on how to avoid an angry alligator.

Possible required skill sets are good things to learn as well. If I am venturing out hiking or hunting, I like to know how to read a map and use a compass, I have used my GPS before, and I also have a rough idea of the terrain I am likely to encounter. If I am with others, I like to know that my first aid qualifications are up to date and that I have a first aid kit ready with items I know how to use properly.

Learning new skills is always a good idea. Not only could they prove useful in an unexpected situation, they also keep your mind and body active. Stretching yourself is the best way to improve yourself. It might be a case of reading about something in the library or online. Perhaps you'll take an evening class or join a class at the gym. Whatever it is, give it a go.

Personally, I learn best when I have a teacher. I like someone to show me the ropes and then guide me as I try things out. There are many good teachers ready to impart their knowledge on a whole range of subjects. Look for them online, in the newspaper, or at your local community center.

There are a lot of people who claim to be an expert at something, so be careful whom you choose to be your mentor. I would suggest going with a reputable company or someone who has good ratings, rather than someone who offers the cheapest price. I do believe that when it comes to learning and being trained, you get what you pay for.

Practice the skills that you learn. Keep pushing yourself, and review your knowledge so that you don't get rusty. That way, when everything is going wrong, you are far more likely to remember what to do, having tried it and mastered it before. It is also better to make those learning mistakes at a time when your life doesn't depend on it.

FEARS AND FACTS

Most of our fears are based on false beliefs or lack of knowledge. There are two main ways to develop fears. One way is to have experienced something that has led you to fear it. The other way is to have them instilled in you by someone else. There is a third one where people tend to have absolutely no idea why they fear something, but that is usually quite rare.

If you have been in a plane crash, it is very understandable that you would be scared of flying. If you have been bitten by a dog, it is understandable that you might not like dogs. These are cases where you have experienced something traumatic, and now it scares you.

More common is having fear instilled in you. This sounds much more traumatic than it is. I'm not talking about the "if you don't behave, the boogeyman will get you" sort of instilling. I am talking about the fears of the people around us being passed on to us. Usually it will be from our parents. We generally want to be like the people we idolize while we are growing up. This includes liking what they like, not liking what they don't, and fearing what they do. How many of you fear something that your mother is scared of as well?

I often saw this when I was working as a rock-climbing instructor. I would sometimes work at an indoor wall and do kids' parties. This involved belaying (holding the rope) and keeping the kids safe while they clambered up the climbing wall. These kids were so safe. They had the most experienced people in the gym tying them into their harnesses and making sure they made it up and down the wall without a problem. We would chat to the kids as a group and make sure that they felt reassured before the whole process began.

Kids are natural climbers. They don't fear getting on that wall, but time and time again, I would see this scenario: kid is happily climbing up the wall. It may be his or her second or third time. Their parent has missed the intro talk and wanders into the gym to see how their child is doing. They see the child halfway up the wall and panic. They begin to call up to their child, asking them if they are okay and telling them it's okay if they don't want to go to the top. The parent's attitude and fear of the situation begins to influence the child, and before long, the kid is in tears and saying they want to come down. I lower the child to the ground, and the kid decides that climbing is way too scary and doesn't want to give it another try. This may be the beginning of a fear of heights or a fear of trying new things or a fear of taking risks. One such experience can potentially manifest in multiple ways throughout an individual's lifetime.

Are fears limiting your life? How many of your fears are based on fact? It may be time to do some research. With fears, as with most other things, it is better to be acting from a position of knowledge rather than rumor or hearsay. Educating yourself can empower you in an emergency and free you from fears in a survival scenario.

THE COMFORT ZONE

The comfort zone is a behavioral state within which a person operates in an anxiety-neutral condition. It's usually a situation without a sense of risk—a mental space where nothing is challenging or threatening to your physical state or your mental well-being. Survival scenarios are rarely within our comfort zones.

The thing with comfort zones is that their boundaries are actually fluid. As people age, their comfort zone usually becomes smaller, but you can also deliberately expand your comfort zone, and by doing so, find that things that previously would have made you anxious don't affect you adversely at all.

The way that I do this is by engaging the things I fear. For example, for a long time I was, like a lot of people, scared of spiders. That position, initially, seemed very logical. After all, in Australia there are several species of spider that can kill you. However, as I spent more time in the Australian outdoors and encountered quite a number of big hairy spiders (and the smaller but still dangerous ones), I knew I had to do something to get rid of my fear otherwise, on every camping trip I would be a bundle of nerves, which would not only make the trip less fun but also impair my decisions, as I would always be thinking about the potential for a spider encounter. I read up on all the different spiders, learning about where they are most likely to be found, their typical behaviors, and their distinctive markings. I made myself watch them and eventually hold them. Doing all of this empowered me. Now I can pick up most spiders to get them out of the house or the tent.

If something has happened to you out of the blue, we can assume that you have experienced a state outside your comfort zone. You may also have specific fears that challenge you when they occur, or maybe just the thought of them happening challenges you. Take courage in this state, and make decisions that will ensure your success and mean you can keep expanding your comfort zone. It will undoubtedly make you a stronger person and mean that, if the unforeseen does happen to you, your past fears will be one less thing for you to worry about.

EDUCATION IN YOUR SITUATION

Once you are in your survival situation, it is not too late to educate yourself. In fact, it is vital that you continue to do so. Observe your environment, your situation, and your response to what is going on. The faster you can learn about the assets and liabilities of your environment, the more likely you are to survive. What animal signs are there? Food or foe? Where is your nearest drinkable water? What are likely to be the weather patterns in your area? Is cold or heat going to be your biggest issue? The more you can learn from your surroundings, the better prepared you can be to adapt to them and the faster they will become familiar to you. This will aid in your long-term survival and help to make your time out there more comfortable.

3.2

BE PREPARED

This next attitude is a critical step that most people miss after educating themselves. It's about acting on the information that you have just learned. You have done the research about what you need to know or do, and now you need to learn it or do it. Book that first aid course, restock your first aid kit, clean out your leaf-filled gutters, and learn how to navigate with a map and compass if your GPS batteries run out.

MAKE A LIST

Tasks might seem overwhelming at first, but writing lists tends to break a massive, seemingly impossible task into manageable, bite-size chunks. Rather than putting a task such as fireproofing your house as a list item, you could write something along these lines:

1. **Clean out the gutters.**

2. **Cut away overhanging branches.**

3. **Clean away undergrowth around the house.**

4. **Make sure all hoses are functional and reach the house roof.**

5. **Learn all roads that lead away from the house—prioritize an escape route.**

6. **Ensure that all valuable possessions are in one place and easily transportable.**

DO THE LIST

These items individually won't take much time, and over a couple of weekends are easily achieved. The advantage of lists is that there is a sense of accomplishment when we tick things off lists, which encourages us to do more.

"Be prepared" isn't the Boy Scouts' motto for no reason. Having the right gear with you if you get lost can be the difference between survival and perishing. Knowledge of the terrain you are traveling into and how best to source your basic needs in that terrain, should the worst happen, can save your life. I am a fan of thinking positively and hoping for the best, but I also am aware that I can't control the world around me, so I am going to prepare for the worst, just in case. To be the best prepared for the challenges and goals ahead of me, I try to do at least one thing on my list a day. It can be a big, full-day task, or it can be one that takes five minutes, depending on the time I have available, but simply setting and achieving that goal makes me the most prepared I can be for any given challenge.

PUSH YOUR LIMITS

People often stop before they have reached their limits of trying. It's more commonly known as "giving up."

I helped organize, and participated in, an adventure called Hike for Survival. A fellow survivalist and I hiked over a hundred miles across the Sierra Nevada mountains with only a pocketknife, We carried no food, water, or shelter and lived only on what the surroundings provided. By the third day, I was exhausted and thought that I could not go on. There were times when I stood up and almost fell again straightaway. I felt that I would have to back out of the challenge we had set ourselves. But I persevered, and by the fifth day I felt better. By the eighth day, I felt like I could have conquered the world.

Our bodies adapt. They can take much more punishment and can provide much more energy than we give them credit for. It is our minds that interfere, suggesting (often simply out of habit) that we are tired and hungry and that we can't do something because we have never done it before. Know your limits, but also know that what you perceive to be your limits is probably just the beginning of your strength and resilience. A limit is somewhere you start to push from, not where you finish.

In a situation where your survival depends on your ability to gather one more armload of firewood or hike across one more valley before dark, chances are you have it in you to keep going, no matter how exhausted you feel.

A good time to begin to practice knowing what you are capable of is when you are not in a survival situation. When you are out for a run, take a break at the top of the hill instead of the middle. Do one more rep in the gym when your muscles are burning. You will probably manage it, and the rush you get from achieving more than you thought you could is a great reward. Such achievements also demonstrate to you (and your body) that the notion of limits is pretty fluid, and something that you can directly affect by your own efforts. Once you have broken through what you thought was your maximum potential, there is nothing to stop you pushing and getting past the new "limit." Think about training to run a half marathon. You don't do it straightaway on day one; you build up to it, pushing yourself a little more each time, gradually making progress developing your abilities. What seemed impossible at first (because it was beyond your "limit") becomes achievable.

It's the same with the power of your brain. By challenging yourself mentally, you can improve upon what you thought was the limit of your knowledge. And you can keep doing this, expanding your cognitive power—there is no limit to knowledge!

I have pushed my body and mind in some situations far beyond what I had previously thought they could do. I have not yet found a situation in which I have fallen and absolutely cannot go on. I may have needed to rest and regroup for a moment, but I have always been able to get up again. I believe that we all have that ability within us, and practicing breaking your limitations barrier before you need to in a survival situation is a great way of preparing for an unexpected scenario, should you find yourself in one.

BEING PREPARED IN YOUR SITUATION

Having observed and educated yourself about your environment, being proactive about making changes is the next step. What can you do today that makes your situation better for tomorrow? In the Amazon, I knew that at dusk and dawn, clouds of hungry mosquitoes were going to flood my shelter and make my life miserable. All those bites and buzzing were driving me crazy. I observed that the sap from the copal tree was a deterrent for the mosquitoes, so I made sure that I collected the sap during the day and had piles of it ready around my shelter for when dusk came. I would light the sap at the first sign of the mosquitoes and keep it burning through that critical time as the sun set. This meant that at night, I only had one or two mosquitoes in there with me, instead of hundreds, and I could get a better sleep. I educated myself and acted on that education. Observe, plan, and act.

3.3

BE POSITIVE

How often do we hear this saying? It comes out of the mouth of every single motivational speaker I've ever heard. Be positive. It's a catchphrase that people often throw at you without a thought for telling you how to be positive when times are tough. But it is a popular phrase for a reason. It really can turn your life and a situation around, and becoming negative has been proven to hasten someone toward giving up, especially in a dire scenario.

ACKNOWLEDGE THE SITUATION

The first thing I do when I have found myself in a less-than-ideal situation is to acknowledge it. Imagine that your plane has crashed, and you are the only survivor. That's an awful situation to be in. Denial of a situation is a short-term solution and often ends badly when reality sets in, so it is important to take a realistic look at what has happened and where you are. Unfortunately, this is where most people then sit and dwell, but this is where you need to move on from.

Choosing to be negative about the situation you are in brings the focus onto, and enhances the perception of, the bad things about the circumstances. If you are in a survival situation, you may be cold, tired, and hungry, but focusing on those things will not make them go away. By concentrating on them, you can make them seem worse than they are. Choose instead to focus on what you do have, like the fact that you are alive and coherent. Looking at the things that are working for you will help you figure out how best to deal with the situation. It will allow you to discover your strengths and then use them to your advantage.

ASSESS YOUR ASSETS

Take stock of what is working for you in the situation: Are you injured? Can you function? What resources do you have? Do you know where you are? Can you build a shelter? Are you near water? The more things that you can find that are in your favor, the less you will focus on the dire scenario.

There is a difference between focusing on the negatives and assessing your weaknesses. Focusing on the negatives is complaining that you are cold. Assessing your weaknesses is realizing that you are sitting on top of a cold mountain and that, by being on that mountain, you are exposing your body to the elements, and wind and rain can exacerbate the low temperatures and make you more uncomfortable. Noting that this is a weakness in your survival plan will allow you to make a strategy and act—by moving to a warmer position out of the wind, for example.

KNOW THE DIFFERENCE BETWEEN A WANT AND A NEED

A need is something that will cause you to die if you don't have it. A want is everything else.

I was once on a television show with another person where we were placed in an extreme survival situation. He spent a lot of time focusing on things that he wanted that we were never going to be able to get access to, like hamburgers and pancakes. His constant chatter about these things kept me focused on the lack we had in the situation. I did much better mentally if I focused on what we had around us and satisfied my basic needs, rather than wishing for the impossible.

I think the Serenity Prayer says it best when it talks about having the strength to do without the things you can't have, the courage to fight for the things you can have, and the knowledge to know the difference between the two. At least that's my interpretation of it, anyway.

BE PRODUCTIVE

A question I ask myself when I am in extreme survival scenarios is "What can I do today to make tomorrow better?" Not only does it help me improve my current conditions, but it keeps me proactive and in success mode. The problem-solving aspect of the question keeps my mind from wandering to dark places and distracts me from focusing on what I don't have.

THIS TOO SHALL PASS

I have used this saying to get me through all sorts of situations where I have felt discomfort or pain, or faced something challenging, ranging from getting through a particularly hard workout in the gym to

Serenity Prayer

God grant me the serenity to accept the things I cannot change, courage to change the things I can, and wisdom to know the difference.

being so cold that I thought my toes were going to need to be amputated at the end of an expedition.

The thing to remember about discomfort is that, in most cases, it is only temporary. If you are cold, there are things you can do to become warmer. If you are overheating, there are things you can do to cool down. This saying is not a passive statement, however. It is a recognition of a situation and a starting point from which your actions can make the discomfort or danger pass and lead to a more positive mindset.

WHAT'S DONE IS DONE

Mistakes happen, plans go awry, and we all do things that we wish we had never done. It's how we get back up and keep moving afterward that defines our future moments.

In a survival scenario, time spent on regrets is time that is not spent on making the current situation better. I always try to look objectively at what has happened and say to myself, "Okay, that happened. Now what?" Time spent yelling, screaming, or throwing things about wastes valuable calories, and sulking, crying, or lamenting wastes valuable time. I reassess and make a new plan based on the outcome of what has happened.

When I was on the Hike for Survival, we experienced a GPS malfunction that took us off the edge of the maps we had. We were exhausted, it was the ninth day of living off the land, and we had about half a liter of water between the two of us. It was close to dark when we found out that we were on the edge of a deep canyon, and our exit was on the other side. We had thought we were almost home, but it turned out we had about five more hours of hiking to go, most of it in the dark. I remember that moment when we realized how much more we had to do. It took all of my strength not to cry. It wouldn't have changed anything. My next response was to stay sitting down. I didn't want to walk anymore. I was angry at my partner, as the GPS was his responsibility, but yelling at him wouldn't change the outcome either. Instead, I stood up and put one foot in front of the other. This got me out eventually and maintained the best possible relations with my partner.

I'm not saying to suppress your emotions. That's not a healthy way of doing things either. But I am saying that you shouldn't dwell on them. Acknowledge that something happened, that it wasn't ideal, and that you feel angry, upset, and disappointed. Then figure out a proactive way to move forward. Life gets better faster this way.

3.4

BE ADAPTABLE

> "It's not necessary to change.
> Survival isn't mandatory."
>
> W. EDWARDS DEMING

THE FIGHT-OR-FLIGHT MECHANISM

What is fight or flight? The sympathetic nervous system discharges when animals, including humans, are threatened, filling the body with catechol-amine hormones, the most common of which is known as adrenaline. This surge of adrenaline is a survival response, giving you a burst of energy that will hopefully result in getting away from the threat. We see this in wildlife documentaries where the speedy lion races after the not-so-agile wilde-beest, and the wildebeest is spurred by a huge burst of almost inconceivable energy and manages to get away.

Humans are no different. This was effective back in prehistoric times, when we were faced with threats such as saber-toothed cats and angry woolly mammoths, but it's not so effective in today's society, where we are rarely faced with life-threatening situations. Often, our fight-or-flight response fires off when someone almost opens a door in our face or honks their horn at us when we are standing on the side of the road. You will know that this response has happened because you will get such physical reactions as sweaty armpits, rapid breathing, an elevated heart rate, and shaking.

If your life is in immediate danger, then capitalize on the burst of adrena-line that fight or flight provides and get out of harm's way. But remember that fight or flight is designed to take over from the brain for a moment and trigger a purely physical reaction. It could end up turning into something akin to panic. Panic can be your deadliest enemy. It is the response that sends you off into the darkness in the middle of the night without a flashlight while fleeing a random noise, or leads you to believe that climbing that steep cliff without a rope is your only route to safety.

STOP, LOOK, AND LISTEN

In an unexpected situation, if your life is not in immediate danger, stop, look, and listen. From my many years in the outdoors and in the stunt world, I have this response so ingrained within me that it overrules my fight-or-flight mechanism. The first thing I do when something seems unusual is to stop. This "unusual" something could be an unexpected noise in the bushes, something crawling on my skin, or something that catches my attention out of the corner of my eye. Once I've stopped, I then look and listen. Do I recognize what I am seeing? Does the noise happen again?

If it is something crawling on my skin, how big does it feel? How fast is it moving? Is it similar to something I have felt before? Most bugs in the outdoors, even the venemous ones, will not bite or sting unless they feel threatened. Most people get stung or bitten when they are trying to get the insect off them. Identify what it is and try to remove it without causing it or you harm. In most cases, a short, sharp flick works.

Is it something bigger, like a large animal moving through the woods? Is the sound coming closer or going away? Can you work out which direction the noise is coming from? Is this a sound that you usually hear at night? If not, what does it sound like? The growl of a predator or merely the mating call of a frog?

If you learn to make stop, look, and listen your first response, rather than reacting in panic, you are taking an important step toward ensuring your survival.

FIRST ASSESSMENT

After pausing rather than reacting, the first thing to do is to assess the situation. Consider your strengths and weaknesses within that scenario. Then figure out a way to make the strengths work for you.

PROPER PLANNING PREVENTS POOR PERFORMANCE
(OR UNDESIRED OUTCOME)

Always make a plan. By weighing the pros and cons of the situation you are in, you will be able to find the best course of action.

By making a plan, you will avoid wasting time and energy trying avenues of action that will not be effective. It may seem that taking the time to plan delays action and therefore prolongs an outcome. This may be the case sometimes (like when you need to move fast to avoid an oncoming obstacle), but usually sitting down and planning saves time in the long run.

Taking time to make a plan will make you will feel proactive. In a survival situation, a feeling of helplessness can be just as deadly as the environment you are in.

Your plan should assess the seriousness of the current situation. Was it an earthquake that shook your house for a few minutes? Did your fight-or-flight mechanism take you to the street, where you joined your neighbors for a quick chat, and then you were able to return to your home, straighten the pictures, and all was okay? Was it a hurricane that has left you without power and cut you off from the nearest town for three days? In that case, you will need to be thinking about how to keep yourself warm, hydrated, and fed until power can be reestablished.

Your plan should take into consideration your personal "tool kit." This is composed of the lessons and skills that you have learned through life. The more education and skills that you bring into whatever situation life throws your way, the better your chance of coming out the other side with a positive result.

Some examples that can be considered part of your personal tool kit are:

- The knots that you know how to tie

- Whether you can read a topographic map instead of relying on the GPS

- Whether you have taken a first aid course at any point

- Whether you know methods of purifying water

You never know what may come in handy in any given situation, so count every skill as a possible bonus.

Here is the tricky part—I can't tell you what to plan. There are more possible scenarios of what life may throw your way than there are people on the planet. All I can do is tell you that by slowing down and making a plan, you are more likely to live to tell your tale than someone who runs off in a blind panic through the woods.

RISK VERSUS REWARD

When making a plan, I always consider the risk of doing that plan versus the reward I would gain. The greater the risk to my survival, the greater the reward needs to be for me to take that action. If the risk hastens me toward my death faster than the reward would stave off my death, then I won't take that course of action. Climbing a high coconut tree for the calories and energy I would gain from a single coconut isn't worth the risk. Burning more calories than I would gain, and also risking my physical safety from a fall, means that I wouldn't choose that course of action in order to survive. However, if there was no water on the island and that coconut was the difference between me dying today or lasting another day, then I would probably devise a way to climb that tree. Risk versus reward is a great way to evaluate the logic of your plan.

TAKE ACTION

From the second you realize things are looking grim, begin to do what you can to assist your survival and improve your situation. Not only will this increase the chances of making it out alive, but it will also enable you to be in better condition when you finally do get out. So once your plan is in place, take action.

Don't wait till it gets dark before trying to secure somewhere warm and safe for the night. Shelters take time to construct, and fire making can take hours, particularly without matches. Plan ahead. Find water if you can before you are thirsty. Sitting down, doing nothing, and waiting for someone to find you is a good strategy if you are lost, but it will only work in the outdoors if someone finds you before dark. (Important: I'm not telling you to travel from your last known location; I'm just asking you to be active within that area.)

CHANGE IS OKAY

It is important to remember that even though you have made a plan, it does not have to be set in stone. If it is not working for you, or the situation changes for some reason, reassess and make a new plan don't stubbornly persist with a plan that is not working or no longer working.

An example of this in a survival setting may be trying to move a heavy boulder in order to flatten out a sleeping area. It's not giving up to stop moving the boulder and find another place to sleep, if continuing to try to move the boulder wastes precious energy.

Changing something that is making a situation worse is not giving up, it is assessing a set of circumstances and acting appropriately to ensure your survival.

I CAN'T VERSUS I WON'T

I can't flap my arms and fly. That is the truth, and I am not going to jump off a cliff to test that truth.

I won't eat brussels sprouts. I say I can't eat them, but I just don't like them.

Do you see the difference between these two statements?

How many things in your life do you say that you can't do, when it's just that you haven't done them before? Are there things that you feel are not possible, but you haven't even tried them to know? In a survival situation, you may have to do a lot of things that you wouldn't do in your everyday life to get through, so I recommend being a little more open to trying things that you wouldn't normally do. No one is going to punish you for being a vegan, but you might have to eat a rabbit to get by if your life depends on it. No one is going to mock you for trying to make friction fire with wood you don't know will work, if you manage to keep yourself warm for days.

Bottom line: if you don't try, you have no chance at all of succeeding. I personally would rather try and fail than never try at all. At least if I try and fail, I have learned what not to do next time and can move on to trying something else.

CHECK FOR YOURSELF

The "experts," including me, might not have all the answers. Don't assume that because someone has told you they can do something that they can actually do it, or that if something doesn't work, that it doesn't. I personally have debunked many survival "facts" presented to me as absolutes. And things that I have never managed to make work, I have seen others succeed in.

Your attitude in a survival scenario has a huge effect on the outcome of your situation. Only you can control your attitude, but the key is knowing that you can change it for the better and begin to take the steps toward ensuring your survival.

4

Basic Needs

THE DIFFERENCE BETWEEN A WANT AND A NEED is that a need is something that if you don't have it, you will eventually die. A want is everything else. The basic needs in a survival situation are:

• Shelter   • Water   • Food   • Fire

Before I begin to delve into these needs, I am going to discuss a want that most survival guides assume you will have. It is something that makes life much easier in an emergency: a blade.

If I am asked to choose one item to take into an extreme scenario with me, it will always be a blade. A sharp and enduring edge is the most useful tool you can have with you, but it is one of the hardest things to procure in an outdoor survival scenario. For this reason, I tend to have a variety of blades scattered throughout my possessions and generally always carry at least one, depending on the activity I am participating in. My everyday carry, or EDC, generally is a Benchmade Bugout folding knife with a 3.24-inch stainless-steel blade. The reason for this is I have found that the Benchmade retains a sharp edge and is a good size for everything from gutting fish and skinning animals to finer woodworking for making traps. It is a light and subtle carry. If I am choosing a fixed-blade EDC, I would probably go no further than the Mora Bushmaster. This is a 4-inch carbon-blade knife that again is very versatile in the wilderness, extremely durable, and affordable.

There is a difference between choosing a stainless-steel or high-carbon blade, and it will come down to personal choice. Stainless steel is averse to rusting but usually doesn't retain an edge as well as high-carbon steel. However, high-carbon steel does require a bit more maintenance, such as oiling and drying in wet conditions.

If you don't have a blade, I recommend creating a sharp-edged tool in order to improve your situation. It will assist with most of your other needs. Stone edges are the most effective primitive blades, and the art of creating tools out of stone is called flint knapping. This skill requires an intrinsic understanding of the composition of rocks and a high level of technical skill that comes with many hours of practice. I don't want this to put you off trying to create blades out of rocks, though, because you aren't trying to create something pretty; you need something practical. Certain rocks will create a usable edge simply by smashing one rock against another and shattering. The rocks that work best are usually:

- **Fine grained or nongrained**
- **Somewhat brittle**
- **Uniform in texture and structure**
- **Lacking flaws**

A single-sided edge won't be as sharp as a double edge, but with a little practice, you can create a durable edge that will be able to cut cordage or slice open an animal. And you can sharpen your blade's edge by rubbing it on coarse- to fine-grained flat rocks.

Don't limit your thinking to metal or stone for a blade edge. Other materials that can work well are:

- **Shells**
- **Sharp teeth**
- **Fire-hardened wood**
- **Bone**

You can attach any of these to a wooden handle to make it safer for you to wield. Bush glue combined with some natural cordage will secure the sharp object in place.

We are a species that relies on being able to work with tools to make our situation better, and there is evidence of toolmaking that reaches back hundreds of thousands of years prior to metal knives. So don't despair if you don't have your favorite field knife on you. Get creative and know that our ancestors managed to survive without metal, and so will you.

Bone blade

Bush Glue

My favorite bush glue is a combination of tree sap (usually pine or grass tree) with some crushed charcoal and some dried, powdered herbivore animal dung. Heat the sap, mix in the other ingredients, and use it as glue.

Termite mounds can also be crushed up and mixed with water. Termite saliva contains trace amounts of a glue-like substance to create the mounds, though this is a much weaker glue and I wouldn't rely on it for my blades or weapons.

SHELTER

Exposure can kill you faster than dehydration or starvation. You can last up to three days without water, but one night in cold temperatures can be the end of you. The night temperature does not need to drop below freezing to be deadly. Even a seemingly warm night with a little bit of rain and a fresh breeze can potentially lead to hypothermia. My worst bouts of hypothermia were in the tropical Amazon jungle on a windy, rainy night where the air temperature didn't drop below 59°F.

A shelter will also prevent excess exposure to heat by providing relief from the sweltering sun.

Besides giving protection from the elements, a shelter provides a refuge, a place to gather your thoughts and to plan your next move. Having a roof over your head is going to make you feel a lot better about your situation.

Because of this, I highly recommend that if you can't get a fire going on the first day of your survival situation, you make sure that you have a shelter constructed before it gets dark.

Your body loses its heat to the environment in five different ways:

1. RESPIRATION

This happens when your body inhales cold air and works to warm it by heating that air before breathing it out. This results in a loss of body heat via your breath.

2. RADIATION

This happens when your body temperature is higher than your environment's and your body heat will exit your exposed skin to warm your environment. Your head, neck, wrists, and ankles contribute up to 60 percent of a loss of body heat, due to their increased blood flow compared to other areas of the body, so it's important to try to keep them covered.

3. EVAPORATION

This happens when the skin has expelled moisture, such as sweat, and this evaporates, causing a cooling of the skin's surface. This usually happens in hot climates, but working up a sweat in a cold climate can result in hypothermia if the skin is not covered up and dried off quickly.

4. CONVECTION

This happens with heat loss by air or water moving across the skin's surface. This includes exposure to one or more of the following: cold air, rain, and wind.

5. CONDUCTION

This happens when heat loss occurs by direct contact with an object. Heat exits the warmer object to equalize the temperatures between the two objects. This can occur when sitting or lying on cold ground or up against cold rocks.

A good shelter will take into consideration as many of these methods of heat loss as possible and work to combat them.

CHOOSING YOUR SHELTER LOCATION

In survival, calories are your greatest asset. Maintaining them is the difference between life and death, so it is imperative to use as few of them as possible. One way people tend to waste calories is by rushing into building their shelter and making the wrong type in the wrong area. This leads to having to construct another one at some stage. Taking the time to explore your options before building is essential. Locations, priorities, and materials all vary, but there are some hard rules I stick to when choosing my location.

Apart from trying to ensure that where you lie is going to be flat, make sure that the shelter:

- Isn't on or close to any insect nests or pathways.

- Isn't on or close to animal pathways or homes.

- Isn't below any tidal or flood marks.

- Isn't located on dry creek beds; even if you can't see any rain, distant rain can still cause flooding from hundreds of miles away.

- Isn't under any dead or heavy-looking tree branches.

- Has the door or entrance facing away from prevailing winds.

As a general rule, if you are on high, exposed ground, try to get down lower to a less exposed location, and, conversely, if you are on low, wet ground, try to get to higher ground. Also look for an area that has good access to water without being so close that you will suffer from the insects that usually also inhabit those areas.

Shelter location rules at a glance:

Avoid insect nests
or pathways.

Avoid animal pathways
or homes.

Avoid areas below tidal
or flood marks.

Avoid dry
creek beds.

Avoid dead or heavy-
looking tree branches.

Face entrance away from
prevailing winds.

MAKING YOUR ENVIRONMENT WORK FOR YOU

The less effort something takes for you to do, the longer you will survive in an emergency scenario. This doesn't mean being lazy with what you do, because a badly built shelter isn't really a shelter at all. This simply means that wherever you can, let nature do your job. In most environments, you will find a partially ready emergency shelter already created for you. Remember that you need to get out of the wind and rain and off the ground for a shelter to help save your life.

Some things to look out for that will make building a shelter easier:

A. **Fallen trees**
B. **Hollow logs**
C. **Root systems**
D. **Caves and overhangs**
E. **Natural hollows**
F. **Stone barriers**
G. **Snow trenches**

These types of natural occurrences can be made into a cozy home with little effort from you. You end up closing gaps and adding material to the roof, sides, and floor rather, than building an entire shelter from scratch.

You will need to ensure that a couple things are okay before inhabiting your already created shelter:

1. Make sure that it doesn't already have locals. This includes checking caves for recent animal signs and making sure any insects and spiders that share the space are friendly.

2. Make sure that it has sufficient air flow and ventilation. Although we are trying to prevent wind from moving through the shelter, carbon dioxide poisoning can occur if you don't allow some oxygen to circulate.

PROPERTIES OF A GOOD SHELTER

Creating a bad shelter is almost worse than creating no shelter at all. There is something demoralizing about making an effort to build something to protect you from the environment if it lets in the wind and rain, and you shiver through the night. A shelter will probably require daily maintenance to ensure it retains these properties, but it's easier to do five minutes of upkeep a day than to rebuild from scratch over and over.

In the Amazon, the palm leaves I used to keep my shelter waterproof in monsoon storms would wilt within days, and if I didn't put twenty fresh palms on each day, the rain would pour in. I made this maintenance part of my morning routine. It didn't take much time at all, yet ensured the integrity of my shelter.

The properties of a good shelter are as follows:

1. **Flat area to lie on:** Sleep is a very important part of your mental well-being, so the better you can make your bedding area, the better sleep you will have.

2. **Sized to fit all required occupants:** Quite often people get carried away with making large shelters, but remembering that physical work requires calories to complete, you are best off building a small shelter; it will also be easier to warm the space if it is smaller.

3. **No other inhabitants:** One way to ensure this is to clear the ground beneath your whole shelter; insects love leaf litter and will tend to be more prolific if you haven't cleared the ground.

4. **Structural integrity:** Make sure that the frame is solid and strong; you will be piling layers of sticks, leaves, and other thatching material onto that frame, and you don't want it collapsing midbuild or when you are asleep underneath it.

5. **Windproof:** Ensure that all openings are facing away from prevailing winds and, where possible, protected from the elements; build your shelter in a way that the materials you use for the walls and roof don't blow away in a storm and are thick enough to prevent most of the wind from moving through your shelter.

6. **Waterproof:** You will need far more materials than you think to keep the rain from coming in when it is stormy out. A good rule of thumb is that if you can see sunlight coming in through the shelter's roof in the daytime, the rain will get in. See thatching methods (page 70) to learn good tips on waterproofing.

DIFFERENT TYPES OF SHELTERS

There are many different types of survival shelters. If it can protect you from the chill of the earth and the elements of the sky, it can be called a survival shelter. The first form of shelter is the clothes on your back, so if you have nothing else and no time to make something, try to cover your wrists, ankles, head, and neck and sit with your back to the wind if you are in an exposed position. Anything more than this is a bonus. Keeping in mind the ways your body loses heat to the environment, pile up some leaves or grasses to get off the ground and stuff some in your shirt and pants (making sure that it is not poisonous, prickly, or occupied). This will store heat in pockets like a makeshift down jacket and prevent all your heat from escaping. The following pages feature increasingly advanced types of shelters.

The Leaf Box, see page 62

The Lean-To, see page 64

The Tepee/Humpy, see page 67

THE LEAF BOX

This is the simplest construction for a shelter and is a good one to know for emergencies. If it was late in the day and I suddenly found myself in need of a shelter to get through the night, I would use this one.

It is quick to assemble, but it is not usually that comfortable or waterproof, so don't use this construction in a long-term survival scenario. However, it will enable you to last through a night out in the wilderness. Its primary function is to get you off the ground and protect you from the wind.

The leaf box requires about eight body-length and six body-width pieces of wood. They are laid down in a crosshatch box form. Alternatively, you can do this in a ready-made hollow or ditch.

You will then need to fill the box with as much leaf litter and grass as possible, remembering that when you lie on the leaves and branches, they will squash quite flat. The idea is that you will crawl into the middle of the leaves, so you will need enough to insulate the ground and also to completely cover you to protect you from the elements. If done properly, this has the potential to keep you dry in a rain shower and warm in freezing temperatures.

One thing to be careful of is what types of critters you invite into your leaf box for the night. Some piles of leaf litter may house an ant nest, scorpions, spiders, or other creatures that will make for an uncomfortable night's sleep. Remember, at the end of the day, we are looking at survival, not comfort, so the more foliage you can pile into your box, the better.

THE LEAN-TO

A lean-to is a little more labor intensive than a leaf box, but if done properly, it is more waterproof and windproof and better for a long-term survival
scenario. Although it seems very open sided, you can fill in the ends of the
lean-to to add further protection from the wind and rain. I usually position my fire along the open edge of the lean-to, which allows me to access
a full-body warmth that bounces off the back of the lean-to and adds a
reflective heat.

To conserve energy, look for a place where the frame has partly constructed
itself. Examples of this include a fallen tree or a hollowed-out tree trunk.
Anywhere one windproof wall is already built will cut down on the labor required. One thing to note is that rock faces do not usually make good walls,
as they generally get very cold at night and suck the warmth away from
your body, rather than helping to keep you warm.

If you are unable to find a suitable natural portion for your shelter, you will
need to find two supports, such as stumps or suitably placed crooks of a
tree branch, to rest the main beam on. Make sure the main beam is long
enough so you can lie down completely underneath. Then use sticks to make
struts on one side of the main branch, securing them with string or grasses where possible. Cover these sticks with whatever thatching material is
available to you. This could be leaves, grasses, moss, bark, or even clay and
mud. The important thing to keep in mind is that you want it to be able to
withstand wind and rain.

This is also the best shelter to build for shade in extreme heat, as it will allow some wind flow as well as keep you out of the sun.

SURVIVE: THE ALL-IN-ONE GUIDE TO STAYING ALIVE IN EXTREME CONDITIONS

THE TEPEE/HUMPY

This shelter is the most labor intensive, but it is the one I would build if I found myself in a long-term survival scenario in a colder climate.

When built properly, it is waterproof and tall enough to sit in, and it gives you the option to have a fire inside that will keep you snug through a very cold night.

There are many ways of building tepees, but the best way I know is to find three long branches (around six feet long works well) that each have a fork in the end. Prop the sticks into the ground and intertwine the forks so that each of the three sticks is holding up the others, resulting in a structure that stand strong on its own. Place them wide enough apart that you can lie down within the circle they make, and ensure that they are tall enough that you can sit underneath them comfortably.

The next step is to find other sticks and fill in the gaps between your three main sticks. Then cover with branches, leaves, and other natural materials, placing them over the frame you've made. Keep going until you can sit inside and not see any daylight through the walls. Make sure that you leave a hole to crawl in and out of.

The trick with having a fire in the structure is allowing for a breathing hole in the roof of the tepee for the smoke to escape. If you are in a rainy location, you can waterproof this hole by making a cover from intertwined branches and leaves and placing it over the protruding ends of your frame, so it rests above the hole.

In a space as small as a tepee, you will only require a tiny twig fire to warm the space during the night. Locate the fire at the center of the tepee and keep it small, or else you may end up burning down your shelter, destroying all your hard work.

A humpy, or wurly, is the Australian Indigenous form of a tepee and tends to be similar in design, but with a more rounded rooftop. I would choose to make a whirly over a tepee if I was unable to find long, solid struts for the three main supporting beams.

THE A-FRAME

I can almost hear every survivalist screaming at me: "But what about the A-frame?" This shelter tends to be at the top of most survival shelter lists, but there is a good reason that I don't recommend it in my top three. In fact, I wouldn't even mention it at all except for the fact it is such a popular design, and I feel like I need to warn people away from it being their go-to. I was one of those people who thought it was the best design to build, but then on two occasions it almost resulted in my death from hypothermia, so this advice is coming from very personal experiences.

I think that the fact it looks like a tent or a house is a comfort to people, and because it has walls on more sides, there is the added psychological aspect of feeling safer.

With the A-frame, unless you have some form of man-made material like a poncho or a tarp, the roof is very hard to make waterproof at its peak. It's not impossible, and there are a few methods of weaving and thatching with an additional building piece that can help, but it is an added complication. In addition, due to its shape, it is very hard to warm the space, as a fire needs to be at one end, and this results in either very cold feet or a very cold head. By the time the heat has circulated enough to warm the space, it has leaked out through the natural roof.

I believe that when we are looking at survival skills, we need to be looking at the ancient skills our ancestors used thousands of years ago. There are very few, if any, examples of A-frame shelters in primitive societies. The lean-to, tepee, and humpy were the most common designs for a reason, and my own experiences have proven why.

NATURAL CORDAGE

This is one of those areas where bushcraft and survival share some crossover. There are books written solely about the art of making rope and cord using natural materials, and if it interests you, there are courses about it that would be a valuable addition to your personal tool kit of skills. Rope can be invaluable for many things, including building shelters, making traps and snares, and making shoes to protect your feet. I'm only going to touch on the basics of making natural cordage, as you won't die if you don't know this, but it can come in handy, especially with making a solid shelter.

Leaves for cordage

Just about any strong, flexible fiber can be used as cordage. This includes:

- Leaves
- Roots
- Stems
- Vines
- Outer bark
- Inner bark
- Grasses
- Hair
- Wool
- Animal intestines
- Animal sinew
- Animal skin

Cordage from leaves

Outer bark for cordage

Animal intestine cord

Inner bark for cordage

Cord from animal skin

Cordage from wool

Animal sinew cord

Certain types of each of these things are better for making cord than others. Your best bet is to experiment with the resources around you. Grab some grasses, and try to tie a piece around something. If it holds, it works. If it doesn't, try something else.

LEAVES Although any long, thin leaf can be utilized as cord if it is strong enough, the best leaves for cord are from plants such as aloes and yuccas that have juicy, fibrous leaves. By placing the leaf on a flat surface and scraping the juicy flesh away with a flat edge, you are left with bundles of thin fibers that can be plaited together to create strong rope.

ROOTS If you are in a swamp or wetland area, you may be able to reach under the water and into the mud to access root systems. Some roots are too brittle to use, but water-soaked ones work perfectly.

STEMS Ideal plants to use will have long, string-like fibers when you split them. You can use some stems when they are green, but most of these types of plants work best when they are dry.

VINES The woodier a vine is, the less likely it is to be good for cord. Look for a flexible vine that you can tie in a knot without it snapping. Vines work best when fresh. The drier a vine is, the more brittle it becomes.

OUTER BARK Outer bark works best when fresh. A way to find suitable outer bark is to bend a twig on the tree. When the stick breaks, check to see if the outer layer of bark is still attached on one side. Pull the inner bits apart, and see if the bark easily peels away from the inner branch. If it does, then it should make good rope. Just make sure you don't harvest bark from around the whole tree, because it will kill the tree. Instead, just remove it in patches or from branches.

INNER BARK Inner bark is best harvested and processed from dry wood. If you break a branch apart and you can peel the bark from the inner wood in long strips, then it will be good for rope. Simply peel the inner layer off the bark you have removed. It will be in long fibers and perfect to be used as is or to be reverse wrapped for extra durability.

GRASSES These include most kinds of rushes, such as bullrush and cattail. They are best used when green. If possible, try to harvest the longest leaves and cut at the base rather than pull out at the roots, so as not to destroy the resource.

HAIR/WOOL Look for the carcasses of hairy or wooly animals, or use the fur or wool from those that you hunt for food. Nothing needs to go to waste out there.

ANIMAL SKIN Again, it's best used if wet or processed to leather. Cut it into strips, and reverse wrap for a good, solid rope.

ANIMAL SINEW It's best to use sinew when it's wet. This means it doesn't need processing, and you can use it straight out of the animal. If it has dried out, then a bit of water will bring it back to a usable state. Our ancestors used to pop it in their mouth and chew it before they used it, when they didn't have an excess of water available. The good thing about sinew is that it shrinks as it dries, so it cinches even tighter, creating a good bond.

ANIMAL INTESTINES I have experimented with smaller animals and have personally found that with any animal smaller than a pig, the intestines are too weak to work well as rope. I have heard of people using smaller animals, but I have not seen it myself. The intestines require cleaning, drying, and salting to be used as rope, but if you happen to be by an ocean or salt lake, then you are in luck and can create solid rope. The intestines work best if you use the reverse wrap to create your rope (see page 77).

I don't tend to process the fibers I use for rope with shelter building; I use it in its purest form. This is because processing enough plant fibers for the amount of cordage required to tie together all beams and joins of a shelter takes a lot of time, and shelter is a priority that needs to be taken care of quickly in a survival situation. It is also possible to build a good shelter without using any rope, so if materials are scarce, don't get hung up on the need for it; just use friction and balance to make your shelter strong.

ADDING STRENGTH TO YOUR FIBERS

A simple way of remembering how to strengthen fibers is to recall that two is better than one. If I have one cord and it is breaking, by adding another strand of fiber, I am making it stronger. At a very basic level, if you have one leaf and it is breaking as you try to tie your shelter up, add another leaf to the bundle and see if it holds. Twisting the two together also adds another level of strength.

Plaiting or reverse wrapping will make your rope or cord more durable and reusable. It takes some time and resources to do, but in a long-term survival situation, rope can assist in making things to make your time out there more comfortable. The only time you should focus on making cordage first in a survival situation is making a short piece of cordage for a bow drill, if you need to get a fire going and this method is your best option.

PLAITING

The reason I recommend this as one way of making rope is that it is a technique that most of us have used at some stage in our lives, so it isn't a new skill to learn. It does the job of adding strength to fibers, and its only disadvantage is that it results in a flat rope that doesn't slide over itself nicely. This means it isn't great to use with traps and snares. As I'm all for keeping survival as simple as possible, if you can only remember how to plait, then do that to strengthen your rope.

For those who have never done a plait before, or if it has been a while, you need three strands of fiber. Tie a knot with them all at the top, and then take the outside right strand and feed it over the middle strand. Then take the outside left strand and feed it over the middle strand. Repeat until you have the length of rope you require, and tie a knot on the end.

THE REVERSE WRAP

Take a length of fibers in both hands. Start with your hands a few inches apart, and twist your hands in opposite directions until a loop forms in the fibers. Usually, I then place that loop in my mouth, but you can also pinch it between your thumb and forefinger. If you are holding it in your mouth, hold the two lengths of fibers so you have one in each hand. Twist the lengths both in the same direction until the fibers tighten, and then wrap the two lengths around each other in the opposite direction.

If you are twisting and wrapping in the same direction, your rope will unravel when you let it go. If you are twisting and wrapping in the opposite direction, the rope will pinch into itself, and this is what you want. Keep doing this until your rope is at your required length.

One thing to remember about natural fibers is that they tend to be shorter than the length of rope you require, so rather than end your rope when the fibers run out, you can splice in more fibers.

Splicing Natural Fibers

Splicing simply involves adding lengths of fiber to existing threads when they begin to get too short to wrap. It is best to add new fibers in when the existing threads are between an inch and an inch and a half long. You place the new fibers along the length of the existing fibers and continue to wrap, incorporating the new fibers in with the old. Another tip is to only add one length of thread in at a time and allow for a couple of inches of wrap before adding another length in; otherwise you will end up with a weak spot in your rope.

KNOTS

Knots are another area where bushcraft and survival overlap in such a way that I feel obligated to make the distinction. Do you need a knowledge of knots in order to survive? Absolutely not. Will it help you survive? Maybe. I firmly believe that if you know how to tie your shoelaces, then you know enough knots to survive. We've all heard the saying "if you don't know knots, then tie lots," and that sums it up for me. I have survived for over a hundred days in various locations around the world with no resources and never tied anything more complex than a reef knot–right over left and then left over right. In fact, most natural fibers won't take a complex knot in their pure form, so that knowledge wouldn't help at all. But, as I have also stated, the more knowledge in your personal tool kit, the better, so I am going to cover what I consider to be the more useful knots for a survival situation.

THE OVERHAND KNOT

It is the simplest of all knots, but the most useful in a survival situation for tying off the top of fibers if you are making cordage. Make a loop and pass the end through.

THE REEF KNOT

This is a very secure knot that is easily untied. When tying a reef knot, tie right over left, and then, instead of going right over left again, you go left over right. This knot is useful for tying the ends of rope or cordage together.

TRUCKER'S HITCH

This knot is great for cinching something tight. Tie a loop in one end of a rope (any way you like), and then feed the other end of the rope through the loop and pull down hard, tying this loose end off with a couple of half hitches.

HALF HITCH

The half hitch is a valuable knot to finish off the ends of other knots, to assist in making them secure. It's a simple overhand knot where the working end of a line is brought over and under the standing part.

Knots don't need to be fancy, and you don't have to know their names—they just need to work. If something needs to be made secure, no one will be judging you on your knot tying when they rescue you. Do whatever you can to make things safe and secure.

LASHING

Another skill that will assist with making a strong and secure shelter is the art of lashing. Lashing is the technique of winding rope in such a way that it secures two or more items together. There are many different lashing techniques, but the most important one for shelter building is square lashing. This is for lashing two branches or beams that cross.

Secure one end of the cord to one of the branches; then weave the line alternatively above and below both branches in a complete clockwise circuit. Make a loop around one of the branches before weaving the rope over and under the branches in a counterclockwise direction. Do this a few times before tying off the end of the rope with two half hitches. The more firmly you can do the looping, the more secure the lashing will be.

THATCHING

There are many different types of thatching used to make the roof of a primitive structure waterproof. I stick with the most basic method for my shelters, and that is to always start from the bottom and work upward, like the tiles of a roof. This will ensure that the overlapping layers push water to the outside of the shelter, rather than funneling it into the shelter.

SHELTER TIPS

Once your shelter is built, it is important to make sure it functions well for you in your survival situation, so here are a few final shelter tips:

Keep your shelter organized If your shelter is a mess, then it's hard to find the things you need. This may not seem like a big deal during the day, but if your fire goes out at night and you can't find more wood, being able to lay your hands on your flashlight or tinder in the dark could save your life.

Don't eat or prepare food in your shelter Your shelter needs to be a safe and comfortable place for you to sleep. Predators are usually drawn into a camp by food smells, so choose an area fifty to a hundred yards from where you sleep to make your kitchen area. Even if you don't attract the larger animals into the area, uncomfortable nuisances like ants and mice can also be drawn in by food smells, so keep your shelter as clean as possible.

Have your toilet area away from your shelter For sanitary reasons, and a level of your comfort, choose an area away from camp to make your toilet area. My only exception to this is in areas where creating a circle of urine around your camp may assist in deterring predators. But even then, make it a large circle.

Make sure you keep the things you need dry inside the shelter Seems like common sense, but sometimes I have left fire-starting tinder or items of clothing outside my shelter if it doesn't look stormy, only for a storm to soak everything. I always make sure I store a little stash of dry fire-making materials in my shelter for emergencies.

Realize you are effectively camouflaged from rescue You have made a solid shelter entirely out of natural materials. Nothing about that shelter will stand out to people searching for you, and they may pass right by you in a ground search if you happen to be sleeping. Find some way to make your location stand out to the people looking for you.

WATER

Water makes up about 70 percent of our body. It circulates through the blood and is responsible for transporting essential nutrients and oxygen to our organs. It then takes the toxins and waste from those organs and gets it out of our bodies in the form of sweat and urine. Basically, if you don't drink enough water, you are not getting good things to your organs and cells, and you aren't getting bad things out of your body.

What is enough water? Everyone has their own thoughts on this topic, and it ranges from two liters a day to six liters a day. Even scientists have trouble agreeing on this one, as every person's water needs are different, depending on such things as their height, weight, gender, and propensity to sweat, and even the different ways an individual processes water.

Personally, I work on three liters a day, but I have survived for twenty-one days on less than a liter a day with no lasting adverse side effects.

Dehydration occurs when your body loses more fluids than it consumes. Most people don't consume enough water, and when dehydration symptoms occur, we often misdiagnose them and combat them with diuretics (tea or coffee) and medication that can further exacerbate the problem.

(opposite) Digging for water; see page 90.

Next time you exhibit any of the following symptoms, try drinking a big glass of water and waiting for ten minutes to see if it helps.

Dehydration symptoms include:

- Dry mouth
- Tiredness or fatigue
- Thirst
- Lack of urination (you should be peeing once every few hours)
- Dark-colored urine
- Headache
- Dizziness

If untreated, dehydration can progress into foggy thinking, the inability to make rational decisions, and eventually seizures, brain damage, and death.

It is largely accepted that you can live approximately three days without water, but this can change rapidly, depending on your circumstances. If it is hot, you can die without water in less than a day. If you are exerting a large amount of effort and sweating a lot, you may last less than that. Even if it is cold and windy, you may be losing more moisture than you think.

Ways to prevent water loss:

- Don't exert yourself.

- Keep cool; stay in the shade where possible.

- Do not lie on hot ground.

- Keep talking to a minimum.

- Don't eat, or eat very little, as digestion requires water.

My first rule about water: always carry more water than you think you will need. It is your most precious resource. All your other equipment won't mean anything if you can't get enough water.

If we are sticking to the rule of threes, where we agree that we can last three minutes without oxygen, three hours in extreme cold, and three days without water, then water quickly becomes a priority after making sure that we can shelter ourselves sufficiently to stay warm.

There are many different methods of sourcing and purifying water. I will go into greater detail in the climate sections for ones that are specific to locations, but in this section, I will discuss the most successful and popular methods that can be utilized in most areas. I will divide the purification into techniques that don't require any specialized equipment, and also popular ones that rely on you being prepared the moment that an outdoor trip turns into a survival scenario.

Vegetation can provide water.

FINDING WATER

- **Collect rainfall** If you happen to be in a location that does get some rain, your best bet for collecting pure, drinkable water is from the sky. Craft containers out of anything you can find. There is a lot of garbage in the world, so if you can find old water bottles or cans, cut the top off and use large leaves to funnel the water into these vessels. Get creative. Bamboo cut in half can work as gutters on your shelter and can direct water into bamboo containers. Bark works just as well. Natural divots in rocks will catch water in pools, and some plants catch water at the base of their leaves. A rainstorm can be a great asset if you are prepared for it.

- **Observe vegetation** Vegetation cannot grow without a water source; however, some desert plants have adapted to survive with very little. If you can get to a high point, try to locate an area where the vegetation grows larger, lusher, and greener than its surroundings. This is a good indicator that water may be in that area.

- **Dig for water** Look for damp mud or soil patches, and dig there. Soon your hole should start to fill with muddy water. Allow the sediment to settle before drinking. You can also drain the water through your clothing if you are in desperate need. If there are no moist patches, try digging on the outside of the bends in a dry riverbed. When the river did have surface water, these areas were where it was slowest moving, so water is more likely to have seeped into the underlying ground. You may need to dig for over a foot before water appears. If it hasn't appeared by then, try a hole in another location.

- **Look at the landscape** Water always flows downhill, so lower-lying areas and valleys are a good place to look if there are not obvious areas of vegetation.

- **Observe animal tracks** Most animals need water to survive as much as we do and, over the course of days, will make their way to the closest water source to slake their thirst. Well-worn animal paths are a good indication that water is nearby. Animals may be scattered to feed, but their paths will merge on the way to water, creating an arrow-like pattern to guide you. It's a good idea to note if the tracks are fresh, because animal paths may stay obvious for a long time in dry areas after the water source has dried up. It might also take a moment to figure out which direction to travel, but following the arrow pattern will give you a good indication as soon as a fork in the road is discovered. One major exception to this rule is reptiles. They don't require a water source, as they are able to access enough water to survive from dew and their food. So following snakes and lizards, especially in a desert setting, probably won't help you at all.

- **Bird behavior** A lot of seed-eating birds require a drink every day, so observing bird flight patterns can also be a good indicator of water. If the birds are flying in a tight formation or line, they are generally heading toward water. If they are flying in a wide, more relaxed formation, they are generally flying away from water. It's also good to note that smaller birds need to be closer to a water source, so finding smaller birds such as wrens and bee-eaters is a good sign.

- **Insect activity** Bees are a great indication of water nearby, although they will travel up to two and a half miles to get it if they need to. Many types of wasps also require a water source nearby, as they build their nests predominantly out of mud. Keeping an eye out for the direction bees and wasps are traveling may give you some idea of a direction to travel if your water situation is dire.

COLLECTING WATER

Most of these methods involve having some kind of plastic bag or plastic sheet with you in order to collect water. They also require you to be in an area where there is an abundance of green leafy trees. The first method works well in desert conditions, where you have hot days but clear, cooler nights, and requires no plastic.

- **DEW COLLECTING** Dew forms as temperatures drop and objects cool down. This forces water vapor in the air around cooling objects to condense. This then collects on the objects. Leaving clothing outside at night may result in being able to wring out some moisture in the morning. Tying clothing around your legs and walking through the grass and bushes will also transfer this moisture to your clothes, and you should be able to wring out enough to keep you sated.

- **LEAF CONDENSATION** If you have a clear plastic bag of any sort, then this method is a good way to collect drinking water. It is a passive collection method, meaning that you don't have to do much work to gain the water. This is important, keeping in mind that some methods of procuring water can burn more water than they obtain.

In the early morning, place a small stone in the bottom of the plastic bag and wrap your bag around a bunch of leaves on a tree branch. You need to choose a branch that extends beyond the main canopy; you are looking for one that will be in full sun during the day. Tie the top of the bag tight around the branch, and leave it over the course of the day. If the area is heavily wooded, you may need to change the branch halfway through the day if it becomes covered in shade.

Water naturally travels from the trunk of the tree to the leaves, where it transpires into the air. Covering the leaves with the bag means this water condenses in the plastic and will collect in the bottom of the bag. You may want to swap branches and leaf bundles as the day progresses to sure a constant supply.

16

- **SOLAR STILL** This method of water collection will require a clear plastic
sheet and a container to collect water in. Dig a hole about three feet long
and a foot deep in a place that gets the most sun throughout the day.
Place the container in the center of the hole, and surround it with green
leafy material. The fleshier the vegetation, the more moisture it is likely
to contain. Place the plastic sheet over the hole, making sure that you
seal the sides. Place a stone in the center of the sheet, so that it forms a
low point in the plastic over the container. The sun will cause the moisture to evaporate from the vegetation and condensate on the plastic,
where it will form drops of pure, drinkable water that will slide into the
waiting container.

  This method can be used to distill the salt out of seawater and the impurities out of urine. It can also be used where the ground is moist but not
puddling, to draw the moisture out of wet soil.

- **SALTWATER STILL** There are many different and complex ways to desalinate salt water. The basic idea is that you need to heat the salt water so that the pure water rises from it as steam. This steam then needs to be collected and cooled in such a way that it reverts to liquid form, this time without the salt in it. If you have a complex array of pipes and collection pots and perhaps some duct tape, you could rig up an efficient system to keep many people satisfied with drinking water indefinitely. However, this is a lot of equipment to rely on having, and you can achieve a smaller version of this with a clear water bottle and a can. You won't be able to process as much water at a time, but it will help to keep you alive.

Cut the bottom off the water bottle and the top off the can. Fold the bottom sides of the water bottle up into itself to create a gutter to catch the desalinated water. Fill the can with salt water, and place it inside of the water bottle. Make sure the lid is on the water bottle, and place your still in the full sun. The water will evaporate from the can in the heat and re-form on the inside of the water bottle, sliding down the sides to be caught in the gutter. This method takes time and sunny weather, so make sure you set this up way before dehydration sets in. If possible, make multiple setups.

PURIFICATION TECHNIQUES

If you are ever asking yourself about whether you need to purify ground-water before you drink it, the answer is yes. Ninety percent of the world's groundwater is polluted in some way, including from chemicals, bacteria, viruses, parasites, or salts. And that pollution may not be obvious. The idea of drinking clear, bubbly, running water may be more appealing than drink-ing out of a muddy puddle, but you never know what is upstream from you. If something has died in a lovely pool and its rotting bacteria is floating down that clear, cool water, it will make you very sick. Always purify water if you can.

This is where I need you to get flexible with your thinking. If not drinking that water WILL lead to your death but drinking it MIGHT save your life, drink the water. Just exhaust all other options first.

Most water pollutants will act as poison in your body. When your body is poisoned, it wants to purge the poison out, and it does so by making you vomit, sweat, and have diarrhea. These are all things that quickly dehydrate your body and hasten you toward death if you can't replenish your fluids. By drinking the water, you may feel like you are saving your life when in fact you are ending it faster.

It is crucial for you to remember that if you drink water without purifying it, you run the risk of becoming sick. If you have any way of purifying the water, do so before consuming.

(opposite, above) Purification by straining; see page 98.
(opposite, below) Purification by boiling; see page 102.

WATER PURIFICATION—WITHOUT GEAR

- **STRAINING** The absolute minimum you should do with murky water is to strain it. It also should be the start of any other technique if your water has chunks in it. This simply involves passing it through some clothing so that the larger impurities are filtered out. This only removes floating particulates; it doesn't take out any poisons.

- **WATER WELL** This water-straining technique is often referred to as a gypsy well. It's simply the method of digging a hole a few yards from a murky water source and allowing the ground to do the filtering for you. If you are there for a while, you can line the well with sticks to prevent the sides from falling in. Over time, all sediment should sink to the bottom, leaving you with clear water to drink. Just remember, this is an emergency water source and can't be trusted not to contain impurities.

  This method can also be tried on the coast to source fresh water by the ocean. Dig a hole behind the first layer of sand dunes above the high tide mark. The sand hills trap rainwater behind them, and it tends to float on top of the denser layer of salt water beneath it. The hole only needs to be deep enough to expose the first inch or so of water; otherwise, salt water will flood in and pollute the fresh water.

- **STRAINING WITH CHARCOAL** If you are unable to get a fire burning to purify your water but have had a fire in the past or happen to be in an area that a bushfire has swept through, you can use the fire's by-product of charcoal to fashion a homemade water filter. This should not be your first choice, as it may not be completely effective, but it is better than sucking the water straight out of the stream or puddle. Simply crush up the charcoal and layer it in the fabric you are straining through. Charcoal has the amazing property of being able to absorb toxins from water.

  Charcoal is also a good remedy for upset stomachs and bloating. Crumble it into a powder, and mix it with water. Ingest it to help eliminate toxins, if you suspect you have consumed something that may have poisoned your system.

Grass

Pebbles

Sand

Charcoal

Natural Water Filter

- **NATURAL WATER FILTER** In an open-ended container, place alternating layers of pebbles, sand, grass, and charcoal. It works best when the container tapers to a smaller end. Passing the water through the pebbles, sand, and grass will remove the sediment from the water, and the charcoal should kill any bacteria.

  The container can be created with bamboo or flexible strips of bark.

What if you don't have a container?

The answer to this is the hot-rock boiling technique. You will need a fire for this method, but other than that, all you need is a waterproof vessel (a large bamboo stem or bark bowl works nicely) and some rocks a little smaller than your fist. Place the rocks in the fire to heat them up. If you have some plastic, you can also dig a pit, line it with plastic, and fill the pit with water. Place the hot rocks into this pit, making sure that you do not get the rocks on dry plastic.

Be aware that river rocks have the tendency to explode, due to tiny pockets of air or water trapped in them that expand when heated. This can be dangerous, with small, hot shards showering in all directions.

Once the rocks are red hot, use two sticks to pull them out of the fire and put them in the water in your vessel. You may need to repeat this several times to get a rolling boil, but eventually the rocks will boil the water.

WATER PURIFICATION—WITH GEAR

Assuming that you were prepared when you headed into the outdoors or a disaster struck, here are some of the more popular ways to purify water:

- **BOILING** Boiling is the most effective way of making your water fit to drink. That's why a pot or steel cup is always in my top-four items to bring into a survival scenario. If you have something to boil water in and a fire, then you can make water safe to drink. Bringing the water to a rolling boil (where the bubbles are continuously moving from the bottom of the water to the top) will kill any bacteria, viruses, or parasites that could make you sick.

If you don't have a pot to boil water in, it is possible to boil water in a plastic container. Don't put the plastic container directly on the fire, as the plastic will melt; but if you can suspend the bottle above the fire, the water will boil before the plastic melts. This is because the melting point of plastic is higher than the boiling point of water. This is not an ideal method of water purification, as heating the plastic releases carcinogens into the water, but it will save your life, so it is worth doing for the short term. Keep in mind that you may not see bubbling when the water is at the boiling point due to the lid being on the bottle, so keep an eye out for small bubbles forming on the bottom to indicate it has reached that stage.

- **WATER FILTER** There are many water filters on the market, and they are a great way of removing impurities from your water source. They usually work by either a pumping action or gravity, and send the water over a filter designed to specifically remove impurities from water. They can purify large amounts of water quickly and can last years when maintained correctly. They are a great asset to carry in your pack, as they will allow you to carry less water if you know you will come across water sources.

- **LIFE STRAW** This is the smaller version of a water filter. The advantage of the straw is that it is lighter and smaller but is really designed for emergency use only. It works as a normal straw does, so you can only drink what you can take in at the time, whereas a larger filter allows you to pump enough to store for later.

- **WATER PURIFICATION TABLETS** These tablets typically contain chlorine, chlorine dioxide, or iodine. These chemicals deactivate bacteria, viruses, and parasites and make the water safe to drink. They usually require some kind of resting period between putting in the water and being able to drink. Make sure that you always follow the instructions, and be aware that they are not necessarily good for your body with long-term use.

  Iodine is commonly found in first aid kits, as it is great for disinfecting cuts. It can also be used to clean your water, but it can leave it tasting strange. A good rule of thumb is five to ten drops per liter, leave for five minutes, and then drink. Iodine is not recommended for people with thyroid issues, so use other methods if this applies to you.

Finally, **never drink your own urine**. This theory has been made popular by a famous survivalist, but very rarely works. If you are going to drink your own pee, it needs to be before you are dehydrated, when your pee is a majority water rather than full of toxic waste products. Usually, people resort to drinking their own pee when the situation has gotten dire and they are so thirsty that they see no other option. By then, their urine is dark and full of toxins and bacteria that the kidneys have filtered out. Introducing this back into your system leads to you becoming more dehydrated and stresses your kidneys, which can cause them to shut down. This leads to you dying faster than you would have without drinking the pee.

If your life depends upon it and you have no way to purify the water you have found, drink sparingly the clearest, most rapidly flowing water you can find.

FOOD

Out of all your survival needs, food might be the most confusing one to come to terms with. There is a comfort to having three solid meals a day, and we are taught that to have any less is to be "starving." Food is the one need that you can last the longest without. On average, people can last up to three weeks without food. This will depend on your body type and how many calories you are burning in a day, but it does give you plenty of time to take care of your other needs before worrying about filling your stomach. I find that I am most effective without food on days one and two, and then again on days five to twelve in an extreme survival scenario. Days three and four seem to fall under detoxing and getting used to a new normal. No matter how healthy our diet is prior to an extreme survival scenario, our bodies are used to all sorts of chemical additives that can cause fatigue, headaches, and nausea when we are deprived of them.

A healthy body can survive for some time on the reserves in its tissues, but a lack of food eventually makes it increasingly difficult to make good decisions, keep warm, recover from hard work, and fight off infections.

The bad news is that food can be quite an elusive thing in a survival scenario, if you don't know what you are looking for or how to get it. There are millions of different plants and animals throughout the world, so I am going to make things as simple as I can to help you make good eating choices in your location.

There are two different types of food groups in the wild: flora (plants) and fauna (animals). While plants may be easier to gather since they don't run away, animals provide far more energy when consumed. It becomes a calories-in-versus-calories-out equation that you need to assess for yourself. If you can trap or hunt animals without burning too many calories, then the reward in energy is worth the effort. If you will burn an excess of calories chasing down your prey, then it may be best to gather wild edible plants instead. What best suits your situation?

SURVIVE: THE ALL-IN-ONE GUIDE TO STAYING ALIVE IN EXTREME CONDITIONS

4.3.1

PLANTS

As always, there are exceptions to every rule of thumb in survival, so if you are 100 percent certain of your plant identification and you know something is edible even if it goes against the advice of my general rules of what not to eat, eat it. **If you can't positively identify it as something you can eat, don't eat it until you have worked through my toxin testing steps, especially if it has any of the characteristics of the items on my list of what to avoid.**

WHAT TO AVOID

Time and time again, people will hold up examples of edible, nutritious plants that have some of the following characteristics. I understand and agree that there are plants that won't kill you that fit these rules. However, most of the time plants that are on the list have the potential to make you sick or hasten your death. Since we all must start somewhere in a disaster scenario, I recommend you avoid consuming all plants that you can't identify that fit in these categories:

- Mushrooms or fungi

- Milky or discolored sap

- Beans, bulbs, or seeds inside pods

- Spines, fine hairs, or thorns

- An almond or peachy scent

- Grains with pink, purple, or black spikes on them

- Red plants

- Fruit that divides into five segments

- Three-leaf growth patterns, i.e., three leaves on the same twig stem

- Trumpet- or bell-shaped flowers

- Stems with leaves on opposite sides

The next move to finding out what is edible in the plant kingdom around you is to experiment. The important thing about experimenting with eating plants is that you take your time and **do all the toxin testing steps**.

Beans, bulbs, seed pods:
Rosary Peas

Mushrooms or fungi:
Death Cap Mushroom

Three leaves:
Poison Ivy

Five-segment fruit:
Jamaican Ackee

Trumpet-shaped flowers:
Angel's Trumpet

Leaves on opposite sides:
Poison Sumac

TESTING FOR TOXINS

There is a myth that if an animal is eating a certain plant, then we can eat that plant. This is false information and could get you killed. Animals have very different digestive tracts to ours, and some have evolved to remove certain toxins from plants to survive eating them. The animal that has the closest digestive system to our own is the monkey, and even then, monkeys can consume certain things we can't. I personally have survived in the jungle eating the fruits I have observed monkeys eating. They will even be so good as to throw some at you or drop it to the ground to save you the trouble of climbing the tree yourself. I always put that fruit through my test for toxins before eating.

THE TOXIN TEST

1. **Inspect:** Make sure it doesn't look rotten or moldy; remove any insects or insect casings.

2. **Smell:** You are looking for an almond or peachy smell; if it smells like marzipan or peach, discard immediately.

3. **Skin irritation:** Wipe the plant on the inside of your wrist, which is delicate and more likely to react to an irritant; if your skin gets red or swollen, or develops a rash, discard the plant.

4. **Lips:** Wipe the plant on the inside of your lip; if irritation occurs, wash the area thoroughly and discard the plant.

5. **Swallow:** Take a small piece of the plant, consume it, and do not eat anything else for five hours; monitor your body reaction for nausea, vomiting, diarrhea, faintness, or excess fatigue.

6. **Eat:** Consume small amounts at first, gradually building up if there are no adverse effects.

This might seem like a long process for each plant, but these steps could save your life. I was once advised by an "expert" that a certain heart of palm was safe to eat. I had never heard of a heart of palm that wasn't edible, so

I consumed the plant. After a few mouthfuls, my throat felt tight and my tongue was fuzzy. I ceased eating the palm and wiped my hands on my legs to get rid of the sap. Immediately, my fingerprints became raised and swollen patterns appeared on my legs. The sap had irritated my skin. If only I had followed my toxin test steps, I never would have consumed that plant and risked my life.

If you do become sick from something you have eaten, the following actions may provide you with some relief:

- Drink a lot of water if you have it to spare

- Induce vomiting

- Eat some crushed charcoal

- Mix some white wood ash to a paste with water and consume

The charcoal possesses properties that bind toxins to its particles and aid in elimination from the body. White wood ash can have an alkalizing effect on the stomach.

Don't limit yourself to certain parts of the plant. A lot of edible plants can be consumed from tip to root. Experiment with:

- Leaves and stems (the younger, the better)

- Roots and tubers

- Fruits

- Nuts (may need boiling to get out all of the tannins)

- Seeds and grains

- Flowers

- Inner bark (raw, boiled, or roasted)

- Lichen (soaked overnight and boiled thoroughly)

Although it is hard to know what will be in your specific area, there are some easily identifiable plants that are prolific around the world and are good to know and be on the lookout for.

COMMON EDIBLE PLANTS

COCONUTS Found on over 65 percent of the world's coastlines, coconuts are easily identifiable and hard to confuse with any other plant. Mature, ripe coconuts contain a clear liquid that is great for hydration, and the flesh of the coconut can be consumed both from the green coconuts and the dried brown nut. Rather than climbing the tree, see if you can find a long, forked stick to knock the coconuts to the ground.

PALMS Heart of palm is the edible inner bark found in the top of the tree between where the oldest leaves begin and the youngest leaves end. The trunk is usually a darker brown color, and the indicator is a clearly defined line between there and a lighter green area where the leaves begin. Cut this area off with a knife or sharp rock, and peel off the outer layers. The super-soft white part in the center is the edible part. Make sure to run through the toxin testing steps first to see if that palm is edible for you.

BAMBOO Easily recognizable, as most species look very similar, long, straight bamboo stalks are jointed and hollow and often grow in thick stands. You can consume the young shoots found at the base of the plant. Cut them off at the base, and peel away the outer layers to expose the white inner flesh. While it is okay to eat bamboo shoots raw for a little while, it is best to boil or roast them if possible, as the raw bamboo contains traces of cyanide that can eventually lead to weakness, confusion, loss of consciousness, and death.

STINGING NETTLES This is one of those plants that goes against my rules of thumb about what to avoid. It is found alongside most rivers and creeks in temperate climates all over the world. Stinging nettles have small hairs that act as an irritant if they come in contact with skin, but these hairs are easily neutralized by scraping or boiling. Nettles are one of the most nutritious wild edibles, containing more iron than spinach and high levels of calcium, fiber, and vitamin C. It will be hard to avoid getting stung in the harvesting process, but the sap of the nettle actually provides a soothing relief from the sting. It's best to harvest the nettles when they are young and not flowering.

CATTAILS This plant can be found in wetlands all over the world. The green seed head can be consumed raw but is best boiled and eaten like corn on the cob. When the seed head is pollinating, collect the pollen, add water, and make it into dense, nutritious cakes to cook by the fire. The young shoots can be gathered, peeled, and eaten raw or boiled. The roots can be dug up and cooked like potatoes, or dried and ground down into a flour that can be used for making flatbreads or added to stews as a nutritious thickener.

SEAWEEDS If you happen to find yourself by the coast, it is good to know that there are no poisonous seaweeds. There are some that may act as a slight laxative or diuretic, but none of them will result in your death when consumed. Eating a small amount and increasing the serving over time will show you which ones may have this effect. It's best to eat seaweeds fresh rather than if they have been lying on the beach for a while, and consume them quickly or dry them for future use when you pick them, as their composition changes quite rapidly once harvested. Seaweeds can be high in iodine, so if you have a thyroid problem, it is best to consume them in small doses.

FAUNA

As a general rule, the flesh of all land mammals is edible. This means if you can catch it and kill it, you don't have to be worried about knowing exactly what it is or subjecting it to any toxin tests.

I like to divide the animals around me into two simple groups: predators and prey. This is another version of my risk-versus-reward calculation. If something is likely to kill me, it's the predator and I'm the prey. These animals feature as a high risk compared to reward. If I can kill an animal without much danger to myself, then it is low risk, high reward. Once I have distinguished between my predators and prey, I can then look at what animal food source I have around me.

Keep in mind that in a lot of countries, harvesting certain animals is illegal either all year-round or during parts of the year without a permit. Trapping and snaring animals is also illegal in some countries, as it is an indiscriminate form of hunting. This means you can't choose the animal that your trap will catch. Know the local laws surrounding hunting and trapping, but remember that in a survival situation, these laws are waived if you have broken any of them in order to save your life.

EDUCATE YOURSELF

The worst thing you can do when hunting in a survival scenario is to throw yourself into the situation without educating yourself. You risk scaring away your viable food sources (perhaps for good) and also wasting valuable time and energy on failed hunts.

Moving silently and slowly through your surroundings, listening for sounds, following game trails, and checking out prints by water sources will provide you with valuable information about what animals may be in the area. Animals tend to be creatures of habit and will often frequent the same watering holes, feeding areas, and bedding-down areas. This will enable you to learn how best to make a kill or what traps to set.

The information you are trying to gather will include:

- **What animals are in your area—size of groups and type**

- **Where they drink**

- **Where they eat**

- **Where they hang out during the day**

- **The paths they follow**

- **How aggressive they are**

- **Their strengths and weaknesses**

Most mammals move at first and last light, choosing to bed down in the heat of the day.

Signs that will help you find the animals in your area include:

TRACKS Pay careful attention to the ground around you. Mud by watering holes usually gives a clear indication of what is drinking there. Animals like to move through the bush the same way as humans do—on unobstructed paths and walkways. They will often follow the same path, leaving clear trails for you to follow. Depending on the weather and soil type, you can get a sense for when an animal last went down that path. Things to be aware of are:

- **When it last rained; if the track has raindrop marks evident on it or if that track was made since the last rain.**

- **How windy it is; if the soil is loose or sandy, the wind will soon erase all signs, so a track could have been made very recently if it is obvious in the sand.**

- **If the track is dry or wet; an animal exiting water recently will leave a wet track.**

To start to understand the time frame of tracks in your area and weather conditions, place an obvious footprint of your own in the ground and observe what happens to it over time.

DROPPINGS Animal scat can reveal some of the most valuable information about the animals in the area. Don't be squeamish. You will have to get in there and have a good look to find out the information you need. Droppings can tell you:

- **The animal type, if you know what types of animals leave what type of droppings.**

- **What they eat:** Is there hair in the droppings, suggesting a carnivore or omnivore, or are they mainly vegetarian? This information can also help you know what to bait traps with.

- **The size of animal.**

- **When they were around:** If the droppings are very fresh, they will have a coat of moisture or slime on them; after an hour or so, they can still be wet but flies are usually buzzing around the droppings at this stage; dry droppings are usually a day or so old, depending on your environment.

OTHER SIGNS Some animals make it obvious that they have passed by. This includes destruction to the vegetation from feeding or rubbing against it. Clawed climbing animals will leave holes and claw marks on the tree trunks. Pigs and deer will wallow and "root" around in the grass and mud, leaving dig marks with obvious hoof prints in them. Burrowing animals will test the ground for new digs, leaving scrapings with paw marks in them as well as their obvious burrow homes. Animals may also be digging for food, such as termites and ant nests. Grubs burrow into tree trunks and branches, leaving perfectly round holes as a clue to their whereabouts. Any signs of disturbance that aren't from your habitation may be a clue to what you could eat.

4.3.2.2

KEEP YOUR OPTIONS OPEN

Mammals tend to be the obvious food of choice in a survival situation, since most people are used to eating them, but there are all sorts of animals that will keep you alive out there:

REPTILES

Snakes and lizards can be a great food source. Treat all snakes as if they are venomous, unless you are 100 percent certain they are not. Many venomous and nonvenomous snakes look alike, and the myth about their pupil shape is a dangerous misconception that can lead to you getting killed.

A long, forked stick is a good method of pinning down a snake. Make sure that you pin down the snake close behind its head, as they are extremely flexible and can spin back and bite you if not properly pinned. If you have a blade, cutting off the snake's head is the quickest way to dispose of the snake, but a rock to the head is as effective. Just make sure the snake is dead, not stunned, before processing it further.

A snake's fangs can retain their venom for a long time after the snake is dead; make sure you dispose of the head, fangs down, so no one will accidentally puncture themselves.

Personally, having lived off snake for quite some time in a survival scenario, I prefer the taste of the venomous snakes to the nonvenomous, but in a risk-versus-reward scenario, the nicer taste isn't worth risking your life over.

When preparing larger snakes and lizards to eat, slice them from anus upwards, and remove the guts before cooking. You can place the whole reptile on the coals, cut into pieces, and kebab, or cut into chunks and boil for a nutritious soup. Sometimes you will have the added bonus of eggs, which are usually creamy and delicious cooked on a hot rock or boiled. Smaller lizards can go straight on the fire or kebab style on sticks and don't require gutting before consumption if you cook them well.

Turtles and tortoises are generally a little easier to catch than other reptiles and are not venomous, but in my experience, there isn't a lot of meat on land turtles. They tend to be mostly hollow under the shell, but if the turtle has good, chunky legs and a long fleshy neck, then it will be worth your while. The shells will make valuable pots for you to catch water in or use for storage.

Frogs are edible and easy to catch, once you get the hang of it. Some people like the grabbing-hand method, but other people prefer a thin spear with multiple prongs on the end as their frogging weapon of choice. While there is not much meat on a frog, their legs are a delicacy in some countries for a reason. If you get good at frogging, you will be able to provide a decent meal for yourself. They are best hunted at night, which makes it harder if you don't have a light source, but they will also be prevalent during and after rains, so it is worth venturing out from your shelter to take a look if you are in a swampy or tropical region. Some toads can be eaten, but they usually secrete a toxin from their skins that make them best avoided.

Avoid toads.

Toads have shorter legs and tend to have lumpy backs.

If you are unsure if what you have is a toad or a frog, the main way to tell them apart is that frogs have long legs in relation to their body and tend to jump, whereas toads have shorter legs and prefer to crawl around. Frogs also have smooth back skin, whereas toad's backs are lumpy. However, there are exceptions to this rule, so if in doubt, don't eat it. **Avoid brightly colored frogs, as they can be extremely poisonous.**

BIRDS

If you can manage to find a nesting site for birds or a place where flocks gather, you can be assured of a good meal. Bird flocks can be hard to sneak up on because there are so many eyes watching for predators, but if you can figure out a pattern on where they roost or hang out during the day, you can make your way to the area before they get there and set up a hide. A hide is merely a place of camouflage where you can sit and your prey can't tell that you are there. If you build a hide, try to build it when the birds are not in the area, and then give them a few days to get used to it before you use it. I find that throwing a heavy stick into a flock of birds is the best way to hunt them in a primitive setting. If the stick is weighted heavier on one end, it will spin into the flock and have a greater chance of hitting one and either injuring it or killing it.

If I want to preserve the feathers for further use (they can greatly contribute to warmth and comfort), I generally skin the bird as I would any mammal. The skin comes off with the feathers still attached, which makes them much more manageable, and you can gut and cook the bird over an open fire. You can also pluck the bird, gut it, and cook it. Remember, everything can be an asset to you in a survival situation, so don't throw away the feathers.

If you can find a roosting area, don't forget to check for eggs. They can be consumed raw or cooked. Don't take all the eggs. Leave some to hatch in case your survival scenario stretches into the long term.

INSECTS

Eighty percent of the world's population eats insects on a regular basis. They are a very good replenishable source of protein. If you can get your mind around using them as a food source, they can be what gets you out of your situation alive.

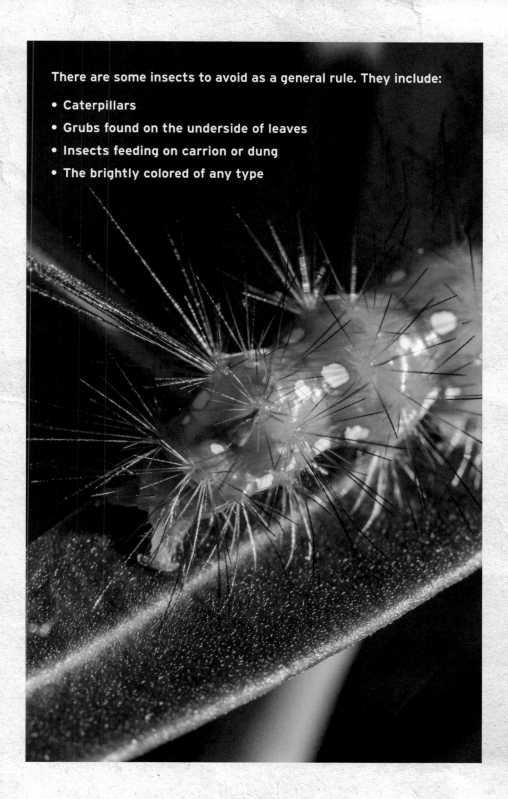

There are some insects to avoid as a general rule. They include:

- Caterpillars
- Grubs found on the underside of leaves
- Insects feeding on carrion or dung
- The brightly colored of any type

Go-to insects:

- **Grasshoppers, locusts, crickets, and cicadas**
These can be eaten whole, but I usually pull off the head, as the guts comes out with it, and thread the bodies on a small twig to roast over the fire. The easiest way to catch them is to swat them from a distance with a leafy branch. This stuns them and makes them much easier to catch. Be aware that if you have an allergy to shellfish, you may also have an allergy to crickets, grasshoppers, and cockroaches, so eat with care.

- **Grubs** These can range from small firefly larvae in the Amazon to the large wood moth larvae found in most parts of Australia. As awful as they sound to eat, grubs are a classic case of "you are what you eat." If the grubs are located inside nuts or still-living trees and roots, they tend to have a nutty flavor when eaten raw, and akin to buttery nut popcorn when eaten cooked. If the grubs are in rotten logs or dirt, they will have a woodier flavor. They are all still amazingly high in protein and a good source of fat, which can be hard to come by in a survival situation. The best way to figure out if a grub is in a tree or nut is to look for a hole. If there is one hole, the grub is generally still in there. If there are two close together, then the grub has probably hatched and left. Breaking open rotten logs is also a good way to locate them.

- **Bees** Most active during the day, bees return to the hive at night. If you locate a hive (watching the common direction bees are flying can be an indicator), then wait until it is near dusk and find a way to transport smoky fire to the entrance. This could be on water-soaked bark or in a container, if you have one. If possible, you can build a smoky fire close to the entrance of the hive. The smoke needs to be blowing into the hive to confuse the bee's pheromone production. It eventually causes them to become sleepy and pass out. You can then collect the bees, the honey, and the bee larvae. All are delicious and edible. The larvae can be eaten raw or cooked. The honey is best raw, and the bees are best cooked with the stinger removed. European bees roam as far as two miles from their hives, but Australian native bees will be no more than 500 yards from their hives when foraging. Wasps are also edible but have a small risk versus reward factor, due to their multiple sting ability and the fact they do not produce honey.

- **Termites** Usually found in mounds on the ground or in trees, or in dead wood, termites can be harvested by breaking off a chunk of the mound and shaking them free. Eat them raw or roast them in a pan. You can also eat their larvae. If you find a dead branch with termites living in it, you can put one end of the branch on the fire and catch them as they retreat from the heat. Termites are also amazing for a variety of other things. They can help you find north, as they tend to make their nests on the sunniest side of the tree. This is the north in the Southern Hemisphere and the south in the Northern Hemisphere. Regardless of the specifics of this knowledge, you can make sure that you are not going around in circles simply by making sure you keep the termite nests consistently on one side in the direction you are traveling. Crushing termites between your hands and rubbing them on your exposed skin can help deter insects, and wetting down the termite nest itself will provide you with a sticky clay that is great for making pots and bowls, as well as providing a weak bush glue (see page 49).

- **Mollusks** In the ocean, these usually can be located between the high and low tide mark, on rocks or under the beach sand where holes or divots will give them away. Dig a foot down into the wet sand where you see those clues. You may need a sharp edge to pry them off the rocks, or just smash the outer shell and scoop it out with a sharpened twig. Avoid any mollusks that are brightly colored, and do not eat them if the following occurs:

- They remain partially open when you touch them.

- They are easy to remove from the rocks or have fallen off by themselves.

- They smell bad.

- They don't open when cooked in boiling water.

- They are located in water with a reddish algae tinge.

With land snails and slugs, it's best to purge them for a few days in case they have been eating any vegetation that is toxic to you, so put them in a container with some fresh grass if possible. Wash them thoroughly and boil; cook them in their shells on the open fire or roast them on skewers.

Do not eat mollusks that are bright in color or shaped like cones.

One species of cone shell is one of the most venomous creatures on the planet. There are over 400 different species of cone shells, and not all of them are deadly, but most of them will deliver an envenomated barb that will range from extremely painful to life threating if it pierces your skin, so they are best avoided entirely.

- **Worms** Worms can be eaten immediately and raw but generally are quite gritty. Roasting on skewers can make them a little more palatable.

My biggest recommendation with wild meats is to cook them well. Overcook them if in doubt. Unlike store-bought meats, wild meats can contain parasites and diseases that could make you sick if consumed raw. The best way to kill these is by boiling or roasting.

Hunting can be broken down into two different types: passive and active. Passive hunting is when you put a mechanism in place and wait for it to secure the animal for you. This includes traps and snares. Active hunting is when you are in pursuit of an animal and kill it through some force exhibited by you. This includes chasing it down on foot and using weapons.

PASSIVE HUNTING

The advantage of passive hunting is that you can set multiple traps and snares, exponentially increasing the chances of getting a meal. Scatter the surrounding area with as many traps and snares as you can make. Then you can use your time and energy for other activities, such as collecting wood and maintaining your shelter.

As mentioned previously, traps and snares are illegal in a lot of countries, because they can't choose which animal to snare and which not to, and you are as likely to end up with a pangolin as you are with a rabbit. In a survival scenario, that doesn't matter, because meat is meat, and if it gets you through to a rescue, then no court in the world would charge you. Just remember that if you are practicing traps and snares, or if you get rescued, dismantle them before you leave. If you are in a survival situation with multiple people, make sure everyone knows where the traps and snares are set so that no one gets unnecessarily injured.

SETTING TRAPS AND SNARES

Once a human has moved into an environment, most likely the animals will move out. Your scent, movement, and fire will scream predator, and your prey will take their family elsewhere. Important things about setting snares and traps are:

- Build the traps and snares a good distance away from your shelter.

- Don't disturb the environment too much; it will cause some animals to avoid the area.

- Locate your traps and snares close to areas with animal signs, such as burrows and game trails.

- Camouflage the traps and snares the best you can, using natural materials.

- Make them strong—an animal struggling for its life will fight a lot harder than you can anticipate.

- Bait the trap with something you know the animal eats or has been eating; their droppings will give you an idea of some of their favorite foods.

- Check your traps regularly; not only is it inhumane to leave an animal suffering needlessly, they also may figure out a way of escaping the trap if they have enough time.

I could do a whole book on traps and snares, but I am only going to provide you with a few examples in order to get you thinking about how and why they work. You will need to be creative in your environment to figure out what will work for you. Look at the terrain you have around you. Do you have an abundance of rocks and hard ground? Don't dig a pitfall, but instead use a deadfall. Can you create strong natural cordage easily? Consider snares your best option.

THE BASIC SNARE

SURVIVE: THE ALL-IN-ONE GUIDE TO STAYING ALIVE IN EXTREME CONDITIONS

EXAMPLES OF SNARES

Snares work by trapping an animal by a body part. The rope or cord is usually set in such a way that the more the animal struggles, the tighter the cord becomes. For all my snares, I use a simple noose knot, where one end of the rope is threaded through a loop tied in the other end.

THE BASIC SNARE

This works best where you have located some burrows or clear game trails of smaller animals. You need:

- **At least three feet of cord or rope**
- **Two small, forked sticks**
- **A strong anchor point**

The anchor can be the base of an existing tree or shrub or a thick stick that you bang into the ground. Make sure you put the anchor stick beside the burrow rather than behind it, as you may cave in the entrance. If you are setting up on a game trail, have the anchor off to the side. Make the loop about four to five inches wide, and set it about four fingers, width off the ground, using the two small, forked sticks to support it. The idea is that the head of the animal will pass into the loop, but the rest of the body won't, and as the animal moves forward, the loop will squeeze around the animal's neck. It's important to picture how the snare will work to set it properly for the type of game you are after.

If you are setting these snares by burrows, remember that an animal will usually have multiple exits to their burrow, so search around the area and set a snare on every burrow you can find.

THE TENSION SNARE

For a quicker kill and to remove your prey from other ground predators, consider a tension snare. You will need:

- **At least three feet of rope**
- **A trigger stick/anchor bar setup made of two pieces of wood, each the width of your thumb**
- **A sapling or branch you can pull downward for tension**
- **Two small, forked sticks**

The snare part of the setup is the same as for the simple snare. The tricky part of this is to locate the perfect tension branch. It also needs to be flexible and long enough to suspend the prey off the ground, yet also needs enough rigidity that it will snap back into place once triggered. It needs to be positioned by a game trail or burrow.

The trigger bar needs to be notched or forked so that it interlocks with the anchor bar. The anchor bar gets hammered into the ground, and the trigger bar is tied to roughly the middle of the rope. One end of the rope is tied around the tensioned branch, and the other end of the rope forms the snare or noose. I find it easier to take care of the tensioned branch first, setting the trigger stick and then delicately positioning the snare on the game trail or in front of the burrow, perched on the small, forked sticks. Just make sure you have threaded your noose knot first before tying the other end to the tree. Test your snare by triggering it with a stick. This will enable you to see if the trigger stick is sensitive enough and if the tension branch will work.

THE TENSION SNARE

THE PLATFORM SNARE

THE PLATFORM SNARE

This can be used for bigger game, with the idea that you will catch them and hold them in place by a leg rather than their neck. The concept is similar to the tension snare. You will need:

- **Three to five feet of rope, depending on your target animal**
- **A branch or sapling that you can pull down for tension**
- **Two thick anchor sticks with forks**
- **Two thinner, longer sticks to aid the trigger mechanism**
- **A trigger stick**
- **Thin twigs and leaf matter to build and disguise a platform**

Hammer the two anchor sticks on either side of the game trail, with the forks facing downward. Place one of the trigger aids between the two anchor sticks under the fork. The other trigger aid will be placed near the ground on the opposite side. The trigger stick needs to be long enough to reach between the two. Make your noose and attach the trigger stick close to the noose end, with enough slack for the noose to lie on the path to one side of the snare. The other side of the rope is then attached to the branch and tensioned. The trigger stick feeds under and to one side the top trigger aid. The bottom trigger aid is then positioned to keep the trigger stick in position. I like having my trigger stick to the side of the snare that the tensioned branch is on, so as not to deter the animal from its path.

A platform is then made with light sticks and leaves over the bottom trigger aid. Be careful not to make the platform material too heavy, or else the weight will trigger the snare. Place the noose on top of the platform.

It's a good idea to test this snare before building the platform by pressing down on the bottom trigger aid. Some common mistakes are to have the trigger aid too close to the ground to create enough movement to trigger the snare, or to have the trigger stick too long, and so it catches on the ground rather than freely triggers.

EXAMPLES OF TRAPS

The most common survival traps are deadfalls. As suggested by the name, these are traps that kill an animal by having something heavy fall on them. While they are usually set for smaller game, historically there are examples of larger animals, such as leopards, being killed with them. Smaller deadfalls can be set up by one person, but the larger ones will require more than one person to set up safely.

While deadfall traps have quickly become the bushcraft trap of choice, as they are fun to demonstrate and easy to set up, it is important to note that most of them are demonstrated in a way that would lead them to fail in a real-life scenario. The characteristics that contribute to their success or failure are:

- **The weight of the deadfall**
- **The density of the ground below the deadfall**
- **The speed of the trigger mechanism**

I have seen many deadfalls set up in a way that the weight would be insufficient to kill the target prey, leading to the animal being able to squeeze out from under the trap. If the ground below the deadfall is soft or uneven, this will also provide an escape route for your food. The trigger mechanism can be ungainly or hesitant, and this will allow the critter time to dash out from under the deadfall once it starts to move. All of these things will be the difference between eating dinner and going hungry.

While a heavy, flat rock is ideal for a deadfall, if your prey of choice is middle- to larger-sized, or there are no suitable rocks available, you can strap logs together like a raft and load the top of the logs with heavy material, such as dirt or smaller rocks, in order to add some weight.

FIGURE-FOUR DEADFALL

This is one of the more popular deadfall traps, due to the limited materials required to make one. You will need:

- **A heavy, flat rock or deadfall**
- **Three pieces of wood as thick as your thumb**
- **Bait**

One piece of wood is the bait stick. It needs a square notch on one side and a 7 notch at one end. One stick is the anchor stick. It needs to have a matching square notch on its side to marry to the bait stick and the top end sharpened on one side. The pivot stick then has a V notch that marries to the top of the anchor stick and a double sharpened end to marry into the 7 notch. The deadfall rests on the other end of the pivot stick. Sounds complicated, but it is quite simple once you have an understanding of how it goes together. The bait is placed on the short end of the bait stick under the deadfall.

Some things to be aware of are making sure that the anchor stick is located on the outside of the deadfall; otherwise, the deadfall will get stuck on the anchor stick when triggered. It's also important to keep the end of the bait stick short, so it doesn't get in the way of the deadfall. Practice triggering the deadfall until the trigger mechanism is sensitive and swift.

V notch

Square notch

7 notch

FIGURE-FOUR DEADFALL TRAP

PAIUTE DEADFALL TRAP

PAIUTE DEADFALL

I find that the trigger mechanism with this deadfall trap can be a little faster than the figure four, but it does require some extra equipment. You will need:

- **A heavy, flat rock or deadfall**
- **An anchor stick**
- **A thin trigger stick**
- **A pivot stick**
- **A toggle**
- **Some cord or rope**
- **Bait**

For a smaller version of this trap, the cord does not need to be very strong. I have used an unprocessed palm leaf in its place and it worked perfectly, so don't get hung up on needing to have or create the perfect piece of rope.

Some people like their anchor stick to have a fork in the end, but I find this has the potential to slow down the trigger mechanism. I find it works best to make a sharpened V shape on the end of the anchor stick and have a matching V notch in the pivot stick. Flatten one end of the pivot stick so the deadfall sits on it more easily, and tie the rope to the other end of the pivot stick. The toggle is tied around the middle to the other end of the rope and wrapped around the anchor stick about an inch or two off the ground. I like to make my toggle flat on one side and carve a divot in it where the trigger stick sits. Bait is then placed in the middle of the trigger stick that sits under the deadfall, or on the ground underneath it. The other end of the trigger stick uses the underside of the deadfall in opposition to the toggle.

Make sure the anchor stick isn't preventing the deadfall from hitting the ground, by locating it outside the lip of the deadfall. While setting up this deadfall, I like to prop up the deadfall with something that prevents it from crushing my hands if it accidentally triggers.

Be wary that the meat from deadfalls can be polluted by burst digestive tracts. If in doubt, do not eat the meat, or wash it thoroughly and overcook it, as it can make you very sick.

ARAPUCA TRAP

This is a bird trap that I have found to be very effective in North America with catching birds such as ravens and jays. Since it is a live capture trap, they were released unharmed but, in a survival scenario, they would have made a good meal. It requires quite a bit of assembly but can be used multiple times, so it is worth the effort. You can use a variety of trigger mechanisms for this trap. The figure four and Paiute triggers work well, but I will add in another mechanism to expand your tool kit of trap triggers. You will need:

- **Twenty-four thumb-width sticks, with six sets of four varying sizes**
- **Two pieces of rope or cord about two feet in length**
- **A short length of cord**
- **A finger-width trigger stick about ten inches long**
- **Bait**

Place the two longest sticks side by side, and attach the two pieces of cord from one end of each stick to the other to create a square. Twist the two sticks once in opposite directions so the rope forms a cross. Slide the next two longest sticks, log-cabin style, between the ropes and begin to fill in the slack. Eventually you will end up with a tensioned pyramid. This is your cage. You may need to fill in the top of the pyramid with sticks to ensure that there isn't an escape route for the bird. These are also the sticks that you will remove in order to get the bird out without it escaping. Break the trigger stick in half in such a way that you can put the pieces back together again. Tie the short length of the cord to the inside of the trap, and loop it around the break in the trigger stick with tension. Lean the trap on the trigger stick. Place the bait inside the trap. When a bird enters the trap, it will disturb the cord, which will trigger the trap. I find that it is necessary to put a weight on top of the trap to make sure that the bird doesn't manage to overturn the trap or wriggle out from under it.

With traps and snares, create a natural flow or path to funnel the animal into the trap and make it hard for them to go around the trap. Do this by building up the pathway on the sides leading to the trap or making the clearest path through the undergrowth the one that passes by the trap. This is best done with the material in the area, so as not to alert the animal to anything suspicious.

Make sure that you are cautious when approaching triggered traps and snares. Wild animals can be extremely vicious when trapped and injured. Approach slowly, and have a backup weapon such as a knife, club, or spear in case you need to finish the job. Don't grab an animal with your bare hands until you have made sure it's dead.

A basic knowledge of the way traps and snares operate could save your life. If one trap doesn't work, try another. Even if you can't remember an exact trap, just an understanding of how traps work could be enough for you to make your own and provide yourself with food to survive.

ARAPUCA TRAP

ACTIVE HUNTING

There are a lot of things to think about when trying to get close to an animal. They include:

- Wind direction; is it blowing your scent to the animal or away from it?

- How noisy you are; are there dead leaves underfoot, or can you move quietly?

- What usually hunts your prey; are they expecting an attack?

- When are they most distracted from keeping an eye out for danger?

- Will they see you; can you disguise yourself or remain hidden?

- It might take you a while to develop the skills necessary to get close enough to actively hunt the animals in your area.

- My two favorite primitive hunting weapons are the spear and the throwing stick.

Fire-hardened spear   Stone tip spear   Fishing/crabbing spear

Throwing stick

Club

SPEAR

All you need for a basic spear is a long, strong, straight piece of wood. I prefer to cut one from a sapling, as it is easier to process while green, but any wood that fits that description will do. Sharpen one end to a point, and you have a workable spear. Any modifications moving forward will make a versatile, stronger, and more durable spear.

- **Fire-hardened spears:** After sharpening the stick to a point, poke the stick into the flames or over coals until it steams but doesn't burn. Remove and allow to cool. Repeat the process until you have the desired hardness.

- **Stone tips:** This gets a little more complicated, as you will need to have some knowledge of flint knapping or stonework. For me, I smash two fine-grained stones together until I get some workable sharp flakes. The most durable way to attach these to the top of your spear is with some bush glue and animal sinew.

- **Fishing or crabbing spear:** Cut the end of your stick into four segments. Sharpen each of these segments individually. Tie two opposing short sticks in the middle of these four segments to create some space between them.

THROWING STICK

The most advanced form of throwing stick is the boomerang, but you don't need to make one that comes back. Find a dense piece of wood about two feet long, with a slight bend in it and one side heavier than the other. Sending this out so that it flies end over end can make a deadly weapon. If you have the time and the blade, you can flatten the top and bottom side to make it more aerodynamic, but it's not necessary. It is perfect for taking out individual birds in a flock, either on the ground or on the wing. It is also great for smaller ground-dwelling mammals.

CLUB

A stick with a heavier knot of wood on the end of it works perfectly for a club. This is a good weapon to finish off injured animals or as a form of defense.

BREAKING DOWN A KILL

Once you have managed to kill an animal, you need to know how to break it down, or process it, to get the maximum value from that kill. You don't want anything useful to go to waste.

This should be done at a location away from your shelter area, so as not to attract predators to your camp.

With most animals, except the very small ones, I recommend removing the digestive tract first. If the stomach or intestines are punctured, the animal's waste will pollute your meat and can lead to you getting sick if you eat it. There are a lot of different ways to process an animal, but I like to keep it simple. You will find the method that suits you if you do it often enough. Every animal is different on the inside, but the steps to my processing remain the same.

The first cut.

Gutting a kill.

1. Skin the animal. I'm not really fussy about how this happens, as I'm not looking to mount it on my wall. Make a shallow cut in the hide, usually in the middle of the belly. You will find that there is a distinct difference between skin and meat, and that it is separated by a layer of fascia. Cut between the skin and meat to remove the hide. I try to make sure that there is not much meat left on the skin and that there are not too many holes in the hide. This will take practice.

2. Find the anus of the animal, and do a shallow cut of the inner skin layer toward the throat until you reach the rib cage. Empty out the digestive cavity.

3. Remove the organs, and place them on the inside of the hide.

4. Cut off as much of the meat as you can see. I'm not going for special cuts like a butcher; I am going for quantity.

5. Collect the sinew. Sinew is the tendons or ligaments of an animal. The best sinew can be found around the legs, or the tail if the animal has a long, muscular one. It comes out in strands and can be wrapped around a twig to store.

6. Remove the bones at the joints.

7. Collect the brain. This may involve crushing the skull with a heavy implement.

8. If the animal has horns or any other defining feature, collect that as well.

Nutrition-wise, you are able to consume:

- Meat
- Blood
- Liver
- Kidneys
- Lungs
- Heart
- Brain
- Bones (roasted and then boiled)

Some of these pieces may not appeal to you, but remember that you are looking for maximum energy gain for the minimum effort, so don't let any of your hunt go to waste. Blood is best consumed fresh, but I would recommend cooking the rest of the animal well to eliminate the parasites that can be found in wild meat.

STORING YOUR MEAT

If you have hunted more than you can consume in one sitting, you will need to figure out a method of storing the meat. It's good to note that unless your meat is sitting in full sun or has attracted flies, fresh meat can last for about three days without being treated. Methods to store meat include:

SUN DRYING Cut the meat into thin strips, and lay them across rocks or a rack of branches. You will need to have the meat in the full sun for about eight to sixteen hours, depending on the intensity of the sun in your location. Be prepared to have to defend your meat from scavengers during the process.

SMOKING Cut the meat into thin strips, and lay them across a rack suspended above a smoky fire. Punk wood (rotten wood that has dried out) is good for making a smoky fire. To speed up the process, build a tepee around the fire and cover the outside of the tepee with some kind of blanketing material. This will direct more heat and smoke toward the meat.

FREEZING This will only work in colder climates. Digging a hole in the cold ground, layering it with leaves, and then covering it with an insulated lid will act as a cooler to extend the life of your meat. If you have access to snow, dig a hole in the snow, layer the hole with vegetation, and cover over. Don't place meat directly on the snow or else the meat can get spoiled by "freezer burn."

Don't keep meat close to camp. This will attract predators. Tie your meat into a bundle and suspend it from a tall branch away from camp, or create a meat safe (from rocks or frozen ground) that keeps animals out of your food stash.

Unless you know how to process the skin to turn it into leather (a method called tanning), the hide you cut off will become stiff as it dries. Keeping that in mind, try to lay the hide flat to dry, as it will be more useful that way. If there is excess meat on the hide, use a sharp edge to scrape it off before drying. This will prevent the hide from becoming rotten.

FISHING

If you are fortunate enough to have ended up next to a body of water in your survival situation, fishing should be your best chance of procuring a food source. If you don't have hooks and nylon line, it will be a little trickier, but there are all kinds of ancient fishing techniques to try.

FISHING LINE If you happen to have some paracord on you, then pulling the inner threads out and tying them together creates a great line. Assuming that you are starting from scratch, you will need to create some natural cordage to be your fishing line (see page 70). It can be kind of tricky to create a tough enough line for the fish not to break or chew through, but you may have some local fibers in your area that will work, so experiment with what you have.

HOOKS Primitive hooks were shaped out of bones, antlers, shells, thorns, and even hardwood. Look for something that you can carve or shape into a hook-like structure that can be sharpened and that maintains its strength.

I have seen people have success with a small, straight, sharpened piece of wood as a hook. This works well for catfish, eels, and any type of bottom-feeder fish. Sharpen both ends of a small, strong stick the length of a toothpick, and attach it to the end of your line. Tie the bait on the stick in a way that it holds the stick parallel to the line, but so that the stick will open out when the bait is consumed. Once the fish swallows the bait and hook, the stick lodges in its gullet.

Fishing hook

FLOAT Any porous or buoyant wood will work. Tie it to your line so the hook dangles in the water rather than sits on the bottom. This will increase your chances of attracting a bite.

BAIT Get creative. Most of the best baits we purchase from shops are gathered from nature. Worms, shellfish, grubs, crickets, innards, and sometimes even berries will all work. If you are in an area with termite mounds, you can break off a chunk and shake it over your fishing area. The termites falling onto the water surface will chum the water and can create a feeding frenzy.

SPEARS For fishing or crabbing, cut the end of a stick into four segments. Sharpen each of these segments. Tie two opposing short sticks in the middle of these four segments to create some space between them.

Fishing spear

TRAPS Some of the oldest man-made structures discovered are coastal fish traps believed to have been constructed over sixty-thousand years ago. If you are in a tidal area, a rock pool fish trap is a good one to consider. Create an area at low tide where a pool of water becomes isolated from the ocean water by a raised wall of rocks. At high tide, the fish will have access to the area, but will become stranded in there as the water retreats. This will make them easier to spear or catch.

FISH DAM If you are by a stream, you can use a similar technique of building rock walls to trap fish. Shape a funnel of rocks across part or all the stream that ends in a rock wall and catchment area on the downstream side.

Fish dam

Fishing basket

FISHING BASKETS Fish traps can also be made of small saplings or vines. The classic one involves making a two- to three-foot-long cylinder that tapers to a dead end. I find it is useful to put a couple of circles of saplings inside this structure, to help give it some shape. A smaller funnel-shaped piece goes in the opening, providing an entrance for the fish but making it impossible to exit. This can be baited and placed in an area of the stream where water naturally funnels through. Or you can create an area that will funnel the fish into the trap you have placed by building up the rocks along most of your stream except for where your trap is.

TICKLING OR NOODLING These are two hand-fishing techniques, but I really have only seen them work in very specific environments with very specific fish types.

Tickling works best on trout that tend to rest under shallow overhangs by the banks of the river. The technique can be done in the water or from the bank. I find it works best for me if I'm in the water. Walk slowly sideways along the river's edge, with your hands in the water and your fingers wiggling. If you feel a fish with your fingers, slowly keep feathering your fingers underneath it until you can locate the head and tail. Swiftly grab the fish and squeeze your hands toward each other. This will compress the spine of the fish so it doesn't wiggle.

Noodling is the art of catching catfish in swamps. Locate a catfish hole, and then place your bare hand inside the hole. The catfish swims forward and latches onto your hand in a defensive maneuver that then allows you to grab the gills of the fish from the inside of its mouth. Pull the catfish free of the hole.

Never eat dead fish that you find floating on the surface, even if it seems like easy food. Dead fish harbor bacteria, parasites, and diseases that can make you very sick. Also be wary of the water you found it in, and don't drink it if you have other choices.

It might take you some time to learn the habits of the fish in your area. Be persistent and try different methods, different times of day, and different baits.

ANIMAL CONFRONTATIONS

Hunting is a risk-versus-reward activity that you will need to assess in your own survival situation. It may open you up to the possibility of an increased number of animal confrontations, but it is important to remember that very few animals will attack a human, except in self-defense.

Some tips on what to do if confronted by a wild animal:

- Avoid eye contact.

- Freeze; if they aren't charging you, don't run.

- Slowly back off.

- Avoid sudden movements.

- If an animal charges, dodge out of the way; you could be blocking their escape route.

- If the animal attacks, shout, make a loud noise, and try to make yourself look bigger; drop whatever you are carrying, as it may distract them; zigzag run away from them, if you run; climb a tree, if a big enough one is available.

WILD PREDATORS

Educate yourself about the predators in your area and in the regions and countries that you are intending to visit. A little knowledge goes a long way and can prevent a dangerous confrontation. Learn what the predators look like, their common behaviors, how to avoid them, and the best way to deter an attack. In the unlikely event of such an incident, what you do could profoundly affect the outcome.

The first tactic when confronted with most predators is to stay still and use the "stop, look, and listen" approach. This communicates to the animal that you are not a threat and are not one of their normal prey species, which flee on sight of the predator. Often, this will mean the animal will move on. However, if they don't, there are other tactics you can use to deter an attack. They are different for all large predators. Some quick examples are:

- **Make noise to scare away a black bear, but play dead to deter a grizzly attack.**

- **Act loud and scary for a mountain lion attack.**

- **Dodge out of the way at the last minute for a rhino attack and then stand still; they aren't very agile, have trouble with quick direction changes, and have very bad eyesight. They may never find you again.**

- **Stand as tall as you can to make yourself appear as big as possible if confronted by an aggressive dog; this should intimidate the animal.**

You should always try to keep your distance from potential predators. Respect the fact that you are intruding into their natural environment, where they act according to their instinctive behaviors. The vast majority of wild animals will avoid confrontation unless threatened or cornered. But in case the worst happens, learn the difference between each tactic. It could save your life.

FIRE

There are many reasons why fire is in the basic needs section of survival. It contributes to all the other basic needs in some way and adds so much more to your survival on its own. Fire will help you survive longer than three hours in exposed conditions, it is one of the best methods of purifying your water to make it potable, and it can make the food you have found safer and more palatable to eat. It can also help keep large predators and insects at bay and signal for help. It is one of the essentials that may make the difference between you surviving and not.

There is one thing that all animals fear: fire. With the exception of the fire-fighting rhinoceros in Africa, most animals will avoid the heat of a flame. In a survival situation, make it a priority to have a fire burning before the sun sets, and make sure you have enough wood stockpiled to ensure that the fire is kept burning throughout the night. The fire doesn't need to be a big one. In most cases, simply the smell of the wood burning will be an ample deterrent.

Fires are also great for morale. They add a feeling of warmth and safety in a situation that can otherwise feel out of control and scary.

There are many methods for getting a fire going in the outdoors. Almost every group of Indigenous people had a different method or variation of how best to make fire in their region. This being a book about survival, not bushcraft, I am going to focus on the ones that you will most likely need to try if you are thrust into a survival situation rather than if you came prepared, although I will touch on some of the more popular man-made ones.

The key to getting a good fire going is preparation. It doesn't matter if you have fire-lighting methods on you or if you have to improvise; what you do before even making a spark, flame, or coal will be the difference between getting a roaring fire going or wasting valuable resources, energy, and time.

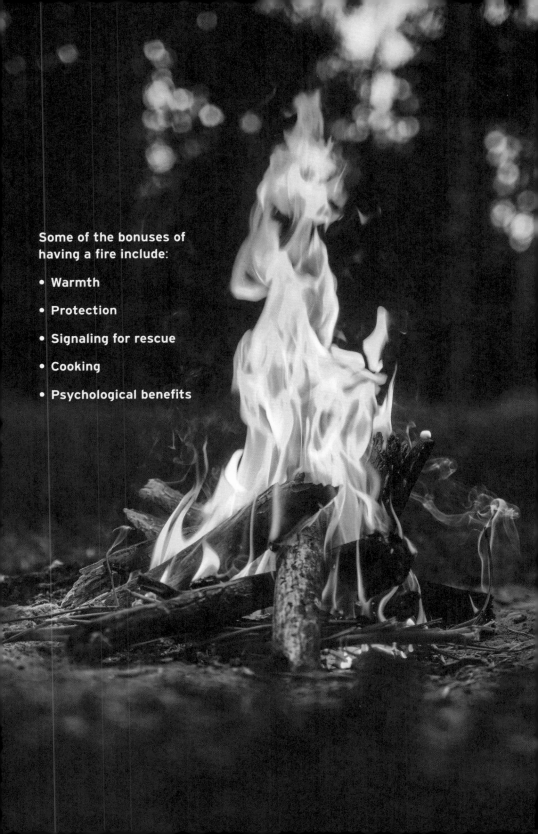

Some of the bonuses of having a fire include:

- Warmth

- Protection

- Signaling for rescue

- Cooking

- Psychological benefits

FIRE PREPARATION

The three things needed to make a flame are **fuel, a heat source, and oxygen**.

Fuel is the main thing that you need to prepare before making a heat source. I have seen many people put in a huge effort to make a friction fire coal, only to have it smolder out while they are frantically searching around for materials to ignite it in. Be aware that most methods of primitive fire making don't finish with you having a flame; they finish with you having a coal, which you then have to nurse into a flame.

A heat source will take resources or time to make. Even if you have matches or a lighter on you, be aware that these resources are finite, and make sure that you make the most of every match or strike of the lighter.

Oxygen is fortunately all around us with the air we breathe, so apart from avoiding accidentally smothering the heat source and locating the fire out of the wind, the preparation for this is minimal.

FUEL

Fire fuel can be broken down into three different types:

1. Tinder

2. Kindling

3. Fuel

TINDER

This is any material that takes a minimal amount of heat to make it catch on fire. The key to good tinder is that it must be dry. Look for fine-grain fibers that can fluff up easily when rubbed between your hands. Its purpose is to be a coal or spark extender. This means that it should take the heat from the heat source and be able to either turn it into a flame or make a bigger, hotter coal. Some materials ignite well but burn too quickly to be useful on their own. Dry cattail heads are a good example of this. They work great when combined with other materials, but burn out too quickly on their own.

The best way to collect tinder ready for your heat source is to make a tinder bundle or bird nest. When a bird makes its nest, it has bigger materials on the outside to keep the structure of the nest and then smaller materials on the inside to protect the baby bird. The finest materials should be on the inside, ready to amp up the heat source, and the larger materials should be on the outside, ready to fuel the flame.

The outer layer of a tinder bundle should also be mostly fine, dry, combustible material. I find that dry grass tied into a knot, creating a nest for the smaller materials, works well. You can also use bark, palm fibers, or coconut husk. It's a good idea to experiment in your area to see what works for you. Some dry fibers seem like they might work but don't have the combustible properties to ensure success, so they could lead to you wasting time and energy. One of my favorite tinder finds is white punk fungus. It can be found in Australia, New Zealand, and South America, and if you send a small spark onto the fungus directly, it will catch easily and roll a coal until the whole fungus is consumed.

White punk fungus

The idea of a tinder bundle is that once you have your coal or heat source, you place it in the center of the bundle and fold over the edges of the bundle so the coal is touching as much fuel as possible. By firmly (but not wildly) blowing into the bundle, you add enough oxygen for that coal to ignite. This is where preparation of kindling comes in; without prior preparation, your tinder bundle will quickly burn out, and you will have to begin again.

Good inner material should almost be the consistency of fluff or dust. Things that work great for this are:

- Dry grasses or the inner bark of some trees, rubbed between your hands

- Bracket fungus pounded into a fine dust

- Palm fibers

- Cattail heads

- Dry dung from grass-eating animals, ground to a fine dust

KINDLING

This is the wood used to extend the flames of the tinder bundle into a useful fire. I always think of kindling as being the size of anything from a toothpick to a thumb. Make sure that this wood is also dry, as the tinder bundle flame won't burn long enough or hot enough to dry out wood. I discuss how to find dry wood in wet conditions in the relevant climate chapters, but for now, gather a handful of toothpick-sized wood, two handfuls of pencil-sized wood, and two handfuls of thumb-sized wood.

There are many and varied methods of setting up a fire lay (the structure made with kindling). Some people like to dig a hole to contain the fire, and others like to make a ring of stones. I do like to have some clearly defined fire area so that the fire doesn't sprawl, but that is a personal choice. Just remember that if you line your fire with rocks, you need to make sure that they are not river rocks. Wet rocks or river rocks tend to explode when heated and can cause nasty injuries. To avoid this, bang the rocks together and discard any rocks that sound hollow or are brittle.

I will give you a few different examples of log lays, but the main things to remember are:

- **Try to find a location out of the wind.**

- **Clear the area around where you intend to make your fire.**

- **Make sure the ground isn't damp, and if it is, lay down a branch platform to keep your fire base dry.**

- **Leave an area at the base of your wood pile to place your tinder bundle in; fire burns upward, so it will seek its fuel above it.**

- **Go from smaller wood to larger wood**: toothpicks at the bottom of your pile where the tinder bundle will be placed, to thumb-sized wood on top.

- **Don't pack the wood on too thickly or too thinly; too much wood will smother the flame, and too little won't provide enough fuel, and the flame will burn out.**

THE TEPEE LAY

This is exactly what the name suggests. Prop the toothpick-sized twigs on your cleared ground first, and then layer the outside of them with the pencil-sized twigs and lastly the thumb-sized branches. I make sure that I don't use all my kindling in the structure, so that I will have some to feed into the fire if I have misjudged how much of each size I will need. Your on-fire tinder bundle is then inserted beneath the toothpick-sized twigs. As the flame burns upward, it will light the toothpicks, which in turn will provide enough sustained heat to light the pencils, etc.

If you have a ready flame such as a match or lighter, you can skip the tinder-bundle stage and head straight to making the log lay. Just make sure you compensate by filling the space under the toothpick-sized twigs with some smaller, highly flammable material to get burning first.

THE LOG CABIN LAY

Again, collect your handfuls of toothpick-, pencil-, and thumb-sized twigs. You will also need two bigger pieces of wood laid out parallel to each other. Scrape out a hole to place the tinder bundle into, and lay the toothpick-sized twigs across the hole, with a handful running one way and a handful running perpendicular (at right angles) to them. The next pencil-sized layer should sit on your two parallel logs, again crisscrossing a layer each, and, finally, the same with the thumb-sized branches. With this method, you can stack your thicker fuel at the top of the cabin structure early in the fire-making process, because it won't collapse in on itself and smother the fire, as can sometimes happen if you put big wood on the tepee structure too soon.

Place the tinder bundle or flame under the toothpick-sized twigs, and you should soon have a fire.

FUEL

This is the wood that you use to keep your fire going. How well it burns will depend on where you are and the types of wood you have access to. As a general rule, hardwoods burn hotter and longer than softwoods and produce bigger coals. These are the kind of fuels you are looking for to keep your fire going through the night. The less you have to tend your fire, the better sleep you will get.

Assuming you don't have an ax or saw with you, the best way to break up these larger pieces of wood is by smacking them over a rock or bending them between two solid objects (boulders or large tree trunks work). If they are too large to break, you can either place them over the fire and let the fire burn each piece in half for you, or you can feed an end in at a time. This allows you to burn quite large logs that will sustain the fire for a good length of time, and it also conserves the energy you may burn from trying to break the wood.

Make sure you avoid the dead wood from poisonous plants such as poison oak or the stinging tree. Smoke from burning poisonous plants can be toxic and cause death or damage to lungs and eyes.

As always, you are trying to conserve energy. Do not make a massive fire unless you are trying to signal for help. A small fire will keep you just as warm if positioned properly, and it doesn't take much of a flame to boil water.

Try to find dry standing wood or wood that is off the ground, as it will generally be a more solid wood. Any wood that has sat on the ground for a while will tend to be rotten or full of termites and will burn faster than standing wood.

Make sure to collect more fuel than you think you will need. You don't want to blunder around in the dark to get more wood if your fire has gone out and you are freezing. Find a way to store wood that will keep it dry or dry it out. I often build a small shelter near the fire that houses my collected wood. I make sure that the wood is off the ground and covered. That way I'm never caught out if it rains.

If you are trying to dry wet wood, place it either around the fire or on a rack over the fire. Just make sure it is not so close that it catches on fire before you want it to.

FEATHER STICK

No fire preparation section would be complete without mentioning a feather stick. It is tinder, kindling, and fuel all in one and a popular method of starting fires, especially in adverse weather. If you make one well enough, you can even light it from a spark.

To create a feather stick, choose a straight, dry stick with no knots. Lay your blade flat on the stick and then tilt the angle of the blade slightly toward the wood. Run the blade all the way down the stick, stopping just before the bottom of the stick so that the shaving remains attached to the stick. Turn the stick around and repeat. Keep repeating until you end up with a thin stick with shavings attached. Place this inside your fire lay, and add an ignition source.

Once you have sufficient tinder, kindling, and fuel for your fire, it is time to decide how best to make your fire.

WAYS TO MAKE FIRE

I'm sure that the first thing most people imagine when they think about making a fire in a survival situation is the friction fire method, or what's better known as rubbing two sticks together. It is a very physically demanding and technical process, and I have seen many gifted survivalists not get a fire going after hours of trying this method under pressure. Before embarking on the friction method, try one of these other techniques if you have the requisite tools—they are much simpler and will burn fewer calories.

REFRACTION METHODS

One of the less strenuous methods of making a fire is to allow the sun to shine through something that will magnify the sun's heat. The most obvious is a magnifying glass. If you have one on you, that's a bonus, but there are a few ways of re-creating the effects of a magnifying glass in a survival scenario.

Human beings have managed to pollute just about everywhere in the world with our garbage, so you can usually manage to find these types of things in quite remote locations. The most obvious is a piece of glass from such things as a broken bottle or a camera lens, but a piece of a plastic bottle will work also. I have made fire using the following methods of refraction:

- **Magnifying glass—your compass usually has a little one incorporated into it.**

- **Reading glasses—if they have a magnifying lens.**

- **Clear plastic water bottle—if it's filled with water, you can use the base to concentrate the sun's rays into a point.**

It can also be done with a clear plastic bag full of water and a piece of ice; however, conditions must be ideal for both.

This method will not work at night for obvious reasons, and the closer the sun gets toward the horizon, the less direct heat there is. This method is best tried in the middle of the day, when the sun is at its peak. Aim the heat spot you are creating for the smallest material at the center of your tinder bundle.

BATTERY METHOD

This method works if you have a flashlight or something that runs on batteries (like a camera). You will also need two pieces of wire; perhaps there is a fence nearby or the inside of an electrical cord, such as a phone charger.

Attach one wire to the positive end of the battery and one wire to the negative end. When you bring the two wires close together, a spark will jump between them. If you can place your tinder between the wires, you should be able to light it from the spark.

FERRO RODS

Although this is technically a friction fire method, since the spark is caused by friction between a rod and a striker, this method needs a whole section of its own, because in the survival world it is one of the most popular yet misunderstood methods of fire making.

These handy little gadgets are often called a "flint and steel," which is not accurate to describe them but is a reflection of their past. Historically, people would hit a rock called flint with their steel knives to create a spark to make a fire. As time went by, the ferro rod was invented, combining a mixture of metal alloys into what is called mischmetal. When struck with a steel striker, this mischmetal ignites with a spark that burns hotter and longer than a spark caused by simply striking two natural rocks together, or a rock and a knife.

The problem is that many survivalists and outdoors people put these gadgets in their packs believing that they have fire sorted, when in reality they only have a method of getting a spark. The process needs to go one step further to knowing how to get the hottest, most sustained spark and what material will ignite with that spark. I have seen many people aiming their ferro rod at a bundle of twigs and wondering why nothing is igniting.

The best way to use a ferro rod is to position the rod so it is facing low and central to your tinder. In the hand holding the striker, brace your knuckles on the ground or your shoe and then sharply pull back the hand with the ferro rod in it. The striker should be at about a 30-degree angle to the rod for best results. If you push the striker toward the bundle, you risk displacing your tinder before the spark reaches it. As with any survival kit, if you choose to have a ferro rod in your bag, make sure you know how to use it and what tinder ignites best with a spark in your area or the area you're visiting.

PERCUSSION FIRE METHODS

All around the world, there are rocks that will create a spark when hit off each other or off a knife with a high carbon content. The spark is generally cooler and faster burning than one produced by a ferro rod, so it is essential to have a good, flammable tinder bundle ready. This method saved my life when I was racing *First Man Out* survivalist Ed Stafford out of a high-altitude mountain pass in Sichuan Province in China. We spent a fair amount of our time above the snow line, and just below the snow line was mostly rain-soaked wood, not ideal for friction fire. I knew that pyrite was native to that area and kept my eye out for some among the thick rockpiles on the edges of the mountain streams. I was lucky enough to find some with a high iron content and was able to get a spark into some dried and ground-up chaga fungus. This created a coal that I could make a fire out of. The weather got down to below -25°F that night, and I would have died had I not been able to get a fire going.

As previously noted, the technique was popularly known as the flint-and-steel method. This is because flint is found in most places in the world, and it dependably produces good sparks when hit with a high-carbon-content metal. Flint tends to be a chalky-looking, fine-grained rock that is either light gray or white in color if you can find it, but most fine-grained rocks that can be broken to have a sharp edge will usually work if flint isn't readily available.

If you are unsure about how to identify flint, try a variety of rocks lying around to see if one produces a spark. Even if you can't see the spark, sometimes you will smell a distinctive match smell on the rocks after striking. You have to hit the rock quite hard and sharply to get the spark, but once you get the hang of it, it's an easy and reliable fire-lighting method.

Quartz also works with a metal striker, and its white color makes it fairly easy to identify.

The only stone that I have found that will deliver a workable spark when struck off itself is iron pyrite. This is less readily found around the world, but there is evidence that some of the most primitive cultures carried with them pieces of this rock specifically to make fire with.

Pyrite

Flint

Quartz

FRICTION FIRE METHODS

There are many different forms of friction fire, but they all usually involve rapidly rubbing two pieces of wood together to create enough heat and dust to make a hot coal. I would recommend learning one or some of these techniques before you take off on your extreme outdoor adventure, because they are very difficult to learn on the fly. However, necessity is the mother of invention, so if you understand the theory behind what works and what doesn't, you may be able to make it work if your life depends on it.

There are certain woods that work better for friction fire making than others. Rather than having you learn all the best friction fire woods in the world, I am going to give you a set of properties to look for that work best:

- **Dry**

- **Soft, lightweight wood—but not punky or rotten**

- **Sourced from faster-growing trees or weeds**

- **Straight—free from bends or knots**

It is better if you choose a slightly softer piece of wood for your spindle with a slightly harder piece of wood for your baseboard, but wood of the same density will work too.

Over the years, I have made friction fires with types of wood that people have told me will not work, so don't get hung up on what someone else has told you; try everything for yourself. One of the most important things to remember is that both bits of wood must be bone dry. Any dampness in either will probably result in failure. Be aware of how damp the ground you are working on is. Any moisture on the ground will be absorbed into the drier wood and lead to a lack of success as well.

With most of these methods, you will need a notch to keep your spindle or drill piece moving in the same place. This will be a hole for the hand drill and bow drill methods and a horizontal notch for the fire saw and fire plow methods. You will also need a catchment area for the "dust" you produce.

This dust will be the main indicator of how well your method is working. It needs to be a dark brown, almost-black color. If your dust is light in color, you either need to change the pressure of the strokes or the speed of the strokes, usually increasing it rather than decreasing it. This dust is what will combust to form a coal, so make sure it doesn't blow away or fall out of the notch.

This can be a very physically demanding way to get a fire going, so start slowly with your strokes. With the right amount of pressure, you can get heat without rapid movement. As smoke starts to be seen, increase the pace of your strokes and for longer than you think.

Once you have a smoking coal, take your time and transfer it to your tinder bundle. You will have created an excess of dust that will help the coal increase its size over a minute or so, which means you don't have to rush.

These are just the basics of friction fire methods. Each method has different specifics that I will outline further in the following pages. If you are unsure if a wood will work, just give it a go. If the wood heats up, changes color, or produces dust or smoke, it is worth putting in a bit of effort with.

HAND DRILL

This is the simplest of friction fire methods, given that it only needs two pieces of wood. It is also one of the hardest methods, because it requires fairly specific wood types and some good upper-body strength to be successful. You will need a straight, thin spindle about a foot and a half long with a half-inch diameter and a baseboard about three-quarters of an inch thick. Carve one end of the spindle into an arch. The arched side rests on the baseboard.

Carve a divot into the baseboard to keep the spindle in place, and place your hands flat on either side of the spindle. When you first start learning this technique, you will need to anchor the baseboard in place with your foot. Push your hands together, and spin the spindle with a downward pressure to help generate the heat required. If you are creating enough friction, the baseboard will start to smoke, and you will burn a circle into the baseboard. Using a sharp edge, cut a notch into the side of the baseboard, making the circle look like Pac-Man. Place a leaf or a piece of bark under the notch to catch your dust. Repeat the spinning motion until the notch fills up with black dust and begins to smoke. With enough heat and friction, this dust will ignite into a coal.

This action of burning in a hole, cutting a notch, and filling the notch with dust is consistent with both the strap drill and bow drill methods as well.

SURVIVE: THE ALL-IN-ONE GUIDE TO STAYING ALIVE IN EXTREME CONDITIONS

STRAP DRILL

This personally is one of my favorite methods of friction fire making. It is also one of the friction fire methods that requires the least amount of strength or exertion, and I have seen children as young as five master it. This method requires only two additional pieces of equipment from the hand drill, but it is a two-person method, so if you are flying solo, then it's not the method for you.

You will need a piece of rope or cordage and a bearing block. I have used a shoelace for this method, so if you are wearing laced shoes, then you are in luck. If you are not and do not have any ready-made cord with you, make natural cordage (see page 70). The cord only needs to be as long as a shoelace. The bearing block needs to have a hole or divot in it. If you are using wood, the wood needs to be of a harder wood than the spindle. You can use bone, antler, rocks, or shells for your bearing block. As long as the spindle can spin freely in the hole, and you can exert some downward pressure without it slipping off the top of the spindle, it should work.

The spindle should be thicker for the strap drill and bow drill; about the thickness of an adult thumb is a good estimate. One end should be carved to a point, and the other end carved into an arch. The pointy end goes into the bearing block, and the arched end goes onto the baseboard. The baseboard can also be a little thicker—anything up to an inch.

One person will put their foot on the baseboard and exert a downward pressure on the top of the spindle with the bearing block. The other person will wrap the cord around the spindle three or four times and then pull one side of the cord and then the other, keeping a firm pressure between their hands and allowing the friction of the cord to spin the spindle. As before, carve a divot into the baseboard, burn in the hole, and then cut your notch before putting in a big effort for the coal. Place a leaf or a piece of bark under the notch to catch your dust. The longer and smoother the strokes of the cord, the faster you will get a coal.

BOW DRILL

This is the next-most-efficient method of friction fire, after the strap drill. The difference is that it can be done with one person, and your piece of cord needs to be stronger than for the strap drill, as it has more pressure on it through the bow. Your shoelace should still work, but certain types of natural cordage won't be strong enough to withstand the pressure, so you may need to experiment with different types to find one that works.

You will need a slightly bent stick that you tie the cord to each end of. I have seen people that prefer small bows, I have seen people who prefer a bow with a big bend in it, and I have seen people with very long bows. My personal preference is a stick about two feet long that is almost straight. The reason for this is because I can still do nice, long strokes with the bow, but it is manageable and not ungainly. Your bow should be made of a rigid wood, as a flexible wood will lead to your cord slipping on the spindle.

The spindle and baseboard can be prepared as for the strap drill.

The cord needs to be fairly firm between the bow ends, as you want it to grip on to the spindle. Twist the spindle so that the cord is wrapped around it once. If the spindle wants to flip out but can be wrapped, that is a perfect tension. The spindle should be on the outside of the cord, with the arched end on the baseboard and the pointed end in the bearing block.

Place your foot on the baseboard, and anchor the inside of your left forearm to the side of your shin (assuming you are right-handed). This hand will hold the bearing block firmly in place. With your right arm, move the bow in a long, smooth motion back and forth. If you do this slowly at first, you will conserve energy as you build up heat. Once you see lots of smoke from your dust, put in a final big effort.

Fire saw

Fire plow

SURVIVE: THE ALL-IN-ONE GUIDE TO STAYING ALIVE IN EXTREME CONDITIONS

FIRE SAW

Bamboo is the wood of choice for a fire saw, so this will be your go-to if you are lucky enough to find bamboo in your environment. The bamboo must be dead and dry. You will need about a two-foot-long piece, ideally two inches wide. Cut the bamboo in half. Using another piece of bamboo, scrape a handful of dry shavings off of the outside of the bamboo. This will be your tinder bundle. Cut a small notch perpendicular to the sides of the bamboo on the top of one round surface. Place the bamboo facedown with the tinder bundle under this notch. Match the edge of the unscored piece with the notch, press down firmly, and saw back and forth to create friction. If you are successful, the ignited dust will fall onto the tinder bundle, and you will be able to blow it to flame.

FIRE PLOW

Out of all the friction fire methods, I would probably recommend this one last. I have successfully made a fire using this method a few times, but as simple as it looks, it requires a level of angle experimentation that other friction fires lack. It also requires a fair bit of stamina. But if you have no tools and can't make cordage, it is a good one to try. For materials, it just requires a softer wood baseboard and a harder wood "plough," or you can try it with the same wood. The plough is a piece of straight wood with a flattened, sharpened end of about 30 degrees. The baseboard needs a long, straight groove in it and needs to be on a solid surface or able to be anchored down somehow. I find it's best to keep both hands on the plough and your arms straight when ploughing. Moving from the waist and pushing forward on the plough means you will have more stamina to keep going longer. Push the plough back and forth in the groove, creating dust at the far side of the groove. As darker dust forms, speed up and give it your all until the dust pile is smoking on its own.

Good preparation before you begin your fire-making method will enable you to create a sustainable fire to assist in your survival situation.

SUSTAINING FIRE

In a survival situation, it's always best to keep a fire burning constantly. This way you don't have to worry about taking the time to light one every night, and you have a signal ready at any time if a plane flies overhead or a ship passes by your island. You should have a pile of wood that you keep specifically for signaling, so that you're not unprepared if your rescuers come close by. Green boughs work best for creating thick smoke to help attract attention.

In order to sustain a fire without having to constantly attend to it, you will need to set your fire in such a way that it burns slowly but has access to fuel when it needs it.

This largely depends on what type of wood you use, but can also depend on how you set your fire. As mentioned previously, hardwood burns hotter and for longer, and soft wood burns colder and quickly. But there are certain types of wood that hold heat and smolder. Mallee roots in Australia are a good example of this. They will rarely ignite fully but will glow and maintain a coal that you can blow to a flame by adding kindling when you need it. It's good to be observant of the woods you are able to access and use on the fire and what properties they have. Choose the ones that burn hot and bright to bring water to a boil quickly, and the ones that smolder to keep the fire going during the day.

Punk wood, wood that has gotten soft and rotten and then dried out, is fantastic for creating a smoky fire if you want to smoke meats or hides, or keep insects away.

Placing a large hardwood log into a fire will keep it burning for a while, and you can also place logs in a star formation and feed them inward when necessary.

Building a solid crosshatch structure and lighting a small fire on top of that will allow the fire to slowly burn downward through the wood without it burning upward quickly.

If your fire has gone out while you were away from it, try digging down into the ash and coals with some small flammable material handy. Chances are there is enough heat left to ignite your tinder in the hot coals below the surface.

TRANSPORTING FIRE

Many ancient civilizations valued fire so much that it was one person's specific job to take care of it when the tribes traveled from place to place. It is way easier to blow a fire alight from a coal than exert the effort required to start a fire from scratch. Transporting fire was done in a variety of ways, but the theory was the same: allow a coal to have just enough oxygen and fuel that it stays lit, without it being smothered from a lack or burning itself out from consuming it all.

The design was fairly similar to a tinder bundle, with small material around a hot coal wrapped tightly to prevent too much oxygen from getting in. Depending on what you have on hand in your survival scenario, you can use such things as punk wood, charcoal, bracket fungus, dry moss, dry dung (of grass eaters), dry cattail heads, or teased dry grass as the first layer. Then have another layer of thicker material around that, and finish with something to hold it all together tightly. A large animal horn works well, but you can also use some kind of flexible bark tied together with a strip of inner bark.

When traveling with coals, it is a good idea to check on them every now and then to see if they need more fuel or oxygen. It's also a good idea to carry a dry tinder bundle with you, so you can fuel the coal immediately to flame when you get to your next campsite.

REFLECTIVE FIRES

Usually, the best thing to do in a survival situation is to stay put and wait for rescuers to come to you. If you do have to be on the move, you can use a reflective fire to keep safe and warm at night. This is less labor intensive than a shelter and can be much warmer.

The key is to find a flat wall surface at least three feet high. Lie between this and a low-burning, body-length fire that you've built a wind break on the other side of. This is not a good option if you think it may rain (definitely build or seek shelter if this is the case), and you must also make sure you have enough wood to last the night, as a 3:00 a.m. wood collection run is never a good thing.

A reflector wall can also be built if you have a permanent shelter. Simply build a windbreak on the opposite side of your fire. Although most heat rises, some heat will bounce off the wall and into your shelter, and it will also cut back on the heat that gets pushed away by the wind.

If you choose to locate your fire inside your shelter due to extreme cold or an abundance of biting insects, make sure that your roof is high enough that it doesn't catch fire and that you maintain a low, cooler fire. In the Amazon, I had my fire safely inside my shelter for twenty-one days. The roof of my shelter was four feet high and never even got singed.

AND FINALLY

Some fire rules to remember:

- **Clear an area around your fire.**

- **Don't light a fire you can't control.**

- **Don't light a fire at the base of a standing tree.**

- **Always make sure your fire is fully out before permanently leaving an area.**

Reflector wall

Reflective fire

RESCUE

Although the four basic needs of survival are commonly thought of as shelter, water, food, and fire, I include rescue under my basic needs. The reason for this is because the sooner your survival situation ends successfully, the better for you. This will either happen by you figuring out how to get out of the situation, or by someone finding you.

It is recommended in a survival situation to remain where you are when your disaster strikes. If it is a threat to your life to remain in that spot, then move to somewhere your life isn't in immediate danger. Examples of this might be a capsized boat, bushfire, or lack of water.

If your life isn't in immediate danger, staying where you are will present you with your best chance of survival. Not only will you be closer to where rescuers might start to look for you, you won't be potentially moving away from rescuers as they search for you. It also gives you time to create an environment that you could survive in long term if you have to.

I have put myself in challenges where I am moving and trying to survive and where I am staying in one area and trying to survive, and it is always easier to stay put. When you are on the move, you are burning a lot of calories for something other than your immediate survival, and you are lacking the time to ensure that you have adequate shelter, water, and food for the night.

Once you have decided that you need rescuing, and you have taken steps to ensure that shelter, water, and warmth are taken care of, it is time to think about making yourself as visible as possible. How you do this will depend on what resources you have around you and on you. You will need to get inventive. The more visible you can make yourself, the more likely you are to be rescued. Try everything. As silly as it seems, people really have been rescued by putting messages in bottles and floating them out to sea.

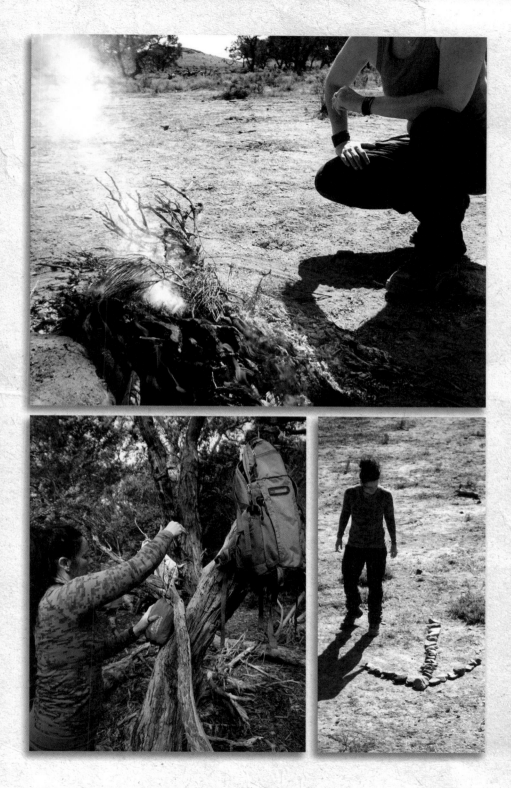

SIGNALING

Your rescue is likely to come by means of air, land vehicle, or a rescue mission on foot. You will need to prepare something visible for all these scenarios. Even if you think that you will hear someone who passes by you on foot, you may be sleeping or out collecting water, and they need to know you are around. Generally, you will have about two minutes from the time you hear an aircraft to the time it is out of range, so any signaling needs to be thought out beforehand and ready to go.

Things that will make you more visible to rescuers include:

- **Bright colors**
- **Reflective surfaces**
- **Straight lines and arrows**
- **Words on the ground**
- **Thick smoke**
- **Bright flames**
- **Torch trees**
- **Lights in the dark**

BRIGHT COLORS Assuming you have spare gear or clothing with you, hang it from the branches of a high tree, ensuring the leaves don't block the item from view. Place it out in the middle of a clearing, anchored so it doesn't blow away. Use branches or rocks to make an arrow to indicate the location of your shelter. Use bright green vegetation on darker surfaces to write a message for aerial search parties. Building a tepee structure to hang your bright and colorful pieces from is also a good idea, as the tepee structure itself will draw the eye.

REFLECTIVE SURFACES While a signal mirror is ideal, assuming you don't have one on you, any reflective surface will do. Utilize garbage that you might find around you, such as polished cans or glass bottles. These will catch the sun's rays, causing a flash of bright light observable from up to two miles away. Hang these in trees around your location. When the wind blows, they will move and signal without you needing to tend to them. Have a polished surface on you at all times in case you hear a vehicle. The front of a mobile phone will work even if you are out of signal or your battery has died. Practice reflecting the sun's rays until you know how to aim them.

AERIAL RESCUE hold your hand to the sky where the plane is and direct the light from the sun to your hand; remove your hand, and you know that the light should be visible from the plane.

GROUND RESCUE reflect the light to the ground, and then direct it in a straight line to the vehicle or person.

Keep signaling until you know that you have been seen. You will know this when you receive some kind of acknowledgment from the rescue party. It may be in the form of a signal back, a change of course, or a low flyover of the aircraft.

Straight lines and arrows Nature rarely constructs in straight lines, so any structure with straight lines stands out; lines and arrows made of rocks, branches, or leaves pointing to your location or the direction you are traveling will all attract attention.

Words on the ground SOS was accepted as the worldwide signal for distress in 1906. Although many people believe it is an acronym for something, it was chosen because it translates easily in Morse code (three dots, three dashes, three dots). HELP would also work, but would require knowledge of the English language. If you are writing words on the ground, make sure you do them in a cleared area, easily visible from above. Make them as large as you can, and try to distinguish them in some way from the ground you are creating them on. Straight-line letters work best, as they don't blend in with nature as easily. Make sure you destroy your words when you are rescued, to ensure people don't think someone still needs saving.

Thick smoke During the day, thick white or black smoke will get attention. If you have managed to get a fire started for your camp, make sure that you keep it burning all day, every day. Have separate fires set up for signal fires, with dry, extremely flammable fuel ready to go. These fires should be out in the open and large. Fires under trees will be hard to see and may start a forest fire if they get out of control. It's best if you can prepare more than one fire area with three fires, which is a universally accepted number for a distress signal. Green leaves will burn with a thick white smoke, and anything rubber will burn with a thick black smoke.

Bright flames At night it's best to have a fire that burns brightly rather than produces smoke. Dry wood and dead leaves will flare up brightly in the dark to shine a light on your location.

Torch trees Build a fire in a tree by filling the lower limbs with flammable kindling. When you light the lower branches, the whole tree will catch on fire, sending out a signal that will last for longer than your average fire. Just make sure you choose a tree that is separate from the forest, so you don't cause a wildfire.

Lights in the dark If you do have a flashlight with you, save the battery for when you truly need it. Signaling for help is going to be way more useful than having it on for comfort during the night. Your phone screen lights up, and most phones today have a flashlight function, so save your battery if you don't have service. Amplify these lights at night by shining them off something reflective, such as tin cans or shiny surfaces. Three short flashes followed by three long flashes and three short flashes will indicate your distress to anyone in the area. Pause for a minute and signal again.

We have all seen the movies where the hero runs to signal the rescue ship or plane as it moves past their location, only to be too late and for rescue to pass them by. As focused as you need to be on your basic needs, your overall aim is to get out of there, so spend the time in the early days of your scenario to be prepared to make the most of any sign of possible help.

NAVIGATION

If you have decided that a rescue is not coming or that to stay in an area is risking your life, you will need to leave your initial location. Make a plan about the direction you want to head in, based on your best chance of being rescued or making it to civilization. If you had familiarized yourself with your area prior to your emergency, you may have an exact or rough idea of which direction to travel. If you are unsure, heading to a high point to check out the surrounding terrain is a good idea. Try to locate signs of civilization, such as fences, windmills, and rail tracks. Follow your best hope for survival if you are unsure of where to start. In a desert, this will mean following water signs, and in a swamp, this may mean heading inland or toward signs of dry land.

If you are on foot, you will need a system to ensure you walk in a straight line. Humans have a natural tendency to walk veering to the left or right if they don't have a point to walk toward. This means that you will end up wasting a lot of energy walking in circles. Scientists have a lot of theories behind this, but no answer yet. If you don't have a compass and are trying to walk in a set direction, there are a few ways of achieving this. The first is to sight something in the distance in the direction you want to go and walk to that. Once you get to that object, place it at your back and find another object to aim for. This will work in relatively clear terrain but isn't so effective in heavily wooded areas. Another method is using catchment features and "aiming off." This means that you sight a feature you are trying to head toward that has an obvious feature that funnels toward it. This may be a valley pass with a river in front or a farmer's water tank along a fence line. Purposely head to one side of the landmark so that when you are "caught" by the feature, you know that you have to head in a certain direction to get to the landmark.

If you know which direction you want to head in but are unsure how to find that direction or how to stay walking in that direction, there are some good clues in nature.

DAY NAVIGATION

At its very simplest, the sun rises in the east and sets in the west. It then gets a little more complicated, as the rest depends on whether you are located in the Southern or Northern Hemisphere. At the equator, the sun's path will draw a perfect line in the sky overhead. The farther away you go from the equator, the less overhead the sun will be and the more south or north tending it will be, depending on the season or time of year.

In the Southern Hemisphere, the sun follows a path that tends southerly in winter and northerly in summer; in the Northern Hemisphere, the sun follows a path that tends northerly in winter and southerly in the summer. This means that walking with the sun on your back or at your shoulder will only give you a very rough idea of a direction to walk in, and you will need to be aware of when the sun has hit its peak and begins heading down, to prevent you from getting turned around.

To make a basic compass, stand in the sun as it rises and draw a line that runs parallel to your shadow. That is east-west. Put an E at the side closest to you and a W to the side farthest from you. Draw a perpendicular bisecting line, and label the end of the one to your right with an N and the end of the one to your left with an S. You now have a compass. Sight a landmark in the direction you wish to head in, based on this compass, and walk there.

If you don't know what time of day it is or want to recheck the bearing that you are walking on, you will need to set up a sundial.

SUNDIAL This requires a straight stick and two rocks. Plant the stick upright in the ground, and place a stone at the tip of the shadow. As the sun moves, so will the shadow. Wait at least half an hour, and place a second rock at the tip of the shadow. Mark a line between the two rocks, and lay a stick to perpendicularly bisect it. This will be your compass. Stand with your back to the upright stick and your feet on either side of the stick on the ground, and you will be facing a northerly direction.

NIGHT NAVIGATION

Many stars are different in the Northern and Southern Hemispheres. Most stars move through the sky at night, changing position and visibility quite rapidly. This means you shouldn't pick just any star in the sky and follow it for the night.

In the Northern Hemisphere, the only visible star in the night sky that remains in the same spot is Polaris, or the North Star. This is because it is in the center of the star field, and Earth's axis points almost directly toward it. It may be difficult to locate the North Star because it isn't the brightest star in the night sky, but the Big Dipper and Cassiopeia are two very obvious constellations nearby that can help guide you to Polaris.

Polaris is not visible in the Southern Hemisphere, and there are no stars that remain constant. To find south, you will need to locate the Southern Cross and its two Pointer stars. Draw a line between the two long points of the cross, and then create a line that does a perpendicular bisection of a line between the two pointers. Where these two lines meet in the sky, draw a line down to the horizon, and that will always be south.

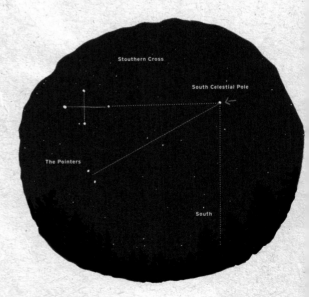

NATURAL INDICATORS

Again, these natural indicators will change sides of the compass, depending on which hemisphere you are in, but if you know that they will always be on a specific side, it might save you from walking in circles.

Moss likes cooler, damper environments, so it tends to grow on the side of the tree that gets less sun. Termite mounds tend to be on the side that gets more sun. Snow and ice will thaw faster on the sunny side of rocks, and the prevailing winds will shape the trees in the area, helping you to head on a bearing. Use as many natural clues as you can to piece together which direction to head in, because there are always exceptions to these rules that can get you turned around.

If you are by a river, follow it downstream. Bigger rivers tend to have villages or towns on their banks, and where they empty into the ocean, there may be ports and cities.

To decide how much daylight you have left, hold up three fingers to the sun-side horizon. Each three fingers that the sun is above the horizon signals an hour of time. Always make sure that you set up a shelter and establish fire before it gets dark when you are traveling.

Hopefully you came prepared with a GPS, compass, and map of the area and familiarized yourself with your surroundings. If you didn't, utilizing any or all of the above navigational aids may help you make your way to safety and quickly end your survival scenario.

5

Ecosystems

The right survival tip in the wrong situation could kill you.

HAVING EXPLORED THE BASIC NEEDS that you require to endure in any given survival scenario, we are now going to take a closer look at the different ecosystems that you may encounter and some specific techniques that will assist with those respective environments. This will help you to prepare for your particular ecosystem or if you are venturing into a new one.

Ecosystems are regions that can be clearly defined by distinctive weather patterns, terrain, plants, and animals over a long period of time. The more common extremes are:

1. Tropical   3. Swamp   5. Marine

2. Arid   4. Polar   6. Highland

These ecosystems all over the world will have common characteristics that you can identify and utilize in order to survive.

HIGHLAND

SWAMP

MARINE

POLAR

ARID

TROPICAL

TROPICAL

A tropical ecosystem is defined as an area that has high average temperatures year-round and two clear seasons: the wet season and the dry season.

The tropics, commonly known as jungles, are characterized by having an abundance of plants and animals and the likelihood that it will rain at any time of year, including the dry season. They are thought of as one of the most extreme ecosystems in which to survive, in spite of, or perhaps as a result of, the abundance of water and animals.

In a tropical survival scenario, water is usually easily accessible, and shelter and fire become the primary concern. Jungles are hard to navigate in, and even ducking away from your campsite to get more wood can result in getting lost, as every patch of jungle looks like the other. It is hot and humid and full of biting, sucking, and stinging insects that sometimes want to lay eggs under your skin. The ground is usually damp due to the lack of sunlight able to penetrate the canopy, and making sure you can get your body and clothing dried out regularly is a priority, as trench foot, skin rashes, and skin fungus can be serious issues.

To add to the variety of insects attacking you, the plants in jungles have developed their own self-defense against being eaten, in the form of stinging hairs or thorns that catch on your skin and clothing as you pass by them. Every plant is fighting for its little patch of sun, leading to very little light making it down to ground level. This can make your environment seem dense and oppressive, which can increase feelings of hopelessness and despair.

At night, even the moonlight and starlight cannot penetrate the canopy, leading to not even being able to see your hand in front of your face.

Despite all of this, the tropics can be survived in if you focus on the positives of the situation and work to remove the negatives. The first thing to do is to educate yourself about the patch of tropics you have ended up in. Some assets in your location may be:

- **Easy access to multiple water sources**
- **An abundance of edible fruits and palms**
- **An abundance of animal life to hunt**
- **Lots of shelter-building material**

Edible fruits and palms

Shelter-building material

Take stock of your environment, and make a plan that best suits you. Although jungles may seem warm and humid during the day, the dampness of the ground, plus the likelihood of rain, means that making a shelter is a priority. I personally have gone hypothermic in a jungle environment more than once, due to wet and windy conditions overnight, when I didn't have an adequate shelter built in time. The wet season in the Amazon has to be experienced to be believed. The rain pours down like someone is aiming a firehose at you from above, and the wind howls along the ground, sucking any warmth out of your body. A shelter that would usually be considered waterproof in any other part of the world eventually started to drip, and then water cascaded through. My fire quickly went out due to the abundance of water, and all I could do was crawl to the back of my shelter

and curl up into the smallest ball I could to try to keep my vital organs functioning. I ceased to shiver at some stage during the night, which is a bad sign, and just kept an eye on the sky to calculate how long I'd have to wait for dawn. As soon as a sun patch appeared on the jungle floor, I crawled over to it and began to rewarm. That day, I made shelter my priority and put twice as many leaves on the roof as I had the night before. Eventually the shelter became thick enough to withstand the monsoon rains, and I stayed dry during the daily storms.

If your environment is full of biting insects or large predators, you may want to make fire your next priority, but clean drinking water should be close behind, due to the hot, humid nature of the environment. Stay flexible with your thinking, and analyze your situation.

TROPICAL SHELTER

Whenever I am looking at what kind of shelter to build in a region, I look at what the primitive societies used to build there. Almost every survival guide-book tells you to build a shelter off the ground in a jungle. This is a modern way of thinking, based on modern equipment such as hammocks and mosqui-to nets that are quickly and easily strung up and protect the user from most of the insects and creepy-crawlies in the area. The only tribe that was record-ed to live in rain forest trees was the Korowai, who built houses high in the treetops. However, when researchers looked into this, it was discovered that this tribe had only built their homes this way for a particular documentary and usually dwelled on the forest floor.

Most tribes lived in huts on the ground, made from materials found in their local area. Having spent a long time in survival scenarios in jungles, I have found that the most effective way of making sure that you don't get too many creepy-crawlies is to take away their habitat. They love the abundant leaf litter found on the jungle floor, and by simply clearing this away down to the soil layer, you will deter most of the crawling insects from entering your shelter. I have also found that a circle of white ash on the ground around a shelter helps with this.

If you build a raised platform shelter, you are inviting all of these insects into your house. For some reason, a lot of the ants and spiders that are found in these environments love getting off the ground too, and I find that whenev-er I build a platform, it isn't long before it is teeming with the very creatures I was hoping to avoid.

Another reason stated for the raised platform is to stay safe from pred-ators. Most of the larger predators in jungles are cats who wouldn't find it a challenge to jump up to your platform. Fire is your best method of deterring them. And although some of the more venomous snakes are ground dwellers, they tend to move away from humans more often than toward them, and the biggest danger of encountering them is when you are moving around the jungle, not when you are in your shelter at night.

My favorite jungle shelter is one that I learned about from a tribe in the Amazon. I call it a squirrel tail shelter, for lack of a better name. It is a bigger version of the temporary shelter they erect when hunting, and it kept me dry even through the tail end of the wet season.

The key things to remember when building shelters in tropical environments are:

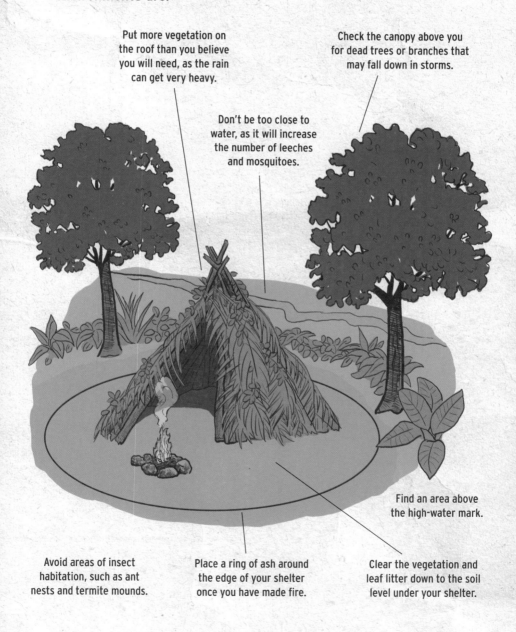

Put more vegetation on the roof than you believe you will need, as the rain can get very heavy.

Check the canopy above you for dead trees or branches that may fall down in storms.

Don't be too close to water, as it will increase the number of leeches and mosquitoes.

Find an area above the high-water mark.

Avoid areas of insect habitation, such as ant nests and termite mounds.

Place a ring of ash around the edge of your shelter once you have made fire.

Clear the vegetation and leaf litter down to the soil level under your shelter.

THE SQUIRREL TAIL SHELTER

The best palm to use for this is one that has feather-shaped leaves rather than fan shaped. Make a crossbeam between two trees, about four feet off the ground. This crossbeam needs to be about four feet in length and thick and strong, as it will be supporting the full weight of your shelter. Cut a lot of palm leaves at the base of the leaf. Then stick the base of the leaf in the ground about three feet away from the crossbeam and draped over the beam to create a squirrel tail effect. Repeat this process until you have a thick covering over you. You will need to make sure you put new leaves on the shelter regularly, as they will wilt, but I have survived monsoons in this type of shelter, and not a drop made it through to my sleeping area.

By clearing the leaf litter from under the shelter, I may have gotten a little dirtier in my sleep, but I only once got woken up with an ant bite in over twenty days of sleeping on the ground there.

Your shelter will blend in seamlessly with your environment and make it impossible for even you to find without making it obvious. In a jungle, you can walk ten feet from a location and never find that location again. Ways of marking your paths and shelter are by breaking branches or twigs, scoring trees (cutting marks into them or rubbing charcoal on them), and making arrows or piles of rocks that can guide you back to your shelter.

You can make yourself a very cozy shelter in tropical ecosystems, so long as you learn how to work with the environment rather than be terrified of it.

TROPICAL WATER

This is one of the few ecosystems where you are almost guaranteed to have a good supply of water. The problem is making sure that the water is safe to drink. You will be tempted by the clear-running streams and sweet-looking rock pools, but if you want to ensure your survival, you will need to find a way to purify all river water before drinking it.

One of the best methods of having safe drinking water is to collect rainfall, and the best method of water purification without a pot or container to boil in will be water wells and natural water filters.

WATER WELL This water-straining technique is often referred to as a gypsy well. It's simply the method of digging a hole a few yards from a murky water source and allowing the ground to do the filtering for you. If you are there for a while, you can line the well with sticks to prevent the sides from falling in. Over time, all sediment should sink to the bottom, leaving you with clear water to drink. Just remember, this is an emergency water source and can't be trusted not to contain impurities.

NATURAL WATER FILTER In an open-ended container, place alternate layers of pebbles, sand, grass, and charcoal. It works best when the container tapers to a smaller end. Passing the water through the pebbles, sand, and grass will remove the sediment from the water, and the charcoal should kill any bacteria. The container can be created with bamboo or flexible strips of bark.

As well as crafting as many collection containers as you can and funneling rainwater through leaves and bark, you can find areas where fresh water has pooled in rocks and plants. But only drink this straight after the rain, when there is no chance it has gone stagnant or collected toxins.

Tropical areas can also have an abundance of vegetation that collects and stores water in its structure. Vines and bamboo are good examples of this.

VINES A lot of the thicker vines in rain forests will supply you with drinking water. You can either cut a section of the vine and blow the moisture out into a container, or you can cut a notch at a high point in a vine and another at a low point in the vine and put your mouth or water container under the lower notch to collect the water. **Do not drink the liquid if it comes out sticky, milky, or bitter tasting.** Take note of that type of vine and try a different one.

BAMBOO You will need to locate one of the larger species of bamboo, where the stalks regularly grow to the size of small trees. Tap the sections of the bamboo. There is more likely to be water in the green bamboo than the dead stalks, but try them all, because sometimes you will find water in the older stalks as well. Sections without water in them will sound hollower than those with water inside of them. Cut a small hole at the top of the section, and then make a cut near the bottom. Drink from the bottom cut. If the water tastes or smells funny, don't drink it, and try another section.

Bamboo will also provide you with some good collection containers, as their sections are watertight. Just cut below two notches to cut out a segment. These containers can also provide you with a pot to boil water in if you can't locate bamboo with water in it already or want to make a soup. Simply fill the container and suspend it over hot coals, or position it next to them. Although the bamboo will eventually burn and crack, there should be ample time for the water to heat up and boil before that happens.

TROPICAL FIRE

Being one of the dampest places on Earth, where rainfall up to seventy-eight inches per annum has regularly been recorded, fire is one of the trickiest needs to gain and maintain. There are few sources of dry fuel, and dry tinder must be sought out and quickly used after processing, as it absorbs the moisture from the air and becomes useless.

Fire is essential in the jungle to help purify water, protect you from predators, repel insects, and provide some light at night. Although I haven't had much success with smoky fires keeping mosquitoes at bay, other survivalists swear by it; smoky fires can be created by adding green boughs to your fire. The ash from your fire (the white powdery by-product) can also be rubbed on your skin to act as a natural repellant or sunscreen. It can be rubbed on wounds to stop bleeding, and it also has some antibacterial properties that can speed healing. This is essential in a jungle environment, where wounds tend to fester and are prone to infection. Fire will also help you dry out your clothes and skin so that they don't begin to rot.

TINDER The best material I have found for tinder in the jungle is the dried stalks of fan palms, but I'm sure that any palm will do. Use your blade to scrape shavings from the dead (but not rotten) stalk. The waxy coating on the dead stalk protects the underneath from the damp and adds an element of combustion to the tinder. Good tinder can also be found on the underside of logs and underneath the outer layer of bark on some trees.

FUEL Locate dead standing wood, and shave off the outer wet layer for the first fire. After that, ensure you have a system of layering the wood around the fire to dry it out before you need it. Building a specific smaller shelter for wood you have collected is invaluable in the tropics. Termite mounds also make for good fuel, and the smoke from burning them can deter flying insects.

Friction fire methods are very tricky in the tropics, since most of the dead wood is damp and rotten. If you can find driftwood on some of the more exposed, sunny riverbanks, it would be worth trying, but your best option would be finding bamboo and using the fire saw method.

THE FIRE SAW

The bamboo must be dead and dry. You will need about a two-foot-long piece, ideally two inches wide. Cut the bamboo in half. Using another piece of bamboo, scrape a handful of dry shavings off the outside of the bamboo. This will be your tinder bundle. Cut a small notch perpendicular to the sides of the bamboo on the top of one round surface. Place the bamboo facedown with the tinder bundle under this notch. Match the edge of the unscored piece with the notch, press firmly down, and saw back and forth to create friction. If you are successful, the ignited dust will fall onto the tinder bundle, and you will be able to blow it to flame.

Keep in mind that you are trying to create fire in an environment that is wet, so don't beat up on yourself if you can't. There are ways to keep warm, get drinking water, and provide yourself with food in the jungle that don't involve fire, so if you can't figure it out after trying everything you can, move on and work on the things you can change.

Fire saw
(see page 185)

TROPICAL FOOD

As well as an abundance of water, the tropics can supply an abundance of food. Depending on the time of year, you may have a wealth of fruit in the trees; just make sure to test for toxins (see page 110), no matter how tempting they look or delicious they smell. There will be palms of some description that you should be able to eat the heart of palm from, and ferns can supply fiddleheads (the small, closed fronds of new leaves). With all the lushness of vegetation will come a variety of insects, grubs, termites, snails, and worms. Although probably not your first food of choice, they can sustain you until you can catch larger game. Remember to avoid the brightly colored insects and snails, as this is a warning system developed to let predators know that they are not good to eat, and we humans should pay attention to such markings as well. With land snails and slugs, it's best to purge them for a few days in case they have been eating any vegetation that is toxic to you, so put them in a container with some fresh grass if possible. Wash them thoroughly and boil them, cook them in their shells on the open fire, or roast them on skewers.

Fuzzy caterpillars are to be avoided. Not only are they not good to eat, but some will leave your skin irritated on contact and even deliver an electric-shock-type sting that can be severe enough to trigger a sudden reduction in blood pressure, vomiting, and/or seizures that may result in death.

There will be a large variety of tropical birds, though they will probably spend most of their time in the canopy, and a throwing stick will not work in such conditions. Try setting up a few arapuca traps on the forest floor to see if you can tempt them out of the treetops.

Heart of palm

Fiddleheads

Snails

Grubs

ARAPUCA TRAP
You will need:

- Twenty-four thumb-width sticks, with six sets of four varying sizes

- Two pieces of rope or cord about two feet in length

- A short length of cord

- A finger-width trigger stick about ten inches long

- Bait

Place the two longest sticks side by side, and attach the two pieces of cord from one end of each stick to the other to create a square. Twist the two sticks once in opposite directions so the rope forms a cross. Slide the next two longest sticks, log-cabin style, between the ropes and begin to fill in the slack. Eventually you will end up with a tensioned pyramid. This is your cage. Fill in the top of the pyramid with sticks to ensure that there isn't an escape route for the bird. These are also the sticks that you will remove in order to get the bird out without it escaping. Break the trigger stick in half in such a way that you can put the pieces back together again. Tie the short length of the cord to the inside of the trap, and loop it around the break in the trigger stick with tension. Lean the trap on the trigger stick. Place the bait inside the trap. When a bird enters the trap, it will disturb the cord, which will trigger the trap. I find that it is necessary to put a weight on top of the trap to make sure that the bird doesn't manage to overturn the trap or wriggle out from under it.

Try a throwing stick on the riverside, mornings and evenings, when certain wading birds will be concentrating on fishing and are not as alert to predators. But be aware that a lot of tropical locations have large predators, such as caimans and alligators, in their waterways. If you wing a bird and it lands on the water, it will attract these predators faster than you can retrieve it, and you may end up becoming the prey if you head in to get it.

It is worth setting up traps and snares on the jungle floor; however, baited traps are not as effective in areas where food is abundant. If your prey has access to the food they like everywhere, they are less likely to be tempted by food that is in an area filled with strange scents.

Although many guides recommend the figure-four deadfall (see page 138) for jungle environments, I have found it to be one of the least effective traps, due to the fact that it can be hard to find good, heavy, flat rocks in the rain forests I have been in, and the floor of the jungle tends to be spongy and soft, which cushions the blow of the deadfall, meaning that the prey can escape. I have had more success with snares set at burrow entrances and on game trails.

In the wet season, mammals can forage and drink in many different areas, so it is hard to determine a pattern in their behavior. In the dry season, the water will retreat, and animals will be forced to travel to certain places for water. This will make them more predictable and easier to hunt. Tracking animals in the jungle is trickier due to the amount of leaf litter on the ground, though the edges of rivers tend to be quite muddy and will enable you to figure out what is in your area.

Due to the abundance of food for animals in a jungle environment, they are not forced into certain areas to survive. This means when you "move in," they can and probably will move to another area. You will need to roam away from your shelter area to set traps and hunt. Make sure you mark your trail clearly so you can find your way back.

The vegetation in these areas tends to grow fast and straight, utilizing any break in the canopy to shoot up in search of sunlight. This means that the wood of most small saplings and palms is perfect for making a quick, strong spear. To make such a spear stronger, harden it in a fire. There are several methods of fire-hardening spears. The first method simply involves running the sharp tip of the spear through the flames until the moisture is removed and the outer layer is slightly charred. This changes its structure and material properties, making the wood harder and more durable.

The second method is to bury or insert the spearhead under the fire until the moisture has been removed from the wood. Evidence of humans using this technique to make their spears stronger dates back to over 400,000 years ago.

The good news is that you will probably be near a body of water that will provide you with good fishing. If the water source is a smaller, flowing river, you can try fish traps. If the stream has lots of rocks in it, the damming technique is worth trying, and there should be a lot of materials to make some good fishing baskets.

FISH DAM If you are by a stream, you can use a similar technique of building rock walls to trap fish. Shape a funnel of rocks across part or all of the stream that ends in a rock wall and catchment area on the downstream side.

FISHING BASKETS Fish traps can also be made of small saplings or vines. The classic one involves making a two- to three-foot-long cylinder that tapers to a dead end. I find it is useful to put a couple of circles of saplings inside this structure, to help give it some shape. A smaller funnel-shaped piece goes in the opening, providing an entrance for the fish but making it impossible to exit. This can be baited and placed in an area of the stream where water naturally funnels through. Or you can create an area that will funnel the fish into the trap you have placed by building up the rocks along most of your stream except for where your trap is located.

If you are by a large, slow-flowing body of water, experiment with making some cordage and hooks. Baiting with grubs or innards should lead to success, as these are a delicacy to the fish.

I have had success in areas such as these with night fishing, but it is definitely a risk-versus-reward decision. Predators such as caimans tend to be more active at night and harder to see, and they also are trying to get a meal in the shallows. You will need a light source and a large knife or spear. The fish in these areas tend to move into the shallows to sleep for the night. You can see them with the light source and have time to spear or club them before they wake up.

Eels can also provide you with a good meaty food source. They prefer low-lying swampy streams and lagoons. They are bottom dwellers and hide in burrows or root systems. You can catch them by hand, with hooks and line, or with a fish spear. Be aware of the region you are in: electric eels populate the waterways in northern regions of South America and can deliver a powerful shock that can travel through the water you are standing in, even if you aren't touching the eel. The shock can register up to 860 volts, which is about seven times the amount of a shock from an electrical socket. It won't kill a healthy individual, but it may stun you into inactivity. Some types of eels can also deliver up to three shocks in a row. If you are in an area with electric eels, the trick is to kill them without getting into the water or touching them. And know that they can deliver a charge for up to eight hours after their death. It is important to cook eels thoroughly, as their blood can be toxic to humans.

You should never starve in a tropical location. But you might need to adjust your idea of what food is and get creative with your foraging.

TROPICAL RESCUE

Highlighting your location and signaling to rescuers are going to be incredibly difficult in tropical locations. The canopy of the jungle will mask and diffuse the smoke from your fire, and the lack of sun that makes it to the ground will render signal mirrors useless. Make the most of any break in the canopy by placing signal fires and eye-catching objects in them. Place signals on river bends or even on floats attached to the shore.

If you decide that rescue is not going to come to you, you may need to try to make your way out. Direction finding is very difficult in the jungle, and it's easy to get turned around, wasting time and energy. The dense vegetation can be hard to move through, and following game trails can lead away from civilization rather than to it. Instead of heading through the jungle, follow larger rivers downstream. Not only will you always have a water source, but villages tend to be built on the edge of wider rivers or at the points where rivers hit the coast.

Leave messages and clues for rescuers about where you are headed and when you left, and also leave a clear trail for them to find you.

DANGERS

Jungles can be home to large predatory cats, venomous snakes and insects, and also any variety of caimans, alligators, and crocodiles.

CATS Large cats have similar instincts to house cats. They like to play with their prey and don't need to be hungry to kill; they will do it for the fun of the chase. If you are confronted with a large cat, do not run. Make yourself look as large as you can and act bold. This will confuse the cat, as it is used to prey running. If you can grab a stick or rock for a weapon, do so, but slowly. Back away slowly, especially if you have the animal cornered. If the cat attacks, drop anything you are carrying; it may confuse them into thinking that what you have dropped is their prey. Defend yourself with your weapon, if you have one. A spear is best for keeping distance between you and these large predators. I make one the minute I find myself in a survival scenario and always carry it with me in the jungle.

SNAKES Venomous snakes in jungles tend to behave a little differently from venomous snakes elsewhere. They are ambush predators, blending in with the leaf litter, allowing prey to get close to them before they strike. This means that making noise moving through the brush won't make them move out of your path. The only way to avoid them is to always pay attention to where you are walking. I move slowly through a jungle environment for a few reasons—it allows me time to find assets in the dense vegetation but also allows me to make sure of my path.

CROCODILES, ALLIGATORS, AND CAIMANS These reptiles are the ultimate water predators, perfecting their techniques over 37 million years. The scales on their backs are designed to limit water movement as they swim, so you will have no signs of their approach until they launch at you. Their powerful tail is designed to propel them through the water like a torpedo, and they have the strongest bite of any animal, with large crocodiles being able to bite down with a force over 5,000 pounds per square inch. They are also smart and take note of your movements in order to best hunt you. If you always get water from the same spot or swim at a certain spot in the river, they will lie in wait at that exact spot the next day to ambush you. Your best defense against them is to be aware of them and, if possible, avoid them. Some species are less aggressive than others and prefer fish as their source of food, so knowing what type of crocodile frequents your area might help you know what you can get away with, but if you can, it's best to avoid their habitat and mating areas.

Try to get your water from shallow river areas, where you can see what is in the water in front of you. Bathe in these same areas. Avoid steep banks that drop off into deep water.

Their mode of killing usually involves a grab-and-roll technique. If you have been grabbed by a crocodile or alligator, you will not be able to push open its jaws, and there are very few weak spots on this animal. If you are in the middle of the rolling, you will have to ride it out until the beast pauses and then try to get your fingers in its eyes. This is the only weak spot on a crocodile or alligator.

If you are on the edge of a waterway and see an alligator moving rapidly toward you, chances are you can avoid it by running as fast as you can in a straight line, as they are not able to move with speed on land.

Crocodile

Alligator

Caiman

Insects Leeches, ticks, mosquitoes, and ants are just some of the little critters that will make your life uncomfortable in tropical ecosystems. Ticks and mosquitoes are notorious for bearing diseases that can make you very sick. Unfortunately, they are very hard to avoid.

Ticks tend to be in areas where there are animals for them to feed on, so if you are looking to build your shelter in an area where it looks like other animals have bedded down, it might be worth choosing somewhere else. Once a tick has attached itself to you, it is important that you remove it in such a way that the head doesn't get left in your body. Ticks will also regurgitate toxins into your body if squeezed or threatened, so don't grab and pull them out by their body or try to remove them by burning them. Find two strong, thin thorns or sticks and slide them under the tick's head and pull upward.

Leeches are not dangerous, but once they drop off, they leave an open wound that can be subject to infection. Make sure you rub the area with some white ash if you have it, or clean the area thoroughly. Leeches will fall off if you touch their body with the heated end of a small stick, or you can slide a fingernail or sharp edge sideways along your skin and dislodge them.

Ants in tropical places can come with a hell of a bite. Fire ants in the Amazon almost incapacitated me once, as a large number swarmed my feet when I disturbed a nest. The resulting bites, which were like electric shocks, gave me a pins-and-needles feeling leading to panic, and I couldn't do anything else until I got them all off me. Some jungle ants have been used as rites of passage for tribesmen who subject themselves to multiple bites in order to prove they can withstand great pain. Ant nests have also been used as torture and murder devices with people being tied to them with the idea it is the worst way to die. It is impossible to avoid ants and biting insects in the jungle. It is rare to have a moment when nothing is crawling on you. Swatting and slapping out at them can result in getting stung, and most ants release a pheromone that will summon more ants if they die or feel threatened. My advice is to flick or brush them off if you can. And some won't bite. My rule of thumb in the jungle is to leave something for thirty seconds if it is crawling on me. If it hasn't stung or bitten me in that time, it is free to stay.

You will need to find some kind of Zen mindset with mosquitoes and insects in the jungle. There are a few natural repellants, but they don't tend to be effective against the number of insects you are likely to encounter. Smoky fires at dusk and dawn, when mosquitoes are most active, might help. Any plants that smell like citronella (a lemon-type smell), camphor (mothballs), or tea tree (eucalyptus) may help if rubbed on your skin; always test a small amount on the inside of your wrist first to make sure it's not toxic to you. Ash from your fire may help as well. I have never had any success with rubbing mud on my skin in any location I have tried, but it is a popular idea for avoiding mosquito bites. All that happens for me is that mosquitoes are attracted to the moisture in the mud and find the gaps where the mud isn't fully applied. Then the mud dries and cracks, and the mosquitoes attack through the cracks.

Smoky fires can be hit or miss too. Green material, dung, termite mounds, and punk wood will all create a smoky fire. The Indigenous people in the north of Australia were able to combat the abundance of mosquitoes by creating shelters that were then sealed and filled with smoke. They would sleep with their mouths positioned by small breathing holes in order to get some fresh air.

I have found some success in the Amazon with burning the sap from the copal tree in my shelter in the morning and night to deter the swarms of mosquitoes from moving in. You will need to experiment with all these techniques and more to find the solution that works best for you. It may be that you will need to relocate your shelter to a position farther from water.

The trick to surviving in tropical environments is to learn to work with the jungle rather than fight against it. You will need to be practicing all your survival attitudes, probably the most important one being focusing on what you can change and ignoring what you cannot. Be adaptable, stay aware, and try to work every day to make your situation better.

ARID

Arid ecosystems are defined by their severe lack of water, to the extent that it hinders or prevents the growth and development of plant and animal life. It is almost impossible for any life to sustain itself in arid regions. People generally associate arid regions with extreme heat. In fact, deserts tend to be areas with the greatest fluctuations between daytime temperatures and nighttime temperatures, meaning that in some locations you will have to contend with both scorching and freezing temperatures. The polar regions are technically defined as arid ecosystems, but I will cover them in their own section.

The cold temperatures are caused by clear skies and wide-open spaces that allow the daytime heat to escape into the atmosphere at night. These open spaces also allow for winds to rage without obstacles, creating dust and sandstorms that can be disorienting and debilitating.

During the day, the sun's rays reflect off the earth and drive temperatures high, causing the unprepared to suffer from extreme dehydration and heatstroke. This means that survival tasks need to be limited to early mornings and evenings, and seeking cover and resting in the heat of the day are essential.

I personally think that an arid ecosystem is one of the hardest to survive. In tropical ecosystems, there is an abundance of things that might kill you; in arid areas, it is the lack of things that might kill you. It is one of the only survival locations where I would recommend you keep moving. Unless you have landed in your survival scenario with resources such as a broken-down vehicle or crashed plane, your best bet for survival in a desert scenario is to get to a water source as soon as possible.

In these conditions, you can die in a day from heat exposure and dehydration. Your survival will depend on your ability to seek shelter and source water.

ARID SHELTER

The clothes on your back are your first line of shelter in the desert. Resist the urge to take off clothing as you get hot. Bare skin can burn quickly, which will heat up your entire body and cause you to lose more fluids. Also, sweat dries faster on bare skin. This can produce a temporary cooling effect, but if you sweat and your clothes get wet, they will help cool you for longer as they retain the moisture. A majority of people who live in deserts wear head-to-toe flowing clothing. This is because it protects them from the sun and allows them to create and take advantage of any breeze. Make sure if you have any spare material that you craft a head covering that protects as much of your head and neck as possible.

This material will also protect you from the cold at night. If you are unable to create or find shelter, scrape a trench in the ground to get out of the wind and try to cover as much of your bare skin with your clothing as possible. If you can find some vegetation around you that isn't filled with thorns, stuff it in your clothing to add an insulating layer, and put a layer of it on the ground beneath you to prevent losing heat to the cooling sand.

In these regions, your whole survival mindset should be focused on doing the least amount of physical exertion you need to do in order to survive. To this end, try to find ready-made natural shelters instead of constructing one from scratch. You are looking for something that will protect you from the sun rather than needing it to be waterproof. Overhangs and shallow caves can provide shade and coolness during the day and retain some heat during the night. Building a wall of rocks can protect you from relentless winds.

Small bushes can provide some shade. Quite often the local animals will scrape out a trench beneath a bush and curl up there in the heat of the day.

Any way to get out of the direct, scorching sun should be considered. Don't lie directly on the hot sand or ground during the day. Scoop away the first few layers to get to the cooler ground below.

These regions tend to have a lack of vegetation, so building an elaborate shelter is usually out of the question, but if you do find yourself in an area with some resources, building a lean-to either in the early morning or late evening is a good idea. Face the back of the lean-to in the direction that the sun tends to move across the sky. If you are on the equator, the sun goes directly overhead, but to either side of the equator, depending on the time of year, the sun will either be trending on the southern side of the sky or the northern side. This will give you the maximum amount of shade during the day. A lean-to will allow you to capitalize on any breeze that flows through your area.

Lean-to shelter
(see page 64)

Do not set up your shelter in a dried-up creek bed. Although it may look like it hasn't rained in forever, sometimes deserts get their annual rainfall in one go. You may not see a cloud in the sky, but then flash flooding can send massive debris and huge volumes of water through your campsite without warning.

Keep an eye on the sky. Quite often clouds can give you a clue as to what weather is headed your way. Without needing to learn different cloud names and what each cloud means, remember that wispy, string-like clouds signal that strong winds are on the way. Wind comes down through the atmosphere in layers, so if there are clouds like that in the sky, the winds will be at ground level by the next day. If you are on the move, this will be a signal for you to find a good shelter where you can be protected from sand and dust.

Seeking shelter in the heat of the day could save your life from day one in arid regions; however, water needs to be one of the priorities as well. If you have found yourself in an area with no water sources, don't waste valuable hydration by constructing an elaborate shelter. Create a simple one to get you through that day, and as the day cools, get on the move to find a place that may help support life.

ARID WATER

If you are unable to get access to a good water source, you will need to move to an area with the hope of improving your situation, and you will need to do it as soon as possible, while you are still able to think clearly.

In normal, everyday life, it is recommended that you drink about a gallon of water a day to operate at your best. I personally have survived on less than a quarter of a gallon a day for an extended period of time, but it was in a humid location, so that could have been why. In dry, arid conditions, you are going to need to be able to access water within a day to get through in a survival situation. If you have come prepared and have some water with you, you will need to assess how long that water will last and decide when you will need to leave to seek more. It's probably better to leave sooner rather than later, while you are still functioning optimally. Ration half a gallon a day per person. If you have a gallon, you have a day to rest and a day to seek out more water, or two days of travel.

There are a few theories about sipping water versus taking a big drink. The latest research, which makes the most sense to me, suggests that you should drink less often but more at a time. Scientists state that any less than 250 milliliters isn't actually effective at staving off dehydration, as most of your small sips will be absorbed first by your stomach, liver, and kidneys, leaving none to make its way to your brain. I certainly have found this to be more effective in extreme heat situations.

Dehydration symptoms include:

- Dry mouth
- Tiredness or fatigue
- Thirst
- Lack of urination (you should be peeing once every few hours)
- Dark-colored urine
- Headache
- Dizziness

If untreated, dehydration can progress into foggy thinking, inability to make rational decisions, and eventually seizures, brain damage, and death.

Travel during the cooler periods of the day, and seek shelter during the heat of the day. Unless you have sufficient light, I never recommend traveling at night. It is very easy to get disoriented, and losing your footing and spraining an ankle can mean certain death in the desert.

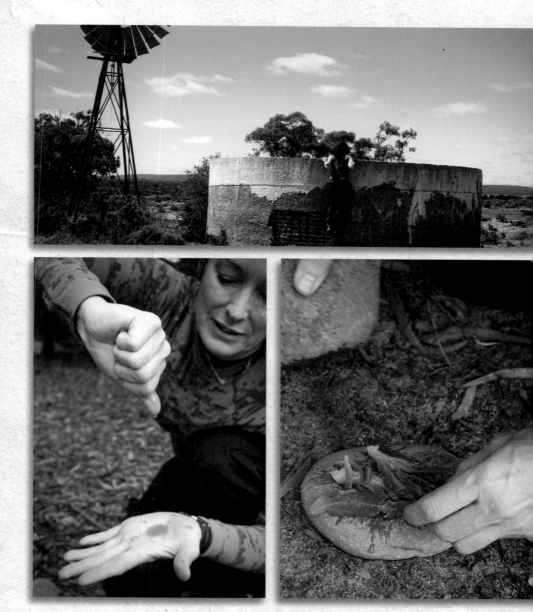

There are a few clues as to where water might be located in arid areas, but you will probably need to seek a high point. Look for:

- Vegetation (the greener, denser, and lusher it is, the more likely there will be water, but any vegetation is worth seeking out)

- Dry creek beds

- Rocky areas

- Animal tracks

- Man-made structures

VEGETATION If the ground at the base of the roots is damp, try digging a hole to see if it fills up with water. If this doesn't work or if the base of the tree is dry, you can try to access water by digging out the root systems. Start as close to the tree as you can. Cut the roots into three-foot segments and prop them up on a container. This will allow the water in the roots to drain out.

If you have access to clear plastic bags or a plastic sheet, you can try the leaf condensation or solar still methods (see pages 92 and 94, respectively), but remember to leave the digging of any holes to the cooler times of the day. Choosing when to exert yourself can be the difference between life and death in arid areas.

DRY CREEK BEDS Dig on the outer bends of dry creek beds, because this is where the water moves more slowly when the creeks are flowing, so the water has more time to absorb into the ground. If you aren't successful, head downstream and try again.

ROCKY AREAS When it does rain in deserts, it can pool in rocky areas. If these areas are relatively deep and shaded, they can store water year round. This can also be an area to find food, as all of the animals from miles around will also use this as their water source. Make sure that you purify the water if you can before consuming it.

ANIMAL TRACKS If an animal is large enough to leave an obvious trail, it is going to need a water source close by. Look for game trails, and follow them to water. Game trails will start wide and branch inward as they get closer to water, creating an arrow pattern to guide you in the right direction.

MAN-MADE STRUCTURES Humans have tried to settle in the harshest of places. In deserts and arid areas, wells and windmills were put in place to suck the water out of underground basins. These structures can be seen from a distance and are worth heading to if you can see them. Not only will they provide a source of water, but they are usually checked fairly regularly on stations and could lead to your rescue. If the windmill pumps to a tank or trough, you can access water from those. Make sure you purify the water if at all possible, due to the number of animals that also have access to these water sources. If the trough and tank are dry, there may still be water at the base of the windmill. Tie your clothing together, and lower it down into the hole. If it touches the waterline, you will be able to pull it up and wring it out, collecting water that way.

If you are unable to locate a high point, then seek out signs of life around you. Look for game trails or tracks, bird life, and insect activity to signal that there may be water around. You may also be able to extract water from a few other sources.

DEW The large temperature difference between daytime and nighttime in arid ecosystems means that dew drops may be your best source of water. Lay out whatever clothing you can spare overnight under the clear skies and wring it out in the morning. You can also tie your T-shirt to your legs and walk through the sparse vegetation first thing in the morning to gather what has collected on their leaves overnight.

SUCCULENTS In Australia, there is a succulent called pigface that can be found along a lot of the coastlines, but also in the desert. It is a low-growing creeping plant with hard, succulent, pricker-free leaves. There are many varieties of similar succulents found in deserts all over the world. If you crush up the leaves and squeeze them in your hand with your thumb pointing downward, drinkable moisture will trickle along your thumb. If you are trying any variety other than the pigface found in Australia, do the toxin test first. **Make sure you do not drink the liquid if it comes out sticky or milky.**

Water is your greatest commodity in arid environments. The best way to stave off dehydration is to conserve your moisture rather than have to collect it, as water sources are scarce in this harsh ecosystem. Being smart about when you move and what you move for, and staying under shelter as much as possible in the heat of the day, will help get you out of a dire situation and make sure you survive.

WARNING:

You will need to be careful using cactus as a water source. There is a myth that drinking from the barrel cactus provides a good source of hydration. The reality is that of the five species of barrel cactus, only one, the fishhook barrel cactus, will provide you with drinkable fluid. The other four will make you very sick with vomiting and diarrhea, leading to further dehydration. Even with the fishhook barrel cactus, the fluid contains alkalis that your body has to work hard to process. It's best to leave all cactus alone when looking for water.

WARNING:

Unfortunately, reality TV has glorified drinking your own urine as a good thing in a survival scenario. Unless you are drinking your urine when you are very hydrated and it is clear, you are drinking toxins and bacteria that your body is getting rid of. To reintroduce these into your body will stress your kidneys and can lead to further dehydration and kidney failure. Do not drink your own urine in a survival scenario. The only exception to this would be that if you have a solar still set up, you can add your urine to the moisture in the still and allow the sun to filter out the drinkable fluid.

ARID FIRE

Fire can become a priority if you are in a desert area where the temperatures drop severely when the sun goes down. One bonus of being in such arid areas is that if you have access to any vegetation, it is likely to be dry, which will help with getting a fire going and maintaining it. Dried dung and termite mounds can act as fuel if you can't find any wood.

It will be harder to find good friction firewood in arid areas, as the vegetation tends to grow slowly. This means that the wood is often crooked and dense, which isn't ideal for friction fires. However, it will be very dry, so if you can find anything that resembles a straight spindle and a flat baseboard, it is worth giving one of those methods a try. I would recommend trying the strap drill or the bow drill if you have access to some rope or cord, because the spindle for the hand drill is less forgiving and needs to be long, straight, and lightweight.

I have had luck with friction fires using Australian desert pines and eucalyptus, even though I have been told by multiple sources that these woods were too dense and full of resin to work. Give everything a go before deciding for yourself what will work or not.

Refraction fires will be your best chance of making fire in arid ecosystems. Anything that can direct and amplify the sun's rays will help. Remember to try your water bottle, glass, or even the polished-up bottom of old drink cans. One person's trash might be your treasure.

Refraction method
(see page 170)

Strap drill
(see page 181)

Bow drill
(see page 182)

ARID FOOD

A side effect of being in a hot, dry climate is that you might not feel as hungry as you normally would. This is one of your body's survival mechanisms, because if you don't have access to water, then you shouldn't be eating. Food digestion uses up precious water supplies in your body and can cause dehydration if you don't have access to enough. You can last up to three weeks without food, so don't force yourself to eat.

Most desert plants have evolved to protect themselves from consumption and will have thorns or spikes as a result. Fortunately, you can work around these and make the most of what vegetation you find. Using the toxin test (see page 110) and the list of what to avoid, try all of the following with any vegetation you find:

- **Flowers**
- **Fruits**
- **Seeds**
- **Inner bark**
- **Young leaves**
- **Roots**

CACTUS While cactus fluids are toxic to drink, cacti are a great food source. Their fruits and leaves can be consumed. Unfortunately, the cacti protect themselves with large and micro thorns and hairs that can cause extreme irritation in your skin and throat. The only way to make sure of removing them all is to cook the fruit and leaves over the fire. If you are consuming them raw, cut off the thorn heads or remove the skin entirely. Excess consumption may cause diarrhea or a diuretic effect, so start with small amounts and monitor the effect on your body.

SUCCULENTS Many desert succulents are edible and can provide the body with some moisture. Do the toxin test on them prior to consumption. The smaller leaves will be nicer to eat, with the larger leaves tending to be a little saltier or bitter.

GRUBS As you are checking the vegetation for edible parts, also take note of any holes in the bark and roots. These are signs of grubs that may be living in the trunk, branches, or roots. If there is one hole, the grub is probably still in the wood. If there are two holes close together, the grub has probably turned into a moth and left. The bigger grubs will create a bulge in the surface of the wood. Cut a hole at this bulge, and fish out the grub with a small, hook-shaped stick. For the smaller grubs, break open the wood to get them out. They are usually located in dead and rotten wood, so it is easy to do. Eat the grubs raw or cook them straight on the coals or on a skewer over the flames.

ANIMAL TRACKS Even the smallest of lizards will leave obvious tracks in the dirt or sand in arid environments. Follow snake or lizard trails to find where they are hiding. Reptiles will hide under rocks or bury themselves in the sand in the heat of the day, so dig where the tracks end. If you are following snake tracks, assume the snake is venomous until proven otherwise. Always use a forked stick to expose its hiding spot and pin the snake behind its head before cutting off the head or killing it with a heavy object. Even when dead, the snake's venom is still toxic; be careful of the fangs and bury the head, fangs down, so you won't accidentally be scratched by them.

If tackling larger lizards such as monitors, it's good to note that while they are not venomous, their mouths are full of bacteria that can cause a bite to turn septic, and they have sharp claws that can inflict a lot of damage. Weigh up your risk versus reward carefully. Although they will provide a good source of protein, infections are hard to manage in arid environments.

Most desert mammals are tiny, fast, and nocturnal. These are the creatures than can live off dew as their water source. Arid ecosystems are where Paiute deadfall traps can really work well. Just make sure they are set to fall onto a solid surface. Set as many as you can, and leave them overnight to do your hunting work for you.

Paiute deadfall (see page 141)

As the animal tracks get bigger, so will your chances of finding a good water source. Most larger mammals in arid environments will require regular water, so bigger tracks are a good sign for both food and water.

Once you have located a good water source, it won't take long to establish what animals are in the area and when they drink. Most animals are creatures of habit and will wake up, drink, and eat at the same time every day unless their patterns are disturbed. For this reason, make sure you set up your camp at least 200 yards from your water source. Don't rush into hunting this bigger game without making a plan. Observe and educate yourself about the prevailing winds, how best to hide yourself to get in close, what time your game drinks, and what animals are the slowest and easiest to hunt. Keep in mind that animals tend to be faster and flightier before drinking and less agile with a belly full of water, so waiting until they have watered might increase your chances of getting a kill.

Depending on your resources, spears, throwing sticks, and clubs will be your best weapons of choice with bigger mammals. Snares will work best with smaller animals, if you can make rope or have some with you.

5.2.5

ARID RESCUE

With their wide-open spaces, arid ecosystems present the best opportunities for rescue. Any structures or words that you make will stand out for miles, so make as many as you can with rocks and branches. Reflective surfaces will have plenty of sun to work with; tie as many to branches or tripod structures as you can find.

Smoke will be obvious during the day, and flames will shine bright during the night. If you are able to get a fire going, make sure you have several signal fires set up that will easily take a flame if you spot any sign of rescue.

If you have a vehicle, stay by the vehicle, if you have enough water to do so. A vehicle will be much easier to spot from a plane than a single person, so this will increase your chances of rescue. If you are with a car, make sure it is obvious that you are in distress by having the hood of the car raised and SOS written in the ground nearby.

Do not try to shelter in the vehicle, as metal surfaces absorb and amplify heat. Construct a shelter outside or nearby your vehicle.

Since there is a good chance that you will be moving from your initial survival site to a more hospitable one, make sure you leave a clear message about the time and date you left and which direction you were planning on traveling in. Leave arrows and rock piles to mark your passage.

Try to find high ground to see which direction will be best to go. Head toward any signs of animal tracks, water clues, and/or anything that looks man-made.

Water clues include:

- Green, lush, dense vegetation

- Animal tracks in the shape of arrows

- Birdlife

- Insects

- Creek beds heading downhill

- Windmills or tanks

DANGERS:

SUN BLINDNESS The sun reflecting off the sand can amplify the glare, causing the corneas in your eyes to become "sunburnt." This can cause a temporary blindness, which can be both scary and debilitating. Wearing or creating a hat with a brim can combat this, but you can also fashion some "glasses" out of strips of bark that cover your eyes, leaving small slits to see through.

HEAT EXHAUSTION This is a condition that is the result of your body over-heating. Signs and symptoms of heat exhaustion include:

- **Cool, moist skin with goose bumps when in the sun**
- **Heavy sweating**
- **Faintness**
- **Dizziness**
- **Fatigue**
- **Weak, rapid pulse**
- **Low blood pressure**
- **Muscle cramps**

The best cure for heat exhaustion is to cool down the body. The best way to do this is to stop activity, seek shelter, and drink water if you have it. Prevention is better than having to cure it, so minimize activity in the heat of the day.

HEATSTROKE If heat exhaustion is untreated, it will lead to heat stroke. This is the most serious heat-related illness, and it occurs when the body becomes unable to control its temperature. The body temperature may rise to 106°F or higher in the space of ten to fifteen minutes. Signs and symptoms of heatstroke include:

- **Throbbing headache**
- **Lack of sweating despite the heat**
- **Red, hot, and dry skin**
- **Nausea and vomiting**
- **Rapid heartbeat**
- **Rapid, shallow breathing**
- **Confusion and disorientation**
- **Seizures**
- **Unconsciousness**

Cool down the body as soon as possible. Stop activity, seek shade, and use water to wet the skin while actively fanning to reduce the core temperature.

PRICKLY HEAT This is an itchy inflammation of the skin that is common in hot weather when you have been sweating a lot. It can be extremely uncomfortable and lead to infections and open sores. Treat with the white ash from your fire, and try to keep the areas dry.

DUST AND SANDSTORMS These kinds of storms can move rapidly, so begin to prepare the second you see one coming. Take shelter in a cave or overhang on the leeward side of the storm (the opposite side to where the storm is coming from). If you can't find a cave or overhang, any object that you can get behind will help. Cover your mouth, eyes, and nose with a breathable clothing layer. Cover as much of your skin as possible. The sand and dust can become as abrasive as sandpaper in the strong winds. Stay in one spot until the storm has passed. It can be very disorienting trying to move through these types of storms, and there is a high risk of injury due to the lack of visibility.

FOOTWEAR Some kind of footwear is essential in the desert, so if your flip-flops have broken, do not attempt to continue barefoot. Thorns and extremely hot surfaces can quickly render you unable to walk, and if you can't walk, the chances of survival rapidly diminish. Strapping other items of clothing to your feet will work, as will bark or animal hide.

Arid ecosystems can be some of the hardest in which to survive. Remember that prevention is better than a cure, and keep your activity to an absolute minimum. Make sure that you seek shelter in the heat of the day and keep activities to early morning and late evening. Move from your location quickly if you do not have water or a viable water source, and mark your trail clearly for rescuers to follow. Keeping a clear head and making proactive decisions early in your survival scenario will aid in a successful outcome.

SWAMP

Swamps can exist in many different climates, from the very cold to the very warm, but they are all characterized by being low-lying wetlands that are dominated by woody plants such as shrubs or trees. Swamplands are predominately saturated with water, and the difference between a patch of dry ground and a river could be one good rain.

Swamps can be put into two categories: freshwater and saltwater. Freshwater swamps are characterized by having impassable, thorny undergrowth, abundant reeds and grasses, scattered small palms, and towering trees. Saltwater swamps are coastal, and therefore subject to the tides, some as changeable as thirty-six feet in depth. They are often thick with mangroves, and passage through them is difficult, with the ground being mostly deep, stinking mud.

Although swamps can be rich sources of plant and fish life, they can be filled with bacteria, parasites, and biting, sucking insects. These can carry and inflict diseases that have devastating physical, and sometimes neurological, side effects. Depending on where you are in the world, they can also be home to large predators such as tigers, alligators, and venomous snakes. You need to watch every step, as these dangerous animals are masters of disguise and blend in well with their surroundings.

Swamps often have higher, drier areas known as hummocks, but some of the areas that may appear to be high ground are actually floating, unstable grass islands.

Swamp ecosystems regularly get lumped in with tropical areas with their survival advice, but, having spent time in both, I can tell you that although some of your basic needs will be covered in the same way, they are very different survival scenarios.

Bear Grylls once described the Louisiana swamps as "hell on earth" and said the only thing you should do in them is get out of them as soon as possible. This may be true, but just in case you do need to spend some time in them, these are my suggestions for making it out alive.

SWAMP SHELTER

Depending on your specific swamp location, shelter may be high on the priority list or lower down. Personally, I have survived for five days in the Louisiana swamps without one, ensuring I had a fire to sleep next to and water to drink rather than expending the effort that building a shelter would require. It's your survival, so you need to be analyzing where you are, the time of year, and what your priorities are.

As always, I look to the local tribes who lived in those areas for clues to the best shelter I should build. Tribes that thrived in swampy areas built structures on stilts, made floating platforms to have their homes on, or headed for the highest ground possible and made lean-tos or humpy-style homes, depending on their climate.

If you are in coastal swamps, some kind of platform to get you off the ground at night will be essential. Assess the high tide mark to make sure you can get higher than that. The high tide mark is usually obvious by where the debris sits in the branches of the trees. It also can be marked by a change in color on tree trunks. Sometimes the debris field will mark the last flood, so match up the clues to see where the waterline regularly stops in your area.

This will not be a place that you set up as a base. It will be an area that you will try to move out of to a better survival position. This means that your survival shelter doesn't need to be fancy; it just needs to get you through a night.

TRIANGLE PLATFORM

Find three strong beams. The bonus of being on the coast is that although the wood in mangroves tends to be stunted, there can be a lot of driftwood suitable for building purposes. Use natural cordage, or find forks in branches to support the beams in a triangle shape. Lash each branch separately to create more strength. This platform only needs to be big enough for you to curl up on. Layer the triangle with crossbeams, and pile on branches and leaves to make a platform for you to sleep on. If possible, make a similar triangle above you, or layer some branches through the canopy above you to provide some shelter from the wind and possible rain.

A smaller version of this would work if you find yourself in a survival scenario close to nightfall. Creating a seat above the high tide mark will provide you some comfort and rest throughout the night. Covering yourself with branches will protect you from the elements and some insect life.

FLOATING PLATFORM

Rather than being a raft you intend to float to safety on, this raft is just a safe sleeping platform. Lash buoyant logs together with rope or natural cordage. Make sure that the logs you choose can float by trying them in some knee-deep water before the tide starts to come in. The platform only needs to be big enough to ensure you can lie down on it. Create a tether that can attach from your raft to a tree above the high tide mark. As the tide rises, you will float with it. Jetties and piers all over the world are designed this way. Cover your platform with branches and grasses for you to crawl under for shelter and warmth.

Coastal areas experience two high tides and two low tides every twenty-four hours and fifty minutes. This means that the high and low tides are different every day, but they will happen usually once a day and once a night.

Once the tide has retreated enough for you to be able to walk through the swamp, head inland to try to find higher ground.

If you are in freshwater swamps or have managed to make your way farther inland from the coast, you should find good resources for shelter building. Palms, grasses, and reeds are all common in swamp areas and will provide great roofing material.

A super-simple shelter would be a version of the leaf box shelter (see page 62). Stack up a large pile of dried reeds to make a comfy, warm bed for the night. You can tuck inside the pile, and you will have insulation below you for the cold ground and above you to keep in some body heat.

One material to be aware of and keep away from is poison ivy. Poison ivy grows on almost every continent and loves moist areas. It can grow as both a shrub and a vine, which means it may be tempting to use as lashing material. It can usually be identified by its three-pointed leaf cluster, but there are times of year when the leaves have fallen off and it looks like a vine. Poison ivy has an oily resin on it that causes an allergic reaction for three out of four people who come in contact with it. The reaction can range anywhere from a slight rash to weepy welts, depending on the severity of the allergy. If you are unsure about a vine in a swampy region (particularly in swamps in North America), use something else.

Try to situate your shelter on the highest ground you can find and away from the water's edge. If possible, 600 feet is a good distance, as this will mean fewer biting insects and less likelihood of running into an alligator or crocodile at night. This is close enough to water that you won't have to expend too many calories collecting water.

If you are unable to find high ground but have low-lying dry ground, consider building a raised bed platform. In some of these regions, it only takes one rain for low-lying areas to become part of the river. Often fallen trees can be rolled into place and covered with branches and leaves to provide a comfy platform. Build a lean-to over this platform to keep off the rain. Likewise, a larger platform lashed to suitable trees would work to keep you off the ground.

Moss can also be found in sheets in these areas and can be quite good for roofing and bedding as well.

If you have found high ground that looks like it rarely gets flooded, building a solid shelter is a good idea. If you are in a colder region, consider building a tepee or humpy (see page 67) to conserve as much heat as possible, and if you find yourself in a warmer swamp, a lean-to (see page 64) with a fire in front works perfectly.

The biggest difference I find between the tropics and the swamps is that in the tropics, you know it will rain on a regular basis, and so you prepare for it. In the swamps, it might not rain every day, but you should definitely prepare for it, because it will lull you into a false sense of security and has the potential to wipe you out in one downpour. Make sure that you can't see any daylight coming through the roof of your shelter, and if in doubt, add more material to en sure you can ride out a storm.

WARNING

I was told once that chiggers don't live in dead moss and happily gathered a bunch of it for my bedding. Chiggers are part of the mite family. They bite and leave their mouthpiece embedded in the skin, which causes severe itching and welts. Chiggers do live in dead moss. They love it. The only way to make sure that chiggers aren't in your mossy bedding is to soak it in water for twenty-four hours and then dry it off before use.

SWAMP WATER

Being prepared to collect rainfall is always good in wetlands. It's not a method that you can rely on, since rainfall is not always regular in these areas, but it is a good backup for drinkable water that doesn't require purifying.

Do not collect water from the same area twice if your swamplands are inhabited by alligators or crocodiles. They are intelligent hunters, will learn your habits, and will be waiting for you next time. Try to avoid collecting water from areas with steep banks and sudden drop-offs. Instead, collect water from the shallow areas where you can see what is in the water in front of you.

Due to the large amount of stagnant water and rotting vegetation in swampy areas, purifying water is more important than ever. The most effective method of purifying water in a swamp is by boiling. If you don't have a pot, boil water in a plastic bottle or segment of bamboo suspended over the fire. Don't put the plastic container directly on the fire, as the plastic will melt, but if you can suspend the bottle above the fire, the water will boil before the plastic melts. This is because the melting point of plastic is higher than the boiling point of water. This is not an ideal method of water purification, as heating the plastic releases carcinogens into the water, but it will save your life, so it is worth doing for the short term. Keep in mind that you may not see bubbling when the water is at the boiling point due to the lid being on the bottle, so keep an eye out for small bubbles forming on the bottom to indicate it has reached that stage.

BAMBOO While bamboo may be present in some wetlands, it is not to be expected or relied upon. Bamboo requires soil that is moist but not soggy and that is able to drain well, something that is found in the tropics but not so much in swamps. However, it may be found on drier hummocks and islands among the wetter ground. If you are lucky enough to find some larger bamboo, there may be water stored in the stem. Tap the greener sections to see if there are some that sound duller than other, hollower-sounding ones. The duller ones might have some water in them. Just cut a hole at the top of one of the segments and a notch at the bottom, and collect the water as it drains out. Do not drink the water if it smells funny or tastes off. Should this happen to you, try a different section of bamboo.

WATER WELL The only time I would consider this an effective filtering method in a swamp is if the dry ground that I have managed to find is sandy and fine grained. This method involves digging a hole away from the water's edge and drinking the water that seeps into that hole. Since most of the ground is rotting vegetation, it is rife with bacteria and parasites. It would not act as an efficient filter to get clean drinking water.

WATER FILTER If you have been able to get a fire going but can't boil water, or you have found traces of a fire through the area, gather the charcoal and make a natural filter. It involves layering pebbles, sand, grass, and charcoal in some kind of containment system, such as rolled-up bark or bamboo, and passing the water through the contraption in order to filter it. This system won't remove all of the contaminants from the water, but it is better than trying to drink straight from the swamp.

Keep in mind that, due to the amount of water around you, the air will tend to be quite moist, and you may not need as much water as you would in other ecosystems. It would be quite possible to last three or more days here without consuming water. Keep an eye on your physiology to see how you are doing. Are you getting foggy? Do you have a headache? Is your mouth dry? Are you beginning to stagger as you walk? It will be hard to be surrounded by cool water and not drink your fill, but drinking without being able to purify the water will possibly lead more quickly to your death. If you are unable to find any way of purifying your water, you are unable to move to a location with a good water source, and you feel like your symptoms of dehydration are heading toward fatal, drink sparingly the clearest, fastest-running water you can find.

SWAMP FIRE

Wetland water will always be cooler than body temperature, so prolonged exposure, even in hot weather, can result in hypothermia. Being surrounded by water also has a refrigerating effect on the air and can drastically reduce the ground temperature in areas with a thick canopy. This means that even in the warmer times of year, you might need a fire going to stave off hypothermia during the night. There is also an abundance of biting and stinging insects whose effects may be reduced by having a fire.

Fuel will be hard to come by in wetlands. The best source for dry wood will be dead standing wood and wood that was deposited in the treetops from the last floods. Tinder will need to be sourced from under dead logs, in tree hollows, or from beneath outer bark. Some good tinder tricks are dry cattail heads (although they will burn out quickly); dry, powdered bracket fungus; and scraping the outer layer of dead palm stems into shavings. Tinder will need to be used quickly, as it will absorb moisture from the air and become too damp to take a coal or spark.

A wood shelter is a must to help dry off wood to use for the fire. It will need to be built off the ground so that the wood doesn't absorb moisture.

If you are located in a low-lying swamp area, you will need to make a fire platform in case of flooding. Make a boxed area contained by four pieces of wood or rock. Pile mud or dirt into the center. I would suggest making the platform at least a foot high. Cover the dirt with sticks and dry bark, and light the fire on top of those.

If you are in an area with bamboo, select the driest pieces you can find and use the fire saw method of friction fire to try to start your fire..

THE FIRE SAW

You will need about a two-foot-long piece of bamboo, ideally two inches wide. Cut the bamboo in half. Using another piece of bamboo, scrape a handful of dry shavings off the outside of the bamboo. This will be your

Cut a small notch perpendicular to the sides of the bamboo on the top of one round surface. Place the bamboo facedown with the tinder bundle under this notch.

Match the edge of the unscored piece with the notch, press down firmly, and saw back and forth to create friction.

tinder bundle. Cut a small notch perpendicular to the sides of the bamboo on the top of one round surface. Place the bamboo facedown with the tinder bundle under this notch. Match the edge of the unscored piece with the notch, press down firmly, and saw back and forth to create friction. If you are successful, the ignited dust will fall onto the tinder bundle, and you will be able to blow it to flame.

If you can't find any bamboo, select the driest and straightest pieces of wood from any standing deadwood or driftwood and try the strap drill or bow drill method of fire making (see pages 181 and 182, respectively). A large majority of coastal areas around the world have beach hibiscus, and its dry branches are one of the most effective friction fire woods available. It can be identified by its iconic yellow flowers and glossy, deep green leaves, both of which are also edible.

Fire will be an essential part of your survival plan in the swamps. It will add much-needed warmth, stave off any rashes or infections caused by the continual dampness, and keep predators at bay (both large and small). It is a big challenge getting and keeping a fire going in a swamp, and if you are unable to do so, plans should be made to move to an area with a greater chance of survival.

SWAMP FOOD

Both saltwater swamps and freshwater swamps can provide a good variety of plants and animals to eat.

SALTWATER SWAMPS In saltwater regions, crabs, fish, and mollusks are abundant in the mangroves. You might also find some varieties of stingray that have come to forage in the muddy waters, as well as freshwater turtles in the estuaries.

FISH DAM If the tidal variance is low in your area, try building a dam fish trap in the shallows. Mangroves are known as fish nurseries, due to the abundance of smaller fish that hide out in their root systems until they get big enough to venture into open water. Creating pools that fill up in high tide but trap fish as the tide retreats is a great way to catch these smaller fish. You can "fish" in your dam either by hand or with a pronged fishing spear.

FISHING HOOKS AND LINES Primitive hooks were shaped out of bones, antlers, shells, thorns, and even hardwood. Look for something that you can carve or shape into a hook-like structure that can be sharpened and that maintains its strength. I have seen people have success with a small, straight, sharpened piece of wood as a hook. This works well for catfish, eels, and any type of bottom feeder. Sharpen both ends of a small, strong stick the length of a toothpick and attach it to the end of your line. Tie the bait on the stick in a way that it holds the stick parallel to the line, but so that the stick will open out when the bait is consumed. Once the fish swallows the bait and hook, the stick lodges in its gullet.

If you happen to have some paracord, then pulling out the inner threads and tying them together creates a great line. Assuming that you are starting from scratch, you will need to create some natural cordage to be your fishing line (see page 70). It can be kind of tricky to create a tough enough line for the fish not to break or chew through, but you may have some local fibers in your area that will work, so experiment with what you have.

CRABBING SPEAR Create a pronged spear by slicing the end of a strong, straight stick into four pieces still attached to the main stick. Sharpen each of the points, and then lash in two crossbeam small sticks at the base of the cut. Crabs in the mangroves will generally dig into the mud, leaving obvious holes. Depending on the size of the hole, you can either use your hands to dig the surrounding area to unearth the crab, or use a separate digging stick. Once the crab is pinned down, make sure to avoid the claws and grab the crab from the back shell. This crabbing spear is also good for stingrays. Make sure you pin them down well and avoid the tail. While the barbs on a stingray are rarely fatal, they can deliver a painful sting and should be avoided.

THROWING STICK Quite often flocks of birds congregate on the shoreline, digging for worms and crabs. A throwing stick is perfect for throwing at a flock in the hope to wing one for a meal. They are easy to make, requiring a single piece of wood, about two feet long, with a slight bend in it and one end heavier than the other. These are great for freshwater swamp wading birds as well.

Some mangroves have edible fruit, but most of the fruit that is edible requires cooking to be palatable. Check the fruit of the mangrove in your area using the toxin test (see page 110) to determine if you should eat it.

FRESHWATER SWAMPS

Freshwater ecosystems are usually abundant with fish, frogs, snakes, snails, birds, and insects. You should also have access to some good flora options as well. Some more common plants include:

CATTAILS Located on most continents, cattails are usually found in dense stands on the edge of waterways; you can eat the green head of the cattail, the root, the young stems, and also the yellow pollen, depending on the time of year.

BERRIES Blueberries and blackberries love wetland environments; if you are not 100 percent sure of the berry you are eating, do the toxin test to determine if it is edible (see page 110).

STINGING NETTLES Located on most continents, they like to grow in damp, fertile soil, so look for them on the low-lying edges of river systems; they are best boiled and eaten like spinach, but you can eat them raw so long as you disable the sting by crushing them between some rocks first.

PALMS Most palms have an edible center in their leaf head; cut the palm off just above the line where the brown trunk ends and the green leaves start, and peel off the outer layers until you get to a white, soft core—this is heart of palm and is edible, though do the toxin test (see page 110) before eating.

Swamps tend to have an abundance of rotten wood in them. Check the wood for grub holes. Even if there aren't any obvious holes, it is worth breaking the wood apart to check. Grubs can be eaten raw or cooked on the fire.

Always be careful of the brighter-colored reptiles, insects, and mollusks. Snails and slugs should be purged by keeping them away from any unknown vegetation for a few days prior to cooking, since they are immune to the poisons found in a lot of plants and fungi.

REPTILES Snakes are a good source of food in swamps. They like sunning themselves in the heat of the day and quite often will choose the top of a log or fallen tree to do so, making them easy to spot. Use a forked stick to pin down their head before cutting it off or crushing it as an effective method of killing them. Treat every snake as venomous unless you are positive it is not. Do not try to hunt snakes in the water. They can vanish beneath the murky surface and swim rapidly without a trace. They are also harder to pin down in the mud. Always use a risk-versus-reward calculation before attempting to hunt snakes for food. Snake venom stays in the fangs long after the snake is dead, so dispose of the head carefully.

AMPHIBIANS Frogs are abundant in swamp ecosystems. A version of the crabbing spear (see page 147) works well to spear them, but they can also be caught by hand. Avoid the brightly colored ones, and make sure you don't have a toad. Toads have rough skin on their backs and a tendency to have shorter, squat legs, meaning they crawl more than they hop. Some toads are edible, but you need to be careful how you prepare them, so it is best to avoid them all. The best meat on frogs is their legs. Remove these, and boil or cook them over an open fire on skewers.

FISH The river systems in swamps tend to be wider and slower moving, so fish traps are not ideal in these scenarios. Fishing cord and fishhooks are definitely worth a try (see page 152). Make sure you don't eat fish raw from swampy areas. Fish from slow-moving water are more likely to be filled with parasites. You can get rid of these parasites by making sure that you gut the fish and cook them well.

BIRDS Throwing sticks are great for wading birds, but it is also worth setting up a few arapuca traps on the swamp floor to see if you can attract any of the canopy birds to take the bait.

ARAPUCA TRAP
You will need:

- Twenty-four thumb-width sticks, with six sets of four varying sizes

- Two pieces of rope or cord about two feet in length

- A short length of cord

- A finger-width trigger stick about ten inches long

- Bait

Place the two longest sticks side by side, and attach the two pieces of cord from one end of each stick to the other to create a square. Twist the two sticks once in opposite directions so the rope forms a cross. Slide the next two longest sticks, log-cabin style, between the ropes and begin to fill in the slack. Eventually you will end up with a tensioned pyramid. This is your cage. Fill in the top of the pyramid with sticks to ensure that there isn't an escape route for the bird. These are also the sticks that you will remove in order to get the bird out without it escaping. Break the trigger stick in half in such a way that you can put the pieces back together again. Tie the short length of the cord to the inside of the trap, and loop it around the break in the trigger stick with tension. Lean the trap on the trigger stick. Place the bait inside the trap. When a bird enters the trap, it will disturb the cord, which will trigger the trap. I find that it is necessary to put a weight on top of the trap to make sure that the bird doesn't manage to overturn the trap or wriggle out from under it.

If you have managed to locate a larger bit of dry land, you may also have some larger land mammals to hunt. Keep an eye out for tracks in the mud that may show you what else is occupying your area. If you are lucky enough to have some larger game nearby, observe and educate yourself about their habits. Employ hunting techniques to get close to them, and either snare or spear them. Smaller mammals can be taken out with a throwing stick, but larger ones will need a spear.

What food you will have access to depends on the swamp you end up in and the time of year. Keep your options open, and know that so long as you're willing to eat it, you will have access to food that crawls, hops, and slithers at most times of the year.

5.3.5

SWAMP RESCUE

Thick, bushy terrain and woody canopies make being spotted from the air almost an impossibility in most swamplands. Multiple channels that snake and wind around to dead ends and back on themselves make rescue by boat a challenge, and marshy grounds and quagmires make traveling on foot a chore. If you find yourself in swampy terrain with no sign of rescue, you will need to make your way out to more populated, hospitable terrain.

If you manage to find a base that can cover your basic needs, build signal fires in clearings and next to open rivers. Place any bright and eye-catching objects in clearings, with clear indications of the direction of your shelter from there. If you are in open grasslands, flatten down or harvest the grasses to spell SOS.

If you move from your location, leave messages about what day and time you left and the direction you are heading in.

Rafts can be a great mode of transport if you have a lot of deeper rivers and waterways in your swamp. They don't need to be large, just enough to support your body weight. A smaller raft will be more maneuverable and easier to carry over shallow water. Simply find four or five suitable logs that float and lash them together with rope, vines, or natural cordage. Always make sure they are lashed together more firmly than you think you will need. The movement of the water will wriggle the logs apart if they are not secure. Paddles can be made of bamboo cut in half or any broad, strong surface you can find. Even a forked branch with some material tied between the forks will work. You can move quite rapidly on a raft, and it will protect you from an arduous slog through thick mud and brush, but you will be subject to where the river goes.

DANGERS

CROCODILES AND ALLIGATORS Depending on your location, these ancient reptiles will either be aggressive hunters or opportunistic hunters. In the coastal swamps of Australia's north, the saltwater crocodile is a fearsome predator and to be avoided at all costs. The best advice for dealing with saltwater crocodiles is to stay out of the water and away from the water's edge. Freshwater crocodiles and American alligators generally prefer to eat fish and will usually get out of your way, but it always pays to be cautious in areas where you know they reside. If you have to travel in waterways with these reptiles, move slowly through the water, sliding your feet along the bottom. Carry a spear in case you encounter an aggressive one, and aim to ram the spear into its mouth if you can, as this is their most vulnerable area apart from their eyes. Crocodiles and alligators can stay underwater for over an hour. Sometimes you may see bubbles coming up to the surface to indicate they are there, but this isn't always the case. If you feel an alligator or crocodile with your feet under the water, back away slowly and exit the water or climb a tree as soon as you can. If the water is deep and you have to swim, try to swim slowly beneath the surface, as thrashing around on the surface will attract their attention.

VENOMOUS SNAKES Swamps are always full of snakes, due to the abundance of food such as frogs and small fish. Treat every snake as venomous unless you are 100 percent certain otherwise. You will need to move carefully and watch every step as you navigate through the swamps. Especially watch out for the tops of logs and fallen trees in the heat of the day.

QUAGMIRES These are the swamp version of quicksand, but made of soggy mud rather than sand. Quagmires are rarely deep enough to swallow you, but they can make walking tough and sometimes are deep enough to get stuck in. If you get stuck in deep mud, sprawl out like you would for quicksand and try to get your body flat on the surface. Use any solid objects on the edge of the bog to pull yourself out or crawl to the edge.

FLUCTUATING WATER LEVELS If you are in a coastal swamp, the water levels can rise and fall by as much as thirty-six feet in some areas. Take note of the shoreline and the tide marks on the vegetation, so you don't get caught out by incoming tides. Know that the biggest tide of the month will occur on the full moon, so take this into consideration when building a shelter by the coast. In freshwater swamp ecosystems, be aware of the weather around you and know that heavy rains in the distance may influence the water levels around you, even if you don't get wet at your camp. Have a plan B temporary shelter built off the ground in case of nighttime flooding.

TRENCH FOOT, RASHES, INFECTIONS Being constantly damp and moving through water filled with bacteria means that trench foot becomes an issue. This is where your feet begin to rot off due to being wet all of the time. Having experienced this before in the Louisiana swamps when my camp was flooded for nine days in a foot of water, I can tell you that your feet begin to feel unbearably hot, and all you want to do is immerse them in the cold water. This is the worst thing you can do for them. You need to keep them as dry as possible, and dry your socks and shoes off whenever you get the opportunity. Keep rashes and sores as clean and dry as possible to deter infections. Use white ash from your fire to coat any sores or rashes.

INSECTS, TICKS, AND LEECHES There are a lot of things in the swamp that will want to bite you and suck your blood. There may be natural deterrents in your ecosystem, so try rubbing on your skin any tree that smells like citronella, camphor, or tea tree. Always do a toxin test first to make sure you don't have an allergic reaction (see page 110). You can try a smoky fire or burying yourself under a pile of vegetation, but mosquitoes in swamps can be relentless. I have never found that mud works to deter mosquitoes, nor have I spoken with anyone who has tried it successfully, yet many survival guides suggest trying it, so perhaps it works in some swamps. Try not to scratch mosquito bites, as open wounds can become infected. When removing ticks, be careful not to leave the head in your body. You can do this by sliding two sharp thorns or thin sticks under the body of the tick and pulling upward. Leeches can be removed by sliding something sharp along your skin under where they are attached to your body. Clean the entry wounds with purified water if you have any and pat on some white ash.

Swamps can vary from Southern Australian swamps, where your greatest predator will be a mosquito, to the African swamps such as the Okavango Delta, where you will be dodging animals like lions, hippos, and crocodiles. They can be freezing or humid and sweltering. Your biggest concern will not be a lack of water, but how to deal with an excess of it. If you can safely exit a swamp ecosystem to seek rescue, then do so as soon as possible; however, know that with the right understanding of your environment and a good attitude, you can provide for all of your basic needs for as long as it takes for someone to find you.

5.4

POLAR

Polar ecosystems, along with deserts, are one of the most extreme ecosystems to survive in. They have long, cold winters and short summers. Many areas will stay below freezing year-round, and winds of up to 110 mph have commonly been recorded. These winds send temperatures plummeting to -94°F and can freeze unprotected skin within minutes.

Most of the soil is covered with ice or snow, so both plant and animal resources are rare. Your body is burning calories faster than it normally would in an attempt to keep you warm, which means that the average person requires about 5,000 calories a day to survive in these regions. This is where the three-hour part of the rule of threes (see page 89) comes into play—you can last up to three hours in extreme cold, if you can't find a way to stay warm. If you are wet, you may last less than fifteen minutes.

People have lived in these climates for thousands of years, and they have adapted to it; however, it is a harsh environment to be dropped into to start from scratch. It is rare that a survival scenario happens in a polar ecosystem without the person starting in that area to begin with, so there is hope that if it happens, you will be prepared. To this end, I will assume that at a minimum you have the right clothing to be in a polar environment.

An exception to this would be a plane crash. A plane crash would allow you to have access to a variety of equipment, emergency transmission devices, and resources. It would also have had a flight path, and people expecting it at a destination at a set time, so rescue is more likely. If you have crashed in a polar region in a plane, stay with or by the aircraft. Take stock of all your assets, and use them to cover your basic needs until rescue arrives. Be inventive. Seat covers can be used as waterproof boot covers or sleeping bags. The soft material inside the seats can be used to stuff your clothing for insulation. Build a shelter outside of the plane, as metal will conduct the cold and add to your discomfort.

The key to surviving the extreme cold is to be proactive about your warmth. As soon as you feel cold, think about how you can warm yourself. In a survival scenario, it is much easier to prevent hypothermia and frostbite than it is to manage it.

POLAR SHELTER

Your clothing is going to be your first shelter from the elements. Make sure that you head into the cold with a good layering system on. The aim is that the first layer wicks moisture from your body and helps with temperature regulation. The next layers aim to trap the warm air coming off your body, to provide insulation. The outer layer should be windproof but allow for some ventilation. A lot of waterproof outer layers have no ventilation, and this creates too much heat when moving around that then translates to sweat. It is important to limit your sweating, as sweating is designed to help cool down the body but can have the effect of cooling it too much in freezing locations, making it hard to warm up again. If you are exerting yourself, open some of the areas of ventilation on your clothing, like zips or drawstrings. If you are still hot, remove a layer. As soon as you have stopped your exertion, replace the layer and close the ventilation.

In a cold environment, cotton clothing can be a killer. Not only does it lose its ability to insulate you, but any dampness on your skin also rapidly cools your body on contact with colder weather, leading quickly to hypothermia.

Natural fabrics are still some of the best fabrics to combat cold environments. Wool retains its thermal properties when wet, and fur worn around your face prevents your breath from freezing on your skin. Skins make ideal outer clothing, but you must wear them fur side in to gain the most warming properties, not fur side out like an expensive mink coat.

Cover every piece of exposed skin that you can. If you don't have gloves or a face covering, improvise with other pieces of clothing or fabric. In China, I once killed a pheasant with a throwing stick and wore its skin feather side in to protect my face while climbing over a freezing mountain pass. I did this by skinning the pheasant as I would a mammal, rather than plucking the feathers off like I usually would with birds. This meant that the feathers all stayed attached to the skin and retained the shape of a face mask, instead of being loose and requiring some kind of casing to use them for warmth. I have also worn my spare socks on my hands when I didn't have gloves and I got hit by an unexpected storm on a mountain. Try to prevent the heat from leaving your clothing by tightening any loose edges, such as sleeves and collars.

Don't wear restrictive clothing or shoes that you can't wiggle your toes in. A lack of ability to move the blood around your body can lead to frostbite and hypothermia.

Your shoes should be waterproof with an insulated liner. Wearing plastic bags inside your boots on the outside of your socks can help in a pinch, as can seat covers over your boots if you are with a vehicle. Make sure you can dry your socks and shoes at night to prevent freezing.

The next level of shelter would be finding a natural shelter that you can improve on. The top priorities are being out of the wind and off the ground, so something as simple as behind a rock on some tree branches or on top of your pack will help keep you warmer. Avoid the lee side (the sheltered side) of cliffs, where snow could drift to cover you or a rockfall or an avalanche is likely. Don't rest by tree trunks if they have snow-laden branches, unless the lower boughs are resting on the snow line. If they are resting on the snow line, they may be hiding a perfect shelter, the tree well shelter.

TREE WELL SHELTER

This shelter is a natural cavern that forms when snow accumulates around the base of a tree but not under its lowest branches or by the trunk. Dig a small entrance and climb down into the tree well. Break off branches from the opposite side of the tree or other trees to insulate the floor of your shelter, and bring in extra to cover yourself with if it is dry. Make sure that you leave a branch sticking out of your shelter entrance to dig yourself out if snow covers the entrance, and also to be able to poke out a ventilation hole. Although it might be tempting to cover every air hole to keep the heat in, you need somewhere that carbon dioxide can escape from and fresh oxygen can get in, or else you may die of poisoning. Snow is an excellent insulator, as it is mainly composed of trapped air rather than water. This slows the heat transference from the inside of your shelter to the outside air. Your body heat alone can heat up a snow cave by up to 7°F. Adding a small candle of animal fat or marrow can ensure you will be warm throughout the night.

SNOW SCREEN SHELTER

If you have found a natural overhang or small cave, pile up a snow wall in front of the cave opening to stop the heat from leaving and the wind from entering. I have slept in freezing conditions with a fire at the entrance to a cave, and I have found it very cozy. But if I had to leave suddenly, I could have risked injury climbing over the fire, so, if possible, it is best to position the fire at the back of the cave. The smaller the cave or overhang, the less space to warm. Pile any warm, insulating material you have on the ground. I slept on my climbing rope, but your pack, leaves, or moss will also do nicely.

SNOW CAVE

There are a few methods of building a snow cave. You can find a suitable deep, solid snowdrift and burrow in, or you can create a small iglu, or igloo. I prefer to build an igloo, as burrowing into a snowdrift can lead to a shelter that may collapse if the snow doesn't have the right consistency. It is best that you have some kind of cutting tool to create the snow blocks that you will need for this shelter. Once, when I was in the Four Sisters mountain range in the Sichuan Province of China, I managed to find the pelvis bone of a yak farther down the mountain, and this worked perfectly. Test the solidity of your snow. If it is too cold, the snow will be too fluffy to make perfect blocks, and if it is too warm, the snow will be too slushy to work. This is a Goldilocks shelter, where the snow needs to be just right to work. If you can slice the snow into blocks, find a patch of snow where it is about waist deep or more, and start to build the walls of your shelter. It is best to make a dome shape, as it will hold the integrity of the roof better. The shelter only needs to be big enough for you to curl up in. Once the dome is done, tunnel down and then up into the shelter. This will ensure that no heat is lost to the entrance, as heat rises. I like to smooth down the walls on the inside, since it makes me feel like they are a little more solid, but that is purely psychological. Insulate the floor of your shelter with whatever material you can find. I even managed to create a "door" with some stray vegetation that was poking up through the snow. The branches kept in a little more of the heat without entirely blocking my ventilation. A small bone-marrow candle helped me get through the freezing night with only the clothes on my back.

SOD HUTS

If you are closer to the tundra areas and it is summer, you may be able to fashion a small hut out of sod. Sod is the combination of soil and grass that can be cut off in chunks. Use an existing structure and fill in the gaps, or create a lean-to and cover it with sod to act as insulation against the cold.

Anything more than the clothes on your back will be a bonus—sleeping bags, emergency blankets, bivy bags, and other human bodies will all assist in making this scenario way more endurable.

Although it might not be comfortable, there are many ways to survive the night in polar regions without a fire for warmth, so the important thing is not to panic. Every step that you can move toward ensuring that you have somewhere out of the wind and insulated is a step to surviving these frigid landscapes.

POLAR WATER

For being made of frozen water, polar ecosystems receive very little rain. If there is water vapor in the air, it might snow, but when the temperature decreases dramatically, there is less water vapor in the air, and therefore it is less likely to snow as well.

Never try to eat snow or ice in these environments. Your body uses valuable heat and energy to process these substances, and this can cause your core temperature to drop dangerously, as well as using more moisture to process the water than what you gain by consuming it. It is better to gather ice for water than snow, as ice is denser and will give you more water per mass as it melts. Melting ice in a pot over a fire is ideal, but if you don't have access to a fire, you can put ice in a water bottle or container and carry it between the layers of your clothing while walking or working to melt it. Since the water has been frozen, there is little chance of any bacteria surviving, so it is fairly safe to drink the melted water if a method of purification isn't available.

Keep all water in your clothing or sleeping layers, as any water left out will freeze. If you have access to a fire, heat up water for your water bottle to add an extra bit of warmth between your clothing layers overnight.

If the temperatures are getting warmer, you may be able to find rivers of glacial melt. If you are collecting water from frozen rivers, be careful of the edges. A lot of frozen river edges are covered in slick ice that may not be obvious but could easily send you into the freezing water. If you fall into a freezing river, you need to get out of the water as soon as possible. You have about three minutes in freezing water before your body becomes incapacitated, and about fifteen minutes before your body shuts down. If you can get out of the river, roll in the snow to get rid of any excess moisture (the snow absorbs the moisture with a wicking effect), get to your shelter, and change into dry clothing if you have it.

If the ice is at least four inches thick, you should be able to venture out on frozen rivers and lakes. If you have a sharpened stick or rock, chip a hole in the ice to get drinking water out of. This hole would also be an asset for fishing (see page 152).

On the tundra, you should be able to find water holes to drink out of, but make sure you boil this water before drinking it or use the natural water filter to get rid of any toxins that may be in the water, as it may be stagnant and full of bacteria.

Natural water filter
(see page 99)

POLAR FIRE

Tinder, kindling, fuel, and the ability to make a flame are all lacking in polar ecosystems. There may be some areas where you have access to trees and shrubs, and on the coast, there might be some driftwood, but for the most part, you will have to use your shelter design to keep you warm. Some exceptions to this would be making a kill or finding a kill and using the fat from the animal to create candles.

Fat and old bone-marrow candles will heat up a small space, but you need to have a source of flame on you to make these work for you, as well as some material to make a wick. The inside of a piece of shoelace might work, or some strips of cotton. I've used the nylon from the inside of a climbing rope. Some natural cordage might also work, but this would depend on the trees and bark you have access to.

If you are on the coast, gather all the driftwood you can. If you can find small enough pieces, dry them out the best you can and try a bow drill friction fire. Wood can float for thousands of miles, so you never know what species you have and if it will work or not.

Although I have been told that trees with high resin don't work for the bow drill, I have had success with some desert pines, so I recommend that you try any dry branches you can find to see if you can successfully get a friction fire.

If you are in an area with trees, gather fallen or dead branches and strip away the icy, wet outer layer for kindling. Once you have a fire going, dry the remaining wood around the edge of the flames.

In the tundra, you will find small shrubs with high resin content to burn for fuel, and perhaps even the dry dung of some of the bigger grazing animals. Fuel will be at a premium, so it is best to reserve it for when you need it the most.

Although we are conditioned to believe that without fire we will freeze to death in cold climates, that is not necessarily the case. If you are fortunate enough to have flammable vegetation in your polar ecosystem, then a fire will be a great advantage. If not, spend more time making your shelter the very best heat insulator possible.

Bow drill
(see page 182)

POLAR FOOD

Food can be very scarce in a polar environment, and as your body burns calories to stay warm, it is important that you work to replace them. On the coastlines, you may be able to find clams and mussels, both of which can be consumed raw straight out of their shells. Do not eat mollusks if:

- **They remain partially open when you touch them.**

- **They are easy to remove from the rocks or have fallen off by themselves.**

- **They smell bad.**

- **They don't open when cooked in boiling water.**

- **They are located in water with a reddish algae tinge.**

You may also be able to find colonies of coastal birds nesting on the rocky shoreline. Try a driftwood throwing stick for the flying birds, but if you come across a colony of penguins, you should be able to walk among them and catch them by hand. A quick flick can break their neck, or use a rock or a piece of hardwood as a club. Skin them to be able to make the most of their feather layer, gut them, and cook them well on an open fire. Don't forget to gather their eggs if they have any. These can be consumed raw or cooked.

Seals may also have colonies on the shorelines, leaving the baby seals alone during the day while they head out fishing. The baby seals make easy targets for spears or clubs. Approach them with caution if there are adult seals present. Avoid walruses, as they can be aggressive. If you are on top of an ice floe, seals may have made breathing holes to come up for air while they are fishing under the ice. With a bit of patience, you might get lucky as a seal comes up for air. Spearing or clubbing is the best method for hunting at these air holes. Process as you would any large mammal (see page 148). Seals can provide good food, skins for clothing, and fat for fires. **Don't eat seals' livers, as they are so high in vitamin A that it can be deadly.**

You can use these breathing holes to catch fish from as well. Bone hooks will probably work best, if you can find any carcasses in the area. You may need to get inventive to source some natural cordage. The carcass may have dried skin you can cut into strips, or the inner bark from trees might work.

To carve your own fishing hole, make sure the ice is at least four inches thick before walking on it; gouge out a hole in the ice, using a sharpened rock or hardened piece of wood. The hole doesn't need to be big, just enough to pull an average-sized fish through. If you have enough materials, you can set several holes with bait. Just use two good-sized sticks about a foot long. Tie them together in a cross, and tie the other side of the line to them. When the fish takes the bait, it will drag the sticks to the hole but not down the hole, so you will know if you have a bite. Make sure that the sticks are long enough that they can't be dragged through the hole.

As you move toward more vegetated areas and onto the tundra, you may find some lichens and edible moss. Lichens are best soaked for a few days or boiled before eating, but can be consumed raw. There are a few varieties of poisonous lichens, so make sure you do the toxin test (see page 110) before consuming. Depending on the time of year, there may also be some edible berries.

During the warmer months, you may see some larger grazing mammals, ranging from caribou to musk ox. These animals are easy to track in the snow but hard to sneak up on. Signs that they are in the area include bark and greenery stripped from trees, hoof diggings in the shallow snow, and droppings. It is better to target smaller mammals, such as squirrels, Arctic hares, and lemmings. Locating their dens and burrows and setting snares would be a good way to hunt them. Observing squirrels will help you find their winter stash of edibles. Quite often the nuts they store will be good to eat after soaking the tannins out of them by boiling them through a few fresh pots of water.

Birds such as ptarmigans, ravens, and jays can be caught with an arapuca trap (see page 142), but it uses a lot of wood to make, so if wood is scarce, lure them close to you with some bait and try for one with a throwing stick (see page 147).

Although some of the choices of food are not politically correct, polar ecosystems will require a survival mindset to make it out alive.

POLAR RESCUE

If at all possible, remain with the vehicle that brought you into this environment. It generally will be the most obvious thing on the landscape for rescuers to find, will have an abundance of resources for you to utilize, and will help create a shelter from the weather.

Make the vehicle and the area as obvious as possible from the air. Anything that contrasts to the white landscape will be seen from miles away, so make large SOS signs in the snow using any materials or debris that you don't need for your direct survival. Try using the vehicle's communication devices to send out Maydays and find all possible methods of signaling, including reflective surfaces and flares. For signaling out to sea, erect a tripod with reflective surfaces and bright colors attached by cords to catch the sun's rays. Prepare a pile of flammable material that you can save for a signal fire if you catch sight of a rescue vehicle.

If you are traveling out by water vessel, avoid traveling close to sea cliffs, as thousands of tons of ice can shear off without warning. Don't try to dock to or climb on icebergs. While most of the weight of an iceberg is below water, it can flip without warning.

A decision to walk out will need to be based on proximity to civilization and hope of rescue. If no Mayday signal was delivered and no one knows that the vehicle might be in that area, you may need to rescue yourself. This is not a decision to be made lightly. Polar weather and terrain can be treacherous and navigation difficult because compasses do not tend to work reliably at the poles.

If you do decide to leave your vehicle, strip it of everything that may be of use. Make a sled so that you can take with you more than you could carry on your back. The more resources you have with you, the better your chances of survival. A sled just needs to have two runners that can slide along the snow and a platform for your gear. Set it up so you can drag this behind you.

Snowshoes need to be an inch wider than your shoe.

SNOWSHOES Create some kind of snowshoes for yourself. If you have access to driftwood or trees, use four thin, flexible, strong lengths of wood and six smaller lengths for crossbeams. This is the minimum material; you can always add more struts, crossbeams, or branches to help with buoyancy on the snow. Tie two long sticks to a point at one end, and then attach three crossbeams about a third of the way down. Snowshoes need to be about an inch wider than your shoe. You can either tie up the pointy end of the snow-shoe in a curve so that it is more maneuverable, or you can leave it long, depending on how flexible your wood is. Tie your shoe to the first crossbeam, leaving the other two there for support on the down step. The theory is that it spreads your weight across a greater surface of snow, so that you don't sink as deeply. This will conserve energy. I find that having walking sticks helps, and they can double as probe sticks or spears.

Choose your path carefully Snowfall can disguise dangerous crevasses and slippery slopes and can trigger avalanches. Stay away from the base of steep valleys, and probe the ground in front of you as you walk, making sure it is solid. Do not venture out in a blizzard, as it can get easy to lose your way and sense of direction. If you are following frozen rivers, keep to the smoother ice on the edges and to the outer curve on bends, as the ice tends to be thicker in these areas.

Reflections on the underside of clouds can help roughly keep track of where you are headed. Clouds over woodlands or snow-free ground might appear darker on the bottom, whereas clouds over sea ice or snow might be whiter on the bottom.

DANGERS

HYPOTHERMIA This is a condition that occurs when the body loses heat faster than it can produce it. It is better to prevent hypothermia than to try to cure it in the field, so always begin to try to warm up again when you start to feel cold.

Signs and symptoms of hypothermia include:

- Shivering

- Slurred speech or mumbling

- Slow, shallow breathing

- Weak pulse

- Clumsiness or lack of coordination

- Drowsiness

- Confusion

- Loss of consciousness

Someone with hypothermia usually isn't aware of their condition, because it comes on gradually. Eventually it can lead to risk-taking behavior and a feeling of euphoria. Quite often people who have died of cold exposure are found naked, as they begin to feel overheated and take all of their clothes off in the final stages of the condition.

When you start to feel cold, add layers or remove damp clothing and replace it with dry items. Move around; seek shelter and warmth. Do not attempt to warm hypothermia victims quickly, since this will lead to cold blood in the extremities rushing to the core and dropping the core temperature dangerously. Warm drinks and a hot water bottle on top of a layer of clothing by their core will help. Avoid alcohol, caffeine, and tobacco. It is not recommended to strip off and join them, because this may lead to two cold people instead of two warm people, but if you are having trouble warming them, keep your warm layer on and get close.

FROSTBITE This is a condition where the skin and the tissue just below the skin freeze. It mostly affects exposed body parts or extremities. Signs and symptoms include:

- **Very cold flesh**
- **Numbness**
- **Hard and pale skin**

To treat frostbite, rewarm slowly in tepid water and wrap. This flesh may turn black, rot, and fall off. It is important to keep the wound as clean and sterile as possible. Any flesh that has been frostbitten in the past will be more susceptible to it in the future.

SNOW BLINDNESS This happens when the sun reflects off the white snow and ice and burns the cornea. It can produce temporary, partial, or full vision loss. It is best to predict when this might happen and act pro-actively to prevent it. Covering sunglasses with tape to restrict light to a thin crack can help. If you don't have glasses, thin strips of bark covering the eyes will work. The idea is to restrict the amount of light entering the eye, so whatever you have on you that will achieve that will prevent this affliction. If you have snow blindness, the best thing you can do is to rest your eyes with a cold compress on them.

CONSTIPATION Quite often people will not want to go to the bathroom because it is so cold and they hold it in. This can make you very sick. If possible, dig a hole at the entrance to your shelter so you don't have to go far. The lack of flying insects and the extreme cold will make sure that this doesn't become too unsanitary.

TRENCH FOOT If the weather is warmer, the ground underfoot may be slushy or boggy. If you don't find a way to dry your feet, the constant moisture will rot the tissue of your feet, and they will become painful to walk on and subject to infection. If you can't waterproof your shoes, try to find a way to dry your socks and feet every night.

POLAR BEARS The Artic has bears; the Antarctic has no bears. Polar bears are opportunistic hunters and have been known to follow and stalk humans. They are powerful beasts and best avoided if possible. Some people who have managed to avoid being attacked by them have suggested that you make yourself bigger and louder if you are confronted by them. I can't confirm this as a method of best dealing with them, but I would certainly try it if avoiding eye contact and backing off wasn't working.

INSECTS For the brief period that the tundra melts in polar ecosystems, all the stinging, biting insects come out. These can include mosquitoes, black flies, deer flies, and midges, and they swarm in such numbers as to almost drive you mad. Since their larvae live in water, choose a shelter site away from water. Smoky fires at night might work, but covering yourself with piles of thick grasses or reeds to sleep will keep a majority off you.

Make sure if you have ended up in a survival situation in a polar ecosystem that you conserve your energy for important tasks, and keep thinking about how you can better your circumstances. The cold can be very demoralizing, but if you can make small, positive changes to your environment each day, you might be able to wait it out until rescue arrives.

Deer fly

Black fly

Mosquito

MARINE

A marine environment is probably one of the better ecosystems to end up in, if your life depends upon it. Although they can be quite different, ranging across diverse, extreme weather conditions, there is usually an abundance of resources available that can make your life a lot easier. Garbage from all over the world ends up in oceans and regularly gets deposited on the shorelines, making your environment a treasure trove of useful material. Every day someone's trash could become your treasure. Check regularly along your tide marks and get inventive with what you find. No resource is useless, so gather it all together for future possibilities. I have found nylon line and fishhooks tangled together with seaweed, as well as tons of rope, water bottles, and even unopened cans of food.

If you are marooned on an island, make sure that you explore the whole island if it isn't that large. Quite often people have been there before you and left behind resources. Sometimes early explorers "seeded" islands they found on their travels with domesticated food sources, and it might be possible to find chickens and pigs at home in the bushlands. The only difficulty with the smaller islands is finite resources. If you have thoroughly exploited the resources on your island, you may need to leave in order to assure your survival.

If you are adrift on the water, the sea itself offers very few resources, so head toward land as soon as possible.

Coastal areas can be smooth, sandy, and tropical, or they can be rocky, desolate, and freezing. Depending on your location, you'll have to determine your priorities accordingly. If you have arrived on the rocky shores of Europe in winter, cold exposure will be a threat to your life. If you are in the Maldives in summer, you are going to be looking to hydrate and stay out of the sun. Observe, assess, and make a plan accordingly. Be flexible with your thinking, and adapt to your environment.

MARINE SHELTER

Exposure to wind is going to be one of your biggest concerns in a coastal location. Afternoon sea breezes are common and usually add a chill to the moist air, coming straight off a body of colder water. Tides are also something that you need to pay close attention to. Make sure that you have an escape route to get out of your shelter if you need to, allowing for access away from it if the tide has come in.

CAVES AND OVERHANGS Sea cliffs will often provide natural shelters in the form of caves and overhangs, but make sure that there is no evidence of the water level rising to the cave floor. This can be in the form of seaweed or other debris. If there are barnacles or other shellfish on the rocks in your cave, you know that the tide reaches it, as these creatures live between the high and low tide level. Even if the tide mark doesn't look fresh, don't risk it, as once a month on a full moon the tide gets fuller, and if the wind direction is pushing the water toward the shore, it can rise even higher than usual.

If you can find an overhang or shelter that is safe to get to and out of the tide mark, check to make sure it is not already occupied, and build a wind break in front of it to keep out the chill. These sea cliff caves may even provide fresh water in the form of seepage through the rock. Pile up dry seaweed and vegetation on the cave floor for warmth and comfort.

LEAN-TO If you have found yourself in a tropical marine environment, a lean-to is the perfect shelter. It will provide shade from the sun and protection from tropical rainstorms, as well as allowing for maximum wind flow on balmy nights. As tempting as it will be to build your lean-to on the sandy beach, build it inland, where you will be protected from the weather and any sandflies, mosquitoes, and other biting insects that may live in the sand or seaweed. Face the lean-to away from the ocean to protect yourself from onshore winds. Even though tropical areas may seem like paradise, don't get lazy with your shelter roof. Waterproof it as you would for a rain forest (see page 110). Tropical coastal storms can be wild, unpredictable, and sudden.

ROCK HUTS In less hospitable coastal areas, make use of whatever resource is abundant to create your shelter. Rock walls are strong and windproof if built well and can be roofed with driftwood and seaweed to keep the heat in and the weather out.

MARINE WATER

Small islands will either have a water source, or they won't. Try the center of the island for fresh springs. Dig above the high tide mark and behind the first layer of dunes. Check for rock pools and signs of drainage into the ocean. Look for signs of recent rain, and assess what you know of the rainfall patterns in the area. If you have exhausted all your options and still not found a water source, you will need to find a way off that island and onto a more hospitable location as soon as possible.

DO NOT DRINK SALT WATER Consuming salt water causes your kidneys to work hard to purge the body of excess salts. This leads to liquid being expelled faster than it can be replaced and can result in death by dehydration.

FRESHWATER STREAMS Coastal areas will generally have estuaries or locations where inland water empties into the ocean. If there is not one close to you, explore the coast in both directions to see if you can find one. A clue to their location may be muddy water in the ocean. The water may be brackish (a mix of fresh and salt) close to the ocean, but it will become fresher as you follow it upstream. Make sure that you purify it before drinking, as you do not know where the water has come from before it reaches you.

FRESHWATER SEEPAGE This is where fresh water is making its way to the ocean underground. This can often be seen in the sand as rivulets or branches of sand flowing toward the ocean as the tide retreats. Dig behind these signs above the high tide mark to access this water.

FRESHWATER WELLS Rainwater has a different density to salt water and will float on top of the saltier water if undisturbed. Digging behind the first layer of sand dunes, above the high tide mark, may expose a fresh water source. Skim the top inch off the water, trying not to disturb the well. This should be fresh and drinkable.

ROCK POOLS Rock pools by the water's edge will be salty. Even if the high tide doesn't reach them, they will be affected by salt spray. On top of higher cliffs and sometimes on rock ledges, rainfall can pool and provide a fresh source of water. Clues that it might be fresh include ferns or moss growing. If the pool has been there awhile, the water may be stagnant. Make sure to boil it before drinking.

VEGETATION Some coastal succulents can provide fluids to stave off dehydration. Simply gather in handfuls, pound them slightly between two rocks, and squeeze in your hand with your thumb pointed downward to your mouth. Make sure that the succulent is not toxic first by using the toxin test (see page 110). **Do not drink the liquid if it comes out sticky or milky.**

Coconuts are a good source of hydration. The liquid inside coconuts at all stages is consumable and will provide you with valuable natural electrolytes that water is lacking. Coconuts are a risk-versus-reward gather. A lot of the time, they will be lying on the ground or the high tide mark, which makes them low risk. If the coconut palms are not too tall, you should be able to find a long, forked stick and use it to knock them down. Again, pretty low risk. It is when you are required to climb the coconut palm in order to get the nuts that the risk grows in opposition to the reward gained. Your physicality is one of your greatest assets in a survival scenario, and even a sprained ankle can diminish your chances of survival. If you have some good cordage or rope, make a loop that is just big enough to wrap around the soles of your feet with a few spare inches between your feet. Wrap your arms around the palm, and place the soles of your feet, on the palm so that the material is flattened taut against the bark. With your knees splayed like a frog, push upward until your legs straighten, pull the tree toward you with your arms, and when you are able to support your weight on your arms alone, bring your feet up higher on the tree and secure another foothold. Repeat until you are by the coconuts. It may be tempting to simply slide down the tree, but the bark can be rough and the landing hard, so avoid injury by using the same method to get you down.

She-oaks, or casuarinas, can be found on a lot of deserted islands. They can often hold a reservoir of water in their trunks. An indicator of this is a trail of ants disappearing into the trunk of the tree. You may need to fashion a straw or dip some material into the trunk to access the water. Enlarge the hole with a stone or your knife, but don't chop into the trunk, because doing so will result in losing a future source of water, as it will replenish after you use it. You can also chop off some of the roots of the she-oak into three-foot-long segments and prop them into a container to drain the water out of them.

SALTWATER STILL There are many different and complex ways to remove the salt from salt water. The basic idea is that the salt water needs to be heated so that the pure water rises from it as steam. This steam then needs to be collected and cooled in such a way that it reverts back to liquid form, this time without the salt in it. If you have a complex array of pipes and collection pots and perhaps some duct tape, you could rig up an efficient system to keep many people satisfied with drinking water indefinitely. However, that is a lot of equipment to rely on having, and you can achieve a smaller version of this with a clear water bottle and a can. You won't be able to process as much water at a time, but it may just keep you alive.

Cut the bottom off the water bottle and the top off the can. Fold the bottom sides of the water bottle up into itself to create a gutter to catch the desalinated water. Fill the can with salt water, and place it inside of the water bottle. Make sure the lid is on the water bottle, and place your still in the full sun. The water will evaporate from the can in the heat and re-form on the inside of the water bottle, sliding down the sides to be caught in the gutter. This method takes time and sunny weather, so make sure you set this up way before dehydration sets in. If possible, make multiple setups.

MARINE FIRE

On smaller islands, wood could be sparse and should only be used when you really need it, such as for emergency signaling or if required to purify water. All driftwood should be collected. Not having wood will not be a reason to leave a location, unless fire is a necessity for you to achieve your basic needs. On larger islands, you may have more vegetation, and this should not be an issue.

Coconut husks make great tinder to put a spark or coal into. Work it between your hands until it is soft; this makes it even easier to light.

There are some amazing coastal plants that work very well for friction fire. This is because they grow quickly and straight, with soft, lightweight wood. Choose the dry, dead branches, and try any of the friction fire methods to see if you can get some smoke and eventually a coal. Beach hibiscus works very well to get friction fire coals and is easily identified by its bright yellow flower and bright green leaves (both of which are edible).

Driftwood is also worth trying as a source of friction fire. Even though it can be hard to identify what plant it came from, it might be one that works. Remember, the best wood for friction fire is:

- **Dry**

- **Soft and lightweight but not punky or rotten**

- **Straight and free from bends and knots**

Scour the beach for any garbage that may work for a refraction fire method (see page 170). Plastic water bottles filled with water can help direct the sun's rays into a hot pinpoint that may combust. The polished bottoms of soda cans can get bright enough to direct heat onto a tinder bundle. Any glass is worth testing if it can concentrate the sun's rays. With all of these methods, move the object closer and farther away from your tinder bundle to see what works best. The smaller the point of light that you can make, the more heat you will generate in a concentrated area, and the more likely you are to get a flame.

Bow drill
(see page 182)

Fire plow
(see page 185)

Fire saw
(see page 185)

Strap drill
(see page 181)

MARINE FOOD

Fortunately, most coastlines will provide you with an abundance of food, both in the shallows and above the waterline. Be flexible with your idea of what food is, and you should have no reason to starve.

Don't eat anything that you find already dead. A lot of sea life absorbs toxins from the water, and you cannot be sure what killed whatever it is you found.

You can use salt water to boil your food, and it will add some much-needed salts to your meal. Salt is also great for when you are drying or smoking excess meat, as it helps to enhance and preserve the flavor, as well as preventing spoilage by speeding up the preservation process.

Pebble beaches can be the least food abundant, but a lot of edible species make their homes under rocks, so you will need to turn them over to discover your main food source.

Do not eat mollusks that are bright in color or shaped like cones.

One species of cone shell is one of the most venomous creatures on the planet. There are over 400 different species of cone shells, and not all of them are deadly, but most of them will deliver an envenomated barb that will range from extremely painful to life threating if it pierces your skin, so they are best avoided entirely.

SEAWEED While there are no inedible seaweeds, some definitely taste better than others. They may have a laxative or diuretic effect if consumed in large quantities, so take your time with them and only eat small quantities at first until you know the effect they have on you, if any. Make sure that you only eat seaweed that is fresh and growing, as bacteria can breed quickly in dead seaweed. Seaweed can be eaten raw, cooked, or dried.

MOLLUSKS These can be found clinging to rocks or buried in the sand. On sandy beaches, look for breathing holes, divots in the sand, or opened, empty shells to indicate what might be under the surface. They are found between the high and low tide mark, and to locate them, you can either dig with your hands or wiggle your feet into the sand as the water goes out. Most of the shellfish in the sandy areas will be less than a foot below the sand surface. This is also a good way to find crabs.

In rock pools, the mollusks will also be found clinging to rocks between the high and low tide mark. Do not eat mollusks if the following occurs:

- **They remain partially open when you touch them.**
- **They are easy to remove from the rocks or have fallen off by themselves.**
- **They smell bad.**
- **They don't open when cooked in boiling water.**
- **They are located in water with a reddish algae tinge.**

Mollusks filter the toxins out of the water and can store them in their system. This is usually of greater concern when you are in urban and industrial areas. In a very isolated area, I would eat mollusks raw from the ocean, unless there was evidence of algae bloom. Otherwise, cook by boiling, steaming, or placing them directly on the coals.

Sea urchins A risk-versus-reward food, sea urchins are covered in spines that can deliver an extremely painful sting and can remain lodged under the skin, causing extensive damage to skin, tissue, and bone. Using a combination of rocks and sticks, you can fashion some tools to safely break open the urchin, shake out the guts, and scoop out and eat the remaining orangey insides. You can also eat the roe if you are lucky enough to find some. Do not eat them if their spines don't move when you touch them, or if they smell bad.

Sea cucumbers Personally, I haven't had much success with eating sea cucumbers, but they are edible. Slice them up the bottom middle and remove the insides; you will be left with a hard outer shell. It is extremely difficult to chew when raw. It is best to cut it into thin slices and boil.

Crabs, prawns, lobsters Depending on the region you are in, crabs will either leave very obvious traces of their presence or nothing at all. Some signs include holes on the beach, small balls of sand on the beach, or tracks in the sand. Most crabs are nocturnal, so if you are hunting them during the day, they will be hidden away. Crabs can be very fast once exposed to the daylight. Crabbing spears are very effective to pin them down. This can be as simple as a forked stick, or as complex as a multi-barbed fishing spear. Make sure you grab the crab from the back to avoid its claws. They can be cooked over the fire or boiled. They need to be eaten as soon as they are killed, as their meat spoils quickly.

Octopus Most active at night, octopuses retreat into holes during the day. Their holes can sometimes be discovered by looking for a pile of empty shells. A fishing spear is the best method for getting them out of the hole. If the octopus is small and develops blue rings when agitated, leave it alone. This is the blue-ringed octopus, and it has a deadly venom that can cause respiratory failure in minutes.

Fish If you are lucky enough to find line and something that will double as a hook, then hand-line fishing will be a good option. The best time to fish is with an incoming tide. Mollusks make great bait, as do sand worms and animal guts. Rock pools trap larger fish in them when the tide goes out. You can try to flip them onto dry land with your hands or make a fishing spear (see page 152). You can create your own fish traps by damming areas above the low tide mark with rocks. A circle shape will work, but an arrow shape is more effective, as the fish will become trapped more easily. Avoid the fins of fish if you aren't sure of what they are, since some fish can have sharp or venomous spines. **Never eat a puffer fish.** Fish should be gutted before eating. Saltwater fish are better to eat raw than freshwater fish, but if you have a fire going, it's best to cook them.

Birds Flocks of birds will often roam the seashores, looking for crabs and mollusks. A throwing stick made from a two- to three-foot-long piece of driftwood with a slight bend in it is a good weapon for hunting them. It will work best if one side is heavier than the other, and you can modify it by carving it flatter so it moves through the air faster. Check cliffs for nesting sites; this can be a great source of eggs. But don't risk your life climbing steep, unstable cliffs in search of them.

Turtles If you are lucky enough to be in an area where turtles come to land or graze on seagrass in the shallows, make the most of this meal. Sea turtles can be cooked in their shell over an open fire and will provide a large amount of meat. You can also follow their obvious trail along the beach sand to their nests and dig up their eggs. The average sea turtle lays one-hundred and ten eggs, so you will have enough food to last you a while. Don't collect all of the eggs at once; rebury to protect them from predators, and collect more when you run out.

Mammals Make sure you don't forget to explore inland areas for signs of larger prey.

Coconuts As well as the liquid providing a good source of hydration, the inside of the nuts (the meat) is edible. You can cook it or eat it raw. Heating it up can release the oils in the nut that can be used for cooking and to soothe sunburns. The meat is edible in the green and brown nut forms and if the nut is sprouting; the small, growing shoots are edible. Just remember that although an average coconut tree can grow thirty nuts a year, they are a finite resource, as they take a while to grow, so ration coconuts to make sure they last.

Succulents and fruits A lot of coastal succulents are edible, as are tropical fruits. Be sure you use the toxin test (see page 110) before consuming, however, no matter how safe they look. In the Bahamas, there is a tree called manzanilla de la muerte, or apple of death. The fruit looks like an apple, but it is one of the most toxic trees in the world, and eating that fruit can be fatal. The first indication of its toxicity is the milky sap that will cause blistering on impact with your skin.

The food possibilities will be as numerous as the locations where you could become stranded. Take your time and explore all available options.

MARINE RESCUE

If your coastal area is a paradise of useful resources and infinite possibilities, then make the most of your signaling capabilities and wait for rescue to come to you. If you have ended up on a barren coastline or an island without resources, you will need to figure out the best way to get out of there fast.

On sandy beaches, use seaweed, driftwood, and rocks to create large SOS letters above the high tide mark. The more contrast you can create with your letters when compared with the ground, the more likely someone will be able to see them.

Use the washed-up debris to make tripods of hanging reflective surfaces that can catch the sun and shine out to sea and to air. Place these tripods in clearings and areas that are likely to get the most sun all day.

Have signal fires ready to be lit, if you have an abundance of wood available. Make sure you have a stash of dry, highly flammable material to light the fires and a plan on how best to get a flame. You have about two minutes to get a pilot's attention when they fly overhead. Green leaves will make a smoky fire, as will any washed-up rubber you have found.

If your island is uninhabitable and you decide to head off, leave a message and clearly mark the direction you intend to travel and when you left.

Building a raft would be ideal, but if you are leaving due to a lack of resources, you may not have enough materials to create one. Often the ocean has washed-up items you can use to keep you buoyant, including plastic bottles, old buoys, drums, and logs. Test everything in the water to see how well it floats before lashing it to your raft. If you can see land from where you are and it isn't a long journey, the raft doesn't have to be large or fully resourced, just big enough to keep you out of the water and to be able to direct in some way. Even strapping some coconuts together may be enough to keep you afloat as you head to your next piece of land.

Carry whatever resources you can find with you, in case there isn't anything at your next destination either. Strap everything buoyant together well, and create a platform over it for you to sit on. A paddle is important to help with direction and speed if you are sitting on the raft, but you can also direct it by kicking or swimming if you are mostly in the water.

You will need to be able to propel the raft away from the coast in seas that will be trying to beach you back on the sand again. Some kind of sail rig could help with this. It doesn't have to be fancy, just something that can catch the wind on the end of a solid branch attached to your raft. Plastic, cloth, or even a woven mat of leaves would do the trick. This could also double as a sunshade in the heat of the day. Always plan to head off the island with the outgoing tide, as this will give you greater success in moving past the wave line and out to sea.

If no land is in sight, use clues such as watching which direction sea birds head and if they come back at night. If they don't, they may be flying to other areas of land. Cumulus clouds often form over land, so if you see them in the distance, it is worth heading toward them.

If you are deciding whether or not to leave a coastal area rather than wait for rescue, it is useful to consider the following:

- Does my land have resources?

- What information did I manage to get to someone prior to being stranded?

- Is my position known?

- Is there favorable weather for a search?

- Am I stranded in a popular or remote place?

If you have the resources and decide to leave rather than wait for rescue, try to ensure that the vessel you make has the following:

- Protection from the elements

- A way of attracting rescue

- Water or a method of catching rainfall

- Food or a way of catching food

- A steering method

Remember that you are always going to be better off on land than you are at sea, so as soon as viable landfall is sighted, try to steer toward it. Avoid high sea cliffs, as they can be unclimbable, and this can be deadly if the tides leave no dry land. The ideal landing point will be one with a gently sloping beach and a small swell. An ingoing tide will help you make it to land. If you have to swim to shore, keep your clothing and shoes on, even if you feel like they are weighing you down. Keep your legs in front of you with your knees bent if the shoreline is rocky, and try to absorb any hits by compressing your legs.

DANGERS

SUN EXPOSURE In tropical climates, stay out of the sun in the heat of the day. Create some kind of shelter to lie under, if shade is limited. Use vegetation to craft a head covering. Sun exposure can lead to dehydration, and with fresh water being a commodity in these environments, it's important to limit any activity that will lead to you losing water to the environment. The glare off the water will exacerbate the heat of the sun, so restrict fishing to mornings and evenings.

RIPTIDES AND TIDAL CURRENTS Riptides can knock you off your feet in knee-deep water and drag you out into the depths. They are unpredictable and can occur in previously safe waters. Some indicators of riptides include:

- **A steeply sloping beach**

- **Sand in the waves, stretching into the ocean**

- **Waves forming heading away from the beach as well as toward it**

If you get caught in a riptide and cannot get your feet down or easily make it to shore, do not fight it, as you will end up getting exhausted and possibly drown. Save your energy and float with the current out until the rip finishes. This may be up to 400 yards but is usually less than that. You will know when it ends, as you will stop being dragged out to sea. Swim parallel to the shore, testing to see where the riptide is. Most riptides are no more than 40 yards long, so you should soon be able to find where it ends and swim to shore.

It is best in a survival situation to never swim out beyond your depth.

DEADLY SEA CREATURES Jellyfish, men o' war, stingrays, cone shells, stone fish, sea snakes, blue-ringed octopus: these and many more could deliver a painful, even deadly hit of venom and are all best avoided if possible. This includes not putting your hands in crevices and holes in the ocean that you can't see into.

The high tide line will sometimes give you clues as to what dangerous sea creatures lurk in your part of the ocean, but also keep an eye out when you are in the water. Most marine venoms are best treated with as much hot water as the patient can bear. I will cover more in the wilderness first aid chapter (see page 548), but if hot water doesn't ease the pain, try urine or cold water. If the venom is deadly and requires medical assistance to survive, chances are you won't. None of these other treatments will endanger your life; they will either help or they won't.

SHARKS A majority of shark attacks happen close to shore or near areas with nearby deep drop-offs, such as sandbars and reefs. This is because it is close to where their prey is often located. If you are sharing your location with seals, it is best to avoid going into the water as much as possible, as baby seal is among a shark's favorite meals. River mouths are also places where sharks tend to hang out, as freshwater fish become sluggish and easy to catch when they hit the salt water. Avoid getting into water that is not clear enough for you to see what is around you, and don't fish when you see sharks in the area.

If you are in the water and you can see a shark near you, don't panic. Rapid movements in water can mimic a fish in distress and attract their attention. Watch how the shark is moving. If their movements are sharp and rapid, they are in hunting mode. If they are slow and relaxed, then they are merely coming by for a look. Keep facing the direction of the shark so you can see them. If the shark approaches you calmly, push the snout of the shark away from you. If the shark approaches menacingly, try to punch or kick at the snout, avoiding the mouth and teeth. If you have a paddle or stick, put it between you and the shark and try to push it away. If the shark has you in its jaws, punch at its snout or try to gouge its eyes to get away. Get out of the water as soon as possible if you have encountered a shark.

CROCODILES Saltwater crocodiles will often be found near estuaries where rivers empty into the ocean. If you are in a coastal tropical location, make sure you keep an eye out for these creatures. They are not likely to be on island locations but have been spotted swimming up to thirty miles out to sea. They are the ultimate predator, so stay out of murky water if you know they are in the area. If you are grabbed by a crocodile, their only vulnerable spot is their eyes, so try to stick your fingers in their eyes in the hope they will let you go.

Being creative and utilizing all resources will be key to survival in a marine location. Depending on your location, you could make yourself quite comfortable while waiting for a rescue. Stay busy, create a routine, and try to improve your situation every day with what you have around you.

HIGHLAND

Highland ecosystems consist of mountainous or elevated regions. They are characterized by snow and ice, rocky terrain, and an absence of trees and large bushes. Weather is usually unpredictable and able to turn from extreme heat to freezing cold in a matter of minutes.

Anything above 1,500 feet is classified as highlands, so you may have a mix of snow, bare timber, rocky outcrops, and, lower down, forests and woodland areas with an abundance of resources. It is your aim in a survival situation to make your way safely down to these forests and woodlands in order to access the assets required to stay alive. If you need to cross high mountain passes, the lower forests may give a much-needed rest and provide you with food and water to help make a successful crossing.

The higher elevation you are at, the less resources you will have access to, including oxygen. Altitude sickness can hit at around 8,000 feet and can dramatically reduce your ability to function.

Avalanches, crevasses, steep cliffs, and icefall are all dangers you will need to be constantly aware of and navigate around. Whiteout conditions can happen suddenly and leave you stuck and disoriented without shelter in precarious positions. Keep a close eye on the clouds, and be prepared for anything.

HIGHLAND SHELTER

Exposure is going to be your number one concern in a highland environment. Keeping in mind that exposed, wet flesh can freeze in under thirty minutes and cold exposure can kill in about three hours, cover up and shelter as soon as possible when inclement weather sets in.

If you are with a vehicle, stay with the vehicle. Use whatever resources you have with you to create shelter and keep you warm. Wrapping yourself in canvas or plastic will prevent your body heat from escaping, and any layers of warm material that you can add to your cocoon will get you through the night. If you can't insulate an area of the vehicle, make a shelter next to the vehicle in the snow, using salvaged materials. Snow holds heat much better than metal does, so digging a snow cave and lining it with plastic and seat stuffing will be much warmer than sleeping in a metal container.

If you are on foot, getting off the mountain will be your first priority, but if night or bad weather is approaching, you will need to seek shelter and try to find a way out in the morning.

Your clothing will be your first line of defense against the cold. Make sure you are wearing layers that are warm but not restricting. Cover all areas of bare flesh, including your face. I have used socks on my hands and a bandana on my head when I was caught out on a mountain unprepared. It doesn't have to be much; just try to cover anywhere that you could lose heat to the environment. Close any clothing openings, including sleeves and collars. Remove cotton layers if possible, as they suck the heat out of your body if they get wet.

Stuff your clothing with any leaves or moss-like material that you can find. This creates layers with air pockets that will catch and hold heat lost from your body. Don't sit on the cold ground. Sit on your pack, or pad the ground with leaves and branches.

Mountaintops may have no resources to make shelters. Find a place out of the wind. If you are in the snow, push up a wall of snow to protect you. Use rocks, if you can find any, or look for a natural overhang or cave out of the weather. Make sure that the entrance doesn't become completely blocked by snow. You will be tempted to prevent all the air and wind from entering the shelter, but if there is no ventilation in your shelter, you can quickly be overcome by carbon dioxide poisoning and die. If you have a walking pole or stick with you, make sure that you keep clearing a hole in the snow buildup so fresh air can get in.

Without any resources or natural shelter, the best chance of survival on a mountain is to build a snow cave.

SNOW CAVE

There are a few methods of building a snow cave. You can find a suitable deep, solid snowdrift and burrow in, or you can create a small iglu, or igloo. I prefer the igloo, as it can be more structurally sound than a snow-drift. It is best that you have some kind of cutting tool to create the snow blocks that you will need for this shelter. I once managed to find the pelvis bone of a yak farther down the mountain, and this worked perfectly. Test the solidity of your snow. If it is too cold, the snow will be too fluffy to make perfect blocks, and if it is too warm, the snow will be too slushy to work. This is a Goldilocks shelter, where the snow needs to be just right to work. If you can slice the snow into blocks, find a patch of snow where it is about waist deep or more, and start to build the walls of your shelter. It is best to make a dome shape, as it will hold the integrity of the roof better. Your shelter only needs to be big enough for you to curl up in. Once the dome is done, tunnel down and then up into the shelter. This will ensure that no heat is lost to the entrance, as heat rises. I like to smooth down the walls on the inside, since it makes me feel like they are a little more solid, but that is purely psychological. Insulate the floor of your shelter with whatever material you can find. I even managed to create a "door" with some stray vegetation that was poking up through the snow. The branches kept a little more of the heat in without entirely blocking my ventilation. A small bone-marrow candle helped me get through the freezing night with only the clothes on my back.

If you are down into the tree line but still snowed in, try to find a solid tree well to bed down in. These occur when the lower branches of the tree are resting on the snowbanks, and no snow has gathered below the branches beside the trunk. It creates a hole that you can crawl into and insulate with branches and leaves. Your body heat will keep the temperature at a surviv-able level, and you will be out of the wind and weather. Make sure you keep an air passage clear so that the space has ventilation.

Below the snow line and into the forest area, there should be an abundance of resources to make shelters with. If you are in a cold mountain area, try to make a tepee or humpy (see page 67) to limit the wind exposure and to conserve as much of the heat you create as possible. If you are in a warmer mountain area or time of year, a lean-to (see page 64) with a fire in front of it will suffice.

If you are on the move through the mountain areas, conserve energy as much as possible each day by using natural shelters to sleep in. Caves, tree hollows, tree root systems, and fallen trees and big branches can all provide structures that require very little modification to be good shelters. If you are able to carry fire with you or create fire easily, these shelters will get you through nights when the temperatures will drop below freezing. If you can't make a fire, keep your shelter small and add as much insulation as you can, in the form of grasses, moss, leaves, and branches. Crawl inside this insula-tion, so that you have some below you to protect you from the cold ground and some above you to keep your body heat in.

Remember the five ways that your body loses heat to the atmosphere, and do everything you can to prevent this from happening. The most important ones in this environment are:

RESPIRATION When your body inhales cold air, it works to warm it by heating that air before breathing it out. This results in a loss of body heat via your breath.

RADIATION When your body temperature is greater than your environment, heat will exit your exposed skin in an attempt to warm your environment's. Your head, neck, wrists, and ankles contribute up to 60 percent of a loss of body heat, due to their increased blood flow compared to other areas of the body, so it's important to try to keep them covered.

CONVECTION Heat loss by air or water moving across the skin's surface; this includes exposure to one or more of the following: cold air, rain, or wind.

CONDUCTION Heat loss by direct contact with an object; heat exits the warmer object in an attempt to equalize the temperatures between the two objects. This can occur when sitting or lying on cold ground or up against cold rocks.

HIGHLAND WATER

In cooler climates and at altitude, it is easy to forget to drink. Although you are not losing moisture to the heat, you are losing moisture due to increased urine output, drier air, and more rapid breathing. Your body loses water through respiration twice as fast at altitude than it does at sea level, so it is very important to keep up your water intake, even if you do not feel thirsty.

Above the snow line, your main source of water will be ice and snow melt. Ice is denser than snow, and therefore will provide you with more water per volume when melting it. Do not eat snow and ice in an effort to stay hydrated. Your body uses valuable heat and energy to process these substances, and this can cause your core temperature to drop dangerously, as well as using more moisture to process the water than what you gain by consuming it. Use a fire and container to melt the snow and ice, if you have them. If you have a container but no fire, place the container full of ice inside your clothing (not directly on your skin) while you are moving. Your body heat will melt the ice. It is also a good idea to keep your water under your clothing layers at night so that it doesn't freeze overnight in the open.

Collect water from snow and ice melt in the heat of the day. If the sun is strong, you may be able to find areas in full sun that are melting in rivulets, despite the chill and altitude. Soak these up with a piece of material and squeeze into your mouth or a container.

It may be tempting to drink from the cool, fresh mountain streams, but you never know what is upstream, so always purify water if you are able to.

BOILING WATER Water has a lower boiling point at altitude, but even that lower boiling point is enough to kill most pathogens in less than a minute, so once those bubbles are coming up from the bottom, it is safe to drink. If you can get a fire going but don't have a pot to boil in, you can use a plastic water container as the pot. Water boils at a lower temperature than the plastic will melt. Don't put the bottle directly onto the fire; suspend it over the flames. Watch it carefully, as the water won't obviously boil in a closed container. As soon as little bubbles form in the water, it should be ready.

Boiling water

Water filter

WATER FILTER If you have access to some charcoal from a previous bush-fire or perhaps a fire you had the night before, you can use the charcoal for a natural water filter. Layer it in a piece of material, and pour the unfiltered water through the material over the charcoal, in the hope that the charcoal will absorb a majority of the toxins. If the water is murky and full of debris, you can fashion a water filter to drain out the particles as well by adding layers of grass, sand, and pebbles above the charcoal. This works best if you have a spare container or some bark to wrap them in to pour the water through.

WATER WELL If you are lower down in the highlands or have hit some warmer summer weather, you should have access to streams, rivers, and lakes. Without a fire, a good method of purifying the water is to dig a hole three feet away from the water's edge and drink the water that seeps into the hole. It doesn't remove a majority of waterborne pathogens, but it is better than drinking straight from the stream.

As always, be adaptable and make decisions based on the situation that you find yourself in. If you aren't able to purify or filter the water in any way, avoid drinking from standing pools of water, and drink from the clearest, swiftest-flowing stream you can find.

HIGHLAND FIRE

Above the snow line, there will be very limited resources for making and sustaining fire. If you have trees available, you may be able access some dead standing branches and peel off the wet outer layer to see if the underneath is dry enough to help start a fire. Trees above snow lines tend to have quite resinous sap, which means that they may be able to take a flame when wet. Use pine needles or sticks covered in sap for the kindling phase of your fire. Feather sticks (see below) are a great option in this environment to create kindling or even tinder out of fuel-sized sticks.

Feather stick To create a feather stick, choose a straight, dry stick with no knots. Lay your blade flat on the stick, and then tilt the angle of the blade slightly toward the wood. Run the blade all the way down the stick, stopping just before the bottom of the stick so that the shaving remains attached to the stick. Turn the stick around and repeat. Keep repeating until you end up with a thin stick with shavings attached. Place this inside your fire lay, and add an ignition source.

Feather stick

Fatwood Another asset you can look for in these environments is fatwood, or lighter knot. This occurs when a pine tree falls over and dies or is chopped down. All the resin concentrates in its base and produces a highly flammable wood that can be identified by a strong turpentine smell. Make small cuts into any dead pine trunks you find. The strong smell will let you know when you have found some. Carrying a piece of fatwood with you will make fire making in the alpine a much easier task. It can also be used to make torches to see and signal at night. Simply cut into one end over and over until it is "fluffy," and this will hold a flame for a length of time. I have used this wood and method to night fish for lobster when I didn't have access to any other light.

Animal fat If you have managed to harvest any animals, make sure that you collect their fat. If you are starving, eat it, as it will provide much-needed fuel for your body, but if you are intending to head back into the snow, collect it. This can be done by rolling it up in leaves or pieces of bark. Rubbing animal fat on exposed skin can prevent it from freezing. If you get enough of it, you can make a candle by preparing a natural cordage wick or using a small piece of your shoelace. In the high-altitude mountains of the Sichuan Province, I once found some old bones that had the marrow left in them. The marrow had turned into a fatty, waxy substance, and with a bit of the inside of my climbing rope as a wick, the candle kept me alive the whole night in a snow cave with only the clothes on my back for additional warmth. You will need a way to make fire with you as well. I carried a dry tinder bundle, some iron pyrite, and some chaga mushroom as my fire kit, which allowed me to make a flame for the candle.

Animal fat
candle

Percussion fire Mountain areas are great places to find rocks that will create a spark when struck against each other or a piece of steel. There are usually piles of rocks to choose from, and it is worth spending time hitting some together to see what you can find. Iron pyrite will make a spark when hit off another piece of iron pyrite. It is sometimes called fool's gold, so you are looking for a gold rock or a black rock with some gold flecks or sparkles distributed through it. If you can't find any pyrite, look for fine-grained or no-grained rocks, and try hitting them with a piece of high-carbon-content metal. You may not see the spark in the daytime, but you might be able to smell something like a burnt match, which will let you know that rock will work. The sparks created by percussion are usually colder sparks that die out quickly, so you need a good tinder that acts as a coal extender to eventually create a flame. In forest areas, dry bracket fungus will sometimes work. Crush the fungus into a fine powder, and aim your spark into the center of the pile. The powder should catch hold of the spark and enlarge it to a coal to be able to put it into a tinder bundle. If one type of fungus doesn't work, try another.

Friction fire Find the straightest, driest, lightest wood you have in your area and have a go at the bow drill (see page 182) or fire plow (see below). It is highly doubtful that you will find any wood suitable for a hand drill unless it is summer, and you have an abundance of tall, straight weeds with a solid stem. I have been told that dense, resin-filled wood will not work for a bow drill, and I have managed to get a coal from a cypress pine, so try with what-ever wood you have at hand.

Fire plow I have successfully made a fire using this method a few times, but as simple as it looks, it actually requires a level of angle experimentation that other friction fires lack. It also requires a fair bit of stamina, but if you have no tools and can't make cordage, it is a good one to try. For materials, it just requires a softer wood baseboard and a harder wood "plough," or you can give it a go with the same wood. The plough is just a piece of straight wood with a flattened, sharpened end of about 30 degrees. The baseboard needs a long, straight grove in it. The baseboard needs to be on a solid surface or able to be anchored down somehow. I find it's best to keep both hands on the plough and your arms straight when ploughing. Moving from the waist and pushing forward on the plough means you will have more stamina to keep going longer. Push the plough back and forth in the groove, creating dust at the far side of the groove. As darker dust forms, speed up and give it your all until the dust pile is smoking on its own.

Fire plow

A refraction fire can be made with a convex piece of ice, but the ice must be perfectly clear and free from bubbles and cracks. I personally have not been able to make it happen, but I know people who have managed to, so it is possible.

Fuel will likely be damp, so you will need to make sure you have a wood, storing area out of the weather, and that you dry your firewood around the edge of your fire before putting it on the flames.

HIGHLAND FOOD

Although game can be abundant in highland ecosystems, the higher in the mountains you are, the scarcer it will get. If you need to cross high, snowy mountain passes on your way to safety, try to spend a few days in lower-altitude forested areas, stocking up on valuable calories before you begin your trek. The difference between scarce food options and all the food options is going to be the snow line. It is tricky to know what your food choices are going to be below the snow line, because you could be in any location on Earth, and all would present you with different food options. Take your time, try to remember what you know about plants and animals in that part of the world, and observe and experiment with your environment.

EDIBLE VEGETATION Just above the snow line will be where your chances for food begin to increase exponentially. Many trees will have nuts that can be boiled and processed to eat. One exception to this is the pine tree. The nuts found in pine cones can be eaten raw, straight out of the cone. If all the pine cones on the tree are closed, the nuts are not ready to eat. Look for a tree with some open and some closed. They are not easy to harvest, but they are high in fat and worth the effort. Smash open the cones, and pick out the nuts. Most pine trees have edible nuts; some species just have larger, tastier ones. You can also eat the inner bark on most pines, but be aware that yew is a poisonous exception and very common in the United States. Pine needles can be boiled into a tea to deliver a good dose of vitamin C, which can also help with disinfecting wounds and soothing sore throats.

Pine nuts

A variety of berries and wild greens can usually be found in these areas as well. Make sure you do the toxin test (see page 110) to establish if they are edible, if you are not 100 percent certain of what plant they are.

RODENTS AND SMALL MAMMALS Snow is fantastic for sighting tracks to let you know what is in the area. The easiest animal food source will be the abundance of small mammals and rodents that populate these snow line forests. This is where deadfall traps really come in handy. Place them along popular game trails, and bait them with berries or nuts, if you can find them. Depending on whether you have cordage or need to make some, you can either set a Paiute deadfall or a figure-four deadfall (see page 138). Make sure you set multiple traps. The more traps you can have working for you, the more likely you are to get a meal. Be aware that the weight of the deadfall can puncture internal organs, so make sure the meat isn't polluted by stomach waste before you eat it. Wash the meat and always cook it well.

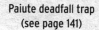

Paiute deadfall trap
(see page 141)

FIGURE-FOUR DEADFALL This is one of the more popular deadfall traps, due to the limited materials required to make one. You will need:

- **A heavy, flat rock or deadfall**
- **Three pieces of wood as thick as your thumb**
- **Bait**

One piece of wood is the bait stick. It needs a square notch on one side and a 7 notch at one end. One stick is the anchor stick. It needs to have a matching square notch on its side to marry to the bait stick and the top end sharpened on one side. The pivot stick then has a V notch that marries to the top of the anchor stick and a double sharpened end to marry into the 7 notch. The deadfall rests on the other end of the pivot stick. Sounds complicated, but it is quite simple once you have an understanding of how it goes together. The bait is placed on the short end of the bait stick under the deadfall.

Some things to be aware of are making sure that the anchor stick is located on the outside of the deadfall; otherwise, the deadfall will get stuck on the anchor stick when triggered. It's also important to keep the end of the bait stick short, so it doesn't get in the way of the deadfall. Practice triggering the deadfall until the trigger mechanism is sensitive and swift.

V notch

Square notch

7 notch

FIGURE-FOUR DEADFALL TRAP

Arapuca trap
(see page 142)

Birds You should have a variety of ground-dwelling and tree-dwelling birds to choose from. I found that the ground-dwelling pheasants in China would quite often be in groups with a male and his harem of up to six hens. They were focused on digging up the ground for bugs, and these enabled me to get quite close to them and hit one with a throwing stick (see page 147). Birds like this quite often roost in trees for the night and can start moving into position in the early evening. Get to know the birds in your area and their habits. Throwing sticks are great for flocks on the ground, and an arapuca trap is great for coaxing canopy-dwelling birds down to the forest floor. Skin or pluck the birds to save the feathers for warmth. Gut and cook them whole on a rotating stick over an open fire, or skewer pieces for a faster meal. Keep an eye out for where the birds head to nest at night, and check those areas for eggs. Don't take all the eggs from each nest.

Mammals Quite often deer and large grazing animals will make mountainous regions their home. It is very challenging to hunt these animals in highland conditions. There is a prestige to a successful mountain hunt that many professional hunters seek, because even with all the right gear and a high-scope rifle, it can be almost impossible. Unless your survival scenario stretches from days to months, choose the smaller mammals and fish for a food source. If you are armed with a hunting weapon and some previous hunting experience, check the edges of creeks and lakes for tracks. Watch for these animals at water sources in the early mornings and late evenings. If you can establish a pattern, make a hide and lie in wait.

Fish dam
(see page 154)

Fishing basket
(see page 154)

Fish Mountain lakes and streams will be a good source of fish. If you can create hooks out of strong wood or bone and have a supply of natural cordage (stinging nettle is common in these areas and works great for rope), set a hand line in a water source and see what you can catch. Fish traps and dams would be good to set up in the shallower streams. Keep in mind that the water will be frigid snow melt, so be sure to always have some quick rewarming method available to you after wading in the rivers to make them. The forest should provide long, straight wood for fishing spears (see page 152).

If your plan is to try to cross a snowy mountain pass, try to hunt extra food and preserve it by smoking it on a rack over your fire. Dry meat, roasted nuts, and water will be a good start for traveling supplies.

Highland environments can also provide habitats for some large, dangerous predators, including bears, wolves, and mountain lions. Always process your kill away from camp, and store any excess meat either suspended in a tree or inside a makeshift meat safe (see page 150) away from where you sleep.

5.6.5

HIGHLAND RESCUE

If you have ended up in an emergency situation with a vehicle and a last-known destination, stay with your vehicle and make the most of the resources you have with you. Make your position as clear as possible for would-be rescuers. Large letters in the snow and arrows pointing to your location are good ideas. Have fires ready to be lit with fuel from your vehicle if a plane or helicopter is spotted. Black rubber will burn with thick, black smoke, if you can salvage your vehicle's tires. Use any emergency communication devices to broadcast your position and condition. Remember that your phone's GPS will work even if you don't have service at your location, so preserve the battery life as much as you can. Phones are traceable once they have powered down, but only to your last-known location, which may have been before you went off grid.

If your position is above 25,000 feet, you are too high to be rescued by a helicopter, as the air is too thin for them to maintain flight. If no one is aware of your location or you have been severely knocked off course by a storm, you may need to leave your vehicle in order to get to a place where you can survive until rescued.

Never try to move at night or in a whiteout in highland ecosystems. The ground will become icier, and there are multiple unseen obstacles that can result in severe injury or death. Try to create or find shelter the best you can to get through the night, and get on the move at first light.

In the mountains, high ground is ideal for signaling to rescue parties, as there tends to be few trees and more open spaces to attract attention, but you will be exposed to high winds and inclement weather, and the terrain is often covered in snow and ice. If no rescue is likely, the first aim will be to get to lower ground. Low ground is where you will be able to establish a base for long-term survival. Staying just below the snow line will allow you to have access to both of these areas. Place your signals and messages in the open snow fields, with clear arrows pointing toward your shelter location.

Moving across snow and ice can be hazardous and extremely taxing. If the slope is steep, walk up in a zigzag pattern to enable you to safely ascend. Dig your toes into the snow when moving upward and your heels into the snow when moving downward.

One way to conserve energy is building a set of snowshoes. Short-term snowshoes can be as simple as strapping a leafy branch to the bottom of your feet. If you have more time and resources, you can create a pair that will be durable and reusable (see below).

SNOWSHOES Use four thin, flexible, strong lengths of wood and six smaller lengths for crossbeams. This is the minimum material; you can always add more struts, crossbeams, or branches to help with buoyancy on the snow. Tie two long sticks to a point at one end, and then attach three crossbeams about a third of the way down. They just need to be about an inch wider than your shoe. You can either tie up the pointy end of the snowshoe in a curve so that it is more maneuverable, or you can leave it long, depending on how flexible your wood is. Tie your shoe to the first crossbeam, leaving the other two there for support on the down step. The theory is that it spreads your weight across a greater surface of snow, so that you don't sink as deeply. This will conserve energy. I find that having walking sticks helps, and they can double as probe sticks or spears.

CRAMPONS If you have to travel across ice, it is a good idea to create more friction on the bottom of your shoes. This can be done by hammering nails through the soles of the shoes (sharp end on the outside) or by tying some cordage around your shoes and making knots on the bottom of them. Anything that adds a rough, uneven surface to the bottom of your shoes will help.

ICE AX Walking poles are essential for moving through mountainous terrain. They will provide you with extra support, allow you to probe the ground in front to see if it is solid, and also act as a defensive weapon, should a large predator appear. If you are going to be moving through some steep snowy or icy terrain on your way over a mountain pass, it is a good idea to also fashion a pair of ice axes. They can be made out of a strong, forked branch or a combination of wood and sharpened bone. Simply cut the handle to about a foot and a half in length and have the other end about eight inches long and sharpened at the end. You can still use it to probe the ground in front of you, but if you start to slip or the ground gives way beneath you, fling yourself backward and onto your stomach, and dig the sharp point of the ax into the ground to slow or stop you. They can also be useful to provide extra holds if you are forced to climb up a steep slope. Hit the sharp end into the ground in front of you and pull upward.

Be cautious in route finding, as it can be hard to see what is below you. Avoid steep terrain as much as possible, and try to follow spurs to the valley floor. Spurs are ridges of land that descend from a hill, mountain, or crest of a ridge. They tend to offer a more gradual slope to the valley floor.

Climbing rock and negotiating ice and snow fields require special skills and technical knowledge. These are obstacles to go around if at all possible. If you are confronted with a rock cliff, know that the rock will probably be loose and unstable. This will be a risk-versus-reward endeavor. If climbing the rockface isn't challenging and will save you a lot of time, you may want to take the risk. But at the end of the day, if you are unsure, it is better to go around, as injuries severely decrease your chances of survival. If you choose to climb, here are some things to make it safer:

- **Work out a route before leaving the ground.**

- **Don't climb up something that you can't climb down if you get stuck.**

- **Maintain three points of contact at all times.**

- **Keep your weight in your feet, and push yourself up the cliff rather than trying to use your arms to pull yourself up.**

- **Test all hand- and footholds before committing your weight to them.**

- **Make sure that you are never directly above or below someone else if there is more than one of you, as loose rocks can be deadly when falling from above.**

- **If you are climbing down steep terrain, face toward the rock and test your footing and handholds before committing to them. Steep or high cliffs should never be attempted. It is best to walk around or find another way down.**

DANGERS

AVALANCHE An avalanche is a rapid flow of snow down a slope. There will always be the danger of an avalanche when a fresh layer of snow sits on top of a weak layer. There is an increased chance of avalanches under the following conditions:

- **Snow falling as crystals**

- **Loose, dry snow that doesn't settle**

- **Slopes without trees and rocks**

- **Soft, newly fallen snow more than a foot deep**

- **Snowdrifts that sound hollow**

- **Rain or a rise in temperature**

- **Lee slopes (sheltered or protected from the wind) where snow has accumulated**

- **Snow-filled gullies**

In order to avoid potential avalanches, travel across slopes with rocky out-crops and trees. Stick to ridges and high ground above avalanche paths, if possible. This way, if you trigger an avalanche, you will be above it and have a greater chance of survival. If you have to cross a steep slope, choose your path carefully and try to cross early in the day, before the sun hits the snow. Make a loud noise, and throw rocks at the slope to see if you can trigger the avalanche before you head off. Move carefully but swiftly through the avalanche zone.

If there is more than one of you, go through an avalanche zone one at a time, so that, if someone is caught in an avalanche, there will be someone who was safe to try to rescue them. If you see someone caught in an ava-lanche, try to watch and take note of where they last were seen, as this will be the first place that you will need to dig for them.

The upper snow layer loses its support and slides.

Temperature increase in upper layer of snow.

Temperature difference between the two layers.

Evaporation under snow.

If you get caught in the path of an avalanche:

- **Try to move to the side; the bulk of the force of an avalanche will be flowing down the middle, and you will not be able to outrun it.**

- **Grab something sturdy to anchor yourself.**

- **Make a swimming motion to try to propel yourself to the top of the snow.**

- **Get rid of any equipment that might drag you down: snowshoes, walking sticks, etc.**

If you are buried in an avalanche:

- **Move your head back and forth to create an air pocket to breathe in.**

- **Dribble out some spit to see which way is up; it can be very disorienting to be surrounded by snow.**

- **Try to punch your way to the surface.**

- **Try to dig your way out.**

If you are alone and trapped under the snow, your chances of survival rapidly diminish. Prevention is better than dealing with the aftermath, so if in doubt, do not take the risk.

ALTITUDE SICKNESS The higher you ascend from sea level, there is less oxygen in the atmosphere. Eventually your body will feel the effects of this lack of oxygen, and you will develop altitude sickness. It happens at different heights for different people and can present in different ways.

Signs and symptoms of altitude sickness include:

- Headache
- Nausea
- Shortness of breath
- Difficulty sleeping
- Elevated heart rate
- Blue-tinged skin and nails

If untreated, there can be a buildup of fluid on the brain and lungs, and this can be life threatening. Making sure that you are hydrated can help stave off altitude sickness, but unless you are carrying oxygen, the only cure for altitude sickness is to descend at once, as fast as is safe.

CREVASSES These are deep, open cracks, often found on glaciers. Open crevasses are not as dangerous, as you can generally see them, but once they get covered by a thin layer of snow or ice, they can be deadly. It is important when moving across glaciers or ice fields that you probe the ground in front of you with a stick to test how solid it is. It is better to cross a glacier field very early in the morning, when the ice bridges will be stronger. If you are unsure if an ice bridge will hold your weight, go around if at all possible. If you fall into a crevasse:

- **Try to walk out; sometimes the crevasse may lead to accessible lower ground.**

- **Try to climb out; the sides may have ledges or footholds to make your way up and out.**

- **If you can't get out, try to make yourself as visible as possible; throw something up and over the lip of the crevasse to attract attention, or make a flag with a stick that you can wave out of the top, if it is long enough.**

- **Make yourself as comfortable as possible; remember the basic needs of survival, and do what you can to cover the ones that you can.**

WATER CROSSINGS As you descend, there may be rapid-flowing rivers or streams that you will need to ford to get to rescue. Never underestimate the power of water. Rapidly flowing water a foot deep is enough to move a car. Find the safest place to cross, ideally an area of shallow water or a ready-made bridge. Never cross white water or rivers that have flooded. Water depth can be deceptive, so make sure you carry a strong stick and probe the water ahead to gauge the depth. Take off your clothing, and bundle it on your shoulders to prevent it from getting wet. Keep your shoes on to prevent any foot injuries from sharp objects under the water. Face upstream and move sideways in the water, using your stick as a brace to assist you in maintaining your footing.

HYPOTHERMIA This is a condition that occurs when the body loses heat faster than it can produce it. It is better to prevent hypothermia than to try to cure it in the field, so always begin to try to warm up again when you start to feel cold.

Signs and symptoms of hypothermia include:

- Shivering
- Slurred speech or mumbling
- Slow, shallow breathing
- Weak pulse
- Clumsiness or lack of coordination
- Drowsiness
- Confusion
- Loss of consciousness

Someone with hypothermia usually isn't aware of their condition, because it comes on gradually. Eventually it can lead to risk-taking behavior and a feeling of euphoria. Quite often people who have died of cold exposure are found naked, as they begin to feel overheated and take all their clothes off in the final stages of the condition.

When you start to feel cold, add layers or remove damp clothing and replace it with dry. Move around; seek shelter and warmth. Do not attempt to warm hypothermia victims quickly, since this will lead to cold blood in the extremities rushing to the core and dropping the core temperature dangerously. Warm drinks and a hot water bottle on top of a layer of clothing by their core will help. Avoid alcohol, caffeine, and tobacco. It is not recommended to strip off and join them, because this may lead to two cold people instead of two warm people, but if you are having trouble warming them, keep your warm layer on and get close.

Predators Larger predators that can reside in highland ecosystems include bears, mountain lions, and wolves. When confronted with a large predator:

- **Avoid eye contact.**
- **Freeze; if they aren't charging you, don't run.**
- **Slowly back off.**
- **Avoid sudden movements.**

If an animal charges, dodge out of the way—you could be blocking their escape route.

If the animal attacks, shout, make a loud noise, and try to make yourself look bigger. Drop whatever you are carrying, as it may distract them. Zigzag rug away from them, if you run. Climb a tree, if a big enough one is available.

Survival in the highlands will most probably depend on your ability to safely make your way to lower ground. Take your time when choosing a route, and always minimize risk taking where possible.

6

Natural Disasters

ACCIDENTS OR HUMAN ERROR are not the only ways you could end up in a life-or-death struggle. Natural disasters cause great damage or loss of human life. They can produce emergency scenarios that will demand the same survival attitudes and techniques you would use when lost in the woods. Disasters can happen anywhere and at any time, whether you are in remote locations or close to home.

Natural disasters occur all of the time all around the world, year after year. These disasters result in tens of thousands of deaths per year. Hundreds of millions of people are affected, whether through injury, loss, or damages. While the events themselves may not be preventable, the deaths and damage can be drastically reduced through:

- **Early prediction**

- **Emergency preparedness**

- **Good response systems**

Your first seconds, minutes, and hours count, and they can set you up for success or struggle.

The most important thing you can do in the first few minutes of a disaster is to stay calm. This may feel impossible to do as chaos reigns around you, but it will ensure a better outcome.

REMOVE YOURSELF FROM HARM'S WAY

If a car is coming toward you, get out of its path. If an earthquake is happening, get down low and take cover under something solid. If a tornado warning is sounding, head for the nearest storm shelter or safe room.

ASSESS YOUR CONDITION

Always remember that you will be no help to anyone if you haven't first taken care of yourself. It's the whole airplane strategy of making sure that you put your oxygen mask on before helping others. Are you injured? How badly? Can you fix it yourself? Do you need medical help? If you do need urgent attention, see to that first before assisting others.

The next appropriate response to a disaster is going to depend on what disaster you are facing. This is where the survival attitude of being adaptable becomes critical. It will be up to you to make the crucial decisions in the moment. I can't give you the answers to every possible scenario, but I can give you some steps to follow so that you will be able to make more educated and informed decisions.

People spend too much time dwelling on the fact the disaster has happened. Take a second to acknowledge the disaster; then move from seeing that it is happening to figuring out what you can do about it. Survival is largely about seeing a problem and finding a solution as quickly as possible.

ACTION PLAN

If you are okay, then your next priorities are as follows:

1. Stop to assess the situation. Some things to consider are:

- **Where are your loved ones?** Is it safe to get to them? If so, how?

- **Can you help others, or will it endanger you?** How do you judge what is dangerous? Look for immediate and obvious threats, such as downed power lines, swift-flowing water, thick smoke, increased agitation, or armed attackers. You will need to use common sense and err on the side of caution, if your survival comes down to it.

- **What are authorities saying?** How can you even gather information if the electricity and Wi-Fi are down? If the situation is serious enough, authorities will be making their presence and wishes felt with door-to-door evacuations.

- **What is the mood of the people around you?** Are tensions high, or are people banding together to help?

- **Is the danger over or just beginning?**

2. Make your location safe, or move to a safe place.

- Check to see if it's structurally sound

- Have the ability to survey your surroundings

- Know your best evacuation path, and always have a plan B

- Be able to fortify the area to prevent undesirable entry

- Regulate temperature and access critical survival needs

3. Once you have reached a safe place, and you have decided to hunker down, do an emergency needs assessment, which includes an inventory of the following:

- Food

- Shelter

- Safe drinking water

- Total access to water, including containers for storage and carrying

- Essential items to moderate temperature, such as blankets and extra warm clothing

- Sanitation and waste disposal

- Medication and medical care, including a first aid kit

- Psychosocial support (entertainment and communication)

4. Figure out how to improve your situation without compromising your safety, to turn your weaknesses or shortfalls into assets or strengths. Being proactive can stave off panic and a feeling of helplessness.

PANIC IS YOUR ENEMY

The first thing to remember about panic is that it can escalate a situation and spread to those around you.

Panic causes many symptoms, including a rapid heart rate and shortness of breath or tightness in your throat. Simply pausing and taking a few deep breaths can dramatically calm your nervous system and reduce these symptoms, leading to a reduction in the feeling of panic. Finding purpose can also reduce the feeling of panic, so either taking charge of the situation or finding tasks to assist in making the situation better eases this fear of impending doom.

Your calmness and take-charge attitude will spread, allowing the people around you to find a greater sense of calm as well. Speak firmly where needed, assign tasks even if they seem to be impractical, and listen to people's fears to address and alleviate them.

BE PREPARED

While some natural disasters can come out of nowhere, some destinations will experience certain types of disasters more often than others. Wildfires are the most common type of natural disasters, closely followed by floods. Research the history of natural disasters in your area, and take steps to prevent and prepare for them in and around your home. Make a go bag that can be filled with everything you need to survive an emergency, along with the things that you would be devastated to lose (see page 348). Have an action plan, and make sure all your loved ones know the plan, should the worst happen.

THE AFTERMATH

Sometimes the aftermath of a natural disaster can be worse than the actual disaster itself, as it can have wide-ranging and long-term consequences on infrastructure and ecosystems. You should be prepared to be able to survive independently for at least three days after a natural disaster. The chapter on urban survival (see page 420) will address how to survive an extended scenario in your own home.

There is a saying that natural disasters happen when hazards meet vulnerabilities. The aim of the next section of *Survive* is to decrease your vulnerabilities so that you won't become another casualty that could have been avoided.

GO BAG

A go bag, or bug out bag, is one of the more fiercely debated and personal methods of preparation for an emergency. For every "survival expert" on-line, there will be a different suggestion for how best to pack one and what it should contain. For me personally, I have a go bag packed with the idea that it will sustain me for an indefinite amount of time, should the worst come to be. This means that it needs to provide me with the ability to cover my basic survival needs of food, fire, water, and shelter for an extended peri-od and assist me with rescue. The items need to be reusable and sustaining, rather than single use and disposable. It does mean that the contents of my bag require some level of education and skill to use, but I don't ever put anything in my go bag without knowing how to use it.

My go bag is specifically designed for a zombie-like apocalypse event where all of civilization has collapsed, but your go bag doesn't need to reflect such extremes. If you are in an urban environment where your greatest fear may be a bushfire, then your bag could contain precious, irreplaceable items and a few changes of underwear, should you need to flee your house for a few days. Ask yourself: What would I grab first if a fireman knocked on my door and gave me two minutes to evacuate? I know people who have photo albums, hard drives, and jewelry in their go bags. Keep in mind that you may be evacuated to a center that can't provide for your needs, so always have some water, long-life food, and a change of underwear in case it takes a while for the situation to revert to normal.

A go bag needs to be able to be quickly accessed and light enough to carry easily. For this reason, I recommend a large daypack or duffel bag that has two shoulder straps. We've all seen the movies where the trained operative carries out their most important possessions in a duffel that they sling over a shoulder, and that's fine when you can move straight into a waiting vehicle, but if you have to walk for any distance, something that fits comfortably on your back is preferable.

I will now list my go bag contents, along with a quick explanation about each item. All these things fit into a snug 40L pack. Feel free to add or take out different items to your own personal preference, and use this as a guide rather than something set in stone.

GO BAG

WATER

- **Water-carrying vessel**

  You can survive for about two to three days without water, but you will start to lose cognitive function before then. It's important if you are going to be processing water that you have something to process and carry it in. It is my preference that this vessel is stainless steel, so it can also be used as a pot to boil water if that becomes the only purification method available.

- **Water purification straws/tablets**

  These methods of purification will help make water drinkable on the go, or for times when making a fire to boil water may compromise your safety.

- **All-weather lighter x 2**

  Can I make fire by rubbing two sticks together? Yes. Does this fire-making method burn up unnecessary time and calories? Yes. My idea of survival is making things as efficient and fast as possible, so I will most definitely include a few foolproof methods for fire making.

- **Ferro rods x 2**

  Lighters will eventually run out of fuel and have moving parts that can malfunction, so ferro rods are also a must, with the average rod offering between 8,000 and 12,000 sparks or possible fires and being impervious to weather conditions.

SHELTER

- **Emergency blankets x 2**

  Amazing for containing body heat, should temperatures plummet or water immersions occur.

- **Plastic ponchos x 2**

  Durable to keep dry during the wet, but can also double as a waterproof roof for a shelter; they usually fold down smaller than a waterproof jacket and can be used for other purposes, such as water containment and food gathering.

- **Small tarp**

  Great for shelter building, keeping in body warmth, general waterproofing, and also as a carrying tool.

- **Thermal tops and bottoms x 2**

  Always good to have warm layers for those colder times.

- **Socks x 2**

  Fresh socks can aid in keeping your feet in good condition; if your feet begin to deteriorate, then your chances of survival go down dramatically.

- **Underwear x 2**

  Not a necessity, but luxuries are always good for survival mental health.

- **Warm hat x 1**

  Contrary to popular belief, we don't lose a majority of our heat from our head, but we do lose about 7 to 10 percent, so it's worth having a hat for cold nights.

- **Pot/cup/mess tin**

  Makes dinnertime a little easier; make sure it's stainless steel or similar, to allow for cooking and boiling water in if necessary.

- **Spork x 2**

  Building your own chopsticks is the best option for eating utensils in the outdoors, but sporks, which are a luxury item, don't weigh much or take up much room, and they make life a little easier.

- **Ration packs for three days**

  You can last twenty-one days without food, so this really is a luxury item; however, having access to something to fill your stomach until you can establish a food source can help with a good mental state of mind.

- **Paracord**

  The problem with cord is that it is a finite resource. For that reason, I tend not to use it for shelter building, as that requires a lot of cord for a single purpose. Where possible, I will use natural resources to hold my shelter together, but I will save paracord for such things as traps and snares; it is a wonderful resource for passive hunting techniques.

- **Fishing line and hooks**

  The line is useful for snares and traps, and durable hooks are incredibly tricky to make out of natural materials; they are reusable, and if you are by water, they are an incredibly efficient way of procuring food.

- **Multitool**

  A good multitool will have the versatility to aid you in a variety of situations. I personally find the saw blade and screwdriver heads to be the most useful. It can help you remain adaptable both in an urban environment and in the backcountry.

GENERAL

- **Field knife**

  If I am asked to choose only one survival item ever, then it will always be a knife. With the right ingenuity, skills, and problem-solving abilities, I can create everything I need with just a knife. This is possibly the most important item in this kit, so take your time in deciding on the right knife for you. I always have a minimum of a four-inch fixed-steel, full-tang blade that I have field-tested to make sure it works well for me.

- **Small first aid kit**

  I always travel with a stocked first aid kit, and my go bag is no exception; make sure it has any prescription medication that you can't live without.

- **Headlamp**

  After having spent a lot of time in the outdoors at night without a source of light, I can tell you that not being able to see at night is a huge safety risk, and having accessible light can help immensely on a mental comfort level; it's best to have a headlamp with rechargeable batteries, but take spare batteries just in case.

- **Spare medicines**

  Best stored in the first aid kit.

- **Hand sanitizer/gloves/masks**

  For interaction with other people outside of your family unit, especially if your survival situation has come about during, or because of, a pandemic.

- **Spare batteries**

  In case the survival scenario becomes prolonged.

- **Dynamo radio/charger**

  This handy gadget allows you to crank a handle to create electricity to charge it and other items; it will also give you some access to news regarding your situation, if all other means of communication have failed.

- **Flashlight**

  Always good to have a backup light source.

- **Glow sticks**

  To be used for signaling for rescue, marking locations at night, or communication over distances.

- **Signal mirror**

  To be used to signal for rescue during the day; a flash from a mirror can be seen from up to a mile away.

- **Compass**

  Always valuable for wayfinding, if your survival situation requires you to travel any distances; a modern compass will also usually have a magnifying glass that will aid in fire making, should the weather be sunny.

- **Duct tape**

  I would use this more for repairs in an urban survival scenario, but no one can dispute the usefulness of duct tape; it is a finite resource, so use it sparingly.

- **Small solar charger**

  We all have a variety of devices that require charging to function; a solar charger allows for the longevity of these items.

- **Spare cash**

  If the survival scenario is urban and access to card transactions has failed, it's always good to have some cash on you to barter your way out of situations or buy supplies you need.

- **Photocopies of relevant documentation**

  Such paperwork as birth certificates, passports, and credit cards should be photocopied and carried in the go bag, in case the originals are lost and proof of identity needs to be established or money needs to be accessed.

As I said, these are my preferences from my experiences. Take your go bag out into the wilderness before a survival scenario strikes and see if you can sustain yourself for a short period of time with what you have chosen. Make notes, add and subtract items according to what you feel you would need, and get comfortable with your choices. A good go bag could save your life.

FIRES

Fires can start suddenly and without warning. They can destroy homes, properties, and lives. One out of every one hundred people will experience a fire in their lifetime. The devastating effects of a fire decrease dramatically if you are prepared and act early.

Fire requires heat, fuel, and oxygen to stay burning. The more of these things a fire has access to, the more intense and damaging it will be.

Fires spread through three methods:

1. **Conduction:** where there is direct contact between materials

2. **Convection:** when the air around the fire becomes hot enough to start new fires, if there is enough oxygen and a fuel source

3. **Radiation:** when heat travels in rays similar to sunrays, in straight lines and away from the fire

Smoke, heat, and toxic gases are all products of fire. Some are more obvious, but it can be the ones that are not so visible that take you by surprise and lead to your death. More people die from toxic fumes and smoke inhalation than from burns. During a fire, and in the aftermath, you may experience a variety of symptoms, including:

- **Confusion**
- **Inability to breathe properly**
- **Disorientation**

- **Tiredness**
- **Fear**
- **Thirst**

It is important to try to stay calm and take actions to ensure your survival. Having an action plan in place prior to the disaster will help you move through proactive steps, even if you are experiencing these symptoms.

Your initial response to a fire will depend on the time it has been burning and the ferocity of the flames. For instance, if your campfire jumps its boundary and catches nearby grass alight, you may be able to smother the fire with some dirt or put it out with your water bottle. If your house is in the path of a massive firestorm that is being pushed by gale-force winds, it is best to evacuate early, knowing that human lives are more important than staying to defend possessions.

What you do next will depend on where you are, the intensity of the fire, and your ability to get to safety quickly.

WILDERNESS FIRES

Being out in the middle of nowhere when a forest fire starts can be terrifying. Chances are you will be surrounded by fuel and on foot, with very few options for your escape route. Trying to outrun a forest fire can be impossible; fire is able to travel up to 14 miles per hour in grasslands. If the fire is on an upward slope, it can double that speed, as the flames can reach more unburnt fuel faster. The heat radiating from the fire also preheats the fuel on a slope, which in turn causes the fuel to burn faster. A fire can also spread in any direction and change direction in seconds. A change in wind direction is one of the most dangerous factors in how a fire behaves. Many people who die in wildfires do so after a change in wind direction, so you will need to have a backup plan in case conditions change.

If you are present when the fire begins, or when it starts to get out of control, it is important to try to put it out if you can do so safely. Use any available water, or smother the fire to deprive it of oxygen. This can be done with such things as wool blankets, jackets, or dirt. If you don't have access to these things, try a branch of thick green leaves and beat the fire to squash it out. Just be careful that your efforts are not adding more oxygen to the situation by fanning the flames.

To ensure your campfire doesn't get out of control:

- Don't build a fire at sites with dry conditions.
- Build your fire away from your tent, trees, and bushes.
- Keep your fire small and manageable.
- Allow your fire to burn to ash before you leave.
- Pour water on the ashes until the hissing stops.
- Scatter dirt on the fire if you don't have water; make sure the coals remain exposed, and don't leave until they are cool to the touch.
- Don't cover your fire with dirt or sand, as this subdues it rather than smothering, it and the fire may catch back to life in windy conditions.

Once a fire is out of your ability to control it, you need to focus your energy on how to get to safety. Get safe, and then take a moment to make a plan. Your plan will be based on the following information:

- **The fire's access to fuel:** Are you surrounded by dry, dense forest, or are you in a wet, rocky area with very little vegetation?
- **Wind speed and direction:** Is the wind going toward you or away from you? The faster the wind, the faster the fire will travel; if the wind is strong, the flames can leap bigger fire breaks.
- **Your method of transport:** Are you on foot, or do you have a vehicle?
- **The terrain:** Where is the fire likely to spread to? Can you move quickly and easily to safety? Do you need to go uphill or downhill to safety?
- **Fire breaks:** Are there any natural fire breaks, including roadways, rivers, or lack of vegetation?

DO NOT RUN WILDLY. TAKE YOUR TIME, AND CHOOSE YOUR BEST ESCAPE ROUTE BASED ON ALL AVAILABLE INFORMATION.

If the fire doesn't start near you, some clues that a fire is approaching can be the smell of smoke, seeing smoke, or unusual animal behavior. Animals will flee ahead of a fire front and will be less cautious about human interaction. There will be a combination of animals that are not usually traveling together, and their movements can be agitated.

Do not think that because you can smell smoke but not see it that you have a lot of time to get out. Fire can reach you in under ten minutes from the time you smell the smoke.

To check which way the fire may be going if you can't see the flames, look high in the sky to see which direction the smoke is traveling. Wind can swirl in many directions on the ground, especially in mountainous terrain, but the smoke direction high up should be a good indicator of the way the fire is traveling.

If you are unable to outrun a forest fire, you can either find the best defensive position and hunker down or try to make it through the fire to the other side. These techniques are last-resort options. Always try to make your way to safety if possible.

DEFENSIVE POSITION

Search your immediate area for a natural fire break. This can be a river, a
road, or an area with very little to no vegetation. Clear the area of flammable materials the best you can with the time you have. Scoop out a trench
in the ground on the opposite side to the fire, if you are able to. Cover all
exposed skin with clothing, including your head and face. Dampen down the
clothing, if you have water available. Drink to ensure you are hydrated. Lie in
the trench with your feet facing the fire, and cover yourself with dirt. Try to
stay calm and prepare your mind for what is to come. It may be loud, dark,
and hot, but survivable. A deep gully might also work for a good defensive
position. Lie low and flat against the rock wall closest to the fire; cover
yourself with clothing and dirt the best you can. If the gully has dirt sides,
try to dig a hole in the wall closest to the fire and crawl into it. Use a branch
or stick to make digging easier.

Direction of fire

OFFENSIVE POSITION

Run through the fire. If the fire is a slower, cooler fire, it may be possible to run through the fire to safety on the other, already-burnt side. This is not to be attempted for intense fires with a lot of fuel and high winds. It may be possible in a large clearing or with a low grass fire. Assess your position and your type of fire, and make a decision. If you decide to choose this option:

1. Cover as much skin as possible with material, and wet it down if you can.

2. Remove anything you are wearing that conducts heat, such as jewelry or a belt buckle.

3. Cover your nose and mouth with material.

4. Choose your spot carefully, aiming for an area where the flames are sparse and low.

5. Once you have made your decision and picked your route, don't delay.

6. Run as fast as you can until clear of the fire.

7. The ground on the burnt side may be hot enough to melt the soles of your shoes, so keep going until you reach a patch of cooler ground.

Create your own backburn. If the wind is blowing the fire toward you, and you have some time before it will reach you, consider creating your own backburn. This works well with grass fires and low-lying brush. Determine the wind direction and consistency, stand with your back to the wind, and light a wide line of fire in front of you. As this burns, it will deprive the following fire of its fuel and create a safe haven for you. Make sure that you have enough time for your fire to burn out a large enough area before the main fire reaches you, or else you will be trapped between two fires.

Being prepared for a fire in the wilderness means educating yourself about the terrain you are about to enter. Is it fire ban season? Has there been a drought in the area? Are you surrounded by flammable tinder waiting for a spark? Is the weather predicted to be hot and windy? If the answer to any of these questions is yes, then maybe consider changing your plans. If you choose to head out anyway, make sure you have appropriate clothing (natural fibers versus nylons, which are made of plastics that will melt and stick to your skin), bring plenty of water, and have an escape plan ready in case you need it.

Wind

VEHICLES AND FIRES

Whether you get stuck in your vehicle during a fire, or your vehicle catches on fire, you need to be aware that you are traveling in something that could be either your best form of survival shelter, or a fueled bomb waiting to explode. Knowing when to leave the vehicle and when to stay could be the difference between a fire being deadly or an inconvenience.

DRIVING THROUGH FIRE

If you try to escape a wildfire in your vehicle or come across a fire while driving, it is important to know what to do to ensure your best chance of survival. Try to drive out of the danger zone if possible, but if you can't:

1. Call 911, and let them know where you are and that you are in trouble.

2. Park the vehicle behind a solid structure, if available.

3. If no structure is available, find a clear area away from trees and bushes.

4. Park off the road with the front of the car facing the fire.

5. Turn off the engine.

6. Put on the headlights and hazard lights.

7. Stay inside the vehicle.

8. Shut the windows.

9. Close all air vents.

10. Get below the level of the windows.

11. Cover yourself with whatever you can find. Seat covers and car mats will work.

12. Drink water.

Stay down and inside the vehicle until the fire has passed. This may take between five and fifteen minutes. Once the fire has passed you, cover your mouth and nose with a cloth and carefully exit the car. Any metal will be hot, so take care when touching the car's surface.

6.2.2.2

VEHICLE ON FIRE

The first thing to do with a vehicle fire is to stop the car and turn off the engine. Get everyone out of the car quickly.

It is always important to have a fire extinguisher in your vehicle. Make sure it is inside the car rather than inside the trunk, in case the car has crashed and you cannot exit the vehicle quickly, or the trunk has been damaged and is unable to open.

If possible, it is important to control a vehicle fire to prevent it from reaching the fuel tank. If the fire is small and inside the vehicle, use a fire extinguisher to put it out, or try to smother it with whatever material you have at hand. Coats and bags will work well. Move away quickly after you have extinguished the flames, so you don't get overwhelmed by toxic fumes.

If the car has crashed and there is fuel leaking out, get out of the vehicle as soon as possible. If the fuel catches on fire, quickly move to a safe distance, at least one hundred feet or more from the vehicle. Call 911, and allow first responders to control the fire.

6.2.3

FIRES OUTSIDE THE HOUSE

It is always good to have your house wildfire ready, regardless of where you live, but especially if you reside in a high-risk area. Your home is at risk if:

- **The local area has a history of wildfires.**
- **You live near forests or bushland.**
- **There are many trees and bushes around your home.**
- **Your house is built on a slope.**
- **You need to travel through forest or grasslands to leave home.**
- **You reside where cities, towns, or suburbs meet grasslands.**
- **Your house is near coastal brush.**
- **You live close to grass or among paddocks.**

A well-prepared house is more likely to survive a wildfire even if you aren't there. It can also be easier to defend and can offer more protection if fire threatens suddenly and you become trapped.

6.2.3.1

PREPARATION AND PREVENTION

ESTABLISH A SURVIVAL PLAN

It is important to develop a plan of what to do if a wildfire threatens your home *before* one does. Talk this plan over with all the members of your household. Details will include:

- **Meeting places, if you become separated**

- **Lines of communication**

- **When to evacuate**

- **Escape routes (always have a plan B)**

- **What to do with pets and animals**

- **What to take—have a go bag ready (see page 348) and a list of things to grab**

Your list of last-minute things to grab should include:

- Driver's license
- Passport
- Photos/hard drives
- Will
- Jewelry

- Insurance papers
- Medical prescriptions
- USB containing important files
- Phone and phone charger

Some of these items can be stored together and ready with your go bag, if they are not needed on a day-to-day basis.

MAKE A FIRE EMERGENCY KIT

This is different from a go bag and need only be prepared if you are in a high-fire-danger area. Have the bag easily accessible and always ready. It should include:

1. Working battery-operated radio

2. Protective clothing: loose-fitting long pants and long-sleeve shirts made out of natural fibers, gloves, heavy-soled boots, protective eyewear, hat, and bandanna

3. Wool blankets

4. Water

PREPARE YOUR HOUSE

The time to prepare your house for wildfires is before the fire season hits. In most areas, fires rage in the hotter months of the year, so get organized in the cooler months before. Some things you can do to lower your chance of losing your house to a wildfire are to:

1. Clean out the gutters.

2. Repair any holes in the roof and/or replace missing shingles or tiles.

3. Enclose all areas under the house.

4. Clear surroundings of debris and undergrowth.

5. Maintain greenery by keeping it trimmed and to a minimum.

6. Know where your shovel and fire extinguisher are.

7. Ensure you have solid hoses that can reach all areas of the house.

8. Attach a fire sprinkler system to the gutters.

9. Establish a fire break if you live on a remote property.

10. Establish a water source that doesn't rely on electricity from the power grid.

Most people die in wildfires because they leave their home too late. By the time you smell smoke or see flames, the fire may be five to ten minutes away, and all your escape routes might be cut off. You can expect embers and spot fires moving ahead of an intense firestorm. There will be smoke, heat, and noise. You will be hampered by a lack of visibility and darkness, with fires approaching from any direction. Roads may be blocked by fallen trees, downed power lines, or emergency vehicles.

On extremely high-risk fire days, you should prepare as if a fire has already been announced:

- If the plan was to leave early, then evacuate.

- Keep an eye on local emergency service announcements.

- Move livestock to a safe area.

- Keep pets in a safe place and ready to be moved.

- Pack personal items and put them in the car.

- Face the car in the direction you will drive out.

- Remove anything from around the house that will burn easily.

- Turn off gas to the house.

- Block down pipes and partially fill gutters with water.

- Have your fire emergency bag ready.

- Close and lock all doors and windows.

- Unlock any side and rear gates to allow first responder access if needed.

RESPONSE

Remember that the first thing you should do when a natural disaster strikes is to get out of harm's way. Listen to what authorities are saying; don't think you know best. If an evacuation order is in place, take your valuables and get out. Leaving early means getting away before there are signs of fire. Don't wait for a warning or siren. Don't wait to smell or see smoke. Enact your survival plan, and head for safer ground. If you can't leave your home safely, do the following:

1. **Let someone know you are staying.**

2. **Get into protective clothing (see page 362).**

3. **Turn on the sprinklers.**

4. **Remove anything flammable from the outside of the house, e.g., outdoor furniture or doormats.**

5. **Shut doors and windows.**

6. **Tape across windows so they don't shatter everywhere if they break.**

7. **Keep an eye out for embers and put out spot fires. Burning twigs, leaves, and pieces of debris can float ahead of a fire, and sometimes precede it by hours, and they are the most common way homes catch fire in wildfires.**

8. **Decide on your best refuge in the house.**

9. **Locate a flashlight or headlamp.**

10. **Stay calm.**

Out of the three ways a fire spreads, radiant heat is the main cause of people dying. This is because temperatures in front of a fire can soar to almost 3,000°F. The good news is that it only radiates in straight lines, so this lethal heat can be blocked by a solid object. Your best chance of survival if you are caught in a wildfire is to shelter in a solid brick building that has two points of exit. Your best refuge in your house will be a room that:

- **Is on the opposite side of the house to the approaching fire**
- **Is on the ground floor**
- **Has two exits, including one that leads directly outside in case the house begins to burn**
- **Has a clear field of vision toward the direction of the fire**
- **Allows you to stay away from windows**

Traditionally, people have filled the bathtub and sheltered in the bathroom. Bathrooms usually only have one exit, and it isn't to the outdoors. They also have frosted glass windows, so you can't keep an eye on the fire to know what is happening. Bathrooms also tend to be smaller rooms and more vulnerable to carbon monoxide poisoning, so they shouldn't be your first choice.

Once the fire front arrives at your house, seek shelter and actively defend the house from the inside by putting out embers and spot fires. Know that the fire will be very loud and very hot, and it will get dark. A single fire front normally passes within five to fifteen minutes.

Do not shelter in dams, swimming pools, or tanks. Radiant heat and smoke can still damage your face, head, and lungs. If you seek shelter in a large body of water, make sure you have something to float on or that supports your weight, as you may need to tread water for some time until it is safe to return to land.

6.2.3.3

AFTERMATH

Survival is also about how you will recover in the days, weeks, and months after the fire. If you have evacuated, do not return home until authorities tell you it is safe to do so. Be careful of hazards on the road, including downed power lines, fallen branches, and escaped livestock. Look out for potential hazards when entering your home, as the fire may have compromised the structural integrity. Depending on the severity of the natural disaster, your survival scenario will be shaped by what you managed to bring with you in your go bag and the grace of others.

Above all, remember that things can be replaced but people cannot, so if you are standing in the wreckage of your place but you have all your loved ones with you, you made the right decisions.

6.2.4

FIRES INSIDE THE HOUSE

Cooking fires are the leading cause of home fires, with electrical appliances and faults being the next. Cigarettes, heaters, and candles round out the top-five causes. Unlike wildfires, each of these methods of ignition requires a different method of extinguishing, and not knowing the difference could fan the flames rather than putting out the fire. House fires can happen in any house at any time, and there is no one location that is more prone to them than another.

6.2.4.1

PREPARATION AND PREVENTION

Keeping an eye on any flame inside is a must, whether it is on the stove, by your bathtub, or on the end of your cigarette. In the United States, over 500 deaths per year would be prevented if more people made sure that their house wiring was up to code. You are twice as likely to die in a house fire if you don't have working smoke alarms, so make sure they are replaced every ten years and batteries are replaced whenever necessary. Always have a fire extinguisher in an accessible location, and know what type of fire the extinguisher is meant for. Most residential fire extinguishers are multipurpose and labeled ABC, but it is important to verify this before using it on different types of fires.

Types of fire extinguishers include:

- **Class A—for ordinary combustibles, such as wood and paper**
- **Class B—for flammable liquids, such as grease, gasoline, and oil**
- **Class C—for electrical fires**
- **Class ABC—multipurpose**

HOW TO USE AN EXTINGUISHER:

1. Pull or release the lock.

2. Aim at the base of the fire.

3. Squeeze or press the trigger.

4. Sweep it from side to side.

RESPONSE

If you have caught the fire while it is small, attempt to extinguish it. This can be done by depriving the fire of oxygen, fuel, or heat. You can smother it with clothing, a heavy blanket, or sand. Only use water to try to put it out if it isn't caused by grease or electricity.

COOKING FIRES

These are usually only seriously ignited when caused by oil or grease. When your cooking oil becomes hotter than 375°F, it will start smoking and burst into flames. If you have a grease fire in the kitchen:

1. **Remove the source of heat by turning off the stove.**

2. **Remove the oxygen by covering the lit oil with a metal lid, if it is contained in a pot or pan.**

3. **Pour baking soda over smaller grease fires; this will smother the flames.**

4. **Use a Class ABC or Class B fire extinguisher to put out the fire.**

Do not use water on a cooking fire, as the water will sink to the bottom of the pan, become very hot, and explode, splattering burning oil into the air. Do not try to transfer the pot anywhere, since this may spill the burning oil onto the floor or more flammable surfaces.

ELECTRICAL FIRES

One-third of all home fires stem from an electrical fault. They tend to be difficult to identify, and therefore are more dangerous and destructive than other household fires. If your fire stems from an electrical fault:

1. **Cut off the electricity—either at the plug or at the fuse box.**

2. **Remove the oxygen source by smothering it with clothing or a heavy blanket.**

3. **Use a Class ABC or Class C fire extinguisher to extinguish the flames.**

Do not throw water on an electrical fire, as water is a natural conductor of electricity, and you may get shocked or electrocuted. Even if the electricity has been turned off, the appliance itself can store enough electricity to deliver a shock.

If the fire is too big to fight, it is important to evacuate immediately. If you have a go bag packed and accessible, grab it on the way out. Move away from the house, and call emergency services. Do not waste time collecting your valuables. No possession is worth dying for.

Smoke and toxic gas inhalation kill three times more people in house fires than burns do, so even if the flames are not threatening you, cover your nose and mouth with some material, get low to the ground, and head for the nearest exit. You may need to feel your way along the walls to find the door, if the smoke is thick. Feel the door with the back of your hand. If the door is hot or there is smoke billowing under the door, find another exit.

Trapped inside. If you cannot escape the building, go to a room as far from the fire as possible on the lower levels. Close all doors behind you and, wherever possible, put a solid object between you and the radiant heat. It may be tempting to flee upstairs away from the fire, but flames move faster upward than downward, so the lower you can get, the safer you'll be. If you can get to a room on the lower level that has windows but no doors, smash the windows to create an escape route. Use a heavy object rather than a body part to do this, as the glass will smash into jagged sections that can cause deadly bleeds. Make sure you remove the shards from the top of the window, and place some clothing or blankets over the lower ledge before crawling out.

If you have to escape through a room that is on fire:

- Remove any metal, including jewelry and your belt buckle.

- Cover all bare skin and your head with flame-retardant material, such as cotton or wool.

- Wet your clothing and coverings, if possible.

- Cover your nose and mouth with breathable material.

- Make a route plan, and avoid rooms with only one exit.

- Get down low.

- Don't hesitate once you have committed to going.

If your clothing catches on fire, exit the flames and immediately stop, drop, and roll. If you continue to run, this will fan the flames. If you are with someone who has caught on fire, encourage them to stop, drop, and roll, and try to help them smother the flames with extra clothing or blankets. Do not try to smother them with your body, as this may set you alight.

If you are trapped on the second floor, do not retreat into a room with no windows or doors to the outside. Get to a room that has the safest landing below its window or balcony. Look for a soft surface such as grass, try to avoid hard, uneven surfaces like rock gardens. Close the door behind you, and fill any gaps around the door with thick material, such as curtains or mats. Wet them if you can. Check the room to see if there is anything that you can tie together to make a rope—bed linen, curtains, and towels will all work. Use a reef knot (right over left, left over right) to tie them together, and test by putting some weight on the rope before you commit your full weight to it. If there is nothing in the room to make a rope out of, prepare yourself to drop from the windowsill or balcony.

People have died on the second floor of buildings believing they are too high up to get to the ground safely. The reality is that if you drop from a windowsill or a balcony on the second floor of a building, the average person is dropping less than six feet to the ground. A normal human body is able to survive the impact from a drop of up to thirty feet. Don't let your fear of heights lead to your death.

Throw any extra padding out of the room onto the ground below to add extra cushioning for your landing. Lower yourself out of the window backward, and hang from the windowsill facing toward the building. Push away from the building with one foot, and bend your knees on the landing. Use your arms to protect your head, and roll with the impact.

Only jump out face first if instructed to do so by emergency services with specialized equipment.

6.2.4.3

AFTERMATH

Do not enter your home until instructed that it is safe to do so by first responders. Be aware that the fire may have compromised the structural integrity of your house.

6.2.5

SKYSCRAPERS

If you work or live in a multistory building, take time to familiarize yourself with the escape routes. Take care to note the difference between an ordinary stairwell and a fire escape stairwell, and always prioritize using the fire escape. Avoid elevators in a fire, as they are designed to drop to the first floor and disengage once a building's fire alarm is activated. Do not hesitate once the fire alarm is raised. Your best chance of survival is to get out quickly, before the fire takes hold.

People who wait to take action when a fire starts are late to evacuate, have little to no protection, and end up sheltering in an unsafe environment. Know your fire danger, have a plan, prepare your home to best defend itself from flames, and prepare yourself for evacuation. Listen to authorities, and when in doubt, evacuate. No possession is worth losing your life or loved ones for.

FLOODS

Floods are the deadliest type of severe weather. They occur where there is an overflow of a large amount of water beyond its normal limits, and usually dry land becomes covered or submerged in water. Floods can happen both in coastal areas and inland, and can be anywhere from a few inches deep to over twenty feet deep. There are so many casualties associated with flooding because it can happen rapidly, and the power of the water is usually underestimated. It takes only six inches of water to knock you off your feet, and a foot of rapidly flowing water is enough to move a car.

Floods are usually caused by one or more of the following:

- **Heavy rainfall**
- **Overflowing rivers**
- **Broken dams**
- **Storm surge and tsunamis**
- **Lack of vegetation**
- **Melting snow and ice**

The effects of floods can be devastating, with loss of lives, property destruction, and far-reaching economic impact. Even just a few inches of floodwater can do a lot of damage.

TYPES OF FLOODS

There are five different types of floods:

1. River floods: When the water rises above the level of the riverbanks: It usually happens because of excessive rainfall from tropical storm fronts, persistent thunderstorms, or combined rain and snowmelt; it can happen slowly or rapidly.

2. Coastal floods: When seawater encroaches on areas of land that usually stay dry: They are typically the result of a combination of tidal surges and strong winds caused by storms out at sea or tsunami events.

3. Storm surges: An abnormal rise in water levels in coastal areas usually caused by storms that create higher-than-normal tides due to a combination of high winds, big waves, and low atmospheric pressure, a storm surge is one of the more dangerous types of flooding, as it can happen very quickly and affect large areas at the same time; when a storm surge happens at the same time as a high tide, flooding as deep as twenty feet can occur.

4. Inland floods: Occur inland rather than on the coast. Usually caused by persistent rainfall over a few days or heavy rainfall over a short period of time, they can be catastrophic in urban areas, as there is nowhere for the water to go.

5. Flash floods: Can occur when there is intense rainfall over a short period of time They are the deadliest of all the floods, as they are extremely powerful and have enough force to move large boulders and cars, tear trees from the ground, and destroy buildings and bridges; these floods usually begin between three to six hours after rain.

It is important to know whether the area you live in, or are planning to travel to, has a history of flooding. Some terrain features that may be subject to flooding include:

- **River valleys**
- **Flood plains**
- **Low-lying coastal areas**

If you are spending time in these areas, it is best to make sure you are prepared for the possible chance of flooding.

6.3.1

WILDERNESS FLOODS

Deaths caused by flooding on camping trips are usually the result of poor planning and a general lack of knowledge of what to do when these disasters strike.

Before heading into any wilderness area, check the weather forecast for the week prior. Floods are usually caused by heavy, persistent rainfall after long periods of dry weather. If your trip is taking you into areas with low-lying, river-filled valleys after such weather, it would be worth postponing the trip or heading elsewhere.

Study the map, looking not only at the route you have planned but also at the general terrain in the area and possible alternate routes out, should your initial plan become too dangerous.

Never make your camp in any of the following areas:

- **Next to the water's edge**
- **In dry creek beds or washes**
- **Below a high water mark**
- **At the bottom of a hill or ravine**
- **In a ditch**

Even if you can't see storm clouds and don't get a drop of rain at your camp, high rainfall in areas around you can funnel large amounts of water and debris your way quickly.

If possible, camp on spurs or at least 200 yards away from the edge of the water. If the water level starts rising, move to higher ground.

Flash floods may sound like a train or thunder coming toward you. If you hear this, immediately evacuate. You may have a matter of seconds to get to high ground before a wall of water and debris hits. Leave all belongings, and move as fast as you can.

If you get swept away in a flash flood, the important thing is not to panic. Turn onto your back and face your feet downstream. Keep your knees slightly bent to push off any objects or obstacles in front of you. Try to scull with your hands to move you toward the edge of the water, as this will not be moving as fast or as powerfully as the middle section. If you hit an obstacle, try to go over it rather than under it, as you may get trapped under the obstacle with a wall of water forcing you down. As soon as you can, make your way to the edge of the flood. If you have managed to get out of the floodwater by climbing a tree, stay in the tree as long as it is safe and wait for the floodwaters to recede. When it is safe, climb down and make your way to safety.

Shock and hypothermia may set in, depending on your location. Assess your basic needs to make sure that you can meet them. If you have lost all your gear, you may need to make your way out of the wilderness and to safety as soon as possible. Remember that all animals seek out higher ground when their land floods, so keep an eye out for panicked animals and predators out of their usual habitat.

Although you can never predict when flash flooding will occur, you can watch out for the weather signs that suggest it might happen. Never wait to evacuate. If you are unsure about the weather, err on the side of caution and move to higher, protected ground.

6.3.2

URBAN FLOODS

The hard surfaces usually found in urban areas, such as roofs, roads, driveways, and sidewalks, make it harder for an excess of water to drain away. This means that less water is required to create flooding, and it may pool for longer than it would in rural areas.

6.3.2.1

FLOODS ON THE ROADS

Never attempt to drive through floodwaters, if you are unsure of how deep they are. It is best to reverse away from the water and find another way to your destination. It only takes a foot of fast-flowing water to sweep away your car into deeper waters. Even if the water isn't moving rapidly, once water enters the tailpipe of a vehicle, it can flood the engine and cause the car to stall. Unless your car has a special snorkel for your exhaust, this means it will probably stall in a foot or so of standing water.

Do not drive across any bridges if they have water flooding over them. It is hard to tell how structurally sound the bridge is if you cannot see it.

As soon as your car stalls in floodwaters or begins to be swept away, you need to be making plans on how to exit the vehicle. **Do not call emergency services at this stage.** You may have a matter of seconds to act, and in this moment, you are the only one who can be proactive about your safety.

1. **Put down all windows and unlock doors. This needs to happen before your car goes underwater, as once water pressure builds up on the outside of windows and doors, they become impossible to open until the car is fully submerged.**

2. **Take off your seat belt; it is best to keep a blade or scissors in the glove box in case the belt has locked shut.**

3. **Exit the vehicle however you can; this may be through the door, window, or sunroof.**

If the vehicle is sinking, you will need to swim to safety. If the vehicle is remaining partially submerged, stay on the roof of the vehicle and wait for rescue. This would be the time to make the call to emergency services if you have your phone. If the water is less than knee-deep, you can try to walk to safety. Face upstream and shuffle sideways with your feet wide apart and your knees bent.

SUBMERGED VEHICLE If your vehicle has become submerged to the stage that you are unable to open any doors and windows, you will either need to break the glass or wait until the vehicle is fully submerged to open the doors. I suggest trying the former first, as it can be a very scary ordeal to wait for a car to fill up with water as it sinks. You will also need to be capable of relaxing and holding your breath for at least forty-five seconds as the final air leaves the interior of the vehicle and allows the outside to equalize with the inside.

The front windshield tends to be double-paned to withstand an impact, so your energy is best spent trying to break a side window. Use your foot, aiming for the upper edge, to see if you can smash the top of the glass away from its lower anchor points. If this doesn't work, remove the seat headrests and use the sharp underside to try to puncture the glass. A blade or scissors will also have sharp, solid points on them, which could be used to shatter glass. Aim at the top corners of the window. Keep your face averted to avoid getting shattered glass in your eyes. Car windows are made of tempered glass and will shatter in small squares that are less likely to cause deadly bleeds than large, jagged panes of glass. If you are unable to break the glass, take a moment to calm yourself. You will need to save your breath to wait to fully submerge.

One thing to be aware of is that a car can take two or three minutes to sink. As soon as you break the seal of the window or open the door, the car will sink more rapidly, so it is important that you exit the vehicle as soon as you have managed to secure an escape route. Do not wait for the vehicle to hit the bottom if it hasn't already. If multiple people are in the vehicle, make sure everyone is ready to leave before you open the door or smash the window. Once you have exited the submerged vehicle, swim for the surface and to safety.

Over 50 percent of flash flood deaths are caused by people trying to drive their vehicle through floodwaters. If you can't tell the depth of the water and/or if it is flowing rapidly across the road, do not attempt to cross. Not only does it put you and your loved ones in danger, but it also endangers those who may try to rescue you as well. Turn around and seek higher, safer ground.

PREPARATION

If you are aware that the area you live in has a history of flooding, there are some things you can do to make sure that the damage to you and your property is minimal if history repeats itself:

- **Make an evacuation plan; have two planned routes to high ground, designated meeting places if you get separated from those in your group, emergency contacts, etc.**

- **Sign up for flood notifications on your phone.**

- **Make a flood emergency go bag. Include such things as:**

  - Phone charger

  - Flashlight and spare batteries

  - Blankets

  - Tarp/ponchos and/or emergency blanket

  - First aid kit

  - Rubber boots and gloves

  - Drinking water

  - Long-life food snacks

  - A signaling device (mirror or flares)

  - Radio to get accurate updates on flood

- **Fill some sandbags or plastic bags to have on hand.**

- **Clean all gutters and drains so they flow freely.**

- **Create a plan for your pets.**

RESPONSE

Always listen to the authorities. If they say to evacuate immediately, grab your go bag and leave the area for higher ground. If they say you have a few hours to prepare to evacuate, make your home flood ready and leave.

The aftermath of floods can be devastating to a home, but there are many things you can do to ensure that the damage is minimal.

1. Monitor the radio to keep an eye on the severity of the flood warning; you may need to stop what you are doing and leave at once.

2. Roll up any rugs and move furniture, electrical items, and valuables to higher ground; if your home doesn't have a second level, stack things on tables or benches—anything to get them off the ground.

3. Place important documents, USBs, and hard drives in waterproof cases; doubled-up resealable plastic bags work fine if you don't have anything else.

4. Empty fridges and freezers; take the food with you if you can.

5. Turn off the power, water, and gas.

6. Put sandbags in the toilet, and any drain holes in the bathrooms and laundry to prevent sewage from coming back up the pipes into your home.

7. Shut windows and doors, and seal up any areas that allow ventilation into your house.

8. Line sandbags along the bottoms of your doors.

9. Bring all outdoor furniture inside, along with any other items that may wash away.

If you are evacuating on foot, make sure that you do not cross any floodwaters that go above your knees. Find a stick or pole to use as a stabilizer and a depth probe. If the water is flowing rapidly, face toward where the water is coming from and walk sideways using the stick as a brace on the ground in front of you. Avoid drains and culverts, as a current can form near them that is strong enough to act like a vacuum that could suck you into them. If the water conditions are too deep and too strong or become that way, return to your home and establish a safe survival environment there.

If you are evacuating in a vehicle, do not attempt to cross floodwaters. If you are unable to find a route that doesn't require a water crossing, return home and establish a safe survival environment there.

SURVIVING A FLOODED BUILDING

If it is too risky to evacuate, stay where you are. Make sure that the gas and electricity are turned off. Shut all doors and windows, and sandbag the entrances. Grab your emergency flood go bag and some warm clothing, and move toward the upper levels of your building. This could be to the second story or the rooftop.

If you are seeking safety on the roof of your building, make sure that you are safely secured if the roof is steeply sloping. Use rope or sheets to tether yourself and others to strong, sturdy structures, such as chimneys. If you are able, establish some kind of shelter. Keeping in mind that clothing is your first line of shelter, this can be a poncho, or an emergency blanket wrapped around you.

Unless water rises so high that it forces you off this high ground, stay until the floodwaters have safely receded. Use your phone or emergency signaling devices to let people know you require assistance. Know that they may be dealing with more urgent cases than yours, so stay calm and get comfortable if your life isn't in immediate danger.

SWEPT AWAY If you find yourself swept up in floodwaters, do not panic. Turn onto your back, and face your feet in the direction you are going. Keep your knees slightly bent to help you push off any objects you might encounter in front of you, and try to scull with your hands to direct your body to safety.

Use rope or sheets to tether yourself and others to strong, sturdy structures, such as chimneys.

Unless water rises so high that it forces you off this high ground, stay until the floodwaters have safely receded.

AFTERMATH

If you managed to evacuate before the flooding, do not return to your house until authorities have deemed it safe to do so. Be aware that the flood may have left your house structurally unsound, so be careful when entering the building and moving around until you have determined the severity of the damage.

Stay away from rooms where water still covers the electrical sockets, as water is a great conductor of electricity and may deliver a life-threatening shock.

Be aware that contaminated water may have penetrated the groundwater supply, and this will mean that your tap water is no longer safe to drink. Boil or purify all tap water until authorities have declared supplies safe to use again.

Do not eat food that has been in floodwaters, as the waters can be filled with bacteria, toxins, and chemicals that can make you very sick. You should also take care when cleaning up, making sure you wear rubber gloves and boots to minimize contact with any potential poisons.

Floodwaters can leave scenes of devastation, with debris, destruction, and corpses (animal and human). They are breeding grounds for stagnation, bacteria, and disease. Be prepared, listen to authorities, and evacuate sooner rather than later. It could be the difference between life and death.

6.4

EARTHQUAKES

Earthquakes are the least predictable of the natural disasters, which makes them very hard to prepare for. They can come suddenly and with very little warning.

An earthquake is the sudden and violent shaking of the ground, caused by two blocks of earth slipping past one another at what becomes known as the epicenter. The sudden release of stored energy as this happens creates seismic waves that ripple through the earth's crust. They can be felt over large areas of land, decreasing in magnitude from the epicenter. Although earthquakes usually last less than a minute, their aftermath is devastating and has been responsible for thousands of deaths.

Fault Scrap

Epicenter

Focus

Fault

Wave Fronts

Reverse fault   Normal fault   Strike-slip fault

The effects of earthquakes can include:

- Ground shaking

- Surface faulting—when cracks appear in the ground

- Ground failure—sinkholes and unstable ground

- Tsunamis

The main causes of death are collapsing buildings and landslides, with over 3.5 million people worldwide being affected by earthquakes annually.

Earthquakes are fairly common, with over half a million earthquakes recorded globally each year. They range from subtle tremors to violent shaking, but only twenty will cause serious damage. Modern science still hasn't managed to find a way to predict earthquakes.

Earthquake severity is graded as follows:

2.5–5.4	May be felt slightly, but only causes minor damage
5.5–6.0	Slight damage to buildings and structures
6.1–6.9	May cause a lot of damage in populated areas
7.0–7.9	Can cause serious damage
8.0 >	Can destroy communities near its epicenter

The most powerful earthquake ever recorded was a 9.4–9.6 in Chile in 1960, but the deadliest earthquake on record was in China in 1556, with 830,000 casualties.

Minor tremors can happen anywhere, but major quakes are confined to known earthquake belts. There are over five hundred fault lines in California alone, and most people there live within thirty miles of one. It is important to find out if you live on one of these earthquake belts, in order to do what little preparation you can for these potentially catastrophic events.

6.4.1

WILDERNESS EARTHQUAKES

If you are out in the wilderness when an earthquake happens, immediately move away from cliffsides and tall trees. Make your way to a clearing if you can, and lie flat; don't try to run. Cover your head with your arms. If you are on a hillside, it is safer to get to the top, as slopes may become landslides. Once the quake has stopped, make your way carefully to a place of safety.

6.4.2

PREPARATION

The main thing you can do to prepare for an earthquake is to prepare for the aftermath. You can do this by having a go bag set up that will allow for you to last indefinitely without a functioning infrastructure (see page 348).

Some other things you can do are:

- **Identify solid safe zones in your house and place of work; these need to be areas that are structurally sound or will provide a solid roof over your head if the building (or part of it) collapses. Solid wooden tables or desks would work, as well as your bed. Down low against the inside corners of rooms and solid interior walls are also good options. Avoid any walls with windows or glass surfaces. Do not shelter under doorjambs. This advice worked when houses were built differently years ago, but doesn't work with today's building techniques and materials.**

- **Identify potential weaknesses and hazards in your home, so you know the areas to avoid.**

- Repair deep plaster cracks in ceilings and foundations.

- Attach large, heavy pieces of furniture to the foundation of your home.

- Use earthquake-proof putty to attach pictures and frames to the walls.

- Remove fragile items from high shelves, and place them in low cupboards.

- Ensure your shelves have lips on them, so things can't slide off.

- Make an emergency plan, so everyone in your household knows what to do and where to go if an earthquake happens.

6.4.3

RESPONSE

Where you are when the earthquake strikes will determine your course of action, but the main idea, no matter where you are, is to:

1. **Stop: Do not try to keep moving, or you may fall and get injured.**

2. **Drop: Get close to the ground for more stability.**

3. **Cover: Seek cover under something solid, or cover your head if you can't find anywhere to get under.**

4. **Hold on: Grab on to something solid if the ground is buckling.**

As with any survival scenario, your ability to stay calm and think clearly will also help.

IN A VEHICLE

Once you are clear of underpasses and large trees, pull over and stop the car. Remain in your vehicle and try to get below window level. This will give you some protection if debris hits the roof of your car.

IN BED

If you are in bed, stay there. Turn onto your stomach, and cover your head with a pillow to protect yourself from projectiles and glass. If you have assessed your bed to be a safe place to take cover under, crawl under there as soon as the quake starts.

INSIDE A BUILDING

If you are inside a building, stay inside. A majority of deaths and injuries occur when someone is inside and they try to flee. If you are at home, head to your predetermined safe place. If you are at work, get beneath your desk or underneath something solid. Keep away from glass displays and shelving if you are in a shop. If you are in a high-rise building, stay where you are; never go into an elevator or try to escape down the stairwell until after the main tremor has ceased.

OUTSIDE A BUILDING

If you are outside, stay outside. Move away from anything that might fall on you, and if you can, relocate to an open area. Lie flat on the ground and cover your head. Keep away from tall buildings and large trees, and do not deliberately go underground or into a tunnel.

6.4.4

AFTERMATH

As soon as the main tremors cease and debris stops moving around, check yourself and others for injuries. **If you live in coastal areas, make your way to high ground as soon as possible, as there is a chance a tsunami may follow.** Don't wait for authorities to advise you on this matter, because by the time you realize a tsunami is on its way, it's too late.

If you are in your home, check the water, gas, and power lines for damage. Stay out of affected areas of your house, and avoid or clean up any broken glass and debris. Turn on the radio to see what authorities are saying, and make sure you follow their instructions. Open cupboards carefully, and filter and boil all water until you have been told it is safe to drink.

If you are outside, do not enter or seek shelter in damaged buildings. Be aware of and avoid downed power lines and still-falling buildings.

TRAPPED

If you are trapped under large pieces of debris or have fallen down a sink-hole, cover your mouth and nose with some breathable material. See if you can move. If you are able to move, do so slowly to avoid causing further structural collapse, and try to make your way to safety. If you are unable to get out, try to find ways to make a lot of noise. Banging on exposed pipes, using a whistle, or smashing metal pieces together are all good ways of getting noticed by rescuers. Save your voice until you hear someone nearby.

The aftermath of an earthquake can stretch into days and weeks. The rupture of sewage systems, contamination of water, dead bodies trapped in wreckage, and disruption of infrastructure can be as deadly as the earthquake itself. Make sure that your go bag has enough resources to ensure your basic needs can be met indefinitely, and be aware that while you will be able to rebuild your life, you cannot replace it.

6.5

HURRICANES

Depending on where you are in the world, the words "hurricane," "cyclone," and "typhoon" all describe the same phenomenon—an extremely deadly tropical storm with wind speeds in excess of seventy-four miles per hour.

They are called:

- **Hurricanes in the North Atlantic, central North Pacific, and eastern North Pacific**
- **Cyclones in the South Pacific and Indian Ocean**
- **Typhoons in the Northwest Pacific**

Hurricanes are destructive storms that are powered by strong winds cir-
cling around a center of low pressure, or the eye of the storm. They bring
torrential rain and can occur at any time of year in any location, but
usually occur in the Northern Hemisphere between June and November
and in the Southern Hemisphere between November and April.

Hurricanes usually build up force out at sea and travel as fast as thirty miles
per hour, wreaking devastation on islands and shorelines, and then slow
down when they encounter land and the storm is cut off from the heat and
moisture that fuels it.

There are different categories of hurricanes, based on the intensity of their wind speeds:

Category 1 (74-95 mph winds): Results in falling debris that may injure humans or animals. Older homes may be destroyed, and there might be short-term power outages.

Category 2 (96-110 mph winds): Extremely dangerous winds with greater risk of injury to humans and animals. Some houses may be damaged, and trees will be uprooted. There may be power outages that last anywhere from a few days to two weeks.

Category 3 (111-129 mph winds): Devastating damage will occur. There is a high risk that flying debris will result in injury and death. Well-built apartment buildings, individual houses, and industrial buildings will be damaged, and many trees will be uprooted.

Category 4 (130-156 mph winds): Catastrophic damage will occur, with a high risk of death and injury. All buildings will experience damage and power can be out for weeks or months. Infrastructure becomes severely damaged.

Category 5 (157 mph or higher): Massive destruction occurs. Only three such hurricanes have made landfall since 1924.

The problem with these categories is that they only take into consideration the wind speed of the event, not the expected rainfall or storm surge. This means that even a Category 1 hurricane can bring with it serious damage and risk, even more so because people underestimate its severity based on the category rating. Take all hurricane warnings seriously, and do the same for a Category 1 as you would for a Category 5.

Meteorologists can see hurricanes developing far out in the ocean, using satellite surveillance systems. This means that they can provide the public with a warning up to twenty-four hours prior to the storm making landfall. Hurricanes have been known to move erratically, though, so it is important to continue to listen for hourly updates once a warning has been issued.

WILDERNESS HURRICANES

It is always important to check the weather forecast before you start a trip into the wilderness and to have some kind of method to check the updates if you are planning on being out for a long time. If you live in a place that is susceptible to hurricanes and you are heading out in hurricane season, carry a method to check weather updates no matter how long you are out for. Twenty-four hours' warning should be enough time for you to evacuate the area you are in and head for safety. Unless you can seek solid shelter where you are camping, you should never try to ride out a hurricane in the woods.

If you get caught unawares, you need to find the best place to shelter from strong winds, torrential rains, and possible lightning strikes. Stay away from the edges of water sources, as there may be flash flooding. Don't head for the highest ground, though, because this is where you are most exposed to the strong winds and lightning strikes. A deep cave would be ideal, as it allows you to move in far from the possibility of lightning strikes, out of the wind and rain. Do not shelter in overhangs or shallow caves, as lightning travels along vertical surfaces to seek the ground and can electrocute you as it jumps the gap.

If you can't find a cave, sit on the lee side (out of the wind) of any large object. Just make sure it is not the tallest object in your vicinity. If it is, you are better off lying facedown, flat on the ground with your hands covering your head. This will provide some protection from the debris flying around. Avoid small trees and fences, as they could be uprooted.

LIGHTNING

If your storm contains a lot of lightning, keep away from hilltops, ridgelines, tall trees, and lone boulders. Make for lower ground (being aware of the potential for flooding), and lie flat. If you cannot make it to low ground, find a dry insulating object and crouch on it with your head down, hugging your knees to your chest. **Do not sit or stand on anything wet.** If you have nothing to insulate you, lie as flat as you can.

If you see a flash of lightning and count before you hear the thunder, it will give you an idea of how far away the storm is. Simply count the seconds and divide by five to get the miles. Count "one hippopotamus, two hippopotamus," etc. to get the number of kilometers.

I have been very close to being struck by lightning while hiking on a ridge-line in the Blue Mountains in New South Wales, Australia. You can sometimes sense it coming when it is close by. My skin started tingling, and my hair stood up on end. I was also holding a fork that started tingling. These seconds of warning gave me enough time to drop the metal I was holding and hit the deck. The strike happened about thirty yards from me and was deafening, but I didn't receive a direct strike and was able to make it to cover for the remainder of the storm.

If you feel your skin tingle in a lightning storm, the best thing to do is to drop straight to your hands and knees. If you get struck, hopefully it will channel through your arms and into the ground rather than flowing through your torso and affecting your heart. As soon as you can, lie flat. Keep away from metal objects or structures. Proximity to large metal objects can be dangerous even without contact, because the shock waves caused by the heated air as lightning passes can cause damage to your lungs. An exception to this is your vehicle. If no buildings are available to shelter in but you have a car, this is the next best thing. Get inside, shut all the windows, and get down low, making sure you are not coming in contact with the metal exterior of the vehicle.

If you are on a boat, drop anchor and get as low as possible. If you can see a storm approaching, get out of the water as soon as you can. A significant lightning strike can stretch anywhere from six to ten miles from the base of the storm.

Education about the area and the weather conditions, plus a bit of preparation, could prevent loss of equipment, injury, or death. If possible, stay clear of wilderness areas until the threat of hurricanes has passed.

PREPARATION

Even though meteorologists can give twenty-four-hour warnings prior to a hurricane making landfall, some preparations should be done well in advance. Tropical locations are more likely to be prone to hurricanes, and you can do some research to see the history of hurricanes in your area.

LONG-TERM PREPARATION

If you live in a place that may experience hurricane activity, you should:

- Make a household emergency evacuation plan; have multiple planned escape routes to high and sheltered ground if authorities issue an evacuation warning.

- Install storm shutters on your windows and glass doors.

- Buy a generator, and have about twenty-five gallons of fuel on hand.

- Trim trees and large shrubs around the home.

- Clean and clear all gutters and downpipes.

- Stockpile enough long-life food and water for seven days (one gallon of water per person per day).

- Install a bolted-down safe for important documents and valuables.

- Identify the best room to shelter in if you don't evacuate.

- Prepare a hurricane emergency bag (see sidebar).

- Prepare a go bag.

- Make a plan for your pets and livestock.

SAFE ROOM

This should be the room you shelter in to ride out the storm. It should be an interior room, with no windows or glass doors and very little furniture on the lower level. A cellar is perfect. If your accommodation is not very structurally sound, make plans to go to the nearest hurricane shelter, or bunk with friends or relatives until the danger has passed.

Once the hurricane warning has been issued, the most important thing to do is to listen to the authorities. If they tell you to evacuate, then do your final preparations and get out. It is important that you leave far in advance of the hurricane making landfall, as travel in a hurricane is extremely dangerous and to be avoided. **Do not drive unless you must.** If you do need to drive, never attempt to drive through floodwaters, if you are unsure of how deep they are. It is best to reverse away from the water and find another way to your destination. It only takes a foot of fast-flowing water to sweep your car away into deeper waters. Even if the water isn't moving rapidly, once water enters the tailpipe of a vehicle, it can flood the engine and cause the car to stall.

If authorities are telling you to get ready but shelter on-site, do the final preparations and make your way to your safe room.

A hurricane emergency bag should contain the following:

- Battery-powered or hand-crank radio

- A NOAA weather radio with tone alert

- Flashlight

- Spare batteries

- First aid kit

- Whistle

- Charger and power pack for cell phone

Final preparations include:

- Stay informed, as hurricane updates could change at any moment; have the TV or a battery-operated radio tuned to the local news channel.

- Fill cars with gas, and move them to higher ground or put them in the garage if you are planning to stay.

- Charge all phones and devices; ensure power packs are fully charged.

- Bring all outdoor furniture inside, and secure any loose outdoor items.

- Place all important documents and valuables in the safe, or remove them from the premises.

- Fill all tubs and sinks with water in case water supplies become polluted or compromised.

- Unplug electrical appliances.

- Close all interior doors; this will help compartmentalize the pressure in the home into smaller areas, which reduces the overall force on the roof during a storm.

- If you don't have storm shutters on glass doors and windows, buy some $5/8$-inch plywood from a hardware store and bolt it to the frames. Cover the whole window with a few inches of overlap on each side.

RESPONSE

During the hurricane:

- Stay away from all windows, skylights, and glass doors.

- Don't walk outside to feel the strength of the wind, as even small debris can be dangerous.

- Don't use electronics that are plugged in, since there may be power surges.

- Do not watch the storm through the window, as flying debris and shattering glass could cause injury.

- Don't use running water if there is lightning, because if the house is struck, the pipes might conduct the electricity and travel it through the water.

- Stay inside until given the all clear from authorities. Hurricanes have a lull in them when the eye of the storm is passing over. It may feel like the storm is over, but it will start up again. Also, there may be hazards like downed power lines and fallen trees that need to be cleared before it is safe to venture out.

- Do not use your cell phone unless it is an emergency. Cell towers can get overwhelmed during natural disasters, and there may be someone trying to get through to emergency services with a life-or-death situation while you are calling your mom to say you are okay. Text your loved ones instead.

- Don't use charcoal or gas grills, generators, or propane stoves inside. This is because they release carbon monoxide that can quickly build up in unventilated spaces.

AFTERMATH

If you have evacuated, return home only once you have been given the all clear from authorities. Avoid downed power lines and fallen trees as well as any other debris that may be hazardous to your vehicle.

If you have sheltered in place, administer any first aid required and cautiously move from your safe room when told it is okay by authorities. Assess the damage to your home, board up broken windows, clean up glass and hazards, and check for any damage done to your gas pipes. Find temporary accommodation if your home is unsafe. If major flooding has taken place, do not drink the tap water until it has been checked by a specialist. Filter and boil all water.

In severe weather events, you need to be prepared to lose electricity, fresh water, and sewage services for days and sometimes even weeks. You should have the right equipment in your go bag to be able to be self-sufficient until such time as repairs can be done and infrastructure reestablished. A majority of casualties occur when people do not want to prepare for the worst and then ignore warnings and evacuation orders. Expect the best, but prepare for anything.

6.6

TORNADOES

A tornado is a tube of violently spinning air that touches the ground. It usually has the appearance of a funnel-shaped cloud and advances beneath a large storm system. Tornadoes can be among the most violent of storms, with a larger number of casualties than other storms, due to their unpredictable and extreme behavior, allowing for very little time to act. Falling and flying debris are responsible for the most deaths, as winds have been recorded at up to 350 miles per hour during a tornado.

Scientists are still not 100 percent sure what causes a tornado, but they surmise it is a change in wind direction and wind speed at high altitudes. This causes the wind to swirl horizontally. Rising air from the ground then pushes up on the swirling air and tips it over. The funnel of swirling air begins to suck up more warm air from the ground, and when the funnel touches the ground, it becomes a tornado. This mostly happens during strong thunderstorms called supercells.

Tornadoes can come in different sizes and shapes. Some may appear as wide, funnel-shaped clouds, and others like thin, rope-like swirls stretching from the ground to the sky. You cannot always see a tornado before it hits, and not all tornadoes will be visible. Some that are small or form in drier climates might not develop their funnels. These will look like swirling debris on the ground.

Tornadoes form in minutes and destroy large buildings, uproot trees, and send cars flying hundreds of yards. Most tornadoes last about ten minutes and travel approximately four miles, but there have been cases where tornadoes have lasted for several hours and traveled more than 150 miles. Their trail of destruction can be up to a mile wide. They can cross cities, mountains, and bodies of water and can occur anywhere in the world, but they are usually found in areas where warm, moist air meets cold, dry air.

Springtime usually brings the conditions that most commonly cause tornadoes, but they can happen at any time of year. Of the 1,400 tornadoes that occur on average worldwide every year, 1,000 of them occur in the United States.

Tornadoes are ranked according to wind speed on the Fujita Scale:

- **F0**: <73 mph wind speed, resulting in light damage

- **F1**: 73–112 mph wind speed, resulting in moderate damage

- **F2**: 113–157 mph wind speed, resulting in considerable damage

- **F3**: 158–206 mph wind speed, resulting in severe damage

- **F4**: 207–260 mph wind speed, resulting in devastating damage

- **F5**: 261–318 mph wind speed, resulting in catastrophic damage

Tornadoes are graded after they have passed through an area, based on the damage they have caused to human-built structures and vegetation.

Although tornadoes are hard to predict, these are some indicators that could suggest one is on the way:

- **Dark-, orange-, or green-colored sky**

- **Large, dark overhanging clouds**

- **Humidity**

- **Strong winds**

- **Large hail**

- **A loud roar**

If you encounter these conditions in an area that has a history of tornadoes, seek shelter immediately, regardless of whether an alarm has sounded or not.

WILDERNESS TORNADOES

Facing a tornado out in the wilderness has the potential to be deadly. Escaping a tornado requires solid shelter or the ability to get out of the way. Tornadoes can move up to seventy miles per hour and have unlimited energy, so never attempt to outrun one. Use what time you have to find the best shelter option and hunker down. A cave would be the top option, but if you are unable to find one, seek low ground and try to create or find a ditch or depression to lie in. Place your arms over your head. Remember that most injuries happen from flying debris, so any way you can cover yourself will help.

If you have a vehicle, try to drive out of the way of the tornado, but if it is too late, buckle your seat belt and bend forward below the level of the windows. Cover yourself with a jacket or blanket, if available. Vehicle glass is made for impact, so it tends to be sturdier than house glass, but it will break with a direct hit from something heavy. Your seat belt will prevent you from being thrown around, should the strong winds move your vehicle.

Try to avoid going out in wilderness areas if storms are predicted, and always make sure you carry some form of communication device that will allow you to get weather updates if you plan on being out in the backcountry for a while.

PREPARATION

It is always a good idea to check the local natural disaster history in your area or an area that you're planning on visiting. If you are living in a region renowned for tornadoes, some important things to do before a tornado strikes are:

- **Make an emergency plan for your household. Include where to shelter outside the home, what to do when a tornado strikes, emergency numbers, and a safe meeting place once the tornado has passed.**

- **Get to know your local tornado emergency siren and what the alerts mean.**

- **Create a safe room or storm shelter. If you live in an area where tornadoes are common, creating an underground shelter is a good investment; this can be a purpose-built room outside of your house, or simply modifying the basement, if you have one.**

- **Identify where the local tornado shelters are in close proximity to your location. If you are caught outside your home when a warning is issued, it may be easier to make your way to your nearest shelter than trying to make it home.**

- **Create a tornado emergency bag:**

  - First aid kit
  - Flashlight
  - Spare batteries
  - Signal light
  - Battery-operated or hand-crank radio
  - Long-life food and water for three days

- **Create a go bag (see page 348).**

- **Make a plan for your pets and livestock.**

If you do not create a safe room, identify a room in your house that everyone knows will be the safe room. It would be ideal if this room is an interior room with no glass windows or doors. The less furniture in the room, the better. Bathrooms work well as the safe room for tornadoes, as they are usually fortified by pipes, and you can lie in the bathtub and cover yourself with a mattress, pillows, or blankets.

6.6.3

RESPONSE

Tornadoes are extremely hard to predict. If an evacuation order is issued, you may only have minutes to get out. Always have your go bag ready and in an accessible place, and leave everything else behind.

Tornado alerts are issued as follows:

- **TORNADO WATCH:** Watch and prepare for severe weather.

- **TORNADO WARNING:** Get to shelter now; you may have only minutes.

- **TORNADO EMERGENCY:** There is a tornado confirmed in the area.

When a tornado watch is issued:

- **Secure all outdoor furniture and moveable objects.**

- **Close all doors and windows:** The myth that opening some or all windows helps in a tornado has been disproven, and it is recommended that you keep them closed; open windows can create a pressure vacuum that may result in strong winds lifting your house off its foundations, and it also lets in debris that can cause more damage.

- **Close blinds and curtains.**

- **Turn off all utilities.**

- **Park vehicles in the garage, if possible.**

- **Grab your emergency bag and go bag, and make your way to your safe room.**

- **If you are on the road, drive to your nearest shelter if you are not close to home.**

- **If you live in a mobile home, it is best to make your way to the nearest storm shelter.**

When a tornado warning is issued, you should already be in your safe room. Get down low, and cover yourself with a blanket. Stay calm and positive for those around you. Keep the radio tuned to your local news station, and do not leave the room until authorities have declared it safe to do so.

If you are not home when a tornado warning is issued:

- **Take shelter in the most solid structure available.**

- **Go to the smallest central room on the lowest floor of the structure (staying out of elevators).**

- **Keep away from windows and glass doors.**

- **Do not go outside.**

- **Do not try to outdrive a tornado in an urban area; seek shelter instead.**

- **Do not shelter under overpasses or bridges in your vehicle; the wind can become more intense under these structures and funnel in debris.**

If driving has become dangerous, pull over away from any trees or structures, stay in your vehicle, keep your seat belt on, and lean forward to try to get your head beneath window height; cover yourself with a coat or blanket, if you have one.

Although it is frequently said that you can hear a tornado coming, the wind often only picks up before the tornado arrives, so do not wait until you hear it to act, as that may already be too late.

6.6.4

AFTERMATH

Always wait until given the all clear by authorities to leave your shelter or return to your house if you have evacuated. Be aware of any hazards that may have been caused by the strong winds, such as downed power lines and uprooted trees.

When leaving your safe room or returning to your house, take care to avoid any broken glass or structural damage. If your house is no longer structurally sound, seek shelter elsewhere. Check all utilities to see if there is any damage to gas or power lines. Do not use an open flame if you suspect there may be damage to gas lines.

Be aware that you may be without power for a few days or weeks, depending on the severity of the tornado. Ensure that your go bag has everything you require to meet your basic needs over this period.

Tornadoes can be very scary to contemplate if you have never experienced one before, but for many people in certain parts of the United States, they are simply part of life. Being proactive before one hits, and staying calm during, can increase your chances of making it out alive.

TSUNAMI

A tsunami is the deadliest of all ocean disasters, with the potential to level entire cities. Tsunamis can travel up to five hundred miles per hour and reach heights of over one hundred feet before piling up against the coastline. They can strike without warning, and there is little that can be done to prepare and defend against a moving wall of water. Tsunamis produce unusually strong currents, rapidly flood land, and devastate communities.

A tsunami is a series of ocean waves, usually caused by one of three things:

1. **Earthquakes**

2. **Landslides**

3. **Volcanic eruptions**

Epicenter

The wave will start at the epicenter and radiate outward in all directions. The first wave to hit the shore is usually not the strongest. The successive waves will get bigger and stronger. A tsunami can be up to a hundred miles in length, and the waves can continue for days, resulting in loss of life, mass injuries, and damage and destruction of homes, infrastructure, and facilities.

Tsunami Waves

There are two types of tsunamis:

1. Local: These are large waves that have a source close to shore and can arrive in less than an hour; they are more dangerous, as there is less time to evacuate and get to safety.

2. Distant: These are large waves that have a source farther out to sea; they are less dangerous, as authorities have more time to issue warnings, and people have more time to respond and get to safety.

Most damage in a tsunami is caused by:

- **Flooding**
- **Wave impact**
- **Strong currents**
- **Erosion**
- **Debris**

Although tsunamis can happen anywhere, there are well-known, high-risk areas along the coasts in the Pacific Ocean. On average, there are two tsunamis per year that are destructive, and about 80 percent of all tsunamis happen in the "Ring of Fire," a chain of active volcanoes that runs for almost 25,000 miles (40,000 kilometers) around the Pacific Ocean.

Be aware if you are choosing to travel to or live in an area that has been impacted by a tsunami in the past. Areas to have a good emergency plan if you are spending time in them include:

- Beaches
- Bays
- Lagoons
- Harbors
- River mouths
- Low-lying coastal areas

Scientists have developed early warning systems that can accurately predict when a tsunami can make landfall, based on the depth of water, the distance from one place to another, and the time the trigger occurred. However, this does rely on them having sensors in the right place on the ocean floor when the trigger goes off, so it is important for you to know what to look for in nature that may indicate a tsunami is on its way.

Some of the indicators in nature include:

- **A significant earthquake felt along the coast**
- **Rapid rise and fall of water on the shorelines**
- **Pets and animals acting strangely**

After noticing these signs, you may have less than twenty minutes to get to high ground, so move swiftly.

6.7.1

PREPARATION

Surviving a tsunami is going to be all about how quickly you can mobilize and retreat to higher ground. This means that you will need to have your best evacuation routes from home, school, and work memorized, along with a backup if traffic is jammed.

A safe place will be at 150 feet above sea level or two miles inland. Plan both vehicle routes and ones you can travel on foot. If you don't have a plan, simply head uphill however you can.

It's also a good idea to:

- Have an emergency plan for your whole household, and make sure everyone is familiar with it; know where your safe area is, map out routes from home, school, and work, and aim to meet during or after the event if you are separated.

- Educate yourself about tsunami warnings in your area, official and natural.

- Have a go bag packed and easily accessible (see page 348).

- Have a plan for pets and livestock.

6.7.2

RESPONSE

If your tsunami is preceded by an earthquake, follow earthquake protocol (see page 392) until tremors cease, and then follow tsunami protocol.

It is always better to be safe than sorry, so don't take any chances in tsunami areas if any of the warning signs occur. Get out, and get out quickly. Head to higher ground by whatever means you can as fast as you can. Stay out of the water, away from beaches, and avoid waterways.

Most buildings are not designed to withstand the impact of a tsunami; however, the upper stories of some buildings may be able to provide protection if no other options are available.

The levels of authority warning are:

Tsunami watch: This is when a tsunami may later impact the area; begin to gather your family members and valuables together, and have radio updates going all the time in case the status changes.

Tsunami advisory: This is when a tsunami with the potential to generate widespread damage is imminent, expected, or coming; evacuate low-lying coastal areas immediately.

Tsunami warning: Take the same actions as with an advisory.

If you get caught in a tsunami, do not try to swim. Grab hold of any passing floating object, and let the current carry you. Turn so that your feet are facing downcurrent, and keep your knees slightly bent to allow you to push off any objects that you encounter under the water. Try to go over objects you come up against rather than under them. If you see any high ground or a place of refuge, use your hands to scull toward it. Be aware of debris in the water with you.

Once the forward energy is spent, the water may retreat back into the ocean if it has nowhere else to go. This will produce an outgoing wave that can be as dangerous as the ingoing one, so make sure you try to find a secure position before this occurs and hold tight.

If you are in a boat during a tsunami warning, head out to sea. The deeper the ocean, the lesser the wave.

6.7.3

AFTERMATH

Do not return to low ground until authorities have given you the all clear. Tsunami waves can last as long as a few days and have hours between them.

Depending on the severity of the tsunami, your home may range from having no impact, to flooding, to complete destruction. Take care to avoid hazards such as downed power lines and uprooted trees as you make your way home. In the event of a major tsunami, be prepared for infrastructure to be compromised and the possibility of a survival scenario that may stretch into weeks.

EMERGENCY PLANNING

What you choose to include in your emergency plan can be as varied as what you decide to put in your go bag. However, a good emergency plan for all natural disasters should include:

Hazard identification and assessment: What is your most likely natural disaster, and how serious could it be?

What can you do to prepare or prevent the disaster?

Emergency resources: What infrastructure is in place in your local community to help combat the disaster?

Communication systems: Have all relevant phone numbers stored, emergency contacts established, and an alternate means of communication, should phones be lost or batteries die.

Emergency response procedure: What are the steps you will follow if you are evacuating, or if you are staying in place? Have at least two evacuation routes established and rehearsed, and two meeting places established if the household gets separated. Have routes planned from your workplace, home, and school.

Communication of the procedure: It is important that the whole family knows the plan. Awareness of a threat shouldn't lead to fear of a threat. Being prepared and letting everyone know how prepared you are can ease the fear of the unknown.

Create a go bag: Make sure it can cover all your basic needs for the whole family for at least three days or more (see page 348).

AFTER THE DISASTER

A natural disaster doesn't end when the event burns itself out or loses momentum. For most people, this is when the true survival scenario begins. You and your loved ones may be safe from harm, but what if you return to a site of devastation and destruction? And you are not alone? The emergency services may be overwhelmed as your neighbors and community, and perhaps even the state or country, battle to come to terms with what has happened. The demand on emergency resources will be high, and people can react with fear, shock, and anger to such an event. This is when you will need to stay calm and make proactive decisions, relying on your good preparation and knowledge of your basic needs to get you through. You are now in an urban survival scenario, and you need to know how to manage it for the immediate future, and what your priorities will be if it takes weeks or months to rebuild.

7

Urban
Survival

ALTHOUGH YOUR BASIC NEEDS WILL STAY the same, urban survival is a completely different scenario from surviving in the wilderness. You may have access to more resources, but you will likely be competing with scared, desperate, and hungry individuals and groups of people that may become violent and threatening when they feel like their life is on the line. Limited supplies quickly turn friendly faces in the streets against one another, and anything accessible is considered fair game.

You may need to use your urban survival skills in the days and weeks following a natural disaster, in a pandemic, and in times of war and civil unrest. These skills will also be helpful if the power grid goes down for a few days in extreme heat or storms have downed power lines in your region, leaving you without utilities for weeks. It doesn't take long for your home to become an icebox in a blizzard without access to heating, and the exposure rules of three hours of extreme cold before death apply in cities as well as out in the woods.

If you survive through a natural disaster, you may be lucky enough to find that your house is still standing with minimal damage and all utilities are still functioning. You may also return after an evacuation to devastation, but have a place to retreat to while you rebuild your home and life. The situation gets dire if you return to your house to find it damaged or destroyed, but you have nowhere else to go. This may be because it is a widespread catastrophe, and infrastructure is not functioning for days leading into weeks. The people around you have been impacted as well, and the demand for emergency relief far outweighs the help available.

Power will be one of the first things to go that will make communication and staying informed difficult. Society is so dependent on technology to help with these things that it is almost incomprehensible to consider that there may not be access to devices once batteries are dead. Always have a charger pack in your go bag as well as another method of renewable energy, such as a small solar panel. If you live in an area that has a history of losing power during natural weather events, it is worth investing in a generator and keeping thirty gallons of fuel in storage for it. This should last at least five days if you are running it for eight hours a day, so use it sparingly if it looks like you may need it for longer than that.

Your go bag should also contain a battery-operated or rechargeable radio. This will help you stay informed by listening to local news channels.

You will need to make your home your own personal life raft and work to ensure the survival of all those who are a part of your team. It will be time to get creative. One person's trash is another person's treasure; be adaptable, and stay positive for those who are struggling with the dire change of living conditions.

7.1

GETTING HOME

Your emergency plan will have covered where your household should meet when disaster strikes. Hopefully you all made it out together, but if you didn't, call each other, call emergency contacts, and check all meetup locations to band together. Wait until authorities declare it safe to return to your area before traveling back to your house. Be aware of hazards from the disaster, making sure to avoid flooded areas, downed power lines, and fallen trees.

Your car should be equipped with a car emergency kit, as well as having your go bag, in case you are required to spend a few days away from home before returning. These kits will ensure that you can take care of yourself and your loved ones in whatever emergency shelter situation you end up in.

7.2

SHELTER

Once you have made it back to your house, assess the damage from the outside first. How badly is your home affected? If the disaster has left your residence structurally damaged to the point of collapse, do not try to shelter inside.

This being the worst-case scenario, salvage materials from your house and yard to build a shelter outside of your house. Sheets of plywood, beams, bricks, and furniture will all contribute to building a sturdy shelter for you and your family. Depending on your disaster, you may need to cover your shelter with a tarp to stop the rain from getting in or use a table to get off the ground. Build the shelter at the back of the house if possible, as it will be easier to fortify and will also shield you from opportunistic looters.

If your house has some damage but is structurally sound, choose the best room for everyone to bunk in and make that your base. Keeping everyone together will be safer but also use fewer resources to warm if heating is an issue. In extreme cold, choose the smallest room in the house, and cover windows and doors with sheets and blankets to prevent the heat from escaping. Place mattresses together, and cover them with as many blankets and duvets as you can find.

Assuming access to electricity, water, and gas has been cut off, you will need to begin to make provisions for basic sanitation, as toilets will not flush in these scenarios. If you have access to a large water supply, such as a swimming pool or rainwater tank, you may keep using your toilet, but you will have to throw a bucket of water down into the bowl after use. In order to save water, only "flush" when you need to, rather than every time you urinate, and only use minimal toilet paper.

If you have limited access to water, you will need to find an alternative. One option would be digging a hole in your backyard. It would be best if it was one deep hole and filled in as people use it, rather than multiple holes each

time you need the bathroom. Another option is a
bucket lined with a plastic bag. Some suggest lining
the top with a pool noodle for comfort and using kitty
litter to sprinkle on as you go. The only problem with
this method is disposing of it once you are done, as
garbage collection usually vanishes if a town's infrastructure does. It is, however, the best method for
apartment buildings or places without a backyard.

Disease becomes rife in these kinds of scenarios, so make sure you use hand
sanitizer after each toilet visit, especially if you don't have access to water
to wash your hands.

7.3

WATER

If you are located in an area that has a history of natural disasters, you
should have at least three days' worth of water stored somewhere in your
house for such an emergency.

Natural disasters have the potential to contaminate the groundwater that is
fed into your plumbing. This means that until local authorities have declared
it safe to consume municipal water, you shouldn't use it for drinking, cooking,
washing your hands, or bathing without purifying it first. If your electricity is
off, chances are your water supply will be too. Unless your house is gravity
fed, water requires electricity to pump into your house and out your taps.

Water that has been contaminated by toxic chemicals or fuel cannot be
made safe to drink by adding disinfectants or by boiling, so if you suspect
that this is the case, find water from elsewhere.

It is a good idea to familiarize yourself with your closest bodies of water
prior to an emergency. These could be lakes, rivers, dams, or a local swimming pool. All water will need to be purified before drinking, and if there are
chunks, I suggest filtering it as well. If you are using it for toilet water, you
can use it as you find it.

In a shorter-term urban survival scenario, it is good to ration half a gallon per person per day for drinking water and half a gallon for cooking, washing, and sanitation. Some places to access water around the home will be:

- **The toilet tank**: Don't use water from the bowl, as that water will be polluted by bacteria. But the tank that supplies the bowl will hold about four gallons on average, and that can keep a family of four going for a day; make sure that there are no deodorizers or chemicals in the tank before purifying and consuming.

- **Hot water heater**: The average water heater will hold anywhere from six to a hundred gallons of water. Just be careful that the water isn't scalding hot when you access it.

- **The bathtub**: If you managed to fill it before the power went out, the average bathtub can hold forty-two gallons of water.

- **Water tanks**: You may have a method of catching and storing rainwater, which will ensure a good supply of water.

- **Swimming pools**: This water is good for flushing the toilet and washing clothing but will need to be purified and distilled to make it drinkable, depending on how maintained it is and the method of treatment used to keep it clean. If the chlorine levels are less than four parts per million, the water will be safe to drink after bringing it to a boil. Anything more than that will need to be filtered using a purpose-built water filter, then distilled using evaporation to separate the pure water from the chemical impurities. There are many different and complex ways to distill water. The basic idea is that you need to heat the water so that the pure water rises from it as steam. This steam then needs to be collected and cooled in such a way that it reverts to liquid form, this time without the impurities in it. If you have some pipes and collection pots and perhaps some duct tape, you could rig up an efficient system to keep many people satisfied with drinking water indefinitely.

A simple water still could be put together by collecting the pool water in a pot and devising a cover for the pot that has a pipe rising from it and traveling to another container. Place the pot over a heat source. When the water begins to steam, the system should allow the steam to rise from the pot and travel through the pipe, where it cools back to liquid form and runs downward into the collecting container. This water will be good to drink.

Toilet tank

Bathtub

Hot water heater

Swimming pool

Water tank

Some other simple water stills are mentioned below.

RAIN If your disaster is accompanied by rainy weather, it is a good idea to try to catch and store as much of the rain as possible. This can be done by redirecting gutter downpipes and/or creating catchment areas with buckets or any other containers you can find.

PURIFYING

The best way to ensure that the water you drink is safe is by boiling it. This requires using electricity, wood fire, or fuel for your stove in your go bag. If the electricity is off, wood and fuel may be limited in an urban survival scenario. Your go bag should be equipped with at least two other methods of purifying water, including a water filter and/or purification tablets. If you don't have access to either of these, you can create your own urban distillation process.

WATER STILL

There are a couple of ways to do this, but they both require direct sunlight or heat, so if you are experiencing cloudy weather or want to save fuel, choose another method to purify your water.

Solar still

Fill a tub with the water to be distilled; this still works on the same principle as a wilderness solar still. Place an empty container in the center of the tub; weigh it down so it doesn't float. The water in the tub should not be high enough to flow into the empty container. Cover the tub with clear plastic, and place a rock in the center of the plastic so it dips down where the empty container is, without touching it. The water will evaporate and recondense on the surface of the plastic, where it will drip into the empty container. This water will be drinkable. If the tub is metal, or you have a larger metal container to use, you can apply heat to the bottom of the tub to speed up the process.

Another method requires a clear water bottle and a can. Cut the bottom off the water bottle and the top off the can. Fold the bottom sides of the water bottle up into itself to create a gutter to catch the distilled water. Fill the can with pool water, and place it inside the water bottle. Make sure the lid is on the water bottle, and place the still in the full sun. The water will evaporate from the can in the heat and re-form on the inside of the water bottle, sliding down the sides to be caught in the gutter. This method takes time and sunny weather, so make multiple setups, if possible.

CHEMICAL PURIFICATION

If you do not have specific water purification tablets, you are able to safely use bleach as an alternative. Add eight drops to a gallon of water and wait thirty minutes, and then it will be safe to drink.

Iodine also works, if there is any in your first aid kit. Add thirty drops to a gallon of water, and wait thirty minutes before drinking. Iodine aggravates thyroid conditions, so avoid this method if you have any issues.

Do not drink radiator water under any circumstances. Quite often this water is mixed with coolants or antifreeze, both of which are toxic to humans.

7.4

FOOD

Your go bag should be stocked with three days' worth of emergency rations. This is the average time that it takes for services to resume after a disaster. Take stock of what long-life food you have in the house, and create a meal plan that will enable you to make it last for as long as possible.

If electricity is compromised, your refrigerator and freezer will not work. Eat the food that will spoil first. Do not eat refrigerated perishables after one day in hot climates and two days in cooler climates.

You can extend the time that your fridge stays cool by not opening the door very often or for long periods of time. This will keep the colder air in for longer. You can also put food from the freezer into the fridge. The frozen goods will act like ice blocks and allow you to get an extra day out of your perishable foods.

This is one of the areas that survival is easier in the outdoors as the days stretch into weeks. It is much easier to forage for wild edibles in most wilderness areas. There are some common weeds that grow in urban environments that are great edible weeds, but make sure that you harvest them from areas that you know haven't been subjected to weed killer or other toxic chemicals.

It is a good idea to wash them thoroughly before consuming, due to human and animal pollutants as well.

Some plants you may find in urban areas are:

MUSTARD A common plant found all over the side of the road, its edible yellow flowers have quite a spicy kick, and the young leaves are good for a salad. The mustard plant belongs to the same family as vegetables like cabbage and broccoli. As such, it has many of the same nutrients; it is very high in vitamins A and C and serves as an antioxidant.

SUNFLOWERS The raw seeds of sunflowers are very high in protein, and the flower buds (before they bloom) can be cooked and eaten like artichokes. The hulls of the seeds are a good source of fiber but need to be ground up to avoid sharp pieces damaging your mouth and throat.

DANDELIONS High in calcium, magnesium, and iron, dandelions are also used medicinally and are helpful if you are having digestive trouble. The green leaves can be eaten raw in salads or sandwiches and have a tangy, slightly bitter taste. You can also boil them briefly to remove some of the bitterness. The root, stripped of its outer fibrous layer, can be eaten raw if taken from young plants, or dried and ground to make a good substitute for coffee.

THISTLES These are among the hardest wild plants to gather, on account of their spines, but they are edible. The stalk can be peeled to rid it of its spines, and then boiled before eating. The roots can be dug up and eaten raw or cooked, while the leaves should be stripped of their spiny green parts to leave the edible "rib" down the middle. Eat raw or cooked.

STINGING NETTLES Wear gloves to make sure you aren't stung collecting the leaves, but once nettle leaves are boiled, the irritant is gone and they taste a lot like spinach.

Remember, there are far more edible plants in the world than there are poisonous ones, but you only need to make one mistake and it can be fatal. Make sure you know you have the right plant before eating.

In urban survival scenarios, it is better for you to remain in your home if possible, as society can descend into a chaos of lawlessness and looting. Do not go out until your life depends on it.

If weeks stretch into months and there is no end in sight, you may need to head into your local wilderness areas to hunt for bigger game. My local park is filled with rabbits and is a five-minute walk away. The local bird life would also become a good, targeted food source. Be vigilant with your weapon safety, and ensure you have a safe backstop before firing a weapon in an urban area.

Assume that most food stores will have been stripped of all available consumables by the time you need to start seeking food if your disaster preparation was solid, but it is a good idea to scavenge what you can from your immediate area. This isn't looting; it is survival. If your neighbors haven't returned and a month has gone by, raiding their cupboards for your family's survival is forgivable.

7.5

FIRE

In an urban environment, you should be able to find enough warm materials to see you through the night without a fire, if the temperatures don't drop way below zero. Unless you live by a wilderness area or have a wood-fueled fireplace with a stock of winter fuel, wood will be a limited resource. You may need to make a fire to cook on or purify water. If this is the case, keep it small and contained.

Methods of lighting fire should be easy to come by, although they may be finite materials such as matches and lighters. Make sure you do not waste them even if it seems that you have plenty, because you don't know for how long you will need them.

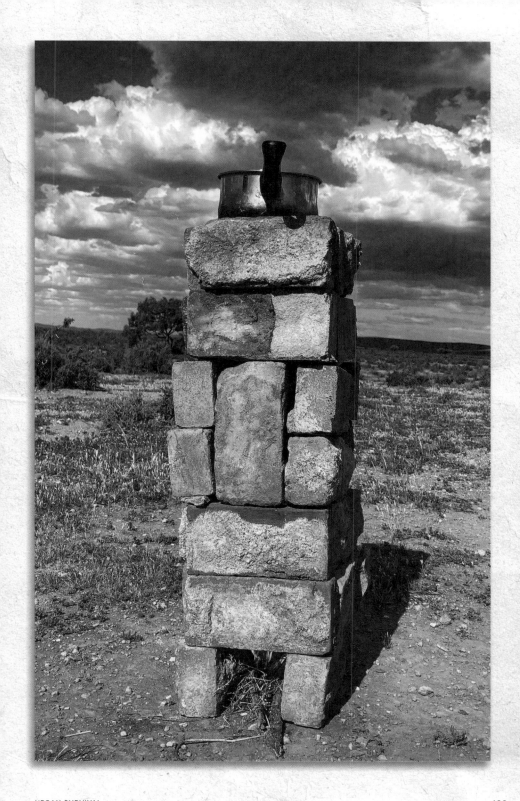

BATTERY METHOD

A good urban fire-lighting method is the battery-and-wire method, as you should have access to both of these resources. You will need two pieces of wire or a gum wrapper and a battery. Attach one wire to the positive end of the battery and one wire to the negative end. When you bring the two wires close together, a spark will jump between them. If you can place your tinder between the wires, you should be able to light it from the spark. Steel wool is an excellent tinder for this method.

Having light at night will also be an issue. I encourage you not to keep lanterns and flashlights on, to conserve your batteries in case you need them for future emergencies. A candle will provide a comforting light if you need it, but be sure to never leave a candle burning unattended. Putting the candle inside a glass jar will give it some stability and prevent the wind from blowing it out. Again, these are finite resources, so try to sleep and conserve energy during the night rather than doing activities that require light.

BRICK ROCKET STOVE

If you do not have a cooking stove in your go bag or a gas grill at home, you will need to find some method of cooking food. A brick rocket stove allows you to get the maximum heat from the minimum firewood. Simply make a small, two-foot-high chimney of bricks (one brick width per side), making sure that you leave a gap at the bottom. Place the fire at the base of the chimney and feed it with small twigs and sticks. The fire will funnel up the bricks and allow you to cook on top.

KEEPING COOL

We are so used to modifying our surrounding temperature with the flick of a switch that we are no longer adapted to extreme temperatures or able to cope when we cannot avoid them. Many people die in their homes in unseasonably warm weather if their electricity gets shut off or if they don't have a decent cooling system set up. Some ways you can cool down without electricity include to:

- Limit time in the sun.

- Stay hydrated.

- Find or create shade.

- Wear light, loose-fitting cotton clothing.

- Seal off the hottest rooms in the house, and avoid them.

- Sleep downstairs or in the basement.

- Open windows at night when it is cooler, and close them during the day.

- Keep curtains closed during the day.

- Minimize opening and closing outside doors.

- Use rechargeable battery-operated fans.

- Wet a bandanna, and cover your face and neck.

- Dampen wrists and ankles.

- Refrain from cooking inside.

If you are still struggling to cool down, go to a place that you know will be cooler, such as a shopping mall (if it is open) or the local pool or swimming area.

URBAN SAFETY

In disaster scenarios, people usually take one of two roads: they band to-gether, or they develop an "every man for himself" attitude. Building a community of people who have your back will aid in ensuring your safety and survival. It will enable you to pool resources, both physically and mentally, and potentially barter for items you may not have. Having a good relationship with your neighbors prior to finding yourself in a survival scenario will help with this.

It is important to have your shelter out of sight and your resources stored in a locked area, if at all possible. Do not draw attention to where you are staying and to the fact that you have resources that may help others through this time of disaster. Fortify your shelter or house in any way you can. This may mean boarding up some exits and windows, finding alternative ways of locking an area, and establishing some weapons. If you do not have access to guns and ammunition, think outside the box. If your safety is threat-ened, a wood-chopping ax, heavy hammer, and baseball bat are all effective close-contact weapons. Keep these nearby at all times. You don't want to be paranoid and look for an attacker around every corner, but you are not in a position to assume that everyone is a friend. Such people might believe that their life depends on taking what you have, and if you present an easy target, it may be taken advantage of.

Spend your time cleaning and fixing up your home to the best of your ability. Improving your situation will help you feel proactive and stave off feelings of helplessness and despair.

Fuel will be at a premium during these times, so try to avoid using your car. Save the fuel for if you need to flee or evacuate again. Move around on foot or by bike.

It is important that you do not venture out from your base unless it is absolutely necessary. If you decide that you need to leave, try to gather a group of people to join you. There is safety in numbers when you venture out. Be calm, but be alert and maintain good situational awareness. Avoid any encounters that feel like they might be threatening or dangerous. Urban self-defense includes:

- **Backing down**: Do not escalate an argument; if someone is aggressive, try to defuse the situation by staying calm and moving away.

- **Don't look like a target**: Wear old clothes and carry an old bag to scavenge what you can while you are out. Predators will generally prey on those they feel are weaker than them, so do not look weak or scared, and walk as if you have a purpose.

- **Have a weapon ready**: Part of carrying a weapon is also being in the headspace to use it. If you are uncertain whether you can use a weapon to inflict harm when your life is threatened, you are better not to carry one at all. It will only end up being used against you. Understand the consequences of the weapon you carry, and visualize doing what you need to do to return home safely. Do not hesitate if your life is in danger.

- **If you can limit your exposure to others and scavenge essential resources, your chances of survival go up exponentially in an urban survival scenario.**

7.7

RIOTS

A riot is a violent disturbance of the peace by a crowd. Riots can be as dangerous and as unpredictable as natural disasters. Thousands of people are killed in riots each year worldwide. They are usually the result of a protest. There are two different types of protests: peaceful and violent. A peaceful protest has the potential to become violent at any stage. Anytime emotional, volatile groups of people gather in large numbers, there is the possibility it may become lethal.

Whether you are a willing participant, an observer, or just a passerby, it is important to always keep an eye on crowd dynamics. A peaceful protest might be hiding violence at its core. The safest course of action is to bypass violent crowds altogether and identify points of potential danger before they erupt. Skirt around a large crowd instead of making your way through it. If you are caught in the crowd, flow with it until you can move calmly and slowly to the edge. Make your way home or to a point of safety. If you are traveling with friends or loved ones, grab hands or grip elbows to ensure you stay together.

If you have been caught up in a violent protest, avoid the following areas:

- The space between groups of people with opposing views
- The front line of protests
- Places where people have been pushed up against barricades
- Lines between protestors and law enforcement

If possible, avoid approaching law enforcement, as they will be in defensive mode and may perceive anyone moving toward them as a threat.

It is very difficult to de-escalate violence in an already-agitated crowd. It is best to:

- **Avoid confrontation by keeping your head down.**
- **Walk away, instead of running; you do not want to draw attention to yourself.**
- **Not take sides; be neutral or support anyone who asks whose side you are on, and move on quickly.**
- **Move to the edge of the crowd.**
- **Seek shelter inside or on the back side of a building.**
- **Get to elevated ground.**

Avoid confrontation by keeping your head down.

Move to the edge of the crowd.

Walk away, instead of running.

STAMPEDE

This can occur when crowd control is overwhelmed, and crushing injuries or fatal suffocation occurs. It is important to maintain control over your personal space if you get caught in a stampede. Widen your stance, bend your knees, and keep your weight above your feet. Bring your arms up to a boxing position, in order to help widen the gap between you and others and protect your head. Try to avoid being pushed to the ground, as it is very difficult to get up again once you have been pushed down by a crowd of panicking people. Try to move to the edges of the crowd, as there is less pressure and force there. If you do get knocked down, assume a defensive position with your knees bent, your body curled over your knees, and your arms protecting your head until there is a gap in the crowd big enough to find your feet again.

Widen your stance.

Bring arms up to a boxing position.

If knocked down, assume defensive postion with knees bent and arms protecting your head.

Riots most commonly happen on the streets and out in public, so move to a safe, enclosed area. Lock doors and windows and stay away from them. Move to rooms that do not directly lead to the outside, and look for at least two exits in case you need to get out. Stay informed by listening to the local news or following social media, and stay in place until the danger has passed.

If you are in a vehicle:

- **Stay in the car.**

- **Keep driving as calmly as possible; do not stop to assess the situation.**

- **If someone tries to block your car, honk and keep driving toward them at a moderate speed; do not hit them if they do not give way, but be assertive.**

- **Do not let a few angry people stop you from driving.**

- **Keep going unless you absolutely can't.**

As with all dangerous scenarios, prevention is better than having to deal with a life-threatening scenario, so observe locally enforced curfews and regulations, and if you feel like tensions are mounting, calmly but quickly exit the crowd and make your way home.

LOOTING

A by-product of riots can be looting. This is the act of stealing or taking goods by force in the middle of a crisis. It is an illegal act, and usually looters don't take items of necessity but luxury items. Do not get dragged along with the crowd momentum to think this is an act of survival. Scavenging and looting are two very different actions. One comes with a penalty of fines or imprisonment after the excitement has settled, and the other is accepted if the items of value have no clear ownership, (such as supplies that are found in an abandoned or burnt-out store), and they will sustain your life.

TERRORIST ATTACKS

These are violent, criminal acts committed by individuals or Predicting of where these acts may occur is almost impossible, and so your ability to prepare is minimal.

Communities can defeat terrorist attacks by looking for anything out of the ordinary and reporting it to authorities straightaway. This includes:

1. **People in stationary vehicles watching public areas or buildings for long periods of time**

2. **Vehicles moving slowly near public buildings or monuments**

3. **People using cameras or making notes of security movements**

4. **Suspicious-looking people examining entry and exits points to public buildings**

5. **People loitering for no apparent reason**

6. **People asking suspicious questions about the operations of buildings or monuments**

7. **Anyone in restricted areas without permission**

"See something, say something" has foiled planned terrorist attacks and saved thousands of lives.

If you are living in or traveling to areas of civil unrest, you should have an emergency plan organized in case you get caught up in acts of terror. This would include establishing a meeting place for your loved ones and traveling companions and making sure you have everyone's number and emergency contacts.

If an act of terrorism occurs near you:

- Try to stay calm.

- Administer medical care to yourself first and then others, if needed.

- Leave the area as soon as possible for your home or a safe space.

- Walk but do not run, unless there is an active shooter.

- Follow the advice of local authorities.

- Listen to the news for up-to-date information on action required.

- Contact friends and relatives to let them know you are okay.

EVACUATION

If you are asked to leave your home due to a terrorist attack, you will need to leave immediately, and you should:

- **Change into long sleeves and pants, and put on with sturdy shoes; this clothing will act as protection if you need to have bare skin covered for any reason.**

- **Grab your go bag.**

- **Lock up your home.**

- **Go where authorities say; don't use shortcuts or think you know better.**

After a terrorist attack, it is important to band together with your community to help and heal. These are shocking events that have the potential to divide nations, but if you allow them to force you to live in fear, they have won. Repair, rebuild, and come back stronger.

ACTIVE SHOOTER

In the United States, terrorist attacks tend to be gunfire rather than suicide vests or pipe bombs. If you encounter an active shooter, you should:

1. **Immediately duck down to a squat or to hands and knees.**

2. **Establish the location of the shooter and move in the opposite direction.**

3. **Move to an area of cover, if you are not already behind cover. Cover is defined as an area that will stop or slow down bullets, like concrete walls or solid objects. Things like curtains may prevent the shooter from seeing you but will not stop bullets, so they are not a good choice.**

4. **Run from cover to cover to get to safety. If there is no cover available, run in a zigzag pattern, as it is harder to hit.**

5. **Hide somewhere you can lock and barricade the entrances. Stay clear of the doors when locating yourself inside this room. Shooters will often shoot through doors, as they tend to be the most penetrable surface available.**

Remember to always look for an escape route. In the heat of the moment, you can feel trapped in a situation that you aren't actually trapped in, because of panic. People have died from being shot while huddled up against glass windows that they could have broken to escape through long before the shooter made their way to them. Just because something isn't traditionally thought of as an exit doesn't mean you can't break your way out to safety if you have to.

If all else fails, you may need to stand and fight. Team up, find any weapons or improvised weapons you can, and fight hard and with aggression. Your life may depend upon it.

Simply put: run, hide, fight.

PANDEMICS

A pandemic is defined as an outbreak of a new disease that becomes prevalent in a country or across the world. There are usually a number of fatalities associated with pandemics. It is hard to predict when a pandemic will occur or whom it will affect.

Some things you can do to prepare for a pandemic are to:

- **Learn how diseases spread, to help protect yourself and others. Viruses can spread from person to person, from a nonliving object to a person, and by people who may be infected but don't have any symptoms.**

- **Gather supplies—such as cleaning supplies, nonperishable foods, feminine hygiene products, prescriptions, bottled water, and food for pets—in case you need to stay home for several days or weeks; buy supplies slowly to ensure that everyone has the opportunity to buy what they need.**

- **Stock up on disinfectant wipes, hand sanitizer, gloves, and masks.**

- **Ensure you have some form of inside entertainment, including books and games.**

- **Make sure your go bag is stocked.**

One of the reasons people end up panic buying is there tends to be denial about how a virus could have a large and lasting impact on society. Many people think it won't affect them. They do not bother preparing for it when they have plenty of time and resources, and then find themselves nervous about their supplies at the last minute. This is an example of when you need to hope for the best but prepare for the worst.

If you do end up in the last-minute crowds, it is important to prioritize what you should be putting in your shopping cart. Any nonperishable food items will take priority over luxury items such as toilet paper. You need to be thinking about food, water, shelter, and fire even when you are still able to go out shopping. Toilet paper, although nice to have, can be replaced by any number of other options, such as a bidet, newspaper, or tissues. (But remember to only flush toilet paper, because it can be hard to get a plumber to visit in a pandemic if you clog up the system.)

DURING A PANDEMIC

It is important to listen to what your health authorities have to say during a pandemic. There is a lot of misinformation and fearmongering that can take place, so check the sources of your information before trusting it as fact.

Some things that can help prevent the spread of a pandemic:

- **Stay home as much as possible.**

- **Cover coughs and sneezes.**

- **In public, wear a mask that covers your nose and mouth.**

- **Wash hands often with soap and water.**

- **Use hand sanitizer.**

- **Clean and disinfect high-touch objects and surfaces often.**

- **Keep six feet away from people who aren't in your household.**

- **If you have symptoms or believe you may have been exposed to the virus, contact your nearest testing site.**

- **If you do get sick, isolate so you don't pass on the virus to friends and loved ones; seek medical care if necessary.**

- **Know that it is normal to feel anxious or stressed, and talk to someone if you need help.**

- **Stay connected to friends and loved ones via virtual communication.**

AFTER A PANDEMIC

Continue taking protective actions:

- **Stay home when you are sick (except to get medical care).**

- **Follow the guidance of your health care provider.**

- **Cover coughs and sneezes.**

- **Wash your hands with soap and water often.**

FORTIFYING YOUR HOME

The more difficult your home is to penetrate, the more likely a criminal will choose an easier target. There are some simple solutions that will increase your safety and help you protect your family. They include:

SECURITY CAMERAS There are many different types of cameras, ranging from quite cheap ones that can be set up with relative ease to more complicated ones that will require a company to install. You can choose to have some scattered around the house or focusing on the main entry point. Anything is better than nothing, and simply knowing that they may be caught committing a crime on camera will be enough to deter some criminals.

MOTION SENSOR LIGHTS It has been proven that motion-triggered lights deter many would-be intruders, and they are cheap and simple to install. They can be bought from a hardware store and placed at outside entry points. Be aware that they can be triggered by all motion, so having a dog in the backyard at night or large branches in the sensors' range on a windy night may continually set them off. It may take some experimenting to get the positioning right for you.

FORTIFY YOUR HOME'S ENTRY POINTS Thirty-four percent of intruders enter a house through the front door. Most of the time it was unlocked, but other times the door was kicked in. Make sure to lock your front door, especially at night. Install good security screen doors and safety chains, with double locks on the main door. Some intruders will knock to make sure no one is home. Always keep the screen door locked, so that, if you answer the door, you have one line of defense between you and a possible home invader.

SECURE YOUR WINDOWS The next-most-common entry points are windows. Make sure that your windows have locks and that you use them. Window alarms work when the intruder slides the window but not when they break them. A simple way to fortify them is security window film. It's a transparent film that makes windows harder to break or shatter.

BELLS OR CHIMES Install them on your doors so that they are set off whenever the door is opened or closed. If you know that you are alone in the house and you hear the sound, you know to take action to deal with an intruder.

DOGS When interviewed, most thieves say they would be deterred if a house had a large dog in residence. This should never be a reason to get a dog, as they require care and attention, but if you love dogs and have the time to care for them, they can help keep intruders away.

TREES AND SHRUBS These are a long-term plan, as they will take time to grow once planted, but if people can't see the target, they will be less temped to rob it.

CACTUSES Planted under your first-floor windows, they will prevent would-be intruders from breaking and entering in these locations, due to the painful, prickly barrier these plants present.

WEAPONS What type of weapon you have in your house will depend on the laws in your country, but arming yourself and making sure you are educated to competently use your weapon of choice will allow you to protect yourself if all else has failed.

Urban survival is all about your ability to survive a widespread disaster while remaining in a densely populated urban environment. You will need all your survival attitudes to help yourself and others through these often life-changing events, remaining positive and adaptable while being proactive to make the situation better for everyone. One step at a time, one job at a time, make today better than yesterday to rebuild your future.

8

Outdoor Recreation

ANYTIME YOU VENTURE INTO THE OUTDOORS by choice, you have the chance to ensure the outcome of your trip will be the best it can be. You know where you are going, you know what some of the possible dangers are, and you have time to prepare for them. You can make a choice as to what to bring in case the worst happens. You can have those emergency items that you dream of in extreme, unexpected survival scenarios, and you can make sure that whatever happens, you can deal with it proactively and to the best of your ability.

I always encourage anyone heading into the outdoors to get some form of first aid qualification. It is usually injury in the outdoors that is the cause of most life-or-death scenarios. Being able to deal with a first aid scenario quickly, competently, and efficiently could save someone's life, including your own. This is a duty of care that you owe to your fellow adventurers. You can choose to do a basic first aid course with CPR that will take a day or two of your time, or a wilderness first aid course, which usually runs from three to seven days. It is good knowledge to have even if you aren't venturing into the outdoors. Who knows when you may encounter a kid drowning in a swimming pool or an elderly man having a heart attack? What you do in those first few minutes is vital to saving their lives.

If I have a choice, I am the one carrying all the gear. People will laugh, asking, "Can't you survive with just a knife?" And the answer to that is yes, but why would I make life harder for myself if I have a choice? Survival is about making smart decisions and trying to save calories wherever you can when your life is on the line. Can I make a friction fire? Yes. Will I save valuable time and energy if I have a ferro rod or a lighter on me? Yes. Work smarter, not harder.

A few people have been made famous in books about their extreme survival scenarios. In most cases, their challenges could have been prevented by following some simple safety rules prior to departure. Be inspired by those who did all the right things and managed to survive as a result, rather than those who were irresponsible and created a survival scenario that easily could have been prevented. The repercussions of their bad choices led to other people putting their lives at risk to save them, concern and grief from loved ones, and sometimes irreparable damage to their mind and body, or even death.

There are many hobbies that take you into the outdoors, too numerous for me to name, so I have chosen the more popular ones to help you prepare for. Hiking can simply be any activity that is in the outdoors for one or more days with a pack on your back. Boating can be any water sport, and hunting is any armed outdoor activity. I have also chosen backcountry skiing for a colder-climate hobby, but this could be snowshoeing, mountaineering, or ice climbing. Among all of these, you should be able to get a good idea of the priorities for preparation and how best to survive most incidents that may happen.

HIKING

The most common cause of a hiking trip turning deadly is a lack of preparation. I've lost count of the times I have been out for a hike and come across groups of people, red faced in the heat of the day, with inappropriate footwear, no water, no food, and no idea how far they have come and how far they have left to go. Sometimes I have had to cut short my plan in order to ensure they make it safely back to their accommodation or vehicle, using my valuable resources to keep them healthy. Other times they have continued to walk, and I have wondered if and how they made it back alive.

Even if you plan to head out for only a day, I recommend bringing a few extra items in case something unexpected happens. A badly twisted ankle on a day hike is as likely to keep you outside for the night as getting lost on a longer hike.

PREPARATION:

There are some things that should always happen as part of your hike preparation, whether you are going out for a day or you are going out for multiple days. It is important for you to:

RESEARCH THE TRAIL There are all types of apps specifically designed for avid hikers. They have trail notes, including the length of the trail, expected walking time, and difficulty, and sometimes even downloadable maps that you can GPS track on while you walk. If you don't want to purchase an app, you can usually find downloadable information for free on various websites that you can print off. I like doing this, as it usually gives a history of the track and what you might be able to see when you walk it. This can add a richness to the experience. You should also be able to find a hard copy of walking maps at the ranger's station or tourist information center. I like to have a physical copy of a map as well as using GPS or my phone, in case the technology fails. If I am going on a multiday trip, I will bring a topographic map of the area and a compass.

CHECK THE WEATHER It is always important to know what the weather will be before heading out. Don't let a little bit of rain deter your plans, but pack accordingly. If you are going to be out for multiple days, bring a portable NOAA radio; this is a radio designed specifically to broadcast weather and national emergency announcements. Keep an eye on the sky, and err on the side of caution if you see thunderstorms or strong winds approaching.

KNOW YOUR CAPABILITIES I am the first person to encourage people to push their limits, but I always do a gradual build if I am starting a new activity. There is no point in pushing too hard on a hike and not being able to walk for three days afterward, as it usually discourages you from trying again. Setting achievable hikes is also more rewarding, since you have time to make the summit or see the waterfall, rather than having to turn around before dark. Some hikes will have some rock scrambling along the trail or even chained areas. If you are not a confident climber, it is not worth taking the risk, remembering that if you go up, you usually have to come back down.

Mileage: Everyone will be different with the number of miles they can cover in a day. Factors to consider will include:

- Fitness level

- Level of experience

- Terrain

- Weather

- Condition of trail

- How much gear you are carrying

- Altitude of the trail (add one hour per two thousand feet above sea level)

- Elevation gains or change (uphill requires more time and effort, but downhill can have more impact on your feet and joints)

- Motivation

The average person can hike about three miles per hour with a daypack. The longer the hike, the fewer miles per hour as fatigue sets in, and in total they will average about twelve miles per day.

Hiking with a group: If you are hiking with a group, you need to take into consideration the abilities of the entire group. It is always easier for someone to slow down rather than speed up, if they are trying their hardest already. A good leader will position their slowest person at the front, with a helpful motivating personality nearby. The leader should be at the back of the group, in order to be able to assess the way the group is moving and make decisions about rest stops and group safety. It is always best for a group to walk together, unless it is understood that individuals have different goals for the hike.

PREPARE A TRIP PLAN Once you have determined your route, it is important to leave a copy of your trip plan with someone who isn't going on the hike. This means that if you don't return, an alarm will be raised sooner rather than later, and the rescue operation will have a general idea of where to start looking. If people are not aware you are missing, it could take days before a rescue is mounted, and if they don't know where you are going, it could take weeks to find you. Your trip plan should include:

- **Your name and the name of all hikers with you**

- **Emergency contact info**

- **The date and time of departure**

- **The expected time of return (always allow a few extra hours, so that an alarm isn't raised simply because you had a long lunch)**

- **The route plan**

This information should also be left at any trailheads that have a register, or with the ranger station if you are going remote.

HAVE A PLAN B Always make sure that you have a turnaround time or an alternate route mapped out, in case you can't make your destination or are forced to evacuate.

HIKE WITH SOMEONE It is my favorite thing in the world to be out in the wilderness alone, but I acknowledge that it is much safer if you have someone with you. It allows you to double-check any navigation queries, and if one person is injured, the other can help them out or go for help.

DRESS APPROPRIATELY There is a saying in the outdoors: "Cotton kills." Personally, I am all for a cotton top in a hot environment, but only if you understand the choice you are making. Cotton absorbs and retains up to seven times its weight in moisture, which means it loses all its thermal properties when wet, dries slowly, and can chafe. This means it only needs a cooler wind on a sunny day to begin to drive your core temperature toward hypothermia. Synthetic clothes specifically designed for the outdoors regulate temperatures, allowing you to remain cooler on hot days and warmer on cold days. It is important to have layers that you can remove or put on, depending on your level of exertion and changes in weather conditions.

- **Base layer**: Should be sweat wicking and breathable, and help regulate body temperature

- **Mid-weight layer**: Something to keep you warm, such as an insulated jacket or fleece

- **Outer layer**: A lightweight raincoat

BOOTS

There are many new and varied trains of thought about what footwear is appropriate for hiking, with a trend toward "barefoot" shoes. Shoes are one of the most important parts of your gear, considering that your mode of transport relies on your feet being in good condition.

BAREFOOT SHOES AND HIKING

I agree with the theory behind reverting back to a more natural way of moving through our shoe choice. You should wear the lightest-weight boot that you can get away with, depending on the nature of your hike. On a day hike, where I want to travel fast and light, I wear a barefoot hiker because it allows for a more natural rhythm of movement. But I had to train my feet and ankles to get used to the lack of support. Most shoes we hike in are focused on ankle support, so we don't twist or break an ankle moving across uneven terrain. This in turn means our ankles begin to depend on that level of support from the boot and become weaker, needing more support. If you want to wear a barefoot hiker, do so only when hiking with a light daypack, and work up to a long day on the trail to give your ankles time to adjust to the lack of support. If you are carrying a heavy pack, I would recommend wearing a solid boot with good ankle support, because your body will need support to compensate for the extra load on your frame.

CHOOSING THE BOOT THAT'S RIGHT FOR YOU

There are many different options and alternatives for hiking boots, and I recommend going into a shop and trying them on if you don't know what brand will suit you. I am always looking for a light, sturdy boot with good ankle support for my longer trips. Lugging around a heavy weight on your feet will end in more fatigue and joint aches. No need to buy a mountaineering boot if you are staying in the lowlands. The fit is important as well. The store should have a ramp for you to try your shoes on. If they don't, tie up the laces tight and kick your feet forward on the ground. If your toes touch the end of the boots at all, that's going to lead to blisters and lost toenails; get the next size up. Same with width; if you are snug in width, go for a wider shoe or vice versa. Make sure you try on the boots with thick woolen socks. These are the type of socks that you should be wearing on hikes to prevent blisters, so the shoes need to fit with the socks that you will be wearing.

DON'T TAKE NEW BOOTS ON LONG HIKES

Make sure you break in your boots before going on a long hike. Boots will usually take some time to mold to the shape of your feet. This will help avoid pain and discomfort once you are on the trail.

KNOW HOW TO NAVIGATE I'm not suggesting that you take a course on compass use (although that would be helpful), but be sure you know what you are seeing when you look at a trail map. Before you start, figure out where you are. A lot of trails have a map at the trailhead with a "You Are Here" sign to help with that, but if they don't, locate where you are on whatever map or device you have with you. Knowing where you started is important for helping you keeping track of where you are as you go. Most maps will be orientated in a north-south direction or will have a diagram of a compass on them, allowing you to see the orientation. If you have a compass with you, you can align the map north with the compass north and gauge the general direction you are headed in. A lot of smartphones have a compass as a standard app, but be aware that they may not be accurate if you put them on a metal surface. If you have a GPS, know how to use it properly, but don't rely on it, and always carry spare batteries.

CARRY EXTRA FOOD AND WATER I carry a minimum of half a gallon of water if I am going on a day hike. For an overnight hike, I try to carry an extra days' worth of food and water. I also bring a method of purifying water.

RECOGNIZE SIGNS AND SYMPTOMS OF FATIGUE AND DEHYDRATION Most accidents and injuries happen when people try to make their destination when they are not in the right frame of mind or physical health. This is called "summit fever" and can result in being out longer than anticipated and getting "knighted," or rushing getting down, and making errors of judgment.

Signs and symptoms of fatigue and dehydration include:

- Headache

- Dizziness

- Sore or aching muscles

- Slowed reflexes and responses

- Tripping often

- Moodiness and irritability

- Impaired decision-making and judgment

These are all things that can cause accidents or injuries on the trail. If you recognize any of these symptoms in yourself or others, slow down, take a rest, drink water, have something to eat, and move cautiously when you continue.

It is important to drink before you are thirsty; have your water bottle accessible, so you can regularly drink before dehydration becomes an issue. Many people end up dehydrated simply because they don't want to stop to get their water bottle out of their bag.

8.1.2

DAY HIKES

Even if your day hike doesn't turn deadly, you will have a far more enjoyable experience if you take a small pack and a few things to ensure your comfort and safety. The gear in my pack for a day hike will include provisions for all my basic needs, in case something unexpected arises. I carry:

1. **Navigation equipment: GPS plus hard copy of maps and a compass**

2. **Headlamp and spare batteries: even if I don't plan to be out at dark**

3. **Small first aid kit, consisting of the following:**

   - Pressure bandages x 2
   - A roller bandage
   - A triangular bandage
   - Gauze or cotton pads
   - Strapping tape
   - Band-Aids
   - Antiseptic cream

4. **Pain relief**

5. **Knife** (see page 48 for my preference)

6. **Lighter**

7. **Ferro rod**

8. **Whistle**

9. **At least half a gallon of water (drink a good amount before you hike, and refill your bottles before you set off; being hydrated from the start puts you ahead of the game)**

10. **Meals, plus extra snacks**

11. **Extra layers of warm clothing**

12. **Waterproof jacket**

13. **Emergency bivy bag or small tarp**

14. **Life straw or water purification tablets**

15. **Hat and sunscreen**

16. **Phone and portable charger**

This might seem like a lot of gear, but most of it is light and compact and can make the difference between life or death, should an unexpected scenario arise. It can all fit into a small daypack. Make sure you familiarize yourself with all the equipment you choose to carry before you venture outside with it.

WALKING POLES An optional piece of gear that divides hikers with its usefulness, or lack thereof, is the walking pole. People will either love them or hate them. Walking poles can take the pressure off your knees, give you more power when going up slopes, and help you maintain your balance in rocky terrain. They are also great for river crossings and can assist in creating splints or carry systems in first aid scenarios. Try them out if you want, and make up your own mind.

OVERNIGHT HIKES

Obviously, you need to carry more for an overnight hike than for a day hike. Some people pack as light as they can and trade comfort for minimalization. If you like this approach, be careful that you do not compromise your safety in the aim to cut down on weight. You may get away with it most of the time, but you only need one inclement event for your survival to be on the line. My minimum overnight bag contains:

- **A cooking system:** stove plus extra fuel, and a pot or large cup to cook in

- **Half a gallon of water/day plus spare empty water bag**

- **Water purification:** filter plus tablets

- **Sleeping bag (down is lighter, but synthetic retains heat when wet)**

- **Sleeping mat**

- **Shelter:** tarp for ultralight, hammock in the right environment, or tent

- **Knife:** field knife plus multitool for the extra gadgets

- **Headlamp plus extra batteries**

- **First aid kit:** expedition style, rather than ultralight

- **Food plus an extra day's worth of meals**

- **Fire:** lighter, waterproof matches, and ferro rod

- **Trowel and toilet paper**

- **Navigation:** maps, compass, and GPS backup

- **Phone, phone charger, and small solar charger (phones will die faster when it is cold or when they are continually going in and out of signal)**

- **Repair kit**
  - duct tape
  - paracord
  - cable ties
  - spare buckles
  - bandanna
  - plastic bags

- **Emergency shelter:** small tarp, emergency bivy bag, or space blanket

- **Signaling devices:** mirror and whistle

- **Extra set of clothing plus insulating layer for coldest possible temperature**

Although some people might list some of these as luxury items, they are all necessities to me that will assist in comfortably surviving just about anything unexpected that could occur while I am out. It is important that you know how to use everything you put in your pack, so you should set up the equipment in your house or backyard before you go to ensure that you have all the pieces you need and that all your gear functions properly.

CHOOSING A PACK

Choosing the right backpack can mean the difference between enjoying your time out in the wilderness or hating every minute of it. If your pack breaks or becomes dysfunctional in the middle of a multiday trip, it could compromise the condition of your other gear or result in lost essentials.

Always make sure the pack you choose is durable. Check:

- **Straps—Are they good quality, with double stitching?**

- **Material—Sewn together well with no gaps in the stitching; is it waterproof or does it have a waterproof cover?**

- **Zippers—Open and close them to see if they move smoothly; waterproof zippers are a bonus.**

- **Buckles—Are they solid? Avoid any that look like they will snap easily.**

- **Ventilation or netting—Does it have a system to keep the pack cool on your back?**

- **Waist belt and chest strap—These help keep the weight of the pack off your shoulders and keep the pack in the most effective position for carrying your load. I recommend that both your daypack and your overnight pack have this system.**

Your pack should fit your body. This will allow you to stay comfortable and use less energy on the trail. There are frames of all sizes to suit all body types. The pack should sit with the top of the hip belt just above your iliac crest, and the shoulder straps should wrap down to about three inches below the top of your shoulders. Most packs will be a certain frame size, and then the good ones will allow for some adjustment of the frame within those measurements.

The shoulder straps should wrap down to about three inches below the top of your shoulder.

The pack should sit with the top of the hip belt just above your iliac crest.

Packs come in a lot of different sizes. The size you choose is important. Some people will pack until the space is full, so having a big pack means a heavy pack full of luxuries. I like to have a bigger pack so that I can pack extra items if I need them, such as when if I'm responsible for the safety of a large group of people or I'm going to be in different extreme climates within one trip. But if I don't need the space, I can cinch in the buckles and travel light. If your pack is too small, you may end up leaving essential items at home. As a general rule, my daypacks are usually 25L to 40L packs, and my overnight packs are 65L to 80L packs.

Multiday packs come in front loading or top loading and with internal or external frames. This will come down to your preference. I will explain mine and why I choose it, and I will let you make up your own mind.

TOP-LOADING PACKS When you are walking a trail with a heavy pack on, it is important that the pack fits snug to your body. If it is wide or bulky and ill fitting, it will cause excess movement, and your muscles will have to work harder to stabilize the weight on your back. I have a small frame, and top-loading packs tend to be more streamlined, so I can save energy by using them. It is important that you establish a pattern of how you pack them, though, so you don't have to unpack your whole bag to get items during the day. Your first aid kit should always be on or near the top of your pack, as should water, snacks, and a warm layer. A good top-loading pack will have external pockets to help with this organization. Front-zip packs are great for backpacking and touring when you won't be carrying your bag for extended lengths of time.

INTERNAL FRAME For the same reason I prefer a top-loading pack, I prefer an internal frame when hiking. It's a different story when I'm hunting (see page 490). Internal frames are designed to be loaded with more weight between the small of the back to the shoulders and to fit snug against your frame. This reduces the excess movement. They also are less likely to snag on rocks or branches, and I don't like the idea of losing anything that I may have strapped to the outside of my pack if it comes untied or breaks off without me noticing. An external frame allows for more flexibility to add an extra-bulky load if I get lucky on a hunt.

WEARING A PACK CORRECTLY A majority of people I see walking with large packs are wearing them in such a manner that will cause extra discomfort and fatigue on the body. These few handy hints will add comfort and decrease fatigue.

Load-lifter straps.

When you first put on your pack, lean forward so that the load on your back moves upward, and tighten your waist strap firmly. Pull on the shoulder straps so they hug your shoulders without constricting movement. The last important straps are the load-lifter straps. They are found above the shoulder straps, and these are usually the ones that people forget about but that can make a big difference to how your load sits. If they are too loose, they will cause the load to pull backward and cause muscle fatigue. Too tight, and they will have you bent over as you walk. Loosen them off until you feel like you are being pulled backward, and then tighten slightly. This will keep your pack load firmly over your center of balance. The chest strap should be firm but not distort the shape of your shoulder straps or inhibit your breathing.

BLISTERS

Your feet are one of your most valuable assets in a survival scenario, and you will need them to walk out of a hike safely.

Blisters are one of the most common, preventable injuries that occur while hiking. They are caused by skin being damaged by friction. The four stages of blisters are:

- **Hot spot**
- **Roof intact**
- **Roof torn**
- **Deroofed**

The time to deal with blisters is when they are a hot spot. Any time you have an injury that compromises a layer of skin, you are opening yourself up to the possibility of an infection, so it is best to prevent this from happening, rather than having to treat it. A hot spot forms due to rubbing. As soon as you feel one, stop hiking and deal with it, as it doesn't take long for a blister to develop from there. Cover the area that is hot with an adhesive bandage or piece of tape and continue.

If a blister has formed but is small, cover it with an adhesive bandage. If the blister is large, you will need to make a donut bandage to take the pressure off it. Whatever you do, don't pop the blister, as the fluid-filled blister is keeping the skin underneath clean, which will promote healing and prevent infection. If the roof of the blister is torn or completely gone, clean and disinfect the area and cover it with an adhesive bandage.

Your feet are prone to bacteria and infections from being in dirty, sweaty socks, so change the dressing and clean the blister often. If the clear fluid becomes creamy and yellow, or the area around it becomes raised and red, it has become infected, and you will need to take extra care of the area and plan to hike out.

Wearing good, clean, thick wool socks can help prevent blisters, as can the double-sock method. This is where you wear a very thin inner sock under a thicker hiking sock. It allows the material of the socks to rub against each other, rather than against your skin.

8.1.6

SANITATION

Whether you are on a day hike or an extended trip into the wilderness, there is usually a lack of public facilities available once you have headed out. How you choose to toilet in the wilderness can affect your experience, as well as the experience of those around you and those who come after you. It is a huge pet peeve of mine to have an area ruined by someone else's thoughtlessness. You have come out to enjoy a pristine experience, so leave the area that way for others who follow.

URINE Urine is actually very sanitary. It contains ammonia, which is a common disinfectant used in a lot of household cleaners. Many African tribes urinate on their wounds in order to sterilize them and to prevent infection. Wilderness first aid courses still teach such practices today, if the need is dire enough. However, if you feel the need to use a modern-day cleanser on your hands after peeing, then carrying around a small hand sanitizer will do the trick.

FECES This waste product can contain bacteria and disease. It needs to be disposed of properly. There are protected areas of the outdoors where you are not allowed to leave anything behind, and in those areas, you are required to do your business in a bag or a specially designed box and carry it out with you. There are also some enthusiasts who believe that we shouldn't leave anything behind in nature that wasn't there when we went in. And that's great. I'm not one of them, however. I believe that poop is nature's fertilizer, and it's actually contributing to nature when I leave.

However, in order to avoid spreading disease and ruining other people's outdoor experience, it does need to be buried and covered with the soil, as opposed to filling the hole with leaves or grass. It should also be done a good distance from your main camp and any running water or dry creek beds.

For this you will need a trowel in your wilderness kit. Your toilet hole needs to be at least eight inches deep. Any shallower and it is easily dug up by animals or exposed by the elements. Putting a rock pile on top of your covered hole will help prevent this from happening and warn fellow campers from digging in the same area.

After you've finished, wash your hands! This is not optional. Poor hygiene can spread disease through your friends and family. If you have run out of soap, a good scrubbing with sand or dirt and some water works just as well. Disinfect your hands afterward if possible.

Many people in stressful situations don't end up going to the bathroom. This is largely due to the fact that the brain and the digestive system are intimately linked and regulated by many of the same hormones and other elements of the nervous system. There are many people who can't even do a number two in a public toilet because of embarrassment or fear or self-consciousness.

Not having bowel movements is very detrimental to your health. There are more and more studies being published that show that the digestive system helps regulate the overall well-being of your body. Constipation leads to a buildup of toxins in your body, and eventually you will get sick. If you don't have a bowel movement for long enough, a hard plug of waste matter will form in your colon, and you will soon be unable to go at all. Then the only way to get better is to insert your finger up your bottom (or have someone else do it!) and break it up, which can be way more embarrassing than finding a nice private spot to squat in the woods. So please make sure you try to have a bowel movement at least once a day.

PAPER As part of the planning for your trip, you should factor in a sufficient number of sheets of toilet paper. The paper will need to be carried out with you. You would (I hope) take your garbage out of the wilderness, so why leave your toilet paper? Some people prefer to burn it, but coming from Australia, I am a little wary of lighting paper in the outdoors in case I set the whole bush alight, so I prefer the paper in the plastic bag method. Carry a small plastic bag to put used toilet paper in until you find a trash can where it can be disposed of properly. Now you may find the thought of this unappealing, but how many of you walk around with dog feces in a similar plastic bag when you are out with your pet? I'm thinking that a little piece of toilet paper isn't all that bad.

If you get caught out without toilet paper, there are a few good outdoor alternatives. Some people will use rocks to wipe with. Don't use sharp crystalline ones. A better option is to use a leaf or other form of vegetation, but you have to exercise some caution as to which ones you choose, to avoid an irritating result. Anything that may have poison or fine prickles should be avoided. What you have available will depend on the environment you are in, of course, but I have found that a good handful of sage bush works best.

PERIODS I have only one suggestion for pads and tampons—take them out of the wilderness with you. Even if you dig a deep hole to bury them, the smell of blood will draw the attention of some little carnivore, and soon the countryside will be littered with regurgitated tampons.

For an extended trip into the outdoors, store your tampons in a couple of airtight resealable bags.

Time to dispel a popular myth: the idea that women should stay out of the outdoors when menstruating. Many studies have been done to try to discover whether bears are more attracted to women who are menstruating than women who are not. They have concluded that it is not a significant factor.

Being prepared for the worst but expecting the best will ensure the best possible outcome for your hiking trip. It won't prevent all disasters or emergencies from happening, but it will ensure that you are in the best possible position to manage those disasters and live to tell the tale.

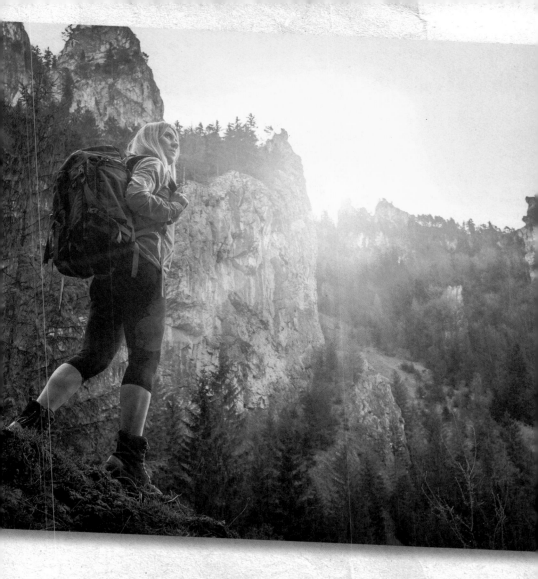

8.1.7

POSSIBLE SCENARIOS

An ideal hike is a day out in nature, enjoying the scenery and the company, providing you with some time away from every day life. But, you should always be prepared to deal with the unexpected.

GETTING LOST

On average, 2,000 hikers get lost in the United States per year. They were lost anywhere from half a day to ninety days before they were rescued. Some didn't make it back. Of those who survived, most of them attributed being prepared before their hike as the reason they made it out alive.

Things you can do to help prevent getting lost include:

- Research your route before you head out; look at features on the map, the general direction you will be heading, and where civilization is from your route.

- Know how to use a map and compass as well as a GPS; never rely on technology, and always have a backup.

- Pay attention as you walk, observe landmarks, and remember forks in the road and which way you traveled; look backward every now and then to note how the trail will look on the way back.

- Stay on the marked trail, follow the cairns (rock piles) or markers where the trail may not be obvious, and don't take shortcuts; most people get lost because they leave the trail.

- Never go walking alone; if you need to go off the path to go to the bathroom, have one person stay on the trail to guide you back to it.

STOP

Getting lost can be as easy as stepping off the trail to check out something interesting and then getting turned around and being unable to find your path again. The most important thing to do the second you realize you are lost is to stop moving. Think about the direction you came from. If you can retrace your steps to your last known point, do so. If you are not sure which direction this might be in, stay where you are.

Two-thirds of people who became lost kept moving after they realized it. Only a quarter of those people made it out by themselves, and 75 percent were rescued anyway. Your best chance of being rescued is by staying where you first are when you realize you are lost. If you continue to move, you may be moving farther away from your last known location and from rescuers searching for you.

ASSESS

The only reasons to leave this area would be if it is dangerous to stay or if you can't meet your basic needs. If you have materials for a shelter, a way to keep warm, and enough food and water for a few days, it is time to get comfortable.

TAKE ACTION

Once you have decided to stay in place, if you have access to phone service, call 911 to let them know you need help. If you have an emergency beacon, set it off.

Hopefully you were with a group of people who will miss you, or you left a trip plan with an emergency contact. In these cases, your chance of a quick rescue increases. See how you can make your position visible by tying brightly colored objects to tree branches and bushes, and make as much noise as you can. If you came prepared, you should have a whistle in your pack. Blow in short, sharp bursts to attract attention. Listen after each round of three whistles to hear if someone has heard you. I don't encourage yelling unless you hear someone calling out for you. Save your voice until rescuers are within earshot.

Don't wait until it gets dark to make a shelter or fire. Begin to gather materials together after you have planned to stay. Being proactive and keeping busy will help to stave off panic.

LONG TERM

If you haven't been rescued after a few days, assess your ability to stay in the location you are in. Do you have a good potable water source? Will your shelter protect you from all weather? Have you gotten a fire going? Is there a food source that you can access? If you can keep meeting all your basic needs, stay in that location. If you cannot, it may be time to move to a better location. If you do move on, make sure you leave a note or make clear the direction you are headed in, and mark an obvious path so rescuers can track you if they find your initial camp.

A successful rescue happens sooner if you have left a plan with someone reliable and have come prepared with some basic equipment.

8.1.7.2

ANIMAL ATTACK

Any time you venture into the wild, you are removing yourself from a controlled environment and entering into a realm where it is hard to predict the behavior of the animals you might encounter. It is important to remember that very few animals will attack a human except in self-defense.

If you are confronted by a wild animal:

- **Avoid eye contact.**

- **Freeze; if they aren't charging you, don't run.**

- **Slowly back away.**

- **Avoid sudden movements.**

- **If an animal charges, dodge out of the way; you could be blocking their escape route.**

- **If the animal attacks, shout, make a loud noise, and try to make yourself look bigger; drop whatever you are carrying, as it may distract them; zigzag run away from them, if you run; climb a tree, if a big enough one is available.**

Educate yourself about the predators that live in the region you are visiting. A little knowledge goes a long way and can prevent a dangerous confrontation. Learn what the predators look like, their common behaviors, how to avoid them, and the best way to deter an attack. In the unlikely event of such an incident, your immediate response to the situation will determine the outcome.

The first tactic when confronted with most predators is to stay still and use the stop-look-and-listen approach. (The exceptions are crocodiles and alligators, which don't tend to chase their prey on land; run away from them.) This communicates to the animal that you are not a threat and are not one of their normal prey species, which flee on sight of the predator. Often, this will mean the animal will move on. However, if they don't, there are other tactics you can use to deter an attack. They are different for all large predators. Some quick examples are to:

- **Make noise to scare away a black bear, but play dead to deter a grizzly attack.**

- **Act loud and scary to prevent a mountain lion attack.**

- **Dodge out of the way at the last minute from a rhino attack, and then stand still; they aren't very agile, have trouble with quick direction changes, and have very bad eyesight, so they may never find you again.**

- **Stand as tall as you can to make yourself appear as big as possible if confronted by an aggressive dog; this should intimidate the animal.**

You should always try to keep your distance from potential predators. Respect the fact that you are intruding into their natural environment, where they act according to their instinctive behaviors. The vast majority of wild animals will avoid confrontation unless threatened or cornered. But in case the worst happens, learn the difference between each tactic. It could save your life.

If you are attacked and injured but the animal has appeared to leave the area, administer first aid and make your way to safety as soon as possible. Some animals may leave but then come back to finish the job, so it is important that you make your way to help as quickly and safely as possible.

INJURED HIKER

The most important thing to do as soon as an injury occurs is to assess the danger. If the injury is to yourself and you are still in danger of more injury, remove yourself from that position, if possible. If a fellow hiker is injured, assess the danger to yourself if you rush in to help. If you can assist your fellow hiker without any danger to you, do so and move on to assessing the injury and administering first aid.

The last thing you want in a wilderness setting is for the uninjured person rushing in to help to get injured. You see this often when a swimmer is caught in a riptide and a family member drowns rushing in to save them. You need to look after yourself first and then see to others. I am not saying don't attempt to rescue someone. But take a second to assess the situation and make a plan rather than rushing in panicking.

Once everyone is safe, administer first aid. Wilderness first aid is covered in a separate section (see page 548), but common hiking injuries include twisted ankles, broken ankles, heat exhaustion, and dehydration.

TWISTED ANKLE This can range from a slight twist, easily walked off, to more extreme tendon and ligament damage. Assess the severity of the sprain. If you are not far from your exit and the injured person is able to put weight on the ankle, do not remove the boot. It is acting as a compression bandage and supporting the injury. Provide some aid in the form of a walking stick or shoulder to lean on, and slowly make your way to safety. If the victim is unable to put weight on the injured foot, take the weight off, remove the boot, apply a compression bandage, and have them rest with their foot elevated. If you have cold water available, soak a bandanna in the water and cover the foot with a cooling compress.

BROKEN ANKLE It may be hard to tell the difference between a sprained ankle and a broken one. Some things to look for will be deformities, numbness, and whether the victim heard a cracking noise when the injury occurred. Sprains will usually be associated with a popping noise. Depending on which bone is broken, the victim may be able to walk out unaided or will not be able to support their weight at all. Treat as for a severe twisted ankle.

DEHYDRATION Signs and symptoms include:

- **Dry mouth**
- **Tiredness or fatigue**
- **Thirst**
- **Lack of urination (you should be peeing once every few hours)**
- **Dark-colored urine**
- **Headache**
- **Dizziness**

If untreated, dehydration can progress into foggy thinking, inability to make rational decisions, and, eventually, seizures, brain damage, and death. Stop, rest in the shade, and hydrate until symptoms begin to ease.

HEAT EXHAUSTION This condition results from your body overheating. Signs and symptoms of heat exhaustion include:

- **Cool, moist skin with goose bumps when in the heat**
- **Heavy sweating**
- **Faintness**
- **Dizziness**
- **Fatigue**
- **Weak, rapid pulse**
- **Low blood pressure**
- **Muscle cramps**

The best cure for heat exhaustion is to cool down the body, so stop activity, seek shelter, and drink water if you have it. Prevention is better than having to cure it, so try not to be active in the heat of the day.

If the injured hiker is mobile but needing further medical attention, slowly and carefully walk to safety.

If the injured hiker is not mobile and requires medical assistance, call emergency services or set off your emergency beacon, and make them as comfortable as you can until help arrives.

If you are out of cell range, without an emergency beacon, or need emergency help fast, assess your victim. Can you transport them to help faster than help can get to you? Are you able to build a stretcher? Can you carry assist them out? Will it compromise their condition by moving them? If you have the ability to move them and can do so safely, mobilize them, keeping their comfort in mind.

If you are unable to move the victim and unable to contact emergency services, make them as comfortable and safe as you can and hike out to a place where you can get help. This will involve setting up a temporary shelter and making sure the injured person has access to warmth, water, and food. Make sure you find some way of remembering exactly where they are to relay the message to authorities.

If you are injured and alone, you will need to assess your ability to become mobile. What will it take for you to get to safety, and are you capable of doing that? Can you make an emergency call? If you are unable to move and out of service, do what you can to treat your injury. Make yourself as comfortable as possible and visible to any passersby or potential rescuers.

ENSURING RESCUE

Before heading out, always make sure to tell a responsible person about your plans. This will ensure that an alarm is raised quickly, and the rescue will be directed to the right location.

Your rescue is likely to come from a few different sources: by air, land vehicle, or foot. You will need to prepare something visible for all the scenarios. Even if you think that you will hear someone who passes by you on foot, you may be sleeping or out collecting water, and they need to know you are around. Generally, you will have about two minutes from the time you hear an aircraft to the time it is out of range, so any signaling needs to be thought out beforehand and ready to go.

Things that will make you more visible to rescuers include:

Bright colors: Hang items on trees, or place them in the middle of clearings.

Reflective surfaces: Tie your signal mirror to a tepee structure to blow in the breeze, or use any reflective garbage you can find.

Straight lines and arrows: Try to use contrasting colors to the ground and point toward your location.

Words on the ground: SOS is the worldwide signal for distress.

Thick smoke: Green leaves on a fire create thick, visible smoke during the day.

Bright flames: Use dry wood to create a bright fire at night.

Lights in the dark: Use a flashlight amplified by a shiny surface or signal mirror to attract attention.

Torch trees: Build a fire in a tree, and light it when a rescue vehicle is sighted.

Your signals should be clear and well thought out. When thinking about where to locate them, keep in mind the specific terrain. The signals need to be easily accessible for you and on high spots or ridgelines, or in clearings.

Most incidents that occur while hiking can be prevented by paying attention to where you are walking, wearing appropriate hiking clothing, and monitoring your fatigue and hydration levels. Prevention is always better than having to deal with an emergency in the outdoors.

HUNTING

Being prepared for a hunting trip is very similar to being prepared for a hiking trip. The exception to this is the fact that most hunting trips occur off trails and off the beaten path by choice. Hunters can be so focused on tracking and following prey that they forget to keep an eye on their surroundings and where they are in relation to their vehicle or campsite. Priorities when packing can be weapons and ammunition, and how they are going to break down and carry back an animal if they are successful, rather than planning for an emergency. I am always surprised at how few of my hunting friends carry a first aid kit or any survival items when they head out into the woods. Mixing weapons, the wilderness, and wounded animals always seems to me like the perfect time to be preparing for something unexpected.

There are over a thousand hunting accidents a year in the United States, and about a hundred of them are fatal. That is a high percentage of deaths to injuries. They are mostly attributed to hunters' lack of judgment, with faulty tree stands and poor firearm management being the top causes. I am not going to tell you how to be a better hunter in this section, but I am going to examine the safety issues and survival techniques relevant to hunters.

PREPARATION

It is important to anticipate any potential problems that may occur and make plans to deal with them. Before you head out on your hunting trip, you should:

- **Educate yourself about the game you are hunting and the environment where that game lives.** This will help you to understand the wilderness that you will be interacting with and enable you to wear the appropriate clothing and bring the right equipment.

- **Check the legalities of what you plan to do.** Aside from getting caught and charged for illegal activity, you want to make sure the area that you are in isn't filled with other recreational visitors that may get caught in your cross fire.

- **Wear appropriate clothing for the environment.** Just because it is camouflaged doesn't mean it is great for the outdoors. Make sure you aren't wearing anything made of cotton, and gauge what is best for the weather at that time of year. As a hunter, you may not want to wear sunscreen because of the smell, so make sure you are wearing lightweight long sleeves and a hat for sun protection if it is hot. In colder weather, employ a layering system that will allow you to take off layers as you travel and add layers when you are stationary.

  - **Base layer:** should be sweat wicking and breathable, and should help regulate body temperature

  - **Midweight layer:** something to keep you warm, such as an insulated jacket or fleece

  - **Outer layer:** a lightweight raincoat

- **Wear sturdy shoes.** You may be more focused on what is ahead of you than where you are putting your feet; you need to trust that your shoes will provide you with the support you need. Even if you are packing in light, you will hopefully be packing out heavy, so you'll need good foot support by the end of the trip.

- **Wear some kind of visible fluorescent marker to help hunters distinguish you from prey.** If you are doing a good job stealthily stalking your prey, chances are you will be invisible to any other hunters as well.

- **Do a reconnaissance trip.** Scope out the area that you plan to hunt in before you go out hunting. This will help you recognize features and know the terrain when your focus is elsewhere. It will also enable you to tag catchment features in your mind, identifying such things as when I hit that fence line, if I go left I will eventually get back to my car.

- **Make sure your weapons are well maintained and working properly.**

- **Take time to perfect your skills at a range before heading out on a hunt.** The more efficient you are at loading your weapon and hitting a target, the more successful your hunt will be.

- **If you are a beginner, seek guidance from experienced hunters on initial hunts.** There is a lot to think about when you head out on your first hunting trips. It can be overwhelming. Going with someone who knows the terrain and your quarry will allow you to focus on safe weapon management and hitting your prey, rather than all the other details that go into a successful hunt.

- **Get into shape.** Unless you are hunting in a blind or tree stand, spot and stalkers can end up walking many miles in a day through rugged terrain in pursuit of their quarry. It won't be until later in the day when you turn to head home that you realize how exhausted you have become. During a hunt, physical fitness can allow you to walk faster, breathe better, avoid exhaustion, and overall take a better shot when you have your prey in sight. Some conditions that may affect your hunt include:

  - Asthma
  - Allergies
  - Excess weight
  - Heart conditions
  - Impaired vision or hearing
  - Poor physical condition

  These aren't reasons not to hunt, but it may be necessary to modify plans to compensate.

- **Tell someone reliable your plans.** Let them know where you are going, whom you will be there with, and when you expect to be back. Let them know the directions to the route and alternate places you may go, and then do not deviate from that plan without letting someone know.

- **Check the weather before you go out.** Not only will it give you some indication of what your quarry might be doing, it will be a good indicator of what you should do. Avoid hunting on stormy days and on days with high fire risk.

If you are planning on a day hunt, your pack should include the following:

1. Navigation equipment—GPS plus hard copy of maps and a compass

2. Headlamp and spare batteries, even if you don't plan to be out at dark

3. Small first aid kit consisting of the following:

- Pressure bandages x 2
- A roller bandage
- A triangular bandage
- Gauze or cotton pads

- Strapping tape
- Band-Aids
- Antiseptic cream
- Pain relief

4. Knife—your field knife of choice

5. Lighter

6. Ferro rod

7. Whistle

8. At least half a gallon of water (drink a good amount before you hike and refill your bottles before you set off; being hydrated from the start puts you ahead of the game)

9. Meals plus extra snacks

10. Extra warm layers of clothing

11. Waterproof jacket

12. Emergency bivy bag or small tarp

13. Life straw or water purification tablets

14. Sun protection—hat and sunscreen

15. Phone and portable charger

As a hiker, you can get away with basic navigational skills if you are careful to follow the clearly marked trail. As a hunter, good navigational skills are an important asset. An experienced map reader can:

- Read terrain

- Determine direction

- Follow features

- Find your location in relation to your vehicle and camp

- Identify areas preferred by prey

If you are hunting in a group, it may be a good idea to delegate a navigator. Quite often it will be the goal for a certain person in the group to take the first shot on sighted animals. If this is the case, allow that hunter to focus on the hunt, and have another member of the group focus on the trail. It is also a good idea for all members of the hunting party to have a GPS on them in case anyone breaks off for a solo stalk. Try to keep an eye on terrain features as you stalk, so you have an idea how to backtrack once the hunt is over.

The weapons that are carried on a hunt are lethal. It is important that they are managed safely and proficiently:

- Always transport weapons and ammunition in appropriate carrying cases or holsters.

- Always keep the firearm muzzle pointed in a safe direction, even if you think it is empty and/or the safety is on.

- When moving in and out of tree stands or blinds, safely unload the firearm and have the safety on.

- Pass the firearm to someone else to hold when climbing through or over fences, or place it safely on the other side before scaling the obstacle if you are by yourself.

- Never shoot in the direction of another hunter.

When situating in a tree stand, make sure you inspect the stand to ensure that it is in good condition. Check to see if it is rusty or unstable and if you can attach to a secondary support or not. Most hunting accidents happen when a tree stand fails, so before you trust your weight to the platform, make sure you won't become a statistic by checking the stand.

If you are going on a multiday hunting trip, I would recommend bringing the following items:

- **A cooking system:** stove plus extra fuel, and a pot or large cup to cook in

- **Hydration:** half a gallon of water per day plus spare empty water bag

- **Water purification:** filter plus tablets

- **Sleeping bag (down is lighter but synthetic retains heat when wet)**

- **Sleeping mat**

- **Shelter:** tarp for ultralight, hammock in the right environment, or tent

- **Knife:** field knife plus multitool for the extra gadgets

- **Sharpening stone**

- **Headlamp plus extra batteries**

- **First aid kit:** expedition style rather than ultralight

- **Food plus an extra day's worth of meals**

- **Fire:** lighter, waterproof matches, and ferro rod

- **Trowel and toilet paper**

- **Navigation:** maps, compass, and GPS backup

- **Phone, phone charger, and small solar charger (phones die faster when it is cold or when they are continually going in and out of signal)**

- **Repair kit**
  - duct tape
  - paracord
  - cable ties
  - spare buckles
  - bandanna
  - plastic bags

- **Emergency shelter:** small tarp, emergency bivy bag, or space blanket

- **Signaling devices:** mirror and whistle

I would recommend the external frame pack for a hunting trip, as it allows you to strap extra weight on the frame while keeping it in a good position that will have the least impact on your body. It also means you can carry meat, skulls, and hides on the outside of your pack without getting bodily fluids on your camping gear.

When carrying out your kill, make sure that you:

- **Break it down into manageable loads.** The glory of carrying the whole kill on your back will be dampened by any strain injuries you incur while trying to do so.

- **Be aware of predators.** You now seem like an easy target to any predators who want to save the hassle of hunting an animal themselves. You will smell like blood and injured animal, and this will attract carnivores from miles around. Be cautious when returning to your stash, if you have decided to pack the animal out in multiple trips.

- **Carry your basic survival kit on every lap in and out with the meat.** Being tired at the end of a hunt can result in a lack of focus, and this is when you are more likely to lose the trail or become injured.

Consider learning some survival skills before you head off on your next hunt. Being able to confidently make good choices in the wilderness will always lead to a more positive experience.

8.2.2

POSSIBLE SCENARIOS

8.2.2.1

GETTING LOST

A hunter is more likely to get lost than your average hiker, due to the fact that they are rarely following clearly marked trails or in areas with a good infrastructure. They are also focused on something other than a set route or the path they are being led down following game signs. However, the response to being lost is the same, no matter who you are and why you are out there.

The steps are as follows:

STOP

The most important thing to do the second you realize you are lost is to stop moving. Think about the direction you came from. If you can retrace your steps to your last known point, do so. If you are not sure which direction this might be in, stay where you are. Your best chance of being rescued is by staying where you first are when you realize you are lost.

ASSESS

The only reasons to leave this area would be if it is dangerous to stay or if you can't meet your basic needs. If you have materials for a shelter, a way to keep warm, and enough food and water for a few days, it is time to get comfortable.

TAKE ACTION

Once you have decided to stay in place, if you have access to your phone service, call 911 to let them know you need help. If you have an emergency beacon, set it off.

If you came prepared, you should have a whistle in your pack. Blow in short, sharp bursts to attract attention.

Hopefully you were with a group of people who will miss you, or you left a trip plan with an emergency contact. In these cases, your chance of a quick rescue increases. See how you can make your position visible by tying brightly colored objects to tree branches and bushes, and make as much noise as you can. If you came prepared, you should have a whistle in your pack. Blow in short, sharp bursts to attract attention. Listen after each round of three whistles to hear if someone has heard you. I don't encourage yelling unless you hear someone calling out for you. Save your voice until rescuers get within earshot.

Don't wait until it gets dark to make a shelter or fire. Begin to gather materials after you have planned to stay. Being proactive and keeping busy will help to stave off panic.

LONG TERM

If you haven't been rescued after a few days, assess your ability to stay in the location you are in. Do you have a good drinkable water source? Will your shelter protect you from all weather? Have you gotten a fire going? Is there a food source that you can access? If you can keep meeting all your basic needs, stay in that location. If you cannot, it may be time to move to a better location. If you do move on, make sure you leave a note, indicate the direction you are headed, and mark an obvious path so rescuers can track you if they find your initial camp.

A successful rescue happens sooner if you have left a plan with someone reliable and have come prepared with some basic equipment.

ANIMAL ATTACK

Any time you venture into the wild, you are removing yourself from a controlled environment and entering into a realm where it is hard to predict the behavior of the animals you might encounter. This is even more relevant when you are actually seeking out interactions with animals, and when encounters with these animals can lead to blood in the air and the echoing calls of wounded animals. If you aren't efficient with your hunting, you could also be faced with wounded and terrified animals fighting for their lives. It is important to remember that very few animals will attack a human except in self-defense.

If you are confronted by a wild animal:

- Avoid eye contact.

- Freeze; if they aren't charging you, don't run.

- Slowly back away.

- Avoid sudden movements.

- If an animal charges, dodge out of the way; you could be blocking their escape route.

- If the animal attacks, shout, make a loud noise, and try to make yourself look bigger; drop whatever you are carrying, as it may distract them; zigzag run away from them, if you run; climb a tree, if a big enough one is available.

Educate yourself about the predators that live in the region you are visiting. A little knowledge goes a long way and can prevent a dangerous confrontation. Learn what the predators look like, their common behaviors, how to avoid them, and the best way to deter an attack. In the unlikely event of such an incident, your immediate response to the situation will determine the outcome.

The first tactic when confronted with most predators is to stay still and use the stop-look-and-listen approach. (The exceptions are crocodiles and alligators, which don't tend to chase their prey on land; run away from them.) This communicates to the animal that you are not a threat and are not one of their normal prey species, which flee on sight of the predator. Often, this will mean the animal will move on. However, if they don't, there are other tactics you can use to deter an attack. They are different for all large predators. Some quick examples are:

- **Make noise to scare away a black bear, but play dead to deter a grizzly attack.**

- **Act loud and scary to prevent a mountain lion attack.**

- **Dodge out of the way at the last minute from a rhino attack, and then stand still; they aren't very agile, have trouble with quick direction changes, and have very bad eyesight, so they may never find you again.**

- **Stand as tall as you can to make yourself appear as big as possible if confronted by an aggressive dog; this should intimidate the animal.**

You should always try to keep your distance from potential predators unless you are hunting them. Respect the fact that you are intruding into their natural environment, where they act according to their instinctive behaviors. The vast majority of wild animals will avoid confrontation unless threatened or cornered. But in case the worst happens, learn the difference between each tactic. It could save your life.

If you are attacked and injured but the animal has appeared to leave the area, administer first aid and make your way to safety as soon as possible. Some animals may leave but then come back to finish the job, so it is important that you make your way to help as quickly and safely as possible.

INJURED HUNTER

The most important thing to do as soon as an injury has occurred is to assess the danger. If the injury is to yourself and you are still in danger of more injury, remove yourself from that position if possible. If the injury is to a fellow hunter, assess the danger to yourself before you rush in to help, and the danger to them if they stay where they are. If you can assist your fellow hunter without any danger to you, do so and move on to assessing the injury and administering first aid.

In a hunting scenario, you may only have a second to analyze the situation if the danger is from a wounded or wild animal attack. How you respond will be up to you and your perception of your ability to deter the attack. If you have a weapon at hand and feel confident you can make a difference by stepping into the scenario, then that choice is yours. If stepping into the scenario will result in you both becoming injured, it is best to try to deter the attack from afar and prepare to administer first aid as soon as possible.

As most hunting accidents involve blunt force trauma from falls out of unsafe tree stands, deadly bleeds from firearm incidents, or fatigue-related accidents, these are the wilderness first aid scenarios I will cover in this section. For more wilderness first aid knowledge, check out the full section on wilderness first aid (see page 548). The knowledge here is an abbreviated version of what you would learn in a first aid course. I highly recommend getting professional training before venturing into the outdoors.

BLUNT FORCE TRAUMA

There is a significant difference in the type of injury acquired in a fall from a tree stand, depending on the height of the fall and type of landing. Most often falls from a height in wilderness areas result in soft tissue injuries, such as sprains and strains. If the fall was from a significant height or onto a hard surface, always suspect a spinal injury and treat it as such until the possibility can be ruled out. If the person has hit their head, treat them for a spinal injury until the possibility can be ruled out.

As soon as the accident happens, assess the potential for further injury. Has the victim fallen to the ground? Are they suspended in the air? Is anything going to fall down on you from the tree stand? Do not rush into danger. Once you have established that there is no danger to you, remove the victim from danger. If they are suspended, work to get them safely to the ground before administering first aid.

If the victim is on the ground, assess their level of consciousness by asking questions. If they are unconscious, you will need to establish if they are breathing or not. If they are not breathing, send for help or call for help and commence CPR. If they are breathing but not conscious, turn them on their side, being careful to keep their spine straight. If they are conscious, you can begin to ask them questions to assess the seriousness of their condition.

SPINAL INJURY

Be aware that immediately after an accident, a victim may be flooded with adrenaline, which may mask symptoms of whatever injury they have sustained. I love this adrenaline because it enables me to finish whatever task I'm trying to complete before dealing with the injury, but it can also mean that you may miss serious conditions in your first aid assessment.

If they have an obvious head injury, immobilize them, paying attention to keeping the spine in a neutral position. Spinal injuries can present symptoms such as:

- **Extreme back pain or pressure in the head, neck, or back**
- **Weakness or paralysis in any part of the body**
- **Numbness, tingling, or loss of sensation in extremities**
- **Loss of bladder or bowel control**

Do not attempt to move someone who is displaying any of these symptoms. Call 911 if you have service, or set off your emergency beacon. If you cannot reach anyone, make the victim as comfortable as possible and have someone head out to where they can contact emergency services. If you are the victim and you are alone, do not attempt to make your way out, as you have the potential to cause permanent damage. Try not to panic, make yourself as visible as possible, and wait for rescue.

CONCUSSION

This is another serious injury caused by blunt force trauma. There is a mistaken idea that concussions only happen with a direct head hit, but landing on your feet from a high fall can also jar your cranium and result in a concussion. Signs and symptoms to look for include:

- **Confusion**
- **Headache**
- **Lack of coordination**
- **Memory loss**
- **Nausea**

- **Vomiting**
- **Dizziness**
- **Ringing in the ears**
- **Sleepiness**
- **Excessive fatigue**

The decision to self-evacuate or wait for rescue will depend on the severity of these symptoms. Usually, the treatment for a concussion is absolute rest from any physical or mental stimulation until signs and symptoms reside. You will need to assess how far you need to walk to get to safety, what the terrain is like, the time of day, and weather conditions. If you decide to evacuate, make sure you allow for the fact that the person's balance and coordination may be compromised, and carry their pack and support them through rough terrain. If you decide to stay put, make sure you wake the concussed person every few hours to assess their level of consciousness. If it is deteriorating, call emergency services and evacuate immediately.

BROKEN BONE

It may be hard to tell the difference between a sprained ankle and a broken one. Some things to look for will be deformities, numbness, and whether the victim heard a cracking noise when the injury occurred. Sprains will usually be associated with a popping noise. Depending on which bone is broken, the victim may be able to walk out unaided, or will not be able to support their weight at all. If the victim is unable to put weight on the injured limb, take the weight off, apply a compression bandage, and have them rest in the position most comfortable to them. If you have cold water available, soak a bandanna in the water and cover the injured area with a cooling compress.

TWISTED ANKLE

This can range from a slight twist, easily walked off, to more extreme tendon and ligament damage. Assess the severity of the sprain. If you are not far from your exit and the person is able to put weight on the ankle, do not remove the boot. It is acting as a compression bandage and providing support to the injury. Provide some support in the form of a walking stick or shoulder to lean on, and slowly make your way to safety. If the victim is unable to put weight on the injured foot, take the weight off, remove the boot, apply a compression bandage, and have them rest with their foot elevated. If you have cold water available, soak a bandanna in the water and cover the foot with a cooling compress.

DEADLY BLEEDS

These are wounds where the blood is pumping from the wound, the bleeding doesn't slow down or stop with pressure, and/or the blood is quickly soaking through the bandage. Deadly bleeds can be internal or external, but the ones most often associated with hunting will be external bleeding. For all deadly bleeds, immediate evacuation and medical assistance will be required. Treat the wound first before dialing emergency services, if it is just you or one other person.

Assign someone else to dial or head out for help immediately if you are in a group.

If the projectile is still in the body, do not attempt to remove in the field. If it is an arrow, immobilize it in place with a bandage so it doesn't move around and create further damage internally. Removing projectiles in the field could open up arteries, and the victim can bleed out in minutes.

On the surface: If the wound is superficial (mainly on the surface of the body), treat it as you would any other puncture wound and apply pressure, dress the wound, and apply a bandage.

Wounded limb: If the wound is deep and to a limb, apply pressure, elevate the area above the heart, and cover it with a circulation bandage, making sure that it is firm but not tight enough to cut off pressure to the extremities. You want a firm bandage but not a tourniquet. If the wound bleeds through the dressing, do not remove the initial dressing; simply apply another layer of absorbent material and another bandage.

Abdominal wound: If the wound is in the abdomen, and there are no internal organs visible, treat it as above. If there are internal organs visible or protruding, **do not try to stuff them back in the cavity**. Cover the wound with a moist, sterile dressing and bandage it firmly. Make the victim comfortable, but do not give them anything to eat or drink.

Chest wound: If the wound is in the chest and a wheezing noise can be heard through the wound, assume that a lung has been punctured. Cover the hole with a dressing to create a pressure seal. This can be a resealable plastic bag or something similar. Tape around three edges of the square, allowing one side to remain free. Immobilize until help can arrive.

TOURNIQUET

Unless a limb has been completely shattered or torn off, or the femoral artery (the main one in your leg) has been compromised, try to avoid applying a tourniquet. A tourniquet is a last resort, as it will probably result in the loss of a limb once applied in the field. If your choice is to lose a life or lose a limb, apply a tourniquet and do not take it off. A tourniquet is a bandage that restricts all blood flow to a body part. Write the time and date that you applied it. The only person who should remove a tourniquet is a medical professional, once the person has made it to a medical facility.

FATIGUE

Signs and symptoms of fatigue include:

- Headache
- Dizziness
- Sore or aching muscles
- Slowed reflexes and responses

- Tripping often
- Impaired decision making and judgment
- Moodiness and irritability

These are all things that can cause accidents or injuries out on a hunt. If you recognize any of these symptoms in yourself or others, slow down, take a rest, drink water, have something to eat, and move cautiously when you continue.

If you are injured and alone, you will need to assess your ability to become mobile. What will it take for you to get to safety, and are you capable of doing that? Can you make an emergency call? If you are unable to move and are out of service, do what you can to treat your injury. Make yourself as comfortable as possible and visible to any passersby or potential rescuers.

8.2.3

ENSURING RESCUE

Before heading out, always make sure to tell a responsible person about your plans. This will ensure that an alarm is raised quickly, and the rescue will be directed to the right location.

Your rescue is likely to come from a few different sources: by air, land vehicle, or foot. You will need to prepare something visible for all the scenarios. Even if you think that you will hear someone who passes by you on foot, you may be sleeping or out collecting water, and they need to know you are around. Generally, you will have about two minutes from the time you hear an aircraft to the time it is out of range, so any signaling needs to be thought out beforehand and ready to go.

Things that will make you more visible to rescuers include:

- **Bright colors:** Hang items on trees or place them in the middle of clearings.

- **Reflective surfaces:** Tie your signal mirror to a tepee structure to blow in the breeze, or use any reflective garbage you can find.

- **Straight lines and arrows:** Try to use contrasting colors to the ground and point toward your location.

- **Words on the ground:** SOS is the worldwide signal for distress.

- **Thick smoke:** Green leaves on a fire create thick, visible smoke during the day.

- **Bright flames:** Use dry wood to create a bright fire at night.

- **Torch trees:** Build a fire in a tree and light it when a rescue vehicle is sighted.

- **Lights in the dark:** Use a flashlight amplified by a shiny surface or signal mirror to attract attention.

Your signals should be clear and well thought out. When thinking about where to locate them, keep in mind the specific terrain. The signals need to be easily accessible for you and on high spots or ridgelines, or in clearings.

Regardless of the potential for a whole range of variables to become emergency scenarios, hunting can be a safe and enjoyable pastime, with a little preparation and education prior to heading out.

BOATING

This chapter is not designed to teach you how to captain a boat or sail a ship. There are courses and other books designed for that. This chapter is intended to look at how best you can prepare for your boating experience to prevent accidents from happening, and what to do if you end up in a worst-case scenario. As this falls under the outdoor recreation section, there is going to be an assumption that the boat you are in is a personal-use vessel rather than a cruise ship, where there are people in charge of your safety and the emergency equipment.

The majority of boating accidents can be avoided by proper preparation and safe operation of the vessel. Since alcohol consumption is responsible for over 23 percent of fatalities in the boating world, it would seem that simply choosing not to drink excessively while operating a boat would prevent over two hundred deaths per year in the United States alone.

Other leading causes of boating accidents include:

- **Operator distraction**
- **Improper lookout**
- **Operator inexperience**
- **Excessive speed**

Drowning is the leading cause of death in boating accidents worldwide, with the majority of those fatalities being people who were not wearing a life jacket. This means that most of these fatalities could have been prevented by wearing a life jacket and not drinking.

Research has also been done to suggest that taking a boater safety course before heading out on the water reduces accidents by 80 percent.

8.3.1

PREPARATION

A day on the river or lake is a little different from heading out in the ocean, but in order to properly prepare for any boating experience, you should:

- **Ensure that your vehicle is well maintained; get it serviced regularly, and have any issues repaired as soon as they are noticed.**

- **Double-check that the bung is in prior to launching; this is the leading cause of boats sinking and can happen to experienced sailors and novices alike.**

- **Check the fuel and oil levels; make sure to bring spare fuel with you.**

- **Check propellers and running gear.**

- **Make sure lights, horns, and pumps are working.**

- **Check all electronics.**

- **Check safety gear, including:**

  - Life jackets for everyone on board
  - A working fire extinguisher
  - Fully stocked first aid kit in a dry bag
  - Functional flares
  - A working sound signal
  - All appropriate documentation in a waterproof bag
  - Binoculars
  - Anchor with sufficient rope or chain
  - A bailing device
  - Extra mooring lines or fenders
  - A boat hook or pole

If you are heading out in the ocean, even if for a little offshore fishing, you should assemble a "ditch bag." This is a go bag designed for marine environments. Your ditch bag is as personal as your go bag. I have recommendations for what you should have in it, but it's important that you fill it according to your boat and the possible emergency situation, taking into account the location and time of year. As with every go bag, you should have your basic needs covered with shelter, water, food, and fire. A ditch bag will also include items for dealing with being adrift on the ocean and requiring rescue. It should be in a waterproof bag and stowed securely above deck where you can get to it without having to reenter your vessel. I recommend having it next to your EPIRB (Emergency Position Indicating Radio Beacon) device, so you can set off the beacon and grab the bag at the same time. Items for your ditch bag should include:

- A waterproof VHF radio
- A waterproof GPS
- Compass and charts
- Flashlight
- Spare batteries
- Marine whistle
- Signal mirror
- Flares and/or a strobe light
- Sea dye marker that marks your location for up to three hours
- Nylon cord
- Duct tape
- Emergency blanket
- Small tarp
- Plastic bags
- Weatherproof lighter
- Ferro rod
- Water filter
- Water purification tablets
- Three days' worth of emergency rations and water
- Thermal top and bottom and warm hat
- Bandanna
- First aid kit
- Spare prescription meds
- Sunglasses
- Sunscreen
- Field knife
- Multitool
- Fishing kit: hooks, lines, sinkers
- Photocopies of important documents in a waterproof bag
- Cash

If you are going on a long-haul trip, you should also ensure that you have:

- **EPIRB (Emergency Position Indicating Radio Beacon)**

- **Life raft**

- **Man overboard recovery system**

- **Radar**

- **NOAA radio for accurate weather updates**

The life raft should be sturdy, brightly colored, and stocked for any emergency. It should have:

- **A durable canopy**

- **An external light**

- **A food-and-water dry bag containing**
  - Fishing gear
  - Fishing net
  - Long-life food
  - Bottled water

- **A shelter dry bag containing**
  - Ponchos
  - Emergency blankets
  - Sunscreen
  - Sunglasses
  - Thermal layers

Prior to leaving your initial location, it is important that you pick a destination, plan your route, and check the weather. Let someone reliable know where you are going and when you intend to be back. Once you are on board your vessel, it is important to familiarize everyone on the trip with emergency safety procedures, in case you are the one who falls overboard or has a first aid situation. Things to let passengers know are:

- **How to put on a life jacket and where they are located**
- **Location and operation of fire extinguishers**
- **Location of first aid kit**

- **Docking and anchoring procedures**
- **Garbage handling and sanitation**
- **Safety rules particular to your boat**

As well as boating accidents, there are common scenarios that lead to boaters requiring a rescue. These are all 100 percent preventable and include:

- **Running out of gas**
- **Running aground**
- **Falling overboard**
- **Sinking due to bung not being inserted or the bilge pump not working**
- **Catching on fire**

- **Breaking down**
- **Lacking proper safety gear**
- **Speeding at night**
- **Ignoring weather reports**
- **Failing to maintain a lookout**

The consequences of poor preparation when boating can be disastrous. There is not a lot of room for error when you are venturing out into the open ocean, relying on your vessel to keep you safe. Proper maintenance and safety checks prior to leaving, and being focused and conscious of your responsibility to those on board when on your journey, can prevent almost all fatalities or required rescues.

POSSIBLE SCENARIOS

MAN OVERBOARD

If you go overboard, your best chance of rescue is in the immediate few seconds after hitting the water. Try your best to attract attention. Shout, splash, and wave one hand over your head. If no one has noticed and your boat moves out of sight, it is important for you to conserve energy, so relax and assess your situation. Is land in sight? If so, can you slowly make your way toward it? If not, what is around you? If there is anything buoyant floating by, grab hold of it. If you are wearing pants, take them off and tie the bottoms of the legs in knots. Lift the waistband out of the water, and fling it forward before submerging to fill them with air. Whatever air you managed to trap will flood up the leg sections and get trapped at the knots, providing you with a makeshift floatation device. This works best before you are fully in the water, but anything you can do to remain a little buoyant will conserve energy. If you know the best direction to head to be rescued, float on your back and slowly kick toward that direction. If you are unsure of a direction to go, just float and save your energy for attracting the attention of a rescue party.

Try your best to attract attention. Shout, splash, and wave one hand over your head.

If you are wearing pants, take them off and tie the bottoms of the legs in knots.

Lift the waistband out of the water, and fling it forward before submerging to fill them with air.

Whatever air you managed to trap will flood up the leg sections and get trapped at the knots, providing you with a makeshift floatation device.

CAPSIZE

The average time at sea to get rescued after a Mayday call is sent out is about four and a half hours. It is important to have a plan in place in case you capsize, so that you can survive this length of time in potentially freezing water. It takes only twenty minutes in water 45°F or less for a person to succumb to extreme hypothermia, but even water temperatures upward of 75°F can lead to someone becoming hypothermic.

If your vessel is sinking, set off the EPIRB or personal emergency beacon and locate your ditch bag. Put on warm clothing layers if you can easily access them. These extra layers will not drag you down as it can be suggested; rather air gets trapped in the clothing layers and helps combat the extra weight with extra buoyancy. They will also help maintain your body heat. Make sure you are wearing your life jacket, and locate any buoyant objects you can find.

Do not panic, and stay with your vessel until it goes completely underwater. Quite often there will be a pocket of water in the boat that will mean it doesn't completely sink, and this could provide you with a life raft until rescue arrives.

The exception to this is if you are in a large ship or superyacht. As large ships sink, they create a suction vacuum that can pull you under the water with them. If you are in one of these vessels, throw something into the water that floats and jump off close to it. Grab your floatation device, and swim away from the sinking vessel. These boats should be equipped with life rafts, so as soon as the boat has sunk well below the surface, locate and make your way to the nearest life raft.

If your sinking boat is equipped with a life raft, deploy the life raft and relocate safely before your boat has become flooded.

If you don't have a life raft and your boat has sunk completely, use whatever buoyant items you have managed to gather to get as much of your body out of the water as possible. Tie the items together to create a raft if possible. Being able to get out of the water a little will stave off hypothermia.

If you haven't managed to send out an emergency alert, this will be your priority. Hopefully you have some method of communication that is waterproof and working.

If your boat has caught on fire, try to extinguish it if the fire is small. If the fire has gotten out of control, jump into the water upwind of the fire and swim into the wind. Fuel sitting on the water can burn, resulting in the water around you being on fire. If this is the case, try to dive underneath the flames and surface in an area that isn't alight. You can also try to push the flaming fuel away from you by splashing the flames. It is important to move away from the vessel, as it may explode. Diving underwater will help protect you from projectiles if the boat explodes, but be wary of what is above you when you resurface.

ADRIFT

Your boat or vessel may still be afloat, or it may have sunk and you are now in a lifeboat or makeshift raft. Being adrift means you are now no longer able to direct your craft or are unsure which direction to go. The ocean is one of the most extreme survival environments to find yourself in, as resources are scarce if you have no way to harvest them, and reliable drinking water is a commodity. Depending on your craft and its condition, you may be exposed to elements that could result in death in less than twenty-four hours.

If you have managed to send out a distress signal, it is best to maintain your position if possible, unless you can see land. If you are afloat in any kind of craft, you can do this by making a sea anchor. Some boats are equipped with them already, but if you don't have one, the theory is to attach something that will apply drag to the bow of your boat or raft. This could be a piece of plastic or canvas attached in such a way that it parachutes out in the water and creates drag, slowing your craft and keeping it closer to where your boat sank.

If you are within sight of land, begin to head toward it however you can. This may be by paddling or creating a makeshift sail. If the tide is going out, don't try to fight against it. You may need to wait until the tide is going in to float to land.

If you cannot see land, take a moment to assess your situation before acting. If you do not know where you are or where to head toward to best attract a rescue, allow the ocean currents to carry you along, saving your energy for more useful tasks.

Take stock of the resources you have. If you are on your boat still, you should have access to everything you need to survive until rescued. If you are in a life raft or on a makeshift raft, you will need to immediately begin to ration your supplies and see to your basic needs.

SHELTER

If you are partially submerged or have been in the water, it is important to dry your clothes off as soon as possible. If you are in a warmer climate, the sun may do this for you. If you are not, take off your clothes, wring out as much water as you can, and put them back on again. Try to maintain body heat by wrapping up in any materials available or huddling together for warmth if there is a group of you. Extreme hypothermia can kill in under three hours if you are wet and the wind is blowing, even in warmer climates, so try to rig up a windbreak or locate to a position where you are out of the wind. This windbreak can also act as a roof and collect drinking water if it rains, and provide shade from the sun if it is scorching hot.

If it is hot, take off all unnecessary clothing, but keep your body covered or in the shade. You will be trying to keep cool and prevent unnecessary moisture loss. Remaining inactive during the heat of the day will help with this. If you cannot construct any type of shade, try to keep your head and neck covered to avoid sunstroke. During the day, dampen any clothing with seawater to keep cool, making sure it has time to dry before dark. If you get in the water to cool off, tie the raft to yourself before you get in and make sure you can get back on your raft. A larger object can get caught in the current and be swept away from you faster than you can swim to keep up with it.

You will also need to protect your eyes from sun blindness. This happens when the reflection of sun off the water burns your corneas and results in sore eyes and temporary blindness. Wearing sunglasses will help prevent this. If you do not have sunglasses, wearing a hat or creating some kind of eye cover with slits in it to reduce the glare hitting your eyes will also help.

WATER

Water will be your next priority. Ration what you have until such time as you are rescued or find a reliable source. If you have managed to bring your ditch bag with you, it should be stocked with three days' worth of drinking water to allow for plenty of time to be rescued. Do not take this for granted, though, and immediately begin to put plans in place to collect water if it rains. Collect all containers, plastic bags, and waterproof coverings, such as tarps or canvases. Place them in such a way to allow the maximum water to pool in them, while also protecting you from the weather. If the inside of your boat is dry and relatively salt free, you could also drink the water that pools in the bottom of the boat. Never under any circumstances drink salt water. Your kidneys are unable to deal with the amount of salt in the water and will shut down. There is some moisture in fish eyes, so make sure you eat them if you have managed to catch a fish, but it is not a lot, and the protein in the flesh of the fish requires more water to digest than is available in the eyes, so only eat the fish if you also have access to other water.

If you have access to a plastic water bottle and a soft drink can, you can make a small portable saltwater still. Cut the bottom off the water bottle and the top off the can. Fold the bottom sides of the water bottle up into itself to create a gutter to catch the desalinated water. Fill the can with salt water, and place it inside the water bottle. Make sure the lid is on the water bottle, and place your still in the full sun. The water will evaporate from the can in the heat and re-form on the inside of the water bottle, sliding down the sides to be caught in the gutter. This method takes time and sunny weather, so make sure you set this up way before dehydration sets in, and if possible, make multiple setups. It will not make a lot at a time, but it may make enough to keep you alive.

Saltwater Still

FOOD

The main food source when you are adrift will be whatever you can get from the ocean. Hopefully you will have fishing tackle in your emergency kit, but if you don't, improvise a hook out of any piece of metal you may have in your raft. The inside filament of paracord can provide a fine fishing line, as can floss, if you have access to either of these things.

Seaweed is edible, and there are some types of seaweed that float on the surface of the water. These weeds can sometimes be filled with a variety of small sea critters hitching a ride, so make sure you pull the weed onto your raft and shake it to see what other food sources you can find. You may be able to coax seabirds to land on your raft by luring them with bait such as fish guts. Snaring them or winging them will provide you with a bigger meal. Even if you have food in your emergency kit, start trying to get fresh food straightaway, as it may take some time to catch something.

SHARKS

A majority of shark attacks happen close to shore or near areas with nearby deep drop-offs, such as sandbars and reefs. This is because these areas are close to where their prey is often located. Avoid getting into water that is not clear enough for you to see what is around you, and don't fish when you see sharks in the area.

If you are in the water and you can see a shark near you, don't panic. Rapid movements in water can mimic a fish in distress and attract their attention. Watch how the shark is moving. If their movements are sharp and rapid, they are in hunting mode. If they are slow and relaxed, then they are merely coming by for a look. Keep facing the direction of the shark so you can see them. If the shark approaches you calmly, push the shark's snout away from you. If the shark approaches menacingly, try to punch or kick at the snout, avoiding the mouth and teeth. If you have a paddle or stick, put it between you and the shark and try to push it away. If the shark has you in its jaws, punch at its snout or try to gouge its eyes to get away. Get out of the water as soon as possible if you have encountered a shark.

RESCUE

Hopefully, you have been able to trigger an alarm, whether it is from a personal beacon, a Mayday signal, or missing a return deadline, and someone has sent help. Have your emergency signal equipment ready to go, as you may have only two minutes from the time you see a plane to attract its attention. Don't set off flares or dyes until you sight a rescue vehicle. It can be very difficult to spot a small object floating on a big body of water, so think about how you can be as visible as possible. Movement, reflection, and color are going to catch the eye of rescuers.

If you are with a group of people, always assign watches. You need to keep an eye out for rescue, land, ships, or resources.

Even if you can't see land, there are some indicators that land may be nearby. They include:

- **Cumulus clouds on the horizon, with an otherwise clear sky.**

- **The direction birds fly in the afternoon; some seabirds sleep on the ocean, but a majority of them fly back to land for the evening.**

- **The continuous sound of bird calls, which indicates nesting sites on land.**

- **Driftwood; although driftwood can be found out at sea, it tends to gather closer to shorelines.**

- **Muddy- and murky-looking ocean water; this could indicate a river mouth nearby.**

Always try to head toward land if you can. Be aware of what type of coastline you encounter. Rocky shores with wild waves can be dangerous to land on. Try to locate a gently sloping beach with quiet waves. It will be easier to make landfall on the ingoing tide. If possible, bring your craft onto land with you, as it will enable you to have some resources with which to create camp. At the very least, take your ditch bag if you abandon ship to try to swim in. If the waves are rough and you can't see what is under the surface, keep your feet in front of you and your knees bent to push off objects under the water.

INJURED BOATER

As mentioned before, 86 percent of boating fatalities are a result of drowning. Doing a first aid course is one of the most valuable skills to learn before heading out in a boat with passengers on board. Even a single-day CPR course could save a loved one's life. Read the following advice, but know that in the heat of the moment, practicing and learning the information in a professionally taught session will leave you better prepared for dealing with it in real life.

A single-day CPR course could save a loved one's life.

DROWNING VICTIM

If you come across someone who is drowning, get the person out of the water if you can do so safely without compromising yourself or others. If they are unconscious, place them on their side, with their top leg bent forward and their top arm at a right angle to their body to help maintain the position. Their head should be tilting toward the ground to allow their tongue to remain clear of their airway and any fluids in their throat to drain out. This is called the recovery position. If you are able to delegate someone to contact emergency services, do so. If you are alone, call emergency services or send out a Mayday signal and then check to see whether the victim's airway is clear. If there is an obstruction, clear the obstruction, then place your hand on their chest to see if you can feel their chest rise and fall, or the back of your hand by their mouth to see if you can feel a rush of air. If they are not breathing, turn the person on their back and begin to do chest compressions. There are different suggestions for how many pushes to do,

If they are unconscious, place them on their side, with their top leg bent forward and their top arm at a right angle to their body to help maintain the position.

Check to see if their airway is clear.

Place your hand on their chest to see if you can feel their chest rise and fall.

but at the end of the day, as long as you are doing any at all, it is better than none. You should be aiming to compress the chest by a third. This is quite a solid push on an adult and less on a teenager and child. Use both hands for an adult and large teen, and one hand for a younger teen and child. You should be aiming at doing about a hundred thrusts in a minute. Famously, and ironically, the song beat that works for the chest compressions is "Stay-in' Alive" by the Bee Gees, if that helps you get a rhythm.

In these times of airborne viruses, medical professionals are leaving it up to you as to whether you want to do assisted breathing or not. Chest compressions will also move the lungs of the victim enough to get some oxygen circulating to the brain. If you know the victim and feel confident about their health status, pinch the victim's nostrils, tilt their head back slightly, and deliver two long, slow breaths into their mouth for every thirty chest compressions. Continue to do so until the victim starts breathing or medical help arrives.

Being a wilderness first aid scenario, it may be some time before medical help arrives. Continue to administer CPR until the victim starts breathing or until it compromises your health and safety.

Once the victim is breathing, place them into the recovery position and continue to monitor them. If they stop breathing again, place them on their back and commence CPR. If they recover, get them comfortable and look at evacuating. Seek medical help as soon as possible, as water in the lungs may lead to respiratory conditions even if the victim seems fine.

HYPOTHERMIA

This is a condition that occurs when the body loses heat faster than it can produce it. It is better to prevent hypothermia than to try to cure it in the field, so always begin to try to rewarm when you start to feel cold.

Signs and symptoms of hypothermia include:

- **Shivering**
- **Slurred speech or mumbling**
- **Slow, shallow breathing**
- **Weak pulse**
- **Clumsiness or lack of coordination**
- **Drowsiness**
- **Confusion**
- **Loss of consciousness**

Someone with hypothermia usually isn't aware of their condition, as it comes on gradually. Eventually it can lead to risk-taking behavior and a feeling of euphoria. Quite often people who have died of cold exposure are found naked, as they begin to feel overheated and take off all their clothes in the final stages of the condition.

When you start to feel cold, add layers or remove damp clothing and replace them with dry. Move around, and seek shelter and warmth. Do not attempt to warm hypothermia victims quickly, as this will lead to cold blood in the extremities rushing to the core and dropping the core temperature dangerously. Warm drinks and a hot water bottle on top of a layer of clothing by their core will help. Avoid alcohol, caffeine, and tobacco. It is not recommended to strip off and join them, because this may lead to two cold people instead of two warm people, but if you are having trouble warming them, keep your warm layers on and get close.

EXTREME WEATHER

With today's access to accurate and up-to-date weather forecasting, there should be no reason for a boating enthusiast to be caught out in a storm. If in doubt, stay home. If you are hit with a storm out of the blue, there are three classic storm strategies:

1. **Run for cover. Only head toward land if you are sure that you will make cover before the storm hits. Waves and submerged objects can make for treacherous waters close to land if you have misjudged your timing and get caught out.**

2. **Keep away from land. Head out to sea and take your chances with the open ocean. This is a better scenario than trying to run close to land if time is tight.**

3. **Sail (or drive) away from the path of the storm. See if you can get around it or make it to the edges where the storm front may not be as severe.**

Make sure if a storm picks up that you:

- **Put on life jackets (if they are not already on)**

- **Take note of emergency equipment**

- **Call the coast guard and tell them where you are and why you are concerned**

ENSURING RESCUE

A rogue wave can swamp a boat in the blink of an eye. What you have on you or close at hand can be the difference between drifting at sea for days or being picked up by the coast guard in hours. Some things that can help speed this along are to:

1. **Make sure you tell someone where you are going and what time you intend to return.**

2. **Have your boating emergency kit attached on deck and close to an EPIRB or personal location beacon.**

3. **Have a fully-stocked life raft, on larger vessels**

4. **Wear a life jacket.**

5. **Send out a Mayday signal as soon as it looks like you are in trouble.**

6. **Have methods of communication in a waterproof bag.**

7. **Stay with the boat until the boat sinks completely.**

8. **Be as visible as possible. Use flares and sea dye markers when a rescue vehicle is spotted, not before when they may not attract attention. Reflect any shiny object off the sun toward ships, planes, or the shore.**

9. **Wave brightly colored material in the air, which will catch the eye of a potential rescuer.**

Boating can be an extremely safe and enjoyable pastime, with a little bit of preparation and responsible safe practices. Know the weather, wear a life jacket, pack an emergency bag, and limit alcohol consumption until you are back in a safe harbor, and this will help prevent almost all emergency boating scenarios.

Send out a Mayday signal as soon as it looks like you are in trouble.

Wear a life jacket.

Use flares and sea dye markers when a rescue vehicle is spotted, not before when they may not attract attention.

BACKCOUNTRY SKIING

Regardless of whether you hike, snowshoe, skin, ride a lift, or take a helicopter there, any time you are outside of the maintained boundaries of a resort, you are in the backcountry, and you need to make sure you are properly equipped to deal with it. In the backcountry, you lose the added bonuses of medically qualified ski patrollers, quick-response medevac, and avalanche-controlled slopes that come with a well-run mountain. Sporting enthusiasts heading into the backcountry are usually seeking untracked snow and challenging terrain, but if you head out often enough, it's not a question of if you will encounter an avalanche, but when and how big. Sixty-nine percent of deaths in the alpine backcountry are caused by avalanche, with cardiac arrest coming in second.

Carrying an avalanche beacon, show shovel, and probe into the backcountry with you is not enough; you must be trained on how to use them with no hesitation when minutes make the difference between life and death. Knowledge of the mountains and snow conditions is vital as you break tracks and choose your trail. Although most backcountry skiing trips are day trips, it is easy to lose your way in terrain that can change its appearance overnight. A wrong turn could have you in a deep gully or dead end on a cliff edge, requiring extra time to find your way back on track. Always head out for the day with an emergency survival kit that can keep you alive through a night in freezing conditions.

AVALANCHE

An avalanche is a rapid flow of snow down a slope. There will always be the danger of an avalanche when a fresh layer of snow sits on top of a weak layer. There is an increased chance of avalanches with:

- **Snow falling as crystals**

- **Loose, dry snow that doesn't settle**

- **Slopes without trees and rocks**

- **Soft, newly fallen snow more than a foot deep**

- **Snowdrifts that sound hollow**

- **Rain or a rise in temperature**

- **Lee slopes (sheltered or protected from the wind) where snow has accumulated**

- **Snow-filled gullies**

In order to avoid potential avalanches, travel across slopes with rocky out-crops and trees. Stick to ridges and high ground above avalanche paths if possible. This way, if you trigger an avalanche, you will be above it and have a greater chance of survival. If you have to cross a steep slope, choose your path carefully and try to cross early in the day, before the sun hits the snow. Make a loud noise, and throw rocks at the slope to see if you can trigger the avalanche before you head off. Move carefully but swiftly through the avalanche zone.

If there is more than one of you, go through an avalanche zone one at a time, so if someone is caught in one, there will be someone who was safe to try to rescue them. If you see someone caught in an avalanche, try to watch and take note of where they last were seen, as this will be the first place that you will need to dig for them.

The upper snow layer loses its support and slides.

Temperature increase in upper layer of snow.

Temperature difference between the two layers.

Evaporation under snow.

If you get caught in the path of an avalanche:

- **Try to move to the side; the bulk of the force of an avalanche will be flowing down the middle, and you will not be able to outrun it.**

- **Grab something sturdy to anchor yourself.**

- **Make a swimming motion to try to propel yourself to the top of the snow.**

- **Get rid of any equipment that might drag you down: snowshoes, walking sticks, etc.**

If you are buried in an avalanche:

- **Move your head back and forth to create an air pocket to breathe in.**

- **Dribble out some spit to see which way is up; it can be very disorienting to be surrounded by snow.**

- **Try to punch your way to the surface.**

- **Try to dig your way out.**

- **If you are alone and trapped under the snow, your chances of survival rapidly diminish.**

If you are traveling with someone else who gets caught in an avalanche, keep your eye on them the best you can. The last place you saw them go under the snow will be a good first place to look, if you are not wearing beacons. Make sure that the snow has stabilized before heading into the avalanche zone. You will be no good to your partner if you get taken by a secondary slide. If you are wearing a beacon, turn the setting to receive and track their signal. Look for surface clues like gloves, boots, or other equipment. Always probe before you dig to save time and energy.

Prevention is better than dealing with the aftermath, so if in doubt, do not take the risk.

8.4.2

PREPARATION

Being a backcountry rider is as much about preparation as it is about freedom. Before you head into the backcountry, it is vital that you learn how to prepare for and deal with avalanches. The best way to do this is to take an accredited course. Buy an avalanche beacon, snow probe, and snow shovel, and learn how to use them. These three items are your critical gear for backcountry skiing. Each year, before you go on your first trip, take out your gear, check the batteries, and have a practice run to see if you can still remember how to use everything.

Some other things you can do to prepare are:

- **Scope your lines before it snows:** Hike the area so you can identify potential hazards that may get buried under the snow; identify any areas that may encourage a buildup of unsafe snow conditions.

- **Purchase appropriate clothing:** Unlike downhill skiing, where time on the lifts requires an extra-thick layer of padding, alpine touring will work up a sweat regardless of the cold temperatures. Good layering systems will help prevent the onset of hypothermia. Have a base layer that can wick away sweat and help regulate temperatures, an insulating mid layer, and a lightweight waterproof shell, and add and remove depending on your level of exercise. Don't wait to cool down when you stop. Immediately layer up to prevent excess heat loss.

- **Assess your skill level:** Backcountry skiing requires a good level of fitness and an experienced skier. Unlike groomed slopes, you will come across a lot of different snow conditions, sometimes within minutes of each other. You also may end up in extreme terrain by accident. Knowing how to ski a variety of snow conditions and grades is a good idea before you head out. For your first few trips into the backcountry, find someone to mentor you. Knowledge comes with time on the mountain and going out with experienced partners.

- **Make a route plan.**

- **Partner up:** Never head into the backcountry alone. Make sure your partner has first aid qualifications, has done an avalanche course, and is carrying the proper emergency equipment. Your life may come down to how well they are prepared, and you have a duty of care to do the same.

- **Follow the local avalanche or weather patterns:** Knowing the temperatures, rain, and snowfall in the area you plan to travel in will give you an understanding of the layers of snow you may encounter. Avalanche training will give you an understanding of the snowpack layers that are most likely to split and what conditions produce them; this will help you decide when the conditions are ideal for heading out.

- **Maintain equipment:** Assess potential problems with your gear; look at what could break and what needs changing or repairing, and do it prior to it becoming an issue; take spare pieces of kit with you that may require regular maintenance or are prone to breaking; make sure you have fresh batteries in your radios and beacons.

- **Create a survival kit to carry:** (see below).

- **Always let someone reliable know of your plans:** Let them know where you are planning on going, who is with you, and how long you will be there for.

A good backcountry survival kit should have a way to cover your basic needs in conditions that may drop below freezing during the day and well below freezing at night. These conditions are not the ones to play around with, so don't cut corners in order to pack light, as mistakes will be less forgiving in this climate. Experiment with what suits you best, but I would recommend:

- **Avalanche transceiver**

- **Avalanche probe**

- **Snow shovel**

- **Personal locator beacon**

- **Two-way radio**

- **Water bottle (avoid bladders or hoses, as they will freeze)**

- **Water purification tablets**

- **Water filter (life straws work well in this environment)**

- **High-energy food with enough for an extra meal**

- **Extra warm layers in addition to your three standard layers**

- **Extra gloves and hat**

- **Emergency shelter or space blanket**

- **First aid kit**

- **Headlamp**

- **Spare batteries**

- **Map of area and compass (great to have if you get off track)**

- **Cell phone plus battery pack (cell phone batteries die faster in cold air, so it is good to have a backup)**

- **All-weather lighter**
- **Ferro rod/fire starter**
- **Knife**
- **Multitool**
- **Signal mirror**
- **Whistle**
- **Duct tape**
- **Zip ties**
- **Paracord**

It is a good idea to carry both an avalanche beacon and a personal locator beacon because, while they both aid in search and rescue, they provide different services. An avalanche beacon can send and receive a signal to another beacon, to enable you to find someone buried in the snow. A personal locator beacon will send out a signal to emergency services to request help.

Make sure that you are using your avalanche beacon correctly. It should be worn on a harness attached to your body above your base layer of clothing. Avalanches can be violent if you are caught up in them, and having the beacon in your pack or pocket might result in it getting ripped away from you in the slide. Always have the beacon on and in send mode while you are traveling.

POSSIBLE SCENARIOS

GETTING LOST/CAUGHT IN A STORM

As soon as you realize you are lost, take a second to assess the situation. Fortunately, there should be fresh tracks in the snow indicating where you came from, so take a moment to orientate yourself from where you came, to where you wanted to go. If you can head back along your tracks to gauge your intended destination, do so. If you have headed far from where you wanted to go and are unsure how to make your way back, stop and take stock. Do you have cell service? If so, make a call to emergency services and explain your position. If not, are you wearing a personal locator beacon? If it is getting dark and your situation is looking serious, get to a safe, sheltered site; set off the beacon; and get as comfortable as you can.

If you are unable to communicate to anyone the seriousness of your circumstances, it is a good idea to immediately set about making your situation better. Do not wait until nightfall to construct some form of shelter.

Your clothing will be your first line of defense against the cold. Make sure you are wearing layers that are warm but not restricting. Cover all areas of bare flesh, including your face. I have used socks on my hands and a bandanna on my head when I was caught out on a mountain unprepared. It doesn't have to be much; just try to reduce anywhere that you could lose heat to the environment. Close any clothing openings, including sleeves and collars.

Don't sit on the cold ground. Sit on your pack or pad the ground with leaves or branches.

Alpine environments may have no resources to make shelters. Find a place out of the wind. If you are in the snow, push up a wall of snow to protect you. Use rocks if you can find any, or look for a natural overhang or cave out of the weather. Make sure that your entrance doesn't become completely blocked by snow. You will be tempted to block all the air and wind from entering your shelter, but if your shelter has no ventilation, you can quickly be overcome by carbon dioxide poisoning and die. If you have a walking pole or stick with you, make sure that, if the snow is accumulating, you keep clearing a hole for fresh air to get in.

Without any resources or natural shelter, the best bet to surviving on a cold mountain is to build a snow cave.

SNOW CAVE

There are a few methods for building a snow cave. You can find a suitable deep, solid snowdrift and burrow in, or you can create a small igloo. Use your snow shovel to create the snow blocks that you will need for this shelter. Test the solidity of your snow. If it is too cold, the snow will be too fluffy to make perfect blocks, and if it is too warm, the snow will be too slushy to work. This is a Goldilocks shelter, where the snow needs to be just right to work. If you can slice the snow into blocks, find a patch of snow where it is at least waist deep, and start to build the walls of your shelter. It is best to make a dome shape, as it will hold the integrity of the roof better. Your shelter only needs to be big enough for you to curl up in. Once the dome is done, tunnel down from the outside and then up into the shelter. This will ensure that no heat is lost to the entrance, as heat rises. I like to smooth down the walls on the inside, as it makes me feel like they are a little more solid, but that is purely psychological.

TREE WELL

If you are down into the tree line, try to find a solid tree well to bed down in. These occur when the lower branches of the tree are resting on the snowbanks, and no snow has gathered below the branches beside the trunk. It creates a hole that you can crawl into and insulate with branches and leaves. Your body heat will keep the temperature at a survivable level, and you will be out of the wind and weather. Make sure you keep an air passage clear so that the space has ventilation.

Hopefully you have left a plan with a reliable person who will alert emergency services when you fail to return, and rescue parties will be on their way at first light.

INJURED SKIER

AVALANCHE

With avalanches being the leading cause of death and injury to backcountry skiers, there are many possible wilderness first aid scenarios that you may be dealing with. Even with prompt and proper avalanche rescue techniques being employed, the chance of surviving an avalanche is slim. The most extreme will be an unconscious victim, who may not have a heartbeat, as well as impact injuries, many of which could be internal and not presenting on initial examination.

Always assess the danger to yourself and others before entering a first aid situation. If you are unable to see the victim, call emergency services or set off your personal locator beacon quickly before conducting your search, as time is of the essence.

If you manage to locate the victim in the snow, dig them out carefully but quickly. Assess their level of consciousness. Are they responding to your questions? If they are unconscious, place them in the recovery position for further diagnosis (see page 522). Check for breathing and pulse, and begin CPR if they are absent. Know that in cold conditions, breathing and heart rate slow down considerably, so take a little longer than usual to make sure they are absent before beginning resuscitation. **Do not begin CPR if you suspect that the victim may be hypothermic (body core temperature of less than 95°F).** This is due to the possible fragile electrical state of the heart. Evacuate and work to slowly and carefully to rewarm their core.

If they are conscious, do a secondary assessment to check for any further injuries.

Anyone who has been buried in an avalanche should be evacuated to medical professionals as soon as possible.

CARDIAC ARREST

A lack of physical preparation and fitness, and underestimating the effort required for backcountry touring, add to cardiac arrest being a common cause of fatalities in the backcountry. Cardiac arrests can come on gradually or hit quickly. Symptoms include:

- **Sudden collapse**
- **No pulse**

- **No breathing**
- **Loss of consciousness**

Signs of an impending issue can be:

- **Chest discomfort**
- **Shortness of breath**

- **Weakness**
- **Fast-beating, fluttering, or pounding heart**

If you or your friends are experiencing any signs of a possible heart attack, stop activity immediately and assess. How far are you from your vehicle or base? What is the terrain like? How serious are the signs? If you can make your way out to medical help, take your time and get out as quickly and safely as possible. If signs are escalating and you are unable to self-evacuate, make the victim comfortable in a seated position and call for help, or head out to get help.

If they are unconscious, place them on their side, with their top leg bent forward and their top arm at a right angle to their body to help maintain the position. Their head should be tilting toward the ground to allow their tongue to remain clear of their airway and any fluids in their throat to drain out. This is called the recovery position. If you are able to delegate someone to contact emergency services, do so. If you are alone, call emergency services or send out a Mayday signal and then check to see whether the victim's airway is clear. If there is an obstruction, clear the obstruction, then place your hand on their chest to see if you can feel their chest rise and fall, or the back of your hand by their mouth to see if you can feel a rush of air. If they are not breathing, turn the person on their back and begin to do chest compressions. There are different suggestions for how many pushes to do, but at the end of the day, as long as you are doing any at all, it is better than none. You should be aiming to compress the chest by a third. This is quite a solid push on an adult and less on a teenager and child. Use both hands for an adult and large teen, and one hand for a younger teen and child. You should be aiming at doing about a hundred thrusts in a minute. Famously, and ironically, the song beat that works for the chest compressions is "Stayin' Alive" by the Bee Gees, if that helps you get a rhythm.

In these times of airborne viruses, medical professionals are leaving it up to you as to whether you want to do assisted breathing or not. Chest compressions will also move the lungs of the victim enough to get some oxygen circulating to the brain. If you know the victim and feel confident about their health status, pinch the victim's nostrils, tilt their head back slightly, and deliver two long, slow breaths into their mouth for every thirty chest compressions. Continue to do so until the victim starts breathing or medical help arrives.

Being a wilderness first aid scenario, it may be some time before medical help arrives. Continue to administer CPR until the victim starts breathing or until it compromises your health and safety.

Once the victim is breathing, place them into the recovery position and continue to monitor them. If they stop breathing again, place them on their back and commence CPR. If they recover, get them comfortable and look at evacuating.

HYPOTHERMIA

This is a condition that occurs when the body loses heat faster than it can produce it. It is better to prevent hypothermia than to try to cure it in the field, so always begin to try to rewarm when you start to feel cold.

Signs and symptoms of hypothermia include:

- Shivering
- Slurred speech or mumbling
- Slow, shallow breathing
- Weak pulse
- Clumsiness or lack of coordination
- Drowsiness
- Confusion
- Loss of consciousness

Someone with hypothermia usually isn't aware of their condition, as it comes on gradually. Eventually it can lead to risk-taking behavior and a feeling of euphoria. Quite often people who have died of cold exposure are found naked, as they begin to feel overheated and take off all their clothes in the final stages of the condition.

When you start to feel cold, add layers or remove damp clothing and replace them with dry. Move around, and seek shelter and warmth. Do not attempt to warm hypothermia victims quickly, as this will lead to cold blood in the extremities rushing to the core and dropping the core temperature dangerously. Warm drinks and a hot water bottle on top of a layer of clothing by their core will help. Avoid alcohol, caffeine, and tobacco. It is not recommended to strip off and join them, because this may lead to two cold people instead of two warm people, but if you are having trouble warming them, keep your warm layers on and get close.

ENSURING RESCUE

Being prepared before heading out into alpine conditions is the best way to ensure that you will be rescued. Being as visible as possible will help a rescue party locate you.

1. **Wear an avalanche beacon and know how to use it; carry a probe and shovel as part of your essential gear.**

2. **Leave your plan with a responsible person, including an expected return time.**

3. **Have multiple methods of communication, including a personal locator beacon, two-way radio, and cell phone.**

4. **Make your position as clear as possible for rescuers. Large contrasting letters in the snow and arrows pointing to your location are good ideas, as well as brightly colored material tied to trees or planted in the snow on the end of a pole.**

5. **Movement on the ground is easier to spot from the air. If you hear a rescue vehicle, make yourself as large as you can and wave your arms in the air. Perhaps wave a branch or make a flag out of a ski pole with brightly colored material on it.**

6. **Use a whistle in short, sharp blasts; make sure you pause in between to listen for a response.**

It is important to mentally prepare yourself before backcountry skiing. This will allow you to make good decisions and manage risks. Learn what to do in case of an avalanche, and get familiar with knowing how to access skiable terrain. These things will all contribute to an amazing, safe adventure.

9

Wilderness First Aid

NO SURVIVAL BOOK WOULD BE COMPLETE without a section on wilderness first aid. But keep in mind that reading about how to do something is no substitute for hands-on experience in a course taught by professionals. This section is here for emergencies, or to jog your memory if you have forgotten what to do in the heat of the moment.

Recommended procedures are constantly changing, as research finds more effective ways of administering first aid in both urban and wilderness settings, so it is good to update your CPR qualifications every year and your wilderness first aid every three. They also differ from country to country, so if you are in charge of a group of people, make sure you are qualified for the country that you are working in.

I have over thirty years of first aid and wilderness first aid course experience, in three different countries. I have always kept my qualifications up to date, and I have never once learned all the same things in any course. I always learn something new, and the recommended procedures always change. I have used my knowledge often in both urban and wilderness environments. I wouldn't go so far as to say that I have saved anyone's life, but I have made them comfortable and ensured that they were in the best condition they could be once professional medical care arrived.

Your initial response to the scene of an accident will be the same regardless of whether you are in an urban or wilderness setting and if you have brought a first aid kit or not. That is the DRS ABC of being a first responder.

DRS ABC

This is a handy acronym to help you remember your order of priorities in a first aid scenario.

DANGER

The last thing that you want in an emergency scenario is to put a healthy person in danger. Once you also become a victim, chances of survival diminish. As soon as you see a person in trouble or if you come across someone who looks injured, check the area for danger. What was the mechanism of injury? Is it something that will cause injury to you? Has the danger passed, or can you safely remove the victim from danger?

If you have seen someone fall to the ground because a branch broke, it should be safe for you to move in to help them immediately. If someone has fallen because of a rockslide, wait until the slide has settled before you move in to help them.

Always take a moment to assess the scene. You may want to jump in and rescue someone from danger, but acting proactively will usually have a better result than acting impulsively. This can be seen with the amount of people who drown trying to rescue loved ones from riptides in the ocean. If they took a moment to grab a floatation device before entering the water, their success would almost be guaranteed. Diving in without one ends up putting two lives in danger.

RESPONSE

Once you have established that there is no danger to either party, it is time to assess their level of consciousness. If the person is yelling or screaming, their trachea (the body's largest airway) is clear, and they have a pulse. Move on to your secondary assessment.

If the person is still, try to get a response from them. Don't shake them violently, because you are still unsure what else may be wrong with them.

Simply touch their shoulder and say things like: "Hello," "Can you hear me?" "What's your name?" and "Can you squeeze my hand?" Give them a moment to respond. If they moan, open their eyes, or answer a question, you can move on to your secondary assessment.

If there is no response, assume they are unconscious and roll them into the recovery position. If the mechanism of injury was a fall from a height or a head hit, assume that the spine may be damaged, and take extra care when moving them into the recovery position to keep the spine straight, if possible.

THE RECOVERY POSITION

An unconscious person is placed in this position, as it allows the airways to stay open and fluids to drain out if need be. The tongue muscle may fall back and block the airways of an unconscious person on their back. To move someone into the recovery position, lie them on their back, bend the arm nearest to you so that their hand cushions their head, and bend the opposite knee to you. Pull the person over onto their side so that their knee holds them on their side. Tilt their head back slightly to ensure their airways are open.

SEND FOR HELP

This was a more recent addition to first aid teachings, because it was a step that people in urban environments kept forgetting to do. If you are with a group of people and have access to cell phone service, this is the moment when you delegate someone to call 911. If you are by yourself, take a second to dial, put the phone on speaker, and continue with your assessment.

In a wilderness environment, it can get tricky. If you have cell service, dial 911. If you don't have service where you are, continue with your assessment. It is best to get more information before you send for help.

AIRWAY

Look for any obstructions in the mouth. Check and scoop out anything that you see inside their mouth that shouldn't be there. If their breathing is wheezy or noisy, there may be something blocking their airway. Do not shove your fingers too far down their throat to try to clear it out, as this will trigger the gag reflex. If you can't see anything, check their breathing.

BREATHING

If the airway is clear, check for breathing. This can be done by listening, looking, and feeling. Place the back of your hand by their mouth to see if you can feel air moving by. Place your hand high on their chest to see if you can feel a rise and fall. Listen to see if you can hear their breath moving in and out.

If the person is breathing, keep them on their side and continue to do your secondary assessment.

If the person isn't breathing, turn them onto their back and commence CPR. This would be the time I would recommend sending someone for help, if you are out of cell phone range. If you are alone with the victim, set off your personal locator beacon or stay with the patient and continue to the next step if neither of these options is available.

If they are unconscious, place them on their side, with their top leg bent forward and their top arm at a right angle to their body to help maintain the position.

Check to see if their airway is clear.

Place your hand on their chest to see if you can feel their chest rise and fall.

COMPRESSIONS

There are many schools of thought as to how many compressions per minute and how many rescue breaths, but as long as you are doing compressions and breaths so that blood is continuing to circulate through the body and oxygen can get to the brain, you are doing more than nothing. Thirty compressions to two breaths is considered fairly standard. In times of airborne pathogens, choosing whether or not to do rescue breaths will be up to you. If you know the person and know their health status, you may make a choice to do assisted breathing. If the patient is a stranger, it is okay to just give chest compressions, knowing that some air will be moving in and out of their lungs while you are massaging their heart.

How to do chest compressions:

- **Kneel by the person's side.**
- **Place the heel of one hand in the center of the person's chest.**
- **Place the heel of your other hand on top of the first hand.**
- **Interlock your fingers.**
- **Position yourself vertically above the person's chest.**
- **Keep your arms straight, and press down on the sternum about three inches.**
- **Keep a pace of approximately one hundred compressions per minute.**

How to do assisted breathing:

- **Pinch the soft part of the patient's nose closed.**
- **Tilt their head back slightly.**
- **Use a pinch grip to raise up their chin.**
- **Take a normal breath, and place your lips around the person's lips, creating a seal.**
- **Blow steadily into their mouth while watching to see if the chest rises.**
- **Remove your mouth, and let the chest fall.**
- **Take another normal breath, and blow into the patient's mouth.**

If the chest isn't rising when you breathe into their mouth, try tilting the head back a little more, or look for an obstruction in their airway.

You will need to continue CPR until such time as the person is breathing on their own, a medical professional has arrived to take over, or your health and safety are compromised. You may be able to swap in and out with other people if you aren't alone, allowing for some rest between rounds.

If you are in an urban environment, there is a good chance that a defibrillator is somewhere nearby and someone has managed to access it for you. Using one of these would be the next step, if this is available and they haven't responded to the first few rounds of CPR.

A person will either recover and start breathing, or they won't. In a wilderness setting, if they recover, you will need to get this person to medical attention as soon as possible. Either get help to come to you or assess and evacuate on your own. It is important to understand that chances of resuscitation are slim without intervention from either a defibrillator or a professional medical team. Do not feel like you have failed if you are unable to resuscitate someone. The failure would have been in not possessing the knowledge to at least try.

You can manage to get through the first few minutes of a first responder incident without needing any equipment. This is why it will be similar procedures wherever you are. It is when dealing with further injuries that having a first aid kit available may be the difference between competently dealing with a situation and managing to get someone to safety, or having to improvise and risk incomplete healing or infection. Always carry a first aid kit into the outdoors, and know how to use it.

SURVIVAL FIRST AID

In a survival scenario, I will assume that you don't have a first aid kit with you and make suggestions as to some alternative things you can try. This is where you will need to get inventive and be adaptable. Think about what would solve the problem if you were in civilization, and then explore your environment to figure out what you can use that might deliver a similar result. I am also going to assume that you are unable to get help, because you would have gotten out of your survival scenario if that was an option. This is why I emphasize a risk-versus-reward analysis of every task you undertake while trying to survive. Something like a small cut that you effortlessly and routinely tend to at home can kill you if you can't keep it clean in the wilderness.

SECONDARY ASSESSMENT

If the person is conscious or unconscious but breathing, you will need to check to see what else has to be done to keep them alive. This is where the scenarios become too numerous for me to list off. There are situations that need to be dealt with immediately or the person will deteriorate, such as deadly bleeds and venomous snakebites, and situations that are not so urgent, like blisters and splinters. Generally, a conscious person will be able to describe what has happened to them, which will cut down the guesswork of what you need to treat. It will also be easier if you are around them when they became unconscious. It is only when you come across an unconscious patient that you will need to do some investigation as to the possible cause.

Be aware that immediately after an accident, a patient may be flooded with adrenaline, which might mask symptoms of whatever injury they have sustained. I love this adrenaline because it enables me to finish whatever task I'm trying to complete before dealing with the injury, but it can also mean that you may miss serious conditions in your first aid assessment.

I will discuss some of the more common scenarios that you may encounter while interacting with the outdoors and how best to deal with them. I have divided them up into injuries and illnesses.

9.2

INJURIES

DEADLY BLEEDS

A severed artery can lead to someone bleeding out in minutes. It doesn't take much. I have lost count of the times I have seen people cutting something with a knife while resting the object on their leg. Fatigue and momentary lapses in concentration can have disastrous consequences when combined with sharp objects or projectiles.

Deadly bleeds are wounds where the blood is pumping from the wound, the bleeding doesn't slow down or stop with pressure, and/or the blood is quickly soaking through the bandage. Deadly bleeds can be internal or external. External ones are more obvious, as there will be blood soaking clothing or flowing from the wound. Internal bleeds can generally be observed as swelling or bruising at an impact site. If the swelling or bruising is in the abdominal region, call for help and evacuate as soon as possible.

For all deadly bleeds, immediate evacuation and medical assistance will be required. Treat the wound first before dialing emergency services, if you are alone or if it is just you and the victim. Assign someone else to dial, or head out for help immediately if you are in a group.

If the object is still in the body, do not attempt to remove it. If it is protruding from the wound, immobilize it in place so it doesn't move around and create further damage internally. Removing projectiles in the wilderness could open up arteries, and the patient can bleed out in minutes.

The first thing to do with a massive bleed is to apply pressure to the wound. Grab some absorbent material if you have any available, or use your hands to try to stem the bleeding. In some cases, wounds will stop bleeding when pressure is applied to them. Elevate the wound above the level of the heart if possible. If you have absorbent dressing and a bandage available, place the dressing on the wound and wrap it in place with a bandage. You want a firm bandage but not a tourniquet. If the wound bleeds through the dressing, do not remove the initial dressing; simply apply another layer of absorbent material and another bandage.

STRAIGHT-SIDED DEEP CUT

If the wound is a slice cut, hold the two sides of the wound together as you apply pressure. Once bleeding has slowed, flush out the wound and check the depth of the wound and whether it looks like it will continue to bleed. If the wound requires stitches, use butterfly stitches from your first aid kit to hold the sides of the wound together, and cover it with a clean nonadhesive dressing.

WOUNDED LIMB If the wound is deep and to a limb, apply pressure, elevate the area above the heart, and cover it with a pressure bandage, making sure that it is firm but not tight enough to cut off circulation to the extremities. You want a firm bandage but not a tourniquet. If the wound bleeds through the dressing, do not remove the initial dressing; simply apply another layer of absorbent material and another bandage.

ABDOMINAL WOUND If the wound is in the abdomen, and there are no internal organs visible, treat it as above. If there are internal organs visible or protruding, **do not try to stuff them back in the cavity**. Cover the wound with a moist, sterile dressing and bandage it firmly. Make the victim comfortable, but do not give them anything to eat or drink.

CHEST WOUND If the wound is in the chest and a wheezing noise can be heard through the wound, assume that a lung has been punctured. Cover the hole with a dressing to create a pressure seal. This can be a resealable plastic bag or something similar. Tape around three edges of the square, allowing one side to remain free. Immobilize until help can arrive.

Treating an abdominal wound.

Treating a chest wound.

TOURNIQUET

Unless a limb has been completely shattered or torn off, or the femoral artery (the main one in your leg) has been compromised, try to avoid applying a tourniquet. A tourniquet is a last resort, as it will probably result in the loss of a limb once applied in the field. If your choice is to lose a life or lose a limb, apply a tourniquet and do not take it off. A tourniquet is a bandage that restricts all blood flow to a body part. Write the time and date that you applied it. The only person who should remove a tourniquet is a medical professional, once the person has made it to a medical facility.

SURVIVAL SCENARIO

If a deadly bleed occurs, apply pressure to the wound. If you have any spare absorbent material, place it over the wound and use whatever cordage you have to keep it firmly in place. If the bleeding stops, try to keep the wound clean by washing it out with purified water twice a day and keeping it covered.

Once you have dealt with DRS ABC and deadly bleeds, you should be able to take your time with further assessment.

BLUNT FORCE TRAUMA

This is most often associated with falls from a height in wilderness areas. If the fall was from a significant height or onto a hard surface, always suspect a spinal injury and treat it as such until the possibility can be ruled out. If the person has hit their head, treat them for a spinal injury until the possibility can be ruled out.

SPINAL INJURY

If they have an obvious head injury, immobilize them, paying attention to keeping the spine in a neutral position. Spinal injuries can present symptoms such as:

- **Extreme back pain or pressure in the head, neck, or back**

- **Weakness or paralysis in any part of the body**

- **Numbness, tingling, or loss of sensation in extremities**

- **Loss of bladder or bowel control**

Do not attempt to move someone who is displaying any of these symptoms. Call 911 if you have service, or set off your emergency beacon. If you cannot reach anyone, make the patient as comfortable as possible, and have someone head out to where they can contact emergency services. If you are the patient and you are alone, do not attempt to make your way out, as you have the potential to cause more permanent damage. Try not to panic, make yourself as visible as possible, and wait for rescue.

SURVIVAL SCENARIO

Immobilize and rest. Assess the injury daily and act accordingly. If you are able to heal through rest, take it slowly until there is no pain associated with movement.

Concussion: This is another serious injury caused by blunt force trauma. There is a mistaken idea that concussions only happen with a direct head hit, but landing on your feet from a high fall can also jar your cranium and result in a concussion. Signs and symptoms to look out for include:

- **Confusion**
- **Headache**
- **Lack of coordination**
- **Memory loss**
- **Nausea**

- **Vomiting**
- **Dizziness**
- **Ringing in the ears**
- **Sleepiness**
- **Excessive fatigue**

The decision to self-evacuate or wait for rescue will depend on the severity of these symptoms. Usually the treatment for a concussion is absolute rest from any physical or mental stimulation until signs and symptoms reside. You will need to assess how far you need to walk to get to safety, what the terrain is like, the time of day, and weather conditions. If you decide to evacuate, make sure you allow for the fact that the person's balance and coordination may be compromised, and carry their pack and support them through rough terrain. If you decide to stay, make sure you wake the concussed person every few hours to assess their level of consciousness. If it is deteriorating, call emergency services and evacuate immediately.

SURVIVAL SCENARIO

Concussions will generally fix themselves with rest and time. Do not try to do any physical activities for the first couple of days, and rest when you are dizzy or nauseous. If you are looking after someone with concussions, make sure you wake them every few hours for the first twenty-four hours, and keep them resting for a few days until symptoms subside.

Broken bone: It may be hard to tell the difference between a sprained joint and a broken bone. Some things to look for will be deformities, numbness, and whether the patient heard a cracking noise when the injury occurred. Sprains will usually be associated with a popping noise. Depending on which bone is broken, the patient may be able to walk out unaided, or will not be able to support their weight at all. If the patient is unable to put weight on the injured limb, take the weight off, apply a compression bandage, and have them rest in the position most comfortable to them. If you have cold water available, soak a bandanna in the water and cover the injured area with a cooling compress.

SURVIVAL SCENARIO

If the break is internal and minor, treat as for a sprain and rest, cool, and elevate. Immobilize the limb in whatever position is most comfortable for the patient, and rest until it feels better. Do not try to reset a disfigured fractured bone in the field. The sharp ends of the bone can cut vital arteries and result in a deadly bleed. Splint the limb in whatever position is most comfortable to the patient, and strap it to the body or to the other limb to immobilize it. If bone is exposed, rinse it with purified water and try to keep the wound clean and covered to prevent infection.

Twisted ankle: This can range from a slight twist, easily walked off, to more extreme tendon and ligament damage. Assess the severity of the sprain. If you are not far from your exit and the person is able to put weight on the ankle, do not remove the boot. It is acting as a compression bandage and supporting the injury. Provide some aid in the form of a walking stick or shoulder to lean on, and slowly make your way to safety. If the patient is unable to put weight on the injured foot, take the weight off, remove the boot, apply a compression bandage, and have them rest with their foot elevated. If you have cold water available, soak a bandanna in the water and cover the foot with a cooling compress.

SURVIVAL SCENARIO

Rest, cool down, and elevate. Hopefully the limb will get better on its own with rest, but add support if necessary. Crafting a pair of crutches out of tree limbs or a walking stick may help.

BITES AND STINGS

If something bites you and you get ill, it is venomous. If you bite something and you get ill, it is poisonous. This section will look at how to deal with venom.

SNAKES

When a snake strikes, usually the venom will enter the body in the lymphatic system. Lymph only moves rapidly through the body when you move your muscles. This means the first action in dealing with a snakebite is to stay calm and still. Get out of the way of the snake and away from danger, and then lie down in a comfortable position with the heart higher than the bite site, if possible. Immobilize the limb that has the bite on it. If you are close to help, do not wash the venom off the wound, as medical professionals will use this sample to help identify the antivenom they will use to treat the victim. Simply cover the wound with a nonadhesive dressing and, using a compression bandage, wrap from the bite site up to the joint above the bite and then down to the joint below the bite. The bandage should be firm but not cut off circulation. Mark on the bandage where the bite is. Call or send for help. Do not attempt to move the patient.

SURVIVAL SCENARIO

There are countless examples of Australian Indigenous people surviving snakebites from some of the deadliest snakes in the world. They would simply find a place in the shade, make sure they have access to water, and lie down to ride it out. They would either battle a fever and sickness for a few days and be able to continue on their way afterward, or they would die. Your best chance of survival without compression bandages will be to wash the bite site, drink some water, and lie down, letting your body fight the venom slowly.

ALL OTHER BITES AND STINGS

Monitor the site of the injury for changes. If you have been bitten or stung by a land insect, put a cooling compress on the more serious stings. Having an insect bite relief cream or spray in your first aid kit is a good idea.

If there are any signs or symptoms of an allergic reaction, such as swelling of the throat or wheezing, rashes, hives, or severe swelling at the bite site, take an antihistamine and look to evacuate. I carry an EpiPen for more extreme allergic reactions such as anaphylaxis, but this is generally only available from pharmacists with a prescription for people with known allergies. If you are traveling with anyone who has a known extreme allergic reaction, make sure that they bring their EpiPen and keep it at the top of their pack.

Most marine animal stings are best treated with water that is as hot as you can bear. This can be applied with a wet cloth, or the body part can be submerged in a container, depending on the size of the area affected and where the sting is located. If you are in a marine environment, it is a good idea to carry white vinegar if you know there might be jellyfish about. This will help remove the tentacles and neutralize the venom. Marine animals have some of the most toxic venom in the world, so if you have been stung in a marine environment, evacuate and seek professional medical help as soon as possible.

SURVIVAL SCENARIO

For land stings and bites, apply cold water compresses. For marine stings, use hot water compresses. For jellyfish stings, pee on the area to remove the tentacles, and then apply hot water. This is a highly debated subject, but if your urine is acidic, which it will be if you are slightly dehydrated, then urine will work. If your urine is alkaline, which happens when you are hydrated, then it won't work. Never use salt water to remove the tentacles.

Be aware that a lot of venom from marine animals works to paralyze the respiratory system, so if you are not alone, twenty-four hours of assisted breathing for the patient will allow the venom time to work its way out of their system, and they may recover.

DROWNING

If you come across someone who is drowning, get the person out of the water if you can do so safely without compromising yourself or others.

If they are unconscious, place them on their side in the recovery position. If you are able to delegate someone to contact emergency services, do so. If you are alone, call emergency services or send out a Mayday and then check to see whether the patient's airway is clear. Place your hand on their chest to see if you can feel their chest rise and fall, or the back of your hand by their mouth to see if you can feel a rush of air. If they are not breathing, turn the patient on their back and begin to do chest compressions. There are different suggestions for how many pushes to do, but at the end of the day, as long as you are doing any at all, it is better than none. You should be aiming to compress the chest by a third. This is quite a solid push on an adult and less on a teenager and child. Use both hands for an adult and large teen, and one hand for a younger teen and child. You should be aiming at doing about one hundred thrusts in a minute.

In these times of airborne viruses, medical professionals are leaving it up to you as to whether you want to do assisted breathing or not. Chest compressions will also move the lungs of the patient enough to get some oxygen circulating to the brain, if you are uncertain. If you know the patient and feel confident about their health status, pinch the patient's nostrils, tilt their head back slightly, and deliver two long, slow breaths into their mouth for every thirty chest compressions. Continue to do so until the patient starts breathing or medical help arrives.

Being a wilderness first aid scenario, it may be some time before medical help arrives. Continue to administer CPR until the patient starts breathing or until it compromises your health and safety.

Once the patient is breathing, place them into the recovery position until they are conscious. Seek medical help as soon as possible, as water in the lungs may lead to respiratory conditions even if the patient seems fine.

Survival scenario As above. If the patient recovers, advise rest and monitor for signs of respiratory infections.

CARDIAC ARREST

Cardiac arrests can come on gradually or hit quickly.

Symptoms include:

- **Sudden collapse**
- **No pulse**
- **No breathing**
- **Loss of consciousness**

Signs of an impending issue can be:

- **Chest discomfort**
- **Shortness of breath**
- **Weakness**
- **Fast-beating, fluttering, or pounding heart**

If you or your friends are experiencing any signs of a possible heart attack, stop activity immediately and assess. How far are you from your vehicle or base? What is the terrain like? How serious are the signs? If you can make your way out to medical help, take your time and get out as quickly and safely as possible. If signs are escalating and you are unable to self-evacuate, make the patient comfortable in a seated position and call for help, or head out to get help.

If the patient collapses, immediately begin the DRS ABC procedures.

Survival scenario

As above. Be aware that getting a heart started in a wilderness setting is a hard task. Usually CPR is recommended until such time as a defibrillator or medical help arrives. Cease CPR if it begins to compromise your health and safety by continuing.

BURNS

Most wilderness experiences come with the idea of sitting around an open campfire at night. It is easy to forget that a pot is hot if you pick it up, or that a burning log can roll out of the fire and make contact with skin. Depending on the severity of the burn, you may need to evacuate to medical help immediately, or simply holding it under running cold water for ten minutes could ease the pain and you can continue on your trip.

The important thing to remember with burns is that the layers of skin continue to burn after the heat source is removed, so skin that is burnt requires immediate cooling, preferably under running cold water for at least ten minutes. Keep cooling the area until removing it from the water doesn't lead to an increase in pain or until it isn't providing any further relief.

Burns extending over 50 percent or more of the body are usually fatal. Call or send for emergency help, and try to submerge the patient in cool running water for at least ten minutes.

Different types of burns:

- **First degree:** These are superficial burns that are mild compared to other burns; they cause pain and reddening of the outer layer of skin.

- **Second degree:** These are partial-thickness burns that affect the outer layer and the lower layer of skin; they cause pain, redness, swelling, and blistering.

- **Third degree:** These are full-thickness burns that go through the skin layers and affect deeper tissues; they result in white or blackened, charred skin that may be numb.

- **Fourth degree:** These go deeper than third degree and can affect your muscles and bones; nerve endings are also damaged or destroyed, so there is no feeling in the burned area.

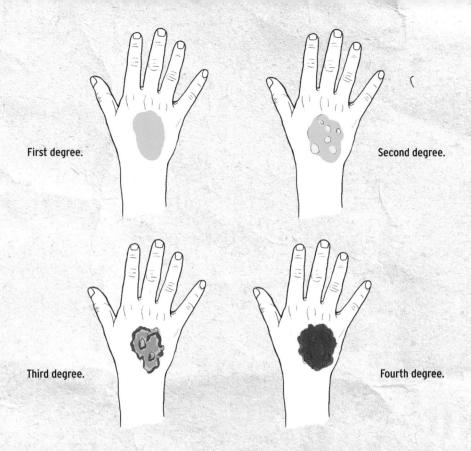

First degree.

Second degree.

Third degree.

Fourth degree.

Third- and fourth-degree burns require immediate evacuation. Cool with running water for ten minutes, and cover area with a dry, nonstick adhesive dressing. Do not apply anything else to the burn. Hydrate the patient by ensuring they continue to sip small amounts of water.

Second-degree burns will require assessment. Any burn that is larger than an inch in diameter or widespread should be cooled in running water and covered with a dry sterile dressing, and then the victim should be evacuated to medical help. If you have a burn-specific dressing or gel, it is okay to apply this if you don't have cold running water or when you are evacuating. Do not burst blisters. They are keeping the burn site sterile and reducing the chance of infection.

First-degree burns can be cooled under cold running water and monitored. Do not apply any oil-based products, as these can heat up and "cook" the area further.

SURVIVAL SCENARIO

Cool the burned area and then keep it dry and clean in order to prevent infection.

ENVIRONMENT-RELATED INJURY

These are any injuries to your body that are caused by the climate or eco-system you are in. The treatment is the same, regardless of whether you are in a backcountry or survival scenario.

Dehydration:

- **Dry mouth**
- **Tiredness or fatigue**
- **Thirst**
- **Headache**
- **Lack of urination (you should be peeing once every few hours)**
- **Dark-colored pee**
- **Dizziness**

If untreated, dehydration can progress into foggy thinking, inability to make rational decisions, and eventually seizures, brain damage, and death.

Heat exhaustion This is a condition that is the result of your body over-heating. Signs and symptoms of heat exhaustion include:

- **Cool, moist skin with goose bumps when in the heat**
- **Heavy sweating**
- **Faintness**
- **Dizziness**
- **Fatigue**
- **Weak, rapid pulse**
- **Low blood pressure**
- **Muscle cramps**

The best cure for heat exhaustion is to cool the body down, so stop activity, seek shelter, and drink water if you have it. Prevention is better than having to cure it, so try not to be active in the heat of the day.

Heat stroke If heat exhaustion is untreated, it will lead to heat stroke. This is the most serious heat-related illness and occurs when the body becomes unable to control its temperature. Body temperature may rise to 106°F or higher in the space of ten to fifteen minutes. Signs and symptoms of heat stroke include:

- Throbbing headache
- Lack of sweating despite the heat
- Red, hot, and dry skin
- Nausea and vomiting

- Rapid heartbeat
- Rapid, shallow breathing
- Confusion and disorientation
- Seizures
- Unconsciousness

Cool the body down as soon as possible. Stop activity, seek shade, and use water to wet the skin while actively fanning to reduce the core temperature.

HYPOTHERMIA

This is a condition that occurs when the body loses heat faster than it can produce it. It is better to prevent hypothermia than to try to cure it in the field, so always begin to try to rewarm when you start to feel cold.

Signs and symptoms of hypothermia include:

- Shivering
- Slurred speech or mumbling
- Slow, shallow breathing
- Weak pulse

- Clumsiness or lack of coordination
- Drowsiness
- Confusion
- Loss of consciousness

Someone with hypothermia usually isn't aware of their condition, as it comes on gradually. Eventually it can lead to risk-taking behavior and a feeling of euphoria. Quite often people who have died of cold exposure are found naked, as they begin to feel overheated and take off all their clothes in the final stages of the condition.

When you start to feel cold, add layers or remove damp clothing and replace them with dry. Move around, and seek shelter and warmth. Do not attempt to warm hypothermia victims quickly, as this will lead to cold blood in the extremities rushing to the core and dropping the core temperature dangerously. Warm drinks and a hot water bottle on top of a layer of clothing by their core will help. Avoid alcohol, caffeine, and tobacco. It is not recommended to strip off and join them, because this may lead to two cold people instead of two warm people, but if you are having trouble warming them, keep your warm layers on and get close.

Frostbite This is a condition where the skin and the tissue just below the skin freeze. It mostly affects exposed body parts or extremities. Signs and symptoms include:

- **Very cold flesh**
- **Numbness**
- **Hard, pale skin**

To treat frostbite, rewarm slowly in tepid water and wrap. This flesh may turn black, rot, and fall off. It is important to keep the wound as clean and sterile as possible. Any flesh that has been frostbitten in the past will be more susceptible to it in the future.

Sun or snow blindness The sun reflecting off the sand or snow can amplify the glare, causing the corneas in your eyes to become "sunburnt." It can produce temporary partial or full vision loss. It is best to predict when this might happen and act proactively to prevent it. Covering sunglasses with tape to restrict light to a thin crack can help. If you don't have glasses, thin strips of bark covering the eyes will work. The idea is to restrict the amount of light entering the eyes, so whatever you have on you that will achieve that will prevent this affliction. If you have snow or sun blindness, the best thing you can do is to rest your eyes with a cold compress on them.

Altitude sickness The higher you ascend from sea level, the less oxygen is in the atmosphere. Eventually your body will feel the effects of this lack of oxygen, and you will develop altitude sickness. It happens at different heights for different people and can present in different ways.

Signs and symptoms of altitude sickness include:

- **Headache**
- **Difficulty sleeping**
- **Nausea**
- **Elevated heart rate**
- **Shortness of breath**
- **Blue-tinged skin and nails**

Eventually there can be a buildup of fluid on the brain and lungs, and this can be life threatening. Making sure that you are hydrated can help stave off altitude sickness, but unless you are carrying oxygen, the only cure for altitude sickness is to descend at once, as fast as is safe.

FOOT INJURIES

Your feet are essential in a wilderness or survival scenario. They are usually your method of transport and will allow you to do the tasks you need to do to get home or keep you alive.

BLISTERS

If left untreated, even the smallest blisters can become a life-threatening infection. They are usually caused by skin being damaged by friction or heat. The four stages of friction blisters are:

- **Hot spot**
- **Roof intact**
- **Roof torn**
- **Deroofed**

The time to deal with blisters is when they are a hot spot. Any time you have an injury that compromises a layer of skin, you are opening yourself up to the possibility of an infection, so it is best to prevent this from happening, rather than having to treat it. A hot spot is exactly as it sounds: a hot spot that begins due to rubbing. As soon as a hot spot forms, stop doing the activity that is causing it and deal with it, as it doesn't take long for a blister to form after that. Cover the area that is hot with a Band-Aid or piece of tape and continue.

If a blister has formed but is small, cover it with a Band-Aid. If the blister is large, you will need to make a donut bandage to take the pressure off it. Whatever you do, don't pop the blister, as the fluid-filled blister is keeping the skin underneath clean, which will promote healing and prevent infection.

If the roof of the blister is torn or completely gone, clean and disinfect the area and cover it with a Band-Aid. Your feet are prone to bacteria and infections from being in dirty, sweaty socks, so change the dressing and clean the blister often. If the clear fluid becomes creamy and yellow, or the area around becomes raised and red, it has become infected, and you will need to take extra care of the area and plan to hike out.

Wearing good, clean, thick woolen socks can help prevent blisters, as can the double-sock method. This is where you wear a very thin inner sock under your thicker hiking sock. This allows the material of the socks to rub against each other, rather than on your skin.

SURVIVAL SCENARIO

Keep the blistered area dry and clean. Try to avoid breaking the skin.

TRENCH FOOT

This occurs when your feet are constantly damp from sweat or submerged in water. If you don't find a way to dry your feet, the constant moisture will rot the tissue of your feet, and they will become painful to walk on and subject to infection. Dry out boots and socks at night or during the day when you are resting. Make sure you carry a spare pair of dry socks.

SURVIVAL SCENARIO

Find ways to get your feet out of the water, and keep them dry as much as possible.

POISONS

A poison is anything you consume that is toxic to your system. If you know that you have consumed a poison, immediately try to vomit it up. This can be done by putting your fingers down your throat to trigger your gag reflex.

Poisons will generally produce an eliminating effect on your body, which will include vomiting and diarrhea. Combat the dehydrating effects of these by consuming as much water as you can keep down. First aid kits may contain hydration salts or electrolytes that can be added to your water to help replace essential salts that your body is expelling. It is important that your body passes the poison out of its system, so try to avoid any tablets that prevent the vomiting or diarrhea for the first few hours, and only take them if you need to travel or the expulsion of fluids isn't slowing down.

Ground-up charcoal can also help bind the toxins in your stomach and pass them through your system, so the minute you begin to feel nauseous, mix some with water and drink it down.

SURVIVAL SCENARIO

Try to vomit up the poison if possible. Drink water mixed with ground charcoal and/or white ash paste; keep hydrated.

SHOCK

This is a life-threatening condition that occurs when the body is not getting enough blood flow. There are many different medical emergencies that can trigger shock. They include:

- **Heart problems**
- **Deadly bleeds**
- **Allergic reactions**
- **Poisons**
- **Infections**
- **Damage to the nervous system**

It is important to know what the signs and symptoms of shock are, because one in five people who experience shock will die from it. Signs and symptoms include:

- **Anxiety or agitation**
- **Bluish lips and fingernails**
- **Chest pain**
- **Confusion**
- **Dizziness or light-headedness**

- **Pale, cool, clammy skin**
- **Profuse sweating**
- **Rapid, weak pulse**
- **Shallow breathing**
- **Feeling faint**
- **Unconsciousness**

Follow the DRS ABC (see page 550), and then, if the person is conscious and responding, have the patient lie on their back with their legs slightly raised, unless some other injury prevents this. Monitor every five minutes for a change in their condition. You will need to call emergency services to arrange for an evacuation if you suspect a person is in shock, as their condition can deteriorate rapidly.

SURVIVAL SCENARIO

Follow the DRS ABC, and then, if the person is conscious and responding, have them lie on their back with their legs slightly raised unless some other injury prevents this. Monitor every five minutes for a change in their condition, and treat accordingly. Rest until all symptoms have ceased, and then take it easy for a few days.

9.3

ILLNESSES

Becoming ill in a wilderness setting is never an ideal scenario. Illnesses affect physicality, quite often leaving you feeling weak, tired, and confused. I recommend not heading into the wilderness if you do not have to and you are under the weather, as these symptoms could lead to more serious errors in judgment. Rest and fluids are usually the recommended treatment for most ailments, and the physical exertion required in the outdoors will quite possibly make the illness worse. If you get ill while in the outdoors, consider cutting your trip short and heading out until you feel better.

SURVIVAL SCENARIO

There are many different potential causes of illnesses in wilderness settings. Rest and hydration will be the best treatment you can find out there, unless you know some natural medicines. If it is a stomach virus, treat as for a poison (see page 575).

9.4

EVACUATION TECHNIQUES

If you have assessed that the ill or injured person is stable but requires further medical help, you may need to self-evacuate. This should only be done if you are unable to get medical help to you and/or moving the individual will not compromise their life or their injury. It can also be done if not moving them will compromise their life.

You will have to take into consideration:

- **The type of injury sustained**

- **The distance you need to travel to get to help**

- **The type of terrain you need to move through**

- **The people you have available to help**

- **The individual's weight**

- **The resources available to make a carrying device**

- **The fitness of the people evacuating**

Always test your evacuation system with a healthy person, if possible, before using it with the person who needs to be evacuated.

There are many different methods of creating a support for someone incapable of walking out of the wilderness on their own. You may need to get creative. And keep in mind that it needs to be strong and as comfortable as you can make it to prevent secondary injuries.

9.4.1

SOLO EVACUATION

If there are only two people—one healthy person and one who is not—you will need to assess the weight and build of the victim compared to the weight and build of the healthy person. Injuring a healthy person or dropping an injured person makes the first aid scenario worse. I don't recommend carrying someone in your arms or across your shoulders unless you don't have far to go, the terrain is flat, or the individual is a young child or toddler.

BACKPACK CARRY

If you have a backpack with you, even a large daypack, you have a frame capable of supporting heavy weight in a position that will create the least impact on the person carrying. Loosen the arm straps of the pack all the way, and have the person in need of help step through the arm loops with the bag at their back. Lean forward, and have that person get on your back, threading your arms through the arm loops. Tighten the waist strap around your waist, and cinch in the arm straps so they are between you and the backpack and their weight is mostly on your waist strap. Walk out.

SLING CARRY

You will need something long enough to go around both you and the person who needs to be carried, and wide enough that it doesn't cut into your skin. A tarp or sleeping sheet works. Roll it into a line, and tie the ends together, forming a loop. Have one side of the loop sitting under the person's buttocks and one across their back. Loop your arms through so that the person being carried is in a supported piggyback position on your back.

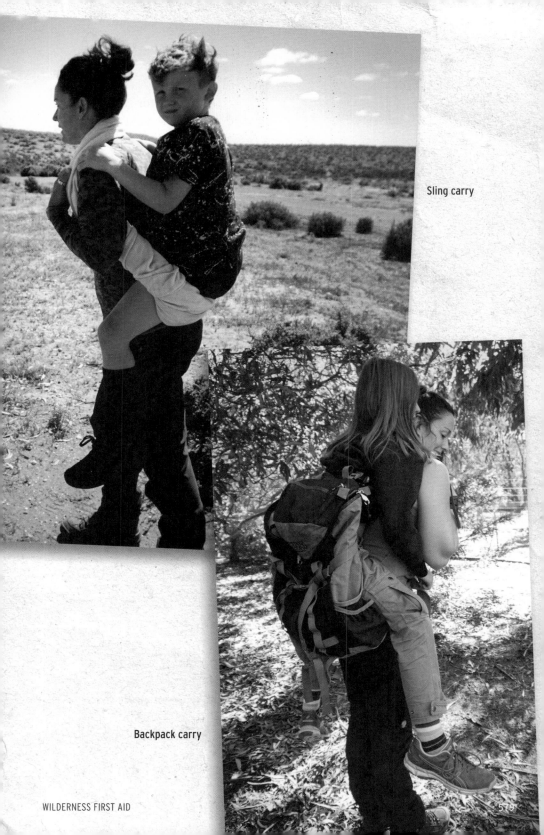

Sling carry

Backpack carry

EVACUATION WITH MORE THAN TWO PEOPLE

Having just one other person to help with the evacuation eases the load immensely. The two-person carrying methods I recommend for a conscious patient are the arm seat or the backpack assist. Only use the arm seat method if you don't have far to travel. If the person is unconscious or unable to support themselves, you will have to build a stretcher. If you have a larger group, take turns being the carriers and take rest breaks as needed.

ARM SEAT

The two carriers grip hand to wrist, creating a square "seat" for the patient. The patient sits with an arm over each of the carriers' shoulders.

BACKPACK ASSIST

If there are two backpacks available, have the two carriers put on the packs and tuck a solid stick above the waist straps of the packs, suspended between the two carriers. The patient will sit on the stick and sling an arm over each of the carriers' shoulders.

STRETCHER

The aim with a stretcher is that you make it as light and as strong as you can. If you only have two people to carry it, you don't want to add any more weight to the structure than you have to, as carrying a stretcher is a very physically demanding task. You will need two poles about two feet longer than the patient's body length. The middle support can be any number of things, from backpacks to jackets or sweaters, with the poles threaded through. If you have rope, you can weave a hammock for the middle, and duct tape can work great as well. Get creative, but make sure that it is wide enough to fit the victim's shoulders. Ensure their comfort by lining the stretcher with sleeping bags or extra clothes.

Evacuations present all kinds of risks for both the injured party and the healthy people assisting. Only perform one if you don't have far to travel, or it is your last resort.

Arm seat

Backpack assist

FIRST AID KITS

A first aid kit should be an essential on every trip into the outdoors and top on your list when packing your go bag (see page 348). I take a smaller first aid kit on personal day trips and a more extensive kit if I am doing a multi-day trip or leading expeditions. My kit also changes depending on where I am traveling and what sort of conditions I may face.

A first aid kit is designed to deliver the first line of aid in a medical emergency, supposing that you will be able to hand over to medical professionals if need be. This may not always be the case with wilderness first aid scenarios, and so I do carry a few things that will help me through if it takes a little longer to get to professional care.

Simply buying a first aid kit is not enough, though. You need to be thoroughly familiar with what your kit contains and how to use all the kit's contents. In the ultimate test of whether or not I am prepared, I have grabbed my first aid kit out of my car, and I will go through everything to see if I have all I should. I will also let you know why I have chosen to carry each item.

My first aid kit is red and clearly marked as a first aid kit. On the outside, it has a clear window detailing the DRS ABC steps, in case I forget them in an emergency (see page 550). Everything is clearly labeled as to what each pouch and pocket contains. It includes:

- **CPR kit:** including a hygienic face covering to allow for safe emergency breaths, and a pair of gloves

- **Major wound dressing:** which has a thick, absorbent pad attached to a bandage, ready to place and apply pressure on a deadly wound

- **2 triangular bandages:** to create slings, help apply pressure, and aid in head bandaging; they can also be soaked in cold water and used for a cold compress

- **2 pressure bandages** (usually my kit contains only one, but living and traveling in the Outback of Australia, I want a backup in case of snakebites)

- **Roller bandage:** probably don't need the extra, but it is smaller and better for sprains and strains than my large pressure bandages

- **6 safety pins:** to fasten slings or bandages

- **Hypoallergenic sports tape:** to provide support for injuries

- **6 small conforming bandages:** to keep dressings in place

- **10 nonadherent wound dressings:** for burns and abrasions

- **Combine dressings:** for major wounds

- **5 cotton gauze swabs:** for wound cleaning

- **Butterfly sutures:** for closing wounds

- **Adhesive dressings:** for minor scrapes, cuts, and blisters

- **Blister kit:** including moleskin and thin foam for making donut dressings

- **Antiseptic wipes:** to clean minor wounds and scrapes

- **Hydro gel:** for cooling down burns and scalds if I don't have access to cold running water

- **Ice pack:** for applying to sprains or breaks, or to help cool down burns and scalds if I don't have access to cold running water

- **4 eye pads:** for eye injuries
- **2 saline solutions:** for washing wounds or irrigating eyes
- **9 skin-cleaning wipes:** for cleaning dirt or blood from around a wound
- **4 sets of plastic gloves:** to prevent the exchange of bodily fluids and to keep the injury site as clean as possible
- **Emergency blanket:** for cold exposure

- **Tweezers:** for removing small, embedded objects
- **Fever strips:** to test temperature
- **Hydrolyte:** to aid in rehydration

- **EpiPen:** in case of a severe anaphylactic shock
- **Thermometer**
- **Splinter probes**
- **Hand sanitizer**

- **Sanitary items:** in case anyone in my group needs them unexpectedly
- **Pain medication:** ibuprofen to help manage pain if I am on my own and need to get back to help
- **Lip balm:** handy, but purely a comfort item
- **Pen and paper:** to record all vital information in case of an emergency

Make sure to include any prescription medication that you require.

This is a large, well-stocked wilderness first aid kit for an expedition leader. I want to make sure that I am fully able to take care of whatever emergency arises, to the best of my ability and for the long term if required. Add or take away any items you wish, but I would take a minimum of the following:

- **Pressure bandages x 2**
- **Roller bandage**
- **Triangular bandage**
- **Gauze or cotton pads**
- **Strapping tape**
- **Adhesive dressings**
- **Antiseptic wipes**
- **Pain relief**

I can't stress enough the importance of doing a first aid course and carrying a first aid kit into the outdoors with you. Chances are, it won't be you that benefits from your training, but it could mean the difference between life and death for someone that you care about.

10

Travel

10.1

FOREIGN TRAVEL

SOME PEOPLE WHO TRAVEL ABROAD will experience a mugging, robbery, or scam. Travelers to foreign countries stick out like a sore thumb, and a lack of understanding of cultural differences, problem areas, and common cons can lead to them becoming easy targets.

I have backpacked, mostly on my own, in over sixty countries, most of them developing countries. I have never been mugged or robbed, and the most I've been scammed out of is a few dollars when I paid for a ring I thought was silver and it turned out to be nickel. This is because I stick to a few easy rules and always make sure my travel survival kit is stocked with items that make my travel experiences safer.

Some problems that may be encountered when traveling are:

- **Fake police:** Just because someone is wearing a police uniform and shows you a badge, it doesn't mean they are official. If something seems suspicious, ask to be taken to the nearest police station to deal with the matter. If they are reluctant, call for the police yourself.

- **Drugged food or drink:** Do not accept opened food or drink from strangers or people that you aren't traveling with. Make sure you never leave your drink unattended. It is a common occurrence for people to be drugged and wake up to find they have been stripped of all their belongings. Certain drugs also make you more susceptible to suggestion, which means you will happily go into the back alley with your mugger rather than putting up any resistance.

- **Back-alley deals:** Everyone on vacation is looking for a bargain, but do your haggling in public spaces. Don't be tempted by someone who says they can get you a better deal at their friend's shop that is just down the road. This is an attempt to lead you to an area where you will be vulnerable to attack.

- **Fake money changers:** Street corner money launderers will offer you a deal on exchanging money and leave you with far less than you bargained for. Make sure that you exchange money at hotels or established businesses, and take a photo of what you give them and count what you get in return before leaving the premises. Put the money in a safe place before heading out into public. Muggers hang around money exchange places, knowing that people walking out of them have cash on them.

- **Transport scams:** Always decide on a price for your travel before you get in a taxi or car for hire. Even if the car has a meter, the driver may not turn it on and will charge exorbitant prices once you have reached your destination. Only use transportation that is recommended by the establishment you are staying with or that you find at official taxi bays at places like airports, train stations, and hotels.

- **Getting mugged:** If you find yourself in a situation where you are being threatened in return for handing over your money and possessions, don't fight back. Muggers may be desperate, and life may be cheap in their country. Your watch might keep their family fed for a year, and they want it more than you. Don't panic, give them what they want, and report it to the local police. Hopefully you haven't put all your possessions in one place and can recover quickly.

- **Being robbed:** Wandering through a packed crowd can lead to opportunistic thieves pickpocketing your phone or wallet or removing items from your bag or backpack. Try to avoid large, busy crowds, and be suspicious if someone slows you down. Be aware of your surroundings, and keep an eye out for anyone who may be following you. If you are carrying a small daypack, move it to the front of your body on jam-packed public transport and make sure all the zippers are shut. Don't carry anything in open pockets.

The best protection against to many of these common travel issues is preparation and prevention. Some ways to prepare for a good travel experience are:

- **Check the advisory warnings of a country before you book a ticket or board your plane.**
- **Ensure you have the proper visas required to travel to the country; make sure that your passport isn't about to expire.**
- **Check what vaccinations are required to either enter a country or return to your own.**

Carry a travel first aid kit with prescription drugs for any illnesses you may have to deal with on the road; these can be bought at traveler's medical clinics and come with a doctor's note granting permission to carry them. Have more than you think you will need of any prescription meds you regularly take.

Sew hidden pockets into loose-fitting travel clothes for emergency cash and passport storage.

Photocopy all important documents, including passports, visas, and credit cards, and store them somewhere safe in your luggage and daypack. I always put them in a waterproof bag with some extra cash and a spare credit card and stash them in the padding of my backpack frame.

Always get travel and medevac insurance. It may seem like a waste of money, but the second anything goes wrong, you will be glad that you have it. It can pay for itself easily if you leave your phone at the hotel or twist an ankle on a hike.

Learn the local customs and laws. Don't risk unintentionally offending someone with a simple gesture. You are visiting their country; you should respect the way they choose to do things there, even if it doesn't seem right to you. Learn some of the language, even if it is just the local word for "hello."

Make sure you have your passwords memorized or written somewhere safe. If you lose your phone and must try to access emails and banking information from a public computer, you will not have access to the device that they will text a change of password confirmation to.

Let your bank know you are traveling, or they will lock your cards when transactions begin in foreign countries.

Staying safe while you are in a foreign country is largely common sense, with a little bit of luck thrown in. Some things to think about are:

- **Don't allow substances to cloud your judgment:** Stay away from excess alcohol and illicit drugs when traveling in a foreign country; not only do they lead to being taken advantage of, depending on the substance, they could lead to a jail sentence.

- **Don't go out late if you are alone:** If I am alone, I try to be back in my hotel room by dark; luckily, all the exciting things I want to do usually happen in the daytime, but if I want to head out at night, I make sure I have company as a backup.

- **Don't wear expensive clothing or jewelry:** Anything that screams you have a lot of money puts a target on your back; unless you are traveling for the purpose of extravagance, dress down and leave precious pieces at home.

- **Blend in with the locals:** Travelers can be easy to spot a mile away and can make easy marks because of it; buy a few cheap items of clothing that help you blend in, and leave the fanny pack at home and use a casual daypack instead.

- **Always look like you know where you are going:** Walk with purpose in unsafe neighborhoods. Prey in the wilds acts nervous and jumpy. This signals to predators that they might be an easy meal. Think of the difference between the way a rabbit moves and the way a cat stalks. Don't give off prey signals, and it may just make a predator pause and choose someone else to target.

- **Always have your passport with you, and store money in several places:** I keep a small amount of cash and a credit card where I can access them easily, and then I have most of my money, my passport, and another credit card hidden somewhere less obvious on my person.

- **Chat with other travelers before booking tours, or read the reviews:** I personally have been stranded out on an island for four more days than I was meant to be there when the boat didn't come to pick me up. This meant I had to pay the island hotel for three nights I wasn't intending to stay with them. Apparently, this was a well-known scam in this area.

- **Ask multiple people for directions:** I always ask at least three people for directions before taking a route. In some cultures, it is seen as a bad thing not to know something when asked. This means that sometimes people will make up things if they don't know. If two people give me the same directions, I follow those directions.

- **Be cautious of friendly strangers:** Meeting people is one of the wonderful things about traveling, but remember that trust must be earned; if someone is too friendly or too insistent on you spending time with them, be wary.

- **Never carry packages for anyone, not even people you think you know well:** Drug traffickers play a long game, carefully grooming their drug mules over a matter of days, weeks, and months. You may feel like you are doing them a lovely favor by taking something back to their relatives in your country, but it is never worth risking your freedom over. Only ever carry your own personal belongings when traveling.

Depending on the country I am traveling in, I will also only drink bottled water and eat cooked food. This includes the water I use to brush my teeth. Nothing spoils a holiday faster than not being able to leave the bathroom because the chef washed your salad with the local water.

TRAVEL EMERGENCY KIT

Some items that help me deal with unexpected situations when I am traveling away from home include:

- **Multitool:** because it has a knife and a lot of handy tools in one device
- **Travel adaptor:** a universal one, allowing for any electrical socket connection
- **Duct tape:** great for fixing just about anything
- **Cable ties:** great for running repairs
- **Portable charger**
- **Bike lock:** I have used this to tie my backpack to a seat while I slept and for securing it on trains and buses.
- **Luggage lock:** makes it a little harder for thieves to get to your gear
- **Hand sanitizer**
- **Toilet paper:** because it's never a guarantee in some countries
- **Headlamp and batteries:** in case you get stranded somewhere at night
- **Small collapsible daypack**
- **Resealable plastic bags:** good for waterproofing
- **Long-life bars:** sometimes it's hard to find anything safe to eat
- **Rubber doorstop:** if the door lock is faulty or you are worried about security
- **Safety pins**
- **Paracord:** comes in handy for all sorts of situations
- **Sewing kit:** for running repairs

Duct tape

Toilet paper

Bike lock

Cable ties

Luggage lock

Paracord

Safety pins

Batteries

Hand sanitizer

HAND SANITIZER

Headlamp

Hand sanitizer

10.2

DOMESTIC TRAVEL

With over 69 million car breakdowns and over 30,000 car-related fatalities occurring in the United States annually, being prepared to face emergency situations in your vehicle is a must. Whether it is being first on the scene to an accident or having to deal with extreme weather conditions when you have broken down in remote locations, your knowledge and preparation can prevent the situation from turning deadly.

10.2.1

CAR EMERGENCY KIT

As with all emergency kits, I suggest that you think about your needs, your terrain, the roads you are planning on traveling, and the environment you will be in. Make the kit all-purpose, but tailor it with specific items. For example, if you are heading off-road in the desert, carry extra water. If you are going to a ski resort for the day, have extra blankets and an ice scraper in the car. I stock my car with at least three days' worth of food and water, as I tend to go on some remote backroads often, but the very least it should contain is a one-day supply of both.

My car emergency kit is always in the trunk or on the roof of my car and contains the following:

- **Gas can:** full; breakdowns can occur when you misjudge the distance between gas stations, especially at night when your nearest gas station may be closed

- **Jumper cables**

- **Spare tire and jack:** know where they are located and how to use your jack; this includes knowing the best place to position it under the car when changing a tire

- **First aid kit:** know what's in it and how to use it; I have been first on the scene of three vehicle accidents, and this has been an important part of helping out until the first responders arrived

- **Glow sticks:** these will help illuminate you and your vehicle if you are broken down on the side of the road at night

- **Water and long-life food:** in case help takes a while to get there or the radiator needs more fluid

- **Multitool:** has a knife and a multitude of other possibly useful gadgets

- **Small tool kit:** some basic tools that can be used to fix a variety of issues, like a screwdriver, pliers, vise grips, adjustable wrench, and tire pressure gauge

- **Flashlight and spare batteries**

- **Small solar charger:** to charge devices if the car battery dies

- **Small foldable shovel:** to help dig the car out if it gets stuck in mud or snow

- **Car escape tool:** keep in the glove box or somewhere accessible in the vehicle

- **Duct tape:** good for all types of repairs

- **Blanket:** helpful for comfort if you are first on the scene of an accident, or if you end up spending the night in your car

- **Small tarp:** allows you to easily rig up a shelter outside the vehicle

- **Car fire extinguisher:** keep inside the vehicle, somewhere easily accessible

- **Antifreeze:** to add to the radiator fluid if temperatures get below freezing and to prevent overheating

- **Motor oil:** to prevent the engine seizing up if there is an oil leak

- **Fix-a-Flat:** this is a foam substance that can be squirted into a flat tire to temporarily fix it until you can get to a safe place to change the tire

- **Pen and paper:** to record accurate information about incidents that occur, or for writing directions and notes to rescuers if you leave your vehicle for any reason

- **Phone charger and cords:** for emergency use only

- **Hard copy of maps:** in case technology fails, especially out on the backroads

Decide what is important to you, and make sure that your car emergency kit provides items to ensure that all your basic needs are met and to help fix smaller problems to get you on your way.

Spare tire and jack

Duct tape

Batteries

Flashlight

Small foldable shovel

Jumper cables

ANTIFREEZE

Phone charger

Antifreeze

Glow sticks

Gas can

SAFETY LIGHTS

Fire extinguisher

BREAKDOWNS

If your car breaks down in an urban environment, it is easy enough to call your local emergency roadside assistance or mechanic to come and take a look or tow you to the nearest help. Most call services promise to be out within the hour, and you will probably be home in time for dinner. But if you are traveling out of town, there is no guarantee of cell phone service, and in remote areas, no guarantee of rescue.

Whenever you are traveling in remote areas, it is a good idea to make sure that you let someone reliable know of your plan and expected arrival time at your destination. This will allow for an alarm to be raised sooner if you break down somewhere on the road.

Any extreme weather breakdowns will require proactive behavior in order to safely navigate the situation.

In any breakdown scenario:

1. **Put on your hazard lights to let the cars around you know that you have a car that isn't functioning as it should.**

2. **If you have stopped completely in traffic, you may need to get help to push the vehicle off the road. Put the car in neutral, take off the parking brake, and make sure someone is by the driver's side window or in the driver's seat to steer the vehicle to safety.**

3. **If the car is still moving, slowly drive to the side of the road as soon as you can find a large, flat shoulder. It is best if this is on a long, straight stretch of road, rather than on a curve.**

4. **Put on the parking brake, and assess the situation. Is it something you can fix yourself, or do you require assistance?**

5. **Fix it if you can. Call for help if you need to.**

COLD WEATHER

A dead battery, stalled engine, or flat tire is bad enough to deal with on a good day. In a blizzard or snowstorm, they could turn into a survival scenario. The top causes of vehicle emergencies in winter include:

- **Dead battery:** The cold weather makes it more difficult for the battery to charge itself; this means that when you turn the key, the car may not produce enough charge to start.

- **Bald or flat tires:** If your car doesn't have enough grip on the road, it is easy to lose control in icy or slippery road conditions.

- **Engine issues:** In cold weather, your radiator can freeze or crack; your engine can also overheat if the motor oil becomes thicker and doesn't circulate properly throughout the engine.

Some things you can do to prevent these cold-weather emergencies from happening are:

- Check the weather forecast, and do not travel if a storm warning is in effect.

- Change your battery every five years; batteries more than five years old will tend to struggle in colder weather, so check when your battery was last replaced.

- Allow for more gas than you think you will need, always have at least a quarter tank, and fill up if you are getting low; disruptive weather and slower traffic will mean an increased amount of time on the road.

- Check the coolant level on a regular basis; make sure it is at the correct level, and top up with antifreeze if it isn't.

- Check tires regularly. With slippery or icy conditions, you need to have a minimum of 3 mm of tread on all tires. If you live in snow conditions, consider getting a set of winter tires for the colder seasons, or carry a set of snow chains.

If you know you may be traveling through areas with storms and blizzards, you can prepare and:

1. Make sure that your car is filled with fuel, especially if you are not sure where the next gas station may be.

2. Let someone reliable know of your plans and an estimated time of arrival at your destination; this way if something goes wrong, you will be looked for sooner rather than later.

3. Charge your cell phone, and carry a car charger and extra battery pack.

4. Pack extra supplies of food and water.

5. Pack a blanket and warmer layers of clothing.

6. Pack a car emergency kit (see page 594).

Cold temperatures, early nightfall, and low visibility can make for a swift descent into an emergency situation once your car is not working. It is important to:

- Move as far off the road as you can to avoid other traffic on the road.

- Make your car as visible as possible so that other traffic is aware that it is there; this can be done with glow sticks, traffic cones, and hazard lights, if your battery is still working.

- Clean the snow off your car to the best of your ability, if it is snowing.

- Call for assistance, if you have phone service; hopefully someone will be able to come and either get your car started or take you to a place that can.

- Don't leave your car, unless staying in the car puts your life at risk or there is a building you can take shelter in nearby; your car is providing shelter out of the wind and snow, and it will keep you warm until help arrives.

- If you are unable to call for help, make it obvious that you need help by raising the hood of your car and turning on the hazard lights.

- If your engine is working, clear the snow from the inside and outside of the exhaust pipe, and wind down the window an inch if you turn the engine on to warm the car. Do not have the engine going the whole time. Turn the engine on for ten to fifteen minutes every hour to warm up. This will prevent carbon monoxide poisoning.

- Keep warm by adding extra layers or covering up with a blanket before you get cold. If you don't have these items in your car, get inventive. Car mats or removable seat covers can be wrapped around you to keep in body warmth. Anything that will act as insulation will help. If you are not traveling solo, get in the back seat and get close to share body warmth. Light exercises and movement will also help you stay warm.

- Make sure the windows are clear of snow, so that someone driving past can see that there is someone in the car.

- Don't try to dig your car out of the snow if it is firmly entrenched. It is better to conserve your energy, keep as dry as possible, and protect your body from the cold winter air.

- Try not to fall asleep. Your body may become hypothermic if you get too cold, or excess carbon dioxide could fill the small space. If you need a nap, set an alarm so that you wake up once an hour, and reasses your health status.

- Drink fluids to prevent dehydration; this will help combat the hazards of cold weather health problems.

- Do not eat snow if you are thirsty; eating snow will cause your core temperature to drop and takes more moisture to process than you will gain by consuming it.

If you are in a remote area and rescue is unlikely, you will need to assess whether it will be best for you to remain with the vehicle or try to walk to safety. You will need to take into consideration the distance you are away from civilization, the terrain, if you know where you are and where to go, and what supplies you have with you.

If you are close to somewhere you can access help from, wait until morning, take extra clothing, food, and water, and walk out.

If you are too far to walk to help or safety in a day, begin to assess your resources and take care of your basic needs. Cold and exposure will be your biggest concerns, but you have a great resource with the vehicle and whatever is in it to assist with warmth. Metal conducts the cold, so it may be better to start to construct a shelter next to the car to stay warmer at night. Weigh up the benefits of the solid structure versus the cooling effect of the metal. A snow cave lined with car seat covers will keep you warmer than the inside of a car. Ration your food and water supplies, and begin to think about where you can access water from.

Rescue will be a priority, so make sure you are as visible as possible, and make it clear you are in distress.

Stay calm, and ensure you are out of the way of traffic and highly visible. Only travel well-maintained roads in the winter months, and make sure you always let someone know where you are going and when to expect you back in inclement weather.

10.2.2.2

HOT WEATHER

Every year, people die in hot conditions because of vehicle breakdowns. Although this is usually in remote locations, working in extreme heat adds stress to the cooling systems of the car, causing the engine temperature to soar and putting the engine at risk of serious damage. Some causes of vehicle breakdowns in hot weather include:

- **Water leaks:** Heat can cause seals to dry out and crack, creating small leaks that can be enough to drain the radiator fluids over time.
- **Low oil pressure:** Oil can become quite watery when it gets hot, and this means it doesn't lubricate the engine parts as well, leading to failure.
- **Fan belts snapping:** Fan belts need to work harder in the hotter weather, both to cool down the car engine and to run the air conditioner; this may lead to belt failure.

- **Brakes and clutch failing:** These are friction components in a car, and when they get too hot, their surface texture changes, meaning they may not grip as well as they should.

- **Tires blowing out:** High road temperatures can aggravate existing tire damage and can cause punctures and blowouts.

If your engine begins to overheat, put down your windows and turn on your heater to pull the heat out of the engine. If you can, keep driving at about 30 miles per hour, keeping a good distance between you and the car in front. This will allow air to run through the engine bay and over the radiator. If the car still doesn't cool down, pull over as soon as it is safe, and allow the engine time to cool. Whatever you do, don't try to take the radiator cap off immediately. This will result in scalding water spraying out under pressure and possibly causing nasty burns. Allow the radiator to cool completely, and then check the water levels by removing the radiator cap. Top up your coolant and radiator fluids if necessary and continue driving, keeping an eye on your temperature gauge.

Some things you can do to prevent hot-weather breakdowns include to:

- **Check your battery:** Hot temperatures can put a strain on batteries. Even though most batteries purchased today should be maintenance free, check whether the battery casing has cracked or is leaking, and make sure that the terminals are clear of corrosion. Make sure the connections are tight and the battery is securely mounted.

- **Always carry extra gas:** Make sure that you never run your tank low in hot weather.

- **Replace coolant regularly:** Ensure that your radiator fluids are replaced at least every six months, and be sure to check coolant and radiator levels before a long trip; make sure the engine is cold if you are checking the radiator.

- **Check all car fluids:** Hot-weather driving puts a strain on all fluids that ensure your car functions properly, so check the engine, transmission, power steering, and brake fluids regularly and before long trips.

- **Check tire pressure:** Underinflated tires flex more on the road, which causes more heat buildup; this means any weaknesses in the tires or potential punctures could lead to blowouts.

Remote hot areas can be some of the most dangerous places to break down in the world. If you know you are traveling through areas where you might encounter soaring temperatures, you can prepare and:

- **Make sure that your car is filled with fuel, especially if you are not sure where the next gas station may be.**

- **Let someone reliable know of your plans and an estimated time of arrival at your destination; this way if something goes wrong, you will be looked for sooner rather than later.**

- **Charge your cell phone, and carry a car charger and extra battery pack.**

- **Download offline maps, and carry hard-copy maps of the roads you intend to be traveling on.**

- **Check that the spare tire is in good condition.**

- **Pack extra supplies of food and water.**

- **Pack a blanket and warmer layers of clothing, as hot places can get very cold overnight.**

- **Pack a car emergency kit.**

- **Pack a tarp or some sort of shade.**

If your vehicle breaks down or gets stuck in an extremely hot environment, move over to the side of the road to get out of the way of other traffic, and make sure that you are not in danger. If you are in a remote location, it is important to:

- Stay with your vehicle unless you do not have the resources to survive in that location.

- Call for assistance. If you do not have cell service where you are, head for a high point only if it is close by. If you are unable to get service, conserve your energy and take stock of your resources.

- Make it obvious that you require help. Raise the hood of your car, have the hazard lights on, or make a large SOS or HELP sign that can be sighted from the air.

- Shelter outside of your vehicle. Find shade close by, or create shade next to your vehicle by constructing a tarp shelter or something similar. Being made of metal, your vehicle will conduct heat and create an oven-like environment that will dehydrate and exhaust you.

- Stay in the shade in the heat of the day, and conserve your water and energy.

Assess your situation. If you are not far from help and safety, it is okay to try to walk there, but remember to restrict movements to the cooler hours of the early morning and later evening, and seek shade in the heat of the day. Carry more water than you think you will need, and ensure you have sun protection for your head and neck. Leave a note on the car detailing your situation and plans.

It is hard to determine distance in the heat with flat plains. Mirages can appear, making buildings seem closer than they are, so if you are unsure of how far you will need to go for help, it is best to stay with your vehicle.

Take stock of your resources. How long will you survive if you choose to stay with your vehicle? Water will be your main concern. If you have three days' or more worth of water, construct a shelter next to your vehicle and try to conserve your energy and hydration by minimizing your movements. Create a fire, and burn something rubber from the car on it. This could be the spare tire, if you are certain you won't be able to get the car started again or if it has a blowout. This will create a thick black smoke that may attract attention from a distance. Burning a tire every hour creates a pattern that may raise curiosity.

If you are low on water and there is none to be found in your immediate surroundings, you may need to make a plan to head out toward help. Again, only walk in the cooler times of day and stick to the road you followed in. It may be tempting to head across country if you feel like you know the way, but a road's surface is usually easier to navigate than uneven terrain. Also, if you descend into confusion from dehydration, following the road is a clear path that doesn't require problem solving.

Always carry more water than you think you will need, as it will be the key to survival if you have broken down in hot weather.

ESCAPING A VEHICLE

The main reason you would need to escape your vehicle is if it is swept into floodwaters or is accidentally driven into a large body of water.

SUBMERGED VEHICLE

As soon as your car stalls in floodwaters or begins to be swept away, you need to be making plans on how to exit the vehicle. **Do not call emergency services at this stage.** You may have a matter of seconds to act, and you are the only one who can be proactive about your safety in this moment.

Put down all windows, and unlock the doors. This needs to happen before your car goes underwater, as once water pressure builds up on the outside of windows and doors, they become impossible to open until the car is fully submerged.

Take off your seat belt. It is best to keep a knife or belt cutter in the glove box, in case the belt has locked shut.

Exit the vehicle however you can; this may be through the window or sunroof.

If the vehicle is sinking, you will need to swim to safety. If the vehicle is remaining partially submerged, stay on the roof of the vehicle and wait for rescue. This would be the time to make the call to emergency services if you have your phone. If the water is less than knee deep, you can try to walk to safety. Face upstream, and shuffle sideways with your feet wide apart and your knees bent.

If your vehicle has become submerged to the stage you are unable to open any doors and windows, you will either need to break the glass or wait until the vehicle is fully submerged to open the doors. I suggest trying the former first, as it can be a very scary ordeal to wait for a car to fill up with water as it sinks. You will also need to be capable of relaxing and holding your breath for at least forty-five seconds, while the final air leaves the interior of the vehicle and allows the outside to equalize with the inside.

The front windshield tends to be double-paned to withstand an impact, so your energy is best spent trying to break a side window. Use your foot, aiming for the upper edge, to see if you can smash the top of the glass away from its lower anchor points. If this doesn't work, remove the seat headrests and use the sharp underside to try to puncture the glass. Belt cutters will also have sharp, solid points on them, designed to shatter glass. Aim at the top corners of the window. Keep your face averted, so that you avoid shattered glass getting in your eyes. Car windows are made of tempered glass and will shatter in small squares that are less likely to result in deadly bleeds than large, jagged panes of glass. If you are unable to break the glass, take a moment to calm yourself down. You will need to save your breath to wait to fully submerge.

One thing to be aware of is that a car can take two or three minutes to sink. As soon as you break the seal of the window or open the door, the car will sink more rapidly, so it is important that you exit the vehicle as soon as you have managed to secure an escape route. Do not wait for the vehicle to hit the bottom if it hasn't already. If multiple people are in the vehicle, make sure everyone is ready to leave. Once you have exited the submerged vehicle, swim for the surface and to safety.

Never try to cross floodwaters or water that you can't gauge the depth of. It only takes a foot of running water to move a vehicle, so it is best to reverse and find another way around to your destination.

CAR CRASH

Another reason you may need to escape your vehicle is if your vehicle has crashed and the doors are jammed shut. Use belt cutters or a knife to remove your seat belt, if it is jammed. Find something heavy and solid to smash the side windows. The end of the belt cutter will usually have a solid, sharp point on it that is designed to shatter glass. The pointed ends of seat headrests can also be effective. Make sure you face away from the glass you are shattering, to avoid getting glass chips in your eyes. Clear as much glass from the shattered window as possible, and lay a blanket or item of clothing on the lip of the window as you crawl out, to avoid getting cut.

If you have come across someone who is stuck in their car, communicate with them to move away from the window you are going to smash, or smash one away from where they are sitting. Get them to avert their face and cover any bare skin.

10.2.4

CHANGING A TIRE

Changing a tire is an important skill that can prevent a small inconvenience from turning into a big deal. Anyone who is driving a car should be able to change a tire.

Your vehicle should come with the following equipment:

- **Jack**
- **Lug wrench**

- **Fully inflated spare tire**
- **Vehicle owner's manual**

Make sure you know where they are and how to access them. If you have misplaced any of these items, or if your car did not come with these items, purchase new ones right away. You should also have a headlamp and spare batteries stashed in your glove box, in case your flat happens at night.

The steps to changing a tire are as follows:

1. **Find a safe location. As soon as you realize you have a flat tire, do not abruptly brake or turn. Slowly reduce speed, and scan your surroundings for a level, straight stretch of road with a wide shoulder. An empty parking lot would be an ideal place. Level ground is good because it will prevent your vehicle from rolling. Also, straight stretches of road are better than curves, because oncoming traffic is more likely to see you. Never attempt to change your tire on a narrow shoulder near oncoming traffic. Keep moving slowly until you**

find a safer spot. While driving on a flat tire risks ruining your rim, replacing a rim is better than being hit by an inattentive driver.

2. Turn on your hazard lights. Your hazard lights will help other drivers see you on the side of the road. To avoid an accident, turn them on as soon as you realize you need to pull over.

3. Apply the parking brake. Always use the parking brake when changing a flat tire, as it will minimize the possibility of your vehicle moving.

4. Locate your jack, lug wrench, and spare tire.

5. Remove the hubcap. If your car has a hubcap covering the lug nuts, it is easier to remove the hubcap before lifting the vehicle with the jack. You can use the flat end of your lug wrench to remove it.

6. Loosen the lug nuts. Using the lug wrench, turn the lug nuts counterclockwise until you break their resistance. It may be tough, as they will have been machine tightened. Use your foot or whole body weight if necessary. Do not remove the lug nuts yet; just back them off half a turn.

7. Place the jack under the vehicle. The best place for the jack is usually beneath the vehicle's metal frame, alongside the flat tire. Do not place the jack on any areas of molded plastic, as this will not support the weight of the vehicle. Get down to ground level, and scope out the best place to put it.

8. Raise the vehicle with the jack. If the ground is wet, muddy, or sandy, you may need to place something under the jack to prevent it from sinking. I find that a solid, flat piece of wood or a flat rock does the trick. Raise the vehicle about six inches off the ground. Do not put any part of your body under the car while it is raised on the jack.

9. Unscrew the lug nuts the whole way.

10. Remove the flat tire.

11. Mount the spare tire on the lug bolts.

SURVIVE: THE ALL-IN-ONE GUIDE TO STAYING ALIVE IN EXTREME CONDITIONS

12. Tighten the lug nuts by hand.

13. Lower the vehicle, and tighten the lug nuts again, this time with the wrench; use your full body weight to get them as tight as possible.

14. Replace the hubcap, and return all equipment to where you found it.

It is important to get your flat tire fixed as soon as possible, as some spare tires aren't designed to drive long distances or at high speeds. They also may have a different tread wear and can throw out your wheel alignment, causing other problems in the long run.

It shouldn't take longer than half an hour to change a tire, and even less once you have done it a few times. It is worth having a look at all the steps and trying it out in your garage before you need to do it in an emergency.

Traveling can be an amazing adventure, whether overseas or in your home country. Part of the adventure is dealing with unexpected situations as they arise, and being prepared will always ensure that you will be able to be proactive and get back on track quickly.

11

Survival and Kids

EDUCATING YOUR FAMILY about what to do in times of emergency can seem alarmist, and many people choose not to because they do not want their children to grow up in fear. In fact, educating your children about what to do if the worst should happen is the best thing to do to combat fear. It empowers them to feel confident about venturing out into the world, knowing that if the worst should happen, they have a plan. And it doesn't have to be about life-or-death scenarios; you can make it a fun activity that encourages logical problem-solving skills and adaptability.

The outdoors is also great for developing resilience in children, giving them opportunities to push through challenges and see the reward of a little bit of hard work. The key for working with kids in the outdoors is making it fun for them and helping them through the harder times by making it an adventure. There are many interesting activities that you can do with children that will begin to have them looking at the world in a different way and knowing what they need to do if an emergency presents itself.

SURVIVE: THE ALL-IN-ONE GUIDE TO STAYING ALIVE IN EXTREME CONDITIONS

OUTDOOR SURVIVAL ACTIVITIES

Growing up in the outdoors, I didn't realize that the games I was playing were preparing me for my life in the world of extreme survival expeditions. I was always making forts and tree houses, with the idea of running away to live in them. I loved getting close to wildlife and observing their habits, and was always happy to get outside and play no matter what the weather was doing. Learning through play and fun activities is key for children, and if you frame it right, they will learn to survive without a fear of events that might lead to them needing those skills.

SHELTER

CAMPING OUT IN THE BACKYARD I started my niece camping when she was three. We set up the tent in the living room at her house and made it into a fairy palace. I made sure that she slept in a sleeping bag and on a camp mat like we were outside, but all else was fun and luxurious. I explained how the poles went together, and she helped thread them into the sleeves on the tent so she could see how it all worked. From there, we progressed to sleeping in the backyard. We chose a nice summer night and made a campfire. Although we only cooked marshmallows on the fire and slept on a nice mattress, it was adjusting her to the idea of sleeping outside and out of a bed. Encouraging kids to help with the tent setup is a big part of this activity. Explain how the poles go together and why you put them where you do, if certain poles have to go into certain sleeves. Treating the tent like a playroom encourages them to adjust to the idea that they can be comfortable while camping, rather than it being a situation where they are deprived of everything they enjoy.

MAKING A SHELTER If you have access to the woods or a large backyard with some scrap timber, you can start looking at making a shelter from scratch. Ask them what they think makes a good house. Eventually you want answers such as "keeps the rain out" and "stays warm," although most of their other suggestions are probably valid too. Talk about how most shelters don't look like a house, and get them to draw up some colored-pencil designs before you begin. Talk about how big it needs to be, and discuss with them what types of materials would work to make the shelter. If you are in suburban area, you may want to bring in some suitable building materials. Have your child come with you to get them or purchase them, so they can be a part of the choosing process.

Talk about the qualities of a good shelter—they need to be windproof, because if the wind can get in, it will be colder in there. Look at the roof, and talk about how if they can see daylight, it isn't waterproof. Find ways to fix that together. Kids get very creative when it comes to building shelters, and they will want chairs and tables and bed areas. Allow them the chance to figure out how to create these things and help make their shelter into a "home."

If you can, it is a good idea to get the shelter in your backyard to the stage where you can camp out a night in it. Make it cozy with air mattresses and sleeping bags, and line it with a mosquito net if bugs are a bother. It is the next step up from tenting, because it isn't an enclosed structure, and they helped make it themselves.

As a kid, I was always building "cubbies" or forts in our local woods. I would spend days out at a time making it solid and modifying the design. They were always a great place to hang out, and the more involved I was in creating them, the more time I wanted to spend in them.

FINDING READY-MADE SHELTERS When you go walking in nature, start to make a game out of finding good places to make a shelter. Check out fallen trees and hollow trunks, and talk about what would need to be done to them to be able to spend a night in them. Look at the materials you have around you, and talk about which ones would make great insulation and which ones would work to build a shelter roof. Look at the other creatures that may be in that space, and talk about ones you could live with and ones that mean you should find somewhere else to sleep if you find them. See if you can find five suitable ready-made shelters on your walk.

WATER

WATER COLLECTION The next time it rains, set a challenge to see who can collect the most rainfall, using only items found in a certain place. This could be a shed or in a particular cupboard. The person who manages to collect the most rainwater wins the challenge. Encourage them to look at ways to funnel water from larger surfaces or even construct elaborate designs that will maximize the potential water collected from a small shower.

GETTING WATER FROM TREES This can be an interesting lesson on how trees "breathe." Talk about how amazing it is that trees are able to access water that we can't even see below the ground and funnel it up to their leaves, where it then enters the atmosphere. We are able to collect this water if we have a sunny day and some clear plastic bags. Look at areas on the tree that might be better for collecting water than others. Talk about why you would choose a certain bunch of leaves over another. Things such as insects or insect casings might influence your decision, as well has how big the bunch of leaves is and the leaves' position in the sun. Try tying bags over different leaves to see which ones produce the most water, and try to figure out why that might be.

WATER PURIFICATION A fun activity to demonstrate how a water purifier works is adding food coloring to a glass of water and then using the water filter to pump water from that glass into another glass. Talk about how some water has bugs in it that can make you sick, and those bugs are the food coloring. Then demonstrate how the water filter can pull those bugs out of the water, leaving it clear and safe to drink. Life straws are the smaller version of these water filters. Have one for each child's daypack when you are out hiking.

FIRE

MAKING A TINDER BUNDLE I use this activity often with students as a way of beginning to get them to understand how to find flammable material. Talk about how a bird shapes its nest from thicker material on the outside to the finer fluff on the inside. Talk about finding suitable tinder material, emphasizing the need for it to be dead and dry. Look at how to "fluff" up tinder materials, using your hands to rub it over itself. Depending on the environment I am in, I will either show how to harvest a long handful of grass and tie a knot as the outside of the tinder bundle, or just create a basketlike structure with some coconut husk, cabbage palm fiber, or dry bark and fill the inside with finer materials. Dried cattails are great for the inside of tinder bundles as spark enhancers, as are dried rabbit dung and finer, fluffy grasses. This tinder bundle can then be used to demonstrate and practice a wide variety of fire-making methods, including ferro rod fires and magnifying glass fires, and as a base for a log lay.

FERRO RODS Ferro rods are a great way to get kids to start exploring lighting fires in survival scenarios. If you set up some rules and make sure you are supervising the use of them, they can be a safe, exciting experiment for kids as young as four or five. My niece has been making ferro rod sparks since she was four and loves to light our outdoor fires using the ferro rod instead of matches. It is a skill that takes failure and persistence to get right, and therefore there is a feeling of great accomplishment that comes along with getting a spark and lighting a tinder bundle. My rules for using a ferro rod include:

- **Only use the ferro rod when there is an adult present.**

- **Never make a spark at someone else.**

- **Never make a spark inside.**

- **Only make a spark on a designated tinder bundle in a cleared area.**

- **Always sit with their back to the wind, so that the flame will be protected or blow away from their body when lit.**

- **Sit in a kneeling or squatting position, so they can move quickly if the fire flares high.**

- **Always have long hair tied back when making a ferro rod fire.**

- **Always have a method of putting the fire out handy.**

Demonstrate the correct hand position and striking technique. The best way to use a ferro rod is to position the rod so it is facing low and central to your tinder. Brace the knuckles of the hand holding the striker on the ground or your shoe, and then pull the hand with the ferro rod in it back sharply. The striker should be at about a 30-degree angle to the rod for best results. If you push the striker toward the bundle, you risk displacing your tinder before the spark reaches it. The dried head of a cattail is fantastic to put a spark into for beginners, as it catches a spark easily and flares up brightly, but then extinguishes quickly.

MAGNIFYING-GLASS FIRES On a sunny day, use a magnifying glass to demonstrate how to make fire through refraction. Explain how it focuses the light and therefore the heat into a small spot. Show how the circle of light expands and contracts when you move the magnifying glass closer and farther away from the target tinder. See if they can get smoke and then a flame from a tinder bundle. I have made this part of a team-building activity with students, where they race other groups to make a viable tinder bundle and get a flame. Make sure it is done in a controlled environment with methods of extinguishing flames available. Explain that it should only be done under adult supervision.

SETTING UP A LOG LAY This can be done as a one-match challenge or a ferro rod challenge. Depending on your preference, you can either demonstrate the tepee method or the log cabin method of fire lays.

Get the children to gather two big handfuls each of toothpick-thickness wood, pencil-thickness wood, and thumb-thickness wood. Explain that it needs to be dry wood, not green. Dry wood makes a crackling noise when it breaks.

Have them create a tinder bundle as in Fire Activity 1. Place it on a dry surface where you intend to have your fire. Build one of the following log lays around the tinder bundle:

THE TEPEE LAY

This is exactly what the name suggests. Prop the toothpick-sized twigs on your cleared ground first, then layer the outside of them with the pencil-sized twigs, and lastly the thumb-sized branches. As the flame burns upward, it will light the toothpicks, which in turn will provide enough sustained heat to light the pencils, etc.

THE LOG CABIN LAY

As well as your various-sized twigs, you will need two bigger pieces of wood laid out parallel to each other. You will need to scrape out a hole to place your tinder bundle into, and then lay the toothpick-sized twigs across the hole, with a handful running one way and a handful running perpendicular (at right angles) to them. The next pencil-sized layer should sit on your two parallel logs, again crisscrossing a layer each, and finally, the same with the thumb-sized branches.

If you have taught your children how to light matches safely, allow them one match to see if they have done a good job at the fire lay. If set correctly, one match or one spark of the ferro rod should be all it takes to get your fire going.

FOOD

TRACKING Take some paper and pencils out into nature areas, and look for animal tracks. Sand and mud make for great places to look for clear prints. Copy what the prints look like onto the paper, and try to guess what may have made them. Look at the size, shape, and characteristics of the prints. Bird, reptile, mammal? How many? What does it look like they were doing there? Have a look at the animals you can see in the area. Did any of them make the print? If you can't figure out the animal that made the print, do some research on the computer when you get home and see if you can figure it out.

STALKING Teaching kids to move silently through the woods is a fun activity. Not only will it be a beneficial skill if they decide to hunt their own food later in life, it also allows them to get closer to animals for observation and photos. Have a look at the ground you will be walking on. Ask the kids which surfaces are noisy and which ones will be quiet to walk on. Look at the difference between green leaves and grasses and dead leaves and grasses. Talk about walking on dirt and rocky surfaces. Look at how you should place your feet on the ground. Good stalkers place their feet toe first and then let the rest of their foot touch the ground. Try to walk from a point A to point B without making a sound.

The next challenge will be to see how close they can get to a flock of birds or the pet dog without the animals noticing. Have the children try one at a time to sneak up, and see if they can get closer each time.

FISHING If you live near a body of water, fishing is a great way to introduce kids to catching and processing their own food. Small children's rods are just as effective to catch all kinds of fish as large adult rods are. Kids are absolute sponges for information, and the more they understand about the activities you are doing with them, the more interested they become. Make sure you share why you are making certain fishing choices with them. If you are choosing to fish in the ocean, explain why you are going out when the tide is coming in, rather than when the tide is going out. Talk about the bait you are choosing to use in each setting and what you are hoping to catch with it. Show them how to set up their own rod, and talk about how best to manage hook safety. Have them bait their own rod, and teach them how to safely cast and what to aim for. Teach them how to safely reel in the fish and how to hold the fish to avoid the potentially sharp spines.

Fish are also good for learning how to gut and clean an animal, as they are very simple and not very messy. If the child you are working with knows how to use a knife, encourage them to descale and gut their own fish. This leads to a greater feeling of ownership of the process and a feeling of being able to provide for the family.

TRAPPING This is a fun activity to do with a group of children. I usually lead into it by talking about the fact that they can last a long time without food, and then ask about what food types they think they could eat in the outdoors. It's a good way to introduce the idea of not eating things that they can't identify in the outdoors. Reinforce that berries and mushrooms can be poisonous, as this will be the food that looks most familiar to them out there. When they mention animals, ask them how they would get an animal for food. They will probably mention weapons first, but you can guide them around to traps. Most children will be familiar with the idea of traps and snares from certain cartoons. Get them to work in small groups with a pencil and paper to design the best way that they think they could trap an animal. Have one of the group present their trap idea, and explain how it works. Discuss the features of a good trap.

The next step in this process is to have them try to build a successful trap or snare. I always have some paracord and duct tape available and maybe some sticks if the area I am working in is bare. Send them off in their groups to build a trap, using what they can find. Once the exercise is finished, have the groups talk through their design and explain why they chose to do what they did.

An addition to this activity would be to build and demonstrate a working trap to the children, explaining what the trap is for and why it works. Two good traps for this are a deadfall and an arapuca bird trap.

For the Paiute deadfall, you need:

- A heavy, flat rock or deadfall
- An anchor stick
- A thin trigger stick
- A pivot stick
- A toggle
- Some cord or rope
- Bait

Make a sharpened V shape on the end of the anchor stick and have a matching V notch in the pivot stick. Flatten one end of the pivot stick so the deadfall sits on it more easily, and tie the rope to the other end of the pivot stick. The toggle is tied around the middle to the other end of the rope and wrapped around the anchor stick about an inch or two off the ground. I like to make my toggle flat on one side and carve a divot in it where the trigger stick sits. Bait is then placed in the middle of the trigger stick that sits under the deadfall or on the ground underneath it. The other end of the trigger stick uses the underside of the deadfall in opposition to the toggle.

Make sure the anchor stick isn't preventing the deadfall from hitting the ground, by locating it outside the lip of the deadfall. When setting up this deadfall, I like to prop the deadfall up with something that prevents it from crushing my hands if it accidentally triggers. Have a child trigger the deadfall with a long stick.

The arapuca trap: It requires quite a bit of assembling but can be used multiple times, so it is worth the effort. You will need:

- **24 thumb-width sticks, withsix sets of four varyingsizes**
- **2 pieces of rope or cord about 2 feet in length**
- **A short length of cord**
- **A finger-width trigger stick about 10 inches long**
- **Bait**

Place the two longest sticks side by side, and attach the two pieces of cord from one end of each stick to the other to create a square. Twist the two sticks once in opposite directions, so the rope forms a cross. Slide the next two longest sticks, log-cabin style, between the ropes, and begin to fill in the slack. Eventually you will end up with a tensioned pyramid. This is your cage. Since this is a live capture trap, it can be a fun exercise to bait the trap and watch it to see if any of the local birds will take the bait.

You may need to fill in the top of the pyramid with sticks to ensure that there isn't an escape route for the bird. These are also the sticks that you will remove in order to get the bird out without it escaping. Break the trigger stick in half in such a way that you can put the pieces back together again. Tie the short length of the cord to the inside of the trap, and loop it around the break in the trigger stick with tension. Lean the trap on the trigger stick. Place the bait inside the trap. When a bird enters the trap, it will disturb the cord, which will trigger the trap. Release the bird unharmed by either lifting the trap up or removing it through the top of the trap.

Weapons This can be a divisive idea, due to the fact that children can be tempted to do battle with each other once the weapons are made. Rules need to be established about how to handle the weapons. A spear is the easiest and best option for weapon making. I like showing kids how to make a weapon, because if a child is lost, sometimes finding a sharp stick can make a huge psychological difference in how safe they feel while waiting for rescue. How you manage this activity will depend on what knife work the child has done in the past and how you feel about introducing them to a sharp knife. I like to use long, straight, pointed sticks while the child is young, and then work up to sharpening them.

To take this one step further, you can set up a target with a controlled backdrop and throw your spear sticks at the target to see who can score "dinner."

Foraging This is an activity that can be done in the backyard or in any nature area. Challenge the children to find and identify ten different species of plants. Ways to identify plants include leaf pattern and type, height, flowers, nuts or seeds, and bark. They can either take photos of these things or sketch them, and use a computer or plant book to help identify them. Once the plant has been positively identified, do some research to see if there are any useful properties of the plant. Are they medicinal, nutritious, or helpful in any way? Are they poisonous and to be avoided?

If you live in an area where there are edible plants that you can identify, have the children help gather them and make something delicious with them for you all to share.

11.1.5

RESCUE

NAVIGATION Create a treasure map. Depending on the age of your children, you can use symbols and drawings to mark the map, or have them follow a compass and directions. With a four-year-old, start drawing the structures and features almost cartoonlike. Put bushes and obvious trees or landmarks, as well as a path for them to follow. Leave little "treasures" along the way so that they can't go all the way to the end first. As the children get older, make it more complex. Add a key to it that put symbols in places of the drawings. For example, use a circle for a bush and a triangle for a chair. This will get them used to the idea that sometimes on maps, symbols are used to let you know where certain landmarks and features are. Eventually add in the idea of the compass. I usually keep it very simple, showing how the red needle on the compass will always point to the north and explaining that most maps are drawn in such a way that the top of the map is usually in a northerly direction. Keep treasure hunt directions to a simple north, south, east, or west, and have them walk on a bearing to get to the checkpoints. I might even add in pacing, which will require them to "walk twenty steps east" to get to a marked spot.

Quite often we underestimate a child's willingness and ability to be responsible for "adult" tasks. On a hike, it is a great idea to work with children to take responsibility for where you are and the direction you are traveling in. It also turns questions like "How much farther?" and "Are we there yet?" into a game. When they ask, you can ask them to figure it out. Have the kids carry a copy of the map, and ask them every now and then where you are on the map and help them find geographical clues to figure it out.

GETTING LOST Any time you venture into the wilderness with kids, you should make sure they know what to do if they get lost. If you have been talking to them about other basic needs of survival, you could make this into a "what would you do here?" game. The most important thing for a child to know about getting lost is that they have to stop and stay where they are. Children will be missed far sooner than adults will and usually have a spot where they were last seen. If they stop moving the second they become lost, they have a far greater chance of being rescued quickly than if they keep moving to try to find their way home. The next important information to share with them is how to shelter for the night. I like to challenge children to start thinking about it on breaks. When you are all stopped for water or snacks, ask, "How would you make this area your home?" Prioritize how they would shelter for the night and encourage them to get creative.

USING A SIGNAL MIRROR Show kids how to refract light from the sun, using a signal mirror. Have them aim the light at certain targets on the ground and in trees. Make sure they know not to aim the mirror into other people's eyes when doing this exercise. Get some old soda cans and use sandpaper to buff the bottom of them. Challenge the children to see how far they can refract a beam of light across the ground with the bottom of the can. The winner is the kid who manages to have the brightest beam. Explain that this could be a way to let people know where you are when you are lost, by beaming the light toward any vehicles you see.

GENERAL SKILLS

USING A KNIFE There are a lot of trains of thought about when it is appropriate to teach children how to use a knife. Whatever the age is that you feel comfortable, it is important to show them how to use one properly and to lay down some ground rules. At first, emphasize how important it is that the knife is only used when supervised by an adult. Other important information to communicate to kids about knife handling is:

- **Concentration** Make sure children know that they need to focus when handling knives. If something is distracting them, pause until the distraction has passed, and then return to using the knife.

- **Grip** There are a few different ways of gripping a knife, depending on what task you are performing. The most common grip is the hammer grip. This will work best for most types of cutting for survival. Wrap the hand around the handle like you would with a hammer, and cover your fingers with your thumb.

- **Cutting** It is important to always cut away from themselves and not toward others. Demonstrate how this works and how you can change the position of the object to make sure this can always be done.

- **Positioning** Never cut onto a body part. Sounds like common sense, but I have seen a number of adults brace an item they are cutting on their leg. Show the child how to create leverage by bracing the blunt side of the knife against their knee and moving the wood to create cuts rather than their arm.

- **Passing the knife** Always pass the knife to someone else handle first. Grasp the dull edge of the knife in your fingers and palms, and offer it to them so they can safely grasp the handle without cutting you.

- **Keeping the knife sheathed** Always keep the knife sheathed if not in use. Never leave the knife unsheathed on the ground nor stab it into the ground or wood while not in use. Not only will this dull the knife, but someone may accidentally touch it and get cut. The second the child isn't using the knife, it goes back in the sheath.

These guidelines will assist with children being knife aware and being able to move into more advanced bushcraft skills.

MAKING CORDAGE This is a great activity to show children how our ancestors used to make their belongings with natural fibers. I always ask them first if they have any ideas about what can be used to make rope in nature. If you have access to any inner bark or leaf fibers, you can demonstrate how strong they can be, coming straight out of something natural. If you don't have access to any great natural cordage plants, you can purchase raffia from a craft store for this activity. The cool thing about raffia is that it is actually a natural fiber made from the leaves of a palm.

Demonstrate how to reverse braid the cord to make it even stronger. Kids love making things for themselves that they can wear or use, so help them reverse braid enough cordage for a bracelet or necklace. You can even collect shells or nuts for them to thread on the bracelet for added decoration.

The Reverse Wrap

Take a length of fibers in both hands. Start with your hands a few inches apart, and twist your hands in opposite directions until a loop forms in the fibers. Place that loop in your mouth. Hold the two lengths of fibers so you have one in each hand. Twist the lengths both in the same direction until the fibers tighten, and then wrap the two lengths around each other in the opposite direction. If you are twisting and wrapping in the same direction, your rope will unravel when you let it go. If you are twisting and wrapping in the opposite direction, the rope will pinch into itself, and this is what you want. Keep doing this until your rope is at your required length. One thing to remember about natural fibers is that they tend to be shorter than the length of rope you require, so rather than end your rope when the fibers run out, you can splice in more fiber.

Splicing Natural Fibers

Splicing simply involves adding lengths of fiber to existing threads when they begin to get too short to wrap. I find that it is best to add new fibers in when the existing threads are between an inch and an inch and a half long. You place the new fibers along the length of the existing fibers and continue to wrap, incorporating the new fibers in with the old. Another tip is to only add one length of thread in at a time and allow for a couple of inches of wrap before adding another length in; otherwise, you will end up with a weak spot in your cord.

There are many other games and activities that can get children excited and interested in spending time in the outdoors. The more time they spend out there, the less foreign it will seem if something does go wrong. Building trust in their capabilities and developing adaptability and problem-solving techniques is valuable for developing confidence in all aspects of their lives. It will also be reassuring for you to know that if the worst does happen, you have instilled some skills that will make a difference to the outcome of a search party.

URBAN SURVIVAL

Preparing your children for urban disasters becomes less of a game and a little more about learning safety procedures. There are certain pieces of information and skill sets that will become invaluable to keep them safe in cities and towns.

SHARE THE EMERGENCY PLAN Depending on the age of your children, involve them in making an emergency plan. Make sure they know what to do if a natural disaster occurs while they are away from home. Have an address for a safe meeting point and a route planned from their school for them to be able to make their way there. Have emergency phone numbers programmed into their phone or written down in something that they always have on them. Include a phone number of a family member or close friend who lives in a different town, in case the disaster has affected the entire town or city.

Involve them in the home emergency plan. Assign tasks that will be theirs, should a disaster strike. A task may be as simple as locating the cat and putting her in her traveling cage. Anything to make them feel involved and to pull the focus from potential feelings of panic.

MAKE THEIR OWN PERSONAL GO BAG
Explain the role of a go bag (see page 348) and give each child a small daypack for them to fill with items that they feel would be important to them if they had to leave home suddenly, knowing they may not be back for a few days. Include some essentials like a bottle of water, their favorite snack, and some changes of clothes. I find that children love the idea of making the bag their own and taking responsibility for the items in it, and that they also have some suggestions for the larger family go bag too.

DRS ABC Rather than explaining the whole first responder process (see page 550), keep it simple, but understand that a child who comes across an unconscious adult can save their life as easily as an adult would. Explain that if the adult doesn't respond when the child calls their name or shakes them , the child should immediately call 911, and the operator will tell them what to do.

STRANGER DANGER Unfortunately, we live in a world where strangers can present a level of danger to children rather than a community that protects them. In order for adults to allow children to have a sense of freedom, children need to be educated on how to make safe decisions for themselves.

Basic stranger danger rules include:

- **Never go anywhere with a stranger.**

- **Never accept gifts or sweets from a stranger.**

- **Never get in a car with a stranger.**

- **Never go off on your own without telling your parents or a trusted adult.**

- **Tell your child that it is okay to break the rules if they are in danger.**

- **Tell them to yell, kick, scream, lie, or run away if they feel they are in danger.**

- **Give your child a code word or sign that only you and your child know; they can trust anyone who knows that word.**

In this digital day and age, education of stranger danger needs to include online dangers. Some things for children to be aware of online include:

- **Don't give out personal information:** No one should give out their name, age, address, school name, phone number, or photos of themselves online, in chat rooms, by email, by instant message, or in clubs online.

- **Don't talk to strangers:** Tell children they should avoid befriending strangers online in almost all circumstances. If they don't know the person, they should not friend them on Facebook, and don't let them follow or be a follower on Instagram.

- **Never meet with an online "friend" in person:** Children should be reminded to never meet in real life with someone they met on the internet. Dangerous strangers can easily pretend online to be someone they are not.

- **Don't respond to strange requests:** If a child receives an instant message from a stranger that seems inappropriate in some way, tell them to log off and notify an adult immediately.

- **Never share passwords:** Children should never share a password with anyone other than their parents. Even close friends should not know a child's passwords.

Although there is a fear that communicating with children about these matters will inspire anxiety, when done properly, it can create a feeling of safety for the child. It gives them the tools to know what to do in certain situations to keep themselves and others safe and contributes to them feeling responsible for their own well-being.

ABOUT THE AUTHOR

FROM SUPERHERO STUNTS in Hollywood blockbuster movies to extreme survival feats in the world's most challenging wilderness, Ky Furneaux's incredible achievements have all been kickstarted by two words: "you can't." Her determination to defy the impossible has fueled a remarkable career as survivalist, stuntwoman, TV host, and motivational speaker.

At the age of 19, Furneaux's quiet life in rural South Australia was over-turned when a car accident broke her back. Doctors told her she'd never be physically active again.

She fought her way back to full health, and while rock climbing as part of her rehabilitation, discovered a deep love for the wilderness. She became a qualified kayaking, sailing, hiking, and rock-climbing guide, sharing this passion with others while pushing the limits of her own survival skills. Furneaux has kept people safe in some of the most extreme climates in the world, from the remote and dangerous West Coast trail in the far reaches of British Columbia to the depths of the Amazon jungle and the barren, deadly high-altitude slopes of Nepal.

Furneaux pursued a dream career in stunt performing and traveled to Canada for three years of intense martial arts, stunt driving, and weapons training. She worked hard and eventually landed the job of Sharon Stone's stunt double in the movie *Catwoman*. For the next sixteen years she doubled stars such as Jennifer Garner in *Elektra* and Jaimie Alexander in *Thor* and the NBC series *Blindspot*. Her professional, calm attitude on set had her working with the likes of Anne Hathaway, Ellen DeGeneres, Hugh Jackman, Arnold Schwarzenegger, and Chris Hemsworth. In 16 years at the top of the stunt game, her many achievements included winning Best Female Stunt Performer in the world in the 2012 Taurus Awards (the Oscars of the stunt industry).

Despite the red-carpet glamour, the outdoors remained Furneaux's first love. Following the call of the wild, she challenged herself to new extreme survival expeditions, ditching all the gear and heading out with only a knife.

She produced and documented an extraordinary hundred-mile hike across the Sierra Nevada mountain range. She featured in three episodes of Discovery's *Naked and Afraid* and was the only female in season two of Discovery's *Ed Stafford: First Man Out*, braving a twelve-thousand-foot mountain climb and -22°F temperatures.

Although she's conquered grueling terrain in over sixty-five countries, Furneaux is passionate about her country's unique landscape and wildlife, and she shared the beauty of the Aussie bush in her Discovery and 7Mate series *Outback Lockdown*. She's a wilderness warrior in the tradition of the late, great Steve Irwin and in her own words a "true survival nerd."

Already a published author, her book, *Girls' Own Survival Guide*, shared her survival attitudes with women everywhere, and her motivational speaking frequently focuses on empowering and supporting people to achieve their potential. She inspires them to tune out the "you can't" voices and reach for the stars, just as she did.